CHILD DEVELOPMENT

With special appreciation to my wife, Mary Jo;
my children, Tracy and Jennifer;
and my grandchildren, Jordan and Alex.

ABOUT THE AUTHOR

JOHN W. SANTROCK

John Santrock received his Ph.D. from the University of Minnesota in 1973. He taught at the University of Charleston and the University of Georgia before joining the Program in Psychology and Human Development at the University of Texas at Dallas, where he currently teaches a number of undergraduate courses.

John has been a member of the editorial boards of *Child Development* and *Developmental Psychology.* His research on father custody is widely cited and used in expert witness testimony to promote flexibility and alternative considerations in custody disputes. John also has authored these exceptional McGraw-Hill texts: *Psychology* (7th edition), *Children* (9th edition), *Adolescence* (11th edition), *Life-Span Development* (10th edition), and *Educational Psychology* (2nd edition).

For many years, John was involved in tennis as a player, teaching professional, and coach of professional tennis players. He has been married for more than 35 years to his wife, Mary Jo, who is a realtor. He has two daughters—Tracy, who is studying to become a financial planner at Duke University, and Jennifer, who is a medical sales specialist at Medtronic. He has one granddaughter, Jordan, age 14, and one grandson, Alex, age 1. Tracy recently completed the New York Marathon, and Jennifer was in the top 100 ranked players on the Women's Professional Tennis Tour. In the last decade, John also has spent time painting expressionist art.

John Santrock (*center*) teaching an undergraduate psychology course.

BRIEF CONTENTS

CONTENTS

Section 1 THE NATURE OF CHILD DEVELOPMENT 2

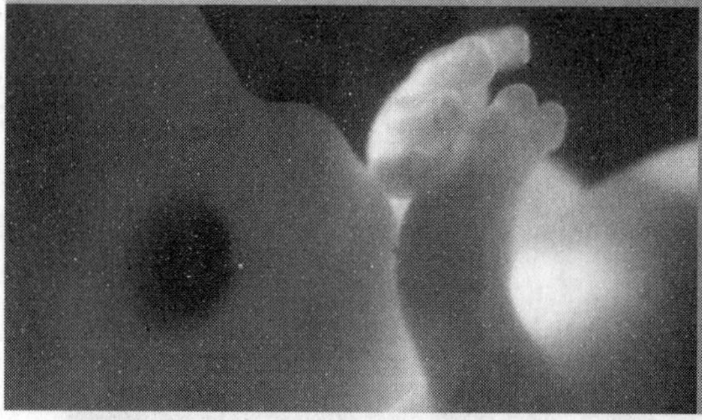

Section 2

BIOLOGICAL PROCESSES, PHYSICAL DEVELOPMENT, AND PERCEPTUAL DEVELOPMENT 72

Section 3
COGNITION AND LANGUAGE 206

Section 5
SOCIAL CONTEXTS OF DEVELOPMENT 452

PREFACE

Preparing a new edition of *Child Development* is both a joy and a challenge. I enjoy revising this text because I continue to learn more about children and because the feedback from students and instructors has been consistently enthusiastic. The challenge of revising a successful text is always to continue meeting readers' needs and expectations, while keeping the material fresh and up to date. To meet this challenge, I have made a number of key changes, which I describe below.

NEW TO THIS EDITION

For the eleventh edition of *Child Development*, I wrote two new chapters, expanded coverage in a number of key areas, incorporated the latest research and applications, and fine-tuned the aspects of the book that make learning easier and more engaging.

Two New Chapters

At the request of adopters and reviewers, I added two new chapters to the book by significantly rearranging and revising the discussion of physical development. In the tenth edition, the two physical development chapters were primarily organized in a chronological manner with chapter 5 focusing on infancy and chapter 6 describing childhood and adolescence. In the eleventh edition, these two chapters have a much stronger topical, process emphasis.

In the eleventh edition, chapter 5 is now titled "Physical Development and Health." In the tenth edition, much of this material was in chapter 6, and it included no discussion of infancy. In the eleventh edition, the main headings in chapter 5 are "Body Growth and Change"; "The Brain"; "Sleep"; and "Health." Developmental changes from infancy through adolescence are now discussed within each of these topics.

The coverage of motor, sensory, and perceptual development has been expanded and chapter 6 is now devoted to these topics. The result is a far more cohesive discussion that follows from the increased interest in viewing perceptual and motor development as integrated.

Placing the discussion of motor, sensory, and perceptual development after physical development also provides a better connection of both of these chapters to material in adjacent chapters. Thus, the coverage of body growth and change in chapter 5 now immediately follows the discussion of birth, and the information on perceptual development now immediately precedes the coverage of cognitive processes.

Research and Applications

Above all, a text on child development must include a solid research foundation as well as applied examples. In this edition, I have updated and expanded the coverage of research and applications.

Recent Research This edition of *Child Development* presents the latest research on the biological, cognitive, and socioemotional aspects of children's lives and includes more than 1,800 citations from the twenty-first century, including more than 600 from 2004, 2005, and 2006. The new research discussions include information from chapters in the sixth edition of the *Handbook of Child Psychology* (Damon & Lerner, 2006). Later in the preface I highlight the main content changes on a chapter-by-chapter basis.

NEW! Research in Child Development Interludes New to this edition are the Research in Child Development interludes. Appearing in each chapter, these interludes provide a more in-depth look at research related to a topic in the chapter. In most cases, they describe a research study, including the identity of the participants, the methods used to obtain data, and the main results. Most of the highlighted studies were conducted after 2000. Because students often have more difficulty reading about research studies than other text material, I wrote these in a way that students will understand them. Examples of the new Research in Child Development interludes are:

Chapter 6 (Motor, Sensory, and Perceptual Development): Studying the Newborn's Perception
Chapter 8 (Information Processing): Suggesting False Events to Children
Chapter 12 (The Self and Identity): A Possible Selves Intervention to Enhance School Involvement
Chapter 15 (Families): Marital Conflict, Individual Hostility, and the Use of Physical Punishment
Chapter 16 (Peers): Aggressive Victims, Passive Victims, and Bullies
Chapter 18 (Culture): Multiple Risks of Children Living in Poverty

Expert Research Consultants Child development has become an enormous, complex field and no single author, or even several authors, can possibly be an expert in many different areas of child development. To solve this problem, I sought the input of leading experts in many different research areas of child development. The experts provided me with detailed evaluations and recommendations for chapters in their areas of expertise. The expert consultants for *Child Development*, eleventh edition, are:

Ross Thompson, *University of California–Davis*
Tiffany Field, *University of Miami (Florida)*
Douglas Frye, *University of Virginia*
Cynthia Hudley, *University of California–Santa Barbara*
Kenneth Rubin, *University of Maryland*
Elizabeth Vera, *Loyola University–Chicago*
John Reiser, *Vanderbilt University*
Vera John-Steiner, *University of New Mexico*
John Gibbs, *Ohio State University*
Barbara McCombs, *University of Denver*

Applications Applied examples give students a sense that the field of life-span development has personal meaning for them. This edition retains the well-received Careers in Child Development inserts and also includes a new application titled Caring for Children.

New! Caring for Children Interludes In addition to giving special attention throughout the text to health and well-being, parenting, and educational applications, the eleventh edition of *Child Development* includes Caring for Children interludes, which describe important strategies for nurturing and improving the lives of children. Among the topics of the Caring for Children interludes are:

Chapter 1: (Introduction): Improving Family Policy
Chapter 3: (Biological Beginnings): Parenting Adopted Children
Chapter 11: (Emotional Development): Helping Children Cope with Stressful Events
Chapter 16: (Peers): Appropriate and Inappropriate Strategies for Making Friends

Careers in Child Development Instructors and students have provided extremely positive feedback about the emphasis on careers in child development in the text. The eleventh edition continues this emphasis. Each Careers in Child Development insert profiles an individual whose career relates to the chapter's content. Most of these inserts include a photograph of the person at work. A number of new Careers inserts appear in the eleventh edition of *Child Development*.

In addition, a Careers in Child Development section in chapter 1 encourages students to consider a career that involves working with children. The Careers in Child Development section describes a number of careers in education/research, clinical/counseling, medical/nursing/physical development, and family/relationships categories. Numerous Web links provide opportunities to read about these careers in more detail.

Diversity I made every effort to explore diversity issues in a sensitive manner in each chapter of the eleventh edition of *Child Development*. The book continues to have an entire chapter devoted to culture, and I expanded the coverage of diversity in a number of places in this edition. New or expanded coverage of diversity includes:

Chapter 1 (Introduction): New section on socioeconomic status and poverty
Chapter 3 (Biological Beginnings): New discussion of the increased diversity of adopted children and adoptive parents
Chapter 9 (Intelligence): Much expanded coverage of cross-cultural comparisons of intelligence and new discussion of stereotype threat
Chapter 12 (The Self and Identity): New section, Sociocultural Contexts and new chapter opening story: Maxine Hong Kingston, Bridging Cultural Worlds
Chapter 13 (Gender): Coverage of very recent research on the gender socialization of Latino and Latina adolescents
Chapter 15 (Families): New section, Parenting Styles
Chapter 18 (Culture): Extensive new material on cross-cultural comparisons of health and well-being, gender, family, school, peers, and use of time; much expanded coverage of poverty and immigration

ACCESSIBILITY AND INTEREST

The new edition of this text should be accessible to students because of the careful attention to clarity, the changes in organization, and the learning system.

Writing and Organization

Every sentence, paragraph, section, and chapter of this book was carefully examined and when appropriate revised and rewritten. The result is a much clearer, better organized presentation of material in this edition.

The Learning System

I strongly believe that students not only should be challenged to study hard and think more deeply and productively about child development, but should also be provided with effective learning aids. Instructors and students alike have commented that this book is very student-friendly.

Now more than ever, students struggle to find the main ideas in their courses, especially in courses like child development, which includes so much material. The book's learning system centers on learning goals that, together with the main text headings, keep the key ideas in front of the reader from the beginning to the end of the chapter. Each chapter has no more than five main headings and corresponding learning goals, which are presented side by side in the chapter-opening spread. At the end of each main section of a chapter, the learning goal is repeated in a feature called "Review and Reflect," which prompts students to review the key topics in the section and poses a question to encourage them to think critically about what they have read. At the end of the chapter, under the heading "Reach Your Learning Goals," the learning goals guide students through the bulleted chapter review.

In addition to the verbal tools just described, maps that link up with the learning goals are presented at the beginning of each major section in the chapter. At the end of each chapter, the section maps are assembled into a complete map of the chapter that provides a visual review guide. The complete learning system, including many additional features not mentioned here, is presented in a section following the preface titled "To the Student."

CHAPTER-BY-CHAPTER CHANGES

I made a number of changes in all 18 chapters of *Child Development,* eleventh edition. The highlights of these changes follow.

Chapter 1
INTRODUCTION

- New Research in Child Development interlude: Early Childhood TV Viewing and Adolescent Behavior
- New Caring for Children interlude: Improving Family Policy
- New section on socioeconomic status (SES) in the coverage of Sociocultural Contexts, including the main points in a recent review of research on poverty and children's development (Brooks-Gunn, 2003)
- Movement of Careers in Child Development to become the last main section of chapter 1 from its previous location as an appendix to improve the probability that students will read it
- Two new Careers in Child Development inserts: Valerie Pang, Professor of Teacher Education, and Katherine Duchen Smith, Nurse and Child Care Health Consultant

Chapter 2
THE SCIENCE OF CHILD DEVELOPMENT

- New opening section on the foundations of child development as a science, including subsections on why research in child development is important and the scientific research approach
- New section on psychophysical methods
- New example of a case study focused on Erikson's analysis of Mahatma Gandhi's life
- Added assimilation and accommodation to discussion of Piaget's theory
- Updated, clarified description of information-processing theory
- New Caring for Children interlude: Mesosystem Connection: Family and School Communication
- New section on Thinking Critically About Research on Child Development

Chapter 3
BIOLOGICAL BEGINNINGS

- Extensive rewriting and reorganization of chapter
- Inclusion of a number of new introductions to topics and transitions between topics for improved clarity and understanding
- New section on evolutionary developmental psychology
- New figure 3.1 on the brain sizes of various primates in relation to the length of the juvenile period
- New section, The Epigenetic View
- Major revision and update of material on adoption, including dramatic increases in the diversity of adopted children and adopted parents
- New Caring for Children interlude: Parenting Adopted Children

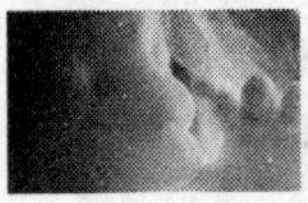

Chapter 4
PRENATAL DEVELOPMENT AND BIRTH

- Expanded discussion of alcohol effects on the fetus, including recent research linking moderate drinking to preterm risk and birth size
- Updated coverage of cocaine use by pregnant women, including increasing evidence of its negative effects
- New discussion of links between eating certain fish by pregnant women and risks to the fetus and child
- New Caring for Children interlude: Prenatal Care in the United States and Around the World, including new figure 4.6 on the use of timely prenatal care by women from different ethnic groups in the United States
- Updated research on low birth weight infants, including new figure 4.8
- New section on kangaroo care, including recent research of its positive effects on preterm infants
- New Research in Child Development interlude: Tiffany Field's Research on Massage Therapy
- Much expanded coverage of postpartum depression, including new figure 4.11

Chapter 5
PHYSICAL DEVELOPMENT AND HEALTH

- Completely new focus on chapter with emphasis on physical development and health in one chapter at the

request of instructors (previously, this material was spread across two chapters); the new organization of this chapter provides a much stronger topical focus to the material on physical development and health
- Substantial rewriting of chapter for improved clarity and understanding
- Expanded, updated coverage of puberty, especially in terms of adrenarche, gonadarche, and hormonal changes
- Substantially revised organization of coverage of the brain with a much improved introduction of basic aspects of brain physiology to help set the stage for improved understanding of the developmental changes in the brain; updated, expanded coverage of developmental changes in the brain during adolescence
- Expanded coverage of developmental changes in sleep, including updated research coverage of SIDS with the reasons why sleeping in a prone position is linked with SIDS and a new section on changes in sleep during adolescence

Chapter 6
MOTOR, SENSORY, AND PERCEPTUAL DEVELOPMENT

- New chapter focused on motor, sensory, and perceptual development that involves expanded and more integrated coverage of these topics that in the previous edition were disconnected across two chapters; creating this new chapter provides a much stronger emphasis on the important topic of perceptual motor coupling
- Topics extensively revised and rewritten with special attention to providing more examples of concepts and explanations of challenging concepts, such as dynamic systems theory and ecological theory; movement of dynamic systems theory to beginning of chapter to emphasize its importance
- Much expanded and more detailed discussion of research techniques for studying infant perception in the Research in Child Development interlude, including the visual preference method, habituation, and tracking
- New chapter opening story on Stevie Wonder and Andrea Bocelli and their ability to adapt to their visual impairment, as well as expanded coverage of visual impairment in the chapter
- New discussion of binocular vision and its emergence at 3 to 4 months of age, providing a powerful cue to depth
- Expanded coverage of hearing in infancy to include changes in the perception of loudness, pitch, and sound localization, and new coverage of hearing in adolescence

Chapter 7
COGNITIVE DEVELOPMENTAL APPROACHES

- Extensive rewriting of chapter for improved flow and student understanding
- Revised and expanded coverage of Piaget's concept of schemes
- New figure 7.1 that summarizes the main characteristics of Piaget's four stages
- Expanded coverage in the Research in Child Development insert with discussion of the violated-expectations method and new figure 7.4 to show the procedures used in the study of object permanence
- Provided extensive example of the zone of proximal development
- Expanded material on description of private speech with examples and research
- Updated coverage of Barbara Rogoff's ideas on cognitive apprenticeship
- Added criticisms of Vygotsky's approach

Chapter 8
INFORMATION PROCESSING

- Extensively revised and reorganized chapter to give a stronger focus to developmental changes in children's attention, memory, thinking, and metacognition
- New figure 8.2 showing a simplified version of information processing to improve students' understanding of this approach
- New coverage of the explanations for increased processing speed in childhood
- Completely revised, updated coverage of developmental changes in attention in terms of selective attention, divided attention, and sustained attention
- New Research in Child Development interlude: Suggesting False Events to Children
- Expanded and updated coverage of false memories in children
- New section on the role of content knowledge in memory
- New material on the developmental shift to flexible, goal-directed problem solving in early childhood

Chapter 9
INTELLIGENCE

- Extensive rewriting and reorganization of the chapter for better student understanding

- Brief discussion and definition of factor analysis added to help students understand the factor analytic approach to intelligence
- New section on the Sternberg Triarchic Abilities Test (STAT)
- Much expanded coverage of the influence of heredity and environment on intelligence
- New coverage of a leading expert's conclusions on what research indicates about the role of intervention in improving children's intelligence
- New section, Group Comparisons, with new material on gender comparisons
- Much expanded coverage of cross-cultural comparisons of intelligence, including recent research
- New coverage of the concept of stereotype threat and the intelligence of ethnic minority individuals (Aronson, Fried, & Good, 2002; Steele & Aronson, 1995)

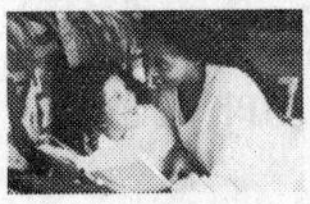

Chapter 10
LANGUAGE DEVELOPMENT

- Extensive rewriting and reorganization of chapter with the development of language now preceding the section on biological and environmental influences
- Updated material on change in language in early childhood and middle and late childhood
- New Research in Child Development interlude: Family Environment and Young Children's Language Development
- New figure 10.4 showing the research setting in Patricia Kuhl's studies of infants changing from being universal linguists to specializing in the speech of their native language
- New section on preparing for literacy
- New Careers in Child Development: Beverly Gallagher, elementary school teacher

Chapter 11
EMOTIONAL DEVELOPMENT

- Extensively revised and rewritten chapter for better student understanding
- New discussion of biological foundations and experience in emotions, including early development in the brain and culture
- New photographs in figures 11.2 and 11.4 from Michael Lewis' laboratory showing seven different emotions being displayed by infants
- Expanded, revised, and updated coverage of emotion in adolescence
- New figure 11.7 on what to do and what not to do when you suspect that someone is about to attempt suicide
- Expanded, updated material on coping with death in childhood, including coping with stressful events involving death, such as September 11, 2001
- New Caring for Children interlude on helping children cope with stressful events
- Much expanded coverage of biological and experiential factors in temperament
- Updated coverage of the National Institute of Child Health and Development's longitudinal study of child care in the new Research in Child Development interlude
- New material on strategies parents can use in selecting quality child care based on expert Kathleen McCartney's ideas

Chapter 12
THE SELF AND IDENTITY

- New chapter opening story: The Story of Maxine Hong Kingston, Bridging Cultural Worlds, and reference to the opening story at various points in the chapter
- New section on sociocultural contexts and the self
- New Research in Child Development interlude: A Possible Selves Intervention to Enhance School Involvement, based on the research of Daphina Oyserman and her colleagues with African American middle school students
- New discussion of how self-esteem does not always involve perceptions that match reality
- Revised and updated coverage of the controversy about whether self-esteem changes with age
- New section, Variations in Self-Esteem, with new coverage of research on the extent self-esteem is linked to school performance, initiative, physical appearance, happiness, depression, and other problems (Baumeister & others, 2003)
- New discussion of Susan Harter's research on links between self-esteem and physical appearance, including a new research figure
- New Caring for Children interlude: Increasing Children's Self-Esteem
- Revised and updated coverage of culture, ethnicity, and identity

Chapter 13
GENDER

- New Research in Child Development interlude: Young Children's Gender Schemas of Occupations
- Expanded, updated, rewritten discussion of the evolutionary psychology view of gender
- New material on whether same-sex education benefits boys and/or girls

- Discussion of recent study on gender stereotyping by young children and their mothers and commentary about how children construct their understanding of gender
- Much expanded and updated discussion of developmental changes in gender stereotyping
- Updated coverage of gender differences in the brain
- Extensively rewritten and improved coverage of cognitive influences on gender, including updated material on gender and visuospatial skills
- Criticism of Tannen's ideas on gender differences in communication, including recent research documenting more similarities than differences in men and women in their talk about relationship problems and a meta-analytic review of research documenting the importance of context in gender differences
- Updated description of gender and relational aggression
- New section on gender differences in prosocial behavior
- Updated coverage of gender and emotion, including descriptions of developmental changes
- Updated discussion of gender controversy based on a recent review of meta-analyses of gender differences and similarities
- Recent research on gender-role classification and academic self-efficacy
- Coverage of recent research on differences in the gender socialization of Latino and Latina adolescents in the United States
- New Caring for Children interlude: Guiding Children's Gender Development

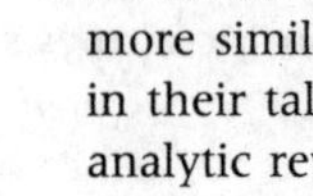

Chapter 14 MORAL DEVELOPMENT

- Substantial rewriting of chapter on a line-by-line basis for improved student understanding and clarity
- Major new section on moral personality that includes the recent surge of interest in moral identity, moral character, and moral exemplars
- New material on the distinction between moral/conventional issues and personal issues
- New Research in Child Development interlude on the consistency and development of prosocial behavior
- New sections on relational quality, proactive strategies, and conversational dialogue in the discussion of parenting and moral development
- Recent research documenting the role of secure attachment as a precursor for a link between positive parenting and a child's conscience
- Discussion of new parenting recommendations based on Ross Thompson's analysis of parent-child relations and children's moral development
- Expanded and updated coverage of character education
- Expanded coverage of service learning with new discussion of Connie Flanagan's research
- Discussion of recent study linking father absence and incarceration of youth
- Description of recent research on peers and delinquency
- New Caring for Children interlude on strategies for reducing youth violence

Chapter 15 FAMILIES

- New introduction in Family Processes section involving Bronfenbrenner's ecological theory and reference to it at different points in the chapter
- New section on Parenting Styles and Ethnicity, including recent research on Mexican American parenting styles
- New Research in Child Development interlude: Marital Conflict, Individual Hostility, and the Use of Physical Punishment
- Much expanded coverage of child maltreatment, including more in-depth discussion of types of abuse, recent research, and an effective prevention program
- New Caring for Children interlude: Communicating with Children About Divorce
- Inclusion of information from the recent NICHD Early Childhood Research Care Network Study of five types of before- and after-school care
- New coverage of study on the importance of paternal warmth and involvement in infancy when mothers were depressed
- Description of recent review of the use of nonabusive physical punishment by parents in African American families and child outcomes
- Coverage of longitudinal study showing a link between spanking in infancy and later behavioral problems
- Inclusion of recent research on sibling relations
- Discussion of recent study on divorce and attachment (Brockmeyer, Treboux, & Crowell, 2005)
- Updated coverage of father involvement in chidren's lives

Chapter 16 PEERS

- Expanded and updated discussion of developmental changes in peer interaction
- Expanded, updated coverage of peer statuses, including description of average children
- New discussion of emotion in peer relations, including recent research on the emotional aspects of information in highly aggressive boys

- New Research in Child Development interlude: Aggressive Victims, Passive Victims, and Bullies
- Inclusion of John Coie's recent view on the reasons peer-rejected aggressive boys have problems in social functioning and may engage in antisocial behavior over time
- Much expanded discussion of peer-rejected children, including a recent successful intervention study
- Much expanded recommendations for teachers and parents in reducing bullying
- New section on the role of culture in peer relations
- New discussion of recent longitudinal research on the outcomes of not having a friend
- Updated and expanded coverage of gender differences in friendship
- New Caring for Children interlude: Appropriate and Inappropriate Strategies for Making Friends
- New description of developmental changes in crowds
- Expanded and updated coverage of the sequence of relationships in sexual minority youth
- Description of research on a link between dating and lower social anxiety in adolescents
- Coverage of recent research on the role of mixed-gender peer groups in romantic relationships in early adolescence

Chapter 17 SCHOOLS AND ACHIEVEMENT

- Extensive rewriting and updating of chapter
- New chapter title that now includes achievement to reflect the expanded, updated, and revised material on achievement in the chapter
- New section on accountability in education as a major issue, including recent material on No Child Left Behind (NCLB)
- New discussion of controversy in early childhood education regarding academic emphasis
- Coverage of current consideration by the U.S. Congress of infusing Project Head Start with a stronger academic focus and commentary by early childhood experts about some concerns with this academic emphasis
- Inclusion of information from recent review of effective school dropout programs and new discussion of gender differences in school dropout rates and revised estimates of the dropout rate for Native American youth
- Updated and expanded coverage of the "I Have a Dream Program"
- More precise, updated explanation of how stimulants work in children with ADHD
- New sections on the identification of learning disabilities and the causes of learning disabilities
- New coverage of the 2004 reauthorization of the Individuals with Disabilities Act and its alignment with No Child Left Behind legislation
- New discussion of James Kauffman and his colleagues' views that in some cases inclusion has become too extreme and that too often children with disabilities are not challenged to become all they can be
- New section on attribution and achievement
- Inclusion of recent study linking mastery motivation to higher math and reading grades in elementary school students

Chapter 18 CULTURE

- Extensive new material on cross-cultural comparisons in the areas of health and well-being, gender, family, school, peers, and adolescents' use of time
- Much expanded coverage of poverty and children's development, including information from a recent research review
- New Research in Child Development interlude: Multiple Risks of Children Living in Poverty, including two new research figures
- Coverage of recent study on parents' educational aspirations and adolescents' educational outcomes in low-income families
- New Caring for Children interlude: The Quantum Opportunities Program
- New discussion of collectivist orientation of many recent immigrant families to the United States and their emphasis on family obligation and duty
- New section on media use by children and adolescents, including recent surveys
- New section on television and sex that focuses on the influence of TV on adolescents' sexual attitudes and behavior
- New discussion of violent video games and children's aggression
- Updated and modified conclusions about links between television viewing and children's creativity, mental ability, and achievement
- Coverage of recent national study on media use by U.S. 8- to 18-year-olds, including new figure 18.6
- Recent update of Internet access at home by different ethnic groups

ACKNOWLEDGMENTS

I very much appreciate the support and guidance provided to me by many people at McGraw-Hill. Mike Sugarman, Executive Editor, brought a wealth of publishing knowledge and vision to bear on this edition. Judith Kromm, Senior Developmental Editor, did a superb job of organizing and monitoring the many tasks necessary to move the book through the editorial and production process. Kate Russillo,

Editorial Coordinator, has once again done a marvelous of job of obtaining reviewers and handling many editoral chores. Melissa Caughlin, Marketing Manager, has contributed in numerous positive ways to this book. Special thanks also go to Marcie Mealia, Field Publisher in psychology, for coming home. I especially appreciate her extensive knowledge of psychology and her infectious enthusiasm. Project Manager Rick Hecker very competently managed the production of the book. Kim Menning, Senior Designer, provided a beautiful design, and Laurie McGee once again did a stellar job in copyediting the book. I also thank freelance project manager Marilyn Rothenberger for her excellent work pulling everything together. Finally, I wish to thank my incredibly talented freelance developmental editor, Kathy Field, for imparting her words and wisdom to this book.

REVIEWERS

I owe much gratitude to the reviewers who provided detailed feedback about the book.

Expert Consultants

A list of the expert consultants appears earlier in the preface. These experts provided detailed recommendations of new research to include in their areas of expertise.

General Text Reviewers

I also owe a great deal of thanks to the instructors teaching the child development course who have provided feedback about the book. Many of the changes in *Child Development*, eleventh edition, stem from their input. For their help, I thank these individuals:

Prerevision Reviewers

Christy Kimpo, *University of Washington*
Jerry Dusek, *Syracuse University*
Margaret Szewczyk, *University of Chicago*
Marjorie M. Battaglia, *George Mason University*
Marlene DeVoe, *Saint Cloud State University*
Pamela Ludemann, *Framingham State College*
Robin Yaure, *Pennsylvania State–Mont Alto*
Stephen B. Graves, *University of South Florida*
Susan Shonk, *SUNY–College of Brockport*

Eleventh Edition Manuscript Reviewers

Barba Patton, *University of Texas–Victoria*
Brad Morris, *Grand Valley State University*
Carrie Mori, *Boise State University*
Judy Payne, *Murray State University*
Lisa Caya, *University of Wisconsin–LaCrosse*
Oney Fitzpatrick, Jr., *Lamar University*
Pamela Ludemann's, *Framingham State College*
Robin Harwood, *Texas Tech University*
Saramma T. Mathew, *Troy State University*
William Curry, *Wesleyan College*
Winnie Mucherah, *Ball State University*

Reviewers of Previous Editions

Ruth L. Ault, *Davidson College*
Mary Ballard, *Appalachian State University*
William H. Barber, *Midwestern State University*
Wayne Benenson, *Illinois State University*
Michael Bergmire, *Jefferson College*
David Bernhardt, *Carleton University*
Kathryn Norcross Black, *Purdue University*
Elain Blakemore, *Indiana University*
Susan Bland, *Niagara County Community College*
Amy Booth, *Northwestern University*
Marc Bornstein, *National Institute of Child Health and Human Development*
Megan E. Bradley, *Frostburg State University*
Maureen Callahan, *Webster University*
D. Bruce Carter, *Syracuse University*
Elaine Cassel, *Marymount University, Lord Fairfax Community College*
Steven Ceci, *Cornell University*
Theodore Chandler, *Kent State University*
Dante Cicchetti, *University of Rochester*
Audry E. Clark, *California State University, Northridge*
Debra E. Clark, *SUNY–Cortland*
Robert Cohen, *The University of Memphis*
John D. Coie, *Duke University*
Cynthia Garcia Coll, *Wellesley College*
W. Andrew Collins, *University of Minnesota*
Robert C. Coon, *Louisiana State University*
Roger W. Coulson, *Iowa State University*
Fred Danner, *University of Kentucky*
Denise M. DeZolt, *Kent State University*
K. Laurie Dickson, *Northern Arizona University*
Daniel D. DiSalvi, *Kean College*
Diane C. Draper, *Iowa State University*
Beverly Brown Dupré, *Southern University at New Orleans*
Glen Elder, Jr., *University of North Carolina*
Claire Etaugh, *Bradley University*
Dennis T. Farrell, *Luzerne County Community College*
Saul Feinman, *University of Wyoming*
Tiffany Field, *University of Miami*
Jane Goins Flanagan, *Lamar University*
L. Sidney Fox, *California State University–Long Beach*
Janet A. Fuller, *Mansfield University*
Irma Galejs, *Iowa State University*
Mary Gauvain, *University of California, Riverside*
Colleen Gift, *Highland Community College*
Margaret S. Gill, *Kutztown University*
Hill Goldsmith, *University of Wisconsin–Madison*

Cynthia Graber, *Columbia University*
Nira Grannott, *University of Texas at Dallas*
Donald E. Guenther, *Kent State University*
Julia Guttmann, *Iowa Wesleyan College*
Robert A. Haaf, *University of Toledo*
Susan Harter, *University of Denver*
Craig Hart, *Brigham Young University*
Elizabeth Hasson, *Westchester University*
Rebecca Heikkinen, *Kent State University*
Joyce Hemphill, *University of Wisconsin*
Shirley-Anne Hensch, *University of Wisconsin*
Stanley Henson, *Arkansas Technical University*
Alice Honig, *Syracuse University*
Helen L. Johnson, *Queens College*
Kathy E. Johnson, *Indiana University–Purdue University Indianapolis*
Seth Kalichman, *Loyola University*
Kenneth Kallio, *SUNY–Geneseo*
Maria Kalpidou, *Assumption College*
Daniel W. Kee, *California State University–Fullerton*
Melvyn B. King, *SUNY–Cortland*
Claire Kopp, *UCLA*
Deanna Kuhn, *Columbia University*
John Kulig, *Northern Illinois University*
Janice Kupersmidt, *University of North Carolina*
Michael Lamb, *National Institute of Child Health and Human Development*
Daniel K. Lapsley, *University of Notre Dame*
David B. Liberman, *University of Houston*
Robert Lickliter, *Florida International University*
Marianna Footo Linz, *Marshall University*
Kevin MacDonald, *California State University–Long Beach*
Virginia A. Marchman, *University of Texas at Dallas*
Dottie McCrossen, *University of Ottawa*
Sheryll Mennicke, *Concordia College, St. Paul*
Carolyn Meyer, *Lake Sumter Community College*
Dalton Miller-Jones, *NE Foundation for Children*
Marilyn Moore, *Illinois State University*
John P. Murray, *Kansas State University*
Dara Musher-Eizenman, *Bowling Green State University*
José E. Nanes, *University of Minnesota*
Sherry J. Neal, *Oklahoma City Community Center*
Larry Nucci, *University of Illinois at Chicago*
Daniel J. O'Neill, *Briston Community College*
Randall E. Osborne, *Southwest Texas State University*
Margaret Owen, *University of Texas at Dallas*
Robert Pasnak, *George Mason University*
Elizabeth Pemberton, *University of Delaware*
Herb Pick, *University of Minnesota*
Kathy Lee Pillow, *Arkansas State University, Beebe*
Nan Ratner, *University of Maryland*
Brenda Reimer, *Southern Missouri State University*
Cosby Steele Rogers, *Virginia Polytechnic Institute and State University*
Kimberly A. Gordon Rouse, *Ohio State University*
Alan Russell, *Flinders University*
Carolyn Saarni, *Sonoma State University*
Douglas B. Sawin, *University of Texas, Austin*
Krista Schoenfeld, *Colby Community College*
Ed Scholwinski, *Southwest Texas State University*
Dale Schunk, *Purdue University*
Bill M. Seay, *Louisiana State University*
Matthew J. Sharps, *California State University, Fresno*
Marilyn Shea, *University of Maine, Farmington*
Susan Siaw, *California Polytechnic Institute–Pomona*
Robert Siegler, *Carnegie Mellon University*
Evelyn D. Silva, *Cosumnes River College*
Mildred D. Similton, *Pfeiffer University*
Dorothy Justus Sluss, *Virginia Polytechnic Institute and State University*
Janet Spence, *University of Texas–Austin*
Melanie Spence, *University of Texas–Dallas*
Richard Sprott, *California State University, East Bay*
Mark S. Strauss, *University of Pittsburgh*
Donna J. Tyler Thompson, *Midland College*
Marion K. Underwood, *University of Texas–Dallas*
Cherie Valeithian, *Kent State University*
Jaan Valsiner, *Clark University*
Lawrence Walker, *University of British Columbia*
Kimberlee L. Whaley, *Ohio State University*
Belinda M. Wholeben, *Northern Illinois University*
Frederic Wynn, *County College of Morris*

SUPPLEMENTS

The supplements listed here may accompany *Child Development,* eleventh edition. Please contact your McGraw-Hill representative for details concerning policies, prices, and availability as some restrictions may apply.

For the Instructor

Instructor's Manual

Cosby Steele Rogers, Sarah Rogers, and Bonnie C. Graham, Virginia Polytechnic Institute and State University

Each chapter of the *Instructor's Manual* contains a Total Teaching Package Outline, a fully integrated tool to help instructors better use the many resources for the course. This outline shows instructors which supplementary materials can be used in the teaching of a particular chapter topic. In addition, there is a chapter outline, suggested lecture topics, classroom activities and demonstrations, suggested student research projects, essay questions, critical thinking questions, and implications for guidance.

Test Bank and Dual Platform Computerized Test Bank on CD-ROM

Marilyn Moore, Illinois State University

This comprehensive test bank includes more than 2,000 factual, conceptual, and applied multiple-choice questions, as well as approximately 75 essay questions per chapter. Available on the Instructor's Resource CD-ROM as Word files and in computerized EZ Test format, the test bank is compatible with Macintosh and Windows platforms. McGraw-Hill's EZ Test is a flexible and easy-to-use electronic testing program. The program allows instructors to create tests from book-specific items. It accommodates a wide range of question types, and instructors may add their own questions. Multiple versions of the test can be created, and any test can be exported for use with course management systems such as WebCT, BlackBoard, or PageOut. EZ Test Online is a new service that gives you a place to easily administer your EZ Test–created exams and quizzes online. The program is available for Windows and Macintosh environments.

PowerPoint Slide Presentations

Anita Rosenfield, Yavapai College

This resource offers the instructor an array of PowerPoint slides for each chapter of *Child Development.* The slides can be downloaded from the instructor's side of the Online Learning Center or from the Instructor's Resource CD-ROM.

Instructor's Resource CD-ROM (IRCD)

This CD-ROM offers instructors a convenient tool for customizing the McGraw-Hill materials to prepare for and create lecture presentations. Included on the IRCD are the Instructor's Manual, Test Bank, and PowerPoint slides.

McGraw-Hill's Visual Assets Database (VAD) for Life-span Development

Jasna Jovanovic, University of Illinois–Urbana-Champaign

McGraw-Hill"s Visual Assets Database is a password-protected online database of hundreds of multimedia resources for use in classroom presentations, including original video clips, audio clips, photographs, and illustrations—all designed to bring to life concepts in human development. In addition to offering multimedia presentations for every stage of the life span, the VAD's search engine and unique "My Modules" program allows instructors to select from the database's resources to create customized presentations, or "modules." These customized presentations are saved in an instructor's folder on the McGraw-Hill site, and the presentation is then run directly from the VAD to the Internet-equipped classroom. For information about this unique resource, contact your McGraw-Hill representative.

Taking Sides: Clashing Views on Controversial Issues in Childhood and Society

Taking Sides is a debate-style reader designed to introduce students to controversial viewpoints on some of the most critical issues in the field. Each issue is framed for the student, and the pro and con essays represent the arguments of leading scholars and commentators in their fields. An instructor's guide containing testing materials is available.

Annual Editions: Child Growth and Development

Published by Dushkin/McGraw-Hill, this is a collection of articles on topics related to the latest research and thinking in child development. These editions are updated regularly and contain useful features, including a topic guide, an annotated table of contents, unit overviews, and a topical index. An instructor's guide, containing testing materials, is also available.

Online Learning Center (OLC)

This extensive website, designed specifically to accompany this edition of *Child Development,* offers a wide variety of resources for instructors and students. The password-protected instructor's side of the site includes the *Instructor's Manual,* PowerPoint lecture slides, images, and a link to McGraw-Hill's Visual Asset Database of brief film clips, audio clips, and photographs. These resources and more can be found by logging on to the text website (www.mhhe.com/santrockcd11).

For the Student

Study Guide

Megan E. Bradley, Frostburg State University

This comprehensive study guide integrates the learning system found in the textbook. Designed to promote active learning, it includes true-false, multiple-choice, matching, critical thinking, and short-answer exercises. An answer key is included so that students can assess their comprehension of the text content.

Online Learning Center (OLC)

This companion website for this edition of *Child Development* offers a wide variety of resources for instructors and students. For students, the website includes a Career Appendix, learning goals, chapter outlines, and multiple-choice and true-false quizzes. In addition, it offers interactive scenarios and short video clips from McGraw-Hill's Visual Assets Database for Life-span Development, and Web links to additional sources of information about the topics discussed in the book. These resources and more can be found by logging on to the website (www.mhhe.com/santrockcd11).

Multimedia Courseware for Child Development

Charlotte J. Patterson, University of Virginia

This interactive CD-ROM includes video footage of classic and contemporary experiments, detailed viewing guides, challenging preview, follow-up and interactive feedback, graphics, graduated developmental charts, a variety of hands-on projects, related websites. and navigation aids. The CD-ROM is programmed in a modular format. Its content focuses on integrating digital media to better explain physical, cognitive, social, and emotional development throughout childhood and adolescence. It is compatible with both Macintosh and Windows computers.

TO THE STUDENT

This book provides you with important study tools to help you more effectively learn about life-span development. Especially important is the learning goals system that is integrated throughout each chapter. In the visual walk-through of features, pay special attention to how the learning goals system works.

THE LEARNING GOALS SYSTEM

Using the learning goals system will help you to learn the material more easily. Key aspects of the learning goals system are the learning goals, chapter maps, Review and Reflect sections, and Reach Your Learning Goals sections, which are all linked together.

At the beginning of each chapter, you will see a page that includes both a chapter outline and three to six learning goals that preview the chapter's main themes and underscore the most important ideas in the chapter. Then, at the beginning of each major section of a chapter, you will see a minichapter map that provides you with a visual organization of the key topics you are about to read in the section. At the end of each section is a Review and Reflect section, which restates the learning goal for the section and poses review questions related to the minichapter map as well as a question that encourages you to think critically about a topic related to the text you just read. At the end of the chapter, you will come to a section titled Reach Your Learning Goals. This includes an overall chapter map that visually organizes all of the main headings, a restatement of the chapter's learning goals, and a summary of the chapter's content that is directly linked to the chapter outline at the beginning of the chapter and the review questions asked in the Review and Reflect sections within the chapter. The summary essentially answers the questions asked in the chapter Review sections.

CHAPTER OUTLINE AND LEARNING GOALS

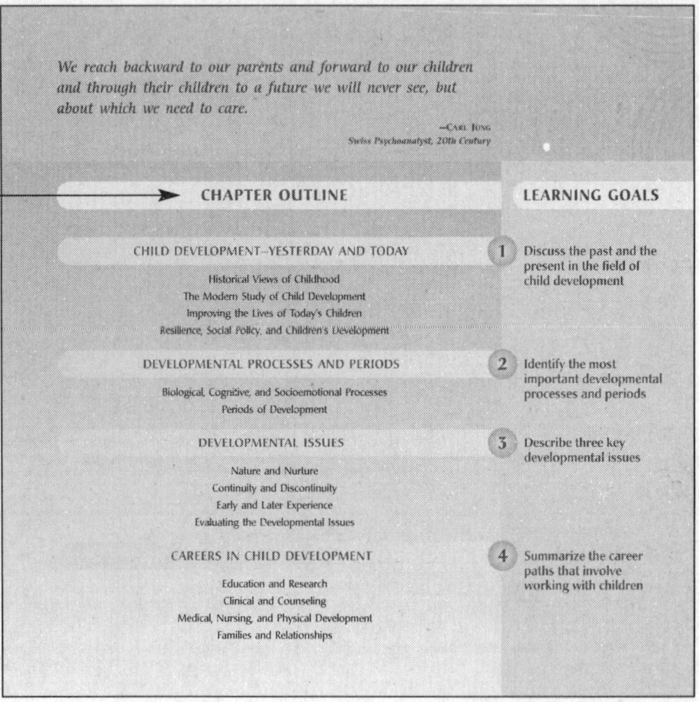

We reach backward to our parents and forward to our children and through their children to a future we will never see, but about which we need to care.

—Carl Jung
Swiss Psychoanalyst, 20th Century

CHAPTER OUTLINE	LEARNING GOALS
CHILD DEVELOPMENT–YESTERDAY AND TODAY Historical Views of Childhood The Modern Study of Child Development Improving the Lives of Today's Children Resilience, Social Policy, and Children's Development	1 Discuss the past and the present in the field of child development
DEVELOPMENTAL PROCESSES AND PERIODS Biological, Cognitive, and Socioemotional Processes Periods of Development	2 Identify the most important developmental processes and periods
DEVELOPMENTAL ISSUES Nature and Nurture Continuity and Discontinuity Early and Later Experience Evaluating the Developmental Issues	3 Describe three key developmental issues
CAREERS IN CHILD DEVELOPMENT Education and Research Clinical and Counseling Medical, Nursing, and Physical Development Families and Relationships	4 Summarize the career paths that involve working with children

MINI-CHAPTER MAP

1 CHILD DEVELOPMENT—YESTERDAY AND TODAY

Historical Views of Childhood
Improving the Lives of Today's Children
The Modern Study of Child Development
Resilience, Social Policy, and Children's Development

What do we mean when we speak of an individual's development? **Development** is the pattern of change that begins at conception and continues through the life span. Most development involves growth, although it also includes decay. Anywhere you turn today, the development of children captures public attention. Historically, though, interest in the development of children has been uneven.

Historical Views of Childhood

Childhood has become such a distinct period that it is hard to imagine that it was not always thought of as markedly different from adulthood. However, in medieval Europe, laws generally did not distinguish between child and adult offenses. After analyzing samples of art along with available publications, historian Philippe Ariès (1962) concluded that European societies prior to 1600 did not give any special status to children (see figure 1.1).

Were children actually treated as miniature adults with no special status in medieval Europe? Ariès primarily sampled aristocratic, idealized subjects, which might have been misleading. Childhood probably was recognized as a distinct phase of life more than Ariès believed, but his analysis helped to highlight cultural differences in how children are viewed and treated.

Throughout history, philosophers have speculated at length about the nature of children and how they should be reared. The ancient Egyptians, Greeks, and Romans held rich conceptions of children's development. More recently in European history, three influential philosophical views portrayed children in terms of original sin, tabula rasa, and innate goodness:

- In the **original sin view,** especially advocated during the Middle Ages, children were perceived as being born into the world as evil beings. The goal of child rearing was to provide salvation, to remove sin from the child's life.
- Toward the end of the seventeenth century, the **tabula rasa view** was proposed by English philosopher John Locke. He argued that children are not innately bad but, instead, are like a "blank tablet." Locke believed that childhood experiences are important in determining adult characteristics. He advised parents to spend time with their children and to help them become contributing members of society.
- In the eighteenth century, the **innate goodness view** was presented by Swiss-born French philosopher Jean-Jacques Rousseau. He stressed that children are inherently good. Because children are basically good, said Rousseau, they should be permitted to grow naturally, with little parental monitoring or constraint.

Today, the Western view of children holds that childhood is a highly eventful and unique period of life that lays an important foundation for the adult years and is markedly different from them. Most current approaches to childhood identify distinct periods in which children master specific skills and tasks that prepare them for adulthood. Childhood is no longer seen as an inconvenient waiting period during which adults must suffer the incompetencies of the young. Instead, we protect children from the stresses and responsibilities of adult work through strict child

FIGURE 1.1 **Historical Perception of Children.** European paintings centuries ago often depicted children as miniature adults. *Do these artistic creations indicate that earlier Europeans did not view childhood as a distinct period?*

development The pattern of change that begins at conception and continues through the life span.

original sin view Advocated during the Middle Ages, the belief that children were born into the world as evil beings and were basically bad.

tabula rasa view The idea, proposed by John Locke, that children are like a "blank tablet."

innate goodness view The idea, presented by Swiss-born philosopher Jean-Jacques Rousseau, that children are inherently good.

REVIEW AND REFLECT

Review and Reflect • LEARNING GOAL 1

1 Discuss the past and the present in the field of child development

Review
- What is development? How has childhood been perceived through history?
- What are the key characteristics of the modern study of child development?
- What are some contemporary concerns about today's children?
- What is social policy, and what is its status in regard to America's children?

Reflect
- Imagine what your development as a child would have been like in a culture that offered fewer or distinctly different choices from your own. How might your development have been different if your family had been significantly richer or poorer than it was?

2 DEVELOPMENTAL PROCESSES AND PERIODS

Biological, Cognitive, and Socioemotional Processes
Periods of Development

Each of us develops in certain ways like all other individuals, like some other individuals, and like no other individuals. Most of the time, our attention is directed to a person's uniqueness, but psychologists who study development are drawn to our shared characteristics as well as what makes us unique. As humans, we all have traveled some common paths. Each of us—Leonardo da Vinci, Joan of Arc, George Washington, Martin Luther King, Jr., and you—walked at about the age of 1, engaged in fantasy play as a young child, and became more independent as a youth. What shapes this common path of human development, and what are its milestones?

Biological, Cognitive, and Socioemotional Processes

The pattern of human development is created by the interplay of several processes—biologial, cognitive, and socioemotional. **Biological processes** produce changes in an individual's body. Genes inherited from parents, the development of the brain, height and weight gains, motor skills, and the hormonal changes of puberty all reflect the role of biological processes in development.

Cognitive processes refer to changes in an individual's thought, intelligence, and language. The tasks of watching a mobile swinging above a crib, putting together a two-word sentence, memorizing a poem, solving a math problem, and imagining what it would be like to be a movie star all involve cognitive processes.

PEANUTS © United Features Syndicate, Inc.

biological processes Changes in an individual's body.

cognitive processes Changes in an individual's thought, intelligence, and language.

REACH YOUR LEARNING GOALS

REACH YOUR LEARNING GOALS

INTRODUCTION

1 CHILD DEVELOPMENT–YESTERDAY AND TODAY
- Historical Views of Childhood
- Improving the Lives of Today's Children
- The Modern Study of Child Development
- Resilience, Social Policy, and Children's Development

2 DEVELOPMENTAL PROCESSES AND PERIODS
- Biological, Cognitive, and Socioemotional Processes
- Periods of Development

3 DEVELOPMENTAL ISSUES
- Nature and Nurture
- Early and Later Experience
- Continuity and Discontinuity
- Evaluating the Developmental Issues

4 CAREERS IN CHILD DEVELOPMENT
- Education and Research
- Medical, Nursing, and Physical Development
- Clinical and Counseling
- Families and Relationships

SUMMARY

1 Discuss the past and the present in the field of child development
- Development is the pattern of movement or change that occurs throughout the life span. The history of interest in children is long and rich. Prior to the nineteenth century, philosophical views of childhood were prominent, including the notions of original sin, tabula rasa, and innate goodness.
- Today, we conceive of childhood as an important time of development. The modern era of studying children spans a little more than a century, an era in which the study of child development has become a sophisticated science. Methodological advances in observation as well as the introduction of experimentation and the development of major theories characterize the achievements of the modern era.
- Five important contemporary concerns in children's development are health and well-being; families and parenting; education; the sociocultural contexts of culture, ethnicity, and socioeconomic status; and gender.
- Social policy is a government's course of action designed to promote the welfare of its citizens. The poor conditions of life for a significant percentage of U.S. children and the lack of attention to prevention point to the need for revised social policies.

2 Identify the most important developmental processes and periods
- Development is influenced by an interplay of biological, cognitive, and socioemotional processes.
- Development is commonly divided into the following periods from conception through adolescence: prenatal, infancy, early childhood, middle and late childhood, and adolescence.

3 Describe three key developmental issues
- The nature-nurture issue focuses on the extent to which development is mainly influenced by nature (biological inheritance) or nurture (experience).
- Some developmentalists describe development as continuous (gradual, cumulative change); others describe it as discontinuous (a sequence of abrupt stages).
- The early-later experience issue focuses on whether early experiences (especially in infancy) are more important in development than later experiences.
- Most developmentalists recognize that extreme positions on the nature-nurture, continuity-discontinuity, and early-later experience issues are unwise. Despite this consensus, these issues continue to be spiritedly debated.

4 Summarize the career paths that involve working with children
- Education and research careers include college/university professor, researcher, elementary or secondary teacher, exceptional children teacher, early childhood educator, preschool/kindergarten teacher, family and consumer science educator, educational psychologist, and school psychologist.
- Clinical and counseling careers include clinical psychologist, psychiatrist, counseling psychologist, school counselor, career counselor, social worker, and drug counselor.
- Medical, nursing, and physical development careers include obstetrician/gynecologist, pediatrician, neonatal nurse, nurse-midwife, pediatric nurse, audiologist, speech therapist, and genetic counselor.
- Families and relationships careers include child welfare worker, child life specialist, and marriage and family therapist.

OTHER LEARNING SYSTEM FEATURES

IMAGES OF CHILD DEVELOPMENT

Each chapter opens with a high-interest story that is linked to the chapter's content.

The Stories of Jeffrey Dahmer and Alice Walker

Jeffrey Dahmer. What are some possible causes of the brutal acts of violence that he commited?

Alice Walker. What might be some reasons that she overcame trauma in her childhood to develop in positive ways?

Jeffrey Dahmer had a troubled childhood. His parents constantly bickered before they divorced, his mother had emotional problems and doted on his younger brother, and he felt that his father neglected him. When he was 8 years old, Jeffrey was sexually abused by an older boy. But most individuals who suffer through such childhood pains never go on to commit Dahmer's grisly crimes.

In 1991, a man in handcuffs dashed out of Dahmer's bizarrely cluttered apartment in a tough Milwaukee neighborhood, called the police, and stammered that Dahmer had tried to kill him. At least 17 other victims did not get away.

Alice Walker was born in 1944. She was the eighth child of Georgia sharecroppers who earned $300 a year. When Walker was 8, her brother accidentally shot her in the left eye with a BB gun. By the time her parents got her to the hospital a week later (they had no car), she was blind in that eye and it had developed a disfiguring layer of scar tissue.

Despite the counts against her, Alice Walker went on to become an essayist, a poet, and an award-winning novelist. She won the Pulitzer Prize for her book *The Color Purple*. Like her characters, especially the women, Alice Walker overcame pain and anger to celebrate the human spirit. Walker writes about people who "make it, who come out of nothing. People who triumph."

What leads one child to grow up and commit brutal acts of violence and another to turn poverty and trauma into a rich literary harvest? How can we explain how one child picks up the pieces of a life shattered by tragedy, while another becomes unhinged by life's stress? Why is it that some children are whirlwinds—full of energy, successful in school, and able to get along well with their peers—while others stay on the sidelines, mere spectators of life? If you ever have wondered about why children turn out the way they do, you have asked yourself the central questions we will explore in this book.

Why study children? Perhaps you are or will be a parent or teacher, and responsibility for children is or will be a part of your everyday life. The more you learn about children, the better you can guide them. Perhaps you hope to gain an understanding of your own history—as an infant, as a child, and as an adolescent. Perhaps you accidentally came across the course description and found it intriguing. Whatever your reasons, you will discover that the study of child development is provocative, intriguing, and informative.

RESEARCH IN CHILD DEVELOPMENT INTERLUDE

One Research in Child Development interlude appears in each chapter. The research interludes each describe a research study or program. They are designed to acquaint you with the methods used to study child development.

90 Chapter 3 Biological Beginnings

babies will have life-threatening and costly problems, such as extremely low birth weight (Appelman & Furman, 2005).

The creation of families by means of the new reproductive technologies raises important questions about the psychological consequences for children. To read about a recent study that addresses these consequences, see the Research in Child Development interlude that follows.

RESEARCH IN CHILD DEVELOPMENT

In Vitro Fertilization and Developmental Outcomes in Early Adolescence

A longitudinal study examined 34 in vitro fertilization families, 49 adoptive families, and 38 families with a naturally conceived child (Golombok, MacCallum, & Goodman, 2001). Each type of family included a similar portion of boys and girls. Also, the age of the young adolescents did not differ according to family type (their mean age was 11 years, 11 months).

Children's socioemotional development was assessed by (1) interviewing the mother and obtaining detailed descriptions of any problems the child might have, (2) administering a Strengths and Difficulties questionnaire to the child's mother and teacher, and (3) administering the Social Adjustment Inventory for Children and Adolescents, which examines functioning in school, peer relationships, and self-esteem.

No significant differences between the children from the in vitro fertilization, adoptive, and naturally conceiving families were found. The results from the Social Adjustment Inventory for Children and Adolescents are shown in figure 3.9. Thus, this study, as well as others (Hahn & DiPietro, 2001), support the idea that "test-tube" babies function well.

FIGURE 3.9 Socioemotional Development at Adolescence of Children in Three Family Types: In Vitro Fertilization, Naturally Conceived, and Adopted. In this study, there were no significant differences in socioemotional development at the beginning of adolescence in terms of school functioning, peer relations, and self-esteem (Golombok, MacCallum, & Goodman, 2001). The mean scores shown for the different measures are all in the normal range of functioning.

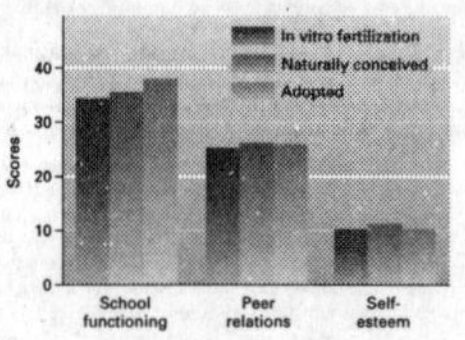

CARING FOR CHILDREN INTERLUDE

One Caring for Children interlude appears in each chapter. These interludes focus on applications for improving the lives of children.

Child Development–Yesterday and Today 15

and elected officials, the nation's economic strengths and weaknesses, and partisan politics all influence the policy agenda.

When concern about broad social issues is widespread, comprehensive social policies often result. Child labor laws were established in the early twentieth century to protect not only children but also jobs for adults; federal child-care funding during World War II was justified by the need for women laborers in factories; and Head Start and other War on Poverty programs in the 1960s were implemented to decrease intergenerational poverty.

Out of concern that policymakers are doing too little to protect the well-being of children, researchers increasingly are undertaking studies that they hope will lead to wise and effective decision making about social policy (Benson & others, 2006; Maccoby, 2001; Selman & Dray, 2006). When more than 17 percent of all children and almost half of all ethnic minority children are being raised in poverty, when between 40 and 50 percent of all children born today can expect to spend at least five years in a single-parent home, when children and young adolescents are giving birth, when the use and abuse of drugs are widespread, and when the specter of AIDS persists, our nation needs revised social policy (Mahoney, Larson, & Eccles, 2005; Pittman & others, 2003). To read more about improving the lives of children through social policies, see the Caring for Children interlude that follows.

If our American way of life fails the child, it fails us all.

–Pearl Buck
American Author, 20th Century

CARING FOR CHILDREN

Improving Family Policy

In the United States, the national government, state governments, and city governments all play a role in influencing the well-being of children (Linver & others, 2004). At the national and state levels, policymakers for decades have debated whether helping poor parents ends up helping their children as well. Researchers are providing some answers by examining the effects of specific policies.

For example, the Minnesota Family Investment Program (MFIP) was designed in the 1990s primarily to affect the behavior of adults—specifically, to move adults off the welfare rolls and into paid employment. A key element of the program was that it guaranteed that adults who participated in the program would receive more money if they worked than if they did not. When the adults' income rose, how did that affect their children? A study of the effects of MFIP found that increases in the incomes of working poor parents were linked with benefits for their children (Gennetian & Miller, 2002). The children's achievement in school improved, and their behavior problems decreased.

Developmental psychologists and other researchers have examined the effects of many other government policies, and they have offered many suggestions for improving those policies. One frequent criticism is that the family policies of the United States are overwhelmingly treatment oriented: only those families and individuals who already have problems are eligible. Few preventive programs are available. For example, families in which the children are on the verge of being placed in foster care are eligible, and often required, to receive counseling; families in which problems are brewing but are not yet full-blown usually cannot qualify for public services.

CAREERS IN CHILD DEVELOPMENT PROFILE

Every chapter has at least one Careers in Child Development profile featuring a person working in a child development field related to the chapter's content.

Careers in Child Development 23

College/University Professor Courses in child development are taught in many programs and schools in colleges and universities, including psychology, education, nursing, child and family studies, social work, and medicine. The work that college professors do includes teaching courses either at the undergraduate or graduate level (or both), conducting research in a specific area, advising students and/or directing their research, and serving on college or university committees. Some college instructors do not conduct research as part of their job but instead focus mainly on teaching. Research is most likely to be part of the job description at universities with master's and Ph.D. programs.

A Ph.D. or master's degree almost always is required to teach in some area of child development in a college or university. Obtaining a doctoral degree usually takes four to six years of graduate work. A master's degree requires approximately two years of graduate work. The training involves taking graduate courses, learning to conduct research, and attending and presenting papers at professional meetings. Many graduate students work as teaching or research assistants for professors in an apprenticeship relationship that helps them to become competent teachers and researchers.

If you are interested in becoming a college or university professor, you might want to make an appointment with your instructor in this class on child development to learn more about his or her profession and work. To read about the work of one college professor, see the Careers in Child Development insert.

Researcher Some individuals in the field of child development work in research positions. In most instances, they have either a master's or Ph.D. in some area of child development. The researchers might work at a university, in some cases in a university professor's research program, in government at such agencies as the National Institute of Mental Health, or in private industry. Individuals who have full-time research positions in child development generate innovative research ideas, plan studies, carry out the research by collecting data, analyze the data, and then interpret it. Then, they will usually attempt to publish the research in a scientific journal. A researcher often works in a collaborative manner with other researchers on a project and may present the research at scientific meetings. One researcher might spend much of his or her time in a laboratory while another researcher might work out in the field, such as in schools, hospitals, and so on.

CAREERS in CHILD DEVELOPMENT

Valerie Pang
Professor of Teacher Education

Valerie Pang is a professor of teacher education at San Diego State University and formerly an elementary school teacher. Like Dr. Pang, many professors of teacher education have a doctorate and have experience in teaching at the elementary or secondary school level.

Dr. Pang earned a doctorate at the University of Washington. She has received a Multicultural Educator Award from the National Association of Multicultural Education for her work on culture and equity. She also was given the Distinguished Scholar Award from the American Educational Research Association's Committee on the Role and Status of Minorities in Education.

Pang (2005) believes that competent teachers need to:

- Recognize the power and complexity of cultural influences on students.
- Be sensitive to whether their expectations for students are culturally biased.
- Evaluate whether they are doing a good job of seeing life from the perspective of students who come from different cultures.

Valerie Pang is a professor in the School of Teacher Education of San Diego State University and formerly an elementary school teacher. Valerie believes it is important for teachers to create a caring classroom that affirms all students.

KEY TERMS AND GLOSSARY

Key terms appear in boldface. Their definitions appear in the margin near where they are introduced.

issues in the study of children's development include nature and nurture, continuity and discontinuity, and early and later experience.

Nature and Nurture

The **nature-nurture issue** involves the debate about whether development is primarily influenced by nature or by nurture (Kagan & Fox, 2006; Kagan & Herschkowitz, 2005; Lippa, 2005). *Nature* refers to an organism's biological inheritance, *nurture* to its environmental experiences. Almost no one today argues that development can be explained by nature alone or by nurture alone. But some ("nature" proponents) claim that the most important influence on development is biological inheritance, and others ("nurture" proponents) claim that environmental experiences are the most important influence.

According to the nature proponents, just as a sunflower grows in an orderly way—unless it is defeated by an unfriendly environment—so does a person. The range of environments can be vast, but a genetic blueprint produces commonalities in growth and development. We walk before we talk, speak one word before two words, grow rapidly in infancy and less so in early childhood, and experience a rush of sexual hormones in puberty. Extreme environments—those that are psychologically barren or hostile—can stunt development, but nature proponents emphasize the influence of tendencies that are genetically wired into humans.

By contrast, other psychologists emphasize the importance of nurture, or environmental experiences, to development. Experiences run the gamut from the individual's biological environment (nutrition, medical care, drugs, and physical accidents) to the social environment (family, peers, schools, community, media, and culture). For example, a child's diet can affect how tall the child grows and even how effectively the child can think and solve problems. Despite their genetic wiring, a child born and raised in a poor village in Bangladesh and a child in the suburbs of Denver are likely to have different skills, different ways of thinking about the world, and different ways of relating to people.

FIGURE 1.7 Continuity and Discontinuity in Development. Is human development more like that of a seedling gradually growing into a giant oak or more like that of a caterpillar suddenly becoming a butterfly?

Continuity and Discontinuity

Think about your own development for a moment. Did you become the person you are gradually, like the seedling that slowly, cumulatively grows into a giant oak? Or did you experience sudden, distinct changes, like the caterpillar that changes into a butterfly (see figure 1.7)?

The **continuity-discontinuity issue** focuses on the extent to which development involves gradual, cumulative change (continuity) or distinct stages (discontinuity). For the most part, developmentalists who emphasize nurture usually describe development as a gradual, continuous process, like the seedling's growth into an oak. Those who emphasize nature often describe development as a series of distinct stages, like the change from caterpillar to butterfly.

Consider continuity first. As the oak grows from seedling to giant oak, it becomes more oak—its development is continuous. Similarly, a child's first word, though seemingly an abrupt, discontinuous event, is actually the result of weeks and months of growth and practice. Puberty, another seemingly abrupt, discontinuous occurrence, is actually a gradual process occurring over several years.

Viewed in terms of discontinuity, each person is described as passing through a sequence of stages in which change is qualitatively rather than quantitatively different. As the caterpillar changes to a butterfly, it is not more caterpillar, it is a different kind of organism—its development is discontinuous. Similarly (as discussed in chapters 2 and 7), at some point a child moves from not being able to think abstractly about the world to being able to do so. This is a qualitative, discontinuous change in development, not a quantitative, continuous change.

nature-nurture issue Nature refers to an organism's biological inheritance, nurture to environmental influences. The "nature" proponents claim biological inheritance is the most important influence on development; the "nurture" proponents claim that environmental experiences are the most important.

continuity-discontinuity issue The issue regarding the extent to which development involves gradual, cumulative change (continuity) or distinct stages (discontinuity).

CRITICAL THINKING AND CONTENT QUESTIONS IN PHOTOGRAPH CAPTIONS

Most photographs have a caption that ends with a critical thinking or knowledge question in italics to stimulate further thought about a topic.

What is the nature of the early and later experience issue?

Early and Later Experience

The **early-later experience** issue focuses on the degree to which early experiences (especially in infancy) or later experiences are the key determinants of the child's development. That is, if infants experience harmful circumstances, can those experiences be overcome by later, positive ones? Or are the early experiences so critical—possibly because they are the infant's first, prototypical experiences—that they cannot be overridden by a later, better environment? To those who emphasize early experiences, life is an unbroken trail on which a psychological quality can be traced back to its origin (Kagan, 1992, 2000). In contrast, to those who emphasize later experiences, development is like a river, continually ebbing and flowing.

The early-later experience issue has a long history and continues to be hotly debated among developmentalists (Caspi, 2006; Gottlieb, 2004; Gottlieb, Wahlsten, & Lickliter, 2006; Thompson, 2006). Plato was sure that infants who were rocked frequently become better athletes. Nineteenth-century New England ministers told parents in Sunday afternoon sermons that the way they handled their infants would determine their children's later character. Some developmentalists argue that, unless infants experience warm, nurturing care during the first year or so of life, their development will never quite be optimal (Carlson, Sroufe, & Egeland, 2004; Sroufe & others, 2005).

In contrast, later-experience advocates argue that children are malleable throughout development and that later sensitive caregiving is just as important as earlier sensitive caregiving. A number of life-span developmentalists (developmentalists who focus on the entire life span) stress that too little attention has been given to later experiences in development (Baltes, 2003). They accept that early experiences are important contributors to development, but no more important than later experiences. Jerome Kagan (2000) points out that even children who show the qualities of an inhibited temperament, which is linked to heredity, have the capacity to change their behavior. In his research, almost one-third of a group of children who had an inhibited temperament at 2 years of age were not unusually shy or fearful when they were 4 years of age (Kagan & Snidman, 1991).

People in Western cultures, especially those influenced by Freudian theory, have tended to support the idea that early experiences are more important than later experiences (Chan, 1963; Lamb & Sternberg, 1992). The majority of people in the world do not share this belief. For example, people in many Asian countries believe that experiences occurring after about 6 to 7 years of age are more important to development than are earlier experiences. This stance stems from the long-standing belief in Eastern cultures that children's reasoning skills begin to develop in important ways during middle childhood.

KEY TERMS AND GLOSSARY

Key terms are alphabetically listed, defined, and page-referenced in a glossary at the end of the book.

GLOSSARY

A

AB̄ error The Piagetian object-permanence concept in which an infant progressing into substage 4 makes frequent mistakes, selecting the familiar hiding place (A) rather than the new hiding place (B).

accommodation (culture) Occurs when children adjust their knowledge to fit new information and experience.

accommodation Piagetian concept of adjusting schemes to fit new information and experiences.

active (niche-picking) genotype-environment correlations Correlations that exist when children seek out environments they find compatible and stimulating.

adolescence The developmental period of transition from childhood to early adulthood, entered at approximately 10 to 12 years of age and ending at 18 to 22 years of age.

adolescent egocentrism The heightened self-consciousness of adolescents, which is reflected in adolescents' beliefs that others are as interested in them as they are in themselves, and in adolescents' sense of personal uniqueness and invincibility.

adoption study A study in which investigators seek to discover whether, in behavior and psychological characteristics, adopted children are more like their adoptive parents, who provided a home environment, or more like their biological parents, who contributed their heredity. Another form of the adoption study is to compare adoptive and biological siblings.

affordances Opportunities for interaction offered by objects that are necessary to perform activities.

altruism An unselfish interest in helping another person.

amnion The life-support system that is a bag or envelope that contains a clear fluid in which the developing embryo floats.

androgens The main class of male sex hormones.

androgyny The presence of masculine and feminine characteristics in the same person.

anger cry A cry similar to the basic cry but with more excess air forced through the vocal cords (associated with exasperation or rage).

animism A facet of preoperational thought, the belief that inanimate objects have "lifelike" qualities and are capable of action.

anorexia nervosa An eating disorder that involves the relentless pursuit of thinness through starvation.

Apgar Scale A widely used method to assess the health of newborns at one and five minutes after birth. The Apgar Scale evaluates infants' heart rate, respiratory effort, muscle tone, body color, and reflex irritability.

aphasia A loss or impairment of language ability caused by brain damage.

assimilation (Piaget) Occurs when children incorporate new information into their existing knowledge (schemes).

assimilation (culture) The absorption of ethnic minority groups into the dominant group, which often means the loss of some or virtually all of the behavior and values of the ethnic minority group.

associative play Play that involves social interaction with little or no organization.

attachment A close emotional bond between two people.

attention Concentrating and focusing mental resources.

attention deficit hyperactivity disorder (ADHD) A disability in which children consistently show one or more of the following characteristics: (1) inattention, (2) hyperactivity, and (3) impulsivity.

attributions Attributions are explanations people give for behavior; one way to classify these explanations is whether they are internal or external.

authoritarian parenting This is a restrictive, punitive style in which the parent exhorts the child to follow the parent's directions and to respect their work and effort. Firm limits and controls are placed on the child, and little verbal exchange is allowed. This style is associated with children's socially incompetent behavior.

authoritative parenting This style encourages children to be independent but still places limits and controls on their actions. Extensive verbal give-and-take is allowed, and parents are warm and nurturant toward the child. This style is associated with children's socially competent behavior.

automaticity The ability to process information with little or no effort.

autonomous morality The second stage of moral development in Piaget's theory, displayed by older children (about 10 years of age and older). The child becomes aware that rules and laws are created by people and that, in judging an action, one should consider the actor's intentions as well as the consequences.

average children Children who receive an average number of both positive and negative nominations from their peers.

B

basal metabolism rate (BMR) The minimum amount of energy an individual uses in a resting state.

basic cry A rhythmic pattern usually consisting of a cry, a briefer silence, a shorter inspiratory whistle that is higher pitched than the main cry, and then a brief rest before the next cry.

basic-skills-and-phonics approach An approach that emphasizes that reading instruction should teach phonics and its basic rules for translating written symbols into sounds.

Bayley Scales of Infant Development Developed by Nancy Bayley, these scales are widely used in assessing infant development. The current version has three parts: a Mental Scale, a Motor Scale, and the Infant Behavior Profile.

KEY TERMS AND GLOSSARY

Key terms also are listed with page references at the end of each chapter.

KEY TERMS

QUOTATIONS

These appear at the beginning of each chapter and occasionally in the margins to stimulate further thought about a topic.

Ah! What would the world be to us
If the children were no more?
We should dread the desert behind us
Worse than the dark before.

—Henry Wadsworth Longfellow
American Poet, 19th Century

labor laws. We handle their crimes in a special system of juvenile justice. We also have provisions for helping children when families fail. In short, we now value childhood as a special time of growth and change, and we invest great resources in caring for and educating children.

The Modern Study of Child Development

The modern era of studying children began with some important developments in the late 1800s (Cairns, 1983, 1998, 2006). Since then the study of child development has evolved into a sophisticated science with major theories as well as elegant techniques and methods of study that help organize our thinking about children's development (Lerner, 2002, 2006; Thomas, 2005). This new era began during the last quarter of the nineteenth century when a major shift took place—from a strictly philosophical approach to human psychology to an approach that includes systematic observation and experimentation.

KEY PEOPLE

The most important theorists and researchers discussed in the chapter are listed and page-referenced at the end of the chapter.

KEY TERMS

development 7
original sin view 7
tabula rasa view 7
innate goodness view 7
genetic epistemology 9
culture 12
ethnicity 12
ethnic identity 12
socioeconomic status (SES) 13
gender 13
social policy 14
biological processes 16
cognitive processes 16
socioemotional processes 17
prenatal period 17
infancy 17
early childhood 17
middle and late childhood 17
adolescence 17
nature-nurture issue 19
continuity-discontinuity issue 19
early-later experience issue 20

KEY PEOPLE

Philippe Ariès 7
John Locke 7
Jean-Jacques Rousseau 7
G. Stanley Hall 8
Arnold Gesell 8
Charles Darwin 8
Sigmund Freud 9
John Watson 9
James Mark Baldwin 9
Jean Piaget 9
Jeanne Brooks-Gunn 15
Jerome Kagan 20

WEB LINKS

Web icons appear a number of times in each chapter. They direct you to the book's website, where you will find connecting links that provide additional information on the topic discussed in the text. The labels under the Web icon appear as Web links on the text's Online Learning Center under the heading *More Resources* for each chapter (www.mhhe.com/santrockcd11).

www.mhhe.com/santrockcd11

Family and Consumer Science Education
Educational Psychology
School Psychology

degree. The training involves taking a wide range of courses with a major or concentration in education as well as completing a supervised practice-teaching internship.

Exceptional Children (Special Education) Teacher A teacher of exceptional children spends concentrated time with individual children who have a disability or are gifted. Among the children a teacher of exceptional children might work with are children with learning disabilities, ADHD (attention deficit hyperactivity disorder), mental retardation, or a physical disability such as cerebral palsy. Some of this work will usually be done outside of the student's regular classroom, some of it will be carried out when the student is in the regular classroom. The exceptional children teacher works closely with the student's regular classroom teacher and parents to create the best educational program for the student.

E-LEARNING TOOLS

Taking It to the Net, which appears at the end of each chapter, asks questions that you can answer by exploring the Internet. By going to the text's Online Learning Center and looking in the *Quizzes* section for a given chapter for Taking It to the Net exercises, you will be able to connect to other websites, where you can find information that will help you think more deeply about the question posed.

E-Learning Tools 33

E-LEARNING TOOLS

To help you master the material in this chapter, visit the Online Learning Center for *Child Development*, eleventh edition (**www.mhhe.com/santrockcd11**), where you'll find these additional resources:

Taking It to the Net

1. George is teaching fourth grade. He wants his students to learn about the difficulties and challenges of being a child in colonial America. What was life like for children in the early history of our country?
2. Janice thinks that better and stricter gun control laws will help decrease violent crime among children. Her husband, Elliott, disagrees. Janice found a March, 2000, Department of Justice study that provides support for her argument. What facts in the report can she point to in order to convince Elliott?
3. For his political science class, Darren has to track federal funding appropriations in the most recent Congress for any issue of his choice. He has chosen children's issues. What happened with funding for the No Child Left Behind Act in congressional appropriations in the first half of the 109th Congress?

Nursing, Parenting, and Teaching Exercises

Build your decision-making skills by trying your hand at the scenarios on the Online Learning Center.

Video Clips

The Online Learning Center includes the following videos for this chapter:

- Career in Child Development
  Dr. Lerner gives a humorous account of a decision to major in psychology in college.
- Career in Developmental Psychology
  Dr. Weinraub, one of the leading researchers on the NICHD Early Childcare Study, describes how she became interested in developmental psychology.

VIDEO CLIPS

At the end of each chapter, you will find a list of short video clips that illustrate key topics from the chapter. These video clips are available on the Online Learning Center.

NURSING, PARENTING, AND TEACHING EXERCISES

At the end of each chapter, you are directed to the text's Online Learning Center, where nursing, parenting, and teaching exercises will give you an opportunity to practice your decision-making skills.

Section 1

THE NATURE OF CHILD DEVELOPMENT

In every child who is born, under no matter what circumstances, and of no matter what parents, the potentiality of the human race is born again.

—James Agee
American Writer, 20th Century

Examining the shape of childhood allows us to understand it better. Every childhood is distinct, the first chapter of a new biography in the world. This book is about children's development, its universal features, its individual variations, its nature at the beginning of the twenty-first century. *Child Development* is about the rhythm and meaning of children's lives, about turning mystery into understanding, and about weaving together a portrait of who each of us was, is, and will be. In Section 1, you will read two chapters: "Introduction" (chapter 1) and "The Science of Child Development" (chapter 2).

Chapter 1 INTRODUCTION

We reach backward to our parents and forward to our children and through their children to a future we will never see, but about which we need to care.

—Carl Jung
Swiss Psychoanalyst, 20th Century

CHAPTER OUTLINE

CHILD DEVELOPMENT—YESTERDAY AND TODAY

Historical Views of Childhood
The Modern Study of Child Development
Improving the Lives of Today's Children
Resilience, Social Policy, and Children's Development

DEVELOPMENTAL PROCESSES AND PERIODS

Biological, Cognitive, and Socioemotional Processes
Periods of Development

DEVELOPMENTAL ISSUES

Nature and Nurture
Continuity and Discontinuity
Early and Later Experience
Evaluating the Developmental Issues

CAREERS IN CHILD DEVELOPMENT

Education and Research
Clinical and Counseling
Medical, Nursing, and Physical Development
Families and Relationships

LEARNING GOALS

1. **Discuss the past and the present in the field of child development**
2. **Identify the most important developmental processes and periods**
3. **Describe three key developmental issues**
4. **Summarize the career paths that involve working with children**

The Stories of Jeffrey Dahmer and Alice Walker

Jeffrey Dahmer. *What are some possible causes of the brutal acts of violence that he committed?*

Alice Walker. *What might be some reasons that she overcame trauma in her childhood to develop in positive ways?*

Jeffrey Dahmer had a troubled childhood. His parents constantly bickered before they divorced, his mother had emotional problems and doted on his younger brother, and he felt that his father neglected him. When he was 8 years old, Jeffrey was sexually abused by an older boy. But most individuals who suffer through such childhood pains never go on to commit Dahmer's grisly crimes.

In 1991, a man in handcuffs dashed out of Dahmer's bizarrely cluttered apartment in a tough Milwaukee neighborhood, called the police, and stammered that Dahmer had tried to kill him. At least 17 other victims did not get away.

Alice Walker was born in 1944. She was the eighth child of Georgia sharecroppers who earned $300 a year. When Walker was 8, her brother accidentally shot her in the left eye with a BB gun. By the time her parents got her to the hospital a week later (they had no car), she was blind in that eye and it had developed a disfiguring layer of scar tissue.

Despite the counts against her, Alice Walker went on to become an essayist, a poet, and an award-winning novelist. She won the Pulitzer Prize for her book *The Color Purple*. Like her characters, especially the women, Alice Walker overcame pain and anger to celebrate the human spirit. Walker writes about people who "make it, who come out of nothing. People who triumph."

What leads one child to grow up and commit brutal acts of violence and another to turn poverty and trauma into a rich literary harvest? How can we explain how one child picks up the pieces of a life shattered by tragedy, while another becomes unhinged by life's stress? Why is it that some children are whirlwinds—full of energy, successful in school, and able to get along well with their peers—while others stay on the sidelines, mere spectators of life? If you ever have wondered about why children turn out the way they do, you have asked yourself the central questions we will explore in this book.

Why study children? Perhaps you are or will be a parent or teacher, and responsibility for children is or will be a part of your everyday life. The more you learn about children, the better you can guide them. Perhaps you hope to gain an understanding of your own history—as an infant, as a child, and as an adolescent. Perhaps you accidentally came across the course description and found it intriguing. Whatever your reasons, you will discover that the study of child development is provocative, intriguing, and informative.

PREVIEW

This chapter previews the themes and issues that we will explore throughout our study of children's development. First, we will familiarize ourselves with how children were thought of and studied in the past and how they are perceived and studied today. Then we will examine the processes and periods that characterize children's development. Next, we will study the primary issues that developmentalists debate, issues that will come up repeatedly in the text. Finally, we describe some of the many careers related to child development.

1 CHILD DEVELOPMENT–YESTERDAY AND TODAY

- Historical Views of Childhood
- The Modern Study of Child Development
- Improving the Lives of Today's Children
- Resilience, Social Policy, and Children's Development

What do we mean when we speak of an individual's development? **Development** is the pattern of change that begins at conception and continues through the life span. Most development involves growth, although it also includes decay. Anywhere you turn today, the development of children captures public attention. Historically, though, interest in the development of children has been uneven.

Historical Views of Childhood

Childhood has become such a distinct period that it is hard to imagine that it was not always thought of as markedly different from adulthood. However, in medieval Europe, laws generally did not distinguish between child and adult offenses. After analyzing samples of art along with available publications, historian Philippe Ariès (1962) concluded that European societies prior to 1600 did not give any special status to children (see figure 1.1).

Were children actually treated as miniature adults with no special status in medieval Europe? Ariès primarily sampled aristocratic, idealized subjects, which might have been misleading. Childhood probably was recognized as a distinct phase of life more than Ariès believed, but his analysis helped to highlight cultural differences in how children are viewed and treated.

Throughout history, philosophers have speculated at length about the nature of children and how they should be reared. The ancient Egyptians, Greeks, and Romans held rich conceptions of children's development. More recently in European history, three influential philosophical views portrayed children in terms of original sin, tabula rasa, and innate goodness:

- In the **original sin view,** especially advocated during the Middle Ages, children were perceived as being born into the world as evil beings. The goal of child rearing was to provide salvation, to remove sin from the child's life.
- Toward the end of the seventeenth century, the **tabula rasa view** was proposed by English philosopher John Locke. He argued that children are not innately bad but, instead, are like a "blank tablet." Locke believed that childhood experiences are important in determining adult characteristics. He advised parents to spend time with their children and to help them become contributing members of society.
- In the eighteenth century, the **innate goodness view** was presented by Swiss-born French philosopher Jean-Jacques Rousseau. He stressed that children are inherently good. Because children are basically good, said Rousseau, they should be permitted to grow naturally, with little parental monitoring or constraint.

Today, the Western view of children holds that childhood is a highly eventful and unique period of life that lays an important foundation for the adult years and is markedly different from them. Most current approaches to childhood identify distinct periods in which children master specific skills and tasks that prepare them for adulthood. Childhood is no longer seen as an inconvenient waiting period during which adults must suffer the incompetencies of the young. Instead, we protect children from the stresses and responsibilities of adult work through strict child

FIGURE 1.1 Historical Perception of Children. European paintings centuries ago often depicted children as miniature adults. *Do these artistic creations indicate that earlier Europeans did not view childhood as a distinct period?*

development The pattern of change that begins at conception and continues through the life span.

original sin view Advocated during the Middle Ages, the belief that children were born into the world as evil beings and were basically bad.

tabula rasa view The idea, proposed by John Locke, that children are like a "blank tablet."

innate goodness view The idea, presented by Swiss-born philosopher Jean-Jacques Rousseau, that children are inherently good.

Ah! What would the world be to us
If the children were no more?
We should dread the desert behind us
Worse than the dark before.

—Henry Wadsworth Longfellow
American Poet, 19th Century

labor laws. We handle their crimes in a special system of juvenile justice. We also have provisions for helping children when families fail. In short, we now value childhood as a special time of growth and change, and we invest great resources in caring for and educating children.

The Modern Study of Child Development

The modern era of studying children began with some important developments in the late 1800s (Cairns, 1983, 1998, 2006). Since then the study of child development has evolved into a sophisticated science with major theories as well as elegant techniques and methods of study that help organize our thinking about children's development (Lerner, 2002, 2006; Thomas, 2005). This new era began during the last quarter of the nineteenth century when a major shift took place—from a strictly philosophical approach to human psychology to an approach that includes systematic observation and experimentation.

www.mhhe.com/santrockcd11
History of Childhood

Methods for a New Science Most of the influential early psychologists were trained either in the natural sciences such as biology or medicine or in philosophy. The natural scientists valued experiments and reliable observations; after all, experiments and systematic observation had advanced knowledge in physics, chemistry, and biology. But these scientists were not at all sure that people, much less children or infants, could be studied in this way. Their hesitation was due, in part, to a lack of examples to follow in studying children. In addition, philosophers of the time debated, on both intellectual and ethical grounds, whether the methods of science were appropriate for studying people.

The deadlock was broken when some daring thinkers began to try new methods of studying infants, children, and adolescents. For example, near the turn of the century, French psychologist Alfred Binet invented many tasks to study attention and memory. He used them to study his own daughters, other normal children, children with mental retardation, extremely gifted children, and adults. Eventually, he collaborated in the development of the first modern test of intelligence (the Binet test). At about the same time, G. Stanley Hall pioneered the use of questionnaires with large groups of children. In one investigation, Hall tested 400 children in the Boston schools to find out how much they "knew" about themselves and the world, asking them such questions as "Where are your ribs?"

Later, during the 1920s, many child development research centers were created, and their professional staffs began to observe and chart a myriad of behaviors in infants and children. Research centers at the Universities of Minnesota, Iowa, California at Berkeley, Columbia, and Toronto became famous for their investigations of children's play, friendship patterns, fears, aggression and conflict, and sociability. This work became closely associated with the so-called child study movement, and a new organization, the Society for Research in Child Development, was formed at about the same time.

FIGURE 1.2 Gesell's Photographic Dome. Cameras rode on metal tracks at the top of the dome and were moved as needed to record the child's activities. Others could observe from outside the dome without being seen by the child.

Another ardent observer of children was Arnold Gesell. With his photographic dome (shown in figure 1.2), Gesell (1928) could systematically observe children's behavior without interrupting them. He strove for precision in charting what a child is like at specific ages.

The direct study of children, in which investigators directly observe children's behavior, conduct experiments, and obtain information about children by questioning their parents and teachers, had an auspicious start in the work of these child study experts. The flow of information about children, based on direct study, has not slowed since that time.

Theories for a New Science Gesell not only developed sophisticated strategies for studying children, but also had provocative views on children's development. His views were strongly influenced by Charles Darwin's evolutionary theory.

(Darwin had made the scientific study of children respectable when he developed a baby journal for recording systematic observations of children.) Gesell argued that certain characteristics of children simply "bloom" with age because of a biological, maturational blueprint.

Evolutionary theory also influenced G. Stanley Hall. Hall (1904) argued that child development follows a natural evolutionary course that can be revealed by child study. He theorized that child development unfolds in stages, with distinct motives and capabilities at each stage.

Stages are also a feature of Sigmund Freud's portrait of child development. According to Freud's psychoanalytic theory, children are rarely aware of the motives and reasons for their behavior and the bulk of their mental life is unconscious. Freud's ideas were compatible with Hall's, emphasizing conflict and biological influences on development, although Freud stressed that a child's experiences with parents in the first five years of life are important determinants of later personality development. Freud envisioned the child moving through a series of stages, filled with conflict between biological urges and societal demands. Since the early part of the twentieth century, Freud's theory has had a profound influence on the study of children's personality development and socialization.

A competing view that gained prominence during the 1920s and 1930s was John Watson's (1928) theory of behaviorism. Watson argued that children can be shaped into whatever society wishes by examining and changing the environment. He believed strongly in the systematic observation of children's behavior under controlled conditions. Watson had some provocative views about child rearing as well. He claimed that parents are too soft on children. Quit cuddling and smiling at babies so much, he told parents.

Whereas Watson was observing the environment's influence on children's behavior and Freud was probing the depths of the unconscious mind to discover clues about our early experiences with our parents, others were more concerned about the development of children's conscious thoughts—that is, the thoughts of which they are aware. James Mark Baldwin was a pioneer in the study of children's thought (Cairns, 1998, 2006). He gave the term **genetic epistemology** to the study of how children's knowledge changes over the course of their development. (The term *genetic* at that time was a synonym for "developmental," and the term *epistemology* means "the nature or study of knowledge.")

Baldwin's ideas initially were proposed in the 1880s. Later, in the twentieth century, Swiss psychologist Jean Piaget adopted and elaborated on many of Baldwin's themes, keenly observing the development of his own children and devising clever experiments to investigate how children think. Piaget became a giant in developmental psychology. Some of you, perhaps, are already familiar with his view that children pass through a series of cognitive, or thought, stages from infancy through adolescence. According to Piaget, children think in a qualitatively different manner than adults do.

This introduction to several theories of children's development has been brief, designed to give you a glimpse of some of the different ways children have been viewed as the study of child development unfolded. (You will read more about theoretical perspectives in chapter 2 and in later chapters.) These theories helped push forward the scientific study of child development. New knowledge about children—based on direct observation and testing—is accumulating at a breathtaking pace.

Improving the Lives of Today's Children

Consider some of the topics you read about every day in newspapers, magazines, and on the Internet: health and well-being, families and parenting, education, culture and ethnicity, and gender. What child development researchers are discovering about each of these topics has direct and significant consequences for understanding children and for improving their lives, an important theme of this book (Bornstein, 2006; Ramey, Ramey, & Lanzi, 2006; Renninger & Sigel, 2006).

Children are the legacy we leave for the time we will not live to see.

—Aristotle
Greek Philosopher, 4th Century B.C.

www.mhhe.com/santrockcd11

Children's Issues
Prevention Programs

genetic epistemology The study of how children's knowledge changes over the course of their development.

CAREERS in CHILD DEVELOPMENT

Luis Vargas
Clinical Child Psychologist

Luis Vargas is Director of the Clinical Child Psychology Internship Program and a professor in child and adolescent psychiatry at the University of New Mexico School of Medicine. Luis obtained an undergraduate degree in psychology from Trinity University in Texas and a Ph.D. in clinical psychology at the University of Nebraska–Lincoln.

Luis' work includes assessing and treating children, adolescents, and their families, especially when a child or adolescent has a serious mental disorder. Luis also trains mental health professionals to provide culturally responsive and developmentally appropriate mental health services. In addition, he is interested in cultural and assessment issues with children, adolescents, and their families.

Luis' clinical work is heavily influenced by contextual and ecological theories of development (which we will discuss in chapter 2, "The Science of Child Development"). His first undergraduate course in human development, and subsequent courses in development, contributed to his decision to pursue a career in clinical child psychology.

At the end of this chapter you can read about many careers in child development, including more about the field of child clinical psychology. Also, at appropriate places throughout the book we will provide profiles of individuals in various child development careers.

Luis Vargas (*left*) conducting a child therapy session.

Health and Well-Being Around the world the health and well-being of children are jeopardized by many factors, including poverty, AIDS, starvation, poor health care, inadequate nutrition and exercise, alcohol and drug abuse, and sexual abuse. Asian physicians around 2600 B.C. and Greek physicians around 500 B.C. recognized that good habits are essential for good health. At the beginning of the twenty-first century, once again we recognize the power of lifestyles and psychological states in promoting health and well-being (Hales, 2006; Payne, Hahn, & Mauer, 2005; Robbins, Powers, & Burgess, 2005). We are returning to the ancient view that the ultimate responsibility for our health and well-being, both ours and our children's, rests in our hands. Parents, teachers, nurses, physicians, and other adults can serve as models of healthy habits for children, communicate strategies for health and well-being to children, and monitor whether children follow these strategies (Crane & Marshall, 2005; DuBois & Karcher, 2005; Hoeger, 2006).

Developmental psychologists contribute to the health and well-being of children through direct work with children as well as through research. For example, Luis Vargas is a child clinical psychologist who helps children get their lives back on track. (You can read about Luis Vargas and his work in the Careers in Child Development insert.) Tiffany Field is a researcher who has explored the effects of massage therapy on the health and well-being of premature infants. Field and her colleagues (2001, 2003; Field & others, 2004) have found that massage therapy can facilitate weight gain in premature infants. Massaged infants also show improved social and motor skills. We will further discuss Field's massage therapy in chapter 4, "Prenatal Development and Birth."

Families and Parenting Parents want their children to grow into healthy, happy, socially mature individuals, but they often are not sure how to help their children reach this goal. One reason for parents' frustration is that they receive conflicting messages about how to deal with their children. One "expert" urges them to be more permissive with their children. Another warns that their children will become spoiled brats unless they control and discipline them.

Understanding how children develop can help you become a better parent (Cowan & others, 2005; Lamb & Lewis, 2005; Parke & Buriel, 2006; Powell, 2005, 2006). Many parents learn parenting practices from their parents. Unfortunately, when parenting practices are passed from one generation to the next, both desirable and undesirable ones are usually perpetuated. This book and your instructor's lectures in this course can help you become much more knowledgeable about children's development and sort through which practices in your own upbringing you should continue with your own children and which you should abandon.

Good parenting takes time. It means committing yourself day after day, week after week, month after month, and year after year to providing your children with a warm, supportive, safe, and stimulating environment that will make them feel secure and allow them to reach their full potential. But contemporary families face many pressures that add to the difficulties of devoting time and effort to parenting (Garbarino, Bradshaw, & Kostelny, 2005; Harvey & Fine, 2004; Luster & Okagaki, 2005). Researchers have documented that the number of U.S. families in which both parents work has increased (Crouter & Booth, 2004; Crouter & McHale, 2005). With more children being raised by two working parents, the time parents have to spend with their children is being squeezed and the quality of child care is of concern to many (Lamb & Ahnert, 2006; Lowe, Weisner, & Geis, 2005; Randolph & Kochanoff, 2004; Zaslow, 2004).

Are working parents more effectively using the decreased time with their children? Do child-care arrangements provide high-quality alternatives for parents? How concerned should we be about the increasing number of *latchkey children*—those at home alone after school? Answering these questions requires several different kinds of information obtained by research in child development. For example, information comes from studies of how working parents use time with their children, studies of how various child-care arrangements influence children, and examination of the consequences of a child being without adult supervision for hours every day after school (Lamb & Ahnert, 2006).

One issue examined by researchers focuses on links between how children are treated by their parents and how they relate to their peers (Ladd & Pettit, 2002; Parke & others, 2004; Collins & Steinberg, 2006; Robin, Bukowski, & Parker, 2006). In one study of maltreated children (children who have been abused) and nonmaltreated children, the maltreated children were more likely to be repeatedly rejected by peers (Bolger & Patterson, 2001). The main reason for the rejection was the aggressive behavior by the children who had been abused by their parents. Why do you think abuse by parents is linked to increased aggression toward their peers by the children? We will have more to say about maltreated children in chapter 15, "Families."

Education Like parenting, education is an extremely important dimension of children's lives (Morrison, 2006; Santrock, 2006a). There is widespread agreement that something needs to be done to improve the education of our nation's children (Pressley & Hilden, 2006; Silberman, 2006; Wiles, 2005). What can we do to make schools more productive and enjoyable contexts for children's development? Should we make the school days longer or shorter? Should teachers have higher expectations for students and tougher standards? Should we emphasize memorization more or less? Should schools focus only on developing the children's knowledge and cognitive skills, or should they pay more attention to their socioemotional and physical development? Can mentors help children who are doing poorly in school?

These are just a few of the questions being asked about U.S. schools. You might look back at your own education and think of ways your schools could have been better. For systematic evaluations of specific proposals for improving education, however, you can look to researchers in child development.

For example, can mentoring programs improve the achievement of children and adolescents who are at risk for failure? Mentoring involves a more experienced, usually older individual acting as a guide, role model, or teacher to help someone who is less experienced become more competent (Hamilton & Hamilton, 2004). One study examined 959 adolescents who had applied to the Big Brothers/Big Sisters program (Rhodes, Grossman, & Resch, 2000). Half of the adolescents were mentored through extensive discussions about school, careers, and life, as well as participation in leisure activities with other adolescents. The other half were not mentored. Those who were mentored had fewer unexcused absences from school, improved their performance in class, and had better relationships with parents. In

ERIC Database
Education Resources
Diversity
Trends in the Well-Being of Children and Youth
Children Now
Children and Advocacy

Shown here are two Korean-born children on the day they became U.S. citizens. Asian American children are the fastest-growing group of ethnic minority children.

culture The behavior patterns, beliefs, and all other products of a group that are passed on from generation to generation.

ethnicity A characteristic based on cultural heritage, nationality characteristics, race, religion, and language.

ethnic identity A sense of membership in an ethnic group, based on shared language, religion, customs, values, history, and race.

sum, mentoring may be an important avenue for improving the education of many children.

Sociocultural Contexts: Culture, Ethnicity, and Socioeconomic Status Schools and families are just two of the important contexts of development. A *context* is a setting, and every child's development occurs in numerous contexts—including homes, schools, peer groups, churches, neighborhoods, communities, cities, and countries. Each of these settings is influenced by historical, social, and economic factors (Matsumoto, 2004; Secada, 2005). Each may reflect the influence of culture, ethnicity, and socioeconomic status. These three concepts are central to our discussion of children's development.

Culture encompasses the behavior patterns, beliefs, and all other products of a particular group of people that are passed on from generation to generation. The products result from the interaction between groups of people and their environment over many years. A cultural group can be as large as the United States or as small as an isolated Italian village. Whatever its size, the group's culture influences the identity, learning, and social behavior of its members (Cole, 2005, 2006; Shweder & others, 2006).

Ethnicity refers to characteristics that are rooted in cultural heritage, including nationality, race, religion, and language. (The word *ethnic* comes from the Greek word for "nation.") Ethnicity is central to the development of an **ethnic identity,** which is a sense of membership in an ethnic group, based on shared language, religion, customs, values, history, and race. You are a member of one or more ethnic groups. Your ethnic identity reflects your deliberate decision to identify with an ancestor or ancestral group (Phinney, 2003; Umana-Taylor & Fine, 2004). If you are of Irish and African ancestry, you might choose to align yourself with the traditions of African Americans even though (if you look White and have an Irish surname) people might think that your identity is Irish American.

Race and ethnicity are sometimes confused. *Race* is a controversial classification of people according to real or imagined biological characteristics such as skin color and blood group (Corsini, 1999). An individual's ethnicity can include his or her race but also many other characteristics (Chun, Organista, & Marin, 2003). Thus, an individual might be White (a racial category) and a fifth-generation Texan who is Catholic and speaks English and Spanish fluently.

The tapestry of American culture has changed dramatically in recent years as the ethnic diversity of America's citizens has increased. Non-White ethnic groups (African American, Latino, Native American, and Asian American, for example) made up only a fifth of all children and adolescents under the age of 17 in 1989 but one-third of all school-age children at the beginning of the twenty-first century. This changing demography promises to bring to us both a richer culture and many challenges in extending the American dream to individuals of all ethnic groups (Cooper & others, 2005; Diaz, Pelletier, & Provenzo, 2006; Garcia Coll, Szalacha, & Palacios, 2005; McLoyd, 2005).

Of course, each ethnic group is also diverse (Banks, 2006; Pang, 2005). Not all English American children come from middle- and upper-income families; not all Latino children are members of the Catholic Church; not all Asian American children are academically gifted; and so on. As we describe children from ethnic groups, keep in mind that each group is heterogeneous.

Historically, however, immigrant and non-White ethnic groups have shared at least one feature: they found themselves at the bottom of the economic and social order. They have been disproportionately represented among the poor and the inadequately educated (Leyendecker & others, 2005). Half of all African American children and one-third of all Latino children live in poverty. School dropout rates for minority youth reach the alarming rate of 60 percent in some urban areas. In other words, members of ethnic minorities tend to have a low socioeconomic status.

Socioeconomic status (SES) refers to the grouping of people with similar occupational, educational, and economic characteristics. Socioeconomic status implies certain inequalities. Generally, members of a society have (1) occupations that vary in prestige, and some individuals have more access than others to higher-status occupations; (2) different levels of educational attainment, and some individuals have more access than others to better education; (3) different economic resources; and (4) different degrees of power to influence a community's institutions. These differences in the ability to control resources and to participate in society's rewards produce unequal opportunities for children.

The fact that a disproportionate number of minority individuals are at the bottom of the socioeconomic ladder produces an imperative for social institutions (Banks, 2006; Cushner, 2006; Diaz, Pelletier, & Provenzo, 2006; Sheets, 2005). Schools, social services, health and mental health agencies, and other programs need to provide improved services to ethnic minorities (Koppelman, 2005). There is a special concern about children who grow up in poverty (Bernstein, 2004; Blumenfeld & others, 2005; Weiss & others, 2005). How does poverty influence a child's development?

In a review of research, Jeanne Brooks-Gunn and her colleagues (2003) concluded that poverty in the first few years of life is a better predictor of school completion and achievement at 18 than poverty in the adolescent years. However, she also found that early intervention for two or three years doesn't permanently reduce socioeconomic disparities in children's achievement, because poor children are likely to continue facing obstacles to success. They continue to go to inadequate schools and to live in neighborhoods plagued by violence with no safe places to play. Thus, intervention may be needed into the elementary school years and even adolescent years to improve the lives of children living in poverty.

Some of the detrimental effects of poverty on children's development occur because of poverty's effects on children's home life. Because so many members of ethnic minority groups are poor, however, distinguishing the effects of poverty and those of ethnicity can be difficult. For example, suppose researchers find that the homes of children whose development is lagging have few toys or books and little conversation between children and parents. Are those characteristics tied to the culture of particular ethnic groups or to poverty or to neither?

One study examined the home environments of three ethnic groups: European American, African American, and Latino (Bradley & others, 2001). At five points in children's lives from infancy through early adolescence researchers assessed their home environments through observations and interviews with the mothers. There were some ethnic differences, but the most consistent results involved poverty, which was a more powerful indicator of the type of home environment children experienced than ethnicity was (see figure 1.3).

Gender Few aspects of our development are more central to our identity and social relationships than gender (Hyde, 2004; Lippa, 2005; Poelmans, 2005; Ruble, Martin, & Berenbaum, 2006). **Gender** involves the psychological and sociocultural dimensions of being female or male. (*Sex* refers to the biological dimension of being female or male.) Our society's attitudes about gender are changing, but how much?

One cross-cultural study of more than 2,000 second- to sixth-graders from a number of European countries, Russia, Japan, and the United States found that girls consistently earned higher grades in school than boys (Stetsenko & others, 2000). However, even though they were aware that they made better grades than boys, the girls did not report stronger beliefs in their own ability. Why might girls have less confidence in their academic ability than their performance warrants? The answer might be that despite some changes in attitudes, the stereotype that boys are smarter than girls still reigns in many societies, including our own. In chapter 13 (on gender), we will examine current stereotypes about gender.

socioeconomic status (SES) Refers to the grouping of people with similar occupational, educational, and economic characteristics.

gender The psychological and sociocultural dimensions of being male or female.

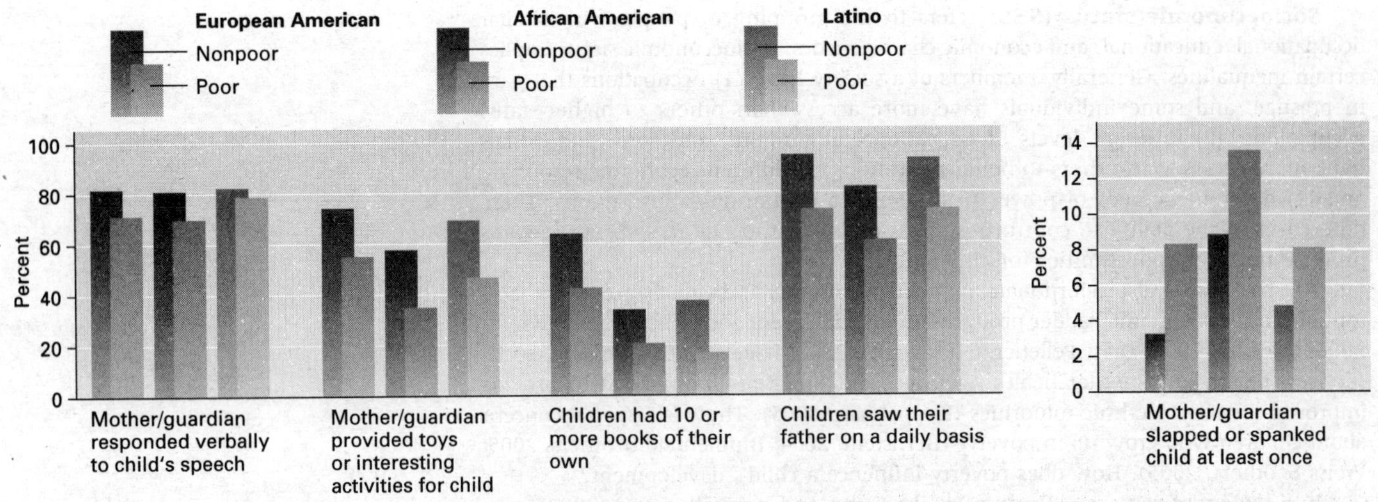

FIGURE 1.3 Home Environments of Infants by Ethnicity and Poverty Status. The above data are based on home observations and maternal interviews obtained in the first three years of children's lives. Although there were some differences across ethnic groups, the most consistent differences were found between families classified as poor and nonpoor. For example, regardless of their ethnic group, children growing up in nonpoor home environments were more likely to have their speech responded to, be provided with toys or interesting activities, have 10 or more books of their own, see their father on a daily basis, and be less likely to be slapped or spanked. Similar findings occurred when children were older.

Source	Characteristic
Individual	Good intellectual functioning Appealing, sociable, easygoing disposition Self-confidence, high self-esteem Talents Faith
Family	Close relationship to caring parent figure Authoritative parenting: warmth, structure, high expectations Socioeconomic advantages Connections to extended supportive family networks
Extrafamilial Context	Bonds to caring adults outside the family Connections to positive organizations Attending effective schools

FIGURE 1.4 Characteristics of Resilient Children and Their Contexts

Resilience, Social Policy, and Children's Development

Some children develop confidence in their abilities despite negative stereotypes about their gender or their ethnic group. And some children (like Alice Walker, discussed in the opening of this chapter) triumph over poverty or other adversities. They show *resilience.*

Are there certain characteristics that make children resilient? After analyzing research on this topic, Ann Masten and her colleagues (Masten, 2001, 2004; Masten & Coatsworth, 1998; Roisman & others, 2004) concluded that resilient children and adolescents do tend to share a number of individual factors, such as good intellectual functioning. In addition, as figure 1.4 shows, their families and extrafamilial contexts tend to show certain features. For example, resilient children are likely to have a close relationship to a caring parent figure and bonds to caring adults outside the family.

Thus factors outside the individual child may act as buffers to adversity, helping the child to show resilience. Norman Garmezy (1993) described a setting in a Harlem neighborhood of New York City that demonstrated the adult competence and concern for children that might bolster resilience. In the entranceway of a walk-up apartment building, there is a large frame on a wall. It displays the photographs of children. With the photographs is a written request that if anyone sees any of the children endangered on the street, they bring them back to the apartment house.

Should governments also take action to improve the contexts of children's development and aid their resilence? **Social policy** is a government's course of action designed to promote the welfare of its citizens. The shape and scope of social policy related to children are tied to the political system. The values held by citizens

social policy A government's course of action designed to promote the welfare of its citizens.

and elected officials, the nation's economic strengths and weaknesses, and partisan politics all influence the policy agenda.

When concern about broad social issues is widespread, comprehensive social policies often result. Child labor laws were established in the early twentieth century to protect not only children but also jobs for adults; federal child-care funding during World War II was justified by the need for women laborers in factories; and Head Start and other War on Poverty programs in the 1960s were implemented to decrease intergenerational poverty.

Out of concern that policymakers are doing too little to protect the well-being of children, researchers increasingly are undertaking studies that they hope will lead to wise and effective decision making about social policy (Benson & others, 2006; Maccoby, 2001; Selman & Dray, 2006). When more than 17 percent of all children and almost half of all ethnic minority children are being raised in poverty, when between 40 and 50 percent of all children born today can expect to spend at least five years in a single-parent home, when children and young adolescents are giving birth, when the use and abuse of drugs are widespread, and when the specter of AIDS persists, our nation needs revised social policy (Mahoney, Larson, & Eccles, 2005; Pittman & others, 2003). To read more about improving the lives of children through social policies, see the Caring for Children interlude that follows.

If our American way of life fails the child, it fails us all.

—Pearl Buck
American Author, 20th Century

Caring for Children

Improving Family Policy

In the United States, the national government, state governments, and city governments all play a role in influencing the well-being of children (Linver & others, 2004). At the national and state levels, policymakers for decades have debated whether helping poor parents ends up helping their children as well. Researchers are providing some answers by examining the effects of specific policies.

For example, the Minnesota Family Investment Program (MFIP) was designed in the 1990s primarily to affect the behavior of adults—specifically, to move adults off the welfare rolls and into paid employment. A key element of the program was that it guaranteed that adults who participated in the program would receive more money if they worked than if they did not. When the adults' income rose, how did that affect their children? A study of the effects of MFIP found that increases in the incomes of working poor parents were linked with benefits for their children (Gennetian & Miller, 2002). The children's achievement in school improved, and their behavior problems decreased.

Developmental psychologists and other researchers have examined the effects of many other government policies, and they have offered many suggestions for improving those policies. One frequent criticism is that the family policies of the United States are overwhelmingly treatment oriented: only those families and individuals who already have problems are eligible. Few preventive programs are available. For example, families in which the children are on the verge of being placed in foster care are eligible, and often required, to receive counseling; families in which problems are brewing but are not yet full-blown usually cannot qualify for public services.

At the beginning of the twenty-first century, the well-being of children is one of America's foremost concerns (Renninger & Sigel, 2006). Children, after all, are the future of any society. Children who do not reach their potential, who are unable to contribute effectively to society, and who do not take their place as productive adults diminish society's future (Horowitz & O'Brien, 1989).

Review and Reflect **LEARNING GOAL 1**

1 Discuss the past and the present in the field of child development

Review
- What is development? How has childhood been perceived through history?
- What are the key characteristics of the modern study of child development?
- What are some contemporary concerns about today's children?
- What is social policy, and what is its status in regard to America's children?

Reflect
- Imagine what your development as a child would have been like in a culture that offered fewer or distinctly different choices from your own. How might your development have been different if your family had been significantly richer or poorer than it was?

2 DEVELOPMENTAL PROCESSES AND PERIODS

Biological, Cognitive, and Socioemotional Processes

Periods of Development

Each of us develops in certain ways like all other individuals, like some other individuals, and like no other individuals. Most of the time, our attention is directed to a person's uniqueness, but psychologists who study development are drawn to our shared characteristics as well as what makes us unique. As humans, we all have traveled some common paths. Each of us—Leonardo da Vinci, Joan of Arc, George Washington, Martin Luther King, Jr., and you—walked at about the age of 1, engaged in fantasy play as a young child, and became more independent as a youth. What shapes this common path of human development, and what are its milestones?

Biological, Cognitive, and Socioemotional Processes

The pattern of human development is created by the interplay of several processes—biologial, cognitive, and socioemotional. **Biological processes** produce changes in an individual's body. Genes inherited from parents, the development of the brain, height and weight gains, motor skills, and the hormonal changes of puberty all reflect the role of biological processes in development.

Cognitive processes refer to changes in an individual's thought, intelligence, and language. The tasks of watching a mobile swinging above a crib, putting together a two-word sentence, memorizing a poem, solving a math problem, and imagining what it would be like to be a movie star all involve cognitive processes.

PEANUTS © United Features Syndicate, Inc.

biological processes Changes in an individual's body.

cognitive processes Changes in an individual's thought, intelligence, and language.

Socioemotional processes involve changes in an individual's relationships with other people, changes in emotions, and changes in personality. An infant's smile in response to her mother's touch, a young boy's attack on a playmate, a girl's development of assertiveness, and an adolescent's joy at the senior prom all reflect socioemotional development.

Biological, cognitive, and socioemotional processes are intricately intertwined. Consider a baby smiling in response to its mother's touch. Even this simple response depends on biological processes (the physical nature of the touch and responsiveness to it), cognitive processes (the ability to understand intentional acts), and socioemotional processes (smiling often reflects positive emotion and smiling helps to connect infants with other human beings).

We typically will study each type of process in separate sections of the book. However, keep in mind that you are studying the development of an integrated human child who has only one interdependent mind and body (see figure 1.5).

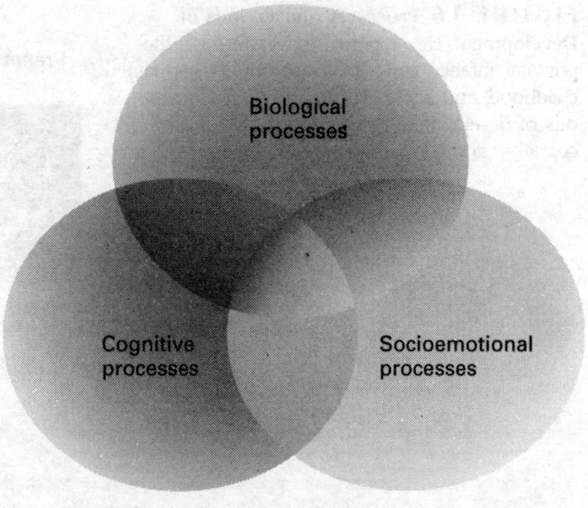

FIGURE 1.5 Changes in Development Are the Result of Biological, Cognitive, and Socioemotional Processes. The processes interact as individuals develop.

Periods of Development

For the purposes of organization and understanding, a child's development is commonly described in terms of periods, which are given approximate age ranges. The most widely used classification of developmental periods describes a child's development in terms of the following sequence: the prenatal period, infancy, early childhood, middle and late childhood, and adolescence.

The **prenatal period** is the time from conception to birth, roughly a nine-month period. During this amazing time a single cell grows into an organism, complete with a brain and behavioral capabilities.

Infancy is the developmental period that extends from birth to about 18 to 24 months of age. Infancy is a time of extreme dependence on adults. Many psychological activities are just beginning—the ability to speak, to coordinate sensations and physical actions, to think with symbols, and to imitate and learn from others.

Early childhood is the developmental period that extends from the end of infancy to about 5 to 6 years of age; sometimes this period is called the preschool years. During this time, young children learn to become more self-sufficient and to care for themselves, they develop school readiness skills (following instructions, identifying letters), and they spend many hours in play and with peers. First grade typically marks the end of this period.

Middle and late childhood is the developmental period that extends from about 6 to 11 years of age; sometimes this period is referred to as the elementary school years. Children master the fundamental skills of reading, writing, and arithmetic, and they are formally exposed to the larger world and its culture. Achievement becomes a more central theme of the child's world, and self-control increases.

Adolescence is the developmental period of transition from childhood to early adulthood, entered at approximately 10 to 12 years of age and ending at 18 to 22 years of age. Adolescence begins with rapid physical changes—dramatic gains in height and weight; changes in body contour; and the development of sexual characteristics such as enlargement of the breasts, development of pubic and facial hair, and deepening of the voice. The pursuit of independence and an identity are prominent features of this period of development. More and more time is spent outside of the family. Thought becomes more abstract, idealistic, and logical.

Today, developmentalists do not believe that change ends with adolescence (Baltes, 2003; Santrock, 2006b). They describe development as a lifelong process. However, the purpose of this text is to describe the changes in development that take place from conception through adolescence. All of these periods of development are produced by the interplay of biological, cognitive, and socioemotional processes (see figure 1.6).

socioemotional processes Changes in an individual's relationships with other people, emotions, and personality.

prenatal period The time from conception to birth.

infancy The developmental period that extends from birth to about 18 to 24 months.

early childhood The developmental period that extends from the end of infancy to about 5 to 6 years of age, sometimes called the preschool years.

middle and late childhood The developmental period that extends from about 6 to 11 years of age, sometimes called the elementary school years.

adolescence The developmental period of transition from childhood to early adulthood, entered at approximately 10 to 12 years of age and ending at 18 to 22 years of age.

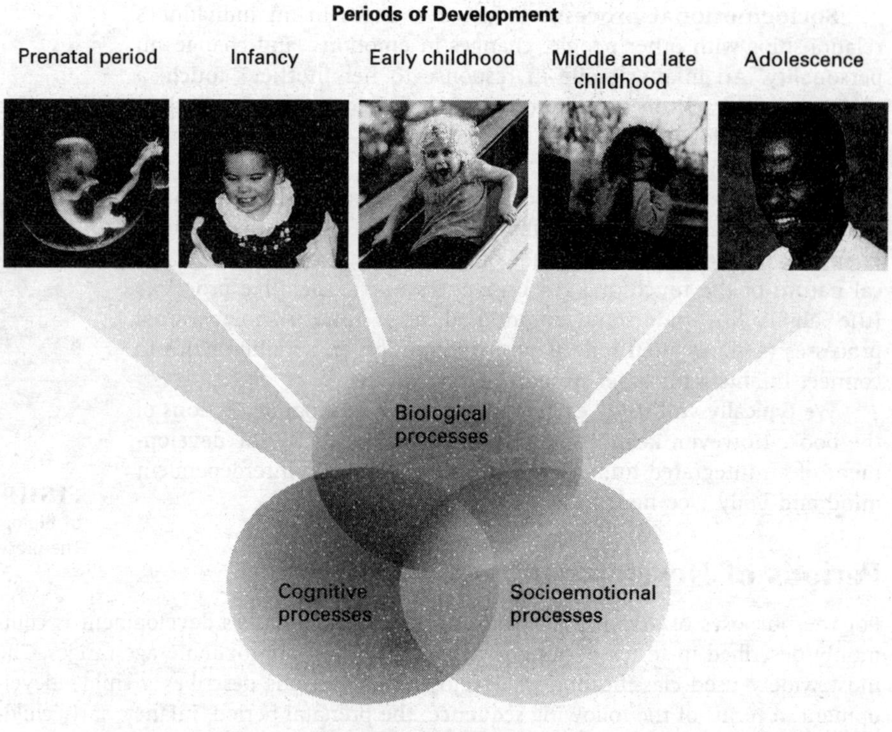

FIGURE 1.6 Processes and Periods of Development. Development moves through the prenatal, infancy, early childhood, middle and late childhood, and adolescence periods. These periods of development are the result of biological, cognitive, and socioemotional processes.

Review and Reflect • **LEARNING GOAL 2**

2 Identify the most important developmental processes and periods

Review

- What are three key developmental processes?
- What are five main developmental periods?

Reflect

- At what age did you become an adolescent? Were you physically, cognitively, and socioemotionally different when you became an adolescent? If so, how?

3 DEVELOPMENTAL ISSUES

- Nature and Nurture
- Continuity and Discontinuity
- Early and Later Experience
- Evaluating the Developmental Issues

Many questions about children's development remain unanswered. For example, what exactly drives the biological, cognitive, and socioemotional processes of development, and how does what happens in infancy influence middle childhood or adolescence? Despite all of the knowledge that developmentalists have acquired, debate continues about the relative importance of factors that influence the developmental processes and about how the periods of development are related. The most important issues in the study of children's development include nature and nurture, continuity and discontinuity, and early and later experience.

Nature and Nurture

The **nature-nurture issue** involves the debate about whether development is primarily influenced by nature or by nurture (Kagan & Fox, 2006; Kagan & Herschkowitz, 2005; Lippa, 2005). *Nature* refers to an organism's biological inheritance, *nurture* to its environmental experiences. Almost no one today argues that development can be explained by nature alone or by nurture alone. But some ("nature" proponents) claim that the most important influence on development is biological inheritance, and others ("nurture" proponents) claim that environmental experiences are the most important influence.

According to the nature proponents, just as a sunflower grows in an orderly way—unless it is defeated by an unfriendly environment—so does a person. The range of environments can be vast, but a genetic blueprint produces commonalities in growth and development. We walk before we talk, speak one word before two words, grow rapidly in infancy and less so in early childhood, and experience a rush of sexual hormones in puberty. Extreme environments—those that are psychologically barren or hostile—can stunt development, but nature proponents emphasize the influence of tendencies that are genetically wired into humans.

By contrast, other psychologists emphasize the importance of nurture, or environmental experiences, to development. Experiences run the gamut from the individual's biological environment (nutrition, medical care, drugs, and physical accidents) to the social environment (family, peers, schools, community, media, and culture). For example, a child's diet can affect how tall the child grows and even how effectively the child can think and solve problems. Despite their genetic wiring, a child born and raised in a poor village in Bangladesh and a child in the suburbs of Denver are likely to have different skills, different ways of thinking about the world, and different ways of relating to people.

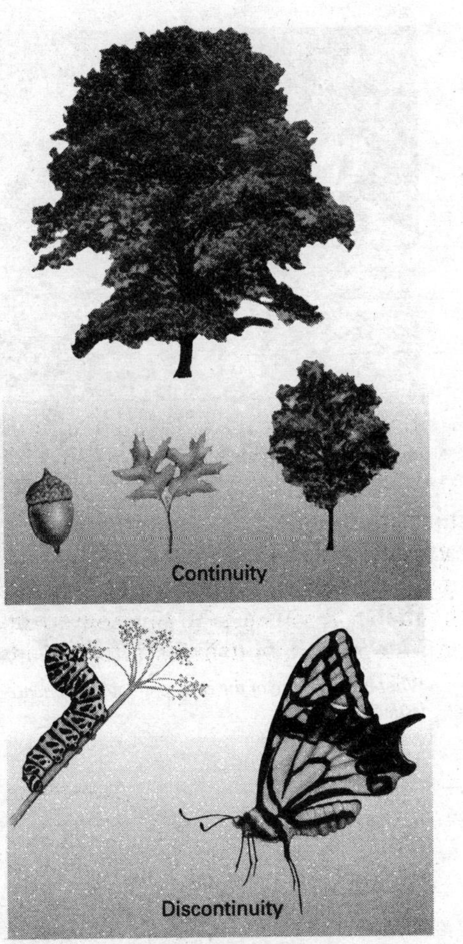

FIGURE 1.7 Continuity and Discontinuity in Development. Is human development more like that of a seedling gradually growing into a giant oak or more like that of a caterpillar suddenly becoming a butterfly?

Continuity and Discontinuity

Think about your own development for a moment. Did you become the person you are gradually, like the seedling that slowly, cumulatively grows into a giant oak? Or did you experience sudden, distinct changes, like the caterpillar that changes into a butterfly (see figure 1.7)?

The **continuity-discontinuity issue** focuses on the extent to which development involves gradual, cumulative change (continuity) or distinct stages (discontinuity). For the most part, developmentalists who emphasize nurture usually describe development as a gradual, continuous process, like the seedling's growth into an oak. Those who emphasize nature often describe development as a series of distinct stages, like the change from caterpillar to butterfly.

Consider continuity first. As the oak grows from seedling to giant oak, it becomes more oak—its development is continuous. Similarly, a child's first word, though seemingly an abrupt, discontinuous event, is actually the result of weeks and months of growth and practice. Puberty, another seemingly abrupt, discontinuous occurrence, is actually a gradual process occurring over several years.

Viewed in terms of discontinuity, each person is described as passing through a sequence of stages in which change is qualitatively rather than quantitatively different. As the caterpillar changes to a butterfly, it is not more caterpillar, it is a different kind of organism—its development is discontinuous. Similarly (as discussed in chapters 2 and 7), at some point a child moves from not being able to think abstractly about the world to being able to do so. This is a qualitative, discontinuous change in development, not a quantitative, continuous change.

nature-nurture issue Nature refers to an organism's biological inheritance, nurture to environmental influences. The "nature" proponents claim biological inheritance is the most important influence on development; the "nurture" proponents claim that environmental experiences are the most important.

continuity-discontinuity issue The issue regarding the extent to which development involves gradual, cumulative change (continuity) or distinct stages (discontinuity).

What is the nature of the early and later experience issue?

Early and Later Experience

The **early-later experience** issue focuses on the degree to which early experiences (especially in infancy) or later experiences are the key determinants of the child's development. That is, if infants experience harmful circumstances, can those experiences be overcome by later, positive ones? Or are the early experiences so critical—possibly because they are the infant's first, prototypical experiences—that they cannot be overridden by a later, better environment? To those who emphasize early experiences, life is an unbroken trail on which a psychological quality can be traced back to its origin (Kagan, 1992, 2000). In contrast, to those who emphasize later experiences, development is like a river, continually ebbing and flowing.

The early-later experience issue has a long history and continues to be hotly debated among developmentalists (Caspi, 2006; Gottlieb, 2004; Gottlieb, Wahlsten, & Lickliter, 2006; Thompson, 2006). Plato was sure that infants who were rocked frequently become better athletes. Nineteenth-century New England ministers told parents in Sunday afternoon sermons that the way they handled their infants would determine their children's later character. Some developmentalists argue that, unless infants experience warm, nurturing care during the first year or so of life, their development will never quite be optimal (Carlson, Sroufe, & Egeland, 2004; Sroufe & others, 2005).

In contrast, later-experience advocates argue that children are malleable throughout development and that later sensitive caregiving is just as important as earlier sensitive caregiving. A number of life-span developmentalists (developmentalists who focus on the entire life span) stress that too little attention has been given to later experiences in development (Baltes, 2003). They accept that early experiences are important contributors to development, but no more important than later experiences. Jerome Kagan (2000) points out that even children who show the qualities of an inhibited temperament, which is linked to heredity, have the capacity to change their behavior. In his research, almost one-third of a group of children who had an inhibited temperament at 2 years of age were not unusually shy or fearful when they were 4 years of age (Kagan & Snidman, 1991).

People in Western cultures, especially those influenced by Freudian theory, have tended to support the idea that early experiences are more important than later experiences (Chan, 1963; Lamb & Sternberg, 1992). The majority of people in the world do not share this belief. For example, people in many Asian countries believe that experiences occurring after about 6 to 7 years of age are more important to development than are earlier experiences. This stance stems from the long-standing belief in Eastern cultures that children's reasoning skills begin to develop in important ways during middle childhood.

What can research tell us about the early-later experience issue? If we narrow our focus to examine specific experiences, there is a great deal of informative research. The interlude that follows focuses on whether certain television viewing experiences (during early childhood) are linked with competencies later, during adolescence. (This is the first of the Research in Child Development interludes that will appear in each chapter to provide a sense of how research in child development is carried out.)

early-later experience issue The issue of the degree to which early experiences (especially infancy) or later experiences are the key determinants of the child's development.

RESEARCH IN CHILD DEVELOPMENT

Early Childhood TV Viewing and Adolescent Behavior

Many researchers have examined how watching television influences children. One study examined the long-term relation between the television viewing of 570 U.S. young children and their behavior as adolescents (Anderson & others, 2001).

Information about TV viewing when the children were 5 years old was obtained through viewing diaries. If the child was in the room while the TV was turned on, parents were asked to indicate in the diary what channel and program the TV was tuned to. Information about the children when they were adolescents was obtained by interviewing them by phone about their academic achievement, book reading, creativity, and aggression. In addition, high school transcripts were obtained for most participants.

What did the researchers find? The more often children viewed educational programs like *Sesame Street* and *Mr. Rogers' Neighborhood* when they were 5 years old, the higher their grades and creativity, the more they emphasized achievement, the more books they read, and the lower their aggression when they were in high school. The findings were stronger for boys than girls. Figure 1.8 shows the relationship between boys' viewing of educational television during early childhood and their grade point average in high school. The high school girls who had viewed violent programs more often in preschool had lower grades than those who had watched these types of programs less frequently in preschool.

The results of this study support the view that early experiences can have important implications for later development. They also document that watching educational television during childhood is linked with positive outcomes and that exposure to violent television during childhood is associated with negative outcomes.

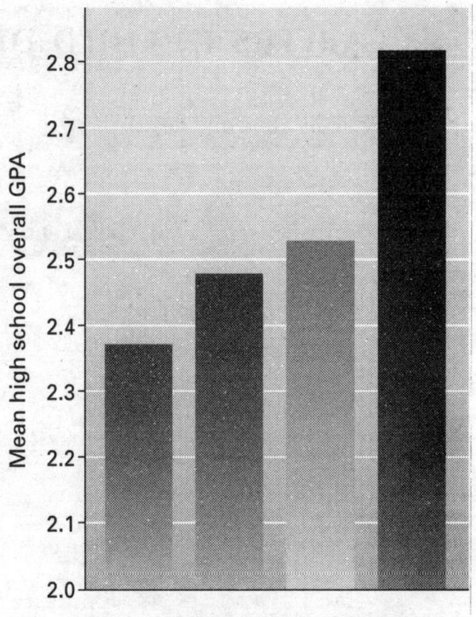

FIGURE 1.8 Educational TV Viewing in Early Childhood and High School Grade Point Average for Boys. When boys watched more educational television (especially *Sesame Street*) as preschoolers, they had higher grade point averages in high school. The graph displays the boys' early TV viewing patterns in quartiles and the means of their grade point averages. The bar on the left is for the lowest 25 percent of boys who viewed educational TV programs, the next bar the next 25 percent, and so on, with the bar on the right for the 25 percent of the boys who watched the most educational TV shows as preschoolers.

Evaluating the Developmental Issues

Most developmentalists recognize that it is unwise to take an extreme position on the issues of nature and nurture, continuity and discontinuity, and early and later experiences. Development is not all nature or all nurture, not all continuity or all discontinuity, and not all early or later experiences (Gottlieb, Wahlsten, & Lickliter, 2006; Overton, 2004). Nature and nurture, continuity and discontinuity, and early and later experiences all play a part in development through the human life span.

Along with this consensus, there is still spirited debate about how strongly development is influenced by each of these factors (Baltes, Lindenberger, & Stavdinger, 2006; Caspi, 2006; Conger, Lorenz, & Wickrama, 2004; Elder & Shanahan 2006; Waters, 2001). Are girls less likely to do well in math mostly because of inherited characteristics or because of society's expectations and because of how girls are raised? Can enriched experiences during adolescence remove deficits resulting from poverty, neglect, and poor schooling during childhood? The answers have a bearing on social policy decisions about children and adolescents, and consequently on each of our lives.

Review and Reflect • LEARNING GOAL 3

3 Describe three key developmental issues

Review

- What is the nature and nurture issue?
- What is the continuity and discontinuity issue?
- What is the early and later experience issue?
- What is a good strategy for evaluating the developmental issues?

Reflect

- Can you identify an early experience that you believe contributed in important ways to your development? Can you identify a recent or current (later) experience that you think had (is having) a strong influence on your development?

4 CAREERS IN CHILD DEVELOPMENT

- Education and Research
- Clinical and Counseling
- Medical, Nursing, and Physical Development
- Families and Relationships

Each of us wants to find a rewarding career and enjoy the work we do. The field of child development offers an amazing breadth of career options that can provide extremely satisfying work.

If you decide to pursue a career in child development, what career options are available to you? There are many. College and university professors teach courses in areas of child development, education, family development, nursing, and medicine. Teachers impart knowledge, understanding, and skills to children and adolescents. Counselors, clinical psychologists, nurses, and physicians help parents and children of different ages to cope more effectively with their lives and well-being. Various professionals work with families to improve the quality of family functioning.

Although an advanced degree is not absolutely necessary in some areas of child development, you usually can expand your opportunities (and income) considerably by obtaining a graduate degree. Many careers in child development pay reasonably well. For example, psychologists earn well above the median salary in the United States. Also, by working in the field of child development you can guide people in improving their lives, understand yourself and others better, possibly advance the state of knowledge in the field, and have an enjoyable time while you are doing these things.

If you are considering a career in child development, would you prefer to work with infants? Children? Adolescents? Parents? As you go through this term, try to spend some time with children of different ages. Observe their behavior. Talk with them about their lives. Think about whether you would like to work with children of this age in your life's work.

Another important aspect of exploring careers is to talk with people who work in various jobs. For example, if you have some interest in becoming a school counselor, call a school, ask to speak with a counselor, and set up an appointment to discuss the counselor's career and work.

Something else that should benefit you is to work in one or more jobs related to your career interests while you are in college. Many colleges and universities have internships or work experiences for students who major in such fields as child development. In some instances, these jobs earn course credit or pay; in others, they are strictly on a volunteer basis. Take advantage of these opportunities. They can provide you with valuable experiences to help you decide if this is the right career for you and they can help you get into graduate school, if you decide you want to go.

In the upcoming sections, we will profile careers in four areas: education and research; clinical and counseling; medical, nursing, and physical development; and families and relationships. These are not the only career options in child development, but they should provide you with an idea of the range of opportunities available and information about some of the main career avenues you might pursue. In profiling these careers, we will address the amount of education required, the nature of the training, and a description of the work.

www.mhhe.com/santrockcd11

Careers in Psychology
Elementary and Secondary School Teaching
Exceptional Children Teachers
Early Childhood Education

Education and Research

Numerous career opportunities in child development involve education or research. These range from a college professor to child-care director to school psychologist.

College/University Professor Courses in child development are taught in many programs and schools in colleges and universities, including psychology, education, nursing, child and family studies, social work, and medicine. The work that college professors do includes teaching courses either at the undergraduate or graduate level (or both), conducting research in a specific area, advising students and/or directing their research, and serving on college or university committees. Some college instructors do not conduct research as part of their job but instead focus mainly on teaching. Research is most likely to be part of the job description at universities with master's and Ph.D. programs.

A Ph.D. or master's degree almost always is required to teach in some area of child development in a college or university. Obtaining a doctoral degree usually takes four to six years of graduate work. A master's degree requires approximately two years of graduate work. The training involves taking graduate courses, learning to conduct research, and attending and presenting papers at professional meetings. Many graduate students work as teaching or research assistants for professors in an apprenticeship relationship that helps them to become competent teachers and researchers.

If you are interested in becoming a college or university professor, you might want to make an appointment with your instructor in this class on child development to learn more about his or her profession and work. To read about the work of one college professor, see the Careers in Child Development insert.

CAREERS in CHILD DEVELOPMENT

Valerie Pang
Professor of Teacher Education

Valerie Pang is a professor of teacher education at San Diego State University and formerly an elementary school teacher. Like Dr. Pang, many professors of teacher education have a doctorate and have experience in teaching at the elementary or secondary school level.

Dr. Pang earned a doctorate at the University of Washington. She has received a Multicultural Educator Award from the National Association of Multicultural Education for her work on culture and equity. She also was given the Distinguished Scholar Award from the American Educational Research Association's Committee on the Role and Status of Minorities in Education.

Pang (2005) believes that competent teachers need to:

- Recognize the power and complexity of cultural influences on students.
- Be sensitive to whether their expectations for students are culturally biased.
- Evaluate whether they are doing a good job of seeing life from the perspective of students who come from different cultures.

Valerie Pang is a professor in the School of Teacher Education of San Diego State University and formerly an elementary school teacher. Valerie believes it is important for teachers to create a caring classroom that affirms all students.

Researcher Some individuals in the field of child development work in research positions. In most instances, they have either a master's or Ph.D. in some area of child development. The researchers might work at a university, in some cases in a university professor's research program, in government at such agencies as the National Institute of Mental Health, or in private industry. Individuals who have full-time research positions in child development generate innovative research ideas, plan studies, carry out the research by collecting data, analyze the data, and then interpret it. Then, they will usually attempt to publish the research in a scientific journal. A researcher often works in a collaborative manner with other researchers on a project and may present the research at scientific meetings. One researcher might spend much of his or her time in a laboratory while another researcher might work out in the field, such as in schools, hospitals, and so on.

Elementary School Teacher The work of an elementary or secondary school teacher involves teaching in one or more subject areas, preparing the curriculum, giving tests, assigning grades, monitoring students' progress, conducting parent-teacher conferences, and attending in-service workshops. Becoming an elementary or secondary school teacher requires a minimum of an undergraduate

www.mhhe.com/santrockcd11

Family and Consumer Science Education
Educational Psychology
School Psychology

degree. The training involves taking a wide range of courses with a major or concentration in education as well as completing a supervised practice-teaching internship.

Exceptional Children (Special Education) Teacher A teacher of exceptional children spends concentrated time with individual children who have a disability or are gifted. Among the children a teacher of exceptional children might work with are children with learning disabilities, ADHD (attention deficit hyperactivity disorder), mental retardation, or a physical disability such as cerebral palsy. Some of this work will usually be done outside of the student's regular classroom, some of it will be carried out when the student is in the regular classroom. The exceptional children teacher works closely with the student's regular classroom teacher and parents to create the best educational program for the student.

Becoming a teacher of exceptional children requires a minimum of an undergraduate degree. The training consists of taking a wide range of courses in education and a concentration of courses in educating children with disabilities or children who are gifted. Teachers of exceptional children often continue their education after obtaining their undergraduate degree and attain a master's degree.

Early Childhood Educator Early childhood educators work on college faculties and have a minimum of a master's degree in their field. In graduate school, they take courses in early childhood education and receive supervisory training in child-care or early childhood programs. Early childhood educators usually teach in community colleges that award an associate degree in early childhood education.

Preschool/Kindergarten Teacher Preschool teachers teach mainly 4-year-old children, and kindergarten teachers primarily teach 5-year-old children. They usually have an undergraduate degree in education, specializing in early childhood education. State certification to become a preschool or kindergarten teacher usually is required. Some early childhood teachers have a two-year associate degree. To read about one early childhood teacher, see the Careers in Child Development insert.

Family and Consumer Science Educator Family and consumer science educators may specialize in early childhood education or instruct middle and high school students about such matters as nutrition, interpersonal relationships, human sexuality, parenting, and human development. Hundreds of colleges and universities throughout the United States offer two- and four-year degree programs in family and consumer science. These programs usually include an internship requirement. Additional education courses may be needed to obtain a teaching certificate. Some family and consumer educators go on to graduate school for further training, which provides a background for possible jobs in college teaching or research.

Educational Psychologist An educational psychologist most often teaches in a college or university and conducts research in such areas of educational psychology as learning, motivation, classroom management, and assessment. Most educational psychologists have a doctorate in education, which takes four to six years of graduate work. They help to train students who will take various positions in education, including educational psychology, school psychology, and teaching.

School Psychologist School psychologists focus on improving the psychological and intellectual well-being of elementary and secondary school students. They may work in a centralized office in a school district or in one or more schools. They give psychological tests, interview students and their parents, consult with teachers, and may provide counseling to students and their families.

School psychologists usually have a master's or doctoral degree in school psychology. In graduate school, they take courses in counseling, assessment, learning, and other areas of education and psychology.

Clinical and Counseling

A wide variety of clinical and counseling jobs are linked with child development. These range from child clinical psychologist to adolescent drug counselor.

Clinical Psychologist Clinical psychologists seek to help people with psychological problems. They work in a variety of settings, including colleges and universities, clinics, medical schools, and private practice. Some clinical psychologists only conduct psychotherapy, others do psychological assessment and psychotherapy, and some also do research. Clinical psychologists may specialize in a particular age group, such as children (child clinical psychologist).

Clinical psychologists have either a Ph.D. (which involves clinical and research training) or a Psy.D. degree (which only involves clinical training). This graduate training usually takes five to seven years and includes courses in clinical psychology and a one-year supervised internship in an accredited setting toward the end of the training. In most cases, they must pass a test to become licensed in a state and to call themselves a clinical psychologist.

Psychiatrist Like clinical psychologists, psychiatrists might specialize in working with children (child psychiatry) or adolescents (adolescent psychiatry). Psychiatrists might work in medical schools in teaching and research roles, in a medical clinic, or in private practice. In addition to administering drugs to help improve the lives of people with psychological problems, psychiatrists also may conduct psychotherapy.

Psychiatrists obtain a medical degree and then do a residency in psychiatry. Medical school takes approximately four years and the psychiatry residency another three to four years. Unlike psychologists (who do not go to medical school) in most states, psychiatrists can administer drugs to clients.

Counseling Psychologist Counseling psychologists work in the same settings as clinical psychologists and may do psychotherapy, teach, or conduct research. In many instances, however, counseling psychologists do not work with individuals who have a severe mental disorder. A counseling psychologist might specialize in working with children, adolescents, and/or families.

Counseling psychologists go through much of the same training as clinical psychologists, although in a graduate program in counseling rather than clinical psychology. Counseling psychologists have either a master's degree or a doctoral degree. They also must go through a licensing procedure. One type of master's degree in counseling leads to the designation of licensed professional counselor.

School Counselor School counselors help to identify students' abilities and interests, guide students in developing academic plans, and explore career options with students. They may help students cope with adjustment problems. They may work with students individually, in small groups, or even in a classroom. They often

www.mhhe.com/santrockcd11

Clinical and Counseling
Clinical Psychology
Psychiatry
Counseling Psychology
School Counseling
Social Work
Drug Counseling

consult with parents, teachers, and school administrators when trying to help students with their problems.

High school counselors advise students on choosing a major, admissions requirements for college, taking entrance exams, applying for financial aid, and on appropriate vocational and technical training. Elementary school counselors are mainly involved in counseling students about social and personal problems. They may observe children in the classroom and at play as part of their work. School counselors usually have a master's degree in counseling.

Career Counselor Career counselors help individuals to identify their best career options and guide them in applying for jobs. They may work in private industry or at a college/university. They usually interview individuals and give them vocational or psychological tests to help them provide students with information about careers that fit their interests and abilities. Sometimes they help individuals to create résumés or conduct mock interviews to help them feel comfortable in a job interview. They may create and promote job fairs or other recruiting events to help individuals obtain jobs.

Social Worker Social workers often are involved in helping people with social or economic problems. They may investigate, evaluate, and attempt to rectify reported cases of abuse, neglect, endangerment, or domestic disputes. They can intervene in families if necessary and provide counseling and referral services to individuals and families.

Social workers have a minimum of an undergraduate degree from a school of social work that includes course work in various areas of sociology and psychology. Some social workers also have a master's or doctoral degree. They often work for publicly funded agencies at the city, state, or national level, although increasingly they work in the private sector in areas such as drug rehabilitation and family counseling.

In some cases, social workers specialize in a certain area, as is true of a medical social worker, who has a master's degree in social work (M.S.W.). This involves graduate course work and supervised clinical experiences in medical settings. A medical social worker might coordinate a variety of support services to people with a severe or long-term disability. Family care social workers often work with families who need support services.

Drug Counselor Drug counselors provide counseling to individuals with drug abuse problems. They may work on an individual basis with a substance abuser or conduct group therapy sessions. They may work in private practice, with a state or federal government agency, with a company, or in a hospital setting. Some drug counselors specialize in working with adolescents or families. Most states provide a certification procedure for obtaining a license to practice drug counseling.

At a minimum, drug counselors go through an associates or certificate program. Many have an undergraduate degree in substance-abuse counseling, and some have master's and doctoral degrees.

www.mhhe.com/santrockcd11

Obstetrics and Gynecology
Pediatrics
Nurse-Midwife
Neonatal Nursing
Pediatric Nursing

Medical, Nursing, and Physical Development

This third main area of careers in child development includes a wide range of careers in the medical and nursing areas, as well as jobs pertaining to improving some aspect of the child's physical development.

Obstetrician/Gynecologist An obstetrician/gynecologist prescribes prenatal and postnatal care and performs deliveries in maternity cases. The individual also treats diseases and injuries of the female reproductive system. Obstetricians may work in private practice, in a medical clinic, a hospital, or in a medical school. Becoming an obstetrician/gynecologist requires a medical degree plus three to five years of residency in obstetrics/gynecology.

Pediatrician A pediatrician monitors infants' and children's health, works to prevent disease or injury, helps children attain optimal health, and treats children with health problems. Pediatricians may work in private practice, in a medical clinic, in a hospital, or in a medical school. As medical doctors, they can administer drugs to children and may counsel parents and children on ways to improve the children's health. Many pediatricians on the faculty of medical schools also teach and conduct research on children's health and diseases. Pediatricians have attained a medical degree and completed a three- to five-year residency in pediatrics.

Neonatal Nurse A neonatal nurse is involved in the delivery of care to the newborn infant. The neonatal nurse may work to improve the health and well-being of infants born under normal circumstances or be involved in the delivery of care to premature and critically ill neonates.

A minimum of an undergraduate degree in nursing with a specialization in the newborn is required. This training involves course work in nursing and the biological sciences, as well as supervisory clinical experiences.

Nurse-Midwife A nurse-midwife formulates and provides comprehensive care to selected maternity patients, cares for the expectant mother as she prepares to give birth and guides her through the birth process, and cares for the postpartum patient. The nurse-midwife also may provide care to the newborn, counsel parents on the infant's development and parenting, and provide guidance about health practices. Becoming a nurse-midwife generally requires an undergraduate degree from a school of nursing. A nurse-midwife most often works in a hospital setting.

Pediatric Nurse Pediatric nurses have a degree in nursing that takes from two to five years to complete. Some also may obtain a master's or doctoral degree in pediatric nursing. Pediatric nurses take courses in biological sciences, nursing care, and pediatrics, usually in a school of nursing. They also undergo supervised clinical experiences in medical settings. They monitor infants' and children's health, work to prevent disease or injury, and help children attain optimal health. They may work in hospitals, schools of nursing, or with pediatricians in private practice or at a medical clinic. To read about the work of one pediatric nurse practitioner, see the Careers in Child Development insert.

CAREERS in CHILD DEVELOPMENT

Katherine Duchen Smith
Nurse Practitioner and Child-Care Health Consultant

Katherine Duchen Smith has a master's degree in nursing and works as a child-care health consultant. She lives in Ft. Collins, Colorado, and in 2004 was appointed as the public relations chair of the National Association of Pediatric Nurse Practitioners (NAPNAP), which has more than 6,000 members.

Smith provides health consultation and educational services to child-care centers, private schools, and hospitals. She also teaches in the Regis University Family Nurse Practitioner Program. Smith developed an interest in outreach and public relations activities during her five-year term as a board member for the Fort Collins Poudre Valley Hospital System. Later, she became the organization's outreach consultant.

As child-care health consultants, nurse practitioners might provide telephone consultation and link children, families, or staff with primary-care providers. In underserved areas, they might also be asked to administer immunizations, help chronically ill children access specialty care, or develop a comprehensive health promotion or injury prevention program for caregivers and families.

Katherine Duchen Smith with a child at the child-care center where she is a consultant on health care.

Audiologist

An audiologist has a minimum of an undergraduate degree in hearing science. This includes courses and supervisory training. Audiologists assess and identify the presence and severity of hearing loss, as well as problems in balance. Some audiologists also go on to obtain a master's and/or doctoral degree. They may work in a medical clinic, with a physician in private practice, in a hospital, or in a medical school.

Speech Therapist

Speech therapists are health-care professionals who are trained to identify, assess, and treat speech and language problems. They may work with physicians, psychologists, social workers, and other health-care professionals as a team to help individuals with physical or psychological problems that include speech and language problems. Speech pathologists have a minimum of an undergraduate degree in the speech and hearing science or communications disorders area. They may work in private practice, in hospitals and medical schools, and in government agencies with individuals of any age. Some specialize in working with children or with a particular type of speech disorder.

Audiology and Speech Pathology
Genetic Counseling

Genetic Counselor

Genetic counselors work as members of a health-care team, providing information and support to families who have members with birth defects or genetic disorders and to families who may be at risk for a variety of inherited conditions. They identify families at risk and provide supportive counseling. They serve as educators and resource people for other health-care professionals and the public. Almost half work in university medical centers, and another one-fourth work in private hospital settings.

Most genetic counselors enter the field after majoring in undergraduate school in such disciplines as biology, genetics, psychology, nursing, public health, and social work. They have specialized graduate degrees and experience in medical genetics and counseling.

Families and Relationships

A number of careers are available for working with families and relationship problems. These range from being a child welfare worker to a marriage and family therapist.

Child Welfare Worker
Child Life Specialist
Marriage and Family Therapist

Child Welfare Worker

A child welfare worker is employed by the child protective services unit of each state. The child welfare worker protects the child's rights, evaluates any maltreatment the child might experience, and may have the child removed from the home if necessary. A child social worker has a minimum of an undergraduate degree in social work.

Child Life Specialist

Child life specialists work with children and their families when the child needs to be hospitalized. They monitor the child's activities, seek to reduce the child's stress, help the child cope effectively, and assist the child in enjoying the hospital experience as much as possible. Child life specialists may provide parent education and develop individualized treatment plans based on an assessment of the child's development, temperament, medical plan, and available social supports.

Child life specialists have an undergraduate degree. As undergraduates, they take courses in child development and education and usually take additional courses in a child life program.

Marriage and Family Therapist

Marriage and family therapists work on the principle that many individuals who have psychological problems benefit when psychotherapy is provided in the context of a marital or family relationship. Marriage and family therapists may provide marital therapy, couples therapy to individuals in a relationship who are not married, and family therapy to two or more members of a family.

Marriage and family therapists have a master's or doctoral degree. They go through a training program in graduate school similar to that of a clinical psychologist but with the focus on marital and family relationships. To practice marital and family therapy in most states it is necessary to go through a licensing procedure.

Review and Reflect • LEARNING GOAL 4

4 Summarize the career paths that involve working with children

Review

- What are some education and research careers that involve working with children?
- What are some clinical and counseling careers that involve working with children?
- What are some medical, nursing, and physical development careers that involve working with children?
- What are some family and relationship-oriented careers that involve working with children?

Reflect

- Which of the careers that were described are the most interesting to you? Choose three of these careers and go to the related website connections to learn more about them.

REACH YOUR LEARNING GOALS

INTRODUCTION

- **1 CHILD DEVELOPMENT—YESTERDAY AND TODAY**
  - Historical Views of Childhood
  - The Modern Study of Child Development
  - Improving the Lives of Today's Children
  - Resilience, Social Policy, and Children's Development
- **2 DEVELOPMENTAL PROCESSES AND PERIODS**
  - Biological, Cognitive, and Socioemotional Processes
  - Periods of Development
- **3 DEVELOPMENTAL ISSUES**
  - Nature and Nurture
  - Continuity and Discontinuity
  - Early and Later Experience
  - Evaluating the Developmental Issues
- **4 CAREERS IN CHILD DEVELOPMENT**
  - Education and Research
  - Clinical and Counseling
  - Medical, Nursing, and Physical Development
  - Families and Relationships

SUMMARY

1 Discuss the past and the present in the field of child development

- Development is the pattern of movement or change that occurs throughout the life span. The history of interest in children is long and rich. Prior to the nineteenth century, philosophical views of childhood were prominent, including the notions of original sin, tabula rasa, and innate goodness.
- Today, we conceive of childhood as an important time of development. The modern era of studying children spans a little more than a century, an era in which the study of child development has become a sophisticated science. Methodological advances in observation as well as the introduction of experimentation and the development of major theories characterize the achievements of the modern era.
- Five important contemporary concerns in children's development are health and well-being; families and parenting; education; the sociocultural contexts of culture, ethnicity, and socioeconomic status; and gender.
- Social policy is a government's course of action designed to promote the welfare of its citizens. The poor conditions of life for a significant percentage of U.S. children and the lack of attention to prevention point to the need for revised social policies.

2 Identify the most important developmental processes and periods

- Development is influenced by an interplay of biological, cognitive, and socioemotional processes.
- Development is commonly divided into the following periods from conception through adolescence: prenatal, infancy, early childhood, middle and late childhood, and adolescence.

3 Describe three key developmental issues

- The nature-nurture issue focuses on the extent to which development is mainly influenced by nature (biological inheritance) or nurture (experience).
- Some developmentalists describe development as continuous (gradual, cumulative change); others describe it as discontinuous (a sequence of abrupt stages).
- The early-later experience issue focuses on whether early experiences (especially in infancy) are more important in development than later experiences.
- Most developmentalists recognize that extreme positions on the nature-nurture, continuity-discontinuity, and early-later experience issues are unwise. Despite this consensus, these issues continue to be spiritedly debated.

4 Summarize the career paths that involve working with children

- Education and research careers include college/university professor, researcher, elementary or secondary teacher, exceptional children teacher, early childhood educator, preschool/kindergarten teacher, family and consumer science educator, educational psychologist, and school psychologist.
- Clinical and counseling careers include clinical psychologist, psychiatrist, counseling psychologist, school counselor, career counselor, social worker, and drug counselor.
- Medical, nursing, and physical development careers include obstetrician/gynecologist, pediatrician, neonatal nurse, nurse-midwife, pediatric nurse, audiologist, speech therapist, and genetic counselor.
- Families and relationships careers include child welfare worker, child life specialist, and marriage and family therapist.

KEY TERMS

KEY PEOPLE

E-LEARNING TOOLS

To help you master the material in this chapter, visit the Online Learning Center for *Child Development*, eleventh edition (**www.mhhe.com/santrockcd11**), where you'll find these additional resources:

Taking It to the Net

1. George is teaching fourth grade. He wants his students to learn about the difficulties and challenges of being a child in colonial America. What was life like for children in the early history of our country?
2. Janice thinks that better and stricter gun control laws will help decrease violent crime among children. Her husband, Elliott, disagrees. Janice found a March, 2000, Department of Justice study that provides support for her argument. What facts in the report can she point to in order to convince Elliott?
3. For his political science class, Darren has to track federal funding appropriations in the most recent Congress for any issue of his choice. He has chosen children's issues. What happened with funding for the No Child Left Behind Act in congressional appropriations in the first half of the 109th Congress?

Nursing, Parenting, and Teaching Exercises

Build your decision-making skills by trying your hand at the scenarios on the Online Learning Center.

Video Clips

The Online Learning Center includes the following videos for this chapter:

- Career in Child Development
  Dr. Lerner gives a humorous account of a decision to major in psychology in college.
- Career in Developmental Psychology
  Dr. Weinraub, one of the leading researchers on the NICHD Early Childcare Study, describes how she became interested in developmental psychology.

Chapter 2 THE SCIENCE OF CHILD DEVELOPMENT

There is nothing quite so practical as a good theory.

—Kurt Lewin
American Social Psychologist, 20th Century

CHAPTER OUTLINE

LEARNING GOALS

SCIENCE AND THE STUDY OF CHILD DEVELOPMENT

The Importance of Research in Child Development
The Scientific Research Approach

1 Discuss the importance of research and the scientific method in the study of child development

THEORIES OF CHILD DEVELOPMENT

Psychoanalytic Theories
Cognitive Theories
Behavioral and Social Cognitive Theories
Ethological Theory
Ecological Theory
An Eclectic Theoretical Orientation

2 Describe the main theories of child development

RESEARCH METHODS IN CHILD DEVELOPMENT

Methods for Collecting Data
Research Designs
Time Span of Research
Methods and Theories

3 Explain how research on child development is conducted

CHALLENGES IN CHILD DEVELOPMENT RESEARCH

Conducting Ethical Research
Minimizing Bias
Thinking Critically About Research on Children's Development

4 Discuss research challenges in child development

The Stories of Erik Erikson and Jean Piaget

The overview of theories of development that was presented in chapter 1 gave a hint of how different these theories can be. What explains these differences? In part, the answer may come from many varying ideas that theorists encounter during their training. But theoretical differences may also in part reflect differing life experiences. Two important developmental theorists, whose views will be described later in the chapter, are Erik Erikson and Jean Piaget. Let's examine a portion of their lives as they were growing up to discover how their experiences might have contributed to the theories they developed.

Erik Homberger Erikson (1902–1994) was born near Frankfurt, Germany, to Danish parents. Before Erik was born, his parents separated, and his mother left Denmark to live in Germany. At age 3, Erik became ill, and his mother took him to see a pediatrician named Homberger. Young Erik's mother fell in love with the pediatrician, married him, and renamed Erik after his new stepfather.

Erik attended primary school from the ages of 6 to 10 and then the gymnasium (high school) from 11 to 18. He studied art and a number of languages. Erik did not like formal schooling, and this attitude was reflected in his grades. Rather than going to college at age 18, the adolescent Erikson wandered around Europe, keeping a diary about his experiences. After a year, he returned to Germany and enrolled in art school, became dissatisfied, and enrolled in another. Later he traveled to Florence, Italy. According to psychiatrist Robert Coles (1970, p. 15), to the Italians Erikson "was the young, tall, thin Nordic expatriate with long, blond hair"; to his family and friends, he was "a wandering artist who was trying to come to grips with himself."

Erikson would later become known for his theory of identity development. Contrast his experiences with those of Jean Piaget. Piaget (1896–1980) was born in Neuchâtel, Switzerland. Jean's father was an intellectual who taught young Jean to think systematically. Jean's mother was also very bright. His father had an air of detachment from his mother, whom Piaget described as prone to frequent outbursts of neurotic behavior.

In his autobiography, Piaget described why he chose to study cognitive development:

> I started to forego playing for serious work very early. Indeed, I have always detested any departure from reality, an attitude which I relate to . . . my mother's poor health. It was this disturbing factor which at the beginning of my studies in psychology made me keenly interested in psychoanalytic and pathological psychology . . . I have never since felt any desire to involve myself deeper in that particular direction, always much preferring the study of normalcy and of the workings of the intellect to that of the tricks of the unconscious. (Piaget, 1952, p. 238)

These snapshots of Erikson and Piaget illustrate how personal experiences might influence the direction that a particular theorist takes. Erikson's wanderings and search for self contributed to his theory of identity development, and Piaget's intellectual experiences with his parents and schooling contributed to his emphasis on cognitive development.

Like the theories of Erikson and Piaget, all theories are created by people, not computers, and any theory bears the stamp of its creator. And like any human creation, theories should be approached critically, not accepted blindly. The theories we discuss in this chapter, however, have proven to be more than personal reflections of their creators. They have played an important role in the growth of the field of child development.

PREVIEW

This chapter introduces the theories and methods that are the foundation of the science of child development. Toward the end of the chapter we will explore some of the ethical challenges and biases that researchers must guard against to protect the integrity of their results and respect the rights of the participants in their studies.

1 SCIENCE AND THE STUDY OF CHILD DEVELOPMENT

The Importance of Research in Child Development | The Scientific Research Approach

Is the field of child development really a science? Some individuals have difficulty thinking of child development as a science like physics, chemistry, and biology. Can a discipline that studies how parents nurture children, how peers interact, the developmental changes in children's thinking, and whether watching TV hour after hour is linked with being overweight be equated with disciplines that study the molecular structure of a compound and how gravity works? The answer is yes. Science is defined not by *what* it investigates, but by *how* it investigates. Whether you're studying photosynthesis, butterflies, Saturn's moons, or children's development, it is the way you study that makes the approach scientific or not.

The Importance of Research in Child Development

It sometimes is said that experience is the most important teacher. We get a great deal of knowledge from personal experience. We generalize from what we observe and frequently turn memorable encounters into lifetime "truths." But how valid are these conclusions? Sometimes we err in making our observations or misinterpret what we see and hear. Chances are, you can think of many situations in which you thought other people read you the wrong the way, just as they may have felt that you misread them. When we base information only on personal experiences, sometimes we make judgments that protect our ego and self-esteem (McMillan, 2004).

We get information not only from personal experiences but also from authorities and experts. You may hear experts spell out a "best way" to parent children or educate them, but the authorities and experts don't always agree. You may hear one expert proclaim that one strategy for interacting with children is the best and, the next week, see that another expert advocates another strategy. How can you tell which one to believe? One way to clarify the situation is to carefully examine research.

The Scientific Research Approach

Researchers take a skeptical, scientific attitude toward knowledge. When they hear someone claim that a particular method is effective in helping children cope with stress, they want to know if the claim is based on *good* research. The science part of child development seeks to sort fact from fancy by using particular strategies for obtaining information (McMillan & Schumacher, 2006; Salkind, 2003; Wiersma & Jurs, 2005).

Scientific research is objective, systematic, and testable. It reduces the likelihood that information will be based on personal beliefs, opinions, and feelings (Rosnow & Rosenthal, 2005). Scientific research is based on the **scientific method,** an approach for discovering accurate information. It includes these steps: conceptualize the problem, collect data, draw conclusions, and revise research conclusions and theory.

scientific method An approach that can be used to obtain accurate information. It includes these steps: (1) conceptualize the problem, (2) collect data, (3) draw conclusions, and (4) revise research conclusions and theory.

Science refines everyday thinking.

—ALBERT EINSTEIN
German-born American Physicist, 20th Century

The first step, *conceptualizing a problem,* involves identifying the problem. For example, suppose a team of researchers decides that they want to study ways to improve the achievement of children from impoverished backgrounds. The researchers have *identified a problem,* but as part of the first step, they must go beyond a general description of the problem and isolate specifically what they hope to study.

To isolate their specific topic and thus conceptualize the problem, researchers often draw on theories and develop hypotheses (Thomas, 2005). A **theory** is an interrelated, coherent set of ideas that helps to explain and to make predictions. A **Hypothesis** *(plural hypotheses)* is a specific testable assumption or prediction. For example, researchers decide to discover if mentoring children from impoverished backgrounds can improve their academic performance. A theory on mentoring might attempt to explain and predict why mentoring makes a difference in the lives of children from impoverished backgrounds. The theory might hold that positive outcomes from mentoring are a result of giving children many opportunities to observe and imitate the behavior and strategies of mentors, or the theory might hold that giving children from impoverished backgrounds sustained individual attention produces improved academic performance. Each of these theories suggests hypotheses—testable predictions—that the researchers might examine.

At this point, even more narrowing and focusing needs to take place in order to conceptualize the problem to be examined. What specific strategies do the researchers want to test? How often will the mentors see the children? How long will the mentoring program last? What aspects of the children's achievement will the researchers assess?

The second step is to *collect information (data).* In the study of mentoring, the researchers might decide to conduct the mentoring program for six months. Their data might consist of classroom observations, teachers' ratings, and achievement tests given to the mentored children before the mentoring began and at the end of six months of mentoring.

Once data have been collected, child development researchers use *statistical procedures* to understand the meaning of the data and try to draw *conclusions.* For example, statistics help researchers determine whether or not their observed results are due to chance.

After data have been collected and analyzed, researchers compare their findings with those of other researchers on the same topic. The final step in the scientific method is *revising research conclusions and theory.*

Notice that we mentioned theories in the description of both the first and final steps of the scientific method. Theories help to inspire research, generating specific questions that are tested, but theories also are tested, revised, rejected, and themselves inspired by research. In the study of child development, there are a wealth of theories, as we discuss in the next section.

Review and Reflect • LEARNING GOAL 1

1 Discuss the importance of research and the scientific method in the study of child development

Review

- Why is research on child development important?
- What is the scientific method? What are its four main steps?

Reflect

- Imagine that a friend says she saw an ad on TV claiming a particular toy is something all parents need to buy to ensure their child is getting adequate learning opportunities. Based on what you have read in this section, why might you be skeptical of this claim?

theory An interrelated, coherent set of ideas that helps to explain and to make predictions.

hypothesis *(plural hypotheses)* Specific assumptions and predictions that can be tested to determine their accuracy.

2 THEORIES OF DEVELOPMENT

- Psychoanalytic Theories
- Cognitive Theories
- Behavioral and Social Cognitive Theories
- Ethological Theory
- Ecological Theory
- An Eclectic Theoretical Orientation

The diversity of theories makes understanding children's development a challenging undertaking. Just when you think one theory has the most helpful explanation of children's development, another theory crops up and makes you rethink your earlier conclusion. To keep from getting frustrated, remember that child development is a complex, multifaceted topic. No single theory has been able to account for all aspects of child development. Each theory contributes an important piece to the child development puzzle. Although the theories sometimes disagree, much of their information is complementary rather than contradictory. Together they let us see the total landscape of development in all its richness.

We will briefly explore five major theoretical perspectives on development: psychoanalytic, cognitive, behavioral and social cognitive, ethological, and ecological. As you will see, these theoretical approaches examine in varying degrees the three major processes involved in children's development: biological, cognitive, and socioemotional.

Psychoanalytic Theories

Psychoanalytic theory describes development as primarily unconscious (beyond awareness) and colored by emotion. Psychoanalytic theorists believe that behavior is merely a surface characteristic and that a true understanding of development requires analyzing the symbolic meanings of behavior and the deep inner workings of the mind. Psychoanalytic theorists also stress that early experiences with parents extensively shape development. These characteristics are highlighted in the psychoanalytic theory of Sigmund Freud.

Sigmund Freud, the pioneering architect of psychoanalytic theory. *What are some characteristics of Freud's theory?*

www.mhhe.com/santrockcd11

Freud's Theory

psychoanalytic theory Describes development as primarily unconscious and heavily colored by emotion. Behavior is merely a surface characteristic, and the symbolic workings of the mind have to be analyzed to understand behavior. Early experiences with parents are emphasized.

Freud's Psychosexual Theory Freud (1856–1939) developed his ideas about psychoanalytic theory while working with mental patients. He was a medical doctor who specialized in neurology. He spent most of his years in Vienna, though he moved to London near the end of his career because of Nazi anti-Semitism.

Structures of Personality Freud (1917) believed that personality has three structures: the id, the ego, and the superego. The *id,* he said, consists of instincts, which are an individual's reservoir of psychic energy. For Freud, one of the primary instincts, and the primary source of psychic energy, is sexual. In Freud's view, the id is totally unconscious; it has no contact with reality.

As children experience the demands and constraints of reality, a new part of personality emerges—the *ego,* which is the Freudian personality structure that deals with the demands of reality. The ego is called the *executive branch* of personality because it uses reasoning to make decisions.

The id and the ego have no morality. They do not take into account whether something is right or wrong. The *superego* is the Freudian structure of personality that is the moral branch of personality; it decides whether something is right or wrong. Think of the superego as what we often refer to as our "conscience."

You probably are beginning to sense that both the id and the superego make life rough for the ego. Your ego might say, "I will have sex only occasionally and be sure to take the proper precautions because I don't want the intrusion of a child in the development of my career." However, your id is saying, "I want to be satisfied;

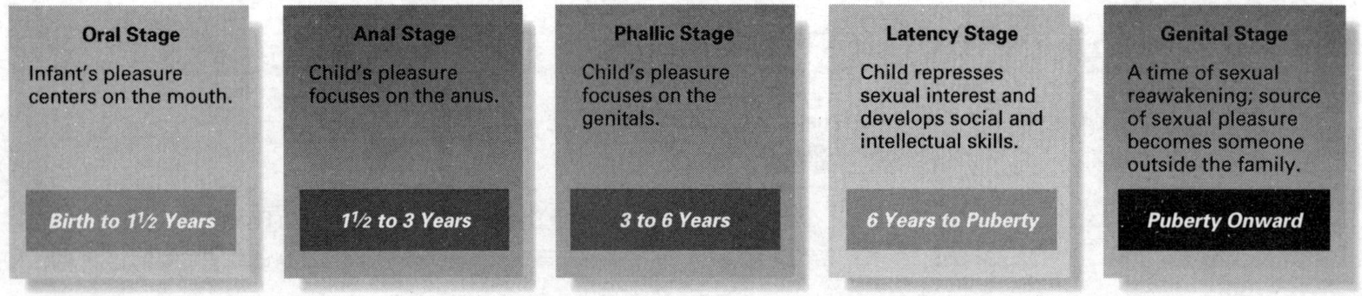

FIGURE 2.1 Freudian Stages

sex is pleasurable." Your superego is at work, too: "I feel guilty about having sex." In Freud's view, such conflict is a constant theme in our lives.

Stages of Development As Freud listened to, probed, and analyzed his patients, he became convinced that their problems were the result of experiences early in life. Freud proposed that we go through five stages of development, and that at each stage we experience pleasure in one part of the body more than in others. Our adult personality, according to Freud, is determined by the way we resolve conflicts between these early sources of pleasure—the mouth, the anus, and then the genitals—and the demands of reality. If the need for pleasure at any stage is either undergratified or overgratified, an individual may become *fixated*, or locked in, at that stage of development.

Because Freud emphasized sexual motivation, his stages are known as *psychosexual stages* of development. Figure 2.1 summarizes the five Freudian psychosexual stages: oral, anal, phallic, latency, and genital.

The *oral stage* is the first Freudian stage of development, occurring during the first 18 months of life, in which the infant's pleasure centers around the mouth. Chewing, sucking, and biting are the chief sources of pleasure. These actions reduce tension in the infant.

The *anal stage* is the second Freudian stage of development, occurring between 1½ and 3 years of age, in which the child's greatest pleasure involves the anus or the eliminative functions associated with it. In Freud's view, the exercise of anal muscles reduces tension.

The *phallic stage* is the third Freudian stage of development. The phallic stage occurs between the ages of 3 and 6; its name comes from the Latin word *phallus*, which means "penis." During the phallic stage, pleasure focuses on the genitals as both boys and girls discover that self-manipulation is enjoyable.

In Freud's view, the phallic stage has a special importance in personality development because it is during this period that the Oedipus complex appears. This name comes from Greek mythology, in which Oedipus, the son of the King of Thebes, unwittingly kills his father and marries his mother. The *Oedipus complex*, according to Freudian theory, is the young child's development of an intense desire to replace the same-sex parent and enjoy the affections of the opposite-sex parent.

How is the Oedipus complex resolved? At about 5 to 6 years of age, children recognize that their same-sex parent might punish them for their incestuous wishes. To reduce this conflict, the child identifies with the same-sex parent, striving to be like him or her. If the conflict is not resolved, though, the individual may become fixated at the phallic stage.

The *latency stage* is the fourth Freudian stage of development, which occurs between approximately 6 years of age and puberty. During this period, the child represses all interest in sexuality and develops social and intellectual skills. This activity channels much of the child's energy into emotionally safe areas and helps the child forget the highly stressful conflicts of the phallic stage.

The *genital stage* is the fifth and final Freudian stage of development, occurring from puberty on. The genital stage is a time of sexual reawakening; the source of sexual pleasure now becomes someone outside of the family. Freud believed that unresolved conflicts with parents reemerge during adolescence. When these conflicts have been resolved, the individual is capable of developing a mature love relationship and functioning independently as an adult.

Freud's theory has undergone significant revisions by a number of psychoanalytic theorists (Eagle, 2000). Many contemporary psychoanalytic theorists place less emphasis on sexual instincts and more emphasis on cultural experiences as determinants of an individual's development. Unconscious thought remains a central theme, but most contemporary psychoanalysts believe that conscious thought makes up more of the mind than Freud envisioned.

Erikson's Psychosocial Theory Erik Erikson recognized Freud's contributions but believed that Freud misjudged some important dimensions of human development. Erikson (1950, 1968) said we develop in *psychosocial* stages, rather than in *psychosexual* stages. For Freud, the primary motivation for human behavior was sexual in nature, for Erikson it was social and reflected a desire to affiliate with other people. Erikson emphasized developmental change throughout the human life span, whereas Freud argued that our basic personality is shaped in the first five years of life.

In **Erikson's theory,** eight stages of development unfold through the life span (see figure 2.2). Each stage consists of a unique developmental task that confronts individuals with a crisis that must be resolved. According to Erikson, this crisis is not a catastrophe but a turning point of increased vulnerability and enhanced potential. The more successfully an individual resolves the crises, the healthier development will be (Hopkins, 2000).

Trust versus mistrust is Erikson's first psychosocial stage, which is experienced in the first year of life. A sense of trust requires a feeling of physical comfort and a minimal amount of fear and apprehension about the future. Trust in infancy sets the stage for a lifelong expectation that the world will be a good and pleasant place to live.

Autonomy versus shame and doubt is Erikson's second stage of development. This stage occurs in late infancy and toddlerhood (1–3 years). After gaining trust in their caregivers, infants begin to discover that their behavior is their own. They start to assert their sense of independence, or autonomy. They realize their *will.* If infants are restrained too much or punished too harshly, they are likely to develop a sense of shame and doubt.

Initiative versus guilt, Erikson's third stage of development, occurs during the preschool years. As preschool children encounter a widening social world, they are challenged more than when they were infants. Active, purposeful behavior is needed to cope with these challenges. Children are asked to assume responsibility for their bodies, their behavior, their toys, and their pets. Developing a sense of responsibility increases initiative. Uncomfortable guilt feelings may arise, though, if the child is irresponsible and is made to feel too anxious. Erikson has a positive outlook on this stage. He believes that most guilt is quickly compensated for by a sense of accomplishment.

Industry versus inferiority is Erikson's fourth developmental stage, occurring approximately in the elementary school years. Children's initiative brings them in contact with a wealth of new experiences. As they move into middle and late childhood, they direct their energy toward mastering knowledge and intellectual skills. At no other time is the child more enthusiastic about learning than at the end of early childhood's period of expansive imagination. The danger in the elementary school years is that the child can develop of a sense of inferiority—feeling incompetent and unproductive. Erikson believed that teachers have a special responsibility for children's development of industry. Teachers should "mildly but firmly coerce children into the adventure of finding out that one can learn to accomplish things which one would never have thought of by oneself" (Erikson, 1968, p. 127).

Erikson's Stages	Developmental Period
Integrity versus despair	Late adulthood (60s onward)
Generativity versus stagnation	Middle adulthood (40s, 50s)
Intimacy versus isolation	Early adulthood (20s, 30s)
Identity versus identity confusion	Adolescence (10 to 20 years)
Industry versus inferiority	Middle and late childhood (elementary school years, 6 years to puberty)
Initiative versus guilt	Early childhood (preschool years, 3 to 5 years)
Autonomy versus shame and doubt	Infancy (1 to 3 years)
Trust versus mistrust	Infancy (first year)

FIGURE 2.2 **Erikson's Eight Life-Span Stages**

Erikson's theory Includes eight stages of human development. Each stage consists of a unique developmental task that confronts individuals with a crisis that must be faced.

Erikson's Theory

Erik Erikson with his wife, Joan, an artist. Erikson generated one of the most important developmental theories of the twentieth century. *Which stage of Erikson's theory are you in? Does Erikson's description of this stage characterize you?*

Identity versus identity confusion is Erikson's fifth developmental stage, which individuals experience during the adolescent years. At this time, individuals are faced with finding out who they are, what they are all about, and where they are going in life. Adolescents are confronted with many new roles and adult statuses—vocational and romantic, for example. Parents need to allow adolescents to explore many different roles and different paths within a particular role. If the adolescent explores such roles in a healthy manner and arrives at a positive path to follow in life, then a positive identity will be achieved. If an identity is pushed on the adolescent by parents, if the adolescent does not adequately explore many roles, and if a positive future path is not defined, then identity confusion reigns.

Intimacy versus isolation is Erikson's sixth developmental stage, which individuals experience during the early adulthood years. At this time, individuals face the developmental task of forming intimate relationships with others. Erikson describes intimacy as finding oneself yet losing oneself in another. If the young adult forms healthy friendships and an intimate relationship with another individual, intimacy will be achieved; if not, isolation will result.

Generativity versus stagnation is Erikson's seventh developmental stage, which individuals experience during middle adulthood. A chief concern is to assist the younger generation in developing and leading useful lives—this is what Erikson means by generativity. The feeling of having done nothing to help the next generation is stagnation.

Integrity versus despair is Erikson's eighth and final stage of development, which individuals experience in late adulthood. During this stage, a person reflects on the past and either pieces together a positive review or concludes that life has not been spent well. Through many routes, the older person may have developed a positive outlook in most or all of the previous stages of development. If so, the retrospective glances will reveal a picture of a life well spent, and the person will feel a sense of satisfaction—integrity will be achieved. If the older adult resolved many of the earlier stages negatively, the retrospective glances likely will yield doubt or gloom—the despair Erikson talks about.

Erikson did not believe that the proper solution to a stage crisis is always completely positive. Some exposure or commitment to the negative side of the crisis is sometimes inevitable—you cannot trust all people under all circumstances and survive, for example. Nonetheless, in the healthy solution to a stage crisis, the positive resolution dominates. We will discuss Erikson's theory again on a number of occasions in the chapters on socioemotional development.

Evaluating the Psychoanalytic Theories

The psychoanalytic theories focus on the socioemotional processes of development; they have much less to tell us about biological or cognitive processes. The contributions of psychoanalytic theories include the following:

- The theories highlight the role of early experiences in development.
- Family relationships are examined as a central aspect of development.
- Psychoanalytic theories take a developmental approach to personality and provide a developmental framework for understanding it.
- Freud's theory championed the idea that the *mind* is not all conscious and brought attention to the unconscious aspects of the mind.
- Erikson showed that changes take place in adulthood as well as in childhood.

The criticisms of psychoanalytic theories include the following:

- The main concepts of psychoanalytic theories have been difficult to test scientifically.
- Much of the data used to support psychoanalytic theories come from individuals' reconstruction of the past, often the distant past, and are of unknown accuracy.

- The sexual underpinnings of development are given too much importance (especially in Freud's theory).
- The unconscious mind is given too much credit for influencing development.
- Psychoanalytic theories (especially Freud's) present an image of humans that is too negative.
- Psychoanalytic theories are culture- and gender-biased. For example, sexual repression characterized the late-nineteenth- and early-twentieth-century Vienna society in which Freud lived and this likely contributed to his overemphasis on sexual motivation in his theory. Feminist critics stress that Freud underestimated the importance of relationships and positive emotions in women's development.

Jean Piaget, the famous Swiss developmental psychologist, changed the way we think about the development of children's minds. *What are some key ideas in Piaget's theory?*

Cognitive Theories

Whereas psychoanalytic theories stress the importance of children's unconscious thoughts, cognitive theories emphasize their conscious thoughts. Three important cognitive theories are Piaget's cognitive development theory, Vygotsky's sociocultural cognitive theory, and information-processing theory.

Piaget's theory will be covered in detail later in this book, when we discuss cognitive development in infancy, early childhood, middle and late childhood, and adolescence. Here we briefly present the main ideas of his theory.

Piaget's Cognitive Developmental Theory

Piaget's theory states that children actively construct their understanding of the world and go through four stages of cognitive development. Two processes underlie this cognitive construction of the world: organization and adaptation. To make sense of our world, we organize our experiences. For example, we separate important ideas from less important ideas. We connect one idea to another. In addition to organizing our observations and experiences, we *adapt* our thinking to include new ideas.

Piaget's Theory

Piaget (1954) believed that we adapt in two ways: assimilation and accommodation. **Assimilation** occurs when children incorporate new information into their existing knowledge. **Accommodation** occurs when children adjust their knowledge to fit new information and experiences. Consider an 8-year-old girl who is given a hammer and nails to hang a picture on the wall. She has never used a hammer, but from experience and observation she realizes that a hammer is an object to be held, that it is swung by the handle to hit the nail, and that it is usually swung a number of times. Recognizing each of these things, she fits the current task into her existing knowledge (assimilation). However, the hammer is heavy, so she holds it near the top. She swings too hard and the nail bends, so she adjusts the pressure of her strikes. These adjustments reveal her ability to alter her knowledge (accommodation).

Piaget also believed that we go through four stages in understanding the world (see figure 2.3). Each of the stages is age-related and consists of distinct ways of thinking. It is the *different* way of understanding the world that makes one stage more advanced than another; knowing *more* information does not make the child's thinking more advanced, in the Piagetian view. This is what Piaget meant when he said the child's cognition is *qualitatively* different in one stage compared to another (Vidal, 2000). What are Piaget's four stages of cognitive development like?

The *sensorimotor stage,* which lasts from birth to about 2 years of age, is the first Piagetian stage. In this stage, infants construct an understanding of the world by coordinating sensory experiences (such as seeing and hearing) with physical, motoric actions—hence the term *sensorimotor.* At the beginning of this stage, newborns have little more than reflexive patterns with which to work. At the end of the stage, 2-year-olds have complex sensorimotor patterns and are beginning to operate with primitive symbols.

Piaget's theory States that children actively construct their understanding of the world and go through four stages of cognitive development.

assimilation Occurs when children incorporate new information into their existing knowledge.

accommodation Occurs when children adjust their knowledge to fit new information and experience.

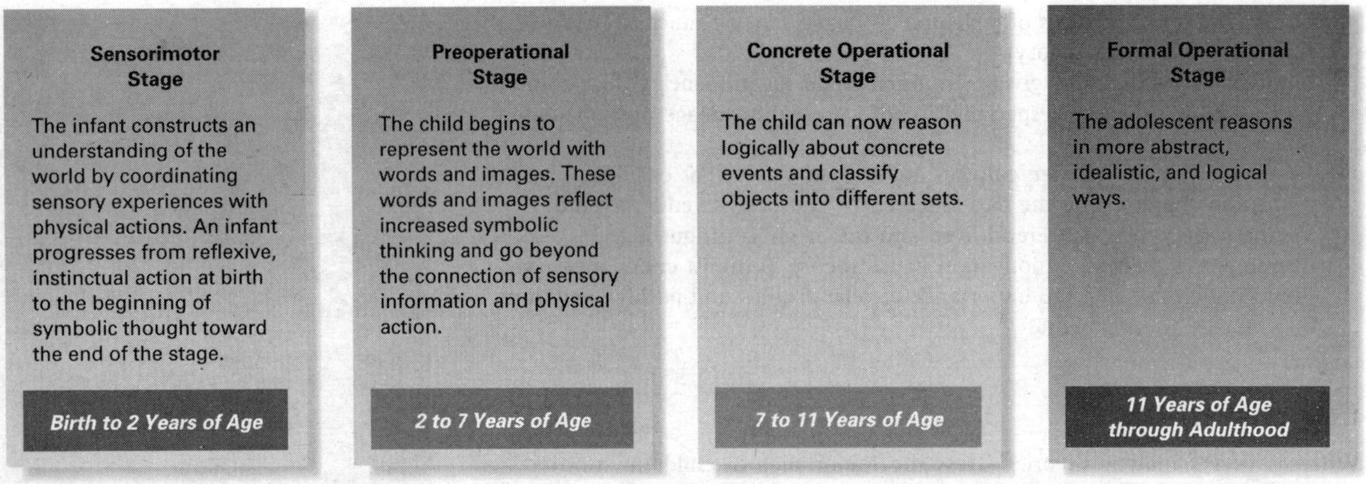

FIGURE 2.3 Piaget's Four Stages of Cognitive Development

The *preoperational stage,* which lasts from approximately 2 to 7 years of age, is the second Piagetian stage. In this stage, children begin to represent the world with words, images, and drawings. However, according to Piaget, preschool children still lack the ability to perform *operations,* the Piagetian term for internalized mental actions that allow children to do mentally what they previously did physically.

The *concrete operational stage,* which lasts from approximately 7 to 11 years of age, is the third Piagetian stage. In this stage, children can perform operations, and logical reasoning replaces intuitive thought as long as reasoning can be applied to specific or concrete examples. For instance, concrete operational thinkers cannot imagine the steps necessary to complete an algebraic equation, which is too abstract for thinking at this stage of development.

The *formal operational stage,* which appears between the ages of 11 and 15, is the fourth and final Piagetian stage. In this stage, individuals move beyond concrete experiences and think in abstract and more logical terms. As part of thinking more abstractly, adolescents develop images of ideal circumstances. They might think about what an ideal parent is like and compare their parents to this ideal standard. They begin to entertain possibilities for the future and are fascinated with what they can be. In solving problems, formal operational thinkers are more systematic, developing hypotheses about why something is happening the way it is, then testing these hypotheses in a deductive manner. We will examine Piaget's cognitive developmental theory further in chapter 7, "Cognitive Developmental Approaches."

www.mhhe.com/santrockcd11

Vygotsky's Theory

Vygotsky's Sociocultural Cognitive Theory Like Piaget, the Russian developmentalist Lev Vygotsky (1896–1934) also believed that children actively construct their knowledge. However, Vygotsky gave social interaction and culture far more important roles in cognitive development than Piaget did. **Vygotksy's theory** is a sociocultural cognitive theory that emphasizes how culture and social interaction guide cognitive development.

Vygotsky portrayed the child's development as inseparable from social and cultural activities (Rowe & Wertsch, 2004). He believed that the development of memory, attention, and reasoning involves learning to use the inventions of society, such as language, mathematical systems, and memory strategies. In one culture, this might consist of learning to count with the help of a computer. In another, it might consist of counting on one's fingers or using beads.

Vygotsky's theory has stimulated considerable interest in the view that knowledge is *situated* and *collaborative* (John-Steiner & Mahn, 2003; Rogoff, 2003). In this view, knowledge is not generated from within the individual but rather is constructed

Vygotsky's theory A sociocultural cognitive theory that emphasizes how culture and social interaction guide cognitive development.

through interaction with other people and objects in the culture, such as books. This suggests that knowing can best be advanced through interaction with others in cooperative activities.

Vygotsky emphasized that children's social interaction with more skilled adults and peers is indispensable in advancing cognitive development. It is through this interaction that less-skilled members of the culture learn to use the tools that will help them adapt and be successful in the culture. When a skilled reader regularly helps a child learn how to read, this not only advances a child's reading skills but also communicates to the child that reading is an important activity in the culture.

Vygotsky was born the same year as Piaget, but he died much earlier, at the age of 37. Both Piaget's and Vygotsky's ideas remained virtually unknown to American scholars until the 1960s. In the past several decades, American psychologists and educators have shown increased interest in Vygotsky's (1962) unique ideas. In chapter 7, "Cognitive Developmental Approaches," we will further explore Vygotsky's contributions to our understanding of children's development.

There is considerable interest today in Lev Vygotsky's sociocultural cognitive theory of child development. *What were Vygotsky's basic ideas about children's development?*

Information-Processing Theory Machines may be the best candidate for the title of "founding father" of information-processing theory. Although a number of factors stimulated the growth of this theory, none was more important than the computer. Psychologists began to wonder if the logical operations carried out by computers might tell us something about how the human mind works. They drew analogies between a computer's hardware and the brain and between computer software and cognition. The physical brain is said to be analogous to the computer's hardware; cognition is said to be analogous to its software.

This line of thinking helped to generate **information-processing theory,** which emphasizes that individuals manipulate information, monitor it, and strategize about it. According to this theory, individuals develop a gradually increasing capacity for processing information, which allows them to acquire increasingly complex knowledge and skills (Birney & others, 2005; Munakata, 2006).

Unlike Piaget's theory but like Vygotsky's theory, information-processing theory does not describe development as stagelike. Instead, Robert Siegler (1998, 2006; Siegler & Alibali, 2005), a leading expert on children's information processing, suggests that learning good strategies for processing information is especially important to cognitive development. For example, becoming a better reader might involve learning to monitor the key themes of the material being read (McCormick, 2003).

Evaluating the Cognitive Theories The contributions of cognitive theories include the following:

- The cognitive theories present a positive view of development, emphasizing conscious thinking.
- The cognitive theories (especially Piaget's and Vygotsky's) emphasize the individual's active construction of understanding.
- Piaget's and Vygotsky's theories underscore the importance of examining developmental changes in children's thinking.
- Information-processing theory offers detailed descriptions of cognitive processes.

The criticisms of cognitive theories include the following:

- Piaget's stages don't accurately portray children's cognitive development. Children's thinking at a particular age is more varied than Piaget proposed and the timing of the stages is different than Piaget envisioned.
- The cognitive theories do not give adequate attention to individual variations in cognitive development.
- Information-processing theory does not provide an adequate description of developmental changes in cognition.
- Psychoanalytic theorists argue that the cognitive theories do not give enough credit to unconscious thought.

information-processing theory A theory that emphasizes that individuals manipulate information, monitor it, and strategize about it. The processes of memory and thinking are central.

Behavioral and Social Cognitive Theories

At about the same time as Freud was interpreting patients' unconscious minds through their early childhood experiences, Ivan Pavlov and John B. Watson were conducting detailed observations of behavior in controlled laboratory settings. Their work provided the foundation for the behavioral view that we can study scientifically only what can be directly observed and measured. According to behaviorists, development consists of observable behaviors that are learned through experience with the environment. The three versions of the behavioral approach that we will explore are Pavlov's classical conditioning, Skinner's operant conditioning, and social cognitive theory.

Pavlov's Classical Conditioning In the early 1900s, Russian physiologist Ivan Pavlov (1927) knew that dogs innately salivate when they taste food. He became curious when he observed that dogs salivate to various sights and sounds before eating their food. For example, if a bell rang when the dog was given food, the dog subsequently salivated when the bell rang by itself. Pavlov had discovered the principle of *classical conditioning:* after a neutral stimulus (in our example, ringing a bell) has been paired with a stimulus (in our example, food) that automatically produces a response, that response will be elicited by the previously neutral stimulus on its own.

In the 1920s, John Watson applied classical conditioning to human beings. He showed a little boy named Albert a white rat to see if he was afraid of it. He was not. As Albert played with the rat, Watson sounded a loud noise behind Albert's head. As you might imagine, the noise caused little Albert to cry. After only several pairings of the loud noise and the white rat, Albert began to fear the rat even when the noise was not sounded (Watson & Rayner, 1920).

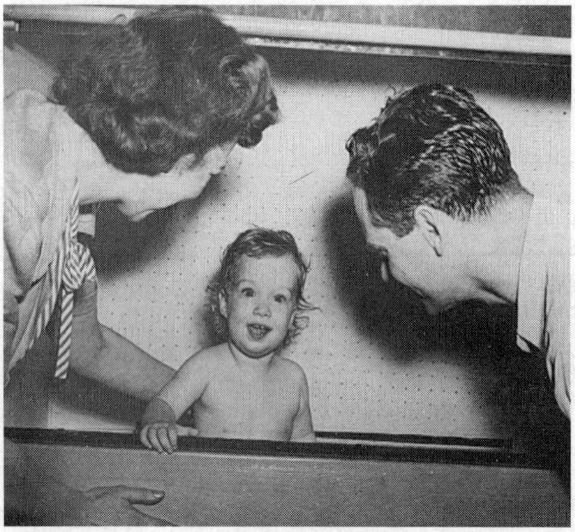

B. F. Skinner was a tinkerer who liked to make new gadgets. The younger of his two daughters, Deborah, was raised in Skinner's enclosed Air-Crib, which he invented because he wanted to control her environment completely. The Air-Crib was soundproofed and temperature-controlled. Debbie, shown here as a child with her parents, is currently a successful artist, is married, and lives in London. *What do you think about Skinner's Air-Crib?*

Similarly, many of our fears can be learned through classical conditioning. For instance, we might learn fear of the dentist from a painful dental experience, fear of driving from being in an automobile accident, fear of heights from falling off a high chair when we were infants, and fear of dogs from being bitten. Classical conditioning explains how we develop many involuntary responses, such as these fears, but B. F. Skinner showed how many of our actions might be explained by a different type of learning known as operant conditioning.

Skinner's Operant Conditioning In Skinner's (1938) *operant conditioning,* the consequences of a behavior produce changes in the probability of the behavior's occurrence. A behavior that is followed by a rewarding stimulus is more likely to recur, but a behavior that is followed by a punishing stimulus is less likely to recur. For example, a child is more likely to repeat a behavior if it is greeted with a smile than if it is met with a nasty look.

For Skinner, such rewards and punishments shape individuals' development. For example, according to Skinner, a child learns to be shy as a result of experiences with the environment; if the environment is rearranged, the child can learn to enjoy social interaction.

Social Cognitive Theory Some psychologists found that although conditioning could explain some aspects of behavior, it was inadequate because of its failure to consider how people think. **Social cognitive theory** is a type of behavioral theory that does take thinking into account. It holds that behavior, environment, and person/cognition are important factors in development. *Person/cognition* refers to personal characteristics (for example, being introverted or extraverted and believing that one can effectively control one's experiences) and to cognitive processes (for example, thinking and planning) that mediate connections between environment and behavior.

social cognitive theory The view of psychologists who emphasize that behavior, environment, and cognition are the key factors in development.

American psychologists Albert Bandura (1986, 2000, 2001, 2004) and Walter Mischel (1973, 1995, 2004) are the main architects of contemporary social cognitive theory, which Mischel (1973) initially labeled cognitive social learning theory. Bandura's early research focused heavily on *observational learning*—learning that occurs through observing what others do. Observational learning is also referred to as *imitation* or *modeling*. In observational learning, people cognitively represent the behavior of others and then sometimes adopt this behavior themselves. For example, a young boy who regularly observes his father's aggressive outbursts and hostile interchanges with people might also be very aggressive with his peers. A girl who adopts the dominating, sarcastic style of her teacher might say to her younger brother, "You are so slow! How can you do this work so slowly?" People acquire a wide range of behaviors, thoughts, and feelings through observing others' behavior.

In his recent work, Bandura (2000, 2001, 2004) emphasizes interactions among behavior, the person/cognition, and the environment, as shown in figure 2.4. Behavior can influence person/cognitive factors and vice versa. The person's cognitive activities can influence the environment, the environment can change the person's cognition, and so on.

Let's consider how Bandura's model might work in the case of a college student's achievement behavior. As the student diligently studies and gets good grades, her behavior produces positive thoughts about her abilities. As part of her effort to make good grades, she plans and develops strategies to make her studying more efficient. In these ways, her behavior has influenced her thought and her thought has influenced her behavior. At the beginning of the term, her college made a special effort to involve students in a study skills program. She decided to join. Because of her success, along with that of other students in the program, the college is expanding the program next semester. In these ways, environment influenced behavior, and behavior changed the environment. And the college administrators' expectations that the study skills program would work made it possible in the first place. The program's success has spurred expectations that this type of program could work in other colleges. In these ways, cognition changed the environment and the environment changed cognition.

Albert Bandura has been one of the leading architects of social cognitive theory. *What is the nature of his theory?*

Behavioral and Social Cognitive Theories
Albert Bandura

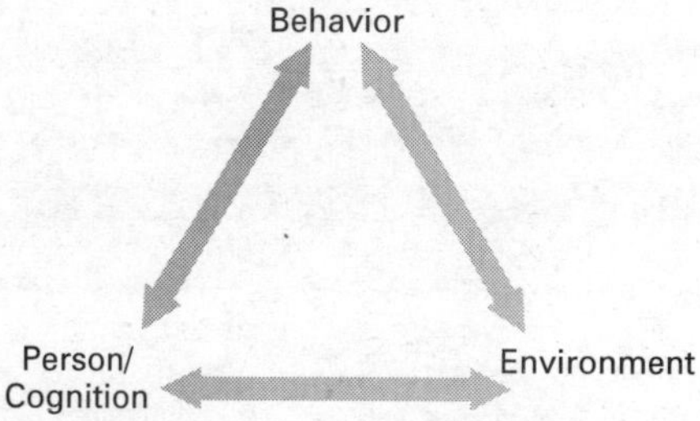

FIGURE 2.4 Bandura's Social Cognitive Model. The arrows illustrate how relations between behavior, person/cognition, and environment are reciprocal rather than unidirectional.

Evaluating the Behavioral and Social Cognitive Theories Behavioral and social cognitive theories have much to say about socioemotional processes in development, and social cognitive theory deals with cognitive processes, but these approaches have little to say about biological processes (Bugental & Grusec, 2006). Contributions of the behavioral and social cognitive theories include the following:

- Their emphasis on the importance of scientific research.
- Their focus on the environmental determinants of behavior.
- The explanation of observational learning in Bandura's theory.
- The emphasis on person/cognitive factors in social cognitive theory.

Criticisms of the behavioral and social cognitive theories include the following:

- Skinner's theory places too little emphasis on cognition.
- The theories place too much emphasis on environmental determinants.
- They give inadequate attention to developmental changes.
- Their consideration of human spontaneity and creativity is inadequate.

Ethological Theory

In striking contrast to the behavioral and social cognitive theories, another approach to development grew out of *ethology*, a scientific discipline that studies animal behavior. The **ethological theory** of development holds that behavior is strongly influenced by biology and evolution (Hinde, 1992; Rosenzweig, 2000). It also emphasizes that our sensitivity to different kinds of experience varies during our life span. In other words, there are critical or sensitive periods for some experiences. If we fail to have these experiences during this sensitive period, ethological theory argues that our development is not likely to be optimal.

ethological theory Stresses that behavior is strongly influenced by biology, is tied to evolution, and is characterized by critical or sensitive periods.

Konrad Lorenz, a pioneering student of animal behavior, is followed through the water by three imprinted greylag geese. Describe Lorenz's experiment with the geese. *Do you think his experiment would have the same results with human babies? Explain.*

www.mhhe.com/santrockcd11

Exploring Ethology

Ethology emerged as an important contributor to theories of human development because of the work of European zoologists, especially Konrad Lorenz (1903–1989). Working mostly with greylag geese, Lorenz (1965) studied a behavior pattern that was thought to be programmed by the birds' genes. A newly hatched gosling seemed to be born with the instinct to follow its mother. Observations showed that the gosling was capable of such behavior as soon as it hatched. Is this behavior "programmed" into the gosling?

In a remarkable set of experiments, Lorenz proved that inherited programming is too simple an explanation for the gosling's behavior. Lorenz separated the eggs laid by one goose into two groups. One group he returned to the goose to be hatched by her. The other group was hatched in an incubator. The goslings in the first group followed their mother as soon as they hatched. However, those in the second group, which saw Lorenz when they first hatched, followed him everywhere, as though he were their mother. Lorenz marked the goslings and then placed both groups under a box. Mother goose and "mother" Lorenz stood aside as the box lifted. Each group of goslings went directly to its "mother." Lorenz called this process *imprinting:* the rapid, innate learning within a limited critical period of time that produces attachment to the first moving object seen.

The ethological view of Lorenz and other European zoologists forced American developmental psychologists to recognize the importance of the biological basis of behavior. However, the research and theorizing of ethology still lacked some ingredients that would elevate it to the ranks of the other theories discussed so far in this chapter. In particular, there was little or nothing in the classical ethological view about the nature of social relationships across the human life span, something that any major theory of development must explain. Classical ethological theory was weak in simulating studies with humans. Also, its concept of *critical period,* a fixed time period very early in development during which certain behaviors optimally emerge, seemed to be overdrawn.

Recent expansion of the ethological view has improved its status as a viable developmental perspective. One important change is that instead of emphasizing a rigid, narrow critical period, current ethological theory proposes a longer *sensitive period.*

One of the most important applications of ethological theory to human development involves John Bowlby's (1969, 1989) theory of attachment. Bowlby argues that attachment to a caregiver over the first year of life has important consequences throughout the life span. In his view, if this attachment is positive and secure, the individual has a foundation for developing into a competent individual who has positive social relationships and is emotionally mature. If this relationship is negative and insecure, according to Bowlby, as the child grows he or she is likely to encounter difficulties in social relationships and dealing with emotions. In chapter 11,

"Emotional Development," we will explore the concept of infant attachment in much greater detail.

Evaluating Ethological Theory The contributions of ethological theory include the following:

- It increased the focus on the biological and evolutionary basis of development.
- It uses careful observations in naturalistic settings.
- It emphasizes sensitive periods of development.

The criticisms of ethological theory include the following:

- The concepts of critical period and sensitive period may still be too rigid.
- It places too much emphasis on biological foundations.
- It gives inadequate attention to cognition.
- The theory has been better at generating research with animals than with humans.

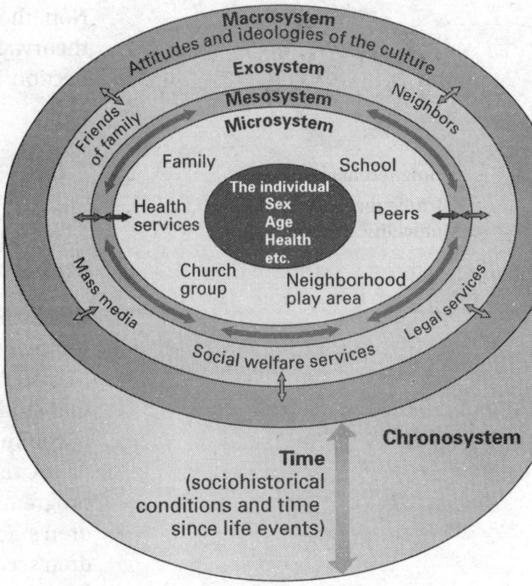

FIGURE 2.5 Bronfenbrenner's Ecological Theory of Development. Bronfenbrenner's ecological theory consists of five environmental systems: microsystem, mesosystem, exosystem, macrosystem, and chronosystem.

Ecological Theory

Unlike ethological theory, which stresses biological factors, ecological theory emphasizes environmental contexts. One ecological theory that has important implications for understanding development was created by Urie Bronfenbrenner (1917–).

Ecological theory is Bronfenbrenner's view that development is influenced by five environmental systems, ranging from the fine-grained contexts of direct interactions with people to the broad-based contexts of culture. The five systems in Bronfenbrenner's ecological theory are the microsystem, mesosystem, exosystem, macrosystem, and chronosystem (Bronfenbrenner, 1986, 2000, 2004; Bronfenbrenner & Morris, 1998, 2006) (see figure 2.5):

- The *microsystem* is the setting in which the individual lives. It includes the person's family, peers, school, and neighborhood. It is in the microsystem that the most direct interactions with social agents take place—with parents, peers, and teachers, for example.
- The *mesosystem* involves relationships between microsystems, or connections between contexts. Examples are the relation of family experiences to school experiences, school experiences to church experiences, and family experiences to peer experiences.
- The *exosystem* is involved when experiences in another social setting—in which the individual does not have an active role—influence what the individual experiences in an immediate context. For example, work experiences can affect a woman's relationship with her husband and their child. The mother might receive a promotion that requires more travel, which could increase marital conflict and change patterns of parent-child interaction.
- The *macrosystem* involves the culture in which individuals live. *Culture* refers to the behavior patterns, beliefs, and all other products of a group of people that are passed on from generation to generation.
- The *chronosystem* involves the patterning of environmental events and transitions over the life course. For example, the negative effects of divorce on children often peak in the first year after the divorce (Hetherington, 1993, 2000). By 2 years after the divorce, family interaction is less chaotic and more stable. With regard to sociocultural circumstances, women today are much more likely to be encouraged to pursue a career than they were 20 or 30 years ago.

Urie Bronfenbrenner developed ecological theory, a perspective that is receiving increased attention. *What is the nature of ecological theory?*

Bronfenbrenner (2000, 2004; Bronfenbrenner & Morris, 1998, 2006) recently added biological influences to his theory and now describes it as a *bioecological* theory.

ecological theory Bronfenbrenner's environmental systems theory that focuses on five environmental systems: microsystem, mesosystem, exosystem, macrosystem, and chronosystem.

www.mhhe.com/santrockcd11

Bronfenbrenner's Theory
Bronfenbrenner and a Multicultural Framework

Nonetheless, ecological, environmental contexts still predominate in Bronfenbrenner's theory. For a closer look at one of these contexts, the important mesosystem connection between family and school, see the Caring for Children interlude.

CARING FOR CHILDREN

Mesosystem Connection: Family and School Communication

Researchers have consistently found that successful students benefit from having both competent teachers in school and supportive parents at home (Cowan & others, 2005; Mattanah, 2005; Piata, Hamre, & Stuhlman, 2003; Pressley & others, 2003). To ensure that students receive support for school at home, it is important to maintain channels of communication between schools and families (Epstein, 2001; Epstein & others, 2002).

A recent review of research on links between schools and families revealed that programs and special efforts to engage families can often make a difference in children's achievement (Henderson & Mapp, 2002). Parental involvement in their children's education is related to higher grade point averages, better attendance, and improved behavior at school and home. Successful strategies include teachers meeting face-to-face with parents and keeping in touch with parents on a regular basis about students' progress.

Joyce Epstein (2001; Epstein & others, 2002) stresses that these activities can be especially helpful in improving school-family connections:

- *Provide assistance to families.* For example, schools can provide parents with information about child-rearing skills, family support, and child and adolescent development.
- *Encourage parents to be volunteers.* In some schools, parents are extensively involved in educational planning and assisting teachers.
- *Involve families with their children in learning activities at home.* This can include homework and curriculum-linked activities.
- *Include families as participants in school decisions.* Parents can be invited to be on PTA/PTO boards, various committees, councils, and other parent organizations.
- *Coordinate community collaboration.* Schools can connect the work and resources of community businesses, agencies, colleges, and other groups to strengthen school programs, family practices, and student learning. Schools can alert families to community programs and services that may benefit them.

Let's look at two programs that have been developed to enhance communication between schools and families. The first program involves the school system of Lima, Ohio, where the main goal is for each school to establish a personal relationship with every parent. At an initial parent-teacher conference, parents are given a packet that is designed to increase their likelihood of engaging in learning activities with their children at home. Conferences, regular phone calls, and home visits establish an atmosphere of mutual understanding that makes other types of communication (progress reports, report cards, activity calendars, and discussions about problems that arise during the year) more welcome and successful. The second program is at Hanshaw Middle School in California's Stanislaus County. The program created a resource center for students' families where parents can take classes in many subjects, including parenting and computers. They can also take courses toward earning a high school equivalency degree. Latino parents find assistance in communicating with the school's teachers and administrators. The center also features a case management team and referral service that is available for students and their families.

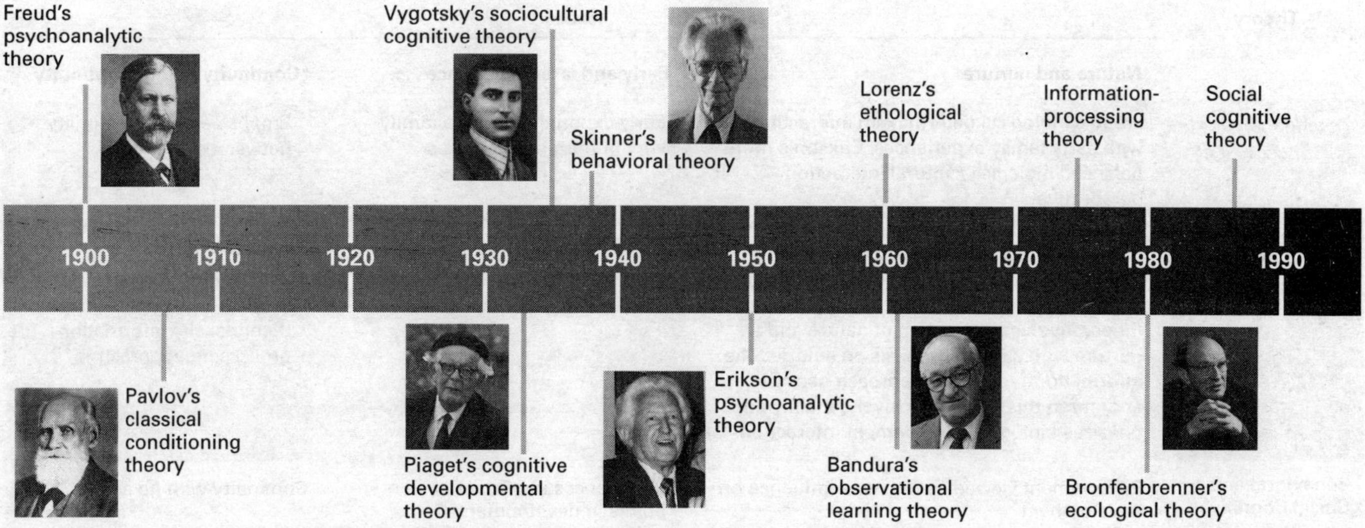

FIGURE 2.6 Time Line for Major Developmental Theories

Evaluating Ecological Theory Contributions of ecological theory include the following:

- It systematically examines macro and micro dimensions of environmental systems.
- It pays attention to connections between environmental settings (mesosystem).
- It considers sociohistorical influences on development (chronosystem).

Criticisms of ecological theory include the following:

- Even with the added discussion of biological influences in recent years, it still gives too little attention to biological foundations of development.
- It does not pay enough attention to cognitive processes.

An Eclectic Theoretical Orientation

The theories that we have discussed were proposed at different points in the twentieth century, as figure 2.6 shows. Figure 2.7 compares the main theoretical perspectives in terms of the three developmental issues discussed in chapter 1—nature and nurture, continuity and discontinuity, and early versus later experience.

No single theory described in this chapter can entirely explain the rich complexity of children's development. Each of the theories, however, has made important contributions to our understanding of development. Psychoanalytic theory best explains the unconscious mind and Erikson's theory best describes the changes that occur throughout the life span. Piaget's, Vygotsky's, and the information-processing views provide the most complete descriptions of cognitive development. The behavioral and social cognitive and ecological theories have been the most adept at examining the environmental determinants of development. The ethological theories have made us aware of biology's role and the importance of sensitive periods in development.

It is important to recognize that, although theories are helpful guides, it would probably be a mistake to rely on a single theory to explain development. An **eclectic theoretical orientation** does not follow any theoretical approach but rather selects and uses what is considered the best in each theory. This is the

eclectic theoretical orientation An orientation that does not follow any one theoretical approach, but rather, selects from each theory whatever is considered the best in it.

Theory	Issues		
	Nature and nurture	Early and later experience	Continuity and discontinuity
Psychoanalytic	Freud's biological determinism interacting with early family experiences; Erikson's more balanced biological/cultural interaction perspective	Early experiences in the family very important influences	Emphasis on discontinuity between stages
Cognitive	Piaget's emphasis on interaction and adaptation; environment provides the setting for cognitive structures to develop. Vygotsky's theory involves interaction of nature and nurture with strong emphasis on culture. The information-processing approach has not addressed this issue extensively; mainly emphasizes biological/environment interaction.	Childhood experiences important influences	Discontinuity between stages in Piaget's theory; no stages in Vygotsky's theory or the information-processing approach
Behavioral and Social Cognitive	Environment viewed as the main influence on development	Experiences important at all points in development	Continuity with no stages
Ethological	Strong biological view	Early experience very important, which can contribute to change early in development; after early critical or sensitive period has passed, stability likely to occur	Discontinuity because of early critical or sensitive period; no stages
Ecological	Strong environmental view	Experiences involving the five environmental systems important at all points in development	No stages but little attention to the issue

FIGURE 2.7 A Comparison of Theories and Issues in Child Development

approach that will be maintained throughout the book. In this way, you can view the study of development as it exists—with different theorists making different assumptions, stressing different empirical problems, and using different strategies to discover information.

Review and Reflect • LEARNING GOAL 2

2 Describe the main theories of child development

Review

- How can the psychoanalytic theories be defined? What are the two main psychoanalytic theories? What are some strengths and weaknesses of psychoanalytic theories?
- What are the three main cognitive theories? What are some strengths and weaknesses of the cognitive theories?
- What are the three main behavioral and social cognitive theories? What are some of the strengths and weaknesses of these theories?
- What is ethological theory? What are some strengths and weaknesses of the theory?
- What is ecological theory? What are strengths and weaknesses of the theory?
- What is an eclectic theoretical orientation?

Reflect

- Which of the theories do you think best explains your own development? Why?

3 RESEARCH METHODS IN CHILD DEVELOPMENT

Methods for Collecting Data | Time Span of Research | Research Designs | Methods and Theories

If you take an eclectic approach, how do you decide what is "best" in different theories? Scientific research is the answer. All scientific knowledge stems from a rigorous, systematic method of research. Through research, theories are modified to reflect new data.

How are data about children's development collected? What types of research designs are used to study children's development? If researchers want to study children of different ages, what research designs can they use? To what extent are theories and methods linked? These are the questions that we will examine next.

Methods for Collecting Data

Whether we are interested in studying attachment in infants, children's cognitive skills, or pubertal change in adolescents, we can choose from several ways of collecting data. Here we outline the measures most often used, including their advantages and disadvantages, beginning with observation.

Observation Scientific observation requires an important set of skills. Unless we are trained observers and practice our skills regularly, we might not know what to look for, we might not remember what we saw, we might not realize that what we are looking for is changing from one moment to the next, and we might not communicate our observations effectively.

For observations to be effective, they have to be systematic (Kantowitz, Roediger, & Elmes, 2005; Gall, Gall, & Borg, 2005). We have to have some idea of what we are looking for. We have to know whom we are observing, when and where we will observe, and how the observations will be made. In what form they will be recorded: In writing? Tape recording? Video? Where should we make our observations? We have two choices: a **laboratory**, which is a controlled setting with many of the complex factors of the "real world" removed, and the everyday world.

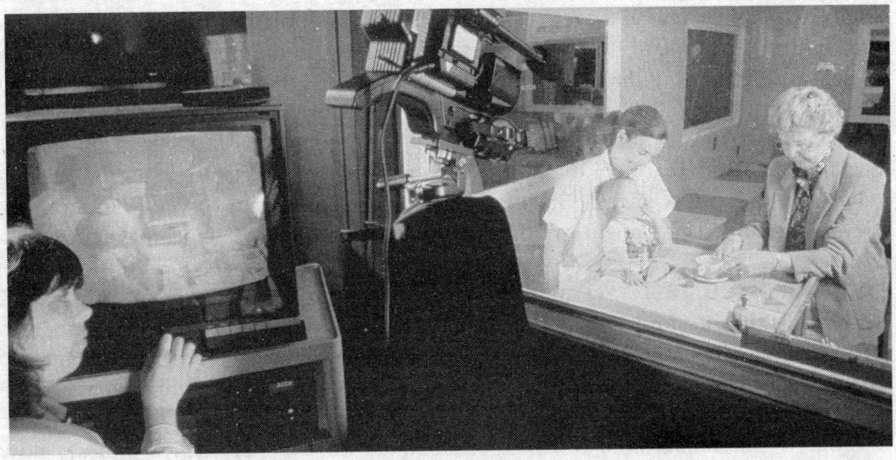

In this study, a 6-month-old infant's behavior is being videotaped during a research study. Later, researchers will code the infant's behavior using precise categories.

laboratory A controlled setting in which many of the complex factors of the "real world" are removed.

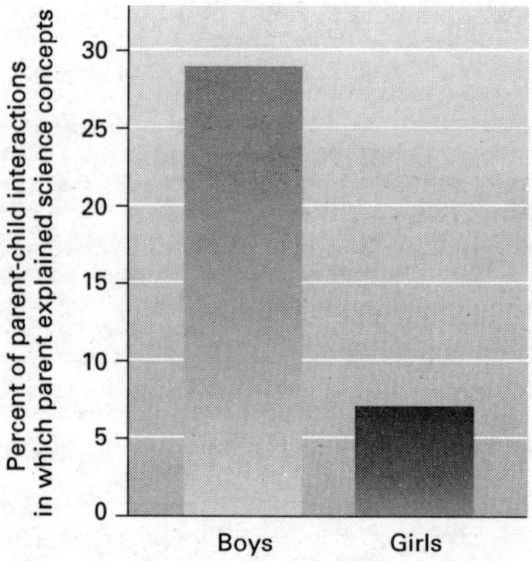

FIGURE 2.8 Parents' Explanations of Science to Sons and Daughters at a Science Museum. In a naturalistic observation study at a children's science museum, parents were three times more likely to explain science to boys than to girls (Crowley & others, 2001). The gender difference occurred regardless of whether the father, the mother, or both parents were with the child, although the gender difference was greatest for fathers' science explanations to sons and daughters.

Making observations in a laboratory allows us to control certain factors that influence behavior but are not the focus of our inquiry (Kantowitz, Roediger, & Elmes, 2005). However, laboratory research does have some drawbacks (Beins, 2004). First, it is almost impossible to conduct research without the participants' knowing they are being studied. Second, the laboratory setting is unnatural and therefore can cause the participants to behave unnaturally. Third, parents and children who are willing and able to come to a university laboratory may not fairly represent the population we are interested in studying. Those who are unfamiliar with university settings, and with the idea of "helping science," may be intimidated by the setting. Finally, some aspects of child development are difficult if not impossible to examine in the laboratory.

Naturalistic observation provides insights that we sometimes cannot achieve in the laboratory (Billman, 2003). **Naturalistic observation** means observing behavior in real-world settings, making no effort to manipulate or control the situation. Child development researchers conduct naturalistic observations at homes, day-care centers, schools, playgrounds, malls, and other places children live in and frequent.

Figure 2.8 shows the results of a study using naturalistic observation. In this case, researchers observed how mothers and fathers interacted with their sons and daughters in a children's science museum (Crowley & others, 2001). Parents were three times more likely to engage boys than girls in explanatory talk while visiting exhibits at the science museum, suggesting a gender bias that encourages boys to be more interested in science than girls.

Survey and Interview Sometimes the best and quickest way to get information about people is to ask them for it. One technique is to *interview* them directly. A related method that is especially useful when information from many people is needed is the *survey*, sometimes referred to as a questionnaire. A standard set of questions is used to obtain people's self-reported attitudes or beliefs about a particular topic. In a good survey, the questions are clear and unbiased, allowing respondents to answer unambiguously (Babbie, 2005; Tourangeau, 2004).

Surveys and interviews can be used to study a wide range of topics from parenting attitudes to perceptions of friends to whether or not individuals use drugs. Surveys and interviews can be conducted in person, over the telephone, or over the Internet.

Some survey and interview questions are unstructured and open-ended, such as "Tell me about your relationship with your child?" or "What is your school like?" They allow for unique responses from each person surveyed. Other survey and interview questions are more structured and specific. For example, one national poll on beliefs about what needs to be done to improve U.S. schools asked: "Of the following four possibilities, which one do you think offers the most promise for improving public schools in the community: a qualified, competent teacher in every classroom; free choice for parents among a number of private, church-related, and public schools; rigorous academic standards; the elimination of social promotion; or don't know?" (Rose & Gallup, 2000). More than half of the respondents said that the most important way to improve schools is to have a qualified, competent teacher in every classroom.

One problem with surveys and interviews is the tendency of participants to answer questions in a way that they think is socially acceptable or desirable rather than telling what they truly think or feel (Babbie, 2005). For example, on a survey or in an interview some adolescents might say that they do not take drugs even though they do.

naturalistic observation Observing behavior in real-world settings.

standardized test A test with uniform procedures for administration and scoring. Many standardized tests allow a person's performance to be compared with the performance of other individuals.

Standardized Test Yet another method of collecting data is the **standardized test,** which has uniform procedures for administration and scoring. One example is the Stanford-Binet intelligence test, which is described in chapter 9, "Intelligence." Many standardized tests allow a person's performance to be compared with the performance of other individuals (Aiken, 2003; Gregory, 2004).

Scores on standardized tests are often stated in *percentiles,* which indicate how much higher or lower one person's score is than the scores of people who previously took the test. If you scored in the 92nd percentile on the SAT, 92 percent of a large group of individuals who previously took the test received scores lower than yours.

The main advantage of standardized tests is that they provide information about individual differences among people (Gregory, 2004; Walsh & Betz, 2001). One problem with standardized tests is that they do not always predict behavior in nontest situations. Another problem is that standardized tests are based on the belief that a person's behavior is consistent and stable, yet personality and intelligence—two primary targets of standardized testing—can vary with the situation. For example, a child may perform poorly on a standardized intelligence test in a school psychologist's office but score much higher at home, where he or she is less anxious. This criticism is especially relevant for members of minority groups, some of whom have been inaccurately classified as mentally retarded on the basis of their scores on intelligence tests (Valencia & Suzuki, 2001).

In addition, cross-cultural psychologists caution that many psychological tests developed in Western cultures might not be appropriate in other cultures (Cole, 2006; Cushner, 2003, 2006; Shweder & others, 2006). People in other cultures may have had experiences that cause them to interpret and respond to questions much differently from the people on whom the test was standardized.

Psychophysiological Measures To collect data about an individual's biological functioning, *psychophysiological measures* may be the most useful method. These measures are used to assess the functioning of the central nervous system (CNS), the autonomic nervous system(ANS), and the endocrine system.

The *central nervous system* consists of the brain and spinal cord. Both neuroimaging techniques and the electroencephalograph provide information about the brain and its functioning. *Neuroimaging techniques* include several methods that produce varying types of images of the brain's structure or its activity or both. Especially useful is *magnetic resonance imaging (MRI)*, which creates magnetic fields around a person and uses radio waves to construct very clear images of the brain's tissues. A particular type of MRI also provides images of the brain's biochemical activities (see figure 2.9).

The *electroencephalogram (EEG)* records the brain's electrical activity. Electrodes placed on the scalp detect brain-wave activity, which is recorded on a chart known as an electroencephalograph. EEGs have been used to assess the brain's functioning during performance on memory tasks and to measure brain damage (Nelson, 2003).

The *autonomic nervous system* takes messages to and from the body's internal organs, monitoring such processes as heart rate, breathing, and digestion. Heart rate and breathing can be measured even in very young infants, and they can give useful indicators of an infant's capacities. For example, "heart rate indicates whether an infant is simply staring blankly at a stimulus (heart rate is stable) or is actually attending to and processing the stimulus (heart rate slows during periods of concentration)" (Lamb, Bornstein, & Teti, 2002, p. 81).

The *endocrine system* consists of a set of glands that regulate the activities of certain organs by producing and releasing the chemical products known as *hormones* into the bloodstream. Measuring hormone concentrations in the blood can provide information about many aspects of a person's emotional and physical status, such as stress levels and pubertal change (Gunnar & Davis, 2003; Susman & Rogol, 2004). For example, the hormone cortisol is secreted in times of stress, such as when an infant is awakened by a loud noise. And levels of estrogens and androgens change as girls and boys go through puberty.

Caution needs to be exercised in interpreting data obtained using psychophysical measures. "Many factors determine responses, and thus there is never an exact one-to-one correspondence between a

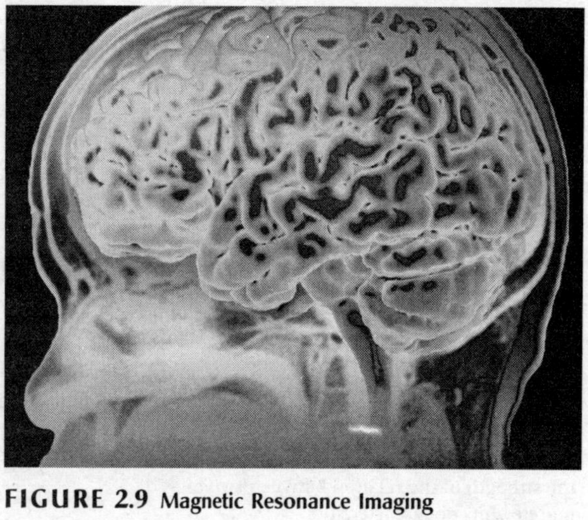

FIGURE 2.9 Magnetic Resonance Imaging

Mahatma Gandhi was the spiritual leader of India in the middle of the twentieth century. Erik Erikson conducted an extensive case study of his life to determine what contributed to his identity development. *What are some limitations of the case study approach?*

physiological index (such as heart rate acceleration or cortisol level) and a psychological state (such as fear)" (Lamb, Bornstein, & Teti, 2002, p. 84).

Case Study A **case study** is an in-depth look at a single individual. Case studies are performed mainly by mental health professionals when, for either practical or ethical reasons, the unique aspects of an individual's life cannot be duplicated and tested in other individuals (Dattilio, 2001). A case study provides information about one person's fears, hopes, fantasies, traumatic experiences, upbringing, family relationships, health, or anything that helps the psychologist understand the person's mind and behavior.

One famous case study is Erik Erikson's (1969) analysis of India's spiritual leader Mahatma Gandhi. Erikson studied Gandhi's life in great depth to discover insights about how Gandhi's spiritual identity developed, especially during his youth. In putting the pieces of Gandhi's identity development together, Erikson described the contributions of culture, history, family, and various other factors that might affect the way other people develop an identity.

Case histories provide dramatic, in-depth portrayals of people's lives, but we must be cautious when generalizing from this information (Leary, 2004). The subject of a case study is unique, with a genetic makeup and personal history that no one else shares. In addition, case studies involve judgments of unknown reliability. Psychologists who conduct case studies rarely check to see if other psychologists agree with their observations.

Research Designs

Suppose you want to find out whether the children of permissive parents are more likely than other children to be rude and unruly. What method would you use to collect your data? The data-collection method that researchers choose often depends on the goal of their research Best & Kahn, 2006; Fraenkel & Wallen, 2006. The goal may be simply to describe a phenomenon, or to describe relationships between phenomena, or to determine the causes or effects of a certain phenomenon.

Perhaps you decide to observe both permissive and strict parents with their children and compare them. How would you do that? In addition to a method for collecting data, you would need a research design. There are three main types of research design: descriptive, correlational, and experimental.

Descriptive Research All of the data-collection methods that we have discussed can be used in **descriptive research,** which aims to observe and record behavior. For example, a researcher might observe the extent to which children are altruistic or aggressive toward each other. By itself, descriptive research cannot prove what causes some phenomena, but it can reveal important information about people's behavior.

Correlational Research In contrast to descriptive research, correlational research goes beyond describing phenomena to provide information that will help us to predict how people will behave. In **correlational research,** the goal is to describe the strength of the relationship between two or more events or characteristics. The more strongly the two events are correlated (or related or associated), the more effectively we can predict one event from the other (Whitley, 2002).

For example, to study whether children of permissive parents have less self-control than other children, you would need to carefully record observations of parents' permissiveness and their children's self-control. The data could then be

case study An in-depth look at a single individual.

descriptive research This type of research aims to observe and record behavior.

correlational research The goal is to describe the strength of the relation between two or more events or characteristics.

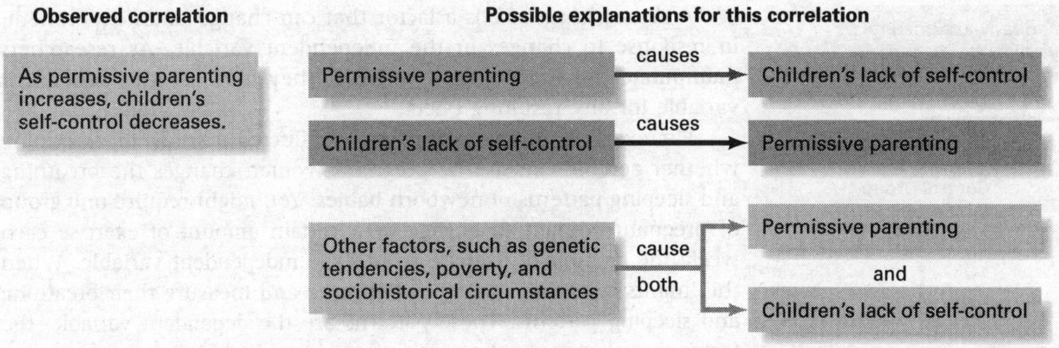

FIGURE 2.10 Possible Explanations for Correlational Data. An observed correlation between two events cannot be used to conclude that one event caused the other. Some possibilities are that the second event caused the first event or that a third, unknown event caused the correlation between the first two events.

analyzed statistically to yield a numerical measure, called a **correlation coefficient,** which is a number based on a statistical analysis that describes the degree of association between two variables.

Correlation coefficients range from +1.00 to −1.00. A negative number means an inverse relation. For example, researchers often find a *negative* correlation between permissive parenting and children's self-control. By contrast, they often find a *positive* correlation between parental monitoring of children and children's self-control. The higher the correlation coefficient (whether positive or negative), the stronger the association between the two variables. A correlation of 0 means that there is no association between the variables. A correlation of −.40 is stronger than a correlation of +.20 because we disregard whether the correlation is positive or negative in determining the strength of the correlation.

A caution is in order, however. Correlation does not equal causation (Rosnow & Rosenthal, 2005). The correlational finding just mentioned does not mean that permissive parenting necessarily causes low self-control in children. It could mean that, but it also could mean that a child's lack of self-control caused the parents to simply throw up their arms in despair and give up trying to control the child. It also could mean that other factors, such as heredity or poverty, caused the correlation between permissive parenting and low self-control in children. Figure 2.10 illustrates these possible interpretations of correlational data.

Throughout this book you will read about numerous correlational research studies. Keep in mind how easy it is to assume causality when two events or characteristics merely are correlated (Christensen, 2004; Rowntree, 2004).

Experimental Research

To study causality, researchers turn to **experimental research.** An **experiment** is a carefully regulated procedure in which one or more factors believed to influence the behavior being studied are manipulated while all other factors are held constant. If the behavior under study changes when a factor is manipulated, we say that the manipulated factor has caused the behavior to change. In other words, the experiment has demonstrated cause and effect. The cause is the factor that was manipulated. The effect is the behavior that changed because of the manipulation. Nonexperimental research methods (descriptive and correlational research) cannot establish cause and effect because they do not manipulate factors in a controlled way (Martin, 2004).

Independent and Dependent Variables Experiments include two types of changeable factors, or variables: independent and dependent. An *independent variable* is a manipulated, influential, experimental factor. It is a potential cause. The label *independent* is used because this variable can be manipulated independently of other factors to determine its effect. One experiment may include several independent variables.

www.mhhe.com/santrockcd11

Correlational Research
Experimental Research

correlation coefficient A number based on a statistical analysis that is used to describe the degree of association between two variables.

experimental research Research involving experiments that permit the determination of cause.

experiment A carefully regulated procedure in which one or more of the factors believed to influence the behavior being studied is manipulated and all other factors are held constant.

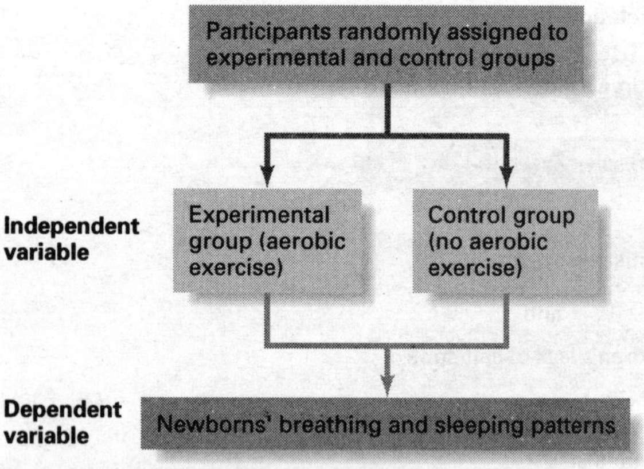

FIGURE 2.11 Principles of Experimental Research. Imagine that you decide to conduct an experimental study of the effects of aerobic exercise by pregnant women on their newborns' breathing and sleeping patterns. You would randomly assign pregnant women to experimental and control groups. The experimental group women would engage in aerobic exercise over a specified number of sessions and weeks. The control group would not. Then, when the infants are born, you would assess their breathing and sleeping patterns. If the breathing and sleeping patterns of newborns whose mothers were in the experimental group are more positive than those of the control group, you would conclude that aerobic exercise caused the positive effects.

A *dependent variable* is a factor that can change in an experiment, in response to changes in the independent variable. As researchers manipulate the independent variable, they measure the dependent variable for any resulting effect.

For example, suppose that you conducted a study to determine whether aerobic exercise by pregnant women changes the breathing and sleeping patterns of newborn babies. You might require one group of pregnant women to engage in a certain amount of exercise each week; the amount of exercise is thus the independent variable. When the infants are born, you would observe and measure their breathing and sleeping patterns. These patterns are the dependent variable, the factor that changes as the result of your manipulation.

Experimental and Control Groups Experiments can involve one or more experimental groups and one or more control groups. An *experimental group* is a group whose experience is manipulated. A *control group* is a comparison group that is as much like the experimental group as possible and that is treated in every way like the experimental group except for the manipulated factor (independent variable). The control group serves as a baseline against which the effects of the manipulated condition can be compared.

Random assignment is an important principle for deciding whether each participant will be placed in the experimental group or in the control group (Kantowitz, Roediger, & Elmes, 2005). *Random assignment* means that researchers assign participants to experimental and control groups by chance. It reduces the likelihood that the experiment's results will be due to any preexisting differences between groups. In the example of the effects of aerobic exercise by pregnant women on the breathing and sleeping patterns of their newborns, you would randomly assign half of the pregnant women to engage in aerobic exercise over a period of weeks (the experimental group) and the other half to not exercise over the same number of weeks (the control group). Figure 2.11 illustrates the elements of experimental research.

Time Span of Research

Developmentalists must deal with some additional issues when they design research. Often, they want to focus on the relation of age to some other variable. The time span of a research investigation is a special concern to them (Hartmann & Pelzel, 2005). Researchers can study different individuals of different ages and compare them or they can study the same individuals as they age over time.

Cross-Sectional Approach

The **cross-sectional approach** is a research strategy in which individuals of different ages are compared at one time. A typical cross-sectional study might include a group of 5-year-olds, 8-year-olds, and 11-year-olds. The different groups can be compared with respect to a variety of dependent variables: IQ, memory, peer relations, attachment to parents, hormonal changes, and so on. All of this can be accomplished in a short time. In some studies data are collected in a single day. Even in large-scale cross-sectional studies with hundreds of subjects, data collection does not usually take longer than several months to complete.

cross-sectional approach A research strategy in which individuals of different ages are compared at one time.

The main advantage of the cross-sectional study is that the researcher does not have to wait for the individuals to grow up or become older. Despite its time efficiency, the cross-sectional approach has its drawbacks. It gives no information about how individuals change or about the stability of their characteristics. The increases and decreases of development—the hills and valleys of growth and development—can become obscured in the cross-sectional approach. For example, in a cross-sectional study of self-esteem, average increases and decreases might be revealed.

But the study would not show how the self-esteem of individual adults waxed and waned over the years.

Longitudinal Approach The **longitudinal approach** is a research strategy in which the same individuals are studied over a period of time, usually several years or more. For example, if a study of self-esteem were conducted longitudinally, the same children might be assessed three times—at 5, 8, and 11 years of age. Some longitudinal studies take place over shorter time frames, even just a year or so.

Longitudinal studies provide a wealth of information about such important issues as stability and change in development and the importance of early experience for later development, but they are not without their problems (Raudenbush, 2001). They are expensive and time-consuming. Also, the longer the study lasts, the more participants drop out. For example, children's families may move, get sick, lose interest, and so forth. Those who remain in the study may be dissimilar to those who drop out, biasing the results. Those individuals who remain in a longitudinal study over a number of years may be more compulsive and conformity-oriented, for example, or they might have more stable lives.

longitudinal approach A research strategy in which the same individuals are studied over a period of time, usually several years or more.

Methods and Theories

A point that is important to make is that theories often are linked with a particular research method or methods. Thus, methods that researchers use are associated with their particular theoretical approach. Figure 2.12 illustrates the connections between research methods and theories.

Research Method	Theory
Observation	• All theories emphasize some form of observation. • Behavioral and social cognitive theories place the strongest emphasis on laboratory observation. • Ethological theory places the strongest emphasis on naturalistic observation.
Interview/survey	• Psychoanalytic and cognitive studies (Piaget, Vygotsky) often use interviews. • Behavioral, social cognitive, and ethological theories are the least likely to use surveys or interviews.
Standardized test	• None of the theories discussed emphasize the use of this method.
Physiological measures	• None of the theories discussed address psychophysiological measures to any significant degree.
Case study	• Psychoanalytic theories (Freud, Erikson) are the most likely to use this method.
Correlational research	• All of the theories use this research method, although psychoanalytic theories are the least likely to use it.
Experimental research	• The behavioral and social cognitive theories and the information-processing theories are the most likely to use the experimental method. • Psychoanalytic theories are the least likely to use it.
Cross-sectional/ longitudinal methods	• No theory described uses these methods more than any other.

FIGURE 2.12 Connections of Research Methods to Theories

Whatever a researcher's theory or method, he or she should be willing to take one further step: to submit the study and results to the judgment of his or her peers. Then the study can be criticized, compared with other findings, perhaps replicated, perhaps discredited. This openness to testing and additional evidence is at the heart of science. The main forum through which this judgment by others in the scientific community can occur is the research journal, which is the subject of the Research in Child Development interlude that follows.

RESEARCH IN CHILD DEVELOPMENT

www.mhhe.com/santrockcd11

Developmental Psychology
Child Development

Research Journals

Regardless of whether you pursue a career in child development, education, psychology, nursing, or a related field, you can benefit by learning about research journals. Possibly as a student you will be required to look up original research in journals as part of writing a term paper. As a parent, teacher, or nurse you might want to consult journals to obtain information that will help you understand and work more effectively with children. And, as an inquiring person, you might want to look up information in journals after you have heard or read something that piqued your curiosity.

A *journal* publishes scholarly and academic information, usually in a specific domain, such as physics, math, sociology, or, in the case of our interest, child development. Scholars in these fields publish most of their research in journals, which are the core information source in virtually every academic discipline.

Research journals are the core of information in virtually every academic discipline. Those shown here are among the increasing number of research journals that publish information about child development. *What are the main parts of a research article that presents findings from original research?*

Journal articles are usually written for other professionals in the same field as the journal's focus—such as geology, anthropology, or child development. Because the articles are written for other professionals, they often contain technical language. You have probably already had one or more courses in psychology, and you will be learning a great deal more about the specialized field of child development in this course, which should improve your ability to understand journal articles in this field.

An increasing number of journals publish information about children's development. Among the leading journals of child development are *Child Development, Developmental Psychology, Infant Behavior & Development, Pediatric Nursing, Pediatrics, Early Childhood Research Quarterly,* and *Journal of Research on Adolescence.* Also, a number of journals that do not focus solely on development include articles on children's development, such as *Journal of Educational Psychology, Sex Roles, Journal of Cross-Cultural Psychology, Journal of Marriage and the Family,* and *Journal of Consulting and Clinical Psychology.*

In psychology and the field of child development, most journal articles are reports of original research. Many journals also include review articles that present an overview of different studies on a particular topic, such as a review of day care, a review of the transition to elementary school, or a review of adolescent depression.

Many journals are highly selective about what they publish. Every journal has a board of experts that evaluates articles submitted for publication. One or more of the experts carefully examine the submitted paper and accept or reject it based on such factors as its contribution to the field, its theoretical relevance, its methodological excellence, and its clarity of writing. Some of the most prestigious journals reject as many as 80 to 90 percent of the articles submitted because they fail to meet the journal's standards.

Where can you find research journals? Your college or university library likely has one or more of the journals listed. Some public libraries also carry journals. An increasing number of research journals can be accessed on the Internet.

An *abstract* is a brief summary that appears at the beginning of a journal article. The abstract lets readers quickly determine whether the article is relevant to their interests and if they want to read the entire article. The *introduction,* as its title suggests, introduces the problem or issue that is being studied. It includes a concise review of research relevant to the topic, theoretical ties, and one or more hypotheses to be tested. The *method* section consists of a clear description of the subjects evaluated in the study, the measures used, and the procedures followed. The method section should be sufficiently clear and detailed so that, by reading it, another researcher could repeat, or replicate, the study. The *results* section reports the analysis of the data collected. In most cases, the results section includes statistical analyses that are difficult for nonprofessionals to understand. The *discussion* section describes the author's conclusions, inferences, and interpretation of the findings. Statements are usually made about whether the hypotheses presented in the introduction were supported, the limitations of the study, and suggestions for future research. The last part of a journal article is called *references,* which lists bibliographic information for every source cited in the article. The references section is often a good source for finding other articles relevant to the topic you are interested in.

Review and Reflect • **LEARNING GOAL 3**

3 Explain how research on child development is conducted

Review

- How are data on children's development collected?
- What are the main research designs used in studying development?
- What are some ways that researchers study the time span of people's lives?
- To what extent are theories and methods connected?

Reflect

- You have learned that correlation does not equal causation. Develop an example of two variables (two sets of observations) that are correlated but that you believe certainly have no causal relationship.

4 CHALLENGES IN CHILD DEVELOPMENT RESEARCH

- Conducting Ethical Research
- Minimizing Bias
- Thinking Critically About Research on Children's Development

The scientific foundation of research in child development helps to minimize the effect of individual researchers' biases and to maximize the objectivity of the results. Still, some subtle challenges remain. One is to ensure that research is conducted in an ethical way; another is to recognize, and try to overcome, researchers' deeply buried personal biases.

www.mhhe.com/santrockcd11

Psychologists' Ethical Principles

Conducting Ethical Research

Even if you have no formal exposure to child development beyond this course, you will find that scientific research in this field and related disciplines affects your everyday life. For one thing, decision makers in government, schools, and many other institutions use the results of research in child development to help children and the adults who care for them lead happier, healthier, more productive lives. The results of research, however, can also create ethical questions.

For example, the same line of research that enables previously sterile couples to have children might also let prospective parents "call up and order" the characteristics they prefer in their children and someday tip the balance of males and females in the world. Should embryos left over from procedures for increasing fertility be saved or discarded? Research that enables previously sterile couples to have children has also led to the spectacle of frozen embryos being passed about in the courts as a part of divorce settlements.

Ethics in research may affect you more personally if you serve as a participant in a study. In that event, you need to know about your rights as a participant and about the responsibilities researchers have to safeguard these rights. If you become a researcher in child development, you will need an even deeper understanding of ethics. Even if you only conduct one or more studies in this course or other courses, you must consider the rights of the participants who serve in studies. A student might think, "I volunteer at home several hours a week for children who are mentally retarded. I can use these children in my study to see if a particular treatment helps their memory for everyday tasks." But without proper permissions, the most well-meaning, kind, and considerate studies still violate the rights of the participants.

Safeguarding the rights of participants is a challenge because the potential harm is not always obvious. The failure to consider participants' well-being can have life-altering consequences for them. For example, one investigation of young dating couples asked them to complete a questionnaire (Rubin & Mitchell, 1976). One year later, when the researchers followed up with the original sample, 9 of 10 participants said they had discussed their answers with their dating partner. In most instances, the discussions helped to strengthen the relationships. In some cases, though, the participants used the questionnaire as a springboard to discuss previously hidden concerns. One participant said, "The study definitely played a role in ending my relationship with Larry." In this case, the couple had different views about how long they expected to be together. Their answers to the questions brought the disparity in their views to the surface and led to the end of their relationship. Researchers have a responsibility to anticipate the personal problems their study might cause and to at least inform the participants of the possible fallout.

Today colleges and universities have review boards that evaluate the ethical nature of research conducted at their institutions. Proposed research plans must pass the scrutiny of a research ethics committee before the research can be initiated.

In addition, the American Psychological Association (APA) has developed ethics guidelines for its members. The code of ethics instructs psychologists to protect their participants from mental and physical harm. The participants' best interests need to be kept foremost in the researcher's mind (Beins, 2004). APA's guidelines address four important issues:

- **Informed Consent.** All participants, if they are old enough (typically 7 years or older), must give their consent to participate. If they are not old enough, their parents' or guardians' consent must be attained. Informed consent means that the participants (and/or their parents or legal guardians) have been told what their participation will entail and any risks that might be involved. For example, if researchers want to study the effects of conflict in divorced families on children's self-esteem, the participants should be informed that in some instances discussion of a family's experiences might improve family relationships, but in other cases might raise unwanted stress. After informed consent is given, participants have the right to withdraw at any time.

- **Confidentiality.** Researchers are responsible for keeping all of the data they gather on individuals completely confidential and when possible, completely anonymous.
- **Debriefing.** After the study has been completed, participants should be informed of its purpose and the methods that were used. In most cases, the experimenter also can inform participants in a general manner beforehand about the purpose of the research without leading participants to behave in a way they think that the experimenter is expecting. When preliminary information about the study is likely to affect the results, participants at least can be debriefed after the study has been completed.
- **Deception.** This is an ethical issue that psychologists debate extensively (Hoyle & Judd, 2002). In some circumstances, telling the participant beforehand what the research study is about substantially alters the participant's behavior and invalidates the researcher's data. In all cases of deception, however, the researcher must ensure that the deception will not harm the participant and that the participant will be told the complete nature of the study (debriefed) as soon as possible after the study is completed.

Minimizing Bias

Research on children's development also creates another concern—conducting research without bias or prejudice toward any group of people. Of special concern is bias based on gender and bias based on culture or ethnicity.

Gender Bias For decades, society has had a strong gender bias, a preconceived notion about the abilities of females and males that prevented individuals from pursuing their own interests and achieving their potential (Hyde, 2004). But gender bias also has had a less obvious effect within the field of child development (Etaugh & Bridges, 2004). It is not unusual for conclusions to be drawn about females' attitudes and behaviors from research in which males were the only participants.

Florence Denmark and her colleagues (1988) argue as well that when gender differences are found, they sometimes are magnified. For example, a researcher might report that 74 percent of the boys had high achievement expectations versus only 67 percent of the girls and go on to talk about the differences in some detail. In reality, this might be a rather small difference. It might even disappear if the study were repeated or the study might have methodological problems that don't allow such strong interpretations.

Cultural and Ethnic Bias Research on child development needs to include more people from diverse ethnic groups (Garcia Coll & others, 2005; Graham, 1992; Parke & Clarke-Stewart, 2003). Historically, people from ethnic minority groups (African American, Latino, Asian American, and Native American) were excluded from most research in the United States. They were simply thought of as variations from the norm or average. In view of their long exclusion from research on child development, we might reasonably conclude that children's real lives are perhaps more varied than research data have indicated in the past (Ponterotto & others, 2001).

Researchers also have tended to overgeneralize about ethnic groups (Trimble, 1989). **Ethnic gloss** is using an ethnic label such as African American or Latino in a superficial way that portrays an ethnic group as being more homogeneous than it

ethnic gloss A superficial way of using an ethnic label, such as African American or Latino, that portrays an ethnic group as being more homogeneous than it really is.

Look at these two photographs, one of all White male children, the other of a diverse group of girls and boys from different ethnic groups, including some White children. Consider a topic in child development, such as parenting, cultural values, or independence seeking. *If you were conducting research on this topic, might the results of the study be different depending on whether the participants in your study were the children in the left or right photograph?*

really is. For example, a researcher might describe a research sample like this: "The participants were 20 Latinos and 20 Anglo-Americans." A more complete description of the Latino group might be something like this: "The 20 Latino participants were Mexican Americans from low-income neighborhoods in the southwestern area of Los Angeles. Twelve were from homes in which Spanish is the dominant language spoken, 8 from homes in which English is the main language spoken. Ten were born in the United States, 10 in Mexico. Ten described themselves as Mexican American, 5 as Mexican, 3 as American, 2 as Chicano, and 1 as Latino." Ethnic gloss can cause researchers to obtain samples of ethnic groups that are not representative of the group's diversity, which can lead to overgeneralization and stereotyping.

Pam Reid is a leading researcher who studies gender and ethnic bias in development. To read about Pam's interests, see the Careers in Child Development insert.

Thinking Critically About Research on Children's Development

Our society generates a vast amount of information about children in various media ranging from research journals to newspaper and television accounts. The information varies greatly in quality. How can you evaluate this information?

Be Cautious About What Is Reported in the Popular Media Television, radio, newspapers, and magazines frequently report research on child development. Many researchers regularly supply the media with information about children. In some cases, the popular media pick up research that has been published in professional journals or presented at national meetings. In other cases, the press was contacted about the research by the media relations department at a college.

However, not all research on children that is discussed in the media comes from professionals with excellent credentials and reputations. Journalists, television reporters, and other media personnel generally are not scientifically trained. It is not an easy task for them to sort through the avalanche of material they receive and to make sound decisions about which information to report.

Unfortunately, the media often focus on sensational findings. They want you to stay tuned or buy their publication. When the information they gather from research journals is not sensational, they may embellish it and sensationalize it, going beyond what the researcher intended.

Another problem with research reported in the media is a lack of time or space to report important details of a study. The media may summarize complex findings in only a few lines or a few minutes. Too often this means that what is reported is overgeneralized and stereotyped (Stanovich, 2004).

Don't Assume Group Research Applies to an Individual Most research focuses on groups, yet often people want to know how it applies to one individual. Individual variations about how participants respond are usually not the focus of research. For example, if researchers are interested in the effects of divorce on a child's ability to cope with stress, they might conduct a study with 50 children from divorced families and 50 children from intact, never-divorced families. They might find that the children from divorced families, as a group, had lower self-esteem than did the children from intact families. That is a group finding that applies to children from divorced families as a group. But it likely was the case that some of the children from divorced families had higher self-esteem than did the children from intact families—not as many, but some. Indeed, it is entirely possible that, of the 100 children in the study, the 2 or 3 children who had the highest self-esteem were from divorced families, but that was never reported.

Group research provides valuable information about a group of children, revealing strengths and weaknesses of the group. However, in many instances, parents, teachers, and others want to know about how to help one particular child. Unfortunately, the conclusions from group research do not always apply to an individual child.

Don't Overgeneralize About a Small or Clinical Sample In many cases, samples are too small to generalize to a larger population. For example, if a study of children from divorced families is based on only 10 to 20 children, what is found in the study cannot be generalized to all children from divorced families. Perhaps the sample was drawn from families who have substantial economic resources, are Anglo-American, live in a small southern town, and are undergoing therapy. From this study, we clearly would be making unwarranted generalizations if we thought the findings also characterize children from low- to moderate-income families, from other ethnic backgrounds, in a different geographic region, and who are not undergoing therapy.

Don't Generally Take a Single Study as the Defining Word It is extremely rare for a single study to have earth-shattering, conclusive answers that

CAREERS in CHILD DEVELOPMENT

Pam Reid

Educational and Developmental Psychologist

When she was a child, Pam Reid liked to play with chemistry sets. Pam majored in chemistry during college and wanted to become a doctor. However, when some of her friends signed up for a psychology class as an elective, she also decided to take the course. She was intrigued by learning about how people think, behave, and develop—so much so that she changed her major to psychology. Pam went on to obtain her Ph.D. in psychology (American Psychological Association, 2003, p. 16).

For a number of years, Pam was a professor of education and psychology at the University of Michigan, where she also was a research scientist at the Institute for Research on Women and Gender. Her main focus has been on how children and adolescents develop social skills with a special interest in the development of African American girls (Reid & Zalk, 2001). In 2004, Pam became provost and executive vice-president at Roosevelt University in Chicago.

Pam Reid (center, back row) with some of the graduate students she mentored at the University of Michigan.

apply to all children. In fact, when many studies focus on a particular issue, it is not unusual to find conflicting results from one study to the next. Reliable answers about children's development usually emerge only after many researchers have conducted similar studies and have drawn similar conclusions. In the case of divorce, if one study reports that a counseling program for children from divorced families improved their self-esteem, we cannot conclude that the counseling program will work as effectively with all children from divorced families until many studies have been conducted.

Don't Accept Causal Conclusions from Correlational Studies

Drawing causal conclusions from correlational studies is one of the most common mistakes made by the media. Remember that in an experiment participants are randomly assigned to treatments or experiences. In nonexperimental studies, two variables may be related to each other, but we cannot say that one variable causes the other when two or more factors simply are correlated.

Suppose a headline says, "Divorce Causes Children to Have Low Self-Esteem." We read the story and find out that the information is based on the results of a research study. But the study must be correlational, and the causal statement in the headline must be unproved, because researchers cannot, for ethical and practical reasons, randomly assign children to families that either will become divorced or will remain intact. It might well be, for example, that another factor, such as family conflict or economic problems, is typically responsible for both children's poor self-esteem and parents' divorce.

Always Consider the Source of the Information and Evaluate Its Credibility Finally, examine and evaluate the sources of information. As discussed earlier in the chapter, findings published in a research journal have been reviewed by a researcher's colleagues, who decide whether or not to publish them. Though the quality of research in journals is far from uniform, in most cases the research has undergone far more scrutiny than has research or other information that has not gone through the journal process. Within the popular media, reports about research in respected newspapers and magazines, such as the *New York Times* and *Newsweek*, are likely to have passed higher standards than what appears in tabloids, such as the *National Enquirer.*

In this chapter, we examined how children's development is studied from a scientific research perspective. In the next chapter, we will begin tracing the journey of childhood by examining biological beginnings. As you continue your study of children's development, remember to think critically about the research information you read about, hear about, and see in the media.

Review and Reflect • LEARNING GOAL 4

4 Discuss research challenges in child development

Review

- What are researchers' ethical responsibilities to the people they study?
- How can gender, cultural, and ethnic bias affect the outcome of a research study?
- What are some good strategies for thinking critically about research on children's development?

Reflect

- Choose one of the topics in this book and course–such as child care, parenting, or adolescent problems. Find an article in a research journal (for example, *Child Development* or *Developmental Psychology*) and an article in a newspaper or magazine on the same topic. How did the research article on the topic differ from the newspaper or magazine article? What did you learn from this comparison?

REACH YOUR LEARNING GOALS

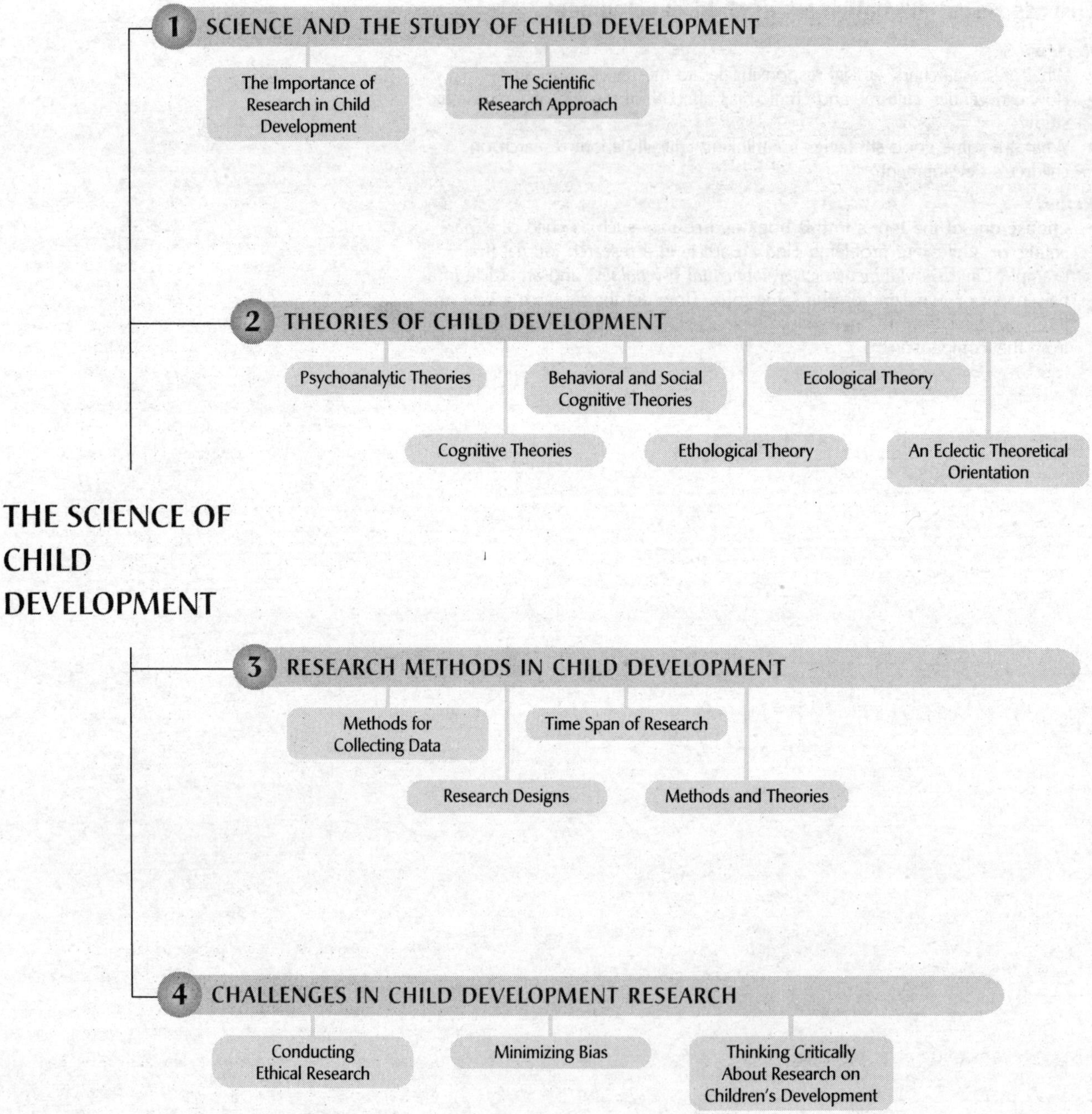

SUMMARY

1 Discuss the importance of research and the scientific method in the study of child development

- When we base information on personal experience, we aren't always objective. Research provides a vehicle for evaluating the accuracy of information.
- Scientific research is objective, systematic, and testable. Scientific research is based on the scientific method, which includes these steps: conceptualize the problem, collect data, draw conclusions, and revise conclusions and theory.

2 Describe the main theories of child development

- Psychoanalytic theories describe development as primarily unconscious and as heavily colored by emotion. Psychoanalytic theorists believe that behavior is merely a surface characteristic and that early experiences with parents shape development. Freud said that personality is made up of three structures—id, ego, and superego—and that individuals go through five psychosexual stages—oral, anal, phallic, latency, and genital. Erikson's theory emphasizes these eight psychosocial stages of development: trust vs. mistrust, autonomy vs. shame and doubt, initiative vs. guilt, industry vs. inferiority, identity vs. identity confusion, intimacy vs. isolation, generativity vs. stagnation, and integrity vs. despair. Contributions of psychoanalytic theories include an emphasis on a developmental approach to personality. One criticism is that they often lack scientific support.
- Cognitive theories emphasize conscious thoughts. Piaget proposed a cognitive developmental theory in which children use the processes of organization and adaptation (assimilation and accommodation) to understand their world. In Piaget's theory, children go through four cognitive stages: sensorimotor, preoperational, concrete operational, and formal operational. Vygotsky's sociocultural cognitive theory emphasizes how culture and social interaction guide cognitive development. Information-processing theory emphasizes that individuals manipulate information, monitor it, and strategize about it. Contributions of cognitive theories include an emphasis on the active construction of understanding. One criticism is that they give too little attention to individual variations.
- Three versions of the behavioral approach are Pavlov's classical conditioning, Skinner's operant conditioning, and Bandura's social cognitive theory. In Pavlov's classical conditioning, a neutral stimulus acquires the ability to produce a response originally produced by another stimulus. In Skinner's operant conditioning, the consequences of a behavior produce changes in the probability of the behavior's occurrence. In Bandura's social cognitive theory, observational learning is a key aspect of life-span development. Bandura emphasizes reciprocal interactions among the person (cognition), behavior, and environment. Contributions of the behavioral and social cognitive theories include an emphasis on scientific research. One criticism is that they give inadequate attention to developmental changes.
- Ethology stresses that behavior is strongly influenced by biology, is tied to evolution, and is characterized by critical or sensitive periods. Contributions of ethological theory include a focus on the biological and evolutionary basis of development. Criticisms include a belief that the critical and sensitive period concepts are too rigid.
- Ecological theory is Bronfenbrenner's environmental systems view of development. It proposes five environmental systems: microsystem, mesosystem, exosystem, macrosystem, and chronosystem. Contributions of the theory include a systematic examination of macro and micro dimensions of environmental systems. One criticism is that it gives inadequate attention to biological and cognitive factors.
- An eclectic theoretical orientation does not follow any one theoretical approach, but rather, selects from each theory whatever is considered best in it.

3 Explain how research on child development is conducted

- Methods for collecting data include observation, interview and survey, standardized test, physiological measures, and case study.
- Three main research designs are descriptive, correlational, and experimental. Descriptive research aims to observe and record behavior. In correlational research, the goal is to describe the strength of the relationship between two or more events or characteristics. Experimental research involves conducting an experiment, which can determine cause and effect. An independent variable is the manipulated, influential, experimental factor. A dependent variable is a factor that can change in an experiment, in response to changes in the independent variable. Experiments can involve one or more experimental groups and control groups. Researchers assign participants to experimental and control groups by chance.

- When researchers decide to study age or changes over time, they can conduct cross-sectional or longitudinal studies.
- The method or methods that a researcher selects are often linked to the theoretical approach of the researcher.

4 Discuss research challenges in child development

- Researchers' ethical responsibilities include protecting participants from mental and physical harm, seeking their informed consent, ensuring their confidentiality, debriefing them about the purpose and potential personal consequences of participating, and avoiding unnecessary deception of participants.
- Gender, cultural, and ethnic bias may lead researchers to exclude certain people from their studies, skewing the results; to magnify differences found between groups; or to overgeneralize about members of ethnic groups.
- Thinking critically about child development research includes being cautious about what is reported in the media, not automatically applying results from group research to one individual, not overgeneralizing about a small or clinical sample, not taking a single study as the defining word, not accepting causal interpretations from correlational studies, and always considering the source of the information and evaluating its credibility.

KEY TERMS

scientific method 37
theory 38
hypothesis 38
psychoanalytic theory 39
Erikson's theory 41
Piaget's theory 43
assimilation 43
accommodation 43
Vygotsky's theory 44
information-processing theory 45
social cognitive theory 46
ethological theory 47
ecological theory 49
eclectic theoretical orientation 51
laboratory 53
naturalistic observation 54
standarized test 54
case study 56
descriptive research 56
correlational research 56
correlation coefficient 57
experimental research 57
experiment 57
cross-sectional approach 58
longitudinal approach 59
ethnic gloss 63

KEY PEOPLE

Sigmund Freud 39
Erik Erikson 41
Jean Piaget 43
Lev Vygotsky 44
Robert Siegler 45
Ivan Pavlov 46
B. F. Skinner 46
Albert Bandura 46
Walter Mischel 46
Konrad Lorenz 48
Urie Bronfenbrenner 49

E-LEARNING TOOLS

To help you master the material in this chapter, visit the Online Learning Center for *Child Development,* eleventh edition (**www.mhhe.com/santrockcd11**), where you'll find these additional resources:

Taking It to the Net

1. Erika has never put much faith in Freud's theories, especially the one about the "Oedipus Complex" and how it accounts for differences in male and female moral development. Her child development teacher challenged her to find out if there is any empirical evidence to back up Freud's claims. Is there empirical evidence to back up Freud's claims?
2. Matilda is giving a presentation in her psychology class on memory aids. She knows the theory of information processing covers memory extensively. Find information for Matilda from work on this theory on elaboration techniques used in the teaching/learning process to help her prepare her presentation (and memorize it!).
3. For her senior psychology project, Doris wants to study the effect on self-esteem of mandatory school uniforms. She wants to limit her study to fourth graders. She has located a school with a mandatory uniform policy and one without such a policy. What type of research design will she use?

Nursing, Parenting, and Teaching Exercises

Build your decision-making skills by trying your hand at the scenarios on the Online Learning Center.

Video Clips

The Online Learning Center includes the following videos for this chapter:

- Attachment Theory
  Renowned attachment researcher L. Alan Sroufe defines attachment theory and how it relates to children's social and emotional development. He states that attachment theory led to a revolution in developmental psychology. He uses examples from his own research to illustrate the significance of attachment relationships.
- Ethical Issues in Studying Infants
  Renowned infant researcher Albert Yonas, Department of Psychology, University of Minnesota, discusses the ethical issues he faces when studying infants.

Section 2

BIOLOGICAL PROCESSES, PHYSICAL DEVELOPMENT, AND PERCEPTUAL DEVELOPMENT

What endless questions vex the thought, of whence and whither, when and how.

—Sir Richard Burton
British Explorer, 19th Century

The rhythm and meaning of life involve beginnings, with questions raised about how, from so simple a beginning, complex forms develop, grow, and mature. What was this organism, what is this organism, and what will this organism be? In Section 2, you will read four chapters: "Biological Beginnings" (chapter 3), "Prenatal Development and Birth" (chapter 4), "Physical Development and Health" (chapter 5), and "Motor, Sensory, and Perceptual Development" (chapter 6).

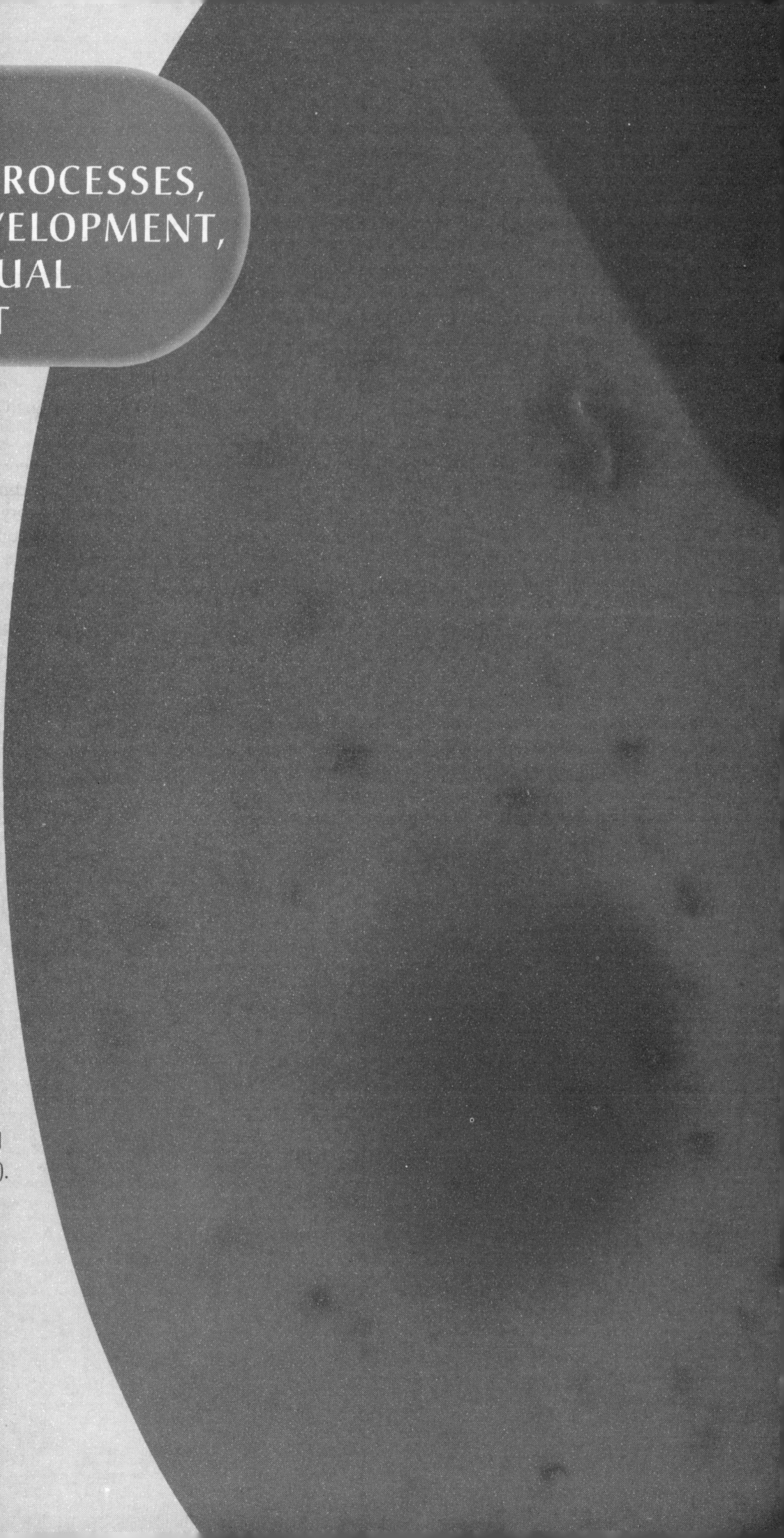

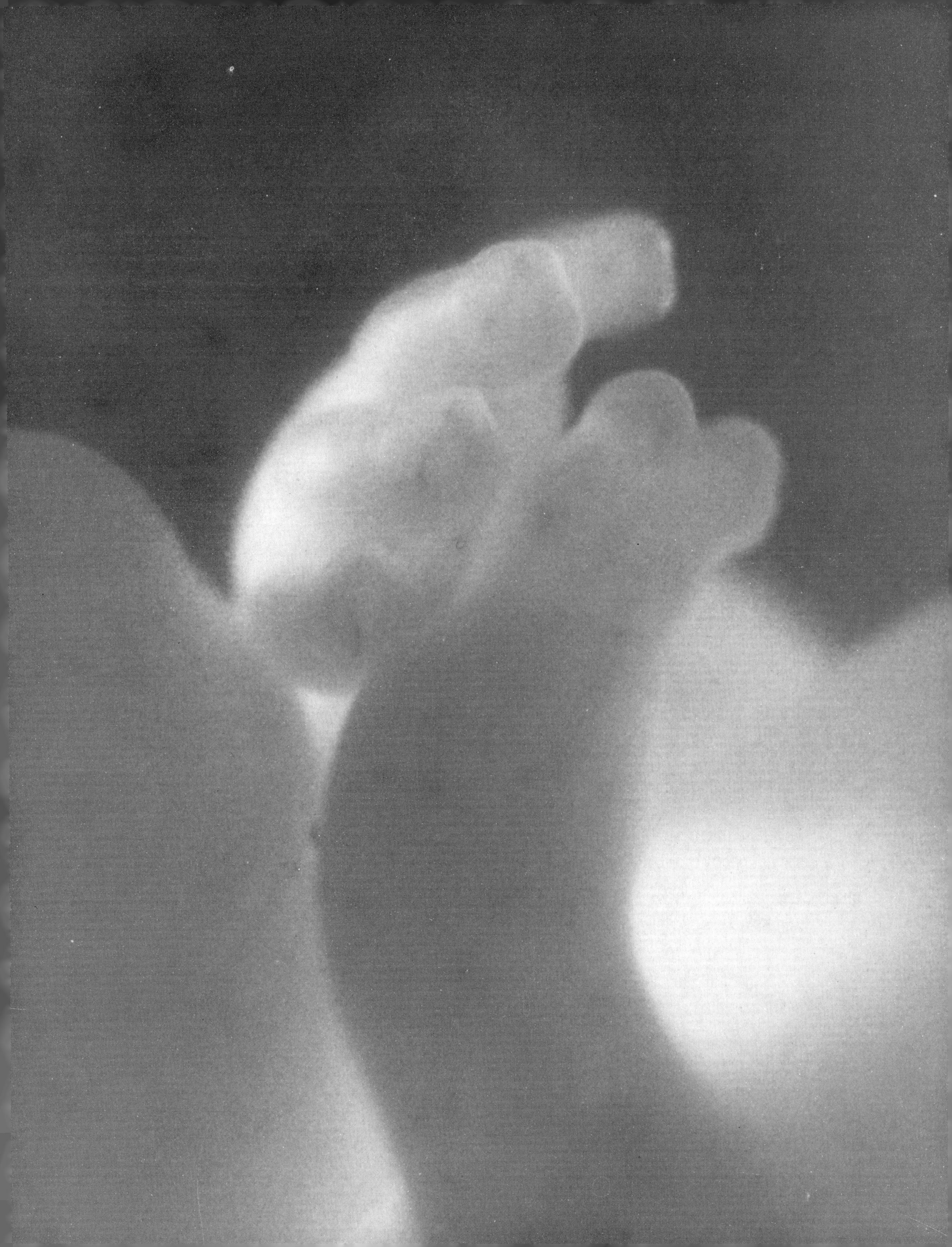

Chapter 3 BIOLOGICAL BEGINNINGS

There are one hundred and ninety-three living species of monkeys and apes. One hundred and ninety-two of them are covered with hair. The exception is the naked ape, self-named Homo sapiens.

—DESMOND MORRIS
British Zoologist, 20th Century

CHAPTER OUTLINE

THE EVOLUTIONARY PERSPECTIVE

Natural Selection and Adaptive Behavior
Evolutionary Psychology

GENETIC FOUNDATIONS

The Genetic Process
Genetic Principles
Chromosome and Gene-Linked Abnormalities

REPRODUCTIVE CHALLENGES AND CHOICES

Prenatal Diagnostic Tests
Infertility and Reproductive Technology
Adoption

HEREDITY AND ENVIRONMENT INTERACTION: THE NATURE-NURTURE DEBATE

Behavior Genetics
Heredity-Environment Correlations
Shared and Nonshared Environmental Experiences
The Epigenetic View
Conclusions About Heredity-Environment Interaction

LEARNING GOALS

1. **Discuss the evolutionary perspective on development**
2. **Describe what genes are and how they influence human development**
3. **Identify some important reproductive challenges and choices**
4. **Characterize some of the ways that heredity and environment interact to produce individual differences in development**

The Stories of the Jim and Jim Twins

Jim Lewis (*left*) and Jim Springer (*right*).

Jim Springer and Jim Lewis are identical twins. They were separated at 4 weeks of age and did not see each other again until they were 39 years old. Both worked as part-time deputy sheriffs, vacationed in Florida, drove Chevrolets, had dogs named Toy, and married and divorced women named Betty. One twin named his son James Allan, and the other named his son James Alan. Both liked math but not spelling, enjoyed carpentry and mechanical drawing, chewed their fingernails down to the nubs, had almost identical drinking and smoking habits, had hemorrhoids, put on 10 pounds at about the same point in development, first suffered headaches at the age of 18, and had similar sleep patterns.

Jim and Jim do have some differences. One wears his hair over his forehead, the other slicks it back and has sideburns. One expresses himself best orally; the other is more proficient in writing. But, for the most part, their profiles are remarkably similar.

Jim and Jim were part of the Minnesota Study of Twins Reared Apart, directed by Thomas Bouchard and his colleagues. The study brings identical twins (identical genetically because they come from the same fertilized egg) and fraternal twins (who come from different fertilized eggs) from all over the world to Minneapolis to investigate their lives. There the twins complete personality and intelligence tests, and they provide detailed medical histories, including information about diet and smoking, exercise habits, chest X-rays, heart stress tests, and EEGs (brain-wave tests). The twins are asked more than 15,000 questions about their family and childhood, personal interests, vocational orientation, values, and aesthetic judgments (Bouchard & others, 1990).

Another pair of identical twins in the Minnesota study, Daphne and Barbara, are called the "giggle sisters" because, after being reunited, they were always making each other laugh. A thorough search of their adoptive families' histories revealed no gigglers. The giggle sisters handled stress by ignoring it, avoided conflict and controversy whenever possible, and showed no interest in politics.

Two other identical twin sisters were separated at 6 weeks and reunited in their fifties. Both had nightmares, which they describe in hauntingly similar ways: both dreamed of doorknobs and fishhooks in their mouths as they smothered to death! The nightmares began during early adolescence and stopped within the past 10 to 12 years. Both women were bed wetters until about 12 or 13 years of age, and their educational and marital histories are remarkably similar.

When genetically identical twins who were separated as infants show such striking similarities in their tastes and habits and choices, can we conclude that their genes must have caused the development of those tastes and habits and choices? Some critics of the Minnesota identical twins study point out that the twins shared not only the same genes but also some experiences. Some of the separated twins were together for several months prior to their adoption, and some of the twins had been reunited prior to testing (in some cases, many years earlier). Furthermore, adoption agencies often place twins in similar homes, and even strangers who spend several hours together and start comparing their lives are likely to come up with some coincidental similarities (Adler, 1991). Still, the Minnesota study of identical twins reflects the interest scientists have recently shown in the genetic basis of human development, and it points to the need for further research on genetic and environmental factors (Bouchard, 1995, 2004).

PREVIEW

The examples of Jim and Jim, the giggle sisters, and the identical twins who had the same nightmares stimulate us to think about our genetic heritage and the biological foundations of our existence. Organisms are not like billiard balls, moved by simple, external forces to predictable positions on life's pool table. Environmental experiences and biological foundations work together to make us who we are. Our coverage of life's biological beginnings focuses on evolution, genetic foundations, challenges and choices regarding reproduction, and the interaction of heredity and environment.

1 THE EVOLUTIONARY PERSPECTIVE

- Natural Selection and Adaptive Behavior
- Evolutionary Psychology

In evolutionary time, humans are relative newcomers to Earth. If we consider evolutionary time as a calendar year, humans arrived here only in the last moments of December (Sagan, 1977). As our earliest ancestors left the forest to feed on the savannahs, and then to form hunting societies on the open plains, their minds and behaviors changed, and they eventually established humans as the most successful and dominant species on earth. How did this evolution come about?

Natural Selection and Adaptive Behavior

Natural selection is the evolutionary process that favors individuals of a species that are best adapted to survive and reproduce. To understand what this means, let's return to the middle of the nineteenth century, when the British naturalist Charles Darwin was traveling around the world, observing many different species of animals in their natural surroundings. Darwin, who published his observations and thoughts in *On the Origin of Species* (1859), noted that most organisms reproduce at rates that would cause enormous increases in the population of most species and yet populations remain nearly constant. He reasoned that an intense, constant struggle for food, water, and resources must occur among the many young born each generation, because many of the young do not survive. Those that do survive and reproduce pass on their characteristics to the next generation. Darwin believed that these survivors are better *adapted* to their world than are the nonsurvivors (Johnson, 2005; Rose & Mueller, 2006). The best-adapted individuals survive to leave the most offspring. Over the course of many generations, organisms with the characteristics needed for survival make up an increased percentage of the population. Over many, many generations, this could produce a gradual modification of the whole population. If environmental conditions change, however, other characteristics might become favored by natural selection, moving the species in a different direction (McKee, Poirier, & McGraw, 2005).

All organisms must adapt to particular places, climates, food sources, and ways of life. An example of adaptation is an eagle's claws, which facilitate predation. *Adaptive behavior* is behavior that promotes an organism's survival in the natural habitat (Cosmides & others, 2003). For example, in the human realm, attachment between a caregiver and a baby ensures the infant's closeness to a caregiver for feeding and protection from danger, thus increasing the infant's chances of survival. Another human example of an evolutionary-based adaptation involves pregnancy sickness (a tendency for women to avoid certain foods and become nauseous during pregnancy) (Schmitt & Pilcher, 2004). Women with pregnancy sickness tend to avoid foods that are higher in toxins, such as coffee, that may harm the fetus. Thus, pregnancy sickness may have been favored as an adaptation in evolution because it enhances the offspring's ability to survive.

Evolutionary Psychology

Although Darwin introduced the theory of evolution by natural selection in 1859, his ideas only recently have become a popular framework for explaining behavior. Psychology's newest approach, **evolutionary psychology,** emphasizes the importance of adaptation, reproduction, and "survival of the fittest" in shaping behavior. "Fit" in this sense refers to the ability to bear offspring that survive long enough to bear offspring of their own. In this view, the evolutionary process of natural selection has favored behaviors that increase our reproductive success, our ability to pass our genes to the next generation (Durrant & Ellis, 2003; Kenrick, Li, & Butner, 2003).

David Buss (1995, 2000, 2004) has been especially influential in stimulating new interest in how evolution can explain human behavior. He believes that just as evolution shapes our physical features, such as body shape and height, it also pervasively influences how we make decisions, how aggressive we are, our fears, and our mating patterns. For example, assume that our ancestors were hunters and gatherers on the plains and that men did most of the hunting and women stayed close to home gathering seeds and plants for food. If you have to travel some distance from your home in an effort to find and slay a fleeing animal, you need not only certain physical traits but also the ability for certain types of spatial thinking. Men born with these traits would be more likely than men without them to survive, to bring home lots of food, and to be considered attractive mates—and thus to reproduce and pass on these characteristics to their children. In other words, some traits would provide a reproductive advantage for males and, over many generations, men with good spatial thinking skills might become more numerous in the population. Critics point out that this scenario might or might not have actually happened.

evolutionary psychology Emphasizes the importance of adaptation, reproduction, and "survival of the fittest" in shaping behavior.

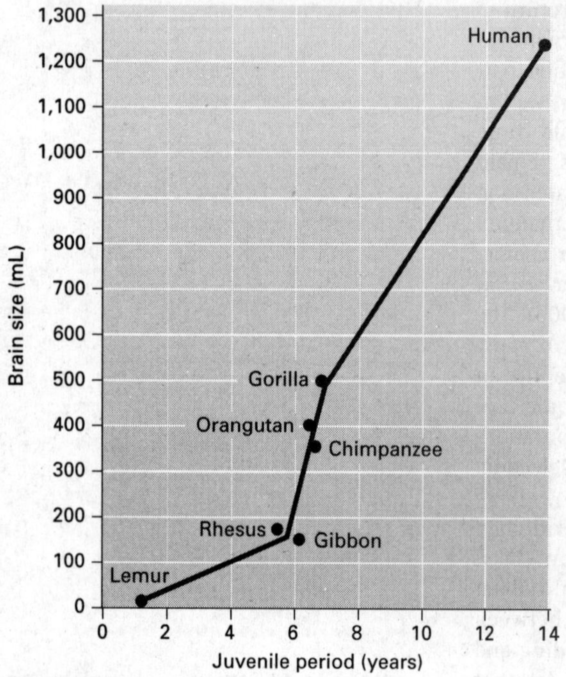

FIGURE 3.1 **The Brain Sizes of Various Primates and Humans in Relation to the Length of the Juvenile Period**

Evolutionary Developmental Psychology

Much of the thinking about evolutionary psychology has not had a developmental focus. Recently, however, interest has grown in applying the concepts of evolutionary psychology to the changes that take place as people develop. Here are a few ideas proposed by evolutionary developmental psychologists (Bjorklund & Pellegrini, 2002, pp. 336–340):

- *An extended "juvenile" period evolved because humans require time to develop a large brain and learn the complexity of human social communities.* Humans take longer to become reproductively mature than any other mammal (see figure 3.1). During this time they develop a large brain and the experiences required for mastering the complexities of human society.
- *"Many aspects of childhood function as preparations for adulthood and were selected over the course of evolution"* (p. 337). Play is one possible example. Beginning in the preschool years, boys in all cultures engage in more rough-and-tumble play than girls. Perhaps rough-and-tumble play prepares boys for fighting and hunting as adults. In contrast to boys, girls engage in play that involves more imitation of parents, such as caring for dolls, and less physical dominance. This, according to evolutionary psychologists, is an evolved tendency that prepares females for becoming the primary caregivers for their offspring.

- *Some characteristics of childhood were selected because they are adaptive at specific points in development, not because they prepare children for adulthood.* For example, some aspects of play may function, not to prepare us for adulthood, but to help children adapt to their immediate circumstances, perhaps to learn about their current environment.
- *Many evolved psychological mechanisms are domain-specific.* That is, the mechanisms apply only to a specific aspect of a person's psychological makeup (Atkinson & Wheeler, 2004; Rubenstein, 2004). According to evolutionary psychology, information processing is one example. In this view, the mind is not a general-purpose device that can be applied equally to a vast array of problems. Instead, as our ancestors dealt with certain recurring problems, specialized modules evolved that process information related to those problems, such as a module for physical knowledge, a module for mathematical knowledge, and a module for language. Also in this view, "infants enter the world 'prepared' to process and learn some information more readily than others, and these preparations serve as the foundation for social and cognitive development" (p. 338).
- *Evolved mechanisms are not always adaptive in contemporary society.* Some behaviors that were adaptive for our prehistoric ancestors may not serve us well today. For example, the food-scarce environment of our ancestors likely led to humans' propensity to gorge when food is available and to crave high-caloric foods, a trait that might lead to an epidemic of obesity when food is plentiful.

Evaluating Evolutionary Psychology Although the popular press gives a lot of attention to the ideas of evolutionary psychology, it remains just one theoretical approach. Like the theories described in chapter 2, it has limitations, weaknesses, and critics. Albert Bandura (1998), whose social cognitive theory was described in chapter 1, acknowledges the important influence of evolution on human adaptation. However, he rejects what he calls "one-sided evolutionism," which sees social behavior as the product of evolved biology. An alternative is a *bidirectional view,* in which environmental and biological conditions influence each other. In this view, evolutionary pressures created changes in biological structures that allowed the use of tools, which enabled our ancestors to manipulate the environment, constructing new environmental conditions. In turn, environmental innovations produced new selection pressures that led to the evolution of specialized biological systems for consciousness, thought, and language.

In other words, evolution gave us bodily structures and biological potentialities; it does not dictate behavior. People have used their biological capacities to produce diverse cultures—aggressive and pacific, egalitarian and autocratic. As American scientist Stephen Jay Gould (1981) concluded, in most domains of human functioning, biology allows a broad range of cultural possibilities.

www.mhhe.com/santrockcd11

Evolutionary Psychology
Handbook of Evolutionary Psychology
Evolutionary Psychology Resources

Review and Reflect • LEARNING GOAL 1

1 Discuss the evolutionary perspective on development

Review
- How can natural selection and adaptive behavior be defined?
- What is evolutionary psychology? What are some basic ideas about human development proposed by evolutionary psychologists? How can evolutionary psychology be evaluated?

Reflect
- Which is more persuasive to you: the views of evolutionary psychologists or their critics? Why?

2 GENETIC FOUNDATIONS

The Genetic Process | Genetic Principles | Chromosome and Gene-Linked Abnormalities

Every species has a mechanism for transmitting characteristics from one generation to the next. This mechanism is explained by the principles of genetics. Each of us carries a "genetic code" that we inherited from our parents, and it is a distinctly human code. Because a fertilized egg carries this human code, a fertilized human egg cannot grow into an egret, eagle, or elephant.

The Genetic Process

Each of us began life as a single cell weighing about one twenty-millionth of an ounce! This tiny piece of matter housed our entire genetic code—instructions that orchestrated growth from that single cell to a person made of trillions of cells, each containing a replica of the original code. That code is carried by our genes. What are genes and what do they do? For the answer, we need to look into our cells.

chromosomes Threadlike structures that come in 23 pairs, one member of each pair coming from each parent. Chromosomes contain the genetic substance DNA.

DNA A complex molecule that contains genetic information.

genes Units of hereditary information composed of DNA. Genes direct cells to reproduce themselves and manufacture the proteins that maintain life.

DNA and the Collaborative Gene The nucleus of each human cell contains **chromosomes,** which are threadlike structures made up of deoxyribonucleic acid, or DNA. **DNA** is a complex molecule that has a double helix shape, like a spiral staircase, and contains genetic information. **Genes,** the units of hereditary information, are short segments of DNA, as you can see in figure 3.2. They direct cells to reproduce themselves and to assemble proteins. Proteins, in turn, are the building blocks of cells as well as the regulators that direct the body's processes (Hartwell & others, 2004; Johnson, 2006).

Each gene has its own function and each gene has its own location, its own designated place on a particular chromosome. Today, there is a great deal of enthusiasm about efforts to discover the specific locations of genes that are linked to certain

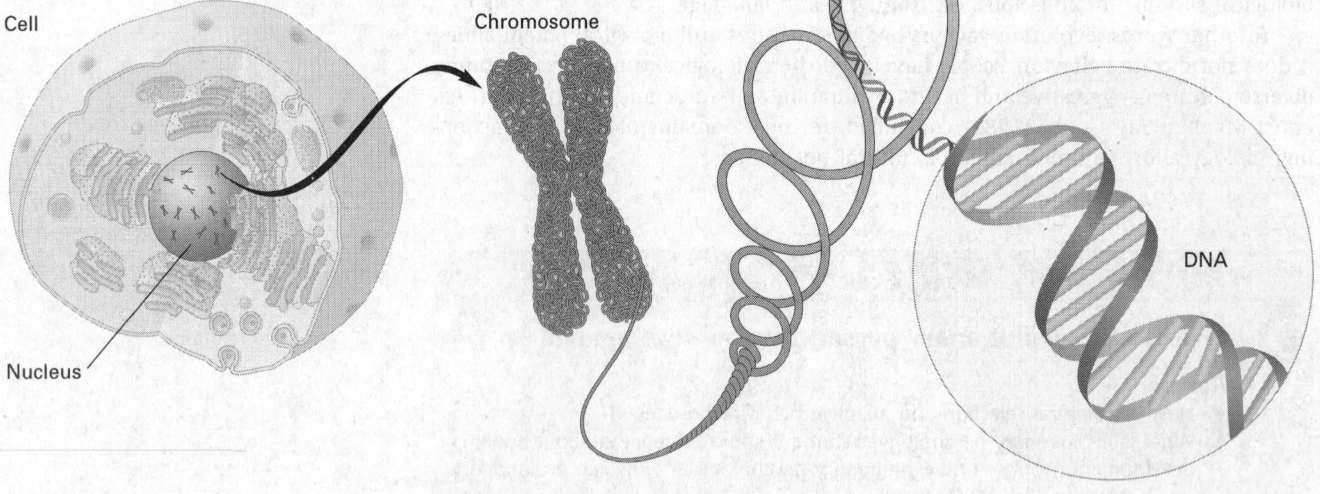

FIGURE 3.2 Cells, Chromosomes, Genes, and DNA. (*Left*) The body contains trillions of cells, which are the basic structural units of life. Each cell contains a central structure, the nucleus. (*Middle*) Chromosomes and genes are located in the nucleus of the cell. Chromosomes are made up of threadlike structures composed of DNA molecules. (*Right*) A gene is a segment of DNA that contains the hereditary code. The structure of DNA is a spiraled double chain of molecules.

functions (Benfey, 2005; Brooker, 2005; Lewin, 2006; Lewis, 2007). An important step in this direction was accomplished when the Human Genome Project and the Celera Corporation completed a preliminary map of the human *genome*—the complete set of instructions for making a human organism (U.S. Department of Energy, 2001).

One of the big surprises of the Human Genome Project was a report indicating that humans have only about 30,000 genes (U.S. Department of Energy, 2001). More recently, the number of human genes has been revised further downward to 20,000 to 25,000 (International Human Genome Sequencing Consortium, 2004). Scientists had thought that humans had as many as 100,000 or more genes. They had also believed that each gene programmed just one protein. In fact, humans appear to have far more proteins than they have genes, so there cannot be a one-to-one correspondence between genes and proteins (Commoner, 2002; Moore, 2001). Each gene is not translated, in automation-like fashion, into one and only one protein. It does not act independently, as developmental psychologist David Moore (2001) emphasized by titling his recent book *The Dependent Gene.*

Rather than being an independent source of developmental information, DNA collaborates with other sources of information to specify our characteristics. The collaboration operates at many points. For example, the cellular machinery mixes, matches, and links small pieces of DNA to reproduce the genes, and that machinery is influenced by what is going on around it. Whether a gene is turned "on," working to assemble proteins, is also a matter of collaboration. The activity of genes (*genetic expression*) is affected by their environment (Gottlieb, 2003, 2004). For example, hormones that circulate in the blood make their way into the cell where they can turn genes "on" and "off." And the flow of hormones can be affected by environmental conditions, such as light, day length, nutrition, and behavior. Numerous studies have shown that external events outside of the cell and the person, as well as events inside the cell, can excite or inhibit gene expression (Gottlieb, Wahlsten, & Lickliter, 1998, 2006; Mauro & others, 1994; Rusak & others, 1990).

In short, a single gene is rarely the source of a protein's genetic information, much less of an inherited trait (Gottlieb, 2003, 2004; Gottlieb, Wahlsten, & Lickliter, 2006; Moore, 2001). Rather than being a group of independent genes, the human genome consists of many collaborative genes.

Genes and Chromosomes

Genes are not only collaborative; they are enduring. How do the genes manage to get passed from generation to generation and end up in all of the trillion cells in the body? Three processes explain the heart of the story: mitosis, meiosis, and fertilization.

Mitosis, Meiosis, and Fertilization

All cells in your body (except the sperm and egg) have 46 chromosomes arranged in 23 pairs. Why pairs? Because you inherited one

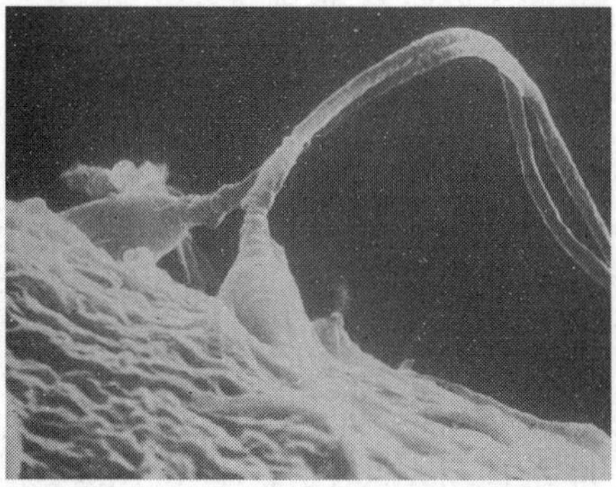

FIGURE 3.3 Union of Sperm and Egg

chromosome from your mother and one from your father. These cells reproduce by a process called **mitosis.** During mitosis, the cell's nucleus—including the chromosomes—duplicates itself and the cell divides. Two new cells are formed, each containing the same DNA as the parent cell, arranged in the same 23 pairs of chromosomes.

However, a different type of cell division—**meiosis**—forms eggs and sperm (or *gametes*). During meiosis, a cell of the testes (in men) or ovaries (in women) duplicates its chromosomes, but then divides *twice,* thus forming four cells, each of which has only half of the genetic material of the parent cell. By the end of meiosis, each egg or sperm has 23 *unpaired* chromosomes.

The next stage in the process of reproduction is **fertilization,** whereby an egg and a sperm fuse to create a single cell, called a **zygote** (see figure 3.3). In the zygote, the unpaired chromosomes from the egg and the unpaired chromosomes from the sperm combine to form one set of paired chromosomes—one member of each pair from the mother's egg and the other member from the father's sperm. In this manner, each parent contributes half of the offspring's genetic material.

Sources of Variability Combining the genes of two parents in offspring increases genetic variability in the population, which is valuable for a species because it provides more characteristics for natural selection to operate on (Klug & Cummings, 2005; Krogh, 2005; Mader, 2006). However, the chromosomes in the zygote are not exact copies of the mother's ovaries and the father's testes. During the formation of the sperm and egg in meiosis, the members of each pair of chromosomes are separated, but which chromosome in the pair goes to the gamete is a matter of chance. In addition, before the pairs separate, pieces of the two chromosomes in each pair are exchanged, creating a new combination of genes on each chromosome. Thus, when chromosomes from the mother's egg and the father's sperm are brought together in the zygote, the result is a truly unique combination of genes (Starr, 2006).

Figure 3.4 shows 23 paired chromosomes of a male and a female. The members of each pair of chromosomes are both similar and different: each chromosome in the pair contains varying forms of the same genes, at the same location on the

mitosis Cellular reproduction in which the cell's nucleus duplicates itself with two new cells being formed, each containing the same DNA as the parent cell, arranged in the same 23 pairs of chromosomes.

meiosis A specialized form of cell division that occurs to form eggs and sperm (or gametes).

fertilization A stage in reproduction whereby an egg and a sperm fuse to create a single cell, called a zygote.

zygote A single cell formed through fertilization.

FIGURE 3.4 **The Genetic Difference Between Males and Females.** The chromosome structures of a male (*left*) and female (*right*). The 23rd pair is shown at bottom right. Notice that the male's Y chromosome is smaller than his X chromosome. To obtain pictures of chromosomes, a cell is removed from a person's body, usually a cheek cell. Cheek cells are found in saliva so a special procedure is not required to obtain them. The chromosomes are photographed under magnification.

chromosome. A gene for hair color, for example, is located on both members of one pair of chromosomes, in the same location on each. However, one of those chromosomes might carry the gene for blond hair; the other chromosome in the pair might carry the gene for brown hair.

Do you notice any obvious differences between the chromosomes of the male and the chromosomes of the female in figure 3.4? The difference lies in the 23rd pair. Ordinarily, in females this pair consists of two chromosomes called *X chromosomes*; in males the 23rd pair consists of an *X* and a *Y chromosome*. The presence of a Y chromosome is what makes an individual male.

All of a person's genetic material makes up his or her **genotype.** However, not all of the genetic material is apparent in our observed and measurable characteristics. A **phenotype** consists of observable characteristics. Phenotypes include physical characteristics (such as height, weight, and hair color) and psychological characteristics (such as personality and intelligence). For each genotype, a range of phenotypes can be expressed, providing another source of variability (Gottlieb, Wahlsten, & Lickliter, 2006; Loos & Rankin, 2005). An individual can inherit the genetic potential to grow very large, for example, but nutrition will influence how much of that potential is achieved. The giggle sisters introduced in the chapter opening might have inherited the same genetic potential to be very tall, but if Daphne had grown up malnourished, she might have ended up noticeably shorter than Barbara.

Yet another source of variability comes from DNA. Chances, a mistake by cellular machinery, or damage from an environmental agent such as radiation may produce a *mutated gene*, which is a permanently altered segment of DNA (Cummings, 2006).

Landmarks in the History of Genetics
Human Genome Project

Genetic Principles

What determines how a genotype is expressed to create a particular phenotype? Much is unknown about the answer to this question (Klug, Cummings, & Spencer, 2006; Lewis, 2005, 2007; Tobin & Dusheck, 2005). However, a number of genetic principles have been discovered, among them those of dominant-recessive genes, sex-linked genes, genetic imprinting, and polygenically determined characteristics.

Dominant-Recessive Genes Principle In some cases, one gene of a pair always exerts its effects; it is *dominant*, overriding the potential influence of the other gene, called the *recessive* gene. This is the *dominant-recessive genes principle*. A recessive gene exerts its influence only if the two genes of a pair are both recessive. If you inherit a recessive gene for a trait from each of your parents, you will show the trait. If you inherit a recessive gene from only one parent, you may never know you carry the gene. Brown hair, farsightedness, and dimples rule over blond hair, nearsightedness, and freckles in the world of dominant-recessive genes.

Can two brown-haired parents have a blond-haired child? Yes, they can. Suppose that in each parent the gene pair that governs hair color includes a dominant gene for brown hair and a recessive gene for blond hair. Since dominant genes override recessive genes, the parents have brown hair, but both are carriers of blondness and can pass on their recessive genes for blond hair. With no dominant gene to override them, the recessive genes can make the child's hair blond. Figure 3.5 illustrates the dominant-recessive genes principle.

Sex-Linked Genes *X-linked inheritance* is the term used to describe the inheritance of an altered (*mutated*) gene that is carried on the X chromosome (Trappe & others, 2001). Most mutated genes are recessive, but remember that males have only one X chromosome. When there is an alteration of the X chromosome, males have no "backup" copy and therefore may carry an X-linked disease. However, females have a second X chromosome, which is likely to be unchanged. As a result,

genotype A person's genetic heritage; the actual genetic material.

phenotype The way an individual's genotype is expressed in observed and measurable characteristics.

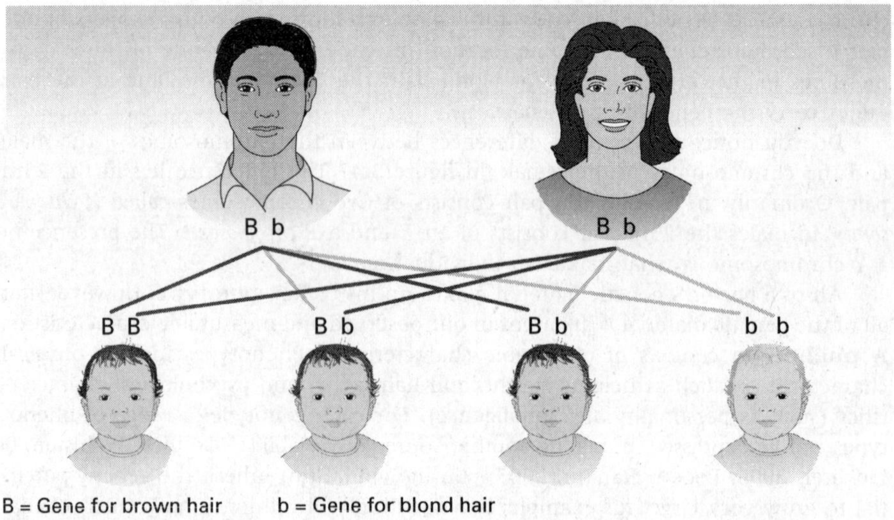

FIGURE 3.5 How Brown-Haired Parents Can Have a Blond-Haired Child. Although both parents have brown hair, each parent can have a recessive gene for blond hair. In this example, both parents have brown hair, but each parent carries the recessive gene for blond hair. Therefore, the odds of their child having blond hair are one in four–the probability the child will receive a recessive gene (*b*) from each parent.

females are not likely to have the X-linked disease. Thus, most individuals who have X-linked diseases are males. Females who have one changed copy of the X gene are known as "carriers," and they usually do not show any signs of the X-linked disease. Hemophilia and fragile X syndrome, which we will discuss later in the chapter, are examples of X-linked inheritance (Gonzalez-del Angel & others, 2000).

Genetic Imprinting *Genetic imprinting* occurs when genes have differing effects depending on whether they are inherited from the mother or the father (Beaudet, 2004; Curley & others, 2004). An imprinted gene dominates one that has not been imprinted. Genetic imprinting may explain why individuals who inherit Turner syndrome (which is characterized by underdeveloped sex organs) from their fathers tend to show better cognitive and social skills than when they inherit the disorder from their mothers (Martinez-Pasarell & others, 1999). We will further discuss Turner syndrome later in this chapter.

Polygenic Inheritance Genetic transmission is usually more complex than the simple examples we have examined thus far (Lewis, 2005; Starr, 2005). Few psychological characteristics are the result of a single gene or pair of genes. Most are determined by the interaction of many different genes; they are said to be *polygenically determined. Polygenic inheritance* occurs when many genes interact to influence a characteristic. There are about 20,000 to 25,000 human genes, so you can imagine that possible combinations are staggering in number.

Chromosome and Gene-Linked Abnormalities

In some cases, abnormalities characterize the genetic process. Some of these abnormalities involve whole chromosomes that do not separate properly during meiosis. Other abnormalities are produced by inheriting harmful genes by mutation of genes.

Genetic Disorders
Prenatal Testing and Down Syndrome

Chromosome Abnormalities Sometimes, when a gamete is formed, the sperm and ovum does not have its normal set of 23 chromosomes. The most notable

Name	Description	Treatment	Incidence
Down syndrome	An extra chromosome causes mild to severe retardation and physical abnormalities.	Surgery, early intervention, infant stimulation, and special learning programs	1 in 1,900 births at age 20 1 in 300 births at age 35 1 in 30 births at age 45
Klinefelter syndrome	An extra X chromosome causes physical abnormalities.	Hormone therapy can be effective	1 in 800 males
Fragile X syndrome	An abnormality in the X chromosome can cause mental retardation, learning disabilities, or short attention span.	Special education, speech and language therapy	More common in males than in females
Turner syndrome	A missing X chromosome in females can cause mental retardation and sexual underdevelopment.	Hormone therapy in childhood and puberty	1 in 2,500 female births
XYY syndrome	An extra Y chromosome can cause above-average height.	No special treatment required	1 in 1,000 male births

FIGURE 3.6 Some Chromosome Abnormalities. Note: Treatment does not necessarily erase the problem but may improve the individual's adaptive behavior and quality of life.

examples involve Down syndrome and abnormalities of the sex chromosomes (see figure 3.6).

Down Syndrome An individual with **Down syndrome** has a round face, a flattened skull, an extra fold of skin over the eyelids, a protruding tongue, short limbs, and retardation of motor and mental abilities (Alfirevic & Neilson, 2004; Egan & others, 2004; Matias, Montenegro, & Blickstein, 2005). The syndrome is caused by the presence of an extra copy of chromosome 21. It is not known why the extra chromosome is present, but the health of the male sperm or female ovum may be involved (Liou & others, 2004). Down syndrome appears approximately once in every 700 live births. Women between the ages of 18 and 38 are less likely to give birth to a child with Down syndrome than are younger or older women. African American children are rarely born with Down syndrome.

Sex-Linked Chromosome Abnormalities Recall that a newborn normally has either an X and a Y chromosome, or two X chromosomes. Human embryos must possess at least one X chromosome to be viable. The most common sex-linked chromosome abnormalities involve the presence of an extra chromosome (either an X or Y) or the absence of one X chromosome in females.

Klinefelter syndrome is a genetic disorder in which males have an extra X chromosome, making them XXY instead of XY (Denschlag & others, 2004; Tyler & Edman, 2004). Males with this disorder have undeveloped testes, and they usually have enlarged breasts and become tall. Klinefelter syndrome occurs approximately once in every 800 live male births.

Fragile X syndrome is a genetic disorder that results from an abnormality in the X chromosome, which becomes constricted and often breaks (Irwin & others, 2005). Mental deficiency often is an outcome but it may take the form of mental retardation, a learning disability, or a short attention span (Lewis, 2005). This disorder occurs more frequently in males than in females, possibly because the second X chromosome in females negates the disorder's negative effects (Chiurazzi, Neri, & Oostra, 2003).

Turner syndrome is a chromosome disorder in females in which either an X chromosome is missing, making the person XO instead of XX, or the second chromosome is partially deleted (Frias & Davenport, 2003). These females are short in stature and have a webbed neck. They might be infertile and have difficulty in

These athletes, many of whom have Down syndrome, are participating in a Special Olympics competition. Notice the distinctive facial features of the individuals with Down syndrome, such as a round face and a flattened skull. *What causes Down syndrome?*

Down syndrome A chromosomally transmitted form of mental retardation, caused by the presence of an extra copy of chromosome 21.

Klinefelter syndrome A chromosomal disorder in which males have an extra X chromosome, making them XXY instead of XY.

fragile X syndrome A genetic disorder involving an abnormality in the X chromosome, which becomes constricted and, often, breaks.

Turner syndrome A chromosome disorder in females in which either an X chromosome is missing, making the person XO instead of XX, or the second X chromosome is partially deleted.

Name	Description	Treatment	Incidence
Cystic fibrosis	Glandular dysfunction that interferes with mucus production; breathing and digestion are hampered, resulting in a shortened life span.	Physical and oxygen therapy, synthetic enzymes, and antibiotics; most individuals live to middle age.	1 in 2,000 births
Diabetes	Body does not produce enough insulin, which causes abnormal metabolism of sugar.	Early onset can be fatal unless treated with insulin.	1 in 2,500 births
Hemophilia	Delayed blood clotting causes internal and external bleeding.	Blood transfusions/injections can reduce or prevent damage due to internal bleeding.	1 in 10,000 males
Phenylketonuria (PKU)	Metabolic disorder that, left untreated, causes mental retardation.	Special diet can result in average intelligence and normal life span.	1 in 14,000 births
Sickle-cell anemia	Blood disorder that limits the body's oxygen supply; it can cause joint swelling, as well as heart and kidney failure.	Penicillin, medication for pain, antibiotics, and blood transfusions.	1 in 400 African American children (lower among other groups)
Spina bifida	Neural tube disorder that causes brain and spine abnormalities.	Corrective surgery at birth, orthopedic devices, and physical/medical therapy.	2 in 1,000 births
Tay-Sachs disease	Deceleration of mental and physical development caused by an accumulation of lipids in the nervous system.	Medication and special diet are used, but death is likely by 5 years of age.	One in 30 American Jews is a carrier.

FIGURE 3.7 Some Gene-Linked Abnormalities

During a physical examination for a college football tryout, Jerry Hubbard, 32, learned that he carried the gene for sickle-cell anemia. Daughter Sara is healthy but daughter Avery (in the print dress) has sickle-cell anemia. *If you were a genetic counselor, would you recommend that this family have more children? Explain.*

XYY syndrome A chromosomal disorder in which males have an extra Y chromosome.

phenylketonuria (PKU) A genetic disorder in which an individual cannot properly metabolize an amino acid. PKU is now easily detected but, if left untreated, results in mental retardation and hyperactivity.

mathematics, but their verbal ability is often quite good. Turner syndrome occurs in approximately 1 of every 2,500 live female births.

The **XYY syndrome** is a chromosomal disorder in which the male has an extra Y chromosome (Monastirli, 2005; Parmar, Muranjan, & Swami, 2002). Early interest in this syndrome focused on the belief that the extra Y chromosome found in some males contributed to aggression and violence. However, researchers subsequently found that XYY males are no more likely to commit crimes than are XY males (Witkin & others, 1976).

Gene-Linked Abnormalities

Abnormalities can be produced by an uneven number of chromosomes; they also can result from harmful genes. More than 7,000 such genetic disorders have been identified, although most of them are rare. Figure 3.7 describes some gene-linked abnormalities.

Phenylketonuria (PKU) is a genetic disorder in which the individual cannot properly metabolize phenylalanine, an amino acid (Brumm & others, 2004; Channon & others, 2004). It results from a recessive gene and occurs about once in every 10,000 to 20,000 live births. If phenylketonuria is left untreated, mental retardation and hyperactivity result. Phenylketonuria accounts for approximately 1 percent of institutionalized individuals who are mentally retarded, and it occurs primarily in Whites. Today, phenylketonuria is easily detected and it is treated by a diet that prevents an excess accumulation of phenylalanine.

The story of phenylketonuria has important implications for the nature-nurture issue. Although phenylketonuria is a genetic disorder (nature), how or whether a gene's influence in phenylketonuria is played out can depend on environmental influences since the disorder can be treated (nurture) (Luciana, Sullivan, & Nelson, 2001; Zaffanello, Maffies, & Zamboni, 2005). That is, the presence of a genetic defect *does not* inevitably lead to the development of the disorder *if* the individual develops in the right environment (one free of phenylalanine).

Sickle-cell anemia, which occurs most often in African Americans, is a genetic disorder that impairs the body's red blood cells. A red blood cell is usually shaped like a disk, but in sickle-cell anemia, a recessive gene causes the cell to become a hook-shaped "sickle." These cells die quickly, causing anemia and early death of the individual because of their failure to carry oxygen to the body's cells (Benz, 2004; De, 2005; Persons & Tisdale, 2004). About 1 in 400 African American babies is affected. One in 10 African Americans is a carrier, as is 1 in 20 Latin Americans.

Other diseases resulting from genetic abnormalities include cystic fibrosis, diabetes, hemophilia, spina bifida, and Tay-Sachs disease. Figure 3.7 provides further information about the genetic abnormalities we have discussed. The work of the Human Genome Project and similar research holds out the promise that someday scientists may identify why these and other genetic abnormalities occur and discover how to cure them. The Human Genome Project has already linked specific DNA variations with increased risk of a number of diseases and conditions (Armstrong & others, 2004; Norremolle & others, 2004).

Dealing with Genetic Abnormalities

Genetic disorders can sometimes be compensated for by other genes or developmental events (Gottlieb, 2004). As a result, it often is the case that not all of the affected individuals show the disorder. Thus, genes are not destiny. However, when they are missing, nonfunctional, or mutated, they can be associated with disorders because the normal gene is not functioning.

Every individual carries DNA variations that might predispose that person to serious physical disease or mental disorder. Identifying the flaws could enable doctors to predict an individual's disease risks, recommend healthy lifestyle regimens, and prescribe the safest and most effective drugs. A decade or two from now, parents of a newborn baby may be able to leave the hospital with a full genome analysis of their offspring that reveals disease risks.

However, this knowledge might bring important costs as well as benefits. Who would have access to a person's genetic profile? An individual's ability to land and hold jobs or obtain insurance might be threatened if it is known that a person is considered at risk for some disease. For example, should an airline pilot or a neurosurgeon who is predisposed to develop a disorder that makes one's hands shake be required to leave that job early?

Genetic counselors, usually physicians or biologists who are well versed in the field of medical genetics, are familiar with the kinds of problems just described, the odds of encountering them, and helpful strategies for offseting some of their effects (Mayeux, 2005; Watson & others, 2005). To read about the career and work of a genetic counselor, see the Careers in Child Development insert.

CAREERS in CHILD DEVELOPMENT

Holly Ishmael
Genetic Counselor

Holly Ishmael is a genetic counselor at Children's Mercy Hospital in Kansas City. She obtained an undergraduate degree in psychology from Sarah Lawrence College and then a master's degree in genetic counseling from the same college.

Genetic counselors have specialized graduate degrees in the areas of medical genetics and counseling. They enter graduate school in these areas with undergraduate backgrounds from a variety of disciplines, including biology, genetics, psychology, public health, and social work. Genetic counselors, like Holly, work as members of a health-care team, providing information and support to families with birth defects or genetic disorders. They identify families at risk by analyzing inheritance patterns and explore options with the family. Genetic counselors may serve as educators and resource people for other health-care professionals and the public. Some genetic counselors also work in administrative positions or conduct research. Some genetic counselors, like Holly, become specialists in prenatal and pediatric genetics; others might specialize in cancer genetics or psychiatric genetic disorders.

Holly says, "Genetic counseling is a perfect combination for people who want to do something science-oriented, but need human contact and don't want to spend all of their time in a lab or have their nose in a book."

There are approximately 30 graduate genetic counseling programs in the United States. If you are interested in this profession, you can obtain further information from the National Society of Genetic Counselors at this website: http://www.nsgc.org.

Holly Ishmael (*left*) in a genetic counseling session.

sickle-cell anemia A genetic disorder that affects the red blood cells and occurs most often in people of African descent.

Review and Reflect • **LEARNING GOAL 2**

2 Describe what genes are and how they influence human development

Review
- How does the genetic process work?
- How can the genetic principles of dominant-recessive genes, sex-linked genes, genetic imprinting, and polygenic inheritance be characterized?
- What are some chromosome and gene-linked abnormalities?

Reflect
- What are some possible ethical issues regarding genetics and development that might arise in the future?

3 REPRODUCTIVE CHALLENGES AND CHOICES

Prenatal Diagnostic Tests | Infertility and Reproductive Technology | Adoption

Earlier in this chapter we discussed several principles of genetics, including the role of meiosis in reproduction. Having also examined a number of genetic abnormalities that can occur, we now have some background to consider challenges and choices facing prospective parents.

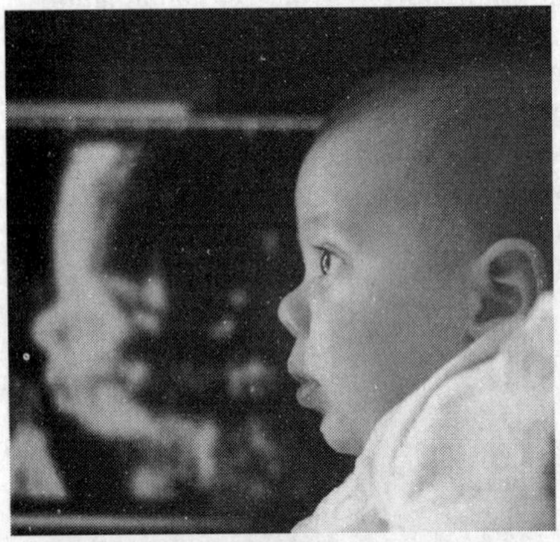

A 6-month-old infant poses with the ultrasound sonography record taken 4 months into the baby's prenatal development. *What is ultrasound sonography?*

Prenatal Diagnostic Tests

One choice open to prospective mothers is the extent to which they should undergo prenatal testing. Scientists have developed a number of tests to determine whether a fetus is developing normally (Murphy, Fowlie, & McGuire, 2004). These tests include ultrasound sonography, chorionic villi sampling, amniocentesis, and maternal blood screening.

An ultrasound test is often conducted 7 weeks into a pregnancy and at various times later in pregnancy. *Ultrasound sonography* is a prenatal medical procedure in which high-frequency sound waves are directed into the pregnant woman's abdomen. The echo from the sounds is transformed into a visual representation of the fetus' inner structures. This technique can detect many structural abnormalities in the fetus, including microencephaly, a form of mental retardation involving an abnormally small brain; it can also determine the number of fetuses and give clues to the baby's sex (Filkins & Koos, 2005).

Amniocentesis
Obstetric Ultrasound
Chorionic Villi Sampling
Infertility Resources
Genetic Counseling

At some point between the 8th and 11th weeks of pregnancy, chorionic villi sampling may be used to detect genetic defects and chromosome abnormalities (Jenkins & others, 2004). Diagnosis takes approximately 10 days. *Chorionic villi sampling* is a prenatal medical procedure in which a small sample of the placenta (the vascular organ that links the fetus to the mother's uterus) is removed.

Between the 8th and 11th weeks of pregnancy, amniocentesis may be performed. *Amniocentesis* is a prenatal medical procedure in which a sample of amniotic fluid is withdrawn by syringe and tested for any chromosome or metabolic disorders (Ramsey & others, 2004). The amnionic fluid is found within the amnion, a thin sac in which the embryo is suspended. Ultrasound sonography is often used during amniocentesis so that the syringe can be placed at the precise location of the fetus in the mother's abdomen. The later amniocentesis is performed, the better its diagnostic potential. The earlier it is performed, the more useful it is in deciding how to handle a pregnancy (Pinette & others, 2004).

Both amniocentesis and chorionic villi sampling provide valuable information about the presence of birth defects, but they also raise difficult issues for parents about whether an abortion should be obtained if birth defects are present (Papp & Papp, 2003). Chorionic villi sampling allows a decision to made sooner, near the end of the first 12 weeks of pregnancy, when abortion is safer and less traumatic than later, but chorionic villi sampling carries greater risks than amniocentesis. Amniocentesis brings a small risk of miscarriage: about 1 woman in every 200 to 300 miscarries after amniocentesis. Chorionic villi sampling brings a slightly higher risk of miscarriage than amniocentesis and is linked with a slight risk of limb deformities.

During the 16th to 18th weeks of pregnancy, maternal blood screening may be performed. *Maternal blood screening* identifies pregnancies that have an elevated risk for birth defects such as spina bifida (a typically fatal defect in the spinal cord) and Down syndrome (Bassett & others, 2004; Benn, Fang, & Egan, 2005; Summers & others, 2004). The current blood test is called the *triple screen* because it measures three substances in the mother's blood: alpha-fetoprotein (AFP), estriol, and human chorionic gonadotropin. After an abnormal triple screen result, the next step is usually an ultrasound examination. If an ultrasound does not explain the abnormal triple screen results, amniocentesis is typically used.

Infertility and Reproductive Technology

Recent advances in biological knowledge have also opened up many choices for infertile people. Approximately 10 to 15 percent of couples in the United States experience *infertility,* which is defined as the inability to conceive a child after 12 months of regular intercourse without contraception. The cause of infertility can rest with the woman or the man (Pasch, 2001). The woman may not be ovulating (releasing eggs to be fertilized), she may be producing abnormal ova, her fallopian tubes (by which ova normally reach the womb) may be blocked, or she may have a disease that prevents implantation of the embyro into the uterus. The man may produce too few sperm, the sperm may lack motility (the ability to move adequately), or he may have a blocked passageway (Oehninger, 2001).

In the United States, more than 2 million couples seek help for infertility every year. In some cases of infertility, surgery may correct the cause; in others, hormone-based drugs may improve the probability of having a child. Of the 2 million couples who seek help for infertility every year, about 40,000 try high-tech assisted reproduction. The three most common techniques are as follows:

- *In vitro fertilization (IVF).* Eggs and a sperm are combined in a laboratory dish. If any eggs are successfully fertilized, one or more of the resulting embryos is transferred into the woman's uterus or womb.
- *Gamete intrafallopian transfer (GIFT).* A doctor inserts eggs and sperm directly into a woman's fallopian tube.
- *Zygote intrafallopian transfer (ZIFT).* This is a two-step procedure. First, eggs are fertilized in the laboratory. Then, any resulting zygotes are transferred to a fallopian tube.

Figure 3.8 shows the success rates for these three assisted reproduction techniques, based on a national study in the United States in 2000 by the Centers for Disease Control and Prevention. IVF is by far the most common technique used (98 percent of all cases in the national study) and had the highest success rate in the national study of slightly more than 30 percent.

One consequence of fertility treatments is an increase in multiple births. Twenty-five to 30 percent of pregnancies achieved by fertility treatments—including IVF—now result in multiple births. Any multiple birth increases the likelihood that the

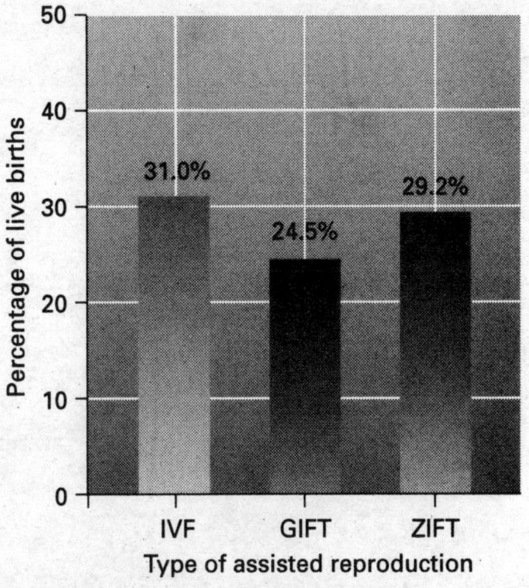

FIGURE 3.8 Success Rates of Three Different Assisted Reproduction Techniques. *Note:* The results were combined across the ages of the couples because there was little variation in success rates based on age.

babies will have life-threatening and costly problems, such as extremely low birth weight (Appelman & Furman, 2005).

The creation of families by means of the new reproductive technologies raises important questions about the psychological consequences for children. To read about a recent study that addresses these consequences, see the Research in Child Development interlude that follows.

RESEARCH IN CHILD DEVELOPMENT

In Vitro Fertilization and Developmental Outcomes in Early Adolescence

A longitudinal study examined 34 in vitro fertilization families, 49 adoptive families, and 38 families with a naturally conceived child (Golombok, MacCallum, & Goodman, 2001). Each type of family included a similar portion of boys and girls. Also, the age of the young adolescents did not differ according to family type (their mean age was 11 years, 11 months).

Children's socioemotional development was assessed by (1) interviewing the mother and obtaining detailed descriptions of any problems the child might have, (2) administering a Strengths and Difficulties questionnaire to the child's mother and teacher, and (3) administering the Social Adjustment Inventory for Children and Adolescents, which examines functioning in school, peer relationships, and self-esteem.

No significant differences between the children from the in vitro fertilization, adoptive, and naturally conceiving families were found. The results from the Social Adjustment Inventory for Children and Adolescents are shown in figure 3.9. Thus, this study, as well as others (Hahn & DiPietro, 2001), support the idea that "test-tube" babies function well.

FIGURE 3.9 Socioemotional Development at Adolescence of Children in Three Family Types: In Vitro Fertilization, Naturally Conceived, and Adopted. In this study, there were no significant differences in socioemotional development at the beginning of adolescence in terms of school functioning, peer relations, and self-esteem (Golombok, MacCallum, & Goodman, 2001). The mean scores shown for the different measures are all in the normal range of functioning.

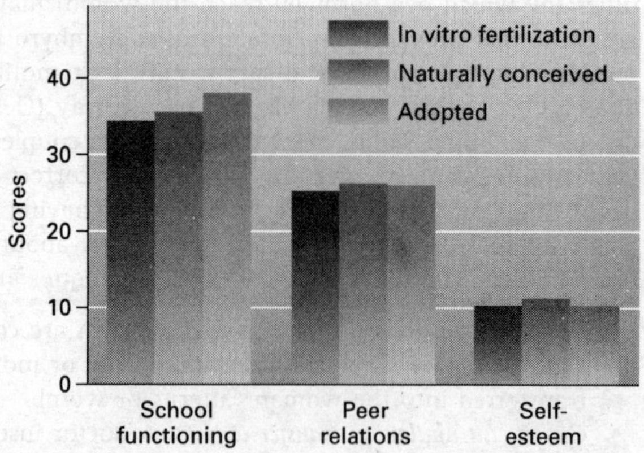

Adoption

Although surgery and fertility drugs can sometimes solve the infertility problem, another choice is to adopt a child (Moody, 2001; Smit, 2002). *Adoption* is the social and legal process by which a parent-child relationship is established between persons unrelated at birth. It is estimated that approximately 2 to 4 percent of children in the United States are adopted (Stolley, 1993).

Several changes occurred during the last several decades of the twentieth century in the characteristics both of adopted children and of adoptive parents (Brodzinsky & Pinderhughes, 2002, pp. 280–282). Until the 1960s, most U.S. adopted children were healthy, European American infants, who were adopted within a few days or weeks after birth. However, in recent decades, an increasing number of unmarried U.S. mothers decided to keep their babies, and the number of unwanted births decreased as contraception became readily available and abortion was legalized. As a result, the number of healthy European American infants available for adoption dropped dramatically. Increasingly, U.S. couples adopted children who were not European Americans, children from other countries, and children in foster care whose characteristics—such as age, minority status, exposure to neglect or abuse, or physical or mental health problems—"were once thought to be barriers to adoption" (p. 281).

Changes also have characterized adoptive parents. Until the last several decades of the twentieth century, most adoptive parents had a middle- or upper-socioeconomic status and were "married, infertile, European American couples, usually in their thirties and forties, and free of any disability. Adoption agencies *screened out* couples who did not have these characteristics" (p. 281). Today, however, many adoption agencies *screen in* as many applicants as possible and have no income requirements for adoptive parents. Many agencies now permit single adults, older adults, and gay and lesbian adults to adopt children (Rampage & others, 2003; Ryan, Pearlmutter, & Groza, 2004).

The changes in adoption practice over the last several decades make it difficult to generalize about the average adopted child or average adoptive parent. But many researchers have provided useful comparisons between adopted children and nonadopted children and their families. How do adopted children fare after they are adopted?

Children who are adopted very early in their lives are more likely to have positive outcomes than children adopted later in life. In one study, the later adoption occurred, the more problems the adoptees had. Infant adoptees had the fewest adjustment difficulties; those adopted after they were 10 years of age had the most problems (Sharma, McGue, & Benson, 1996).

In general, adopted children and adolescents often show more psychological and school-related problems than nonadopted children (Brodzinsky & others, 1984; Brodzinksy, Lang, & Smith, 1995; Brodzinsky & Pinderhughes, 2002). For example, adopted adolescents are referred to psychological treatment two to five times as often as their nonadopted peers (Grotevant & McRoy, 1990). In one study of 1,587 adopted and 87,165 nonadopted adolescents, the adopted adolescents were at higher risk for all problems examined, including problems with school, substance abuse, psychological well-being, and physical health (Miller & others, 2000). Also, the adolescents with the most problems were far more likely to be adopted than nonadopted. In this study, adopted adolescents were more likely to have problems if the adoptive parents had low levels of education.

Research that contrasts adopted and nonadopted adolescents has found positive as well as negative characteristics among the adopted adolescents. In one study, adopted adolescents had more school adjustment problems, were more likely to use illicit drugs, and were more likely to engage in delinquent behavior (Sharma, McGue, & Benson, 1998). However, compared with nonadopted siblings, adopted siblings were also less withdrawn and engaged in more prosocial behavior, such as being altruistic, caring, and supportive of others.

Although adoption is associated with increased academic and psychological difficulties, the vast majority of adopted children (including those adopted at older ages, transracially, and across national borders) adjust effectively, and their parents report considerable satisfaction with their decision to adopt (Brodzinsky & Pinderhughes, 2002). Furthermore, adopted children fare much better than children in long-term foster care or in an institutional environment (Brodzinsky & Pinderhughes, 2002).

Children benefit from adoption if their biological parents could not or would not provide adequate care for them. To read more about adoption, see the Caring for Children interlude in which we discuss effective parenting strategies with adopted children.

Proponents of intercountry adoption emphasize the humanitarian benefits of providing supportive homes for orphaned and needy children. Opponents argue that children have a right to a national identity and that "placing" countries need to make a stronger effort to find homes for these children in their birth country. Research on the adjustment and well-being of adopted children who are placed internationally is mixed (Brodzinsky & Pinderhughes, 2002). Despite challenges, many transracially and internationally placed adopted children and their families show positive adjustment.

CARING FOR CHILDREN

Parenting Adopted Children

Many of the keys to effectively parenting adopted children are no different than those for effectively parenting biological children: be supportive and caring, be involved and monitor the child's behavior and whereabouts, be a good communicator, and help the child to learn to develop self-control. However, there are some unique circumstances that parents of adopted children face. These include recognizing the differences involved in adoptive family life, communicating about these differences, showing respect for the birth family, and supporting the child's search for self and identity.

David Brodzinsky and Ellen Pinderhughes (2002, pp. 288–292) recently discussed how to handle some of the challenges that parents face when their adopted children are at different points in development:

- ***Infancy.*** Researchers have found few differences in the attachment that adopted and nonadopted infants form with their parents, but attachment can be compromised "when parents have difficulty in claiming the child as their own either because of unresolved fertility issues, lack of support from family and friends, and/or when their expectations about the child have not been met" (p. 288). Competent adoption agencies or counselors can help prospective adoptive parents develop realistic expectations, especially if the child has special needs.
- ***Early Childhood.*** During infancy, adoptive parents often focus on integrating the child into the family and develop a strong bond with the child. In early childhood the focus shifts. Early childhood is when most parents begin to talk with their child about adoption. Because many children begin to ask where they came from when they are about 4 to 6 years old, this is a natural time to begin to talk in simple ways to children about their adoption status (Warshak, 2004). Some parents (although not as many as in the past) decide not to tell their children about the adoption. This secrecy may create psychological risks for the child if he or she later finds out about the adoption.
- ***Middle and Late Childhood.*** During the elementary school years, children begin to express "much more curiosity about their origins: *Where did I come from? What did my birthmother and birthfather look like? Why didn't they keep me? Where are they now? Can I meet them?*" (p. 290). As they grow older, children may become more ambivalent about being adopted and question their adoptive parents' explanations. It is important for adoptive parents to recognize that this ambivalence is normal. Also, clinical psychologists report that problems may come from the desire of adoptive parents to make life too perfect for the adoptive child and to present a perfect image of themselves to the child. The result too often is that adopted children feel that they cannot release any angry feelings and openly discuss problems (Warshak, 2004).
- ***Adolescence.*** Adolescents are likely to develop more abstract and logical thinking, to focus their attention on their bodies, and to search for an identity. These characteristics provide the foundation for adopted adolescents to reflect on their adoption status in more complex ways, to become "preoccupied with the lack of physical resemblance between themselves and others in the family" (p. 291), and to explore how the fact that they were adopted fits into their identity. Adoptive parents "need to be aware of these many complexities and provide teenagers with the support they need to cope with these adoption-related tasks" (p. 292).

Review and Reflect • **LEARNING GOAL 3**

3 Identify some important reproductive challenges and choices

Review
- What are some common prenatal diagnostic tests?
- What are some causes of infertility? What types of reproductive technology are used to improve the success rates of having children for infertile couples?
- How does adoption affect children's development?

Reflect
- We discussed a number of studies indicating that adoption is linked with negative outcomes for children. Does that mean that all adopted children have more negative outcomes than all nonadopted children? Explain.

4 HEREDITY AND ENVIRONMENT INTERACTION: THE NATURE-NURTURE DEBATE

Behavior Genetics
Shared and Nonshared Environmental Experiences
Conclusions About Heredity-Environment Interaction
Heredity-Environment Correlations
The Epigenetic View

In each section of this chapter so far we have examined parts of the nature-nurture debate. We have seen how the environment exerts selective pressures on the characteristics of species over generations, examined how genes are passed from parents to children, and discussed how reproductive technologies and adoption influence the course of children's lives. But in all of these situations, heredity and environment interact to produce environment. After all, Jim and Jim (and each of the other pairs of identical twins discussed in the opening of the chapter) have the same genotype, but they are not the same person; each is unique. What made them different? Whether we are studying how genes produce proteins, their influence on how tall a person is, or how PKU might affect an individual, we end up discussing heredity-environment interactions. Is it possible to untangle the influence of heredity from that of environment and discover the role of each in producing individual differences in development? When heredity and environment interact, how does heredity influence the environment, and vice versa?

Behavior Genetics

Behavior Genetics

Behavior genetics is the field that seeks to discover the influence of heredity and environment on individual differences in human traits and development (Eaves & Silberg, 2003; Maxson, 2003; Knafo, Iervolino, & Plomin, 2005; Kuo & others, 2004). What behavior geneticists try to do is to figure out what is responsible for the differences—that is, to what extent do people differ because of differences in genes, environment, or a combination of these (Haig, 2003)?

To study the influence of heredity on behavior, behavior geneticists often use either twins or adoption situations. In the most common **twin study,** the behavioral

behavior genetics The field that seeks to discover the influence of heredity and environment on individual differences in human traits and development.

twin study A study in which the behavioral similarity of identical twins is compared with the behavioral similarity of fraternal twins.

Identical twins develop from a single fertilized egg that splits into two genetically identical organisms. Twin studies compare identical twins with fraternal twins. Fraternal twins develop from separate eggs, making them genetically no more similar than nontwin siblings. *What is the nature of the twin study method?*

similarity of identical twins is compared with the behavioral similarity of fraternal twins. *Identical twins* (called monozygotic twins) develop from a single fertilized egg that splits into two genetically identical replicas, each of which becomes a person. *Fraternal twins* (called dizygotic twins) develop from separate eggs and separate sperm, making them genetically no more similar than ordinary siblings. Although fraternal twins share the same womb, they are no more alike genetically than are nontwin brothers and sisters, and they may be of different sexes.

By comparing groups of identical and fraternal twins, behavior geneticists capitalize on the basic knowledge that identical twins are more similar genetically than are fraternal twins (Rietveld & others, 2003; Wadsworth & others, 2004). A recent study found that conduct problems were more prevalent in identical twins than fraternal twins; the researchers concluded that the study demonstrated an important role for heredity in conduct problems (Scourfield & others, 2004).

However, several issues complicate interpretation of twin studies. For example, perhaps the environments of identical twins are more similar than the environments of fraternal twins. Adults might stress the similarities of identical twins more than those of fraternal twins, and identical twins might perceive themselves as a "set" and play together more than fraternal twins do. If so, the influence of the environment on the observed similarities between identical and fraternal twins might be very significant.

In an **adoption study,** investigators seek to discover whether the behavior and psychological characteristics of adopted children are more like those of their adoptive parents, who have provided a home environment, or more like those of their biological parents, who have contributed their heredity (Haugaard & Hazan, 2004). Another form of the adoption study compares adoptive and biological siblings.

Heredity-Environment Correlations

The difficulties that researchers encounter when they interpet the results of twin studies and adoption studies reflect the complexities of heredity-environment interaction. Some of these interactions are *heredity-environment correlations,* which means that individuals' genes influence the types of environments to which they are exposed. In a sense, individuals "inherit" environments that are related or linked to genetic propensities (Plomin & others, 2003). Behavior geneticist Sandra Scarr (1993) described three ways that heredity and environment are correlated (see figure 3.10):

- **Passive genotype-environment correlations** occur because biological parents, who are genetically related to the child, provide a rearing environment for the child. For example, the parents might have a genetic predisposition to be intelligent and read skillfully. Because they read well and enjoy reading, they provide their children with books to read. The likely outcome is that their children, given their own inherited predispositions from their parents and their book-filled environment, will become skilled readers.
- **Evocative genotype-environment correlations** occur because a child's characteristics elicit certain types of environments. For example, active, smiling children receive more social stimulation than passive, quiet children do. Cooperative, attentive children evoke more pleasant and instructional responses from the adults around them than uncooperative, distractible children do.
- **Active (niche-picking) genotype-environment correlations** occur when children seek out environments that they find compatible and stimulating. *Niche-picking* refers to finding a setting that is suited to one's abilities. Children select from their surrounding environment some aspect that they respond to, learn about, or ignore. Their active selections of environments are related to

adoption study A study in which investigators seek to discover whether, in behavior and psychological characteristics, adopted children are more like their adoptive parents, who provided a home environment, or more like their biological parents, who contributed their heredity. Another form of the adoption study is to compare adoptive and biological siblings.

passive genotype-environment correlations Correlations that exist when the natural parents, who are genetically related to the child, provide a rearing environment for the child.

evocative genotype-environment correlations Correlations that exist when the child's genotype elicits certain types of physical and social environments.

active (niche-picking) genotype-environment correlations Correlations that exist when children seek out environments they find compatible and stimulating.

Heredity-Environment Correlation	Description	Examples
Passive	Children inherit genetic tendencies from their parents and parents also provide an environment that matches their own genetic tendencies.	Musically inclined parents usually have musically inclined children and they are likely to provide an environment rich in music for their children.
Evocative	The child's genetic tendencies elicit stimulation from the environment that supports a particular trait. Thus genes evoke environmental support.	A happy, outgoing child elicits smiles and friendly responses from others.
Active (niche-picking)	Children actively seek out "niches" in their environment that reflect their own interests and talents and are thus in accord with their genotype.	Libraries, sports fields, and a store with musical instruments are examples of environmental niches children might seek out if they have intellectual interests in books, talent in sports, or musical talents, respectively.

FIGURE 3.10 Exploring Heredity-Environment Correlations

their particular genotype. For example, outgoing children tend to seek out social contexts in which to interact with people, whereas shy children don't. Children who are musically inclined are likely to select musical environments in which they can successfully perform their skills.

Scarr believes that the relative importance of the three genotype-environment correlations changes as children develop from infancy through adolescence. In infancy, much of the environment that children experience is provided by adults. Thus, passive genotype-environment correlations are more common in the lives of infants and young children than they are for older children and adolescents; older children and adolescents can extend their experiences beyond the family's influence and create their environments to a greater degree.

Critics argue that the concept of heredity-environment correlation gives heredity too much of a one-sided influence in determining development because it does not consider the role of prior environmental influences in shaping the correlation itself (Gottlieb, 2003, 2004; Gottlieb, Wahlsten, & Lickliter, 2006). Heredity-environment correlation stresses that heredity may influence the types of environments children experience but does not address *how* the correlation comes about developmentally in the first place. How correlation comes about will be described shortly in the discussion of the epigenetic view. Before turning to the epigenetic view, we will examine a view that emphasizes the importance of the non-shared environment of siblings and their heredity as important influences on their development.

Shared and Nonshared Environmental Experiences

Does the concept of heredity-environment correlation downplay the importance of environment in our development? Behavior geneticists have argued that to understand the environment's role in differences between people, we should distinguish between shared and nonshared environments. That is, we should consider experiences that children share in common with other children living in the same home, and experiences that are not shared (Becker-Blease & others, 2004; Feinberg & Hetherington, 2001; Petrill & Deater-Deckard, 2004; Plomin, Asbury, & Dunn, 2001).

shared environmental experiences Siblings' common environmental experiences, such as their parents' personalities and intellectual orientation, the family's socioeconomic status, and the neighborhood in which they live.

nonshared environmental experiences The child's own unique experiences, both within the family and outside the family, that are not shared by another sibling. Thus, experiences occurring within the family can be part of the "nonshared environment."

Shared environmental experiences are siblings' common experiences, such as their parents' personalities or intellectual orientation, the family's socioeconomic status, and the neighborhood in which they live. By contrast, **nonshared environmental experiences** are a child's unique experiences, both within the family and outside the family, that are not shared with a sibling. Even experiences occurring within the family can be part of the "nonshared environment." For example, parents often interact differently with each sibling, and siblings interact differently with parents (Hetherington, Reiss, & Plomin, 1994). Siblings often have different peer groups, different friends, and different teachers at school.

Behavior geneticist Robert Plomin (1993) has found that shared environment accounts for little of the variation in children's personality or interests. In other words, even though two children live under the same roof with the same parents, their personalities are often very different. Further, Plomin argues that heredity influences the nonshared environments of siblings through the heredity-environment correlations we described earlier (Plomin & others, 2003). For example, a child who has inherited a genetic tendency to be athletic is likely to spend more time in environments related to sports while a child who has inherited a tendency to be musically inclined is more likely to spend time in environments related to music.

What are the implications of Plomin's interpretation of the role of shared and nonshared environments in development? In *The Nurture Assumption*, Judith Harris (1998) argued that what parents do does not make a difference in their children's and adolescents' behavior. Yell at them. Hug them. Read to them. Ignore them. Harris says it won't influence how they turn out. She argues that genes and peers are far more important than parents in children's and adolescents' development.

Genes and Parenting

Genes and peers do matter, but Harris' descriptions of peer influences do not take into account the complexity of peer contexts and developmental trajectories (Hartup, 1999). In addition, Harris is wrong in saying that parents don't matter. For example, in the early child years parents play an important role in selecting children's peers and indirectly influencing children's development (Baumrind, 1999). A huge parenting literature with many research studies documents the importance of parents in children's development (Collins & others, 2000, 2001; Maccoby, 2002). We will discuss parents' important roles throughout this book.

The Epigenetic View

The heredity-environment correlation view emphasizes how heredity directs the kind of environmental experiences individuals have. However, earlier in the chapter we discussed how genes are collaborative, not determining an individual's traits in an independent manner, but rather in an interactive manner with the environment. In line with the concept of a collaborative gene, Gilbert Gottlieb (1998, 2003, 2004) emphasizes the **epigenetic view,** which states that development is the result of an ongoing, bidirectional interchange between heredity and the environment. Figure 3.11 compares the heredity-environment correlation and epigenetic views of development.

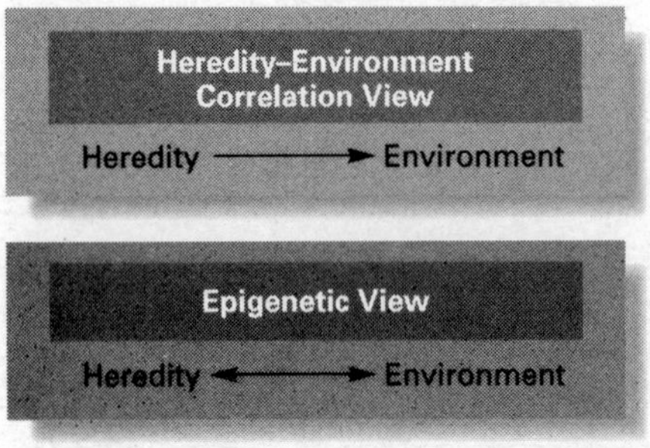

FIGURE 3.11 Comparison of the Heredity-Environment Correlation and Epigenetic Views

Let's look at an example that reflects the epigenetic view. A baby inherits genes from both parents at conception. During prenatal development, toxins, nutrition, and stress can influence some genes to stop functioning while others become stronger or weaker. During infancy, environmental experiences such as toxins, nutrition, stress, learning, and encouragement continue to modify genetic activity.

Conclusions About Heredity-Environment Interaction

Heredity and environment operate together—or collaborate—to produce a person's intelligence, temperament, height, weight, ability to pitch a baseball, ability to read, and so on (Coll, Bearer, & Lerner, 2004; Gottlieb, 2004; Gottlieb, Wahlsten, & Lickliter, 1998, 2006; McClearn, 2004). If an attractive, popular, intelligent girl is elected president of her senior class in high school, is her success due to heredity or to environment? Of course, the answer is both.

The relative contributions of heredity and environment are not additive. That is, we can't say that such-and-such a percentage of nature and such-and-such a percentage of experience make us who we are. Nor is it accurate to say that full

epigenetic view Emphasizes that development is the result of an ongoing, bidirectional interchange between heredity and environment.

genetic expression happens once, around conception or birth, after which we carry our genetic legacy into the world to see how far it takes us. Genes produce proteins throughout the life span, in many different environments. Or they don't produce these proteins, depending in part on how harsh or nourishing those environments are.

The emerging view is that many complex behaviors likely have some *genetic loading* that gives people a propensity for a particular developmental trajectory (Plomin & others, 2003; Walker, Petrill, & Plomin, 2005). However, the actual development requires more: an environment. And that environment is complex, just like the mixture of genes we inherit (Bronfenbrenner & Morris, 2006; Overton, 2004; Spencer, 2006). Environmental influences range from the things we lump together under "nurture" (such as parenting, family dynamics, schooling, and neighborhood quality) to biological encounters (such as viruses, birth complications, and even biological events in cells) (Greenough, 1997, 1999; Greenough & others, 2001).

Imagine for a moment that there is a cluster of genes somehow associated with youth violence. (This example is hypothetical because we don't know of any such combination.) The adolescent who carries this genetic mixture might experience a world of loving parents, regular nutritious meals, lots of books, and a series of masterful teachers. Or the adolescent's world might include parental neglect, a neighborhood in which gunshots and crime are everyday occurrences, and inadequate schooling. In which of these environments are the adolescent's genes likely to manufacture the biological underpinnings of criminality?

The interaction of heredity and environment is so extensive that to ask which is more important, nature or nurture, is like asking which is more important to a rectangle, height or width.

—William Greenough
Contemporary Developmental Psychologist, University of Illinois at Urbana

Review and Reflect • LEARNING GOAL 4

4 *Characterize some of the ways that heredity and environment interact to produce individual differences in development*

Review

- What is behavior genetics?
- What are three types of heredity-environment correlations and what is an example of each?
- What is meant by the concepts of shared and nonshared environmental experiences?
- What is the epigenetic view of development?
- What conclusions can be reached about heredity-environment interaction?

Reflect

- Someone tells you that he or she has analyzed his or her genetic background and environmental experiences and reached the conclusion that environment definitely has had little influence on his or her intelligence. What would you say to this person about his or her ability to make this self-diagnosis?

REACH YOUR LEARNING GOALS

BIOLOGICAL BEGINNINGS

- **1 THE EVOLUTIONARY PERSPECTIVE**
  - Natural Selection and Adaptive Behavior
  - Evolutionary Psychology
- **2 GENETIC FOUNDATIONS**
  - The Genetic Process
  - Genetic Principles
  - Chromosome and Gene-Linked Abnormalities
- **3 REPRODUCTIVE CHALLENGES AND CHOICES**
  - Prenatal Diagnostic Tests
  - Infertility and Reproductive Technology
  - Adoption
- **4 HEREDITY AND ENVIRONMENT INTERACTION: THE NATURE-NURTURE DEBATE**
  - Behavior Genetics
  - Heredity-Environment Correlations
  - Shared and Nonshared Environmental Experiences
  - The Epigenetic View
  - Conclusions About Heredity-Environment Interaction

SUMMARY

1 Discuss the evolutionary perspective on development

- Natural selection is the process that favors the individuals of a species that are best adapted to survive and reproduce. The process of natural selection was originally proposed by Charles Darwin. In evolutionary theory, adaptive behavior is behavior that promotes the organism's survival in a natural habitat. Biological evolution shaped human beings into a culture-making species.
- Evolutionary psychology holds that adaptation, reproduction, and "survival of the fittest" are important in shaping behavior. Ideas proposed by evolutionary developmental psychology include the view that an extended "juvenile" period is needed to develop a large brain and learn the complexity of human social communities. Bandura argues for a bidirectional link between biology and environment. Biology allows for a broad range of cultural possibilities.

2 Describe what genes are and how they influence human development

- The nucleus of each human cell contains 46 chromosomes, which are composed of DNA. Short segments of DNA constitute genes, the units of hereditary information that direct cells to reproduce and manufacture proteins. Genes act collaboratively, not independently. Mitosis and meiosis are two important ways in which new cells are formed. In the process of reproduction, an egg and a sperm unite to form a zygote. Sources of genetic variability include the distinction between a genotype and a phenotype.
- Genetic principles include those involving dominant-recessive genes, sex-linked genes, genetic imprinting, and polygenic inheritance.
- Chromosome abnormalities produce Down syndrome, which is caused by the presence of an extra copy of chromosome 21, as well as sex-linked chromosomal abnormalities such as Klinefelter syndrome, fragile X syndrome, Turner syndrome, and XYY syndrome. Gene-linked disorders include phenylketonuria (PKU) and sickle-cell anemia. Genetic counseling has increased in popularity as more couples desire information about their risk of having a child with defective characteristics.

3 Identify some important reproductive challenges and choices

- Amniocentesis, ultrasound sonography, chorionic villi sampling, and maternal blood screening are used to determine the presence of defects once pregnancy has begun.
- Approximately 15 percent of U.S. couples have infertility problems, some of which can be corrected through surgery or fertility drugs. Additional options include in vitro fertilization and other, less common, more recently developed techniques.
- Although adopted children and adolescents have more problems than their nonadopted counterparts, the vast majority of adopted children adapt effectively. When adoption occurs very early in development, the outcomes for the child are improved. Because of the dramatic changes that occurred in adoption in recent decades, it is difficult to generalize about the average adopted child or average adoptive family.

4 Characterize some of the ways that heredity and environment interact to produce individual differences in development

- Behavior genetics is the field concerned with the degree and nature of behavior's hereditary basis. Methods used by behavior geneticists include twin studies and adoption studies.
- In Scarr's heredity-environment correlations view, heredity directs the types of environments that children experience. She describes three genotype-environment correlations: passive, evocative, and active (niche-picking). Scarr believes that the relative importance of these three genotype-environment correlations changes as children develop.
- Shared environmental experiences refer to siblings' common experiences, such as their parents' personalities and intellectual orientation, the family's socioeconomic status, and the neighborhood in which they live. Nonshared environmental experiences involve the child's unique experiences, both within a family and outside a family, that are not shared with a sibling. Many behavior geneticists argue that differences in the development of siblings are due to nonshared environmental experiences (and heredity) rather than shared environmental experiences.
- The epigenetic view emphasizes that development is the result of an ongoing, bidirectional interchange between heredity and environment.
- Many complex behaviors have some genetic loading that gives people a propensity for a particular developmental trajectory. However, actual development also requires an environment, and that environment is complex. The interaction of heredity and environment is extensive. Much remains to be discovered about the specific ways that heredity and environment interact to influence development.

KEY TERMS

KEY PEOPLE

E-LEARNING TOOLS

To help you master the material in this chapter, visit the Online Learning Center for *Child Development,* eleventh edition (**www.mhhe.com/santrockcd11**), where you'll find these additional resources:

Taking It to the Net

1. Ahmahl, a biochemistry major, is writing a psychology paper on the potential dilemmas that society and scientists may face as a result of the decoding of the human genome. What are some of the main issues or concerns that Ahmahl should address in his class paper?
2. Brandon and Katie are thrilled to learn that they are expecting their first child. They are curious about the genetic makeup of their unborn child and want to know (a) what disorders might be identified through prenatal genetic testing, and (b) which tests, if any, should Katie undergo to help determine this information.
3. Greg and Courtney have three boys. They would love to have a girl. Courtney read that there is a clinic in their state where you can pick the sex of your child. How successful are such efforts? Would you want to have this choice available to you?

Nursing, Parenting, and Teaching Exercises

Build your decision-making skills by trying your hand at the scenarios on the Online Learning Center.

Video Clips

The Online Learning Center includes the following videos for this chapter:

- Interview with Adoptive Parents
  An interview with a couple that adopted a second child. Peggy describes how long ago she decided she would adopt after reading a poignant magazine article. She describes the process of adoption and how the birth mother interviewed her and her husband. They both describe their involvement in the actual birth of the baby, the joys and stresses of that day. Peggy describes that one of the best days of her life was when the adoption became final.

Chapter 4 PRENATAL DEVELOPMENT AND BIRTH

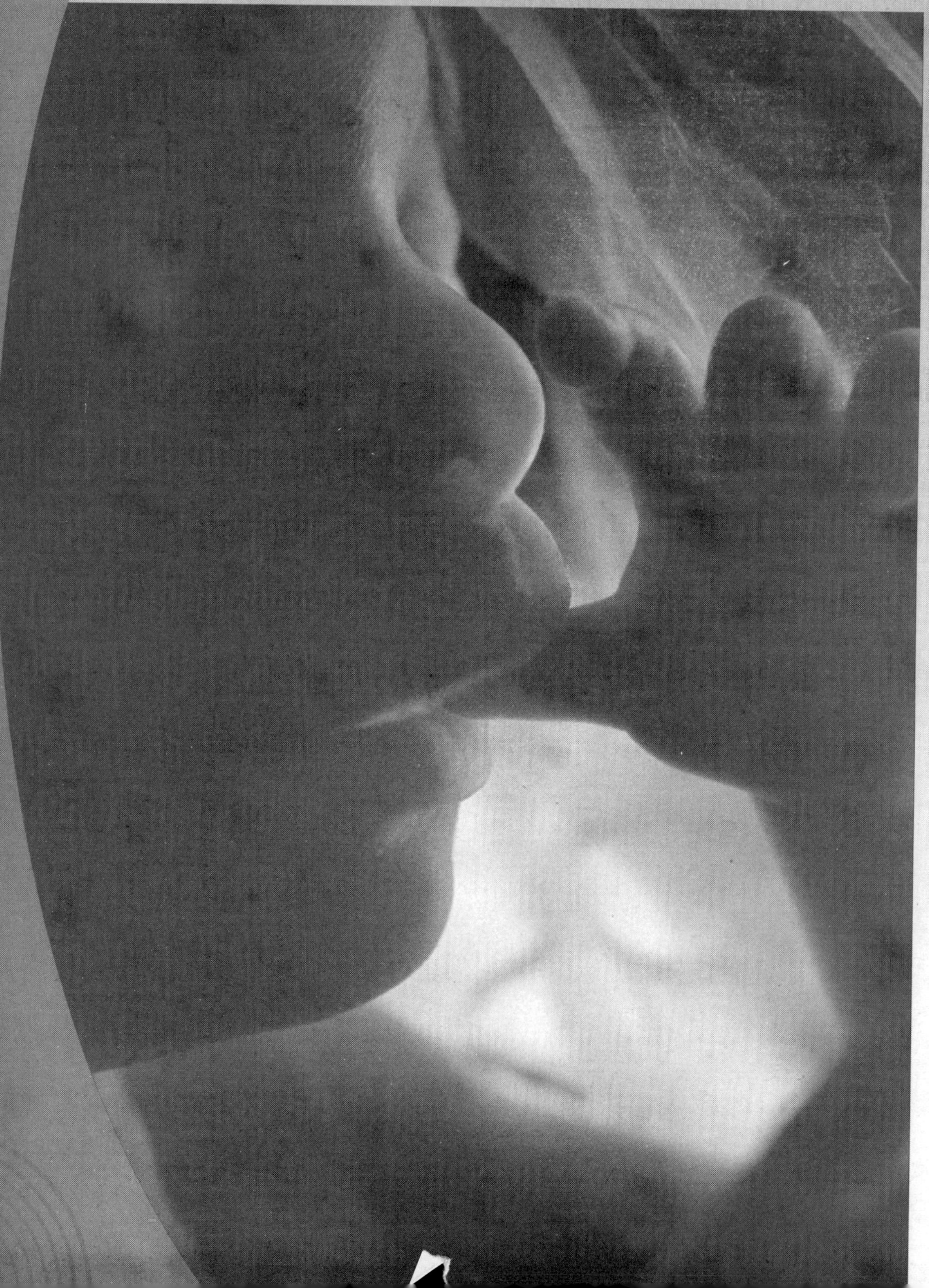

There was a star danced, and under that I was born.

—William Shakespeare
English Playwright, 17th Century

CHAPTER OUTLINE

LEARNING GOALS

PRENATAL DEVELOPMENT

The Course of Prenatal Development
Teratology and Hazards to Prenatal Development
Prenatal Care
Cultural Beliefs About Pregnancy
Normal Prenatal Development

1 Describe prenatal development

BIRTH

The Birth Process
Assessing the Newborn
Low Birth Weight and Preterm Infants

2 Discuss the birth process

THE POSTPARTUM PERIOD

Physical Adjustments
Emotional and Psychological Adjustments
Bonding

3 Explain the changes that take place in the postpartum period

The Story of Tanner Roberts' Birth:
A Fantastic Voyage

Tanner Roberts was born in a suite at St. Joseph's Medical Center in Burbank, California (Warrick, 1992, pp. E1, E11, E12). Let's examine what took place in the hours leading up to his birth.

It is day 266 of his mother Cindy's pregnancy. She is in the frozen-food aisle of a convenience store and feels a sharp pain, starting in the small of her back and reaching around her middle, which causes her to gasp. For weeks, painless Braxton Hicks spasms (named for the gynecologist who discovered them) have been flexing her uterine muscles. But these practice contractions were not nearly as intense and painful as the one she just experienced. After six hours of irregular spasms, her uterus settles into a more predictable rhythm.

At 3 A.M., Cindy and her husband, Tom, are wide awake. They time Cindy's contractions with a stopwatch. The contractions are now only six minutes apart. It's time to call the hospital. A short time later, Tom and Cindy arrive at the hospital's labor-delivery suite. A nurse puts a webbed belt and fetal monitor around Cindy's middle to measure her labor. The monitor picks up the fetal heart rate. With each contraction of the uterine wall, Tanner's heartbeat jumps from its resting state of about 140 beats to 160 to 170 beats per minute. When the cervix is dilated to more than 4 centimeters, or almost half open, Cindy receives her first medication. As Demerol begins to drip in her veins, the pain of her contractions is less intense. Tanner's heart rate dips to 130 and then 120.

Contractions are now coming every three to four minutes, each one lasting about 25 seconds. The Demerol does not completely obliterate Cindy's pain. She hugs her husband as the nurse urges her to "relax those muscles. Breathe deep. Relax. You're almost there."

Each contraction briefly cuts off Tanner's source of oxygen, his mother's blood. However, in the minutes of rest between contractions, Cindy's deep breathing helps rush fresh blood to the baby's heart and brain.

At 8 A.M., Cindy's cervix is almost completely dilated and the obstetrician arrives. Using a tool made for the purpose, he reaches into the birth canal and tears the membranes of the amniotic sac, and about half a liter of clear fluid flows out. Contractions are now coming every two minutes, and each one is lasting a full minute.

By 9 A.M., the labor suite has been transformed into a delivery room. Tanner's body is compressed by his mother's contractions and pushes. As he nears his entrance into the world, the compressions help press the fluid from his lungs in preparation for his first breath. Squeezed tightly in the birth canal, the top of Tanner's head emerges. His face is puffy and scrunched. Although fiercely squinting because of the sudden light, Tanner's eyes are open. Tiny bubbles of clear mucus are on his lips. Before any more of his body emerges, the nurse cradles Tanner's head and suctions his nose and mouth. Tanner takes his first breath, a large gasp followed by whimpering, and then a loud cry. Tanner's body is wet but only slightly bloody as the doctor lifts him onto his mother's abdomen. The umbilical cord, still connecting Tanner with his mother, slows and stops pulsating. The obstetrician cuts it, severing Tanner's connection to his mother's womb. Now Tanner's blood flows not to his mother's body for nourishment, but to his own lungs, intestines, and other organs.

PREVIEW

This chapter chronicles the truly remarkable developments from conception through birth. Imagine . . . at one time you were an organism floating in a sea of fluid in your mother's womb. Let's now explore what your development was like from the time you were conceived through the time you were born.

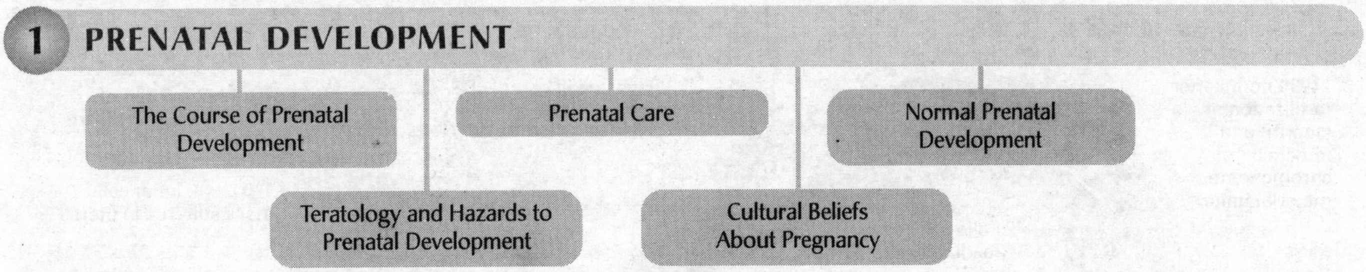

Imagine how Tanner Roberts came to be. Out of thousands of eggs and millions of sperm, one egg and one sperm united to produce him. Had the union of sperm and egg come a day or even an hour earlier or later, he might have been very different—maybe even of the opposite sex. Conception occurs when a single sperm cell from the male unites with an ovum (egg) in the female's fallopian tube in a process called fertilization. Over the next few months the genetic code discussed in chapter 3 directs a series of changes in the fertilized egg, but many events and hazards will influence how that egg develops and becomes tiny Tanner.

The Course of Prenatal Development

The course of prenatal development lasts approximately 266 days, beginning with fertilization and ending with birth. Prenatal development is divided into three periods: germinal, embryonic, and fetal.

The Germinal Period The **germinal period** is the period of prenatal development that takes place in the first two weeks after conception. It includes the creation of the fertilized egg, called a *zygote,* cell division, and the attachment of the zygote to the uterine wall.

Rapid cell division by the zygote begins the germinal period. By approximately one week after conception, the differentiation of these cells—their specialization for different tasks—has already begun. At this stage the group of cells, now called the **blastocyst,** consists of an inner mass of cells that will eventually develop into the embryo and the **trophoblast,** an outer layer of cells that develops during the germinal period. It later provides nutrition and support for the embryo. *Implantation,* the attachment of the zygote to the uterine wall, takes place about 10 to 14 days after conception. Figure 4.1 illustrates some of the most significant developments during the germinal period.

The Embryonic Period The **embryonic period** is the period of prenatal development that occurs from two to eight weeks after conception. During the embryonic period, the rate of cell differentiation intensifies, support systems for cells form, and organs appear.

This period begins as the blastocyst attaches to the uterine wall. The mass of cells is now called an *embryo,* and three layers of cells form. The embryo's *endoderm* is the inner layer of cells, which will develop into the digestive and respiratory systems. The *ectoderm* is the outermost layer, which will become the nervous system, sensory receptors (ears, nose, and eyes, for example), and skin parts (hair and nails, for example). The *mesoderm* is the middle layer, which will become the circulatory system, bones, muscles, excretory system, and reproductive system. Every body part eventually develops from these three layers. The endoderm primarily produces internal body parts, the mesoderm primarily produces parts that surround the internal areas, and the ectoderm primarily produces surface parts.

As the embryo's three layers form, life-support systems for the embryo develop rapidly. These life-support systems include the amnion, the umbilical cord, and the

germinal period The period of prenatal development that takes place in the first two weeks after conception. It includes the creation of the zygote, continued cell division, and the attachment of the zygote to the uterine wall.

blastocyst The inner layer of cells that develops during the germinal period. These cells later develop into the embryo.

trophoblast The outer layer of cells that develops in the germinal period. These cells provide nutrition and support for the embryo.

embryonic period The period of prenatal development that occurs two to eight weeks after conception. During the embryonic period, the rate of cell differentiation intensifies, support systems for the cells form, and organs appear.

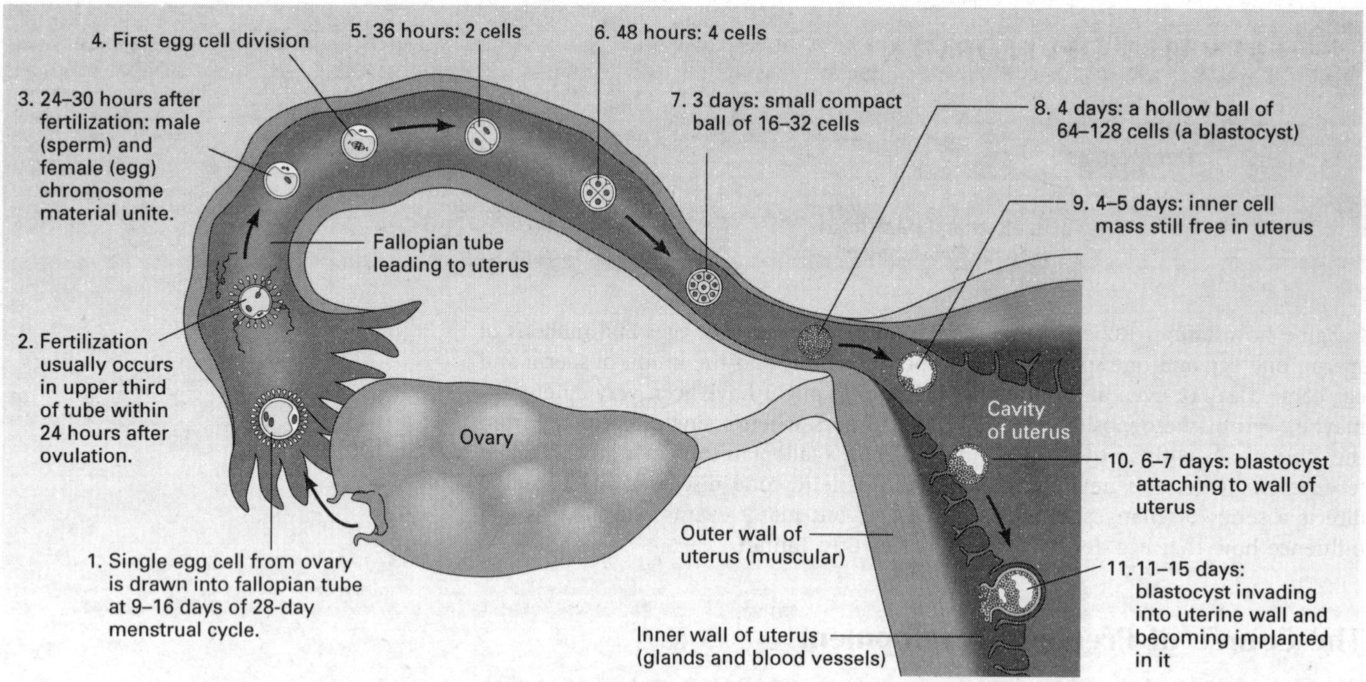

FIGURE 4.1 Significant Developments in the Germinal Period

placenta. The **amnion** is like a bag or an envelope and contains a clear fluid in which the developing embryo floats. The amniotic fluid provides an environment that is temperature- and humidity-controlled, as well as shockproof. The amnion develops from the fertilized egg, not from the mother's own body. The same is true for the **umbilical cord,** which contains two arteries and one vein, and connects the baby to the placenta. The **placenta** consists of a disk-shaped group of tissues in which small blood vessels from the mother and the offspring intertwine but do not join.

Figure 4.2 illustrates the placenta, the umbilical cord, and the blood flow in the expectant mother and developing fetus. Very small molecules—oxygen, water, salt, food from the mother's blood, as well as carbon dioxide and digestive wastes from the embryo's blood—pass back and forth between the mother and infant. Large molecules cannot pass through the placental wall; these include red blood cells and harmful substances, such as most bacteria, maternal wastes, and hormones. The mechanisms that govern the transfer of substances across the placental barrier are complex and are still not entirely understood (Jimenez & others, 2004; Wehrens & others, 2004).

By the time most women know they are pregnant, the major organs have begun to form. **Organogenesis** is the name given to the process of organ formation that takes place during the first two months of prenatal development. While they are being formed, the organs are especially vulnerable to environmental changes. In the third week, the neural tube, which eventually becomes the spinal cord, forms. At about 21 days, eyes begin to appear, and at 24 days the cells for the heart begin to differentiate. During the fourth week, the urogenital system becomes apparent, and arm and leg buds emerge. Four chambers of the heart take shape, and blood vessels appear. From the fifth to the eighth week, arms and legs differentiate further; at this time, the face starts to form but still is not very recognizable. The intestinal tract develops and the facial structures fuse. At 8 weeks, the developing organism weighs about $\frac{1}{30}$ ounce and is just over 1 inch long.

The Fetal Period

The **fetal period** is the prenatal period of development that begins two months after conception and lasts for seven months, on the average. Growth and development continue their dramatic course during this time.

The Visible Embryo
The Trimesters

amnion The life-support system that is a bag or envelope that contains a clear fluid in which the developing embryo floats.

umbilical cord A life-support system containing two arteries and one vein that connects the baby to the placenta.

placenta A life-support system that consists of a disk-shaped group of tissues in which small blood vessels from the mother and offspring intertwine.

organogenesis Organ formation that takes place during the first two months of prenatal development.

fetal period The prenatal period of development that begins two months after conception and lasts for seven months, on the average.

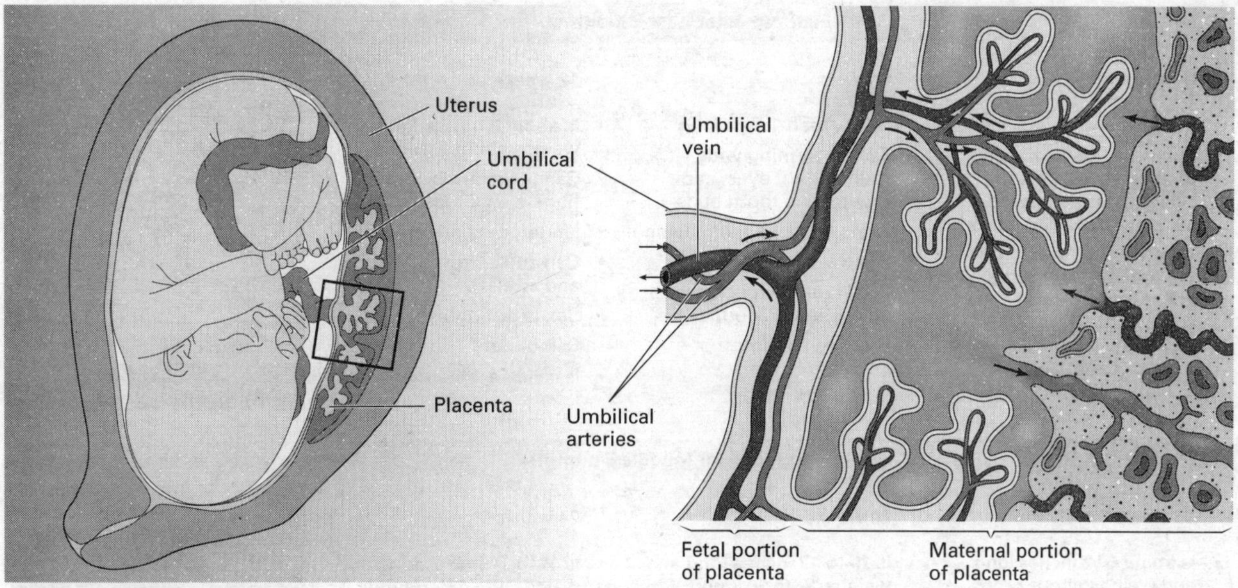

FIGURE 4.2 The Placenta and the Umbilical Cord. Maternal blood flows through the uterine arteries to the spaces housing the placenta, and it returns through the uterine veins to the maternal circulation. Fetal blood flows through the umbilical arteries into the capillaries of the placenta and returns through the umbilical veins to the fetal circulation. The exchange of materials takes place across the layer separating the maternal and fetal blood supplies, so the bloods never come into contact. *Note:* The area bound by the square is enlarged in the right half of the illustration. Arrows indicate the direction of blood flow.

Three months after conception, the fetus is about 3 inches long and weighs about 1 ounce. It has become active, moving its arms and legs, opening and closing its mouth, and moving its head. The face, forehead, eyelids, nose, and chin are distinguishable, as are the upper arms, lower arms, hands, and lower limbs. The genitals can be identified as male or female. By the end of the fourth month, the fetus has grown to 6 inches in length and weighs 4 to 7 ounces. At this time, a growth spurt occurs in the body's lower parts. Arm and leg movements can be felt for the first time by the mother.

By the end of the fifth month, the fetus is about 12 inches long and weighs close to a pound. Structures of the skin have formed—toenails and fingernails, for example. The fetus is more active, showing a preference for a particular position in the womb. By the end of the sixth month, the fetus is about 14 inches long and has gained another half pound to a pound. The eyes and eyelids are completely formed, and a fine layer of hair covers the head. A grasping reflex is present, and irregular breathing movements occur.

At about seven months, the fetus for the first time has a chance of surviving outside of the womb—that is, the fetus is *viable*. But even when infants are born in the seventh month, they usually need help breathing.

During the last two months of prenatal development, fatty tissues develop, and the functioning of various organ systems—heart and kidneys, for example—steps up. By the end of the seventh month, the fetus is about 16 inches long and now weighs about 3 pounds. During the eighth and ninth months, the fetus grows longer and gains substantial weight—about another 4 pounds. At birth, the average American baby weighs 7½ pounds and is about 20 inches long.

Figure 4.3 gives an overview of the main events during prenatal development. Notice that instead of describing development in terms of germinal, embryonic, and fetal periods, figure 4.3 divides prenatal development into equal periods of three months, called *trimesters.* Remember that the three trimesters are not the same as the three prenatal periods we have discussed. The germinal and embryonic periods

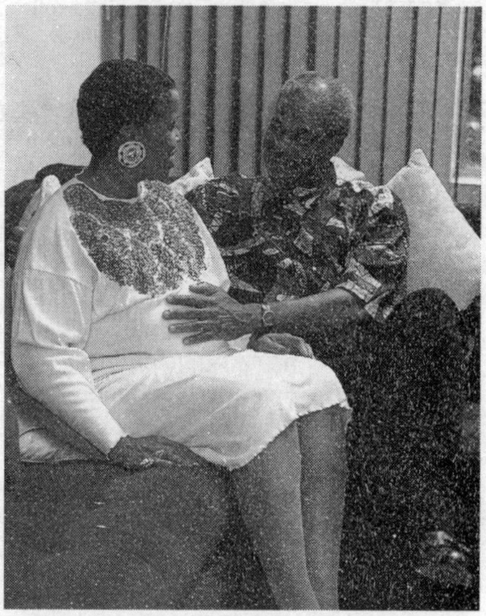

Lines of communication should be open between the expectant mother and her partner during pregnancy. *What are some examples of good partner communication during pregnancy?*

First trimester (first 3 months)			
Prenatal growth	Conception to 4 weeks	8 weeks	12 weeks
	• Is less than 1/10 inch long • Beginning development of spinal cord, nervous system, gastro-intestinal system, heart, and lungs • Amniotic sac envelopes the preliminary tissues of entire body • Is called a "zygote"	• Is less than 1 inch long • Face is forming with rudimentary eyes, ears, mouth, and tooth buds • Arms and legs are moving • Brain is forming • Fetal heartbeat is detectable with ultrasound • Is called an "embryo"	• Is about 3 inches long and weighs about 1 ounce • Can move arms, legs, fingers, and toes • Fingerprints are present • Can smile, frown, suck, and swallow • Sex is distinguishable • Can urinate • Is called a "fetus"

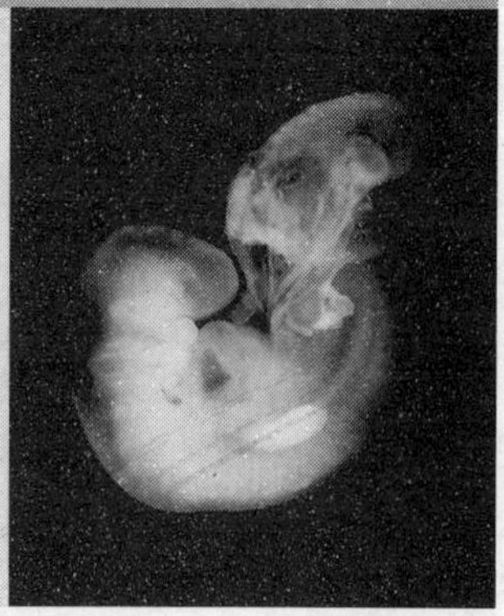

Second trimester (middle 3 months)			
Prenatal growth	16 weeks	20 weeks	24 weeks
	• Is about 5½ inches long and weighs about 4 ounces • Heartbeat is strong • Skin is thin, transparent • Downy hair (lanugo) covers body • Fingernails and toenails are forming • Has coordinated movements; is able to roll over in amniotic fluid	• Is 10 to 12 inches long and weighs ½ to 1 pound • Heartbeat is audible with ordinary stethoscope • Sucks thumb • Hiccups • Hair, eyelashes, eyebrows are present	• Is 11 to 14 inches long and weighs 1 to 1½ pounds • Skin is wrinkled and covered with protective coating (vernix caseosa) • Eyes are open • Waste matter is collected in bowel • Has strong grip

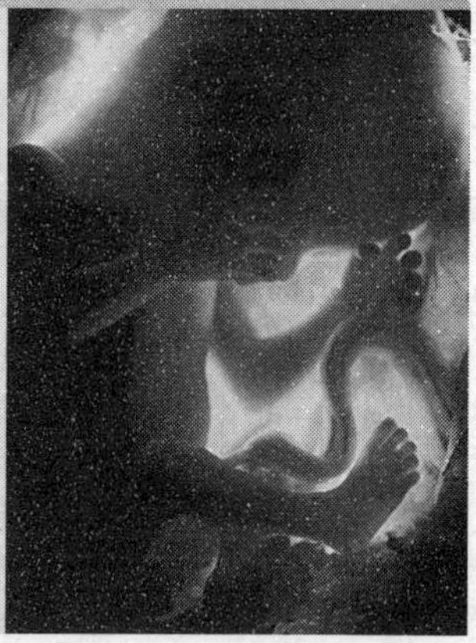

Third trimester (last 3 months)			
Prenatal growth	28 weeks	32 weeks	36 to 38 weeks
	• Is 14 to 17 inches long and weighs 2½ to 3 pounds • Is adding body fat • Is very active • Rudimentary breathing movements are present	• Is 16½ to 18 inches long and weighs 4 to 5 pounds • Has periods of sleep and wakefulness • Responds to sounds • May assume the birth position • Bones of head are soft and flexible • Iron is being stored in liver	• Is 19 inches long and weighs 6 pounds • Skin is less wrinkled • Vernix caseosa is thick • Lanugo is mostly gone • Is less active • Is gaining immunities from mother

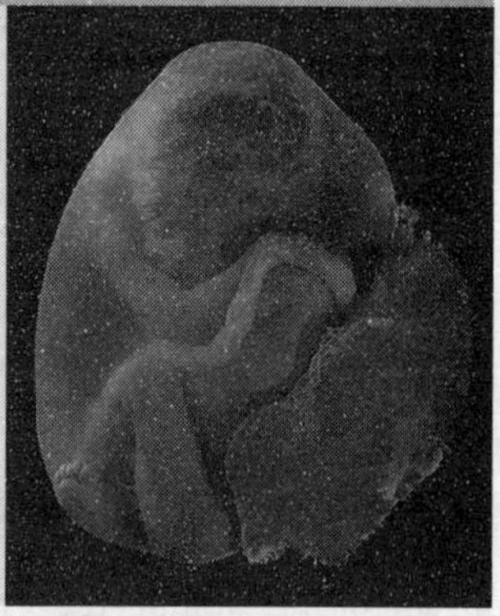

FIGURE 4.3 The Three Trimesters of Prenatal Development

occur in the first trimester. The fetal period begins toward the end of the first trimester and continues through the second and third trimesters. Viability (the chance of surviving outside the womb) occurs at the beginning of the third trimester.

Teratology and Hazards to Prenatal Development

Although the fetus lives in a protected environment, it is not totally immune to the larger world. The environment can affect the child in many well-documented ways.

General Principles A **teratogen** is any agent that causes a birth defect. (The word comes from the Greek word *tera* meaning "monster.") The field of study that investigates the causes of birth defects is called *teratology.* Teratogens include drugs, incompatible blood types, environmental pollutants, infectious diseases, nutritional deficiencies, maternal stress, and advanced maternal and paternal age. In fact, thousands of babies are born deformed or mentally retarded every year as a result of events that occurred in the mother's life as early as one or two months *before* conception (Bailey, Forget, & Koren, 2002). As we further discuss teratogens, you will see that factors related to the father also can influence prenatal development.

So many teratogens exist that practically every fetus is exposed to at least some teratogens. For this reason, it is difficult to determine which teratogen causes which birth defect. In addition, it may take a long time for the effects of a teratogen to show up. Only about half of all potential effects appear at birth.

The dose, genetic susceptibility, and the time of exposure to a particular teratogen influence the severity of the damage to an unborn child and the type of defect:

- *Dose* The dose effect is rather obvious—the greater the dose of an agent, such as a drug, the greater the effect.
- *Genetic Susceptibility* The type or severity of abnormalities caused by a teratogen is linked to the genotype of the pregnant woman and the genotype of the fetus (Lidral & Murray, 2005). For example, how a mother metabolizes a particular drug can influence the degree to which the drug effects are transmitted to the fetus. Differences in placental membranes and placental transport also affect fetal exposure. The extent to which a fetus is vulnerable to a particular teratogen may also depend on the genotype of the fetus (Pellizzer & others, 2004).
- *Time of Exposure* Teratogens do more damage when they occur at some points in development rather than at others (Brent & Fawcett, 2000). Damage during the germinal period may even prevent implantation. In general, the embryonic period is more vulnerable than the fetal period.

Figure 4.4 summarizes additional information about the effects of time of exposure to a teratogen. Sensitivity to teratogens begins about three weeks after conception. The probability of a structural defect is greatest early in the embryonic period, when organs are being formed. Each body structure has its own critical period of formation. Recall from chapter 2 that a *critical period* is a fixed time period very early in development during which certain experiences or events can have a long-lasting effect on development. The critical period for the nervous system (week 3) is earlier than for arms and legs (weeks 4 and 5).

After organogenesis is complete, teratogens are less likely to cause anatomical defects. Exposure during the fetal period is more likely instead to stunt growth or to create problems in the way organs function.

Prescription and Nonprescription Drugs Some pregnant women take prescription and nonprescription drugs without thinking about the possible effects on the fetus (Addis, Magrini, & Mastroiacovo, 2001). Occasionally, a rash of deformed babies is born, bringing to light the damage drugs can have on a developing fetus. This happened in 1961, when many pregnant women took a popular tranquilizer, thalidomide, to alleviate their morning sickness. In adults, the effects of thalidomide are mild; in embryos, however, they are devastating. Not all infants were affected in the same way. If the mother took thalidomide on day 26 (probably before she knew she was pregnant), an arm might not grow. If she took the drug two days later, the arm might not grow past the elbow. The thalidomide tragedy shocked the medical community and parents and taught a valuable lesson: taking the wrong drug at the wrong time is enough to physically handicap the offspring for life (Sorokin, 2002).

The history of man for nine months preceding his birth would, probably, be far more interesting, and contain events of greater moment than all three score and ten years that follow it.

—SAMUEL TAYLOR COLERIDGE
English Poet, Essayist, 19th Century

www.mhhe.com/santrockcd11

Exploring Teratology
High-Risk Situations

teratogen From the Greek word *tera,* meaning "monster." Any agent that causes a birth defect. The field of study that investigates the causes of birth defects is called teratology.

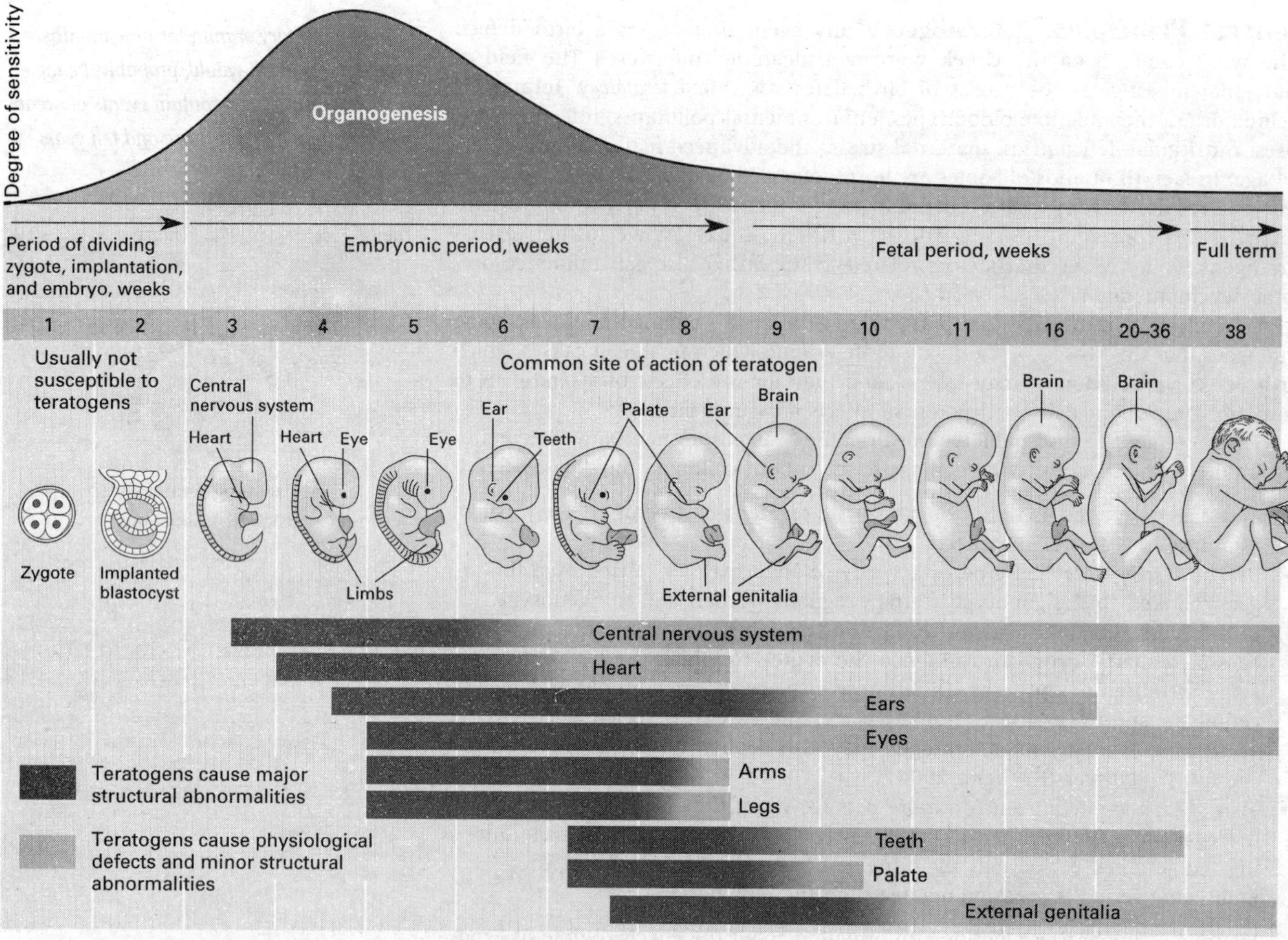

FIGURE 4.4 Teratogens and the Timing of Their Effects on Prenatal Development. The danger of structural defects caused by teratogens is greatest in embryonic development. The period of organogenesis (red color) lasts for about six weeks. Later assaults by teratogens (blue color) mainly occur in the fetal period and instead of causing structural damage are more likely to stunt growth or cause problems in how organs function.

Prescription drugs that can function as teratogens include antibiotics, such as streptomycin and tetracycline; some antidepressants; certain hormones, such as progestin and synthetic estrogen; and Accutane (which often is prescribed for acne) (Committee on Drugs, 2000; Kallen, 2004).

Nonprescription drugs that can be harmful include diet pills, aspirin, and caffeine (Cnattingius & others, 2000). Let's explore the research on caffeine, which people often consume by drinking coffee, tea, or colas, or by eating chocolate. A review of studies on caffeine consumption during pregnancy concluded that a small increase in the risks for spontaneous abortion and low birth weight occurs for pregnant women consuming more than 150 milligrams of caffeine (approximately two cups of brewed coffee or two to three 12-ounce cans of cola) per day (Fernandez & others, 1998). In one study, pregnant women who drank caffeinated coffee were more likely to have preterm deliveries and newborns with a lower birth weight than their counterparts who did not drink caffeinated coffee (Eskenazi & others, 1999). In this study, no effects were found for pregnant women who drank decaffeinated coffee. Taking into account such results, the Food and Drug Administration recommends that pregnant women either not consume caffeine or consume it only sparingly.

Psychoactive Drugs *Psychoactive drugs* are drugs that act on the nervous system to alter states of consciousness, modify perceptions, and change moods. A number of psychoactive drugs, including alcohol and nicotine, as well as illegal drugs such as cocaine, marijuana, and heroin have been studied to determine their links to prenatal and child development (Caulfield, 2001; Fogel, 2001).

Alcohol Heavy drinking by pregnant women can be devastating to offspring (Barr & Streissguth, 2001; Caley, Kramer, & Robinson, 2005; Enoch & Goldman, 2002). **Fetal alcohol syndrome (FAS)** is a cluster of abnormalities that appears in the offspring of mothers who drink alcohol heavily during pregnancy (Archibald & others, 2001). The abnormalities include facial deformities and defective limbs, face, and heart. Figure 4.5 shows a child with FAS. Most of these children are below average in intelligence, and some are mentally retarded (Bookstein & others, 2002; O'Leary, 2004; West & Blake, 2005). One recent study found that prenatal exposure to binge drinking was linked to a greater likelihood of having IQ scores in the mentally retarded range and a higher incidence of acting-out behavior at 7 years of age (Bailey & others, 2004). Although many mothers of FAS infants are heavy drinkers, many mothers who are heavy drinkers do not have children with FAS or have one child with FAS and other children who do not have it.

Is moderate drinking during pregnancy also harmful to the offspring? Serious malformations such as those produced by FAS are not found in infants born to mothers who are moderate drinkers, but even moderate drinking can have an effect on the offspring (Burden & others, 2005; Howell & others, 2005, in press). In one study, children whose mothers drank moderately (one to two drinks a day) during pregnancy were less attentive and alert, even at 4 years of age (Streissguth & others, 1984). Also, a recent study found that moderate alcohol drinking by pregnant women (three or more drinks a day) was linked with increased risk of preterm birth (Parazzini & others, 2003). And in a longitudinal study, the more alcohol mothers drank in the first trimester of pregnancy, the more 14-year-olds fell behind on growth markers such as weight, height, and head size (Day & others, 2002).

What are some guidelines for alcohol use during pregnancy? Moderate drinking of one or two servings of beer or wine or one serving of hard liquor a few days a week can have negative effects on the fetus, although it is generally agreed that this level of alcohol use will not cause fetal alcohol syndrome. The U.S. Surgeon General recommends that *no* alcohol be consumed during pregnancy. And recent research suggests that it may not be wise to consume alcohol at the time of conception. One study revealed that "both male and female alcohol intakes during the week of conception increased the risk of early pregnancy loss" (Henriksen & others, 2004, p. 661).

Nicotine Cigarette smoking by pregnant women can also adversely influence prenatal development, birth, and postnatal development (Pringle & others, 2005; Zdravkovic & others, 2005). Preterm births and low birth weights, fetal and neonatal deaths, respiratory problems, and sudden infant death syndrome (SIDS, also known as crib death) are all more common among the offspring of mothers who smoked during pregnancy (Mathews, Menacker, & MacDorman, 2003; Moore & Davies, 2005).

Prenatal exposure to heavy smoking has been linked in one study to nicotine withdrawal symptoms in newborns (Godding & others, 2004). Another study tied prenatal exposure to cigarette smoking to poorer language and cognitive skills at 4 years of age (Fried & Watkinson, 1990). Yet another study revealed a link between maternal smoking during pregnancy and increased incidence of attention deficit hyperactivity disorder in almost 3,000 children 5 to 16 years of age (Thapar & others, 2003). Intervention programs designed to help pregnant women stop smoking can reduce some of smoking's negative effects, especially by raising birth weights (Klesges & others, 2001).

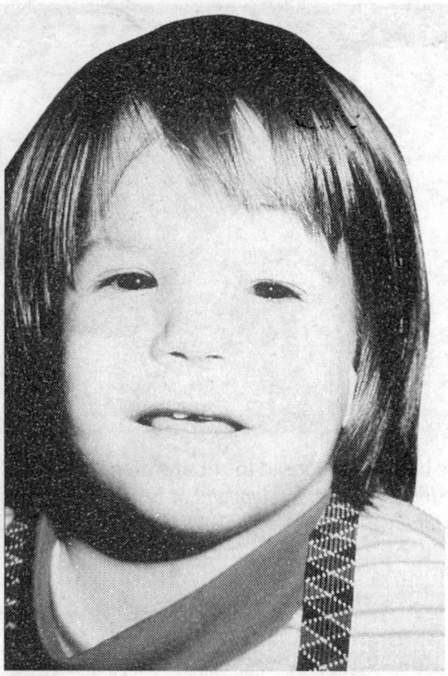

FIGURE 4.5 Fetal Alcohol Syndrome. Notice the wide-set eyes, flat bones, and thin upper lip.

www.mhhe.com/santrockcd11

Fetal Alcohol Syndrome
Smoking and Pregnancy

fetal alcohol syndrome (FAS) A cluster of abnormalities that appears in the offspring of mothers who drink alcohol heavily during pregnancy.

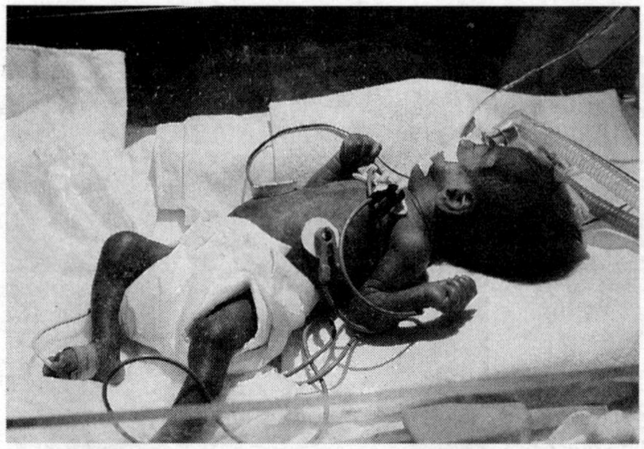

This baby was exposed to cocaine prenatally. *What are some of the possible effects on development of being exposed to cocaine prenatally?*

Cocaine Does cocaine use during pregnancy harm the developing embryo and fetus? The most consistent finding is that cocaine exposure during prenatal development is associated with reduced birth weight, length, and head circumference (Smith & others, 2001). Also, in one study, prenatal cocaine exposure was associated with impaired motor development at 2 years of age (Arendt & others, 1999). In a recent study of 1-month-old infants, those with prenatal exposure to cocaine had lower arousal, less effective self-regulation, higher excitability, and lower quality of reflexes (Lester & others, 2002). Other studies link prenatal exposure to cocaine to impaired information processing and language development (Morrow & others, 2003; Singer & others, 1999).

These findings should be interpreted cautiously (Chavkin, 2001; Vidaeff & Mastrobattista, 2003). Why? Because other factors in the lives of pregnant women who use cocaine (such as poverty, malnutrition, and other substance abuse) often cannot be ruled out as possible contributors to the problems found in their children (Hurt & others, 2005; Kaugers, Russ, & Singer, 2000). For example, cocaine users are more likely than nonusers to smoke cigarettes, use marijuana, drink alcohol, and take amphetamines.

Despite these cautions, the weight of research evidence indicates that children born to mothers who use cocaine are likely to have neurological and cognitive deficits (Mayes, 2003). Cocaine use by pregnant women is not recommended.

Marijuana There has not been extensive research on how marijuana use by pregnant women affects their offspring. A recent review of the research concluded that marijuana use by pregnant women is related to negative outcomes in memory and information processing in their offspring (Kalant, 2004). For example, in a longitudinal study, prenatal marijuana exposure was related to learning and memory difficulties at age 11 (Richardson & others, 2002). However, because of the small numbers of studies, it is difficult to reach conclusions about the effects of marijuana use by mothers during pregnancy. Nonetheless, marijuana use is not recómmended for use by pregnant women.

Heroin It is well documented that infants whose mothers are addicted to heroin show several behavioral difficulties (Hulse & others, 2001). The difficulties include withdrawal symptoms, such as tremors, irritability, abnormal crying, disturbed sleep, and impaired motor control. Many still show behavioral problems at their first birthday, and attention deficits may appear later in development. The most common treatment for heroin addiction, methadone, is associated with very severe withdrawal symptoms in newborns.

Incompatible Blood Types Incompatibility between the mother's and father's blood type poses another risk to prenatal development. Blood types are created by differences in the surface structure of red blood cells. One type of difference in the surface of red blood cells creates the familiar blood groups—A, B, O, and AB. A second difference creates what is called Rh-positive and Rh-negative blood. If a surface marker, called the *Rh factor,* is present in an individual's red blood cells, the person is said to be Rh positive; if the Rh marker is not present, the person is said to be Rh negative. If a pregnant woman is Rh negative and her partner is Rh positive, the fetus may be Rh positive (Harty-Golder, 2005; Weiss, 2001). If the fetus' blood is Rh positive and the mother's is Rh negative, the mother's immune system may produce antibodies that will attack the fetus. This can result in any number of problems, including miscarriage or stillbirth, anemia, jaundice, heart defects, brain damage, or death soon after birth (Moise, 2005; Narang & Jain, 2001).

Generally, the first Rh-positive baby of an Rh-negative mother is not at risk, but with each subsequent pregnancy the risk increases. A vaccine (RhoGAM) may be given to the mother within three days of the child's birth to prevent her body from making antibodies that will attack future Rh-positive fetuses. Also, babies affected by Rh incompatibility can be given blood transfusions before or right after birth (Mannessier & others, 2000).

Maternal Diseases Maternal diseases and infections can produce defects in offspring by crossing the placental barrier, or they can cause damage during birth (Kirkham, Harris, & Grzybowski, 2005). Rubella (German measles) is one disease that can cause prenatal defects (Kobayashi & others, 2005). The greatest damage occurs if a mother contracts rubella in the third or fourth week of pregnancy, although infection during the second month is also damaging. A rubella outbreak in 1964–1965 resulted in 30,000 prenatal and neonatal (newborn) deaths, and more than 20,000 affected infants were born with malformations, including mental retardation, blindness, deafness, and heart problems. Elaborate preventive efforts ensure that rubella will never again have such disastrous effects. A vaccine that prevents German measles is now routinely administered to children, and women who plan to have children should have a blood test before they become pregnant to determine if they are immune to the disease (Signore, 2001; Ward, Lambert, & Lester, 2001).

Syphilis (a sexually transmitted disease) is more damaging later in prenatal development—four months or more after conception. Rather than affecting organogenesis, as rubella does, syphilis damages organs after they have formed. Damage includes eye lesions, which can cause blindness, and skin lesions. When syphilis is present at birth, problems can develop in the central nervous system and gastrointestinal tract (Hollier & others, 2001; Mullick, Beksinska, & Msomi, 2005). Most states require that pregnant women be given a blood test to detect the presence of syphilis.

Another infection that has received widespread attention recently is genital herpes (Rupp, Rosenthal, & Stanberry, 2005). Newborns contract this virus when they are delivered through the birth canal of a mother with genital herpes (Qutub & others, 2001; Thung & Grobman, 2005). About one-third of babies delivered through an infected birth canal die; another one-fourth become brain damaged. If an active case of genital herpes is detected in a pregnant woman close to her delivery date, a cesarean section can be performed (in which the infant is delivered through an incision in the mother's abdomen) to keep the virus from infecting the newborn.

AIDS is a sexually transmitted disease that is caused by the human immunodeficiency virus (HIV), which destroys the body's immune system. A mother can infect her offspring with AIDS in three ways: (1) during gestation across the placenta, (2) during delivery through contact with maternal blood or fluids, and (3) postpartum (after birth) through breast-feeding. The transmission of AIDS through breast-feeding is especially a problem in many developing countries (Mohalla & others, 2005; Thorne & Newell, 2003; UNICEF, 2004). Babies born to HIV-infected mothers can be (1) infected and symptomatic (show AIDS symptoms), (2) infected but asymptomatic (not show AIDS symptoms), or (3) not infected at all. An infant who is infected and asymptomatic may still develop HIV symptoms up until 15 months of age.

In the early 1990s, before preventive treatments were available, 1,000 to 2,000 infants were born with HIV infection each year in the United States. Since then transmission of AIDS from mothers to their fetuses has been reduced dramatically (Blair & others, 2004; Gerrard & Chudasama, 2003). Only about one-third as many cases of newborns with AIDS appear today as in the early 1990s. This decline is due to the increase in counseling and voluntary testing of pregnant women for HIV and to the use of zidovudine (AZT) by infected women during pregnancy, and for the infant after birth (Sullivan, 2003).

Maternal Diet and Nutrition A developing fetus depends completely on its mother for nutrition, which comes from the mother's blood. The nutritional status of the fetus is determined by the mother's total caloric intake and intake of

Because the fetus depends entirely on its mother for nutrition, it is important for the pregnant woman to have good nutritional habits. In Kenya, this government clinic provides pregnant women with information about how their diet can influence the health of their fetus and offspring. *What might the information about diet be like?*

proteins, vitamins, and minerals. Children born to malnourished mothers are more likely than other children to be malformed.

Being overweight before and during pregnancy can also put the fetus at risk. Two studies found that obese women had a significant risk of late fetal death, although the risk of preterm delivery was reduced in these women (Cnattingius & others, 1998; Kumari, 2001).

One aspect of maternal nutrition that is important for normal prenatal development is folic acid, a B-complex vitamin (Bailey & Berry, 2005; Cleves & others, 2004). A lack of folic acid is linked with neural tube defects in offspring, such as spina bifida (a typically fatal defect in the spinal cord in offspring (Evans & others, 2004; Felkner & others, 2005). The U.S. Public Health Service recommends that pregnant women consume a minimum of 400 micrograms of folic acid per day (about twice the amount the average woman gets in one day). Orange juice and spinach are examples of foods rich in folic acid.

Eating fish is often recommended as part of a healthy diet, but pollution has made many fish a risky choice for pregnant women. Some fish contain high levels of mercury, which is released into the air both naturally and by industrial pollution (Fitzgerald & others, 2004). When mercury falls into the water, it can become toxic and accumulate in large fish, such as shark, swordfish, king mackerel, and some species of large tuna. Mercury is easily transferred across the placenta, and the embryo's developing brain and nervous system are highly sensitive to the metal (Patterson, Ryan, & Dickey, 2004; Stephenson, 2004). The U.S. Food and Drug Administration (2004) recently provided the following recommendations for women of childbearing age and young children: don't eat shark, swordfish, king mackerel or tilefish; eat up to 12 ounces (2 average meals) a week of fish and shellfish that are lower in mercury, such as shrimp, canned light tuna, salmon, pollock, and catfish.

PCB-polluted fish also pose a risk. PCBs (polychlorinated biphenyls) are manufacturing chemicals that are harmful to prenatal development (Fitzgerald & others, 2004; Vreugdenhil & others, 2004). Although banned in the 1970s in the United States, PCBs continue to be present in landfills, sediments, and wildlife. One study kept track of the extent to which pregnant women ate PCB-polluted fish from Lake Michigan and subsequently observed their children as newborns, young children, and at 11 years of age (Jacobson & others, 1984; Jacobson & Jacobson, 2002, 2003). The women who had eaten more PCB-polluted fish were more likely to have smaller, preterm infants who were more likely to react slowly to stimuli. As preschool children, their exposure to PCBs was linked with less effective short-term memory, and at age 11 with lower verbal intelligence and reading comprehension.

Maternal Emotional States and Stress Tales abound about how a pregnant woman's emotional state affects the fetus. For centuries it was thought that frightening experiences—such as a severe thunderstorm or a family member's death—leave birthmarks on the child or affect the child in more serious ways. In fact, a mother's stress can be transmitted to the fetus, and we now have a better grasp of how this takes place, although the mechanisms that link fetal health and the mother's emotional states are still far from certain (Federenko & Wadhwa, 2004; Loveland, Cook, & others, 2004; Van den Bergh & others, 2005).

When a pregnant woman experiences intense fears, anxieties, and other emotions, physiological changes occur that may affect her fetus. For example, producing adrenaline in response to fear restricts blood flow to the uterine area and can deprive the fetus of adequate oxygen. Also, maternal stress may increase the level of corticotrophin-releasing hormone (CRH) early in pregnancy (Hobel & others,

1999; Wadhwa, 2005; Weinstock, 2005). CRH, in turn, has been linked to premature delivery. Women under stress are about four times more likely than their low-stress counterparts to deliver babies prematurely (Dunkel-Schetter, 1998; Dunkel-Schetter & others, 2001). A mother's stress may also influence the fetus indirectly by increasing the likelihood that the mother will engage in unhealthy behaviors, such as taking drugs and engaging in poor prenatal care.

The mother's emotional state during pregnancy can influence the birth process, too. An emotionally distraught mother might have irregular contractions and a more difficult labor, which can cause irregularities in the supply of oxygen to the fetus or other problems after birth. Babies born after extended labor also may adjust more slowly to their world and be more irritable.

Positive emotional states also appear to make a difference to the fetus. Pregnant women who are optimistic thinkers have less adverse outcomes than pregnant women who are pessimistic thinkers (Lobel & others, 2002). Optimists are more likely to believe that they have control over the outcomes of their pregnancies.

What are some of the risks for infants born to adolescent mothers?

Maternal Age When possible harmful effects on the fetus and infant are considered, two maternal ages are of special interest: adolescence and the thirties and beyond (Aliyu & others, 2004; Callaghan & Berg, 2003; Spandorfer & others, 2004). Approximately 1 of every 5 births in the United States is to an adolescent; in some urban areas, the figure reaches as high as 1 in every 2 births. Infants born to adolescents are often premature (Ekwo & Morwad, 2000). The mortality rate of infants born to adolescent mothers is double that of infants born to mothers in their twenties. This high rate probably reflects the immaturity of the mother's reproductive system, but poor nutrition, lack of prenatal care, and low socioeconomic status may also play a role (Lenders, McElrath, & Scholl, 2000).

Prenatal care decreases the probability that a child born to an adolescent girl will have physical problems. However, adolescents are the least likely of women in all age groups to obtain prenatal assistance from clinics, pediatricians, and health services.

Maternal age is also linked to the risk that a child will have Down syndrome (Holding, 2002). As discussed in chapter 3, an individual with *Down syndrome* has distinctive facial characteristics, short limbs, and retardation of motor and mental abilities. A baby with Down syndrome rarely is born to a mother 16 to 34 years of age. However, when the mother reaches 40 years of age, the probability is slightly over 1 in 100 that a baby born to her will have Down syndrome, and by age 50 it is almost 1 in 10.

Increased risk for low birth weight is another danger when the mother is 35 years or older (Cleary-Goldman & others, 2005; Mirowsky, 2005). One recent study found that low birth weight delivery increased 11 percent and preterm delivery increased 14 percent in women 35 years and older (Tough & others, 2002).

Fetal death is also more likely to occur in older women. Fetal death was low for women 30 to 34 years of age but increased progressively for women 35 to 39 and 40 to 44 years of age in one recent study (Canterino & others, 2004).

We still have much to learn about the role of the mother's age in pregnancy and childbirth. As women remain active, exercise regularly, and are careful about their nutrition, their reproductive systems may remain healthier at older ages than was thought possible in the past.

Paternal Factors So far, we have discussed how characteristics of the mother—such as drug use, disease, nutrition and diet, emotional states, and age—can influence prenatal development and the development of the child. Might there also be some paternal risk factors? Indeed, there are several. Men's exposure to lead, radiation, certain pesticides, and petrochemicals may cause abnormalities in sperm that lead to miscarriage or diseases, such as childhood cancer (Lindbohm, 1991; Trasler,

2000; Slama & others, 2005; Trasler & Doerksen, 2000). When fathers have a diet low in vitamin C, their offspring have a higher risk of birth defects and cancer (Fraga & others, 1991). Also, it has been speculated that, when fathers take cocaine, it may attach itself to sperm and cause birth defects, but the evidence for this effect is not yet strong. In one study, long-term use of cocaine by men was related to low sperm count, low motility, and a higher number of abnormally formed sperm (Bracken & others, 1990). Cocaine-related fertility appears to be reversible if users stop taking the drug for at least one year.

The father's smoking during the mother's pregnancy also can cause problems for the offspring. In one investigation, the newborns of fathers who smoked around their wives during the pregnancy were 4 ounces lighter at birth for each pack of cigarettes smoked per day than were the newborns whose fathers did not smoke during their wives' pregnancy (Rubin & others, 1986). In another study, in China, the longer the fathers smoked, the stronger the risk that their children would develop cancer (Ji & others, 1997). In such studies, it is very difficult to tease apart prenatal and postnatal effects.

The father's age also makes a difference (Klonoff-Cohen & Natarajan, 2004). About 5 percent of children with Down syndrome have older fathers. The offspring of older fathers also face increased risk for other birth defects, including dwarfism and Marfan's syndrome, which involves head and limb deformities.

There are also risks to offspring when both the mother and father are older (Dunson, Baird, & Columbo, 2004). In one recent study, the risk of an adverse pregnancy outcome, such as miscarriage, was much greater when the woman was 35 years or older and the man was 40 years of age or older (de la Rochebrochard & Thonneau, 2002).

An explosion at the Chernobyl nuclear power plant in the Ukraine produced radioactive contamination that spread to surrounding areas. Thousands of infants were born with health problems and deformities as a result of the nuclear contamination, including this boy whose arm did not form. *Other than radioactive contamination, what are some other types of environmental hazards to prenatal development?*

Environmental Hazards Many aspects of our modern industrial world can endanger the fetus (Bellinger, 2005). Earlier, we mentioned that a fetus may be harmed if the mother's diet includes polluted fish or if the father's exposure to certain chemicals caused abnormalities in his sperm. Some specific hazards to the fetus that are worth a closer look include radiation, toxic wastes, and other chemical pollutants (Blaasaas, Tynes, & Lie, 2004; Grigorenko, 2001; Urbano & Tait, 2004).

Radiation can cause a gene mutation (an abrupt, permanent change in DNA). Chromosomal abnormalities are elevated among the offspring of fathers exposed to high levels of radiation in their occupations (Schrag & Dixon, 1985). X-ray radiation also can affect the developing embryo and fetus, especially in the first several weeks after conception, when women do not yet know they are pregnant (Urbano & Tait, 2004). Possible effects include microencephaly (an abnormally small brain), mental retardation, and leukemia. Women and their physicians should weigh the risk of an X-ray when an actual or potential pregnancy is involved (Brent, 2004; Shaw, 2001). However, a routine diagnostic X-ray of a body area other than the abdomen, with the women's abdomen protected by a lead apron, is generally considered safe.

The low-level electromagnetic radiation emitted by computer monitors has raised the fear that pregnant women who spend long hours in front of monitors might risk adverse effects to their offspring. Researchers have not found exposure to computer monitors to be related to miscarriage (Schnorr & others, 1991).

Environmental pollutants and toxic wastes are also sources of danger to unborn children. Among the dangerous pollutants are carbon monoxide, mercury, and lead. Some children are exposed to lead because they live in houses in which lead-based paint flakes off the walls or near busy highways, where there are heavy automobile emissions from leaded gasoline. Researchers believe that early exposure to lead affects children's mental development (Yang & others, 2003). For example, in one study, 2-year-olds who prenatally had high levels of lead in their umbilical-cord blood performed poorly on a test of mental development (Bellinger & others, 1987).

Prenatal Care

Information about teratogens and other prenatal hazards is one of the many benefits that expectant mothers gain from prenatal care. Prenatal care varies enormously but usually involves a defined schedule of visits for medical care, which typically includes screening for manageable conditions and treatable diseases that can affect the baby or the mother (Parmet, Lynn, & Glass, 2004).

In addition to medical care, prenatal programs often include comprehensive educational, social, and nutritional services. Women who are pregnant can benefit from the information and advice they receive from health-care personnel, such as Rachel Thompson, an obstetrician/gynecologist whose work is described in the Careers in Child Development insert. Information about pregnancy, labor, delivery, and caring for the newborn can be extremely valuable, especially for first-time mothers (Chang & others, 2003). Prenatal care is also very important for women in poverty because it links them with other social services (Lewallen, 2004). The legacy of prenatal care continues after birth, because women who receive this type of care are more likely to seek preventive care for their infants (Bates & others, 1994).

One recent study found that U.S. women who had no prenatal care were far more likely than their counterparts who received prenatal care to have infants who had low birth weight, increased mortality, and a number of other physical problems (Herbst & others, 2003). The prenatal care that women receive depends in part on their attitudes toward pregnancy. Women who have unplanned or unwanted pregnancies, or who have negative attitudes about being pregnant, are more likely to delay prenatal care or to miss appointments (Joseph, 1989). Next, in the Caring for Children interlude, we will compare prenatal care in the United States and other countries.

CAREERS in CHILD DEVELOPMENT

Rachel Thompson

Obstetrician/Gynecologist

Rachel Thompson is the senior member of Houston Women's Care Associates, which specializes in health care for women. She has one of Houston's most popular obstetrics/gynecology (OB/GYN) practices. Rachel's medical degree is from Baylor College of Medicine, where she also completed her internship and residency. Rachel's work focuses on many of the topics we discuss in this chapter on prenatal development, birth, and the postpartum period.

In addition to her clinical practice, Rachel is a clinical instructor in the Department of Obstetrics and Gynecology at Baylor College of Medicine. Rachel says that one of the unique features of their health-care group is that the staff is composed only of women who are full-time practitioners.

Rachel Thompson (*right*), talking with one of her patients at Houston Women's Care Associates.

www.mhhe.com/santrockcd11

Reproductive Health Links
Exploring Pregnancy
Childbirth Classes
Prenatal Care
Health-Care Providers

CARING FOR CHILDREN

Prenatal Care in the United States and Around the World

Statistics such as infant mortality rates and the rates of low birth weight babies indicate that many other nations have healthier babies than the United States (Grant, 1996; Smulian & others, 2002). A lack of prenatal care may contribute to this poor showing. A recent study revealed that low birth weight babies and preterm deliveries were common among U.S. women who received no prenatal care (Maupin & others, 2004). And a recent national study found that in the United States, the absence of prenatal care increased the risk for preterm birth almost threefold for both non-Latino White and African American women (Vintzileos & others, 2002). Another recent study found that the later prenatal care begins, the greater the risk of congenital malformations (Carmichael, Shaw, & Nelson, 2002).

(continued on next page)

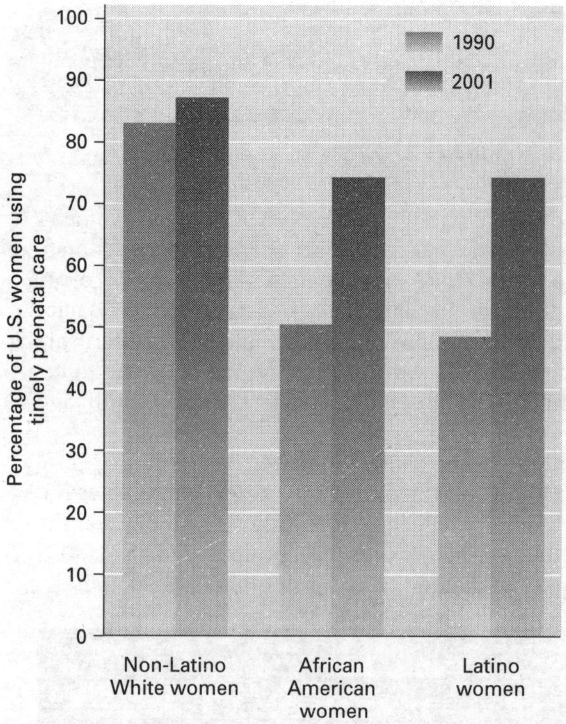

FIGURE 4.6 Percentage of U.S. Women Using Timely Prenatal Care: 1990 to 2001. From 1990 to 2001, the use of timely prenatal care increased by 6 percent (to 88.5) for non-Latino White women, by 23 percent (to 74.5) for African American women, and by 26 percent (to 75.7) for Latino women in the United States (MacDorman & others, 2002).

In many countries that have a lower percentage of low birth weight infants than the United States, either free or very low cost prenatal and postnatal care is available to mothers. This care includes paid maternity leave from work that ranges from 9 to 40 weeks. In Norway and the Netherlands, prenatal care is coordinated with a general practitioner, an obstetrician, and a midwife.

Within the United States, there are striking differences among ethnic groups both in the health of babies and in prenatal care. For example, African American infants are twice as likely as non-Latino White infants to be born prematurely, have low birth weight, and have mothers who received late or no prenatal care. They are three times as likely to have their mothers die in childbirth (Edelman, 1995). In the 1980s, more than one-fifth of all non-Latino White mothers and one-third of all African American mothers did not receive prenatal care in the first trimester of their pregnancy, and 5 percent of White mothers and 10 percent of African American mothers received no prenatal care at all (Wegman, 1987).

The situation is improving. From 1990 to 2001, the use of timely prenatal care increased for women from a variety of ethnic backgrounds in the United States, although non-Latino White women were still more likely to obtain prenatal care than African American and Latino women (MacDorman & others, 2002) (see Figure 4.6). Other researchers also have found that the discrepancy in prenatal care for non-Latino White and African American women is decreasing (Alexander, Kogan, & Nabukera, 2002).

The United States needs more comprehensive medical and educational services to improve the quality of prenatal care and to reduce the number of low birth weight and preterm infants (Bloom & others, 2004; Grady & Bloom, 2004; Laditka & others, 2005).

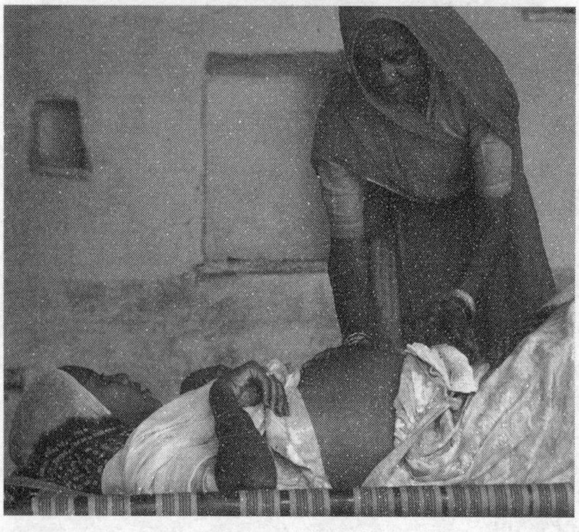

In India, a midwife checks on the size, position, and heartbeat of a fetus. Midwives deliver babies in many cultures around the world. *What are some cultural variations in prenatal care?*

Cultural Beliefs About Pregnancy

All cultures have beliefs and rituals that surround life's major events, including pregnancy. Some cultures treat pregnancy simply as a natural occurrence; others see it as a medical condition. Obtaining medical care during pregnancy may not seem important to a woman whose culture defines pregnancy as a natural condition.

How expectant mothers behave during pregnancy may depend in part on the prevalence of traditional home-care remedies and folk beliefs, the importance of indigenous healers, and the influence of health-care professionals in their culture. For example, some Filipinos will not take any medication during pregnancy. Many Mexican American women seek advice about their pregnancy from their mothers and from older women in the community. They may also call on an indigenous healer known as a *curandero*. In various cultures pregnant women may turn to herbalists, faith healers, root doctors, or spiritualists for help.

When health-care professionals work with expectant mothers, cultural assessment should be an important component of their care. In other words, they should identify beliefs, values, and behaviors related to childbearing. In particular, ethnic background, degree of affiliation with the ethnic group, patterns of decision making, religious preference, language, communication style, and etiquette may all affect a woman's attitudes about the care needed during pregnancy. Health-care workers should assess whether a woman's beliefs or practices pose a threat to her or the fetus. If they do, health-care profesionals should consider a culturally sensitive way to handle the problem.

Normal Prenatal Development

Much of our discussion so far in this chapter has focused on what can go wrong with prenatal development. Prospective parents should take steps to avoid the vulnerabilities to fetal development that we have described. But it is important to keep in mind that most of the time, prenatal development does not go awry and development occurs along the positive path that we described at the beginning of the chapter (Lester, 2000).

Review and Reflect • **LEARNING GOAL 1**

1 Describe prenatal development

Review

- What is the course of prenatal development?
- What are some of the main hazards to prenatal development?
- What are some good prenatal care strategies?
- What are some cultural beliefs about pregnancy?
- Why is it important to take a positive approach to prenatal development?

Reflect

- What can be done to convince women who are pregnant not to smoke or drink? Consider the role of health-care providers, the role of insurance companies, and specific programs targeted at women who are pregnant.

2 BIRTH

- The Birth Process
- Assessing the Newborn
- Low Birth Weight and Preterm Infants

As we saw in the opening story about Tanner Roberts, many changes take place during the birth of a baby. Let's further explore the birth process, examining variations in how it occurs and in its outcomes.

The Birth Process

Nature writes the basic script for how birth occurs, but parents make important choices about conditions surrounding birth. We look first at the sequence of physical steps when a child is born.

Stages of Birth Childbirth—or labor—occurs in three stages. In the first stage, uterine contractions are 15 to 20 minutes apart at the beginning and last up to a minute. These contractions cause the woman's cervix, the opening into the birth canal, to stretch and open. As the first stage progresses, the contractions come closer together, appearing every two to five minutes. Their intensity increases, too. By the end of the first birth stage, contractions dilate the cervix to an opening of about 4 inches, so that the baby can move from the uterus to the birth canal. For a woman

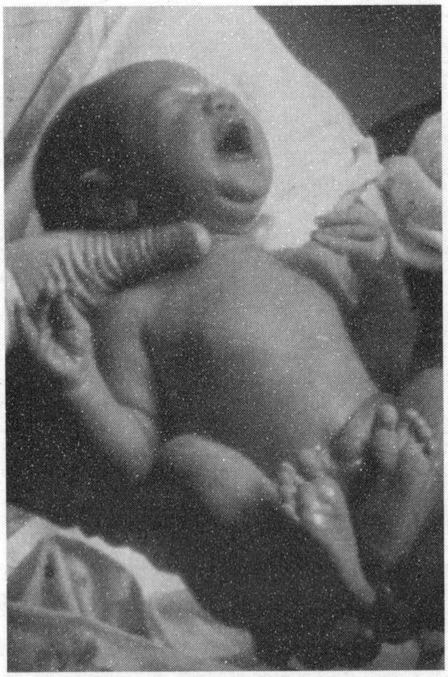

After the long journey of prenatal development, birth takes place. During birth the baby is on a threshold between two worlds. *What is the fetus/newborn transition like?*

having her first child, the first stage lasts an average of 12 to 24 hours; it is the longest of the three stages.

The second birth stage begins when the baby's head starts to move through the cervix and the birth canal. It terminates when the baby completely emerges from the mother's body. For a first birth, this stage lasts approximately 1½ hours. With each contraction, the mother bears down hard to push the baby out of her body. By the time the baby's head is out of the mother's body, the contractions come almost every minute and last for about a minute.

Afterbirth is the third stage, at which time the placenta, umbilical cord, and other membranes are detached and expelled. This final stage is the shortest of the three birth stages, lasting only minutes.

Childbirth Setting and Attendants In the United States, 99 percent of births take place in hospitals (Ventura & others, 1997). Many hospitals replaced the sterile "delivery room" of the early twentieth century with a homelike birthing center. Some women with good medical histories and low risk for problem delivery may choose a home delivery or a delivery in a freestanding birth center, which is usually staffed by nurse-midwives. Births at home are far more common in many other countries; for example, in Holland, 35 percent of the babies are born at home (Treffers & others, 1990).

Who helps a mother during birth varies across cultures. In U.S. hospitals it has become the norm for fathers or birth coaches to be with the mother throughout labor and delivery. In the East African Nigoni culture, men are completely excluded from the childbirth process. When they are ready to give birth, female relatives move into the woman's hut and the husband leaves, taking his belongings (clothes, tools, weapons, and so on) with him. He is not permitted to return until after the baby is born. In some cultures, childbirth is an open, community affair. For example, in the Pukapukan culture in the Pacific Islands, women give birth in a shelter that is open for villagers to observe.

Midwifery is the norm throughout most of the world. In Holland, more than 40 percent of babies are delivered by midwives rather than doctors (Treffers & others, 1990). But more than 90 percent of U.S. births are attended by physicians, and only 6 percent of women who deliver a baby in the United States are attended by a midwife (Tritten, 2004; Ventura & others, 1997). In the United States, most midwives are nurses who have been specially trained in delivering babies (Hyde & Roche-Reid, 2004; O'Dowd, 2004). Compared to physicians, certified nurse-midwives generally spend more time with patients during prenatal visits, place more emphasis on patient counseling and education, provide more emotional support, and are more likely to be with the patient one-on-one during the entire labor and delivery process—characteristics that may explain the more positive outcomes for babies delivered by certified nurse-midwives.

A woman in the African !Kung culture giving birth in a sitting position. Notice the help and support being given by another woman. *What are some cultural variations in childbirth?*

In many countries, a doula attends a childbearing woman. *Doula* is a Greek word that means "a woman who helps." A **doula** is a caregiver who provides continuous physical, emotional, and educational support for the mother before, during, and after childbirth. Doulas remain with the mother throughout labor, assessing and responding to her needs (Lantz & others, 2005). Researchers have found positive effects when a doula is present at the birth of a child (Stein, Kennell, & Fulcher, 2003). In one study, the mothers who received doula support reported less labor pain than the mothers who did not receive doula support (Klaus, Kennell, & Klaus, 1993).

In the United States, most doulas work as independent providers hired by the expectant woman. Doulas typically function as part of a "birthing team" that includes a midwife or the hospital obstetric staff (McGrath & others, 1999; Pascali-Bonaro, 2002). Managed-care organizations are increasingly offering doula support as a part of regular obstetric care.

Methods of Childbirth

U.S. hospitals often allow the mother and her obstetrician a range of options regarding the method of delivery. One choice involves which drugs, if any, to use.

We must respect this instant of birth, this fragile moment. The baby is between two worlds, on a threshold, hesitating . . .

—Frederick Leboyer
French Obstetrician, 20th Century

Medications Three basic kinds of drugs are used for labor: analgesia, anesthesia, and oxytocics.

Analgesia is used to relieve pain. Analgesics include tranquilizers, barbiturates, and narcotics (such as Demerol).

Anesthesia is used in late first-stage labor and during expulsion of the baby to block sensation in an area of the body or to block consciousness. There is a trend toward not using general anesthesia, which blocks consciousness, in normal births because a general anethesia can be transmitted through the placenta to the fetus. However, an epidural anesthesia does not cross the placenta. An *epidural block* is regional anesthesia that numbs the woman's body from the waist down. Even this drug, thought to be relatively safe, has come under recent criticism because it is associated with fever and extended labor (Glantz, 2005).

Oxytocics are synthetic hormones that are used to stimulate contractions. Pitocin is the most commonly used oxytocic (Carbonne, Tsatsaris, & Goffinet, 2001; Durodola & others, 2005, in press; Gard & others, 2002).

Predicting how a drug will affect an individual woman and her fetus is difficult. A particular drug might have only a minimal effect on one fetus yet have a much stronger effect on another. The drug's dosage also is a factor. Stronger doses of tranquilizers and narcotics given to decrease the mother's pain have a potentially more negative effect on the fetus than mild doses. It is important for the mother to assess her level of pain and have a voice in the decision of whether she should receive medication (Young, 2001).

Many husbands, or coaches, take childbirth classes with their wives or friends as part of prepared or natural childbirth. This is a Lamaze training session. *What is the nature of the Lamaze method? Who devised it?*

Natural and Prepared Childbirth For a brief time not long ago, the idea of avoiding all medication and reducing the pain of childbirth through education and special techniques gained favor in the United States. The techniques known as natural childbirth and prepared childbirth became popular. Today, the typical approach to childbirth is to use some medication. But educating pregnant women so that they can be reassured and confident is emphasized, and elements of natural childbirth and prepared childbirth remain popular.

Natural childbirth was developed in 1914 by an English obstetrician, Grantley Dick-Read. Its purpose is to reduce the mother's pain by decreasing her fear through education about childbirth and by teaching her to use breathing methods and relaxation techniques during delivery (Day-Stirk, 2005). Dick-Read believed that the doctor's relationship with the mother plays an important role in reducing her perception of pain and that the doctor should be present, providing reassurance, during her active labor prior to delivery.

Prepared childbirth was developed by French obstetrician Ferdinand Lamaze. The Lamaze method is similar to natural childbirth but includes a special breathing technique to control pushing in the final stages of labor, as well as more detailed education about anatomy and physiology. The Lamaze method has become very popular in the United States. The pregnant woman's husband or a friend usually serves as a coach, who attends childbirth classes with her and helps her with her breathing and relaxation during delivery.

Many other prepared childbirth techniques have been developed (Samuels & Samuels, 1996). They usually include elements of Dick-Read's natural childbirth or Lamaze's method, plus one or more other components. For instance, the Bradley method emphasizes the father's role as a labor coach. Virtually all of the prepared childbirth methods emphasize education, relaxation and breathing exercises, and support. Recently, guided mental imagery, massage, and meditation have been used to teach relaxation.

doula A caregiver who provides continuous physical, emotional, and educational support for the mother before, during, and after childbirth.

natural childbirth Developed in 1914 by Dick-Read, this method attempts to reduce the mother's pain by decreasing her fear through education about childbirth and relaxation techniques during delivery.

prepared childbirth Developed by French obstetrician Ferdinand Lamaze, this childbirth strategy is similar to natural childbirth but includes a special breathing technique to control pushing in the final stages of labor and a more detailed anatomy and physiology course.

In sum, the current belief in prepared childbirth is that, when information and support are provided, women *know* how to give birth. To read about one nurse whose research focuses on discovering ways to prevent and reduce fatigue during childbearing and the use of breathing exercises during labor, see the Careers in Child Development insert.

Cesarean Delivery Normally, as in the case of Tanner Roberts described in the opening of the chapter, the baby's head comes through the vagina first. But if the baby is in a **breech position,** the baby's buttocks are the first part to emerge from the vagina. In 1 of every 25 deliveries, the baby's head is still in the uterus when the rest of the body is out. Breech births can cause respiratory problems (Hannah, 2005). As a result, if the baby is in a breech position, what is called a cesarean section or a cesarean delivery is usually performed. In a *cesarean delivery,* the baby is removed from the mother's uterus through an incision made in her abdomen.

Cesarean deliveries are safer than breech deliveries. Cesarean deliveries also are performed if the baby is lying crosswise in the uterus, if the baby's head is too large to pass through the mother's pelvis, if the baby develops complications, or if the mother is bleeding vaginally. Cesarean deliveries can be life-saving, but they do bring risks. Compared with vaginal deliveries, they involve a higher infection rate, longer hospital stays, and the greater expense and stress that accompany any surgery.

The benefits and risks of cesarean sections continue to be debated (Lee & others, 2005; Sheiner & others, 2005). Some critics believe that too many babies are delivered by cesarean section in the United States. More cesarean sections are performed in the United States than in any other country in the world.

CAREERS in CHILD DEVELOPMENT

Linda Pugh
Perinatal Nurse

Perinatal nurses work with childbearing women to support health and growth during the childbearing experience. Linda Pugh (Ph.D., R.N.C.) is a perinatal nurse on the faculty at the Johns Hopkins University School of Nursing. She is certified as an inpatient obstetric nurse and specializes in the care of women during labor and delivery. Linda teaches nursing to both undergraduate and graduate students. In addition to educating professional nurses and conducting research, Linda consults with hospitals and organizations about women's health issues.

Linda's research interests include nursing interventions with low-income breast-feeding women, discovering ways to prevent and ameliorate fatigue during childbearing, and using effective breathing exercises during labor.

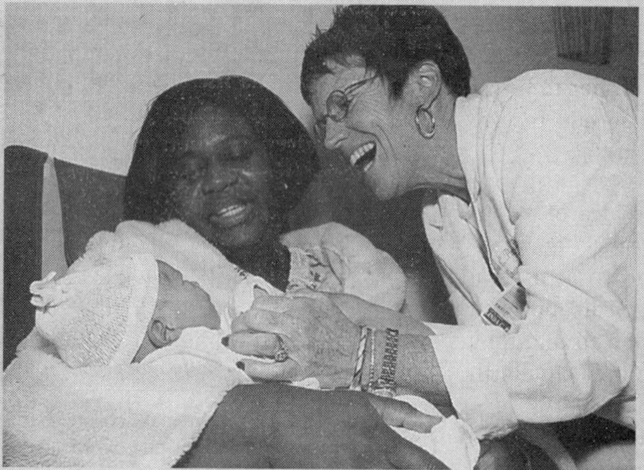

Linda Pugh (*right*) with a mother and her newborn.

The Transition from Fetus to Newborn

Much of our discussion of birth so far has focused on the mother. Being born also involves considerable stress for the baby. During each contraction, when the placenta and umbilical cord are compressed as the uterine muscles draw together, the supply of oxygen to the fetus is decreased. If the delivery takes too long, anoxia can develop (Mohan, Golding, & Paterson, 2001). *Anoxia* is the condition in which the fetus/newborn has an insufficient supply of oxygen. Anoxia can cause brain damage.

The baby has considerable capacity to withstand the stress of birth. Large quantities of adrenaline and noradrenalin, hormones that protect the fetus in the event of oxygen deficiency, are secreted in stressful circumstances. These hormones increase the heart's pumping activity, speed up heart rate, channel blood flow to the brain, and raise the blood-sugar level. Never again in life will such large amounts of these hormones be secreted. This circumstance underscores how stressful it is to be born and also how well prepared and adapted the fetus is for birth (Committee on Fetus and Newborn, 2000; Mishell, 2000; Van Beveren, 2002).

At the time of birth, the baby is covered with what is called *vernix caseosa,* a protective skin grease. This vernix consists of fatty secretions and dead cells, thought to function in protecting the baby's skin against heat loss before and during birth.

Childbirth Strategies
Childbirth Setting and Attendants
Midwifery
Doula
Fathers and Childbirth
Siblings and Childbirth

breech position The baby's position in the uterus that causes the buttocks to be the first part to emerge from the vagina.

As we saw in the case of Tanner Roberts at the beginning of the chapter, immediately after birth, the umbilical cord is cut and the baby is on its own. Before birth, oxygen came from the mother via the umbilical cord, but now the baby is self-sufficient and can breathe on its own. Now 25 million little air sacs in the lungs must be filled with air. The first breaths may be the hardest ones an individual takes.

Assessing the Newborn

Almost immediately after birth, after the baby and mother have become acquainted, a newborn is taken to be weighed, cleaned up, and tested for signs of developmental problems that might require urgent attention. The **Apgar Scale** is widely used to assess the health of newborns at one and five minutes after birth. The Apgar Scale evaluates infants' heart rate, respiratory effort, muscle tone, body color, and reflex irritability. An obstetrician or a nurse does the evaluation and gives the newborn a score, or reading, of 0, 1, or 2 on each of these five health signs (see figure 4.7). A total score of 7 to 10 indicates that the newborn's condition is good. A score of 5 indicates there may be developmental difficulties. A score of 3 or below signals an emergency and indicates that the baby might not survive.

The Apgar Scale is especially good at assessing the newborn's ability to respond to the stress of delivery and the new environment (Decca & others, 2004; Waltman & others, 2004). The Apgar Scale also identifies high-risk infants who need resuscitation.

To evaluate the newborn more thoroughly, the **Brazelton Neonatal Behavioral Assessment Scale (NBAS)** is performed within 24 to 36 hours after birth. It assesses the newborn's neurological development, reflexes, and reactions to people. The newborn is an active participant, and the score is based on the newborn's best performance. Sixteen reflexes, such as sneezing, blinking, and rooting, are assessed, along with reactions to circumstances, such as the infant's reaction to a rattle. (We will have more to say about reflexes in chapter 6, when we discuss motor development in infancy.)

The examiner rates the newborn on each of 27 items. As an indication of how detailed the ratings are, consider item 15: "cuddliness." Nine categories are involved in assessing this item, and scoring is done on a continuum that ranges from the infant's being very resistant to being held to the infant's being extremely cuddly and clinging. In scoring the Brazelton scale, T. Berry Brazelton and his colleagues organize the 27 items into four categories—physiological, motoric, state, and interaction. They also classify the baby in global terms, such as "worrisome," "normal," or "superior," based on these categories (Nugent & Brazelton, 2000).

Apgar Scale A widely used method to assess the health of newborns at one and five minutes after birth. The Apgar Scale evaluates infants' heart rate, respiratory effort, muscle tone, body color, and reflex irritability.

Brazelton Neonatal Behavioral Assessment Scale (NBAS) A test given several days after birth to assess newborns' neurological development, reflexes, and reactions to people.

Score	0	1	2
Heart rate	Absent	Slow—less than 100 beats per minute	Fast—100 to 140 beats per minute
Respiratory effort	No breathing for more than one minute	Irregular and slow	Good breathing with normal crying
Muscle tone	Limp and flaccid	Weak, inactive, but some flexion of extremities	Strong, active motion
Body color	Blue and pale	Body pink, but extremities blue	Entire body pink
Reflex irritability	No response	Grimace	Coughing, sneezing, and crying

FIGURE 4.7 The Apgar Scale

The Brazelton scale is used not only as a sensitive index of neurological competence in the week after birth but also as a measure in many research studies on infant development (Myers & others, 2003; Nakai & others, 2004; Oghi, Akiyama, & Fukuda, 2005). A very low Brazelton score can indicate brain damage, or it can reflect stress to the brain that may heal in time. If an infant merely seems sluggish, parents are encouraged to give the infant attention and become more sensitive to the infant's needs. Parents are shown how the newborn can respond to people and how to stimulate such responses. Researchers have found that the interaction skills of both high-risk infants and healthy, responsive infants can be improved through such communication with parents (Worobey & Belsky, 1982).

Recently, Brazelton, along with Barry Lester and Edward Tronick, developed a new neonatal assessment, the **Neonatal Intensive Care Unit Network Neurobehavioral Scale (NNNS)** (Lester, Tronick, & Brazelton, 2004). Described as an "offspring" of the NBAS, the NNNS provides a more comprehensive analysis of the newborn's behavior, neurological and stress responses, and regulatory capacities (Brazelton, 2004). Whereas the NBAS was developed to assess normal, healthy term infants, the NNNS was created to assess at-risk infants, especially those who are preterm (although it may not be appropriate for those less than 30 weeks' gestational age) or substance-exposed (Miller-Loncar & others, 2005). Nevertheless, according to Brazelton (2004), the NNNS is also appropriate for assessing normal, healthy, full-term infants.

For clinical purposes in assessing high-risk infants, significant features of the NNNS include (Boukydis, Bigsby, & Lester, 2004, p. 680):

- Items that assess the infant's capacity for regulating arousal, "responsiveness to stimulation, self-soothing, and tolerance of handling."
- The Stress/Abstinence Scale, which provides information about the physiological and "behavioral manifestations of drug dependence or environment-related stress."

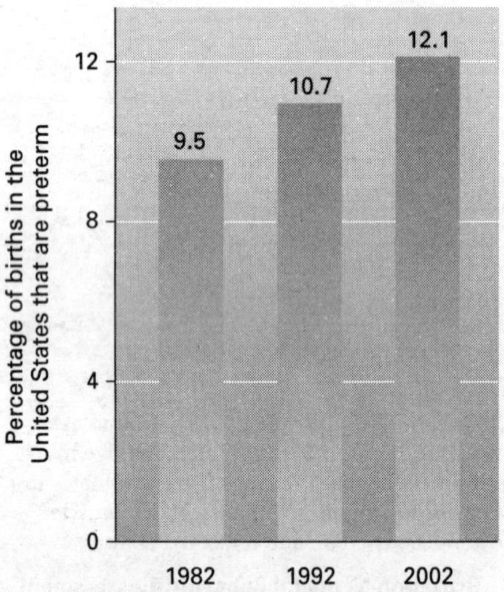

FIGURE 4.8 Preterm Births in the United States: 1982–2002.
Source: National Center for Health Statistics (2004).

Neonatal Intensive Care Unit Network Neurobehavioral Scale (NNNS) An "offspring" of the NBAS, the NNNS provides a more comprehensive analysis of the newborn's behavior, neurological and stress responses, and regulatory capacities.

low birth weight infants An infant that weighs less than 5½ pounds at birth.

preterm infants Those born three weeks or more before the pregnancy has reached its full term.

small for date infants Also called small for gestational age infants, these infants' birth weights are below normal when the length of pregnancy is considered. Small for date infants may be preterm or full term.

Low Birth Weight and Preterm Infants

Three related conditions pose threats to newborns: low birth weight, being preterm, and being small for date. **Low birth weight infants** weigh less than 5 ½ pounds at birth. *Very low birth weight* newborns weigh under 3 pounds and *extremely low birth weight* newborns under 2 pounds (Tang & others, 2004). **Preterm infants** are those born three weeks or more before the pregnancy has reached its full term—in other words, 35 or fewer weeks after conception. **Small for date infants** (also called *small for gestational age infants*) are those whose birth weight is below normal when the length of the pregnancy is considered. They weigh less than 90 percent of all babies of the same gestational age. Small for date infants may be preterm or full term. One recent study found that small for date infants had more than a fourfold risk of death (Regev & others, 2003).

The preterm birth rate in the United States increased 27 percent from 1982 to 2002 (National Center for Health Statistics, 2004). As shown in figure 4.8, approximately 12 percent of U.S. births are now preterm. The increase in preterm birth is likely due to such factors as the increasing number of births to women 35 years and older, increasing rates of multiple births, increased management of maternal and fetal conditions, increased substance abuse (tobacco, alcohol), and increased stress. African American infants are twice as likely as non-Latino White infants to be born preterm. In one recent study, weekly injections of the hormone progesterone, which is naturally produced by the ovaries, lowered the rate of preterm births by one-third (Meis & others, 2003). Researchers are recommending that further research be conducted to determine the safest and most effective way to administer the drug.

A short gestation period does not necessarily harm an infant. The neurological development of the preterm baby continues after birth on approximately the same timetable as if the infant were still in the womb. For example, consider a preterm baby born 30 weeks after conception. At 38 weeks, approximately two months after birth, this infant shows the same level of brain development as a 38-week fetus who is yet to be born. But most preterm babies are also low birth weight babies, and many adverse consequences have been linked with low birth weight, as we discuss shortly. First, however, let's examine the incidence and causes of low birth weight.

Incidences and Causes of Low Birth Weight The incidence of low birth weight varies considerably from country to country. In the United States, there has been an increase in low birth weight infants in the last two decades, and the U.S. low birth weight rate of 7.6 percent is considerably higher than that of many other developed countries (National Center for Health Statistics, 2004; UNICEF, 2001). For example, only 4 percent of the infants born in Sweden, Finland, the Netherlands, and Norway are low birth weight, and only 5 percent of those born in New Zealand, Australia, France, and Japan are low birth weight. In some developing countries, such as Bangladesh, where poverty is rampant and the health and nutrition of mothers are poor, the percentage of low birth weight babies reaches as high as 50 percent.

The causes of low birth weight also vary. In the developing world, low birth weight stems mainly from the mother's poor health and nutrition. Diseases such as diarrhea and malaria, which are common in developing countries, can impair fetal growth if the mother becomes infected while she is pregnant. In developed countries, cigarette smoking during pregnancy is the leading cause of low birth weight (Ashdown-Lambert, 2005; Okah & others, 2005; UNICEF, 2001). In both developed and developing countries, adolescents who give birth when their bodies have not fully matured are at risk for having low birth weight babies (Bacak & others, 2005). In the United States, the increase in the number of low birth weight infants is thought to be due to the increasing number of adolescents having babies, the use of drugs, and poor nutrition (Chan, Keane, & Robinson, 2001; England & others, 2001).

Consequences of Low Birth Weight Although most low birth weight infants are normal and healthy, as a group they have more health and developmental problems than normal birth weight infants (Drake & Walker, 2004; Gale & Martin, 2004; Hintz & others, 2005; Litt & others, 2005; Pietz & others, 2004; Tang & others, 2004). The number and severity of these problems increase as birth weight decreases (Kilbride, Thorstad, & Daily, 2004). Survival rates for infants who are born very early and very small have risen, but with this improved survival rate have come increases in rates of severe brain damage (Yu, 2000). The lower the birth weight, the greater the likelihood of brain injury (Watemberg & others, 2002). Approximately 7 percent of moderately low birth weight infants (3 pounds 5 ounces to 5 pounds 8 ounces) have brain injuries. This figure increases to 20 percent for the smallest newborns (1 pound 2 ounces to 3 pounds 5 ounces). Low birth weight infants are also more likely than normal birth weight infants to have lung or liver diseases.

A "kilogram kid," weighing less than 2.3 pounds at birth. *What are some long-term outcomes for weighing so little at birth?*

At school age, children who were born low in birth weight are more likely than their normal birth weight counterparts to have a learning disability, attention deficit hyperactivity disorder, or breathing problems such as asthma (Saigal & others, 2003; Taylor, Klein, & Hack, 1994). Very low birth weight children have more learning problems and lower levels of achievement in reading and math than moderately low birth weight children. Approximately 50 percent of all low birth weight children are enrolled in special education programs.

Note that not all of these adverse consequences can be attributed solely to being born low in birth weight. Some of the less severe but more common developmental and physical delays occur because many low birth weight children come from disadvantaged environments (Fang, Madhaven, & Alderman, 1999).

Some effects of being born low in birth weight can be reversed. Intensive enrichment programs that provide medical and educational services for both the parents and children can improve short-term outcomes for low birth weight children. Federal

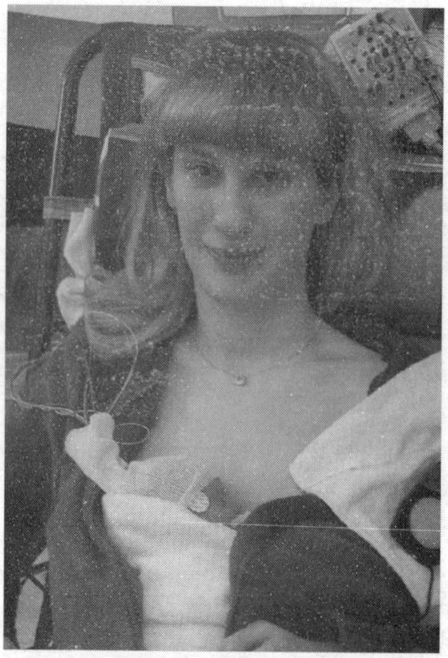

A new mother practicing kangaroo care. *What is kangaroo care?*

laws mandate that services for school-age children be expanded to include family-based care for infants. At present, these services are aimed at children born with severe disabilities. The availability of services for moderately low birth weight children who do not have severe physical problems varies, but most states do not provide these services.

Kangaroo Care and Massage Therapy One recent survey found that 82 percent of neonatal intensive-care units in the United States use kangaroo care (Engler & others, 2002). **Kangaroo care** is a way of holding a preterm infant so that there is skin-to-skin contact (Ludington-Hoe & Golant, 1993). The baby, wearing only a diaper, is held upright against the parent's bare chest. The method is similar to how a baby kangaroo is carried by its mother. Kangaroo care is typically practiced for two to three hours per day, skin-to-skin over an extended time period in early infancy (Feldman & others, 2003).

Why use kangaroo care with preterm infants? Researchers have found many positive results. Preterm infants often have difficulty coordinating their breathing and heart rate, and the close physical contact with the parent provided by kangaroo care can help to stabilize the preterm infant's heartbeat, temperature, and breathing (Dodd, 2005; Ferber & Makhoul, 2004). Further, researchers have found that preterm infants who experience kangaroo care have longer periods of sleep, gain more weight, decrease their crying, have longer periods of alertness, and an earlier hospital discharge (Lehtonen & Martin, 2004; Worku & Kassie, 2005). One recent study compared 26 low birth weight infants who received kangaroo care with 27 low birth weight infants who received standard medical/nursing care (Ohgi & others, 2002). At both 6 and 12 months of age, the kangaroo care infants were able to better regulate their body states, had better orientation, and had a more positive mood. Another recent study found that preterm infants who received kangaroo care had better control of their arousal, more effectively attended to stimuli, and showed sustained exploration in a toy session than a control group of preterm infants who did not receive kangaroo care (Feldman & others, 2002). Increasingly kangaroo care is being recommended for full-term infants as well (Johnson, 2005).

Many preterm infants experience less touch than full-term infants because they are isolated in temperature-controlled incubators (Beachy, 2003). However, the research of Tiffany Field has led to a surge of interest in the role that massage might play in improving the developmental outcomes for preterm infants. To read about her research, see the following Research in Child Development interlude.

RESEARCH IN CHILD DEVELOPMENT

Tiffany Field's Research on Massage Therapy

Throughout history and in many cultures, caregivers have massaged infants. In Africa and Asia, infants are routinely massaged by parents or other family members for several months after birth. In the United States, interest in using touch and massage to improve the growth, health, and well-being of infants has been stimulated by the research of Tiffany Field (1998, 2001, 2003; Field, Hernandez-Reif, & Freedman, 2004; Field & others, 2004), director of the Touch Research Institute at the University of Miami School of Medicine.

In Field's first study in this area, massage therapy consisting of firm stroking with the palms of the hands was given three times per day for 15-minute periods to preterm infants (Field & others, 1986). The massage therapy led to 47 percent greater weight gain than standard medical treatment (see figure 4.9). The massaged

kangaroo care A way of holding a preterm infant so that there is skin-to-skin contact.

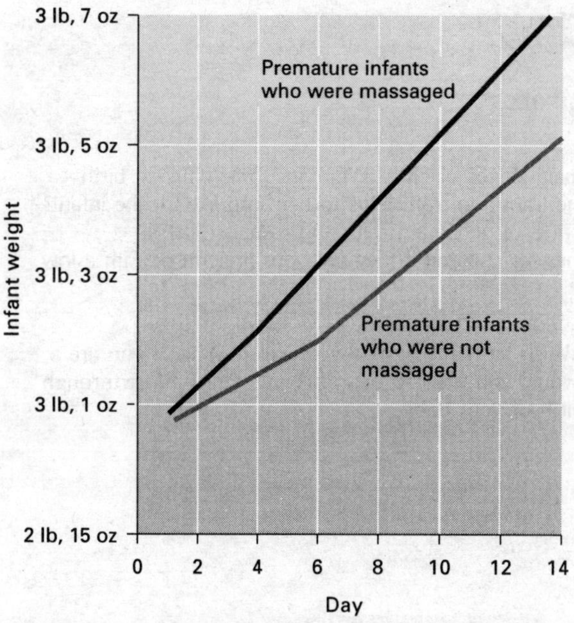

FIGURE 4.9 Weight Gain Comparison of Premature Infants Who Were Massaged or Not Massaged. The graph shows that the mean daily weight gain of premature infants who were massaged was greater than for premature infants who were not massaged.

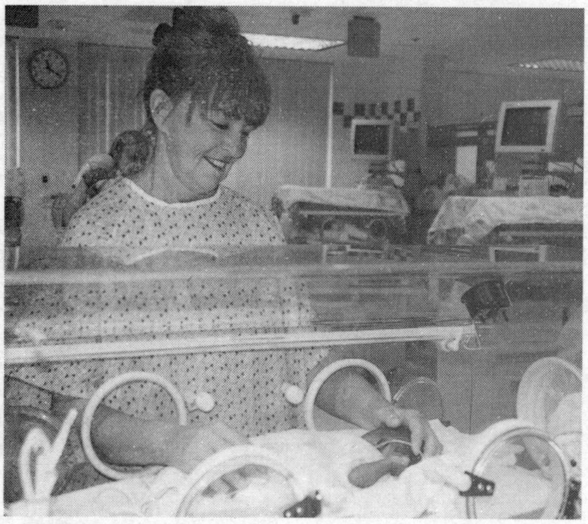

Shown here is Dr. Tiffany Field massaging a newborn infant. *What types of infants has massage therapy been shown to help?*

infants also were more active and alert than preterm infants who were not massaged, and they performed better on developmental tests.

In later studies, Field demonstrated the benefits of massage therapy for infants who faced a variety of problems. For example, preterm infants exposed to cocaine in utero who received massage therapy gained weight and improved their scores on developmental tests (Field, 2002). In another investigation, newborns born to HIV-positive mothers were randomly assigned to a massage therapy group or to a control group that did not receive the therapy (Scafidi & Field, 1996). The massaged infants showed superior performance on a wide range of assessments, including daily weight gain. Another study investigated 1- to 3-month-old infants born to depressed adolescent mothers (Field & others, 1996). The infants of depressed mothers who received massage therapy had lower stress—as well as improved emotionality, sociability, and soothability—compared with the nonmassaged infants of depressed mothers.

In a recent study, Field and her colleagues (2004) taught mothers how to massage their full-term infants. Once a day before bedtime the mothers massaged the babies using either light or moderate pressure. Infants who were massaged with moderate pressure "gained more weight, were greater length, performed better on the orientation scale of the Brazelton, had lower Brazelton excitability and depression scores, and exhibited less agitation during sleep" (p. 435).

In a recent review of the use of massage therapy with preterm infants, Field and her colleagues (2004) concluded that the most consistent findings show (1) increased weight gain and (2) earlier discharge from the hospital, ranging from three to six days earlier.

Infants are not the only ones who may benefit from massage therapy. In other studies, Field and her colleagues have demonstrated the benefits of massage therapy with women in reducing labor pain (Field, Hernandez-Reif, Taylor, & others, 1997), with children who have arthritis (Field, Hernandez-Reif, Seligman, & others, 1997), with autistic children's attentiveness (Field, Lasko, & others, 1997), and with adolescents who have attention deficit hyperactivity disorder (Field, Quintino, & others, 1998).

***Review and Reflect* • LEARNING GOAL 2**

2 Discuss the birth process

Review

- What are the three main stages of birth? What are some different birth strategies? What is the transition from fetus to newborn like for the infant?
- What are three measures of neonatal health and responsiveness?
- What are the outcomes for children if they are born preterm or with a low birth weight?

Reflect

- If you are a female, which birth strategy do you prefer? Why? If you are a male, how involved would you want to be in helping your partner through pregnancy and the birth of your baby?

3 THE POSTPARTUM PERIOD

Physical Adjustments | Emotional and Psychological Adjustments | Bonding

The weeks immediately following childbirth present many challenges for new parents and their offspring. This is the **postpartum period,** the period after childbirth or delivery that lasts for about six weeks or until the body has completed its adjustment and has returned to a nearly prepregnant state. It is a time when the woman adjusts, both physically and psychologically, to the process of childbearing.

Some health professionals refer to the postpartum period as the "fourth trimester." Though the time span of the postpartum period does not necessarily cover three months, the term "fourth trimester" suggests continuity and the importance of the first several months after birth for the mother.

The postpartum period involves a great deal of adjustment and adaptation (Plackslin, 2000). The baby has to be cared for; the mother has to recover from childbirth; the mother has to learn how to take care of the baby; the mother needs to learn to feel good about herself as a mother; the father needs to learn how to take care of his recovering wife; the father needs to learn how to take care of the baby; and the father needs to learn how to feel good about himself as a father. Many health professionals believe that the best way to meet these challenges is with a family-centered approach that uses the family's resources to support an early and smooth adjustment to the newborn by all family members.

Physical Adjustments

A woman's body makes numerous physical adjustments in the first days and weeks after childbirth. She may have a great deal of energy or feel exhausted and let down. Most new mothers feel tired and need rest. Though these changes are normal, the fatigue can undermine the new mother's sense of well-being and confidence in her ability to cope with a new baby and a new family life.

The physical adjustments during the postpartum period are influenced by what preceded it. During pregnancy, the woman's body gradually adjusted to physical changes, but now it is forced to respond quickly. The method of delivery and circumstances surrounding the delivery affect the speed with which the woman's body readjusts.

postpartum period The period after childbirth when the mother adjusts, both physically and psychologically, to the process of childbirth. This period lasts for about six weeks or until her body has completed its adjustment and returned to a near prepregnant state.

After delivery, a woman's body undergoes sudden and dramatic changes in hormone production. When the placenta is delivered, estrogen and progesterone levels drop steeply and remain low until the ovaries start producing hormones again. The woman will probably begin menstruating again in four to eight weeks if she is not breast-feeding. If she is breast-feeding, she might not menstruate for several months to a year or more, though ovulation can occur during this time. The first several menstrual periods following delivery might be heavier than usual, but periods soon return to normal.

Involution is the process by which the uterus returns to its prepregnant size five or six weeks after birth. Immediately following birth, the uterus weighs 2 to 3 pounds. By the end of five or six weeks, the uterus weighs 2 to 3½ ounces. Nursing the baby helps contract the uterus at a rapid rate.

Some women and men want to resume sexual intercourse as soon as possible after the birth. Others feel constrained or afraid. A sore perineum (the area between the anus and vagina in the female), a demanding baby, lack of help, and extreme fatigue affect a woman's ability to relax and to enjoy making love. Physicians often recommend that women refrain from having sexual intercourse for approximately six weeks following the birth of the baby.

If the woman regularly engaged in conditioning exercises during pregnancy, exercise will help her recover her former body contour and strength during the postpartum period (Blum, Beaudoin, & Caton-Lemos, 2005). With a caregiver's approval, the new mother can begin some exercises as soon as one hour after delivery. In addition to recommending exercise in the postpartum period for women, health professionals also increasingly recommend that women practice the relaxation techniques they used during pregnancy and childbirth. Five minutes of slow breathing on a stressful day in the postpartum period can relax and refresh the new mother, as well as the new baby.

Postpartum Adjustment
Postpartum Resources

Emotional and Psychological Adjustments

Emotional fluctuations are common for mothers in the postpartum period. These emotional fluctuations may be due to any of a number of factors: hormonal changes, fatigue, inexperience or lack of confidence with newborn babies, or the extensive time and demands involved in caring for a newborn. For some women, emotional fluctuations decrease within several weeks after the delivery, but other women experience more long-lasting emotional swings (Bloch & others, 2005, in press; Hall, 2005).

"Baby Blues" and Postpartum Depression As shown in figure 4.10, about 70 percent of new mothers have what are called "baby blues." About two to three days after birth, they begin to feel depressed, anxious, and upset. These feelings may come and go for several months after the birth, often peaking about three to five days after birth. Even without treatment, these feelings usually go away after one or two weeks.

For other women, emotional fluctuations persist and can produce feelings of anxiety, depression, and difficulty in coping with stress (Dennis, 2004; Goodman, 2004). Mothers who have such feelings, even when they are getting adequate rest, may benefit from professional help in dealing with their problems. Here are some of the signs that can indicate a need for professional counseling about postpartum adaptation:

- Excessive worrying
- Depression
- Extreme changes in appetite
- Crying spells
- Inability to sleep

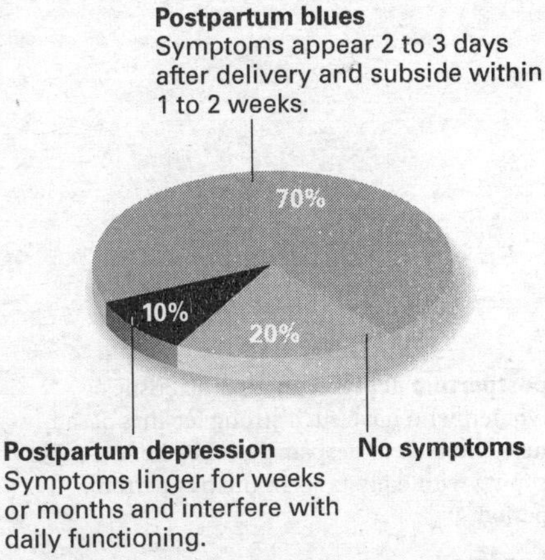

FIGURE 4.10 Percentage of U.S. Women Who Experience Postpartum Blues and Postpartum Depression

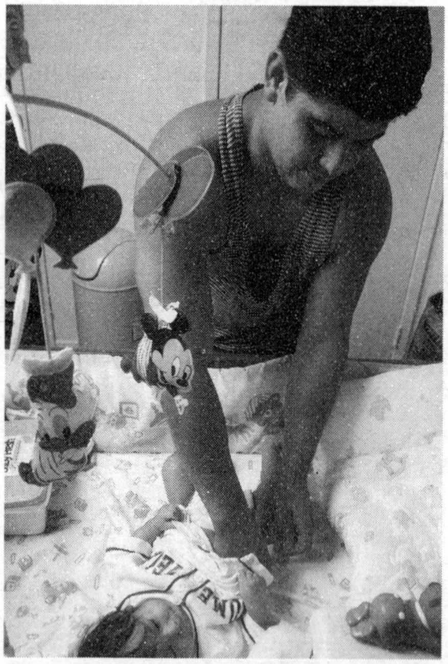

The postpartum period is a time of considerable adjustment and adaptation for both the mother and the father. Fathers can provide an important support system for mothers, especially in helping mothers care for young infants. *As part of supporting the mother, what kinds of tasks might the father of a newborn do?*

Women with **postpartum depression** have such strong feelings of sadness, anxiety, or despair that they have trouble coping with their daily tasks. Postpartum depression involves a major depressive episode that typically occurs about four weeks after delivery. Without treatment, postpartum depression may become worse and last for many months (Bonari & others, 2004; Clay & Seehusen, 2004; Horowitz & Goodman, 2005; Teissedre & Chabrol, 2004). About 10 percent of new mothers experience postpartum depression. Between 25 to 50 percent of these depressed new mothers have episodes that last six months or longer (Beck, 2002). If untreated, approximately 25 percent of these women are still depressed a year later.

The hormonal changes occurring after childbirth are believed to play a role in postpartum depression, but the precise role of hormones has not been identified (Flores & Hendrick, 2002; McCoy, Beal, & Watson, 2003). Estrogen has been shown to have positive effects in treating postpartum depression for some women, but estrogen has some possible problematic side effects (Grigoriadis & Kennedy, 2002; Tsigos & Chrousos, 2002). Several antidepressant drugs are effective in treating postpartum depression and appear to be safe for breast-feeding women (Sharma, 2002). Psychotherapy, especially cognitive therapy, has also been found to be an effective treatment of postpartum depression (Beck, 2002; Kennedy, Beck, & Driscoll, 2002).

One recent study found that postpartum depression may affect not only the new mother but also her child (Righetti-Veltema & others, 2002). A sample of 570 women and their infants were assessed three months after delivery. Ten percent of the mothers were classified as experiencing postpartum depression on the basis of their responses to the Edinburgh Postnatal Depression Scale (Cox & others, 1987). Compared with nondepressed mothers, the depressed mothers had less vocal and visual communication with their infants, touched the infants less, and smiled less at the infants. The negative effects on the infants involved eating or sleeping problems.

A Father's Adjustment Fathers also undergo considerable adjustment in the postpartum period, even when they work away from home all day. One of the husband's most common reactions is the feeling that the baby comes first and gets all of the attention. In some marriages, the man may have had that relationship with his wife and now feels that the baby has replaced him.

One strategy to help the man's postpartum reaction is for the parents to set aside some special time to be together with each other. The father's postpartum reaction also likely will be improved if he has taken childbirth classes with his wife and is an active participant in caring for the baby.

For the father as well as the mother, it is important to put time and thought into being a competent parent of a young infant (Cowan & Cowan, 2000; Hipwell & others, 2005; McVeigh, Baafi, & Williamson, 2002). Both need to become aware of the infant's needs—physical, psychological, and emotional. Both the mother and the father need to develop a sensitive, comfortable relationship with the baby.

Bonding

A special component of the parent-infant relationship is **bonding,** the formation of a connection, especially a physical bond between parents and the newborn in the period shortly after birth. Sometimes hospitals seem determined to deter bonding. Drugs given to the mother to make her delivery less painful can make the mother drowsy, interfering with her ability to respond to and stimulate the newborn. Mothers and newborns are often separated shortly after delivery, and preterm infants are isolated from their mothers even more than full-term mothers.

postpartum depression Characteristic of women who have such strong feelings of sadness, anxiety, or despair that they have trouble coping with daily tasks in the postpartum period.

bonding The formation of a close connection, especially a physical bond between parents and their newborn in the period shortly after birth.

Do these practices do any harm? Some physicians believe that during the period shortly after birth, the parents and newborn need to form an emotional attachment as a foundation for optimal development in years to come (Kennell & McGrath,

1999). Is there evidence that close contact between mothers and infants in the first several days after birth is critical for optimal development later in life? Although some research supports the bonding hypothesis (Klaus & Kennell, 1976), a body of research challenges the significance of the first few days of life as a critical period (Bakeman & Brown, 1980; Rode & others, 1981). Indeed, the extreme form of the bonding hypothesis—that the newborn must have close contact with the mother in the first few days of life to develop optimally—simply is not true.

Nonetheless, the weakness of the maternal-infant bonding research should not be used as an excuse to keep motivated mothers from interacting with their infants in the postpartum period. Such contact brings pleasure to many mothers. In some mother-infant pairs—including preterm infants, adolescent mothers, and mothers from disadvantaged circumstances—early close contact may establish a climate for improved interaction after the mother and infant leave the hospital.

Many hospitals now offer a *rooming-in* arrangement, in which the baby remains in the mother's room most of the time during its hospital stay. However, if parents choose not to use this rooming-in arrangement, the weight of the research evidence suggests that it will not harm the infant emotionally (Lamb, 1994).

Review and Reflect • LEARNING GOAL 3

3 Explain the changes that take place in the postpartum period

Review

- What does the postpartum period involve? What physical adjustments does the woman's body make in this period?
- What emotional and psychological adjustments characterize the postpartum period?
- Is bonding critical for optimal development?

Reflect

- If you are a female, what can you do to adjust effectively in the postpartum period? If you are a male, what can you do to help in the postpartum period?

REACH YOUR LEARNING GOALS

PRENATAL DEVELOPMENT AND BIRTH

1 PRENATAL DEVELOPMENT

- The Course of Prenatal Development
- Prenatal Care
- Normal Prenatal Development
- Teratology and Hazards to Prenatal Development
- Cultural Beliefs About Pregnancy

2 BIRTH

- The Birth Process
- Assessing the Newborn
- Low Birth Weight and Preterm Infants

3 THE POSTPARTUM PERIOD

- Physical Adjustments
- Emotional and Psychological Adjustments
- Bonding

SUMMARY

1 Describe prenatal development

- Prenatal development is divided into three periods: germinal (conception until 10 to 14 days later), which ends when the zygote (a fertilized egg) attaches to the uterine wall; embryonic (two to eight weeks after conception), during which the embryo differentiates into three layers, life-support systems develop, and organ systems form (organogenesis); and fetal (two months after conception until about nine months, or when the infant is born), a time when organ systems mature to the point at which life can be sustained outside of the womb.
- Teratology is the field that investigates the causes of congenital (birth) defects. Any agent that causes birth defects is called a teratogen. The dose, time of exposure, and genetic susceptibility influence the severity of the damage to an unborn child and the type of defect that occurs. Prescription drugs that can be harmful include antibiotics, some depressants, and certain hormones. Nonprescription drugs that can be harmful include diet pills, aspirin, and coffee. Fetal alcohol syndrome (FAS) is a cluster of abnormalities that appear in offspring of mothers who drink heavily during pregnancy. When pregnant women drink moderately (one to two drinks a day), negative effects on their offspring have been found. Cigarette smoking by pregnant women has serious adverse effects on prenatal and child development (such as low birth weight). Illegal drugs that are potentially harmful to offspring include marijuana, cocaine, and heroin. Incompatibility of the mother's and the father's blood types can also be harmful to the fetus. Rubella (German measles) can be harmful. Syphilis, genital herpes, and AIDS are other teratogens. A developing fetus depends entirely on its mother for nutrition. One nutrient that is especially important early in development is folic acid. Recently, there has been concern about pregnant women eating polluted fish. High anxiety and stress in the mother are linked with less than optimal prenatal and birth outcomes. Maternal age can negatively affect the offspring's development if the mother is an adolescent or over 30. Paternal factors that can adversely affect prenatal development include exposure to lead, radiation, certain pesticides, and petrochemicals. Potential environmental hazards include radiation, environmental pollutants, and toxic wastes.
- Prenatal care varies extensively but usually involves medical care services with a defined schedule of visits.
- Specific actions in pregnancy are often determined by cultural beliefs. Certain behaviors are expected if a culture views pregnancy as a medical condition or a natural occurrence. For example, prenatal care may not be a priority for expectant mothers who view pregnancy as a natural occurrence.
- It is important to remember that, although things can and do go wrong during pregnancy, most of the time pregnancy and prenatal development go well. Avoiding teratogens helps ensure a positive outcome.

2 Discuss the birth process

- Childbirth occurs in three stages. The first stage, which lasts about 12 to 24 hours for a woman having her first child, is the longest stage. The cervix dilates to about 4 inches at the end of the first stage. The second stage begins when the baby's head moves through the cervix and ends with the baby's complete emergence. The third stage is afterbirth. Being born involves considerable stress for the baby, but the baby is well prepared and adapted to handle the stress. Anoxia—insufficient oxygen supply to the fetus/newborn—is a potential hazard. Childbirth strategies involve the childbirth setting and attendants. In many countries, a doula attends a childbearing woman. Methods of delivery include medicated, natural and prepared, and cesarean.
- For many years, the Apgar Scale has been used to assess the newborn's health. The Brazelton Neonatal Behavioral Assessment Scale (NBAS) examines the newborn's neurological development, reflexes, and reactions to people. Recently, the Neonatal Intensive Care Unit Network Neurobehavioral Scale (NNNS) was created to assess the at-risk infant.
- Low birth weight infants weigh less than 5½ pounds and they may be preterm (born three weeks or more before the pregnancy has reached full term) or small for date (also called small for gestational age, which refers to infants whose birth weight is below norm when the length of pregnancy is considered). Small for date infants may be preterm or full term. Although most low birth weight infants are normal and healthy, as a group they have more health and developmental problems than normal birth weight infants. Kangaroo care and massage therapy have been shown to have benefits for preterm infants.

3 Explain the changes that take place in the postpartum period

- The postpartum period is the name given to the period after childbirth or delivery. The period lasts for about six weeks or until the body has completed its adjustment. Physical adjustments in the postpartum period include fatigue, involution (the process by which the uterus returns to its prepregnant size five or six weeks after birth), hormonal changes, when to resume sexual intercourse, and exercises to recover body contour and strength.

- Emotional fluctuations on the part of the mother are common in this period, and they can vary a great deal from one mother to the next. Postpartum depression characterizes women who have such strong feelings of sadness, anxiety, or despair that they have trouble coping with daily tasks in the postpartum period. Postpartum depression occurs in about 10 percent of new mothers. The father also goes through a postpartum adjustment.
- Bonding is the formation of a close connection, especially a physical bond between parents and the newborn shortly after birth. Early bonding has not been found to be critical in the development of a competent infant.

KEY TERMS

germinal period 105
blastocyst 105
trophoblast 105
embryonic period 105
amnion 106
umbilical cord 106
placenta 106
organogenesis 106
fetal period 107
teratogen 109
fetal alcohol syndrome (FAS) 111
doula 121
natural childbirth 121
prepared childbirth 121
breech position 122
Apgar Scale 123
Brazelton Neonatal Behavioral Assessment Scale (NBAS) 123
Neonatal Intensive Care Unit Network Neurobehavioral Scale (NNNS) 124
low birth weight infants 124
preterm infants 124
small for date infants 124
kangaroo care 126
postpartum period 128
postpartum depression 130
bonding 130

KEY PEOPLE

Grantley Dick-Read 121
Ferdinand Lamaze 121
T. Berry Brazelton 123
Tiffany Field 126

E-LEARNING TOOLS

To help you master the material in this chapter, visit the Online Learning Center for *Child Development,* eleventh edition (**www.mhhe.com/santrockcd11**), where you'll find these additional resources:

Taking It to the Net

1. Denise's sister, Doreen, is pregnant for the first time. Doreen engages in an unhealthy lifestyle. What particular things can Denise encourage Doreen to do in order to give birth to a healthy baby?
2. Sienne told her fiancé, Jackson, that he had better stop smoking before they begin trying to conceive a child. Why is Sienne concerned about Jackson's smoking and its effect on their children before they even start planning their family?
3. Hannah, who gave birth to a healthy baby boy—her first child—two weeks ago, appears to her husband, Sean, to be sad, lethargic, and is having trouble sleeping. How can Sean determine if Hannah is just going through a natural period of post-baby "blues," or if she might be suffering from postpartum depression?

Nursing, Parenting, and Teaching Exercises

Build your decision-making skills by trying your hand at the scenarios on the Online Learning Center.

Video Clips

The Online Learning Center includes the following videos for this chapter:

- Midwifery
  Here we learn about midwives and how they differ from obstetricians.
- Childbirth Education Alternatives
  A childbirth educator describes the types of childbirth classes that are available to expectant parents and the benefits of childbirth education.
- Breast- vs. Bottle-Feeding
  A discussion of the numerous benefits of breast-feeding over bottle-feeding.

Chapter 5 PHYSICAL DEVELOPMENT AND HEALTH

That energy which makes a child hard to manage is the energy which afterward makes him a manager of life.

—HENRY WARD BEECHER
American Author, 19th Century

CHAPTER OUTLINE

BODY GROWTH AND CHANGE

Growth Patterns
Infancy and Childhood
Puberty

THE BRAIN

Brain Physiology
Infancy
Childhood
Adolescence

SLEEP

Infancy
Childhood
Adolescence

HEALTH

Illness and Injuries Among Children and Adolescents
Nutrition and Eating Behavior
Exercise
Substance Use

LEARNING GOALS

1. Discuss developmental changes in the body
2. Describe how the brain changes
3. Summarize how sleep patterns change as children develop
4. Characterize health in childhood and adolescence

The Story of Latonya and Ramona: Breast- and Bottle-Feeding in Africa

Latonya is a newborn baby in Ghana. During her first days of life she was kept apart from her mother and bottle-fed. Manufacturers of infant formula provided the hospital where she was born with free or subsidized milk powder. Her mother has been persuaded to bottle-feed rather than breast-feed her. When her mother bottle-feeds Latonya, she overdilutes the milk formula with unclean water. Latonya's feeding bottles have not been sterilized. Latonya becomes very sick. She dies before her first birthday.

Ramona was born in Nigeria at a hospital with a "baby-friendly" program. In this program, babies are not separated from their mothers when they are born, and the mothers are encouraged to breast-feed them. The mothers are told of the perils that bottle-feeding can bring because of unsafe water and unsterilized bottles. They also are informed about the advantages of breast milk, which include its nutritious and hygienic qualities, its ability to immunize babies against common illnesses, and its role in reducing the mother's risk of breast and ovarian cancer. Ramona's mother is breast-feeding her. At 1 year of age, Ramona is very healthy.

In recent years, the World Health Organization and UNICEF have tried to reverse the trend toward bottle-feeding infants, which emerged in many impoverished countries. They instituted the "baby-friendly" program in many countries (Grant, 1993). They also persuaded the International Association of Infant Formula Manufacturers to stop marketing their baby formulas to hospitals in countries where the governments support the baby-friendly initiatives. For the hospitals themselves, costs actually were reduced as infant formula, feeding bottles, and separate nurseries become unnecessary. For example, baby-friendly Jose Fabella Memorial Hospital in the Philippines reported saving 8 percent of its annual budget.

Hospitals play a vital role in getting mothers to breast-feed their babies. For many years, maternity units favored bottle-feeding and did not give mothers adequate information about the benefits of breast-feeding (Grant, 1993). With the initiatives of the World Health Organization and UNICEF, things are changing, but there still are many places in the world where the baby-friendly initiatives have not been implemented (UNICEF, 2003).

The advantages of breast-feeding in impoverished countries are substantial. However, these advantages now have to be counterbalanced by the risk of passing HIV to the baby through breast milk if the mothers have the virus; the majority of mothers don't know that they are infected. In some areas of Africa more than 30 percent of mothers have the HIV virus.

PREVIEW

Think about how much you changed physically as you grew up. You came into this life as a small being but grew very rapidly in infancy, more slowly in childhood, and once again more rapidly during puberty. In this chapter, we will explore changes in body growth, the brain, and sleep. We also will examine children's health, including the topic of the opening story: breast- versus bottle-feeding.

1 BODY GROWTH AND CHANGE

Growth Patterns | Infancy and Childhood | Puberty

In the journey of childhood, we go through many bodily changes. Let's begin by studying some basic patterns of growth and then turn to the bodily changes that occur from the time we were infants through the time we were adolescents.

Growth Patterns

During prenatal development and early infancy, the head constitutes an extraordinarily large portion of the total body (see figure 5.1). Gradually, the body's proportions change. Why? Growth is not random. Instead, it generally follows two patterns: the cephalocaudal pattern and the proximodistal pattern.

The **cephalocaudal pattern** is the sequence in which the fastest growth always occurs at the top—the head. Physical growth in size, weight, and feature differentiation gradually works its way down from the top to the bottom—for example, from neck to shoulders, to middle trunk, and so on. This same pattern occurs in the head area; the top parts of the head—the eyes and brain—grow faster than the lower parts, such as the jaw.

Sensory and motor development also generally proceed according to the cephalocaudal principle. For example, infants see objects before they can control their torso, and they can use their hands long before they can crawl or walk. However, one recent study found that infants reached for toys with their feet prior to using their hands (Galloway & Thelen, 2004). On average, infants first touched the toy with their feet when they were 12 weeks old and with their hands when they were 16 weeks old. We will have much more to say about sensory and motor development in chapter 6.

The **proximodistal pattern** is the growth sequence that starts at the center of the body and moves toward the extremities. For example, muscle control of the trunk and arms matures before control of the hands and fingers. Further, infants use their whole hand as a unit before they can control several fingers.

cephalocaudal pattern The sequence in which the greatest growth occurs at the top—the head—with physical growth in size, weight, and feature differentiation gradually working from top to bottom.

proximodistal pattern The sequence in which growth starts at the center of the body and moves toward the extremities.

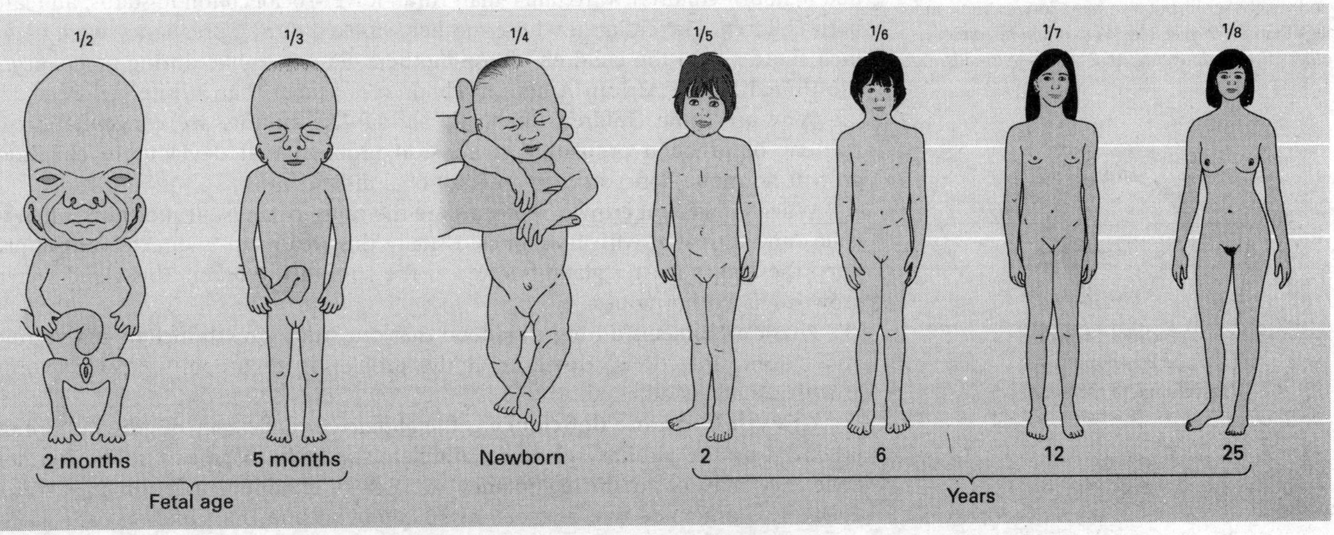

FIGURE 5.1 Changes in Proportions of the Human Body During Growth. As individuals develop from infancy through adulthood, one of the most noticeable physical changes is that the head becomes smaller in relation to the rest of the body. The fractions listed refer to head size as a proportion of total body length at different ages.

Infancy and Childhood

Height and weight increase rapidly in infancy. Then, they take a slower course during the childhood years.

Infancy

The average North American newborn is 20 inches long and weighs 7½ pounds. Ninety-five percent of full-term newborns are 18 to 22 inches long and weigh between 5½ and 10 pounds.

In the first several days of life, most newborns lose 5 to 7 percent of their body weight. Once infants adjust to sucking, swallowing, and digesting, they grow rapidly, gaining an average of 5 to 6 ounces per week during the first month. They have doubled their birth weight by the age of 4 months and have nearly tripled it by their first birthday. Infants grow about 1 inch per month during the first year, reaching approximately 1½ times their birth length by their first birthday.

In the second year of life, infants' rate of growth slows considerably. By 2 years of age, infants weigh approximately 26 to 32 pounds, having gained a quarter to half a pound per month during the second year; now they have reached about one-fifth of their adult weight. The average 2-year-old is 32 to 35 inches tall, which is nearly one-half of adult height.

The bodies of 5-year-olds and 2-year-olds are different. Notice how the 5-year-old not only is taller and weighs more, but also has a longer trunk and legs than the 2-year-old. *What might be some other physical differences in 2- and 5-year-olds?*

Early Childhood

As the preschool child grows older, the percentage of increase in height and weight decreases with each additional year. Girls are only slightly smaller and lighter than boys during these years. Both boys and girls slim down as the trunks of their bodies lengthen. Although their heads are still somewhat large for their bodies, by the end of the preschool years most children have lost their top-heavy look. Body fat declines slowly, but steadily during the preschool years. Girls have more fatty tissue than boys; boys have more muscle tissue.

Growth patterns vary individually. Think back to your preschool years. This was probably the first time you noticed that some children were taller than you, some shorter; some were fatter, some thinner; some were stronger, some weaker. Much of the variation is due to heredity, but environmental experiences also are involved to some extent. A review of the height and weight of children around the world concluded that two important contributors to height differences are ethnic origin and nutrition (Meredith, 1978). Also, urban, middle-socioeconomic-status, and firstborn children were taller than rural, lower-socioeconomic-status, and later-born children. The children whose mothers smoked during pregnancy were half an inch shorter than the children whose mothers did not smoke during pregnancy. In the United States, African American children are taller than White children.

www.mhhe.com/santrockcd11

Preschool Growth and Development
Development Milestones

Why are some children unusually short? The culprits are congenital factors (genetic or prenatal problems), a physical problem that develops in childhood, growth hormone deficiency, or an emotional difficulty.

When congenital growth problems are the cause of unusual shortness, often the child can be treated with hormones. Usually this treatment is directed at the pituitary, the body's master gland, located at the base of the brain. This gland secretes growth-related hormones.

Physical problems during childhood that can stunt growth include malnutrition and chronic infections. However, if the problems are properly treated, normal growth usually is attained.

Growth hormone deficiency is the absence or deficiency of growth hormone produced by the pituitary gland to stimulate the body to grow. Growth hormone deficiency may occur during infancy or later in childhood (Gandrud & Wilson, 2004). It is estimated that as many as 10,000 to 15,000 U.S. children have growth hormone deficiency (Stanford University Medical Center, 2005). Without treatment, most children with growth hormone deficiency will not reach a height of five feet. Treatment for this deficiency involves regular injections of growth hormone and usually lasts several years (Chernausek, 2004; Minczykowski & others, 2005; Radcliffe & others, 2004). Some children receive daily injections; others, several times a week.

growth hormone deficiency The absence or deficiency of growth hormone produced by the pituitary gland to stimulate the body to grow.

Middle and Late Childhood The period of middle and late childhood—from about 6 to 11 years of age—involves slow, consistent growth. This is a period of calm before the rapid growth spurt of adolescence.

During the elementary school years, children grow an average of 2 to 3 inches a year. At the age of 8 the average girl and the average boy are 4 feet 2 inches tall. During the middle and late childhood years, children gain about 5 to 7 pounds a year. The average 8-year-old girl and the average 8-year-old boy weigh 56 pounds (National Center for Health Statistics, 2004). The weight increase is due mainly to increases in the size of the skeletal and muscular systems, as well as the size of some body organs. Muscle mass and strength gradually increase as "baby fat" decreases in middle and late childhood.

The loose movements and knock-knee of early childhood give way to improved muscle tone in middle and late childhood. Children also double their strength capacity during these years. The increase in muscular strength is due to heredity and to exercise. Because they have more muscle cells, boys tend to be stronger than girls.

Changes in proportions are among the most pronounced physical changes in middle and late childhood. Head circumference, waist circumference, and leg length decrease in relation to body height. A less noticeable physical change is that bones continue to harden during middle and late childhood; still, they yield to pressure and pull more than mature bones.

Puberty

After slowing through childhood, growth surges during puberty. **Puberty** is a period of rapid physical maturation involving hormonal and bodily changes that take place in early adolescence. The features and proportions of the body change as the individual becomes capable of reproducing. We will begin our exploration of puberty by describing its determinants and then examine important physical changes and psychological accompaniments of puberty.

Determinants of Puberty Puberty is not the same as adolescence. For virtually everyone, puberty has ended long before adolescence is exited. Puberty is often thought of as the most important marker for the beginning of adolescence.

There are wide variations in the onset and progression of puberty. Puberty might begin as early as 10 years of age or as late as 13½ for boys. It might end as early as 13 years or as late as 17 years.

In fact, over the years the timing of puberty has changed. Imagine a 3-year-old girl with fully developed breasts or a boy just slightly older with a deep male voice. That is what toddlers would be like by the year 2250 if the age at which puberty arrives were to continue decreasing as it did for much of the twentieth century. For example,

puberty A period of rapid physical maturation involving hormonal and bodily changes that take place in early adolescence.

From *Penguin Dreams and Stranger Things*, by Berke Breathed. Copyright © 1985 by The Washington Post Company. By permission of Little, Brown & Company, Inc. Reprinted by permission of International Creative Management, Inc. Copyright © 1985 by Berkeley Breathed.

www.mhhe.com/santrockcd11

Biological Changes

in Norway, **menarche**—a girl's first menstruation—now occurs at just over 13 years of age, compared to 17 years of age in the 1840s (Petersen, 1979). In the United States—where children mature up to a year earlier than in European countries—the average age of menarche dropped an average of 2 to 4 months per decade for much of the twentieth century, to about 12½ years today. Some researchers have found evidence that the age of puberty is still dropping for American girls (Herman-Giddens & others, 1997); others believe the evidence is inconclusive (Rosenfield & others, 2000) or that the decline in age is slowing down (Archibald, Graber, & Brooks-Gunn, 2003). The earlier onset of puberty is likely the result of improved health and nutrition.

The normal range for the onset and progression of puberty is wide enough that, given two boys of the same chronological age, one might complete the pubertal sequence before the other one has begun it. For girls, the age range of menarche is even wider. It is considered within a normal range if it occurs between the ages of 9 and 15. Among the most important factors that influence the onset and sequence of puberty are heredity, hormones, and weight and body fat.

Heredity Puberty is not an environmental accident. It does not take place at 2 or 3 years of age, and it does not occur in the twenties. Programmed into the genes of every human being is a timing for the emergence of puberty (Eaves & others, 2005). Nonetheless, within the boundaries of about 9 to 16 years of age, environmental factors such as health, weight, and stress can influence the onset and duration of puberty.

Hormones Behind the first whisker in boys and the widening of hips in girls is a flood of hormones. **Hormones** are powerful chemical substances secreted by the endocrine glands and carried through the body by the bloodstream. In the case of puberty, the secretion of key hormones is controlled by the interaction of the hypothalamus, the pituitary gland, and the gonads. The *hypothalamus* is a structure in the brain best known for monitoring eating, drinking, and sex. The *pituitary gland* is an important endocrine gland that controls growth and regulates other glands. The *gonads* are the sex glands—the testes in males, the ovaries in females.

How does this hormonal system work? The pituitary gland sends a signal via *gonadotropins* (hormones that stimulate the testes and ovaries) to the appropriate gland to manufacture the hormone. Then the pituitary gland, through interaction with the hypothalamus, detects when the optimal level of hormones is reached and responds by adjusting gonadotropin secretion.

The hormonal changes associated with puberty actually occur in two stages: adrenarche and gonadarche (Susman, Dorn, & Schiefelbein, 2003; Susman & Rogol, 2004). *Adrenarche* involves hormonal changes in the adrenal glands, which are located just above the kidneys. These changes occur from about 6 to 9 years of age, before what we generally consider to be the beginning of puberty. Adrenal androgens are secreted by the adrenal glands during adrenarche and continuing on through puberty.

Gonadarche is what most people think of as puberty, and it involves sexual maturation and the development of reproductive maturity. Gonadarche begins at approximately 9 to 10 years of age in non-Latino White girls, and 8 to 9 years of age in African American girls in the United States (Grumbach & Styne, 1992). Gonadarche begins at about 10 to 11 years of age in boys. The culmination of gonadarche in girls is menarche and in boys **spermarche,** a boy's first ejaculation of semen.

The key hormonal changes of gonadarche involve two classes of hormones that have significantly different concentrations in males and females. **Androgens** are the main class of male sex hormones. **Estrogens** are the main class of female hormones.

Testosterone is an androgen that is key to puberty in boys. Throughout puberty, as their testosterone level rises, external genitals enlarge, height increases, and the voice changes. *Estradiol* is an estrogen that plays an important role in female pubertal development. As estradiol level rises, breast development, uterine development, and skeletal changes occur. In one study, testosterone levels increased eighteenfold in boys but only twofold in girls across puberty; estradiol levels increased eightfold in girls but only twofold in boys across puberty (Nottelman & others, 1987) (see figure 5.2).

menarche A girl's first menstrual period.

hormones Powerful chemical substances secreted by the endocrine glands and carried through the body by the bloodstream.

spermarche A boy's first ejaculation of semen.

androgens The main class of male sex hormones.

estrogens The main class of female sex hormones.

Other hormonal changes involve growth hormones. Not only does the pituitary gland release gonadotropins that stimulate the testes and ovaries, but through interaction with the hypothalamus the pituitary gland also secretes hormones that either directly lead to growth and skeletal maturation or produce growth effects through interaction with the *thyroid gland,* located in the neck region.

Initially, growth hormones are secreted at night during puberty; later they are also secreted during the day, although daytime levels are usually very low (Susman, Dorn, & Schiefelbein, 2003; Susman & Rogol, 2004). Growth can also be influenced by other endocrine factors, such as *cortisol,* which is secreted by the adrenal cortex. Testosterone and estrogen also facilitate growth during puberty.

Are there links between concentrations of hormones and adolescent behavior? Findings are inconsistent. Some studies have found higher levels of testosterone to be related to aggressive behaviors; other studies have not (Susman & others, 1998). Links between high levels of adrenal androgens and antisocial behavior have been found (van Goozen & others, 1998). Few studies have focused on estrogens, but there is some indication that increased levels of estrogens are linked with depression in adolescent girls (Angold, Costello, & Worthman, 1999).

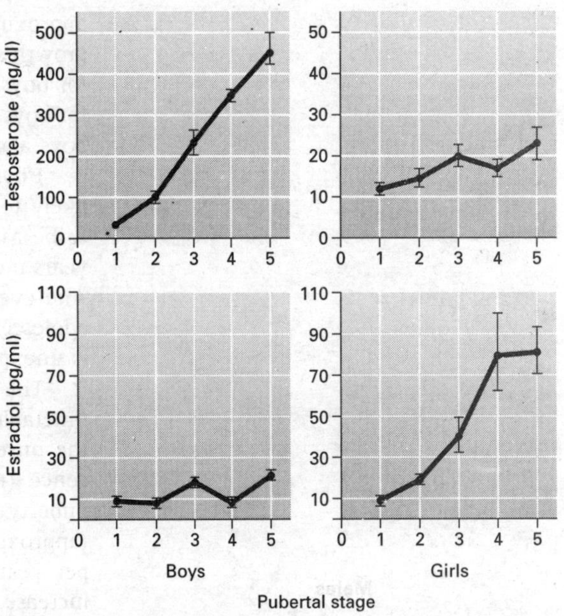

FIGURE 5.2 Hormone Levels by Sex and Pubertal Stage for Testosterone and Estradiol. The five stages range from the early beginning of puberty (stage 1) to the most advanced stage of puberty (stage 5). Notice the significant increase in testosterone in boys and the significant increase in estradiol in girls.

In any event, hormonal factors alone are not responsible for adolescent behavior. For example, one study found that social factors accounted for two to four times as much variance as hormonal factors in young adolescent girls' depression and anger (Brooks-Gunn & Warren, 1989). Another study found little direct connection between testosterone levels in adolescent males and females and their risk-taking behavior or depression (Booth & others, 2003). In contrast, a link with risk-taking behavior depended on the quality of parent-adolescent relations. When the quality of the relationship decreased, testosterone-linked risk-taking behavior and symptoms of depression increased. Hormones do not act independently; hormonal activity is influenced by many environmental factors, including parent-adolescent relationships. Stress, eating patterns, sexual activity, and depression can also activate or suppress various aspects of the hormone system (Archibald, Graber, & Brooks-Gunn, 2003; Graber & Brooks-Gunn, 2002).

Weight and Body Fat Two recent studies found that higher weight was strongly associated with having reached menarche (Anderson, Dallal, & Must, 2003; Mandel & others, 2005). Some researchers have even proposed that a body weight of approximately 106 +/− 3 pounds triggers menarche and the end of the pubertal growth spurt. For menarche to begin and continue, fat must make up 17 percent of the girl's body weight (Friesch, 1984). Both anorexic adolescents whose weight drops dramatically and females in certain sports (such as gymnastics) may become *amenorrheic* (having an absence or suppression of menstrual discharge). Undernutrition also can delay puberty in boys (Susman & Rogol, 2004; Swenne, 2004).

How does the body know that weight or body fat is adequate for the onset of puberty or for menarche? The hormone *leptin,* which is released by fat cells, might be a signal (Grasemann & others, 2004; Li & others, 2005; Plant & Barker-Gibb, 2004). Leptin may be one of the messengers that signal the adequacy of fat stores for reproduction and maintenance of pregnancy at puberty (Misra & others, 2004). Leptin concentrations are higher in girls than in boys. They also are related to the amount of fat in girls and androgen concentrations in boys (Celi & others, 2004).

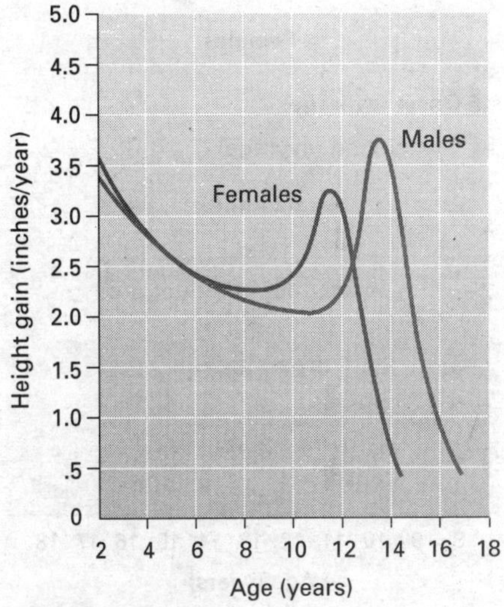

FIGURE 5.3 Pubertal Growth Spurt. On the average, the peak of the growth spurt that characterizes pubertal change occurs two years earlier for girls (11½) than for boys (13½).

In sum, the determinants of puberty include heredity, hormones, and weight and body fat. Next, we will turn our attention to the key changes that characterize puberty, beginning with the growth spurt.

Growth Spurt

Puberty ushers in the most rapid increases in growth since infancy. As indicated in figure 5.3, the growth spurt associated with puberty occurs approximately two years earlier for girls than for boys. The mean beginning of the growth spurt in the United States today is 9 years of age for girls and 11 years of age for boys. Pubertal change peaks at an average of 11½ years for girls and 13½ years for boys. During their growth spurt, girls increase in height about 3½ inches per year, boys about 4 inches.

Boys and girls who are shorter or taller than their peers before adolescence are likely to remain so during adolescence. At the beginning of adolescence, girls tend to be as tall as or taller than boys their age, but by the end of the middle school years most boys have caught up to, or in many cases even surpassed, girls in height. And even though height in elementary school is a good predictor of height later in adolescence, as much as 30 percent of the height of individuals in late adolescence is unexplained by height in the elementary school years.

The rate at which adolescents gain weight follows approximately the same timetable as the rate at which they gain height. Marked weight gains coincide with the onset of puberty. Fifty percent of adult body weight is gained during adolescence (Rogol, Roemmrich, & Clark, 1998). At the peak of weight gain during puberty, girls gain an average of 18 pounds in one year at about 12 years of age (approximately six months after their peak height increase). Boys' peak weight gain per year (20 pounds in one year) occurs at about the same time as their peak increase in height (about 13 to 14 years of age). During early adolescence, girls tend to outweigh boys. But just as with height, by about 14 years of age, boys begin to surpass girls in weight.

In addition to increases in height and weight, body shape changes. Adolescent girls experience a spurt in hip width, and boys undergo an increase in shoulder width. In girls, increased hip width is linked with an increase in estrogen; in boys, increased shoulder width is associated with an increase in testosterone.

The later growth spurt of boys also produces greater leg length in boys than girls. Also, in many cases boys' facial structure becomes more angular during puberty, and girls' becomes more round and soft.

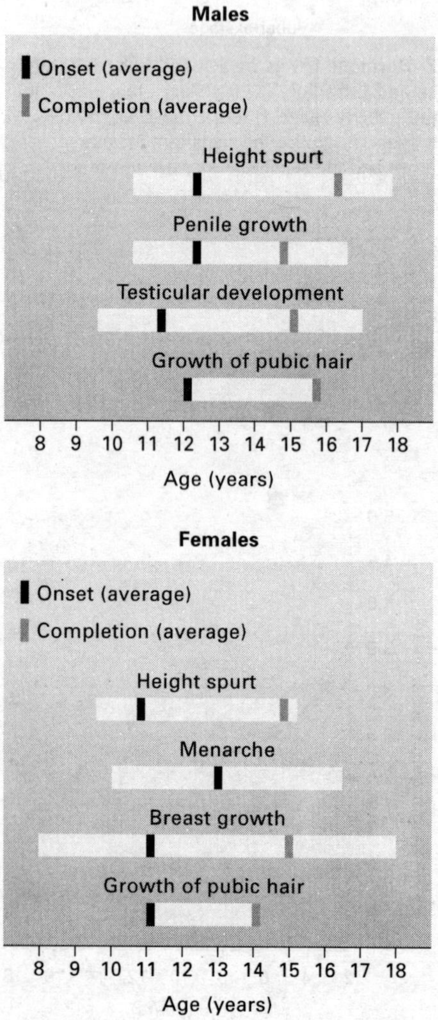

FIGURE 5.4 **Normal Range and Average Development of Sexual Characteristics in Males and Females**

Sexual Maturation Think back to the onset of your puberty. Of the striking changes that were taking place in your body, what was the first change that occurred? Researchers have found that male pubertal characteristics develop in this order: increase in penis and testicle size, appearance of straight pubic hair, minor voice change, first ejaculation (spermarche—this usually occurs through masturbation or a wet dream), appearance of pubic hair, onset of maximum body growth, growth of hair in armpits, more detectable voice changes, and growth of facial hair. Three of the most noticeable areas of sexual maturation in boys are penis elongation, testes development, and growth of facial hair. The normal range and average age of development for these sexual characteristics, along with height spurt, are shown in figure 5.4.

What is the order of appearance of physical changes in females? First either the breasts enlarge or pubic hair appears. These are two of the most noticeable aspects of female pubertal development. Later, hair appears in the armpits. As these changes occur, the female grows in height, and her hips become wider than her shoulders. Her first menstruation (menarche) occurs rather late in the pubertal cycle; as noted earlier, it is considered normal if it occurs between the ages of 9 and 15. Initially, her menstrual cycles may be highly irregular. For the first several years, she might not ovulate during every menstrual cycle. Some girls do not become fertile until two years after their periods begin. Pubertal females do not experience voice changes comparable to those in pubertal males. By the end of puberty, the female's breasts have become more fully rounded.

Body Image One psychological aspect of physical change in puberty is certain: adolescents are preoccupied with their bodies and develop individual images of what their bodies are like. Perhaps you looked in the mirror daily, and sometimes even hourly, to see if you could detect anything different about your changing body. Preoccupation with one's body image is strong throughout adolescence, but it is especially acute during puberty, a time when adolescents are more dissatisfied with their bodies than in late adolescence (Wright, 1989).

There also are gender differences in adolescents' perceptions of their bodies. In general, girls are less happy with their bodies and have more negative body images, compared with boys, throughout puberty (Brooks-Gunn & Paikoff, 1993). Also, as puberty proceeds, girls often become more dissatisfied with their bodies, probably because their body fat increases, whereas boys become more satisfied as they move through puberty, probably because their muscle mass increases (Gross, 1984).

Early and Late Maturation Did you enter puberty early, late, or on time? When adolescents mature earlier or later than their peers, might they perceive themselves differently? In the Berkeley Longitudinal Study conducted some years ago, early-maturing boys perceived themselves more positively and had more successful peer relations than did late-maturing boys (Jones, 1965). The findings for early-maturing girls were similar but not as strong as for boys. When the late-maturing boys were in their thirties, however, they had developed a more positive identity than the early-maturing boys had (Peskin, 1967). Perhaps the late-maturing boys had had more time to explore life's options or, perhaps the early-maturing boys continued to focus on their physical status instead of paying attention to career development and achievement.

What are some outcomes of early and late maturation in adolescence?

In recent years an increasing number of researchers have found that early maturation increases girls' vulnerability to a number of problems (Brooks-Gunn & Paikoff, 1993; McCabe & Ricciardelli, 2004; Sarigiani & Petersen, 2000; Stattin & Magnusson, 1990; Waylen & Wolke, 2004). Early-maturing girls are more likely to smoke, drink, be depressed, have an eating disorder, request earlier independence from their parents, and have older friends; and their bodies are likely to elicit responses from males that lead to earlier dating and earlier sexual experiences. In one study, the early-maturing girls had lower educational and occupational attainment in adulthood (Stattin & Magnusson, 1990). In a recent study, early-maturing girls had a higher incidence of mental disorders than late-maturing girls had (Graber & others, 2004). Apparently as a result of their social and cognitive immaturity, combined with early physical development, early-maturing girls are easily lured into problem behaviors, not recognizing the possible long-term effects of these on their development.

Review and Reflect • **LEARNING GOAL 1**

1 Discuss developmental changes in the body

Review
- What are cephalocaudal and proximodistal patterns?
- How do height and weight change in infancy and childhood?
- What changes characterize puberty?

Reflect
- Did you experience puberty early, late, or on time? How do you think this affected your social relationships and development?

2 THE BRAIN

Brain Physiology | Infancy | Childhood | Adolescence

In every physical change we have described so far, the brain is involved in some way. Structures of the brain help to regulate not only behavior but also metabolism, the release of hormones, and other aspects of the body's physiology. As the rest of the body is changing, what is happening in the brain?

Until recently, little was known for certain about how the brain changes as children develop. Not long ago, scientists thought that our genes determined how our brains were "wired" and that unlike most cells, the cells in the brain responsible for processing information stopped dividing early in childhood. Whatever brain your heredity dealt you, you were essentially stuck with it. This view, however, turned out to be wrong. Instead, the brain has plasticity, and its development depends on context. What you do can change the development of your brain.

The old view of the brain in part reflected the fact that scientists did not have the technology that could detect and map sensitive changes in the brain as it develops. The creation of sophisticated brain-scanning techniques has allowed better detection of these changes (Nelson, Thomas, & de Haan, 2006). Before exploring these changes, let's examine some key structures of the brain and how they function.

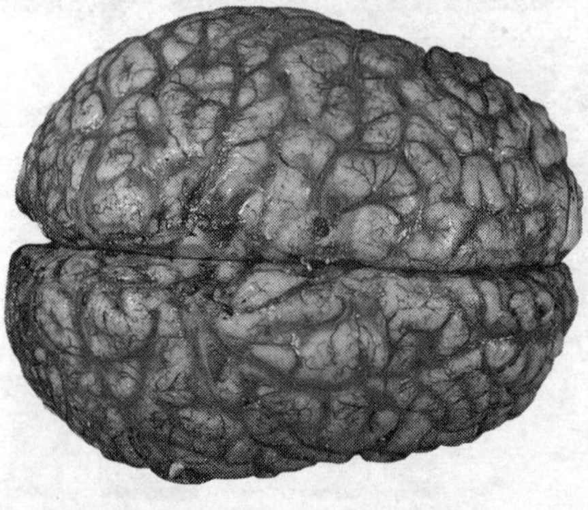

FIGURE 5.5 The Human Brain's Hemispheres. The two halves (hemispheres) of the human brain are clearly seen in this photograph.

Brain Physiology

Looked at from above, the brain has two halves, or *hemispheres* (see figure 5.5). The top portion of the brain, farthest from the spinal cord, is known as the *forebrain*. Its outer layer of cells, the *cerebral cortex*, covers it like a cap. The cerebral cortex is responsible for about 80 percent of the brain's volume and is critical in perception, thinking, language, and other important functions.

Each hemisphere of the cortex has four major areas, called *lobes*. Although the lobes usually work together, each has a somewhat different primary function (see figure 5.6):

- *Frontal lobes* are involved in voluntary movement, thinking, personality, and intentionality or purpose.
- *Occipital lobes* function in vision.
- *Temporal lobes* have an active role in hearing, language processing, and memory.
- *Parietal lobes* play important roles in registering spatial location, attention, and motor control.

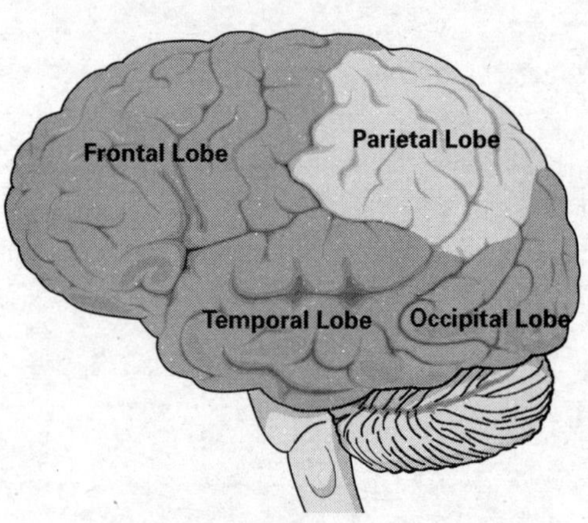

FIGURE 5.6 The Brain's Four Lobes. Shown here are the locations of the brain's four lobes: frontal, occipital, temporal, and parietal.

Deeper in the brain, beneath the cortex, lie other key structures. These include the hypothalamus and the pituitary gland, which we discussed earlier, as well as the *amygdala*, which plays an important role in emotions, and the *hippocampus*, which is especially important in memory and emotion. These structures and parts of others nearby are sometimes referred to as the *limbic system*.

Neurons are the cells in the brain that process information. Figure 5.7 shows some important parts of the neuron, including the *axon* and *dendrites*. Basically an axon sends electrical signals away from the central part of the neuron. At the end of the axon, at tiny gaps called *synapses*, this electrical signal causes the release of chemical substances known as *neurotransmitters*. The neurotransmitters cause a signal to travel up the dendrite of a different neuron to its central portion, or cell body. Thus neurons communicate with each other through the release of neurotransmitters at synapses.

neurons Nerve cells that handle information processing at the cellular level.

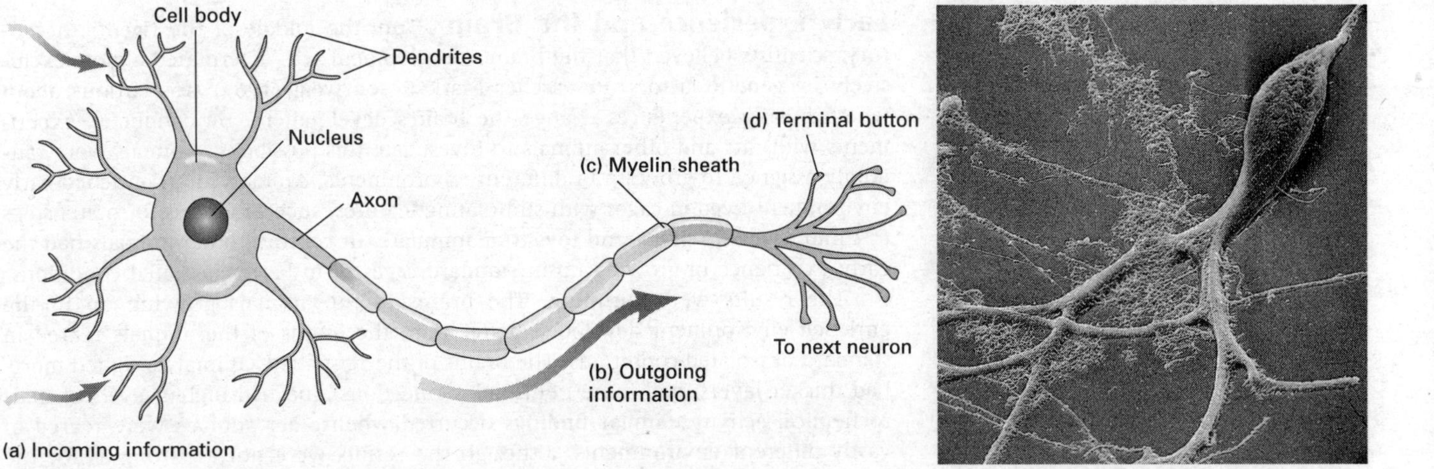

FIGURE 5.7 **The Neuron.** (*a*) The dendrites receive information from other neurons, muscles, or glands. (*b*) Axons transmit information away from the cell body. (*c*) A myelin sheath covers most axons and speeds information transmission. (*d*) As the axon ends, it branches out into terminal buttons. At the right is an actual photograph of a neuron.

As figure 5.7 shows, most axons are covered by a *myelin sheath,* which is a layer of fat cells. The sheath helps impulses travel faster along the axon, increasing the speed with which information travels from neuron to neuron.

Which neurons get which information? Clusters of neurons known as *neural circuits* work together to handle particular types of information. The brain is organized in many neural circuits. For example, one neural circuit is important in attention and *working memory* (the type of memory that holds information for a brief time and is like a "mental workbench" as we perform a task) (Krimel & Goldman-Rakic, 2001). This neural circuit uses the neurotransmitter *dopamine* and lies in the *prefrontal cortex* (see figure 5.8).

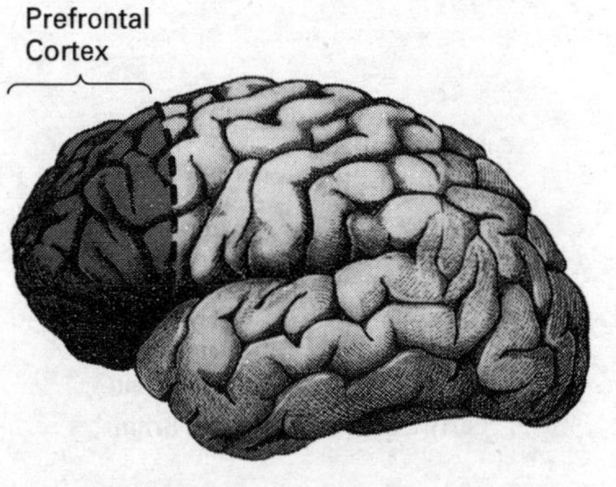

FIGURE 5.8 **The Prefrontal Cortex.** This evolutionarily advanced portion (shaded in purple) of the brain shows extensive development from 3 to 6 years of age and is believed to play important roles in attention and working memory.

To some extent, the type of information handled by neurons depends on whether they are in the left or right hemisphere of the cortex. Speech and grammar, for example, depend on activity in the left hemisphere in most people; humor and the use of metaphors depend on activity in the right hemisphere. This specialization of function in one hemisphere of the cerebral cortex or the other is called **lateralization.** However, complex thinking in normal people is the outcome of communication between both hemispheres of the brain. Labeling people as "left-brained" because they are logical thinkers and "right-brained" because they are creative thinkers does not correspond to the way the brain's hemispheres work.

Researchers have found that the degree of specialization may change through the life span. Let's explore other ways that the brain develops over time.

Infancy

Brain development occurs extensively *in utero* and continues through infancy and later. Because the brain is still developing so extensively in infancy, the infant's head should always be protected from falls or other injuries and the baby should never be shaken. *Shaken baby syndrome,* which includes brain swelling and hemorrhaging, affects hundreds of babies in the United States each year (Harding, Risdon, & Krous, 2004; Minns & Busuttil, 2004; Newton & Vandeven, 2005).

www.mhhe.com/santrockcd11

Neural Processes

As an infant walks, talks, runs, shakes a rattle, smiles, and frowns, changes in its brain are occurring. Consider that the infant began life as a single cell and nine months later was born with a brain and nervous system that contained approximately 100 billion neurons. What determines how those neurons are connected to and communicate with one another?

lateralization Specialization of functions in one hemisphere of the cerebral cortex or the other.

Early Experience and the Brain Until the middle of the twentieth century, scientists believed that the brain's development was determined almost exclusively by genetic factors. Researcher Mark Rosenzweig (1969) was curious about whether early experiences change the brain's development. He conducted experiments with rats and other animals to investigate this possibility. Animals were randomly assigned to grow up in different environments. Animals in an enriched early environment lived in cages with stimulating features, such as wheels to rotate, steps to climb, levers to press, and toys to manipulate. In contrast, other animals had the early experience of growing up in standard cages or in barren, isolated conditions.

The results were stunning. The brains of the animals growing up in the enriched environment developed better than the brains of the animals reared in standard or isolated conditions. The brains of the "enriched" animals weighed more, had thicker layers, had more neuronal connections, and had higher levels of neurochemical activity. Similar findings occurred when older animals were reared in vastly different environments, although the results were not as strong as for the younger animals.

Children who grow up in a deprived environment may also have depressed brain activity (Cicchetti, 2001). As shown in figure 5.9, a child who grew up in the unresponsive and unstimulating environment of a Romanian orphanage showed considerably depressed brain activity compared with a normal child (Begley, 1997).

Are the effects of deprived environments irreversible? There is reason to think the answer is no. The brain demonstrates both flexibility and resilience. Consider 14-year-old Michael Rehbein. At age 7, he began to experience uncontrollable seizures—as many as 400 a day. Doctors said the only solution was to remove the left hemisphere of his brain where the seizures were occurring. Recovery was slow but his right hemisphere began to reorganize and take over functions that normally occur in the brain's left hemisphere, including speech.

Neuroscientists believe that what wires the brain—or rewires it, in the case of Michael Rehbein—is repeated experience. Each time a baby reaches for an attractive object or looks at a face, tiny bursts of electricity shoot through the brain, connecting neurons in circuits. The results are some of the behavioral milestones we discuss in this and other chapters.

In sum, the infant's brain is waiting for experiences to determine how connections are made (Greenough, 2000, 2001; Johnson, 2001, 2005). Before birth, it

www.mhhe.com/santrockcd11

Development of the Brain
Early Development of the Brain
Early Experience and the Brain

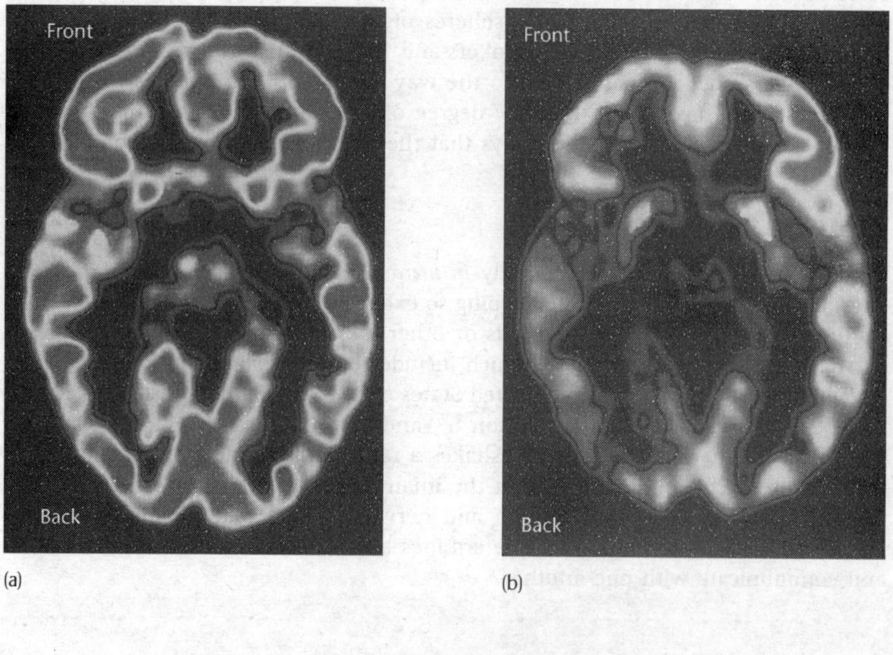

(a) (b)

FIGURE 5.9 Early Deprivation and Brain Activity. These two photographs are PET (positron emission tomography) scans–which use radioactive tracers to image and analyze blood flow and metabolic activity in the body's organs. These scans show the brains of (*a*) a normal child and (*b*) an institutionalized Romanian orphan who experienced substantial deprivation since birth. In PET scans, the highest to lowest brain activity is reflected in the colors of red, yellow, green, blue, and black, respectively. As can be seen, red and yellow show up to a much greater degree in the PET scan of the normal child than the deprived Romanian orphan.

appears that genes mainly direct basic wiring patterns. Neurons grow and travel to distant places awaiting further instructions. After birth, the inflowing stream of sights, sounds, smells, touches, language, and eye contact help shape the brain's neural connections (Graven, 2004; Nelson, 2005; Nelson, Thomas, & de Haan, 2006).

The unfolding of developmental changes in the brain likely holds some important keys to understanding why individuals think and behave the way they do. But the Research in Child Development interlude indicates that studying the brains of babies requires some ingenuity.

Research in Child Development

Studying Babies' Brains

Studying the brain's development in infancy is not easy. Even the latest brain-imaging technologies can't make out fine details—and these technologies can't be used on babies. PET scans (in which the amount of specially treated glucose in various areas of the brain is measured and then analyzed by computer) pose a radiation risk, and infants wriggle too much for an MRI (in which a magnetic field is created around the body and radio waves are used to construct images of brain tissue and biochemical activity).

However, one researcher who is making strides in finding out more about the brain's development in infancy is Charles Nelson (2000, 2001, 2005; Nelson, Thomas, & de Haan, 2006). In his research, he attaches up to 128 electrodes to a baby's scalp. He has found that even newborns produce distinctive brain waves that reveal they can distinguish their mother's voice from another woman's, even while they are asleep. Other research conducted by Nelson found that by 8 months of age babies can distinguish the picture of a wooden toy they were allowed to feel, but not see, from pictures of other toys. This achievement coincides with the development of neurons in the brain's hippocampus (an important structure in memory) that enable the infant to remember specific items and events.

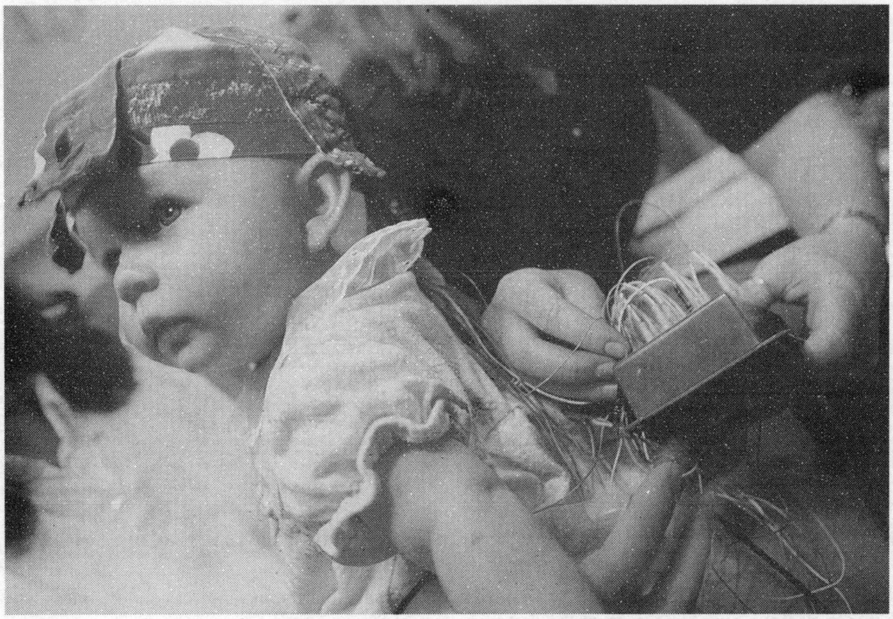

In Charles Nelson's research, electrodes are attached to a baby's scalp to measure the brain's activity to determine its role in the development of an infant's memory. *Why is it so difficult to measure infants' brain activity?*

Changing Neurons At birth, the newborn's brain is about 25 percent of its adult weight. By the second birthday, the brain is about 75 percent of its adult weight. Two key developments during these first two years involve the myelin sheath (the layer of fat cells that speeds up the electrical impulse along the axon) and synaptic connections.

Myelination, the process of encasing axons with a myelin sheath, begins prenatally and continues after birth. Myelination for visual pathways occurs rapidly after birth, being completed in the first six months. Auditory myelination is not completed until 4 or 5 years of age. Some aspects of myelination continue through adolescence. For example, the most extensive increase in myelination in the brain's frontal lobes occurs during adolescence (Nelson, Thomas, & de Haan, 2006).

Dramatic increases in synaptic connections also characterize the development of the brain in the first two years of life (see figure 5.10). Recall that neurons use synapses to transmit information. Nearly twice as many of these connections are made as will ever be used (Huttenlocher & others, 1991; Huttenlocher & Dabholkar, 1997). Synapses bloom—and then they are "pruned"; that is, they disappear.

Figure 5.11 illustrates the growth and later pruning of synapses in the visual, auditory, and prefrontal cortex areas of the brain (Huttenlocher & Dabholkar, 1997). For example, the peak synaptic overproduction in the area concerned with vision occurs about the fourth month after birth, followed by a gradual pruning until the middle to end of the preschool years (Huttenlocher & Dabholkar, 1997). A similar sequence of overproduction and pruning occurs somewhat later in areas of the brain involved in hearing and language. However, in the *prefrontal cortex* (the area of the brain where higher-level thinking and self-regulation occur), the peak of overproduction occurs just after 3 years of age.

Both heredity and environment are thought to influence synaptic overproduction and subsequent pruning. The connections that the child uses become strengthened and survive while the unused ones are pruned (Casey, Durston, & Fossella, 2001).What does all of this blooming and pruning accomplish? Perhaps the blooming of synapses gives the developing brain an increased capacity to interact with the environment. The pruning represents a specialization of the brain, fine-tuning its capacity to interact with the world.

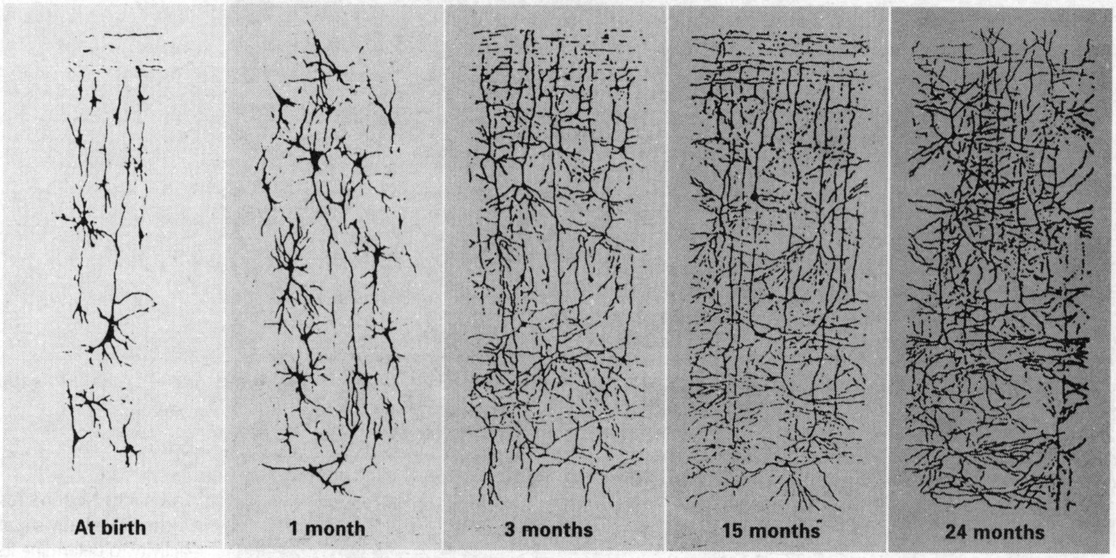

FIGURE 5.10 The Development of Dendritic Spreading. Note the increase in connectedness between neurons over the course of the first two years of life.

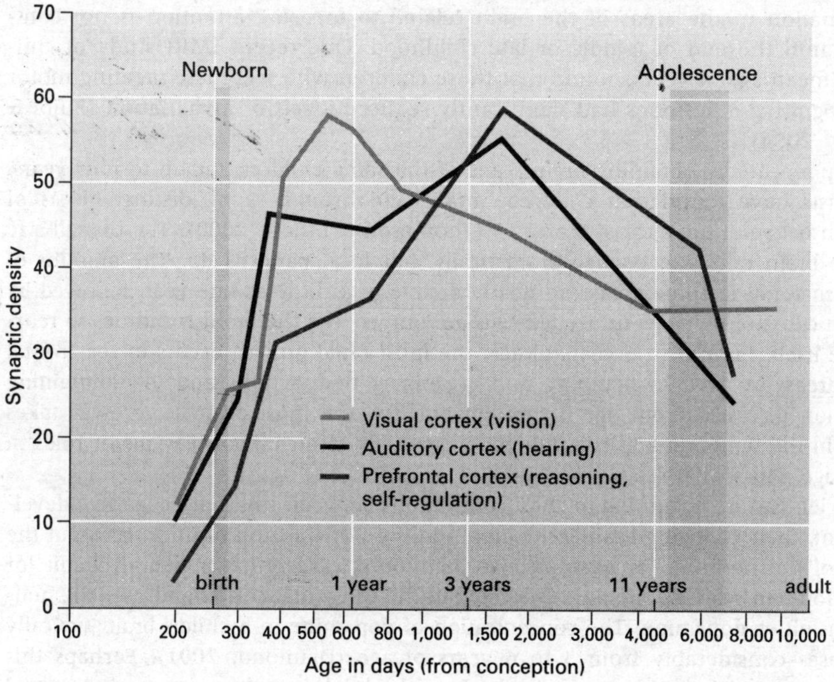

FIGURE 5.11 Synaptic Density in the Human Brain from Infancy to Adulthood. The graph shows the dramatic increase and then pruning in synaptic density for three regions of the brain: visual cortex, auditory cortex, and prefrontal cortex. Synaptic density is believed to be an important indication of the extent of connectivity between neurons.

Changing Structures At birth, the hemispheres already have started to specialize: newborns show greater electrical activity in the left hemisphere than in the right hemisphere when they are listening to speech sounds (Hahn, 1987).

The areas of the brain do not mature uniformly. The frontal lobe is immature in the newborn. However, as neurons in the frontal lobe become myelinated and interconnected during the first year of life, infants develop an ability to regulate their physiological states (such as sleep) and gain more control over their reflexes. Cognitive skills that require deliberate thinking don't emerge until later (Bell & Fox, 1992).

At about 2 months of age, the motor control centers of the brain develop to the point that infants can suddenly reach out and grab a nearby object. At about 4 months, the neural connections necessary for depth perception begin to form. And at about 12 months the brain's speech centers are poised to produce one of infancy's magical moments: when the infant utters its first word. Researchers have found that a spurt in the brain's electrical activity occurs from about 1½ to 2 years of age (Fischer & Bidell, 1998). This surge in activity is likely associated with an increase in conceptual and language development.

Childhood

The brain and other parts of the nervous system continue developing through childhood and adolescence (Byrnes, 2001, 2003). This development along with opportunities to experience a widening world contributes to children's cognitive abilities.

During early childhood, the brain does not grow as rapidly as in infancy; still, the brain and head grow more rapidly than any other part of the body. Some of the brain's increase in size is due to myelination, and some is due to an increase in the number and size of dendrites. Some developmentalists conclude that myelination is important in the maturation of a number of children's abilities (Nagy, Westerberg, & Klingberg, 2004). For example, myelination in the areas of the brain related to hand-eye coordination is not complete until about 4 years of age.

Myelination in the areas of the brain related to focusing attention is not complete until the end of middle or late childhood. One recent fMRI study of children (mean age: 4 years) found that those children who were late meeting motor and cognitive milestones had significantly reduced levels of myelination (Pujol & others, 2004).

By repeatedly obtaining brain scans of the same children for up to four years, scientists have found that children's brains go through rapid, distinct bursts of growth between the ages of 3 and 15 (Thompson & others, 2000). The overall size of the brain does not change dramatically, but local patterns do. The amount of brain material in some areas can nearly double in as little as one year, followed by a drastic loss of tissue as unneeded cells are purged and the brain continues to reorganize itself. From 3 to 6 years of age, the most rapid growth occurs in the frontal lobe areas involved in planning and organizing new actions and in maintaining attention to tasks. From age 6 through puberty, the most dramatic growth takes place in the temporal and parietal lobes, especially in areas that play major roles in language and spatial relations.

Scientists are beginning to chart connections between children's cognitive development, their changing brain structures, and the transmission of information at the level of the neuron. For example, we mentioned earlier that a neural circuit for attention and working memory is located in the prefrontal cortex and uses the neurotransmitter dopamine. The concentration of dopamine in a child's brain typically increases considerably from 3 to 6 years of age (Diamond, 2001). Perhaps this change, as well as rapid growth in the frontal lobe during this same period, is tied to the child's growing cognitive skills. As advances in technology allow scientists to see inside the brain and observe its activity, we will likely understand more precisely how the brain functions in cognitive development.

Adolescence

Until recently, little research had been conducted on developmental changes in the brain during adolescence. Although research in this area is still in its infancy, an increasing number of studies are under way (Walker, 2002). Scientists now believe that the adolescent's brain is different from the child's brain, and that in adolescence the brain is still growing (Keating, 2004; Kuhn & Franklin, 2006; Nelson, Thomas, & de Haan, 2006; Steinberg, 2005).

In one study, researchers used MRIs to discover if brain activity during the processing of emotional information differed in adolescents (10 to 18 years of age) and adults (20 to 40 years of age) (Baird & others, 1999). Participants were asked to view pictures of faces displaying fearful expressions while they underwent an MRI. When adolescents (especially younger ones) processed the emotional information, their brain activity was more pronounced in the amygdala than in the frontal lobe (see figure 5.12). The reverse occurred in the adults. The amygdala is involved in processing information about emotion, while the frontal lobes are involved in higher-level reasoning and thinking. The researchers interpreted their findings to mean that adolescents tend to respond with "gut" reactions to emotional stimuli while adults are more likely to respond in rational, reasoned ways. The researchers also concluded that these changes are linked to growth in the frontal lobe of the brain from adolescence to adulthood. However, more research is needed to clarify these findings (Dahl, 2004; de Bellis & others, 2001; Spear, 2000, 2004). Other researchers have found that the amygdala and hippocampus, both limbic system structures involved in emotion, increase in volume during adolescence (Giedd & others, 1999; Sowell & Jernigan, 1998).

Leading researcher Charles Nelson (2003) points out that while adolescents are capable of very strong emotions, their prefrontal cortex hasn't developed to the point at which they can control these passions. It is as if their brain doesn't have the brakes to slow down their emotions, or as if adolescents combine "early

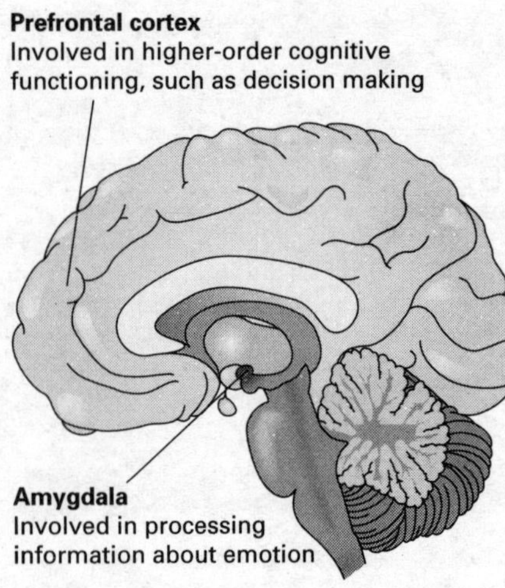

FIGURE 5.12 The Amygdala and the Frontal Lobes

activation of strong 'turbo-charged' feelings with a relatively unskilled set of 'driving skills' or cognitive abilities to modulate strong emotions and motivations" (Dahl, 2004, p. 18).

Laurence Steinberg (2004) emphasizes that areas of the limbic system involved with reward and pleasure may also be involved in adolescents' difficulty in controlling their behavior. The argument is that changes in the limbic system during puberty lead adolescents to seek novelty and to need higher levels of stimulation to experience pleasure (Price, 2005; Spear, 2000, 2004; White, 2005). However, the relatively slow development of the prefrontal cortex, which continues to mature into emerging adulthood, means that adolescents may lack the cognitive skills to effectively control their pleasure seeking. This developmental disjunction may account for an increase in risk taking and other problems in adolescence. Steinberg (2004, p. 56) concludes that a helpful strategy may be to limit adolescents' "opportunities for immature judgment to have harmful consequences. . . . Thus, strategies such as raising the price of cigarettes, more vigilantly enforcing laws governing the sale of alcohol, expanding access to mental health and contraceptive services, and raising the driving age would likely be more effective in limiting adolescent smoking, substance abuse, suicide, pregnancy, and automobile fatalities than strategies aimed at making adolescents wiser, less impulsive, or less shortsighted. Some things just take time to develop, and mature judgment is probably one of them."

Review and Reflect • **LEARNING GOAL 2**

2 Describe how the brain changes

Review

- What is the nature of brain physiology?
- How does the brain change in infancy?
- What characterizes the development of the brain in childhood?
- How does the brain change in adolescence and how might this change be linked to adolescents' behavior?

Reflect

- Numerous claims have been made that elementary and secondary education should be brain based. Some journalists have even suggested that educators should look to neuroscientists for answers about how best to teach children and adolescents. Unfortunately, such bold statements are speculative at best and far removed from what neuroscientists actually know about the brain. Find an article on brain-based education in a magazine or on the Internet. Use your critical thinking skills to evaluate the article's credibility. Does the author present research evidence to support the link between neuroscience and the brain-based method being recommended? Explain.

3 SLEEP

Infancy | Childhood | Adolescence

Sleep restores, replenishes, and rebuilds our brains and bodies. Some neuroscientists believe that sleep gives neurons used while we are awake a chance to shut down and repair themselves. How do sleeping patterns change during the childhood years?

Infancy

How much do infants sleep? Are there any special problems that can develop regarding infants' sleep?

Sleep that knits up the ravelled sleave of care... Balm of hurt minds, nature's second course. Chief nourisher in life's feast.

—William Shakespeare
English Playwright, 17th Century

The Sleep/Wake Cycle When we were infants, sleep consumed more of our time than it does now (Ingersoll & Thoman, 1999). Newborns sleep 16 to 17 hours a day, although some sleep more and others less—the range is from a low of about 10 hours to a high of about 21 hours. Their longest period of sleep is not always at night. Although a young infant's total sleep remains somewhat consistent, the infant might change from sleeping several long bouts of 7 or 8 hours to three or four sessions of just several hours each. By about 1 month of age, most infants have begun to sleep longer at night; by about 4 months of age, they usually have moved closer to adultlike sleep patterns, spending their longest span of sleep at night and their longest span of waking during the day (Daws, 2000).

There are cultural variations in infant sleeping patterns. For example, in the Kipsigis culture in the African country of Kenya, infants sleep with their mothers at night and are permitted to nurse on demand (Super & Harkness, 1997). During the day they are strapped to their mothers' backs, accompanying them on their daily rounds of chores and social activities. As a result, Kipsigis infants do not sleep through the night until much later than American infants. During their first eight months, Kipsigis infants rarely sleep longer than three hours at a stretch, even at night. This contrasts with many American infants, who generally begin to sleep up to eight hours a night by 8 months of age.

REM Sleep A single night's sleep actually has varied stages marked by changes in physiological activity. Researchers are especially interested in *REM (rapid eye movement) sleep,* when brain activity is similar to when we are relaxed but awake and the eyeballs move rapidly. Most adults spend about one-fifth of their night in REM sleep, and REM sleep usually appears about one hour after non-REM sleep. For adults, dreaming mainly occurs during REM sleep (Hobson, 2000). Figure 5.13 illustrates the average number of total hours spent in sleep and the amount of time spent in REM sleep across the human life span.

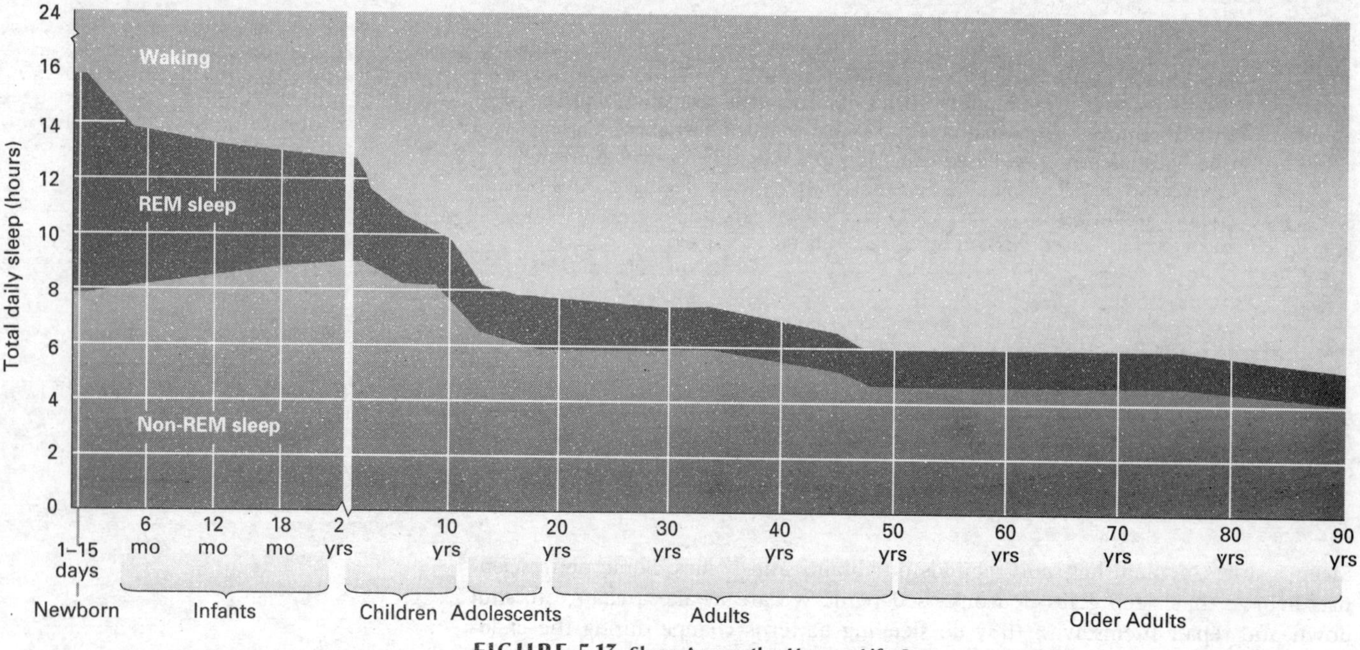

FIGURE 5.13 Sleep Across the Human Life Span

About one-half of an infant's sleep is REM sleep—more than at any other time in life—and infants often begin their sleep cycle with REM sleep rather than non-REM sleep. By the time infants reach 3 months of age, the percentage of time they spend in REM sleep falls to about 40 percent, and REM sleep no longer begins their sleep cycle. The large amount of REM sleep might provide infants with added self-stimulation, because they spend less time awake than older children do. REM sleep also might promote the brain's development in infancy.

Shared Sleeping In many cultures, infants share a bed with their mothers (Cortesi & others, 2004; Jenni & O'Connor, 2005; Owens, 2005). Some child experts believe there are benefits to shared sleeping: it can promote breast-feeding, and it can enable the mother to respond more quickly to the baby's cries and to detect breathing pauses that might be dangerous (McKenna, Mosko, & Richard, 1997). However, shared sleeping remains a controversial issue (Berkowitz, 2004). The American Academy of Pediatrics Task Force on Infant Positioning and SIDS (2000; Cohen, 2000) recommends against shared sleeping. They argue that in some instances bed sharing might lead to sudden infant death syndrome (SIDS), as could be the case if a sleeping mother rolls over on her baby. Two recent studies found significant links between bed sharing and the incidence of SIDS (Alexander & Radisch, 2005; Unger & others, 2003).

SIDS

SIDS **Sudden infant death syndrome (SIDS)** is a condition that occurs when infants stop breathing, usually during the night, and suddenly die without an apparent cause. SIDS remains the highest cause of infant death in the United States, with nearly 3,000 infant deaths. Risk of SIDS is highest at 4 to 6 weeks of age (National Center for Health Statistics, 2002a).

Researchers have found that SIDS decreases when infants sleep on their backs rather than on their stomachs or sides (Alexander & Radisch, 2005; Moon, Oden, & Grady, 2004; Rusen & others, 2004). Perhaps prone sleeping increases the risk for SIDS by impairing arousal from sleep and restricting the ability to swallow effectively (Horne, Parslow, & Harding, 2004; Kahn & others, 2004). Since 1992, when the American Academy of Pediatrics recommended that infants be placed on their backs to sleep in order to reduce the risk of SIDS, the frequency of prone sleeping has decreased from 70 percent to 20 percent of U.S. infants (American Academy of Pediatrics Task Force on Infant Sleep Position and SIDS, 2000).

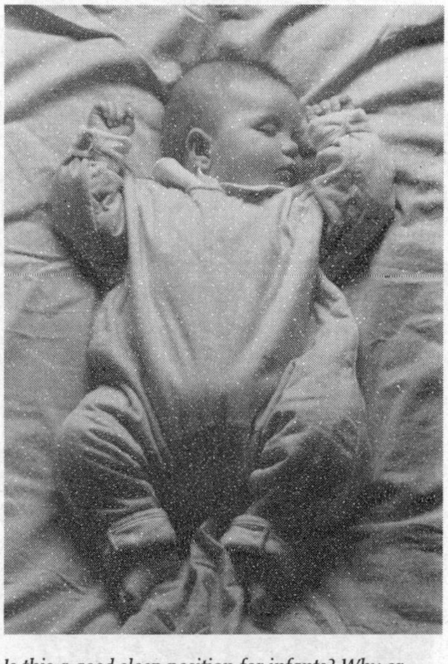

Is this a good sleep position for infants? Why or why not?

In addition to sleeping in a prone position, researchers have identified the following risk factors for SIDS (American Academy of Pediatrics Task Force on Infant Sleep Position and SIDS, 2000; Goldwater, 2001):

- Low birth weight infants are 5 to 10 times more likely to die of SIDS than are their normal-weight counterparts (Horne & others, 2002; Sowter & others, 1999).
- Infants whose siblings have died of SIDS are two to four times as likely to die of it (Lenoir, Mallet, & Calenda, 2000).
- Six percent of infants with *sleep apnea*, a temporary cessation of breathing in which the airway is completely blocked, usually 10 seconds or longer, die of SIDS (McNamara & Sullivan, 2000).
- African American and Eskimo infants are two to six times as likely as all others to die of SIDS (Hauck & others, 2002). One recent study found that prone sleeping was linked to SIDS in African American infants, suggesting educational outreach to African American families regarding the importance of placing infants on their backs while sleeping (Hauck & others, 2002).
- SIDS is more common in lower socioeconomic groups (Mitchell & others, 2000).
- SIDS is more common in infants who are passively exposed to cigarette smoke (Horne & others, 2004; Spitzer, 2005; Tong, England, & Glantz, 2005).
- Soft bedding is not recommended (Flick & others, 2001).

sudden infant death syndrome (SIDS) A condition that occurs when an infant stops breathing, usually during the night, and suddenly dies without an apparent cause.

Childhood

Most young children sleep through the night and have one daytime nap. Sometimes, though, it is difficult to get young children to go to sleep because they drag out their bedtime routine. Helping the child slow down before bedtime often helps reduce his or her resistance to going to bed. Reading the child a story, playing quietly with the child in the bath, or letting the child sit on the caregiver's lap while listening to music are quieting activities.

A recent research review concluded that across many cultures approximately 25 percent of parents report that that their children have sleep problems (Owens, 2005). Many of the sleep problems were similar across cultures, such as resistance in going to bed, waking up at night, being sleepy during the day, and insufficient sleep.

One recent study examined the sleep patterns of children in second, fourth, and sixth grade (Sadeh, Raviv, & Gruber, 2000). Sixth-grade children went to sleep at night about one hour later (just after 10:30 P.M. versus just after 9:30 P.M.) and reported more daytime sleepiness than the second-grade children. Girls spent more time in sleep than boys. Also, family stress was linked with poor sleep, such as nightly wakings, in children.

Nightmares and night terrors are among the sleep problems that children can develop (Boyle & Cropley, 2004; Heussler, 2005; Ivanenko, Crabtree, & Gozal, 2004). *Nightmares* are frightening dreams that awaken the sleeper, often toward the morning. Almost every child has occasional nightmares, but persistent nightmares might indicate that the child is feeling too much stress.

Night terrors are characterized by sudden arousal from sleep and an intense fear, usually accompanied by physiological reactions, such as rapid heart rate and breathing, loud screams, heavy perspiration, and physical movement. In most instances, the child has little or no memory of what happened during the night terror. Night terrors are less common than nightmares and occur more often in deep sleep than do nightmares. Many children who experience night terrors return to sleep rather quickly. These sleep disruptions are not believed to reflect any emotional problems in children.

Adolescence

Adolescents are known for annoying their parents by staying up to all hours and being next to impossible to arouse from bed in the morning. Are they just being difficult? Interest in adolescent sleep patterns has surged recently as researchers have suggested that there are physiological underpinnings to these sleep patterns, that many adolescents are not getting enough sleep, and that these findings have implications for when adolescents learn most effectively in school (Hansen & others, 2005; Lamberg, 2005).

How might changing sleep patterns in adolescents affect their school performance?

Mary Carskadon and her colleagues (2004a, 2004b, 2005; Carskadon, Acebo, & Jenni, 2004; Carskadon, Acebo, & Seifer, 2001) have conducted a number of research studies on adolescent sleep patterns. They found that adolescents sleep an average of 9 hours and 25 minutes when given the opportunity to sleep as long as they like. Most adolescents get considerably less sleep than this, especially during the week. This creates a *sleep debt*, which adolescents often try to make up on the weekend.

The researchers also found that older adolescents are often more sleepy during the day than younger adolescents. Why? Their research suggests that as adolescents age, their biological clocks undergo a hormonal phase shift that pushes the time of wakefulness an hour later. The hormone *melatonin*, which is produced by the brain's pineal gland in preparation for the body to sleep, is the key. Melatonin is secreted at about 9:30 P.M. in younger adolescents but approximately an hour later in older adolescents, which delays the onset of sleep.

Carskadon determined that early school starting times can result in grogginess and lack of attention in class and poor performance on tests. Based on this research, schools in Edina, Minnesota, started classes at 8:30 A.M. instead of 7:25 A.M. Test scores in Edina have improved for high school students, but not for middle school students, which supports Carskadon's idea that older adolescents are more affected by earlier school start times than younger adolescents are. In addition, discipline problems in Edina and the number of students who report an illness or depression have dropped.

A recent longitudinal study further documented the negative outcomes of sleep loss during early adolescence. Katia Fredrikson and her colleagues (2004) examined the sleep patterns of 2,259 students from the sixth through the eighth grade. Over the course of the study, students who engaged in less sleep were more depressed and had lower self-esteem.

Review and Reflect • **LEARNING GOAL 3**

3 Summarize how sleep patterns change as children develop

Review
- How can sleep be characterized in infancy?
- What changes occur in sleep during childhood?
- How does adolescence affect sleep?

Reflect
- Did your sleep patterns start to change when you became an adolescent? Have they changed since you went through puberty? If so, how?

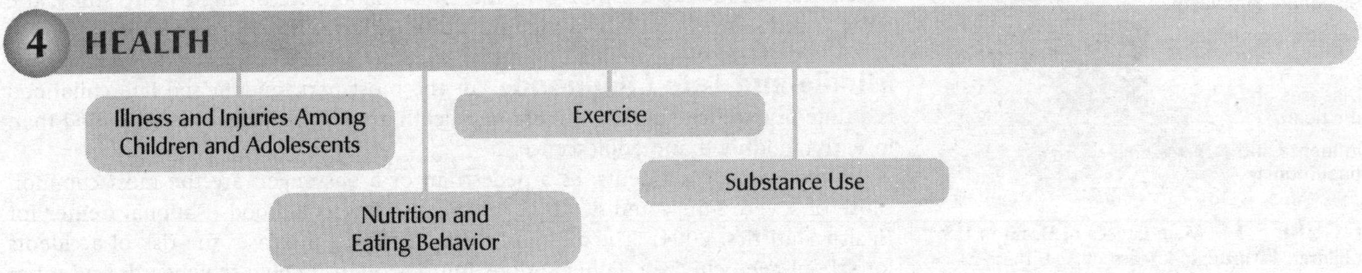

To some extent, the developmental path we have described so far in this chapter is the story of a mythical being, the average child. Whether a child experiences major bumps or detours on this path of physical growth and brain development depends to a great extent on the child's health. What are the major threats to the child's health today? We will look first at the major illnesses and injuries experienced by children and adolescents before turning to less obvious threats to healthy development: poor nutrition and eating habits, lack of exercise, and substance abuse. The formation of healthy habits in childhood, such as eating foods low in fat and cholesterol and engaging in regular exercise, not only has immediate benefits but also contributes to the delay or prevention of the major causes of premature disability and mortality in adulthood—heart disease, stroke, diabetes, and cancer.

Illnesses and Injuries Among Children and Adolescents

To a pediatrician of the 1950s, the medical care available to children and adolescents today might seem like science fiction. New vaccinations and antibiotics as well as new tests and surgical techniques have helped to allow the emphasis in medical care to move toward prevention and outpatient care. Injuries and diseases can be treated far more effectively than in the past. The benefits of these advances, however, are distributed unevenly among the world's children (Bhutta & others, 2005).

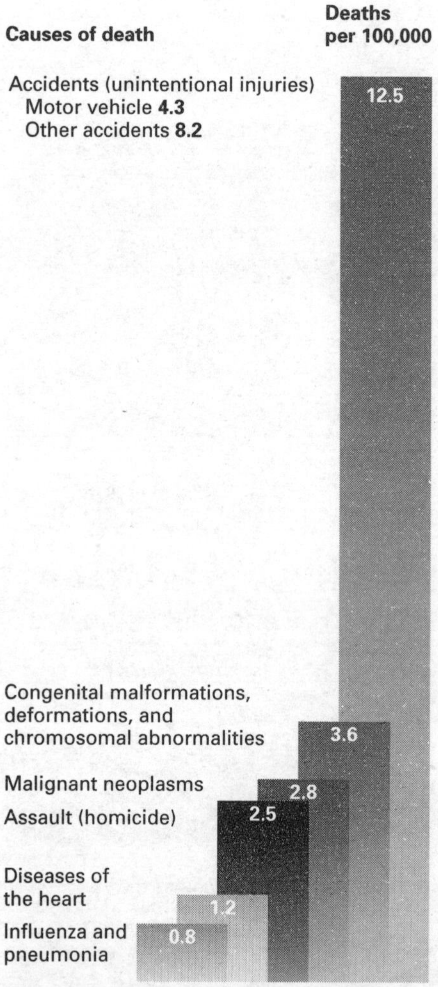

FIGURE 5.14 Main Causes of Death in U.S. Children 1 Through 4 Years of Age. These figures are based on the number of deaths per 100,000 children 1 through 4 years of age in the United States in 1999 (National Vital Statistics Reports, 2001).

In this section, we first examine broad patterns in the causes of illness and death among children and adolescents and then turn to the difficulties faced by poor children in the United States and around the world.

Early Childhood In recent decades, vaccines have nearly eradicated disabling bacterial meningitis and have become available to prevent measles, rubella, mumps, and chicken pox. Although the dangers of many diseases for children have been greatly diminished, it still is important for parents to keep children on an immunization schedule.

From 1950 to the present, there has been a dramatic decline in deaths of children under the age of 5 from preterm birth, birth defects, accidents, cancer, homicide, and heart disease. The disorders still most likely to be fatal during early childhood today are birth defects, cancer, and heart disease.

Accidents are the leading cause of death in young children (National Vital Statistics Reports, 2001) (see figure 5.14). Motor vehicle accidents, drowning, falls, and poisoning are high on the list of causes of death in young children (Brenner & others, 2001; Chen & others, 2005; Schnake, Peterson, & Corden, 2005).

Parental smoking is another major danger to children (Drongowski & others, 2003; Moya, Beaver, & Etzel, 2004). Approximately 22 percent of children and adolescents in the United States are exposed to tobacco smoke in the home. An increasing number of studies conclude that living in a home in which a parent smokes puts children at risk for respiratory problems. They are more likely to experience wheezing symptoms and asthma than are children in nonsmoking homes (Murray & others, 2004). In one study, if the mother smoked, her children were twice as likely to have respiratory problems (Etzel, 1988). Tobacco smoke in the home also affects the amount of vitamin C in the child's blood. According to one study, the more parents smoked, the less vitamin C the children had (Strauss, 2001).

Middle and Late Childhood For the most part, middle and late childhood is a time of excellent health. Disease and death are less prevalent in this period than in early childhood and adolescence.

Motor vehicle accidents, as a pedestrian or a passenger, are the most common cause of severe injury and death in middle and late childhood (National Center for Health Statistics, 2004). The allure of riding a bicycle increases the risk of accidents for school-aged children. Other serious injuries often involve skateboards and other sports equipment.

The most effective strategy for preventing injury (or reducing the severity of an injury) from accidents is to use safety-belt restraints in cars and to educate children about the hazards of risk taking and improper use of equipment. Appropriate safety helmets, protective eye and mouth shields, and protective padding are recommended for children who engage in active sports.

Cancer is the second-leading cause of death in children 5 to 14 years of age. Three percent of all children's deaths in this age period are due to cancer. Currently, 1 in every 330 children in the United States develops cancer before the age of 19. Morover, the incidence of cancer in children is increasing (Negalia & others, 2001).

Child cancers have a different profile from adult cancers. Adult cancers attack mainly the lungs, colon, breast, prostate, and pancreas. Child cancers mainly attack the white blood cells (leukemia), brain, bone, lymph system, muscles, kidneys, and nervous system.

The most common cancer in children is leukemia, a cancer of the tissues that make blood cells. In leukemia, the bone marrow makes an abundance of white blood cells that don't function properly. They crowd out normal cells, making the child susceptible to bruising and infection.

Child life specialists are among the health professionals who try to make the lives of children with diseases such as cancer less stressful. To read about the work of child life specialist Sharon McLeod, see the Careers in Child Development insert.

Adolescence The three leading causes of death in adolescence are accidents, homicide, and suicide. More than half of all deaths in adolescents ages 10 to 19 are due to accidents, and most of those involve motor vehicles, especially for older adolescents. Risky driving habits, such as speeding, tailgating, and driving under the influence of alcohol or other drugs, may be more important causes of these accidents than is lack of driving experience. In about 50 percent of the motor vehicle fatalities involving an adolescent, the driver has a blood alcohol level of 0.10 percent, twice the level needed to be "under the influence" in some states. A high rate of intoxication is also often present in adolescents who die as pedestrians or while using recreational vehicles.

Homicide is the second-leading cause of death in adolescence (National Center for Health Statistics, 2004). Homicide is especially high among African American male adolescents, who are three times more likely to be killed by guns than by natural causes.

Suicide accounts for 6 percent of the deaths in the 10- to 14-year-old age group, a rate of 1.3 per 100,000 population. In the 15- to 19-year-old age group, suicide accounts for 12 percent of deaths or 9 per 100,000 population. Since the 1950s the adolescent suicide rate has tripled.

Health, Illness, and Poverty Among the World's Children The general statistics on children's health in the United States mask the special difficulties faced by the millions of U.S. children who live in poverty. As discussed in chapter 1, in 2003 more than 17 percent of children in the United States were living in poverty, a rate much higher than that in other industrialized nations. An estimated 7 percent of U.S. children have no source of routine health care.

Children in poverty face elevated risks for many threats to health (Flores, Abreu, & Tomany-Korman, 2005; Insel & Roth, 2006; Ramey, Ramey, & Lanzi, 2006; Shi & Stevens, 2005). Lead can get into children's bloodstreams if their food or water is contaminated by lead, if they put lead-contaminated fingers in their mouths, or if they inhale dust from lead-based paint. High lead levels in children's blood have been linked to lower intelligence and achievement, as well as attention deficit hyperactivity disorder (Soong & others, 1999).

What is the best way to improve the health of children who live in poverty? Some experts argue that offering medical care is not enough. If you give an antibiotic to a child with a sore throat who then returns to a home where she will be cold and hungry, have you provided good health care? One approach to children's health aims to treat not only medical problems of the individual child but the conditions of the entire family. In fact, some programs seek to identify children who are at risk for problems and then try to alter the risk factors in an effort to prevent illness and disease. The Caring for Children interlude describes one program that takes this ambitious approach.

CAREERS in CHILD DEVELOPMENT

Sharon McLeod
Child Life Specialist

Sharon McLeod is a child life specialist who is clinical director of the Child Life and Recreational Therapy Department at the Children's Hospital Medical Center in Cincinnati.

Under Sharon's direction, the goals of the Child Life Department are to promote children's optimal growth and development, reduce the stress of health-care experiences, and provide support to child patients and their families. These goals are accomplished through therapeutic play and developmentally appropriate activities, educating and psychologically preparing children for medical procedures, and serving as a resource for parents and other professionals regarding child development and health-care issues.

Sharon says that a course in human growth and development provides the foundation for her profession of child life specialist. She also describes her best times as a student when she conducted fieldwork, had an internship, and experienced the theories and concepts she learned in her courses.

Sharon McLeod, child life specialist, working with a child at Children's Hospital Medical Center in Cincinnati.

Caring for Children

A Healthy Start

The Hawaii Family Support/Healthy Start Program began in 1985 (Allen, Brown, & Finlay, 1992). It was designed by the Hawaii Family Stress Center in Honolulu, which already had been making home visits to improve family functioning and reduce child abuse for more than a decade. Participation is voluntary. Families of newborns are screened for family risk factors, including unstable housing, histories of substance abuse, depression, parents' abuse as a child, late or no prenatal care, fewer than 12 years of schooling, poverty, and unemployment. Healthy Start workers screen and interview new mothers in the hospital. They also screen families referred by physicians, nurses, and others. Because the demand for services outstrips available resources, only families with a substantial number of risk factors can participate.

The Hawaii Family Support/Healthy Start Program provides many home-visitor services for overburdened families of newborns and young children. This program has been very successful in reducing abuse and neglect in families. *What are some examples of the home-visitor services in this program?*

Each new participating family receives a weekly visit from a family support worker. Each of the program's eight home visitors works with approximately 25 families at a time. The worker helps the family cope with any immediate crises, such as unemployment or substance abuse. The family also is linked directly with a pediatrician to ensure that the children receive regular health care. Infants are screened for developmental delays and are immunized on schedule. Pediatricians are notified when a child is enrolled in Healthy Start and when a family at risk stops participating.

The Family Support/Healthy Start Program recently hired a child development specialist to work with families of children with special needs. And, in some instances, the program's male family support worker visits a father to talk about his role in the family. The support workers encourage parents to participate in group activities held each week at the program center located in a neighborhood shopping center.

Over time, parents are encouraged to assume more responsibility for their family's health and well-being. Families can participate in Healthy Start until the child is 5 and enters public school. One recent study found that the Hawaiian Healthy Start program produced a lower incidence of maternal alcohol abuse and partner violence but did not reduce child abuse (Duggan & others, 2004).

Poverty in the United States is dwarfed by poverty in developing countries around the world. The poor are the majority in nearly one of every five nations in the world (UNICEF, 2003). They often experience lives of hunger, malnutrition, illness, inadequate access to health care, unsafe water, and inadequate protection from harm.

Much of the developing world has seen little reduction in children's illnesses. A leading cause of child death in impoverished countries is diarrhea produced by dehydration. Giving the child a large volume of water and liquids usually prevents dehydration. Measles, tetanus, and whooping cough still lead to the deaths of many children around the world, although immunization programs in the last several decades have made progress in reducing deaths due to these diseases (Foege, 2000).

In the last decade, there has been a dramatic increase in the number of children who have died because of HIV/AIDS transmitted to them by their parents (UNICEF, 2003). The uneducated are four times more likely to believe there is no way to avoid AIDS and three times more likely to be unaware that the virus can be transmitted from mother to child (UNICEF, 2003).

Nutrition and Eating Behavior

Poverty influences health in part through its effects on nutrition. The different fates of Latonya and Ramona described in the opening of the chapter dramatized the importance of nutrition for infants, but as our discussion of topics such as height illustrated, nutrition has significant if less obvious effects later in life. From infancy to childhood to adolescence, nutritional needs and the major threats to health shift. Let's begin by exploring the nutritional needs of infants.

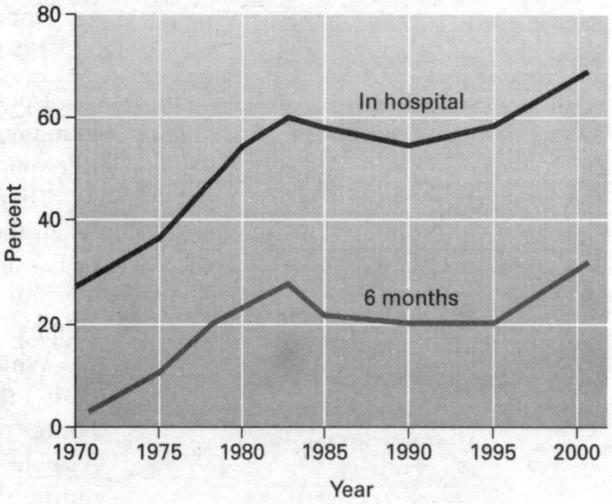

FIGURE 5.15 Trends in Breast-feeding in the United States: 1970–2001. Significant increases in the percentage of U.S. mothers who breast-feed their infants have occurred recently.

Infancy

For the infant, the importance of receiving adequate energy and nutrients in a loving and supportive environment cannot be overstated (DiGiorgio, 2005; Samour, Helm, & Lang, 2000; Thompson, 2005). Recall that from birth to 1 year of age, infants triple their weight and increase their length by 50 percent. Because infants vary in their nutrient reserves, body composition, growth rates, and activity patterns, their nutrient needs vary as well. However, because parents need guidelines, nutritionists recommend that infants consume approximately 50 calories per day for each pound they weigh—more than twice an adult's requirement per pound. For infants in the United States and other industrialized countries, the source of those calories rather than the amount is more likely to be an important concern.

Breast- Versus Bottle-Feeding Either human milk or alternative "formula" is the baby's source of nutrients and energy for the first four to six months of life. In the United States, "formula" was the conventional choice for a while, but breast-feeding is increasing, as shown in figure 5.15 (Ryan, Wenjun, & Acosta, 2002). In fact, some U.S. women today feel guilty if they terminate breast-feeding early (Mozingo & others, 2000). Because it is better than formula for the infant's health, the American Pediatric Association strongly endorses breast-feeding throughout the first year of life (AAP Work Group on Breast-feeding, 1997; James & Dobson, 2005).

What are some of the benefits of breast-feeding? During the first two years of life and later, benefits include the following (AAP Work Group on Breast-feeding, 1997; Eiger & Olds, 1999; Hanson & Korotkova, 2002; Kramer, 2003):

- Appropriate weight gain and lowered risk of childhood obesity (Grummer-Strawn & Mei, 2004). A recent review of 11 studies found that breast-feeding reduces the risk of childhood obesity to a moderate extent (Dewey, 2003). Why? One possible explanation for this lowered risk is early metabolic programming. That is, consuming formula may change how the infant's body responds to carbohydrates, changes that predispose the infant to later obesity.
- Fewer allergies (Friedman & Zeiger, 2005; Host & Halken, 2005).
- Prevention or reduction of diarrhea, respiratory infections (such as pneumonia and bronchitis), bacterial and urinary tract infections, and otitis media (a middle ear infection) (Issacs, 2005; Morrow & Rangel, 2004).
- Denser bones in childhood and adulthood (Gibson & others, 2000; Jones, Riley, & Dwyer, 2000).
- Reduced childhood cancer and reduced incidence of breast cancer in mothers and their female offspring (Eisinger & Burke, 2003; Kwan & others, 2004).
- Lower incidence of sudden infant death syndrome (SIDS) (Horne & others, 2004). In one study, for every month of exclusive breast-feeding, the rate of SIDS was cut in half (Fredrickson, 1993).

Human milk or an alternative formula is a baby's source of nutrients for the first 4 to 6 months. The growing consensus is that breast-feeding is better for the baby's health, although controversy still swirls about the issue of breast-feeding versus bottle-feeding. *Why is breast-feeding strongly recommended by pediatricians?*

- Improved visual acuity and neurological and cognitive development (Brody, 1994; Eidelman & Feldman, 2004; Makrides & others, 1995).

Does breast-feeding also bring psychological benefits? Some researchers have found no psychological differences between breast-fed and bottle-fed infants (Ferguson, Harwood, & Shannon, 1987; Young, 1990).

There are circumstances in which mothers should not breast-feed. They are (1) when the mother is infected with AIDS, which can be transmitted through her milk, or has another infectious disease, (2) if she has active tuberculosis, or (3) she is taking any drug that might not be safe for the infant (AAP Work Group on Breast-feeding, 1997; Jain & Lacy, 2005; Kiarie & others, 2004; Merchant & Lala, 2005).

Which women are least likely to breast-feed? Some women cannot breast-feed their infants because of physical difficulties. Also, if they are not constantly at home, some women are deterred from breast-feeding because they are uncomfortable breast-feeding in public places. Increasingly, mothers who return to work during the infant's first year use a breast pump to extract breast milk that can be stored and later fed to the infant in a bottle when the mother is not present. Still, women least likely to breast-feed include mothers who work full-time outside of the home, mothers under age 25, mothers without a high school education, African American mothers, and mothers in low-income circumstances (DiGiorgio, 2005; Li & others, 2005; Ryan, 1997).

This Honduran child has kwashiorkor. Notice the telltale sign of kwashiorkor—a greatly expanded abdomen. *What are some other characteristics of kwashiorkor?*

In poor countries in particular, breast-feeding may be the only way a mother can feed her infant adequately, and in many of these countries, mothers used to breast-feed their infants for at least two years. To become more modern, some stopped breast-feeding or abandoned it earlier in the infant's life. Sometimes the substitute for breast-fed milk is an unsuitable and unsanitary cow's milk formula; sometimes it is a form of tapioca or rice. Sometimes, as we described in the chapter opening, the substitute is formula diluted with polluted water and used with unsterilized bottles. The result may be malnutrition and even death, as it was for Latonya. Studies in Afghanistan, Haiti, Ghana, Chile, and other countries found that the death rate of bottle-fed infants is as much as five times that of breast-fed infants (Grant, 1997; Piwoz & Ross, 2005; Shanker & others, 2005).

The use of formula by mothers like Latonya's reflected cultural change, and efforts like the "baby-friendly" programs described in the chapter opening aim for new cultural changes to encourage breast-feeding. Similar programs exist in the United States. In one study of low-income mothers in Georgia, interventions such as counseling that focused on the benefits of breast-feeding and the free loan of a breast pump increased the number of mothers who chose breast-feeding (Ahluwalia & others, 2000). However, as described in the chapter opening, in some cases breast-feeding may not be the best choice as when mothers are infected with the HIV virus (Chauma, Adu, & Kyari, 2004; Merchant & Lala, 2005).

Malnutrition in Infancy When they are severely malnourished, infants fail to grow adequately and they are listless. Very severe malnutrition usually takes the form of marasmus or kwashiorkor. **Marasmus** is severe malnutrition due to insufficient caloric intake. Infants with marasmus have a shrunken, wasted, elderly appearance. **Kwashiorkor** is severe malnutrition caused by a deficiency in protein. The child's abdomen and feet swell with water. Otherwise, children with kwashiorkor may look well-fed. In fact, their vital organs are collecting whatever nutrients are present, depriving other parts of the body. The disease usually appears between 1 and 3 years of age. Marasmus and kwarshiorkor are serious problems in developing countries, with as many as 50 percent of deaths under the age of 5 in these countries due to such severe protein-energy malnutrition (UNICEF, 2003).

marasmus A wasting away of body tissues in the infant's first year, caused by severe protein-calorie deficiency.

kwashiorkor A condition caused by a deficiency in protein in which the child's abdomen and feet become swollen with water.

Marasmus and kwashiorkor are rare in the United States, but there is increasing concern that U.S. babies are not eating the right foods. A recent national study of more than 3,000 randomly selected 4- to 24-month-olds documented that many U.S. parents aren't feeding their babies enough fruits and vegetables, but are feeding them too much junk food (Fox & others, 2004). Up to one-third of the babies ate no vegetables and fruit, frequently ate French fries, and almost half of the 7- to 8-month-old babies were fed desserts, sweets, or sweetened drinks. By 15 months, French fries were the most common vegetables the babies ate.

One recent study found low intakes of vitamin D, zinc, and iron, especially at 12 and 18 months in U.S. infants (Nolan & others, 2002). Iron and zinc deficiency also are prevalent during infancy in developing countries. One recent study found that supplements of these minerals benefited the motor development of infants in Bangladesh (Black & others, 2003).

The effects of nutrition in infancy may extend at least into early childhood (Morgan, 2005). One study linked the diets of rural Guatemalan infants with their social development when they entered elementary school (Barrett, Radke-Yarrow, & Klein, 1982). Researchers compared children whose mothers had been given nutrition supplements during pregnancy and who themselves had been given more nutritious, high-calorie foods in their first two years of life with children who had not received nutritional supplements. When they entered elementary school, the children who had received the supplements were more active, more involved, more helpful with their peers, less anxious, and happier.

Nutritional supplements for infants can also improve their cognitive development. In a longitudinal investigation conducted over two decades in rural Guatemala, Ernesto Pollitt and his colleagues (1993) found that giving malnourished infants or children protein supplements and increased calories had long-term effects on cognitive development. Both the socioeconomic status of the children and the period during which the nutritional supplements were given influenced the effects of the supplements. For example, the children in the lowest socioeconomic groups benefited more than the children in the higher socioeconomic groups. Also, when supplements were given only after the children were 2 years old, they still had a positive influence, but the effect on cognitive development was less powerful.

Childhood Malnutrition and even starvation are daily facts of life for children in many developing countries (UNICEF, 2003). In the United States, approximately 11 million preschool children are malnourished. Their malnutrition places their health at risk (Drewnowski & Spector, 2004; Ghosh & Shah, 2004; Richter, 2003). Many of these children do not get essential amounts of iron, vitamins, or protein. Many have poor resistance to diseases—including minor ones, such as colds, and major ones, such as influenza. And in a longitudinal study, U.S. children who were malnourished at 3 years of age showed more aggressive and hyperactive behavior at age 8, had more externalizing problems at age 11, and evidenced more excessive motor behavior at age 17 (Liu & others, 2003).

In the United States, the Special Supplemental Nutrition Program for Women, Infants, and Children (WIC) provides nutritious foods and counseling on nutrition to about 7.5 million low-income participants. Positive influences on young children's nutrition and health have been found for participants in WIC (Black & others, 2004). For example, one recent study found that participating in the WIC program was linked with a lower risk for being overweight in young Mexican American children (Melgar-Quinonez & Kaiser, 2004). In another study, participation in the WIC program was related to improved nutrition in preschool children, including higher intake of fruit and lower intake of added sugar from snacks (Siega-Riz & others, 2004).

For most children in the United States and other developed nations, insufficient food is not the key problem. Instead, poor nutrition as a result of unhealthy eating habits and being overweight threaten their present and future health.

Health and Unhealthy Eating What children eat affects their skeletal growth, body shape, and susceptibility to disease (Brom, 2005; Tershakovec & others, 2003). From the late 1970s through the late 1990s, key dietary shifts took place in the United States not only for adults but also for children as young as 2 years old. According to one national study, the shifts included greater away-from-home consumption, large increases in total energy from salty snacks, soft drinks, and pizza; and large decreases in energy from low- and medium-fat milk and medium- and high-fat beef and pork (Nielsen, Siega-Riz, & Popkin, 2002). Another recent national assessment found that only 27 percent of 2- to 5-year-old children had good diets (Federal Interagency Forum on Child and Family Statistics, 2002). Their diets worsened as they became older—only 13 percent of 6- to 9-year-old children had healthy diets.

Unfortunately, eating fast food may be the key habit that U.S. children are learning today. Many children start eating fast foods in their preschool years (Poulton & Sexton, 1996). The habit of eating on the run and picking up fast-food meals clashes with concerns about the appropriate amount of fat content in children's diets (Troiano & Flegal, 1998). Most fast-food meals are high in protein, but the average American child does not need to be concerned about getting enough protein. What must be of concern is the vast number of children being raised on fast foods that are high in fat. The American Heart Association recommends that no more than 35 percent of daily calories should come from fat.

www.mhhe.com/santrockcd11

Helping an Overweight Child
Harvard Center for Children's Health
Child Health Guide

Obesity How much children should eat depends on their energy needs. These needs can be different even for children of the same age, sex, and size. Their energy requirements depend mostly on their physical activity and their **basal metabolism rate (BMR),** which is the minimum amount of energy a person uses in a resting state. But American culture encourages both adults and children to overeat. Food is everywhere you go. Portion sizes have grown. Fast-food restaurants give people the opportunity to "supersize" a meal at relatively low additional cost.

These trends are producing increasing numbers of overweight children and adults (Bell & Swinburn, 2004; Brom, 2006; Hedley & others, 2004; Jansen & others, 2005; Sizer & Whitney, 2006). The percentage of U.S. children who are overweight has more than doubled since 1980 and almost quadrupled since 1965 (National Center for Health Statistics, 2002a). Although genes contribute to weight problems, this trend cannot be attributed to changes in genetics. Instead, cultural changes have encouraged children to live in ways that make them fat—to eat too much, to eat junk food and fatty food, and to sit around, watch TV, and engage in little exercise.

Fifteen percent of U.S. children 6 to 11 years of age are overweight (Flegal, Ogden, & Carroll, 2004). The extent of the problem varies by gender and ethnic group. Girls are more likely than boys to be obese. Obesity is less common in African American than in White children during childhood, but during adolescence this reverses. And a high percentage of children who are in the 95th percentile among their peers in terms of weight are still likely to be overweight when they are in their thirties (Guo & others, 2002) (see figure 5.16). Obesity at 6 years of age results in approximately a 25 percent probability that the child will be obese as an adult; obesity at age 12 results in approximately a 75 percent chance that the adolescent will be an obese adult. Researchers also recently found that one-third of the mothers of overweight children believed their children were of normal weight (Maynard & others, 2003).

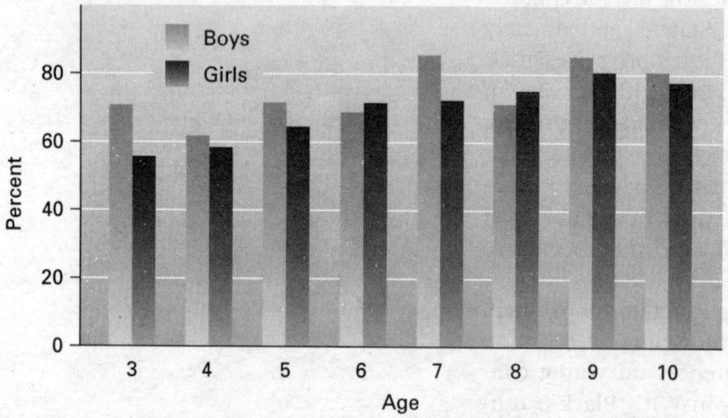

FIGURE 5.16 Relation of Being Overweight in Childhood to Being Overweight in Adulthood. *Note:* Data show the chance that children who are in the 95th percentile among their peers in terms of weight are likely to be overweight when they are 35.

basal metabolism rate (BMR) The minimum amount of energy an individual uses in a resting state.

Being overweight can be a serious problem (Treuth & others, 2003; Wardlaw, 2006). Obesity increases a child's risk of developing many medical and psychological problems. Obese children can develop pulmonary problems, such as sleep apnea (which involves upper airway obstruction) (Li & others, 2003). Hip problems also are common in obese children. Obese children are more likely than nonobese children to develop diabetes (Gaylor & Condren, 2004; Molnar, 2004). Obese children also are prone to have high blood pressure and elevated blood cholesterol levels (Burke & others, 2004; Clinton Smith, 2004). Once considered rare, hypertension in children has become increasingly common in association with obesity; obese children are three times more likely to develop hypertension than nonobese children (Sorof & Daniels, 2002). Low self-esteem and depression also are common outgrowths of obesity (Lumeng & others, 2003). One recent study also found that overweight and obese children were more likely than normal-weight children to be both the victims and perpetrators of bullying (Janssen & others, 2004).

Many experts on childhood obesity recommend a treatment that combines diet, exercise, and behavior modification (Caballero, 2004; Eliakim & others, 2004; Holcomb, 2004). Diets only moderately deficient in calories are more successful over the long term than are those involving extreme deprivation of calories. The context in which children eat also matters. In one recent study, children who ate with their families were more likely to eat low-fat foods (such as low-fat milk and salad dressings and lean meats) and vegetables and to drink fewer sodas than children who ate alone (Cullen, 2001). In this study, overweight children ate 50 percent of their meals in front of the TV, compared to only 35 percent of normal-weight children.

Pediatric nurses play an important role in the health of children, including providing advice to parents about ways to improve their children's eating habits. To read about the work of one pediatric nurse, see the Careers in Child Development insert.

CAREERS in CHILD DEVELOPMENT

Barbara Deloin
Pediatric Nurse

Barbara Deloin is a pediatric nurse in Denver, Colorado. She practices nursing in the Pediatric Oral Feeding Clinic and is involved in research as part of an irritable infant study for the Children's Hospital in Denver. She also is on the faculty of nursing at the Colorado Health Sciences Center. Deloin previously worked in San Diego where she was coordinator of the Child Health Program for the County of San Diego.

Her research interests focus on children with special health-care needs, especially high-risk infants and children and promoting positive parent-child experiences. Deloin was elected president of the National Association of Pediatric Nurse Associates and Practitioners for the 2000–2001 term.

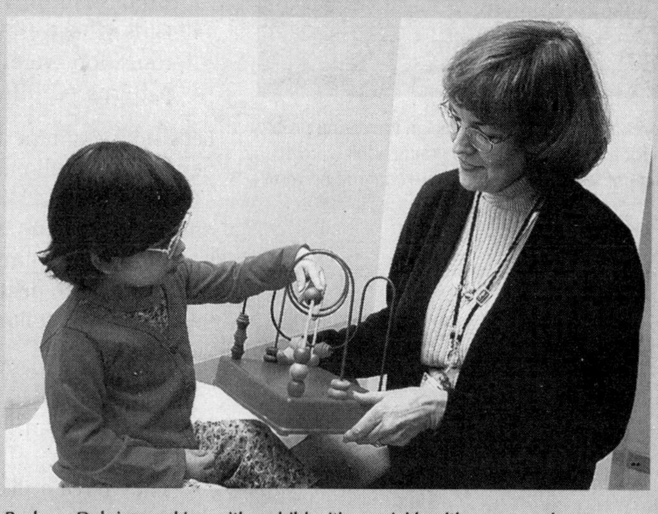

Barbara Deloin, working with a child with special health-care needs.

Adolescence

Adolescence is a critical juncture in the adoption of behaviors relevant to health (Fowler-Brown & Kahwati, 2004). Many of the factors linked to poor health habits and early death in the adult years begin during adolescence. Among U.S. adolescents, nutrition and being overweight are key problems. A comparison of adolescents in 28 countries found that U.S. adolescents ate more junk food than teenagers in most other countries (World Health Organization, 2000). They were also more likely to eat fried food and less likely to eat fruits and vegetables. Not surprisingly, the percentage of overweight adolescents has been increasing. As figure 5.17 shows, African American girls and Latino girls especially have high risks of being overweight in adolescence (National Center for Health Statistics, 2002b). Another study revealed that the higher obesity rate for African American girls is linked with a diet higher in calories and fat, as well as sedentary behavior (Sanchez-Johnsen & others, 2004).

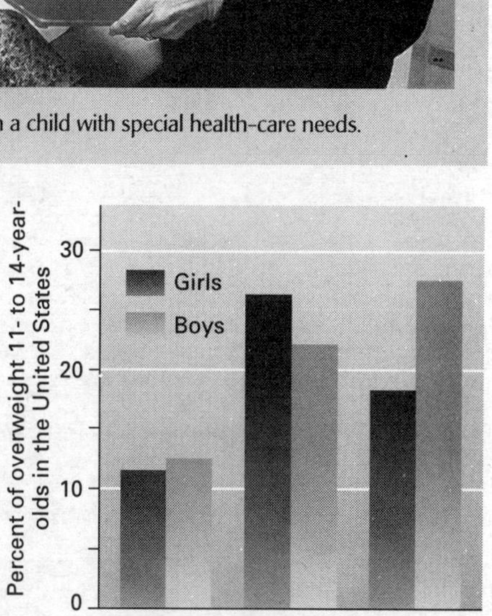

FIGURE 5.17 Percentage of Overweight U.S. Adolescent Boys and Girls in Different Ethnic Groups

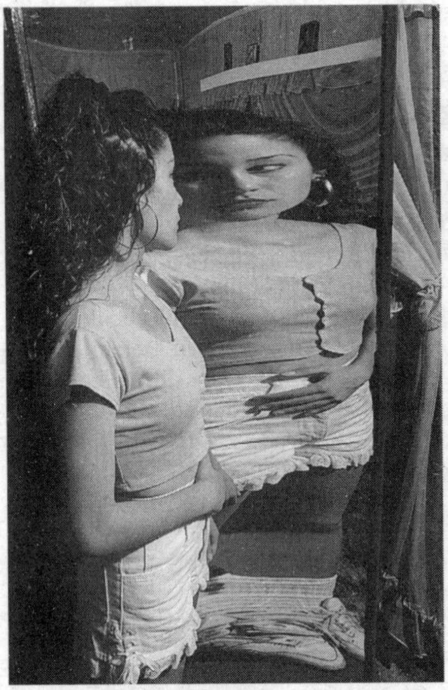

Anorexia nervosa has become an increasing problem for adolescent girls and young adult women. *What are some possible causes of anorexia nervosa?*

Adolescents' problems with weight have been linked with other characteristics of puberty that we discussed earlier: during puberty, adolescents, especially non-Latino White girls, tend to become intensely concerned about their appearance, especially their weight, and this concern may lead to unhealthy eating and excessive dieting.

A number of studies document that adolescent girls have a strong desire to weigh less (Graber & Brooks-Gunn, 2001). Girls who are motivated to try to look like the girls and women they see in the media are especially likely to become very concerned about their weight (Field & others, 2001). Relationships with parents are also related to adolescent girls' eating behavior. One study found that over a one-year period, poor relationships with parents were linked with increased dieting by adolescent girls (Archibald, Graber, & Brooks-Gunn, 1999).

Eating disorders have become an increasing problem among U.S. adolescents (Brom, 2006; Dietz & Robinson, 2005; Lowry & others, 2005; Polivy & others, 2003; Sizer & Whitney, 2006). Research on adolescent eating disorders reveals the following:

- Girls who felt negatively about their bodies in early adolescence were more likely to have developed eating disorders when they were assessed two years later than were girls who did not feel negatively about their bodies (Attie & Brooks-Gunn, 1989).
- Girls who were both sexually active with their boyfriends and in pubertal transition were the most likely to be dieting or engaged in disordered eating patterns (Cauffman, 1994).

Let's now examine two eating disorders that may appear in adolescence: anorexia nervosa and bulimia nervosa.

Anorexia Nervosa **Anorexia nervosa** is an eating disorder that involves the relentless pursuit of thinness through starvation. Anorexia nervosa is a serious disorder that can lead to death. Three main characteristics of people diagnosed with anorexia nervosa are as follows:

- They weigh less than 85 percent of what is considered normal for their age and height.
- They have an intense fear of gaining weight. The fear does not decrease with weight loss.
- They have a distorted image of their body shape (Wiseman, Sunday, & Becker, 2005). Even when they are extremely thin, they see themselves as too fat. They never think they are thin enough, especially in the abdomen, buttocks, and thighs. They usually weigh themselves frequently, often take their body measurements, and gaze critically at themselves in mirrors (Seidenfeld, Sosin, & Rickert, 2004).

Anorexia nervosa typically begins in the early to middle teenage years, often following an episode of dieting and some type of life stress (Lee & others, 2005). It is about 10 times more likely to characterize females than males. When anorexia nervosa does occur in males, the symptoms and other characteristics (such as a distorted body image and family conflict) are usually similar to those reported by females who have the disorder (Ariceli & others, 2005; Olivardia & others, 1995).

Although most U.S. adolescent girls have been on a diet at some point, slightly less than 1 percent ever develop anorexia nervosa (Walters & Kendler, 1994). Most anorexics are White adolescent or young adult females from well-educated, middle- and upper-income families that are competitive and high-achieving (Schmidt, 2003). They set high standards, become stressed about not being able to reach the standards, and are intensely concerned about how others perceive them (Striegel-Moore, Silberstein, & Rodin, 1993). Unable to meet these high expectations, they turn to something they can control: their weight.

anorexia nervosa An eating disorder that involves the relentless pursuit of thinness through starvation.

The fashion image in the American culture that emphasizes that "thin is beautiful" contributes to the incidence of anorexia nervosa (Polivy & others, 2003). This image is reflected in the saying, "You never can be too rich or too thin." The media portrays thin as beautiful in their choice of fashion models, which many adolescent girls want to emulate.

Bulimia Nervosa While anorexics control their eating by restricting it, most bulimics cannot (Mitchell & Mazzeo, 2004). **Bulimia nervosa** is an eating disorder in which the individual consistently follows a binge-and-purge eating pattern. The bulimic goes on an eating binge and then purges by self-inducing vomiting or using a laxative. Many people binge and purge occasionally. A person is considered to have a serious bulimic disorder only if the episodes occur at least twice a week for three months.

As with anorexics, most bulimics are preoccupied with food, have a strong fear of becoming overweight, and are depressed or anxious (Garcia-Alba, 2004; Quadflieg & Fichter, 2003; Ramacciotti & others, 2005; Speranza & others, 2005). Unlike anorexics, people who binge and purge typically fall within a normal weight range, which makes bulimia more difficult to detect (Orbanic, 2001).

Bulimia nervosa typically begins in late adolescence or early adulthood. About 90 percent of the cases are women. Approximately 1 to 2 percent of women are estimated to develop bulimia nervosa (Gotesdam & Agras, 1995). Many women who develop bulimia nervosa were somewhat overweight before the onset of the disorder, and the binge eating often began during an episode of dieting. One recent study of adolescent girls found that increased dieting, pressure to be thin, exaggerated emphasis on appearance, body dissatisfaction, depression symptoms, low self-esteem, and low social support predicted binge eating two years later (Stice, Presnell, & Spangler, 2002). As with anorexia nervosa, about 70 percent of individuals who develop bulimia nervosa eventually recover from the disorder (Agras & others, 2004; Keel & others, 1999).

bulimia nervosa An eating disorder that involves a binge-and-purge sequence on a regular basis.

Exercise

Exercise is linked with many aspects of being physically and mentally healthy in children and adults (Buck & others, 2007). Are children getting enough exercise? A 1997 national poll found that only 22 percent of U.S. children in grades 4 through 12 were physically active for 30 minutes every day of the week (Harris, 1997). Their parents said their children were too busy watching TV, spending time on the computer, or playing video games to exercise much. Boys were more physically active at all ages than girls. In one historical comparison, the percentage of children involved in daily PE programs in schools decreased from 80 percent in 1969 to 20 percent in 1999 (Health Management Resources, 2001) (see figure 5.18). A recent comparison of adolescent health behavior in 28 countries found that U.S. adolescents exercised less than their counterparts in most other countries (World Health Organization, 2000). Just two-thirds of U.S. adolescents exercised at least twice a week, compared to 80 percent or more adolescents in Ireland, Austria, Germany, and the Slovak Republic.

Children become less active as they reach and progress through adolescence (Amisola & Jacobson, 2003; Merrick & others, 2005). In one recent study, activity habits of more than 1,000 African American and more than 1,000 non-Latino White girls were examined annually from 9 to 10 years of age to 18 to 19 years of age (Kimm & others, 2002). The study did not examine boys because it was designed to determine why more African American women than non-Latino White women become obese. At 9 to 10 years of age, most girls reported that they were

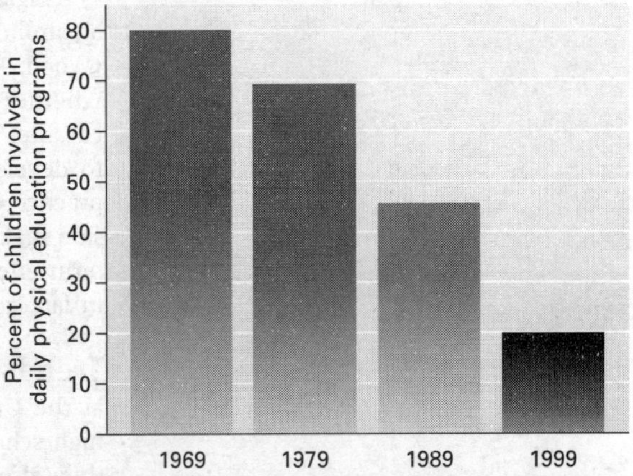

FIGURE 5.18 Percentage of Children Involved in Daily Physical Education Programs in the United States from 1969 to 1999. There has been a dramatic drop in the percentage of children participating in daily physical education programs in the United States from 80 percent in 1969 to only 20 percent in 1999.

engaging in some physical activity outside of school. However, by 16 to 17 years of age, 56 percent of African American girls and 31 percent of non-Latino White girls were not engaging in any regular physical activity in their spare time. By 18 to 19 years of age, the figures were 70 percent and 29 percent, respectively. In sum, substantial declines in physical activity occur during adolescence in girls and are greater in African American than non-Latino White girls (Kimm & Obarzanek, 2002).

Television watching is linked with low activity and obesity in children (Fox & others, 2004). A related concern is the dramatic increase in computer use by children. A recent review of research concluded that the total time that children spend in front of a television or computer screen places them at risk for reduced activity and possible weight gain (Jordan, 2004). A longitudinal study found that higher incidence of watching TV in childhood and adolescence was linked with being overweight, lower physical fitness, and higher cholesterol levels at 26 years of age (Hancox, Milne, & Poulton, 2004).

Some ways to get children and adolescents to exercise more include the following:

- Improve physical fitness classes in schools.
- Offer more physical activity programs run by volunteers at school facilities.
- Have children plan community and school exercise activities that really interest them.
- Encourage families to focus on physical activity and encourage parents to exercise more.

An exciting possibility is that physical exercise might buffer adolescents' stress. In one investigation of 364 females in grades 7 through 11 in Los Angeles, the negative impact of stressful events on health declined as exercise levels increased (Brown & Siegel, 1988). Another investigation found that adolescents who exercised regularly coped more effectively with stress and had more positive identities than did adolescents who engaged in little exercise (Grimes & Mattimore, 1989).

Substance Use

Besides exercising, another important healthy practice is to avoid using substances such as alcohol, cigarettes, and other psychoactive drugs. In chapter 4, we described the negative effects on the fetus and developing child that can result from drug use by the pregnant mother. Here we will examine how drug use affects adolescents.

Cigarette smoking begins primarily in childhood and adolescence, and many alcoholics established their drinking habits during secondary school or college (Wood, Vinson, & Sher, 2001). In fact, most adolescents use drugs at some point, whether limited to alcohol, caffeine, and cigarettes or extended to marijuana, cocaine, and other so-called hard drugs. However, drug use poses a special hazard to development when adolescents use drugs as a way of coping with stress. This practice can interfere with the development of coping skills and responsible decision making. Drug use in childhood or early adolescence has more detrimental long-term effects on the development of responsible, competent behavior than drug use in late adolescence (Newcomb & Bentler, 1988).

Trends in Drug Use Each year since 1975 Lloyd Johnston and his colleagues at the University of Michigan have carefully monitored the drug use of America's high school seniors in a wide range of public and private high schools. Since 1991 they also have surveyed drug use by eighth- and tenth-graders. The University of Michigan study is called the Monitoring the Future Study. In 2004, the study surveyed approximately 50,000 students in nearly 400 secondary schools.

According to this study, the use of drugs among U.S. secondary school students declined in the 1980s but began to increase in the early 1990s (Johnston & others,

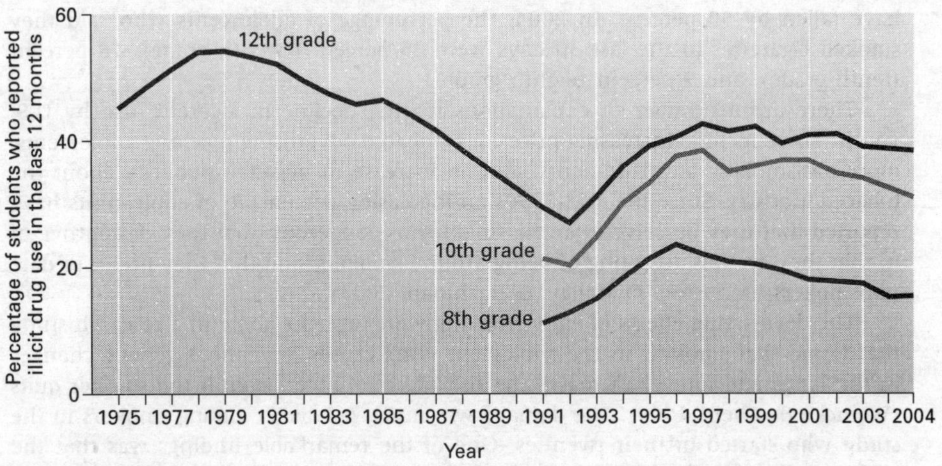

FIGURE 5.19 Trends in Drug Use by U.S. Eighth-, Tenth-, and Twelfth-Grade Students. This graph shows the percentage of U.S. eighth-, tenth-, and twelfth-grade students who reported having taken an illicit drug in the last 12 months from 1991 to 2004 for eighth- and tenth-graders, and from 1975 to 2004 for twelfth-graders (Johnston & others, 2005).

2005). Since the late 1990s the proportions of tenth- and twelfth-grade students who use any illicit drug have been gradually declining (Johnston & others, 2005). In 2004, the proportion of students reporting the use of any illicit drug in the past 30 days declined at all three grade levels (see figure 5.19). Nonetheless, even with the recent declines, the United States still has the highest rate of adolescent drug use of any industrialized nation. Also, the Monitoring the Future survey likely underestimates the percentage of adolescents who take drugs because it does not include high school dropouts, who have a higher rate of drug use than do students who are still in school.

Johnston and his colleagues believe that "generational forgetting" contributed to the rise of adolescent drug use in the 1990s, with adolescents' beliefs about the dangers of drugs eroding considerably (Johnston, O'Malley, & Bachman, 2005). The recent downturn in drug use by U.S. adolescents has been attributed to such factors as an increase in the perceived dangers of drug use and a sobering effect from the terrorist attacks of 9/11.

Alcohol How extensive is alcohol use by U.S. adolescents? Sizable declines have occurred in recent years (Johnston & others, 2005). The percentage of U.S. eighth-graders saying that they had any alcohol to drink in the past 30 days has fallen from a 1996 high of 26 percent to 19 percent in 2004. From 2001 to 2004, 30-day prevalence among tenth-graders fell from 39 to 35 percent. Monthly prevalence among high school seniors was 72 percent in 1980 but had declined to 48 percent in 2004.

Binge drinking (defined in the Monitoring the Future surveys as having five or more drinks in a row in the last two weeks) by high school seniors declined from 41 percent in 1980 to 30 percent in 2002 but increased slightly to 33 percent in 2004. Binge drinking by eighth- and tenth-graders also has dropped in recent years. A consistent sex difference occurs in binge drinking, with males engaging in this more than females. In 1997, 39 percent of male high school seniors said they had been drunk in the last two weeks, compared with 29 percent of their female counterparts.

Cigarette Smoking Cigarette smoking is also decreasing among adolescents. Cigarette smoking peaked in 1996 and 1997 and then gradually declined (Johnston & others, 2005). Following peak use in 1996, smoking rates for U.S. eighth-graders have fallen by 50 percent. In 2004, the percentage of adolescents who said they smoked cigarettes in the last 30 days were 25 percent (twelfth grade), 16 percent (tenth grade), and 9 percent (eighth grade).

There are a number of explanations for the decline in cigarette use by U.S. youth. These include increasing prices, less tobacco advertising reaching adolescents, more antismoking advertisements, and an increase in negative publicity about the tobacco industry. Since the mid-1990s an increasing percentage of adolescents have reported that they perceive cigarette smoking as dangerous, that they disapprove of it, that they are less accepting of being around smokers, and that they prefer to date nonsmokers (Johnston, O'Malley, & Bachman, 2003).

The devastating effects of early smoking were brought home in a research study that found that smoking in the adolescent years causes permanent genetic changes in the lungs and forever increases the risk of lung cancer, even if the smoker quits (Weincke & others, 1999). The damage was much less likely among smokers in the study who started in their twenties. One of the remarkable findings was that the early age of onset of smoking was more important in predicting genetic damage than how much the individuals smoked.

Prescription Painkillers An alarming trend has recently emerged in adolescents' use of prescription painkillers. A 2004 survey revealed that 18 percent of U.S. adolescents had used Vicodin at some point in their lifetime while 10 percent had used Oxycontin (Partnership for a Drug-Free America, 2005). These drugs fall into the general class of drugs called narcotics and they are highly addictive. In this recent national survey, 9 percent of adolescents also said they had abused cough medications to intentionally get high. The University of Michigan began including Oxycontin in its survey of 12th graders in 2002 and adolescents' reports of using it increased from 4 percent to 5 percent from 2002 to 2004 (Johnston & others, 2005).

In the Partnership for a Drug Free America (2005) survey, almost one-half of the adolescents said that using prescription medications to get high was much safer than using street drugs. About one-third of the adolescents erroneously believed that prescription painkillers are not addictive. The adolescents cited the medicine cabinets of their parents or of a friends' parents as the main source for their prescription painkillers.

A recent analysis of data from the National Survey on Drug Use and Health revealed that abuse of prescription painkillers by U.S. adolescents may become an epidemic (Sung & others, 2005). In this survey, adolescents especially at risk for abusing prescription painkillers were likely to already be using illicit drugs, came from low-socioeconomic status families, had detached parents, or had friends who used drugs.

The Roles of Parents and Peers Parents and peers play important roles in preventing adolescent drug abuse (Callas, Flynn, & Worden, 2004; Eitle, 2005; Engels & others, 2005; Nash, McQueen, & Bray, 2005; Windle & Windle, 2003). One recent study revealed that parental control and monitoring were linked with lower drug use by adolescents (Fletcher, Steinberg, & Williams-Wheeler, 2004). In another study, low parental involvement, peer pressure, and associating with problem-behaving friends were linked with higher use of drugs by adolescents (Simons-Morton & others, 2001). Also, in a recent national survey, parents who were more involved in setting limits (such as where adolescents went after school and what they were exposed to on TV and the Internet) were more likely to have adolescents who did not use drugs (National Center for Addiction and Substance Abuse, 2001). Further, one longitudinal study linked the early onset of substance abuse with early childhood predictors (Kaplow & others, 2002). Risk factors at kindergarten for substance use at 10 to 12 years of age included being male, having a parent who abused substances, a low level of verbal reasoning by parents, and low social-problem-solving skills.

Review and Reflect • LEARNING GOAL 4

4 Characterize health in childhood and adolescence

Review

- What are the key health problems facing children?
- What are some important aspects of children's nutrition and eating behavior?
- What role does exercise play in children's development?
- What is the nature of substance use in adolescence?

Reflect

- What were your eating habits like as a child? In what ways are they similar to or different from your current eating habits? Were your early eating habits a forerunner of whether or not you have weight problems today?

REACH YOUR LEARNING GOALS

PHYSICAL DEVELOPMENT AND HEALTH

- **1 BODY GROWTH AND CHANGE**
  - Growth Patterns
  - Infancy and Childhood
  - Puberty
- **2 THE BRAIN**
  - Brain Physiology
  - Infancy
  - Childhood
  - Adolescence
- **3 SLEEP**
  - Infancy
  - Childhood
  - Adolescence
- **4 HEALTH**
  - Illness and Injuries Among Children and Adolescents
  - Nutrition and Eating Behavior
  - Exercise
  - Substance Use

SUMMARY

1 Discuss developmental changes in the body

- Human growth follows cephalocaudal and proximodistal patterns. In a cephalocaudal pattern, growth occurs first at the top and gradually moves to the bottom. In a proximodistal pattern, growth begins at the center of the body and then moves toward the extremities.
- Height and weight increase rapidly in infancy and then take a slower course during childhood. The average North American newborn is 20 inches long and weighs 7½ pounds. Infants grow about 1 inch per month during their first year. In early childhood, girls are only slightly smaller and lighter than boys. Growth is slow and consistent in middle and late childhood.
- Puberty is a rapid maturation involving hormonal and body changes that occur primarily in early adolescence. There are wide individual variations in the age at which puberty begins. Key hormones involved in puberty are testosterone, estradiol, and growth hormones. Key physical changes of puberty include a growth spurt as well as sexual maturation. The growth spurt occurs on the average about two years sooner for girls than for boys. Early maturation favors boys during adolescence, but in adulthood late-maturing boys have a more successful identity. Early-maturing girls are vulnerable to a number of problems.

2 Describe how the brain changes

- Each hemisphere of the brain's cerebral cortex has four lobes (frontal, occipital, temporal, and parietal) with somewhat different primary functions. Neurons are cells in the brain that process information. Communication between neurons occurs through the release of neurotransmitters at gaps called synapses. Communication is speeded by the myelin sheath that covers most axons. Clusters of neurons, known as neural circuits, work together to handle particular types of information. Specialization of functioning does occur in the brain's hemispheres, as in language, but for the most part both hemispheres are at work in most complex functions.
- Researchers have found that experience influences the brain's development. Myelination begins prenatally and continues after birth. In infancy, one of the most impressive changes in the brain is the enormous increase in synaptic connections. These connections are overproduced and later pruned.
- During early childhood, the brain and head grow more rapidly than any other part of the body. Rapid distinct bursts of growth occur in different areas of the brain from 3 to 15 years of age.
- In adolescence, the later development of the frontal lobes (where reasoning is a major function) and the earlier dominance of the amygdala and limbic system (where emotion is a major function) are thought to play important roles in explaining the risk-taking behavior of adolescents.

3 Summarize how sleep patterns change as children develop

- By about 4 months, most infants have sleep patterns similar to those of adults. REM sleep occurs more in infancy than in childhood and adulthood. Sleeping arrangements vary across cultures.
- Most young children sleep through the night and have one daytime nap.
- Many adolescents stay up later than when they were children and are getting less sleep than they need. Research suggests that as adolescents get older, the hormone melatonin is released later at night, shifting the adolescent's biological clock.

4 Characterize health in childhood and adolescence

- In recent decades, vaccines have eradicated many diseases that once were responsible for the deaths of many young children. The disorders most likely to be fatal during early childhood today are birth defects, cancer, and heart disease. Accidents are the number one cause of death in young children, followed by cancer. For the most part, middle and late childhood is a time of excellent health. Adolescence is a critical juncture in health because many health habits are established in adolescence. The three leading causes of death in adolescence are accidents, homicide, and suicide. A special concern is the health of children living in poverty here and abroad. A leading cause of child death in impoverished countries is dehydration produced by diarrhea. There also has been a dramatic increase in low-income countries in the number of children who have died because of HIV/AIDS transmitted to them by their parents.
- The importance of adequate energy intake consumed in a loving and supportive environment in infancy cannot be overstated. Breast-feeding is usually recommended over bottle-feeding. Marasmus and kwashiorkor are diseases caused by severe malnutrition. Concerns about nutrition in childhood focus on fat content in diet and obesity. Slightly more than 20 percent of U.S. children are overweight and 10 percent are obese. Obesity increases a child's risk of developing many medical and psychological problems. Nutrition and being overweight

are also key problems among adolescents. The eating disorders of anorexia nervosa and bulimia nervosa can develop in adolescence.

- Most children and adolescents are not getting nearly enough exercise.
- The United States has the highest rate of adolescent drug use of any industrialized nation. Alcohol and cigarette smoking are special concerns. An alarming trend has recently occurred in the increased use of prescription painkillers by adolescants. Parents and peers play important roles in preventing drug abuse in adolescents.

KEY TERMS

cephalocaudal pattern 139
proximodistal pattern 139
growth hormone deficiency 140
puberty 141
menarche 142
hormones 142
spermarche 142
androgens 142
estrogens 142
neurons 146
lateralization 147
sudden infant death syndrome (SIDS) 155
marasmus 162
kwashiorkor 162
basal metabolism rate (BMR) 164
anorexia nervosa 166
bulimia nervosa 168

KEY PEOPLE

Mark Rosenzweig 148
Charles Nelson 149
Laurence Steinberg 153

E-LEARNING TOOLS

To help you master the material in this chapter, visit the Online Learning Center for *Child Development,* eleventh, ed. **(www.mhhe.com/santrockcd11),** where you will find these additional resources:

Taking It to the Net

1. Juan and Monika are first-time parents. Monika insists that their 2-month-old daughter, Carmen, can tell the difference between her mother and father's face, voice, and touch. Juan says that is ridiculous. Who is correct?
2. Aleysha's mother, Carolyn, who just arrived from out of town and saw her 3-month-old grandson, Cameron, for the first time, exclaimed, "What are you feeding this roly-poly hunk? He looks overweight to me." Aleysha was shocked. She didn't think a baby could be overweight. Should she cut back on his feedings?
3. Tina, who has three children, volunteers to babysit for her friend Natalie's 5-month-old boy so that Natalie can go on a job interview. As Tina is undressing Dylan, she thinks it's odd that he doesn't seem to be able to turn over in his crib. When she cradles him in her arm to bathe him, he feels "floppy" and appears to lack muscle strength. Is Dylan evidencing any motor developmental delays?

Nursing, Parenting, and Teaching Exercises

Build your decision-making skills by trying your hand at the scenarios on the Online Learning Center.

Video Clips

The Online Learning Center includes the following videos for this chapter:

- Brain Development and Cognition
  Renowned infant brain researcher, Charles Nelson, describes findings from his research that show that brain development influences cognitive development.
- Influence of Brain Development in Puberty
  Ronald Dahl, MD, Department of Psychiatry, University of Pittsburgh, emphasizes the importance of considering the influence of brain development on puberty more so than hormones: "Puberty happens at the level of the brain."
- Obesity
  Rebecca Roach, Registered Dietician, discusses reasons for the high rate of obesity in children today.
- Talking About Drugs at Age 14
  Two adolescent girls express their views about drug use among teens. One girl says frankly that smoking a joint is no worse than drinking a glass of wine.

Chapter 6 MOTOR, SENSORY, AND PERCEPTUAL DEVELOPMENT

A baby is the most complicated object made by unskilled labor.

—ANONYMOUS

CHAPTER OUTLINE

MOTOR DEVELOPMENT

The Dynamic Systems View

Reflexes

Gross Motor Skills

Fine Motor Skills

Handedness

SENSORY AND PERCEPTUAL DEVELOPMENT

What Are Sensation and Perception?

The Ecological View

Vision

Hearing

Other Senses

Intermodal Perception

PERCEPTUAL-MOTOR COUPLING

LEARNING GOALS

1. Describe how motor skills develop
2. Outline the course of sensory and perceptual development
3. Discuss the connection of perception and action

The Stories of Stevie Wonder and Andrea Bocelli

Two "sensations": Stevie Wonder and Andrea Bocelli. *How have they adapted to life without sight?*

Blind individuals sometimes achieve greatness through the medium of sound. In 1950, the newly born Steveland Morris was placed in an incubator in which he was given too much oxygen. The result was permanent blindness. In 1962, as 12-year-old singer and musician Stevie Wonder, he began a performing and recording career that has included such hits as "My Cherie Amour" and "Signed, Sealed, Delivered." At the beginning of the twenty-first century, his music is still perceived by some as "wondrous."

At age 12, Andrea Bocelli lost his sight in a soccer mishap. Today, now in his forties and after a brief career as a lawyer, Andrea has taken the music world by storm with his magnificent, classically trained voice.

Although Bocelli's and Stevie Wonder's accomplishments are great, imagine how very difficult it must have been for them as children to do many of the things we take for granted in sighted children. Yet children who lose one channel of sensation—such as vision—often compensate for the loss by enhancing their sensory skills in another area—such as hearing or touch. For example, researchers have found that blind individuals are more accurate at locating a sound source and have greater sensitivity to touch than sighted individuals (Bavelier & Neville, 2002; Levanen & Hamdorf, 2001; Lessard & others, 1998). In one study, blind children were more skillful than blindfolded sighted children at using hearing to detect walls (Ashmead & others, 1998). In this study, acoustic information was most useful when the blind children were within one meter of a wall at which point sound pressure increases.

PREVIEW

Think about what is required for children to find their way around their environment, to play sports, or to create art. These activities require both active perception and precisely timed motor actions. Neither innate, automatic movements nor simple sensations are enough to let children do the things they do every day. How do children develop perceptual and motor abilities? In this chapter, we will focus first on the development of motor skills, then on sensory and perceptual development, and on the coupling of perceptual-motor skills.

1 MOTOR DEVELOPMENT

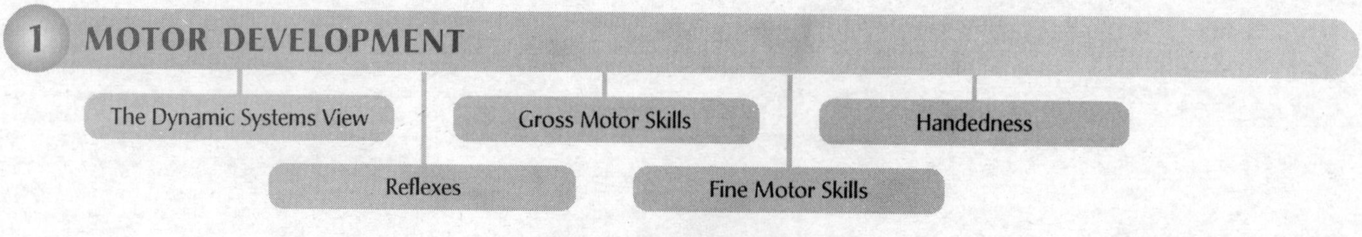

Most adults are capable of coordinated, purposive actions of considerable skill, including driving a car, playing golf, and typing effectively on a computer keyboard. Some adults have extraordinary motor skills, such as those involved in winning an Olympic pole vault competition, performing heart surgery, painting a masterpiece, or in the case of Stevie Wonder, being extraordinarily talented at playing the piano. Look all you want at a newborn infant, and you will observe nothing even remotely approaching these skilled actions. How, then, do the motor behaviors of adults come about?

The Dynamic Systems View

Developmentalist Arnold Gesell (1934) thought his painstaking observations had revealed how people develop their motor skills. He had discovered that infants and children develop rolling, sitting, standing, and other motor skills in a fixed order and within specific time frames. These observations, said Gesell, show that motor development comes about through the unfolding of a genetic plan, or *maturation*.

Later studies, however, demonstrated that the sequence of developmental milestones is not as fixed as Gesell indicated and not due as much to heredity as Gesell argued (Adolph, 2005; Adolph & Berger, 2005, 2006). In the 1990s, the study of motor development experienced a renaissance as psychologists developed new insights about *how* motor skills develop (Thelen & Smith, 1998, 2006). One increasingly influential theory is dynamic systems theory, proposed by Esther Thelen.

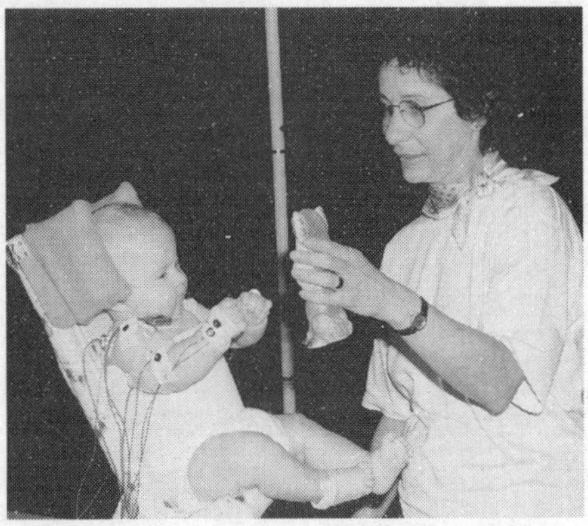

Esther Thelen is shown conducting an experiment to discover how infants learn to control their arms to reach and grasp for objects. A computer device is used to monitor the infant's arm movements and to track muscle patterns. Thelen's research is conducted from a dynamic systems perspective. *What is the nature of this perspective?*

According to **dynamic systems theory,** infants assemble motor skills for perceiving and acting. Notice that perception and action are coupled according to this theory (Thelen, 1995, 2000, 2001; Thelen & Smith, 1998, 2006; Thelen & Whitmeyer, 2005). To develop motor skills, infants must perceive something in the environment that motivates them to act and use their perceptions to fine-tune their movements. Motor skills represent solutions to the infant's goals.

How is a motor skill developed according to this theory? When infants are motivated to do something, they might create a new motor behavior. The new behavior is the result of many converging factors: the development of the nervous system, the body's physical properties and its possibilities for movement, the goal the child is motivated to reach, and the environmental support for the skill. For example, babies learn to walk only when maturation of the nervous system allows them to control certain leg muscles, when their legs have grown enough to support their weight, and when they want to move (Hallemans & others, 2005).

Esther Thelen's Research

Mastering a motor skill requires the infant's active efforts to coordinate several components of the skill (Spencer & others, 2000). Infants explore and select possible solutions to the demands of a new task; they assemble adaptive patterns by modifying their current movement patterns. The first step occurs when the infant is motivated by a new challenge—such as the desire to cross a room—and gets into the "ballpark" of the task demands by taking a couple of stumbling steps. Then, the infant "tunes" these movements to make them smoother and more effective. The tuning is achieved through repeated cycles of action and perception of the consequences of that action. According to the dynamic systems view, even universal milestones, such as crawling, reaching, and walking, are learned through this process of adaptation: infants modulate their movement patterns to fit a new task by exploring and selecting possible configurations (Adolph & Berger, 2006; Thelen & Smith, 2006).

To see how dynamic systems theory explains motor behavior, imagine that you offer a new toy to a baby named Gabriel (Thelen & others, 1993). There is no exact program that can tell Gabriel ahead of time how to move his arm and hand and fingers to grasp the toy. Gabriel must adapt to his goal—grasping the toy—and the context. From his sitting position, he must make split-second adjustments to extend his arm, holding his body steady so that his arm and torso don't plow into the toy. Muscles in his arm and shoulder contract and stretch in a host of combinations, exerting a variety of forces. He improvises a way to reach out with one arm and wrap his fingers around the toy.

Thus, according to dynamic systems theory, motor development is not a passive process in which genes dictate the unfolding of a sequence of skills over time. Rather, the infant actively puts together a skill to achieve a goal within the constraints set by the infant's body and environment. Nature and nurture, the infant and the environment, are all working together as part of an ever-changing system.

As we examine the course of motor development, we will describe how dynamic systems theory applies to some specific skills. First, though, let's examine how the story of motor development begins with reflexes.

dynamic systems theory A theory, proposed by Esther Thelen, that seeks to explain how motor behaviors are assembled for perceiving and acting.

Reflexes

The newborn is not completely helpless. Among other things, it has some basic reflexes. For example, the newborn automatically holds its breath and contracts its throat to keep water out. *Reflexes* are built-in reactions to stimuli; they govern the newborn's movements, which are automatic and beyond the newborn's control. Reflexes are genetically carried survival mechanisms. They allow infants to respond adaptively to their environment before they have had the opportunity to learn.

The rooting and sucking reflexes are important examples. Both have survival value for newborn mammals, who must find a mother's breast to obtain nourishment. The **rooting reflex** occurs when the infant's cheek is stroked or the side of the mouth is touched. In response, the infant turns its head toward the side that was touched in an apparent effort to find something to suck. The **sucking reflex** occurs when newborns automatically suck an object placed in their mouths. This reflex enables newborns to get nourishment before they have associated a nipple with food.

Another example is the **Moro reflex,** which occurs in response to a sudden, intense noise or movement. When startled, the newborn arches its back, throws back its head, and flings out its arms and legs. Then the newborn rapidly closes its arms and legs. The Moro reflex is believed to be a way of grabbing for support while falling; it would have had survival value for our primate ancestors.

Some reflexes—coughing, blinking, and yawning, for example—persist throughout life. They are as important for the adult as they are for the infant. Other reflexes, though, disappear several months following birth, as the infant's brain matures and voluntary control over many behaviors develops. The rooting, sucking, and Moro reflexes, for example, all tend to disappear when the infant is 3 to 4 months old.

The movements of some reflexes eventually become incorporated into more complex, voluntary actions. One important example is the **grasping reflex,** which occurs when something touches the infant's palms. The infant responds by grasping tightly. By the end of the third month, the grasping reflex diminishes, and the infant shows a more voluntary grasp. For example, when an infant sees a mobile turning slowly above a crib, it may reach out and try to grasp it. As its motor development becomes smoother, the infant will grasp objects, carefully manipulate them, and explore their qualities. An overview of the reflexes we have discussed, along with others, is given in figure 6.1.

Although reflexes are automatic and inborn, differences in reflexive behavior are soon apparent. For example, the sucking capabilities of newborns vary considerably. Some newborns are efficient at forceful sucking and obtaining milk; others are not as adept and get tired before they are full. Most infants take several weeks to establish a sucking style that is coordinated with the way the mother is holding the infant, the way milk is coming out of the bottle or breast, and the infant's temperament.

Pediatrician T. Berry Brazelton (1956) observed how infants' sucking changed as they grew older. Over 85 percent of the infants engaged in considerable sucking behavior unrelated to feeding. They sucked their fingers, their fists, and their pacifiers. By the age of 1 year, most had stopped the sucking behavior, but as many as 40 percent of children continue to suck their thumbs after they have started school (Kessen, Haith, & Salapatek, 1970). Most developmentalists do not attach a great deal of significance to this behavior.

Gross Motor Skills

Ask any parents about their baby, and sooner or later you are likely to hear about one or more motor milestones, such as "Cassandra just learned to crawl," "Jesse is finally sitting alone," or "Angela took her first step last week." Parents proudly announce such milestones as their children transform themselves from babies unable

rooting reflex A newborn's built-in reaction that occurs when the infant's cheek is stroked or the side of the mouth is touched. In response, the infant turns its head toward the side that was touched, in an apparent effort to find something to suck.

sucking reflex A newborn's built-in reaction of automatically sucking an object placed in its mouth. The sucking reflex enables the infant to get nourishment before it has associated a nipple with food.

Moro reflex A neonatal startle response that occurs in reaction to a sudden, intense noise or movement. When startled, the newborn arches its back, throws its head back, and flings out its arms and legs. Then the newborn rapidly closes its arms and legs to the center of the body.

grasping reflex A neonatal reflex that occurs when something touches the infant's palms. The infant responds by grasping tightly.

Reflex	Stimulation	Infant's Response	Developmental Pattern
Blinking	Flash of light, puff of air	Closes both eyes	Permanent
Babinski	Sole of foot stroked	Fans out toes, twists foot in	Disappears after 9 months to 1 year
Grasping	Palms touched	Grasps tightly	Weakens after 3 months, disappears after 1 year
Moro (startle)	Sudden stimulation, such as hearing loud noise or being dropped	Startles, arches back, throws head back, flings out arms and legs and then rapidly closes them to center of body	Disappears after 3 to 4 months
Rooting	Cheek stroked or side of mouth touched	Turns head, opens mouth, begins sucking	Disappears after 3 to 4 months
Stepping	Infant held above surface and feet lowered to touch surface	Moves feet as if to walk	Disappears after 3 to 4 months
Sucking	Object touching mouth	Sucks automatically	Disappears after 3 to 4 months
Swimming	Infant put face down in water	Makes coordinated swimming movements	Disappears after 6 to 7 months
Tonic neck	Infant placed on back	Forms fists with both hands and usually turns head to the right (sometimes called the "fencer's pose" because the infant looks like it is assuming a fencer's position)	Disappears after 2 months

FIGURE 6.1 Infant Reflexes

to lift their heads to toddlers who grab things off the grocery store shelf, chase a cat, and participate actively in the family's social life (Thelen, 1995, 2000). These milestones are examples of **gross motor skills,** which are skills that involve large-muscle activities, such as moving one's arms and walking.

The Development of Posture How do gross motor skills develop? As a foundation, these skills, like many other activities, require postural control (Thelen, 1995, 2000; Thelen & Smith, 2006). For example, to track moving objects, you must be able to control your head in order to stabilize your gaze; before you can walk, you must be able to balance on one leg.

Posture is more than just holding still and straight. In Thelen's (1995, 2000) view, posture is a dynamic process that is linked with sensory information from proprioceptive cues in the skin, joints, and muscles, which tell us where we are in space; from vestibular organs in the inner ear that regulate balance and equilibrium; and from vision and hearing (Spencer & others, 2000).

Newborns cannot voluntarily control their posture. Within a few weeks, though, infants can hold their heads erect, and soon they can lift their heads while prone. By 2 months of age, babies can sit while supported on a lap or in an infant seat, but they cannot sit independently until they are 6 or 7 months of age. Standing also develops gradually during the first year of life. By about 8 months of age, infants usually learn to pull themselves up and hold onto a chair, and many can stand alone by about 10 to 12 months of age.

Learning to Walk Locomotion and postural control are closely linked, especially in walking upright (Adolph, 2005; Adolph & Berger, 2005, 2006). To walk upright, the baby must be able both to balance on one leg as the other is swung forward and to shift the weight from one leg to the other (Thelen, 2000).

Even young infants can make the alternating leg movements that are needed for walking. The neural pathways that control leg alternation are in place from a

gross motor skills Motor skills that involve large-muscle activities, such as walking.

Newly crawling infant

Experienced walker

FIGURE 6.2 The Role of Experience in Crawling and Walking Infants' Judgments of Whether to Go Down a Slope. Karen Adolph (1997) found that locomotor experience rather than age was the primary predictor of adaptive responding on slopes of varying steepness. Newly crawling and walking infants could not judge the safety of the various slopes. With experience, they learned to avoid slopes where they would fall. When expert crawlers began to walk, they again made mistakes and fell, even though they had judged the same slope accurately when crawling. Adloph referred to this as the *specificity of learning* because it does not transfer across crawling and walking.

The experiences of the first three years of life are almost entirely lost to us, and when we attempt to enter into a small child's world, we come as foreigners who have forgotten the landscape and no longer speak the native tongue.

—Selma Fraiberg
Developmentalist and Child Advocate, 20th Century

very early age, possibly even at birth or before. Infants engage in frequent alternating kicking movements throughout the first six months of life when they are lying on their backs. Also when 1- to 2-month-olds are given support with their feet in contact with a motorized treadmill, they show well-coordinated, alternating steps. Despite these early abilities, most infants do not learn to walk until about the time of their first birthday.

If infants can produce forward stepping movements so early, why does it take them so long to learn to walk? The key skills in learning to walk appear to be stabilizing balance on one leg long enough to swing the other forward and shifting the weight without falling. This is a difficult biomechanical problem to solve, and it takes infants about a year to do it.

In learning to locomote, infants learn what kinds of places and surfaces are safe for locomotion (Adolph, 2005; Adolph & Berger, 2005, 2006). Karen Adolph (1997) investigated how experienced and inexperienced crawling infants and walking infants go down steep slopes (see figure 6.2). Newly crawling infants, who averaged about 8½ months in age, rather indiscriminately went down the steep slopes, often falling in the process (with their mothers next to the slope to catch them). After weeks of practice, the crawling babies became more adept at judging which slopes were too steep to crawl down and which ones they could navigate safely. New walkers also could not judge the safety of the slopes, but experienced walkers accurately matched their skills with the steepness of the slopes. They rarely fell downhill, either refusing to go down the steep slopes or going down backward in a cautious manner. Experienced walkers perceptually assessed the situation—looking, swaying, touching, and thinking before they moved down the slope. With experience, both the crawlers and the walkers learned to avoid the risky slopes where they would fall, integrating perceptual information with the development of a new motor behavior. In this research, we again see the importance of perceptual-motor coupling in the development of motor skills.

Practice is especially important in learning to walk (Adolph, 2005; Adolph & Berger, 2005, 2006). "Thousands of daily walking steps, each step slightly different from the last because of variations in the terrain and the continually varying biomechanical constraints on the body, may help infants to identify the relevant" combination of strength and balance required to improve their walking skills (Adolph, Vereijken, & Shrout, 2003, p. 495).

www.mhhe.com/santrockcd11

Developmental Milestones
Physical Development in Infancy
Karen Adolph's Research

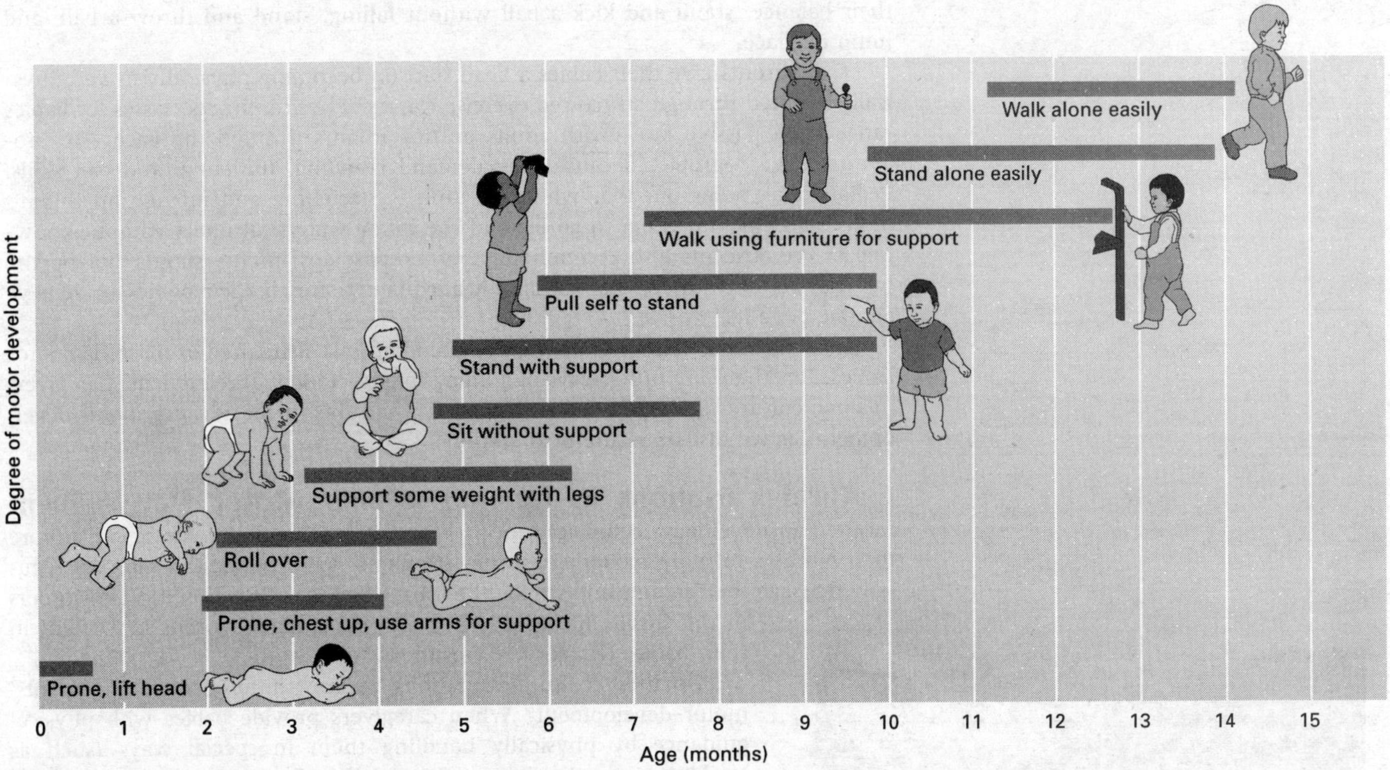

FIGURE 6.3 Milestones in Gross Motor Development

Figure 6.3 summarizes important accomplishments in gross motor skills during the first year, culminating in the ability to walk easily. The timing of these milestones, especially the later ones, may vary by as much as two to four months, and experiences can modify the onset of these accomplishments. For example, since 1992, when pediatricians began recommending that parents keep their infants supine at night, fewer babies crawl and the age of onset of crawling is later (Davis & others, 1998). Also, some infants do not follow the standard sequence of motor accomplishments. For example, many American infants never crawl on their belly or on their hands and knees. They may discover an idiosyncratic form of locomotion before walking, such as rolling, or they might never locomote until they get upright (Adolph, 2005). In the African Mali tribe, most infants do not crawl (Bril, 1999).

A baby is an angel whose wings decrease as his legs increase.

—French Proverb

According to Karen Adolph and Sarah Berger (2005), "the old-fashioned view that growth and motor development reflect merely the age-related output of maturation is, at best, incomplete. Rather, infants acquire new skills with the help of their caregivers in a real-world environment of objects, surfaces, and planes."

Development in the Second Year The motor accomplishments of the first year bring increasing independence, allowing infants to explore their environment more extensively and to initiate interaction with others more readily. In the second year of life, toddlers become more motorically skilled and mobile. They are no longer content in a playpen and want to move all over the place. Child development experts believe that motor activity during the second year is vital to the child's competent development and that few restrictions, except for safety, should be placed on their adventures (Fraiberg, 1959).

By 13 to 18 months, toddlers can pull a toy attached to a string and use their hands and legs to climb up a number of steps. By 18 to 24 months, toddlers can walk quickly or run stiffly for a short distance, balance on their feet in a squat position while playing with objects on the floor, walk backward without losing their balance, stand and kick a ball without falling, stand and throw a ball, and jump in place.

Can parents give their babies a head start on becoming physically fit and physically talented through structured exercise classes? Physical fitness classes for babies range from passive fare—with adults putting infants through the paces—to programs called "aerobic" because they demand crawling, tumbling, and ball skills. Pediatricians point out that when an adult is stretching and moving an infant's limbs, it is easy for them to go beyond the infant's physical limits without knowing it. Pediatricians also recommend that exercise for infants should not be the intense, aerobic variety. Babies cannot adequately stretch their bodies to achieve aerobic benefits.

In short, most infancy experts recommend against structured exercise classes for babies. But there are other ways of guiding infants' motor development. Caregivers in some cultures do handle babies vigorously, and this might advance motor development, as we discuss in the next section.

Cultural Variations in Guiding Infants' Motor Development

Mothers in developing countries tend to stimulate their infants' motor skills more than mothers in more modern countries (Hopkins, 1991). Jamaican mothers regularly massage their infants and stretch their arms and legs (Hopkins, 1991). Mothers in the Gusii culture of Kenya also encourage vigorous movement in their babies (Hopkins & Westra, 1988).

Do these cultural variations make a difference in the infants' motor development? When caregivers provide babies with physical guidance by physically handling them in special ways (such as stroking, massaging, or stretching) or by giving them opportunities for exercise, the infants often reach motor milestones earlier than infants whose caregivers have not provided these activities (Adolph & Berger, 2006). For example, Jamaican mothers expect their infants to sit and walk alone two to three months earlier than English mothers do (Hopkins & Westra, 1990).

Nonetheless, even when infants' motor activity is restricted, many infants still reach the milestones of motor development at a normal age. For example, Algonquin infants in Quebec, Canada, spend much of their first year strapped to a cradle board. Despite their inactivity, these infants still sit up, crawl, and walk within an age range similar to that of infants in cultures who have had much greater opportunity for activity.

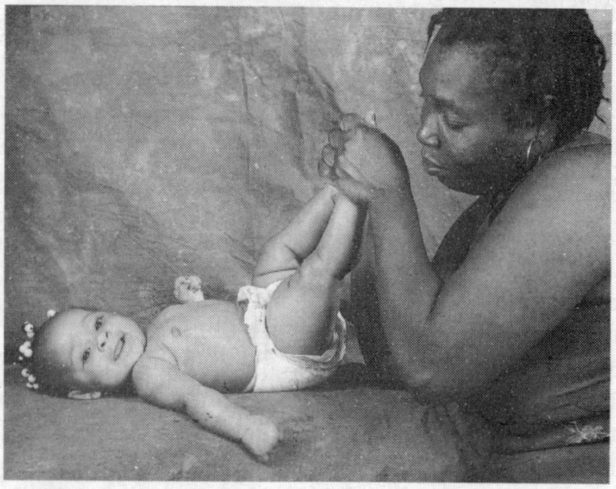

(*Top*) In the Algonquin culture in Quebec, Canada, babies are strapped to a cradle board for much of their infancy. (*Bottom*) In Jamaica, mothers massage and stretch their infants' arms and legs. *To what extent do cultural variations in the activity infants engage in influence the time at which they reach motor milestones?*

Childhood The preschool child no longer has to make an effort to stay upright and to move around. As children move their legs with more confidence and carry themselves more purposefully, moving around in the environment becomes more automatic.

At 3 years of age, children enjoy simple movements, such as hopping, jumping, and running back and forth, just for the sheer delight of performing these activities. They take considerable pride in showing how they can run across a room and jump all of 6 inches. The run-and-jump will win no Olympic gold medals, but for the 3-year-old the activity is a source of pride.

At 4 years of age, children are still enjoying the same kind of activities, but they have become more adventurous. They scramble over low jungle gyms as they display their athletic prowess. Although they have been able to climb stairs with one foot on each step for some time, they are just beginning to be able to come down the same way.

At 5 years of age, children are even more adventuresome than they were at 4. It is not unusual for self-assured 5-year-olds to perform hair-raising stunts on practically any climbing object. They run hard and enjoy races with each other and their parents.

During middle and late childhood, children's motor development becomes much smoother and more coordinated than it was in early childhood. For example, only one child in a thousand can hit a tennis ball over the net at the age of 3, yet by the age of 10 or 11 most children can learn to play the sport. Running, climbing, skipping rope, swimming, bicycle riding, and skating are just a few of the many physical skills elementary school children can master. And, when mastered, these physical skills are a source of great pleasure and a sense of accomplishment. In gross motor skills involving large-muscle activity, boys usually outperform girls.

As children move through the elementary school years, they gain greater control over their bodies and can sit and pay attention for longer periods of time. However, elementary school children are far from being physically mature, and they need to be active. Elementary school children become more fatigued by long periods of sitting than by running, jumping, or bicycling. Physical action is essential for these children to refine their developing skills, such as batting a ball, skipping rope, or balancing on a beam. Elementary school children should be engaged in active, rather than passive, activities.

Organized sports are one way of encouraging children to be active and to develop their motor skills. Schools and community agencies offer programs for children that involve baseball, soccer, football, basketball, swimming, gymnastics, and other sports. These programs may play a central role in children's lives. The Caring for Children interlude that follows examines the role of parents in children's sports.

Caring for Children

Parents and Children's Sports

Participation in sports can have both positive and negative consequences for children (Cary, 2004). Children's participation in sports can provide exercise, opportunities to learn how to compete, increases in self-esteem, and a setting for developing peer relations and friendships. One recent study revealed that participation in sports for three hours per week or more beyond regular physical education classes was related to increased physical fitness and lower fat mass in 9-year-old boys (Ara & others, 2004).

However, sports also can have negative outcomes for children: the pressure to achieve and win, physical injuries, a distraction from schoolwork, and unrealistic expectations for success (Adickes & Stuart, 2004; Demorest & Landry, 2003, 2004; Mafulli, Baxter-Jones, & Grieve, 2005). Few people challenge the value of sports for children when they are part of a school's physical education or intramural program. However, some critics question the appropriateness of highly competitive, win-at-all-costs sports teams; they question intense participation in sports at an early age and the physical strain placed on children's bodies that can result in injuries (Baquet, van Praagh, & Berthoin, 2004; Chen & others, 2005; Lord & Winell, 2004).

High-pressure sports that involve championship play under the media spotlight cause special concern. Some clinicians and child developmentalists believe such activities put undue stress on children and teach them the wrong values—namely, a win-at-all-costs philosophy. Overly ambitious parents, coaches, and community boosters can unintentionally create a highly stressful atmosphere in children's sports. When the prestige of parents, an institution, or a community becomes the focus of the child's participation in sports, the danger of exploitation is clearly present. Programs oriented toward such purposes often require arduous training sessions over many months and years, frequently leading to sports specialization at too early an age. In such circumstances, adults often communicate the distorted view that the sport is the most important aspect of the child's life.

(continued on next page)

What recommendations would you give to parents regarding children's sports?

If parents do not become overinvolved, they can help their children build their physical skills and help them emotionally—for example, by discussing how to deal with a difficult coach, how to cope with a tough loss, and how to put in perspective a poorly played game (Goodman, 2000). Parents should monitor their children as they participate in sports for signs of developing stress. If the problems appear to be beyond the intuitive skills of a volunteer coach or parent, consultation with a counselor or clinician may be needed. Also, the parent should be sensitive to whether a particular sport is the best one for the child and whether the child can handle its competitive pressures.

Here are some guidelines that can benefit both parents and coaches of children in sports (Women's Sports Foundation, 2001):

The Dos

- Make sports fun; the more children enjoy sports, the more they will want to play.
- Remember that it is OK for children to make mistakes; it means they are trying.
- Allow children to ask questions about the sport and discuss the sport in a calm, supportive manner.
- Show respect for the child's sports participation.
- Be positive and convince the child that he or she is making a good effort.
- Be a positive role model for the child in sports.

The Don'ts

- Yell or scream at the child.
- Condemn the child for poor play or continue to bring up failures long after they happen.
- Point out the child's errors in front of others.
- Expect the child to learn something immediately.
- Expect the child to become a pro.
- Ridicule or make fun of the child.
- Compare the child to siblings or to more talented children.
- Make sports all work and no fun.

Fine Motor Skills

Whereas gross motor skills involve large-muscle activity, **fine motor skills** involve finely tuned movements. Grasping a toy, using a spoon, buttoning a shirt, or doing anything that requires finger dexterity demonstrates fine motor skills.

Infancy Infants have hardly any control over fine motor skills at birth, but they have many components of what will become finely coordinated arm, hand, and finger movements (Rosenblith, 1992). The onset of reaching and grasping marks a significant achievement in infants' interactions (McCarty & Ashmead, 1999; Oztop, Bradley, & Arbib, 2004). During the first two years of life, infants refine their reaching and grasping (Smitsman, 2004). Rachel Clifton and her colleagues (1993) demonstrated that infants do not have to see their own hands in order to reach for an object. They concluded that proprioceptive cues from muscles, tendons, and joints, not sight of the limb, guide reaching by 4-month-old infants. Initially, infants move their shoulders and elbows crudely, but later they move their wrists, rotate their hands, and coordinate their thumb and forefinger.

The infant's grasping system is very flexible. Infants vary their grip on an object depending on its size and shape, as well as the size of their own hands relative to the object's size. Infants grip small objects with their thumb and forefinger (and sometimes their middle finger, too), whereas they grip large objects with all of the fingers of one hand or both hands.

Perceptual-motor coupling is necessary for the infant to coordinate grasping (Keen, 2005). Which perceptual system is most likely to be used in coordinating grasping varies with age. Four-month-old infants rely greatly on touch to determine how they will grip an object; 8-month-olds are more likely to use vision as a guide (Newell & others, 1989). This developmental change is efficient because vision lets infants preshape their hands as they reach for an object.

Experience plays a role in reaching and grasping. In one recent study, 3-month-old infants participated in play sessions wearing "sticky mittens" ("mittens with palms that stuck to the edges of toys and allowed the infants to pick up the toys") (Needham, Barrett, & Peterman, 2002, p. 279) (see figure 6.4). Following the mitten sessions, these infants grasped and manipulated objects earlier in their development than a control group of infants who did not receive the "mitten" experience. The experienced infants looked at the objects longer, swatted at them more during visual contact, and were more likely to mouth the objects.

fine motor skills Motor skills that involve more finely tuned movements, such as finger dexterity.

Childhood At 3 years of age, children have had the ability to pick up the tiniest objects between their thumb and forefinger for some time, but they are still somewhat clumsy at it. Three-year-olds can build surprisingly high block towers, each block placed with intense concentration but often not in a completely straight line. When 3-year-olds play with a form board or a simple puzzle, they are rather rough in placing the pieces. When they try to position a piece in a hole, they often try to force the piece or pat it vigorously.

By 4 years of age, children's fine motor coordination is much more precise. Sometimes 4-year-old children have trouble building high towers with blocks because, in their desire to place each of the blocks perfectly, they upset those already stacked. By age 5, children's fine motor coordination has improved further. Hand, arm, and fingers all move together under better command of the eye. Mere towers no longer interest the 5-year-old, who now wants to build a house or a church, complete with steeple. (Adults may still need to be told what each finished project is meant to be.)

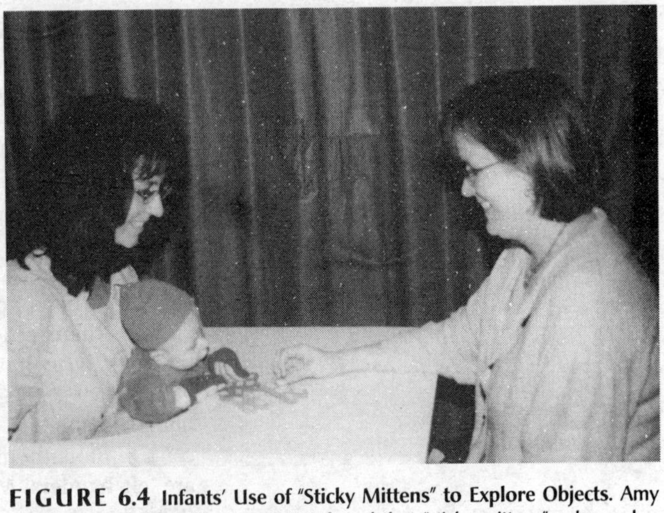

FIGURE 6.4 Infants' Use of "Sticky Mittens" to Explore Objects. Amy Needham and her colleagues (2002) found that "sticky mittens" enhanced young infants' object exploration skills.

Today, most teachers let children write with the hand they favor. *What are the main reasons children became left- or right-handed?*

www.mhhe.com/santrockd11

Handedness

Increased myelination of the central nervous system is reflected in the improvement of fine motor skills during middle and late childhood. Recall from chapter 5 that *myelination* involves the covering of the axon with a myelin sheath, a process that increases the speed with which information travels from neuron to neuron. By middle childhood, children can use their hands adroitly as tools. Six-year-olds can hammer, paste, tie shoes, and fasten clothes. By 7 years of age, children's hands have become steadier. At this age, children prefer a pencil to a crayon for printing, and reversal of letters is less common. Printing becomes smaller. At 8 to 10 years of age, children can use their hands independently with more ease and precision; children can now write rather than print words. Letter size becomes smaller and more even. At 10 to 12 years of age, children begin to show manipulative skills similar to the abilities of adults. The complex, intricate, and rapid movements needed to produce fine-quality crafts or to play a difficult piece on a musical instrument can be mastered. Girls usually outperform boys in fine motor skills.

Handedness

One interesting aspect of motor development is *handedness,* a preference for using one hand rather than the other. For centuries, left-handers have suffered unfair discrimination in a world designed for right-handers. For many years, teachers forced all children to write with their right hand, even if they had a left-hand tendency. Fortunately, today most teachers let children write with the hand they favor.

Origin and Development of Handedness What is the origin of hand preference? Genetic inheritance seems to be a strong influence (Yekin, 2002). In one study, the handedness of adopted children was not related to the handedness of their adopted parents, but it was related to the handedness of their biological parents (Carter-Saltzman, 1980).

Right-handedness is dominant in all cultures (it appears in a ratio of about 9 right-handers to 1 left-hander), and it appears before culture can influence the child. For example, ultrasound observations found that 9 of 10 fetuses were more likely to be sucking their right hand's thumb (Hepper, Shahidullah, & White, 1990). A study of newborns found that 65 percent turned their heads to the right when they were lying on their backs in a crib (Michel, 1981). Fifteen percent preferred to face toward the left and the remaining 20 percent showed no preference. These preferences for the right or the left were linked with handedness later in development.

Handedness and Other Characteristics Researchers have examined whether handedness is linked to lateralization, the specialization of the brain's hemispheres discussed in chapter 5. Approximately 85 to 95 percent of right-handed individuals primarily process speech in the brain's left hemisphere (Khedr & others, 2002; Springer & Deutsch, 1985). However, left-handed individuals show more variation (Knecht & others, 2000; Szaflarski & others, 2002). Almost 75 percent of left-handers process speech in their left hemisphere, just like right-handers (Khedr & others, 2002). However, about 10 percent of left-handers process speech in their right hemisphere, and approximately 15 percent of left-handers process speech equally in both hemispheres (Khedr & others, 2002).

Are there other differences between left- and right-handers? Left-handers are more likely to have reading problems (Geschwind & Behan, 1984; Natsopoulos & others, 1998, 2002). But left-handers also tend to have unusually good visual spatial skills and the ability to imagine spatial layouts (Holtzen, 2000). A higher percentage of mathematicians, musicians, architects, and artists than would be expected are left-handers; Michelangelo, Leonardo Da Vinci, and Picasso were all left-handed (Schachter & Ransil, 1996). In one study of more than 100,000 students taking the Scholastic Aptitude Test (SAT), 20 percent of the top-scoring group was left-handed, twice the rate of left-handedness found in the general population (10 percent) (Bower, 1985).

In sum, while a large majority of people are right-handed, both right-handers and left-handers have a number of strengths. Despite sometimes having to compensate for living in a right-handed world, writing on right-handed desks and cutting with right-handed scissors, overall, being left-handed does not seem to handicap individuals to any significant degree (Porac & Searleman, 2002; Teasdale & Owen, 2001).

Review and Reflect • LEARNING GOAL 1

1 Describe how motor skills develop

Review

- What is the dynamic systems view of motor development?
- What are some reflexes of infants?
- How do gross motor skills develop?
- How do fine motor skills develop?
- How does handedness develop?

Reflect

- How would you evaluate the benefits and drawbacks of allowing an 8-year-old to play Little League baseball?

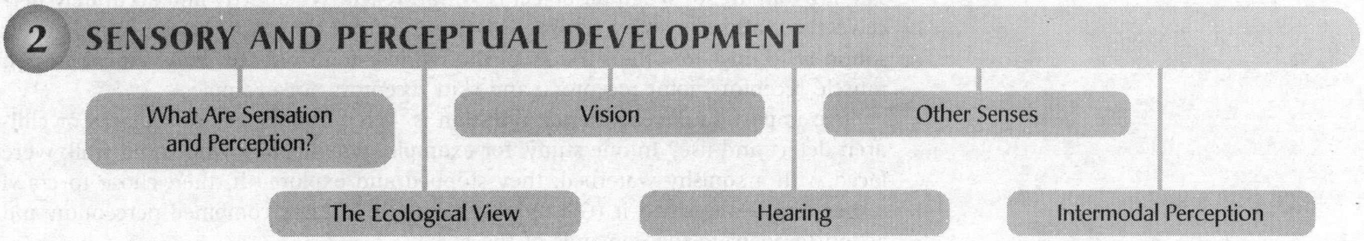

Right now, I am looking at my computer screen to make sure the words are being printed accurately as I am typing them. My perceptual and motor skills are working together. Recall that even control of posture uses information from the senses. And when people grasp an object, they use perceptual information about the object to adjust their motions.

How do these sensations and perceptions develop? Can a newborn see? If so, what can it perceive? What about the other senses—hearing, smell, taste, touch, and pain? What are they like in the newborn, and how do they develop? Can an infant put together information from two modalities, such as sight and sound? These are among the intriguing questions that we will explore in this section.

What Are Sensation and Perception?

How does a newborn know that her mother's skin is soft rather than rough? How does a 5-year-old know what color his hair is? Infants and children "know" these things as a result of information that comes through the senses. Without vision, hearing, touch, taste, smell, and other senses, we would be isolated from the world; we would live in dark silence, a tasteless, colorless, feelingless void.

Sensation occurs when information interacts with sensory *receptors*—the eyes, ears, tongue, nostrils, and skin. The sensation of hearing occurs when waves of pulsating air are collected by the outer ear and transmitted through the bones of the

sensation Reaction that occurs when information contacts sensory receptors—the eyes, ears, tongue, nostrils, and skin.

The infant is by no means as helpless as it looks and is quite capable of some very complex and important actions.

—Herb Pick
Contemporary Developmental Psychologist, University of Minnesota

inner ear to the auditory nerve. The sensation of vision occurs as rays of light contact the eyes, become focused on the retina, and are transmitted by the optic nerve to the visual centers of the brain.

Perception is the interpretation of what is sensed. The air waves that contact the ears might be interpreted as noise or as musical sounds, for example. The physical energy transmitted to the retina of the eye might be interpreted as a particular color, pattern, or shape.

The Ecological View

For the past several decades, much of the research on perceptual development in infancy has been guided by the ecological view of Eleanor and James J. Gibson (E. Gibson, 1969, 1989, 2001; J. Gibson, 1966, 1979). They argue that we do not have to take bits and pieces of data from sensations and build up representations of the world in our minds. Instead, our perceptual system can select from the rich information that the environment itself provides.

According to the Gibsons' **ecological view,** we directly perceive information that exists in the world around us. Perception brings us into contact with the environment in order to interact with and adapt to it. Perception is designed for action. Perception gives people such information as when to duck, when to turn their bodies through a narrow passageway, and when to put their hands up to catch something.

In the Gibsons' view, all objects have **affordances,** which are opportunities for interaction offered by objects that are necessary to perform activities. A pot may afford you something to cook with, and it may afford a toddler something to bang. Adults immediately know when a chair is appropriate for sitting, when a surface is safe for walking, or when an object is within reach. We directly and accurately perceive these affordances by sensing information from the environment—the light or sound reflecting from the surfaces of the world—and from our own bodies through muscle receptors, joint receptors, and skin receptors, for example.

An important developmental question is, What affordances can infants or children detect and use? In one study, for example, when babies who could walk were faced with a squishy waterbed, they stopped and explored it, then chose to crawl rather than walk across it (Gibson & others, 1987). They combined perception and action to adapt to the demands of the task.

Similarly, as we described earlier in the section on motor development, infants who were just learning to crawl or just learning to walk were less cautious when confronted with a steep slope than experienced crawlers or walkers were (Adolph, 1997; Adolph & Avolio, 2000). The more experienced crawlers and walkers perceived that a slope *affords* the possibility for not only faster locomotion but also for falling. Again, infants coupled perception and action to make a decision about what to do in their environment. Through perceptual development, children become more efficient at discovering and using affordances.

Studying the infant's perception has not been an easy task. The Research in Child Development interlude describes some of the ingenious ways researchers study the newborn's perception.

perception The interpretation of sensation.

ecological view The view, proposed by the Gibsons, that people directly perceive information in the world around them. Perception brings people in contact with the environment in order to interact with it and adapt to it.

affordances Opportunities for interaction offered by objects that are necessary to perform activities.

Research in Child Development

Studying the Newborn's Perception

The creature has poor motor coordination and can move itself only with great difficulty. Although it cries when uncomfortable, it uses few other vocalizations. In fact, it sleeps most of the time, about 16 to 17 hours a day. You are curious about this creature and want to know more about what it can do. You think to yourself, "I wonder if it can see. How could I find out?"

You obviously have a communication problem with the creature. You must devise a way that will allow the creature to "tell" you that it can see. While examining the creature one day, you make an interesting discovery. When you move an object horizontally in front of the creature, its eyes follow the object's movement. The creature's head movement suggests that it has at least some vision.

In case you haven't already guessed, the creature you have been reading about is the human infant, and the role you played is that of a researcher interested in devising techniques to learn about the infant's visual perception. After years of work, scientists have developed research methods and tools sophisticated enough to examine the subtle abilities of infants and to interpret their complex actions (Bendersky & Sullivan, 2002; Kellman & Banks, 1998; Kellman & Arterberry, 2006; Menn & Stoel-Gammon, 2005; Slater, 2004).

Visual Preference Method

Robert Fantz (1963) was a pioneer in this effort. Fantz made an important discovery that advanced the ability of researchers to investigate infants' visual perception: infants look at different things for different lengths of time. Fantz placed infants in a "looking chamber," which had two visual displays on the ceiling above the infant's head. An experimenter viewed the infant's eyes by looking through a peephole. If the infant was fixating on one of the displays, the experimenter could see the display's reflection in the infant's eyes. This allowed the experimenter to determine how long the infant looked at each display. Fantz (1963) found that infants only 2 days old look longer at patterned stimuli, such as faces and concentric circles, than at red, white, or yellow discs. Infants 2 to 3 weeks old preferred to look at patterns—a face, a piece of printed matter, or a bull's-eye—longer than at red, yellow, or white discs (see figure 6.5). Fantz's research method—studying whether infants can distinguish one stimulus from another by measuring the length of time they attend to different stimuli—is referred to as the **visual preference method.**

visual preference method A method developed by Fantz to determine whether infants can distinguish one stimulus from another by measuring the length of time they attend to different stimuli.

Habituation and Dishabituation

Another way that researchers have studied infant perception is to present a stimulus (such as a sight or a sound) a number of times. If the infant decreases its response to the stimulus after several presentations, it indicates that the infant is no longer interested in the stimulus. If the researcher now presents a new stimulus, the

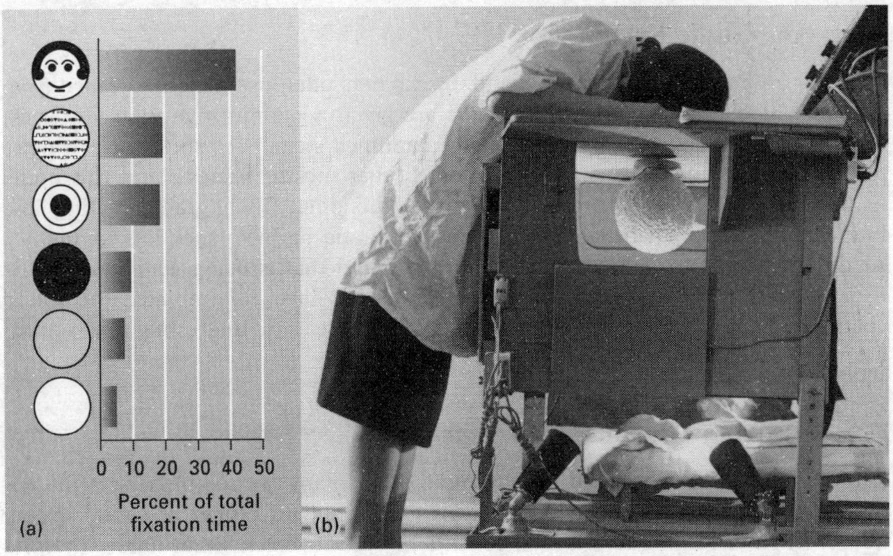

FIGURE 6.5 Fantz's Experiment on Infants' Visual Perception. *(a)* Infants 2 to 3 months old preferred to look at some stimuli more than others. In Fantz's experiment, infants preferred to look at patterns rather than at color or brightness. For example, they looked longer at a face, a piece of printed matter, or a bull's-eye than at red, yellow, or white discs. *(b)* Fantz used a "looking chamber" to study infants' perception of stimuli.

(continued on next page)

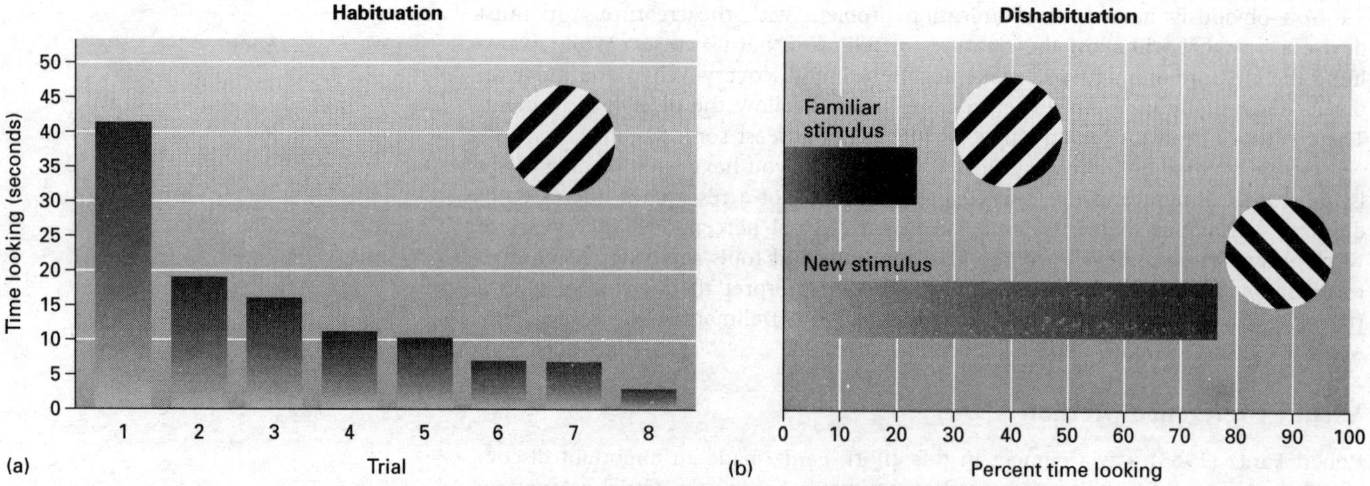

FIGURE 6.6 **Habituation and Dishabituation.** In the first part of one study, 7-hour-old newborns were shown the stimulus in (*a*). As indicated, the newborns looked at it an average of 41 seconds when it was first presented to them (Slater, Morison, & Somers, 1988). Over seven more presentations of the stimulus, they looked at it less and less. In the second part of the study, infants were presented with both the familiar stimulus to which they had just become habituated (*a*) and a new stimulus (shown in *b*, which was rotated 90 degrees). The newborns looked at the new stimulus three times as much as the familiar stimulus.

infant's response will recover—indicating the infant could discriminate between the old and new stimulus.

Habituation is the name given to decreased responsiveness to a stimulus after repeated presentations of the stimulus. **Dishabituation** is the recovery of a habituated response after a change in stimulation. Newborn infants can habituate to repeated sights, sounds, smells, or touches (Rovee-Collier, 2004). Among the measures researchers use in habituation studies are sucking behavior (sucking stops when the young infant attends to a novel object), heart and respiration rates, and the length of time the infant looks at an object. Figure 6.6 shows the results of one study of habituation and dishabituation with newborns (Slater, Morison, & Somers, 1988).

High-Amplitude Sucking

To assess an infant's attention to sound, researchers often use a method called *high-amplitude sucking*. In this method, infants are given a nonnutritive nipple to suck, and the nipple is connected to "a sound generating system. Each suck causes a noise to be generated and the infant learns quickly that sucking brings about this noise. At first, babies suck frequently, so the noise occurs often. Then, gradually, they lose interest in hearing repetitions of the same noise and begin to suck less frequently. At this point, the experimenter changes the sound that is being generated. If the babies renew vigorous sucking, we infer that they have discriminated the sound change and are sucking more because they want to hear the interesting new sound" (Menn & Stoel-Gammon, 2005, p. 71).

habituation Decreased responsiveness to a stimulus after repeated presentations of the stimulus.

dishabituation The recovery of a habituated response after a change in stimulation.

The Orienting Response and Tracking

A technique that can be used to determine if an infant can see or hear is the *orienting response,* which involves turning one's head toward a sight or sound (Keen, 2005). Another technique, *tracking,* consists of eye movements that follow (*track*) a moving object and can used to determine if an infant can see.

Equipment

Technology can facilitate the use of most methods for investigating the infant's perceptual abilities. Videotape equipment allows researchers to investigate elusive behaviors. High-speed computers make it possible to perform complex data analysis in minutes. Other equipment records respiration, heart rate, body movement, visual fixation, and sucking behavior, which provide clues to what the infant is perceiving. For example, some researchers use equipment that detects if a change in infants' respiration follows a change in the pitch of a sound. If so, it suggests that the infants heard the pitch change. Thus, scientists have become ingenious at assessing the development of infants, discovering ways to "interview" them even though they cannot yet talk.

Vision

Some important changes in visual perception with age can be traced to differences in how the eye itself functions over time. These changes in the eye's functioning influence, for example, how clearly we can see an object, whether we can differentiate its colors, at what distance, and in what light.

Infancy

What do newborns see? How does visual perception develop in infancy?

Visual Acuity and Color Vision Psychologist William James (1890/1950) called the newborn's perceptual world a "blooming, buzzing confusion." A century later, we can safely say that he was wrong (Slater, 2004). Even the newborn perceives a world with some order. That world, however, is far different from the one perceived by the toddler or the adult.

Just how well can infants see? At birth, the nerves and muscles and lens of the eye are still developing. As a result, newborns cannot see small things that are far away. The newborn's vision is estimated to be 20/600 on the well-known Snellan chart used for eye examinations (Banks & Salapatek, 1983). In other words, an object 20 feet away is only as clear to the newborn as it would be if it were 600 feet away from an adult with normal vision (20/20). By 6 months of age, though, vision is 20/100 or better, and, by about the first birthday, the infant's vision approximates that of an adult (Banks & Salapatek, 1983). Figure 6.7 shows a computer estimation of what a picture of a face looks like to an infant at different ages from a distance of about 6 inches.

The infant's color vision also improves. At birth, babies can distinguish between green and red (Adams, 1989). All of the eye's color-sensitive receptors (*cones*) function by 2 months of age.

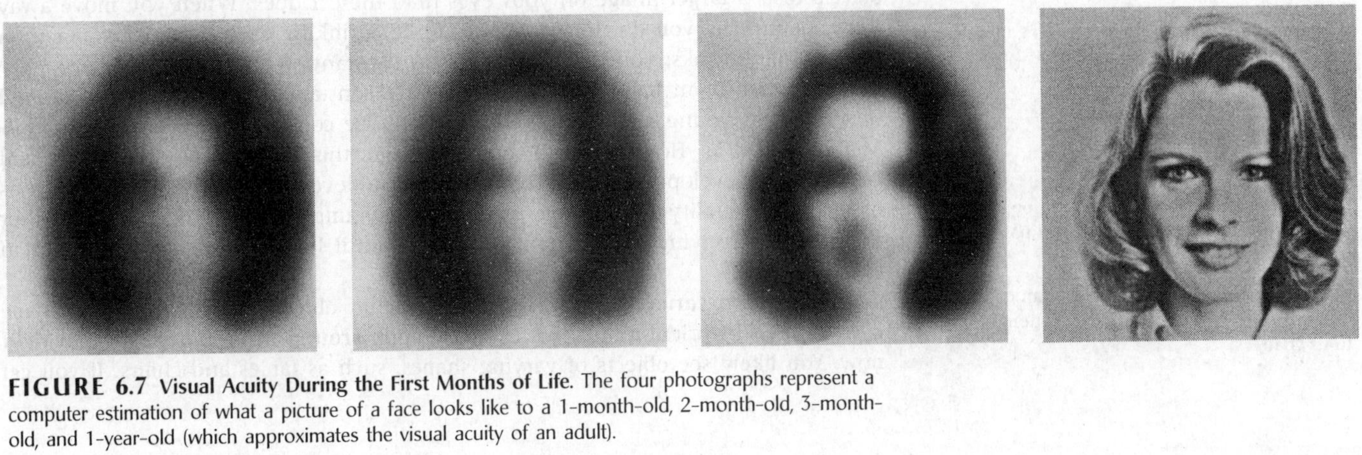

FIGURE 6.7 Visual Acuity During the First Months of Life. The four photographs represent a computer estimation of what a picture of a face looks like to a 1-month-old, 2-month-old, 3-month-old, and 1-year-old (which approximates the visual acuity of an adult).

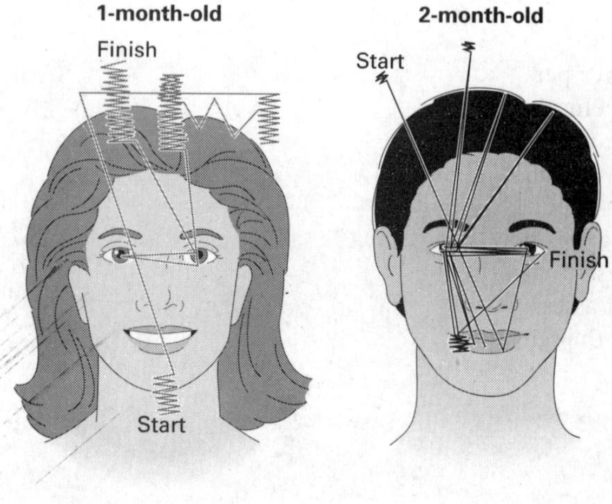

FIGURE 6.8 How 1- and 2-Month-Old Infants Scan the Human Face

Newborns' Senses
Richard Aslin's Research
International Society on Infant Studies

The first few months of life also bring the ability to use cues to depth and distance. One important example is *binocular vision,* which combines into one image the two different views of the world received by our eyes because they are several inches apart. The difference between the images received by the two eyes provides powerful cues for distance and depth. Newborns do not have binocular vision; it develops at about 3 to 4 months of age (Slater, Field, & Hernandez-Reif, 2002).

Perceiving Patterns What does the world look like to infants? Do they recognize patterns? As we saw in the Research in Child Development interlude, with the help of his "looking chamber," Robert Fantz (1963) revealed that infants look at different things for different lengths of time. Even 2- to 3-month-old infants prefer to look at patterned displays rather than nonpatterned displays. For example, they prefer to look at a normal human face rather than one with scrambled features, and they prefer to look at a bulls-eye target or black-and-white stripes rather than a plain circle. Thus, research on visual preferences demonstrates that the newborn's visual world is not the "blooming, buzzing confusion" William James imagined.

Even very young infants soon change the way they gather information from the visual world. By using a special mirror arrangement, researchers projected an image of human faces in front of infants' eyes so that the infants' eye movements could be photographed (Maurer & Salapatek, 1976). As figure 6.8 shows, the 2-month-old scans much more of the face than the 1-month-old, and the 2-month-old spends more time examining the internal details of the face. Thus, the 2-month-old gains more information about the world than the 1-month-old.

Perceptual Constancy Some perceptual accomplishments are especially intriguing because they indicate that the infant's perception goes beyond the information provided by the senses (Bower, 2002; Slater, Field, & Hernandez-Reif, 2002). This is the case in *perceptual constancy,* in which sensory stimulation is changing but perception of the physical world remains constant. If infants did not develop perceptual constancy, each time they saw an object at a different distance or in a different orientation, they would perceive it as a different object. Thus, the development of perceptual constancy allows the infant to perceive its world as stable. Two types of perceptual constancy are size constancy and shape constancy.

Size constancy is the recognition that an object remains the same even though the retinal image of the object changes. The farther away from us an object is, the smaller its image is on our eyes. Thus, the size of an object on the retina is not sufficient to tell us its actual size. For example, you perceive a bicycle standing right in front of you as smaller than the car parked across the street, even though the bicycle casts a larger image on your eyes than the car does. When you move away from the bicycle, you do not perceive it to be shrinking even though its image on your retinas shrinks; you perceive its size as constant.

But what about babies? Do they have size constancy? Researchers have found that babies as young as 3 months of age show size constancy (Bower, 1966; Day & McKenzie, 1973). However, at 3 months of age, this ability is not full-blown and continues to develop. As infants' binocular vision develops between 4 and 5 months of age, their ability to perceive size constancy improves (Aslin, 1987). Further progress in perceiving size constancy continues until 10 or 11 years of age (Kellman & Banks, 1998).

size constancy Recognition that an object remains the same even though the retinal image of the object changes.

shape constancy Recognition that an object remains the same even though its orientation to us changes.

Shape constancy is the recognition that an object remains the same shape even though its orientation to us changes. Look around the room you are in right now. You likely see objects of varying shapes, such as tables and chairs. If you get up and walk around the room, you will see these objects from different sides and angles. Even though your retinal image of the objects changes as you walk and look, you will still perceive the objects as the same shape.

Do babies have shape constancy? As with size constancy, researchers have found that babies as young as 3 months of age have shape constancy (Bower, 1966; Day & McKenzie, 1973). Three-month-old infants, however, do not have shape constancy for irregularly shaped objects, such as tilted planes (Cook & Birch, 1984).

FIGURE 6.9 Examining Infants' Depth Perception on the Visual Cliff. Eleanor Gibson and Richard Walk (1960) found that most infants would not crawl out on the glass, which indicated that they had depth perception.

Depth Perception Decades ago, the inspiration for what would become a classic experiment came to Eleanor Gibson as she was eating a picnic lunch on the edge of the Grand Canyon. She wondered whether an infant looking over the canyon's rim would perceive the dangerous drop-off and back up. She also was worried that her own two young children would play too close to the canyon's edge and fall off. Do even young children perceive depth?

To investigate this question, Eleanor Gibson and Richard Walk (1960) constructed a miniature cliff with a drop-off covered by glass in their laboratory. They placed infants on the edge of this visual cliff and had their mothers coax them to crawl onto the glass (see figure 6.9). Most infants would not crawl out on the glass, choosing instead to remain on the shallow side, indicating that they could perceive depth.

Exactly how early in life does depth perception develop? The 6- to 12-month-old infants in the visual cliff experiment had extensive visual experience. Do younger infants without this experience still perceive depth? Since younger infants do not crawl, this question is difficult to answer. As we noted earlier, infants develop the ability to use binocular cues to depth by about 3 to 4 months of age. Two- to 4-month-old infants show differences in heart rate when they are placed directly on the deep side of the visual cliff instead of on the shallow side (Campos, Langer, & Krowitz, 1970). However, these differences might mean that young infants respond to differences in some visual characteristics of the deep and shallow cliffs, with no actual knowledge of depth.

Visual Expectations By the time they are 3 months of age, infants not only see forms and figures but also develop expectations about future events. For example, Marshall Haith and his colleagues (Canfield & Haith, 1991; Haith, Hazen, & Goodman, 1988) presented pictures to infants in either a regular alternating (such as left, right, left, right) or an unpredictable sequence (such as right, right, left, right). When the sequence was predictable, the 3-month-old infants began to anticipate the location of the picture, looking at the side on which it was expected to appear. However, younger infants did not develop expectations about where a picture would be presented.

What kinds of expectations do infants form? Are we born expecting the world to obey basic physical laws, such as gravity, or when do we learn about how the world works? Experiments by Elizabeth Spelke (1991, 2000; Spelke & Hespos, 2001) have addressed these questions. She placed babies before a puppet stage and showed them a series of actions that are unexpected if you know how the physical world works—for example, one ball seemed to roll through a solid barrier, another seemed to leap between two platforms, and a third appeared to hang in midair (Spelke, 1979). Spelke measured and compared the babies' looking times for unexpected and expected actions. She concluded that, by 4 months of age, even though infants do not yet have the ability to talk about objects, move around objects, manipulate objects, or even see objects with high resolution, they can expect objects to be solid and continuous. However, at 4 months of age, infants do not expect an object to obey gravitational constraints (Spelke & others, 1992).

By 6 to 8 months, infants have learned to perceive gravity and support—that an object hanging on the end of a table should fall, that ball bearings will travel farther when rolled down a longer rather than a shorter ramp, and that cup handles will not fall when attached to a cup (Slater, Field, & Hernandez-Reif, 2002). As infants develop, their experiences and actions on objects help them to understand physical laws.

Childhood Children become increasingly efficient at detecting the boundaries between colors (such as red and orange) at 3 to 4 years of age (Gibson, 1969). When they are about 4 or 5 years old, most children's eye muscles are developed enough for them to move their eyes efficiently across a series of letters. Many preschool children are farsighted, unable to see close up as well as they can see far away. By the time they enter the first grade, though, most children can focus their eyes and sustain their attention effectively on close-up objects.

What are the signs of vision problems in children? They include rubbing the eyes, excessive blinking, squinting, appearing irritable when playing games that require good distance vision, shutting or covering one eye, and tilting the head or thrusting it forward when looking at something. A child who shows any of these behaviors should be examined by an ophthalmologist.

Approximately 1 in every 3,000 children is *educationally blind,* which means they cannot use their vision in learning and must use hearing and touch to learn. Almost one-half of these children were born blind, and another one-third lost their vision in the first year of life. Many children who are educationally blind, like Stevie Wonder and Andrea Bocelli, have normal intelligence and function very well academically with appropriate supports and learning aids. However, many educationally blind students have multiple disabilities and need a range of support services.

Hearing

Can the fetus hear? What kind of changes in hearing take place in infancy?

The Fetus, Infant, and Child During the last two months of pregnancy, the fetus can hear sounds as it nestles in its mother's womb: it hears the mother's voice, music, and so on (Kisilevsky, 1995; Kisilevsky & others, 2005; Smith, Muir, & Kisilevsky, 2001). Two psychologists wanted to find out if a fetus that heard Dr. Seuss' classic story *The Cat in the Hat* while still in the mother's womb would prefer hearing the story after birth (DeCasper & Spence, 1986). During the last months of pregnancy, 16 women read *The Cat in the Hat* to their fetuses. Then shortly after they were born, the mothers read to them either *The Cat in the Hat* or a story with a different rhyme and pace, *The King, the Mice, and the Cheese* (which was not read to them during prenatal development). Using the high-amplitude sucking method described earlier in the chapter, the researchers found that the infants sucked on a nipple in a different way when the mothers read the two stories, suggesting that the infants recognized the pattern and tone of *The Cat in the Hat* (see figure 6.10). This study illustrates that an infant's brain has a remarkable ability to learn even before birth and reflects the ingenuity of researchers in assessing development.

Even newborns show a preference for certain sounds (Fernald, 2004; Saffran, Werker, & Werner, 2006). Through experiments that measure sucking behavior, researchers have found that newborns prefer a recording of their mother's voice to the voice of an unfamiliar woman, their mother's native language to a foreign language, and the classical music of Beethoven to the rock music of Aerosmith (Flohr & others, 2001; Mehler & others, 1988; Spence & DeCasper, 1987).

(a)

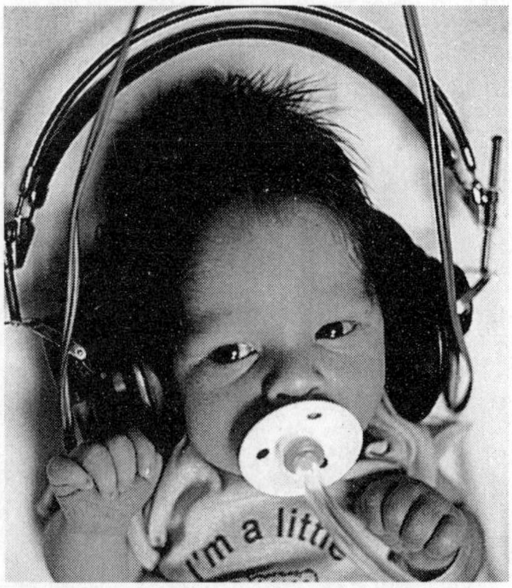

(b)

FIGURE 6.10 **Hearing in the Womb.** (*a*) Pregnant mothers read *The Cat in the Hat* to their fetuses during the last few months of pregnancy. (*b*) When they were born, the babies preferred listening to a recording of their mothers reading *The Cat in the Hat*, as evidenced by their sucking on a nipple that produced this recording, rather than another story, *The King, the Mice, and the Cheese.*

The newborn's hearing abilities are limited in several ways. Changes during infancy involve a sound's loudness, pitch, and localization.

Immediately after birth, infants cannot hear soft sounds quite as well as adults can; a stimulus must be louder to be heard by a newborn than by an adult (Trehub & others, 1991). For example, an adult can hear a whisper from about 4 to 5 feet away, but a newborn requires that sounds be closer to a normal conversational level to be heard at that distance.

Infants are also less sensitive to the pitch of a sound than adults are. *Pitch* is the perception of the frequency of a sound. A soprano voice sounds high pitched, a bass voice low pitched. Infants are less sensitive to low-pitched sounds and are more likely to hear high-pitched sounds (Aslin, Jusczyk, & Pisoni, 1998). By 2 years of age, infants have considerably improved their ability to distinguish sounds with different pitches.

It is important to be able *localize* sounds, detecting their origins. Even newborns can determine the general location that a sound is coming from, but by 6 months of age, they are more proficient at localizing sounds. This ability continues to improve in the second year (Litovsky & Ashmead, 1997; Morrongiello, Fenwick, & Chance, 1990).

Our sensory-perceptual system seems built to give a special place to the sounds of language. Newborns are especially sensitive to the sounds of human speech (Fernald, 2004). Babies are born into the world prepared to respond to the sounds of any human language. Even young infants can discriminate subtle phonetic differences, such as those between the speech sounds of *ba* and *ga*. Experience with the native language, however, has an effect on speech perception. In the second half of the first year of life, infants become "native listeners," especially attuned to the sounds of their native language (Jusczyk, 2002). In chapter 10, "Language Development," we will further discuss development of infants' ability to distinguish the sounds they need for speech.

About 1 in 1,000 newborns are deaf (Mason & Hermann, 1998). Hearing aids or surgery can improve hearing for many of them (O'Gorman, Hamid, & Fox, 2006).

As many as one-third of all U.S. children from birth to 3 years of age have three or more episodes of *otitis media*, a middle-ear infection that can impair hearing temporarily (O'Neill, 2002). If the infection continues too long, it can interfere with language development and socialization (Miceli Sopo, Zorzi, & Calvani, 2004). In some cases, the infection can develop into a more chronic condition in which the middle ear becomes filled with fluid, and this can seriously impair hearing. Treatments for otitis media include antibiotics and placement of a tube in the inner ear to drain fluid (Cruz, Kasse, & Leonhart, 2003; Steinman, Landefeld, & Gonzales, 2003).

Adolescence Most adolescents' hearing is excellent. However, anyone who listens to loud sounds for sustained periods of time runs the risk of developing hearing problems. H.E.A.R (Hearing Education and Awareness for Rockers) was founded by rock musicians whose hearing has been damaged by their exposure to high-volume rock music. Increasingly, rock musicians, such as the group Metallica, wear earplugs when they are playing their music, as do orchestra musicians.

Other Senses

As we develop, we not only obtain information about the world from our eyes and our ears. We also gather information about the world through sensory receptors in our skin, nose, and tongue.

Touch and Pain Do newborns respond to touch? Can they feel pain?

Newborns do respond to touch. A touch to the cheek produces a turning of the head; a touch to the lips produces sucking movements.

If and when you have a son and need to consider whether he should be circumcised, questions about an infant's pain perception probably will become important to you. Circumcision is usually performed on young boys about the third day after birth. Will your young son experience pain if he is circumcised in the days following his birth? An investigation by Megan Gunnar and her colleagues (1987) found that newborn infant males cried intensely during circumcision. The circumcised infant also displays amazing resiliency. Within several minutes after the surgery, they can nurse and interact in a normal manner with their mothers. And, if allowed to, the newly circumcised newborn drifts into a deep sleep, which seems to serve as a coping mechanism.

For many years, doctors performed operations on newborns without anesthesia. This practice was accepted because of the dangers of anesthesia and because of the supposition that newborns do not feel pain. As researchers demonstrated that newborns can feel pain, the practice of operating on newborns without anesthesia is being challenged. Anesthesia now is used in some circumcisions.

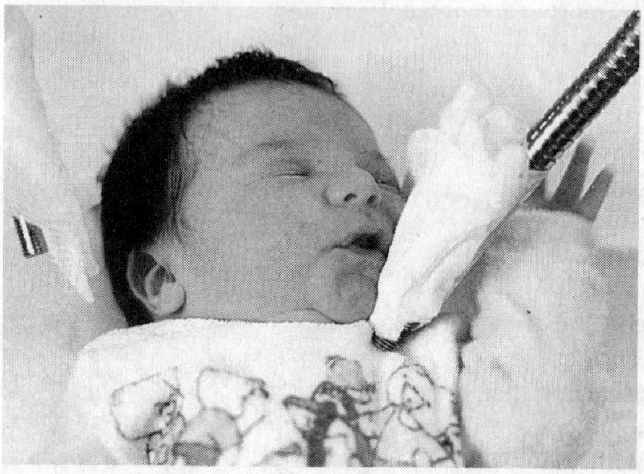

FIGURE 6.11 Newborns' Preference for the Smell of Their Mother's Breast Pad. In the experiment by MacFarlane (1975), 6-day-old infants preferred to smell their mother's breast pad rather than a clean one that had never been used, but 2-day-old infants did not show this preference, indicating that this odor preference requires several days of experience to develop.

Smell and Taste As with the other senses, most research on developmental changes in smell focuses on early infancy and aging. Newborns can differentiate odors. The expressions on their faces seem to indicate that they like the way vanilla and strawberry smell but do not like the smell of rotten eggs and fish (Steiner, 1979). In one investigation, 6-day-old infants who were breast-fed showed a clear preference for smelling their mother's breast pad (MacFarlane, 1975) (see figure 6.11). However, when they were 2 days old, infants did not show this preference, indicating that they require several days of experience to recognize this odor.

Sensitivity to taste might be present even before birth. When saccharin was added to the amniotic fluid of a near-term fetus, swallowing increased (Windle, 1940). In one study, even at only 2 hours of age, babies made different facial expressions when they tasted sweet, sour, and bitter solutions (Rosenstein & Oster, 1988) (see figure 6.12). At about 4 months of age, infants begin to prefer salty tastes, which as newborns they had found to be aversive (Harris, Thomas, & Booth, 1990).

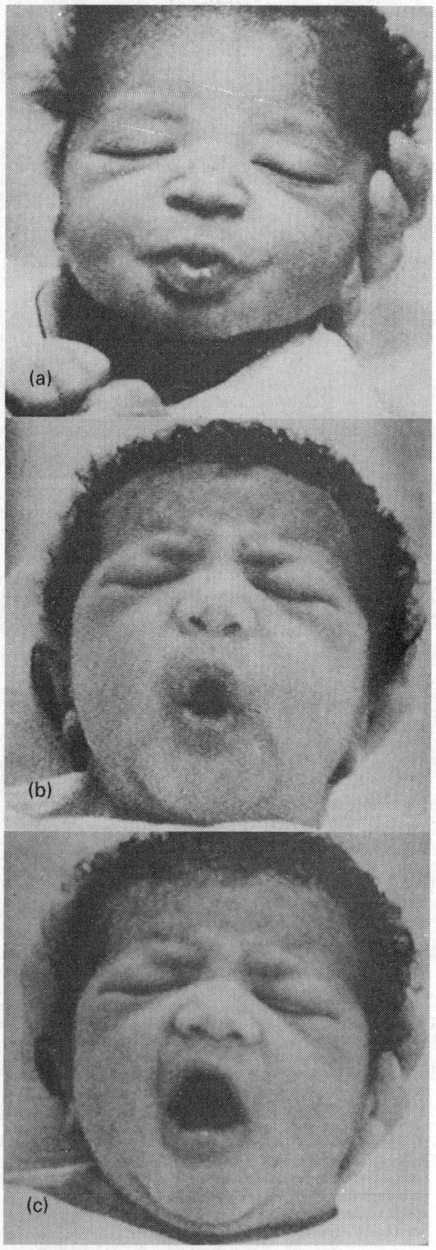

FIGURE 6.12 Newborns' Facial Responses to Basic Tastes. Facial expression elicited by (*a*) a sweet solution, (*b*) a sour solution, and (*c*) a bitter solution.

Intermodal Perception

Imagine yourself playing basketball or tennis. You are experiencing many visual inputs: the ball coming and going, other players moving around, and so on. However, you are experiencing many auditory inputs as well: the sound of the ball bouncing or being hit, the grunts and groans, and so on. There is good correspondence between much of the visual and auditory information: when you see the ball bounce, you hear a bouncing sound; when a player stretches to hit a ball, you hear a groan.

We live in a world of objects and events that can be seen, heard, and felt. When mature observers simultaneously look at and listen to an event, they experience a unitary episode. All of this is so commonplace that it scarcely seems worth mentioning. But consider the task of very young infants with little practice at perceiving. Can they put vision and sound together as precisely as adults do?

Intermodal perception involves integrating information from two or more sensory modalities, such as vision and hearing. To test intermodal perception, Elizabeth Spelke (1979) showed 4-month-old infants two films simultaneously. In each film, a puppet jumped up and down, but in one of the films the sound track matched the puppet's dancing movements; in the other film, it did not. By measuring the infant's gaze, Spelke found that the infants looked more at the puppet whose actions were synchronized with the sound track, suggesting that they recognized the visual-sound correspondence. Young infants can also coordinate visual-auditory information involving people. In one study, 3½-month-old infants looked more at their mother when they also heard her voice and longer at their father when they also heard his voice (Spelke & Owsley, 1979).

Might auditory-visual relations be coordinated even in newborns? Newborns do turn their eyes and their head toward the sound of a voice or rattle when the sound is maintained for several seconds (Clifton & others, 1981), but the newborn can localize a sound and look at an object only in a crude way (Bechtold, Bushnell, & Salapatek, 1979). Improved accuracy at auditory-visual coordination likely requires experience with visual and auditory stimuli.

The ability to connect information about vision with information about touch also develops in infancy. One-year-olds clearly can do this, and it appears that 6-month-olds can, too (Acredolo & Hake, 1982). Whether still younger infants can coordinate vision and touch is yet to be determined.

In sum, crude exploratory forms of intermodal perception exist in newborns. These exploratory forms of intermodal perception become sharpened with experience in the first year of life (Banks, 2005; Hollich, Newman, & Jusczyk, 2005). In the first six months, infants have difficulty connecting sensory input from different modes, but in the second half of the first year they show an increased ability to make this connection mentally. Thus, babies are born into the world with some innate abilities to perceive relations among sensory modalities, but their intermodal abilities improve considerably through experience. As with all aspects of development, in perceptual development, nature and nurture interact and cooperate (Condry, Smith, & Spelke, 2001; Lickliter & Bahrick, 2000).

intermodal perception The ability to relate and integrate information about two or more sensory modalities, such as vision and hearing.

www.mhhe.com/santrockcd11

Elizabeth Spelke's Research

Review and Reflect • LEARNING GOAL 2

2 Outline the course of sensory and perceptual development

Review

- What are sensation and perception?
- What is the ecological view of perception? What are some research methods used to study infant perception?
- How does vision develop?
- How does hearing develop?
- How do touch and pain develop? How does smell develop? How does taste develop?
- What is intermodal perception and how does it develop?

Reflect

- What would you do to effectively stimulate the hearing of a 1-year-old infant?

3 PERCEPTUAL-MOTOR COUPLING

As we come to the end of this chapter, we return to the important theme of perceptual-motor coupling. The distinction between perceiving and doing has been a time-honored tradition in psychology. However, a number of experts on perceptual and motor development question whether this distinction makes sense (Bertenthal, 2005; Gibson, 2001; Lockman, 2000; Pick, 1997; Thelen, 2001; Thelen & Whitmeyer, 2005). The main thrust of research in Esther Thelen's dynamic systems approach is to explore how people assemble motor behaviors for perceiving and acting. The main theme of the ecological approach of Eleanor and James J. Gibson is to discover how perception guides action. Action can guide perception, and perception can guide action. Only by moving one's eyes, head, hands, and arms and by moving from one location to another can an individual fully experience his or her environment and learn how to adapt to it. Perception and action are coupled.

Babies, for example, continually coordinate their movements with perceptual information to learn how to maintain balance, reach for objects in space, and move across various surfaces and terrains (Adolph & Berger, 2005, 2006; Thelen, 2000; Thelen & Smith, 2006). They are motivated to move by what they perceive. Consider the sight of an attractive toy across the room. In this situation, infants must perceive the current state of their bodies and learn how to use their limbs to reach the toy. Although their movements at first are awkward and uncoordinated, babies soon learn to select patterns that are appropriate for reaching their goals.

Equally important is the other part of the perception-action coupling. That is, action educates perception (Adolph & Berger, 2005, 2006; Bertenthal, 2005). For example, watching an object while exploring it manually helps infants to discriminate its texture, size, and hardness. Locomoting in the environment teaches babies about how objects and people look from different perspectives, or whether surfaces will support their weight. Individuals perceive in order to move and move in order to perceive. Perceptual and motor development do not occur in isolation from each other but instead are coupled (Swinnen & others, 2005; Thelen, 1995, 2000; Thelen & Smith, 2006; Thelen & Whitmeyer, 2005).

Review and Reflect • LEARNING GOAL 3

3 Discuss the connection of perception and action

Review

- How are perception and motor actions coupled in development?

Reflect

- Describe two examples, not given in the text, in which perception guides action. Then describe two examples, not given in the text, in which action guides perception.

REACH YOUR LEARNING GOALS

MOTOR, SENSORY, AND PERCEPTUAL DEVELOPMENT

1 MOTOR DEVELOPMENT

- The Dynamic Systems View
- Reflexes
- Gross Motor Skills
- Fine Motor Skills
- Handedness

2 SENSORY AND PERCEPTUAL DEVELOPMENT

- What Are Sensation and Perception?
- The Ecological View
- Vision
- Hearing
- Other Senses
- Intermodal Perception

3 PERCEPTUAL-MOTOR COUPLING

SUMMARY

1 Describe how motor skills develop

- Thelen's dynamic systems theory describes the development of motor skills as the assembling of behaviors for perceiving and acting. Perception and action are coupled. According to this theory, the development of motor skills depends on the development of the nervous system, the body's physical properties and its movement possibilities, the goal the child is motivated to reach, and environmental support for the skill. In the dynamic systems view, motor development is far more complex than the result of a genetic blueprint; the infant or child puts together a skill in order to achieve a goal within constraints set by the body and the environment.
- Reflexes—automatic movements—govern the newborn's behavior. They include the sucking, rooting, and Moro reflexes—all of which typically disappear after three to four months. Some reflexes persist throughout life; components of other reflexes are incorporated into voluntary actions.
- Gross motor skills involve large motor activities. Key skills developed during infancy include control of posture and walking. Gross motor skills improve dramatically in the childhood years.
- Fine motor skills are finely tuned motor actions. The onset of reaching and grasping marks a significant accomplishment. Fine motor skills continue to develop through the childhood years.
- Handedness likely has a genetic link. About 90 percent of children are right-handed, 10 percent left-handed. Left-handers are more likely to process speech in the right hemisphere of the brain than right-handers, and left-handers have more reading problems. Left-handers tend to have unusually good visuospatial skills and often show up in higher than expected numbers as mathematicians, musicians, architects, and artists.

2 Outline the course of sensory and perceptual development

- Sensation occurs when information interacts with sensory receptors. Perception is the interpretation of sensation.
- Created by the Gibsons, the ecological view states that people directly perceive information that exists in the world. Perception brings people in contact with the environment in order to interact and adapt to it. Affordances provide opportunities for interaction offered by objects that are necessary to perform activities.
- Researchers have developed a number of methods to assess the infant's perception, including the visual preference method (which Fantz used to determine young infants' interest in looking at patterned over nonpatterned displays), habituation and dishabituation, high-amplitude sucking, and tracking. The infant's visual acuity increases dramatically in the first year of life. Newborns can distinguish green and red; by 2 months of age all of the color-sensitive receptors function in adultlike ways. Young infants systematically scan human faces. By 3 months of age, infants show size and shape constancy. In Gibson and Walk's classic study, infants as young as 6 months of age had depth perception. As visual perception develops, infants develop visual expectations. After infancy, children's visual expectations continue to develop and further color differentiation occurs from 3 to 4 years of age. A number of children experience vision problems and 1 in every 3,000 children is educationally blind.
- The fetus can hear several weeks prior to birth. Developmental changes in the perception of loudness, pitch, and localization of sound occur during infancy. Most children's hearing is adequate, but one special concern is otitis media. A concern in adolescence is listening to loud rock music for prolonged periods of time, which can damage hearing.
- Newborns can respond to touch and feel pain. Newborns can differentiate odors, and sensitivity to taste may be present before birth.
- Infants as young as 2 months of age have intermodal perception—the ability to relate and integrate information from two or more sensory modalities. Crude, exploratory forms of intermodal perception are present in newborns and become sharpened over the first year of life.

3 Discuss the connection of perception and action

- Perception and action are coupled. Individuals perceive in order to move and move in order to perceive.

KEY TERMS

KEY PEOPLE

E-LEARNING TOOLS

To help you master the material in this chapter, visit the Online Learning Center for *Child Development,* eleventh edition (**www.mhhe.com/santrockcd11**), where you'll find these additional resources:

Taking It to the Net

1. Ten-year-old Kristen is a new member of her soccer league's select team. Kristin's parents are reluctant to allow her to participate in a high-pressure, intensely competitive atmosphere. If they allow her to participate, what can they do to make it a healthy experience for themselves and Kristen?
2. Marianne has obtained a part-time job as a nanny for Jack, a 2-month-old boy. What can Marianne expect to see in terms of the child's sensory and motor development as she interacts with and observes Jack over the next several months?
3. Frank and Elise just received Elise's sonogram results—it's a boy. Frank wants them to circumcise their son. Elise does not want their baby to undergo this painful procedure. Frank was circumcised and assures Elise that he has no memory of the pain—if there was any. Is circumcision medically necessary? If Frank and Elise decide on circumcision, can their baby have some form of anesthesia?

Nursing, Parenting, and Teaching Exercises

Build your decision-making skills by trying your hand at the scenarios on the Online Learning Center.

Video Clips

The Online Learning Center includes the following videos for this chapter.

- Grasping Reflex at 2 Weeks
  The grasping reflex is demonstrated by a 2-week-old infant who holds tightly to an adult's pinky finger.
- Auditory Tracking at 4 Months
  A 4-month-old girl demonstrates auditory perception when she looks up at her mother, after hearing her mother call her name.
- Gross Motor Ability in 2nd Year
  At 18 months, Rose can step up on and off a large block without assistance.
- Copying Shapes at Age 7
  More advanced fine motor skills in middle childhood are demonstrated by this 7-year-old. With careful attention he copies a square, a triangle, and a circle.

Section 3
COGNITION AND LANGUAGE

Learning is an ornament in prosperity, a refuge in adversity.

—ARISTOTLE
Greek Philosopher, 4th Century B.C.

Children thirst to know and understand. In their effort to know and understand, they construct their own ideas about the world around them. They are remarkable for their curiosity and their intelligence. In Section 3, you will read four chapters: "Cognitive Developmental Approaches" (chapter 7), "Information Processing" (chapter 8), "Intelligence" (chapter 9), and "Language Development" (chapter 10).

Chapter 7 COGNITIVE DEVELOPMENTAL APPROACHES

We are born capable of learning.

—Jean-Jacques Rousseau
Swiss-Born French Philosopher, 18th Century

CHAPTER OUTLINE

PIAGET'S THEORY OF COGNITIVE DEVELOPMENT

Processes of Development
Sensorimotor Stage
Preoperational Stage
Concrete Operational Stage
Formal Operational Stage

APPLYING AND EVALUATING PIAGET'S THEORY

Piaget and Education
Evaluating Piaget's Theory

VYGOTSKY'S THEORY OF COGNITIVE DEVELOPMENT

The Zone of Proximal Development
Scaffolding
Language and Thought
Teaching Strategies
Evaluating Vygotsky's Theory

LEARNING GOALS

1. **Discuss the key processes and four stages in Piaget's theory**
2. **Apply Piaget's theory to education and evaluate Piaget's theory**
3. **Identify the main concepts in Vygotsky's theory and compare it with Piaget's theory**

The Stories of Laurent, Lucienne, and Jacqueline

Jean Piaget, the famous Swiss psychologist, was a meticulous observer of his three children—Laurent, Lucienne, and Jacqueline. His books on cognitive development are filled with these observations. Here are a few of Piaget's observations of his children in infancy (Piaget, 1952):

- At 21 days of age, "Laurent found his thumb after three attempts: prolonged sucking begins each time. But, once he has been placed on his back, he does not know how to coordinate the movement of the arms with that of the mouth and his hands draw back even when his lips are seeking them" (p. 27).
- During the third month, thumb sucking becomes less important to Laurent because of new visual and auditory interests. But, when he cries, his thumb goes to the rescue.
- Toward the end of Lucienne's fourth month, while she is lying in her crib, Piaget hangs a doll above her feet. Lucienne thrusts her feet at the doll and makes it move. "Afterward, she looks at her motionless foot for a second, then recommences. There is no visual control of her foot, for the movements are the same when Lucienne only looks at the doll or when I place the doll over her head. On the other hand, the tactile control of the foot is apparent: after the first shakes, Lucienne makes slow foot movements as though to grasp and explore" (p. 159).
- At 11 months, "Jacqueline is seated and shakes a little bell. She then pauses abruptly in order to delicately place the bell in front of her right foot; then she kicks hard. Unable to recapture it, she grasps a ball which she then places at the same spot in order to give it another kick" (p. 225).
- At 1 year, 2 months, "Jacqueline holds in her hands an object which is new to her: a round, flat box which she turns all over, shakes, (and) rubs against the bassinet. . . . She lets it go and tries to pick it up. But she only succeeds in touching it with her index finger, without grasping it. She nevertheless makes an attempt and presses on the edge. The box then tilts up and falls again" (p. 273). Jacqueline shows an interest in this result and studies the fallen box.
- At 1 year, 8 months, "Jacqueline arrives at a closed door with a blade of grass in each hand. She stretches out her right hand toward the (door)knob but sees that she cannot turn it without letting go of the grass. She puts the grass on the floor, opens the door, picks up the grass again, and enters. But when she wants to leave the room, things become complicated. She puts the grass on the floor and grasps the doorknob. But then she perceives that in pulling the door toward her she will simultaneously chase away the grass which she placed between the door and the threshold. She therefore picks it up in order to put it outside the door's zone of movement" (p. 339).

For Piaget, these observations reflect important changes in the infant's cognitive development. Later in the chapter, you will learn that Piaget believed that infants go through six substages of development and that the behaviors you have just read about characterize those substages.

PREVIEW

Cognitive developmental approaches place a special emphasis on how children actively construct their thinking. They also focus heavily on how thinking changes from one point in development to another. In this chapter, we will highlight the cognitive developmental approaches of Jean Piaget and Lev Vygotsky.

1 PIAGET'S THEORY OF COGNITIVE DEVELOPMENT

- Processes of Development
- Sensorimotor Stage
- Preoperational Stage
- Concrete Operational Stage
- Formal Operational Stage

Poet Nora Perry asks, "Who knows the thoughts of a child?" As much as anyone, Piaget knew. Through careful observations of his own three children—Laurent, Lucienne, and Jacqueline—and observations of and interviews with other children, Piaget changed perceptions of the way children think about the world.

Piaget's theory is a general, unifying story of how biology and experience sculpt cognitive development. Piaget thought that, just as our physical bodies have structures that enable us to adapt to the world, we build mental structures that help us to adapt to the world. *Adaptation* involves adjusting to new environmental demands. Piaget stressed that children actively construct their own cognitive worlds; information is not just poured into their minds from the environment. He sought to discover how children at different points in their development think about the world and how systematic changes in their thinking occur.

Piaget with his wife and three children; he often used his observations of his children to provide examples of his theory.

Processes of Development

What processes do children use as they construct their knowledge of the world? Piaget believed that these processes are especially important in this regard: schemes, assimilation, accommodation, organization, equilibrium, and equilibration.

Schemes Piaget (1954) said that as the child seeks to construct an understanding of the world, the developing brain creates **schemes.** These are actions or mental representations that organize knowledge. In Piaget's theory, behavioral schemes (physical activities) characterize infancy and mental schemes (cognitive activities) develop in childhood (Lamb, Bornstein, & Teti, 2002). A baby's schemes are structured by simple actions that can be performed on objects such as sucking, looking, and grasping. Older children have schemes that include strategies and plans for solving problems. For example, a 5-year-old might have a scheme that involves the strategy of classifying objects by size, shape, or color. By the time we have reached adulthood, we have constructed an enormous number of diverse schemes, ranging from how to drive a car to balancing a budget to the concept of fairness.

Assimilation and Accommodation To explain how children use and adapt their schemes, Piaget offered two concepts that we introduced in chapter 2: assimilation and accommodation. Recall that **assimilation** occurs when children incorporate new information into their existing schemes. **Accommodation** occurs when children adjust their schemes to fit new information and experiences.

Think about a toddler who has learned the word *car* to identify the family's car. The toddler might call all moving vehicles on roads "cars," including motorcycles and trucks; the child has assimilated these objects into his or her existing scheme. But the child soon learns that motorcycles and trucks are not cars and fine-tunes the category to exclude motorcycles and trucks, accommodating the scheme.

Assimilation and accommodation operate even in very young infants. Newborns reflexively suck everything that touches their lips; they assimilate all sorts of objects into their sucking scheme. By sucking different objects, they learn about their taste, texture, shape, and so on. After several months of experience, though, they

schemes In Piaget's theory, actions or mental representations that organize knowledge.

assimilation Piagetian concept of the incorporation of new information into existing knowledge (schemes).

accommodation Piagetian concept of adjusting schemes to fit new information and experiences.

construct their understanding of the world differently. Some objects, such as fingers and the mother's breast, can be sucked, and others, such as fuzzy blankets, should not be sucked. In other words, they accommodate their sucking scheme.

Organization

To make sense out of their world, said Piaget, children cognitively organize their experiences. **Organization** in Piaget's theory is the grouping of isolated behaviors and thoughts into a higher-order system. Continual refinement of this organization is an inherent part of development. A boy who has only a vague idea about how to use a hammer may also have a vague idea about how to use other tools. After learning how to use each one, he relates these uses, organizing his knowledge.

Piaget's Theory
Piaget's Stages
The Jean Piaget Society

Equilibration and Stages of Development

Equilibration is a mechanism that Piaget proposed to explain how children shift from one stage of thought to the next. The shift occurs as children experience cognitive conflict, or disequilibrium, in trying to understand the world. Eventually, they resolve the conflict and reach a balance, or equilibrium, of thought. Piaget believed there is considerable movement between states of cognitive equilibrium and disequilibrium as assimilation and accommodation work in concert to produce cognitive change. For example, if a child believes that the amount of a liquid changes simply because the liquid is poured into a container with a different shape—for instance, from a container that is short and wide into a container that is tall and narrow—she might be puzzled by such issues as where the "extra" liquid came from and whether there is actually more liquid to drink. The child will eventually resolve these puzzles as her thought becomes more advanced. In the everyday world, the child is constantly faced with such counterexamples and inconsistencies.

Assimilation and accommodation always take the child to a higher ground. For Piaget, the motivation for change is an internal search for equilibrium. As old schemes are adjusted and new schemes are developed, the child organizes and reorganizes the old and new schemes. Eventually, the organization is fundamentally different from the old organization; it is a new way of thinking, a new stage.

The result of these processes, according to Piaget, is that individuals go through four stages of development. A different way of understanding the world makes one stage more advanced than another. Cognition is *qualitatively* different in one stage compared with another. In other words, the way children reason at one stage is different from the way they reason at another stage (Mooney, 2006).

Each of Piaget's stages is age-related and consists of distinct ways of thinking. Piaget believed that there are four stages of cognitive development: sensorimotor, preoperational, concrete operational, and formal operational (see figure 7.1).

Sensorimotor Stage

The **sensorimotor stage** lasts from birth to about 2 years of age. In this stage, infants construct an understanding of the world by coordinating sensory experiences (such as seeing and hearing) with physical, motoric actions—hence the term "sensorimotor." At the beginning of this stage, newborns have little more than reflexive patterns with which to work. At the end of the sensorimotor stage, 2-year-olds can produce complex sensorimotor patterns and use primitive symbols. We first will summarize Piaget's descriptions of how infants develop. Later we will consider criticisms of his view.

Substages

Piaget divided the sensorimotor stage into six substages: (1) simple reflexes; (2) first habits and primary circular reactions; (3) secondary circular reactions;

organization Piaget's concept of grouping isolated behaviors into a higher-order, more smoothly functioning cognitive system; the grouping or arranging of items into categories.

equilibration A mechanism that Piaget proposed to explain how children shift from one stage of thought to the next. The shift occurs as children experience cognitive conflict or disequilibrium in trying to understand the world. Eventually, they resolve the conflict and reach a balance or equilibrium of thought.

sensorimotor stage The first of Piaget's stages, which lasts from birth to about 2 years of age; infants construct an understanding of the world by coordinating sensory experiences (such as seeing and hearing) with motoric actions.

Stage	Age Range	Description
Sensorimotor	0 to 2 Years	Infants gain knowledge of the world from the physical actions they perform on it. Infants coordinate sensory experiences with these physical actions. An infant progresses from reflexive, instinctual action at birth to the beginning of symbolic thought toward the end of the stage.
Preoperational	2 to 7 Years	The child begins to use mental representations to understand the world. Symbolic thinking, reflected in the use of words and images, is used in this mental representation, which goes beyond the connection of sensory information with physical action. However, there are some constraints on the child's thinking at this stage, such as egocentrism and centration.
Concrete Operational	7 to 11 Years	The child can now reason logically about concrete events, understands the concept of conservation, organizes objects into hierarchical classes (classification), and places objects in ordered series (seriation).
Formal Operational	11 Years Through Adulthood	The adolescent reasons in more abstract, idealistic, and logical (hypothetical-deductive) ways.

FIGURE 7.1 Piaget's Four Stages of Cognitive Development

(4) coordination of secondary circular reactions; (5) tertiary circular reactions, novelty, and curiosity; and (6) internalization of schemes.

Simple reflexes, the first sensorimotor substage, corresponds to the first month after birth. In this substage, sensation and action are coordinated primarily through reflexive behaviors, such as the rooting and sucking reflexes. Soon the infant produces behaviors that resemble reflexes in the absence of the usual stimulus for the reflex. For example, a newborn will suck a nipple or bottle only when it is placed directly in the baby's mouth or touched to the lips. But soon the infant might suck when a bottle or nipple is only nearby. The infant is initiating action and is actively structuring experiences in the first month of life.

First habits and primary circular reactions is the second sensorimotor substage, which develops between 1 and 4 months of age. In this substage, the infant coordinates sensation and two types of schemes: habits and primary circular reactions. A *habit* is a scheme based on a reflex that has become completely separated from its eliciting stimulus. For example, infants in substage 1 suck when bottles are put to their lips or when they see a bottle. Infants in substage 2 might suck even when no bottle is present. A *circular reaction* is a repetitive action.

A *primary circular reaction* is a scheme based on the attempt to reproduce an event that initially occurred by chance. For example, suppose an infant accidentally sucks his fingers when they are placed near his mouth. Later, he searches for his fingers to suck them again, but the fingers do not cooperate because the infant cannot coordinate visual and manual actions.

Habits and circular reactions are stereotyped: that is, the infant repeats them the same way each time. During this substage, the infant's own body remains the infant's center of attention. There is no outward pull by environmental events.

Secondary circular reactions is the third sensorimotor substage, which develops between 4 and 8 months of age. In this substage, the infant becomes more

I wish I could travel by the road that crosses the baby's mind, and out beyond all bounds; where messengers run errands for no cause between the kingdoms of kings of no history; where reason makes kites of her laws and flies them, and truth sets facts free from its fetters.

—Rabindranath Tagore
Bengali Poet and Essayist, 20th Century

object-oriented, moving beyond preoccupation with the self. By chance, an infant might shake a rattle. The infant repeats this action for the sake of its fascination. The infant also imitates some simple actions, such as the baby talk or burbling of adults, and some physical gestures. However, the baby imitates only actions that he or she is already able to produce. Although directed toward objects in the world, the infant's schemes are not intentional or goal-directed.

Coordination of secondary circular reactions is Piaget's fourth sensorimotor substage, which develops between 8 and 12 months of age. To progress into this substage the infant must coordinate vision and touch, hand and eye. Actions become more outwardly directed. Significant changes during this substage involve the coordination of schemes and intentionality. Infants readily combine and recombine previously learned schemes in a coordinated way. They might look at an object and grasp it simultaneously, or they might visually inspect a toy, such as a rattle, and finger it simultaneously, exploring it tactilely. Actions are even more outwardly directed than before. Related to this coordination is the second achievement—the presence of intentionality. For example, infants might manipulate a stick in order to bring a desired toy within reach or they might knock over one block to reach and play with another one.

Tertiary circular reactions, novelty, and curiosity is Piaget's fifth sensorimotor substage, which develops between 12 and 18 months of age. In this substage, infants become intrigued by the many properties of objects and by the many things that they can make happen to objects. A block can be made to fall, spin, hit another object, and slide across the ground. *Tertiary circular reactions* are schemes in which the infant purposely explores new possibilities with objects, continually doing new things to them and exploring the results. Piaget says that this stage marks the starting point for human curiosity and interest in novelty.

Internalization of schemes is Piaget's sixth and final sensorimotor substage, which develops between 18 and 24 months of age. In this substage, the infant develops the ability to use primitive symbols. For Piaget, a *symbol* is an internalized sensory image or word that represents an event. Primitive symbols permit the infant to think about concrete events without directly acting them out or perceiving them. Moreover, symbols allow the infant to manipulate and transform the represented events in simple ways. In a favorite Piagetian example, Piaget's young daughter saw a matchbox being opened and closed. Later, she mimicked the event by opening and closing her mouth. This was an obvious expression of her image of the event.

Object Permanence Imagine how chaotic and unpredictable your life would be if you could not distinguish between yourself and your world. This is what the life of a newborn must be like, according to Piaget. There is no differentiation between the self and world; objects have no separate, permanent existence.

By the end of the sensorimotor period, objects are both separate from the self and permanent. **Object permanence** is the understanding that objects and events continue to exist even when they cannot be seen, heard, or touched. Acquiring the sense of object permanence is one of the infant's most important accomplishments. According to Piaget, infants develop object permanence in a series of substages that correspond to the six substages of sensorimotor development. Figure 7.2 shows how the six substages of object permanence reflect Piaget's substages of sensorimotor development.

How could anyone know whether an infant had a sense of object permanence or not? The principal way that object permanence is studied is by watching an infant's reaction when an interesting object disappears (see figure 7.3). If infants search for the object, it is assumed that they believe it continues to exist.

Object permanence is just one of the basic concepts about the physical world developed by babies. To Piaget, children, even infants, are much like little scientists,

object permanence The Piagetian term for one of an infant's most important accomplishments: understanding that objects and events continue to exist even when they cannot directly be seen, heard, or touched.

FIGURE 7.2 The Six Substages of Object Permanence

Sensorimotor Stage	Behavior
Substage 1	There is no apparent object permanence. When a spot of light moves across the visual field, an infant follows it but quickly ignores its disappearance.
Substage 2	A primitive form of object permanence develops. Given the same experience, the infant looks briefly at the spot where the light disappeared, with an expression of passive expectancy.
Substage 3	The infant's sense of object permanence undergoes further development. With the newfound ability to coordinate simple schemes, the infant shows clear patterns of searching for a missing object, with sustained visual and manual examination of the spot where the object apparently disappeared.
Substage 4	The infant actively searches for a missing object in the spot where it disappeared, with new actions to achieve the goal of searching effectively. For example, if an attractive toy has been hidden behind a screen, the infant may look at the screen and try to push it away with a hand. If the screen is too heavy to move or is permanently fixed, the infant readily substitutes a secondary scheme—for example, crawling around it or kicking it. These new actions signal that the infant's belief in the continued existence of the missing object is strengthening.
Substage 5	The infant now is able to track an object that disappears and reappears in several locations in rapid succession. For example, a toy may be hidden under different boxes in succession in front of the infant, who succeeds in finding it. The infant is apparently able to hold an image of the missing object in mind longer than before.
Substage 6	The infant can search for a missing object that disappeared and reappeared in several locations in succession, as before. In addition, the infant searches in the appropriate place even when the object has been hidden from view as it is being moved. This activity indicates that the infant is able to "imagine" the missing object and to follow the image from one location to the next.

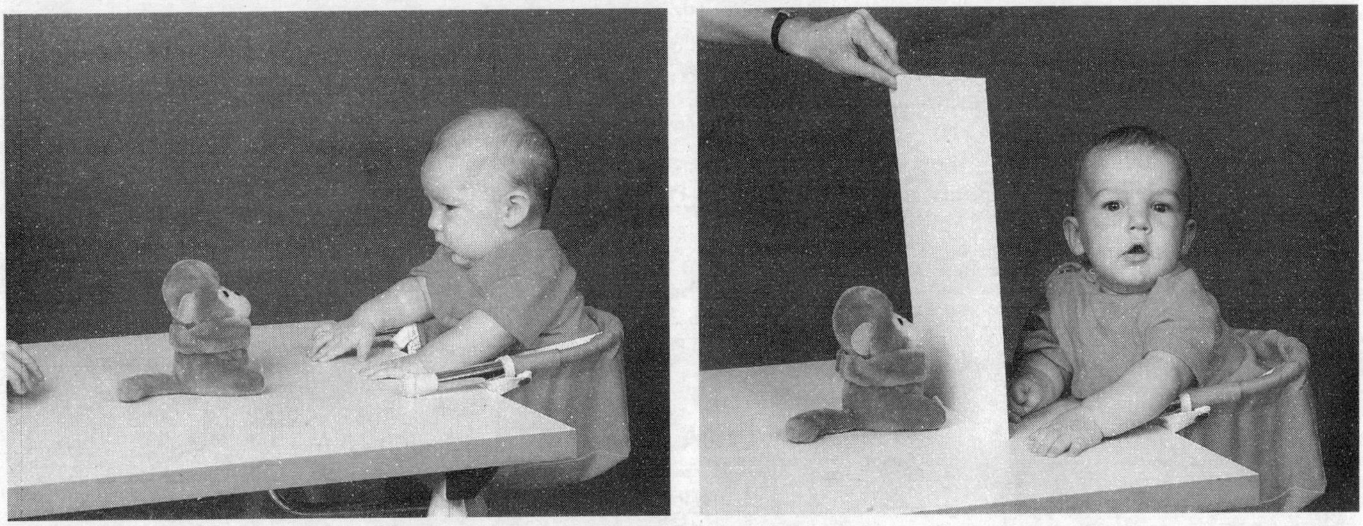

FIGURE 7.3 **Object Permanence.** Piaget thought that object permanence is one of infancy's landmark cognitive accomplishments. For this 5-month-old boy, "out-of-sight" is literally out of mind. The infant looks at the toy monkey (*left*), but, when his view of the toy is blocked (*right*), he does not search for it. Several months later, he will search for the hidden toy monkey, reflecting the presence of object permanence.

examining the world to see how it works. The Research in Child Development interlude describes some of the ways in which adult scientists try to discover what these "baby scientists" are finding out about the world.

RESEARCH IN CHILD DEVELOPMENT

Object Permanence and Causality

Two accomplishments of infants that Piaget examined were the development of object permanence and the child's understanding of causality. Let's examine two research studies that address these topics.

In both studies, Renee Baillargeon and her colleagues used a research method that involves *violation of expectations.* In this method, infants see an event happen as it normally would. Then, the event is changed in a way that violates what the infant expects to see. When infants look longer at the event that violates their expectations it indicates they are surprised by it.

In one study focused on object permanence, researchers showed infants a toy car that moved down an inclined track, disappeared behind a screen, and then reemerged at the other end, still on the track (Baillargeon & DeVoe, 1991) (see figure 7.4a). After this sequence was repeated several times, something different occurred: a toy mouse was placed *behind* the tracks but was hidden by the screen while the car rolled by (b). This was the "possible" event. Then, the researchers created an "impossible event": the toy mouse was placed *on* the tracks but was secretly removed after the screen was lowered so that the car seemed to go through the mouse (c). In this study, infants as young as 3½ months of age looked longer at the impossible event than at the possible event, indicating that they were surprised by it. Their surprise suggested that they remembered not only that the toy mouse still existed (object permanence) but its location.

Another study, illustrated in figure 7.5, focused on the infant's understanding of causality (Kotovsky & Baillargeon, 1994) (see figure 7.5). In this research, a cylinder rolls down a ramp and hits a toy bug at the bottom of the ramp. By 5½ and 6½ months of age, after infants have seen how far the bug will be pushed by a medium-sized cylinder, their reactions indicate that they understand that the bug will roll farther if it is hit by a large cylinder than if it is hit by a small cylinder. Thus, by the middle of the first year of life these infants understood that the size of a moving object determines how far it will move a stationary object that it collides with.

FIGURE 7.4 **Using the Violation of Expectations Method to Study Object Permanence in Infants**

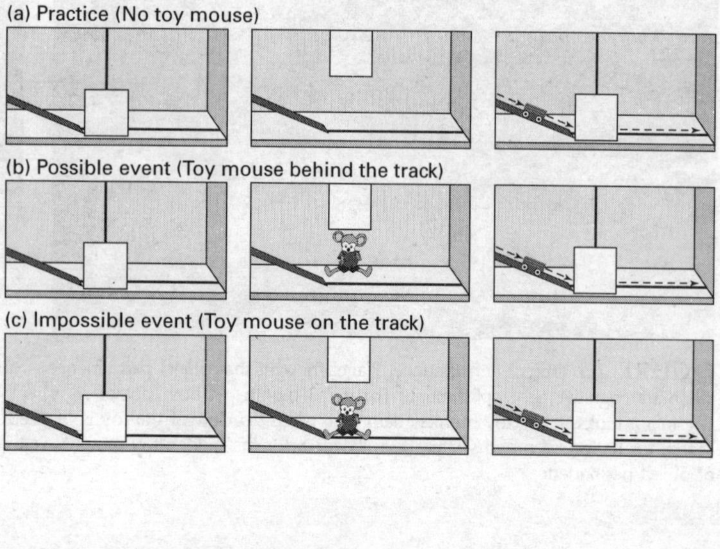

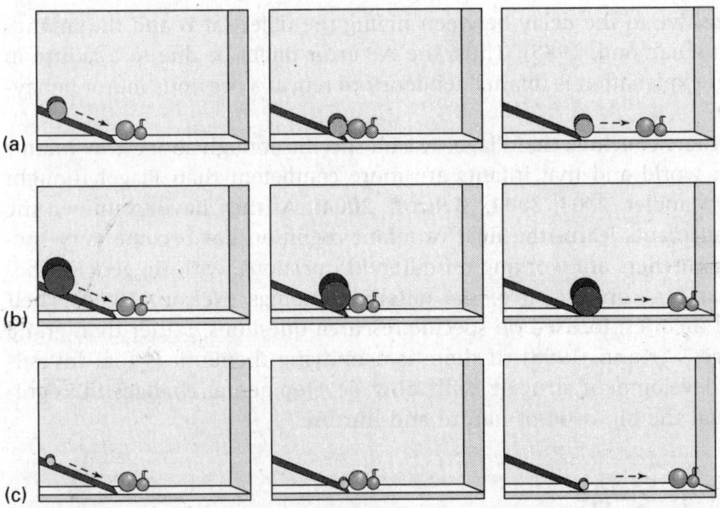

FIGURE 7.5 The Infants' Understanding of Causality. After young infants saw how far the medium-sized cylinder (*a*) pushed a toy bug, they showed more surprise at the event in (*c*) that showed a very small cylinder pushing the toy bug as far as the large cylinder (*b*). Their surprise, indicated by looking at (*c*) longer than (*b*), indicated that they understood the size of a cylinder was a causal factor in determining how far the toy bug would be pushed when it was hit by the cylinder.

Evaluating Piaget's Sensorimotor Stage Piaget opened up a new way of looking at infants with his view that their main task is to coordinate their sensory impressions with their motor activity. However, the infant's cognitive world is not as neatly packaged as Piaget portrayed it, and some of Piaget's explanations for the cause of change are debated (Luo & Baillargeon, 2005; Wang, Baillargeon & Paterson, 2005).

Piaget constructed his view of infancy mainly by observing the development of his own three children. In the past several decades, sophisticated experimental techniques have been devised to study infants, and there have been a large number of research studies on infant development. Much of the new research suggests that Piaget's view of sensorimotor development needs to be modified (Bremner, 2004).

A number of theorists, such as Eleanor Gibson (2001) and Elizabeth Spelke (1991; Spelke & Newport, 1998), believe that infants' perceptual abilities are highly developed very early in development. For example, in chapter 6 we discussed Spelke's research that demonstrated the presence of intermodal perception—the ability to coordinate information from two or more sensory modalities, such as vision and hearing. Research by Renee Baillargeon and her colleagues (1995, 2002, 2004; Aguiar & Baillargeon, 2002) documents that infants as young as 3 to 4 months expect objects to be *substantial* (in the sense that other objects cannot move through them) and *permanent* (in the sense that objects continue to exist when they are hidden).

In sum, researchers believe that infants see objects as bounded, unitary, solid, and separate from their background, possibly at birth or shortly thereafter, but definitely by 3 to 4 months of age, much earlier than Piaget envisioned. Young infants still have much to learn about objects, but the world appears both stable and orderly to them.

Piaget claimed that certain processes are crucial in stage transitions, but the data do not always support his explanations. For example, in Piaget's theory, an important feature in the progression into substage 4, coordination of secondary circular reactions, is an infant's inclination to search for a hidden object in a familiar location rather than to look for the object in a new location. **A$\bar{\text{B}}$ error** (also called A-not-B error) is the term used to describe infants who make the mistake of selecting the familiar hiding place (A) rather than the new hiding place (B) as they progress into substage 4. For example, if a toy is hidden twice, initially at location A and subsequently at location B, 8- to 12-month-old infants search correctly at location A initially but when the toy is subsequently hidden at location B they make the mistake of continuing to search for it at location A. Older infants are less likely to make the A$\bar{\text{B}}$ error. Researchers have found, however, that the A$\bar{\text{B}}$ error does not show up consistently (Corrigan, 1981; Sophian, 1985). The evidence indicates that

A$\bar{\text{B}}$ error The Piagetian object-permanence concept in which an infant progressing into substage 4 makes frequent mistakes, selecting the familiar hiding place (A) rather than the new hiding place (B).

Infants know that objects are substantial and permanent at an earlier age than Piaget envisioned.

—RENEE BAILLARGEON
Contemporary Psychologist, University of Illinois

www.mhhe.com/santrockcd11

Challenges to Piaget

A$\overline{B}$ errors are sensitive to the delay between hiding the object at B and the infant's attempt to find it (Diamond, 1985). Thus, the A$\overline{B}$ error might be due to a failure in memory. Another explanation is infants' tendency to repeat a previous motor behavior (Smith, 1999).

Many researchers conclude that Piaget wasn't specific enough about how infants learn about their world and that infants are more competent than Piaget thought (Bremner, 2004; Mandler, 2003, 2004; Meltzoff, 2004). As they have examined the specific ways that infants learn, the field of infant cognition has become very specialized. Many researchers are working on different questions, with no general theory emerging that can connect all of the different findings (Nelson, 1999). Their theories are local theories, focused on specific research questions, rather than grand theories like Piaget's (Kuhn, 1998). If there is a unifying theme, it is that investigators in infant development struggle with how developmental changes in cognition take place and the big issue of nature and nurture.

Preoperational Stage

The cognitive world of the preschool child is creative, free, and fanciful. The imagination of preschool children works overtime, and their mental grasp of the world improves. Piaget described the preschool child's cognition as *preoperational*. What did he mean?

Because Piaget called this stage preoperational, it might sound unimportant. Not so. Preoperational thought is anything but a convenient waiting period for the next stage, concrete operational thought. However, the label *preoperational* emphasizes that the child does not yet perform **operations,** which are internalized actions that allow children to do mentally what before they could do only physically. Operations are reversible mental actions. Mentally adding and subtracting numbers are examples of operations. *Preoperational thought* is the beginning of the ability to reconstruct in thought what has been established in behavior.

The **preoperational stage,** which lasts from approximately 2 to 7 years of age, is the second Piagetian stage. In this stage, children begin to represent the world with words, images, and drawings. Symbolic thought goes beyond simple connections of sensory information and physical action. Stable concepts are formed, mental reasoning emerges, egocentrism is present, and magical beliefs are constructed. Preoperational thought can be divided into substages: the symbolic function substage and the intuitive thought substage.

The Symbolic Function Substage

The **symbolic function substage** is the first substage of preoperational thought, occurring roughly between the ages of 2 and 4. In this substage, the young child gains the ability to mentally represent an object that is not present. This ability vastly expands the child's mental world (DeLoache, 2001, 2004). Young children use scribble designs to represent people, houses, cars, clouds, and so on; they begin to use language and engage in pretend play. However, although young children make distinct progress during this substage, their thought still has several important limitations, two of which are egocentrism and animism.

Egocentrism is the inability to distinguish between one's own perspective and someone else's perspective. The following telephone conversation between 4-year-old Mary, who is at home, and her father, who is at work, typifies Mary's egocentric thought:

Father: Mary, is Mommy there?
Mary: (Silently nods)
Father: Mary, may I speak to Mommy?
Mary: (Nods again silently)

Mary's response is egocentric in that she fails to consider her father's perspective before replying. A nonegocentric thinker would have responded verbally.

operations Internalized sets of actions that allow children to do mentally what before they had done physically. Operations also are reversible mental actions.

preoperational stage The second Piagetian developmental stage, which lasts from about 2 to 7 years of age; children begin to represent the world with words, images, and drawings.

symbolic function substage The first substage of preoperational thought, occurring roughly between the ages of 2 and 4. In this substage, the young child gains the ability to represent mentally an object that is not present.

egocentrism An important feature of preoperational thought, the inability to distinguish between one's own and someone else's perspective.

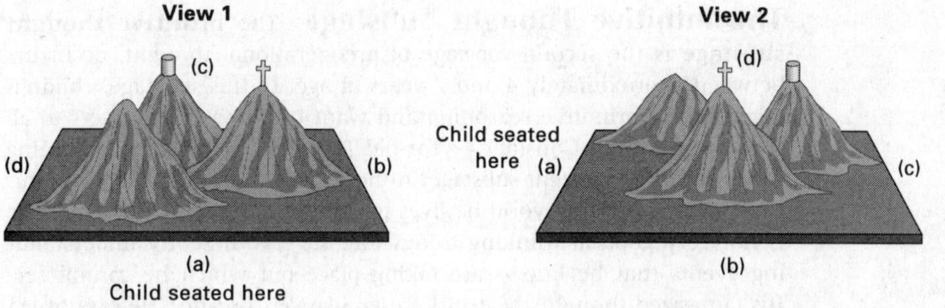

FIGURE 7.6 The Three Mountains Task. View 1 shows the child's perspective from where he or she is sitting. View 2 is an example of the photograph the child would be shown, mixed in with others from different perspectives. To correctly identify this view, the child has to take the perspective of a person sitting at spot (*b*). Invariably, a preschool child who thinks in a preoperational way cannot perform this task. When asked what a view of the mountains looks like from position (*b*), the child selects a photograph taken from location (*a*), the child's view at the time.

Piaget and Barbel Inhelder (1969) initially studied young children's egocentrism by devising the three mountains task (see figure 7.6). The child walks around the model of the mountains and becomes familiar with what the mountains look like from different perspectives, and she can see that there are different objects on the mountains. The child is then seated on one side of the table on which the mountains are placed. The experimenter moves a doll to different locations around the table, at each location asking the child to select from a series of photos the one photo that most accurately reflects the view the doll is seeing. Children in the preoperational stage often pick their own view rather than the doll's view. Preschool children frequently show perspective skills on some tasks but not others.

Animism, another limitation of preoperational thought, is the belief that inanimate objects have lifelike qualities and are capable of action (Gelman & Opfer, 2004). A young child might show animism by saying, "That tree pushed the leaf off, and it fell down," or "The sidewalk made me mad; it made me fall down." A young child who uses animism fails to distinguish the appropriate occasions for using human and nonhuman perspectives.

animism A facet of preoperational thought, the belief that inanimate objects have "lifelike" qualities and are capable of action.

Possibly because young children are not very concerned about reality, their drawings are fanciful and inventive. Suns are blue, skies are yellow, and cars float on clouds in their symbolic, imaginative world. One 3½-year-old looked at a scribble he had just drawn and described it as a pelican kissing a seal (see figure 7.7a). The symbolism is simple but strong, like abstractions found in some modern art. Twentieth-century Spanish artist Pablo Picasso commented, "I used to draw like Raphael but it has taken me a lifetime to draw like young children." In the elementary school years, a child's drawings become more realistic, neat, and precise (see figure 7.7b). Suns are yellow, skies are blue, and cars travel on roads (Winner, 1986).

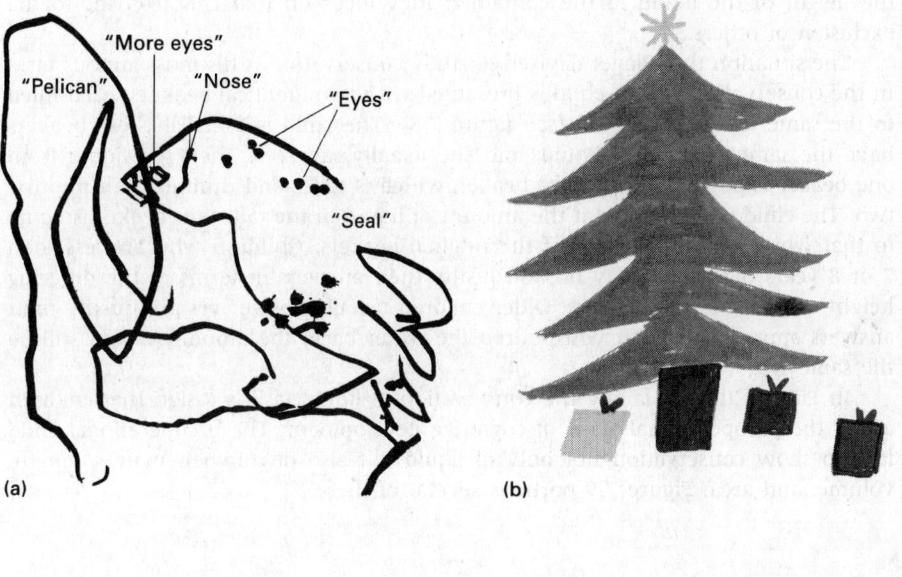

FIGURE 7.7 The Symbolic Drawings of Young Children. (*a*) A 3½-year-old's symbolic drawing. Halfway into this drawing, the 3½-year-old artist said it was "a pelican kissing a seal." (*b*) This 11-year-old's drawing is neater and more realistic but also less inventive.

"I still don't have all the answer, but I'm beginning to ask the right questions."

The Intuitive Thought Substage The **intuitive thought substage** is the second substage of preoperational thought, occurring between approximately 4 and 7 years of age. In this substage, children begin to use primitive reasoning and want to know the answers to all sorts of questions. Consider 4-year-old Tommy, who is at the beginning of the intuitive thought substage. Although he is starting to develop his own ideas about the world he lives in, his ideas are still simple, and he is not very good at thinking things out. He has difficulty understanding events that he knows are taking place but which he cannot see. His fantasized thoughts bear little resemblance to reality. He cannot yet answer the question "What if?" in any reliable way. For example, he has only a vague idea of what would happen if a car were to hit him. He also has difficulty negotiating traffic because he cannot do the mental calculations necessary to estimate whether an approaching car will hit him when he crosses the road.

By the age of 5 children have just about exhausted the adults around them with "why" questions. The child's questions signal the emergence of interest in reasoning and in figuring out why things are the way they are. Following are some samples of the questions children ask during the questioning period of 4 to 6 years of age (Elkind, 1976):

"What makes you grow up?"
"What makes you stop growing?"
"Why does a lady have to be married to have a baby?"
"Who was the mother when everybody was a baby?"
"Why do leaves fall?"
"Why does the sun shine?"

Piaget called this substage *intuitive* because young children seem so sure about their knowledge and understanding yet are unaware of how they know what they know. That is, they know something but know it without the use of rational thinking.

Centration and the Limits of Preoperational Thought One limitation of preoperational thought is **centration,** a centering of attention on one characteristic to the exclusion of all others. Centration is most clearly evidenced in young children's lack of **conservation,** the awareness that altering an object's or a substance's appearance does not change its basic properties. For example, to adults, it is obvious that a certain amount of liquid stays the same, regardless of a container's shape. But this is not at all obvious to young children. Instead, they are struck by the height of the liquid in the container; they focus on that characteristic to the exclusion of others.

The situation that Piaget devised to study conservation is his most famous task. In the conservation task, a child is presented with two identical beakers, each filled to the same level with liquid (see figure 7.8). The child is asked if these beakers have the same amount of liquid, and she usually says yes. Then the liquid from one beaker is poured into a third beaker, which is taller and thinner than the first two. The child is then asked if the amount of liquid in the tall, thin beaker is equal to that which remains in one of the original beakers. Children who are less than 7 or 8 years old usually say no and justify their answers in terms of the differing height or width of the beakers. Older children usually answer yes and justify their answers appropriately ("If you poured the water back, the amount would still be the same").

In Piaget's theory, failing the conservation-of-liquid task is a sign that children are at the preoperational stage of cognitive development. The preoperational child fails to show conservation not only of liquid but also of number, matter, length, volume, and area. Figure 7.9 portrays several of these.

intuitive thought substage The second substage of preoperational thought, occurring between approximately 4 and 7 years of age. Children begin to use primitive reasoning and want to know the answers to all sorts of questions.

centration The focusing of attention on one characteristic to the exclusion of all others.

conservation The idea that an amount stays the same regardless of how its container changes.

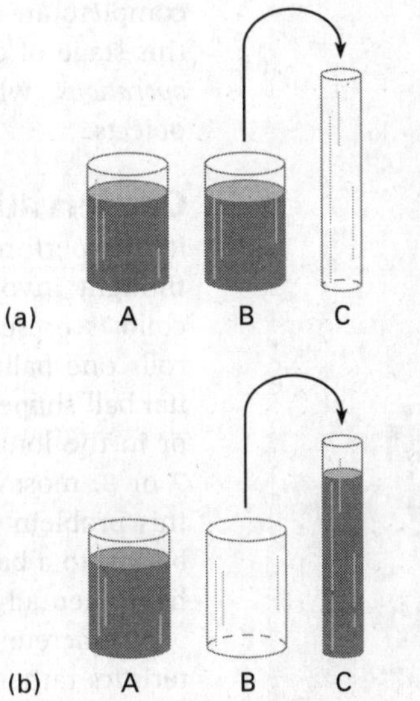

FIGURE 7.8 **Piaget's Conservation Task.** The beaker test is a well-known Piagetian test to determine whether a child can think operationally—that is, can mentally reverse actions and show conservation of the substance. (*a*) Two identical beakers are presented to the child. Then, the experimenter pours the liquid from B into C, which is taller and thinner than A or B. (*b*) The child is asked if these beakers (A and C) have the same amount of liquid. The preoperational child says no. When asked to point to the beaker that has more liquid, the preoperational child points to the tall, thin beaker.

Children often vary in their performance on different conservation tasks. Thus, a child might be able to conserve volume but not number.

Some developmentalists do not believe Piaget was entirely correct in his estimate of when children's conservation skills emerge. For example, Rochel Gelman (1969) showed that when the child's attention to relevant aspects of the conservation task is improved, the child is more likely to conserve. Gelman has also demonstrated that attentional training on one dimension, such as number, improves the preschool child's performance on another dimension, such as mass. Thus, Gelman believes that conservation appears earlier than Piaget thought and that attention is especially important in explaining conservation.

Concrete Operational Stage

The **concrete operational stage,** which lasts approximately from 7 to 11 years of age, is the third Piagetian stage. In this stage, logical reasoning replaces intuitive reasoning as long as the reasoning can be applied to specific or concrete examples. For instance, concrete operational thinkers cannot imagine the steps necessary to

concrete operational stage Piaget's third stage, which lasts from approximately 7 to 11 years of age; children can perform operations, and logical reasoning replaces intuitive reasoning as long as the reasoning can be applied to specific, concrete examples.

Type of Conservation	Initial Presentation	Manipulation	Preoperational Child's Answer
Number	Two identical rows of objects are shown to the child, who agrees they have the same number.	One row is lengthened and the child is asked whether one row now has more objects.	Yes, the longer row.
Matter	Two identical balls of clay are shown to the child. The child agrees that they are equal.	The experimenter changes the shape of one of the balls and asks the child whether they still contain equal amounts of clay.	No, the longer one has more.
Length	Two sticks are aligned in front of the child. The child agrees that they are the same length.	The experimenter moves one stick to the right, then asks the child if they are equal in length.	No, the one on the top is longer.

FIGURE 7.9 **Some Dimensions of Conservation: Number, Matter, and Length**

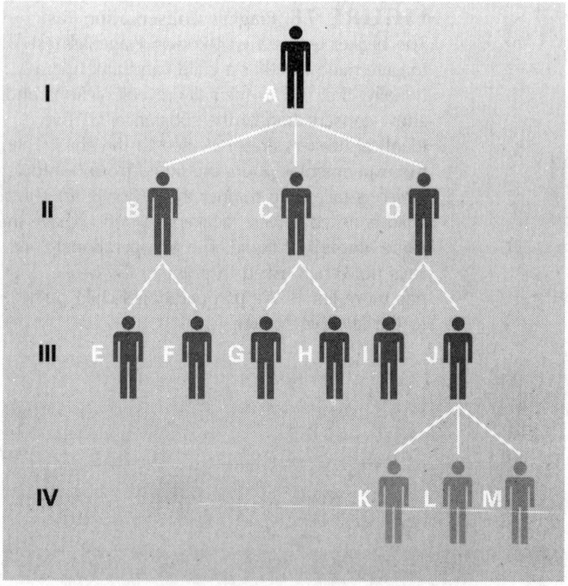

FIGURE 7.10 Classification: An Important Ability in Concrete Operational Thought. A family tree of four generations (*I to IV*): The preoperational child has trouble classifying the members of the four generations; the concrete operational child can classify the members vertically, horizontally, and obliquely (up and down and across). For example, the concrete operational child understands that a family member can be a son, a brother, and a father, all at the same time.

complete an algebraic equation, which is too abstract for thinking at this stage of development. Children at this stage can perform *concrete operations,* which are reversible mental actions on real, concrete objects.

Conservation The conservation tasks demonstrate a child's ability to perform concrete operations. In the test of reversibility of thought involving conservation of matter (shown in figure 7.9), a child is presented with two identical balls of clay. An experimenter rolls one ball into a long, thin shape; the other remains in its original ball shape. The child is then asked if there is more clay in the ball or in the long, thin piece of clay. By the time children reach the age 7 or 8, most answer that the amount of clay is the same. To answer this problem correctly, children have to imagine the clay ball rolling back into a ball after it has been changed into a long, thin shape; they have mentally reversed the action on the ball.

Concrete operations allow children to coordinate several characteristics rather than focus on a single property of an object. In the clay example, a preoperational child is likely to focus on height or width; a concrete operational child coordinates information about both dimensions. Conservation involves recognition that the length, number, mass, quantity, area, weight, and volume of objects and substances are not changed by transformations that merely alter their appearance.

Children do not conserve all quantities or conserve on all tasks simultaneously. The order of their mastery is number, length, liquid quantity, mass, weight, and volume. **Horizontal décalage** is Piaget's concept that similar abilities do not appear at the same time within a stage of development. During the concrete operational stage, conservation of number usually appears first and conservation of volume last. Also, an 8-year-old child may know that a long stick of clay can be rolled back into a ball but not understand that the ball and the stick weigh the same. At about 9 years of age, the child recognizes that they weigh the same, and eventually, at about 11 to 12 years of age, the child understands that the clay's volume is unchanged by rearranging it. Children initially master tasks in which the dimensions are more salient and visible, only later mastering those not as visually apparent, such as volume.

Classification Many of the concrete operations identified by Piaget involve the ways children reason about the properties of objects. One important skill that characterizes concrete operational children is the ability to classify things and to consider their relationships. Specifically, concrete operational children can understand (1) the interrelationships among sets and subsets, (2) seriation, and (3) transitivity.

The ability of the concrete operational child to divide things into sets and subsets and understand their relationship is illustrated by a family tree of four generations (Furth & Wachs, 1975) (see figure 7.10). This family tree suggests that the grandfather (A) has three children (B, C, and D), each of whom has two children (E through J), and that one of these children (J) has three children (K, L, and M). The concrete operational child understands that person J can, at the same time, be father, brother, and grandson. A child who comprehends this classification system can move up and down a level (vertically), across a level (horizontally), and up and down and across (obliquely) within the system.

Seriation is the ordering of stimuli along a quantitative dimension (such as length). To see if children can serialize, a teacher might haphazardly place eight sticks of different lengths on a table. The teacher then asks the children to order the sticks by length. Many young children put the sticks into two or three small groups of "big" sticks or "little" sticks, rather than a correct ordering of all eight sticks. Or they line up the tops of the sticks but ignore the bottoms. The concrete

horizontal décalage Piaget's concept that similar abilities do not appear at the same time within a stage of development.

seriation The concrete operation that involves ordering stimuli along a quantitative dimension (such as length).

operational thinker simultaneously understands that each stick must be longer than the one that precedes it and shorter than the one that follows it.

Transitivity involves the ability to reason about and logically combine relationships. If a relation holds between a first object and a second object, and also holds between the second object and a third object, then it also holds between the first and third objects. For example, consider three sticks (A, B, and C) of differing lengths. A is the longest, B is intermediate in length, and C is the shortest. Does the child understand that if A is longer than B, and B is longer than C, then A is longer than C? In Piaget's theory, concrete operational thinkers do; preoperational thinkers do not.

Formal Operational Stage

So far we have studied the first three of Piaget's stages of cognitive development: sensorimotor, preoperational, and concrete operational. What are the characteristics of the fourth stage?

The **formal operational stage,** which appears between 11 and 15 years of age, is the fourth and final Piagetian stage. In this stage, individuals move beyond concrete experiences and think in abstract and more logical ways. As part of thinking more abstractly, adolescents develop images of ideal circumstances. They might think about what an ideal parent is like and compare their parents to their ideal standards. They begin to entertain possibilities for the future and are fascinated with what they can be. In solving problems, formal operational thinkers are more systematic and use logical reasoning.

Might adolescents' ability to reason hypothetically and to evaluate what is ideal versus what is real lead them to engage in demonstrations, such as this protest related to better ethnic relations? What other causes might be attractive to adolescents' newfound cognitive abilities of hypothetical-deductive reasoning and idealistic thinking?

Abstract, Idealistic, and Logical Thinking

The abstract quality of the adolescent's thought at the formal operational level is evident in the adolescent's verbal problem-solving ability. The concrete operational thinker needs to see the concrete elements A, B, and C to be able to make the logical inference that, if A = B and B = C, then A = C. The formal operational thinker can solve this problem merely through verbal presentation.

Another indication of the abstract quality of adolescents' thought is their increased tendency to think about thought itself. One adolescent commented, "I began thinking about why I was thinking about what I was. Then I began thinking about why I was thinking about what I was thinking about what I was." If this sounds abstract, it is, and it characterizes the adolescent's enhanced focus on thought and its abstract qualities.

Accompanying the abstract thought of adolescence is thought full of idealism and possibilities. While children frequently think in concrete ways, or in terms of what is real and limited, adolescents begin to engage in extended speculation about ideal characteristics—qualities they desire in themselves and in others. Such thoughts often lead adolescents to compare themselves with others in regard to ideal standards. And the thoughts of adolescents are often fantasy flights into future possibilities. It is not unusual for the adolescent to become impatient with these newfound ideal standards and to become perplexed over which of many ideal standards to adopt.

As adolescents are learning to think more abstractly and idealistically, they are also learning to think more logically. Children are likely to solve problems in a trial-and-error fashion. Adolescents begin to think more as a scientist thinks, devising plans to solve problems and systematically testing solutions. They use **hypothetical-deductive reasoning**, which means that they develop hypotheses, or best guesses, and systematically deduce, or conclude, which is the best path to follow in solving the problem.

transitivity If a relation holds between a first object and a second object, and holds between the second object and a third object, then it holds between the first object and the third object. Piaget believed that an understanding of transitivity is characteristic of concrete operational thought.

formal operational stage Piaget's fourth and final stage, which occurs between the ages of 11 and 15; individuals move beyond concrete experiences and think in more abstract and logical ways.

hypothetical-deductive reasoning Piaget's formal operational concept that adolescents have the cognitive ability to develop hypotheses about ways to solve problems and can systematically deduce which is the best path to follow in solving the problem.

The thoughts of youth are long, long thoughts.

—Henry Wadsworth Longfellow
American Poet, 19th Century

One example of hypothetical-deductive reasoning involves a modification of the familiar game Twenty Questions. Individuals are shown a set of 42 color pictures, displayed in a rectangular array (six rows of seven pictures each) and are asked to determine which picture the experimenter has in mind (that is, which is "correct"). The individuals are allowed to ask only questions to which the experimenter can answer yes or no. The object of the game is to select the correct picture by asking as few questions as possible. Adolescents who are deductive hypothesis testers formulate a plan and test a series of hypotheses, which considerably narrows the field of choices. The most effective plan is a "halving" strategy (Q: Is the picture in the right half of the array?).

Assimilation (incorporating new information into existing knowledge) dominates the initial development of formal operational thought, and these thinkers perceive the world subjectively and idealistically. Later in adolescence, as intellectual balance is restored, these individuals accommodate to the cognitive upheaval that has occurred (they adjust to the new information).

Some of Piaget's ideas on formal operational thought are being challenged (Byrnes, 2003; Eccles, Wigfield, & Byrnes, 2003; Keating, 2004; Kuhn & Franklin, 2006). There is much more individual variation in formal operational thought than Piaget envisioned (Kuhn, 2000; Kuhn & Franklin, 2006). Only about 1 in 3 young adolescents is a formal operational thinker. Many American adults never become formal operational thinkers, and neither do many adults in other cultures.

Many adolescent girls spend long hours in front of the mirror, depleting cans of hairspray, tubes of lipstick, and jars of cosmetics. *How might this behavior be related to changes in adolescent cognitive and physical development?*

Adolescent Egocentrism In addition to thinking more logically, abstractly, and idealistically—characteristics of Piaget's formal operational thought stage—in what other ways do adolescents change cognitively? David Elkind (1978) has described how adolescent egocentrism governs the way that adolescents think about social matters. **Adolescent egocentrism** is the heightened self-consciousness of adolescents, which is reflected in their belief that others are as interested in them as they are in themselves, and in their sense of personal uniqueness and invincibility. Elkind believes that adolescent egocentrism can be dissected into two types of social thinking—imaginary audience and personal fable.

The **imaginary audience** refers to the aspect of adolescent egocentrism that involves attention-getting behavior—the attempt to be noticed, visible, and "onstage." An adolescent boy might think that others are as aware of a few hairs that are out of place as he is. An adolescent girl walks into her classroom and thinks that all eyes are riveted on her complexion. Adolescents especially sense that they are "onstage" in early adolescence, believing they are the main actors and all others are the audience.

According to Elkind, the **personal fable** is the part of adolescent egocentrism that involves an adolescent's sense of personal uniqueness and invincibility. Adolescents' sense of personal uniqueness makes them feel that no one can understand how they really feel. For example, an adolescent girl thinks that her mother cannot possibly sense the hurt she feels because her boyfriend has broken up with her. As part of their effort to retain a sense of personal uniqueness, adolescents might craft stories about themselves that are filled with fantasy, immersing themselves in a world that is far removed from reality. Personal fables frequently show up in adolescent diaries.

Adolescents also often show a sense of invincibility—feeling that although others might be vulnerable to tragedies, such as a terrible car wreck, these things won't happen to them. Some developmentalists believe that the sense of uniqueness and invincibility that egocentrism generates is responsible for some of the seemingly wreckless behavior of adolescents, including drag racing, drug use, suicide, and failure to use contraceptives during intercourse (Dolcini & others, 1989). For example,

adolescent egocentrism The heightened self-consciousness of adolescents, which is reflected in adolescents' beliefs that others are as interested in them as they are in themselves, and in adolescents' sense of personal uniqueness and invincibility.

imaginary audience The aspect of adolescent egocentrism that involves attention-getting behavior motivated by a desire to be noticed, visible, and "onstage."

personal fable The part of adolescent egocentrism that involves an adolescent's sense of uniqueness and invincibility.

one study found that eleventh- and twelfth-grade females who were high in adolescent egocentrism were more likely to say they would not get pregnant from engaging in sex without contraception than were their counterparts who were low in adolescent egocentrism (Arnett, 1990).

I check my look in the mirror. I wanna change my clothes, my hair, my face.

—BRUCE SPRINGSTEEN
Contemporary American Rock Star

Review and Reflect • LEARNING GOAL 1

1 Discuss the key processes and four stages in Piaget's theory

Review

- What are the key processes in Piaget's theory of cognitive development?
- What are the main characteristics of the sensorimotor stage?
- What are the main characteristics of the preoperational stage?
- What are the main characteristics of the concrete operational stage?
- What are the main characteristics of the formal operational stage?

Reflect

- Do you consider yourself to be a formal operational thinker? Do you still sometimes feel like a concrete operational thinker? Give examples.

2 APPLYING AND EVALUATING PIAGET'S THEORY

Piaget and Education | Evaluating Piaget's Theory

What are some applications of Piaget's theory to education? What are the main contributions and criticisms of Piaget's theory?

Piaget and Education

Piaget was not an educator, but he provided a sound conceptual framework for viewing learning and education. Following are some ideas in Piaget's theory that can be applied to teaching children (Elkind, 1976; Heuwinkel, 1996):

1. *Take a constructivist approach.* Piaget emphasized that children learn best when they are active and seek solutions for themselves. Piaget opposed teaching methods that treat children as passive receptacles. The educational implication of Piaget's view is that, in all subjects, students learn best by making discoveries, reflecting on them, and discussing them, rather than blindly imitating the teacher or doing things by rote.
2. *Facilitate, rather than direct, learning.* Effective teachers design situations that allow students to learn by doing. These situations promote students' thinking and discovery. Teachers listen, watch, and question students, to help them gain better understanding. Don't just examine what students think and the product of their learning. Rather, carefully observe them and find out how they think. Ask relevant questions to stimulate their thinking, and ask them to explain their answers.
3. *Consider the child's knowledge and level of thinking.* Students do not come to class with empty minds. They have many ideas about the physical and natural world. They have concepts of space, time, quantity, and causality. These ideas differ from the ideas of adults. Teachers need to interpret what a student is saying and respond in a way that is not too far from the student's level.

Also, Piaget suggested that it is important to examine children's mistakes in thinking, not just what they get correct, to help guide them to a higher level of understanding.

4. *Use ongoing assessment.* Individually constructed meanings cannot be measured by standardized tests. Math and language portfolios (which contain work in progress as well as finished products), individual conferences in which students discuss their thinking strategies, and students' written and verbal explanations of their reasoning can be used to evaluate progress.
5. *Promote the student's intellectual health.* When Piaget came to lecture in the United States, he was asked, "What can I do to get my child to a higher cognitive stage sooner?" He was asked this question so often here compared with other countries that he called it the American question. For Piaget, children's learning should occur naturally. Children should not be pushed and pressured into achieving too much too early in their development, before they are maturationally ready. Some parents spend long hours every day holding up large flash cards with words on them to improve their baby's vocabulary. In the Piagetian view, this is not the best way for infants to learn. It places too much emphasis on speeding up intellectual development, involves passive learning, and will not work.
6. *Turn the classroom into a setting of exploration and discovery.* What do actual classrooms look like when the teachers adopt Piaget's views? Several first- and second-grade math classrooms provide some examples (Kamii, 1985, 1989). The teachers emphasize students' own exploration and discovery. The classrooms are less structured than what we think of as a typical classroom. Workbooks and predetermined assignments are not used. Rather, the teachers observe the students' interests and natural participation in activities to determine the course of learning. For example, a math lesson might be constructed around counting the day's lunch money or dividing supplies among students. Often, games are used to stimulate mathematical thinking. For example, a version of dominoes teaches children about even-numbered combinations; a variation on tic-tac-toe replaces *X*s and *O*s with numbers. Teachers encourage peer interaction during the lessons and games because students' different viewpoints can contribute to advances in thinking.

www.mhhe.com/santrockcd11

Piaget and Education

We owe to Piaget the present field of cognitive development with its image of the developing child, who through its own active and creative commerce with its environment, builds an orderly succession of cognitive structures enroute to intellectual maturity.

—John Flavell
Contemporary Psychologist, Stanford University

Jean Piaget, the main architect of the field of cognitive development, at age 27.

Evaluating Piaget's Theory

What were Piaget's main contributions? Has his theory withstood the test of time?

Contributions Piaget was a giant in the field of developmental psychology, the founder of the present field of children's cognitive development. Psychologists owe him a long list of masterful concepts of enduring power and fascination: assimilation, accommodation, object permanence, egocentrism, conservation, and others. Psychologists also owe him the current vision of children as active, constructive thinkers (Vidal, 2000). And they have a debt to him for creating a theory that generated a huge volume of research on children's cognitive development.

Piaget also was a genius when it came to observing children. His careful observations demonstrated inventive ways to discover how children act on and adapt to their world. Piaget showed us some important things to look for in cognitive development, such as the shift from preoperational to concrete operational thinking. He also showed us how children need to make their experiences fit their schemes (cognitive frameworks) yet simultaneously adapt their schemes to experience. Piaget also revealed how cognitive change is likely to occur if the context is structured to allow gradual movement to the next higher level. Concepts do not emerge suddenly, full-blown, but instead develop through a series of partial accomplishments that lead to increasingly comprehensive understanding (Haith & Benson, 1998).

Criticisms Piaget's theory has not gone unchallenged (Byrnes, 2001, 2003; Keating, 2004; Mandler, 2004; Smith, 2004). Questions are raised about estimates of children's competence at different developmental levels, stages, the training of children to reason at higher levels, and culture and education.

Estimates of Children's Competence Some cognitive abilities emerge earlier than Piaget thought (Bjorklund, 2005; Bornstein, Arterberry, & Mash, 2005; Cohen & Cashon, 2006; Mandler, 2004). For example, as previously noted, some aspects of object permanence emerge earlier than he believed. Even 2-year-olds are nonegocentric in some contexts. When they realize that another person will not see an object, they investigate whether the person is blindfolded or looking in a different direction. Some understanding of the conservation of number has been demonstrated as early as age 3, although Piaget did not think it emerged until 7. Young children are not as uniformly "pre" this and "pre" that (precausal, preoperational) as Piaget thought.

Cognitive abilities also can emerge later than Piaget thought. Many adolescents still think in concrete operational ways or are just beginning to master formal operations. Even many adults are not formal operational thinkers. In sum, recent theoretical revisions highlight more cognitive competencies of infants and young children and more cognitive shortcomings of adolescents and adults (Cohen & Cashon, 2006; Keating, 2004; Kellman & Arterberry, 2006; Thomas, 2005).

Stages Piaget conceived of stages as unitary structures of thought. Thus, his theory assumes developmental synchrony; that is, various aspects of a stage should emerge at the same time. However, some concrete operational concepts do not appear in synchrony. For example, children do not learn to conserve at the same time they learn to cross-classify. Thus, most contemporary developmentalists agree that children's cognitive development is not as stagelike as Piaget thought (Bjorklund, 2005; Fischer & Bidell, 2006; Halford, 2004; Kuhn & Franklin, 2006).

Effects of Training Some children who are at one cognitive stage (such as preoperational) can be trained to reason at a higher cognitive stage (such as concrete operational). This poses a problem for Piaget's theory. He argued that such training is only superficial and ineffective, unless the child is at a maturational transition point between the stages (Gelman & Williams, 1998).

Culture and Education Culture and education exert stronger influences on children's development than Piaget believed (Cole, 2005, 2006; Greenfield, 2000). For example, the age at which children acquire conservation skills is related to how much practice their culture provides in these skills. Among Wolof children in the West African nation of Senegal, only 50 percent of the 10- to 13-year-olds understood the principle of conservation (Greenfield, 1966). Comparable studies among cultures in central Australia, New Guinea (an island north of Australia), the Amazon jungle region of Brazil, and rural Sardinia (an island off the coast of Italy) yielded similar results (Dasen, 1977). An outstanding teacher and education in the logic of math and science can promote concrete and formal operational thought.

An outstanding teacher and education in the logic of science and mathematics are important cultural experiences that promote the development of operational thought. *Might Piaget have underestimated the roles of culture and schooling in children's cognitive development?*

An Alternative View **Neo-Piagetians** argue that Piaget got some things right but that his theory needs considerable revision. They give more emphasis to how children use attention, memory, and strategies to process information (Case, 1987, 1999; Case & Mueller, 2001). They especially believe that a more accurate portrayal of children's thinking requires attention to children's strategies, the speed at which children process information, the particular task involved, and the division of problems into smaller, more precise steps (Demetriou, 2001). In chapter 8, we will discuss these aspects of children's thought.

neo-Piagetians Developmentalists who have elaborated on Piaget's theory, believing that children's cognitive development is more specific in many respects than he thought.

Review and Reflect • LEARNING GOAL 2

2 Apply Piaget's theory to education and evaluate Piaget's theory

Review

- How can Piaget's theory be applied to educating children?
- What are some key contributions and criticisms of Piaget's theory?

Reflect

- How might thinking in formal operational ways rather than concrete operational ways help students to develop better study skills?

3 VYGOTSKY'S THEORY OF COGNITIVE DEVELOPMENT

- The Zone of Proximal Development
- Scaffolding
- Language and Thought
- Teaching Strategies
- Evaluating Vygotsky's Theory

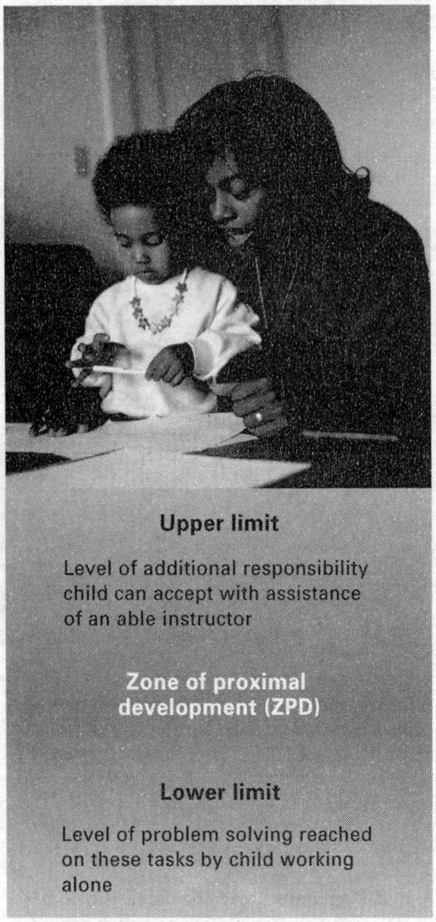

FIGURE 7.11 Vygotsky's Zone of Proximal Development

Like Piaget, Lev Vygotsky emphasized that children actively construct their knowledge. But according to Vygotsky, mental functions have social connections. Vygotsky argued that children develop more systematic, logical, and rational concepts as a result of *dialogue* with a skilled helper. Thus, in Vygotsky's theory, other people and language play key roles in a child's cognitive development (Berninger & others, 2004; Camilleri, 2005; Fidalgo & Pereira, 2005; Stetsenko & Arievitch, 2004).

The Zone of Proximal Development

Vygotsky's belief in the importance of social influences, especially instruction, on children's cognitive development is reflected in his concept of the zone of proximal development. **Zone of proximal development (ZPD)** is Vygotsky's term for the range of tasks that are too difficult for the child to master alone but that can be learned with guidance and assistance of adults or more skilled children. Thus, the lower limit of the ZPD is the level of skill reached by the child working independently. The upper limit is the level of additional responsibility the child can accept with the assistance of an able instructor (see figure 7.11). The ZPD captures the child's cognitive skills that are in the process of maturing and can be accomplished only with the assistance of a more skilled person (Goos, 2004; Gray & Feldman, 2004; Kinginger, 2002; Kulczewski, 2005). Vygotsky (1962) called these the "buds" or "flowers" of development, to distinguish them from the "fruits" of development, which the child already can accomplish independently.

Let's consider an example that reflects the zone of proximal development (Frede, 1995, p. 125):

> A 5-year-old child is pushing a small shopping cart through the house area of his preschool. His teacher notices that he is putting fruit in the small basket and all other groceries in the larger section of the cart. She has watched him sort objects over the past few weeks and thinks that he may now be able to classify along two dimensions at the same time, with some help from her. She goes to the cash register to pretend to be the cashier and says, "We need to be careful how we divide your groceries into bags. We want to use one bag for things that go in the refrigerator, and other bags for things that will go in the cabinet." Together they devise a system with one bag for

each of the following categories: food in cartons that will go into the refrigerator, loose vegetables and fruit for the refrigerator, food cartons that go in the cabinet, and food cans for the cabinet. In this example, the child's unassisted level of classification was fairly gross—fruit versus non-fruit. With the teacher's help, he was able to apply a more sophisticated form of classification.

www.mhhe.com/santrockcd11

Vygotsky's Theory
Vygotsky Links
Scaffolding

Scaffolding

Closely linked to the idea of the ZPD is the concept of scaffolding. **Scaffolding** means changing the level of support. Over the course of a teaching session, a more skilled person (a teacher or advanced peer) adjusts the amount of guidance to fit the child's current performance (de Vries, 2005; Donovan & Smolkin, 2002; John-Steiner & Mahn, 2003; Many, 2002). When the student is learning a new task, the skilled person may use direct instruction. As the student's competence increases, less guidance is given.

Dialogue is an important tool of scaffolding in the zone of proximal development (Tappan, 1998). Vygotsky viewed children as having rich but unsystematic, disorganized, and spontaneous concepts. In a dialogue, these concepts meet with the skilled helper's more systematic, logical, and rational concepts. As a result, the child's concepts become more systematic, logical, and rational. For example, a dialogue might take place between a teacher and a child when the teacher uses scaffolding to help a child understand a concept like "transportation."

Language and Thought

The use of dialogue as a tool for scaffolding is only one example of the important role of language in a child's development. According to Vygotsky, children use speech not only for social communication, but also to help them solve tasks. Vygotsky (1962) further believed that young children use language to plan, guide, and monitor their behavior. This use of language for self-regulation is called *private speech.* For Piaget private speech is egocentric and immature, but for Vygotsky it is an important tool of thought during the early childhood years.

Lev Vygotsky (1896–1934), shown here with his daughter, believed that children's cognitive development is advanced through social interaction with skilled individuals embedded in a sociocultural backdrop.

Vygotsky said that language and thought initially develop independently of each other and then merge. He emphasized that all mental functions have external, or social, origins. Children must use language to communicate with others before they can focus inward on their own thoughts. Children also must communicate externally and use language for a long period of time before they can make the transition from external to internal speech. This transition period occurs between 3 and 7 years of age and involves talking to oneself. After a while, the self-talk becomes second nature to children, and they can act without verbalizing. When this occurs, children have internalized their egocentric speech in the form of *inner speech,* which becomes their thoughts.

Vygotsky believed that children who use a lot of private speech are more socially competent than those who don't (Santiago-Delefosse & Delefosse, 2002). He argued that private speech represents an early transition in becoming more socially communicative. For Vygotsky, when young children talk to themselves, they are using language to govern their behavior and guide themselves. For example, a child working on a puzzle might say to herself, "Which pieces should I put together first? I'll try those green ones first. Now I need some blue ones. No, that blue one doesn't fit there. I'll try it over here."

Piaget believed that self-talk is egocentric and reflects immaturity. However, researchers have found support for Vygotsky's view that private speech plays a positive role in children's development (Winsler, Diaz, & Montero, 1997; Winsler, Carlton, & Barry, 2000). Researchers have found that children use private speech

zone of proximal development (ZPD) Vygotsky's term for tasks too difficult for children to master alone but that can be mastered with assistance.

scaffolding In cognitive development, Vygotsky used this term to describe the changing support over the course of a teaching session, with the more skilled person adjusting guidance to fit the child's current performance level.

more when tasks are difficult, following errors, and when they are not sure how to proceed (Berk, 1994). They also have revealed that children who use private speech are more attentive and improve their performance more than children who do not use private speech (Berk & Spuhl, 1995).

Teaching Strategies

Vygotsky's theory has been embraced by many teachers and has been successfully applied to education (Bearison & Dorval, 2002; Rowe & Wertsch, 2004; Winsler & others, 2002). Here are some ways Vygotsky's theory can be incorporated in classrooms:

1. *Assess the child's ZPD.* Like Piaget, Vygotsky did not believe that formal, standardized tests are the best way to assess children's learning. Rather, Vygotsky argued that assessment should focus on determining the child's zone of proximal development (Meijer & Elshout, 2002). The skilled helper presents the child with tasks of varying difficulty to determine the best level at which to begin instruction.
2. *Use the child's ZPD in teaching.* Teaching should begin toward the zone's upper limit, so that the child can reach the goal with help and move to a higher level of skill and knowledge. Offer just enough assistance. You might ask, "What can I do to help you?" Or simply observe the child's intentions and attempts and provide support when needed. When the child hesitates, offer encouragement. And encourage the child to practice the skill. You may watch and appreciate the child's practice or offer support when the child forgets what to do.
3. *Use more-skilled peers as teachers.* Remember that it is not just adults who are important in helping children learn. Children also benefit from the support and guidance of more-skilled children (John-Steiner & Mahn, 2003).
4. *Monitor and encourage children's use of private speech.* Be aware of the developmental change from externally talking to oneself when solving a problem during the preschool years to privately talking to oneself in the early elementary school years. In the elementary school years, encourage children to internalize and self-regulate their talk to themselves.
5. *Place instruction in a meaningful context.* Educators today are moving away from abstract presentations of material, instead providing students with opportunities to experience learning in real-world settings. For example, instead of just memorizing math formulas, students work on math problems with real-world implications (Santrock, 2006).
6. *Transform the classroom with Vygotskian ideas.* What does a Vygotskian classroom look like? The Kamehameha Elementary Education Program (KEEP) is based on Vygotsky's theory (Tharp, 1994). The ZPD is the key element of instruction in this program. Children might read a story and then interpret its meaning. Many of the learning activities take place in small groups. All children spend at least 20 minutes each morning in a setting called "Center One." In this context, scaffolding is used to improve children's literary skills. The instructor asks questions, responds to students' queries, and builds on the ideas that students generate. Thousands of children from low-income families have attended KEEP public schools—in Hawaii, on an

CAREERS in CHILD DEVELOPMENT

Donene Polson
Elementary School Teacher

Donene Polson teaches at Washington Elementary School in Salt Lake City, Utah. Washington is an innovative school that emphasizes the importance of people learning together as a community of learners. Children as well as adults plan learning activities. Throughout the school day, children work in small groups.

Donene says that she loves working in a school in which students, teachers, and parents work together as a community to help children learn. Before the school year begins, Donene meets with parents at the family's home to prepare for the upcoming year, getting acquainted, and establishing schedules to determine when parents can contribute to classroom instruction. At monthly parent-teacher meetings, Donene and the parents plan the curriculum and discuss how children's learning is progressing. They brainstorm about resources in the community that can be used effectively to promote children's learning.

Arizona Navajo Indian reservation, and in Los Angeles. Compared with a control group of non-KEEP children, the KEEP children participated more actively in classroom discussion, were more attentive in class, and had higher reading achievement (Tharp & Gallimore, 1988).

Cognitive development occurs as new generations collaborate with older generations in varying forms of interpersonal engagement and institutional practices.

—Barbara Rogoff
Contemporary Psychologist, University of California–Santa Cruz

To read about the work of a teacher who applies Vygotsky's theory to her teaching, see the Careers in Child Development on the previous page. The Caring for Children interlude further explores the education of children.

CARING FOR CHILDREN

Guided Participation

Vygotsky's concept of the zone of proximal development—that children learn by interacting with more experienced adults and peers, who help them think beyond the "zone" in which they would be able to perform without assistance—has been applied primarily to academic learning. Barbara Rogoff (1990, 1998, 2003; Rogoff, Turkanis, & Bartlett, 2001) argues that many of Vygotsky's ideas, including the zone of proximal development, are important in understanding children's development beyond the classroom in everyday interactions with adults and peers.

According to Rogoff, children serve a sort of apprenticeship in thinking through *guided participation* in social and cultural activities. Guided participation may occur, for example, when adults and children share activities.

Parents can broaden or limit children's opportunities through their decisions about how much and when to expose children to books, television, and child care. They may give children opportunities to learn about cultural traditions and practices through their routines and play. For example, in the Zambian culture of Chewa, children play numerous games, such as "hide-and-seek, guessing games, complex sand drawing games, imaginative games representing local work and family routines, skill games like jacks and a rule game requiring considerable strategic planning and numerical calculations, and constructing models of wire or clay" (Rogoff, 2003, p. 297). In addition, through observational learning, or as Rogoff calls it, learning by "osmosis," children adopt values, skills, and mannerisms by simply watching and listening to peers and adults.

Guided participation is widely used around the world, but cultures may differ in the goals of development—what content is to be learned—and the means for providing guided participation (Rogoff, 2003). Around the world, caregivers and children arrange children's activities and revise children's responsibilities as they gain skill and knowledge. With guidance, children participate in cultural activities that socialize them into skilled activities. For example, Mayan mothers in Guatemala help their daughters learn to weave through guided participation. Throughout the world, learning occurs, not just by studying or by attending classes, but also through interaction with knowledgeable people.

At about 7 years of age, Mayan girls in Guatemala are assisted in beginning to learn to weave a simple belt, with the loom already set up for them. The young girl shown here is American developmental psychologist Barbara Rogoff's daughter, being taught to weave by a Mayan woman. *What are some other ways that children learn through guided participation?*

Evaluating Vygotsky's Theory

How does Vygotsky's theory compare with Piaget's? We already have mentioned several comparisons, such as Vygotsky's emphasis on the importance of inner speech in development and Piaget's view that such speech is immature. Although both theories are constructivist, Vygotsky's is a **social constructivist approach,** which

social constructivist approach An emphasis on the social contexts of learning and the construction of knowledge through social interaction. Vygotsky's theory reflects this approach.

	Vygotsky	Piaget
Sociocultural Context	**Strong Emphasis**	**Little Emphasis**
Constructivism	Social constructivist	Cognitive constructivist
Stages	No general stages of development proposed	Strong emphasis on stages (sensorimotor, preoperational, concrete operational, and formal operational)
Key Processes	Zone of proximal development, language, dialogue, tools of the culture	Schema, assimilation, accommodation, operations, conservation, classification, hypothetical-deductive reasoning
Role of Language	A major role; language plays a powerful role in shaping thought	Language has a minimal role; cognition primarily directs language
View on Education	Education plays a central role, helping children learn the tools of the culture	Education merely refines the child's cognitive skills that have already emerged
Teaching Implications	Teacher is a facilitator and guide, not a director; establish many opportunities for children to learn with the teacher and more-skilled peers	Also views teacher as a facilitator and guide, not a director; provide support for children to explore their world and discover knowledge

FIGURE 7.12 Comparison of Vygotsky's and Piaget's Theories

emphasizes the social contexts of learning and the construction of knowledge through social interaction (Mooney, 2006).

In moving from Piaget to Vygotsky, the conceptual shift is from the individual to collaboration, social interaction, and sociocultural activity (Rogoff, 1998, 2003). The endpoint of cognitive development for Piaget is formal operational thought. For Vygotsky, the endpoint can differ depending on which skills are considered to be the most important in a particular culture (Elkind, 2004). For Piaget, children construct knowledge by transforming, organizing, and reorganizing previous knowledge. For Vygotsky, children construct knowledge through social interaction (de Vries, 2005; Hogan & Tudge, 1999). The implication of Piaget's theory for teaching is that children need support to explore their world and discover knowledge. The main implication of Vygotsky's theory for teaching is that students need many opportunities to learn with the teacher and more-skilled peers. In both Piaget's and Vygotsky's theories, teachers serve as facilitators and guides, rather than as directors and molders of learning. Figure 7.12 compares Vgotsky's and Piaget's theories.

Even though their theories were proposed at about the same time, most of the world learned about Vygotsky's theory later than they learned about Piaget's theory, so Vygotsky's theory has not yet been evaluated as thoroughly. Vygotsky's view of the importance of sociocultural influences on children's development fits with the current belief that it is important to evaluate the contextual factors in learning (Fidalgo & Pereira, 2005; Kozulin, 2000; Rowe & Wertsch, 2004).

Some critics say Vygotsky overemphasized the role of language in thinking. Also, his emphasis on collaboration and guidance has potential pitfalls. Might facilitators be too helpful in some cases, as when a parent becomes too overbearing and controlling? Further, some children might become lazy and expect help when they might have done something on their own.

Review and Reflect • LEARNING GOAL 3

3 Identify the main concepts in Vygotsky's theory and compare it with Piaget's theory

Review

- What is the zone of proximal development?
- What is scaffolding?
- How did Vygotsky view language and thought?
- How can Vygotsky's theory be applied to education?
- What are some similarities and differences between Vygotsky's and Piaget's theories?

Reflect

- Which theory–Piaget's or Vygotsky's–do you like the best? Why?

REACH YOUR LEARNING GOALS

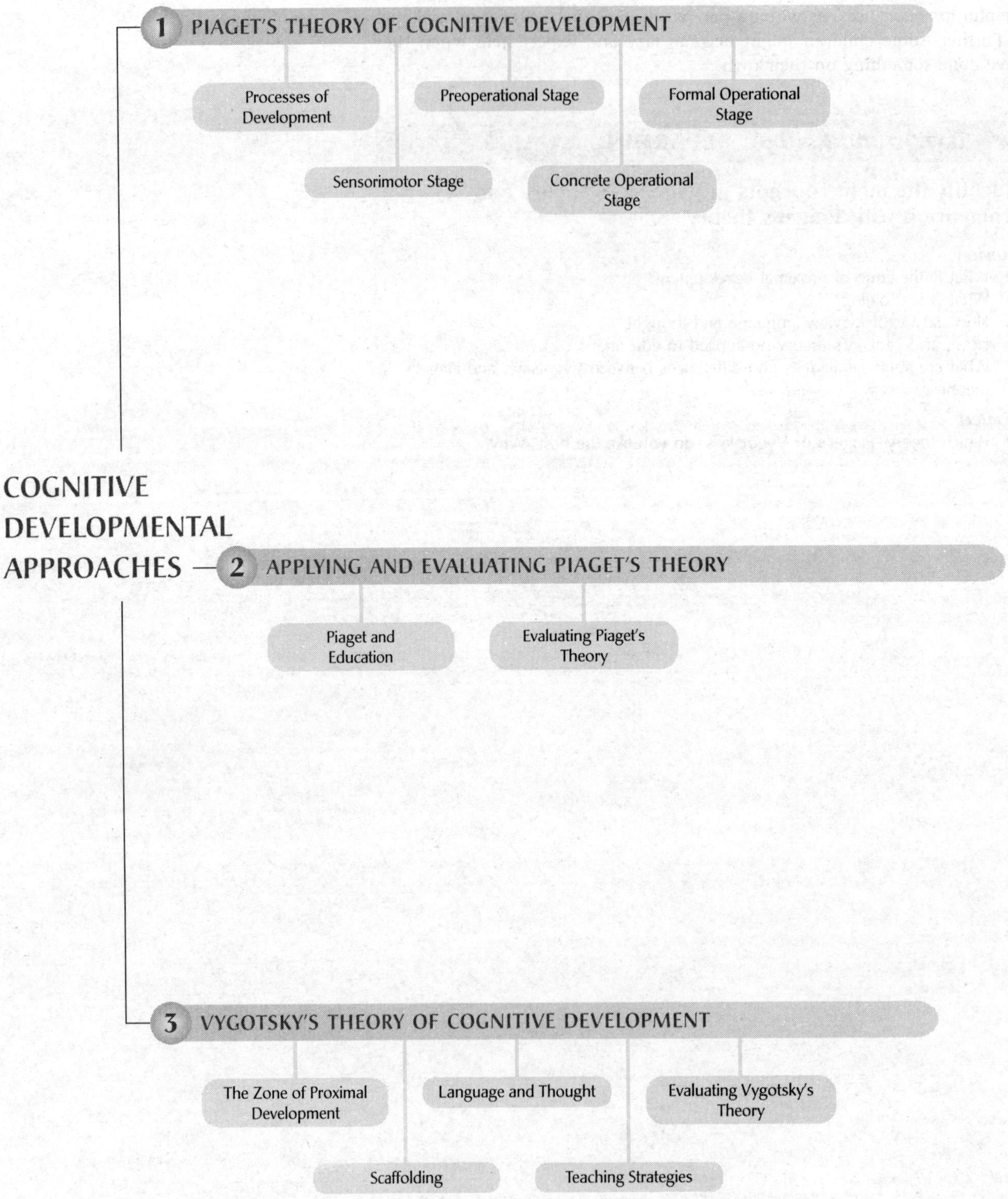

SUMMARY

1 Discuss the key processes and four stages in Piaget's theory

- In Piaget's theory, children construct their own cognitive worlds, building mental structures to adapt to their world. Schemes are actions or mental representations that organize knowledge. Behavioral schemes (physical activities) characterize infancy while mental schemes (cognitive activities) develop in childhood. Adaptation involves assimilation and accommodation. Assimilation occurs when children incorporate new information into existing knowledge. Accommodation refers to children's adjustment to new information. Through organization, children group isolated behaviors into a higher-order, more smoothly functioning cognitive system. Equilibration is a mechanism Piaget proposed to explain how children shift from one cognitive stage to the next. As children experience cognitive conflict in trying to understand the world, they seek equilibrium. The result is equilibration, which brings the child to a new stage of thought. According to Piaget, there are four qualitatively different stages of thought: sensorimotor, preoperational, concrete operational, and formal operational.
- In sensorimotor thought, the first of Piaget's four stages, the infant organizes and coordinates sensations with physical movements. The stage lasts from birth to about 2 years of age and is nonsymbolic throughout, according to Piaget. Sensorimotor thought has six substages: simple reflexes; first habits and primary circular reactions; secondary circular reactions; coordination of secondary circular reactions; tertiary circular reactions, novelty, and curiosity; and internalization of schemes. One key aspect of this stage is object permanence, the ability to understand that objects continue to exist even though the infant is no longer observing them. Another aspect involves infants' understanding of cause and effect. In the past two decades, revisions of Piaget's view have been proposed based on research. For example, researchers have found that a stable and differentiated perceptual world is established earlier than Piaget envisioned.
- Preoperational thought is the beginning of the ability to reconstruct at the level of thought what has been established in behavior. It involves a transition from a primitive to a more sophisticated use of symbols. In preoperational thought, the child does not yet think in an operational way. The symbolic function substage occurs roughly from 2 to 4 years of age and is characterized by symbolic thought, egocentrism, and animism. The intuitive thought substage stretches from 4 to 7 years of age. It is called intuitive because children seem so sure about their knowledge yet they are unaware of how they know what they know. The preoperational child lacks conservation and asks a barrage of questions.
- Concrete operational thought occurs roughly from 7 to 11 years of age. During this stage, children can perform concrete operations, think logically about concrete objects, classify things, and reason about relationships among classes of things. Concrete thought is not as abstract as formal operational thought.
- Formal operational thought appears between 11 and 15 years of age. Formal operational thought is more abstract, idealistic, and logical than concrete operational thought. Piaget believes that adolescents become capable of engaging in hypothetical-deductive reasoning. But Piaget did not give adequate attention to individual variation in adolescent thinking. Many young adolescents do not think in hypothetical-deductive ways but rather are consolidating their concrete operational thinking. In addition, adolescents develop a special kind of egocentrism that involves an imaginary audience and a personal fable about being unique and invulnerable.

2 Apply Piaget's theory to education and evaluate Piaget's theory

- Piaget was not an educator, but his constructivist views have been applied to teaching. These applications include an emphasis on facilitating rather than directing learning, considering the child's level of knowledge, using ongoing assessment, promoting the student's intellectual health, and turning the classroom into a setting of exploration and discovery.
- We owe to Piaget the field of cognitive development. He was a genius at observing children, and he gave us a number of masterful concepts. Critics question his estimates of competence at different developmental levels, his stage concept, and other ideas. Neo-Piagetians, who emphasize the importance of information processing, believe that children's cognition is more specific than Piaget thought.

3 Identify the main concepts in Vygotsky's theory and compare it with Piaget's theory

- Zone of proximal development (ZPD) is Vygotsky's term for the range of tasks that are too difficult for children to master alone but that can be learned with the guidance and assistance of more-skilled adults and peers.
- Scaffolding is a teaching technique in which a more-skilled person adjusts the level of guidance to fit the child's current performance level. Dialogue is an important aspect of scaffolding.

- Vygotsky believed that language plays a key role in cognition. Language and thought initially develop independently, but then children internalize their egocentric speech in the form of inner speech, which becomes their thoughts. This transition to inner speech occurs from 3 to 7 years of age. Vygotsky's view contrasts with Piaget's view that young children's speech is immature and egocentric.
- Applications of Vygotsky's ideas to education include using the child's ZPD and scaffolding, using skilled peers as teachers, monitoring and encouraging children's use of private speech, and accurately assessing the ZPD. These practices can transform the classroom and establish a meaningful context for instruction.
- Like Piaget, Vygotsky emphasized that children actively construct their understanding of the world. Unlike Piaget, he did not propose stages of cognitive development, and he emphasized that children construct knowledge through social interaction. In Vygotsky's theory, children depend on tools provided by the culture, which determines which skills they will develop. Some critics say that Vygotsky overemphasized the role of language.

KEY TERMS

schemes 211
assimilation 211
accommodation 211
organization 212
equilibration 212
sensorimotor stage 212
object permanence 214
A$\bar{\text{B}}$ error 217
operations 218
preoperational stage 218
symbolic function substage 218
egocentrism 218
animism 219
intuitive thought substage 220
centration 220
conservation 220
concrete operational stage 221
horizontal décalage 222
seriation 222
transitivity 223
formal operational stage 223
hypothetical-deductive reasoning 223
adolescent egocentrism 224
imaginary audience 224
personal fable 224
neo-Piagetians 227
zone of proximal development (ZPD) 229
scaffolding 229
social constructivist approach 231

KEY PEOPLE

Jean Piaget 210
Renee Baillargeon 216
Barbel Inhelder 219
Rochel Gelman 222
David Elkind 224
Lev Vygotsky 228

E-LEARNING TOOLS

To help you master the material in this chapter, visit the Online Learning Center for *Child Development*, eleventh edition (**www.mhhe/santrockcd11**), where you'll find these additional resources:

Taking It to the Net

1. Francesca is surveying *Time* magazine's list of the top 100 people of the twentieth century. She notices that Piaget made the list. Why?
2. Ellen is majoring in interdisciplinary studies. She is preparing a report on famous thinkers who engaged in cross-disciplinary study and teaching and how this influenced their theories. She has heard that Piaget was adept at several disciplines. How can she investigate what they were and how they might have influenced his theory of cognitive development?
3. Theo has to write a comparison and contrast paper for his Early Childhood Education class. He wants to compare Vygotsky and Piaget's theories of cognitive development, focusing on implications from these theories for teachers. Would a paper on how these men believed culture influenced cognitive development be a good choice?

Nursing, Parenting, and Teaching Exercises

Build your decision-making skills by trying your hand at the scenarios on the Online Learning Center.

Video Clips

The Online Learning Center includes the following videos for this chapter:

- Categorizing Pictures at Age 4
  A 4-year-old boy is presented with pictures of a lion, bear, zebra, and wagon and asked which one is different from the others. He insists, "They're all different!" The interviewer probes him but he is more interested in adding and subtracting pictures, which he does very well. Another set of pictures is presented to him and again he says that all are different.
- Lacking Concept of Conservation (Liquid) at Age 3
  A 3-year-old girl demonstrates that she lacks an understanding of the concept of conservation when she is presented with Piaget's classic Liquid test. Charlene's explanation for "which has more" is a good example of how preoperational thinking is irreversible.
- Lacking Concept of Conservation (Mass) at Age 4
  A boy who paints his nose a different color every day demonstrates that he lacks an understanding of the concept of conservation when he is presented with Piaget's classic Mass test.
- Understanding Conservation (Liquid) at Age 4
  A girl proves she has an understanding of the concept of conservation when she is presented with Piaget's classic Liquid test. This clip provides a good example of the age variation in the emergence of conservation.

Chapter 8 INFORMATION PROCESSING

The mind is an enchanting thing.

—Marianne Moore
American Poet, 20th Century

CHAPTER OUTLINE

LEARNING GOALS

THE INFORMATION-PROCESSING APPROACH

The Information-Processing Approach to Development
Cognitive Resources: Capacity and Speed of Processing Information
Mechanisms of Change
Comparisons with Piaget's Theory

1 Explain the information-processing approach

ATTENTION

What Is Attention?
Infancy
Childhood and Adolescence

2 Define attention and outline its developmental changes

MEMORY

What Is Memory?
Infancy
Childhood

3 Describe what memory is and how it changes

THINKING

What Is Thinking?
Infancy
Childhood
Adolescence

4 Characterize thinking and its developmental changes

METACOGNITION

What Is Metacognition?
The Child's Theory of Mind
Metacognition in Children and Adolescents

5 Define metacognition and summarize its developmental changes

The Story of Laura Bickford

Laura Bickford, working with students writing papers.

Laura Bickford is a master teacher and chairs the English Department at Nordoff High School in Ojai, California. She recently spoke about how she encourages her students to think:

> I believe the call to teach is a call to teach students how to think. In encouraging critical thinking, literature itself does a good bit of work for us but we still have to be guides. We have to ask good questions. We have to show students the value in asking their own questions, in having discussions and conversations. In addition to reading and discussing literature, the best way to move students to think critically is to have them write. We write all the time in a variety of modes: journals, formal essays, letters, factual reports, news articles, speeches, or other formal oral presentations. We have to show students where they merely scratch the surface in their thinking and writing. I call these moments "hits and runs." When I see this "hit and run" effort, I draw a window on the paper. I tell them it is a "window of opportunity" to go deeper, elaborate, and clarify. Many students don't do this kind of thinking until they are prodded to do so.
>
> I also ask them to keep reading logs so they can observe their own thinking as it happens. In addition, I ask students to comment on their own learning by way of grading themselves. This year a student gave me one of the most insightful lines about her growth as a reader I have ever seen from a student. She wrote, "I no longer think in a monotone when I'm reading." I don't know if she grasps the magnitude of that thought or how it came to be that she made that change. It is magic when students see themselves growing like this.

PREVIEW

What do children notice in the environment? What do they remember? And how do they think about it? These questions illustrate the information-processing approach. Using this approach, researchers usually do not describe children as being in one stage of cognitive development or another. But they do describe and analyze how the speed of processing information, attention, memory, thinking, and metacognition change over time.

1 THE INFORMATION-PROCESSING APPROACH

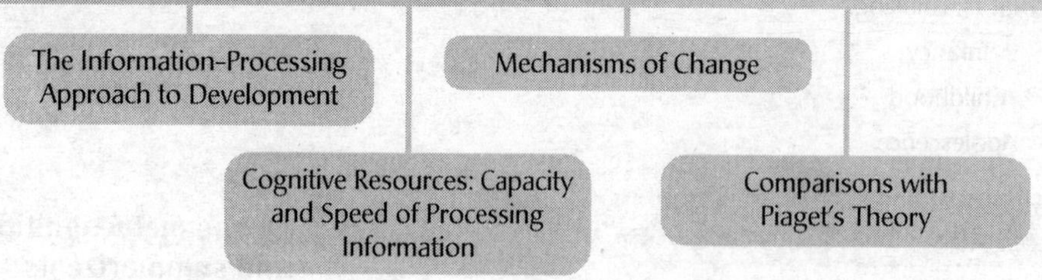

What are some of the basic ideas in the information-processing approach? How is it similar to and different from the cognitive developmental approaches we described in chapter 7?

The Information-Processing Approach to Development

The information-processing approach shares a basic characteristic with the theories of cognitive development that were discussed in chapter 7. Like those theories, the information-processing approach rejected the behavioral approach that dominated

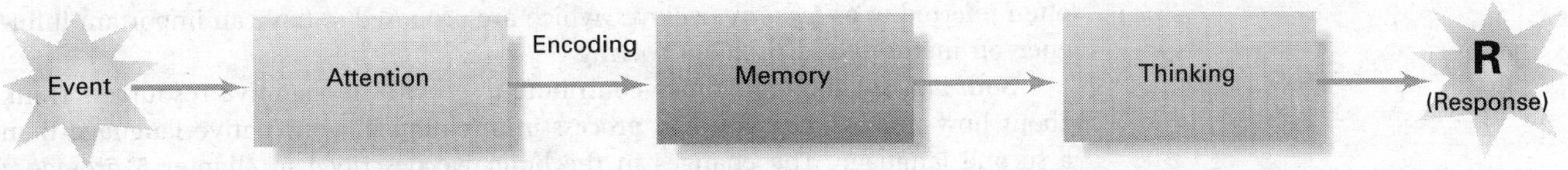

FIGURE 8.1 A Basic, Simplified Model of Information Processing

psychology during the first half of the twentieth century. As we discussed in chapter 2, the behaviorists argued that to explain behavior it is important to examine associations between stimuli and behavior. In contrast, the theories of Piaget and Vygotsky, which were presented in chapter 7, and the information-processing approach focus on how children think.

The **information-processing approach** analyzes how children manipulate information, monitor it, and create strategies for handling it (Munkata, 2006; Siegler, 2001, 2006; Siegler & Alibali, 2005). Effective information processing involves attention, memory, and thinking. To see how these processes work, let's examine a student solving an algebraic equation. The sequence begins with an event in the environment. Suppose the event involves a teacher writing an equation on the chalkboard in a mathematics class with the accompanying instruction: "$2x + 10 = 34$. Solve for x." The student looks up and focuses on what the teacher has written (*attention*). The student determines that the teacher has written a series of numbers, letters, and signs, and—at a higher level of identification—two simple statements: (1) "$2x + 10 = 34$" and (2) "Solve for x." The student must preserve the results of this attention by *encoding* the information and storing it over a period of time (*memory*), even if for only the brief time needed to write the problem on a worksheet. Then, the student begins manipulating and transforming the information (*thinking*). The student might think, "Okay, first I have to collect the information on one side of the equation and the known values on the other side. To do this, I'll leave the $2x$ where it is—on the left. This leaves $2x = 24$. Now I have to express the equation as 'x = something,' and it's solved. How do I do this? I'll divide each side by 2 and that will leave $1x = 12$. That's the answer." The student writes down the answer (response).

Figure 8.1 shows a summary of the basic processes used in solving the algebraic equation. This diagram is a basic, simplified representation of how information processing works, omitting a great deal. In reality, the flow of information takes many routes. For example, the processes may overlap, and they do not always occur in the left-to-right direction indicated. The purpose of the model is to get you to begin thinking in a general way about how people process information. In subsequent sections, we will fill in more of the details about the way children process information and how information processing changes as they develop.

A computer metaphor can illustrate how the information-processing approach can be applied to development. A computer's information processing is *limited* by its hardware and software. The hardware limitations include the amount of data the computer can process—its capacity—and speed. The software limits the kind of data that can be used as input and the ways that data can be manipulated; word processing doesn't handle music, for example. Similarly, children's information processing may be limited by capacity and speed as well as by their ability to manipulate information—in other words, to apply appropriate strategies to acquire and use knowledge. In the information-processing approach, children's cognitive development results from their ability to overcome processing limitations by increasingly executing basic operations, expanding information-processing capacity, and acquiring new knowledge and strategies.

Cognitive Resources: Capacity and Speed of Processing Information

Developmental changes in information processing are likely influenced by increases in both capacity and speed of processing (Frye, 2004). These two characteristics are

information-processing approach An approach that focuses on the ways children process information about their world—how they manipulate information, monitor it, and create strategies to deal with it.

often referred to as *cognitive resources,* which are proposed to have an important influence on memory and problem solving.

Both biology and experience contribute to growth in cognitive resources. Think about how much faster you can process information in your native language than a second language. The changes in the brain we described in chapter 5 provide a biological foundation for increased cognitive resources. Important biological developments occur both in brain structures, such as changes in the frontal lobes, and at the level of neurons, such as the blooming and pruning of connections between neurons. Also, as we discussed in chapter 5, myelination (the process that covers the axon with a myelin sheath) increases the speed of electrical impulses in the brain. Myelination continues through childhood and adolescence.

Most information-processing psychologists argue that an increase in capacity also improves processing of information (Alexander, 2006; Halford, 2004; Keil, 2006). For example, as children's information-processing capacity increases, they likely can hold in mind several dimensions of a topic or problem simultaneously, whereas younger children are more prone to focus on only one dimension.

What is the role of processing speed? How fast children process information often influences what they can do with that information. If an adolescent is trying to add up mentally the cost of items he or she is buying at the grocery store, the adolescent needs to be able to compute the sum before he or she has forgotten the price of the individual items. Children's speed in processing information is linked with their competence in thinking (Bjorklund, 2005; Demetriou & others, 2002). For example, how fast children can articulate a series of words affects how many words they can store and remember. Generally, fast processing is linked with good performance on cognitive tasks. However, some compensation for slower processing speed can be achieved through effective strategies.

Researchers have devised a number of ways for assessing processing speed. For example, it can be assessed through a *reaction-time task* in which individuals are asked to push a button as soon as they see a stimulus such as a light. Or individuals might be asked to match letters or match numbers with symbols on a computer screen.

There is abundant evidence that the speed with which such tasks are completed improves dramatically across the childhood years (Kail, 1988, 2000; Stigler, Nusbaum, & Chalip, 1988). Processing speed continues to improve in early adolescence. Think how much faster you could process the answer to a simple arithmetic problem as an adolescent than as a child. In one study, 10-year-olds were approximately 1.8 times slower at processing information than young adults on such tasks as reaction time, letter matching, mental rotation, and abstract matching (Hale, 1990). Twelve-year-olds were approximately 1.5 times slower than young adults, but 15-year-olds processed information on the tasks as fast as the young adults.

Mechanisms of Change

According to Robert Siegler (1998), three mechanisms work together to create changes in children's cognitive skills: encoding, automatization, and strategy construction.

Encoding is the process by which information gets into memory. Changes in children's cognitive skills depend on increased skill at encoding relevant information and ignoring irrelevant information. For example, to a 4-year-old, an *s* in cursive writing is a shape very different from an *s* that is printed. But a 10-year-old has learned to encode the relevant fact that both are the letter *s* and to ignore the irrelevant differences in their shape.

Automaticity refers to the ability to process information with little or no effort. Practice allows children to encode increasing amounts of information automatically. For example, once children have learned to read well, they do not think about each letter in a word as a letter; instead, they encode whole words. Once a task is automatic, it does not require conscious effort. As a result, as information processing becomes more automatic, we can complete tasks more quickly and handle more

encoding The mechanism by which information gets into memory.

automaticity The ability to process information with little or no effort.

than one task at a time. If you did not encode words automatically but instead read this page by focusing your attention on each letter in each word, imagine how long it would take you to read it.

Strategy construction is the creation of new procedures for processing information. For example, children's reading benefits when they develop the strategy of stopping periodically to take stock of what they have read so far.

In addition, Siegler (1998, 2004; Siegler & Alibali, 2005) argues that children's information processing is characterized by *self-modification*. That is, children learn to use what they have learned in previous circumstances to adapt their responses to a new situation. Part of this self-modification draws on **metacognition,** which means knowing about knowing (Flavell, 1999, 2004; Flavell, Miller, & Miller, 2002). One example of metacognition is what children know about the best ways to remember what they have read. Do they know that they will remember what they have read better if they can relate it to their own lives in some way? Thus, in Siegler's application of the information-processing approach to development, children play an active role in their cognitive development.

www.mhhe.com/santrockcd11

Robert Siegler's Research

Comparisons with Piaget's Theory

How does the information-processing approach compare with Piaget's theory? According to Piaget, as we discussed in chapter 7, children actively construct their knowledge and understanding of the world. Their thinking develops in distinct stages. At each stage, the child develops qualitatively different types of mental structures (or schemes) that allow the child to think about the world in new ways.

Like Piaget's theory, some versions of the information-processing approach are constructivist; they see children as directing their own cognitive development. And like Piaget, information-processing psychologists identify cognitive capabilities and limitations at various points in development. They describe ways in which individuals do and do not understand important concepts at different points in life and try to explain how more advanced understanding grows out of a less advanced one. They emphasize the impact that existing understanding has on the ability to acquire a new understanding of something.

Unlike Piaget, however, developmentalists who take an information-processing approach do not see development as occurring abruptly in distinct stages with a brief transition period from one stage to the next. Instead, according to the information-processing approach, individuals develop a gradually increasing capacity for processing information, which allows them to acquire increasingly complex knowledge and skills (Garton, 2004; Halford, 2004; Siegler, 2004; Mayer, 2003). Compared with Piaget, the information-processing approach also focuses on more precise analysis of change and on the contributions that ongoing cognitive activity—such as encoding and strategies—make to that change.

Review and Reflect • LEARNING GOAL 1

1 Explain the information-processing approach

Review

- What is the information-processing approach to development?
- How do capacity and processing speed change developmentally?
- What are three important mechanisms of change involved in information processing?
- How can the information-processing approach be compared to Piaget's theory?

Reflect

- In terms of ability to learn, are there similarities between how children process information and how a computer does? What might be some differences in the way that children and computers process information?

strategy construction Discovering a new procedure for processing information.

metacognition Cognition about cognition, or "knowing about knowing."

2 ATTENTION

What Is Attention? | Infancy | Childhood and Adolescence

The world holds a lot of information to perceive. Right now, you are perceiving the letters and words that make up this sentence. Now look around you and pick out something to look at other than this book. After that curl up the toes on your right foot. In each of these circumstances you engaged in the process of paying attention. What is attention and what effect does it have? How does it change with age?

What Is Attention?

Attention is the focusing of mental resources. Attention improves cognitive processing for many tasks, from grabbing a toy to hitting a baseball or adding numbers. At any one time, though, children, like adults, can pay attention to only a limited amount of information. They allocate their attention in different ways. Psychologists have labeled these types of allocation as sustained attention, selective attention, and divided attention.

- **Sustained attention** is the state of readiness to detect and respond to small changes occurring at random times in the environment. Sustained attention is also called *vigilance*.
- **Selective attention** is focusing on a specific aspect of experience that is relevant while ignoring others that are irrelevant. Focusing on one voice among many in a crowded room or a noisy restaurant is an example of selective attention. When you switched your attention to the toes on your right foot, you were engaging in selective attention.
- **Divided attention** involves concentrating on more than one activity at the same time. If you are listening to music or the television while you are reading this, you are engaging in divided attention.

Infancy

How effectively can infants attend to something? Even newborns can detect a contour and fixate on it; in other words, they pay attention to it. Older infants scan patterns more thoroughly. Infants as young as 4 months can selectively attend to an object and sustain their attention. For example, in a recent study, 4-month-old infants were more likely to look longer at a dynamic stimulus with an audio track than at a static stimulus that was mute (Shaddy & Colombo, 2004).

Closely linked with attention are the processes of habituation and dishabituation that we discussed in chapter 6, "Motor, Sensory, and Perceptual Development." Recall that *habituation* refers to decreased responsiveness to a stimulus after repeated presentations of the stimulus. When researchers present a sight or sound repeatedly, infants usually pay less attention to it, suggesting they get bored with it. *Dishabituation* is the recovery of a habituated response after a change in stimulation. Researchers study habituation to determine the extent to which infants can see, hear, smell, taste, and experience touch (Slater, 2004). Studies of habituation can indicate whether infants can recognize something they have previously experienced.

Infants' attention is so strongly governed by novelty and habituation that when an object becomes familiar, attention becomes shorter, making infants more vulnerable to distraction (Oakes, Kannass, & Shaddy, 2002). One recent study found that 10-month-olds were more distractible than 26-month-olds, suggesting that with increasing age infants can focus their attention better than younger infants (Ruff &

attention Concentrating and focusing mental resources.

sustained attention The state of readiness to detect and respond to small changes occurring at random times in the environment; also called vigilance.

selective attention Focusing on a specific aspect of experience that is relevant while ignoring others that are irrelevant.

divided attention Concentrating on more than one activity at a time.

Capozzoli, 2003). Another recent study revealed that infants who were labeled "short lookers" because of the brief time they focused attention had better memory at 1 year of age than were "long lookers," who had more sustained attention (Courage, Howe, & Squires, 2004).

Much can be learned by paying attention to a baby's habituation. Habituation provides a measure of an infant's maturity and well-being. Infants who have brain damage do not habituate well. In addition, parents can use knowledge of habituation and dishabituation to improve interaction with their babies. Wise parents sense when the infant shows interest and know that many repetitions of a stimulus may be necessary for the infant to process the information. The parents stop or change their behavior when the infant redirects attention (Rosenblith, 1992).

Childhood and Adolescence

Some important changes in attention occur during childhood. Much of the research on attention has focused on selective attention. One recent study of 5- to 7-year-old children found that the older children and more socially advantaged children in a sample resisted the interference of competing demands and focused their attention better than the younger children and more socially disadvantaged children in the sample (Mezzacappa, 2004).

The toddler wanders around, shifts attention from one activity to another, and seems to spend little time focused on any one object or event. In contrast, the preschool child might watch television for half an hour at a time (Giavecchio, 2001). In one study, researchers who observed 99 families in their homes for 4,672 hours found that visual attention to television dramatically increased in the preschool years (Anderson & others, 1986).

Researchers have found that preschool children's attention is related to their achievement-related and social skills (Ruff & Rothbart, 1996). In regard to achievement-related skills, one recent study of more than 1,000 children found that their sustained attention at 54 months of age was linked to their school readiness (which included achievement and language skills) (NICHD Early Child Care Research Network, 2003). In regard to social skills, young children who have difficulty regulating their attention are more likely than other children to experience peer rejection and engage in aggressive behavior (Eisenberg & others, 2000).

Control over attention shows important changes during childhood (Ruff & Capozzoli, 2003). External stimuli are likely to determine the target of the preschooler's attention; what is *salient* grabs the preschooler's attention. For example, suppose a flashy, attractive clown presents the directions for solving a problem. Preschool children are likely to pay attention to the clown and ignore the directions; they are influenced strongly by the salient features of the environment. After the age of 6 or 7, children pay more attention to features that are relevant to performing a task or solving a problem, such as the directions. This change reflects a shift to *cognitive control* of attention, so that children act less impulsively and reflect more. Instead of being controlled by the most striking stimuli in their environment, older children can direct their attention to more important stimuli.

Attention to relevant information increases steadily through the elementary and secondary school years (Davidson, 1996). Processing of irrelevant information decreases in adolescence.

As children grow up, their abilities both to direct selective attention and to divide attention also improve. Older children and adolescents are better than younger children at tasks that require shifts of attention. For example, writing a good story requires shifting attention among many competing tasks—spelling the words, composing grammar, structuring paragraphs, and conveying the story as a whole. Children also improve in their ability to do two things at once. For example, in one investigation, 12-year-olds were markedly better than 8-year-olds and slightly worse than 20-year-olds at allocating their attention in a situation involving two tasks (divided attention) (Manis, Keating, & Morrison, 1980). These improvements in divided attention might be due to an increase in cognitive resources (through increased processing speed or capacity), automaticity, or increased skill at directing resources.

***Review and Reflect* • LEARNING GOAL 2**

2 Define attention and outline its developmental changes

Review
- What Is attention?
- How does attention develop in infancy?
- How does attention develop in childhood and adolescence?

Reflect
- Imagine that you are an elementary school teacher. Devise some strategies to help children pay attention in class.

3 MEMORY

What Is Memory? | Infancy | Childhood

Twentieth-century American playwright Tennessee Williams once commented that life is all memory except for that one present moment that goes by so quickly that you can hardly catch it going. But just what do we do when we remember something, and how does our ability to remember develop?

memory Retention of information over time.

short-term memory Retention of information for up to 15 to 30 seconds, assuming there is no rehearsal of the information. Using rehearsal, individuals can keep the information in short-term memory longer.

long-term memory A relatively permanent and unlimited type of memory.

What Is Memory?

Memory is the retention of information over time. Without memory you would not be able to connect what happened to you yesterday with what is going on in your life today. Human memory is truly remarkable when you think of how much information we put into our memories and how much we must retrieve to perform all of life's activities.

Processes and Types of Memory Researchers study how information is initially placed or encoded into memory, how it is retained or stored after being encoded, and how it is found or retrieved for a certain purpose later (see figure 8.2). Encoding, storage, and retrieval are the basic processes required for memory. Failures can occur in any of these processes. Some part of an event might not be encoded, the mental representation of the event might not be stored, or even if the memory exists, you might not be able to retrieve it.

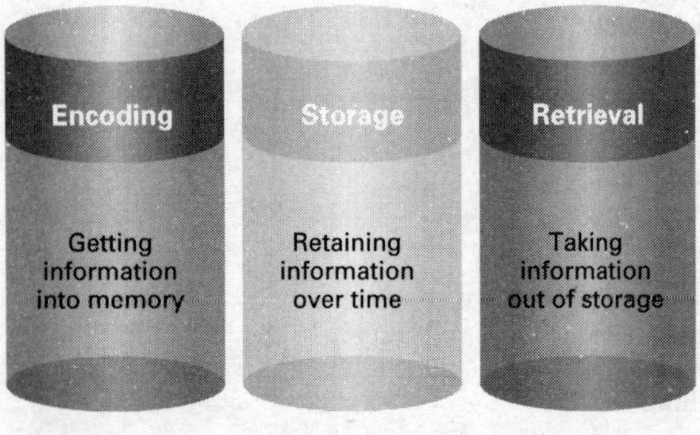

FIGURE 8.2 Processing Information in Memory. As you read about the many aspects of memory in this chapter, think about the organization of memory in terms of these three main activities.

Examining the storage process led psychologists to classify memories based on their permanence (Winkler & Cowan, 2005). **Short-term memory** is a memory system with a limited capacity in which information is usually retained for up to 15 to 30 seconds unless strategies are used to retain it longer. **Long-term memory** is a relatively permanent and unlimited type of memory. People are usually referring to long-term memory when they talk about "memory." When you remember the type of games you enjoyed playing as a child or your first date, you are drawing on your long-term memory. But when you remember the word you just read a few seconds ago, you are using short-term memory.

When psychologists first analyzed short-term memory, they described it as if it were a passive storehouse with shelves to store information until it is moved to long-term memory. But we do many things with the information stored in short-term memory. For example, the words in this sentence are part of your short-term memory, and you are manipulating them to form a meaningful whole.

The concept of working memory acknowledges the importance of our manipulations of the information in short-term memory. **Working memory** is a kind of mental "workbench" where individuals manipulate and assemble information when they make decisions, solve problems, and comprehend written and spoken language (Baddeley, 1990, 1998, 2001). Many psychologists prefer the term working memory over short-term memory to describe how memory works.

"Can we hurry up and get to the test? My short-term memory is better than my long-term memory."
Copyright © 1999. Reprinted courtesy of Bunny Hoest and *Parade*.

Figure 8.3 shows Alan Baddeley's model of working memory. Notice that it includes two short-term stores—one for speech and one for visual and spatial information—as well as a *central executive*. It is the job of the central executive to monitor and control the system—determining what information is stored, relating information from long-term memory to the information in the short-term stores, and moving information into long-term memory. Working memory is linked to many aspects of development (Schneider, 2004; Schneider & others, 2004). For example, children who have better working memory are more advanced in reading comprehension and problem solving than their counterparts with less effective working memory (Bjorklund, 2005; Demetriou & others, 2002).

www.mhhe.com/santrockcd11

Memory Links

Constructing Memories

Memory is not like a tape recorder or a camera or even like computer memory; we don't store and retrieve bits of data in computer-like fashion (Schachter, 2001). Children and adults construct and reconstruct their memories.

Schema Theory According to **schema theory,** people mold memories to fit information that already exists in their minds (Terry, 2003). This process is guided by **schemas,** which are mental frameworks that organize concepts and information. Suppose a football fan and a visitor from a country where the sport isn't played are eating at a restaurant and overhear a conversation about last night's game. Because the visitor doesn't have a schema for information about football, he or she is more likely than the fan to mishear what is said. Perhaps the visitor will interpret the conversation in terms of a schema for another sport, constructing a false memory of the conversation.

Schemas influence the way we encode, make inferences about, and retrieve information. We reconstruct the past rather than take an exact photograph of it, and the mind can distort an event as it encodes and stores impressions of it. Often when we retrieve information, we fill in the gaps with fragmented memories.

In part, our schemas depend on our culture. A culture sensitizes its members to certain objects, events, and strategies, which in turn can influence the nature of memory (Mistry & Rogoff, 1994). If you live on a remote island in the Pacific Ocean and make your living by fishing, your memory about how the weather affects fishing is likely to be highly developed. In contrast, a Pacific Islander might be hard-pressed to encode and recall the details of an hour of MTV.

Fuzzy Trace Theory Another variation of how individuals reconstruct their memories has been proposed by Charles Brainerd and Valerie Reyna (2004; Reyna, 2004; Reyna & Brainerd, 1995). **Fuzzy trace theory** states that when individuals encode information they create two types of memory representations: (1) a *verbatim memory trace,* which consists of precise details, and (2) a *fuzzy trace* or *gist,* which is the central idea of the information. For example, consider a child who is presented with information about a pet store that has 10 birds, 6 cats, 8 dogs, and 7 rabbits. Then

working memory A mental "workbench" where individuals manipulate and assemble information when making decisions, solving problems, and comprehending written and spoken language.

schema theory States that when people reconstruct information, they fit it into information that already exists in their mind.

schemas Mental frameworks that organize concepts and information.

fuzzy trace theory States that memory is best understood by considering two types of memory representations: (1) verbatim memory trace and (2) gist. In this theory, older children's better memory is attributed to the fuzzy traces created by extracting the gist of information.

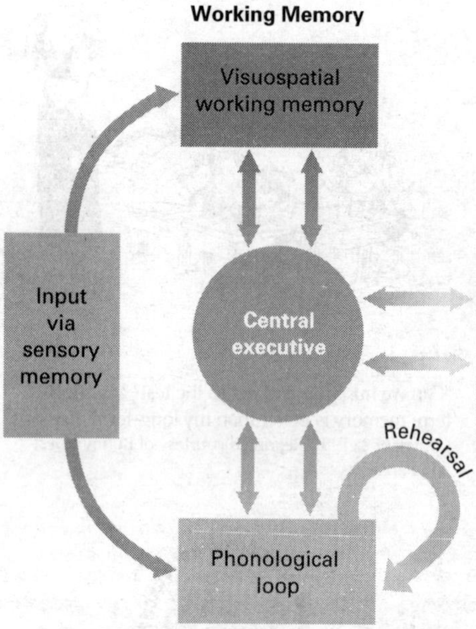

FIGURE 8.3 Working Memory. In Baddeley's working memory model, working memory is like a mental workbench where a great deal of information processing is carried out. Working memory consists of three main components: the phonological loop and visuospatial working memory serve as assistants, helping the central executive do its work. Input from sensory memory goes to the phonological loop, where information about speech is stored and rehearsal takes place, and visuospatial working memory, where visual and spatial information, including imagery, are stored. Working memory is a limited-capacity system, and information is stored there for only a brief time. Working memory interacts with long-term memory, using information from long-term memory in its work and transmitting information to long-term memory for longer storage.

the child is asked (1) verbatim questions, such as: "How many cats are in the pet store, 6 or 8?" and (2) gist questions, such as: "Are there more cats or more dogs in the pet store?" Researchers have found that preschool children tend to remember verbatim information more than gist information, but elementary-school-aged children are more likely to remember gist information (Brainerd & Gordon, 1994). According to Brainerd and Reyna, the increased use of gist by elementary-school-aged children accounts for their improved memory because fuzzy traces are less likely to be forgotten than verbatim traces.

Content Knowledge and Expertise Our ability to remember new information about a subject does depend considerably on what we already know about it (Allen & others, 2004; Mayer, 2004; Rob, 2004). The contribution of content knowledge to memory is especially evident in the memory of individuals who are experts or novices in a particular knowledge domain. An expert is the opposite of a novice (someone who is just beginning to learn a content area). Experts demonstrate especially impressive memory in their areas of *expertise*. One reason children remember less than adults is that they are far less expert in most areas.

What is it, exactly, that experts do so well? They are better than novices at (National Research Council, 1999):

1. Detecting features and meaningful patterns of information.
2. Accumulating more content knowledge and organizing it in a manner that shows an understanding of the topic.
3. Retrieving important aspects of knowledge with little effort.

Experts have superior recall of information in their area of expertise. One way they accomplish this superior recall is through *chunking*, which means grouping bits of information into one higher-order unit that can be remembered as a whole. For example, you probably would have a lot of difficulty remembering a random list of 30 letters but would find it easy to remember the words *hot, city, book, forget, tomorrow,* and *smile,* which also have 30 letters. Putting the letters into words forms a smaller number of more meaningful chunks of information. Similarly, chess masters display impressive memories of the configurations of pieces on a chess board because they "perceive chunks of meaningful information, which affects their memory of what they see. . . . Lacking a hierarchical, highly organized structure for the domain, novices cannot use this chunking strategy" (National Research Council, 1999, p. 21).

In areas where children are experts, their memory is often extremely good. In fact, it often exceeds that of adults who are novices in that content area. This was documented in a study of 10-year-old chess experts (Chi, 1978). These children were excellent chess players, but not especially brilliant in other ways. As with most 10-year-olds, their memory spans for digits were shorter than an adult's. However, when they were presented with chess boards, they remembered the configurations far better than did the adults who were novices at chess (see figure 8.4).

Experts' knowledge is organized around important ideas or concepts more than novices' knowledge is (National Research Council, 1999). This provides experts with a much deeper understanding of knowledge than novices. Experts in a particular area usually have far more elaborate networks of information about that area than novices do. The information they represent in memory has more nodes, more interconnections, and better hierarchical organization.

Experts are more likely than novices to retrieve information in an almost effortless manner (National Research Council, 1999). Consider expert and novice readers.

Expert readers can quickly scan the words of a sentence and paragraph, which allows them to devote attention to understanding what they are reading. However, novice readers' ability to decode words is not yet automatic, so they have to allocate considerable time to this task, which restricts the time they can give to understanding a passage.

We have examined a number of basic processes that are important in understanding children's memory. In several places, we have described developmental changes in these processes. Let's now further explore how memory changes from infancy through childhood.

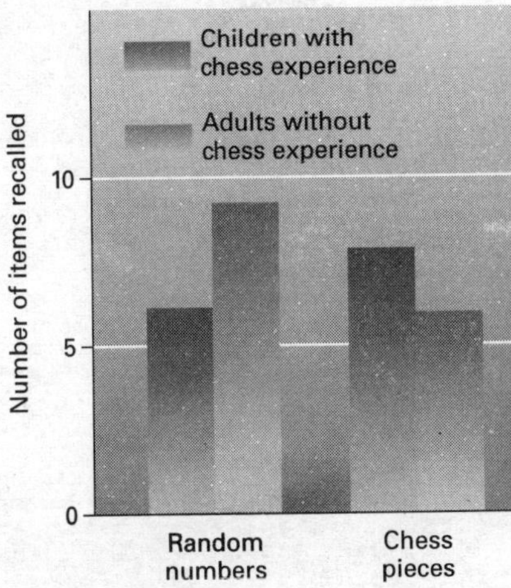

FIGURE 8.4 Memory for Numbers and Chess Pieces

Infancy

Popular child-rearing expert Penelope Leach (1990) told parents that 6- to 8-month-old babies cannot hold in their mind a picture of their mother or father. And historically psychologists believed that infants cannot store memories until they have language skills. Recently, though, child development researchers have revealed that infants as young as 3 months of age show a limited type of memory (Courage, Howe, & Squires, 2004).

First Memories Carolyn Rovee-Collier (1987, 2004; Rovee-Collier & Barr, 2004) has conducted research that demonstrates that infants can remember perceptual-motor information. In a characteristic experiment, she places a baby in a crib underneath an elaborate mobile and ties one end of a ribbon to the baby's ankle and the other end to the mobile. The baby kicks and makes the mobile move (see figure 8.5). Weeks later, the baby is returned to the crib, but its foot is not tied to the mobile. The baby kicks, apparently trying to make the mobile move. However, if the mobile's makeup is changed even slightly, the baby doesn't kick. If the mobile is then restored to being exactly as it was when the baby's ankle was originally tied to it, the baby will begin kicking again. According to Rovee-Collier, even by 2½ months the baby's memory is incredibly detailed.

How well can infants remember? Some researchers such as Rovee-Collier have concluded that infants as young as 2 to 6 months of age can remember some experiences through 1½ to 2 years of age (Rovee-Collier, 2004). However, critics such as Jean Mandler (2000), a leading expert on infant cognition, argue that the infants in Rovee-Collier's experiments are displaying only implicit memory. **Implicit memory** refers to memory without conscious recollection—memories of skills and routine procedures that are performed automatically such as riding a bicycle. In contrast, **explicit memory** refers to the conscious memory of facts and experiences.

When people talk about memory, they are usually referring to explicit memory. Most researchers find that babies do not show explicit memory until the second half of the first year (Mandler & McDonough, 1995). Then, explicit memory improves substantially during the second year of life (Bauer, 2002, 2004, 2005, 2006; Bauer & others, 2003; Carver & Bauer, 2001). In one longitudinal study, infants were assessed several times during their second year (Bauer & others, 2000). Older infants showed more accurate memory and required fewer prompts to demonstrate their memory than younger infants. In sum, most of infants' conscious memories are fragile and short-lived, but their memory of perceptual-motor actions can be substantial (Mandler, 2000).

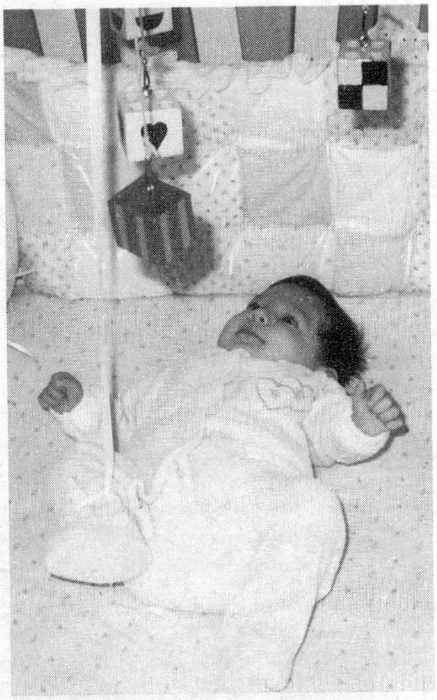

FIGURE 8.5 The Technique Used in Rovee-Collier's Investigation of Infant Memory. In Rovee-Collier's experiment, operant conditioning was used to demonstrate that infants as young as 2½ months of age can retain information from the experience of being conditioned.

Infantile Amnesia Do you remember your third birthday party? Probably not. Most adults can remember little if anything from the first three years of their life. This is called *infantile* or *childhood amnesia.* The few reported adult memories of life at age 2 or 3 are at best very sketchy (Hayne, 2004; Neisser, 2004; Newcombe & others, 2000). Elementary school children also do not remember much of their early child years. In one study, about three years after leaving preschool, children were

implicit memory Memory without conscious recollection; memory of skills and routine procedures that are performed automatically.

explicit memory Conscious memory of facts and experiences.

www.mhhe.com/santrockcd11

Patricia Bauer's Research

much poorer at remembering their former classmates than their teacher was (Lie & Newcombe, 1999). In another study, 10-year-olds were shown pictures of their preschool classmates and they recognized only about 20 percent of them (Newcombe & Fox, 1994).

What is the cause of infantile amnesia? One reason for the difficulty older children and adults have in recalling events from their infant and early child years is the immaturity of the prefrontal lobes of the brain, which are believed to play an important role in memory for events (Boyer & Diamond, 1992).

Childhood

Children's memory improves considerably after infancy. Sometimes the long-term memories of preschoolers seem erratic, but young children can remember a great deal of information if they are given appropriate cues and prompts.

One reason children remember less than adults is that they are far less expert in most areas, but their growing knowledge is one likely source of their memory improvement. For example, a child's ability to recount what she has seen on a trip to the library depends greatly on what she already knows about libraries, such as where books on certain topics are located, how to check out books, and so on. If a child knows little about libraries, she will have a much more difficult time recounting what she saw there.

Fuzzy trace theory suggests another way in which memory develops during childhood (Brainerd & Reyna, 2004). Recall from our earlier discussion that young children tend to encode, store, and retrieve verbatim traces while elementary-school-aged children begin to use gist more. The increased use of gist likely produces more enduring memory traces of information. Other sources of improvement in children's memory include changes in memory span and their use of strategies.

Memory Span Unlike long-term memory, short-term memory has a very limited capacity. One method of assessing that capacity is the *memory-span task*. You simply hear a short list of stimuli—usually digits—presented at a rapid pace (one per second, for example). Then you are asked to repeat the digits.

Research with the memory-span task suggests that short-term memory increases during childhood. For example, in one investigation, memory span increased from about two digits in 2-year-old children to about five digits in 7-year-old children. Between 7 and 13 years of age, memory span increased only by one and a half digits (Dempster, 1981) (see figure 8.6). Keep in mind, though, that individuals have different memory spans.

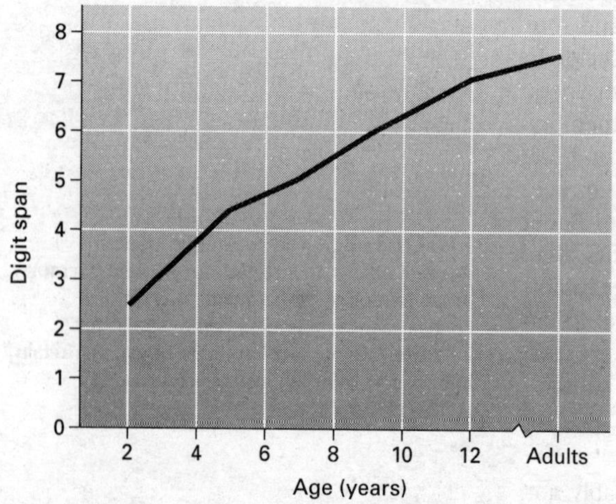

FIGURE 8.6 Developmental Changes in Memory Span. In one study, memory span increased about three digits from 2 years of age to 7 years of age (Dempster, 1981). By 12 years of age, memory span had increased on average another one and a half digits.

Why does memory span change with age? Speed of processing information is important, especially the speed with which memory items can be identified. For example, one study tested children on their speed at repeating words presented orally (Case, Kurland, & Goldberg, 1982). Speed of repetition was a powerful predictor of memory span. Indeed, when the speed of repetition was controlled, the 6-year-olds' memory spans were equal to those of young adults. Rehearsal of information is also important; older children rehearse the digits more than younger children.

Strategies Rehearsal is just one of the strategies that can sometimes aid memory, although rehearsal is a better strategy for short-term memory than long-term memory. In rehearsal, verbatim information is encoded and as we have seen in fuzzy trace theory, gist is more likely to produce a longer memory trace. While fuzzy trace theory emphasizes that children's memory improvement is due to an increased use of gist, children's memory advances also benefit from the use of *strategies*, which involve the use of mental activities to improve the processing of information (Schneider, 2004; Schneider & others, 2004; Siegler, 2004; Siegler & Alibali, 2005). Important strategies that can improve long-term memory include organization, elaboration, and imagery.

Organization If children organize information when they encode it, their memory benefits. Consider this demonstration: Recall the 12 months of the year as quickly as you can. How long did it take you? What was the order of your recall? You probably answered something like "a few seconds" and "in chronological order." Now try to remember the months of the year in alphabetical order. Did you make any errors? How long did it take you? It should be obvious that your memory for the months of the year is organized in a particular way.

Organizing is a strategy that older children (and adults) typically use, and it helps them to remember information. Preschool children usually don't use strategies like organization; in middle and late childhood they are more likely to use organization when they need to remember something (Flavell, Miller, & Miller, 2002).

Elaboration Another important strategy is elaboration, which involves engaging in more extensive processing of information. When individuals engage in elaboration, their memory benefits (Terry, 2003). Thinking of examples is a good way to elaborate information. For example, self-reference is an effective way to elaborate information. Thinking about personal associations with information makes the information more meaningful and helps children to remember it.

The use of elaboration changes developmentally (Pressley, 2003; Schneider & Pressley, 1997). Adolescents are more likely than children to use elaboration spontaneously. Elementary school children can be taught to use elaboration strategies on a learning task but they will be less likely than adolescents to use the strategies on other learning tasks in the future. Nonetheless, verbal elaboration can be an effective strategy even for young elementary school children.

Imagery Creating mental images is another strategy for improving memory. However, using imagery to remember verbal information works better for older children than for younger children (Schneider, 2004; Schneider & Pressley, 1997). In one study, 20 sentences were presented to first- through sixth-grade children to remember—such as, "The angry bird shouted at the white dog" and "The policeman painted the circus tent on a windy day" (Pressley & others, 1987). Children were randomly assigned to an imagery condition (in which they were told to make a picture in their head for each sentence) and a control condition (in which they were told just to try hard). Figure 8.7 shows that the imagery instructions helped older elementary school children (grades 4 through 6) but did not help the younger elementary school children (grades 1 through 3). However, mental imagery can help young schoolchildren to remember pictures (Schneider, 2004; Schneider & Pressley, 1997).

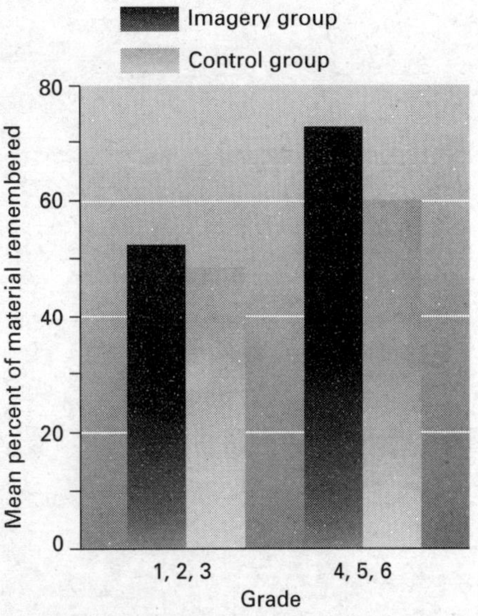

FIGURE 8.7 Imagery and Memory of Verbal Information. Imagery improved older elementary school children's memory for sentences more than younger elementary school children's memory for sentences.

Reconstructive Memory and Children as Eyewitnesses

Children's memories, like those of adults, are constructive and reconstructive. Children have schemas for all sorts of information, and these schemas affect how they encode, store, and retrieve memories. If a teacher tells her class a story about two men and two women who were involved in a train crash in France, students won't remember every detail of the story and will reconstruct the story, putting their own individual stamp on it. One student might reconstruct the story by saying the characters died in a plane crash, another might describe three men and three women, another might say the crash was in Germany, and so on.

Reconstruction and distortion are nowhere more apparent than in clashing testimony given by eyewitnesses at trials. A special concern is susceptibility to

Four-year-old Jennifer Royal was the only eyewitness to one of her playmates being shot to death. She was allowed to testify in open court, and the clarity of her statements helped to convict the gunman. *What are some issues involved in whether young children should be allowed to testify in court?*

www.mhhe.com/santrockcd11

Children's Eyewitness Testimony

suggestion and how this can alter memory. Consider a study of individuals who had visited Disneyland (Pickrell & Loftus, 2001). Four groups of participants read ads and answered questionnaires about a trip to Disneyland. One group saw an ad that mentioned no cartoon characters; the second read the same ad and saw a four-foot-tall cardboard figure of Bugs Bunny; the third read a fake ad for Disneyland with Bugs Bunny on it; and the fourth saw the same fake ad along with cardboard Bugs. Participants were asked whether they had ever met Bugs Bunny at Disneyland. Less than 10 percent of those in the first two groups reported having met Bugs Bunny at Disneyland, but approximately 30 to 40 percent of the third and fourth groups remembered meeting Bugs there. People were persuaded they had met Bugs Bunny at Disneyland even though Bugs is a Warner Brothers character who would never appear at a Disney theme park.

One recent study found that young children were less likely than older children to reject false claims about events (Ghetti & Alexander, 2004). However, the following conclusions about children as eyewitnesses indicate that a number of factors can influence the accuracy of a young child's memory (Bruck & Ceci, 1999):

- *There are age differences in children's susceptibility to suggestion.* Preschoolers are the most suggestible age group in comparison with older children and adults (Ceci & Bruck, 1993; Crossman, Scullin, & Melnyk, 2004). For example, preschool children are more susceptible to believing misleading or incorrect information given after an event (Ghetti & Alexander, 2004). Despite these age differences, there is still concern about the reaction of older children when they are subjected to suggestive interviews (Poole & Lindsay, 1996).
- *There are individual differences in susceptibility.* Some preschoolers are highly resistant to interviewers' suggestions, whereas others immediately succumb to the slightest suggestion. One recent study found that children with more advanced verbal abilities and self-control were more likely to resist interviewers' suggestive questions (Clarke-Stewart, Malloy, & Allhusen, 2004). A recent research review found that the following noncognitive factors were linked to being at risk for suggestibility: low self-concept, low support from parents, and mothers' insecure attachment in romantic relationships (Bruck & Melnyk, 2004).
- *Interviewing techniques can produce substantial distortions in children's reports about highly salient events.* Children are suggestible not just about peripheral details but also about the central aspects of an event (Bruck, Ceci, & Hembrooke, 1998). In some cases, children's false reports can be tinged with sexual connotations. In laboratory studies, young children have made false claims about "silly events" that involved body contact (such as "Did the nurse lick your knee?" or "Did she blow in your ear?"). And these false claims have been found to persist for at least three months (Ornstein & Haden, 2001). A significant number of preschool children have falsely reported that someone touched their private parts, kissed them, and hugged them, when these events clearly did not happen in the research. Nonetheless, young children are capable of recalling much that is relevant about an event (Fivush, 1993; Goodman, Batterman-Faunce, & Kenney, 1992). When children do accurately recall information about an event, the interviewer often has a neutral tone, there is limited use of misleading questions, and there is an absence of any motivation for the child to make a false report (Bruck & Ceci, 1999).

To read further about false memories in children, see the following Research in Child Development interlude.

RESEARCH IN CHILD DEVELOPMENT

Suggesting False Events to Children

As described in Bruck and Ceci (1999, pp. 429–430), a study by Deborah Poole and D. Stephen Lindsay revealed how parents can subtly influence their young children's memory for events. Preschool children participated in four activities (such as lifting cans with pulleys) with "Mr. Science" in a university laboratory (Poole & Lindsay, 1995). Four months later, the children's parents were mailed a storybook with a description of their child's visit to see Mr. Science. The storybook described two of the activities in which the child had participated but it also described two in which the child had not participated. Each description also ended with this fabrication of what had happened when it was time to leave the laboratory: "Mr. Science wiped (child's name) hands and face with a wet-wipe. The cloth got close to (child's name) mouth and tasted real yucky."

Parents read the descriptions to their children three times. Later, the children told the experimenter that they had participated in the activities that actually had only been mentioned in the descriptions read by their parents. For example, when asked whether Mr. Science had put anything yucky in their mouths, more than half of the young children said that he had. Subsequently when asked whether Mr. Science put something in their mouth or their mom just read this to them in a story, 71 percent of the young children said that it really happened.

This study shows how subtle suggestions can influence children's inaccurate reporting of nonevents. If the children's inaccurate reports were pursued in follow-up questioning by an interviewer who suspected that something sexual had occurred, the result could be a sexual interpretation of events that never occurred. This study also revealed the difficulty preschool children have in identifying the source of a suggestion (called *source-monitoring errors*). Children in this study confused their parent reading the suggestion to them with their experience of the suggestion.

Another study revealed age differences in suggestibility. It focused on 329 students in the third/fourth, seventh/eighth, and eleventh/twelfth grades (Lindberg, Keiffer, & Thomas, 2000). Participants saw a short videotape of two boys aged 5 and 11 coming home from school and playing video games. The older boy left to call a friend, at which time the mother came home and dropped a bag of groceries. She asked the younger boy to help her pick them up, but he repeatedly ignored her and continued to play the video game. She then apparently hit him in the head and knocked him to the floor. As he was crying, she picked him up in a rough fashion, dragged him to the kitchen, and apparently hit him again.

The experimenters manipulated a number of factors to determine their effects on the way the children interpreted the video. For example, one question posed to the children was: "How many drops of blood fell from Mark's (the younger boy's) nose?" Actually no drops of blood fell. The children in the third and fourth grades reported more drops of blood than older children did (see figure 8.8), indicating greater suggestibility in the elementary school children. When the question about drops of blood was used, children at all grade levels were more likely to report seeing blood falling from the boy's nose than when the question was not included.

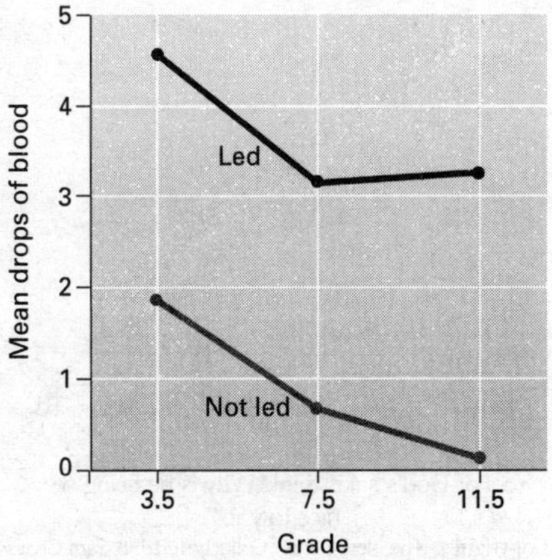

FIGURE 8.8 Suggestibility of Children at Different Grade Levels. The grade levels used in data analysis were combinations of grades (for example, 3.5 = grades 3 and 4 combined). "Led" refers to when the question about drops of blood was used; "Not led" refers to when this question was not used.

In sum, whether a young child's eyewitness testimony is accurate or not may depend on a number of factors such as the type, number, and intensity of the suggestive techniques the child has experienced (Bruck & Ceci, 2004; Crossman, Scullin, & Melnyk, 2004; Ghetti & Alexander, 2004; Gilstrap & Ceci, 2005; Loftus, 2002). It appears that the reliability of young children's reports has as much or more to do with the skills and motivation of the interviewer as with any natural limitations on young children's memory. Because of the possibility that they can be led into saying something falsely, young children should be interviewed by a neutral professional (Hyman & Loftus, 2001).

Review and Reflect • **LEARNING GOAL 3**

3 Describe what memory is and how it changes

Review
- What is memory? What are some important processes and types of memory?
- How does memory develop in infancy?
- How does memory change in childhood?

Reflect
- What is your earliest memory? Why do you think you can remember this particular situation?

4 THINKING

What Is Thinking? | Infancy | Childhood | Adolescence

Attention and memory are often steps toward another level of information processing—thinking. What is thinking? How does it change developmentally? What is children's scientific thinking like, and how do they solve problems? Let's explore these questions.

"For God's sake, think! Why is he being so nice to you?"

What Is Thinking?

Thinking involves manipulating and transforming information in memory; it is the job of the central executive in Baddeley's model of working memory shown in figure 8.3. We can think about the concrete (such as a vacation at the beach or how to win at a video game) or we can think in more abstract ways (such as pondering the meaning of freedom or identity). We can think about the past (what happened to us last month) and the future (what our life will be like in the year 2020). We can think about reality (such as how to do better on the next test) and fantasy (what it would be like to meet Elvis Presley or land a spacecraft on Mars). We think in order to reason, reflect, evaluate ideas, solve problems, and make decisions. Let's explore how thinking changes developmentally, beginning with infancy.

Infancy

Interest in thinking during infancy has especially focused on concept formation and categorization. **Concepts** are categorizes that group objects, events, and characteristics on the basis of common properties. Concepts help us to simplify and summarize information. Imagine a world in which we had no concepts: we would see each object as unique and would not be able to make any generalizations.

Do infants have concepts? Yes, they do, and they form concepts very early in their development (Horst, Oakes, & Madole, 2005; Nelson, 2004; Quinn, 2004). Infants as young as 3 months of age begin to form categories on the basis of perceptual features. How can researchers determine that infants so young can do this? They use the habituation technique discussed earlier in the chapter. For example, in one study 3- and 4-month-olds were shown paired photographs of animals, such as dogs and cats (Quinn & Eimas, 1996). When the infants were presented with paired photographs of dogs across several trials, they habituated to them (that is, over time

thinking manipulating and transforming information in memory, usually to form concepts, reason, think critically, and solve problems.

concepts Categories that group objects, events, and characteristics on the basis of common properties.

they looked at them less). However, when the infants were subsequently shown photographs of a dog paired with a cat, the infants looked longer at the cat, indicating they recognized it as being different from the dogs they had previously seen. Infants less than 6 months of age have also shown the ability to categorize geometric patterns, men's and women's voices, and chairs and tables (Haith & Benson, 1998).

Jean Mandler (2003, 2004) argues that these early categorizations are best described as *perceptual categorization*. That is, the categorizations are based on similar perceptual features of objects, such as size, color, and movement, as well as parts of objects, such as legs for animals. She concludes that it is not until about 7 to 9 months of age that infants form *conceptual* categories that are characterized by perceptual variability. For example, in one study of 7- to 11-year-olds, infants classified birds as animals and airplanes as vehicles even though the objects were perceptually similar—airplanes and birds with their wings spread (Mandler & McDonough, 1993).

Further advances in categorization occur in the second year of life. In Mandler's (2005) analysis, many of infants' "first concepts are broad and global in nature, such as 'animal' or 'indoor thing.' Gradually, over the first two years these broad concepts become more differentiated into concepts such as 'land animal,' then 'dog,' or to 'furniture,' then 'chair'" p. (1).

Childhood

To explore thinking in childhood, we will examine three important types of thinking: critical thinking, scientific thinking, and problem solving.

Critical Thinking Currently, there is considerable interest among psychologists and educators in critical thinking, but it is not a new idea. When educator John Dewey (1933) talked about the importance of getting students to think reflectively and when psychologist Max Wertheimer (1945) talked about the importance of thinking productively rather than guessing at an answer, they were concerned about critical thinking. **Critical thinking** involves thinking reflectively and productively, and evaluating evidence. If you think critically, you will do the following:

- Ask not only what happened but how and why.
- Examine supposed "facts" to determine whether there is evidence to support them.
- Argue in a reasoned way rather than through emotions.
- Recognize that there is sometimes more than one good answer or explanation.
- Compare various answers and judge which is the best answer.
- Evaluate what other people say rather than immediately accepting it as the truth.
- Ask questions and speculate beyond what is known to create new ideas and new information.

According to critics such as Jacqueline and Martin Brooks (1993, 2001), few schools teach students to think critically. Schools push students to give a single correct answer rather than encouraging them to come up with new ideas and rethink conclusions. Too often teachers ask students to recite, define, describe, state, and list rather than to analyze, infer, connect, synthesize, criticize, create, evaluate, think, and rethink. As a result, many schools graduate students who think superficially, staying on the surface of problems rather than becoming deeply engaged in meaningful thinking.

Critical Thinking Resources

One way to encourage students to think critically is to present them with controversial topics or both sides of an issue to discuss. Some teachers shy away from having students debate issues because arguments supposedly are not "polite" or "nice" (Winn, 2004). But debates can motivate students to delve more deeply into a topic and examine issues, especially if teachers refrain from stating their own views so that students feel free to explore multiple perspectives.

Can schools foster critical thinking among children? Anne Brown and Joe Campione (1996; Brown, 1997, 1998) created an innovative program, Fostering a

critical thinking Thinking reflectively and productively, and evaluating the evidence.

Community of Learners (FCL), that is appropriate for encouraging critical thinking among 6- to 12-year-old children. The program focuses on literacy and biology and is set in inner-city elementary schools. Reflection and discussion are key dimensions of the program. Constructive commentary, questioning, and criticism are the norm rather than the exception. Three strategies used by FCL that encourage reflection and discussion are as follows:

- *Online consultation.* In FCL classrooms, both children and adults use e-mail as well as face-to-face communication to share expertise and to build community.
- *Having children teach children.* Cross-age teaching, in which older students teach younger students, occurs both face-to-face and via e-mail in FCL. Older students often serve as discussion leaders. Cross-age teaching provides students with invaluable opportunities to talk about learning, gives students responsibility and purpose, and fosters collaboration among peers. FCL also uses **reciprocal teaching,** in which students take turns leading a small-group discussion. Reciprocal teaching requires students to discuss complex passages, collaborate, and share their individual expertise and perspectives.
- *Using adults as role models.* Visiting experts and classroom teachers introduce the big ideas and difficult principles at the beginning of a unit. The adults model how to think and reflect. The adults continually ask students to justify their opinions and then support them with evidence, to think of counterexamples to rules, and so on. Online experts function as role models of thinking. They wonder, query, and make inferences based on incomplete knowledge. Through e-mail, experts also provide coaching, advice, and commentary about what it means to learn and understand.

One example of a teaching theme used in FCL is "changing populations." Outside experts or teachers introduce this lesson and ask students to generate as many questions about it as possible. It is not unusual for students to come up with more than a hundred questions. The teacher and the students categorize the questions into subtopics according to the type of population they refer to, such as extinct, endangered, artificial, and urbanized populations. About six students make up a learning group, and each group takes responsibility for one subtopic.

A culture of learning, negotiating, sharing, and producing work that is displayed to others is at the heart of FCL. This approach has much in common with what Jerome Bruner (1996) recommended for improving the culture of education. Research evaluation suggests that FCL helps students' thinking skills (Brown, 1998).

Fostering a Community of Learners represents an attempt to apply what is known about children's cognitive development to improving their education (Lehrer & Schauble, 2006; Shulman & Shulman, 2004). To read about one developmental psychologist who used her training in cognitive development to pursue a career in an applied area, see the Careers in Child Development insert.

CAREERS in CHILD DEVELOPMENT

Helen Schwe

Developmental Psychologist and Toy Designer

Helen Schwe obtained a Ph.D. from Stanford University in developmental psychology but she now spends her days talking with computer engineers and designing "smart" toys for children. Smart toys are designed to improve children's problem-solving and symbolic thinking skills.

When she was a graduate student, Helen worked part-time for Hasbro toys, testing its children's software on preschoolers. Her first job after graduate school was with Zowie entertainment, which was subsequently bought by LEGO. According to Helen, "Even in a toy's most primitive stage of development, . . . you see children's creativity in responding to challenges, their satisfaction when a problem is solved or simply their delight when they are having fun" (Schlegel, 2000, p. 50). In addition to conducting experiments and focus groups at different stages of a toy's development, Helen also assesses the age appropriateness of a toy. Most of her current work focuses on 3- to 5-year-old children.

(Source: Schlegel, 2000, pp. 50–51)

Helen Schwe, a developmental psychologist, with some of the "smart" toys she designed.

reciprocal teaching Individuals take turns leading small-group discussions.

Scientific Thinking Some aspects of thinking are specific to a particular domain, such as mathematics, science, or reading. We will explore reading in chapter 10, "Language Development." Here we will examine scientific thinking by children.

Like scientists, children ask fundamental questions about reality and seek answers to problems that seem utterly trivial or unanswerable to other people (such as, Why is the sky blue?). Do children generate hypotheses, perform experiments, and reach conclusions about their data in ways resembling those of scientists (Schunn & Anderson, 2001)?

Scientific reasoning often is aimed at identifying causal relations. Like scientists, children place a great deal of emphasis on causal mechanisms (Frye & others, 1996; Martin & others, 2005). Their understanding of how events are caused weighs more heavily in their causal inferences than even whether the cause happened immediately before the effect.

There also are important differences between the reasoning of children and the reasoning of scientists (Abruscato, 2004; Williams & others, 2004). Children are more influenced by happenstance events than by an overall pattern (Kuhn, Amsel, & O'Laughlin, 1988). Often, children maintain their old theories regardless of the evidence (Kuhn, Schauble, & Garcia-Mila, 1992). Children might go through mental gymnastics trying to reconcile seemingly contradictory new information with their existing beliefs. For example, after learning about the solar system, children sometimes conclude that there are two earths, the seemingly flat world in which they live and the round ball floating in space that their teacher described.

Children also have difficulty designing experiments that can distinguish among alternative causes. Instead, they tend to bias the experiments in favor of whatever hypothesis they began with. Sometimes they see the results as supporting their original hypothesis even when the results directly contradict it (Schauble, 1996).

What are some characteristics of children's scientific thinking?

Science Resources for Teachers

Solving Problems Children face many problems, both in school and out of school. *Problem solving* involves finding an appropriate way to attain a goal. Let's examine two ways children solve problems—by applying rules and by using analogies—and then consider some ways to help children learn effective strategies for solving problems.

Using Rules to Solve Problems During early childhood, the relatively stimulus-driven toddler is transformed into a child capable of flexible, goal-directed problem solving (Zelazo & Muller, 2004; Zelazo & others, 2003). One element in this change is children's developing ability to form representations of reality.

For example, because they lack a concept of perspectives, 3- to 4-year-olds cannot understand that a single stimulus can be redescribed in a different, incompatible way (Perner & others, 2002). Consider a problem in which children must sort stimuli using the rule of *color.* In the course of the color sorting, a child may describe a red rabbit as a *red one* to solve the problem. However, in a subsequent task, the child may need to discover a rule that describes the rabbit as just a *rabbit* to solve the problem. If 3- to 4-year-olds fail to understand that it is possible to provide multiple descriptions of the same stimulus, they persist in describing the stimulus as a red rabbit. In other words, the 3- to 4-year-olds show representational inflexibility. Researchers have found that at about 4 years of age, children acquire the concept of perspectives, which allows them to appreciate that a single thing can be described in different ways (Frye, 1999).

With age, children also learn better rules to apply to problems. Figure 8.9 provides an example; it shows the balance scale problem that has been used to examine children's use of rules in solving problems. The scale includes a fulcrum and an arm that can rotate around it. The arm can tip left or right or remain level, depending on how weights (metal disks with holes in the center) are arranged on the pegs on each side of the fulcrum. The child's task is to look at the configuration of weights

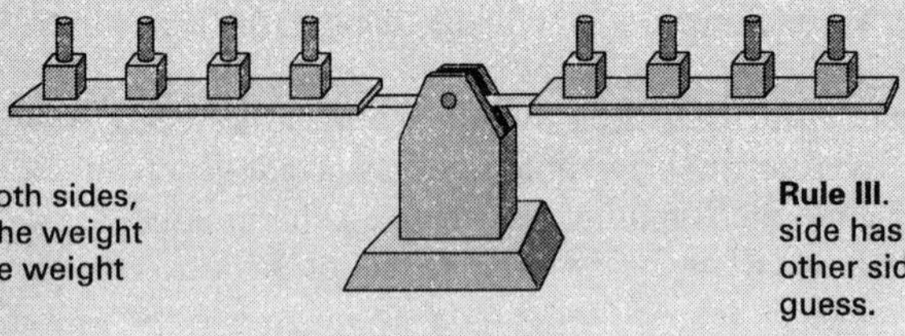

FIGURE 8.9 **The Type of Balance Scale Used by Siegler (1976).** Weights could be placed on pegs on each side of the fulcrum; the torque (the weight on each side times the distance of that weight from the fulcrum) determined which side would go down.

on the pegs on each problem and then predict whether the left side will go down, the right side will go down, or the arm will balance.

Robert Siegler (1976) hypothesized that children would use one of the four rules listed in figure 8.9. He reasoned that presenting problems on which different rules would generate different outcomes would allow assessment of each child's rules. Through a child's pattern of correct answers and errors on a set of such problems, that child's underlying rule could be inferred.

What were the results? Almost all 5-year-olds used Rule I, in which the child considers only the weight on the scales. Almost all 9-year-olds used either Rule II or Rule III, which takes both weight and distance into account, or Rule III, which calls for guessing when the weight and distance dimensions would give conflicting information. Both 13-year-olds and 17-year-olds generally used Rule III.

In other words, the older children performed better at solving the problems because they used a better rule. But even 5-year-old children can be trained to use Rule III if they are taught to pay attention to differences in distance. As children learn more about what is relevant to a problem and learn to encode the relevant information, their ability to use rules in problem solving improves.

Interestingly, despite the 17-year-olds' having studied balance scales in their physics course, almost none of them used the only rule that generated consistently correct answers, Rule IV. Discussions with their teachers revealed why: the balance scale the students had studied was a pan balance, on which small pans could be hung from various locations along the arm, rather than an arm balance, with pegs extending upward. Retesting the children showed that most could consistently solve the problems when the familiar pan balance was used. This example illustrates a set of lessons that frequently emerge from studies of problem solving—learning is often quite narrow, generalization beyond one's existing knowledge is difficult, and even analogies that seem straightforward are often missed.

Using Analogies to Solve Problems An *analogy* involves correspondence in some respects between things that are dissimilar. Even very young children can draw reasonable analogies under some circumstances and use them to solve problems (Freeman & Gehl, 1995). Under other circumstances, even college students fail to draw seemingly obvious analogies (as in the high school students' difficulty in extrapolating from the familiar pan balance to the unfamiliar arm balance).

Anne Brown and her collaborators (Brown, 1990; Brown, Kane, & Echols, 1986) have demonstrated that even 1- and 2-year-olds can use analogical reasoning. When 1- and 2-year-olds are shown that a curved stick can be used as a tool to pull in a toy that is too far away to be reached unaided, they draw the correct analogy in choosing which stick to use the next time. They do not choose sticks on the basis of their being the same color or looking exactly like the stick they saw used before. Instead they identify the essential property and will choose whichever objects have it; for example, they will choose a straight rake as well as the curved cane. The 2-year-olds were more likely than the 1-year-olds to learn the initial task without any help, but once they learned the task, both 1- and 2-year-olds drew the right analogy to new problems.

Analogical problem solving often involves tools more abstract than curved sticks for hauling in objects. Maps and verbal descriptions of routes, for example, often help us to figure out how to get where we want to go (DeLoache, Miller, & Pierroutsakos, 1998). Similarly, Judy DeLoache (1989) showed that young children can use scale models to guide their problem-solving activities.

DeLoache (1989) created a situation in which 2½- and 3-year-olds were shown a small toy hidden within a scale model of a room. The child was then asked to find the toy in a real room that was a bigger version of the scale model. If the toy was hidden under the armchair in the scale model, it was also hidden under the armchair in the real room. Considerable development occurred between 2½ and 3 years of age on this task. Thirty-month-old children rarely could solve the problem but most 36-month-old children could.

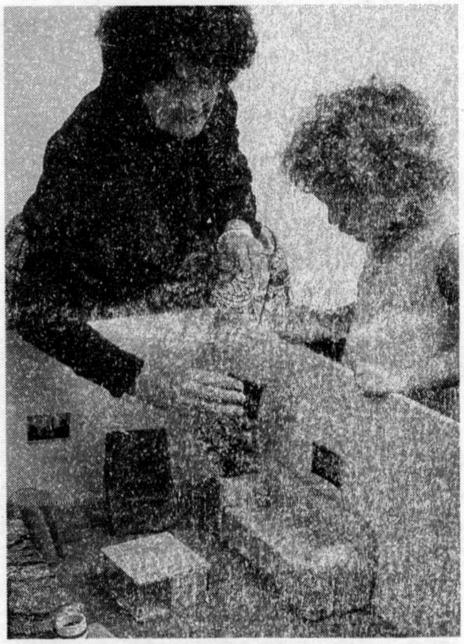

Judy DeLoache *(left)* has conducted research that focuses on young children's developing cognitive abilities. She has demonstrated that children's symbolic representation between 2½ and 3 years of age enables them to find a toy in a real room that is a much bigger version of the scale model.

Why was the task so difficult for the 2½-year-olds? Their problem was not an inability to understand that a symbol can represent another situation. Shown line drawings or photographs of the larger room, 2½-year-olds had no difficulty finding the object. Instead, the difficulty seemed to come from the toddlers' simultaneously viewing the scale model as a symbol of the larger room and as an object in itself. When children were allowed to play with the scale model before using it as a symbol, their performance worsened, presumably because playing with it made them think of it more as an object in itself. Conversely, when the scale model was placed in a glass case, where the children could not handle it at all, more children used it successfully to find the object hidden in the larger room. The general lesson is that young children can use a variety of tools to draw analogies, but they easily can forget that an object is being used as a symbol of something else and instead treat it as an object in its own right (DeLoache, 2004).

Using Strategies to Solve Problems Good thinkers routinely use strategies and effective planning to solve problems (McCormick, 2003; Pressley & Hilden, 2006). Do children use one strategy or multiple strategies in problem solving? They often use more than one strategy (Schneider, 2004; Siegler & Alibali, 2005).

Most children benefit from generating a variety of alternative strategies and experimenting with different approaches to a problem, discovering what works well, when, and where. This is especially true for children from the middle elementary school grades on, although some cognitive psychologists believe that even young children should be encouraged to practice varying strategies (Siegler & Alibali, 2005).

In Michael Pressley's view (Pressley, 2003; Pressley & Hilden, 2006; McCormick & Pressley, 1997), the key to education is helping students learn a rich repertoire of strategies for solving problems. Pressley argues that when children are given instruction about effective strategies, they often can apply strategies that they had not used on their own. Pressley emphasizes that children benefit when the teacher (1) models the appropriate strategy, (2) verbalizes the steps in the strategy, and (3) guides the children to practice the strategy and supports their practice with feedback. "Practice" means that children use the strategy over and over until they perform it automatically. To execute strategies effectively, they need to have the strategies in long-term memory, and extensive practice makes this possible.

Just having children learn a new strategy is usually not enough for them to continue to use it and to transfer the strategy to new situations. Children need to be motivated to learn and to use the strategies. For effective maintenance and transfer, children should be encouraged to monitor the effectiveness of the new strategy by comparing their performance on tests and other assessments.

Let's examine an example of effective strategy instruction. Good readers extract the main ideas from text and summarize them. In contrast, novice readers (for example, most children) usually don't store the main ideas of what they read. One intervention based on what is known about the summarizing strategies of good readers consisted of instructing children to (1) skim over trivial information, (2) ignore redundant information, (3) replace less inclusive terms with more inclusive ones, (4) use a more inclusive action term to combine a series of events, (5) choose a topic sentence, and (6) create a topic sentence if none is given (Brown & Day, 1983). Instructing elementary school students to use these summarizing strategies improves their reading performance (Rinehart, Stahl, & Erickson, 1986).

Adolescence

How does critical thinking change in adolescence? How do adolescents make decisions?

Critical Thinking If a solid basis of fundamental skills (such as literacy and math skills) is not developed during childhood, critical-thinking skills are unlikely to mature in adolescence. For those adolescents who lack fundamental skills, potential gains in adolescent thinking are not likely. For other adolescents, this time is an important transitional period in the development of critical thinking (Keating, 1990). Several cognitive changes occur during adolescence that allow improved critical thinking, including the following:

- Increased speed, automaticity, and capacity of information processing, which frees cognitive resources for other purposes
- More knowledge in a variety of domains
- An increased ability to construct new combinations of knowledge
- A greater range and more spontaneous use of strategies or procedures such as planning, considering alternatives, and cognitive monitoring

In one study of fifth-, eighth-, and eleventh-graders, critical thinking increased with age but still only occurred in 43 percent of even the eleventh-graders. Many adolescents showed self-serving biases in their reasoning (Klaczynski & Narasimham, 1998).

Decision Making Adolescence is a time of increased decision making—about the future, which friends to choose, whether to go to college, which person to date, whether to have sex, whether to buy a car, and so on (Byrnes, 1997, 2003, 2005; Galotti & Kozberg, 1996). How competent are adolescents at making decisions?

Older adolescents appear to be more competent decision makers than younger adolescents, who, in turn, are more competent than children (Keating, 1990, 2004). Compared with children, young adolescents are more likely to generate options, to examine the situation from a variety of perspectives, to anticipate the consequences of decisions, and to consider the credibility of sources.

Most people make better decisions when they are calm rather than emotionally aroused. That may especially be true for adolescents. Recall from our discussion of brain development in chapter 5 that adolescents have a tendency to be emotionally intense. The same adolescent who makes a wise decision when calm may make an unwise decision when emotionally aroused (Dahl, 2004). In the heat of the moment, then, adolescents' emotions may especially overwhelm their decision-making ability.

Being able to make competent decisions does not guarantee that one will make them in everyday life, where breadth of experience often comes into play (Jacobs & Kalczynski, 2002; Jacobs & Potenza, 1990; Keating, 1990, 2004). For example,

How can adolescents' decision making be characterized?

driver-training courses improve adolescents' cognitive and motor skills to levels equal to, or sometimes superior to, those of adults. However, driver training has not reduced adolescents' high rate of traffic accidents (Potvin, Champagne, & Laberge-Nadeau, 1988). An important research agenda is to study the ways adolescents make decisions in actual situations.

Review and Reflect • LEARNING GOAL 4

4 Characterize thinking and its developmental changes

Review
- What is thinking?
- Can children engage in critical and scientific thinking? What are some ways that children solve problems?
- What are some changes in thinking during adolescence?

Reflect
- Some experts lament that few schools teach students to think critically. Does your own experience support this view? If you agree with the experts, why is critical thinking not more widely or effectively taught?

5 METACOGNITION

What Is Metacognition? | The Child's Theory of Mind | Metacognition in Children and Adolescents

As you read at the beginning of this chapter, *metacognition* is cognition about cognition, or "knowing about knowing" (Flavell, 1999, 2004; Flavell, Miller, & Miller, 2002). It is a function of the central executive in Baddeley's model (see figure 8.3).

The developing cognitive competencies that are the most relevant to critical thinking are metacognitive competencies.

—Deanna Kuhn
Contemporary Psychologist, Columbia University

www.mhhe.com/santrockcd11

Metacognition
Metacognition and Reading

What Is Metacognition?

Metacognition helps people to perform many cognitive tasks more effectively (Flavell, 2004; Isquith, Gioia, & Espy, 2004; Kuiper & Pesut, 2004). In one study, students were taught metacognitive skills to help them solve math problems (Cardelle-Elawar, 1992). In each of 30 daily lessons involving math story problems, a teacher guided low-achieving students to recognize when they did not know the meaning of a word, did not have all of the information necessary to solve a problem, did not know how to subdivide the problem into specific steps, or did not know how to carry out a computation. After the 30 daily lessons, the students who were given this metacognitive training had better math achievement and attitudes toward math.

Metacognition can take many forms. It includes knowledge about when and where to use particular strategies for learning or for solving problems. **Metamemory,** individuals' knowledge about memory, is an especially important form of metacognition. Metamemory includes general knowledge about memory, such as knowing that recognition tests (such as multiple-choice questions) are easier than recall tests (such as essay questions). It also encompasses knowledge about one's own memory, such as knowing whether you have studied enough for an upcoming test.

The Child's Theory of Mind

Theory of mind refers to awareness of one's own mental processes and the mental processes of others. Even young children are curious about the nature of the human mind (Flavell, 1999, 2004; Harris, 2006; Wellman, 1997, 2000, 2004). Their theory of mind changes as they go through the childhood years (Flavell, 2004; Flavell, Miller, & Miller, 2002; Wellman, 2004).

When they are 2 to 3 years old, children begin to understand three mental states:

- Perceptions. Children realize that other people see what is in front of their eyes and not necessarily in front of the children's eyes.
- Desires. Children understand that if someone wants something, he or she will try to get it. A child might say, "I want my mommy."
- Emotions. Children can distinguish between positive (for example, "happy") and negative (for example, "sad") emotions. A child might say, "Tommy feels bad."

metamemory Knowledge about memory.

theory of mind Thoughts about how mental processes work, such as a child's becoming aware that the mind exists and understanding cognitive connections to the physical world.

Despite these advances, children who are 2 to 3 years of age have only a minimal understanding of how mental life can be linked to behavior. They think that people are at the mercy of their desires, and they don't understand how beliefs influence behavior.

When they are 4 to 5 years of age, children begin to understand that the mind can represent objects and events accurately or inaccurately. The realization that people have *false beliefs*—beliefs that are not true—develops in a majority of children by the time they are 5 years old (Wellman, Cross, & Watson, 2001) (see figure 8.10). For example, in one study children were shown a Band-Aids box and asked what was inside (Jenkins & Astington, 1996). To the children's surprise, the box contained pencils. When asked what a child who had never seen the box would think was inside, 3-year-olds typically responded "pencils." The 4- and 5-year-olds, grinning in anticipation of other children's false beliefs, were more likely to say "Band-Aids."

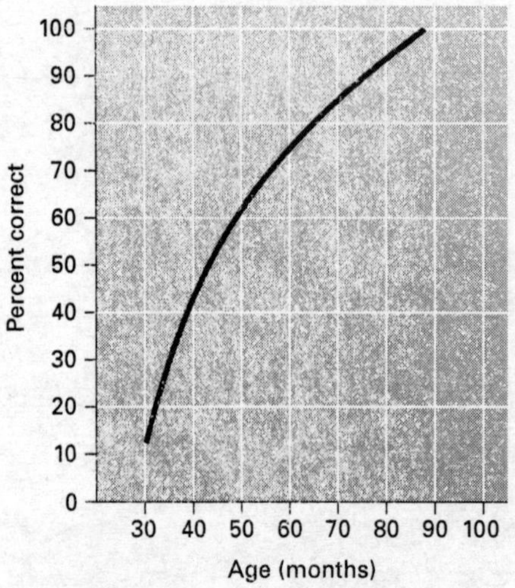

FIGURE 8.10 Developmental Changes in False-Belief Performance. False-belief performance dramatically increases from 2½ years of age through the middle of the elementary school years. In a summary of the results of many studies, 2½-year-olds gave incorrect responses about 80 percent of the time (Wellman, Cross, & Watson, 2001). At 3 years, 8 months, they were correct about 50 percent of the time, and after that, gave increasingly correct responses.

It is only beyond the preschool years that children have a deepening appreciation of the mind itself rather than just an understanding of mental states (Wellman, 2004). Not until middle and late childhood do children see the mind as an active constructor of knowledge or processing center (Flavell, Green, & Flavell, 1995). In middle and late childhood, children move from understanding that beliefs can be false to an understanding of beliefs and mind as "interpretive," exemplified in an awareness that the same event can be open to multiple interpretations (Carpendale & Chandler, 1996).

Metacognition in Children and Adolescents

By 5 or 6 years of age, children usually know that familiar items are easier to learn than unfamiliar ones, that short lists are easier than long ones, that recognition is easier than recall, and that forgetting becomes more likely over time (Lyon & Flavell, 1993). However, in other ways young children's metamemory is limited. They don't understand that related items are easier to remember than unrelated ones or that remembering the gist of a story is easier than remembering information verbatim (Kretuzer, Leonard, & Flavell, 1975). By fifth grade, students understand that gist recall is easier than verbatim recall.

Preschool children also have an inflated opinion of their memory abilities. For example, in one study, a majority of preschool children predicted that they would be able to recall all 10 items of a list of 10 items. When tested, none of the young children managed this feat (Flavell, Friedrichs, & Hoyt, 1970). As they move through the elementary school years, children give more realistic evaluations of their memory skills (Schneider & Pressley, 1997).

Preschool children also have little appreciation for the importance of cues to memory, such as "It helps when you can think of an example of it." By 7 or 8 years of age, children better appreciate the importance of cueing for memory. In general, children's understanding of their memory abilities and their skill in evaluating their performance on memory tasks is relatively poor at the beginning of the elementary school years but improves considerably by 11 to 12 years of age (Bjorklund & Rosenbaum, 2000).

Nonetheless, elementary-school-aged children improve in the metacognitive ability to consciously monitor and control their own thinking processes (Carlson, 2003). **Self-regulatory learning** consists of the self-generation and self-monitoring of thoughts, feelings, and behaviors to reach a goal. These goals might be academic (improving comprehension while reading, becoming a more organized writer, learning how to do multiplication, asking relevant questions) or they might be socioemotional (controlling one's anger, getting along better with peers). Some researchers argue that children's and adolescents' success in academic settings is mainly determined by the degree to which they can become self-regulators of their own learning (Schunk, 2004; Zimmerman & Schunk, 2004). Indeed, compared with low-achieving students, high-achieving students set more-specific learning goals, use more strategies to learn, self-monitor their learning more, and more systematically evaluate their progress toward a goal (Zimmerman & Schunk, 2004). To read further about self-regulation in children, see the following Caring for Children interlude.

CARING FOR CHILDREN

Helping Children Become Self-Regulatory Learners

Teachers, tutors, mentors, counselors, and parents can help children become self-regulatory learners. Barry Zimmerman, Sebastian Bonner, and Robert Kovach (1996) developed a model for turning low-self-regulatory students into students who engage in these multistep strategies: (1) self-evaluation and self-monitoring, (2) goal setting and strategic planning, (3) putting a plan into action and monitoring it, and (4) monitoring outcomes and refining strategies (see figure 8.11).

self-regulatory learning Generating and monitoring thoughts, feelings, and behaviors to reach a goal.

(continued on next page)

FIGURE 8.11 A Model of Self-Regulatory Learning

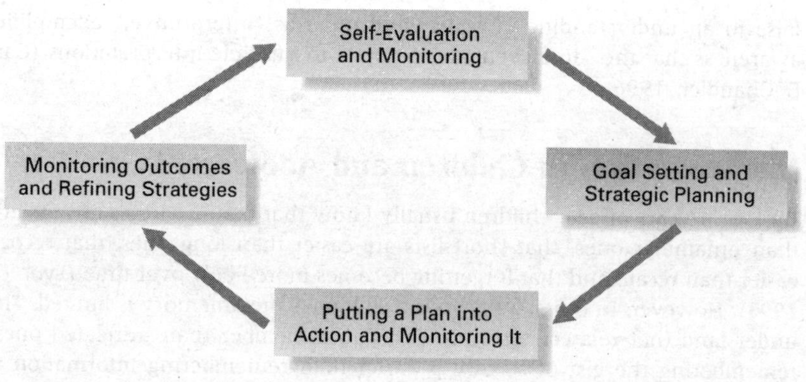

They describe a seventh-grade student who is doing poorly in history and apply their self-regulatory model to her situation. In step 1, she self-evaluates her studying and test preparation by keeping a detailed record of them. The teacher gives her some guidelines for keeping these records. After several weeks, the student turns in the records and recognizes that her poor test performance is due to her inability to understand difficult reading material.

In step 2, the student sets a goal, in this case improving her reading comprehension, and plans how to achieve the goal. The teacher helps her break down the goal into components, such as finding main ideas and setting specific subgoals for understanding a series of paragraphs. The teacher also provides the student with strategies, such as "focusing initially on the first sentence of each paragraph and then scanning the others to see whether any other sentence better captures the meaning of the paragraph" (Zimmerman, Bonner, & Kovach, 1996, p. 14). The teacher might also offer the student tutoring in reading comprehension if it is available.

In step 3, the student puts the plan into action and begins to monitor her progress. Initially, she might need help from the teacher or tutor in discovering the main ideas in the reading. This feedback can help her monitor her reading comprehension.

In step 4, the student monitors her improvement in reading comprehension by evaluating whether it has had any impact on her learning outcomes. Especially important is whether her improvement in reading comprehension led to better performance on history tests.

(Source: Zimmerman, Bonner, & Kovach, 1996, pp. 11, 14–15).

In addition to the metacognition changes in theory of mind, memory, and self-regulation that occur in childhood, important changes in metacognition take place during adolescence (Kuhn & Franklin, 2006). Compared to when they were children, adolescents have an increased capacity to monitor and manage cognitive resources to effectively meet the demands of a learning task. This increased metacognitive ability results in cognitive functioning and learning becoming more effective (Kuhn & Pease, in press).

An important aspect of cognitive functioning and learning is determining how much attention will be allocated to available resources. Evidence is accumulating that adolescents have a better understanding of how to effectively deploy their attention to different aspects of a task than children do (Kuhn & Franklin, 2006). In one investigation, 12-year-olds were markedly better than 8-year-olds, and slightly worse than 20-year-olds, at allocating their attention between two tasks (Manis, Keating, & Morrison, 1980). Adolescents may have more resources available to them than children (through increased processing speed, capacity, and automaticity), or they may be more skilled at directing the resources. Further, adolescents have a better meta-level understanding of strategies—that is, knowing the best strategy to use and when to use it in performing a learning task.

Keep in mind, though, that there is considerable individual variation in adolescents' metacognition. Indeed, some experts argue that individual variation in metacognition becomes much more pronounced in adolescence than in childhood (Kuhn & Franklin, 2006). Thus, some adolescents are quite good at using metacognition to improve their learning, others far less effective.

Review and Reflect • LEARNING GOAL 5

5 Define metacognition and summarize its developmental changes

Review
- What is metacognition?
- How does the child's theory of mind change during the preschool years?
- How does metacognition change during childhood and adolescence?

Reflect
- How might metacognition be involved in the ability of adolescents to have better study skills than children?

REACH YOUR LEARNING GOALS

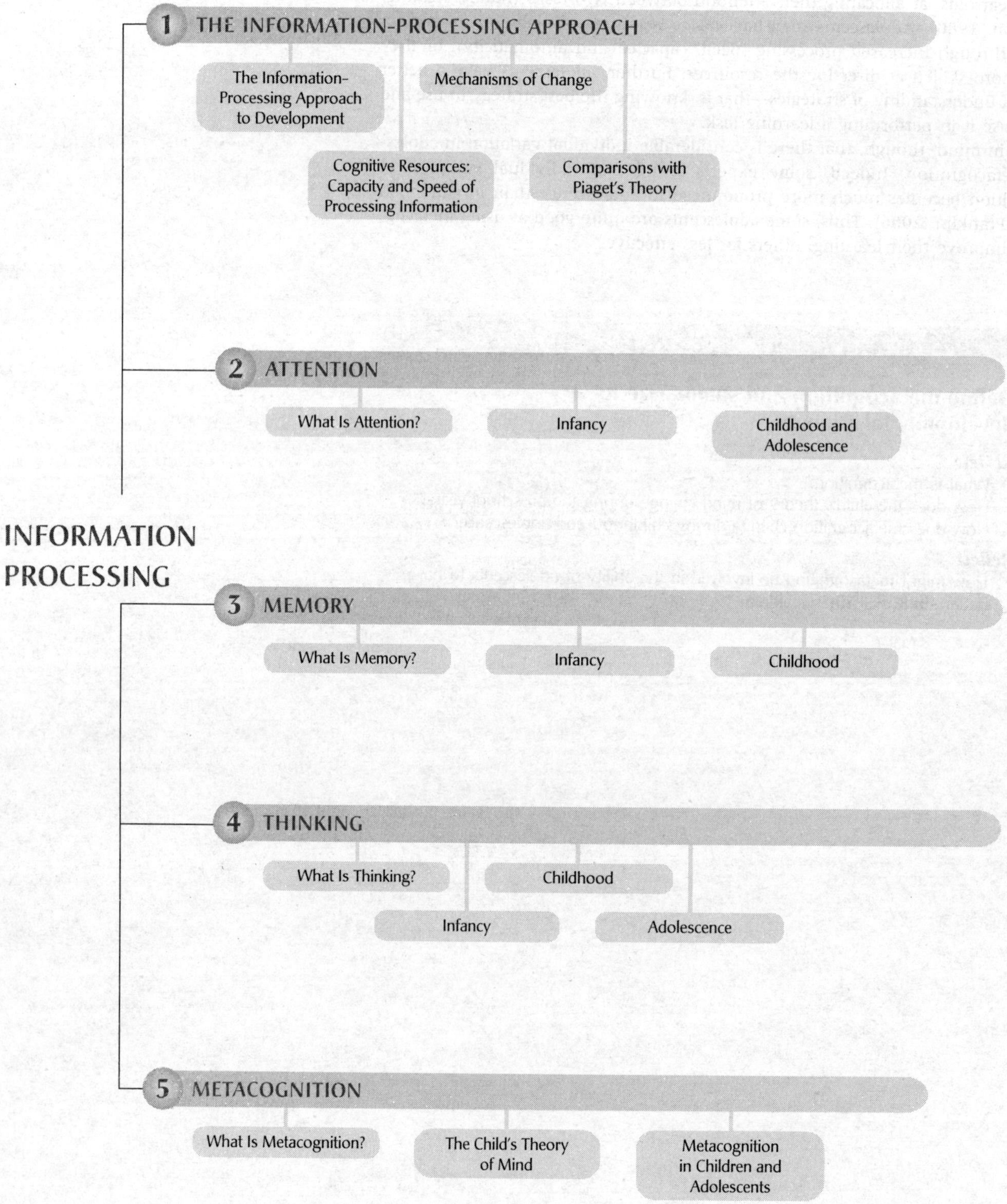

SUMMARY

1 Explain the information-processing approach

- The information-processing approach analyzes how individuals manipulate information, monitor it, and create strategies for handling it. Attention, memory, and thinking are involved in effective information processing. The computer has served as a model for how humans process information. In the information-processing approach, children's cognitive development results from their ability to overcome processing limitations by increasingly executing basic operations, expanding information-processing capacity, and acquiring new knowledge and strategies.
- Capacity and speed of processing speed, often referred to as cognitive resources, increase across childhood and adolescence. Changes in the brain serve as biological foundations for developmental changes in cognitive resources. In terms of capacity, the increase is reflected in older children being able to hold in mind several dimensions of a topic simultaneously. A reaction-time task has often been used to assess speed of processing. Processing speed continues to improve in early adolescence.
- According to Siegler, three important mechanisms of change are encoding (how information gets into memory), automaticity (ability to process information with little or no effort), and strategy construction (creation of new procedures for processing information). Children's information processing is characterized by self-modification and an important aspect of this self-modification involves metacognition, that is, knowing about knowing.
- Unlike Piaget, the information-processing approach does not see development as occurring in distinct stages. Instead, this approach holds that individuals develop a gradually increasing capacity for processing information, which allows them to develop increasingly complex knowledge and skills.

2 Define attention and outline its developmental changes

- Attention is focusing mental resources. Three ways that people can allocate their attention are as follows: sustained attention (the state of readiness to detect and respond to small changes occurring at random times in the environment; also referred to as vigilance), selective attention (focusing on a specific aspect of experience that is relevant while ignoring others that are irrelevant), and divided attention (concentrating on more than one activity at the same time).
- Even newborns can fixate on a contour but as they get older they scan a pattern more thoroughly. Attention in infancy is often studied through habituation and dishabituation.
- Salient stimuli tend to capture the attention of the preschooler. After 6 or 7 years of age, there is a shift to more cognitive control of attention. Selective attention improves through childhood and adolescence.

3 Describe what memory is and how it changes

- Memory is the retention of information over time. Psychologists study the processes of memory: how information is initially placed or encoded into memory, how it is retained or stored, and how it is found or retrieved for a certain purpose later. Short-term memory involves the retention of information for up to 15 to 30 seconds, assuming there is no rehearsal of the information. Long-term memory is a relatively permanent and unlimited type of memory. Working memory is a kind of "mental workbench" where individuals manipulate and assemble information when they make decisions, solve problems, and comprehend written and spoken language. Many contemporary psychologists prefer the term working memory over short-term memory. Working memory is linked to children's reading comprehension and problem solving. People construct and reconstruct their memories. Schema theory states that people mold memories to fit the information that already exists in their minds. Fuzzy trace theory states that memory is best understood by considering two types of memory representation: (1) verbatim memory trace and (2) gist. In this theory, older children's better memory is attributed to the fuzzy traces created by extracting the gist of information. Children's ability to remember new information about a subject depends extensively on what they already know about it. The contribution of content knowledge is especially relevant in the memory of experts. Experts have a number of characteristics that can explain why they solve problems better than novices do.
- Infants as young as 2 to 3 months of age display implicit memory, which is memory without conscious recollection as in memory of perceptual-motor skills. However, many experts believe that explicit memory, which is the conscious memory of facts and experiences, does not emerge until the second half of the first year of life. Older children and adults remember little if anything from the first three years of their lives.

- Young children can remember a great deal of information if they are given appropriate cues and prompts. One method of assessing short-term memory is with a memory span task, on which there are substantial developmental changes through the childhood years. Children's memory improves in the elementary school years as they begin to use gist more, acquire more content knowledge and expertise, develop large memory spans, and use more effective strategies. Organization, elaboration, and imagery are important memory strategies. A current interest focuses on how accurate children's long-term memories are and the implications of this accuracy for children as eyewitnesses.

4 Characterize thinking and its developmental changes

- Thinking involves manipulating and transforming information in memory.
- Studies of thinking in infancy focus on concept formation and categorization. Concepts are categories that group objects, events, and characteristics on the basis of common properties. Infants form concepts early in their development, with perceptual categorization appearing as early as 3 months of age. Mandler argues that it is not until about 7 to 9 months of age that infants form conceptual categories. Infants' first concepts are broad. Over the first two years of life, these broad concepts gradually become more differentiated.
- Critical thinking involves thinking reflectively and productively, and evaluating the evidence. A lack of emphasis on critical thinking in schools is a special concern. Children and scientists think alike in some ways, but not alike in others. Three important aspects of solving problems involve using strategies, using rules, and using analogies. Even young children can use analogies to solve problems in some circumstances.
- Adolescence is an important transitional period in critical thinking. Decision making increases in adolescence.

5 Define metacognition and summarize its developmental changes

- Metacognition is cognition about cognition, or knowing about knowing.
- Young children are curious about the human mind, and this has been studied under the topic of theory of mind.
- Metamemory improves in middle and late childhood, and again in adolescence. Self-regulatory learning consists of the self-generation and self-monitoring of thoughts, feelings, and behaviors to reach a goal. High-achieving students are often self-regulatory learners. One model of self-regulatory learning involves these components: self-evaluation and self-monitoring; goal setting and strategic planning; putting a plan into action; and monitoring outcomes and refining strategies. Self-regulatory learning gives children responsibility for their learning. Self-monitoring increases during adolescence.

KEY TERMS

information-processing approach 241
encoding 242
automaticity 242
strategy construction 243
metacognition 243
attention 244
sustained attention 244
selective attention 244
divided attention 244
memory 246
short-term memory 246
long-term memory 246
working memory 247
schema theory 247
schemas 247
fuzzy trace theory 247
implicit memory 249
explicit memory 249
thinking 254
concepts 254
critical thinking 255
reciprocal teaching 256
metamemory 262
theory of mind 262
self-regulatory learning 263

KEY PEOPLE

Robert Siegler 242
Charles Brainerd and Valerie Reyna 247
Carolyn Rovee-Collier 249
Jean Mandler 249
Jacqueline and Martin Brooks 255
Anne Brown and Joe Campione 255
Judy DeLoache 259
Michael Pressley 259

E-LEARNING TOOLS

To help you master the material in this chapter, visit the Online Learning Center for *Child Development*, eleventh edition (**www.mhhe.com/santrockcd11**), where you'll find these additional resources:

Taking It to the Net

1. Six-year-old Matthew is in the habit of asking his parents to repeat every comment or question. They know he doesn't have a hearing problem—they think he just doesn't pay attention and listen. How can they teach Matthew to pay attention and listen?
2. Fourteen-year-old Nancy, who lives with her grandparents, already has a history of sexual abuse acting-out, substance abuse, and arrests for petty crimes. Her grandmother knows that Nancy's parents physically and sexually abused Nancy before she came to live with her at the age of 5. Might Nancy recall or otherwise be affected by those early traumatic experiences?
3. Bill Harris, grandfather to fourth-grader Kevin and sixth-grader Jocelyn, is looking for a volunteer opportunity at the children's school. A retired chemical engineer, Bill would like to help the school beef up its science education program. How could he help?

Nursing, Parenting, and Teaching Exercises

Build your decision-making skills by trying your hand at the scenarios on the Online Learning Center.

Video Clips

The Online Learning Center includes the following videos for this chapter:

- Memory Ability at Age 4
  Here a 4-year-old girl is presented with a sequence of numbers and asked to repeat them back. She recalls the numbers successfully and then smiles at her accomplishment.
- Memory Ability at Age 7
  A 7-year-old boy is presented with five numbers which are then removed from his view. He recalls all five numbers but is slightly off in the sequence. He states, "2-6-1-4-5." Same numbers, but in a different pattern.
- Children's Eyewitness Testimony
  Stephen Ceci, Department of Psychology, Cornell University, describes his research on children's eyewitness testimony.

Chapter 9 INTELLIGENCE

As many people, as many minds, each in his own way.

—TERENCE
Roman Playwright, 2nd Century B.C.

CHAPTER OUTLINE

THE CONCEPT OF INTELLIGENCE

What Is Intelligence?
Intelligence Tests
Theories of Multiple Intelligences
The Influence of Heredity and Environment
Group Comparisons

THE DEVELOPMENT OF INTELLIGENCE

Tests of Infant Intelligence
Stability and Change in Intelligence Through Adolescence

THE EXTREMES OF INTELLIGENCE AND CREATIVITY

Mental Retardation
Giftedness
Creativity

LEARNING GOALS

1. Explain the concept of intelligence
2. Discuss the development of intelligence
3. Describe the characteristics of mental retardation, giftedness, and creativity

The Story of Project Spectrum

Student in a Spectrum classroom engaged in a science project. *What combinations of materials might you expect to find in other corners of a Spectrum classroom?*

Project Spectrum is an innovative attempt by Howard Gardner (1993; Gardner, Feldman, & Krechevsky, 1998) to encourage the development of a range of intelligences in young children. Spectrum begins with the basic idea that every child has the potential to develop strengths in one or more areas. It provides a context in which to see the strengths and weaknesses of individual children more clearly.

What is a Spectrum classroom like? It has rich and engaging materials that can stimulate a range of skills. For example, a naturalist corner houses biological specimens that children can explore and compare. This area elicits children's sensory capacities, logical analytic skills, and naturalist skills. In a storytelling area, children create imaginative tales with stimulating props and design their own storyboards. This area encourages children to use their skills in language, drama, and imagery. In a building corner, children can construct a model of their classroom and arrange small-scale photographs of the children and teachers in their class. This area encourages the use of spatial and personal skills. In all, the Spectrum classroom has 12 such areas designed to improve children's multiple intelligences.

The Spectrum classroom can identify skills that are typically missed in a regular classroom. In one first-grade Spectrum classroom, a boy whose home was filled with conflict was at risk for school failure. However, when Project Spectrum was introduced, the boy was identified as the best student in the class at taking apart and putting together common objects, like a food grinder or a doorknob. His teacher became encouraged when she found that he possessed this skill, and his overall school performance began to improve.

In addition to identifying unexpected strengths in children, Project Spectrum also can identify weaknesses. Gregory was doing very well in first grade, being especially skilled in computation and conceptual knowledge. However, he performed poorly in several Spectrum areas. He did well only in the areas in which he needed to give the correct answer and a person in authority gave it to him. As a result of the Spectrum program, Gregory's teacher began to search for ways to encourage him to take risks on open-ended tasks, to try things out in innovative ways, and to realize that it is okay to make mistakes.

PREVIEW

The concept of intelligence has generated many controversies, including whether intelligence is more strongly influenced by heredity or by environment, whether there is cultural bias in intelligence testing, and whether intelligence tests are misused. We will explore these controversies in this chapter, as well as these topics: the extent to which children have multiple intelligences, the development of intelligence from infancy through adolescence, and the extremes of intelligence and creativity.

1 THE CONCEPT OF INTELLIGENCE

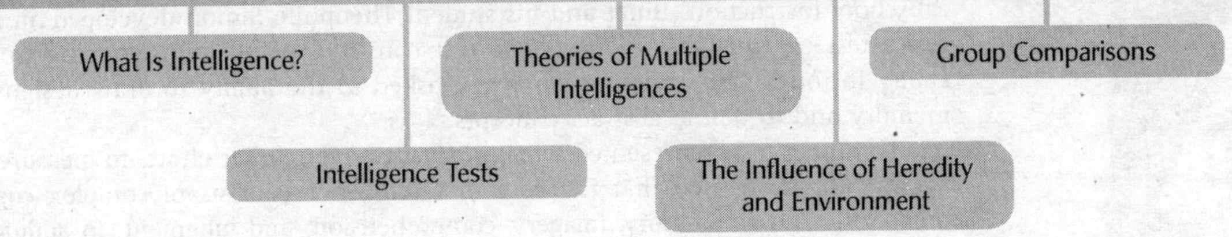

Intelligence is one of our most prized possessions. However, intelligence is a concept that even the most intelligent people have not been able to agree on how to define and how to measure.

What Is Intelligence?

What does the term *intelligence* mean to psychologists? Some experts describe intelligence as the ability to solve problems. Others describe it as the capacity to adapt and learn from experience. Still others argue that intelligence includes characteristics such as creativity and interpersonal skills. We'll use as our definition of **intelligence** the ability to solve problems and to adapt to and learn from experiences.

The problem with intelligence is that, unlike height, weight, and age, intelligence cannot be directly measured. We can't peel back a person's scalp and see how much intelligence he or she has. We can evaluate intelligence only *indirectly* by studying and comparing the intelligent acts that people perform.

The primary components of intelligence are similar to the cognitive processes of thinking and memory that we discussed in chapter 8. The differences in how we described these cognitive processes in chapter 8 and how we will discuss intelligence come from a shift in focus to the assessment of individual differences. *Individual differences* are the stable, consistent ways in which people are different from one another. Individual differences in intelligence generally have been measured by intelligence tests designed to tell us whether a person can reason better than others who have taken the same tests. As you will see shortly, though, the use of intelligence tests to assess intelligence is controversial.

Intelligence Tests

Robert Sternberg (1997) had considerable anxiety about intelligence tests. Because he got so stressed out about taking the tests, he did very poorly on them. Fortunately, a fourth-grade teacher worked with Robert and helped instill the confidence to overcome his anxieties. He not only began performing better on them, but when he was 13, he devised his own intelligence test and began using it to assess classmates—until the school principal found out and scolded him. Sternberg became so fascinated by intelligence that he made its study a lifelong pursuit. He even developed a theory of intelligence that we discuss later in this chapter.

Individual Tests Early psychologists ignored the "higher mental processes," such as thinking and problem solving, that we equate with intelligence today. Sir Frances Galton, an English psychologist who is considered the father of mental tests, believed that sensory, perceptual, and motor processes were the key dimensions of intelligence. In the late nineteenth century, he set out to demonstrate that there are systematic individual differences in these processes. Although his research provided few conclusive results, Galton raised many important questions about intelligence—how it should be measured, what its components are, and the degree to which it is inherited—that we continue to study today.

intelligence Thinking skills and the ability to adapt to and learn from life's everyday experiences.

Alfred Binet constructed the first intelligence test after being asked to create a measure to determine which children could benefit from instruction in France's schools and which could not.

The Binet Tests In 1904, the French Ministry of Education asked psychologist Alfred Binet to devise a method to determine which students would not profit from typical school instruction. Binet and his student Theophile Simon developed an intelligence test to meet this request. The test consisted of 30 items ranging from the ability to touch one's nose or ear when asked to the ability to draw designs from memory and to define abstract concepts.

The Binet tests represented a major advance over earlier efforts to measure intelligence. Binet stressed that the core of intelligence consists of complex cognitive processes, such as memory, imagery, comprehension, and judgment. In addition, he believed that a developmental approach was crucial for understanding intelligence. He proposed that a child's intellectual ability increases with age. Therefore, he tested potential items and determined the age at which a typical child could answer them correctly. Thus, Binet developed the concept of **mental age (MA),** which is an individual's level of mental development relative to others. For an average child, mental age (MA) corresponds to *chronological age (CA),* which is age from birth. A bright child has an MA considerably above CA; a dull child has an MA considerably below CA.

The Binet test has been revised many times to incorporate advances in the understanding of intelligence and intelligence testing. Many revisions were carried out by Lewis Terman, who developed extensive norms and provided detailed, clear instructions for each problem on the test. Terman also applied a concept introduced by William Stern. In 1912, Stern coined the term **intelligence quotient (IQ)** to refer to an individual's mental age divided by chronological age multiplied by 100:

$$IQ = \frac{MA}{CA} \times 100$$

If a child's mental age, as measured by the Binet test, was the same as the child's chronological age, then the child's IQ score would be 100. If the measured mental age was above chronological age, then the IQ score was more than 100. If mental age was below chronological age, the IQ score was less than 100. Although this scoring system is no longer used, the term *IQ* is often still used to refer to a score on a standardized intelligence test.

In 1985, the test, now called the Stanford-Binet (Stanford University is where the revisions were done), was revised to analyze an individual's responses in four content areas: verbal reasoning, quantitative reasoning, abstract/visual reasoning, and short-term memory. A general composite score also is obtained. Today the test is scored by comparing how the test-taker performs compared with other people of the same age. The average score is set at 100.

The current Stanford-Binet is given to individuals from the age of 2 through adulthood. It includes a wide variety of items, some requiring verbal responses, others nonverbal responses. For example, a 6-year-old is expected to complete the verbal task of defining at least six words, such as *orange* and *envelope,* and the nonverbal task of tracing a path through a maze. An adult with average intelligence is expected to define such words as *disproportionate* and *regard,* explain a proverb, and compare the concepts of idleness and laziness.

Over the years, the Binet test has been given to thousands of children and adults of different ages. By administering the test to large numbers of individuals selected at random from different parts of the United States, it has been found that the scores approximate a normal distribution (see figure 9.1). A **normal distribution** is a symmetrical, bell-shaped curve with a majority of the cases falling in the middle of the range of possible scores and few scores appearing toward the extremes of the range. The Stanford-Binet continues to be one of the most widely used individual tests of intelligence.

The Wechsler Scales Besides the Stanford-Binet, the other most widely used intelligence tests are the Wechsler scales, developed by David Wechsler. In 1939, Wechsler introduced the first of his scales, designed for use with adults (Wechsler, 1939). Now

www.mhhe.com/santrockcd11

Alfred Binet
Mental Measurements Yearbook

mental age (MA) An individual's level of mental development relative to others.

intelligence quotient (IQ) An individual's mental age divided by chronological age multiplied by 100; devised in 1912 by William Stern.

normal distribution A symmetrical distribution with a majority of the cases falling in the middle of the possible range of scores and few scores appearing toward the extremes of the range.

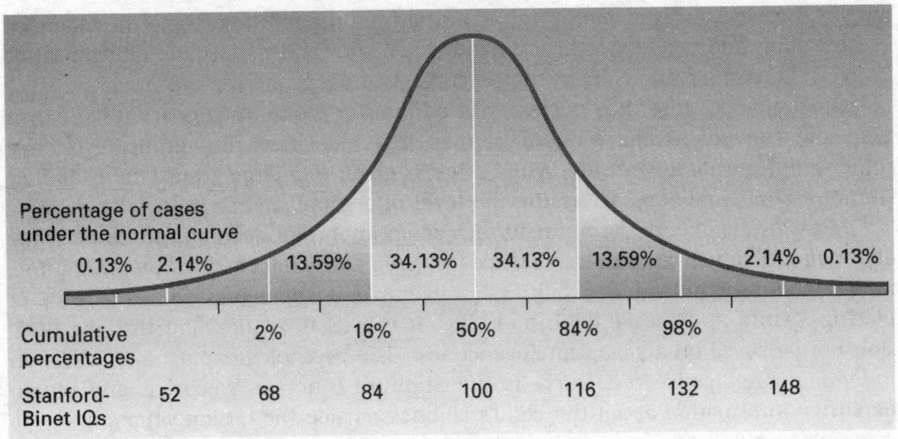

FIGURE 9.1 The Normal Curve and Stanford-Binet IQ Scores. The distribution of IQ scores approximates a normal curve. Most of the population falls in the middle range of scores. Notice that extremely high and extremely low scores are very rare. Slightly more than two-thirds of the scores fall between 84 and 116. Only about 1 in 50 individuals has an IQ of more than 132 and only about 1 in 50 individuals has an IQ of less than 68.

in its third edition, the Wechsler Adult Intelligence Scale-III(WAIS-III), was followed by the Wechsler Intelligence Scale for Children-IV (WISC-IV) for children between the ages of 6 and 16, and the Wechsler Preschool and Primary Scale of Intelligence-III (WPPSI-III) for children from the ages of 4 to 6½.

The Wechsler scales not only provide an overall IQ score but also scores on six verbal and five nonverbal measures. This allows the examiner to separate verbal and nonverbal IQ scores and to see quickly the areas in which the individual is below average, average, or above average. The inclusion of a number of nonverbal subscales makes the Wechsler test more representative of verbal and nonverbal intelligence; the Binet test includes some nonverbal items, but not as many as the Wechsler scales. Several of the Wechsler subscales are shown in figure 9.2.

Group Tests The Stanford-Binet and Wechsler tests are individually administered intelligence tests. The psychologist has an opportunity to sample the behavior of the individual being tested. During testing the psychologist observes the ease with which

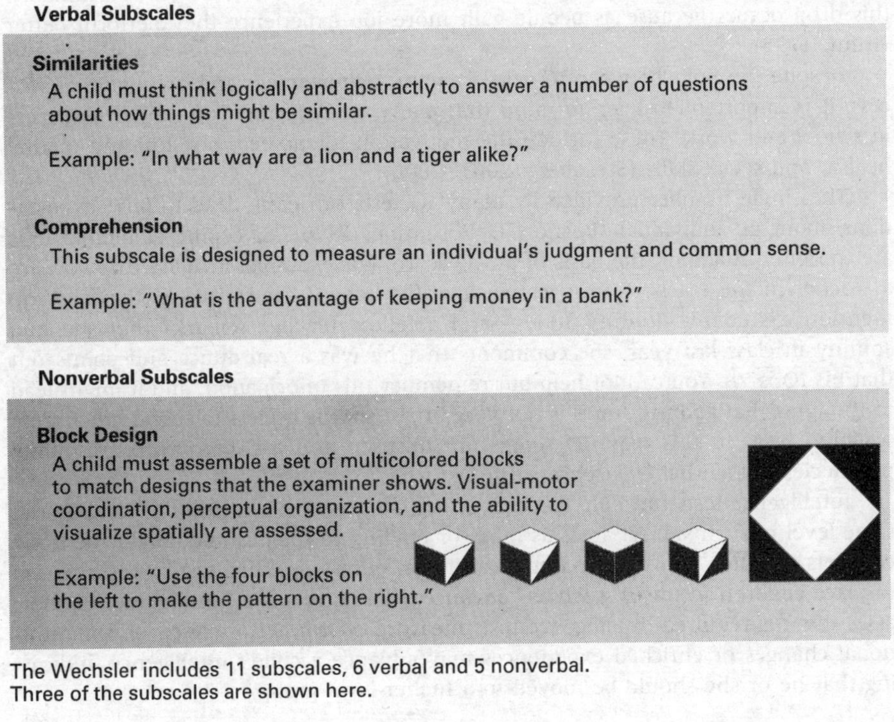

FIGURE 9.2 Sample Subscales of the Wechsler Intelligence Scale for Children (WISC-IV). Simulated items similar to those in the Wechsler Intelligence Scale for Children. *Wechsler Intelligence Scale for Children, Third Edition.* Copyright © 1990 by Harcourt Assessment, Inc. Reproduced with permission. All rights reserved. *"Wechsler Intelligence Scale for Children"* and *"WISC"* are trademarks of Harcourt Assessment, registered in the United States of America and/or other jurisdictions.

rapport is established, the energy and enthusiasm of the individual, and the tolerance of frustration and persistence that the individual shows in performing difficult tasks. Each of these observations helps the psychologist understand the individual.

On some occasions, it is necessary to administer group intelligence tests, which are more convenient and economical than individual tests. But group tests have some significant disadvantages. When a test is given to a large group, the examiner cannot establish rapport, determine the level of anxiety, and so on.

Most testing experts recommend that when important decisions are to be made about an individual, a group intelligence test should be supplemented by other information about the individual's abilities. For example, if a decision is to be made about placing a child in a special education class, it is a legal requirement that the decision not be based on a group intelligence test. The psychologist must administer an individual intelligence test, such as the Stanford-Binet or Wechsler, and obtain extensive information about the child's abilities outside the testing situation.

The Use and Misuse of Intelligence Tests Psychological tests are tools. Like all tools, their effectiveness depends on the knowledge, skill, and integrity of the user. A hammer can be used to build a beautiful kitchen cabinet or it can be used as a weapon of assault. Like a hammer, psychological tests can be used for positive purposes or they can be abused.

Intelligence tests have real-world applications as predictors of school and job success (Brody, 2000). For example, scores on tests of general intelligence are substantially correlated with school grades and achievement test performance, both at the time of the test and years later (Brody, 2000). IQ in the sixth grade correlates about .60 with the number of years of education the individual will eventually obtain (Jencks, 1979).

Intelligence tests are moderately correlated with work performance (Lubinski, 2000). Individuals with higher scores on tests designed to measure general intelligence tend to get higher-paying, more prestigious jobs (Wagner, 1997). However, general IQ tests predict only about one-fourth of the variation in job success; most of the variation in job success is linked to characteristics such as motivation, education, and other factors (Wagner & Sternberg, 1986). Further, the correlations between IQ and achievement decrease the longer people work at a job. Presumably, this drop occurs because as people gain more job experience they perform better (Hunt, 1995).

Despite the links between IQ and academic achievement and occupational success, it is important to keep in mind that many other factors contribute to success in school and work. These include the motivation to succeed, physical and mental health, and social skills (Sternberg, 2003, 2006).

The single number provided by many IQ tests can easily lead to false expectations about an individual (Rosnow & Rosenthal, 1996). Sweeping generalizations are too often made on the basis of an IQ score. For example, imagine that you are a teacher in the teacher's lounge the day after school has started in the fall. You mention a student—Johnny Jones—and a fellow teacher remarks that she had Johnny in class last year; she comments that he was a real dunce and points out that his IQ is 78. You cannot help but remember this information, and it might lead to thoughts that Johnny Jones is not very bright so it is useless to spend much time teaching him. In this way, IQ scores are misused and can become self-fulfilling prophecies (Rosenthal & Jacobsen, 1968).

"How are her scores?"

Intelligence tests can help teachers group children who function at roughly the same level in such subject areas as math or reading so they can be taught the same concepts together. However, extreme caution is necessary when test scores are used to place children in tracks, such as "advanced," "intermediate," and "low." Periodic assessment is required. Intelligence tests measure *current* performance, and maturational changes or enriched experiences may advance a child's intelligence, indicating that he or she should be moved to a higher-level group.

Even though they have limitations, tests of intelligence are among psychology's most widely used tools. To be effective, they should be used in conjunction with other information about an individual. For example, an intelligence test alone should not determine whether a child is placed in a special education or gifted class. The child's developmental history, medical background, performance in school, social competencies, and family experiences should be taken into account, too.

Despite their limitations, when used judiciously, intelligence tests provide valuable information. There are not many alternatives to these tests. Subjective judgments about individuals simply reintroduce the bias that the tests were designed to eliminate.

Theories of Multiple Intelligences

The use of a single score to describe how people perform on intelligence tests suggests that intelligence is a general ability, a single trait. The Wechsler scales provide scores for a number of intellectual skills, as well as an overall score. Do people have some general mental ability that determines how they perform on all of these tests? Or is intelligence a label for a combination of several distinct abilities? And do conventional intelligence tests measure everything that should be considered part of intelligence? Psychologists disagree about the answers to these questions.

Wechsler was not the first psychologist to break down intelligence into a number of abilities. Nor was he the last. A number of contemporary psychologists continue to search for specific components that make up intelligence. Some do not rely on traditional intelligence tests in their conceptualization of intelligence. Let's explore several key alternative conceptions of intelligence, beginning with Wechsler's predecessor, Charles Spearman.

Factor Approaches Some time before Wechsler analyzed intelligence in terms of general and specific abilities, Charles Spearman (1927) proposed that intelligence has two factors. **Two-factor theory** is Spearman's theory that individuals have both general intelligence, which he called *g*, and a number of specific abilities, or *s*. Spearman believed that these two factors account for a person's performance on an intelligence test. Spearman developed his theory by applying a technique called factor analysis to a number of intelligence tests. **Factor analysis** is a statistical procedure that correlates test scores to identify underlying clusters, or factors.

L. L. Thurstone (1938) also used factor analysis in analyzing a number of intelligence tests, but he concluded that the tests measure only a number of specific factors, and not general intelligence. **Multiple-factor theory** is Thurstone's theory that intelligence consists of seven primary mental abilities: verbal comprehension, number ability, word fluency, spatial visualization, associative memory, reasoning, and perceptual speed.

Gardner's Theory of Multiple Intelligences Both Spearman and Thurstone relied on traditional types of intelligence tests in their attempts to clarify the nature of intelligence. In contrast, Howard Gardner argues that these tests are far too narrow. Imagine someone who has great musical skills but does not do well in math or English. The famous composer, Ludwig van Beethoven, was just such a person. Would you call Beethoven "unintelligent"? Unlikely!

According to Gardner, people have multiple intelligences and IQ tests measure only a few of these. These intelligences are independent of each other. For evidence of the existence of multiple intelligences, Gardner points to the ways in which certain cognitive abilities survive particular types of brain damage. He also points to child prodigies and to some individuals who are retarded or autistic but who have extraordinary skill in a particular domain (like the character Dustin Hoffman portrayed in the movie *Rain Man*, who was autistic but had remarkable computing ability).

two-factor theory Spearman's theory that individuals have both general intelligence, which he called *g*, and a number of specific intelligences, referred to as *s*.

factor analysis A statistical procedure that correlates test scores to identify underlying clusters, or factors.

multiple-factor theory L. L. Thurstone's theory that intelligence consists of seven primary mental abilities: verbal comprehension, number ability, word fluency, spatial visualization, associative memory, reasoning, and perceptual speed.

If by 2013 [the 30th anniversary of the publication of Gardner's Frames of Mind*] there is a wider acceptance of the notion that intelligence deserves to be pluralized, I will be pleased.*

—Howard Gardner
Contemporary Psychologist, Harvard University

Gardner (1983, 1993, 2001, 2002) has proposed eight types of intelligence. The following list describes these types along with examples of the occupations in which they are reflected as strengths (Campbell, Campbell, & Dickinson, 2004):

- *Verbal Skills:* The ability to think in words and use language to express meaning.
  Occupations: Authors, journalists, speakers
- *Mathematical Skills:* The ability to carry out mathematical operations.
  Occupations: Scientists, engineers, accountants
- *Spatial Skills:* The ability to think three-dimensionally.
  Occupations: Architects, artists, sailors
- *Bodily-Kinesthetic Skills*: The ability to manipulate objects and be physically adept.
  Occupations: Surgeons, craftspeople, dancers, athletes
- *Musical Skills*: A sensitivity to pitch, melody, rhythm, and tone.
  Occupations: Composers, musicians, and sensitive listeners
- *Interpersonal Skills*: The ability to understand and effectively interact with others.
  Occupations: Successful teachers, mental health professionals
- *Intrapersonal Skills*: The ability to understand oneself.
  Occupations: Theologians, psychologists
- *Naturalist Skills:* The ability to observe patterns in nature and understand natural and human-made systems.
  Occupations: Farmers, botanists, ecologists, landscapers

According to Gardner, everyone has all of these intelligences but to varying degrees. As a result, we prefer to learn and process information in different ways. People learn best when they can apply their strong intelligences to the task.

There continues to be interest in applying Gardner's theory of multiple intelligences to children's education (Campbell, Campbell, & Dickinson, 2004; Hirsh, 2004; Kornhaber, Fierros, & Veenema, 2004; Weber, 2005). In the opening chapter story we profiled Project Spectrum, which applies Gardner's view to schools. The goal in applying Gardner's view to educating children is to allow them to discover and then explore the domains in which they have natural curiosity and talent. According to Gardner, if teachers give students opportunities to use their bodies, imaginations, and different senses, almost every student finds that she or he is good at something. Even students who are not outstanding in any single area will find that they have relative strengths. Thus, at the Key School in Indianapolis, each day every student is exposed to materials that are designed to stimulate a range of

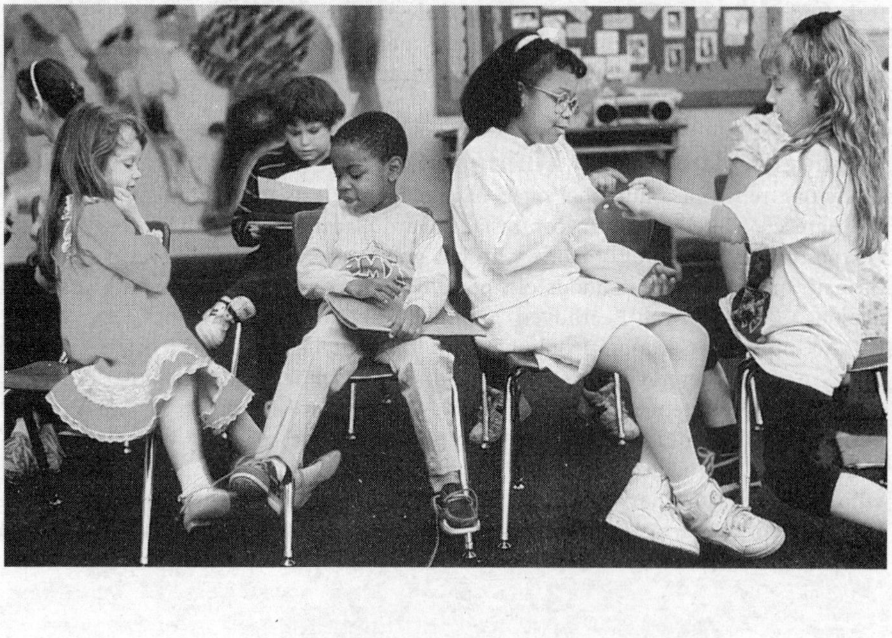

Children in the Key School form "pods," in which they pursue activities of special interest to them. Every day, each child can choose from activities that draw on Gardner's eight frames of mind. The school has pods that range from gardening to architecture to gliding to dancing.

abilities, including art, music, language skills, math skills, and physical games. In addition, attention is given to understanding oneself and others.

Sternberg's Triarchic Theory Like Gardner, Robert J. Sternberg (1986, 1999, 2002, 2003, 2004, 2006) believes that traditional IQ tests fail to measure some important dimensions of intelligence. Sternberg's **triarchic theory of intelligence** proposes that there are three main types of intelligence: analytical, creative, and practical.

To understand what analytical, creative, and practical intelligence mean, let's look at examples of people who reflect these three types of intelligence:

- Consider Latisha, who scores high on traditional intelligence tests such as the Stanford-Binet and is a star analytical thinker. Sternberg calls Latisha's analytical thinking and abstract reasoning *analytical intelligence.* It is the closest to what has traditionally been called intelligence and what is commonly assessed by intelligence tests. In Sternberg's view of analytical intelligence, the basic unit of analytical intelligence is a *component,* which is a basic unit of information processing. Sternberg's components include the ability to acquire or store information; to retain or retrieve information; to transfer information; to plan, make decisions, and solve problems; and to translate thoughts into performance.
- Todd does not have the best test scores but has an insightful and creative mind. The type of thinking at which Todd excels is called *creative intelligence* by Sternberg. According to Sternberg, creative people have the ability to solve new problems quickly, but they also learn how to solve familiar problems in an automatic way so their minds are free to handle other problems that require insight and creativity.
- Finally, consider Emanuel, a person whose scores on traditional IQ tests are low but quickly grasps real-life problems. He easily picks up knowledge about how the world works. Emanuel's "street smarts" and practical know-how indicate that he has what Sternberg calls *practical intelligence.* Practical intelligence includes the ability to get out of trouble and a knack for getting along with people. Sternberg describes practical intelligence as all of the important information about getting along in the world that you are not taught in school.

Sternberg (1997) says that students with different triarchic patterns look different in school. Students with high analytic ability tend to be favored in conventional schools. They often do well in classes in which the teacher lectures and gives objective tests. They often are considered smart students, typically get good grades, do well on traditional IQ tests and the SAT, and later gain admission to competitive colleges.

Students who are high in creative intelligence often are not in the top rung of their class. Creatively intelligent students might not conform to the expectations that teachers have about how assignments should be done. They give unique answers, for which they might get reprimanded or marked down.

Like students high in creative intelligence, students who are practically intelligent often do not relate well to the demands of school. However, these students frequently do well outside the classroom's walls. Their social skills and common sense may allow them to become successful managers, entrepreneurs, or politicians, despite undistinguished school records.

Sternberg (1999) believes that few tasks are purely analytic, creative, or practical. Most tasks require some combination of these skills. For example, when students write a book report, they might (1) analyze the book's main themes, (2) generate new ideas about how the book could have been written better, and (3) think about how the book's themes can be applied to people's lives.

www.mhhe.com/santrockcd11

Multiple Intelligences
Multiple Intelligence Links
Sternberg's Theory

"You're wise, but you lack tree smarts."

triarchic theory of intelligence Sternberg's theory that intelligence consists of compotential intelligence, experiential intelligence, and contextual intelligence.

Sternberg argues that it is important for classroom instruction to give students opportunities to learn through all three types of intelligence.

Sternberg (1993) developed the Sternberg Triarchic Abilities Test (STAT) that assesses analytical, creative, and practical intelligence. The three kinds of abilities are examined through (1) verbal items and essays, (2) quantitative items, and (3) drawings with multiple-choice items. The goal is to obtain a more complete assessment of intelligence than is possible with a conventional test.

The analytical section of STAT is much like a conventional test, with individuals required to provide the meanings of words, complete number series, and complete matrices. The creative and practical sections are much different from conventional tests. For example, in the creative section, individuals are required to write an essay on designing an ideal school. The practical section requires individuals to solve practical everyday problems that involve such matters as planning routes and purchasing tickets to an event.

An increasing number of studies are investigating the effectiveness of the STAT in predicting such important aspects of life as success in school. For example, in one recent study of 800 college students, scores on the STAT were effective in predicting college grade point average (Sternberg & others, 2001a). However, more research is needed to determine the validity and reliability of the STAT.

Emotional Intelligence Both Gardner's and Sternberg's theories include one or more categories related to the ability to understand one's self and others and to get along in the world. In Gardner's theory, the categories are interpersonal intelligence and intrapersonal intelligence; in Sternberg's theory, practical intelligence. Other theorists who emphasize interpersonal, intrapersonal, and practical aspects of intelligence focus on what is called *emotional intelligence*, which was popularized by Daniel Goleman (1995) in his book *Emotional Intelligence*.

The concept of emotional intelligence was initially developed by Peter Salovey and John Mayer (1990). They define **emotional intelligence** as the ability to perceive and express emotion accurately and adaptively (such as taking the perspective of others), to understand emotion and emotional knowledge (such as understanding the roles that emotions play in friendship and marriage), to use feelings to facilitate thought (such as being in a positive mood, which is linked to creative thinking), and to manage emotions in oneself and others (such as being able to control one's anger) (Mayer, Salovey, & Caruso, 2004).

emotional intelligence The ability to perceive and express emotions accurately and adaptively, to understand emotion and emotional knowledge, to use feelings to facilitate thought, and to manage emotions in oneself and others.

Recently, the Mayer-Salovey-Caruso Emotional Intelligence Test (MSCEIT) was developed to measure the four aspects of emotional intelligence just described: perceiving emotions, understanding emotions, facilitating thought, and managing emotions (Mayer, Salovey, & Caruso, 2002). The test consists of 141 items, can be given to individuals 17 years of age and older, and takes about 30 to 45 minutes to administer. Because the MSCEIT has only been available since 2001, few studies have been conducted to examine its ability to predict outcomes (Salovey & Pizarro, 2003). One recent study that used the MSCEIT found that youths with higher emotional intelligence were less likely to have smoked cigarettes or to have used alcohol (Trinidad & Johnson, 2002).

Gardner	Sternberg	Salovey/ Mayer/Goleman
Verbal Mathematical	Analytical	
Spatial Movement Musical	Creative	
Interpersonal Intrapersonal	Practical	Emotional
Naturalistic		

FIGURE 9.3 Comparison of Gardner's, Sternberg's, and Salovey/Mayer/Goleman's Views of Intelligence

Do Children Have One Intelligence or Many Intelligences? Figure 9.3 provides a comparison of Gardner's, Sternberg's, and Salovey/Mayer/Goleman's views. Notice that Gardner includes a number of types of intelligence that are not addressed by the other views and that Sternberg is unique in emphasizing creative intelligence. These theories of multiple intelligence have much to offer. They have stimulated us to think more broadly about what makes up people's intelligence and competence. And they have motivated educators to develop programs that instruct students in different domains.

Theories of multiple intelligences also have many critics (Matthews, Roberts, & Zeidner, 2004; Schulte, Ree, & Carretta, 2004). They conclude that the research base to support these theories has not yet developed. In particular, some critics say that Gardner's classification seems arbitrary. For example, if musical skills represent a type of intelligence, why don't we also refer to chess intelligence, prizefighter intelligence, and so on?

A number of psychologists still support Spearman's concept of *g* (general intelligence) (Bouchard, 2004; Johnson & others, 2004). For example, one expert on intelligence, Nathan Brody (2000) argues that people who excel at one type of intellectual task are likely to excel in other intellectual tasks. Thus, individuals who do well at memorizing lists of digits are also likely to be good at solving verbal problems and spatial layout problems. This general intelligence includes abstract reasoning or thinking, the capacity to acquire knowledge, and problem-solving ability (Brody, 2000; Carroll, 1993).

Some experts who argue for the existence of general intelligence believe that individuals also have specific intellectual abilities (Brody, 2000; Chiappe & MacDonald, 2005). In one study, John Carroll (1993) conducted an extensive examination of intellectual abilities and concluded that all intellectual abilities are related to one another, which supports the concept of general intelligence, but that there are many specialized abilities as well. Some of these specialized abilities, such as spatial abilities and mechanical abilities, are not adequately reflected in the curriculum of most schools. In sum, controversy still characterizes whether it is more accurate to conceptualize intelligence as a general ability, specific abilities, or both (Birney & others, 2005; Kornhaber, Fierros, & Veenema, 2005; Moran & Gardner, 2006; Weber, 2005).

The Influence of Heredity and Environment

We have seen that intelligence is a slippery concept with competing definitions, tests, and theories. It is not surprising, therefore, that attempts to understand the concept of intelligence are filled with controversy. One of the most controversial areas in the study of intelligence centers on the extent to which intelligence is influenced by genetics and the extent to which it is influenced by environment. In chapter 3, we indicated how difficult it is to tease apart these influences, but that has not kept psychologists from trying to unravel them.

Genetic Influences To what degree do our genes make us smart? At one end of the debate, Arthur Jensen (1969) argued that intelligence is primarily inherited and that environment plays only a minimal role in intelligence. Jensen reviewed the research on intelligence, much of which involved comparisons of identical and fraternal twins and used IQ test scores as the indicator of intelligence. Identical twins have exactly the same genetic makeup; if intelligence is genetically determined, Jensen reasoned, the IQs of identical twins should be more similar than the IQs of fraternal twins.

The studies that Jensen examined showed an average correlation between the intelligence test scores of identical twins of .82, a very high positive association. Investigations of fraternal twins produced an average correlation of .50, a moderately high positive correlation. A difference of .32 is substantial. However, a more recent research review that included many studies conducted since Jensen's original review found that the difference in the average correlations for identical and fraternal twins was only .15, substantially less than what Jensen found (Grigorenko, 2000) (see figure 9.4).

Jensen also compared the correlation of IQ scores for identical twins reared together with those reared apart. The correlation for those reared together was .89, and for those reared apart was .78, a difference of .11. Jensen argued that if environmental factors were more important than genetic factors, the difference should have been greater.

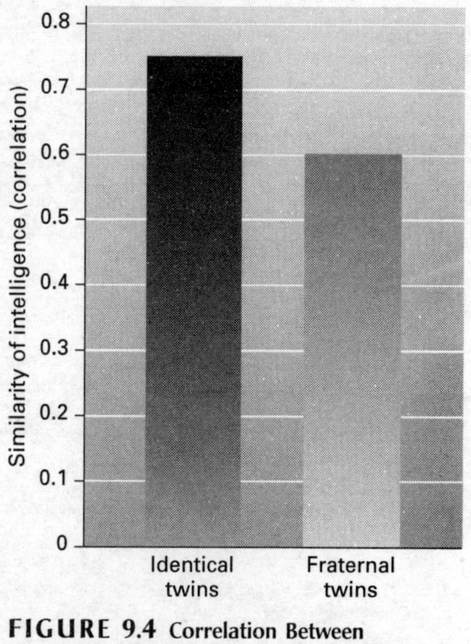

FIGURE 9.4 Correlation Between Intelligence Test Scores and Twin Status. The graph represents a summary of research findings that have compared the intelligence test scores of identical and fraternal twins. An approximate .15 difference has been found, with a higher correlation (.75) for identical twins and a lower correlation (.60) for fraternal twins.

Adoption studies are also used in attempts to analyze the relative importance of heredity in intelligence. In most *adoption studies,* researchers determine whether the behavior of adopted children is more like that of their biological parents or their adopted parents. In two studies, the educational levels attained by biological parents were better predictors of children's IQ scores than were the IQs of the children's adopted parents (Petrill & Deater-Deckard, 2004; Scarr & Weinberg, 1983). But studies of adoption also document the influence of environments. For example, moving children into an adopted family with a better environment than the child had in the past increased the children's IQs by an average of 12 points (Lucurto, 1990).

How strong is the effect of heredity on intelligence? The concept of heritability attempts to tease apart the effects of heredity and environment in a population. **Heritability** is the fraction of the variance within a population that is attributed to genetics. The heritability index is computed using correlational techniques. Thus, the highest degree of heritabilty is 1.00 and correlations of .70 and above suggest a strong genetic influence. A committee of respected researchers convened by the American Psychological Association concluded that by late adolescence, the heritability of intelligence is about .75, which reflects a strong genetic influence (Neisser & others, 1996).

A key point to keep in mind about heritability is that it refers to a specific group (population), *not* to individuals (Okagaki, 2000). Researchers use the concept of heritability to try to describe why people differ. Heritability says nothing about why a single individual, like yourself, has a certain intelligence. Nor does heritability say anything about differences *between* groups.

Most research on heredity and environment does not include environments that differ radically. Thus, it is not surprising that many genetic studies show environment to be a fairly weak influence on intelligence (Fraser, 1995).

Interestingly, researchers have found that the heritability of intelligence increases from as low as .45 in infancy to as high as .80 in late adulthood (McGue & others, 1993; Petrill, 2003; Plomin & others, 1997). Why might hereditary influences on intelligence increase with age? Possibly as we grow older, our interactions with the environment are shaped less by the influence of others and the environment on us and more by our ability to choose our environments to allow the expression of genetic tendencies (Neisser & others, 1996). For example, sometimes children's parents push them into environments that are not compatible with their genetic inheritance (wanting to be a doctor or an engineer, for example), but as adults these individuals may select their own career environments.

The heritability index has several flaws. It is only as good as the data that are entered into its analysis and the interpretations made from it. The data are virtually all from traditional IQ tests, which some experts believe are not always the best indicator of intelligence (Gardner, 2002; Sternberg, 2004). Also, the heritability index assumes that we can treat genetic and environmental influences as factors that can be separated, with each part contributing a distinct amount of influence. As we discussed in chapter 3, genes and the environment always work together. Genes always exist in an environment and the environment shapes their activity.

Environmental Influences Today, most researchers agree that heredity does not determine intelligence to the extent Jensen claimed (Gottlieb & Blair, 2004; Gottlieb, Wahlsten, & Lickliter, 2006; Sternberg & Grigorenko, 2004). For most people, this means modifications in environment can change their IQ scores considerably (Campbell & others, 2001; Ramey, Ramey, & Lanzi, 2006). Although genetic endowment may always influence a person's intellectual ability, the environmental influences and opportunities we provide children and adults do make a difference.

What aspects of the environment influence intelligence? Studies have found significant correlations between socioeconomic status and intelligence (Seifer, 2001). The way that parents communicate with children, the support parents provide, the

heritability The fraction of the variance in a population that is attributed to genetics.

neighborhoods in which families live, and the quality of schools may contribute to these correlations. In one study, researchers went into homes and observed how extensively parents from welfare and middle-income professional families talked and communicated with their young children (Hart & Risley, 1995). They found that the middle-income professional parents were much more likely to communicate with their young children than the welfare parents were. And how much the parents communicated with their children in the first three years of their lives was correlated with the children's Stanford-Binet IQ scores at age 3. The more parents communicated with their children, the higher the children's IQs were.

Schooling also influences intelligence (Ceci & Gilstrap, 2000; Christian, Bachnan, & Morrison, 2001). The biggest effects have been found when large groups of children have been deprived of formal education for an extended period, resulting in lower intelligence. One study examined the intelligence of children in South Africa whose schooling was delayed for four years because teachers were not available (Ramphal, 1962). Compared with children in nearby villages who had teachers, the children whose entry into school was delayed experienced a five-point drop in IQ for every year of delay.

Another possible effect of education can be seen in rapidly increasing IQ test scores around the world (Daley & others, 2003; Flynn, 1999; Kanaya, Scullin, & Ceci, 2003). IQ scores have been increasing so fast that a high percentage of people regarded as having average intelligence at the turn of the century would be considered below average in intelligence today (Howard, 2001) (see figure 9.5). If a representative sample of people today took the Stanford-Binet test used in 1932, about one-fourth would be defined as having very superior intelligence, a label usually accorded to fewer than 3 percent of the population (Horton, 2001). Because the increase has taken place in a relatively short time, it can't be due to heredity. The increase may be due to increasing levels of education attained by a much greater percentage of the world's population or to other environmental factors such as the explosion of information to which people are exposed (Blair & others, 2005). In one recent study, a dramatic IQ increase occurred among children in Kenya over a recent 14-year period that likely was due to improved nutrition and parental emphasis on schooling (Daley & others, 2003). The worldwide increase in intelligence test scores that has occurred over a short time frame has been called the *Flynn effect*, after the researcher who discovered it—James Flynn.

Keep in mind that environmental influences are complex (Neisser & others, 1996; Sternberg, 2001). Growing up with all the "advantages," for example, does not guarantee success. Children from wealthy families may have easy access to

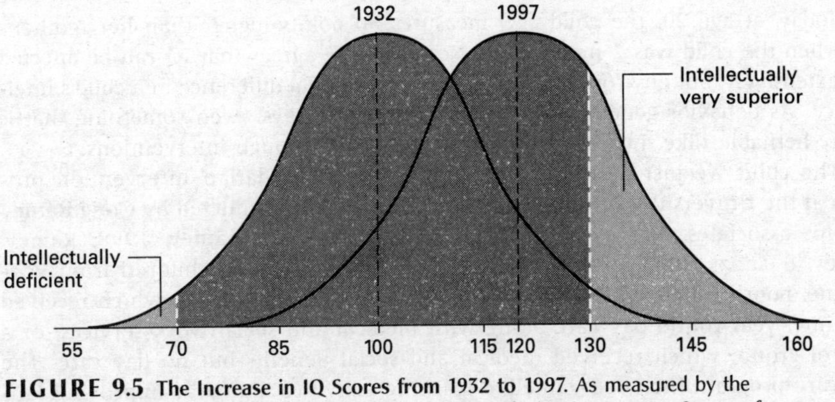

FIGURE 9.5 The Increase in IQ Scores from 1932 to 1997. As measured by the Stanford-Binet intelligence test, American children seem to be getting smarter. Scores of a group tested in 1932 fell along a bell-shaped curve with half below 100 and half above. Studies show that if children took that same test today, using the 1932 scale, half would score above 120. Few of them would score in the "intellectually deficient" range and about one-fourth would rank in the "very superior" range.

The highest-risk children often benefit the most cognitively when they experience early interventions.

—Craig Ramey
Contemporary Psychologist, University of Alabama–Birmingham

excellent schools, books, travel, and tutoring, but they may take such opportunities for granted and fail to develop the motivation to learn and to achieve. In the same way, "poor" or "disadvantaged" does not equal "doomed."

Researchers increasingly are interested in manipulating the early environment of children who are at risk for impoverished intelligence (Ramey, Ramey, & Lanzi, 2001; Sternberg & Grigorenko, 2001). The emphasis is on prevention rather than remediation. Many low-income parents have difficulty providing an intellectually stimulating environment for their children. Programs that educate parents to be more sensitive caregivers and better teachers, as well as support services such as quality child-care programs, can make a difference in a child's intellectual development.

A recent review of the research on early interventions concluded the following (Brooks-Gunn, 2003):

- High-quality center-based interventions are associated with increases in children's intelligence and school achievement.
- The interventions are most successful with poor children and children whose parents have little education.
- The positive benefits continue through adolescence but are not as strong as in early childhood or the beginning of elementary school.
- The programs that are continued into middle and late childhood have the best long-term results.

To read further about environmental influences on intelligence, see the Research in Child Development interlude.

Research in Child Development

The Abecedarian Project

Each morning a young mother waited with her child for the bus that would take the child to school. The child was only 2 months old, and "school" was an experimental program at the University of North Carolina at Chapel Hill. There the child experienced a number of interventions designed to improve her intellectual development—everything from bright objects dangled in front of her eyes while she was a baby to language instruction and counting activities when she was a toddler (Wickelgren, 1999). The child's mother had an IQ of 40 and could not read signs or determine how much change she should receive from a cashier. Her grandmother had a similarly low IQ.

Today, at age 20, the child's IQ measures 80 points higher than her mother's did when the child was 2 months old. Not everyone agrees that IQ can be affected this extensively, but environment can make a substantial difference in a child's intelligence. As behavior geneticist Robert Plomin (1999) says, even something that is highly heritable (like intelligence) may be malleable through interventions.

The child we just described was part of the Abecedarian Intervention program at the University of North Carolina at Chapel Hill conducted by Craig Ramey and his associates (Ramey & Campbell, 1984; Ramey & Ramey, 1998; Ramey, Ramey, & Lanzi, 2006). They randomly assigned 111 young children from low-income, poorly educated families to either an intervention group, which received full-time, year-round day care along with medical and social work services, or a control group, which received medical and social benefits but no day care. The day-care program included gamelike learning activities aimed at improving language, motor, social, and cognitive skills.

The success of the program in improving IQ was evident by the time the children were 3 years of age. At that age, the experimental group showed normal IQs averaging 101, a 17-point advantage over the control group. Recent follow-up results suggest that the effects are long-lasting. More than a decade later at 15, children from the intervention group still maintained an IQ advantage of 5 points over the control-group children (97.7 to 92.6) (Campbell & others, 2001; Ramey, Ramey, & Lanzi, 2001). They also did better on standardized tests of reading and math and were less likely to be held back a year in school. Also, the greatest IQ gains were made by the children whose mothers had especially low IQs—below 70. At age 15, these children showed a 10-point IQ advantage over a group of children whose mothers' IQs were below 70 but did not experience the day-care intervention.

Group Comparisons

For decades, many controversies surrounding intelligence tests have grown from the tendency to compare one group with another. Many people keep asking whether their culture or ethnic group or gender is more intelligent than others.

Cross-Cultural Comparisons Cultures vary in the way they describe what it means to be intelligent (Benson, 2003; Sternberg, 2004; Sternberg & Grigorenko, 2004). People in Western cultures tend to view intelligence in terms of reasoning and thinking skills while people in Eastern cultures see intelligence as a way for members of a community to successfully engage in social roles (Nisbett, 2003). One study found that Taiwanese-Chinese conceptions of intelligence emphasize understanding and relating to others, including when to show and when not to show one's intelligence (Yang & Sternberg, 1997).

"You can't build a hut, you don't know how to find edible roots and you know nothing about predicting the weather. In other words, you do terribly on our I.Q. test."

Robert Serpell (1974, 1982, 2000) has studied concepts of intelligence in rural African communities since the 1970s. He has found that people in rural African communities, especially those in which Western schooling is not common, tend to blur the distinction between being intelligent and being socially competent. In rural Zambia, for example, the concept of intelligence involves being both clever and responsible. Elena Grigorenko and her colleagues (2001) have also studied the concept of intelligence among rural Africans. They found that people in the Luo culture of rural Kenya view intelligence as consisting of four domains: (1) academic intelligence, (2) social qualities such as respect, responsibility, and consideration, (3) practical thinking, and (4) comprehension. In another study in the same culture, children who scored highly on a test of knowledge about medicinal herbs—a measure of practical intelligence—tended to score poorly on tests of academic intelligence (Sternberg & others, 2001b). These results indicated that practical and academic intelligence can develop independently and may even conflict with each other. They also suggest that the values of a culture may influence the direction in which a child develops. In a cross-cultural context, then, intelligence depends a great deal on environment.

Cultural Bias in Testing Many of the early intelligence tests were culturally biased, favoring people who were from urban rather than rural environments, middle-socioeconomic status rather than low-socioeconomic status, and White rather than African American (Miller-Jones, 1989; Provenzo, 2002; Watras, 2002). For example, one question on an early test asked what you should do if you find a 3-year-old child in the street. The correct answer was "call the police." But children from inner-city families who perceive the police as adversaries are unlikely to choose this answer. Similarly, children from rural areas might not choose this answer if there is no police force nearby. Such questions clearly do not measure the knowledge necessary to adapt to one's environment or to be "intelligent" in an inner-city neighborhood or in rural America (Scarr, 1984). Also, members of minority groups

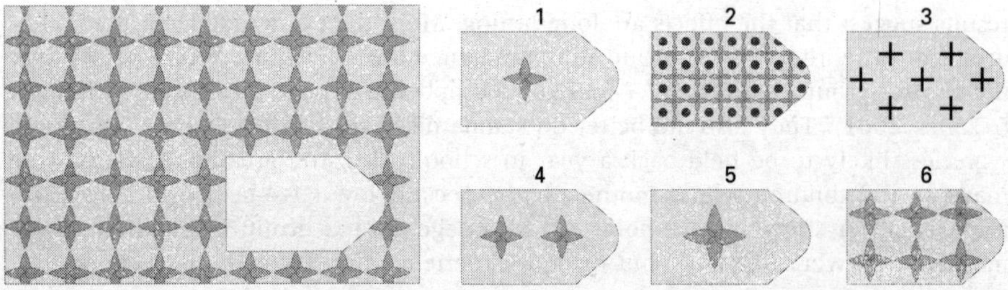

FIGURE 9.6 Sample Item from the Ravens Progressive Matrices Test. Individuals are presented with a matrix arrangement of symbols, such as the one at the left of this figure, and must then complete the matrix by selecting the appropriate missing symbol from a group of symbols.

who do not speak English or who speak nonstandard English are at a disadvantage in trying to understand questions framed in standard English (Gibbs & Huang, 1989).

Gregory Ochoa illustrates how cultural bias in intelligence tests can affect people. When Gregory was a high school student, he and his classmates took an IQ test. Gregory understood only a few words on the test because he did not speak English very well and spoke Spanish at home. Several weeks later, Gregory was placed in a special class for mentally retarded students. Many of the students in the class, it turns out, had last names such as Ramirez and Gonzales. Gregory lost interest in school, dropped out, and eventually joined the navy. In the navy, Gregory took high school courses and earned enough credits to attend college later. He graduated from San Jose City College as an honor student, continued his education, and became a professor of social work at the University of Washington in Seattle.

As a result of cases like Gregory Ochoa's, researchers have developed **culture-fair tests,** which are intelligence tests that aim to avoid cultural bias. Two types of culture-fair tests have been developed. The first includes questions that are familiar to people from all socioeconomic and ethnic backgrounds. For example, a child might be asked how a bird and a dog are different, on the assumption that virtually all children are familiar with birds and dogs. The second type of culture-fair test contains no verbal questions. Figure 9.6 shows a sample question from the Ravens Progressive Matrices Test. Even though tests such as the Ravens Progressive Matrices are designed to be culture-fair, people with more education still score higher than those with less education do (Greenfield, 2003).

Why is it so hard to create culture-fair tests? Most tests tend to reflect what the dominant culture thinks is important (Greenfield, Suzuki, & Rothstein-Fisch, 2006; Greenfield & others, 2003; Merenda, 2004). If tests have time limits, that will bias the test against groups not concerned with time. If languages differ, the same words might have different meanings for different language groups. Even pictures can produce bias because some cultures have less experience with drawings and photographs (Anastasi & Urbina, 1996). Within the same culture, different groups could have different attitudes, values, and motivation, and this could affect their performance on intelligence tests. Items that ask why buildings should be made of brick are biased against children who have little or no experience with brick houses. Questions about railroads, furnaces, seasons of the year, distances between cities, and so on can be biased against groups who have less experience than others with these contexts.

Ethnic Comparisons In the United States, children from African American and Latino families score below children from White families on standardized intelligence tests. On the average, African American schoolchildren score 10 to 15 points lower on standardized intelligence tests than White American schoolchildren do (Brody, 2000; Lynn, 1996). These are *average scores,* however. About 15 to 25 percent of African American schoolchildren score higher than half of White schoolchildren do, and many Whites score lower than most African Americans. The reason is that the distribution of scores for African Americans and Whites overlap.

A controversy erupted in response to the book *The Bell Curve: Intelligence and Class Structure in American Life* (1994) by Richard Herrnstein and Charles Murray.

culture-fair tests Intelligence tests that are intended to not be culturally biased.

Recall that the bell curve is the shape of a normal distribution graph, which represents large numbers of people who are sorted according to some shared characteristic, such as weight, taste in clothes, or IQ. Herrnstein and Murray note that predictions about any individual based exclusively on the person's IQ are virtually useless. Weak correlations between IQ and job success have predictive value only when they are applied to large groups of people. But within large groups, say Herrnstein and Murray, the pervasive influence of IQ on human society becomes apparent. The authors argued that America is developing a huge underclass of intellectually deprived individuals whose cognitive abilities will never match the future needs of most employers. They believe that this underclass, a large proportion of which is African American, may be doomed by their shortcomings to welfare dependency, poverty, and crime.

Significant criticisms have been leveled at *The Bell Curve.* The average score of African Americans is lower than the average score of Whites on IQ tests. However, as we have discussed, many experts question the ability of IQ tests to accurately measure intelligence (Sternberg, Grigorenko, & Kidd, 2005).

Furthermore, as African Americans have gained social, economic, and educational opportunities, the gap between African Americans and Whites on standardized intelligence tests has begun to narrow (Ogbu & Stern, 2001; Onwuegbuzi & Daley, 2001). This gap especially narrows in college, where African American and White students often experience more similar environments than in the elementary and high school years (Myerson & others, 1998). Also, when children from disadvantaged African American families are adopted into more-advantaged middle-socioeconomic-status families, their scores on intelligence tests more closely resemble national averages for middle-socioeconomic-status children than for lower-socioeconomic-status children (Scarr & Weinberg, 1983).

One potential influence on intelligence test performance is *stereotype threat,* the anxiety that one's behavior might confirm a negative stereotype about one's group (Cohen & Sherman, 2005; Helms, 2005; Steele & Aronson, 2004). For example, when African Americans take an intelligence test, they may experience anxiety about confirming the old stereotype that Blacks are "intellectually inferior." In one study, the verbal part of the GRE was given individually to African American and White students at Stanford University (Steele & Aronson, 1995). Half the students of each ethnic group were told that the researchers were interested in assessing their intellectual ability. The other half were told that the researchers were trying to develop a test and that it might not be reliable and valid (therefore, it would not mean anything in relation to their intellectual ability). The White students did equally well on the test in both conditions. However, the African American students did more poorly when they thought the test was assessing their intellectual ability; when they thought the test was just in the development stage and might not be reliable or valid, they performed as well as the White students.

Other studies have confirmed the existence of stereotype threat (Good, Aronson, & Inzlicht, 2003; Steele & Markus, 2003). African American students do more poorly on standardized tests if they believe they are being evaluated. If they believe the test doesn't count, they perform as well as White students (Aronson, 2002; Aronson & others, 1999; Aronson, Fried, & Good, 2002). However, some critics believe the extent to which stereotype threat explains the testing gap has been exaggerated (Cullen, Hardison, & Sackett, 2004; Sackett, Hardison, & Cullen, 2004).

Gender Comparisons The average scores of males and females do not differ on intelligence tests, but variability in their scores does differ (Brody, 2000). For example, males are more likely than females to have extremely high or extremely low scores.

There also are gender differences in specific intellectual abilities (Brody, 2000). Males score better than females in some nonverbal areas, such as spatial reasoning, and females score better than males in some verbal areas, such as the ability to find synonyms for words and verbal memory (Jorm & others, 2004; Lynn & Irwing, 2004; Lynn & others, 2004). However, there often is extensive overlap in the scores of females and males in these areas, and there is debate about how strong the differences are (Brabeck & Shore, 2003; Hyde, 2005). There also is debate about the degree to which the differences are due to heredity or to socialization experiences and bias.

Review and Reflect • LEARNING GOAL 1

1 Explain the concept of intelligence

Review

- What is intelligence?
- What are the main individual tests of intelligence? What are some issues in the use of group tests of intelligence?
- What theories of multiple intelligences have been developed? Do people have one intelligence or many intelligences?
- What evidence indicates that heredity influences IQ scores? What evidence indicates that environment influences IQ scores?
- What is known about the intelligence of people from different cultures and ethnic groups? To what extent are there differences in the intelligence of females and males?

Reflect

- A CD-ROM is being sold to parents for testing their child's IQ. What are some potential problems with parents giving their child an IQ test and interpreting the results?

2 THE DEVELOPMENT OF INTELLIGENCE

- Tests of Infant Intelligence
- Stability and Change in Intelligence Through Adolescence

How can the intelligence of infants be assessed? Is intelligence stable through childhood? These are some of the questions we will explore as we examine the development of intelligence.

Tests of Infant Intelligence

The infant-testing movement grew out of the tradition of IQ testing. However, tests that assess infants are necessarily less verbal than IQ tests for older children. Tests for infants contain far more items related to perceptual-motor development. They also include measures of social interaction. To read about the work of one infant assessment specialist, see the Careers in Child Development insert.

The most important early contributor to the testing of infants was Arnold Gesell (1934). He developed a measure that helped sort out potentially normal babies from abnormal ones. This was especially useful to adoption agencies, which had large numbers of babies awaiting placement. Gesell's examination was used widely for many years and still is frequently employed by pediatricians to distinguish normal and abnormal infants. The current version of the Gesell test has four categories of behavior: motor, language, adaptive, and personal-social. The **developmental quotient (DQ)** combines subscores in these categories to provide an overall score.

developmental quotient (DQ) An overall developmental score that combines subscores on motor, language, adaptive, and personal-social domains in the Gesell assessment of infants.

Bayley Scales of Infant Development Developed by Nancy Bayley, these scales are widely used in assessing infant development. The current version has three parts: a Mental Scale, a Motor Scale, and the Infant Behavior Profile.

The **Bayley Scales of Infant Development** are widely used in assessing infants from 1 to 42 months of age in order to diagnose developmental delays and plan intervention strategies. The scales have three components: a Mental Scale, a Motor Scale, and the Infant Behavior Profile. Initially created by Nancy Bayley (1969), the second edition of the Bayley scales was recently developed (Black & Matula, 1999).

What do the scales measure? On the Bayley Mental Scale, for example, the 6-month-old infant should be able to vocalize pleasure and displeasure, persistently search for objects that are just out of immediate reach, and approach a mirror that is placed in front of the infant. By 12 months of age, the infant should be able to inhibit behavior when commanded to do so, imitate words the examiner says (such as *Mama*), and respond to simple requests (such as "Take a drink").

Overall scores on such tests as the Gesell and the Bayley scales do not correlate highly with IQ scores obtained later in childhood. In one study conducted by Nancy Bayley, no relation was found between the Bayley scales and intelligence as measured by the Stanford-Binet at the ages of 6 and 7 (Bayley, 1943). This is not surprising: remember that the components tested in infancy are not the same as the components tested by IQ tests.

The explosion of interest in infant development has produced many new measures, especially tasks that evaluate the ways infants process information (Rose, Feldman, & Wallace, 1992). The Fagan Test of Infant Intelligence is increasingly being used (Fagan, 1992). This test focuses on the infant's ability to process information in such ways as encoding the attributes of objects, detecting similarities and differences between objects, forming mental representations, and retrieving these representations. For example, it uses the amount of time babies look at a new object compared with the amount of time they spend looking at a familiar object to estimate their intelligence.

The Fagan test elicits similar performances from infants in different cultures and, unlike the Gesell and Bayley scales, is correlated with measures of intelligence in older children. In fact, evidence is accumulating that measures of habituation and dishabituation predict intelligence in childhood and adolescence (Bornstein & Sigman, 1986; DiLalla, 2000; Sigman, Cohen, & Beckwith, 2000). Recall from our discussion in chapter 7 that *habituation* is reduced responsiveness to a stimulus after repeated presentations of the stimuli and *dishabituation* is recovery of a habituated response after a change in stimulation. Quicker habituation and greater amounts of looking in dishabituation reflect more efficient information processing. A recent review concluded that when measured between 3 and 12 months, both habituation and dishabituation are related to higher IQ scores on tests given at various times between infancy and adolescence (average correlation = .37) (Kavšek, 2004).

CAREERS in CHILD DEVELOPMENT

Toosje Thyssen Van Beveren
Infant Assessment Specialist

Toosje Thyssen Van Beveren is a developmental psychologist at the University of Texas Medical Center in Dallas. She has a master's degree in child clinical psychology and a Ph.D. in human development.

Her main current work is in a program called New Connections. This 12-week program is a comprehensive intervention for young children (0 to 6 years of age) who were affected by substance abuse prenatally and for their caregivers.

In the New Connections program, Toosje conducts assessments of infants' developmental status and progress, identifying delays and deficits. She might refer the infants to a speech, physical, or occupational therapist and monitor the infants' therapeutic services and developmental progress. Toosje trains the program staff and encourages them to use the exercises she recommends. She also discusses the child's problems with the primary caregivers, suggests activities they can carry out with their children, and assists them in enrolling their infants in appropriate programs.

During her graduate work at the University of Texas at Dallas, Toosje was author John Santrock's teaching assistant for four years in his undergraduate course on development. As a teaching assistant, she attended classes, graded exams, counseled students, and occasionally gave lectures. Each semester, Toosje returns to give a lecture on prenatal development and infancy. Toosje also teaches part-time in the psychology department at UT-Dallas. She teaches an undergraduate course. "The Child in Society," and a graduate course, "Infant Development."

In Toosje's words, "My days are busy and full. The work is often challenging. There are some disappointments but mostly the work is enormously gratifying."

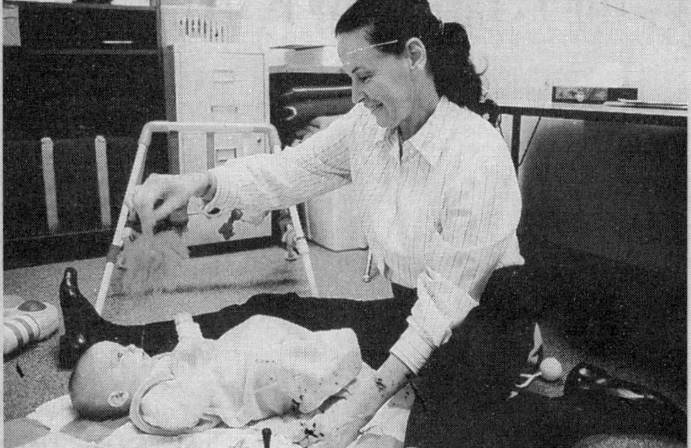

Toosje Thyssen Van Beveren conducting an infant assessment.

www.mhhe.com/santrockcd11

Bayley Scales of Infant Development (2nd ed.)

Stability and Change in Intelligence Through Adolescence

One study examined correlations between IQ at a number of different ages (Honzik, MacFarlane, & Allen, 1948). There was a strong relation between IQ scores obtained at the ages of 6, 8, and 9 and IQ scores obtained at the age of 10. For example, the correlation between IQ at the age of 8 and IQ at the age of 10 was .88. The correlation between IQ at the age of 9 and IQ at the age of 10 was .90. These figures show a very high relation between IQ scores obtained in these years. The correlation between IQ in the preadolescent years and IQ at the age of 18 was slightly less but still statistically significant. For example, the correlation between IQ at the age of 10 and IQ at the age of 18 was .70.

What has been said so far about the stability of intelligence has been based on measures of groups of individuals. The stability of intelligence also can be evaluated through studies of individuals. Robert McCall and his associates (McCall, Applebaum, & Hogarty, 1973) studied 140 children between the ages of 2½ and 17. They found that the average range of IQ scores was more than 28 points. The scores of 1 out of 3 children changed by as much as 40 points.

What can we conclude about the stability and change of intelligence in childhood? Intelligence test scores can fluctuate dramatically across the childhood years. Intelligence is not as stable as the original intelligence theorists envisioned. Children are adaptive beings. They have the capacity for intellectual change, but they do not become entirely new intelligent beings. In a sense, children's intelligence changes but has connections to early points in development.

Review and Reflect • LEARNING GOAL 2

2 Discuss the development of intelligence

Review

- How is intelligence assessed during infancy?
- How much does intelligence change through childhood and adolescence?

Reflect

- As a parent, would you want your infant's intelligence tested? Why or why not?

3 THE EXTREMES OF INTELLIGENCE AND CREATIVITY

Mental Retardation | Giftedness | Creativity

Mental retardation and intellectual giftedness are the extremes of intelligence. Often intelligence tests are used to identify exceptional individuals. Let's explore the nature of mental retardation and giftedness. Then, we'll explore how creativity differs from intelligence.

Mental Retardation

The most distinctive feature of mental retardation is inadequate intellectual functioning. Long before formal tests were developed to assess intelligence, individuals with mental retardation were identified by a lack of age-appropriate skills in learning and caring for themselves. Once intelligence tests were developed, they were used to identify degrees of mental retardation. But of two individuals with mental retardation having the same low IQ, one might be married, employed, and involved in the community and the other require constant supervision in an institution. Such differences in social competence led psychologists to include deficits in adaptive behavior in their definition of mental retardation.

Mental retardation is a condition of limited mental ability in which the individual (1) has a low IQ, usually below 70 on a traditional intelligence test, (2) has difficulty adapting to everyday life, and (3) first exhibits these characteristics by age 18. The age limit is included in the definition of mental retardation because, for example, we don't usually think of a college student who suffers massive brain damage in a car accident, resulting in an IQ of 60, as being "mentally retarded." The low IQ and low adaptiveness should be evident in childhood, not after normal functioning is interrupted by damage of some form. About 5 million Americans fit this definition of mental retardation.

Mental retardation can be classified in several ways (Hallahan & Kaufmann, 2006). Most school systems use the classifications shown in figure 9.7. It uses IQ scores to categorize retardation as mild, moderate, severe, or profound.

Note that a large majority of individuals diagnosed with mental retardation fit into the mild category. However, these categories are not perfect predictors of functioning. The American Association on Mental Retardation (1992) developed a different classification based on the degree of support required for a person with mental retardation to function at the highest level. As shown in figure 9.8, these categories of support are intermittent, limited, extensive, and pervasive.

Some cases of mental retardation have an organic cause (Hardman, Drew, & Egan, 2006). *Organic retardation* is mental retardation caused by a genetic disorder or by brain damage. Down syndrome is one form of organic mental retardation. As discussed in chapter 3, it occurs when an extra chromosome is present.

Other causes of organic retardation include fragile X syndrome, an abnormality in the X chromosome that was discussed in chapter 3; prenatal malformation; metabolic disorders; and diseases that affect the brain. Most people who suffer from organic retardation have IQs between 0 and 50.

When no evidence of organic brain damage can be found, cases of mental retardation are labeled *cultural-familial retardation*. Individuals with this type of retardation have IQs between 55 and 70. Psychologists suspect that these mental deficits often result from growing up in a below-average intellectual environment. Children who are familially retarded can be identified in schools, where they often fail, need tangible

Type of Mental Retardation	IQ Range	Percentage
Mild	55–70	89
Moderate	40–54	6
Severe	25–39	4
Profound	Below 25	1

FIGURE 9.7 Classification of Mental Retardation Based on IQ

This young boy has Down syndrome. *What causes a child to develop Down syndrome? In what major classification of mental retardation does the condition fall?*

Intermittent	Supports are provided "as needed." The individual may need episodic or short-term support during life-span transitions (such as job loss or acute medical crisis). Intermittent supports may be low or high intensity when provided.
Limited	Supports are intense and relatively consistent over time. They are time-limited but not intermittent. Require fewer staff members and cost less than more intense supports. These supports likely will be needed for adaptation to the changes involved in the school-to-adult period.
Extensive	Supports are characterized by regular involvement (e.g., daily) in at least some setting (such as home or work) and are not time-limited (for example, extended home-living support).
Pervasive	Supports are constant, very intense, and are provided across settings. They may be of a life-sustaining nature. These supports typically involve more staff members and intrusiveness than the other support categories.

FIGURE 9.8 Classification of Mental Retardation Based on Levels of Support Needed

www.mhhe.com/santrockcd11

Mental Retardation

mental retardation A condition of limited mental ability in which the individual (1) has a low IQ, usually below 70 on a traditional intelligence test, (2) has difficulty adapting to everyday life, and (3) has an onset of these characteristics by age 18.

rewards (candy rather than praise), and are highly sensitive to what others expect of them. However, as adults, individuals who are familially retarded are usually invisible, perhaps because adult settings don't tax their cognitive skills as sorely. It may also be that individuals who are familially retarded increase their intelligence as they move toward adulthood.

Giftedness

There have always been people whose abilities and accomplishments outshine those of others—the whiz kid in class, the star athlete, the natural musician. People who are **gifted** have high intelligence (an IQ of 130 or higher) or superior talent for something. Programs for the gifted in most school systems select children who have intellectual superiority and academic aptitude. They tend to overlook children who are talented in the arts or athletics or who have other special aptitudes.

Until recently, giftedness and emotional distress were thought to go hand in hand. English novelist Virginia Woolf, Sir Isaac Newton, Vincent van Gogh, Ann Sexton, Socrates, and Sylvia Plath—all had emotional problems. However, these individuals are the exception rather than the rule. In general, no relation between giftedness and mental disorder has been found. Studies support the conclusion that gifted people tend to be more mature and have fewer emotional problems than others, and to grow up in a positive family climate (Feldhusen, 1999; Feldman, 1997).

Characteristics of Children Who Are Gifted What about children who are gifted? Aside from their abilities, do they have distinctive characteristics? Lewis Terman (1925) conducted an extensive study of 1,500 children whose Stanford-Binet IQs averaged 150. Contrary to the popular myth that children who are gifted are maladjusted, Terman found that they were socially well adjusted.

Ellen Winner (1996) described three criteria that characterize gifted children, whether in art, music, or academic domains:

1. *Precocity.* Gifted children are precocious. They begin to master an area earlier than their peers. Learning in their domain is more effortless for them than for ordinary children. In most instances, these gifted children are precocious because they have an inborn high ability.
2. *Marching to their own drummer.* Gifted children learn in a qualitatively different way than ordinary children. For one thing, they need minimal help from adults to learn. In many cases, they resist explicit instruction. They also often make discoveries on their own and solve problems in unique ways.
3. *A passion to master.* Gifted children are driven to understand the domain in which they have high ability. They display an intense, obsessive interest and an ability to focus. They do not need to be pushed by their parents. They motivate themselves, says Winner.

Life Course of the Gifted As a 10-year-old, Alexandra Nechita was described as a child prodigy. She paints quickly and impulsively on large canvases, some as large as 5 feet by 9 feet. It is not unusual for her to complete several of these large paintings in a week's time. Her paintings sell for up to $80,000 apiece. When she was only 2 years of age, Alexandra colored in coloring books for hours. She had no interest in dolls or friends. Once she started school, she would start painting as soon as she got home. And she continues to paint—relentlessly and passionately. It is, she says, what she loves to do.

Is giftedness, like Alexandra Nechita's artistic talent, a product of heredity or environment? Likely both. Individuals who are gifted recall that they had signs of high ability in a particular area at a very young age, prior to or at the beginning of formal training (Howe & others, 1995). This suggests the importance of innate ability in giftedness. However, researchers also have found that individuals with world-class

gifted Having high intelligence (an IQ of 130 or higher) or superior talent for something.

status in the arts, mathematics, science, and sports all report strong family support and years of training and practice (Bloom, 1985). Deliberate practice is an important characteristic of individuals who become experts in a particular domain. *Deliberate practice* is practice that occurs at an appropriate level of difficulty for the individual, provides corrective feedback, and allows opportunities for repetition (Ericsson, 1996). In one study, the best musicians engaged in twice as much deliberate practice over their lives as the least successful ones did (Ericsson, Krampe, & Tesch-Romer, 1993).

An increasing number of experts argue that the education of children who are gifted in the United States requires a significant overhaul, as reflected in the titles of recent books and reports: *Genius Denied: How to Stop Wasting Our Brightest Young Minds* (Davidson & Davidson, 2004) and *A Nation Deceived: How Schools Hold Back America's Brightest Students* (Colangelo, Assouline, & Gross, 2004).

Underchallenged gifted children can become disruptive, skip classes, and lose interest in achieving. Sometimes these children just disappear into the woodwork, becoming passive and apathetic toward school (Rosselli, 1996). It is extremely important for teachers to challenge children who are gifted to reach high expectations (Hargrove, 2005; Tassell-Baska & Stambaugh, 2006; Winner, 2006).

Do gifted children become gifted and highly creative adults? In Terman's research on children with superior IQs, the children typically became experts in a well-established domain, such as medicine, law, or business. However, they did not become major creators (Winner, 2000). That is, they did not create a new domain or revolutionize an old domain.

One reason that some gifted children do not become gifted adults is that they have been pushed too hard by overzealous parents and teachers. As a result, they lose their intrinsic (internal) motivation (Winner, 1996). As adolescents, they may ask themselves, "Who am I doing this for?" If the answer is not for one's self, they may not want to do it anymore.

A number of individuals work with children who are gifted in various capacities in school systems. To read about the work of gifted children specialist Sterling Jones, see the Careers in Child Development insert.

CAREERS in CHILD DEVELOPMENT

Sterling Jones
Supervisor of Gifted and Talented Education

Sterling Jones is program supervisor for gifted and talented children in the Detroit Public School System. Sterling has been working for more than three decades with children who are gifted. He believes that students' mastery of skills mainly depends on the amount of time devoted to instruction and the length of time allowed for learning. Thus, he believes that many basic strategies for challenging children who are gifted to develop their skills can be applied to a wider range of students than once believed. He has rewritten several pamphlets for use by teachers and parents, including *How to Help Your Child Succeed* and *Gifted and Talented Education for Everyone.*

Sterling has undergraduate and graduate degrees from Wayne State University and taught English for a number of years before becoming involved in the program for gifted children. He also has written materials on African Americans, such as *Voices from the Black Experience,* that are used in the Detroit schools.

Sterling Jones with some of the children in the gifted program in the Detroit Public School System.

Creativity

We brought up the term "creative" on several occasions in our discussion of giftedness. What does it mean to be creative? **Creativity** is the ability to think about something in novel and unusual ways and come up with unique solutions to problems.

Intelligence and creativity are not the same thing (Sternberg, 2004; Sternberg, Grigorenko, & Singer, 2004). Most creative people are quite intelligent, but the reverse is not necessarily true. Many highly intelligent people (as measured by high scores on conventional tests of intelligence) are not very creative (Sternberg & O'Hara, 2000). Many highly intelligent people produce large numbers of products but they are not necessarily novel.

creativity The ability to think in novel and unusual ways and come up with unique solutions to problems.

Why don't IQ scores predict creativity? Creativity requires divergent thinking (Guilford, 1967). **Divergent thinking** produces many answers to the same question. In contrast, conventional intelligence tests require **convergent thinking.** For example, a typical item on a conventional intelligence test is, "How many quarters will you get in return for 60 dimes?" There is only one correct answer to this question. In contrast, a question such as, "What image comes to mind when you hear the phrase 'sitting alone in a dark room'?" has many possible answers; it calls for divergent thinking.

Individuals show creativity in some domains more than others (Runco, 2004). For example, a child who shows creativity in mathematics might not be as creative in art. To read about some strategies for helping children become more creative, see the following Caring for Children interlude.

CARING FOR CHILDREN

Guiding Children's Creativity

An important goal is to help children become more creative. What are the best strategies for accomplishing this goal? They include:

- *Have children engage in brainstorming and come up with as many ideas as possible.* **Brainstorming** is a technique in which children are encouraged to come up with creative ideas in a group, play off one another's ideas, and say practically whatever comes to mind. However, some children are more creative when they work alone. Indeed, a recent review of research on brainstorming concluded that for many individuals, working alone can generate more ideas and better ideas than working in groups (Rickards & deCock, 2003). One reason for this is that in groups, some individuals loaf while others do most of the creative thinking. Nonetheless, there may be benefits to brainstorming, such as team building, that support its use.

  Children are usually told to hold off from criticizing others' ideas at least until the end of the brainstorming session. Whether in a group or individually, a good creativity strategy is to come up with as many new ideas as possible. The more ideas children produce, the better their chance of creating something unique. Famous twentieth-century Spanish artist Pablo Picasso produced more than 20,000 works of art; not all of them were masterpieces. Creative children are not afraid of failing or getting something wrong. They may go down 20 dead-end streets before they come up with an innovative idea. They recognize that it's okay to win some and lose some. They are willing to take risks, just as Picasso was.
- *Provide children with environments that stimulate creativity.* Some settings nourish creativity; others depress it (Csikszentmihalyi, 1996; Sternberg, Grigorenko, & Singer, 2004). People who encourage children's creativity often rely on children's natural curiosity. They provide exercises and activities that stimulate children to find insightful solutions to problems, rather than asking a lot of questions that require rote answers. The Spectrum classroom described in the story that opened this chapter is one example. Adults also encourage creativity by taking children to locations where creativity is valued. Howard Gardner (1993) believes that science, discovery, and children's museums offer rich opportunities to stimulate children's creativity.
- *Don't overcontrol.* Teresa Amabile (1993) says that telling children exactly how to do things leaves them feeling that any originality is a mistake and any exploration is a waste of time. Adults are less likely to destroy children's

divergent thinking Thinking that produces many answers to the same question; characteristic of creativity.

convergent thinking Thinking that produces one correct answer; characteristic of the kind of thinking required on conventional intelligence tests.

brainstorming A technique in which children are encouraged to come up with creative ideas in a group, play off one another's ideas, and say practically whatever comes to mind.

natural curiosity if they allow children to select their own interests and support their inclinations rather than dictating activities for the children. Amabile also believes that, when adults constantly hover over children, the children feel they are being watched while they are working. When children are under constant surveillance, their creative risk taking and adventurous spirit wane. Another strategy that can harm creativity is to have grandiose expectations for a child's performance and expect the child to do something perfectly, according to Amabile.

- *Encourage internal motivation.* The excessive use of prizes, such as gold stars, money, or toys, can stifle creativity by undermining the intrinsic pleasure children derive from creative activities. Creative children's motivation is the satisfaction generated by the work itself. Competition for prizes and formal evaluations often undermine intrinsic motivation and creativity (Amabile & Hennesey, 1992).
- *Introduce children to creative people.* Think about the identity of the most creative people in your community. Teachers can invite these people to their classrooms and ask them to describe what helps them become creative or to demonstrate their creative skills. A writer, poet, musician, scientist, and many others can bring their props and productions to the class, turning it into a theater for stimulating students' creativity.

Review and Reflect • LEARNING GOAL 3

3 Describe the characteristics of mental retardation, giftedness, and creativity

Review

- What is mental retardation and what are its causes?
- What makes people gifted?
- What makes people creative?

Reflect

- If you were an elementary school teacher, what would you do to encourage students' creativity?

REACH YOUR LEARNING GOALS

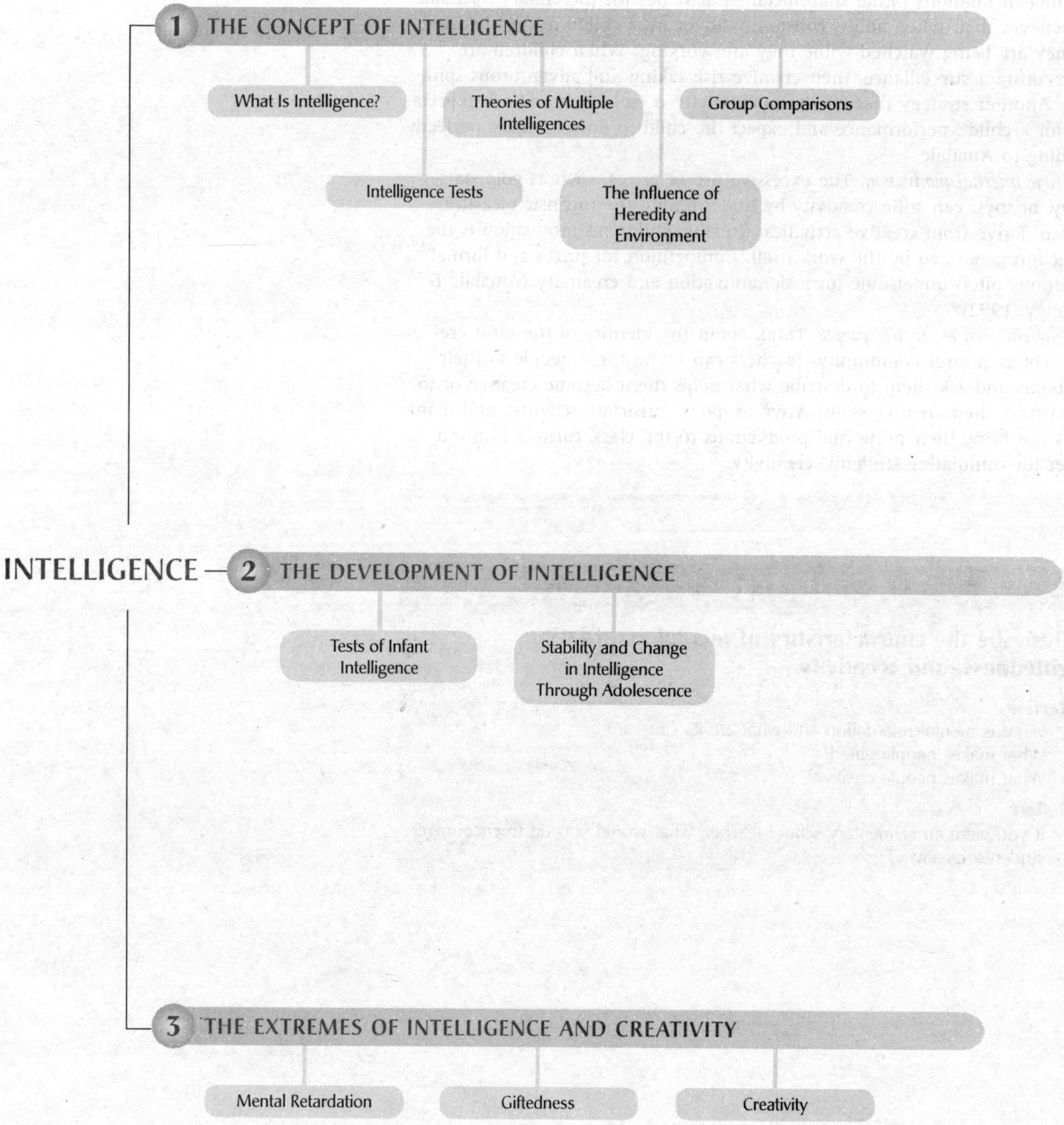

SUMMARY

1 Explain the concept of intelligence

- Intelligence consists of the ability to solve problems and to adapt and learn from everyday experiences. A key aspect of intelligence focuses on its individual variations. Traditionally, intelligence has been measured by tests designed to compare people's performance on cognitive tasks.
- Sir Frances Galton is the father of mental tests. Alfred Binet developed the first intelligence test and created the concept of mental age. William Stern developed the concept of IQ for use with the Binet test. Revisions of the Binet test are called the Stanford-Binet. The test scores on the Stanford-Binet approximate a normal distribution. The Wechsler scales, created by David Wechsler, are the other main intelligence assessment tool. These tests provide an overall IQ, verbal and performance IQs, and information about 11 subtests. Group intelligence tests are convenient and economical, but they do not allow an examiner to monitor the testing closely. When used by a judicious examiner, tests can be valuable tools for determining individual differences in intelligence. Test scores should be only one type of information used to evaluate an individual. IQ scores can produce unfortunate stereotypes and expectations. Ability tests can help divide children into homogeneous groups, but periodic testing should be done to ensure that the groupings are appropriate.
- Factor analysis is a statistical procedure that compares various items or measures and identifies underlying factors that are correlated with each other. Spearman (two-factor theory of *g* and *s*) and Thurstone (multiple-factor theory) used factor analysis in developing their views of intelligence. Gardner believes there are eight types of intelligence: verbal skills, mathematical skills, spatial skills, bodily-kinesthetic skills, musical skills, interpersonal skills, intrapersonal skills, and naturalist skills. Project Spectrum applies Gardner's view to educating children. Sternberg's triarchic theory states that there are three main types of intelligence: analytical, creative, and practical. Sternberg created the Sternberg Triarchic Abilities Test to assess these three types of intelligence and has described applications of triarchic theory to children's education. Emotional intelligence is the ability to perceive and express emotion accurately and adaptively, to understand emotion and emotional knowledge, to use feelings to facilitate thought, and to manage emotions in oneself and others. The multiple intelligences approaches have broadened the definition of intelligence and motivated educators to develop programs that instruct students in different domains. Critics maintain that the multiple intelligence theories include factors that really aren't part of intelligence, such as musical skills and creativity. Critics also say that there isn't enough research to support the concept of multiple intelligences.
- Genetic similarity might explain why identical twins show stronger correlations on intelligence tests than fraternal twins do. Some studies indicate that the IQs of adopted children are more similar to the IQs of their biological parents than to those of their adoptive parents. Many studies show that intelligence has a reasonably strong heritability component. Criticisms of the heritability concept have been made. Intelligence test scores have risen considerably around the world in recent decades—called the Flynn effect—and this supports the role of environment in intelligence. Researchers have found that how much parents talk with their children in the first three years of life is correlated with the children's IQs and that being deprived of formal education lowers IQ scores. Ramey's research revealed the positive effects of educational child care on intelligence.
- Cultures vary in the way they define intelligence. Early intelligence tests favored White, middle-socioeconomic-status urban individuals. Tests may be biased against certain groups because they are not familiar with a standard form of English, with the content tested, or with the testing situation. Tests are likely to reflect the values and experience of the dominant culture. In the United States, children from African American and Latino families score below children from White families on standardized intelligence tests. Males are more likely than females to have extremely high or extremely low IQ scores. There also are gender differences in specific intellectual abilities.

2 Discuss the development of intelligence

- A test developed by Gesell was an important early contributor to the developmental testing of infants. Tests designed to assess infant intelligence include the widely used Bayley scales. The Fagan Test of Infant Intelligence, which assesses how effectively infants process information, is increasingly being used. Infant information-processing tasks that involve attention—especially habituation and dishabituation—are related to standardized scores of intelligence in childhood.
- Although intelligence is more stable across the childhood years than many other attributes are, many children's scores on intelligence tests fluctuate considerably.

3 Discuss the characteristics of mental retardation, giftedness, and creativity

- Mental retardation is a condition of limited mental ability in which the individual (1) has a low IQ, usually below 70, (2) has difficulty adapting to everyday life, and (3) has an onset of these characteristics by age 18. Most affected individuals have an IQ in the 55 to 70 range (mild retardation). Mental retardation can have an organic cause (called organic retardation) or be social and cultural in origin (called cultural-familial retardation).
- People who are gifted have high intelligence (an IQ of 130 or higher) or superior talent for something. Three characteristics of gifted children are precocity, marching to their own drummer, and a passion to master their domain. Giftedness is likely a consequence of both heredity and environment.
- Creativity is the ability to think about something in novel and unusual ways and come up with unique solutions to problems. Although most creative people are intelligent, individuals with high IQs are not necessarily creative. Creative people tend to be divergent thinkers; traditional intelligence tests measure convergent thinking.

KEY TERMS

intelligence 273
mental age (MA) 274
intelligence quotient (IQ) 274
normal distribution 274
two-factor theory 277
factor analysis 277
multiple-factor theory 277
triarchic theory of intelligence 279
emotional intelligence 280
heritability 282
culture-fair tests 286
developmental quotient (DQ) 288
Bayley scales of Infant Development 288
mental retardation 291
gifted 292
creativity 293
divergent thinking 294
convergent thinking 294
brainstorming 294

KEY PEOPLE

Alfred Binet 274
Theophile Simon 274
Lewis Terman 274
David Wechsler 274
Charles Spearman 277
L. L. Thurstone 277
Howard Gardner 277
Robert J. Sternberg 279
Daniel Goleman 280
Peter Salovey and John Mayer 280
John Carroll 281
Arthur Jensen 281
James Flynn 283
Robert Plomin 284
Craig Ramey 284
Robert Serpell 285
Elena Grigorenko 285
Richard Herrnstein and Charles Murray 286
Arnold Gesell 288
Nancy Bayley 289
Robert McCall 290
Lewis Terman 292
Ellen Winner 292

E-LEARNING TOOLS

To help you master the material in this chapter, visit the Online Learning Center for *Child Development*, eleventh edition (**www.mhhe.com/santrockcd11**), where you'll find these additional resources:

Taking It to the Net

1. Terry and Lauren are on a debating team. They have to argue for the proposition, "Intelligence is hereditary." Another pair of members will argue for the opposite proposition, "Intelligence is not related to heredity." What facts do Terry and Lauren need to know as they prepare for the debate?
2. Motabi is from the Congo. He is arguing with his developmental psychology classmates about the meaning of intelligence. Motabi insists that different cultures construct their own paradigms of intelligence and that intelligence in the Congo is a very different concept from intelligence in Illinois. Is there any evidence to support Motabi's argument?
3. Maureen and Harry received a letter from the elementary school principal suggesting that they enroll their daughter, Jasmine, in the gifted program. They know what Jasmine's IQ score is—125—certainly not in the genius category. Is there more to giftedness than IQ score? What talents might Jasmine's teachers have noticed in her that may qualify her as being gifted?

Nursing, Parenting, and Teaching Exercises

Build your decision-making skills by trying your hand at the scenarios on the Online Learning Center.

Video Clips

The Online Learning Center includes the following videos for this chapter:

- Intelligence Testing
  Stephen Ceci, Department of Psychology, Cornell University. Intelligence tests are pervasive in our society—"they are the gatekeepers" to opportunities in our society. Dr. Ceci gives examples of how these tests can underpredict an individual's true abilities.

Chapter 10 LANGUAGE DEVELOPMENT

Words not only affect us temporarily; they change us, they socialize us, and they unsocialize us.

—David Reisman
American Social Scientist, 20th Century

CHAPTER OUTLINE

WHAT IS LANGUAGE?

Defining Language
Language's Rule Systems

HOW LANGUAGE DEVELOPS

Infancy
Early Childhood
Middle and Late Childhood
Adolescence

BIOLOGICAL AND ENVIRONMENTAL INFLUENCES

Biological Influences
Environmental Influences
An Interactionist View of Language

LANGUAGE AND COGNITION

LEARNING GOALS

1 Define language and describe its rule systems

2 Describe how language develops

3 Discuss the biological and environmental contributions to language

4 Evaluate how language and cognition are linked

The Story of Helen Keller

One of the most stunning portrayals of children isolated from the mainstream of language is the case of Helen Keller (1880–1968). At 18 months of age, Helen was an intelligent toddler in the process of learning her first words. Then she developed an illness that left her both deaf and blind, suffering the double affliction of sudden darkness and silence. For the next five years she lived in a world she learned to fear because she could not see or hear.

Even with her fears, Helen spontaneously invented a number of gestures to reflect her wants and needs. For example, when she wanted ice cream, she turned toward the freezer and shivered. When she wanted bread and butter, she imitated the motions of cutting and spreading. But this homemade language system severely limited her ability to communicate with the surrounding community, which did not understand her idiosyncratic gestures.

Alexander Graham Bell, the famous inventor of the telephone, suggested to her parents that they hire a tutor named Anne Sullivan to help Helen overcome her fears. By using sign language, Anne was able to teach Helen to communicate. Anne realized that language learning needs to occur naturally, so she did not force Helen to memorize words out of context as in the drill methods that were in vogue at the time. Sullivan's success depended not only on the child's natural ability to organize language according to form and meaning but also on introducing language in the context of communicating about objects, events, and feelings about others.

Helen Keller eventually graduated from Radcliffe with honors, became a very successful educator, and crafted books about her life and experiences. She had this to say about language: "Whatever the process, the result is wonderful. Gradually from naming an object we advance step by step until we have traversed the vast distance between our first stammered syllable and the sweep of thought in a line of Shakespeare."

PREVIEW

In this chapter, we will tell the remarkable story of language and how it develops. The questions we will explore include these: What is language? What is the developmental course of language? How are language and cognition linked? What does biology contribute to language? How does experience influence language?

1 WHAT IS LANGUAGE?

Defining Language — Language's Rule Systems

In 1799, a nude boy was observed running through the woods in France. The boy was captured when he was 11 years old. He was called the Wild Boy of Aveyron and was believed to have lived in the woods alone for six years (Lane, 1976). When found, he made no effort to communicate. He never learned to communicate effectively. Sadly, a modern-day wild child named Genie was discovered in Los Angeles in 1970. Despite intensive intervention, Genie only has acquired a limited form of spoken language. We will discuss Genie's development in greater detail later in the chapter. Both cases—the Wild Boy of Aveyron and Genie—raise questions about the biological and environmental determinants of language, topics that we also will examine later in the chapter. First, though, we need to define language.

Defining Language

Language is a form of communication—whether spoken, written, or signed—that is based on a system of symbols. Language consists of the words used by a community and the rules for varying and combining them.

Think how important language is in our everyday lives. It is difficult to imagine what Helen Keller's life would have been like if she had never learned language. We need language to speak with others, listen to others, read, and write. Our language enables us to describe past events in detail and to plan for the future. Language lets us pass down information from one generation to the next and create a rich cultural heritage.

All human languages have some common characteristics. These include infinite generativity and organizational rules. **Infinite generativity** is the ability to produce an endless number of meaningful sentences using a finite set of words and rules. When we say "rules" we mean that language is orderly and that rules describe the way language works (Berko Gleason, 2004). Let's further explore what these rules involve.

Language's Rule Systems

When nineteenth-century American writer Ralph Waldo Emerson said, "The world was built in order and the atoms march in tune," he must have had language in mind. Language is highly ordered and organized (Berko Gleason, 2005). The organization involves five systems of rules: phonology, morphology, syntax, semantics, and pragmatics.

Phonology Every language is made up of basic sounds. **Phonology** is the sound system of a language, including the sounds that are used and how they may be combined (Menn & Stoel-Gammon, 2005). For example, English has the sounds *sp, ba,* and *ar,* but the sound sequences *zx* and *qp* do not occur. A *phoneme* is the basic unit of sound in a language; it is the smallest unit of sound that affects meaning. A good example of a phoneme in English is /k/, the sound represented by the letter *k* in the word *ski* and the letter *c* in the word *cat.* The /k/ sound is slightly different in these two words, and in some languages such as Arabic these two sounds are separate phonemes. However, this variation is not distinguished in English, and the /k/ sound is therefore a single phoneme.

Morphology **Morphology** refers to the units of meaning involved in word formation. A *morpheme* is a minimal unit of meaning; it is a word or a part of a word that cannot be broken into smaller meaningful parts. Every word in the English language is made up of one or more morphemes. Some words consist of a single morpheme (for example, *help*), whereas others are made up of more than one morpheme (for example, *helper,* which has two morphemes, *help* + *er,* with the morpheme *-er* meaning "one who," in this case "one who helps"). Thus, not all morphemes are words by themselves; for example, *-pre, -tion,* and *-ing* are morphemes.

Just as the rules that govern phonology describe the sound sequences that can occur in a language, the rules of morphology describe the way meaningful units (morphemes) can be combined in words (Tager-Flusberg, 2005). Morphemes have many jobs in grammar, such as marking tense (for example, she *walks* versus she *walked*) and number (*she* walks versus *they* walk).

Syntax **Syntax** involves the way words are combined to form acceptable phrases and sentences. If someone says to you, "Bob slugged Tom" or "Bob was slugged by Tom," you know who did the slugging and who was slugged in each case because you have a syntactic understanding of these sentence structures. You also understand that the sentence, "You didn't stay, did you?" is a grammatical sentence but that "You didn't stay, didn't you? is unacceptable and ambiguous.

language A form of communication, whether spoken, written, or signed, that is based on a system of symbols.

infinite generativity The ability to produce an endless number of meaningful sentences using a finite set of words and rules.

phonology The sound system of the language, including the sounds that are used and how they may be combined.

morphology Units of meaning involved in word formation.

syntax The ways words are combined to form acceptable phrases and sentences.

FRANK & ERNEST © Thaves. Distributed by Newspaper Enterprise Association, Inc.

If you learn another language, English syntax will not get you very far. For example, in English an adjective usually precedes a noun (as in *blue sky*), whereas in Spanish the adjective usually follows the noun (*cielo azul*). Despite the differences in their syntactic structures, however, the world's languages have much in common. For example, consider the following short sentences:

The cat killed the mouse.
The mouse ate the cheese.
The farmer chased the cat.

In many languages it is possible to combine these sentences into more complex sentences. For example:

The farmer chased the cat that killed the mouse.
The mouse the cat killed ate the cheese.

However, no language we know of permits sentences like the following one:

The mouse the cat the farmer chased killed ate the cheese.

Can you make sense of this sentence? If you can, you probably can do it only after wrestling with it for several minutes. You likely could not understand it at all if someone uttered it during a conversation. It appears that language users cannot process subjects and objects arranged in too complex a fashion in a sentence. That is good news for language learners, because it means that all syntactic systems have some common ground. Such findings are also considered important by researchers who are interested in the universal properties of syntax (Tager-Flusberg, 2005).

Semantics **Semantics** refers to the meaning of words and sentences. Every word has a set of semantic features, or required attributes related to meaning. *Girl* and *women*, for example, share many semantic features but they differ semantically in regard to age.

Words have semantic restrictions on how they can be used in sentences (Pan, 2005). The sentence *The bicycle talked the boy into buying a candy bar* is syntactically correct but semantically incorrect. The sentence violates our semantic knowledge that bicycles don't talk.

Pragmatics A final set of language rules involves **pragmatics,** the appropriate use of language in different contexts. Pragmatics covers a lot of territory. When you take turns speaking in a discussion or use a question to convey a command ("Why is it so noisy in here?" "What is this, Grand Central Station?"), you are demonstrating knowledge of pragmatics. You also apply the pragmatics of English when you use polite language in appropriate situations (for example, when talking to one's teacher) or tell stories that are interesting, jokes that are funny, and lies that convince. In each of these cases, you are demonstrating that you understand the rules of your culture for adjusting language to suit the context.

Pragmatic rules can be complex and differ from one culture to another (Bryant, 2005). If you were to study the Japanese language, you would come face-to-face with countless pragmatic rules about conversing with individuals of various social

www.mhhe.com/santrockcd11
Pragmatics

semantics The meanings of words and sentences.

pragmatics The appropriate use of language in context.

Rule System	Description	Examples
Phonology	The sound system of a language. A phoneme is the smallest sound unit in a language.	The word *chat* has three phonemes or sounds: /ch/ /a/ /t/. An example of phonological rule in the English language is while the phoneme /r/ can follow the phonemes /t/ or /d/ in an English consonant cluster (such as *track* or *drab*), the phoneme /l/ cannot follow these letters.
Morphology	The system of meaningful units involved in word formation.	The smallest sound units that have a meaning are called morphemes, or meaning units. The word *girl* is one morpheme, or meaning unit; it cannot be broken down any further and still have meaning. When the suffix *s* is added, the word becomes *girls* and has two morphemes because the *s* changed the meaning of the word, indicating that there is more than one girl.
Syntax	The system that involves the way words are combined to form acceptable phrases and sentences.	Word order is very important in determining meaning in the English language. For example, the sentence, "Sebastian pushed the bike" has a different meaning than "The bike pushed Sebastian."
Semantics	The system that involves the meaning of words and sentences.	Knowing the meaning of individual words—that is, vocabulary. For example, semantics includes knowing the meaning of such words as *orange*, *transportation*, and *intelligent*.
Pragmatics	The system of using appropriate conversation and knowledge of how to effectively use language in context.	An example is using polite language in appropriate situations, such as being mannerly when talking with one's teacher. Taking turns in a conversation involves pragmatics.

FIGURE 10.1 The Rule Systems of Language

levels and with various relationships to you. Some of these pragmatic rules concern the ways of saying thank you. Indeed, the pragmatics of saying thank you are complex even in our own culture. Preschoolers' use of the phrase *thank you* varies with sex, socioeconomic status, and the age of the individual they are addressing.

At this point, we have discussed five important rule systems involved in language. An overview of these rule systems is presented in figure 10.1.

Review and Reflect • **LEARNING GOAL 1**

1 Define language and describe its rule systems

Review

- What is language?
- What are language's five main rule systems?

Reflect

- How good are your family members and friends at the pragmatics of language? Describe an example in which one of the individuals showed pragmatic skills and another in which he or she did not.

2 HOW LANGUAGE DEVELOPS

Infancy | Early Childhood | Middle and Late Childhood | Adolescence

According to an ancient historian, in the thirteenth century, the emperor of Germany, Frederick II, had a cruel idea. He wanted to know what language children would speak if no one talked to them. He selected several newborns and threatened their caregivers with death if they ever talked to the infants. Frederick never found out what language the children spoke because they all died. As we move forward in the twenty-first century, we are still curious about infants' development of language, although our experiments and observations are, to say the least, far more humane than the evil Frederick's.

Infancy

Whatever language they learn, infants all over the world follow a similar path in language development. What are some key milestones in this development?

Babbling and Other Vocalizations Babies actively produce sounds from birth onward. The purpose of these early communications is to attract attention from caregivers and others in the environment (Lock, 2004; Volterra & others, 2004). Babies' sounds and gestures go through this sequence during the first year:

- *Crying.* Babies cry even at birth. Crying can signal distress, but as we will discuss in chapter 11, there are different types of cries that signal different things.
- *Cooing.* Babies first coo at about 1 to 2 months. These are *oo* sounds such as *coo* or *goo*. They usually occur during interaction with the caregiver.
- *Babbling.* This first occurs in the middle of the first year and includes strings of consonant-vowel combinations, such as "ba, ba, ba, ba."
- *Gestures.* Infants start using gestures, such as showing and pointing, at about 8 to 12 months of age. They may wave bye-bye, nod to mean "yes," show an empty cup if they want more milk, and point to a dog to draw attention to it.

Those deaf infants who are born to deaf parents who use sign language babble with their hands and fingers at about the same age as hearing children babble vocally (Bloom, 1998). Such similarities in timing and structure between manual and vocal babbling indicate that a unified language capacity underlies signed and spoken language (Petitto, Kovelman, & Harasymowycz, 2003).

Recognizing Language Sounds Long before they begin to learn words, infants can make fine distinctions among the sounds of the language (Lock, 2004; Menn & Stoel-Gammon, 2005). Patricia Kuhl (1993, 2000) explored how infants perceive the sounds of speech by piping through a speaker phonemes from languages all over the world for infants to hear (see figure 10.2). A string of identical syllables is played and the sound changes. A box with a toy bear in it is placed where the infant can see it. If the infant turns its head when the sounds of the syllables change, the darkened box lights up and the bear briefly dances and drums. That is, if the infant turns its head to look at the box as soon as it notices the sound changing, the infant is rewarded by getting to see the bear's performance.

Kuhl's research has demonstrated that from birth up to about 6 months of age, infants are "citizens of the world": they recognize when sounds change most of the time no matter what language the syllables come from. But over the next six months, infants get even better at perceiving the changes in sounds from their "own" language, the one their parents speak, and gradually lose the ability to recognize changes in sounds that don't exist in their native tongue.

An example involves the English *r* and *l* sounds, which distinguish words such as *rake* and *lake* (Iverson & Kuhl, 1996; Iverson & others, 2003). In the United States, infants from English-speaking homes detect the changes from *ra* to *la* when they are 6 months old

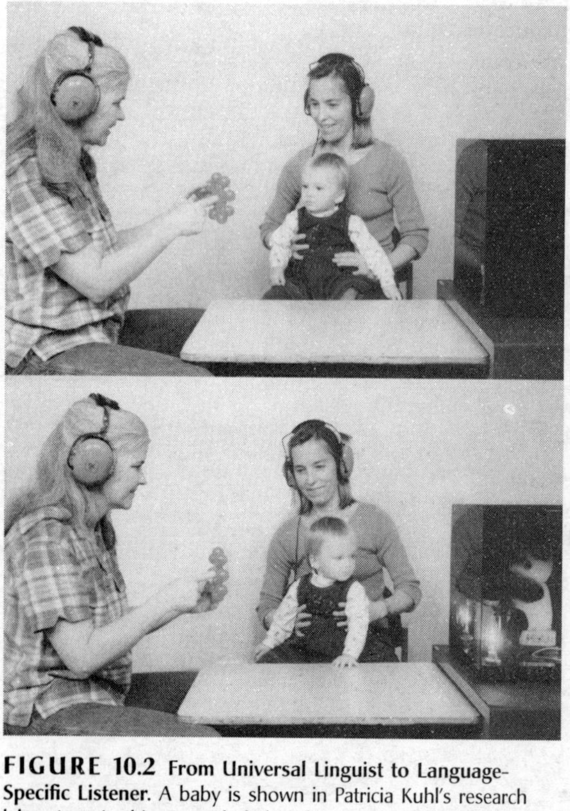

FIGURE 10.2 From Universal Linguist to Language-Specific Listener. A baby is shown in Patricia Kuhl's research laboratory. In this research, babies listen to tape-recorded voices that repeat syllables. When the sounds of the syllables change, the babies quickly learn to look at the bear. Using this technique, Kuhl has demonstrated that babies are universal linguists until about 6 months of age, but in the next six months become language-specific listeners.

and get better at detecting the change by 12 months of age. However, in Japanese there is no such *r* or *l* distinction. In Japan, 6-month-old infants perform as well as their American counterparts in recognizing the *r* and *l* distinction, but by 12 months of age they lose this ability.

Infants have learned the sounds of their native language by the age of six months.

—Patricia Kuhl
Contemporary Psychologist, University of Washington

Infants must fish out individual words from the nonstop stream of sound that makes up ordinary speech (Brownlee, 1998; Jusczyk, 2000). To do so, they must find the boundaries between words, which is very difficult for infants because adults don't pause between words when they speak. Still, infants begin to detect word boundaries by 8 months of age. For example, in one study, 8-month-old infants listened to recorded stories that contained unusual words, such as *hornbill* and *python* (Jusczyk & Hohne, 1997). Two weeks later, the researchers tested the infants with two lists of words, one made up of words in the stories, the other of new, unusual words that did not appear in the stories. The infants listened to the familiar words for a second longer, on average, than to new words.

www.mhhe.com/santrockcd11

Communicating with Babies
Language Milestones
The Naming Explosion

First Words

Between about 8 and 12 months of age, infants often indicate their first understanding of words. The infant's first spoken word is a milestone eagerly anticipated by every parent. This event usually occurs between 10 and 15 months of age and at an average of about 13 months. However, as we have seen, long before babies say their first words, they have been communicating with their parents, often by gesturing and using their own special sounds. The appearance of first words is a continuation of this communication process (Berko Gleason, 2005).

A child's first words include those that name important people (*dada*), familiar animals (*kitty*), vehicles (*car*), toys (*ball*), food (*milk*), body parts (*eye*), clothes (*hat*), household items (*clock*), and greeting terms (*bye*). These were the first words of babies 50 years ago. They are the first words of babies today. Children often express various intentions with their single words, so that "cookie" might mean, "That's a cookie" or "I want a cookie."

On the average, infants understand about 50 words at about 13 months, but they can't say this many words until about 18 months (Menyuk, Liebergott, & Schultz, 1995). Thus, in infancy *receptive vocabulary* (words the child understands) considerably exceeds *spoken vocabulary* (words the child uses).

The infant's spoken vocabulary rapidly increases once the first word is spoken (Camaioni, 2004; Waxman & Lidz, 2006). The average 18-month-old can speak about 50 words, but by the age of 2 years can speak about 200 words. This rapid increase in vocabulary that begins at approximately 18 months is called the *vocabulary spurt* (Bloom, Lifter, & Broughton, 1985).

Like the timing of a child's first word, the timing of the vocabulary spurt varies (Bloom, 1998; Dale & Goodman, 2004). Figure 10.3 shows the range for these two language milestones in 14 children. On average, these children said their first word at 13 months and had a vocabulary spurt at 19 months. However, the ages for the first word of individual children varied from 10 to 17 months and for their vocabulary spurt from 13 to 25 months.

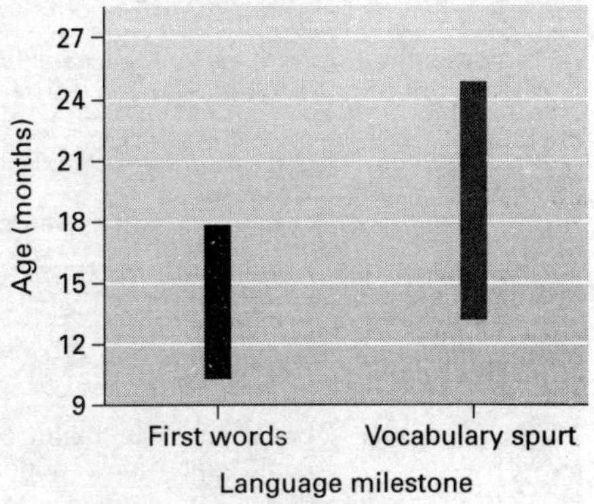

FIGURE 10.3 Variation in Language Milestones

Children sometimes overextend or underextend the meanings of the words they use (Woodward & Markman, 1998). *Overextension* is the tendency to apply a word to objects that are not related to, or are inappropriate for, the word's meaning. For example, children at first may say *"dada"* not only for "father" but also for other men, strangers, or boys. With time, overextensions decrease and eventually disappear. *Underextension* is the tendency to apply a word too narrowly; it occurs when children fail to use a word to name a relevant event or object. For example, a child might use the word *boy* to describe a 5-year-old neighbor but not apply the word to a male infant or to a 9-year-old male.

Two-Word Utterances

By the time children are 18 to 24 months of age, they usually utter two-word utterances. To convey meaning with just two words, the child relies heavily on gesture, tone, and context. The wealth of meaning

Around the world, young children learn to speak in two-word utterances, in most cases at about 18 to 24 months of age. *What implications does this have for the biological basis of language?*

children can communicate with a two-word utterance includes the following (Slobin, 1972):

- Identification: "See doggie."
- Location: "Book there."
- Repetition: "More milk."
- Nonexistence: "All gone thing."
- Negation: "Not wolf."
- Possession: "My candy."
- Attribution: "Big car."
- Agent-action: "Mama walk."
- Action-direct object: "Hit you."
- Action-indirect object: "Give Papa."
- Action-instrument: "Cut knife."
- Question: "Where ball?"

These examples are from children whose first language is English, German, Russian, Finnish, Turkish, or Samoan.

Notice that the two-word utterances omit many parts of speech and are remarkably succinct. In fact, in every language, a child's first combinations of words have this economical quality; they are telegraphic. **Telegraphic speech** is the use of short and precise words without grammatical markers such as articles, auxiliary verbs, and other connectives. Telegraphic speech is not limited to two words. "Mommy give ice cream" and "Mommy give Tommy ice cream" also are examples of telegraphic speech.

We have discussed a number of language milestones in infancy. Figure 10.4 summarizes the time at which infants typically reach these milestones.

telegraphic speech The use of short and precise words without grammatical markers such as articles, auxiliary verbs, and other connectives.

Early Childhood

As children leave the two-word stage, they move rather quickly into three-, four-, and five-word combinations. The transition from simple sentences expressing a single proposition to complex sentences begins between 2 and 3 years of age and continues into the elementary school years (Bloom, 1998).

Young children's understanding sometimes gets way ahead of their speech. One 3-year-old, laughing with delight as an abrupt summer breeze stirred his hair and tickled his skin, commented, "I got breezed!" Many of the oddities of young children's language sound like mistakes to adult listeners. However, from the children's point of view, they are not mistakes. They represent the way young children perceive and understand their world at that point in their development. As children go through their early childhood years, their grasp of the rule systems that govern language increases.

Age	Language Milestones
Birth	Crying
1 to 2 months	Cooing begins
6 months	Babbling begins
6 to 12 months	Change from universal linguist to language-specific learner
8 to 12 months	Use gestures, such as showing and pointing Comprehension of words appears
13 months	First word spoken
18 months	Vocabulary spurt starts
18 to 24 months	Uses two-word utterances Rapid expansion of understanding of words

FIGURE 10.4 Some Language Milestones in Infancy

Understanding Phonology and Morphology

During the preschool years, most children gradually become sensitive to the sounds of spoken words (National Research Council, 1999). They notice rhymes, enjoy poems, make up silly names for things by substituting one sound for another (such as *bubblegum, bubblebum, bubbleyum*), and clap along with each syllable in a phrase.

As they move beyond two-word utterances, there is clear evidence that children know morphological rules. Children begin using the plural and possessive forms of nouns (*dogs* and *dog's*); putting appropriate endings on verbs (*-s* when the subject is third-person singular, *-ed* for the past tense, and *-ing* for the present progressive tense); and using prepositions (*in* and *on*), articles (*a* and *the*), and various forms of the verb *to be* ("I *was going* to the store"). In fact, they *overgeneralize* these rules, applying them to words that do not follow the rules. For example, a preschool child might say "foots" instead of "feet" or "goed" instead of "went."

Children's understanding of morphological rules was the subject of a classic experiment by children's language researcher Jean Berko (1958). Berko presented preschool and first-grade children with cards like the one shown in figure 10.5. Children were asked to look at the card while the experimenter read the words on it aloud. Then the children were asked to supply the missing word. This might sound easy, but Berko was interested not just in the children's ability to recall the right word but also in their ability to say it "correctly" with the ending that was dictated by morphological rules. *Wugs* is the correct response for the card in figure 10.5. Although the children were not perfectly accurate, they were much better than chance would dictate. Moreover, they demonstrated their knowledge of morphological rules not only with the plural forms of nouns ("There are two wugs") but also with the possessive forms of nouns and with the third-person singular and past-tense forms of verbs.

What makes Berko's study impressive is that all of the words were *fictional;* they were created especially for the experiment. Thus, the children could not base their responses on remembering past instances of hearing the words. Instead, they were forced to rely on *rules.* Berko's study demonstrated not only that the children relied on rules, but also that they had *abstracted* the rules from what they had heard and could apply them to novel situations.

FIGURE 10.5 Stimuli in Berko's Study of Young Children's Understanding of Morphological Rules. In Jean Berko's (1958) study, young children were presented cards, such as this one with a "wug" on it. Then the children were asked to supply the missing word; in supplying the missing word, they had to say it correctly too. "Wugs" is the correct response here.

Understanding Syntax Preschool children also learn and apply rules of syntax. After advancing beyond two-word utterances, the child shows a growing mastery of complex rules for how words should be ordered.

Consider *wh-* questions, such as "Where is Daddy going?" or "What is that boy doing?" To ask these questions properly, the child must know two important differences between *wh-* questions and affirmative statements (for instance, "Daddy is going to work" and "That boy is waiting on the school bus"). First, a *wh-* word must be added at the beginning of the sentence. Second, the auxiliary verb must be inverted—that is, exchanged with the subject of the sentence. Young children learn quite early where to put the *wh-* word, but they take much longer to learn the auxiliary-inversion rule. Thus, preschool children might ask, "Where daddy is going?" and "What that boy is doing?"

Advances in Semantics As children move beyond the two-word stage, their knowledge of meanings also rapidly advances (Bloom, 2002; Dale & Goodman, 2004). The speaking vocabulary of a 6-year-old child ranges from 8,000 to 14,000 words (Carey, 1977; Clark, 2000). Assuming that word learning began when the child was 12 months old, this translates into a rate of learning five to eight new word meanings a day between the ages of 1 and 6. The 6-year-old child does not slow down. According to some estimates, the average 6-year-old moves along at the awe-inspiring rate of learning 22 words a day (Miller, 1981). How would you fare if you were given the task of learning 22 new words every day?

Advances in Pragmatics Changes in pragmatics also characterize young children's language development (Bryant, 2005). A 6-year-old is simply a much better conversationalist than a 2-year-old is. What are some of the improvements in pragmatics during the preschool years?

At about 3 years of age, children improve their ability to talk about things that are not physically present: that is, they improve their command of an aspect of language known as *displacement.* Displacement is revealed in games of pretend. Although a 2-year-old might know the word *table,* he is unlikely to use this word to refer to an imaginary table that he pretends is standing in front of him. A child over 3 years of age is more likely to do so. There are large individual differences in preschoolers' talk about imaginary people and things.

Children pick up words as pigeons peas.

—John Ray
English Naturalist, 17th Century

At about 4 years of age, children develop a remarkable sensitivity to the needs of others in conversation. One way in which they show such sensitivity is through their use of the articles *the* and *an* (or *a*). When adults tell a story or describe an event, they generally use *an* (or *a*) when they first refer to an animal or an object, and then use *the* when referring to it later. (For example, "Two boys were walking through the jungle when *a* fierce lion appeared. *The* lion lunged at one boy while the other ran for cover.") Even 3-year-olds follow part of this rule; they consistently use the word *the* when referring to previously mentioned things. However, the use of the word *a* when something is initially mentioned develops more slowly. Although 5-year-old children follow this rule on some occasions, they fail to follow it on others.

Around 4 to 5 years of age children learn to change their speech style to suit the situation. For example, even 4-year-old children speak differently to a 2-year-old than to a same-aged peer; they use shorter sentences with the 2-year-old. They also speak differently to an adult than to a same-aged peer, using more polite and formal language with the adult (Shatz & Gelman, 1973).

Middle and Late Childhood

During middle and late childhood, children make advances in their vocabulary and grammar. As children enter elementary school, they gain skills that make it possible for them to read and write.

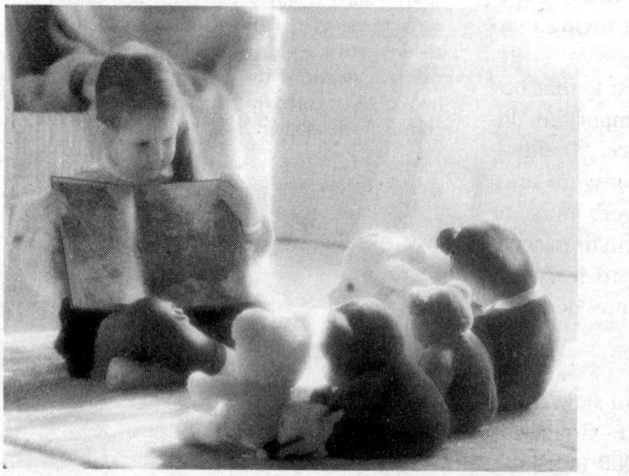

How do children's language abilities develop during early childhood?

Vocabulary and Grammar How children think about words changes during middle and late childhood. They become less tied to the actions and perceptions associated with words, and they become more analytical in their approach to words.

This analytical approach is apparent if children are asked to say the first thing that comes to mind when they hear a word. Preschool children typically respond with a word that often follows the stimulus word in a sentence. For example, when asked to respond to the word *dog*, the young child may say "barks"; to the word *eat*, "lunch." But at about 7 years of age, children may begin to respond with a word that is the same part of speech as the stimulus word. For example, a child may now respond to the word *dog* with "cat" or "horse." To *eat*, the 7-year-old might say "drink." This is evidence that children have begun to categorize their vocabulary by parts of speech (Berko Gleason, 2004).

During the elementary school years, children become increasingly able to understand and use complex grammar—for example, stating sentences such as *The boy who kissed his mother who wore a hat.* They also learn to use language in a more connected way. Now they can produce connected discourse, relating sentences to one another and producing descriptions, definitions, and narratives that hang together and make sense. Children must be able to do these things orally before they can be expected to do them in written assignments.

Metalinguistic Awareness **Metalinguistic awareness** refers to knowledge of language, which allows children "to think about their language, understand what words are, and even define them" (Berko Gleason, 2005, p. 4). Recall from chapter 8 that metacognition is cognition about cognition, or knowing about knowing. Metalinguistic awareness is essentially cognition about language.

Megalinguistic awareness improves considerably during the elementary school years. Defining words becomes a regular part of classroom discourse and children increase their knowledge of syntax as they study and talk about the components of sentences such as subjects and verbs (Ely, 2005). Children also make progress in understanding how to use language in culturally appropriate ways—pragmatics. By the time

metalinguistic awareness Knowledge of language

Stage	Age range/Grade level	Descripton
0	Birth to first grade	Children master several prerequisites for reading. Many learn the left-to-right progression and order of reading, how to identify letters of the alphabet, and how to write their names. Some learn to read words that appear on signs. As a result of TV shows like *Sesame Street* and attending preschool and kindergarten programs, many young children today develop greater knowledge about reading earlier than in the past.
1	First and second grades	Many children learn to read at this time. In doing so, they acquire the ability to sound out words (that is, translate letters into sounds and blend sounds into words). They also complete their learning of letter names and sounds.
2	Second and third grades	Children become more fluent at retrieving individual words and other reading skills. However, at this stage reading is still not used much for learning. The demands of reading are so taxing for children at this stage that they have few resources left over to process the content.
3	Fourth through eighth grades	In fourth through eighth grade, children become increasingly able to obtain new information from print. In other words, they read to learn. They still have difficulty understanding information presented from multiple perspectives within the same story. When children don't learn to read, a downward spiral unfolds that leads to serious difficulties in many academic subjects.
4	High school	Many students become fully competent readers. They develop the ability to understand material told from many perspectives. This allows them to engage in sometimes more sophisticated discussions of literature, history, economics, and politics.

FIGURE 10.6 A Model of Developmental Stages in Reading

they enter adolescence, most children know the rules for the use of language in everyday contexts—that is, what is appropriate to say and what is inappropriate to say.

Reading Children who enter elementary school with a small vocabulary are at risk for developing reading problems (Berko Gleason, 2004; Berninger, 2006; Rubin, 2006). Reading skills develop over many years, as figure 10.6 illustrates. It shows a model that describes five stages in the development of reading (Chall, 1979). The age boundaries are approximate and do not apply to every child, but the stages convey a sense of the developmental changes involved in learning to read.

Before learning to read, children learn to use language to talk about things that are not present; they learn what a word is; and they learn how to recognize and talk about sounds (Berko Gleason, 2004). They also learn the *alphabetic principle*—that letters represent sounds in the language.

How should children be taught to read? Currently, debate focuses on the whole-language approach versus the basic-skills-and-phonics approach (May, 2006; O'Donnell & Wood, 2004; Ruddell, 2006; Vacca & others, 2006).

The **whole-language approach** stresses that reading instruction should parallel children's natural language learning. Reading materials should be whole and meaningful. That is, children should be given material in its complete form, such as stories and poems, so that they learn to understand language's communicative function. Reading should be connected with listening and writing skills. Although there are variations in whole-language programs, most share the premise that reading should be integrated with other skills and subjects, such as science and social studies, and that it should focus on real-world material. Thus, a class might read newspapers, magazines, or books, and then write about and discuss them. In some whole-language classes, beginning readers are taught to recognize whole words or even entire sentences and to use the context of what they are reading to guess at unfamiliar words.

In contrast, the **basic-skills-and-phonics approach** emphasizes that reading instruction should teach phonics and its basic rules for translating written symbols into sounds (Cunningham, 2005; Lane & Pullen, 2004). Early reading instruction should involve simplified materials. Only after they have learned the correspondence rules that relate spoken phonemes to the alphabet letters used to represent them should children be given complex reading materials, such as books and poems (Lane & Pullen, 2004; Smith, 2004).

whole-language approach An approach that stresses that reading instruction should parallel children's natural language learning. Reading materials should be whole and meaningful.

basic-skills-and-phonics approach An approach that emphasizes that reading instruction should teach phonics and its basic rules for translating written symbols into sounds.

Children most at risk for reading difficulties in the first grade are those who began school with less verbal skill, less phonological awareness, less letter knowledge, and less familiarity with the basic purposes and mechanisms of reading.

—Catherine Snow
Harvard University

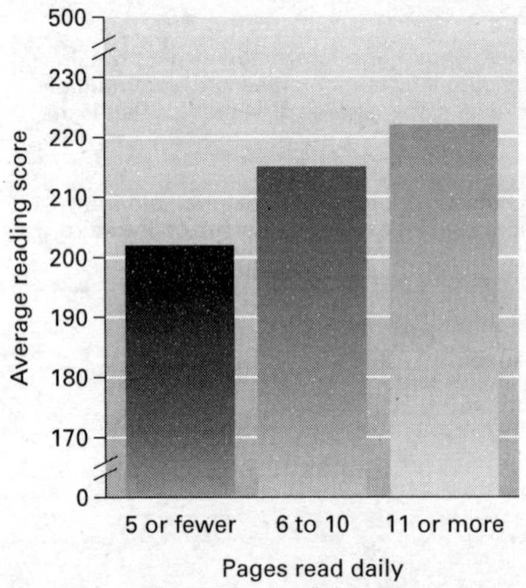

FIGURE 10.7 The Relation of Reading Achievement to Number of Pages Read Daily. In the recent analysis of reading in the fourth grade in the National Assessment of Educational Progress (2000), reading more pages daily in school and as part of homework assignments was related to higher scores on a reading test in which scores ranged from 0 to 500.

Which approach is better? Children can benefit from both approaches. Researchers have found strong evidence that the basic-skills-and-phonics approach should be used in teaching children to read but that students also benefit from the whole-language approach (Durkin, 2004; Fox & Hull, 2002; Silva & Martins, 2003; Temple & others, 2005; Tierney & Readence, 2005). These were the conclusions of the National Reading Panel (2000), which conducted a comprehensive review of research on reading.

Effective training for phonological awareness includes two main techniques:

- *Blending,* which involves listening to a series of separate spoken sounds and blending them, such as /g/ /o/ = go
- *Segmentation,* which consists of tapping out or counting out the sounds in a word, such as /g/ /o/ = go, which is two sounds

In addition, researchers have found that the best training for phonological awareness has three characteristics: the phonological training is integrated with reading and writing, is simple, and is conducted in small groups rather than with a whole class (Stahl, 2002).

Other conclusions reached by the National Reading Panel (2000) suggest that children benefit from *guided oral* reading—that is, from reading aloud with guidance and feedback. Learning strategies for reading comprehension—such as monitoring one's own reading progress and summarizing—also helps children (Pressley, 2003; Pressley & Hilden, 2006).

Reading, like other important skills, takes time and effort (Graves, Juel, & Graves, 2004). In a national assessment, children in the fourth grade had higher scores on a national reading test when they read 11 or more pages daily for school and homework (National Assessment of Educational Progress, 2000) (see figure 10.7). Teachers who required students to read a great deal on a daily basis had students who were more proficient at reading than teachers who required little reading by their students.

Writing Children begin scribbling when they are around 2 to 3 years of age. Their motor skills usually develop enough for them to begin printing letters during early childhood. Most 4-year-olds can print their first name. Five-year-olds can reproduce letters and copy several short words. They gradually learn to distinguish the distinctive characteristics of letters, such as whether the lines are curved or straight, open or closed.

Errors are common when children begin writing. Through the early elementary grades, many children continue to reverse letters such as *b* and *d* and *p* and *q* (Temple & others, 1993). At this age, if other aspects of the child's development are normal, letter reversals do not predict literacy problems. Also, as they begin to write, children often invent spellings. Usually they base these spellings on the sounds of words they hear (Spandel, 2004).

Parents and teachers should encourage children's early writing and not be overly concerned about the formation of letters or spelling (McGee & Richgels, 2004; Wasik, 2004). I once had a conference with my youngest daughter's first-grade teacher when she brought home papers with her printing all marked up and sad faces drawn on the paper. Fortunately, the teacher agreed to reduce her criticism of Jennifer's print skills. Printing errors are a natural part of the child's growth. Corrections of spelling and printing should be selective and made in positive ways that do not discourage the child's writing and spontaneity.

Like becoming a good reader, becoming a good writer takes many years and lots of practice. Children should be given many writing opportunities (McGee & Richgels, 2004). As their language and cognitive skills improve with good instruction, so will their writing skills (Spandel, 2004). For example, developing a more sophisticated understanding of syntax and grammar serves as an underpinning for better writing. So do such cognitive skills as organization and logical reasoning.

Through the course of the school years, students develop increasingly sophisticated methods of organizing their ideas. In early elementary school, they narrate and describe or write short poems. In late elementary and middle school, they can combine narration with reflection and analysis in projects such as book reports. Effective writing instruction provides guidance about planning, drafting, and revising, not only in elementary school but through secondary school and college as well (Graham, 1997; Pressley, 2003).

Anna Mudd is the 6-year-old author of "The Devl and the Babe Goste." Anna has been writing stories for at least two years. Her story includes poetic images, sophisticated syntax, and vocabulary that reflect advances in language development.

Bilingualism

Throughout the world many children speak more than one language. *Bilingualism*—the ability to speak two languages—has a positive effect on children's cognitive development. Children who are fluent in two languages perform better than their single-language counterparts on tests of control of attention, concept formation, analytical reasoning, cognitive flexibility, and cognitive complexity (Bialystok, 1999, 2001). They also are more conscious of the structure of spoken and written language and better at noticing errors of grammar and meaning, skills that benefit their reading ability (Bialystok, 1997).

Learning a Second Language Students in the United States are far behind their counterparts in many developed countries in learning a second language. For example, in Russia, schools have 10 grades, called *forms,* which roughly correspond to the 12 grades in American schools. Children begin school at age 7 in Russia and begin learning English in the third form. Because of this emphasis on teaching English, most Russian citizens under the age of 40 today are able to speak at least some English.

Learning a second language is more readily accomplished by children than by adolescents or adults. Adults make faster initial progress, but their eventual success in the second language is not as great as children's. For example, in one study, Chinese and Korean adults who immigrated to the United States at different ages were given a test of grammatical knowledge (Johnson & Newport, 1991). Those who began learning English when they were 3 to 7 years old scored as well as native speakers on the test, but those who arrived in the United States (and started learning English) in later childhood or adolescence had lower test scores (see figure 10.8). Children's ability to pronounce a second language with the correct accent also decreases with age, with an especially sharp drop occurring after the age of about 10 to 12 (Asher & Garcia, 1969).

In sum, researchers have found that early exposure to two languages is best—not only for learning a second language but also for ensuring the least damage to knowledge of a non-English language spoken in the home (Petitto, Kovelman, & Harasymowycz, 2003).

Bilingual Education A current controversy related to bilingualism involves the millions of U.S. children who come from homes in which English is not the primary language (Adamson, 2004). What is the best way to teach these children?

For the last two decades, the preferred strategy has been *bilingual education,* which teaches academic subjects to immigrant children in their native language while slowly teaching English (Garcia & Willis, 2001; Ovando, Combs, & Collier, 2006; Peregoy & Boyle, 2005). Advocates of bilingual education programs argue that if children who do not know English are taught only in English, they will fall behind in academic subjects. How, they ask, can 7-year-olds learn arithmetic or history taught only in English when they do not speak the language? Critics of bilingual programs come in two main types: some argue that the programs are counterproductive; others contend that existing programs are too brief.

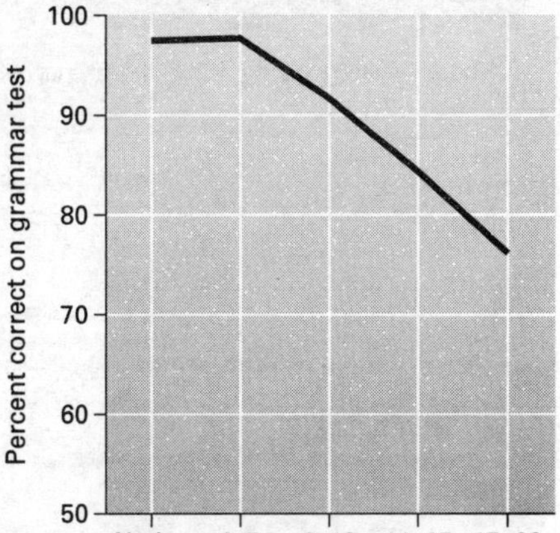

FIGURE 10.8 Grammar Proficiency and Age at Arrival in the United States. In one study, 10 years after arriving in the United States, individuals from China and Korea took a grammar test (Johnson & Newport, 1991). People who arrived before the age of 8 had a better grasp of grammar than those who arrived later.

Critics who oppose bilingual education argue that as a result of these programs, the children of immigrants are not learning English, which puts them at a permanent disadvantage in U.S. society. Some states have eliminated their bilingual education programs. Some states have gone further, passing laws that declare English to be their official language and eliminating the obligation for schools to teach minority children in languages other than English.

What have researchers found regarding outcomes of bilingual education programs? The results generally support bilingual education in that (1) children have difficulty learning a subject when it is taught in a language they do not understand, and (2) when both languages are integrated in the classroom, children learn the second language more readily and participate more actively (Hakuta, 2000, 2001; Pérez, 2004; Pérez & others, 2004; Soltero, 2004).

Some critics of current programs argue that too often it is believed that immigrant children need only one year of bilingual education. However, researchers have found that in general it takes immigrant children approximately three to five years to develop speaking proficiency and seven years to develop reading proficiency in English (Hakuta, Butler, & Witt, 2000). Also, it is important to recognize that immigrant children of course vary in their ability to learn English (Diaz-Rico, 2004; Haley & Austin, 2004; Herrera & Murray, 2005; Lessow-Hurley, 2005). Children who come from lower socioeconomic backgrounds have more difficulty than those from higher socioeconomic backgrounds (Hakuta, 2001; Rivera & Collum, 2006; Snow & Yang, 2006). Thus, especially for immigrant children from low socioeconomic backgrounds, more years of bilingual education may be needed than they currently are receiving. To read about the work of a bilingual education teacher, see the Careers in Child Development insert.

CAREERS in CHILD DEVELOPMENT

Salvador Tamayo
Bilingual Education Teacher

Salvador Tamayo teaches bilingual education in the fifth grade at Turner Elementary School in West Chicago. He recently was given a National Educator Award by the Milken Family Foundation for his work in bilingual education. Salvador especially is adept at integrating technology into his bilingual education classes. He and his students have created several award-winning websites about the West Chicago City Museum, the local Latino community, and the history of West Chicago. His students also developed an "I Want to Be an American Citizen" website to assist family and community members in preparing for the U.S. Citizenship Test. Salvador also teaches a bilingual education class at Wheaton College.

Salvador Tamayo working with bilingual education students.

Adolescence

Language development during adolescence includes increased sophistication in the use of words (Fischer & Lazerson, 1984). As they develop abstract thinking, adolescents become much better than children at analyzing the function a word plays in a sentence.

Adolescents also develop more subtle abilities with words. They make strides in understanding **metaphor,** which is an implied comparison between unlike things. For example, individuals "draw a line in the sand" to indicate a nonnegotiable position; a political campaign is said to be a marathon, not a sprint. And adolescents become better able to understand and to use **satire,** which is the use of irony, derision, or wit to expose folly or wickedness. Caricatures are an example of satire. More advanced logical thinking also allows adolescents, from about 15 to 20 years of age, to understand complex literary works.

Most adolescents are also much better writers than children are. They are better at organizing ideas before they write, at distinguishing between general and specific points as they write, at stringing together sentences that make sense, and at organizing their writing into an introduction, body, and concluding remarks.

metaphor An implied comparison between two unlike things.

satire The use of irony, derision, or wit to expose folly or wickedness.

Everyday speech changes during adolescence, "and part of being a successful teenager is being able to talk like one" (Berko Gleason, 2005, p. 9). Young adolescents often speak a dialect with their peers that is characterized by jargon and slang (Cave, 2002). A **dialect** is a variety of language that is distinguished by its vocabulary, grammar, or pronunciation. Nicknames that are satirical and derisive ("stilt," "refrigerator," "spaz") are part of the dialect of many young adolescents. They might use such labels to show that they belong to the group and to reduce the seriousness of a situation (Cave, 2002).

dialect A variety of language that is distinguished by its vocabulary, grammar, or pronuniciation.

language acquisition device (LAD) Chomsky's term that describes a biological endowment that enables the child to detect the features and rules of language, including phonology, syntax, and semantics.

Review and Reflect • LEARNING GOAL 2

2 Describe how language develops

Review
- What are some key milestones of language development during infancy?
- How do language skills change during early childhood?
- How does language develop in middle and late childhood?
- How does language develop in adolescence?

Reflect
- Should children in the United States be required to learn more than one language?

3 BIOLOGICAL AND ENVIRONMENTAL INFLUENCES

Biological Influences | Environmental Influences | An Interactionist View of Language

We have described how language develops, but we have not examined what makes this amazing development possible. Everyone who uses language in some way "knows" its rules and has the ability to create an infinite number of words and sentences. Where does this knowledge come from? Is it the product of biology? Is language learned and influenced by experiences?

Biological Influences

Some language scholars view the remarkable similarities in how children acquire language all over the world, despite the vast variation in language input they receive, as strong evidence that language has a biological basis. What role does biology play in the child's acquisition of language?

Language Acquisition Device Decades before the idea was popular, linguist Noam Chomsky (1957) argued that humans are biologically prewired to learn language at a certain time and in a certain way. He said that children are born into the world with a **language acquisition device (LAD),** a biological endowment that enables the child to detect the features and rules of language, including phonology, syntax, and semantics. Children are prepared by nature with the ability to detect the sounds of language, for example, and to detect and follow rules such as how to form plurals and ask questions.

Chomsky's LAD is a theoretical construct, not a physical part of the brain. Is there evidence for the existence of a LAD? Supporters of the LAD concept cite the uniformity of language milestones across languages and cultures, evidence that

MIT linguist Noam Chomsky. *What is Chomsky's view of language?*

In the wild, chimps communicate through calls, gestures, and expressions, which evolutionary psychologists believe might be the roots of true language.

children create language even in the absence of well-formed input, and biological substrates of language.

Biological Requirements for Language The ability to speak and understand language requires a certain vocal apparatus as well as a nervous system with certain capabilities. How did these biological foundations for language evolve? The nervous system and vocal apparatus of humanity's predecessors changed over hundreds of thousands or millions of years. Once equipped with these physical requirements for speaking, *Homo sapiens* went beyond grunting and shrieking to develop speech. Although estimates vary, many experts believe that humans acquired language about 100,000 years ago. In evolutionary time, then, language is a very recent acquisition. It clearly gave humans an enormous edge over other animals and increased the chances of human survival (Lachlan & Feldman, 2003; Pinker, 1994).

There is evidence that particular regions of the brain are predisposed to be used for language (Demonet, Thierry, & Cardebat, 2005; Dick & others, 2004). This evidence came to light when studies of brain-damaged individuals revealed two regions involved in language.

In 1861, a patient of Paul Broca, a French surgeon and anthropologist, received an injury to the left side of his brain. The patient became known as Tan because that was the only word he could speak after his brain injury. Tan suffered from **aphasia,** a loss or impairment of language ability caused by brain damage. Tan died several days after Broca evaluated him, and an autopsy revealed the location of the injury. Today, we refer to the part of the brain in which Broca's patient was injured as **Broca's area,** an area of the left frontal lobe of the brain that directs the muscle movements involved in speech production (see figure 10.9).

aphasia A loss or impairment of language ability caused by brain damage.

Broca's area An area of the brain's left frontal lobe that directs the muscle movements involved in speech production.

Wernicke's area An area of the brain's left hemisphere that is involved in language comprehension.

Another place in the brain where an injury can seriously impair language is **Wernicke's area,** a region of the brain's left hemisphere involved in language comprehension (see figure 10.9). Individuals with damage to Wernicke's area often produce fluent but incomprehensible speech and they have difficulty comprehending words (Kellinghaus & Luders, 2004).

Note that both Broca's area and Wernicke's area are in the brain's left hemisphere. Evidence suggests that language processing primarily occurs in the left hemisphere (Gaillard & others, 2004; Gazzaniga, Ivry, & Mangun, 2002; Nagano & Blumstein, 2004). But as discussed in chapter 6, keep in mind that in most activities an interplay occurs between the brain's two hemispheres (Grodzinsky, 2001; Nocentini & others, 2001; Wassenaar & Hagoort, 2005). For example, in reading, most people rely on activity in areas of the left hemisphere for comprehending syntax, but most people rely on activity in the right hemisphere to understand intonation and emotion.

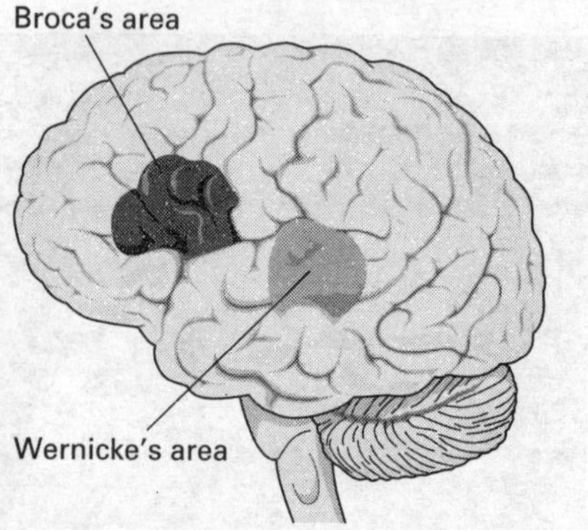

FIGURE 10.9 Broca's Area and Wernicke's Area. Broca's area is located in the frontal lobe of the brain's left hemisphere, and it is involved in the control of speech. Individuals with damage to Broca's area have problems saying words correctly. Also shown is Wernicke's area, a portion of the left hemisphere's temporal lobe that is involved in understanding language. Individuals with damage to this area cannot comprehend words; that is, they hear the words but don't know what they mean.

Is There a Critical Period for Learning Language? Most babies learn a language by a certain age if they are to learn to speak at all. Recall from chapter 2 that a *critical period* is a fixed time period in which certain experiences can have a long-lasting effect on development. It is a time of readiness for learning, after which learning is difficult or impossible. For example, baby white-crowned sparrows learn their song quite well if they are exposed to it during a specific time as a chick. After this time, they can never develop a fully formed song pattern; thus, for these sparrows there seems to be a critical period for learning their song.

Whether the notion of a critical period can be extended to human learning is much less certain. Almost all children learn one or more languages during their early years, so it is difficult to determine whether there is a critical period for language development (Obler, 1993). In the 1960s, Eric Lenneberg (1967) proposed that language depends on maturation and that there is a critical period between about 18 months and puberty during which a first language must be acquired. Lenneberg especially thought that the preschool years were an important time frame because this is when language develops rapidly and with ease.

Are the preschool years a critical period for language acquisition? Evidence for this notion comes from studies of brain development in young children, and from the amount of language learned by preschool children. However, other evidence suggests that we do not have a critical period for language learning. Although much language learning takes place during the preschool years, learning continues well into the later school years and adulthood (Hakuta, Bialystok, & Wiley, 2003). In other words, young children's proficiency in language does not seem to involve a biologically critical period that older children and adults have passed.

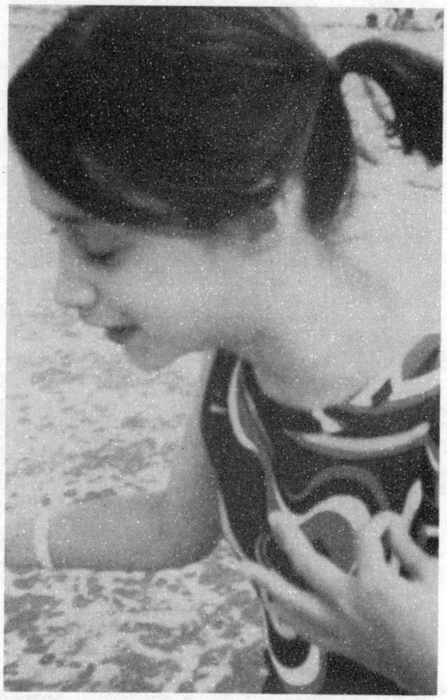

What were Genie's (shown above) *experiences like? What implications do they have for language acquisition?*

Lessons from Genie Does the story of Genie, the modern-day "wild child" described earlier in the chapter, support the idea of a critical period in language development? In 1970, a California social worker made a routine visit to the home of a partially blind woman who had applied for public assistance. The social worker discovered that the woman and her husband had kept their 13-year-old daughter, Genie, locked away in almost total isolation during her childhood. Genie could not speak or stand erect. She had spent every day bound naked to a child's potty seat. She could move only her hands and feet. At night she was placed in a kind of strait-jacket and caged in a crib with wire mesh sides and a cover. Whenever Genie made a noise, her father beat her. He never communicated with her in words; he growled and barked at her instead (Rymer, 1992).

After she was rescued from her parents, Genie spent a number of years in extensive rehabilitation programs, including speech and physical therapy (Curtiss, 1977). She eventually learned to walk, although with a jerky motion, and to use the toilet. Genie also learned to recognize many words and to speak in rudimentary sentences. Eventually, she was able to string together two-word combinations, such as "Big teeth," "Little marble," and "Two hand," then three-word combinations such as "Small two cup." As far as we know, unlike normal children, Genie did not learn to ask questions and did not develop a language system that allowed her to understand English grammar. Four years after she began stringing words together, Genie's speech still sounded like a garbled telegram. As an adult, she speaks in short, mangled sentences, such as "Father hit leg," "Big wood," and "Genie hurt."

www.mhhe.com/santrockcd11

Brain & Language Development
Critical Period Hypothesis in Language
Genie

Children like Genie, who are abandoned, abused, and not exposed to language for many years, rarely speak normally. Some language experts have argued that cases such as Genie support the existence of a critical period for language development, but other issues cloud these cases. Note that these children also suffer possible neurological deficits and severe emotional trauma.

Environmental Influences

As we said earlier, some language scholars view the similarities in children's language acquisition all over the world as strong evidence that language has a biological foundation. However, other language experts, argue that experiences of the child, the particular language to be learned, and the context in which learning takes place can strongly influence language acquisition (Marchman, 2003).

The Behavioral View Behaviorists argued that language represents chains of responses acquired through reinforcement (Skinner, 1957). A baby happens to babble "Ma-ma"; Mama rewards the baby with hugs and smiles; the baby says "Mama" more and more. Bit by bit, the baby's language is built up. According to behaviorists, language is a complex learned skill, much like playing the piano or dancing. This view of language has several problems.

First, the evidence indicates that children learn the syntax of their native language even if they are not reinforced for doing so. Social psychologist Roger Brown (1973) spent long hours observing parents and their young children. He found that parents did not pay attention to the grammatical form of their children's utterances.

They were just as likely to reinforce the ungrammatical utterances of the child as the grammatical ones.

Second, the behavioral view fails to explain the extensive orderliness of language. Because each child has a unique history of reinforcement, the behavioral view predicts that vast individual differences should appear in children's speech development. When children learn a certain aspect of a language, according to the behaviorist view, should depend on whether their parents or someone else has rewarded or punished them for something they have said. But as we have seen, a compelling fact about language is its orderly development. For example, all toddlers produce one-word utterances before two-word utterances.

The behavioral view is no longer considered a viable explanation of how children acquire language. But a great deal of research describes ways in which children's environmental experiences influence their language skills.

Interaction with People Language is not learned in a social vacuum. Most children are bathed in language from a very early age. The Wild Boy of Aveyron did not learn to communicate effectively after living in social isolation for years. Genie's language is rudimentary, even after years of extensive training. The support and involvement of caregivers and teachers greatly facilitate a child's language learning (Berko Gleason, 2005; Snow & Yang, 2006; Tomasello, 2006).

In particular, researchers have found that the quantity of talk that parents direct to their children is linked with the child's vocabulary growth and that the quantity of talk is also linked to the socioeconomic status of the family. To read about these links, see the Research in Child Development interlude that follows.

Research in Child Development

Family Environment and Young Children's Language Development

What characteristics of a family make a difference to a child's language development? Its socioeconomic status has been linked with how much parents talk to their children and with young children's vocabulary. In a study mentioned in chapter 9, Betty Hart and Todd Risley (1995) observed the language environments of children whose parents were professionals and children whose parents were on welfare. Compared with the professional parents, the welfare parents talked much less to their young children, talked less about past events, and provided less elaboration. All of the children learned to talk and acquired all of the forms of English. However, as indicated in figure 10.10 the children of the professional parents had a much larger vocabulary at 36 months of age than the children of the welfare parents.

Janellen Huttenlocher has linked the mother's behavior with characteristics of children's language in a series of studies. In one study, Huttenlocher and her colleagues (1991) observed mothers' speech when interacting with their infants. As indicated in figure 10.11 infants whose mothers spoke more often to them had markedly higher vocabularies. By the second birthday, vocabulary differences were substantial.

In another study, extensive conversations between 22 toddlers and their mothers were taped during the children's typical daily activities (Huttenlocher, Levine, & Vevea, 1998). Tapings were carried out every two to four months when the children were 16 to 26 months of age. The researchers found a remarkable link between the size of a child's vocabulary and the talkativeness of his or her mother. The mothers varied as much as tenfold in how much they talked. The toddler of the most talkative mother had a vocabulary more than four times the size of the vocabulary of the child with the quietest mother. This link might be due at least partly to genetics. However, Huttenlocher believes that is not the case, because the mothers did

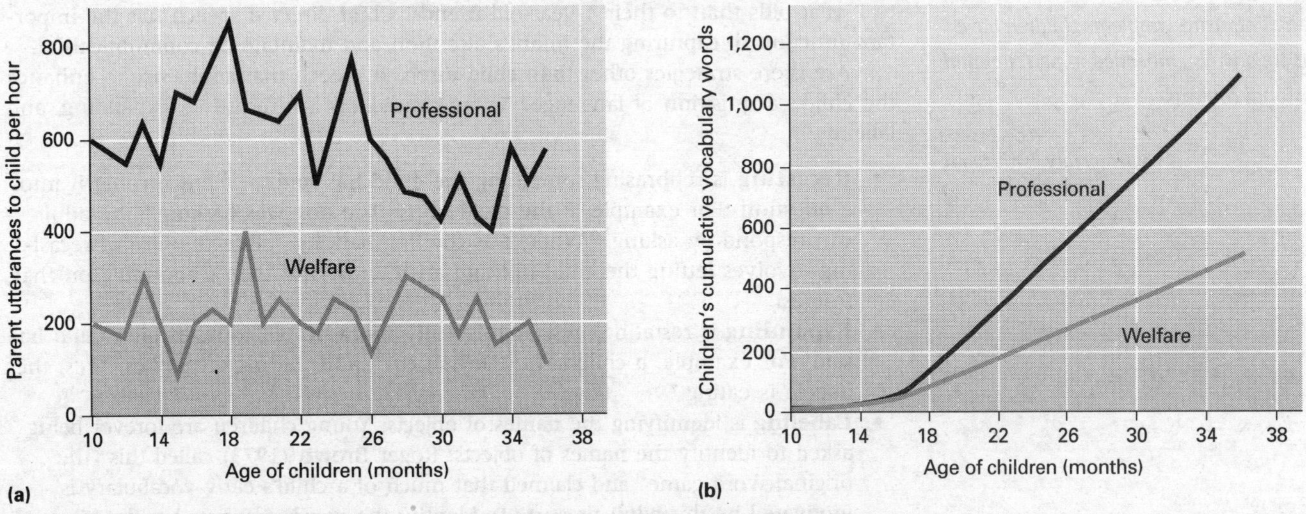

FIGURE 10.10 Language Input in Professional and Welfare Families and Young Children's Vocabulary Development. *(a)* Parents from professional families talked with their young children more than parents from welfare families. *(b)* Children from professional families developed vocabularies that were twice as large as those from welfare families. Thus, by the time children go to preschool, they already have experienced considerable differences in language input in their families and developed different levels of vocabulary that are linked to the socioeconomic context in which they have lived.

not vary much in their verbal IQs. Also, the children clearly were picking up what their mothers were saying, because the words each child used most often mirrored those favored by the mother.

Huttenlocher has also linked the language environment in the home with aspects of the child's language beyond vocabulary. In one study, home language environment was linked to the child's syntax (Huttenlocher & Cymerman, 1999). The speech of 34 parents and their 4-year-old children was taped to determine the proportion of complex, multiclause sentences (such as "I am going to go to the store because we need to get some food") versus that of simple, single-clause ones (such as "Go to your room"). A significant relation was found between the proportion of complex sentences spoken by the parents and the proportion of such sentences spoken by the children (both at home and at school). Such research demonstrates the important effect that early speech input can have on the development of a child's language skills.

What about reading to the child, a practice long advocated by many child development experts? According to a national survey of America's kindergarten class of 1998–1999, parents who read to their kindergarten children three or more times a week had children with better language skills than parents who read to their children less than three times a week (National Center for Education Statistics, 2000).

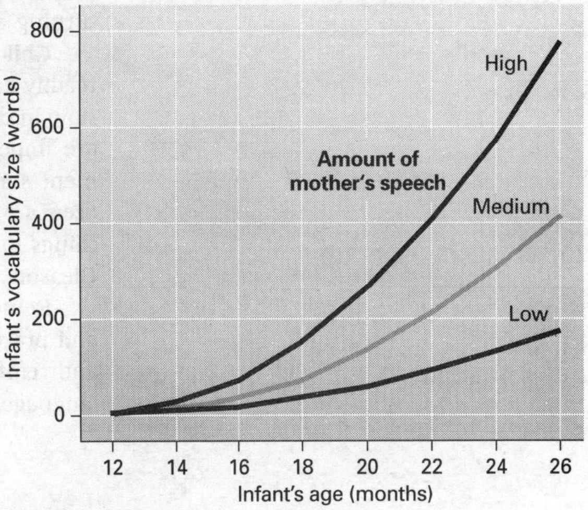

FIGURE 10.11 Amount of Maternal Speech and Infant Vocabulary. The amount of the mother's speech consisted of all utterances directed at the infant.

One intriguing component of the young child's linguistic environment is **child-directed speech,** language spoken in a higher pitch than normal with simple words and sentences. It is hard to use child-directed speech when not in the presence of a baby. As soon as you start talking to a baby, though, you shift into child-directed speech. Much of this is automatic and something most parents are not aware they are doing. Older children also modify their speech when talking to babies and younger children who are learning language. Even 4-year-olds speak in simpler ways

child-directed speech Language spoken in a higher pitch than normal with simple words and sentences.

The linguistics problems children have to solve are always embedded in personal and interpersonal contexts.

—Lois Bloom
Contemporary Psychologist, Columbia University

to 2-year-olds than to their 4-year-old friends. Child-directed speech has the important function of capturing the infant's attention and maintaining communication.

Are there strategies other than child-directed speech that adults use to enhance the child's acquisition of language? Three candidates are recasting, expanding, and labeling:

- **Recasting** is rephrasing something the child has said, perhaps turning it into a question. For example, if the child says, "The dog was barking," the adult can respond by asking, "When was the dog barking?" Effective use of recasting involves letting the child indicate an interest and then elaborating on that interest.
- **Expanding** is restating, in a linguistically sophisticated form, what a child has said. For example, a child says, "Doggie eat," and the parent replies, "Yes, the doggie is eating."
- **Labeling** is identifying the names of objects. Young children are forever being asked to identify the names of objects. Roger Brown (1973) called this "the original word game" and claimed that much of a child's early vocabulary is motivated by this adult pressure to identify the words associated with objects.

Parents use these strategies naturally and in meaningful conversations. Parents do not (and should not) use any deliberate method to teach their children to talk, even for children who are slow in learning language. Children usually benefit when parents guide their children's discovery of language rather than overloading them with language; "following in order to lead" helps a child learn language. If children are not ready to take in some information, they are likely to tell you (perhaps by turning away). Thus, giving the child more information is not always better.

Children vary in their ability to acquire language, and this variation cannot be readily explained by differences in environmental input alone. For children who are slow in developing language skills, however, opportunities to talk and be talked with are important. Children whose parents provide them with a rich verbal environment show many positive benefits. Parents who pay attention to what their children are trying to say, expand their children's utterances, read to them, and label things in the environment are providing valuable, if unintentional, benefits (Berko Gleason, 2004).

Remember, though, that the encouragement of language development, not drill and practice, is the key. Language development is not a simple matter of imitation and reinforcement. To read further about ways that parents can facilitate children's language development, see the Caring for Children interlude.

Caring for Children

How Parents Can Facilitate Infants' and Toddlers' Language Development

In *Growing Up with Language,* linguist Naomi Baron (1992) provided ideas to help parents facilitate their child's language development. A summary of her ideas follows:

Infants

- *Be an active conversational partner.* Initiate conversation with the infant. If the infant is in a daylong child-care program, ensure that the baby receives adequate language stimulation from adults.
- *Talk as if the infant understands what you are saying.* Parents can generate self-fulfilling prophecies by addressing their young children as if they understand what is being said. The process may take four to five years, but children gradually rise to match the language model presented to them.

recasting Rephrasing a statement that a child has said, perhaps turning it into a question.

expanding Restating, in a linguistically sophisticated form, what a child has said.

labeling Identifying the names of objects.

- *Use a language style with which you feel comfortable.* Don't worry about how you sound to other adults when you talk with your child. Your affect, not your content, is more important when talking with an infant. Use whatever type of baby talk with which you feel comfortable.

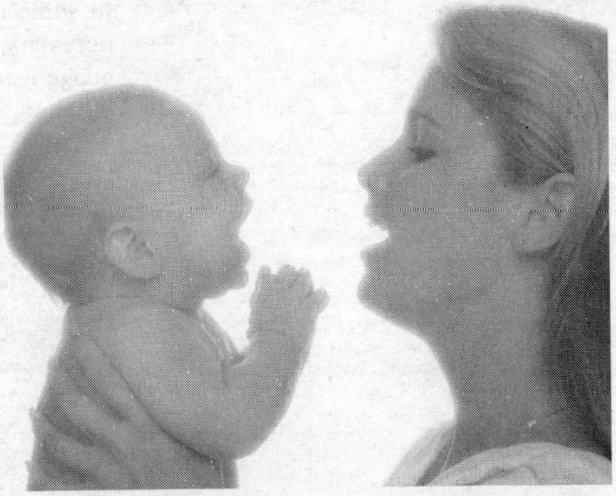

It is a good idea for parents to begin talking to their babies at the start. The best language teaching occurs when the talking is begun before the infant becomes capable of its first intelligible speech.

Toddlers

- *Continue to be an active conversational partner.* Engaging toddlers in conversation, even one-sided conversation, is the most important thing a parent can do to nourish a child linguistically.
- *Remember to listen.* Since toddlers' speech is often slow and laborious, parents are often tempted to supply words and thoughts for them. Be patient and let toddlers express themselves, no matter how painstaking the process is or how great a hurry you are in.
- *Use a language style with which you are comfortable, but consider ways of expanding your child's language abilities and horizons.* For example, using long sentences need not be problematic. Don't be afraid to use ungrammatical language to imitate the toddler's novel forms (such as "No eat"). Use rhymes. Ask questions that encourage answers other than "Yes" and "No." Actively repeat, expand, and recast the child's utterances. Introduce new topics. And use humor in your conversation.
- *Adjust to your child's idiosyncrasies instead of working against them.* Many toddlers have difficulty pronouncing words and making themselves understood. Whenever possible, make toddlers feel that they are being understood.
- *Avoid sexual stereotypes.* Don't let the toddler's sex determine your amount or style of conversation. Many American mothers are more linguistically supportive of girls than of boys, and many fathers talk less with their children than mothers do. Cognitively enriching initiatives from both mothers and fathers benefit both boys and girls.
- *Resist making normative comparisons.* Be aware of the ages at which your child reaches specific milestones (first word, first 50 words, first grammatical combination). However, be careful not to measure this development rigidly against children of neighbors or friends. Such social comparisons can bring about unnecessary anxiety.

An Interactionist View of Language

If language acquisition depended only on biology, then Genie and the Wild Boy of Aveyron (discussed earlier in the chapter) should have talked without difficulty. A child's experiences influence language acquisition. But we have seen that language does have strong biological foundations. No matter how much you converse with a dog, it won't learn to talk. In contrast, children are biologically prepared to learn language. Children all over the world acquire language milestones at about the same time and in about the same order. An interactionist view emphasizes that both biology and experience contribute to language development (Tomasello & Slobin, 2004).

American psychologist Jerome Bruner (1983, 1996) proposed that the sociocultural context is extremely important in understanding children's language development. His view has some similarities with the ideas of Lev Vygotsky that were described in chapter 7. Bruner stresses the role of parents and teachers in constructing what he called a *language acquisition support system (LASS).* The LASS resembles Vygotsky's concept of a zone of proximal development.

Today, most language acquisition researchers believe that children from a wide variety of cultural contexts acquire their native language without explicit teaching.

In some cases, they do so even without encouragement. Thus, very few aids are necessary for learning language. However, caregivers greatly facilitate a child's language learning (Snow & Yang, 2006; Tomasello, 2006).

Review and Reflect • LEARNING GOAL 3

3 Discuss the biological and environmental contributions to language

Review

- What are the biological foundations of language?
- What are the behavioral and environmental aspects of language?
- How does an interactionist view describe language?

Reflect

- How should parents respond to children's grammatical mistakes in conversation? Should parents allow the mistakes to continue and assume their young children will grow out of them, or should they closely monitor their children's grammar and correct mistakes whenever they hear them?

4 LANGUAGE AND COGNITION

As a teenager, Wendy Verougstraete felt that she was on the road to becoming a professional author. "You are looking at a professional author," she said. "My books will be filled with drama, action, and excitement. And everyone will want to read them. I am going to write books, page after page, stack after stack."

Overhearing her remarks, you might have been impressed not only by Wendy's optimism and determination, but also by her expressive verbal skills. In fact, at a young age Wendy showed a flair for writing and telling stories. Wendy has a rich vocabulary, creates lyrics for love songs, and enjoys telling stories. You probably would not be able to immediately guess that she has an IQ of only 49, and cannot tie her shoes, cross the street by herself, read or print words beyond the first-grade level, and do even simple arithmetic.

Wendy Verougstraete has Williams syndrome, a genetic birth disorder that was first described in 1961 and affects about 1 in 20,000 births. The most noticeable features of the syndrome include a unique combination of expressive verbal skills with an extremely low IQ and limited spatial and motor control (Bellugi & George, 2001; Mervis, 2003; Osborne & Pober, 2001; Vicari, Bellucci, & Carlesimo, 2001). Figure 10.12 shows the great disparity in the verbal and motor skills of one person with Williams syndrome. Individuals with Williams syndrome often have good musical skills and interpersonal skills (Doyle & others, 2004). The syndrome also includes a number of physical characteristics as well, such as heart defects and a pixielike facial appearance. Despite having excellent verbal skills and competent interpersonal skills, most individuals with Williams syndrome cannot live independent lives (American Academy of Pediatrics, 2001). For example, Wendy Verougstraete lives in a group home for adults who are mentally retarded.

The verbal abilities of individuals with Williams syndrome are very distinct from those shown by individuals with Down syndrome, a type

Drawing of an Elephant

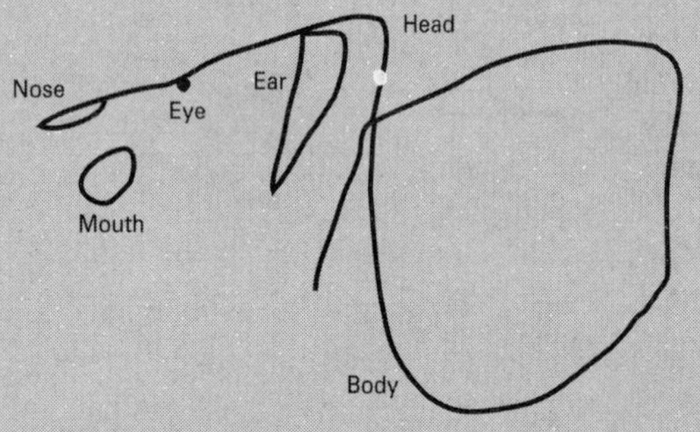

Verbal Description of an Elephant

And what an elephant is, it is one of the animals. And what the elephant does, it lives in the jungle. It can also live in the zoo. And what it has, it has long gray ears, fan ears, ears that can blow in the wind. It has a long trunk that can pick up grass, or pick up hay. . . . If they're in a bad mood it can be terrible. . . . If the elephant gets mad it could stomp; it could charge. Sometimes elephants can charge. They have big long tusks. They can damage a car. . . . It could be dangerous. When they're in a pinch, when they're in a bad mood it can be terrible. You don't want an elephant as a pet. You want a cat or a dog or a bird. . . .

FIGURE 10.12 **Disparity in the Verbal and Motor Skills of an Individual with Williams Syndrome**

of mental retardation that we discussed in chapters 3 and 9 (Bellugi & Wang, 1996). On vocabulary tests, children with Williams syndrome show a liking for unusual words. When asked to name as many animals as they can think of in one minute, Williams children come up with creatures like ibex, chihuahua, saber-toothed tiger, weasel, crane, and newt. Children with Down syndrome give simple examples like dog, cat, and mouse. When children with Williams syndrome tell stories, their voices come alive with drama and emotion, punctuating the dialogue with audience-attention grabbers like "Gadzooks" or "lo and behold!" By contrast, children with Down syndrome tell very simple stories with little emotion.

Aside from being an interesting genetic disorder, Williams syndrome offers insights into the normal development of thinking and language. In our society, verbal ability is generally associated with high intelligence. But Williams syndrome raises the possibility that thinking and language might not be so closely related. Williams disorder is due to a defective gene that seems to protect expressive verbal ability but not reading and many other cognitive skills (Schultz, Grelotti, & Pober, 2001). Thus, cases like Wendy Verougstraete's cast some doubt on the general categorization of intelligence as verbal ability and prompts the question, "What is the relation between thinking and language?"

There are essentially two basic and separate issues involved in exploring connections between language and cognition. The first is this: Is cognition necessary for language? Although some researchers have noted that certain aspects of language development typically follow mastery of selected cognitive skills in both normally developing children and children with mental retardation, it is not clear that language development depends on any specific aspect of cognitive abilities (Lenneberg, 1967). Some experts believe that it is more likely that language and cognitive development occur in parallel but dissociated fashions (Cromer, 1987). Thus, according to research and experts' judgments, cognition is not necessary for language development.

The second issue is this: Is language necessary for (or important to) cognition? This issue is addressed by studies of deaf children. On a variety of thinking and problem-solving skills, deaf children perform at the same level as children of the same age who have no hearing problems. Some of the deaf children in these studies do not even have command of written or sign language (Furth, 1973). Thus, based on studies of deaf children, language is not necessary for cognitive development.

There is, however, some evidence of related activity in the cognitive and language worlds of children (de Villiers & de Villiers, 1999; Goldin-Meadow, 2000; Oates & Grayson, 2004). Piaget's concept of object permanence has been the focus of some research that links cognitive and language development. Piaget believed that children come to learn about the world first and then they learn to label what they know. Infants may need a concept of object permanence before they start to use words for disappearance, such as *all gone* (Gopnik & Meltzoff, 1997).

In sum, thought likely can influence language, and language likely can influence thought. However, there is increasing evidence that language and thought are not part of a single, automated cognitive system, but rather evolved as separate modular, biologically prepared components of the mind.

Review and Reflect • LEARNING GOAL 4

4 Evaluate how language and cognition are linked

Review

- To what extent are language and cognition linked? Are they part of a single, automated cognitive system?

Reflect

- Do children always think in words? Explain.

REACH YOUR LEARNING GOALS

LANGUAGE DEVELOPMENT

1. WHAT IS LANGUAGE?
   - Defining Language
   - Language's Rule Systems
2. HOW LANGUAGE DEVELOPS
   - Infancy
   - Early Childhood
   - Middle and Late Childhood
   - Adolescence
3. BIOLOGICAL AND ENVIRONMENTAL INFLUENCES
   - Biological Influences
   - Environmental Influences
   - An Interactionist View of Language
4. LANGUAGE AND COGNITION

SUMMARY

1 Define language and describe its rule systems

- Language is a form of communication, whether spontaneous, written, or signed, that is based on a system of symbols. Language consists of all the words used by a community and the rules for varying and combining them. Infinite generativity is the ability to produce an endless number of meaningful sentences using a finite set of words and rules.
- Phonology is the sound system of the language, including the sounds that are used and how they may be combined. Morphology refers to the units of meaning involved in word formation. Syntax is the way words are combined to form acceptable phrases and sentences. Semantics involves the meaning of words and sentences. Pragmatics is the appropriate use of language in different contexts.

2 Describe how language develops

- Among the milestones in infant language development are crying (birth), cooing (1 to 2 months), babbling (6 months), making the transition from universal linguist to language-specific listener (6 to 12 months), using gestures (8 to 12 months), comprehension of words (8 to 12 months), first word spoken (13 months), vocabulary spurt (18 months), rapid expansion of understanding words (18 to 24 months), and two-word utterances (18 to 24 months).
- Advances in phonology, morphology, syntax, semantics, and pragmatics continue in early childhood. The transition to complex sentences begins at 2 or 3 years and continues through the elementary school years.
- In middle and late childhood, children become more analytical and logical in their approach to words and grammar. Chall's model proposes five stages in reading, ranging from birth/first grade to high school. Children make advances in metalinguistic awareness, which refers to knowledge about language. Current debate involving how to teach children to read focuses on the whole-language approach versus the basic-skills-and-phonics approach. Many experts recommend a balance of these two approaches. Children's writing emerges out of scribbling. Advances in children's language and cognitive development provide the underpinnings for improved writing. Bilingual education aims to teach academic subjects to immigrant children in their native languages while gradually adding English instruction. Researchers have found that bilingualism does not interfere with performance in either language. Success in learning a second language is greater in childhood than in adolescence.
- In adolescence, language changes include more effective use of words; improvements in the ability to understand metaphor and adult literary works, and improvements in writing.

3 Discuss the biological and environmental contributions to language

- Chomsky argues that children are born with the ability to detect basic features and rules of language. In other words, they are biologically prepared to learn language with a prewired language acquisition device (LAD). In evolution, language clearly gave humans an enormous edge over other animals and increased their chance of survival. A substantial portion of language processing occurs in the brain's left hemisphere, with Broca's area and Wernicke's area being important left-hemisphere locations. The idea that there is a critical period in language development is still controversial.
- The behavioral view—that children acquire language as a result of reinforcement—has not been supported. Adults help children acquire language through child-directed speech, recasting, expanding, and labeling. Environmental influences are demonstrated by differences in the language development of children as a consequence of being exposed to different language environments in the home. Parents should talk extensively with an infant, especially about what the baby is attending to.
- One interactionist view is that both Chomsky's LAD and Bruner's LASS are involved in language acquisition. An interactionist view emphasizes the contributions of both biology and experience in language.

4 Evaluate how language and cognition are linked

- Two basic and separate issues are these: (1) Is cognition necessary for language? (2) Is language necessary for cognition? At an extreme, the answer likely is no to these questions, but there is evidence of linkages between language and cognition. There is increasing evidence that language and thought are not part of a single, automated cognitive system, but rather evolved as separate, modular, biologically prepared components of the mind. The disorder of Williams syndrome supports this modular view.

KEY TERMS

language 303
infinite generativity 303
phonology 303
morphology 303
syntax 303
semantics 304
pragmatics 304
telegraphic speech 308
metalinguistic awareness 310
whole-language approach 311
basic-skills-and-phonics approach 311
metaphor 314
satire 314
dialect 315
language acquisition device (LAD) 315
aphasia 316
Broca's area 316
Wernicke's area 316
child-directed speech 319
recasting 320
expanding 320
labeling 320

KEY PEOPLE

Helen Keller 302
Patricia Kuhl 306
Jean Berko 309
Noam Chomsky 315
Paul Broca 316
Eric Lenneberg 316
Betty Hart and Todd Risley 318
Janellen Huttenlocher 318
Naomi Baron 320
Jerome Bruner 321

E-LEARNING TOOLS

To help you master the material in this chapter, visit the Online Learning Center for *Child Development*, eleventh edition (**www.mhhe.com/santrockcd11**), where you'll find these additional resources:

Taking It to the Net

1. Clarissa wants to be a speech therapist. In her child development class, she learned that Vygotsky believed that linguistic and cognitive development go hand in hand after a certain age. How can she learn more about his theory, so that it might give her some helpful insight in understanding children's language problems?
2. Todd is working in a day-care center after school. He notices that there is a wide range in the children's use of language, even within age groups. Are there any guidelines that Todd can obtain that could help determine if a child is delayed in language development?
3. Jared is concerned because his 7-year-old son, Damion, does not like to read. His second-grade teacher says he is about average for his age, but she has to prod him to do his reading assignments at school. What can Jared do to help Damion become a better reader?

Nursing, Parenting, and Teaching Exercises

Build your decision-making skills by trying your hand at the scenarios on the Online Learning Center.

Video Clips

The Online Learning Center includes the following videos for this chapter:

- Crying at 10 Weeks
  Here a 10-week-old baby boy crys and waves his arms and legs around as his mother attempts to soothe him.
- Babbling at 7.5 Months
  In this clip we see a tired infant babbling to her mother. The mother tries to engage her in play but the infant is uninterested.
- Language Ability at Age 2
  While engaging in a pretend tea party with her mother, 2-year-old Abby demonstrates her advancing language ability.

Section 4

SOCIOEMOTIONAL DEVELOPMENT

I am what I hope and give.

—Erik Erikson
European-Born American Psychotherapist, 20th Century

As children develop, they need the meeting eyes of love. They split the universe into two halves: "me" and "not me." They juggle the need to curb their own will with becoming what they can will freely. They also want to fly but discover that first they have to learn to stand and walk and climb and dance. As they become adolescents, they try on one face after another, looking for a face of their own. In Section 4 you will read four chapters: "Emotional Development" (chapter 11), "The Self and Identity" (chapter 12), "Gender" (chapter 13), and "Moral Development" (chapter 14).

Chapter 11 EMOTIONAL DEVELOPMENT

Blossoms are scattered by the wind
And the wind cares nothing, but
The Blossoms of the heart,
No wind can touch.

—YOUSHIDA KENKO
Buddhist Monk, 14th Century

CHAPTER OUTLINE

EXPLORING EMOTION

What Are Emotions?
A Functionalist View of Emotion
Regulation of Emotion
Emotional Competence

DEVELOPMENT OF EMOTION

Infancy
Early Childhood
Middle and Late Childhood
Adolescence

EMOTIONAL PROBLEMS, STRESS, AND COPING

Depression
Suicide
Stress and Coping

TEMPERAMENT

Describing and Classifying Temperament
Biological Foundations and Experience
Goodness of Fit and Parenting

ATTACHMENT

What Is Attachment?
Individual Differences in Attachment
Caregiving Styles and Attachment
Child Care

LEARNING GOALS

1 Discuss basic aspects of emotion

2 Describe the development of emotion

3 Summarize the nature of depression, suicide, stress, and coping

4 Characterize variations in temperament and their significance

5 Explain attachment and its development

The Story of Tom's Fathering

Many fathers are spending more time with their infants today than in the past.

Tom is a 1-year-old, and his father cares for him during the day. His mother works full-time at a job away from home, and his father is a writer who works at home. Tom's father is doing a great job of caring for him. He keeps Tom nearby while he is writing and spends lots of time talking to him and playing with him. They genuinely enjoy each other.

Tom's father looks to the future and imagines the Little League games Tom will play and the many other activities he can enjoy with Tom. His own father matched the stereotype of 1950s fathers, which portrayed men as emotionally distant, preoccupied with their jobs, and not involved in their children's lives. Remembering how little time his own father spent with him, Tom's father is dedicated to making sure that Tom has an involved, nurturing experience with his father.

When Tom's mother comes home in the evening, she spends considerable time with him. Tom shows a positive attachment to both his mother and his father. His parents have cooperated and have successfully juggled their careers and work schedules to provide 1-year-old Tom with excellent child care.

PREVIEW

For many years, emotion was neglected in the study of children's development. Today, emotion is increasingly important in conceptualizations of development. Even infants show different emotional styles, display varying temperaments, and begin to form emotional bonds with their caregivers. In this chapter, we will study the roles of temperament and attachment in development. But first we will examine emotion itself, exploring the functions of emotions in children's lives and the development of emotion from infancy through adolescence. We also will discuss emotional problems, stress, and coping.

1 EXPLORING EMOTIONS

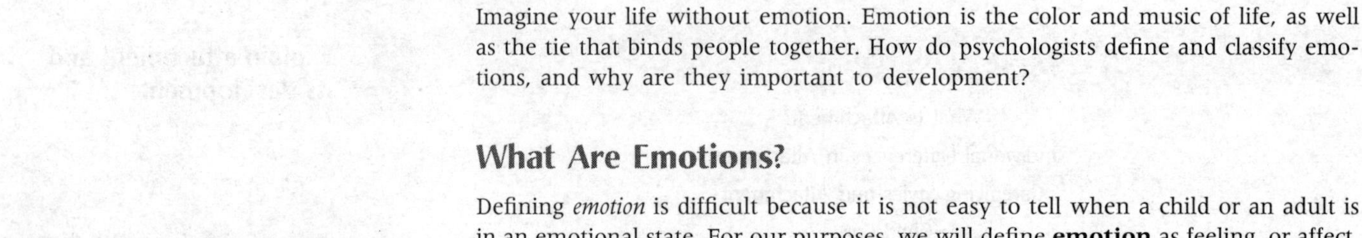

Imagine your life without emotion. Emotion is the color and music of life, as well as the tie that binds people together. How do psychologists define and classify emotions, and why are they important to development?

What Are Emotions?

emotion Feeling, or affect, that occurs when a person is in a state or interaction that is important to him or her. Emotion is characterized by behavior that reflects (expresses) the pleasantness or unpleasantness of the state he or she is in, or the transaction he or she is experiencing.

Defining *emotion* is difficult because it is not easy to tell when a child or an adult is in an emotional state. For our purposes, we will define **emotion** as feeling, or affect, that occurs when a person is in a state or an interaction that is important to him or her, especially to his or her well-being (Campos, 2004; Saarni & others, 2006). Emotion is characterized by behavior that reflects the pleasantness or unpleasantness of a person's state or current transactions. Emotions also can take more specific forms such as joy, fear, anger, and so on, depending on how a transaction affects the person. (For example, is the transaction a threat, a frustration, a relief, a surprise?) And emotions can vary in their intensity. For example, an infant may show intense fear or only mild fear in a particular situation.

When we think about emotions, a few dramatic feelings such as rage or glorious joy spring to mind. But emotions can be subtle as well, such as uneasiness in a new situation or the feeling a mother has when she holds her baby. Psychologists classify the broad range of emotions in many ways, but almost all classifications designate an emotion as either positive or negative. Positive emotions include enthusiasm, joy, and love. Negative emotions include anxiety, anger, guilt, and sadness.

Emotions are influenced by biological foundations and experience. In *The Expression of Emotions in Man and Animals*, Charles Darwin (1872/1965) stated that the facial expressions of humans are innate, not learned; that these expressions are the same in all cultures around the world; and that they evolved from the emotions of animals. Darwin compared human snarls of anger with the growls of dogs and the hisses of cats. Today, psychologists still believe that emotions, especially facial expressions of emotions, have a strong biological foundation (Goldsmith, 2002; Goldsmith & Davidson, 2004). For example, children who are blind from birth and have never observed the smile or frown on another person's face smile and frown in the same way that children with normal vision do. Researchers also have found that facial expressions of basic emotions such as happiness, surprise, anger, and fear are the same across cultures.

These biological factors, however, are only part of the story of emotion. For example, caregivers play a role in the infant's neurobiological regulation of emotions (Thompson, Easterbrooks, & Walker, 2003). By soothing the infant when the infant cries and shows distress, caregivers help infants to modulate their emotion and reduce the level of stress hormones (Gunnar, 2000; Gunnar & Davis, 2003).

To understand when, where, and how emotions are expressed, we need to examine cultural factors. The *display rules* for emotions are not universal (Triandis, 1994). For example, in cultures that are characterized by individuality—such as North America, Western Europe, and Australia—emotional displays tend to be long and intense. In contrast, people in Asian cultures tend to conceal their emotions when in the presence of others. But the rules for emotional expression also vary with the emotion involved. In Asian and other cultures that emphasize social connections, displays of emotions such as sympathy, respect, and shame are more common than in Western countries, but negative emotions that might disrupt communication are rarely displayed in these cultures.

In sum, biology has made human beings emotional creatures, but embeddedness in culture and relationships with others provides diversity in emotional experiences (Saarni, 1999, 2000). As we see next, this emphasis on the role of relationships in emotion is at the core of the functionalist view of emotion.

A Functionalist View of Emotion

The traditional analysis of emotions focused on what was going on inside the individual. Developmentalists today tend to view emotions as the result of individuals' attempts to adapt to the demands of specific contexts (Campos, 1994, 2001; Saarni & others, 2006; Thompson, 2006). Thus, a child's emotional responses cannot be separated from the situations in which they are evoked, which are often interpersonal contexts. In the functionalist view, emotions are *relational* rather than strictly internal, intrapsychic phenomena.

What contextual demands might emotions meet? Emotional expressions serve the important functions of signaling to others how one feels, regulating one's own behavior, and playing pivotal roles in social exchange. Consider some of the ways that emotions function in relationships. The beginnings of an emotional bond between parents and an infant are based on affectively toned interchanges, as when an infant cries and the caregiver sensitively responds. By the end of the first year, a mother's facial expression—either smiling or fearful—influences whether an infant will explore an unfamiliar environment. And when children hear their parents quarreling, they often react with distressed facial expressions and inhibited play (Cummings, 1987). Parents and children may also make each other laugh, creating a light mood to defuse conflict. And when parents put the child in a positive mood, the child is more likely to comply with a parent's directions.

In the functionalist view, emotions are linked with an individual's goals in a variety of ways. A child who overcomes an obstacle to attain a goal experiences happiness. A child who must give up an unattainable goal experiences sadness. And a child who faces difficult obstacles in pursuing a goal often experiences anger. The specific nature of the goal, however, can affect the emotional experience. For example, the avoidance of threat is linked with fear, the desire to atone is related to guilt, and the wish to avoid the scrutiny of others is associated with shame.

Infants' goals are not the same as adults', and neither are infants' emotions. An infant's emotional life develops with age. You might gauge a child's physical development through infancy and childhood by measuring the child's height and weight, but what are the indicators of emotional development? Two key concepts that point to important aspects of emotional development are emotional regulation and emotional competence.

Regulation of Emotion

It is normal for an infant to thrash and cry uncontrollably or for a toddler to throw an occasional tantrum, but you would worry if your parents showed emotion in these ways. The ability to control one's emotions is a key dimension of development (Denham & others, 2003; Rothbart & Bates, 2006; Thompson, 2006). *Emotional regulation* consists of effectively managing arousal to adapt and reach a goal. *Arousal* involves a state of alertness or activation, which can reach levels that are too high for effective functioning. Anger, for example, often requires regulation.

Among the developmental trends in regulating emotion during childhood are (Eisenberg, 1998, 2001):

- *External to internal resources.* Infants primarily rely on external resources, such as their parents, to regulate emotion. As children get older, they are more likely to engage in self-regulation of their emotion.
- *Cognitive strategies.* Cognitive strategies for regulating emotions, "such as thinking about situations in a positive light, cognitive avoidance, and shifting and focusing attention, increase with age" (Eisenberg, 1998, pp. 5–6).
- *Emotional arousal.* With greater maturity, children are able to control their emotional arousal (such as controlling angry outbursts).
- *Choosing and managing contexts and relationships.* As children get older, they are better at selecting and managing situations and relationships in ways that reduce negative emotions.
- *Coping with stress.* As children get older, they become more capable of developing strategies to cope with stress.

Of course, there are wide variations in children's ability to modulate their emotions. Indeed, a prominent feature of children and adolescents with problems is that they often have difficulty managing their emotions.

Parents can help children learn to regulate their emotions (Thompson, 2006). Depending on how they talk with their children about emotion, parents can be described as taking an *emotion-coaching* or an *emotion-dismissing* approach (Katz, 1999). *Emotion-coaching parents* monitor their children's emotions, view their children's negative emotions as opportunities for teaching, assist them in labeling emotions, and coach them in how to deal effectively with emotions. In contrast, *emotion-dismissing parents* view their role as to deny, ignore, or change negative emotions. When interacting with their children, emotion-coaching parents are less rejecting, use more scaffolding and praise, and are more nurturant than are emotion-dismissing parents (Gottman & DeClaire, 1997). Compared with the children of emotion-dismissing parents, the children of emotion-coaching parents are better at physiologically soothing themselves when they get upset, at regulating their negative affect, and at focusing their attention; they also have fewer behavior problems.

www.mhhe.com/santrockcd11

International Society for Research on Emotions

Emotional Competence

In chapter 9, we briefly described the concept of emotional intelligence. Here we will examine a closely related concept, emotional competence, that focuses on the adaptive nature of emotional experience. Carolyn Saarni (1999; Saarni & others, 2006) believes that becoming emotionally competent involves developing a number of skills in social contexts that include:

SKILL	EXAMPLE
• *Awareness of one's emotional states*	Being able to differentiate whether one feels sad or anxious
• *Detecting others' emotions*	Understanding when another person is sad rather than afraid
• *Using the vocabulary of emotion terms in socially and culturally appropriate ways*	Appropriately describing a social situation in one's culture when a person is feeling distress
• *Empathic and sympathetic sensitivity to others' emotional experiences*	Being sensitive to other people when they are feeling distressed
• *Recognizing that inner emotional states do not have to correspond to outer expressions*	Recognizing that one can feel very angry yet manage one's emotional expression so that it appears more neutral
• *Adaptively coping with negative emotions by using self-regulatory strategies that reduce the intensity or duration of such emotional states*	Reducing anger by walking away from an aversive situation and engaging in an activity that takes one's mind off of the aversive situation
• *Awareness that the expression of emotions plays a major role in the nature of relationships*	Knowing that expressing anger toward a friend on a regular basis is likely to harm the friendship
• *Viewing oneself overall as feeling the way one wants to feel*	An individual wants to feel that he or she can and is coping effectively with stress

As children acquire these skills in a variety of contexts, they are more likely to effectively manage their emotions, become resilient in the face of stressful circumstances, and develop positive relationships (Denham & others, 2003; Saarni & others, 2006).

Review and Reflect • LEARNING GOAL 1

1 Discuss basic aspects of emotion

Review
- How is emotion defined?
- What characterizes functionalism in emotion?
- What are some developmental changes in the regulation of emotion?
- What constitutes emotional competence?

Reflect
- Think back to your childhood and adolescent years. How effective were you in regulating your emotions? Give some examples. Has your ability to regulate your emotions changed as you have grown older? Explain.

2 DEVELOPMENT OF EMOTION

Infancy | Middle and Late Childhood | Early Childhood | Adolescence

First appearance	Emotion
Primary Emotions	
3 months	Joy Sadness Disgust
2 to 6 months	Anger
First 6 months	Surprise
6 to 8 months	Fear (peaks at 18 months)
Self-Conscious Emotions	
1½ to 2 years	Empathy Jealousy Embarrassment
2½ years	Pride Shame Guilt

FIGURE 11.1 The First Appearance of Different Emotions

Does an adolescent's emotional life differ from a child's? Does the young child's emotional life differ from an infant's? Does an infant even have an emotional life? In this section, we will sketch an overview of the changes in emotion from infancy through adolescence, looking not only at changes in emotional experience but also at the development of emotional competence.

Infancy

What are some early developmental changes in emotions? What functions do infants' cries serve? When do infants begin to smile?

Early Developmental Changes in Emotion

In research on early emotional development, the classification of emotions into two broad types is useful (Lewis, 2002) (see figure 11.1):

- **Primary emotions,** which appear in humans and other animals. The primary emotions include surprise, interest, joy, anger, sadness, fear, and disgust. They are present in the first six months of life.
- **Self-conscious emotions,** which require cognition, especially consciousness. The self-conscious emotions include empathy, jealousy, and embarrassment, which first appear at about 1½ years (after the emergence of consciousness), and pride, shame, and guilt, which first appear at about 2½ years of age. In developing this second set of self-conscious emotions (referred to as *self-conscious evaluative emotions*), children acquire and are able to use societal standards and rules to evaluate their behavior.

Figure 11.2 shows infants expressing a number of the emotions we have described.

Even when infants experience only the primary emotions, their emotional expressions help create their first relationships. The ability of infants to communicate emotions permits coordinated interactions with their caregivers and the beginning of an emotional bond between them. Not only do parents change their emotional expressions in response to infants' emotional expressions, but infants also modify their emotional expressions in response to their parents' emotional expressions. In other words, these interactions are mutually regulated. Because of this coordination, these interactions are described as *reciprocal* or *synchronous* when all is going well. Cries and smiles are two emotional expressions that infants display when interacting with parents, and they are babies' first forms of emotional communication.

Crying

Crying is the most important mechanism newborns have for communicating with their world. The first cry verifies that the baby's lungs have filled with air. Cries also may provide information about the baby's central nervous system.

Babies have at least three types of cries:

- **Basic cry:** A rhythmic pattern that usually consists of a cry, followed by a briefer silence, then a shorter whistle that is somewhat higher in pitch than the main cry, then another brief rest before the next cry. Some infancy experts believe that hunger is one of the conditions that incite the basic cry.
- **Anger cry:** A variation of the basic cry in which more excess air is forced through the vocal cords.

primary emotions Emotions that are present in humans and animals, including surprise, interest, joy, anger, sadness, fear, and disgust, that appear in the first six months of life.

self-conscious emotions Emotions that require cognition, especially consciousness; they include empathy, jealousy, and embarrassment, which first appear at about 1½ to 2 years and pride, shame, and guilt, which first appear at about 2½ years of age.

basic cry A rhythmic pattern usually consisting of a cry, a briefer silence, a shorter inspiratory whistle that is higher pitched than the main cry, and then a brief rest before the next cry.

anger cry A cry similar to the basic cry but with more excess air forced through the vocal cords (associated with exasperation or rage).

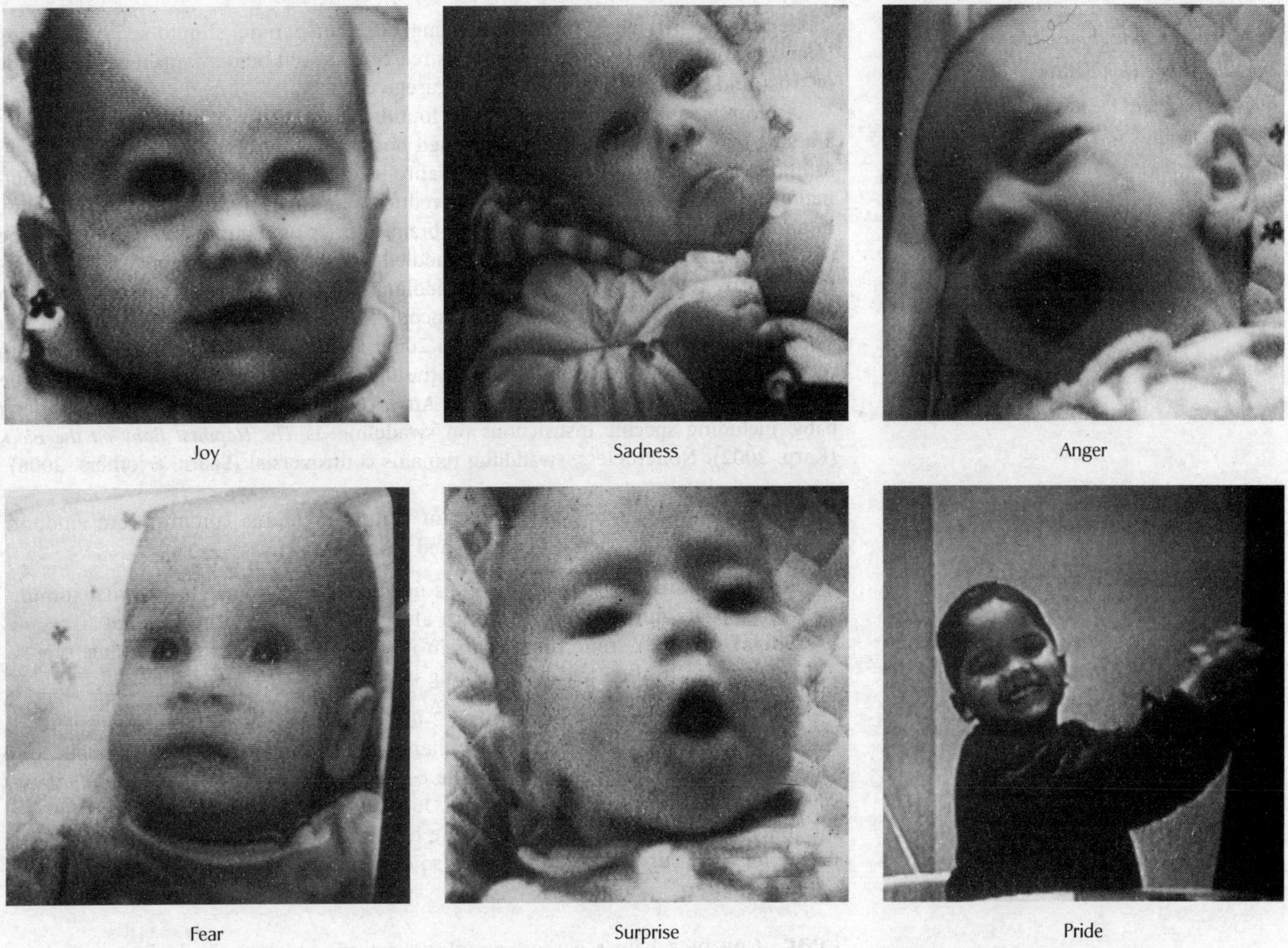

FIGURE 11.2 Expression of Different Emotions in Infants

- **Pain cry:** A sudden long, initial loud cry followed by breath holding; no preliminary moaning is present. The pain cry is stimulated by a high-intensity stimulus.

Most adults can determine whether an infant's cries signify anger or pain (Zeskind, Klein, & Marshall, 1992). Parents can distinguish the cries of their own baby better than those of another baby.

To soothe or not to soothe—should a crying baby be given attention and soothed, or does this spoil the infant? Many years ago, the behaviorist John Watson (1928) argued that parents spend too much time responding to infant crying. As a consequence, he said, parents reward crying and increase its incidence. More recently, behaviorist Jacob Gewirtz (1977) found that a caregiver's quick, soothing response to crying increased crying. In contrast, infancy experts Mary Ainsworth (1979) and John Bowlby (1989) stress that you can't respond too much to infant crying in the first year of life. They believe that a quick, comforting response to the infant's cries is an important ingredient in the development of a strong bond between the infant and caregiver. In one of Ainsworth's studies, infants whose mothers responded quickly when they cried at 3 months of age cried less later in the first year of life (Bell & Ainsworth, 1972).

Controversy still characterizes the question of whether or how parents should respond to an infant's cries (Alvarez, 2004; Hiscock & Jordan, 2004; Lewis & Ramsay, 1999). However, developmentalists increasingly argue that an infant cannot be

www.mhhe.com/santrockcd11

Exploring Infant Crying

pain cry A sudden appearance of loud crying without preliminary moaning and a long initial cry followed by an extended period of breath holding.

He who binds himself to joy
Does the winged life destroy;
But he who kisses the joy as it flies;
Lives in eternity's sun rise.

—William Blake
English Poet, 19th Century

spoiled in the first year of life, which suggests that parents should soothe a crying infant rather than be unresponsive. This reaction should help infants develop a sense of trust and secure attachment to the caregiver.

Researchers and pediatricians have found that some specific behaviors can calm a crying baby. One recent study examined how mothers responded when their 2- to 6-month-old infants were inoculated (Jahromi, Putnam, & Stifter, 2004). A combination of holding and rocking the baby reduced the intensity and duration of crying. In another recent study, newborns with brain injuries were randomly assigned to one of two conditions: they were either swaddled (wrapped in a blanket) or given massage therapy (Ohgi & others, 2004). Swaddling reduced the infants' crying more than massage therapy. Swaddling stops the uncontrolled arm and leg movements that can lead to frenzied crying (Huang & others, 2004; Karp, 2002). Pediatricians and nurses recommend tucking the baby tightly in the blanket so the blanket does not become loose and wrap around the baby's face. An excellent book on how to calm a crying baby, including specific instructions on swaddling, is *The Happiest Baby on the Block* (Karp, 2002). Nonetheless, swaddling remains controversial (Saarni & others, 2006).

Smiling Smiling is another important way that infants communicate emotion. Two types of smiling can be distinguished in infants:

- **Reflexive smile:** A smile that does not occur in response to external stimuli and appears during the first month after birth, usually during sleep.
- **Social smile:** A smile that occurs in response to an external stimulus, typically a face in the case of the young infant.

Social smiling does not occur until 2 to 3 months of age (Emde, Gaensbauer, & Harmon, 1976), although some researchers believe that infants grin in response to voices as early as 3 weeks of age (Sroufe & Waters, 1976). The power of the infant's smiles was captured by British theorist John Bowlby (1969): "Can we doubt that the more and better an infant smiles the better he is loved and cared for? It is fortunate for their survival that babies are so designed by nature that they beguile and enslave mothers."

Fear One of a baby's earliest emotions is fear, which typically first appears at about 6 months of age and peaks at about 18 months. The most frequent expression of an infant's fear involves **stranger anxiety,** in which an infant shows a fear and wariness of strangers. Stranger anxiety usually emerges gradually. It first appears at about 6 months of age in the form of wary reactions. By age 9 months, the fear of strangers is often more intense, and it continues to escalate through the infant's first birthday (Emde, Gaensbauer, & Harmon, 1976).

Not all infants show distress when they encounter a stranger. Besides individual variations, whether an infant shows stranger anxiety also depends on the social context and the characteristics of the stranger.

Infants show less stranger anxiety when they are in familiar settings. For example, in one study, 10-month-olds showed little stranger anxiety when they met a stranger in their own home but much greater fear when they encountered a stranger in a research laboratory (Sroufe, Waters, & Matas, 1974). Also, infants show less stranger anxiety when they are sitting on their mothers' laps than when placed in an infant seat several feet away from their mothers (Bohlin & Hagekull, 1993). Thus, it appears that when infants feel secure, they are less likely to show stranger anxiety.

Who the stranger is and how the stranger behaves also influence stranger anxiety in infants. Infants are less fearful of child strangers than adult strangers. They also are less fearful of friendly, outgoing, smiling strangers than of passive, unsmiling strangers (Bretherton, Stolberg, & Kreye, 1981).

In addition to stranger anxiety, infants experience fear of being separated from their caregivers. The result is **separation protest**—crying when the caregiver leaves. Separation protest tends to peak at about 15 months among U.S. infants. In fact, one

reflexive smile A smile that does not occur in response to external stimuli. It happens during the month after birth, usually during irregular patterns of sleep, not when the infant is in an alert state.

social smile A smile in response to an external stimulus, which, early in development, typically is a face.

stranger anxiety An infant's fear of and wariness toward strangers; it tends to appear in the second half of the first year of life.

separation protest Occurs when infants experience a fear of being separated from a caregiver, which results in crying when the caregiver leaves.

study found that separation protest peaked at about 13 to 15 months in four different cultures (Kagan, Kearsley, & Zelazo, 1978). As indicated in figure 11.3, the percentage of infants who engaged in separation protest varied across cultures, but the infants reached a peak of protest at about the same age—just before the middle of the second year of life. Also, one recent study found that mothers of infants with high separation anxiety were oversensitive to infants' negative signals but undersensitive to infants' positive signals (Hsu, 2004).

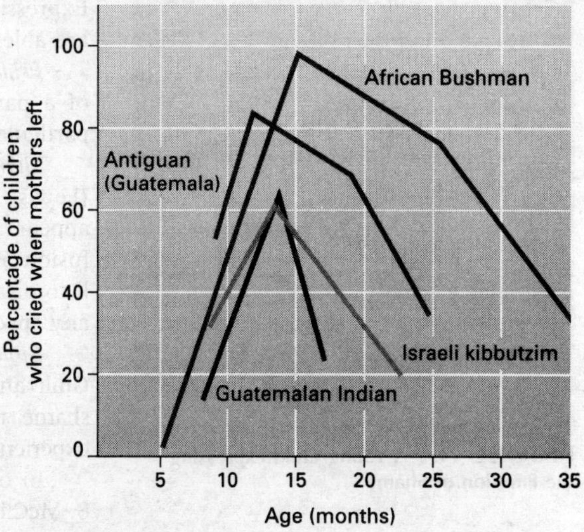

FIGURE 11.3 Separation Protest in Four Cultures. Note that separation protest peaked at about the same time in all four cultures in this study (13 to 15 months of age). However, a higher percentage (100 percent) of infants in an African Bushman culture engaged in separation protest compared to only about 60 percent of infants in Guatemalan Indian and Israeli kibbutzim cultures.

Social Referencing

Infants not only express emotions like fear but "read" the emotions of other people. **Social referencing** involves "reading" emotional cues in others to help determine how to act in a particular situation. The development of social referencing helps infants to interpret ambiguous situations more accurately, as when they encounter a stranger and need to know whether to fear the person (Mumme, Fernald, & Herrera, 1996).

Infants become better at social referencing in the second year of life. At this age, they tend to "check" with their mother before they act; they look at her to see if she is happy, angry, or fearful. For example, in one study, 14- to 22-month-old infants were more likely to look at their mother's face as a source of information for how to act in a situation than were 6- to 9-month-old infants (Walden, 1991).

Emotional Regulation and Coping

During the first year of life, the infant gradually develops an ability to inhibit, or minimize, the intensity and duration of emotional reactions (Eisenberg, 2001; Thompson, 2006). From early in infancy, babies put their thumbs in their mouths to soothe themselves. But at first, infants mainly depend on caregivers to help them soothe their emotions, as when a caregiver rocks an infant to sleep, sings lullabies to the infant, gently strokes the infant, and so on. Many developmentalists believe it is a good strategy for a caregiver to soothe an infant before the infant gets into an intense, agitated, uncontrolled state (Thompson, 1994, 2006).

Later in infancy, when they become aroused, infants sometimes redirect their attention or distract themselves in order to reduce their arousal (Grolnick, Bridges, & Connell, 1996). By 2 years of age, toddlers can use language to define their feeling states and the context that is upsetting them (Kopp & Neufeld, 2002). A toddler might say, "Feel bad. Dog scare." This type of communication may help caregivers to help the child in regulating emotion.

Contexts can influence emotional regulation (Eisenberg, Spinrad, & Smith, 2004; Kopp & Neufeld, 2002; Saarni, 1999). Infants are often affected by fatigue, hunger, time of day, which people are around them, and where they are. Infants must learn to adapt to different contexts that require emotional regulation. Further, new demands appear as the infant becomes older and parents modify their expectations. For example, a parent may take it in stride if a 6-month-old infant screams in a restaurant but may react very differently if a 1½-year-old starts screaming.

Early Childhood

Young children, like adults, experience many emotions during the course of a day. At times, children also try to make sense of other people's emotional reactions and feelings.

Self-Conscious Emotions

Recall our earlier description of *self-conscious emotions,* which require that children be able to refer to themselves and be aware of themselves as distinct from others (Lewis, 2002). We indicated that self-conscious evaluative emotions—pride, shame, and guilt—first appear at about 2½ years of age.

social referencing "Reading" emotional cues in others to help determine how to act in a particular situation.

FIGURE 11.4 A Young Child Expressing the Emotion of Shame

Expression of these emotions indicates that children are beginning to acquire and are able to use societal standards and rules to evaluate their behavior.

Pride is expressed when children feel joy as a result of the successful outcome of a particular action (Lewis, 2002). Pride is often associated with achieving a particular goal.

Shame emerges when children perceive they have not met standards or goals (Lewis, 2002). Children who experience shame often wish they could hide or disappear. Shame typically involves an attack on the entire self and can produce confusion and an inability to speak. The bodies of shamed children seem to shrink as if to disappear from the view of others (see figure 11.4). Shame is not produced by any specific situation but rather by an individual's interpretation of an event.

Guilt emerges when children judge their behavior to be a failure (Lewis, 2002). Guilt and shame have different physical characteristics. When children experience shame, they often try to shrink their bodies in an effort to disappear, but when they experience guilt, they typically move in space as if they are trying to correct their failure.

In one study, girls showed more shame and pride than boys (Stipek, Recchia, & McClintic, 1992). This gender difference is interesting because girls are more at risk for internalizing disorders, such as anxiety and depression, in which feelings of shame and self-criticism are often evident (Cummings, Braungart-Rieker, & Du Rocher-Schudlich, 2003).

The development of evaluative, self-conscious emotions are especially influenced by parents' responses to children's behavior. For example, a young child may experience a twinge of guilt when a parent says, "You should feel bad about biting your sister."

Young Children's Emotion Language and Understanding of Emotion

Among the most important changes in emotional development in early childhood are an increased ability to talk about their own and others' emotions and an increased understanding of emotion (Kuebli, 1994). Between 2 and 4 years of age, children considerably increase the number of terms they use to describe emotions (Ridgeway, Waters, & Kuczaj, 1985). They also are learning about the causes and consequences of feelings (Denham, 1998).

When they are 4 to 5 years of age, children show an increased ability to reflect on emotions. They also begin to understand that the same event can elicit different feelings in different people. Moreover, they show a growing awareness that they need to manage their emotions to meet social standards (Bruce, Olen, & Jensen, 1999). Figure 11.5 summarizes the characteristics of young children's talk about emotion and their understanding of it.

FIGURE 11.5 Some Characteristics of Young Children's Language for Talking About Emotion and Their Understanding of It

Approximate Age of Child	Description
2 to 4 years	Increase emotion vocabulary most rapidly
	Correctly label simple emotions in self and others and talk about past, present, and future emotions
	Talk about the causes and consequences of some emotions and identify emotions associated with certain situations
	Use emotion language in pretend play
5 to 10 years	Show increased capacity to reflect verbally on emotions and to consider more complex relations between emotions and situations
	Understand that the same event may call forth different feelings in different people and that feelings sometimes persist long after the events that caused them
	Demonstrate growing awareness about controlling and managing emotions in accord with social standards

Parents, teachers, and other adults can help children understand and control their emotions (Havighurst, Harley, & Prior, 2004). They can talk with children to help them cope with distress, sadness, anger, or guilt. Learning to express some feelings and mask others is a common, everyday lesson in children's lives. Children who get angry because they have to wait their turn or who laugh at a crying child who has fallen and skinned a knee can be encouraged to consider other children's feelings. Children who boast about winning something can be reminded how sad it feels to lose.

Emotions play a strong role in whether a child's peer relationships are successful or not (Hubbard, 2001). Moody and emotionally negative children experience greater rejection by their peers, whereas emotionally positive children are more popular (Stocker & Dunn, 1990).

Emotional regulation is an important aspect of getting along with peers. In one study conducted in the natural context of young children's everyday peer interactions, self-regulation of emotion enhanced children's social competence (Fabes & others, 1999). Children who made an effort to control their emotional responses were more likely to respond in socially competent ways when they were emotionally provoked by a peer (as when a peer made a hostile comment or took something away from the child). In sum, the ability to modulate their emotions is an important skill that benefits children in their relationships with peers.

Middle and Late Childhood

These are some important developmental changes in emotions during the middle and late childhood years (Kuebli, 1994; Wintre & Vallance, 1994):

- An increased ability to understand such complex emotions as pride and shame (Kuebli, 1994). These emotions become more internalized (self-generated) and integrated with a sense of personal responsibility
- Increased understanding that more than one emotion can be experienced in a particular situation
- An increased tendency to take into fuller account the events leading to emotional reactions
- Marked improvements in the ability to suppress or conceal negative emotional reactions
- The use of self-initiated strategies for redirecting feelings, such as using distracting thoughts

In short, "By middle childhood, children have become more reflective and strategic in their emotional lives. . . . But children of this age are also capable of genuine empathy and greater emotional understanding than ever before" (Thompson & Goodvin, 2005, pp. 401–402).

Adolescence

Adolescence has long been described as a time of emotional turmoil (Hall, 1904). Adolescents are not constantly in a state of "storm and stress," but emotional highs and lows do increase during early adolescence (Rosenblum & Lewis, 2003). Young adolescents can be on top of the world one moment and down in the dumps the next. In many instances, the intensity of their emotions seems out of proportion to events (Steinberg & Levine, 1997). Young adolescents might sulk a lot, not knowing how to express their feelings. With little or no provocation, they might blow up at their parents or siblings, perhaps because they are using the defense mechanism of displacing their feelings onto another person.

Reed Larson and Maryse Richards (1994) found that adolescents reported more extreme emotions and more fleeting emotions than their parents did. For example,

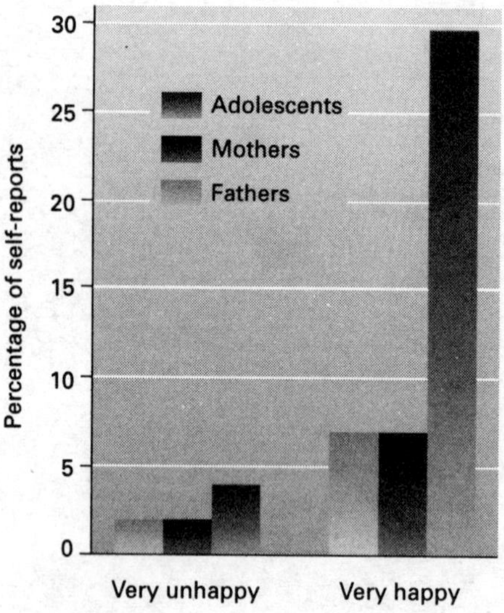

FIGURE 11.6 Self-Reported Extremes of Emotion by Adolescents, Mothers, and Fathers Using the Experience Sampling Method. In the study by Reed Larson and Maryse Richards (1994), adolescents and their mothers and fathers were beeped at random times by researchers using the experience sampling method. The researchers found that adolescents were more likely to report more emotional extremes than their parents.

adolescents were five times more likely to report being "very happy" and three times more likely to report being "very sad" than their parents (see figure 11.6). These findings lend support to the perception of adolescents as moody and changeable (Rosenblum & Lewis, 2003).

It is important for adults to recognize that moodiness is a *normal* aspect of early adolescence, and most adolescents make it through these moody times to become competent adults. Nonetheless, for some adolescents, such emotions can reflect serious problems. Girls are especially vulnerable to depression in adolescence (Nolen-Hoeksema, 2004).

Emotional fluctuations in early adolescence may be related to the variability of hormones during this period. As we saw in chapter 5, significant hormonal changes characterize puberty. Pubertal change is associated with an increase in negative emotions (Archibald, Graber, & Brooks-Gunn, 2003; Dorn, Williamson, & Ryan, 2002). Moods become less extreme as adolescents move into adulthood and this mellowing may be due to adaptation to hormone levels over time (Rosenbaum & Lewis, 2003). However, most researchers conclude that hormonal influences are small and that when they occur they usually are associated with other factors, such as stress, eating patterns, sexual activity, and social relationships (Rosenblum & Lewis, 2003).

Indeed, environmental experiences may contribute more to the emotions of adolescence than hormonal changes. Recall from chapter 5 that in one study, social factors accounted for two to four times as much variance as hormonal factors in young adolescent girls' depression and anger (Brooks-Gunn & Warren, 1989). In sum, both hormonal changes and environmental experiences are involved in the changing emotional landscape of adolescence.

Review and Reflect • **LEARNING GOAL 2**

2 Describe the development of emotion

Review

- How does emotion develop in infancy?
- What characterizes emotional development in early childhood?
- What changes take place in emotion during middle and late childhood?
- How does emotion change in adolescence?

Reflect

- A mother and father of an 8-month-old baby are having difficulty getting any sleep because the baby wakes up in the middle of night crying. How would you recommend that they deal with this situation?

3 EMOTIONAL PROBLEMS, STRESS, AND COPING

Depression | Suicide | Stress and Coping

Sometimes emotions overwhelm children and create major problems. Here we will focus on two of these problems—depression and suicide. We also will explore stress in children's lives and ways they can effectively cope with it.

Depression

Depression is a mood disorder in which the individual is unhappy, demoralized, self-derogatory, and bored. The individual does not feel well, loses stamina easily, often has a poor appetite, and is listless and unmotivated.

Depression in Childhood In childhood, the behaviors linked with depression are often broader than in adulthood, which makes its diagnosis difficult (Weiner, 1980). Many depressed children display aggression, school failure, anxiety, antisocial behavior, and poor peer relations.

Why does depression occur in childhood? Biological, cognitive, and environmental causes have been proposed. Among the views currently being given special attention are Bowlby's developmental theory, Beck's cognitive theory, and Seligman's learned helplessness theory.

John Bowlby (1969, 1989) believes that insecure attachment, a lack of love and affection in child rearing, or the actual loss of a parent in childhood leads the child to develop a negative cognitive schema. This schema is carried forward to influence the way later experiences are interpreted. When the later experiences involve further loss, the child interprets those losses as failures to produce enduring positive relationships, which precipitates depression.

In Aaron Beck's (1973) cognitive view, individuals become depressed because early in their development they acquire cognitive schemas that are characterized by self-devaluation and lack of confidence about the future. Their thoughts are habitually negative thoughts, and these thoughts magnify and expand the person's negative experiences. Depressed children blame themselves far more than is warranted, in Beck's view. In one expansion of Beck's view, depression in children is viewed as growing out of two cognitive tendencies: the children (1) pay attention to negative cues in the environment and (2) identify themselves as the cause of negative outcomes (Quiggle & others, 1992).

Martin Seligman's theory is that depression is learned helplessness; that is, when individuals are exposed to negative experiences over which they have no control, such as prolonged stress and pain, they are likely to become depressed (Seligman, 1975). In a reformulation of this view, depression follows a negative event when individuals explain the event with self-blaming attributions (Abramson, Metalsky, & Alloy, 1989). They blame themselves for causing the event. This explanatory style results in the expectation that no action will control the outcome of similar events in the future, resulting in helplessness, hopelessness, passivity, and depression.

Depression in Parents Depression was traditionally perceived as a problem of the individual, but this view is too limited. Researchers have found an interdependence between depressed persons and their social contexts. This interdependence is especially important in the case of parents' depression and children's adjustment (Downey & Coyne, 1990). Depression is a highly prevalent disorder—so prevalent it has been called the "common cold of mental disorders." Among women of childbearing age, depression occurs at a rate of about 8 percent; the rate is 12 percent for women who have recently given birth. As a result, large numbers of children are exposed to depressed parents.

What are the effects? Depressed mothers show lower rates of behavior and show constricted affect; they adopt less-effortful control strategies with their children; and they sometimes act hostile and negative toward the children. Research on the children of depressed parents clearly documents that depression in parents is associated with problems of adjustment and disorders, especially depression, in their children (Radke-Yarrow & others, 1992). However, marital discord and stress may precede, precipitate, or co-occur with maternal depression. In these instances, marital turmoil may be the key factor that contributes to children's adjustment problems, not parental depression per se (Gelfand, Teti, & Fox, 1992).

When a parent is depressed, it is important for children to develop strong friendships outside the home and find success in school and the community (Beardslee, 2002). Children also benefit from understanding events in the family and developing a capacity for self-reflection and self-understanding.

Depression is more likely to occur in adolescence than in childhood and more likely to characterize female adolescents than male adolescents. *Why might female adolescents be more likely to develop depression than adolescent males?*

Depression in Adolescence Depression is more likely to occur in adolescence than in childhood, and adolescent girls consistently have higher rates of depression than adolescent boys (Blatt, 2004; Graber, 2004; Nolen-Hoeksema, 2004, 2007). Among the reasons for this sex difference are that

- girls tend to ruminate in their depressed mood and amplify it;
- girls' self-images, especially their body images, are more negative than males';
- girls are likely to experience more sexual harassment and abuse than boys do; and
- puberty occurs earlier for girls than for boys, and as a result girls experience a piling up of changes and life experiences in the middle school years, which can increase depression.

Certain family factors place adolescents at risk for developing depression (Blatt, 2004; Graber, 2004; Holmes & Holmes, 2005). These include having a depressed parent, emotionally unavailable parents, parents who have high marital conflict, and parents with financial problems.

Poor peer relationships also are associated with adolescent depression. In particular, depressive tendencies among adolescents have been linked with not having a close relationship with a best friend, having less contact with friends, and experiencing peer rejection.

The experience of difficult changes or challenges also is associated with depressive symptoms in adolescence (Compas, 2004; Compas & Grant, 1993; Mazza, 2005). Parental divorce, for example, increases depressive symptoms in adolescents. Also, when adolescents go through puberty at the same time as they move from elementary school to middle or junior high school, they report being depressed more than do adolescents who go through puberty after the school transition.

Suicide

Suicidal behavior is rare among children but escalates during early adolescence. Suicide is the third-leading cause of death today among adolescents 13 through 19 years of age in the United States (National Center for Health Statistics, 2004). Although the incidence of suicide in adolescence has increased in recent decades, it still is a relatively rare event. In 2002, 1 of every 10,000 individuals from 15 through 24 years of age committed suicide (National Center for Health Statistics, 2004).

Far more adolescents contemplate suicide or attempt suicide unsuccessfully (Borowsky, Ireland, & Resnick, 2001; Cox, Enns, & Clara, 2004; Mazza, 2005). In a national study, 17 percent of U.S. high school students said that they had seriously considered or attempted suicide in the last 12 months (National Center for Health Statistics, 2004). Less than 3 percent reported a suicide attempt that resulted in an injury, poisoning, or drug overdose that had been treated by a doctor.

Which adolescents are more likely to attempt or to commit suicide? The closer a person's genetic relationship to someone who has committed suicide, the more likely that person is to commit suicide (Cerel & Roberts, 2005). Girls are more likely to attempt suicide than boys, but boys are more likely to commit suicide. Boys use more lethal means, such as a gun, in their suicide attempts, while girls are more likely to cut their wrists or take an overdose of sleeping pills, which is less likely to result in death. A recent study revealed that for both male and female adolescents, illegal drug use was associated with an increase in thoughts about suicide and suicide attempts (Hallfors & others, 2004).

Sexual minority (gay male, lesbian, and bisexual) adolescents may be especially vulnerable to suicide. Early reports suggested that these youth were three to seven times more likely to attempt suicide than heterosexual youth (Ferguson, Harwood, & Beautrais, 1999; Herrill & others, 1999). But Rich Savin-Williams (2001) found that gay male and lesbian adolescents were only slightly more likely than heterosexual adolescents to attempt suicide (Savin-Williams, 2001). He argues that the

What to do	What not to do
1. Ask direct, straightforward questions in a calm manner: "Are you thinking about hurting yourself?"	1. Do not ignore the warning signs.
2. Assess the seriousness of the suicidal intent by asking questions about feelings, important relationships, who else the person has talked with, and the amount of thought given to the means to be used. If a gun, pills, a rope, or other means has been obtained and a precise plan developed, clearly the situation is dangerous. Stay with the person until help arrives.	2. Do not refuse to talk about suicide if a person approaches you about it.
3. Be a good listener and be very supportive without being falsely reassuring.	3. Do not react with humor, disapproval, or repulsion.
4. Try to persuade the person to obtain professional help and assist him or her in getting this help.	4. Do not give false reassurances by saying such things as "Everything is going to be OK." Also do not give out simple answers or platitudes, such as "You have everything to be thankful for."
	5. Do not abandon the individual after the crisis has passed or after professional help has commenced.

FIGURE 11.7 What to Do and What Not to Do When You Suspect Someone Is Likely to Attempt Suicide

earlier studies likely exaggerated the suicide rates for gay male and lesbian adolescents because they only surveyed the most disturbed youth who were attending support groups or hanging out at shelters for gay youth. In one recent study of 12,000 adolescents, approximately 15 percent of gay male and lesbian youth said that they had attempted suicide compared to 7 percent of heterosexual youth (Russell & Joyner, 2001).

Several characteristics of the adolescent's social relationships have been linked with suicide attempts or suicide (Holmes & Holmes, 2005; Mazza, 2005). The adolescent might have a long-standing history of family instability and unhappiness. Just as a lack of affection and emotional support, high control, and pressure for achievement by parents during childhood are related to adolescent depression, such combinations of family experiences are also likely to show up as factors in suicide attempts. The adolescent might also lack supportive friendships.

What is the psychological profile of the suicidal adolescent? Suicidal adolescents often have depressive symptoms (American Academy of Pediatrics, 2000; Gadpaille, 1996). Although not all depressed adolescents are suicidal, depression is the most frequently cited factor associated with adolescent suicide. A sense of hopelessness, low self-esteem, and high self-blame are also associated with adolescent suicide (Harter & Marold, 1992; Harter & Whitesell, 2001; Werth, 2004).

A recent concern related to adolescent suicide is a link between the use of antidepressants and suicidal thoughts (Lock & others, 2005). In October 2004, the Federal Drug Administration issued a report based on its review of a number of research studies; the report concluded that 2 to 3 percent of adolescents taking antidepressants experience an increase in suicidal thoughts. It is estimated that antidepressants are prescribed for approximately 1 million U.S. children and adolescents.

To read about what to do and what not to do when you suspect someone is likely to attempt suicide, see figure 11.7.

Stress and Coping

Stress is the response of individuals to the circumstances and events (called stressors) that threaten and tax their coping abilities. Cognitive factors, life events and daily hassles, and sociocultural factors all play roles in children's stress.

stress The response of individuals to the circumstances and events (called stressors) that threaten and tax their coping abilities.

Cognitive Factors

Most of us think of stress as events that place demands on us, events such as an approaching test, being in a car wreck, or losing a friend.

Although these are common sources of stress, not everyone perceives the same events as equally stressful or experiences stress in the same way (Hollon, 2006). For example, one child might perceive an approaching test as threatening, another child might perceive it as challenging. To some degree, then, what is stressful for children depends on how they cognitively appraise and interpret events (Sanders & Wills, 2005). This view has been presented most clearly by stress researcher Richard Lazarus (1996). **Cognitive appraisal** is Lazarus' term for children's interpretations of events in their lives that are harmful, threatening, or challenging, and their determination of whether they have the resources to effectively cope with the event.

In Lazarus' view, events are appraised in two steps:

- In **primary appraisal,** individuals interpret whether an event involves harm or loss that has already occurred, a threat of future danger, or a challenge to be overcome. For example, if a young girl failed a test in school yesterday, she might evaluate the damage that has been done, consider the possibility that the teacher will lower his or her opinion of her and give her a low grade at the end of the year, or develop a commitment not to fail again.
- After children cognitively appraise an event for its harm, threat, or challenge, Lazarus says, they engage in secondary appraisal. In **secondary appraisal,** individuals evaluate their resources and determine how effectively they can cope with the event. This appraisal is called secondary because it comes after primary appraisal and depends on the degree to which the event has been appraised as harmful, threatening, or challenging. Coping involves a wide range of potential strategies, skills, and abilities for effectively managing stressful events. In the example of failing the exam, children who learn that their parents will get a tutor to help them likely will be more confident in coping with the stress than if their parents provide no support.

Lazarus believes a child's experience of stress is a balance of primary and secondary appraisal. When harm and threat are high, and challenge and resources are low, stress is likely to be high. When harm and threat are low, and challenge and resources are high, stress is more likely to be moderate or low.

Martin Seligman (1995) also believes that cognitive factors play an important role in coping with stress. He distinguishes between optimistic and pessimistic children. Compared to optimistic children, pessimistic children are more likely to become depressed, feel hopeless, underachieve at school, and have poor health. Young pessimists believe there are permanent reasons why bad things happen to them. Young optimists perceive bad experiences as temporary. If self-blame is appropriate, the optimists blame their behavior, which is changeable; pessimists are more likely to say that their negative experiences are due to innate qualities in themselves. Figure 11.8 shows how some experiences are interpreted differently by pessimistic and optimistic children.

Seligman believes that pessimistic children can be turned into optimistic ones by adults who model optimistic ways of handling themselves. Also, when pessimistic children falter, adults should provide explanations that encourage further effort. Seligman has developed a program to correct distorted explanations of problems and teach realistic ways of interpreting setbacks. The program includes role playing and discussion. In Seligman's research, this program has been very effective in turning pessimistic thinkers into optimistic ones.

cognitive appraisal Lazarus' term for children's interpretations of events in their lives that are harmful, threatening, or challenging, and their determination of whether they have the resources to effectively cope with the event.

primary appraisal Individuals interpret whether an event involves harm or loss that has already occurred, a threat that involves some future danger, or a challenge to be overcome.

secondary appraisal Individuals evaluate their resources and determine how effectively they can cope with the event.

Life Events and Daily Hassles

Children experience a spectrum of stressors, ranging from ordinary to severe. At the ordinary end are experiences that occur in most children's lives and for which there are reasonably well-defined coping patterns. For example, most parents are aware that siblings are jealous of each other and that when one sibling does well at something the other sibling will be jealous. They know how jealousy works and know ways to help children cope with it. More

Bad Events

Pessimistic	Optimistic
• Teachers are unfair. • I'm a total clod at sports. • Tony hates me and will never hang out with me again. • Nobody will ever want to be friends with me here at a new school. • I got grounded because I'm a bad kid. • I got a C because I'm stupid.	• Mrs. Carmine is unfair. • I stink at kickball. • Tony is mad at me today. • It takes time to make a new best friend when you're at a new school. • I got grounded because I hit Michelle. • I got a C because I didn't study enough.

Good Events

Pessimistic	Optimistic
• I'm smart at math. • I was voted safety patrol captain because the other kids wanted to do a nice thing for me. • Dad is spending time with me because he's in a good mood. • The only reason I won the spelling bee is because I practiced hard this time.	• I'm smart. • I was voted safety patrol captain because the other kids like me. • Dad loves to spend time with me. • I won because I'm a hard worker and I study my lessons.

FIGURE 11.8 Optimistic and Pessimistic Children's Interpretations of Bad and Good Events

severe stress occurs when children become separated from their parents because of divorce, death, illness, or foster placement. Healthy coping patterns for this stressful experience are not as well spelled out. Even more severe are the experiences of children who have been neglected or abused for years (Pfeffer, 1996). Victims of incest also experience severe stress, with few coping guidelines.

Life's daily experiences as well as major events may be the culprits in stress (D'Angelo & Wierzbicki, 2003). The everyday pounding that children take from enduring a tense family life or living in poverty can add up to a highly stressful life and, eventually, psychological disorders or physical illnesses (Pillow, Zautra, & Sandler, 1996).

Sociocultural Factors

Sociocultural factors involved in stress include acculturative stress and poverty. *Acculturative stress* is the negative consequences of cultural change that results from continuous, firsthand contact between two distinctive cultural groups. The young son of recent immigrants may find that none of his schoolmates know his childhood games; he may be teased for his accent or his odd clothes. The teenage daughter who has grown up in the United States but whose parents immigrated from a very traditional, conservative culture may be torn between following the strict dress code and rules imposed by her parents or conforming to her peers' style. If an African American or Latino family moves into a neighborhood in which everyone else is European American, the children may find themselves isolated or targets of hostility.

Poverty imposes considerable stress on children and their families (McLoyd, 2000). Compared with other children, poor children are more likely to experience threatening and uncontrollable events. Inadequate housing, dangerous neighborhoods, burdensome responsibilities, and economic uncertainties are potent stressors in the lives of the poor (Brooks-Gunn, Leventhal, & Duncan, 2000). The incidence of poverty is especially pronounced among ethnic minority children and their families. Many individuals who become poor during their lives remain poor for one or two years. However, African Americans and female family heads are at risk for experiencing persistent poverty.

Coping with Stress

Learning how to cope with stress is an important aspect of children's emotional lives (Bridges, 2003; Folkman & Moskowitz, 2004). In our discussion of stress, we described some strategies that children can use to cope with stress. Among these are Lazarus' ideas about cognitive appraisal and challenge and Seligman's view that children who are optimistic are likely to cope more effectively than those who are pessimistic.

Most researchers also believe that children benefit when they make an effort to take a problem-solving approach to stress rather than avoiding the stress (Bridges, 2003; Folkman & Moskowitz, 2004; Lazarus & Folkman, 1984). For example, children who respond to low test scores by increasing their study time or developing improved study techniques are likely to cope more effectively than children who fake an illness on the day of the next test.

It is important for caregivers to help children cope effectively. In addition, encouraging children to use active, problem-solving strategies, caregivers might (1) remove at least one stressor from the child's life and (2) teach children multiple coping strategies.

When children face several stressors at the same time, the result is likely to be, not the sum of the effect of each stressor, but a multiplication of their impact (Rutter, 1979). One stressor compounds the effects of others. Removing even one stressor can help children feel stronger and more competent. For example, consider Lisa, who had been coming to school hungry each morning. Her teacher arranged for Lisa to have hot breakfasts at school, which improved her concentration in school. This in turn helped Lisa suppress for a time her anxieties about her parents' impending divorce.

Children who have a number of coping techniques have the best chance of adapting and functioning competently in the face of stress. By learning new coping techniques, children might no longer feel as incompetent, and their self-confidence may improve. For example, Kim was relieved when a clinical psychologist helped her anticipate what it would be like to visit her seriously ill sister. She was frightened by the hospital and had withdrawn in order to cope, claiming that she did not want to see her sister, even though she missed her a great deal.

Children tend to apply their coping strategies only in the situations in which stress develops. Adults can show children how to use these coping skills to their best advantage in many other situations as well. For example, Jennifer used altruism to cope when her mother was hospitalized for cancer. She coped with the separation by mothering her father, her little brother, and her classmates. Her classmates quickly became annoyed with her and began to tease her. Jennifer's teacher at school recognized the problem and helped Jennifer express her altruism by taking care of the pet animals in the class and by being responsible for some daily cleanup chores. Her mothering of the children stopped, and so did the teasing.

How can adults help children cope with terrorist attacks, such as 9/11/01?

As children get older, they can appraise a stressful situation more accurately and determine how much control they have over it. Older children generate more coping alternatives to stressful conditions and use more cognitive coping strategies (Compas, 2004; Compas & others, 2001; Saarni, 1999). For example, older children are better than younger children at intentionally shifting their thoughts to something that is less stressful. Older children are better at reframing (changing one's perception of a stressful situation). For example, younger children may be very disappointed that their teacher did not say hello to them when they arrived at school. Older children may reframe the situation and think, "She might have been busy with other things and just forgot to say hello."

By 10 years of age, most children can shift their thoughts and reframe in order to cope with stress (Saarni, 1999). However, if their families have not been supportive and are characterized by turmoil or trauma, children may be so overwhelmed by stress that they do not use such strategies. Children may also fail to use their coping strategies when faced with unusually traumatic events. For advice about how to help children deal with trauma, read the Caring for Children interlude.

Caring for Children

Helping Children Cope with Stressful Events

The terrorist attacks on the World Trade Center in New York City and the Pentagon in Washington, D.C., on September 11, 2001, raised special concerns about how to help children cope with such stressful events. Children who have a number of coping techniques have the best chance of adapting and functioning competently in the face of trauma. Here are some recommendations for helping children cope with the stress of these types of events (Gurwitch & others, 2001, pp. 4–11):

- *Reassure children of their safety and security.* This may need to be done numerous times.
- *Allow children to retell events and be patient in listening to them.*
- *Encourage children to talk about any disturbing or confusing feelings.* Tell them that these are normal feelings after a stressful event.
- *Help children make sense of what happened.* Children may misunderstand what took place. For example, young children "may blame themselves, believe things happened that did not happen, believe that terrorists are in the school, etc. Gently help children develop a realistic understanding of the event" (p. 10).
- *Protect children from reexposure to frightening situations and reminders of the trauma.* This includes limiting conversations about the event in front of the children.

Coping with Death Can children cope with the death of a loved one? The impact of a parent's death can vary with a number of factors, including the quality of the child's relationship with the parent and the nature of the death (such as from AIDS, cancer, suicide, murder) (Hayslip & Hansson, 2003). When children and adolescents experience the death of a parent, their school performance and their relationship with peers often suffer (Worden, 2002). For some children, adolescents, and even adults, a parent's death can bring a hypersensitivity about death, including a fear of losing others close to the individual (Balk & Corr, 2001). Children may also reexperience grief for a parent as they grow older.

Children who have healthy and positive relationships with their parents before a parent dies cope with the death more effectively than children with unhappy prior relationships with the parent. The years of warmth and caring have probably taught the child effective ways of coping with such a traumatic event. Also, children who are given high-quality care by surviving family members during the mourning period, or who are effectively helped by caregivers in other contexts, experience less separation distress (Kastenbaum, 2004).

The effects of the death of a sibling on a child or an adolescent are similar to the effects of a parent's death (Oltjenbruns, 2001). Sometimes, though, the death of a sibling is even more difficult for children to understand and accept than the loss of a parent. Many children believe that only old people die, so the death of a child can stimulate children to think about their own mortality. The majority of children, though, seem to be able to cope with a sibling's death effectively if they are helped through a mourning period.

Knowing what children think about death can help adults understand their behavior after the loss of a parent or sibling. When a 3-year-old boy creeps from his bed every night and runs down the street, searching for his mother who has just died, is he mourning for her? When a 6-year-old girl spends an entire afternoon drawing pictures of graveyards and coffins, is she grieving? When a 9-year-old boy can't wait to go back to school after the funeral so he can tell his classmates about how his sister died, is he denying grief? All of these are ways in which children cope with death. And all follow children's logic.

Children 3 to 5 years old think that dead people continue to live, but under changed circumstances. The missing person is simply missing, and young children expect the person to return at some point. When the person does not come back, they might feel hurt or angry at being abandoned. They might declare that they want to go to heaven to bring the dead person home. They might ask their caregivers where the dead person's house is, where the dead person eats, and why the dead person won't be cold if the person is buried without a coat and hat in winter.

Though children vary somewhat in the age at which they begin to understand death, it is difficult for children younger than 7 or 8 to comprehend death. Young children blame themselves for the death of someone they knew well, believing that they caused the death by disobeying the person. Children under 6 rarely understand that death is universal, inevitable, and final. Instead, young children usually think that only people who want to die, or who are bad or careless, actually do die. At some point around the middle of the elementary school years, children begin to grasp the concept that death is the end of life and is not reversible. They come to realize that they, too, will die someday.

Review and Reflect • LEARNING GOAL 3

3 Summarize the nature of depression, suicide, stress, and coping

Review

- What causes depression in childhood and adolescence?
- Why do adolescents attempt and commit suicide?
- What is the nature of stress and coping in children?

Reflect

- What advice would you give to a parent whose child is experiencing a great deal of stress and having difficulty coping?

4 TEMPERAMENT

Describing and Classifying Temperament | Biological Foundations and Experience | Goodness of Fit and Parenting

Do you get upset a lot? Does it take much to get you angry, or to make you laugh? Even at birth, babies seem to have different emotional styles. One infant is cheerful and happy much of the time; another baby seems to cry constantly. These tendencies reflect **temperament,** which is an individual's behavioral style and characteristic way of responding.

Temperament is closely linked with *personality,* the enduring personal characteristics of an individual. In fact, the lines between temperament and personality are often blurred. Temperament can be thought of as the biological and emotional foundations of personality. A baby's temperament inclines the baby toward a particular style of feeling and reacting, which makes it more likely that the baby's personality will take one shape or another.

Does temperament change as children develop? Does an infant's temperament predict how that infant will behave as a child, adolescent, or young adult? Before these questions can be addressed, we need to examine how researchers describe or classify the temperaments of individuals.

temperament An individual's behavioral style and characteristic emotional response.

Describing and Classifying Temperament

How would you describe your temperament or the temperament of a friend? Researchers have described and classified the temperament of individuals in different ways. Here we will examine three of those ways.

Chess and Thomas' Classification

Psychiatrists Stella Chess and Alexander Thomas (Chess & Thomas, 1977; Thomas & Chess, 1991) identified three basic types, or clusters, of temperament:

- **Easy child:** This child is generally in a positive mood, quickly establishes regular routines in infancy, and adapts easily to new experiences.
- **Difficult child:** This child reacts negatively and cries frequently, engages in irregular daily routines, and is slow to accept change.
- **Slow-to-warm-up child:** This child has a low activity level, is somewhat negative, and displays a low intensity of mood.

In their longitudinal investigation, Chess and Thomas found that 40 percent of the children they studied could be classified as easy, 10 percent as difficult, and 15 percent as slow to warm up. Notice that 35 percent did not fit any of the three patterns. Researchers have found that these three basic clusters of temperament are moderately stable across the childhood years.

"Oh, he's cute, all right, but he's got the temperament of a car alarm."

Kagan's Behavioral Inhibition

Another way of classifying temperament focuses on the differences between a shy, subdued, timid child and a sociable, extraverted, bold child. Jerome Kagan (1997, 2000, 2002, 2003; Kagan & Fox, 2006; Kagan & Snidman, 1991) regards shyness with strangers (peers or adults) as one feature of a broad temperament category called *inhibition to the unfamiliar.* Inhibited children react to many aspects of unfamiliarity with initial avoidance, distress, or subdued affect, beginning about 7 to 9 months of age.

Kagan has found that inhibition shows considerable stability from infancy through early childhood. One recent study classified toddlers into extremely inhibited, extremely uninhibited, and intermediate groups (Pfeifer & others, 2002). Follow-up assessments occurred at 4 and 7 years of age. Continuity was demonstrated for both inhibition and lack of inhibition, although a substantial number of the inhibited children moved into the intermediate groups at 7 years of age.

Rothbart and Bates' Classification

New classifications of temperament continue to be forged (Rothbart & Bates, 2006). Mary Rothbart (2004, p. 495) recently concluded that the following three broad dimensions best represent what she and John Bates have found to characterize the structure of temperament:

- *Extraversion/surgency,* which includes "positive anticipation, impulsivity, activity level, and sensation seeking." Kagan's uninhibited children fit into this category.
- *Negative affectivity,* which includes irritability and fear. These children are easily distressed; they may fret and cry often. Kagan's inhibited children fit this category.
- *Effortful control (self-regulation),* which includes "attentional focusing and shifting, inhibitory control, perceptual sensitivity, and low-intensity pleasure." Infants who are high on effortful control show an ability to keep their arousal from getting too high and have strategies for soothing themselves. By contrast, children low on effortful control are often unable to control their arousal; they become easily agitated and intensely emotional.

easy child A temperament style in which the child is generally in a positive mood, quickly establishes regular routines, and adapts easily to new experiences.

difficult child A temperament style in which the child tends to react negatively and cry frequently, engages in irregular daily routines, and is slow to accept new experiences.

slow-to-warm-up child A temperament style in which the child has low activity level, is somewhat negative, shows low adaptability, and displays a low intensity of mood.

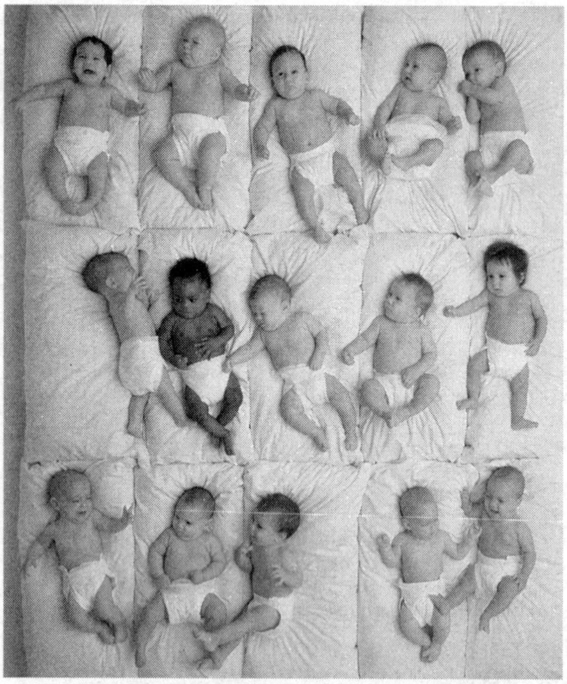

What are some ways that developmentalists have classified infants' temperaments? Which classification makes the most sense to you, based on your observations of infants?

In Rothbart's (2004, p. 497) view, "early theoretical models of temperament stressed the way we are moved by our positive and negative emotions or level of arousal, with our actions driven by these tendencies." The more recent emphasis on effortful control, however, reflects the view that individuals can take a more cognitive, flexible approach to stressful circumstances.

Biological Foundations and Experience

How does a child acquire a certain temperament? Kagan (1997, 2003; Kagan & Fox, 2006) argues that children inherit a physiology that biases them to have a particular type of temperament. However, through experience they may learn to modify their temperament to some degree. For example, children may inherit a physiology that biases them to be fearful and inhibited, but they may learn to reduce their fear and inhibition to some degree.

Biological Influences Physiological characteristics have been linked with different temperaments (Fox & others, 2004; Rothbart & Bates, 1998, 2006). In particular, an inhibited temperament is associated with a unique physiological pattern that includes high and stable heart rate, high level of the hormone cortisol, and high activity in the right frontal lobe of the brain (Kagan, 2003). This pattern may be tied to the excitability of the amygdala, a structure of the brain that plays an important role in fear and inhibition (Kagan, 2003; Kagan & Fox, 2006; LeDoux, 1996, 2000). An inhibited temperament or negative affectivity may also be linked to low levels of the neurotransmitter serotonin, which may increase an individual's vulnerability to fear and frustration (Hariri & others, 2002).

What is heredity's role in the biological foundations of temperament? Twin and adoption studies have found a heritability index for temperament in the range of .50 to .60, suggesting a moderate influence of heredity on differences in temperament within a group of people (Plomin & others, 1994).

Developmental Connections Do young adults show the same behavioral style and characteristic emotional responses as when they were infants or young children? Activity level is an important dimension of temperament. Are children's activity levels linked to their personality in early adulthood? In one longitudinal study, children who were highly active at age 4 were likely to be very outgoing at age 23, which reflects continuity (Franz, 1996). From adolescence into early adulthood, most individuals show fewer emotional mood swings, become more responsible, and engage in less risk-taking behavior, which reflects discontinuity (Caspi, 1998, 2006).

Yet another aspect of temperament involves emotionality and the ability to control one's emotions. In one longitudinal study, when 3-year-old children showed good control of their emotions and were resilient in the face of stress, they were likely to continue to handle emotions effectively as adults (Block, 1993). By contrast, when 3-year-olds had low emotional control and were not very resilient, they were likely to show problems in these areas as young adults.

Is temperament in childhood linked with adjustment in adulthood? Here is what we know based on the few longitudinal studies that have been conducted on this topic (Caspi, 1998, 2006). In one longitudinal study, children who had an easy temperament at 3 to 5 years of age were likely to be well adjusted as young adults (Chess & Thomas, 1977). In contrast, many children who had a difficult temperament at 3 to 5 years of age were not well adjusted as young adults. Also, other researchers have found that boys with a difficult temperament in childhood are less likely as adults to continue their formal education, and girls with a difficult temperament in childhood are more likely to experience marital conflict as adults (Wachs, 2000).

Inhibition is another temperament characteristic that has been studied extensively (Kagan, 2000; Kagan & Fox, 2006). Researchers have found that individuals with an inhibited temperament in childhood are less likely as adults to be assertive or experience social support, and more likely to delay entering a stable job track (Wachs, 2000).

In sum, these studies reveal some continuity between certain aspects of temperament in childhood and adjustment in early adulthood (Caspi, 2006; Rothbart & Bates, 2006). However, keep in mind that these connections between childhood temperament and adult adjustment are based on only a small number of studies and more research is needed to verify these linkages.

www.mhhe.com/santrockcd11

Infant Temperament

Developmental Contexts What accounts for the continuities and discontinuities between a child's temperament and an adult's personality? Physiological and heredity factors likely are involved in continuity. The contemporary view is that "temperament is a biologically based but developmentally evolving feature of behavior. For this reason, temperamental attributes become increasingly more consistent over time as temperamental individuality is enveloped into the network of self-perceptions, behavioral preferences, and social experiences that together shape developing personality" (Thompson & Goodvin, 2005).

Theodore Wachs (1994, 2000) proposed ways that linkages between temperament in childhood and personality in adulthood might vary depending on the intervening contexts in individuals' experience. Figure 11.9 summarizes how one characteristic might develop in different ways depending on the context.

Gender may be an important factor shaping the context that influences the fate of temperament. Parents might react differently to a child's temperament depending on whether the child is a boy or a girl (Kerr, 2001). For example, in one study, mothers were more responsive to the crying of irritable girls than to the crying of irritable boys (Crockenberg, 1986).

Initial Temperament Trait: Inhibition

	Child A	Child B
Intervening Context		
Caregivers	Caregivers (parents) who are sensitive and accepting, and let child set his or her own pace	Caregivers who use inappropriate "low level control" and attempt to force the child into new situations
Physical Environment	Presence of "stimulus shelters" or "defensible spaces" that the children can retreat to when there is too much stimulation	Child continually encounters noisy, chaotic environments that allow no escape from stimulation.
Peers	Peer groups with other inhibited children with common interests, so the child feels accepted	Peer groups consist of athletic extroverts, so the child feels rejected.
Schools	School is "undermanned" so inhibited children are more likely to be tolerated and feel they can make a contribution.	School is "overmanned" so inhibited children are less likely to be tolerated and more likely to feel undervalued.
Personality Outcomes		
	As an adult, individual is closer to extraversion (outgoing, sociable) and is emotionally stable.	As an adult, individual is closer to introversion and has more emotional problems.

FIGURE 11.9 Temperament in Childhood, Personality in Adulthood, and Intervening Contexts. Varying experiences with caregivers, the physical environment, peers, and schools may modify links between temperament in childhood and personality in adulthood. The example given here is for inhibition.

Similarly, the reaction to an infant's temperament may depend in part on culture (Austin & Chorpita, 2004). For example, an active temperament might be valued in some cultures (such as the United States) but not in other cultures (such as China). Indeed, children's temperament can vary across cultures (Putnam, Sanson, & Rothbart, 2002). Behavioral inhibition is more highly valued in China than in North America, and researchers have found that Chinese children are more inhibited than Canadian infants (Chen & others, 1998). The cultural differences in temperament were linked to parents' attitudes and behaviors. Canadian mothers of inhibited 2-year-olds were less accepting of their infants' inhibited temperament while Chinese mothers were more accepting.

In short, many aspects of a child's environment can encourage or discourage the persistence of temperament characteristics. One useful way of thinking about these relationships applies the concept of goodness of fit, which we examine next.

Goodness of Fit and Parenting

Goodness of fit refers to the match between a child's temperament and the environmental demands the child must cope with (Matheny & Phillips, 2001). Consider an active child who is made to sit still for long periods of time or a slow-to-warm-up child who is abruptly pushed into new situations on a regular basis. Both children face a lack of fit between their temperament and environmental demands. Lack of fit can produce adjustment problems for the child.

Some temperament characteristics pose more parenting challenges than others, at least in modern Western societies (Rothbart & Bates, 2006). When children are prone to distress, as exhibited by frequent crying and irritability, their parents may eventually respond by ignoring the child's distress or trying to force the child to "behave." In one research study, though, extra support and training for mothers of distress-prone infants improved the quality of mother-infant interaction (van den Boom, 1989). The training led the mothers to alter their demands on the child, improving the fit between the child and the environment. Also, in a recent longitudinal study, researchers found that a high level of fearlessness on the part of infants, when combined with harsh parenting, was linked with persistent conduct problems at age 8 (Shaw & others, 2003).

Many parents don't become believers in temperament's importance until the birth of their second child. They viewed their first child's behavior as a result of how they treated the child. But then they find that some strategies that worked with their first child are not as effective with the second child. Some problems experienced with the first child (such as those involved in feeding, sleeping, and coping with strangers) do not exist with the second child, but new problems arise. Such experiences strongly suggest that children differ from each other very early in life, and that these differences have important implications for parent-child interaction (Kwak & others, 1999; Rothbart & Putnam, 2002).

What are the implications of temperamental variations for parenting? Although answers to this question necessarily are speculative, these conclusions regarding the best parenting strategies to use in relation to children's temperament were reached by temperament experts Ann Sanson and Mary Rothbart (1995):

- *Attention to and respect for individuality.* One implication is that it is difficult to generate general prescriptions for "good parenting." A goal might be accomplished in one way with one child and in another way with another child, depending on the child's temperament. Parents need to be sensitive and flexible to the infant's signals and needs.
- *Structuring the child's environment.* Crowded, noisy environments can pose greater problems for some children (such as a "difficult child") than others (such as an "easygoing" child). We might also expect that a fearful, withdrawing child would benefit from slower entry into new contexts.

goodness of fit Refers to the match between a child's temperament and the environmental demands the child must cope with.

- *The "difficult child" and packaged parenting programs.* Programs for parents often focus on dealing with children who have "difficult" temperaments. Acknowledging that some children are harder than others to parent is often helpful, and advice on how to handle particular difficult characteristics can be useful. However, whether a particular characteristic is difficult depends on its fit with the environment. To label a child "difficult" has the danger of becoming a self-fulfilling prophecy. If a child is identified as "difficult," people may treat the child in a way that actually elicits "difficult" behavior.

Too often, we pigeonhole children into categories without examining the context (Rothbart & Bates, 1998; Wachs, 2000). Nonetheless, caregivers need to take children's temperament into account. Research does not yet allow for many highly specific recommendations, but, in general, caregivers should (1) be sensitive to the individual characteristics of the child, (2) be flexible in responding to these characteristics, and (3) avoid applying negative labels to the child.

Review and Reflect • LEARNING GOAL 4

4 Characterize variations in temperament and their significance

Review
- How can temperament be described and classified?
- How is temperament influenced by biological foundations and experience?
- What is goodness of fit? What are some positive parenting strategies for dealing with a child's temperament?

Reflect
- Consider your own temperament. We described a number of temperament categories. Which one best describes your temperament? Has your temperament changed as you have gotten older? If your temperament has changed, what factors contributed to the changes?

5 ATTACHMENT

- What Is Attachment?
- Individual Differences in Attachment
- Caregiving Styles and Attachment
- Child Care

So far, we have discussed how emotions and emotional competence change as children develop. We have also examined the role of emotional style; in effect, we have seen how emotions set the tone of our experiences in life. But emotions also write the lyrics because they are at the core of our relationships with others. Foremost among these relationships is attachment.

What Is Attachment?

A small curly-haired girl named Danielle, age 11 months, begins to whimper. After a few seconds, she begins to wail. Soon her mother comes into the room, and Danielle's crying ceases. Quickly, Danielle crawls over to where her mother is seated and reaches out to be held. Danielle has just demonstrated attachment to her mother. **Attachment** is a close emotional bond between two people.

attachment A close emotional bond between two people.

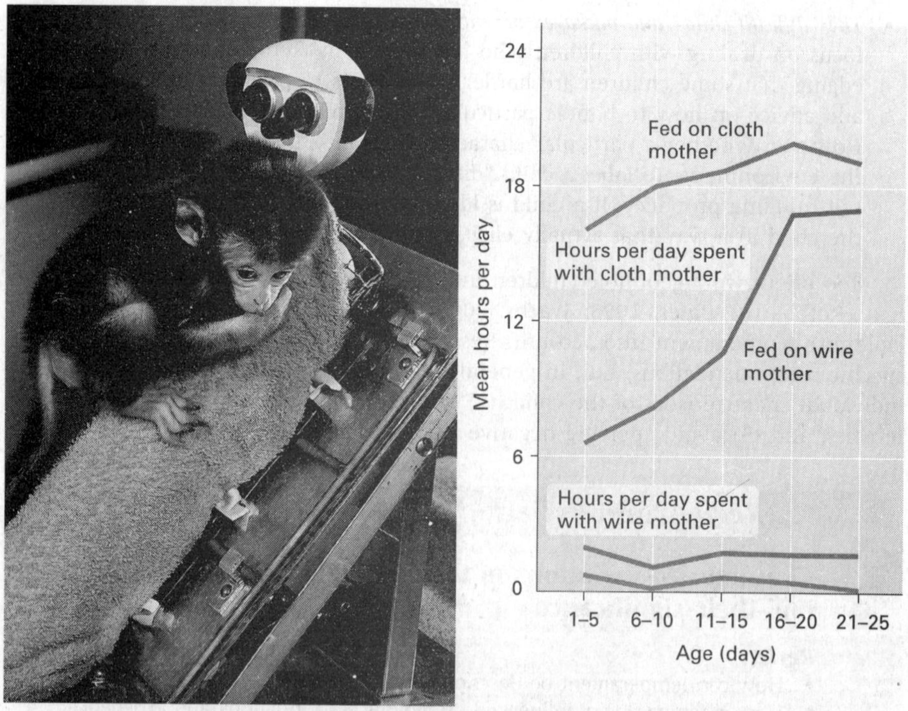

FIGURE 11.10 Contact Time with Wire and Cloth Surrogate Mothers. Regardless of whether the infant monkeys were fed by a wire or a cloth mother, they overwhelmingly preferred to spend contact time with the cloth mother.

There is no shortage of theories about infant attachment. Three theorists discussed in chapter 2—Freud, Erikson, and Bowlby—proposed influential views.

Freud believed that infants become attached to the person or object that provides oral satisfaction. For most infants, this is the mother, since she is most likely to feed the infant. Is feeding as important as Freud thought? A classic study by Harry Harlow (1958) reveals that the answer is no (see figure 11.10). Harlow removed infant monkeys from their mothers at birth; for 6 months they were reared by surrogate (substitute) "mothers." One surrogate mother was made of wire, the other of cloth. Half of the infant monkeys were fed by the wire mother, half by the cloth mother. Periodically, the amount of time the infant monkeys spent with either the wire or the cloth mother was computed. Regardless of which mother fed them, the infant monkeys spent far more time with the cloth mother. This study clearly demonstrated that feeding is not the crucial element in the attachment process and that contact comfort is important.

Physical comfort also plays a role in Erik Erikson's (1968) view of the infant's development. Recall Erikson's proposal (discussed in chapter 2) that the first year of life represents the stage of trust versus mistrust. Physical comfort and sensitive care, according to Erikson (1968), are key to establishing a basic trust in infants. The infant's sense of trust, in turn, is the foundation for attachment and sets the stage for a lifelong expectation that the world will be a good and pleasant place to be.

The ethological perspective of British psychiatrist John Bowlby (1969, 1989) also stresses the importance of attachment in the first year of life and the responsiveness of the caregiver. Bowlby believes that both infants and their primary caregivers are biologically predisposed to form attachments. He argues that the newborn is biologically equipped to elicit attachment behavior (Weizmann, 2000). The baby cries, clings, coos, and smiles. Later, the infant crawls, walks, and follows the mother. The immediate result is to keep the primary caregiver nearby; the long-term effect is to increase the infant's chances of survival.

Attachment does not emerge suddenly but rather develops in a series of phases, moving from a baby's general preference for human beings to a partnership with primary caregivers. Following are four such phases based on Bowlby's conceptualization of attachment (Schaffer, 1996):

- *Phase 1: From birth to 2 months.* Infants instinctively direct their attachment to human figures. Strangers, siblings, and parents are equally likely to elicit smiling or crying from the infant.
- *Phase 2: From 2 to 7 months.* Attachment becomes focused on one figure, usually the primary caregiver, as the baby gradually learns to distinguish familiar from unfamiliar people.
- *Phase 3: From 7 to 24 months.* Specific attachments develop. With increased locomotor skills, babies actively seek contact with regular caregivers, such as the mother or father.
- *Phase 4: From 24 months on.* Children become aware of others' feelings, goals, and plans and begin to take these into account in forming their own actions.

www.mhhe.com/santrockcd11

Forming a Secure Attachment
Attachment Research

Individual Differences in Attachment

Although attachment to a caregiver intensifies midway through the first year, isn't it likely that some babies have a more positive attachment experience than others? Mary Ainsworth thinks so. Ainsworth (1979) created the **Strange Situation,** an observational measure of infant attachment in which the infant experiences a series of introductions, separations, and reunions with the caregiver and an adult stranger in a prescribed order, which is described in figure 11.11. In using the Strange Situation, researchers hope that their observations will provide information about the

Strange Situation Ainsworth's observational measure of infant attachment to a caregiver that requires the infant to move through a series of introductions, separations, and reunions with the caregiver and an adult stranger in a prescribed order.

Episode	Persons present	Duration of episode	Description of setting
1	Caregiver, baby, and observer	30 seconds	Observer introduces caregiver and baby to experimental room, then leaves. (Room contains many appealing toys scattered about.)
2	Caregiver and baby	3 minutes	Caregiver is nonparticipant while baby explores; if necessary, play is stimulated after 2 minutes.
3	Stranger, caregiver, and baby	3 minutes	Stranger enters. First minute: Stranger is silent. Second minute: Stranger converses with caregiver. Third minute: Stranger approaches baby. After 3 minutes caregiver leaves unobtrusively.
4	Stranger and baby	3 minutes or less	First separation episode. Stranger's behavior is geared to that of baby.
5	Caregiver and baby	3 minutes or more	First reunion episode. Caregiver greets and/or comforts baby, then tries to settle baby again in play. Caregiver then leaves, saying "bye-bye."
6	Baby alone	3 minutes or less	Second separation episode.
7	Stranger and baby	3 minutes or less	Continuation of second separation. Stranger enters and gears behavior to that of baby.
8	Caregiver and baby	3 minutes	Second reunion episode. Caregiver enters, greets baby, then picks baby up. Meanwhile stranger leaves unobtrusively.

FIGURE 11.11 **The Ainsworth Strange Situation.** Mary Ainsworth *(left)* developed the Strange Situation to assess whether infants are securely or insecurely attached to their caregiver. The episodes involved in the Ainsworth Strange Situation are described here.

infant's motivation to be near the caregiver and the degree to which the caregiver's presence provides the infant with security and confidence.

Based on how babies respond in the Strange Situation, they are described as being securely attached or insecurely attached (in one of three ways) to the caregiver:

- **Securely attached babies** use the caregiver as a secure base from which to explore the environment. When in the presence of their caregiver, securely attached infants explore the room and examine toys that have been placed in it. When the caregiver departs, securely attached infants might mildly protest, and when the caregiver returns, these infants reestablish positive interaction with her, perhaps by smiling or climbing on her lap. Subsequently, they often resume playing with the toys in the room.
- **Insecure avoidant babies** show insecurity by avoiding the mother. In the Strange Situation, these babies engage in little interaction with the caregiver, are not distressed when she leaves the room, usually do not reestablish contact with her on her return, and may even turn their back on her at this point. If contact is established, the infant usually leans away or looks away.
- **Insecure resistant babies** often cling to the caregiver and then resist her by fighting against the closeness, perhaps by kicking or pushing away. In the Strange Situation, these babies often cling anxiously to the caregiver and don't explore the playroom. When the caregiver leaves, they often cry loudly and push away if she tries to comfort them on her return.
- **Insecure disorganized babies** are disorganized and disoriented. In the Strange Situation, these babies might appear dazed, confused, and fearful. To be classified as disorganized, babies must show strong patterns of avoidance and resistance or display certain specified behaviors, such as extreme fearfulness around the caregiver.

securely attached babies The infant uses the caregiver as a secure base from which to explore the environment.

insecure avoidant babies Babies who show insecurity by avoiding the mother.

insecure resistant babies Babies who might cling to the caregiver, then resist her by fighting against the closeness, perhaps by kicking or pushing away.

insecure disorganized babies Babies who show insecurity by being disorganized and disoriented.

Does the Strange Situation capture important differences among infants? As a measure of attachment, it may be culturally biased. For example, German and Japanese babies often show different patterns of attachment than American infants. As illustrated in figure 11.12, German infants are more likely to show an avoidant attachment pattern and Japanese infants are less likely to display this pattern than U.S. infants (van IJzendoorn & Kroonenberg, 1988). The avoidant pattern in German babies likely occurs because their caregivers encourage them to be independent (Grossmann & others, 1985). Also as shown in figure 11.12, Japanese babies are more likely than American babies to be categorized as resistant. This may have more to do with the Strange Situation as a measure of attachment than with attachment insecurity itself. Japanese mothers rarely let anyone unfamiliar with their babies care for them. Thus, the Strange Situation might create considerably more stress for Japanese infants than for American infants, who are more accustomed to separation from their mothers (Takahashi, 1990). Even though there are cultural variations in attachment classification, however, the most frequent classification in every culture studied so far is secure attachment (van IJzendoorn & Kroonenberg, 1988).

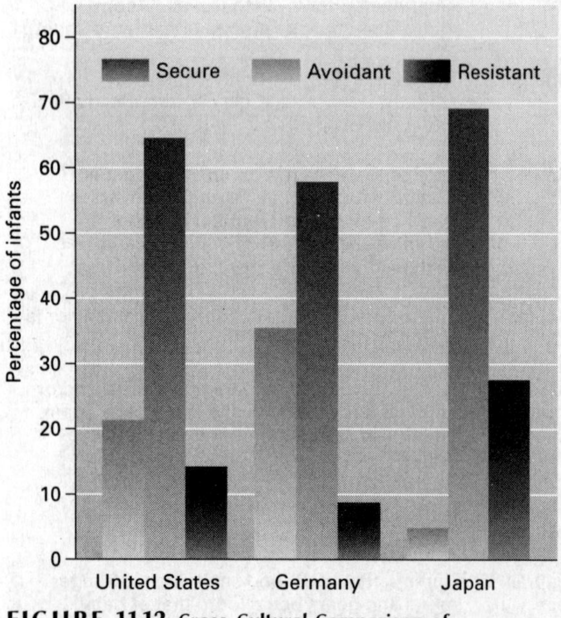

FIGURE 11.12 Cross-Cultural Comparison of Attachment. In one study, infant attachment in three countries—the United States, Germany, and Japan—was measured in the Ainsworth Strange Situation (van IJzendoorn & Kroonenberg, 1988). The dominant attachment pattern in all three countries was secure attachment. However, German infants were more avoidant and Japanese infants were less avoidant and more resistant than U.S. infants.

Some critics stress that behavior in the Strange Situation—like other laboratory assessments—might not indicate what infants do in a natural environment. But researchers have found that infants' behaviors in the Strange Situation are closely related to how they behave at home in response to separation and reunion with their mothers (Pederson & Moran, 1996). Thus, many infant researchers believe the Strange Situation continues to show merit as a measure of infant attachment.

Do individual differences in attachment matter? Ainsworth believes that secure attachment in the first year of life provides an important foundation for psychological development later in life. The securely attached infant moves freely away from the caregiver but keeps track of where she is through periodic glances. The securely attached infant responds positively to being picked up by others and, when put back down, freely moves away to play. An insecurely attached infant, by contrast, avoids the caregiver or is ambivalent toward her, fears strangers, and is upset by minor, everyday separations.

If early attachment to a caregiver is important, it should relate to a child's social behavior later in development. For some children, early attachments do seem to foreshadow later functioning (Carlson, Sroufe, & Egeland, 2004; Egeland & Carlson, 2004; Sroufe & others, 2005). For example, one recent study found that infants who were securely attached at 15 months of age were more cognitively and socioemotionally competent at 4 years of age than their counterparts who were insecurely attached at 15 months of age (Fish, 2004). For other children, there is little continuity (Thompson, 2006; Thompson & Goodvin, 2005). Consistency in caregiving over a number of years is likely an important factor in connecting early attachment and the child's functioning later in development. In one longitudinal study, attachment classification in infancy did not predict attachment classification at 18 years of age (Lewis, 1997). In this study, the best predictor of an insecure attachment classification at 18 was the occurrence of parent divorce in the intervening years.

Some developmentalists believe that too much emphasis has been placed on the attachment bond in infancy. Jerome Kagan (1987, 2000), for example, believes that infants are highly resilient and adaptive; he argues that they are evolutionarily equipped to stay on a positive developmental course, even in the face of wide variations in parenting. Kagan and others stress that genetic characteristics and temperament play more important roles in a child's social competence than the attachment theorists, such as Bowlby and Ainsworth, are willing to acknowledge (Chauhuri & Williams, 1999; Kagan & Fox, 2006; Young & Shahinfar, 1995). For example, if some infants inherit a low tolerance for stress, this, rather than an insecure attachment bond, may be responsible for an inability to get along with peers.

Another criticism of attachment theory is that it ignores the diversity of socializing agents and contexts that exists in an infant's world. In some cultures, infants show attachments to many people. Among the Hausa (who live in Nigeria), both grandmothers and siblings provide a significant amount of care for infants (Harkness & Super, 1995). Infants in agricultural societies tend to form attachments to older siblings, who are assigned a major responsibility for younger siblings' care. Researchers recognize the importance of competent, nurturant caregivers in an infant's development (Bornstein, 2006; Maccoby, 1999; McHale & others, 2001; Parke, 2001; Parke & Buriel, 2006). At issue, though, is whether or not secure attachment, especially to a single caregiver, is critical (Lamb, 2005; Thompson, 2006).

Despite such criticisms, there is ample evidence that security of attachment is important to development (Thompson & Goodvin, 2005; Waters, Corcoran, & Anafara, 2005). Secure attachment in infancy is important because it reflects a positive parent-infant relationship and provides the foundation that supports healthy socioemotional development in the years that follow.

In the Hausa culture, siblings and grandmothers provide a significant amount of care for infants. *How might this practice affect attachment?*

Caregiving Styles and Attachment

Is the style of caregiving linked with the quality of the infant's attachment? Securely attached babies have caregivers who are sensitive to their signals and are consistently available to respond to their infants' needs (Gao, Elliott, & Waters, 1999; Main, 2000). These caregivers often let their babies have an active part in determining the onset and pacing of interaction in the first year of life. One recent study found that maternal sensitivity in parenting was linked with secure attachment in infants in two different cultures: the United States and Colombia (Carbonell & others, 2002).

How do the caregivers of insecurely attached babies interact with them? Caregivers of avoidant babies tend to be unavailable or rejecting (Berlin & Cassidy, 2000). They often don't respond to their babies' signals and have little physical contact with them. When they do interact with their babies, they may behave in an angry and irritable way. Caregivers of resistant babies tend to be inconsistent; sometimes they respond to their babies' needs, and sometimes they don't. In general, they tend not to be very affectionate with their babies and show little synchrony when interacting with them. Caregivers of disorganized babies often neglect or physically abuse them (Barnett, Ganiban, & Cicchetti, 1999; Cicchetti & Toth, 2006). In some cases, these caregivers are depressed.

Child Care

Many U.S. children today experience multiple caregivers. Most do not have a parent staying home to care for them; instead, the children have some type of so-called child care. Does attending child care influence their socioemotional and cognitive development? Many parents worry that child care will reduce their infants' emotional attachment to them, retard the infants' cognitive development, fail to teach them how to control anger, and allow them to be unduly influenced by their peers. How extensive is child care? Are the worries of these parents justified?

Parental Leave Today far more young children are in child care than at any other time in history; about 2 million children in the United States currently receive formal, licensed child care, and more than 5 million children attend kindergarten. Also, uncounted millions of children are cared for by unlicensed baby-sitters.

In part, these numbers reflect the fact that most U.S. adults do not receive paid leave from their jobs to care for their young children. Sheila Kammerman (1989, 2000a, 2000b) has conducted extensive examinations of parental leave policies around the world. Policies vary in eligibility criteria, leave duration, benefit level, and the extent to which parents take advantage of these policies. Europe led the way in creating new standards of parental leave: the European Union (EU) mandated a paid 14-week maternity leave in 1992. Among advanced industrialized countries, the United States grants the shortest period of parental leave and is among the few countries that offers only unpaid leave (Australia and New Zealand are the others).

There are five types of parental leave from employment:

- *Maternity Leave.* In some countries the pre-birth leave is compulsory as is a 6- to 10-week leave following birth.
- *Paternity Leave.* This is usually much briefer than maternity leave. It may be especially important when a second child is born and the first child requires care.
- *Parental Leave.* This is a gender-neutral leave that usually follows a maternity leave and allows either women or men to take advantage of the leave policy and share it or choose which of them will use it. In 1998, the European Union mandated a three-month parental leave.
- *Child-Rearing Leave.* In some countries, this is a supplement to a maternity leave or a variation on a parental leave. A child-rearing leave is usually longer than a maternity leave and is typically paid at a much lower level.
- *Family Leave.* This covers reasons other than the birth of a new baby and can allow time off from employment to care for an ill child or other family members, time to accompany a child to school for the first time, or time to visit a child's school.

Sweden has one of the most extensive leave policies. Paid for by the government at 80 percent of wages, one year of parental leave is allowed (including maternity leave). Maternity leave may begin 60 days prior to the expected birth of the baby and ends six weeks after birth. Another six months of parental leave can be used until the child's eighth birthday (Kammerman, 2000a). Virtually all eligible mothers take advantage of the leave policy, and approximately 75 percent of eligible fathers take at least some part of the leave they are allowed. In addition, employed grandparents now have the right to take time off to care for an ill grandchild. Spain allows a 16-week paid maternity leave (paid at 100 percent of wages) at childbirth with up to 6 weeks prior to childbirth allowed. Fathers are permitted two days of leave.

Variations in Child Care Because the United States does not have a policy of paid leave for child care, child care in the United States has become a major national concern (Lamb & Ahnert, 2006; Marshall, 2004; Randolph & Kochanoff, 2004). The type of child care that young children receive varies extensively (Scarr, 2000). Many child-care centers house large groups of children and have elaborate facilities. Some are commercial operations; others are nonprofit centers run by churches, civic groups, and employers. Child care is frequently provided in private homes, at times by child care professionals, at others by mothers who want to earn extra money.

There is increasing interest in the role of child care in ethnic minority families. Child-care patterns vary by ethnicity. For example, Latino families are far less likely than non-Latino White and African American families to have children in child-care centers (11 percent, 20 percent, and 21 percent, respectively, in one recent study) (Smith, 2002). Despite indicating a preference for center-based care, African American and Latino families often rely on family-based care, especially by grandmothers. However, there has been a substantial increase in the use of center-based care by African American mothers.

Many researchers have examined the role of poverty in the quality of child care (Chase-Lansdale, Coley, & Grining, 2001; Lamb & Ahnert, 2006; McLearn, 2004; Zaslow, 2004). A recent study found that extensive child care was harmful to low-income children only when the care was of low quality (Votruba-Drzal, Coley, & Chase-Lansdale, 2004). Even if the child was in child care more than 45 hours a week, high-quality care was linked with fewer internalizing problems (anxiety, for example) and externalizing problems (aggressive and destructive behaviors, for example).

What constitutes a high-quality child-care program for infants? The demonstration program developed by Jerome Kagan and his colleagues (Kagan, Kearsley, & Zelazo, 1978) at Harvard University is exemplary. The child-care center included a pediatrician, a nonteaching director, and an infant-teacher ratio of 3 to 1. Teachers' aides assisted at the center. The teachers and aides were trained to smile frequently, to talk with the infants, and to provide them with a safe environment, which included many stimulating toys. No adverse effects of child care were observed in this project.

Children are more likely to experience poor-quality child care if they come from families with few resources (psychological, social, and economic) (Lamb, 1994). To read about one individual who provides quality child

CAREERS in CHILD DEVELOPMENT

Rashmi Nakhre
Child-Care Director

Rashmi Nakhre has two master's degrees—one in psychology, the other in child development—and is director of the Hattie Daniels Day Care Center in Wilson, North Carolina. At a recent ceremony, "Celebrating a Century of Women," Rashmi received the Distinguished Women of North Carolina Award for 1999–2000.

Rashmi first worked at the child-care center soon after she arrived in the United States 25 years ago. She says that she took the job initially because she needed the money but "ended up falling in love with my job." Rashmi has turned the Wilson, North Carolina, child-care center into a model for other centers. The Center almost closed several years after Rashmi began working there because of financial difficulties. Rashmi played a major role in raising funds not only to keep it open but to improve it. The Center provides quality child care for the children of many Latino migrant workers.

Rashmi Nakhre, working with young children at her child-care center in Wilson, North Carolina.

www.mhhe.com/santrockcd11

National Child Care Information Center
NICHD Study of Early Child Care

care to individuals from impoverished backgrounds, see the Careers in Child Development insert. In the Research in Child Development interlude below, you can read about an ongoing national study of child care and its effects.

RESEARCH IN CHILD DEVELOPMENT

A National Longitudinal Study of Child Care

In 1991, the National Institute of Child Health and Human Development (NICHD) began a comprehensive, longitudinal study of child-care experiences. Data were collected on a diverse sample of almost 1,400 children and their families at 10 locations across the United States over a period of seven years. Researchers used multiple methods (trained observers, interviews, questionnaires, and testing), and they measured many facets of children's development, including physical health, cognitive development, and socioemotional development. Following are some of the results (NICHD Early Child Care Network, 2001, 2002, 2003, 2005):

- *Patterns of Use.* Many families placed their infants in child care very soon after the child's birth, and there was considerable instability in the child-care arrangements. By 4 months of age, nearly three-fourths of the infants had entered some form of nonmaternal child care. Almost half of the infants were cared for by a relative when they first entered care; only 12 percent were enrolled in child-care centers. Socioeconomic factors were linked to the amount and type of care. For example, mothers with higher incomes and families that were more dependent on the mother's income placed their infants in child care at an earlier age. Mothers who believed that maternal employment has positive effects on children were more likely than other mothers to place their infant in nonmaternal care for more hours. Low-income families were more likely than more affluent families to use child care, but infants from low-income families who were in child care averaged as many hours as other income groups. In the preschool years, mothers who were single, those with more education, and families with higher incomes used more hours of center care than other families. Minority families and mothers with less education used more hours of care by relatives.
- *Quality of Care.* Evaluations of quality of care were based on such characteristics as group size, child-adult ratio, physical environment, caregiver characteristics (such as formal education, specialized training, and child-care experience), and caregiver behavior (such as sensitivity to children). Infants from low-income families experienced lower quality of child care than infants from higher-income families. When quality of caregivers' care was high, children performed better on cognitive and language tasks, were more cooperative with their mothers during play, showed more positive and skilled interaction with peers, and had fewer behavior problems. Caregiver training and good child-staff ratios were linked with higher cognitive and social competence when children were 54 months of age.

  Higher-quality child care was also related to higher-quality mother-child interaction among the families that used nonmaternal care. Further, poor-quality care was related to an increase of insecure attachment to the mother among infants who were 15 months of age, but only when the mother was low in sensitivity and responsiveness. However, child-care quality was not linked to attachment security at 36 months of age.
- *Amount of Child Care.* The quantity of child care predicted some child outcomes. When children spent extensive amounts of time in child care beginning in infancy, they experienced less sensitive interactions with their

mother, showed more behavior problems, and had higher rates of illness (Vandell, 2004). Many of these comparisons involved children in child care for less than 30 hours a week versus those in child care for more than 45 hours a week.

- *Family and Parenting Influences.* The influence of families and parenting was not weakened by extensive child care. Parents played a significant role in helping children to regulate their emotions.

Child care may harm some children more than others. Difficult children and those with poor self-control may be especially at risk in child care (Maccoby & Lewis, 2003). Thus, it may be helpful to teach child-care providers how to foster self-regulatory skills in children (Fabes & others, 2003) and to invest more effort in building children's attachment to their child-care center or school. For example, one study revealed that when children experienced their group, class, or school as a caring community, they showed increased concern for others, better conflict resolution skills, and a decrease in problem behaviors (Solomon & others, 2000).

What are some strategies parents can follow in regard to child care? Child-care expert Kathleen McCartney (2003, p. 4) offered this advice:

- *Recognize that the quality of your parenting is a key factor in your child's development.*
- *Make decisions that will improve the likelihood you will be good parents.* "For some this will mean working full-time"—for personal fulfillment, income, or both. "For others, this will mean working part-time or not working outside the home."
- *Monitor your child's development.* "Parents should observe for themselves whether their children seem to be having behavior problems." They need to talk with child-care providers and their pediatricians about their children's behavior.
- *Take some time to find the best child care.* Observe different child-care facilities and be certain that you like what you see. "Quality child care costs money, and not all parents can afford the child care they want. However, state subsidies, and other programs like Head Start, are available for (most) families in need."

Review and Reflect • LEARNING GOAL 5

5 Explain attachment and its development

Review

- What is attachment?
- What are some individual variations in attachment? What are some criticisms of attachment theory?
- How are caregiving styles related to attachment?
- How does child care affect children?

Reflect

- Imagine that a friend of yours is getting ready to put her baby in child care. What advice would you give to her? Do you think she should stay home with the baby? Why or why not? What type of child care would you recommend?

REACH YOUR LEARNING GOALS

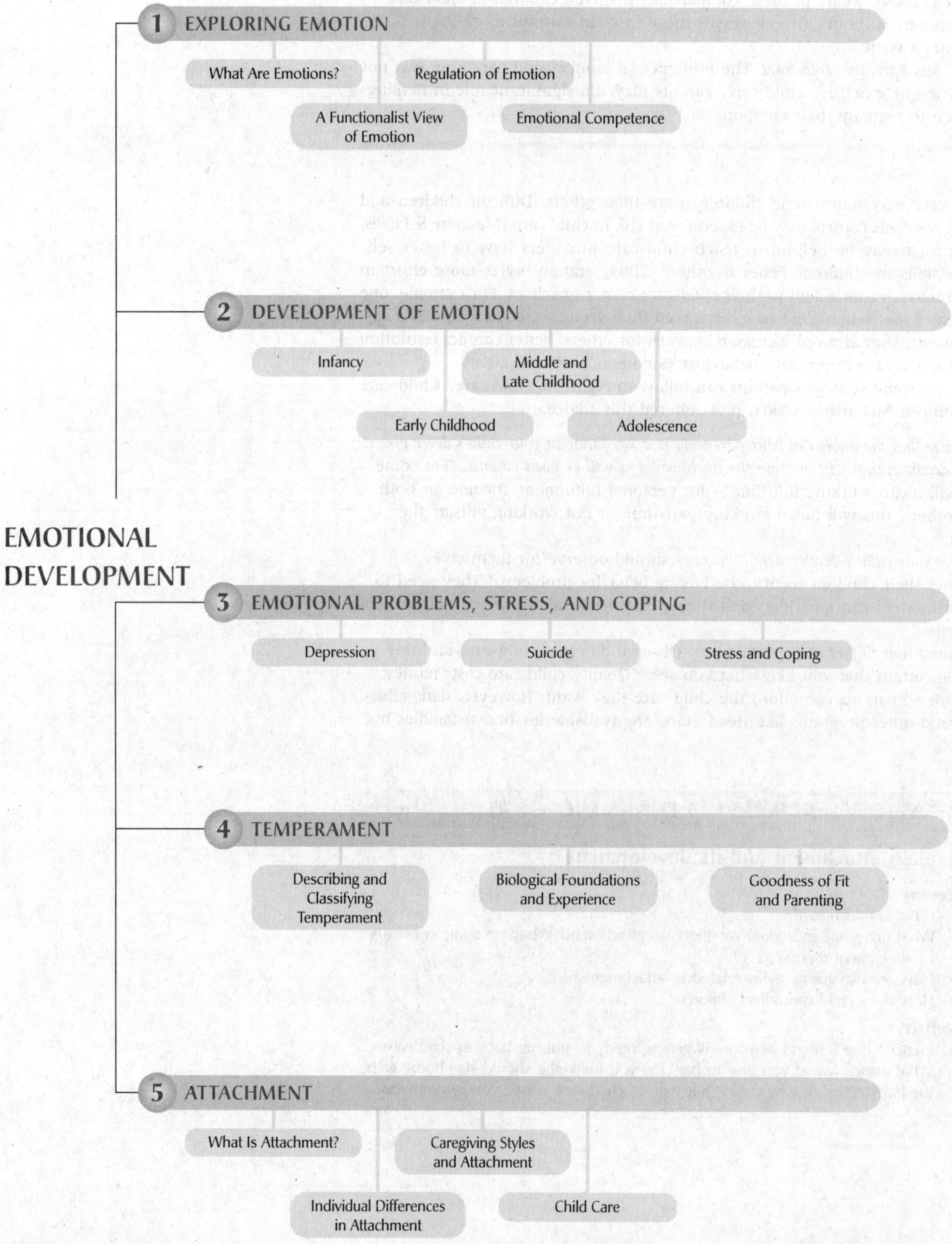

SUMMARY

1 Discuss basic aspects of emotion

- Emotion is feeling or affect that occurs when a person is in a state or an interaction that is important to him or her, especially to his or her well-being. Darwin described the evolutionary basis of emotions and today psychologists believe that emotions, especially facial expressions of emotions, have a biological foundation. Facial expressions of emotion are the same across cultures. However, display rules are not culturally universal. Biological evolution endowed humans to be emotional but embeddedness in culture and relationships provides diversity in emotional experiences.
- The functionalist view of emotion emphasizes the importance of contexts and relationships in emotion. In this view, goals are involved in emotions in a variety of ways.
- Emotional regulation consists of effectively managing arousal to adapt and reach a goal. With increasing age in infancy and early childhood, regulation of emotion gradually shifts from external sources to self-initiated, internal sources. Also with increasing age, children are more likely to increase their use of cognitive strategies for regulating emotion, modulate their emotional arousal, become more adept at managing situations to minimize negative emotion, and choose effective ways to cope with stress. Parents can help children learn to regulate their emotion through emotion coaching.
- Emotional competence focuses on the adaptive nature of emotional experience. Saarni believes that becoming emotionally competent involves developing skills such as being aware of one's emotional states, discerning others' emotions, adaptively coping with negative emotions, and understanding the role of emotions in relationships.

2 Describe the development of emotion

- Two broad types of emotions are primary emotions (surprise, interest, joy, anger, sadness, fear, and disgust, which appear in the first six months of life) and self-conscious emotions (empathy, jealousy, and embarrassment, which appear at 1½ to 2 years, and pride, shame, and guilt, which appear at 2½ years). Crying is the most important mechanism newborns have for communicating with their world. Babies have at least three types of cries—basic, anger, and pain cries. Controversy swirls about whether babies should be soothed when they cry, although increasingly experts recommend immediately responding in a caring way in the first year. Two types of smiling are reflexive and communicative. Two fears that infants develop are stranger anxiety and separation from a caregiver (which is reflected in separation protest). Social referencing increases in the second year of life. As infants develop it is important for them to engage in emotional regulation.
- Preschoolers become more adept at talking about their own and others' emotions. Two- and 3-year-olds substantially increase the number of terms they use to describe emotion and learn more about the causes and consequences of feelings. At 4 to 5 years of age, children increasingly reflect on emotions and understand that a single event can elicit different emotions in different people.
- In middle and late childhood, children show a growing awareness about controlling and managing emotions to meet social standards. Also in this age period, children increasingly understand complex emotions such as pride and shame and realize that more than one emotion can be expressed in a particular situation. They also increasingly take into account the events that led up to an emotional reaction, suppress and conceal their emotions, and initiate strategies to redirect their emotions.
- Moodiness is a normal aspect of early adolescence. Although pubertal change is associated with an increase in negative emotions, hormonal influences are often small and environmental experiences may contribute more to the emotions of adolescence than hormonal changes.

3 Summarize the nature of depression, suicide, stress, and coping

- Depression is more likely to occur in adolescence than in childhood and in girls more than in boys. In childhood, the features of depression often are mixed with a broader array of behaviors than in adulthood. Bowlby's developmental view, Beck's cognitive view, and Seligman's learned helplessness view provide explanations of depression. Depression in parents is linked with children's adjustment problems.
- Adolescent suicide is the third-leading cause of death in U.S. adolescents. Demographic and psychological characteristics as well as social experiences have been linked to suicide.
- Lazarus believes that children's stress depends on how they cognitively appraise and interpret events. Seligman argues that an important aspect of coping with stress is whether the child is optimistic or pessimistic. Sociocultural influences, such as acculturative stress and poverty, can generate stress. Two good strategies for caregivers in helping children cope with stress are to (1) remove at least one stressor from the child's life and

(2) help the child learn to use effective coping strategies. Young children do not understand the nature of death, believing it is not final. In the middle of the elementary school years, they comprehend its final, irreversible nature.

4 Characterize variations in temperament and their significance

- Temperament is an individual's behavioral style and characteristic way of emotional responding. Developmentalists are especially interested in the temperament of infants. Chess and Thomas classified infants as (1) easy, (2) difficult, or (3) slow to warm up. Kagan believes that inhibition to the unfamiliar is an important temperament category. Rothbart and Bates proposed that temperament be classified based on (1) positive affect and approach, (2) negative affectivity, and (3) effortful control (self-regulation).
- Kagan has argued that children inherit a physiology that biases them to have a particular type of temperament but through experience they learn to modify their temperament style to some degree. Physiological characteristics are associated with different temperaments and a moderate influence of heredity has been found in studies of the heritability of temperament. Very active young children are likely to become outgoing adults. Young adults show fewer mood swings, are more responsible, and engage in less risk-taking than adolescents. In some cases, a difficult temperment is linked with adjustment problems in early adulthood. The link between childhood temperament and adult personality depends in part on context, which helps shape the reaction to a child and thus the child's experiences. For example, the reaction to a child's temperament depends in part on the child's gender and on the culture.
- Goodness of fit refers to the match between a child's temperament and the environmental demands the child must cope with. Goodness of fit can be an important aspect of a child's adjustment. Although research evidence is sketchy at this point in time, some general recommendations are that caregivers should (1) be sensitive to the individual characteristics of the child, (2) be flexible in responding to these characteristics, and (3) avoid applying negative labels to the child.

5 Explain attachment and its development

- Attachment is a close emotional bond between two people. In infancy, contact comfort and trust are important in the development of attachment. Bowlby's ethological theory stresses that the caregiver and the infant are biologically predisposed to form an attachment. Attachment develops in four phases during infancy.
- Securely attached babies use the caregiver, usually the mother, as a secure base from which to explore the environment. Three types of insecure attachment are avoidant, resistant, and disorganized. Ainsworth created the Strange Situation, an observational measure of attachment. Ainsworth believes that secure attachment in the first year of life provides an important foundation for psychological development later in life. The strength of the link found between early attachment and later development has varied somewhat across studies. Some critics argue that attachment theorists have not given adequate attention to genetics and temperament. Other critics stress that they have not adequately taken into account the diversity of social agents and contexts. Cultural variations in attachment have been found, but in all cultures studied to date secure attachment is the most common classification.
- Caregivers of secure babies are sensitive to the babies' signals and are consistently available to meet their needs. Caregivers of avoidant babies tend to be unavailable or rejecting. Caregivers of ambivalent-rejecting babies tend to be inconsistently available to their babies and usually are not very affectionate. Caregivers of disorganized babies often neglect or physically abuse their babies.
- Child care has become a basic need of the American family. More children are in child care now than at any earlier point in history. The quality of child care is uneven, and day care remains a controversial topic. Quality child care can be achieved and seems to have few adverse effects on children. In the NICHD child-care study, infants from low-income families were more likely to receive the lowest quality of care. Also, higher quality of child care was linked with fewer child problems.

KEY TERMS

emotion 332
primary emotions 336
self-conscious emotions 336
basic cry 336
anger cry 336
pain cry 337
reflexive smile 338
social smile 338
stranger anxiety 338
separation protest 338
social referencing 339
stress 345
cognitive appraisal 346
primary appraisal 346
secondary appraisal 346
temperament 350
easy child 351
difficult child 351
slow-to-warm-up child 351
goodness of fit 354
attachment 355
Strange Situation 357
securely attached babies 358
insecure avoidant babies 358
insecure resistant babies 358
insecure disorganized babies 358

KEY PEOPLE

Carolyn Saarni 335
John Watson 337
Jacob Gewirtz 337
Mary Ainsworth 337
John Bowlby 337
Richard Lazarus 346
Stella Chess and Alexander Thomas 351
Jerome Kagan 351
Mary Rothbart 351
Theodore Wachs 353
Harry Harlow 356
Erik Erikson 356
Kathleen McCartney 363

E-LEARNING TOOLS

To help you master the material in this chapter, visit the Online Learning Center for *Child Development*, eleventh edition (**www.mhhe.com/santrockcd11**), where you'll find these additional resources:

Taking It to the Net

1. Catherine is conducting a class for new parents at a local clinic. What advice should Catherine give the parents about how parenting practices can affect a child's inborn temperament?
2. Peter and Rachel are adopting a 3-month old infant. What are some practical things they can do to help insure that their child develops a healthy attachment bond with them in the first few months of life?
3. Veronica is anxious about choosing the best child-care center for her child. What are the main things she should consider as she visits the facilities on her list?

Nursing, Parenting, and Teaching Exercises

Build your decision-making skills by trying your hand at the scenarios on the Online Learning Center.

Video Clips

The Online Learning Center includes the following videos for this chapter:

- Describing Best Friend at Age 11
  An 11-year-old girl talks about her best friends and how they helped her through "sad times."
- Adolescent and Parent Emotions
  Reed Larson, Department of Human & Community Development, University of Illinois, U-C, describes adolescents' and parents' emotional behavior, how they differ and how they can clash.
- Adolescent Loneliness
  Dr. Larson discusses the significance of time alone on adolescent emotions.

Chapter 12 THE SELF AND IDENTITY

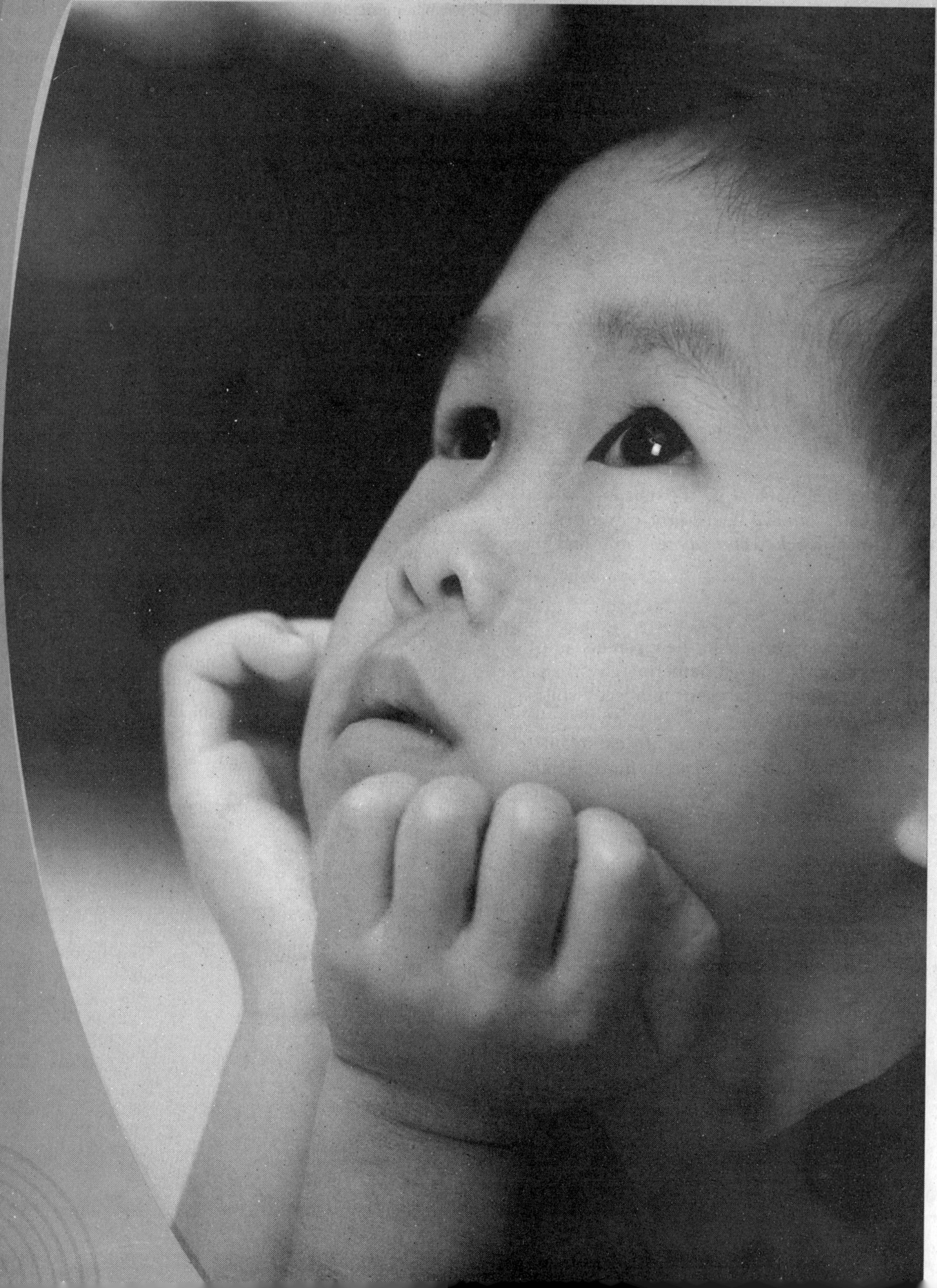

When I say "I," I mean something absolutely unique not to be confused with any other.

—Ugo Betti
Italian Playwright, 20th Century

CHAPTER OUTLINE

SELF-UNDERSTANDING

What Is Self-Understanding?
Developmental Changes
Perspective Taking
Sociocultural Contexts

SELF-ESTEEM AND SELF-CONCEPT

What Are Self-Esteem and Self-Concept?
Assessment
Developmental Changes
Variations in Self-Esteem

IDENTITY

What Is Identity?
Erikson's View
Developmental Changes
Social Contexts

LEARNING GOALS

1. Discuss self-understanding and its development
2. Explain self-esteem and self-concept
3. Describe identity and its development

The Story of Maxine Hong Kingston, Bridging Cultural Worlds

Maxine Hong Kingston

Maxine Hong Kingston's vivid portrayals of her Chinese ancestry and struggles of Chinese immigrants have made her one of the world's leading Asian American writers. Kingston's parents were both Chinese immigrants. Born in California in 1940, she spent many hours working with her parents and five brothers and sisters in the family's laundry. As a youth, Kingston was profoundly influenced by her parents' struggle to adapt to American culture and by their descriptions of their Chinese heritage.

Growing up as she did, Kingston felt the pull of two very different cultures. She was especially intrigued by stories about Chinese women who were perceived as either privileged or degraded.

Her first book is titled *The Woman Warrior: Memoirs of a Girlhood Among Ghosts* (Kingston, 1976). In *The Woman Warrior,* Kingston described her aunt, who gave birth to an illegitimate child. Because having a child outside of wedlock was taboo and perceived as a threat to the community's stability, the entire Chinese village condemned her, pushing her to kill herself and her child. From then on, even mentioning her name was forbidden.

In 1980, Kingston published *China Men,* which won the American Book Award for nonfiction and was runner-up for the Pulitzer Prize. Based on the experiences of her father and several generations of other male relatives, the book examines the lives of Chinese men who left their homeland to settle in the United States. It contains stories of loneliness and discrimination as well as determination and strength.

Kingston currently teaches at the University of California at Berkeley. She says that she doesn't want to be viewed as an exotic writer but as someone who writes and teaches about Americans and what it means to be human. Kingston says she likes to guide people in how to find meaning in their lives, especially by exploring their cultural backgrounds.

PREVIEW

Maxine Hong Kingston's life and writings reflect important aspects of each of our lives as we grew up: our efforts to understand ourselves and to develop an identity that reflects our cultural heritage. This chapter is about these topics: the self and identity. As we examine these topics, reflect on how much you understood yourself at different points in your life as you were growing up and think about how you acquired the stamp of your identity.

1 SELF-UNDERSTANDING

- What Is Self-Understanding?
- Developmental Changes
- Perspective Taking
- Sociocultural Contexts

What is self-understanding? When do children initially develop self-understanding, and how does it develop? What is the role of perspective taking in self-understanding? How is self-understanding linked to sociocultural contexts? We will examine each of these questions.

What Is Self-Understanding?

Self-understanding is a child's cognitive representation of the self, the substance and content of the child's self-conceptions. For example, an 11-year-old boy understands that he is a student, a boy, a football player, a family member, a video game lover, and a rock music fan. A 13-year-old girl understands that she is a middle school student, in the midst of puberty, a girl, a cheerleader, a student council member, and a movie fan. A child's self-understanding is based, in part, on the various roles and membership categories that define who children are (Harter, 1990, 1999). Though not the whole of personal identity, self-understanding provides its rational underpinnings (Damon & Hart, 1988).

www.mhhe.com/santrockcd11

Concepts of Person and Self

self-understanding A child's cognitive representation of the self; the substance and content of a child's self-conceptions.

Developmental Changes

Children are not just given a self by their parents or culture; rather, they find and construct selves (Garcia, Hart, & Johnson-Ray, 1998). As children develop, their self-understanding changes. First, let's examine self-understanding in infants.

Infancy

Studying the self in infancy is difficult mainly because infants cannot tell us how they experience themselves. Infants cannot verbally express their views of the self. They also cannot understand complex instructions from researchers.

Given these restrictions, how would you study infants' self-understanding? One ingenious solution tests infants' visual self-recognition through the mirror technique (Thompson, 2006). An infant's mother puts a dot of rouge on the infant's nose. An observer watches to see how often the infant touches its nose. Next, the infant is placed in front of a mirror, and observers detect whether nose touching increases. Why does this matter? The idea is that increased nose touching indicates that the infant recognizes the self in the mirror and is trying to touch or rub off the rouge because the rouge violates the infant's view of the self. Increased touching indicates that the infant realizes that it is the self in the mirror but that something is not right since the real self does not have a dot of rouge on it.

Figure 12.1 displays the results of two investigations that used the mirror technique. The researchers found that before they were 1 year old, infants did not recognize themselves in the mirror (Amsterdam, 1968; Lewis & Brooks-Gunn, 1979). Signs of self-recognition began to appear among some infants when they were 15 to 18 months old. By the time they were 2 years old, most children recognized themselves in the mirror. In sum, infants begin to develop a rudimentary self-understanding called self-recognition at approximately 18 months of age (Hart & Karmel, 1996; Lewis & others, 1989).

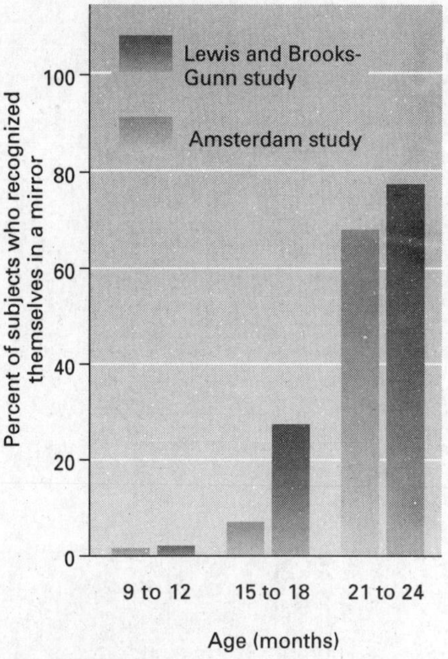

FIGURE 12.1 The Development of Self-Recognition in Infancy. The graph gives the findings of two studies in which infants of different ages showed that they recognized themselves by touching, wiping, or verbally referring to rouge on their faces. Notice that self-recognition did not occur extensively until the second half of the second year of life.

Early Childhood

Because children can verbally communicate, research on self-understanding in childhood is not limited to visual self-recognition, as it is during infancy. Mainly through interviews, researchers have probed many aspects of children's self-understanding. Here are five main characteristics of self-understanding in young children:

- ***Confusion of self, mind, and body.*** Young children generally confuse self, mind, and body (Broughton, 1978). Most young children conceive of the self as part of the body, which usually means the head. For them, the self can be described along many material dimensions, such as size, shape, and color.
- ***Concrete descriptions.*** Preschool children think of themselves and define themselves in concrete terms. A young child might say, "I know my ABC's," "I can count," and "I live in a big house" (Harter, 2006).
- ***Physical descriptions.*** Young children also distinguish themselves from others through many physical and material attributes. Says 4-year-old Sandra, "I'm different from Jennifer because I have brown hair and she has blond hair."

Says 4-year-old Ralph, "I am different from Hank because I am taller, and I am different from my sister because I have a bicycle."

- ***Active descriptions.*** The *active dimension* is a central component of the self in early childhood (Keller, Ford, & Meacham, 1978). For example, preschool children often describe themselves in terms of activities such as play.
- ***Unrealistic positive overestimations.*** Self-evaluations during early childhood are often unrealistically positive and represent an overestimation of personal attributes (Harter, 2006). A young child might say, "I know all of my ABC's" but does not, or might comment, "I'm never scared," which is not the case. These unrealistic positive overestimations of the self occur because: (1) young children have difficulty in differentiating their desired and actual competence, (2) cannot yet generate an ideal self that is distinguished from a real self, and (3) rarely engage in *social comparison*—how they compare with others. *Inability to recognize opposite attributes.* Young children's self-evaluations also reflect an inability to recognize that they can possess opposite attributes, such as "good" and "bad" or "nice" and "mean" (Harter, 2006).

Middle and Late Childhood Children's self-evaluation becomes more complex during middle and late childhood. Five key changes characterize the increased complexity:

- ***Internal characteristics.*** In middle and late childhood, children shift toward defining themselves in terms of internal characteristics. They now recognize the difference between inner and outer states, and they are also more likely than young children to include subjective inner states in their definition of self. For example, in one investigation, second-grade children were much more likely than younger children to name psychological characteristics (such as preferences or personality traits) in their self-definition and less likely to name physical characteristics (such as eye color or possessions) (Aboud & Skerry, 1983). Eight-year-old Todd says, "I am smart and I am popular." Ten-year-old Tina says about herself, "I am pretty good about not worrying most of the time. I used to lose my temper, but I'm better about that now. I also feel proud when I do well in school."
- ***Social descriptions.*** In middle and late childhood, children begin to include *social aspects* such as references to social groups in their self-descriptions (Harter, 2006; Livesly & Bromley, 1973). For example, children might describe themselves as Girl Scouts, as Catholics, or as someone who has two close friends.
- ***Social comparison.*** Children's self-understanding in middle and late childhood includes increasing reference to social comparison (Harter, 2006). At this point in development, children are more likely to distinguish themselves from others in comparative rather than in absolute terms. That is, elementary-school-age children are likely to think about what they can do *in comparison with others.*
- ***Real Self and Ideal Self.*** In middle and late childhood, children begin to distinguish between their real and ideal selves (Harter, 2006). This involves differentiating their actual competencies from those they aspire to have and think are the most important.
- ***Realistic.*** In middle and late childhood, children's self-evaluations become more realistic (Harter, 2006). This may occur because of increased social comparison and perspective taking.

Adolescence The tendency to compare oneself with others continues to increase in the adolescent years. However, when asked whether they engage in social comparison, most adolescents deny it because they are aware that it is somewhat socially undesirable to do so. Let's examine other ways in which the adolescent develops a multifaceted self-understanding that differs from that of a child (Harter, 1998, 1999, 2006):

Know thyself, for once we know ourselves, we may learn how to care for ourselves, but otherwise we never shall.

—SOCRATES
Greek Philosopher, 5th Century B.C.

- *Abstract and Idealistic.* Remember from our discussion of Piaget's theory of cognitive development in chapter 7 that many adolescents begin to think in more *abstract* and *idealistic* ways. When asked to describe themselves, adolescents are more likely than children to use abstract and idealistic labels. Consider 14-year-old Laurie's abstract description of herself: "I am a human being. I am indecisive. I don't know who I am." Also consider her idealistic description of herself: "I am a naturally sensitive person who really cares about people's feelings. I think I'm pretty good-looking." Not all adolescents describe themselves in idealistic ways, but most adolescents distinguish between the real self and the ideal self.
- *Self-Consciousness.* Adolescents are more likely than children to be *self-conscious* about and *preoccupied* with their self-understanding. This self-consciousness and self-preoccupation reflect adolescent egocentrism, which we discussed in chapter 7. A longitudinal study found that from 13 to 18 years of age adolescents' public self-consciousness (involving aspects of the self visible to others, such as appearance, actions, and speech) remained reasonably strong and stable from approximately 13 to 16 years of age and then declined slightly (Rankin & others, 2004). Girls revealed a greater public self-consciousness than boys. Private self-consciousness (involving aspects of the self hidden from view, such as thoughts, emotions, and attitudes) increased from 13 to 18 years of age.
- *The Fluctuating Self.* The adolescent's self-understanding fluctuates across situations and across time (Harter, 1990). Adolescents may not understand why they can be cheerful one moment and sad the next, for example. The adolescent's self continues to be characterized by instability until the adolescent constructs a more unified theory of self, usually not until late adolescence or even early adulthood.
- *Real and Ideal Selves.* The adolescent's emerging ability to construct ideal selves in addition to actual ones can be perplexing and agonizing to the adolescent. In one view, an important aspect of the ideal or imagined self is the **possible self**—what individuals might become, what they would like to become, and what they are afraid of becoming (Dunkel & Kerpelman, 2004; Markus & Nurius, 1986). Thus, adolescents' possible selves include both what adolescents hope to be as well as what they dread they will become (Oyserman & Fryberg, 2004). The attributes of future positive selves (getting into a good college, being admired, having a successful career) can give direction to adolescents' activities. The attributes of future negative selves (being unemployed, being lonely, not getting into a good college) can identify what they will try to avoid.
- *Self-Integration.* In late adolescence, self-understanding becomes more *integrative,* with the disparate parts of the self more systematically pieced together (Harter, 2006). Older adolescents are more likely to detect inconsistencies in their earlier self-descriptions as they attempt to construct a general theory of self, an integrated sense of identity.

Perspective Taking

What drives the changes from infancy through adolescence that we have described? The cognitive development described by Piaget's theory (which we discussed in chapter 7, "Cognitive Developmental Approaches") is one possibility. Recall that according to Piaget, young children are egocentric, which means they are unable to distinguish between their own perspective and someone else's. As they develop, they move away from this self-centeredness and become capable of **perspective taking,** which is the ability to assume another person's perspective and understand his or her thoughts and feelings. These ideas of Piaget served as the foundation for

possible self What an individual might become, what the person would like to become, and what the person is afraid of becoming.

perspective taking The ability to assume another person's perspective and understand his or her thoughts or feelings.

the contemporary belief that perspective taking plays an important role in self-understanding.

Robert Selman (1980) has charted the development of children's perspective-taking abilities. Selman interviews individual children, asking them to comment on such dilemmas as this one:

> Holly is an 8-year-old girl who likes to climb trees. She is the best tree climber in the neighborhood. One day while climbing down from a tall tree, she falls . . . but does not hurt herself. Her father sees her fall. He is upset and asks her to promise not to climb trees anymore. Holly promises.
>
> Later that day, Holly and her friends meet Shawn. Shawn's kitten is caught in a tree and can't get down. Something has to be done right away or the kitten may fall. Holly is the only one who climbs trees well enough to reach the kitten and get it down but she remembers her promise to her father. (Selman, 1976, p. 302)

Subsequently, Selman asks each child a series of questions about the dilemma, such as these:

- Does Holly know how Shawn feels about the kitten?
- How will Holly's father feel if he finds out she climbed the tree?
- What does Holly think her father will do if he finds out she climbed the tree?
- What would you do in this situation?

By analyzing children's responses to dilemmas like this one, Selman (1980) concluded that children's perspective taking follows the developmental sequence described in figure 12.2. He believes perspective taking develops through five stages, ranging from 3 years of age through adolescence. The sequence begins with the egocentric viewpoint in early childhood and ends with in-depth perspective taking in adolescence.

Children's perspective taking can not only increase their self-understanding but also improve their peer group status and the quality of their friendships. For example, one investigation found that the most popular children in the third and eighth grades had competent perspective-taking skills (Kurdek & Krile, 1982). Children who are competent at perspective taking are better at understanding the needs of their companions, so they likely can communicate more effectively with them (Hudson, Forman, & Brion-Meisels, 1982).

Stage	Perspective-taking stage	Ages	Description
0	Egocentric viewpoint	3 to 5	Child has a sense of differentiation of self and other but fails to distinguish between the social perspective (thoughts, feelings) of other and self. Child can label other's overt feelings but does not see the cause-and-effect relation of reasons to social actions.
1	Social-informational perspective taking	6 to 8	Child is aware that other has a social perspective based on other's own reasoning, which may or may not be similar to child's. However, child tends to focus on one perspective rather than coordinating viewpoints.
2	Self-reflective perspective taking	8 to 10	Child is conscious that each individual is aware of the other's perspective and that this awareness influences self's and other's view of each other. Putting self in other's place is a way of judging other's intentions, purposes, and actions. Child can form a coordinated chain of perspectives but cannot yet abstract from this process to the level of simultaneous mutuality.
3	Mutual perspective taking	10 to 12	Adolescent realizes that both self and other can view each other mutually and simultaneously as subjects. Adolescent can step outside the two-person dyad and view the interaction from a third-person perspective.
4	Social and conventional system perspective taking	12 to 15	Adolescent realizes mutual perspective taking does not always lead to complete understanding. Social conventions are seen as necessary because they are understood by all members of the group (the generalized other), regardless of their position, role, or experience.

FIGURE 12.2 Selman's Stages of Perspective Taking

Sociocultural Contexts

The external social world as well as the internal world shapes developmental changes in self-understanding. As the child grows up and constructs multiple selves, self-understanding can vary across relationships and social roles (Keller, 2004). Adolescents, for example, may describe themselves differently depending on whom they are with—mother, father, close friend, romantic partner, or peer—and what role they are describing—student, athlete, or employee. Similarly, adolescents might create different selves depending on their ethnic and cultural background and experiences.

Hazel Markus and her colleagues (Markus & Kitayama, 1994; Markus, Mullally, & Kitayama, 1999) argue that selves emerge as individuals adapt to their cultural environments and are culture-specific. Some cultures emphasize values that subordinate individual goals to the interests of the group; they emphasize interdependence and harmonious relationships. These cultures encourage people to define themselves in terms of their relations to others. In contrast, other cultures are individualistic and give priority to personal goals. In the United States (especially among those in middle-socioeconomic contexts), the culture promotes individualism. When given the opportunity to describe themselves, North Americans often provide not only current portraits but notions of their future selves as well.

What happens if adolescents experience multiple cultures? They might create multiple selves based on their ethnic background. These multiple selves reflect their experiences in navigating their multiple worlds of family, peers, school, and community (Cooper & others, 2002). Research with U.S. youth of African, Chinese, Filipino, Latino, European, Japanese, and Vietnamese descent shows that as these youth move from one culture to another, they can encounter barriers related to language, racism, gender, immigration, and poverty. In each of their different worlds, however, they also can find resources—in institutions, in other people, and in themselves. Youth who find it too difficult to move between worlds can become alienated from their school, family, or peers. However, youth who can navigate effectively between different worlds can develop bicultural or multicultural selves and become "culture brokers" for others.

Sociocultural contexts may also influence the possible selves that the child or adolescent constructs. Are the possible selves of 12-year-old boys in a crime-ridden neighborhood in which few adult men can find a job likely to include getting into an advanced placement class in high school or an engineering program in college? To read further about possible selves, see the Research in Child Development interlude on the next page.

How might sociocultural contexts be involved in children's possible selves?

RESEARCH IN CHILD DEVELOPMENT

A Possible Selves Intervention to Enhance School Involvement

Adolescents construct possible selves by synthesizing what they know about their traits and abilities and what they know about the skills needed to become various future selves. Daphina Oyserman and her colleagues (2002) developed an intervention to promote the development of academically focused possible selves that could help adolescents feel connected and involved with school. The participants in the study were 208 low-income inner-city African American boys and girls in their last year of middle school. Of the 208 participants, 62 received the intervention and 146 (the control group) did not. The intervention was called "Schools-to-Jobs." Students who received the intervention met in small groups weekly after school for nine weeks, with each session lasting 90 minutes. Undergraduates trained by the authors of the study acted as facilitators for these small groups. The intervention had the following elements (Oyserman, Terry, & Bybee, 2002, pp. 317–319):

1. Students were introduced to the skills and abilities needed to succeed in the eighth grade.
2. Students chose among pictures that portrayed adults in the domains of work, family, lifestyle, community service, health, and hobbies.
3. Students drew personal time lines from the present to as far into the future as they could. The time lines were discussed in the group with a focus on connecting current activities with future visions.
4. Students mapped out their next year, possible adult selves, and the strategies that might help them.
5. Students were provided with concrete experience in breaking down everyday school problems into manageable parts.
6. Students developed a list of requirements for high school graduation and getting into college, with facilitators helping them connect these back to their adult visions, time lines, and strategies.
7. Students were guided in organizing their experiences and "walked through" what they had done in each session so far.
8. Students stated their concerns in the coming year, discussed communication skills that might help them handle these concerns, and engaged in role-playing exercises related to these coping efforts.
9. Facilitators identified gaps in students' knowledge about how schooling is linked to careers and provided them with skills to obtain this information.

Students in the intervention and control groups were compared in the fall to establish a baseline and again in the spring. To assess the effects of the intervention, the researchers used the following measures:

1. To assess school bonding, students were asked to rate the extent to which they agreed with three statements: "I feel I really belong at school," "I try hard at school," and "Schoolwork is very important."
2. The students' possible selves were assessed with two measures: (a) Students were asked to generate four or more possible selves in response to two probes: "Next year, I expect to be . . ." and "Next year I want to avoid being . . ." The students' responses were scored in terms of their positive expectation (for example, "Next year I expect to be in high school") "balanced" by a related school-focused concern described as a feared self (for example, "I want to avoid still being in the eighth grade."). (b) After writing in their possible selves, students marked those they were currently working on and wrote what they were doing to try to attain (or avoid) possible selves.
3. Students' effort in school was measured by how often students got into trouble and by how often they were absent from school.

By the end of the school year, the students who received the school-to-jobs intervention "reported more bonding to school, concern about doing well in school, balanced possible selves, plausible strategies to attain these possible selves, better school attendance, and for boys, less trouble at school" (p. 313). Recently, Oyserman found improved academic outcomes two full years after the possible selves–focused intervention (Oyserman & Frybrerg, 2004).

Review and Reflect • LEARNING GOAL 1

1 Discuss self-understanding and its development

Review

- What is self-understanding?
- How does self-understanding change from infancy through adolescence?
- What role does perspective taking play in self-understanding?
- How are sociocultural contexts involved in self-understanding?

Reflect

- If a psychologist had interviewed you at 10 and at 16 years of age, how would your self-understanding have been different?

2 SELF-ESTEEM AND SELF-CONCEPT

- What Are Self-Esteem and Self-Concept?
- Assessment
- Developmental Changes
- Variations in Self-Esteem

Self-conception involves more than self-understanding. Not only do children try to define and describe attributes of the self (self-understanding), but they also evaluate these attributes. These evaluations create self-esteem and self-concept, and they have far-reaching implications for children's development.

What Are Self-Esteem and Self-Concept?

Sometimes the terms self-esteem and self-concept are used interchangeably, or they are not precisely defined (Dusek & McIntyre, 2003; Harter, 2006). Here we use **self-esteem** to refer to a person's self-worth or self-image, a person's global evaluation of the self. For example, a child might perceive that she is not merely a person but a good person. (To evaluate your self-esteem, see figure 12.3.) We use the term **self-concept** to refer to domain-specific evaluations of the self. Children can make self-evaluations in many domains of their lives—academic, athletic, physical appearance, and so on. In sum, self-esteem refers to global self-evaluations, self-concept to more domain-specific evaluations.

Self-esteem reflects perceptions that do not always match reality (Baumeister & others, 2003). A child's self-esteem might reflect a belief about whether he or she is intelligent and attractive, for example, but that belief is not necessarily accurate. Thus, high self-esteem may refer accurate, justified perceptions of one's worth as a person and one's successes and accomplishments but it can also refer to an arrogant, grandiose, unwarranted sense of superiority over others. In the same manner, low self-esteem may reflect either an accurate perception of one's shortcomings or a distorted, even pathological insecurity and inferiority.

self-esteem The global evaluative dimension of the self; also called self-worth or self-image.

self-concept Domain-specific self-evaluations.

FIGURE 12.3 Evaluating Self-Esteem

These items are from a widely used measure of self-esteem, the Rosenberg Scale of Self-Esteem. The items deal with your general feelings about yourself. Place a check mark in the column that best describes your feelings about yourself:
1 = strongly agree, 2 = agree, 3 = disagree, 4 = strongly disagree.

	1	2	3	4
1. I feel that I am a person of worth, at least on an equal plane with others.				
2. I feel that I have a number of good qualities.				
3. All in all, I am inclined to feel that I am a failure.				
4. I am able to do things as well as most other people.				
5. I feel I do not have much to be proud of.				
6. I take a positive attitude toward myself.				
7. On the whole, I am satisfied with myself.				
8. I wish I could have more respect for myself.				
9. I certainly feel useless at times.				
10. At times I think I am no good at all.				

To obtain your self-esteem score, reverse your scores for items 3, 5, 8, 9, and 10. Add those scores to your scores for items 1, 2, 4, 6, and for your overall self-esteem score. Scores can range from 10 to 40. If you scored below 20, consider contacting the counseling center at your college or university for help in improving your self-esteem.

Assessment

Measuring self-esteem and self-concept hasn't always been easy (Dusek & McIntyre, 2003). An example of a useful measure developed to assess self-evaluations by children is Susan Harter's (1985) Self-Perception Profile for Children. It taps general self-worth plus self-concept for five specific domains—scholastic competence, athletic competence, social acceptance, physical appearance, and behavioral conduct.

The Self-Perception Profile for Children is designed to be used with third-grade through sixth-grade children. Harter also developed a separate scale for adolescents, the Self-Perception Profile for Adolescents (Harter, 1989). It assesses global self-worth and the five domains tested for children plus three additional domains—close friendship, romantic appeal, and job competence.

Harter's measures can separate self-evaluations in different domains in one's life. How are these specific self-evaluations related to their general self-esteem? Even children have both a general level of self-esteem and varying levels of self-conceptions in particular domains of their lives (Harter, 1998; Ward, 2004). For example, a child might have a moderately high level of general self-esteem but have these self-conceptions in specific areas: high in athletic competence, high in social acceptance, high in physical appearance, high in behavioral conduct, but low in scholastic competence.

Domain	Harter's U.S. Samples	Other Countries
Physical appearance	.65	.62
Scholastic competence	.48	.41
Social acceptance	.46	.40
Behavioral conduct	.45	.45
Athletic competence	.33	.30

FIGURE 12.4 Correlations Between Global Self-Esteem and Self-Evaluations of Domains of Competence. Note: The correlations shown are the average correlations computed across a number of studies. The other countries in this evaluation were England, Ireland, Australia, Canada, Germany, Italy, Greece, the Netherlands, and Japan. Recall from chapter 2 that correlation coefficients can range from −1.00 to +1.00. The correlations between physical appearance and global self-esteem (.65 and .62) are moderately high.

Self-esteem appears to have an especially strong tie with self-perception in one domain in particular: physical appearance. For example, researchers have found that among adolescents, global self-esteem is correlated more strongly with perceived physical appearance than with scholastic competence, social acceptance, behavioral conduct, or athletic competence (Harter, 1999, 2006; Maeda, 1999) (see figure 12.4). Notice in figure 12.4 that the link between perceived physical appearance and self-esteem has been made in many countries. This association between physical appearance and self-esteem is

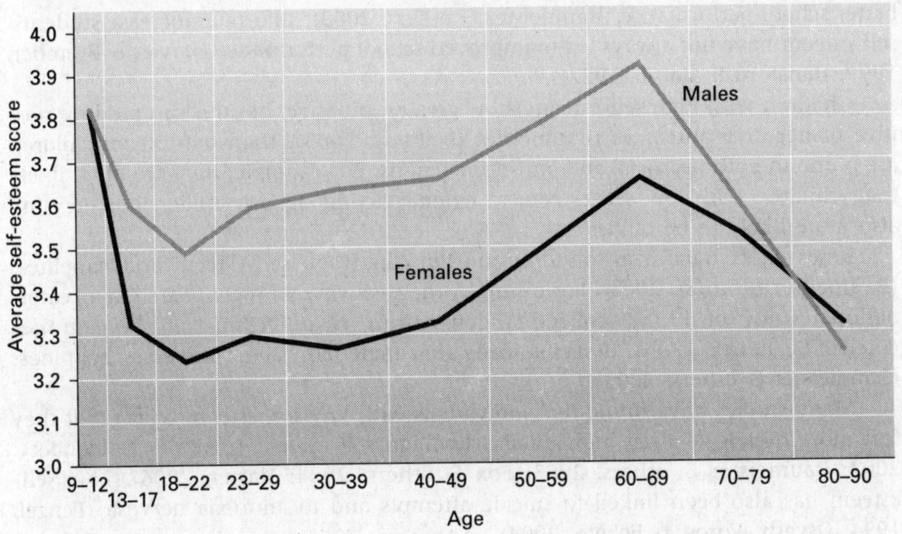

FIGURE 12.5 Self-Esteem Across the Life Span. One large-scale study asked more than 300,000 individuals to rate the extent to which they have high self-esteem on a 5-point scale, 5 being "Strongly Agree" and I being "Strongly Disagree." Self-esteem dropped in adolescence and late adulthood. Self-esteem of females was lower than self-esteem of males through most of the life span.

not confined only to adolescence; it holds across the life span from early childhood through middle age (Harter, 1999, 2006).

Developmental Changes

Researchers disagree about the extent to which self-esteem varies with age. One recent study found that self-esteem is high in childhood, declines in adolescence, and increases in adulthood until late adulthood, when it declines again (Robins & others, 2002) (see figure 12.5). Some researchers argue that although self-esteem may decrease in adolescence, the drop is actually very slight (Harter, 2002, 2006; Kling & others, 1999).

Notice in figure 12.5 that the self-esteem of males was higher than that of females through most of the life span. During adolescence, the self-esteem of girls declined more than that of boys. One explanation for this difference holds that the drop in self-esteem is driven by a negative body image and that girls have more negative body images during pubertal change compared with boys. Another explanation emphasizes the greater interest that adolescent girls take in social relationships and society's failure to reward that interest (Crawford & Unger, 2004). But also note in figure 12.5 that despite the drop in self-esteem among adolescent girls, their average self-esteem score (3.3) was still higher than the neutral point on the scale (3.0).

Might adolescents' self-esteem be influenced by cohort effects? (*Cohort effects* are effects that are due to a person's time of birth or generation but not to actual age.) A recent analysis of studies conducted from the 1960s into the 1990s found that the self-esteem of college students was higher in the 1990s than it was in the 1960s (Twenge & Campbell, 2001). The explanation given for this increase in self-esteem involves the self-esteem movement and the active encouragement of self-esteem in schools.

Variations in Self-Esteem

Variations in self-esteem have been linked with many aspects of children's development. However, much of the research is *correlational* rather than *experimental.* Recall from chapter 2 that correlation does not equal causation. Thus, if a correlational study finds an association between children's low self-esteem and low academic achievement, low academic achievement could cause the low self-esteem as much as low self-esteem causes low academic achievement (Bowles, 1999).

In fact, there are only moderate correlations between school performance and self-esteem, and these correlations do not suggest that high self-esteem produces

The living self has one purpose only: to come into its own fullness of being, as a tree comes into full blossom, or a bird into spring beauty, or a tiger into lustre.

—D. H. Lawrence
English Author, 20th Century

better school performance (Baumeister & others, 2003). Efforts to increase students' self-esteem have not always led to improved school performance (Davies & Brember, 1999; Hansford & Hattie, 1982).

Children with high self-esteem show greater initiative, but this can produce positive or negative outcomes (Baumeister & others, 2003). High-self-esteem children are prone to both prosocial and antisocial actions. For example, they are more likely than children with low self-esteem to defend victims against bullies, but they are also more likely to be bullies.

Researchers have also found strong links between self-esteem and happiness (Baumeister & others, 2003). For example, the two were strongly related in an international study of 13,000 college students from 49 universities in 31 countries (Diener & Diener, 1995). It seems likely that high self-esteem increases happiness (Baumeister & others, 2003).

Many studies have found that individuals with low self-esteem report that they feel more depressed than individuals with high self-esteem (Arndt & Goldenberg, 2002; Baumeister & others, 2003; Fox & others, 2004; Harter, 2006). Low self-esteem has also been linked to suicide attempts and to anorexia nervosa (Fenzel, 1994; Osvath, Voros, & Fekete, 2004).

www.mhhe.com/santrockcd11

An Adolescent Talks About Self-Esteem
Self-Esteem Websites

Are a parent's characteristics and behavior linked to a child's self-esteem? In the most extensive investigation of parent-child relationships and self-esteem, these parenting attributes were associated with boys' high self-esteem (Coopersmith, 1967):

- Expression of affection
- Concern about the child's problems
- Harmony in the home
- Participation in joint family activities
- Availability to give competent, organized help to the boys when they need it
- Setting clear and fair rules
- Abiding by these rules
- Allowing the children freedom within well-prescribed limits

Remember that these findings are correlational, and so we cannot say that these parenting attributes cause children's high self-esteem. Such factors as parental acceptance and allowing children freedom within well-prescribed limits probably are important determinants of children's self-esteem, but we still must say that they are related to rather than that they cause children's self-esteem, based on the available research data. To explore ways that children's low self-esteem might be increased, see the Caring for Children interlude.

CARING FOR CHILDREN

Increasing Children's Self-Esteem

A current concern is that too many of today's children and adolescents grow up receiving empty praise and as a consequence have inflated self-esteem (Graham, 2005; Stipek, 2005). Too often they are given praise for performance that is mediocre or even poor. They may have difficulty handling competition and criticism. The title of a book, *Dumbing Down Our Kids: Why America's Children Feel Good About Themselves but Can't Read, Write, or Add* (Sykes, 1995) vividly captures the theme that the academic problems of many U.S. children, adolescents, and college students stem from unmerited praise aimed at propping up their self-esteem. But it is possible to raise children's self-esteem by (1) identifying the domains of competence important to the child, (2) emotional support and social approval, (3) achievement, and (4) coping.

Harter (1999) believes that intervention must occur at the level of the causes of self-esteem if the individual's self-esteem is to improve significantly. Children have the highest self-esteem when they perform competently in domains that are important to them. Therefore, children should be encouraged to identify and to value areas in which they are competent.

Emotional support and social approval also powerfully influence children's self-esteem. Some children with low self-esteem come from conflicted families or experienced abuse or neglect—situations in which emotional support was unavailable. For some children, formal programs such as Big Brothers and Big Sisters can provide alternative sources of emotional support and social approval; for others, support can come informally through the encouragement of a teacher, a coach, or another significant adult. Peer approval becomes increasingly important during adolescence, but adult as well as peer support continues to be an important influence on self-esteem through adolescence.

Achievement also can improve children's self-esteem. The straightforward teaching of real skills to children often results in increased achievement and enhanced self-esteem. When children know what tasks are necessary to achieve goals and have experience performing these or similar tasks, their self-esteem improves.

Self-esteem also is often increased when children face a problem and try to cope with it, rather than avoid it (Compas, 2004; Folkman & Moskowitz, 2004). If coping rather than avoidance prevails, children often face problems realistically, honestly, and nondefensively. This produces favorable self-evaluative thoughts, which lead to the self-generated approval that raises self-esteem. The converse is true of low self-esteem. Unfavorable self-evaluations trigger denial, deception, and avoidance, which lead to self-generated disapproval.

Review and Reflect • LEARNING GOAL 2

2 Explain self-esteem and self-concept

Review

- What are self-esteem and self-concept?
- How are self-esteem and self-concept assessed?
- How is self-esteem linked with age?
- What are some variations in self-esteem and how are they linked to children's development? What role do parent-child relationships play in self-esteem?

Reflect

- What behaviors would you look for when observing a child to give you an indication that a child has low or high self-esteem?

3 IDENTITY

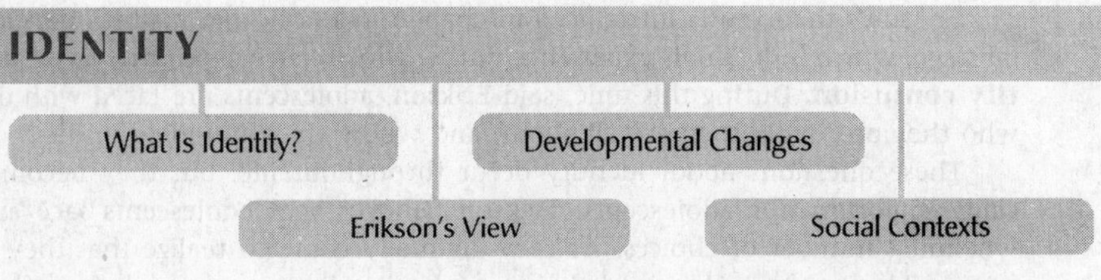

Who am I? What am I all about? What am I going to do with my life? What is different about me? How can I make it on my own? These questions reflect the search for an identity. By far the most comprehensive and provocative theory of identity

"Who are you?" said the caterpillar. Alice replied rather shyly, "I–I hardly know, sir, just at present–at least I know who I was when I got up this morning, but I must have changed several times since then."

—Lewis Carroll
English Writer, 19th Century

development is Erik Erikson's. In this section we examine his views on identity. We also discuss contemporary research on how identity develops and how social contexts influence that development.

What Is Identity?

Identity is a self-portrait composed of many pieces, including these:

- The career and work path the person wants to follow (vocational/career identity)
- Whether the person is conservative, liberal, or middle of the road (political identity)
- The person's spiritual beliefs (religious identity)
- Whether the person is single, married, divorced, and so on (relationship identity)
- The extent to which the person is motivated to achieve and is intellectual (achievement, intellectual identity)
- Whether the person is heterosexual, homosexual, or bisexual (sexual identity)
- Which part of the world or country a person is from and how intensely the person identifies with his or her cultural heritage (cultural/ethnic identity)
- The kind of things a person likes to do, which can include sports, music, hobbies, and so on (interest)
- The individual's personality characteristics (such as being introverted or extraverted, anxious or calm, friendly or hostile, and so on) (personality)
- The individual's body image (physical identity)

At the bare minimum, identity involves commitment to a vocational direction, an ideological stance, and a sexual orientation. We put these pieces together to form a sense of ourselves continuing through time within a social world. Synthesizing the identity components can be a long and drawn-out process, with many negations and affirmations of various roles and faces. Identity development gets done in bits and pieces. Decisions are not made once and for all, but have to be made again and again. Identity development does not happen neatly, and it does not happen cataclysmically (Kroger, 2003).

Erikson's View

Questions about identity surface as common, virtually universal, concerns during adolescence. It was Erik Erikson (1950, 1968) who first understood how central such questions are to understanding adolescent development. That identity is now believed to be a key aspect of adolescent development is a result of Erikson's masterful thinking and analysis. His ideas reveal rich insights into adolescents' thoughts and feelings, and reading one or more of his books is worthwhile. A good starting point is *Identity: Youth and Crisis* (1968). Other works that portray identity development are *Young Man Luther* (1962) and *Gandhi's Truth* (1969).

Erikson's theory was introduced in chapter 2. Recall that his fifth developmental stage, which individuals experience during adolescence, is **identity versus identity confusion.** During this time, said Erikson, adolescents are faced with deciding who they are, what they are all about, and where they are going in life.

identity versus identity confusion Erikson's fifth developmental stage, which individuals experience during the adolescent years. At this time, adolescents examine who they are, what they are all about, and where they are going in life.

psychosocial moratorium Erikson's term for the gap between childhood security and adult autonomy that adolescents experience as part of their identity exploration.

These questions about identity occur throughout life, but they become especially important for adolescents. Erikson believes that adolescents face an overwhelming number of choices. As they gradually come to realize that they will be responsible for themselves and their own lives, adolescents search for what those lives are going to be.

The search for an identity during adolescence is aided by a **psychosocial moratorium,** which is Erikson's term for the gap between childhood security and adult autonomy. During this period, society leaves adolescents relatively free of responsibilities and free to try out different identities. Adolescents in effect search their culture's identity files, experimenting with different roles and personalities. They may want to pursue one career one month (lawyer, for example) and another career the next month (doctor, actor, teacher, social worker, or astronaut, for example). They may dress neatly one day, sloppily the next. This experimentation is a deliberate effort on the part of adolescents to find out where they fit in the world.

As long as one keeps searching, the answers come.

—JOAN BAEZ
American Folk Singer, 20th Century

Many parents and other adults, accustomed to having children go along with what they say, may be bewildered or incensed by the wisecracks, the rebelliousness, and the rapid mood changes that accompany adolescence. It is important for these adults to give adolescents the time and opportunity to explore different roles and personalities. Most adolescents eventually discard undesirable roles.

Youth who successfully cope with these conflicting identities emerge with a new sense of self that is both refreshing and acceptable. Adolescents who do not successfully resolve this identity crisis suffer what Erikson calls *identity confusion*. The confusion takes one of two courses: individuals withdraw, isolating themselves from peers and family, or they immerse themselves in the world of peers and lose their identity in the crowd.

There are hundreds of roles for adolescents to try out, and probably just as many ways to pursue each role. Erikson believes that, by late adolescence, vocational roles are central to identity development, especially in a highly technological society like the United States. Youth who have been well trained to enter a workforce that offers the potential of reasonably high self-esteem will experience the least stress during this phase of identity development.

www.mhhe.com/santrockcd11

Identity Development
The Society for Research on Identity Development

Some youth reject jobs offering good pay and high social status in order to do work that helps people directly, such as in the Peace Corps, in mental health clinics, or in schools in low-income neighborhoods. Some youth prefer unemployment to the prospect of working at a job they feel they could not perform well or would make them feel useless. To Erikson, these choices reflect the desire to achieve a meaningful identity by being true to oneself, instead of burying one's identity in the larger society.

Developmental Changes

Although questions about identity may be especially important during adolescence, identity formation neither begins nor ends during these years. It begins with the appearance of attachment, the development of the sense of self, and the emergence of independence in infancy; the process reaches its final phase with a life review and integration in old age. What is important about identity development in adolescence, especially late adolescence, is that for the first time, physical development, cognitive development, and socioemotional development advance to the point at which the individual can sort through and synthesize childhood identities and identifications to construct a viable path toward adult maturity.

Some decisions made during adolescence might seem trivial: whom to date, whether or not to break up, which major to study, whether to study or play, whether or not to be politically active, and so on. Over the years of adolescence, however, such decisions begin to form the core of what the individual is all about as a human being—what is called his or her identity.

Identity Statuses How do individual adolescents go about the process of forming an identity? Eriksonian researcher James Marcia (1980, 1994) believes that Erikson's theory of identity development contains four statuses of identity, or ways of resolving the identity crisis: identity diffusion, identity foreclosure,

FIGURE 12.6 **Marcia's Four Statuses of Identity**

		Has the person made a commitment? Yes	Has the person made a commitment? No
Has the person explored meaningful alternatives regarding some identity question?	Yes	Identity Achievement	Identity Moratorium
	No	Identity Foreclosure	Identity Diffusion

identity moratorium, and identity achievement. What determines an individual's identity status? Marcia classifies individuals based on the existence or extent of their crisis or commitment (see figure 12.6). **Crisis** is defined as a period of identity development during which the individual is exploring alternatives. Most researchers use the term *exploration* rather than crisis. **Commitment** is personal investment in identity.

The four statuses of identity are:

- **Identity diffusion,** the status of individuals who have not yet experienced a crisis or made any commitments. Not only are they undecided about occupational and ideological choices, they are also likely to show little interest in such matters.
- **Identity foreclosure** is the status of individuals who have made a commitment but not experienced a crisis. This occurs most often when parents hand down commitments to their adolescents, usually in an authoritarian way, before adolescents have had a chance to explore different approaches, ideologies, and vocations on their own.
- **Identity moratorium** is the status of individuals who are in the midst of a crisis but whose commitments are either absent or are only vaguely defined.
- **Identity achievement** is the status of individuals who have undergone a crisis and made a commitment.

To evaluate your identity in different areas of development, see figure 12.7. Let's explore some examples of Marcia's identity statuses. Thirteen-year-old Sarah has neither begun to explore her identity in any meaningful way nor made an identity commitment; she is identity diffused. Eighteen-year-old Tim's parents want him to be a medical doctor so he is planning on majoring in premedicine in college and has not explored other options; he is identity foreclosed. Nineteen-year-old Sasha is not quite sure what life paths she wants to follow, but she recently went to the counseling center at her college to find out about different careers; she is in identity moratorium status. Twenty-one-year-old Marcelo extensively explored several career options in college, eventually getting his degree in science education, and is looking forward to his first year of teaching high school students; he is identity achieved. These examples focused on the career dimension, but remember that identity has a number of dimensions.

In Marcia's terms, young adolescents are primarily in the identity statuses of diffusion, foreclosure, or moratorium. To move to the status of identity achievement, young adolescents need three things (Marcia, 1987, 1996): they must be confident that they have parental support, must have an established sense of industry, and must be able to adopt a self-reflective stance toward the future.

The identity status approach has been sharply criticized by some researchers and theoreticians (Blasi, 1988; Cote & Levine, 1988; Kroger, 2003; Lapsley & Power,

crisis A period of identity development during which the adolescent is choosing among meaningful alternatives.

commitment The part of identity development in which adolescents show a personal investment in what they are going to do.

identity diffusion Marcia's term for the state adolescents are in when they have not yet experienced a crisis (that is, they have not yet explored meaningful alternatives) or made any commitments.

identity foreclosure Marcia's term for the state adolescents are in when they have made a commitment but have not experienced a crisis.

identity moratorium Marcia's term for the state adolescents are in when they are in the midst of a crisis, but whose commitments either are absent or are only vaguely defined.

identity achievement Marcia's term for an adolescent's having undergone a crisis and made a commitment.

Think deeply about your exploration and commitment in the areas listed here. For each area, check whether your identity status is diffused, foreclosed, moratorium, or achieved.

	Identity Status			
Identity Component	Diffused	Foreclosed	Moratorium	Achieved
Vocational (career)				
Political				
Religious				
Relationships				
Achievement				
Sexual				
Gender				
Ethnic/Cultural				
Intersets				
Personality				
Physical				

If you checked diffused or foreclosed for any areas, take some time to think about what you need to do to move into a moratorium identity status in those areas. How much has your identity in each of the areas changed in recent years?

FIGURE 12.7 Exploring Your Identity

1988). They believe that the identity status approach distorts and trivializes Erikson's notions of crisis and commitment. For example, Erikson's idea of commitment loses the meaning of investing oneself in certain lifelong projects and is interpreted simply as having made a firm decision or not. Others still believe that the identity status approach is a valuable contribution to understanding identity (Archer, 1989; Marcia, 1994; Waterman, 1992).

Beyond Erikson Some researchers believe that the most important identity changes do not take place until emerging adulthood (about 18 to 25 years of age). For example, Alan Waterman (1985, 1989, 1992) has found that from the years preceding high school through the last few years of college, the number of individuals who are identity achieved increases while the number of those who are identity diffused decreases. Many young adolescents are identity diffused. College upperclassmen are more likely than high school students or college freshmen to be identity achieved.

The timing of these developmental changes may depend on the particular area of life involved. For example, for religious beliefs and political ideology, many college students have identity-foreclosure and identity-moratorium status; few have reached the identity-achieved status. Many college students are still wrestling with ideological commitments (Arehart & Smith, 1990; Harter, 1990).

In any event, resolution of the identity issue during adolescence does not mean that identity will be stable through the remainder of life. Many researchers believe that a common pattern of individuals who develop positive identities follow what are called "MAMA" cycles of moratorium-achievement-moratorium-achievement (Archer, 1989). These cycles may be repeated throughout life (Francis, Fraser, & Marcia, 1989). Marcia (2002) believes that the first identity is just that—it is not, and should not be expected to be, the final product.

Consider Maxine Hong Kingston's life. When she was 9 years old, she began writing. "All of a sudden," she told an interviewer, "this poem started coming out of me. On and on I went, oblivious to everything. . . . It is a bad habit that doesn't go away." Still, when Kingston enrolled at the University of California, she began an engineering program. Eventually, she changed her major to English literature, became a teacher, and then published her award-winning books. In 1991, however, Kingston's identity was threatened by a catastrophe. Kingston rushed from her father's funeral to a house in flames. Nothing was left of the novel she had been writing. "After the fire," she said, "I just wanted to take care of myself. . . . I had lost my writing" (Alegre & Welsch, 2003). Several years later, however, Kingston reclaimed her identity as an author, again writing fiction for publication.

Questions about identity come up throughout life. An individual who develops a healthy identity is flexible and adaptive, open to changes in society, in relationships, and in careers (Adams, Gulotta, & Montemayor, 1992). This openness assures numerous reorganizations of identity throughout the individual's life.

Social Contexts

Social contexts play important roles in identity. Let's examine how family, culture and ethnicity, and gender are linked to identity development.

Family Influences Parents are important figures in the adolescent's development of identity. Do parenting styles influence identity development? Democratic parents, who encourage adolescents to participate in family decision making, foster identity achievement. Autocratic parents, who control the adolescent's behavior without giving the adolescent an opportunity to express opinions, encourage identity foreclosure. Permissive parents, who provide little guidance to adolescents and allow them to make their own decisions, promote identity diffusion (Enright & others, 1980). One recent study found that poor communication between mothers and adolescents and persistent conflicts with friends were linked to less positive identity development (Reis & Youniss, 2004).

It is during adolescence that the search for balance between the need for autonomy and the need for connectedness becomes especially important to identity. Developmentalist Catherine Cooper and her colleagues (Carlson, Cooper, & Hsu, 1990; Cooper & Grotevant, 1989; Grotevant & Cooper, 1985, 1998) found that the presence of a family atmosphere that promotes both individuality and connectedness are important in the adolescent's identity development:

- **Individuality** consists of two dimensions: self-assertion—the ability to have and communicate a point of view—and separateness—the use of communication patterns to express how one is different from others.
- **Connectedness** also consists of two dimensions: mutuality—which involves sensitivity to and respect for others' views—and permeability—which involves openness to others' views.

In general, Cooper's research indicates that identity formation is enhanced by family relationships that are both individuated, which encourages adolescents to develop their own point of view, and connected, which provides a secure base from which to explore the widening social worlds of adolescence. When connectedness is strong and individuation weak, adolescents often have an identity foreclosure status. When connectedness is weak, adolescents often reveal identity confusion (Archer & Waterman, 1994).

Stuart Hauser and his colleagues (Hauser & Bowlds, 1990; Hauser & others, 1984) also have illuminated family processes that promote identity development. They have found that parents who use enabling behaviors (such as explaining, accepting, and giving empathy) facilitate the adolescent's identity development more than do parents who use constraining behaviors (such as judging and devaluing). In sum, family interaction styles that give the adolescent the right to question and

individuality An important element in adolescent identity development. It consists or two dimensions: self-assertion, the ability to have and communicate a point of view; and separateness, the use of communication patterns to express how one is different from others.

connectedness An important element in adolescent identity development. It consists of two dimensions: mutuality, sensitivity to and respect for others' views; and permeability, openness to others' views.

to be different, within a context of support and mutuality, foster healthy patterns of identity development (Harter, 1990, 1999).

Many ethnic minority youth must bridge "multiple worlds" in constructing their identities.

—Catherine Cooper
Contemporary Psychologist, University of California at Santa Cruz

Culture and Ethnicity "I feel that I have had to translate a whole Eastern culture and bring it to the West," Maxine Hong Kingston told one interviewer, "then bring the two cultures together seamlessly . . ." (Alegre & Welsch, 2003). For Kingston, this melding is "how one makes the Asian American culture." Her efforts illustrate one way of developing an **ethnic identity,** which is an enduring aspect of the self that includes a sense of membership in an ethnic group, along with the attitudes and feelings related to that membership (Phinney, 1996).

ethnic identity An enduring aspect of the self that includes a sense of membership in an ethnic group, along with the attitudes and feelings related to that membership.

Throughout the world, ethnic minority groups have struggled to maintain their ethnic identities while blending in with the dominant culture (Erikson, 1968). Erikson thought this struggle for a separate identity within the larger culture has been the driving force in the founding of churches, empires, and revolutions throughout history.

Many aspects of sociocultural contexts may influence ethnic identity (Davey & others, 2003; Fox & others, 2004; Keller, 2004; Spencer, 2006; Wren & Mendoza, 2004). Ethnic identity tends to be stronger among members of minority groups than among members of mainstream groups. For example, in one study, the exploration of ethnic identity was higher among ethnic minority college students than among White non-Latino college students (Phinney & Alipuria, 1990).

Time is another aspect of the context that influences ethnic identity. The indicators of identity often differ for each succeeding generation of immigrants (Phinney, 2003). First-generation immigrants are likely to be secure in their identities and unlikely to change much; they may or may not develop a new identity. The degree to which they begin to feel "American" appears to be related to whether or not they learn English, develop social networks beyond their ethnic group, and become culturally competent in their new country. Second-generation immigrants are more likely to think of themselves as "American" possibly because citizenship is granted at birth. Maxine Hong Kingston noted, "I have been in America all of my life; Chinese is a foreign culture to me" (Alegre & Welsch, 2003). For second-generation immigrants, ethnic identity is likely to be linked to retention of their ethnic language and social networks. In the third and later generations, the issues become more complex. Broad social factors may affect the extent to which members of this generation retain their ethnic identities. For example, media images may either discourage or encourage members of an ethnic group from identifying with their group or retaining parts of its culture. Discrimination may force people to see themselves as cut off from the majority group and encourage them to seek the support of their own ethnic culture. To read about one individual who guides Latino adolescents in developing a positive identity, see the Careers in Child Development insert.

The immediate contexts in which ethnic minority youth live also influence their identity development (Bryant & LaFromboise, 2005; Newman, 2005; Spencer,

CAREERS in CHILD DEVELOPMENT

Armando Ronquillo
High School Counselor

Armando Ronquillo is a high school counselor and admissions advisor at Pueblo High School in a low-income area of Tucson, Arizona. More than 85 percent of the students have a Latino background. Armando was named the top high school counselor in the state of Arizona for the year 2000.

Armando especially works with Latino students to guide them in developing a positive identity. He talks with them about their Latino background and what it's like to have a bicultural identity—preserving important aspects of their Latino heritage but also pursuing what is important to be successful in the contemporary culture of the United States.

He believes that helping them stay in school and getting them to think about the lifelong opportunities provided by a college education will benefit their identity development. Armando also works with parents to help them understand that their child going to college is doable and affordable.

Armando Ronquillo, counseling a Latina high school student about college.

Researcher Margaret Beale Spencer, shown here talking with adolescents, believes that adolescence is often a critical juncture in the identity development of ethnic minority individuals. Most ethnic minority individuals consciously confront their ethnicity for the first time in adolescence.

1999, 2006; Spencer & others, 2001). In the United States, many ethnic minority youth live in pockets of poverty, are exposed to drugs, gangs, and crime, and interact with youth and adults who have dropped out of school or are unemployed. Support for developing a positive identity is scarce. In such settings, programs for youth can make an important contribution to identity development.

Researchers are also increasingly finding that a positive ethnic identity is related to positive outcomes for ethnic minority adolescents (Fridrich & Flannery, 1995; Lee, 2005; Rieckmann, Wadsworth, & Deyhle, 2004; Umana-Taylor, 2004; Yasui, Dorham, & Dishion, 2004). For example, one recent study revealed that ethnic identity was linked with higher school engagement and lower aggression (Van Buren & Graham, 2003). Another recent study indicated that a stronger ethnic identity was linked to higher self-esteem in African American, Latino, and Asian American youth (Bracey, Bamaca, & Umana-Taylor, 2004). And yet another study with ninth grade students found that the strength of adolescents' ethnic identification was a better predictor of their academic success than the specific ethnic labels they used to describe themselves (Fuligni, Witkow, & Garcia, 2005). In this study, the ethnic groups most likely to incorporate more of their families' national origin and cultural background into their ethnic identifications were Mexican and Chinese immigrant adolescents.

Shirley Heath and Milbrey McLaughlin (1993) studied 60 youth organizations that involved 24,000 adolescents over a period of five years. They found that these organizations were especially good at building a sense of ethnic pride in inner-city youth. Heath and McLaughlin believe that many inner-city youth have too much time on their hands, too little to do, and too few places to go. Organizations that perceive youth as fearful, vulnerable, and lonely but also as capable, worthy, and eager to have a healthy and productive life contribute in positive ways to the identity development of ethnic minority youth.

Gender In Erikson's (1968) classic presentation of identity development, the division of labor between the sexes was reflected in his assertion that males' aspirations were mainly oriented toward career and ideological commitments, while females' were centered around marriage and childbearing. In the 1960s and 1970s researchers found support for Erikson's assertion about gender differences in identity. However, since then, as more women have entered the workforce and gender stereotypes were challenged, these gender differences are disappearing (Waterman, 1985).

The task of identity exploration might be more complex for females than for males, in that females might try to establish identities in more domains than males do. In today's world, the options for females have increased and thus can at times be confusing and conflicting, especially for females who hope to successfully integrate family and career roles (Archer, 1994).

Review and Reflect • **LEARNING GOAL 3**

3 Describe identity and its development

Review

- What is identity?
- What is Erikson's view of identity?
- How do individuals develop their identity? What are the identity statuses that can be used to classify individuals?
- How do the social contexts of family, culture and ethnicity, and gender influence identity?

Reflect

- Do you think that your parents influenced your identity development? If so, how?

REACH YOUR LEARNING GOALS

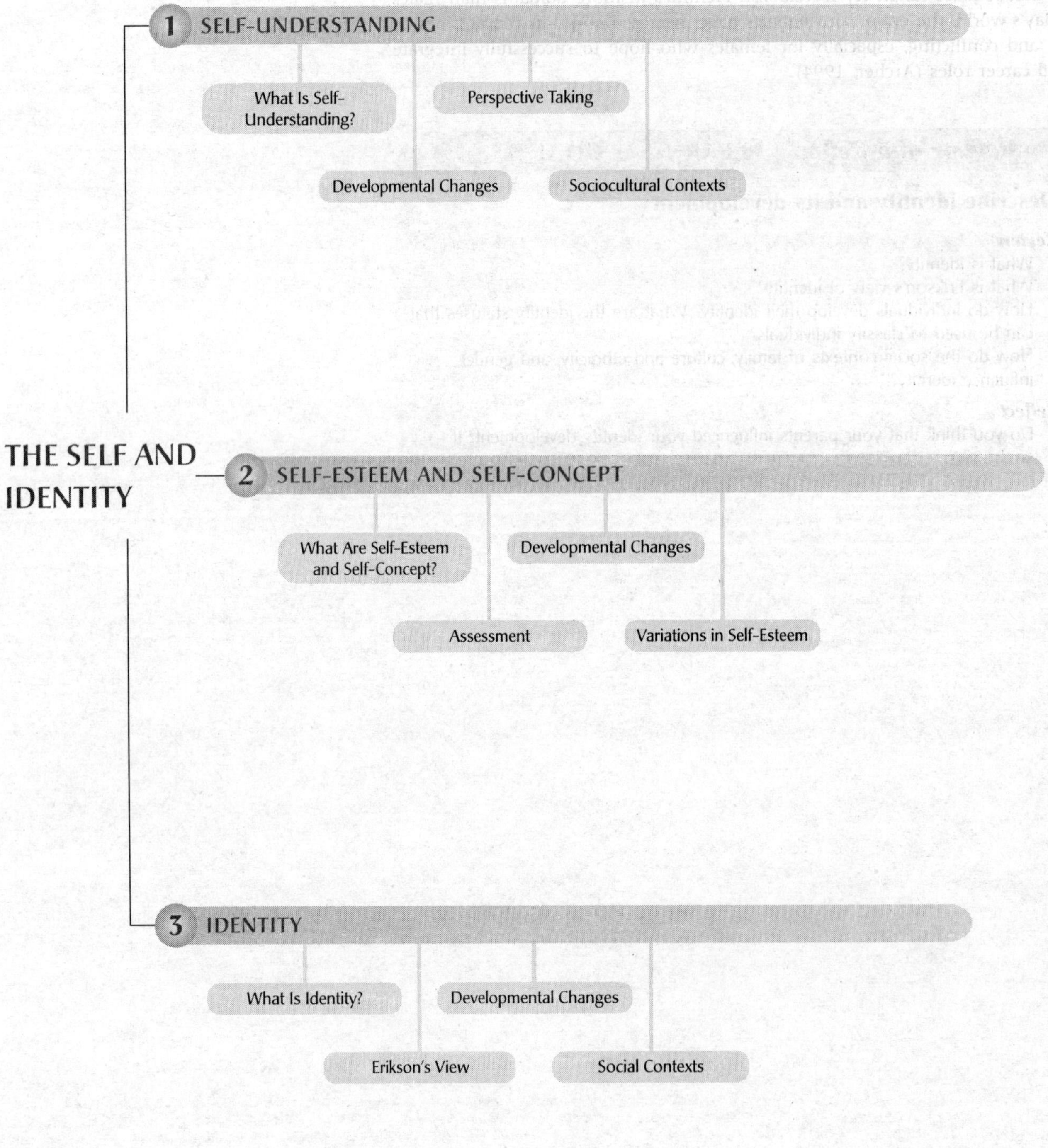

SUMMARY

1 Discuss self-understanding and its development

- Self-understanding is a child's cognitive representation of the self, the substance and content of the child's self-conceptions. It provides the rational underpinnings for identity.
- Infants develop a rudimentary form of self-recognition at approximately 18 months of age. Self-understanding in early childhood is characterized by confusion of self, mind, and body; concrete, physical, and active descriptions; and unrealistic positive overestimations. Self-understanding in middle and late childhood involves an increase in the use of internal characteristics, social descriptions, and social comparison; distinction between the real and ideal self; and an increase in realistic self-evaluations. Adolescents tend to engage in more social comparison, to develop abstract and idealistic conceptions of themselves, and to become self-conscious about their self-understanding. Their self-understanding often fluctuates and they construct multiple selves, including possible selves.
- Perspective taking is the ability to assume another person's perspective and understand his or her thoughts and feelings. Selman proposed a developmental theory of perspective taking that has five stages, ranging from 3 years of age through adolescence. The first stage in early childhood involves an egocentric viewpoint; the last stage in adolescence consists of having an in-depth perspective-taking ability.
- Selves emerge as individuals adapt to their cultural environment. Individualistic and collectivist cultures foster the development of different understandings of the self. Adolescents who experience multiple cultures may develop multiple selves that reflect their experiences in each culture.

2 Explain self-esteem and self-concept

- Self-esteem, also referred to as self-worth or self-image, is the global, evaluative dimension of the self. Self-concept refers to domain-specific evaluations of the self.
- Harter's measures assess self-evaluations in different skill domains as well as general self-worth.
- Some researchers have found that self-esteem drops in adolescence, more so for girls than boys, but there is controversy about how extensively self-esteem varies with age.
- Researchers have found only moderate correlations between self-esteem and school performance. Individuals with high self-esteem have greater initiative than those with low self-esteem, and this can produce positive or negative outcomes. Self-esteem is related to perceived physical appearance and happiness. Low self-esteem is linked with depression, suicide, and anorexia nervosa. In Coopersmith's study, children's self-esteem was associated with parental acceptance and allowing children freedom within well-prescribed limits.

3 Describe identity and its development

- Identity development is complex and is done in bits and pieces.
- Erikson argues that identity versus identity confusion is the fifth stage of the human life span, which individuals experience during adolescence. This stage involves entering a psychological moratorium between the security of childhood and the autonomy of adulthood. Personality and role experimentation are important aspects of identity development. In technological societies like those in North America, the vocational role is especially important.
- Identity development begins during infancy and continues through old age. James Marcia proposed four identity statuses—identity diffusion, foreclosure, moratorium, and achievement—that are based on crisis (exploration) and commitment. Some experts argue the main changes in identity occur in emerging adulthood rather than adolescence. Individuals often follow moratorium-achievement-moratorium-achievement (MAMA) cycles in their lives.
- Parents are important figures in adolescents' identity development. Democratic parenting facilitates identity development; autocratic and permissive parenting do not. Both individuality and connectedness in family relations are related to identity development. Enabling behaviors promote identity development; constraining behaviors restrict it. Throughout the world ethnic minority groups have struggled to maintain their identities while blending into the majority culture. A positive ethnic identity is linked to positive outcomes for ethnic minority adolescents. In Erikson's view, adolescent males have a stronger vocational identity, adolescent females a stronger social identity involving marriage and family roles. Some researchers have found that these gender differences in identity are disappearing.

KEY TERMS

self-understanding 371
possible self 373
perspective taking 373
self-esteem 377
self-concept 377
identity versus identity confusion 382
psychosocial moratorium 382
crisis 384
commitment 384
identity diffusion 384
identity foreclosure 384
identity moratorium 384
identity achievement 384
individuality 386
connectedness 386
ethnic identity 387

KEY PEOPLE

Robert Selman 373
Hazel Markus 374
Susan Harter 377
Erik Erikson 382
James Marcia 383
Alan Waterman 385
Catherine Cooper 386
Stuart Hauser 386
Shirley Heath and Milbrey McLaughlin 388

E-LEARNING TOOLS

To help you master the material in this chapter, visit the Online Learning Center for *Child Development*, eleventh edition (**www.mhhe.com/santrockcd11**), where you'll find these additional resources:

Taking It to the Net

1. Rita's child development teacher wants each student to depict some aspect of child development from infancy to age 6 as a chronological time line represented by descriptions or illustrations. Rita has chosen the development of the self. What behaviors at 6, 12, and 18 months, and at 2, 3, 4, 5, and 6 years of age represent milestones in self-awareness, self-concept, self-understanding, and self-esteem?
2. Margie's psychology professor returned a draft of her class paper on self-esteem indicating that she needed to add more information on how to enhance self-esteem in children. What suggestions can she add to build this part of her paper in accordance with her professor's comments?
3. Thirteen-year-old Amy was adopted out of a Korean orphanage when she was 4 years old. She is now struggling with an identity crisis. Is she Korean or American? She doesn't feel that she is either. How can Amy best resolve this ethnic identity crisis?

Nursing, Parenting, and Teaching Exercises

Build your decision-making skills by trying your hand at the scenarios on the Online Learning Center.

Video Clips

The Online Learning Center includes the following videos for this chapter:

- Parents and Adolescent Self-Esteem
  Susan Harter, Department of Psychology, Denver University. Lessons for parents and teachers on how to help adolescents reconcile the challenges of multiple selves.
- Self-Perception at 10 Years and 8 Years of Age
  Two Mexican-origin siblings, Laura and Jared, are asked to describe themselves. Laura responds that she works hard, tries her best, and talks too much. Jared, however, only responds that he does not talk that much.
- Developing a Sexual Identity
  Ramona Oswald, Department of Human & Community Development, University of Illinois, U-C.
- Ethnic and Racial Identity in Adolescence
  Two African-American girls discuss candidly their feelings about being Black. One describes being Black as being a mixture of many cultures. The other says it's hard to be African American because there is no distinct culture for Blacks.

Chapter 13 GENDER

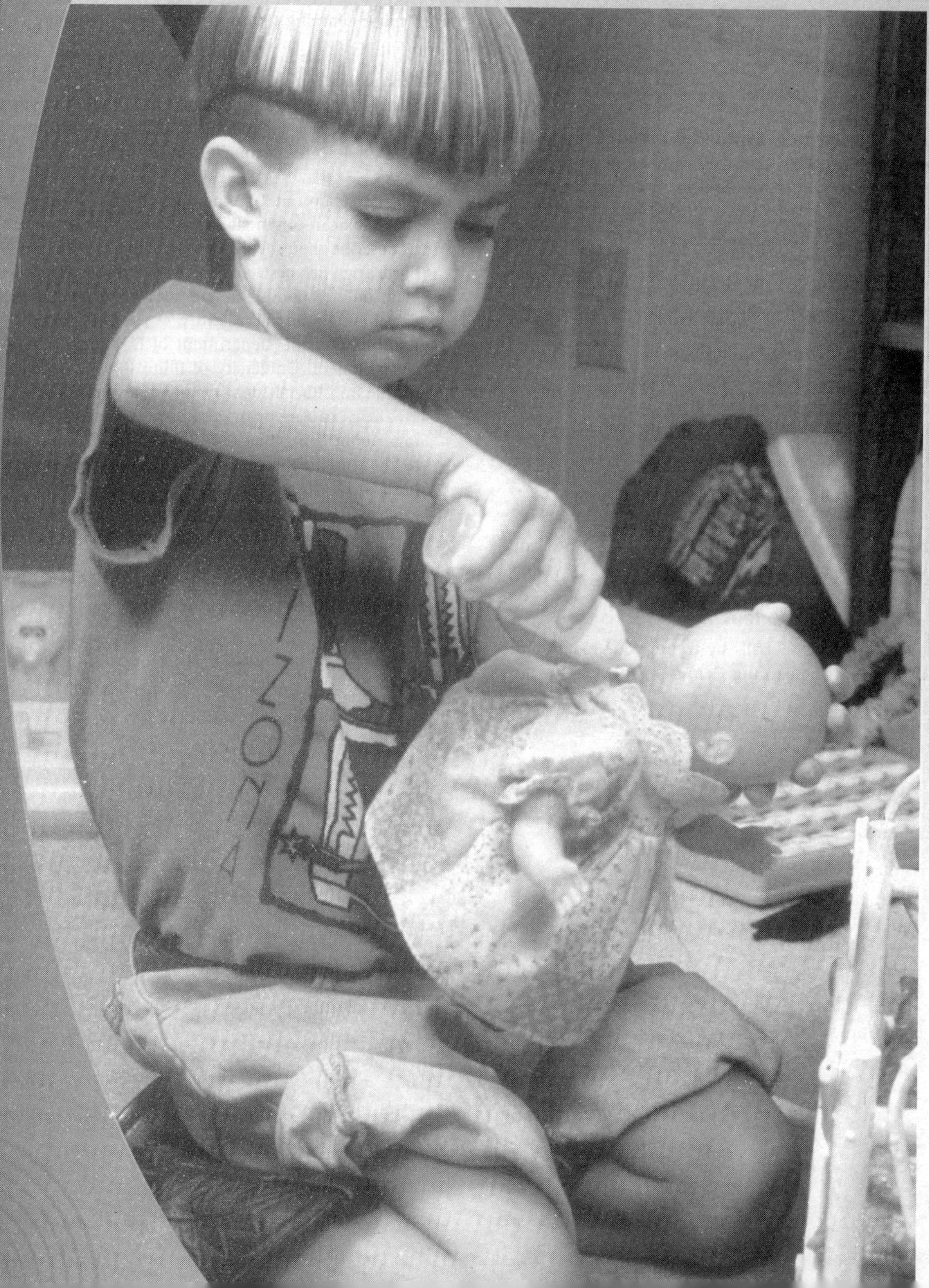

To be meek, patient, tactful, modest, honorable, brave, is not to be either manly or womanly, but is to be humane.

—JANE HARRISON
English Writer, 20th Century

CHAPTER OUTLINE

INFLUENCES ON GENDER DEVELOPMENT

Biological Influences
Social Influences
Cognitive Influences

GENDER STEREOTYPES, SIMILARITIES, AND DIFFERENCES

Gender Stereotyping
Gender Similarities and Differences

GENDER-ROLE CLASSIFICATION

What Is Gender-Role Classification?
Androgyny and Education
Masculinity in Childhood and Adolescence
Gender-Role Transcendence
Gender in Context

LEARNING GOALS

1. Discuss the main biological, social, and cognitive influences on gender
2. Describe gender stereotyping, similarities, and differences
3. Identify how gender roles can be classified

The Story of Jerry Maguire: Gender, Emotion, and Caring

How are gender, emotion, and caring portrayed in the movie Jerry Maguire?

Gender and emotion researcher Stephanie Shields (1998) analyzed the movie *Jerry Maguire* in terms of how it reflects the role of gender in emotions and relationships. In brief, the movie is a "buddy" picture with sports agent Jerry Maguire (played by Tom Cruise) paired with two buddies: the too-short Arizona Cardinals wide receiver Rod Tidwell (played by Cuba Gooding, Jr.) and 6-year-old Ray, son of Jerry's love interest, the accountant Dorothy Boyd (played by Renee Zellweger). Through his buddies, the thinking-but-not-feeling Jerry discovers the right path by connecting to Ray's emotional honesty and Rod's devotion to his family.

The image of nurturing and nurtured males is woven throughout the movie. Through discovering a caring relationship with Ray, Jerry makes his first genuine move toward emotional maturity. The boy is the guide to the man. Chad, Ray's baby-sitter, is a good example of appropriate caring by a male.

Males are shown crying in the movie. Jerry sheds tears while writing his mission statement, when thinking about Dorothy's possible move to another city (which also means he would lose Ray), and at the success of his lone client (Rod). Rod is brought to tears when he speaks of his family. Historically, weeping, more than any emotional expression, has been associated with feminine emotion. However, it has increasingly taken on a more prominent role in the male's emotional makeup.

The movie Jerry Maguire reflects changes in gender roles as an increasing number of males show an interest in improving their social relationships and achieving emotional maturity. However, as we will see later in this chapter, experts on gender argue that overall females are more competent in their social relationships than males are and that large numbers of males still have a lot of room for improvement in dealing better with their emotions.

PREVIEW

What does it mean to be a man or a woman? How a society answers this basic question about gender affects many aspects of a child's life. Gender refers to the psychological and sociocultural dimensions of being female or male. Two aspects of gender bear special mention: gender identity and gender role. Gender identity is the sense of being female or male, which most children acquire by the time they are 3 years old. A gender role is a set of expectations that prescribes how females should think, act, and feel. We will begin this chapter by examining various influences on gender development and then turn our attention to gender stereotypes, similarities, and differences. Next, we will discuss how gender roles are classified.

1 INFLUENCES ON GENDER DEVELOPMENT

Biological Influences | Social Influences | Cognitive Influences

How is gender influenced by biology? By children's social experiences? By cognitive factors?

Biological Influences

To understand biological influences, we need to consider heredity and hormones. We also will explore the theoretical view of Freud, and the more recent view of evolutionary psychologists.

Heredity and Hormones It was not until the 1920s that researchers confirmed the existence of human sex chromosomes, which are called X and Y chromosomes. These chromosomes contain the genetic material that determines our sex. As we discussed in chapter 3, "Biological Beginnings," humans normally have 46 chromosomes arranged in pairs. The 23rd pair may consist of two X chromosomes to produce a female, or it may have both an X and a Y chromosome to produce a male.

In the first few weeks of gestation, female and male embryos look alike. Then ovaries begin developing unless a gene on the Y chromosome directs a small piece of tissue in the embryo to develop into testes. Once the tissue has turned into testes, they begin to secrete testosterone.

Recall from chapter 5, "Physical Development and Health," that testosterone is an androgen, which is one of the two classes of hormones that have the most influence on gender; the other is the estrogens. Both estrogens and androgens occur in both females and males, but in very different concentrations. **Estrogens** are produced mainly by the ovaries and primarily influence the development of female physical sex characteristics and help regulate the menstrual cycle. Estradiol is an example of an estrogen. **Androgens** such as testosterone primarily promote the development of male genitals and secondary sex characteristics. Androgens are produced by the adrenal glands in males and females, and by the testes in males.

Although sex hormones alone, of course, do not determine behavior, researchers have found links between sex hormone levels and certain behaviors. The most established effects of testosterone on humans involve aggressive behavior and sexual behavior (Hyde, 2004). Levels of testosterone are correlated with sexual behavior in boys during puberty (Udry & others, 1985). Violent male criminals have above-average levels of testosterone (Dabbs & others, 1987), and professional football players have higher levels of testosterone than ministers do (Dabbs & Morris, 1990).

Far more direct links occur between sex hormones and physical development. If the fetus is exposed to unusual levels of sex hormones early in development, anatomical anomalies as well as problems in gender development may occur (Reiner & Gearhart, 2004). Here are four examples (Lippa, 2002, pp. 103–105, 114):

- *Congenital adrenal hyperplasia (CAH).* Some girls have this condition, which is caused by a genetic defect that leads to abnormally high levels of androgens. CAH girls, although they are XX females, vary in how much their genitals look like male or female genitals. Often, their genitals are "surgically altered to look more like those of a typical female" (p. 104). Although CAH girls usually grow up to think of themselves as girls and women, they are less content with being a female and show a stronger interest in being a male than other girls (Berenbaum & Bailey, 2003; Ehrhardt, 1987; Hall & others, 2004; Slijper, 1984). "They like participating in rough-and-tumble activities and sports, dressing in clothing that appears more 'masculine,' and playing with boys and boys' toys . . . CAH girls often dislike girl-typical activities such as playing with dolls and wearing makeup, jewelry, and frilly clothes" (Lippa, 2002, p. 104).
- *Androgen-insensitive males.* Because of a genetic error, a small number of genetic XY males do not have androgen receptors; as a result, their bodies look completely female, they think of themselves as females, and most are attracted to males. However, internally they do not develop complete female reproductive structures (Wisniewski & others, 2000).
- *Pelvic field defect.* A small number of newborns have a disorder called pelvic field defect, which in boys involves a missing penis. Prenatally their exposure to hormones was normal, but in the past doctors usually recommended that these genetic boys undergo castration (because they were born with testicles but not a penis) and be raised as girls. According to one study, despite the efforts by parents to rear them as girls, most of the XY children insisted that

gender The psychological and sociocultural dimensions of being male or female.

gender identity The sense of being female or male, which most children acquire by the time they are 3 years old.

gender role A set of expectations that prescribes how females and males should think, act, and feel.

estrogens Hormones, the most important of which is estradiol, that influence the development of female physical sex characteristics and help regulate the menstrual cycle.

androgens Hormones, the most important of which is testosterone, that promote the development of male genitals and secondary sex characteristics.

they were boys (Reiner, 2001). Apparently, normal exposure to androgens prenatally had a stronger influence on their gender identity than being castrated and raised as girls.

- *Boy without a penis.* In another intriguing case, one of two identical twin boys lost his penis due to an errant circumcision. The twin who lost his penis was surgically reassigned to be a girl and to be reared as a girl. "Bruce (the real name of the boy) became Brenda. Although early reports suggested the sex reassignment had been successful, Brenda was never really comfortable as a girl (Diamond & Sigmundson, 1997). In early adulthood, Brenda became Bruce once again, and now lives as a man with a wife and adopted children" (Colapinto, 2000, p. 114).

In sum, research suggests that early hormonal production plays a critical role in gender development.

The Evolutionary Psychology View A theoretical explanation of the role of biological factors such as hormones in gender differences comes from evolutionary psychology, which was described in chapter 3. Evolutionary psychology holds that adaptation during the evolution of humans produced psychological differences between males and females (Buss, 1995, 2000, 2004). Evolutionary psychologists argue that primarily because of their differing roles in reproduction, males and females faced different pressures in primeval environments when the human species was evolving (Janicki, 2004). In particular, because having multiple sexual liaisons improves the likelihood that males will pass on their genes, natural selection favored males who adopted short-term mating strategies. These males competed with other males to acquire more resources in order to gain access to females. Therefore, say evolutionary psychologists, males evolved dispositions that favor violence, competition, and risk taking.

In contrast, according to evolutionary psychologists, females' contributions to the gene pool were increased by securing resources for their offspring, which was promoted by obtaining long-term mates who could support a family. As a consequence, natural selection favored females who devoted effort to parenting and chose mates who could provide their offspring with resources and protection. Females developed preferences for successful, ambitious males who could provide these resources.

This evolutionary unfolding, according to some evolutionary psychologists, explains key gender differences in sexual attitudes and sexual behavior. For example, in one study, men said that ideally they would like to have more than 18 sexual partners in their lifetime, whereas women stated that ideally they would like to have only 4 or 5 (Buss & Schmitt, 1993). In another study, 75 percent of the men but none of the women approached by an attractive stranger of the opposite sex consented to a request for sex (Clark & Hatfield, 1989).

Such gender differences, says David Buss (1995, 2000, 2004), are exactly the type predicted by evolutionary psychology. Buss argues that men and women differ psychologically in those domains in which they have faced different adaptive problems during evolutionary history. In all other domains, predicts Buss, the sexes will be psychologically similar.

Critics of evolutionary psychology argue that its hypotheses are backed by speculations about prehistory, not evidence, and that in any event people are not locked into behavior that was adaptive in the evolutionary past. Critics also claim that the evolutionary view pays little attention to cultural and individual variations in gender differences.

An Interactionist View No one questions the presence of genetic, biochemical, and anatomical differences between the sexes. The importance of biological factors is not at issue. What is at issue is the directness or indirectness of their effects on social behavior (Lippa, 2005). For example, if a high androgen level directly influences the central nervous system, which in turn increases activity level, then the biological effect on behavior is direct. By contrast, if a child's high level of androgen produces strong muscle development, which in turn causes others to expect the child to be a good athlete and, in turn, leads the child to participate in sports, then the biological effect on behavior is indirect.

Although virtually everyone thinks that children's behavior as males or females is due to an interaction of biological and environmental factors, an interactionist position means different things to different people (Maccoby, 1998). For some, it suggests that certain environmental conditions are required before preprogrammed dispositions appear. For others, it suggests that a particular environment will have different effects, depending on the child's predispositions. For still others, it means that children shape their environments, including their interpersonal environment, and vice versa. The processes of influence and counterinfluence unfold over time. Throughout development, in this view, males and females actively construct their own versions of acceptable masculine and feminine behavior patterns.

Social Influences

Many social scientists, such as Alice Eagly (2000, 2001; Eagly & Diekman, 2003; Wood & Eagly, 2002), locate the cause of psychological sex differences not in biologically evolved dispositions but in the contrasting positions and social roles of women and men. In contemporary American society and in most cultures around the world, women have less power and status than men and control fewer resources. Women perform more domestic work than men and spend fewer hours in paid employment. Although most women are in the workforce, they receive lower pay than men and are thinly represented in the highest levels of organizations. Thus, from the perspective of social influences, gender hierarchy and sexual division of labor are important causes of sex-differentiated behavior. As women adapted to roles with less power and less status in society, they showed more cooperative, less dominant profiles than men.

Psychoanalytic and Social Cognitive Theories

Two prominent theories address the way children acquire masculine and feminine attitudes and behaviors from their parents:

- The **psychoanalytic theory of gender** stems from Freud's view that the preschool child develops a sexual attraction to the opposite-sex parent. At 5 or 6 years of age, the child renounces this attraction because of anxious feelings. Subsequently, the child identifies with the same-sex parent, unconsciously adopting the same-sex parent's characteristics. However, today many child developmentalists do not believe gender development proceeds on the basis of identification, at least not through childhood sexual attraction (Callan, 2001). Children become gender-typed much earlier than 5 or 6 years of age, and they become masculine or feminine even when the same-sex parent is not present in the family.
- The **social cognitive theory of gender** emphasizes that children's gender development occurs through observation and imitation of gender behavior and through the rewards and punishments children experience for gender-appropriate and -inappropriate behavior (Bussey & Bandura, 1999). Parents often use rewards and punishments to teach their daughters to be feminine ("Karen, you are being a good girl when you play gently with your doll") and their sons to be masculine ("Keith, a boy as big as you is not supposed to cry"). Peers also extensively reward and punish gender behavior (Lott & Maluso, 2001). And, by observing adults and peers at home, at school, in the

psychoanalytic theory of gender A theory that stems from Freud's view that preschool children develop a sexual attraction to the opposite-sex parent, then at 5 to 6 years of age renounce the attraction because of anxious feelings, subsequently identifying with the same-sex parent and unconsciously adopting the same-sex parent's characteristics.

social cognitive theory of gender This theory emphasizes that children's gender development occurs through observation and imitation of gender behavior, and through rewards and punishments they experience for gender-appropriate and -inappropriate behavior.

FIGURE 13.1 Parents Influence Their Children's Gender Development by Action and Example

Theory	Processes	Outcome
Psychoanalytic theory	Sexual attraction to opposite-sex parent at 3 to 5 years of age; anxiety about sexual attraction and subsequent identification with same-sex parent at 5 to 6 years of age	Gender behavior similar to that of same-sex parent
Social cognitive theory	Rewards and punishments of gender-appropriate and -inappropriate behavior by adults and peers; observation and imitation of models' masculine and feminine behavior	Gender behavior

www.mhhe.com/santrockcd11

Alice Eagly's Research

neighborhood, and on television, children are widely exposed to a myriad of models who display masculine and feminine behavior. Unlike psychoanalytic theory, social cognitive theory argues that sexual attraction to parents is not involved in gender development. (A comparison of the psychoanalytic and social cognitive views is presented in figure 13.1.) Critics of the social cognitive view argue that gender development is not as passively acquired as it indicates. Later, we will discuss the cognitive views of gender development, which stress that children actively construct their gender world.

Parental Influences Once the label girl or boy is assigned by the obstetrician, virtually everyone, from parents to siblings to strangers, begins treating the infant differently (see figure 13.2). In one study, an infant girl, Avery, was dressed in a neutral outfit of overalls and a T-shirt (Brooks-Gunn & Matthews, 1979). People responded to her differently if they thought she was a girl rather than a boy. People who thought she was a girl made comments like "Isn't she cute?" "What a sweet little, innocent thing." By contrast, people who thought the baby was a boy made remarks like "I bet he is a tough little customer. He will be running around all over the place and causing trouble in no time."

In general, parents even hope that their offspring will be a boy. In one investigation in the 1970s, 90 percent of the men and 92 percent of the women wanted their firstborn child to be a boy (Peterson & Peterson, 1973). In a more recent study, parents still preferred a boy as the firstborn child—75 percent of the men and 79 percent of the women had that preference (Hamilton, 1991).

In some countries, a male child is so preferred over a female child that many mothers will abort a female fetus after fetal testing procedures, such as amniocentesis and sonograms, that reveal the fetus's sex. For example, in South Korea, where fetal testing to determine sex is common, male births exceed female births by 14 percent, in contrast to a worldwide average of 5 percent.

Both mothers and fathers are psychologically important in children's gender development (Parke, 2004). Mothers are more consistently given responsibility for nurturance and physical care; fathers are more likely to engage in playful interaction and be given responsibility for ensuring that boys and girls conform to existing cultural norms. And whether or not they have more influence on them, fathers are more involved in socializing their sons than in socializing their daughters (Day & Lamb, 2004; Lamb, 1986). Fathers seem to play an especially important part in gender-role development—they are more likely to act differently toward sons and daughters than mothers are, and thus contribute more to distinctions between the genders (Huston, 1983).

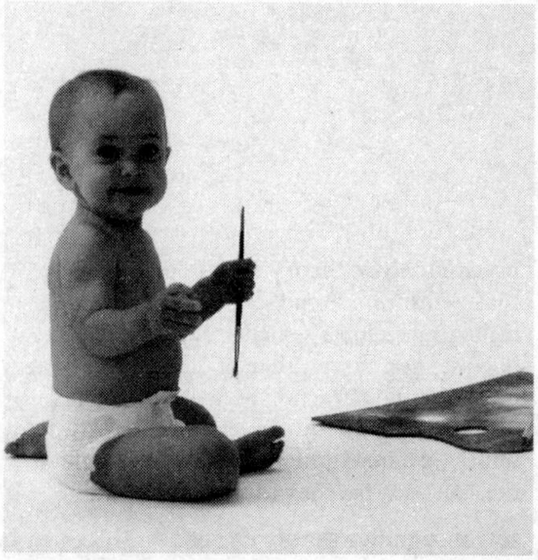

FIGURE 13.2 Expectations for Boys and Girls. First imagine that this is a photograph of a baby girl. What expectations would you have for her? Then imagine that this is a photograph of a baby boy. What expectations would you have for him?

Many parents encourage boys and girls to engage in different types of play and activities (Fagot, Rodgers, & Leinbach, 2000; Ruble, Martin, & Berenbaum, 2006). Girls are more likely to be given dolls to play with during childhood and, when old enough, are more likely to be assigned baby-sitting duties. Girls are encouraged to be more nurturant and emotional than boys, and their fathers are more likely to engage in aggressive play with their sons than with their daughters. As adolescents

increase in age, parents permit boys more freedom than girls, allowing them to be away from home and stay out later without supervision. When parents place severe restrictions on their adolescent sons, it has been found to be especially disruptive to the sons' development (Baumrind, 1999).

In recent years, the idea that parents are the critical socializing agents in gender-role development has come under fire. Parents are only one of many sources through which the individual learns gender roles. Culture, schools, peers, the media, and other family members can also influence a child's gender development. Yet it is important to guard against swinging too far in this direction because—especially in the early years of development—parents are important influences on gender development (Gelman, Taylor, & Nguyen, 2004; Marsiglio, 2004).

Peer Influences Parents provide the earliest discrimination of gender roles in development, but before long, peers join the societal process of responding to and modeling masculine and feminine behavior (Leman, Ahmed, & Ozarow, 2005; Rubin, Bukowski, & Parker, 2006; Underwood, 2004). Children who play in sex-appropriate activities tend to be rewarded for doing so by their peers. Those who play in cross-sexed activities tend to be criticized by their peers or left to play alone. Children show a clear preference for being with and liking same-sex peers, and this tendency usually becomes stronger during the middle and late childhood years (Maccoby, 2002) (see figure 13.3). After extensive observations of elementary school playgrounds, two researchers characterized the play settings as "gender school," pointing out that boys teach one another the required masculine behavior and enforce it strictly (Luria & Herzog, 1985). Girls also pass on the female culture and mainly congregate with one another. Individual "tomboy" girls can join boys' activities without losing their status in the girls' groups, but the reverse is not true for boys, reflecting our society's greater sex-typing pressure for boys (Matlin, 2004).

Peer demands for conformity to gender roles become especially intense during adolescence. While there is greater social mixing of males and females during early adolescence, in both formal groups and in dating, peer pressure is strong for the adolescent boy to be the very best male possible and for the adolescent girl to be the very best female possible.

Schools and Teachers There are concerns that schools and teachers have biases against both boys and girls. What evidence is there that the classroom is biased against boys? Here are some factors to consider (DeZolt & Hull, 2001):

- Compliance, following rules, and being neat and orderly are valued and reinforced in many classrooms. These are behaviors that usually characterize girls more than boys.

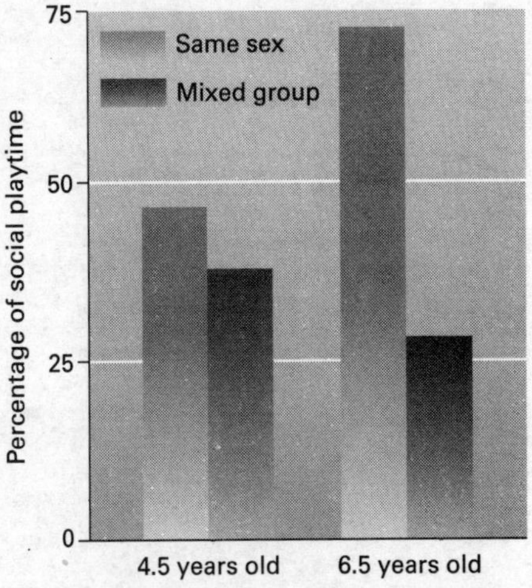

FIGURE 13.3 Developmental Changes in Percentage of Time Spent in Same-Sex and Mixed-Group Settings. Observations of children show that they are more likely to play in same-sex than mixed-sex groups. This tendency increases between 4 and 6 years of age.

- A large majority of teachers are females, especially in the elementary school. This may make it more difficult for boys than girls to identify with their teachers and model their teachers' behavior.
- Boys are more likely than girls to have learning problems.
- Boys are more likely than girls to be criticized.
- School personnel tend to ignore the fact that many boys are clearly having academic problems, especially in the language arts.
- School personnel tend to stereotype boys' behavior as problematic.

What evidence is there that the classroom is biased against girls? Consider the views of Myra and David Sadker (2000, 2005):

- In a typical classroom, girls are more compliant, boys more rambunctious. Boys demand more attention, girls are more likely to quietly wait their turn. Teachers are more likely to scold and reprimand boys, as well as send boys to school authorities for disciplinary action. Educators worry that girls' tendency to be compliant and quiet comes at a cost: diminished assertiveness.
- In many classrooms, teachers spend more time watching and interacting with boys while girls work and play quietly on their own. Most teachers don't intentionally favor boys by spending more time with them, yet somehow the classroom frequently ends up with this type of gendered profile.
- Boys get more instruction than girls and more help when they have trouble with a question. Teachers often give boys more time to answer a question, more hints at the correct answer, and further tries if they give the wrong answer.
- Boys are more likely than girls to get lower grades and to be grade repeaters, yet girls are less likely to believe that they will be successful in college work.
- Girls and boys enter first grade with roughly equal levels of self-esteem. Yet by the middle school years, girls' self-esteem is lower than boys'.
- When elementary school children are asked to list what they want to do when they grow up, boys describe more career options than girls do.

Thus, there is evidence of gender bias against both males and females in schools (DeZolt & Hull, 2001). Many school personnel are not aware of their gender-biased attitudes. These attitudes are deeply entrenched in and supported by the culture. Increasing awareness of gender bias in schools is clearly an important strategy in reducing such bias.

Might same-sex education be better for children than co-ed education? The research evidence related to this question is mixed (Ruble, Martin, & Berenbaum, 2006). Some research indicates that same-sex education has positive outcomes for girls' achievement while other research does not show any improvements in achievement for girls or boys in same-sex education (Mael, 1998; Warrington & Younger, 2003).

Gender and the Media The messages carried by the media about what is appropriate or inappropriate for males and for females also are important influences on gender development (Calvert, 1999; Comstock & Scharrer, 2006; Pike & Jennings, 2005; Purcheco & Hurtado, 2001). A special concern is the way females are pictured on television.

In the 1970s, it became apparent that television was portraying females as less competent than males. For example, about 70 percent of the prime-time characters were males, men were more likely to be shown in the workforce, women were more likely to be shown as housewives and in romantic roles, men were more likely to appear in higher-status jobs and in a greater diversity of occupations, and men were presented as more aggressive and constructive (Sternglanz & Serbin, 1974). Television networks became more sensitive to how males and females are portrayed on television shows, but researchers continued to find that television portrayed males as more competent than females (Durkin, 1985). In one investigation, young adolescent girls indicated that television occupations were more extremely stereotyped than real-life occupations were (Wroblewski & Huston, 1987).

Television directed at adolescents might be the most extreme in its portrayal of the sexes, especially of teenage girls (Beal, 1994). In one study, teenage girls were shown as primarily concerned with dating, shopping, and their appearance (Campbell, 1988). They were rarely depicted as interested in school or career plans. Attractive girls were often portrayed as "airheads" and intelligent girls as unattractive.

Another highly stereotyped form of programming specifically targeted for teenage viewers is rock music videos. What adolescents see on MTV and rock music videos is highly stereotyped and slanted toward a male audience. In music videos, females are twice as likely as in prime-time programming to be dressed provocatively, and aggressive acts are often perpetrated by females.

Gender stereotyping also appears in the print media. Females and males are portrayed with different personalities, and perform different tasks, in children's books (Matlin, 2004). Males are more likely than females to be described and pictured as clever, industrious, and brave. They acquire skills, earn fame and fortune, and explore. By contrast, females are more likely to be described as passive, dependent, and kind. They are more likely to cook and clean up.

In one study, 150 children's books were analyzed for gender-role content (Kortenhaus & Demarest, 1993). It was found that the frequency with which females and males are depicted in the stories has become more equal over the past 50 years. The roles played by females and males in the books have changed in a more subtle way. Girls are now being pictured in more instrumental activities (behavior that is instrumental in attaining a goal), but in the portrayals they are as passive and dependent as they were depicted as being 50 years ago! Boys are occasionally shown as passive and dependent today, but the activities they are pictured in are no less instrumental than they were 50 years ago. However, with effort, parents and teachers can locate interesting books in which girls and women are presented as appropriate models.

Cognitive Influences

Observation, imitation, rewards and punishment—these are the mechanisms by which gender develops according to social cognitive theory. Interactions between the child and the social environment are the main keys to gender development in this view. Some critics argue that this explanation pays too little attention to the child's own mind and understanding and portrays the child as passively acquiring gender roles (Gelman, Taylor, & Nguyen, 2004; Martin, Ruble, & Szkrybalo, 2002). Two cognitive theories—cognitive developmental theory and gender schema theory—stress that individuals actively construct their gender world:

- The **cognitive developmental theory of gender** states that children's gender typing occurs *after* children think of themselves as boys and girls. Once they consistently conceive of themselves as male or female, children prefer activities, objects, and attitudes consistent with this label.
- **Gender schema theory** states that gender typing emerges as children gradually develop gender schemas of what is gender-appropriate and gender-inappropriate in their culture. A *schema* is a cognitive structure, a network of associations that guides an individual's perceptions. A *gender schema* organizes the world in terms of female and male. Children are internally motivated to perceive the world and to act in accordance with their developing schemas.

Initially proposed by Lawrence Kohlberg (1966), the cognitive developmental theory of gender holds that gender development depends on cognition, and it applies the ideas of Piaget that we discussed in chapter 6. As young children develop the

cognitive developmental theory of gender In this view, children's gender typing occurs after they have developed a concept of gender. Once they begin to consistently conceive of themselves as male or female, children often organize their world on the basis of gender.

gender schema theory According to this theory, an individual's attention and behavior are guided by an internal motivation to conform to gender-based sociocultural standards and stereotypes.

FIGURE 13.4 The Development of Gender-Typed Behavior According to the Cognitive Developmental and Gender Schema Theories of Gender Development

Theory	Processes	Emphasis
Cognitive developmental theory	Development of gender constancy, especially around 6 to 7 years of age, when conservation skills develop; after children develop ability to consistently conceive of themselves as male or female, children often organize their world on the basis of gender, such as selecting same-sex models to imitate	Cognitive readiness facilitates gender identity
Gender schema theory	Sociocultural emphasis on gender-based standards and stereotypes; children's attention and behavior are guided by an internal motivation to conform to these gender-based standards and stereotypes, allowing children to interpret the world through a network of gender-organized thoughts	Gender schemas reinforce gender behavior

conservation and categorization skills described by Piaget, said Kohlberg, they develop a concept of gender. What's more, they come to see that they will always be male or female. As a result, they begin to select models of their own sex to imitate. The little girl acts as if she is thinking, "I'm a girl, so I want to do girl things." Therefore, the opportunity to do girl things is rewarding.

Notice that in this view gender-typed behavior occurs only after children develop *gender constancy*, which is the understanding that sex remains the same, even though activities, clothing, and hairstyle might change (Ruble, 2000; Ruble, Martin, & Berenbaum, 2006). However, researchers have found that children do not develop gender constancy until they are about 6 or 7 years old. Before this time, however, most little girls prefer girlish toys and clothes and games, and most little boys prefer boyish toys and games. Thus, contrary to cognitive developmental theory, gender typing does not appear to depend on gender constancy.

Unlike cognitive developmental theory, gender schema theory does not require children to perceive gender constancy before they begin gender typing (see figure 13.4). Instead, gender schema theory states that gender typing occurs when children are ready to encode and organize information along the lines of what is considered appropriate for females and males in their society (Martin & Dinella, 2001; Martin & Halverson, 1981; Ruble, Martin, & Berenbaum, 2006). Bit by bit, children pick up what is gender-appropriate and gender-inappropriate in their culture, and develop gender schemas that shape how they perceive the world and what they remember. Children are motivated to act in ways that conform with these gender schemas. Thus, gender schemas fuel gender typing. To read about how gender schemas extend to young children's judgments about occupations, see the Research in Child Development interlude.

RESEARCH IN CHILD DEVELOPMENT

Young Children's Gender Schemas of Occupations

In one study, researchers interviewed 3- to 7-year-old children about 10 traditionally masculine (airplane pilot, car mechanic) and feminine occupations (clothes designer, secretary), using questions such as these (Levy, Sadovsky, & Troseth, 2000):

Example of a Traditionally Masculine Occupation Item:

> An airplane pilot is a person who "flies airplanes for people." Who do you think would do the best job as an airplane pilot, a man or a woman?

	Boy	Girl
"Masculine Occupations"		
Percentage who judged men more competent	87	70
Percentage who judged women more competent	13	30
"Feminine Occupations"		
Percentage who judged men more competent	35	8
Percentage who judged women more competent	64	92

FIGURE 13.5 Children's Judgments About the Competence of Men and Women in Gender-Stereotyped Occupations

Example of a Traditionally Feminine Occupation Item:

A clothes designer is a person "who draws up and makes clothes for people." Who do you think would do the best job as a clothes designer, a man or a woman?

As indicated in figure 13.5, the children had well-developed gender schemas of occupations. They "viewed men as more competent than women in masculine occupations, and rated women as more competent than men in feminine occupations" (p. 993). Also, "girls' ratings of women's competence at feminine occupations were substantially higher than their ratings of men's competence at masculine occupations. Conversely, boys' ratings of men's competence at masculine occupations were considerably greater than their ratings of women's competence at feminine occupations"(p. 1002). These findings demonstrate that children as young as 3 to 4 years of age have strong gender schemas regarding the perceived competencies of men and women in gender-typed occupations.

The researchers also asked the children to select from a list of emotions how they would feel if they grew up to have each of the 10 occupations. Girls said they would be happy with the feminine occupations and angry or disgusted with the masculine occupations. As expected, boys reversed those choices, saying they would be happy if they grew up to have the masculine occupations but angry and disgusted with the feminine occupations. However, the boys' emotions were more intense (more angry and disgusted) in desiring to avoid the feminine occupations than girls wanting to avoid the masculine occupations. This finding supports other research that indicates gender roles often constrict boys more than girls (Matlin, 2004).

Review and Reflect • LEARNING GOAL 1

1 Discuss the main biological, social, and cognitive influences on gender

Review

- How can gender, gender identity, and gender role be defined? What are some biological influences on gender development?
- What are some social influences on gender development?
- What are some cognitive influences on gender development?

Reflect

- Which theory of gender development do you like best? What might an eclectic theoretical view of gender development be like? (You might want to review the discussion of an eclectic theoretical orientation in chapter 2.)

2 GENDER STEREOTYPES, SIMILARITIES, AND DIFFERENCES

Gender Stereotyping

Gender Similarities and Differences

How pervasive is gender stereotyping? What are the real differences between boys and girls?

Gender Stereotyping

Gender stereotypes are broad categories that reflect our general impressions and beliefs about females and males. How widespread is feminine and masculine stereotyping?

Culture and Stereotyping According to a far-ranging study of college students in 30 countries, stereotyping of females and males is pervasive (Williams & Best, 1982). Males were widely believed to be dominant, independent, aggressive, achievement-oriented, and enduring, while females were widely believed to be nurturant, affiliative, less esteemed, and more helpful in times of distress.

In a subsequent study, women were more likely to perceive similarity between the sexes than men were, and men and women were perceived more similarly in Christian than in Muslim societies (Williams & Best, 1989). Women and men who lived in more highly developed countries perceived themselves as more similar than women and men who lived in less developed countries (Williams & Best, 1989). In the more highly developed countries, the women were more likely to attend college and be gainfully employed. Thus, as sexual equality increases, male and female stereotypes, as well as actual behavioral differences, may diminish. Nevertheless, research continues to find that gender stereotyping is pervasive (Best, 2001; Kite, 2001).

Gender Stereotyping

Developmental Changes in Stereotyping When do children begin to engage in gender stereotyping? A recent study examined the extent to which children of different ages and their mothers engage in gender stereotyping (Gelman, Taylor, & Nguyen, 2004). The researchers videotaped mothers and their 2-, 4-, and 6-year-old sons and daughters as they discussed a picture book with activities that were stereotypical (a boy playing football, for example) and nonstereotypical (a female race car driver, for example). Children engaged in more gender stereotyping than did their mothers. However, mothers expressed gender concepts to their children by referencing categories of gender ("Why do you think only *men* can be firefighters?" for example), labeling gender ("That looks like a Daddy," for example), and contrasting males and females ("Is that a girl job or a boy job?" for example). Gender stereotyping by children was present even in the 2-year-olds, but increased considerably by 4 years of age. This study demonstrated that even when adults don't explicitly engage in gender stereotyping when talking with children, they provide children with information about gender by categorizing gender, labeling gender, and contrasting males and females. Children use these cues to construct an understanding of gender and to guide their behavior (Leaper & Bigler, 2004).

Gender stereotyping continues to change in middle and late childhood, and adolescence (Ruble, Martin, & Berenbaum, 2006). By the time children enter elementary school, they have considerable knowledge about which activities are linked with being male or female. Until about 7 to 8 years of age, gender stereotyping is extensive because young children don't recognize individual variations in masculinity and femininity. By 5 years of age, both boys and girls stereotype boys as powerful and in more negative terms, such as mean, and girls in more positive terms, such as nice

gender stereotypes Broad categories that reflect impressions and beliefs about what behavior is appropriate for females and males.

(Miller & Ruble, 2005). Across the elementary school years, children become more flexible in their gender attitudes (Trautner & others, 2005 in press). In early adolescence, gender stereotyping might increase again. As their bodies change dramatically during puberty, boys and girls are often confused and concerned about what is happening to them. The safe strategy for boys is to become the very best male possible (that is, "masculine"), and the safe strategy for girls is to become the very best female possible (that is, "feminine"). Thus, gender intensification created by pubertal change may produce greater stereotyping in young adolescents, although whether this happens is still debated (Galambos, 2004; Liben & Bigler, 2002). In high school, flexibility in gender attitudes often increases, especially in U.S. adolescents.

Gender Similarities and Differences

Let's now examine some of the differences between the sexes, keeping in mind that (1) the differences are averages—not all females versus all males; (2) even when differences are reported, there is considerable overlap between the sexes; and (3) the differences may be due primarily to biological factors, sociocultural factors, or both. First, we will examine physical differences, and then we will turn to cognitive and socioemotional differences.

Physical Similarities and Differences From conception on, females have a longer life expectancy than males, and females are less likely than males to develop physical or mental disorders. Estrogen strengthens the immune system, making females more resistant to infection, for example. Female hormones also signal the liver to produce more "good" cholesterol, which makes females' blood vessels more elastic than males'. Testosterone triggers the production of low-density lipoprotein, which clogs blood vessels. Males have twice the risk of coronary disease as females. Higher levels of stress hormones cause faster clotting in males, but also higher blood pressure than in females. Women have about twice the body fat of men, most concentrated around breasts and hips. In males, fat is more likely to go to the abdomen. On the average, males grow to be 10 percent taller than females. Male hormones promote the growth of long bones; female hormones stop such growth at puberty.

Does gender matter when it comes to brain structure and function? Human brains are much alike, whether the brain belongs to a male or a female (Halpern, 2001; Hwang & others, 2004). However, researchers have found some differences in the brains of males and females (Goldstein & others, 2001; Kimura, 2000). The differences that have been discovered include the following:

- Female brains are smaller than male brains, but female brains have more folds; the larger folds (called convolutions) allow more surface brain tissue within the skulls of females than males (Luders & others, 2004).
- One part of the hypothalamus responsible for sexual behavior is larger in men than women (Swaab & others, 2001).
- Portions of the corpus callosum—the band of tissues through which the brain's two hemispheres communicate—may be larger in females than males (Driesen & Raz, 1995; Le Vay, 1994), although some studies have found this not to be the case (Bishop & Wahlsten, 1997).
- An area of the parietal lobe that functions in visuospatial skills is larger in males than females (Frederikse & others, 2000).
- The areas of the brain involved in emotional expression show more metabolic activity in females than males (Gur & others, 1995).

Cognitive Similarities and Differences In a classic review of gender differences, Eleanor Maccoby and Carol Jacklin (1974) concluded that males have better math and visuospatial skills (the kinds of skills an architect needs to design a building's angles and dimensions), while females have better verbal abilities.

"So according to the stereotype, you can put two and two together, but I can read the handwriting on the wall."

Subsequently, Maccoby (1987) revised her conclusion about several gender dimensions. She said that the accumulation of research evidence now suggests that verbal differences between females and males have virtually disappeared but that the math and visuospatial differences still exist.

Some experts in gender, such as Janet Shibley Hyde (1993; Hyde & Mezulis, 2001), believe that the cognitive differences between females and males have been exaggerated. For example, Hyde points out that there is considerable overlap in the distributions of female and male scores on math and visuospatial tasks. However, some researchers have found that males have better visual-spatial skills than females (Blakemore, Berenbaum, & Liben, 2005; Ruble, Martin, & Berenbaum, 2006). Despite equal participation in the National Geography Bee, in most years all 10 finalists are boys (Liben, 1995).

In a national study by the U.S. Department of Education (2000), boys did slightly better than girls at math and science. Overall, though, girls were far superior students, and they were significantly better than boys in reading. In another recent national study, females had higher reading achievement and better writing skills than males in grades 4, 8, and 12 with the gap widening as students progressed through school (Coley, 2001).

Socioemotional Similarities and Differences

Five areas of socioemotional development in which gender has been studied are relationships, aggression, emotion, prosocial behavior, and achievement.

Relationships Sociolinguist Deborah Tannen (1990) distinguishes between rapport talk and report talk:

- **Rapport talk** is the language of conversation and a way of establishing connections and negotiating relationships. Girls enjoy rapport talk and conversation that is relationship oriented more than boys do.
- **Report talk** is talk that gives information. Public speaking is an example of report talk. Males hold center stage through report talk with such verbal performances as storytelling, joking, and lecturing with information.

Tannen says that boys and girls grow up in different worlds of talk—parents, siblings, peers, teachers, and others talk to boys and girls differently. The play of boys and girls is also different. Boys tend to play in large groups that are hierarchically structured, and their groups usually have a leader who tells the others what to do and how to do it. Boys' games have winners and losers and often are the subject of arguments. And boys often boast of their skill and argue about who is best at what. In contrast, girls are more likely to play in small groups or pairs, and at the center of a girl's world is often a best friend. In girls' friendships and peer groups, intimacy is pervasive. Turn taking is more characteristic of girls' games than of boys' games. And much of the time, girls simply like to sit and talk with each other, concerned more about being liked by others than jockeying for status in some obvious way.

In sum, Tannen concludes that females are more relationship oriented than males—and that this relationship orientation should be prized as a skill in our culture more than it currently is. Note, however, that some researchers criticize Tannen's ideas as being overly simplified and that communication between males and females is more complex than Tannen indicates (Edwards & Hamilton, 2004). Further, some researchers have found similarities in males' and females' relationship communication strategies. In one recent study, in their talk men and women described and responded to relationship problems in ways that were more similar than different (MacGeorge, 2004).

Further modification of Tannen's view is suggested by a recent *meta-analytic* review of gender differences in talkativeness (general communicative competence),

rapport talk The language of conversation and a way of establishing connections and negotiating relationships; more characteristic of females than of males.

report talk Talk that conveys information; more characteristic of males than females.

affiliative speech (language used to establish or maintain connections with others, such as showing support or expanding on a person's prior remarks), and self-assertive speech (language used to influence others, such as directive statements or disagreements) (Leaper & Smith, 2004). This recent review confirms the criticism that Tannen overemphasizes the size of the gender difference in communication. Gender differences did occur, with girls slightly more talkative and engaging in more affiliative speech than boys, and boys being more likely to use self-assertive speech. But the gender differences were small. Perhaps the most important message from this review is that gender differences in communication often depended on the context:

- *Group size.* The gender difference in talkativeness (girls being more competent in communicating) occurred more in large groups than in dyads.
- *Speaking with peers or adults.* No average differences in talk with peers occurred, but girls talked more with adults than boys.
- *Familiarity.* The gender difference in self-assertive speech (boys using it more) was more likely to occur when talking with strangers than with familiar individuals.
- *Age.* The gender difference in affiliative speech was largest in adolescence. This may be due to adolescent girls' increased interest in socioemotional behavior traditionally prescribed for females.

If you are going to generalize about women, you will find yourself up to here in exceptions.

—Dolores Hitchens
American Mystery Writer, 20th Century

Aggression One of the most consistent gender differences is that boys are more physically aggressive than girls (Dodge, Coie, & Lynam, 2006). The difference occurs in all cultures and appears very early in children's development (White, 2001). The physical aggression difference is especially pronounced when children are provoked. Both biological and environmental factors have been proposed to account for gender differences in aggression. Biological factors include heredity and hormones. Environmental factors include cultural expectations, adult and peer models, and social agents who reward aggression in boys and punish aggression in girls.

Although boys are consistently more physically aggressive than girls, might girls show as much or more verbal aggression, such as yelling, than boys? When verbal aggression is examined, gender differences typically either disappear or are sometimes even more pronounced in girls (Eagly & Steffen, 1986). Also, girls are more likely to engage in *relational aggression,* which involves such behaviors as trying to make others dislike a certain child by spreading malicious rumors about the child or ignoring another child when angry at him or her, than physical aggression (Crick, 2005; Underwood, 2003, 2004). However, it is not clear whether girls engage in relational aggression more than boys do (Underwood & others, 2004).

www.mhhe.com/santrockcd11

Shortchanging Girls, Shortchanging America
Positive Expectations for Girls
Gender and Communication

Emotion and Its Regulation Beginning in the elementary school years, boys are more likely to hide their negative emotions, such as sadness, and girls are less likely to express emotions such as disappointment that might hurt others' feelings (Eisenberg, Martin, & Fabes, 1996). Beginning in early adolescence, girls say they experience more sadness, shame, and guilt, and report more intense emotions, while boys are more likely to deny that they experience these emotions (Ruble, Martin, & Berenbaum, 2006).

An important skill is to be able to regulate and control one's emotions and behavior. Boys usually show less self-regulation than girls (Eisenberg, Spinrad, & Smith, 2004). This low self-control can translate into behavior problems. In one study, children's low self-regulation was linked with greater aggression, teasing of others, overreaction to frustration, low cooperation, and inability to delay gratification (Block & Block, 1980).

Prosocial Behavior Are there gender differences in prosocial behavior? Females view themselves as more prosocial and empathic, and they also engage in more prosocial behavior than males (Eisenberg, Fabes, & Spinrad, 2006; Eisenberg &

What are little boys made of?
Frogs and snails
and puppy dogs' tails.
What are little girls made of?
Sugar and spice
And all that's nice

—J. O. Halliwell
English Author, 19th Century

Morris, 2004). For example, a review of research found that across childhood and adolescence, females engaged in more prosocial behavior (Eisenberg & Fabes, 1998). The biggest gender difference occurred for kind and considerate behavior, with a smaller difference in sharing.

Achievement Although women have made considerable progress in attaining high status in many fields, they still are underrepresented in many areas of technology, math, and science (Wigfield & others, 2006). However, some measures of achievement-related behaviors do not reveal gender differences. For example, girls and boys show similar persistence at tasks.

With regard to school achievement, females earn better grades. For example, recent evidence suggests that boys predominate in the academic bottom half of high school classes (DeZolt & Hull, 2001). That is, although many boys perform at the average or advanced level, the bottom 50 percent academically is made up mainly of boys. Males are more likely than females to be assigned to special/remedial education classes. Females are more likely to be engaged with academic material, be attentive in class, put forth more academic effort, and participate more in class than boys are (DeZolt & Hull, 2001).

Gender Controversy Controversy continues about the extent of gender differences and what might cause them. As we saw earlier, evolutionary psychologists such as David Buss (2004) argue that gender differences are extensive and caused by the adaptive problems they have faced across their evolutionary history. Alice Eagly (2001) also concludes that gender differences are substantial but reaches a very different conclusion about their cause. She emphasizes that gender differences are due to social conditions that have resulted in women having less power and controlling fewer resources than men.

By contrast, Janet Shibley Hyde (1986, 2005 in press) concludes that gender differences have been greatly exaggerated, especially fueled by popular books such as John Gray's (1992) *Men Are from Mars, Women Are from Venus* and Deborah Tannen's (1990) *You Just Don't Understand!* She argues that the research shows that females and males are similar on most psychological factors. In a recent review, Hyde (2005 in press) summarized the results of 44 meta-analyses of gender differences and similarities. In most areas, gender differences either were nonexistent or small, including math ability, communication, and aggression. The largest difference occurred on motor skills (favoring males), followed by sexuality (males masturbate more and are more likely to endorse sex in a casual, uncommitted relationship) and physical aggression (males are more physically aggressive than females).

Hyde's recent summary of meta-analyses is still not likely to quiet the controversy about gender differences and similarities, but further research should continue to provide a basis for more accurate judgments about this controversy.

Review and Reflect • LEARNING GOAL 2

2 Describe Gender Stereotyping, Similarities, and Differences

Review

- How extensive is gender stereotyping?
- What are some gender similarities and differences in the areas of biological, cognitive, and socioemotional development?

Reflect

- How is your gender behavior and thinking similar or different from your mother's and grandmothers' if you are a female? How is your gender behavior and thinking different from your father's and grandfathers' if you are a male?

3 GENDER-ROLE CLASSIFICATION

- What Is Gender-Role Classification?
- Masculinity in Childhood and Adolescence
- Gender in Context
- Androgyny and Education
- Gender-Role Transcendence

Not very long ago, it was accepted that boys should grow up to be masculine and girls to be feminine, that boys are made of "frogs and snails" and girls are made of "sugar and spice and all that's nice." Let's further explore such gender classifications of boys and girls as "masculine" and "feminine."

What Is Gender-Role Classification?

In the past, a well-adjusted boy was supposed to be independent, aggressive, and powerful. A well-adjusted girl was supposed to be dependent, nurturant, and uninterested in power. The masculine characteristics were considered to be healthy and good by society; the feminine characteristics were considered undesirable.

In the 1970s, as both females and males become dissatisfied with the burdens imposed by their stereotypic roles, alternatives to femininity and masculinity were proposed. Instead of describing masculinity and femininity as a continuum in which more of one means less of the other, it was proposed that individuals could have both masculine and feminine traits. This thinking led to the development of the concept of **androgyny,** the presence of masculine and feminine characteristics in the same person (Bem, 1977; Spence & Helmreich, 1978). The androgynous boy might be assertive (masculine) and nurturant (feminine). The androgynous girl might be powerful (masculine) and sensitive to others' feelings (feminine). In one recent study it was confirmed that societal changes are leading females to be more assertive (Spence & Buckner, 2000).

androgyny The presence of masculine and feminine characteristics in the same person.

Measures have been developed to assess androgyny. One of the most widely used measures is the Bem Sex-Role Inventory. To see whether your gender-role classification is masculine, feminine, or androgynous, see figure 13.6.

Gender experts, such as Sandra Bem, argue that androgynous individuals are more flexible, competent, and mentally healthy than their masculine or feminine counterparts. To some degree, though, deciding on which gender-role classification is best depends on the context involved (Woodhill & Samuels, 2004). For example, in close relationships, feminine and androgynous orientations might be more desirable

Androgyny

The following items are from the Bem Sex-Role Inventory. When taking the BSRI, a person is asked to indicate on a 7-point scale how well each of the 60 characteristics describes herself or himself. The scale ranges from 1 (never or almost never true) to 7 (always or almost always true).

EXAMPLES OF MASCULINE ITEMS	EXAMPLES OF FEMININE ITEMS
Defends open beliefs	Does not use harsh language
Forceful	Affectionate
Willing to take risks	Loves children
Dominant	Understanding
Aggressive	Gentle

Scoring: The items are scored on independent dimensions of masculinity and femininity as well as androgyny and undifferentiate classifications.

FIGURE 13.6 The Bem Sex-Role Inventory: Are You Androgynous?

because of the expressive nature of close relationships. However, masculine and androgynous orientations might be more desirable in traditional academic and work settings because of the achievement demands in these contexts. For example, a recent study found that masculine and androgynous individuals had higher expectations for being able to control the outcomes of their academic efforts than feminine or undifferentiated individuals (Choi, 2004).

Androgyny and Education

Can and should androgyny be taught to students? In general, it is easier to teach androgyny to girls than to boys and easier to teach it before the middle school grades. For example, in one study, a gender curriculum was put in place for one year in the kindergarten, fifth, and ninth grades (Guttentag & Bray, 1976). It involved books, discussion materials, and classroom exercises with an androgynous bent. The program was most successful with the fifth-graders, least successful with the ninth-graders. The ninth-graders, especially the boys, showed a boomerang effect, in which they had more traditional gender-role attitudes after the year of androgynous instruction than before it.

Despite such mixed findings, the advocates of androgyny programs believe that traditional sex-typing is harmful for all students and especially has prevented many girls from experiencing equal opportunity. The detractors argue that androgynous educational programs are too value-laden and ignore the diversity of gender roles in our society.

Masculinity in Childhood and Adolescence

Concern about the ways boys have been brought up in traditional ways has been called a "national crisis of boyhood" by William Pollack (1999) in his book *Real Boys*. Pollack says that although there has been considerable talk about the "sensitive male," little has been done to change what he calls the "boy code." He says that this code tells boys they should show little if any emotion as they are growing up. Too often boys are socialized to not show their feelings and act tough, says Pollack. Boys learn the boy code in many different contexts—sandboxes, playgrounds, schoolrooms, camps, hangouts—and are taught the code by parents, peers, coaches, teachers, and other adults. Pollack, as well as many others, believes that boys would benefit from being socialized to express their anxieties and concerns rather than keep them bottled up as well as to learn how to better regulate their aggression.

There also is a special concern about boys who adopt a strong masculine role in adolescence, because this is associated with problem behaviors. Joseph Pleck (1995) believes that what defines traditional masculinity in many Western cultures includes behaviors that do not have social approval but nonetheless validate the adolescent boy's masculinity. That is, in the male adolescent culture, male adolescents perceive that they will be thought of as more masculine if they engage in premarital sex, drink alcohol, take drugs, and participate in illegal delinquent activities.

www.mhhe.com/santrockcd11

Psychological Study of Males

Gender-Role Transcendence

Some critics of androgyny say enough is enough and that there is too much talk about gender. They believe that androgyny is less of a panacea than originally envisioned (Paludi, 2002). An alternative is gender-role transcendence, the view that when an individual's competence is at issue, it should be conceptualized on a personal basis rather than on the basis of masculinity, femininity, or androgyny (Pleck, 1983). That is, we should think about ourselves as people, not as masculine, feminine, or androgynous. Parents should rear their children to be competent boys and girls, not masculine, feminine, or androgynous, say the gender-role critics. They believe such gender-role classification leads to too much stereotyping.

Gender in Context

The concept of gender-role classification involves a personality traitlike categorization of a person. However, it may be helpful to think of personality in terms of person-situation interaction rather than personality traits alone. Thus, in our discussion of gender-role classification, we describe how different gender roles might be more appropriate, depending on the context, or setting, involved.

To see the importance of considering gender in context, let's examine helping behavior and emotion. The stereotype is that females are better than males at helping. However, it depends on the situation. Females are more likely than males to volunteer their time to help children with personal problems and to engage in caregiving behavior (Taylor, 2002). However, in situations in which males feel a sense of competence and involve danger, males are more likely than females to help (Eagly & Crowley, 1986). For example, a male is more likely than a female to stop and help a person stranded by the roadside with a flat tire.

"She is emotional; he is not"—that is the master emotional stereotype. However, like differences in helping behavior, emotional differences in males and females depend on the particular emotion involved and the context in which it is displayed (Shields, 1991). Males are more likely to show anger toward strangers, especially male strangers, when they feel they have been challenged. Males also are more likely to turn their anger into aggressive action. Emotional differences between females and males often show up in contexts that highlight social roles and relationships. For example, females are more likely to discuss emotions in terms of relationships, and they are more likely to express fear and sadness.

The importance of considering gender in context is nowhere more apparent than when examining what is culturally prescribed behavior for females and males in different countries around the world (Gibbons, 2000). In recent decades, roles assumed by males and females in the United States have become increasingly similar—that is, androgynous. In many countries, though, gender roles have remained more gender-specific. For example, in Iran, the division of labor between Iranian males and females is dramatic: Iranian males are socialized to work in the public sphere, females in the private world of home and child rearing. The Islamic religion dictates that the man's duty is to provide for his family, the woman's to care for her family and household (Dickerscheid & others, 1988). Any deviations from this traditional gender-role orientation are severely disapproved of.

Of course, Iran is not the only country in which males and females are socialized to behave, think, and feel in strongly gender-specific ways (Denmark, 2004; Katz, 2004). Kenya and Nepal are two other cultures in which children are brought up under very strict gender-specific guidelines (Munroe, Himmin, & Munroe, 1984). In the People's Republic of China, the female's status has historically been lower than the male's. The teachings of the fifth-century B.C. Chinese philosopher Confucius were used to reinforce the concept of the female as an inferior being. Beginning with the 1949 revolution in China, women began to achieve more economic freedom and more-equal status in marital relationships. However, even with the sanctions of a socialist government, the old patriarchal traditions of male supremacy in China have not been completely uprooted. Chinese women still make considerably less money than Chinese men in comparable positions, and in rural China a tradition of male supremacy still governs many women's lives.

Thus, complete equality remains a distant objective. In many cultures, gender-specific behavior is pronounced, and females are not given access to high-status positions.

Access to education for girls has improved somewhat around the world, but girls' education still lags behind boys' education. For example, according to a recent UNICEF (2003) analysis of education around the world, by age 18, girls have received, on average, 4.4 years less education than boys have. This lack of

Gender Around the World

In China, females and males are usually socialized to behave, feel, and think differently. The old patriarchal traditions of male supremacy have not been completely uprooted. Chinese women still make considerably less money than Chinese men do, and, in rural China (such as here in the Lixian Village of Sichuan) male supremacy still governs many women's lives.

education reduces their chances of developing their potential. Noticeable exceptions to lower participation and completion rates in education for girls occur in Western nations, Japan, and the Phillipines (Brown & Larson, 2002). In most countries more men than women gain advanced training or advanced degrees (Fussell & Greene, 2002).

Although most countries still have gender gaps that favor males, evidence of increasing gender equality is appearing (Brown & Larson, 2002). For example, among upper-socioeconomic-status families in India and Japan, fathers are assuming more child-rearing responsibilities (Stevenson & Zusho, 2002; Verma & Saraswathi, 2002). Rates of employment and career opportunities are expanding in many countries for women. Control over adolescent girls' social relationships, especially sexual and romantic relationships, is decreasing in some countries.

Cultural and ethnic backgrounds also influence how boys and girls are socialized in the United States. In a recent study, Latino and Latina adolescents were socialized differently as they were growing up (Raffaelli & Ontai, 2004). Latinas experienced far greater restrictions than Latinos in curfews, interacting with members of the other sex, getting a driver's license, getting a job, and involvement in after-school activities.

At this point we have discussed many aspects of gender in children's development. The following Caring for Children interlude provides some recommendations for parents and teachers related to children's gender.

CARING FOR CHILDREN

Guiding Children's Gender Development

Boys

1. *Encourage boys to be sensitive in relationships and engage in more prosocial behavior.* An important socialization task is to help boys become more interested in having positive close relationships and become more caring. Fathers can play an especially important role for boys in this regard by being a model who is sensitive and caring.
2. *Encourage boys to be less physically aggressive.* Too often, boys are encouraged to be tough and physically aggressive. A positive strategy is to encourage them to be self-assertive but not physically aggressive.
3. *Encourage boys to handle their emotions more effectively.* This involves helping boys not only to regulate their emotions, as in controlling their anger, but also to learn to express their anxieties and concerns rather than keeping them bottled up.
4. *Work with boys to improve their school performance.* Girls get better grades, put forth more academic effort, and are less likely than boys to be assigned to special/remedial classes. Parents and teachers can help boys by emphasizing the importance of school and expecting better academic effort.

Girls

1. *Encourage girls to be proud of their relationship skills and caring.* The strong interest that girls show in relationships and caring should be rewarded by parents and teachers.
2. *Encourage girls to develop their self-competencies.* While guiding girls to retain their relationship strengths, adults can help girls to develop their ambition and achievement.

3. *Encourage girls to be more self-assertive.* Girls tend to be more passive than boys and can benefit from being encouraged to be more self-assertive.
4. *Encourage girls' achievement.* This can involve encouraging girls to have higher academic expectations and exposing them to a greater range of career options.

Boys and Girls

Help children to reduce gender stereotyping and discrimination. Don't engage in gender stereotyping and discrimination yourself; otherwise, you will be providing a model of gender stereotyping and discrimination for children.

Review and Reflect • LEARNING GOAL 3

3 Identify how gender roles can be classified

Review

- What is gender-role classification?
- What are the effects of teaching androgyny in schools?
- What are some risks of masculinity in childhood and adolescence?
- What is gender-role transcendence?
- How can gender be conceptualized in terms of context?

Reflect

- Several decades ago, the word *dependency* was used to describe the relational orientation of femininity. Dependency took on a negative connotation; for instance, it suggested that females can't take care of themselves while males can. Today, the term *dependency* is being replaced by *relational abilities,* which has more positive connotations (Caplan & Caplan, 1999). Rather than being thought of as dependent, women are now more often described as skilled in forming and maintaining relationships. Make up a list of words that you associate with masculinity and femininity. Do these words have any negative connotations for males and females? For the words that do have negative connotations, think about replacements that have more positive connotations.

REACH YOUR LEARNING GOALS

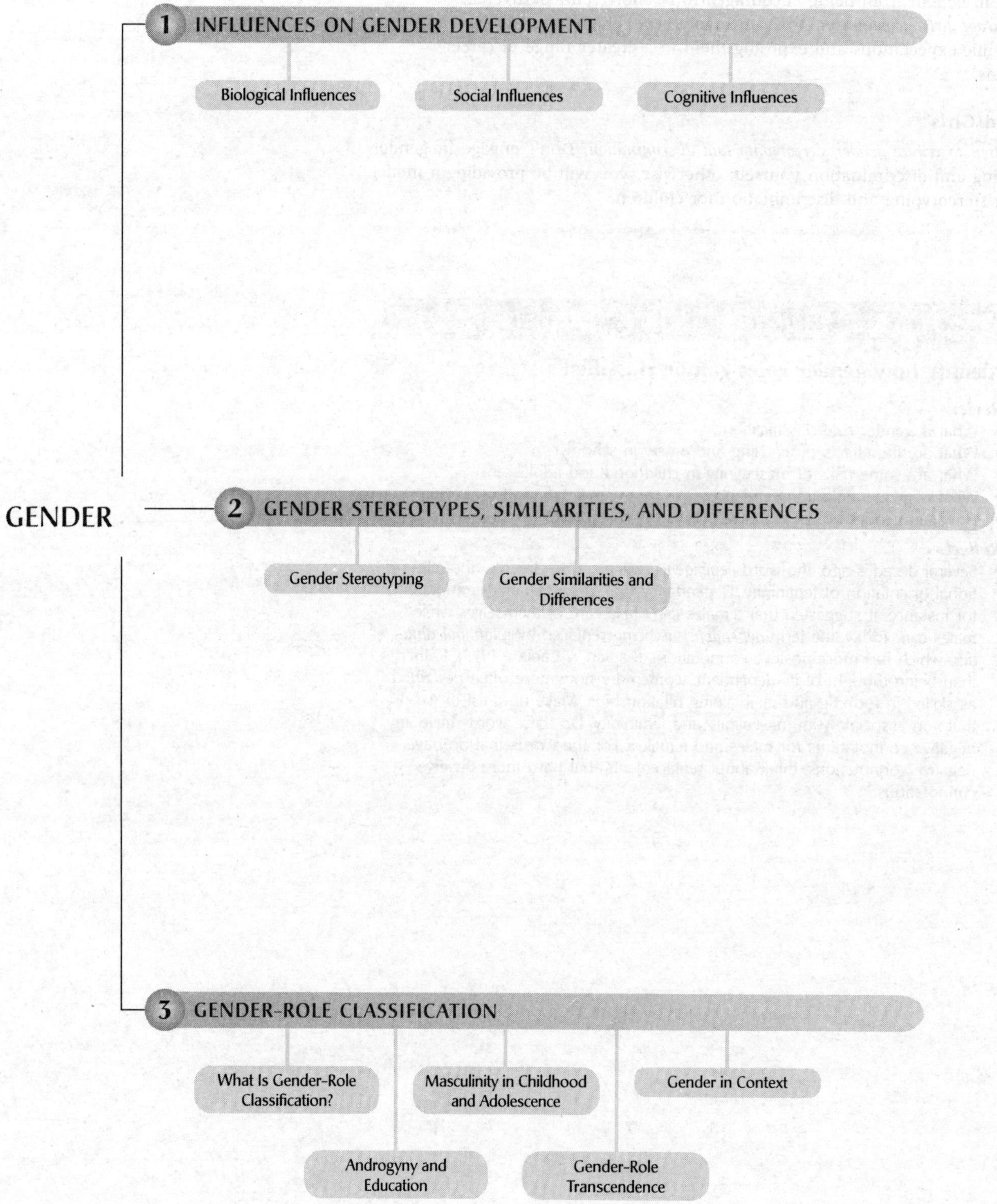

SUMMARY

1 Discuss the main biological, social, and cognitive influences on gender

- Gender refers to the psychological and sociocultural dimensions of being male or female. A gender role is a set of expectations that prescribes how females or males should think, act, and feel. The 23rd pair of chromosomes determines our sex. Ordinarily, females have two X chromosomes, males one X and one Y. Males and females also produce different concentrations of the hormones known as androgens and estrogens. Early hormonal production is linked with later gender development. In the evolutionary psychology view, evolutionary adaptations produced psychological sex differences that are especially present in sexual behavior and mating strategies. Chromosomes determine anatomical sex differences, but culture and society strongly influence gender.
- In the social roles view, women have less power and status than men and control fewer resources, and this gender hierarchy and sexual division of labor are important causes of sex-differentiated behavior. Both psychoanalytic and social cognitive theories emphasize the adoption of parents' gender characteristics. Parents and other adults also might assign gender roles to children and reward or punish behavior along gender lines. Peers are especially adept at rewarding gender-appropriate behavior. Schools and teachers show biases against both boys and girls. Despite improvements, TV still portrays males as more competent than females.
- Both cognitive developmental and gender schema theories emphasize the role of cognition in gender development.

2 Describe gender stereotyping, similarities, and differences

- Gender stereotypes are widespread around the world. They emphasize the male's power and the female's nurturance. Gender stereotyping changes developmentally; it is present even at 2 years of age but increases considerably in early childhood. In middle and late childhood, children become more flexible in their gender attitudes but gender stereotyping may increase again in early adolescence.
- Physical and biological differences between males and females are substantial. Males are often better at math and visuospatial skills. However, some experts, such as Hyde, argue that cognitive differences between males and females have been exaggerated. Males are more physically aggressive and active than females, while females engage in more prosocial behavior, have a stronger interest in social relationships, and are more achievement oriented in school than males. There is considerable controversy about how similar or different females and males are in a number of areas.

3 Identify how gender roles can be classified

- In the past, the well-adjusted male was supposed to show masculine traits; the well-adjusted female, feminine traits. In the 1970s, alternatives to traditional gender roles were introduced. It was proposed that competent individuals could show both masculine and feminine traits. This thinking led to the development of the concept of androgyny, the presence of masculine and feminine traits in one individual. Gender-role measures often categorize individuals as masculine, feminine, androgynous, or undifferentiated. Most androgynous individuals are flexible and mentally healthy, although the particular context and the individual's culture also determine the adaptiveness of a gender-role orientation.
- Androgyny education programs have been more successful with females than males and more successful with children than adolescents.
- A special concern is that boys raised in a traditional manner are socialized to conceal their emotions. Some experts believe that gender-role intensification occurs in early adolescence because of increased pressure to conform to traditional gender roles. Researchers have found that problem behaviors often characterize highly masculine adolescents.
- One alternative to androgyny is gender-role transcendence, which states that there has been too much emphasis on gender and that a better strategy is to think about competence in terms of people rather than gender.
- In thinking about gender, it is important to keep in mind the context in which gender behavior is displayed. In many countries around the world, such as Iran and China, traditional gender roles are still dominant.

KEY TERMS

gender 397
gender identity 397
gender role 397
estrogens 397
androgens 397
psychoanalytic theory of gender 399
social cognitive theory of gender 399
cognitive developmental theory of gender 403
gender schema theory 403
gender stereotypes 406
rapport talk 408
report talk 408
androgyny 411

KEY PEOPLE

Stephanie Shields 396
David Buss 398
Alice Eagly 399
Sigmund Freud 399
Myra and David Sadker 402
Lawrence Kohlberg 403
Eleanor Maccoby 407
Carol Jacklin 407
Janet Shibley Hyde 408
Deborah Tannen 408
Sandra Bem 411
William Pollack 412
Joseph Pleck 412

E-LEARNING TOOLS

To help you master the material in this chapter, visit the Online Learning Center for *Child Development*, eleventh edition (**www.mhhe.com/santrockcd11**), where you'll find these additional resources:

Taking It to the Net

1. Ellen is taking a class in gender psychology. She wants to test the theory of androgyny among her peers in her large geology lecture. She has heard that there is an online version of the test, and thinks people will feel more comfortable taking it online. What conclusions can Ellen draw on the androgyny theory after taking this test?
2. Derek is the program chair for the Men's Focus Group on campus. He is planning a program on the social barriers to men being fully involved fathers. He thinks it has something to do with gender stereotyping that suggests that women are the best nurturers and caregivers. Is there some research Derek ought to share with the group?
3. Professor Lombard told the child development class to find out what the current thinking was on how to treat infants who are born without fully developed male or female genitalia. She said that the old line of thinking was that these children should be surgically altered during infancy so as to be genitally correct females. Are other alternatives being considered today?

Nursing, Parenting, and Teaching Exercises

Build your decision-making skills by trying your hand at the scenarios on the Online Learning Center.

Video Clips

The Online Learning Center includes the following videos for this chapter:

- Sex Typed Play at Age 1
  A 1-year-old girl is shown in a room surrounded by an assortment of toys. She only shows interest in the Barbie dolls, which she examines carefully from every angle.
- Lacking Gender Consistency at Age 4
  A boy is asked to identify the gender of a male doll placed in front of him. After amusing himself by completely rotating the dolls head around, he explains that the doll is a male because of his hair. But when the interviewer puts a skirt on the doll, Sal demonstrates that he lacks an understanding of gender constancy when he explains that the doll is now a girl.
- Sex-Typed Play
  Early sex-typed behavior is demonstrated as we watch a boy and girl make toy selections. The girl quietly plays with an elaborate doll house as the boy excitedly goes from playing with a remote control vehicle to a toy garage. Neither child shows interest in the cross sex-typed toys.
- Girls Engaging in Sex-Typed Play
  Two girls show their preference for a non sex-typed toy as they enthusiastically play with a remote control truck, ignoring the elaborate, colorful dollhouse that sits inches away.

Chapter 14 MORAL DEVELOPMENT

It is one of the beautiful compensations of this life that no one can sincerely try to help another without helping himself.

—CHARLES DUDLEY WARNER
American Essayist, 19th Century

CHAPTER OUTLINE

DOMAINS OF MORAL DEVELOPMENT

What Is Moral Development?
Moral Thought
Moral Behavior
Moral Feeling
Moral Personality

CONTEXTS OF MORAL DEVELOPMENT

Parenting
Schools

PROSOCIAL AND ANTISOCIAL BEHAVIOR

Prosocial Behavior
Antisocial Behavior

LEARNING GOALS

1. Discuss theory and research on the domains of moral development
2. Explain how parenting and schools influence moral development
3. Describe the development of prosocial and antisocial behavior

The Story of Pax, the Make-Believe Planet

Can children understand moral and social problems such as discrimination and economic inequality? Probably not, if you ask them about those terms. But Phyllis Katz (1987) found that children can understand situations that involve those concepts. Katz asked elementary-school-age children to pretend that they had taken a long ride on a spaceship to a make-believe planet called Pax. Once there, the children found problematic situations. For example, citizens of Pax who had dotted noses couldn't get jobs, which went to the people with striped noses. What, Katz asked, would the children do in this situation?

Katz asked the children for their opinions about various situations on this faraway planet. The situations involved conflict, socioeconomic inequality, and civil and political rights. For example, regarding conflict she asked them what a teacher should do when two students were tied for a prize or when they had been fighting. The economic equality dilemmas included a proposed field trip that not all students could afford, a comparable-worth situation in which janitors were paid more than teachers, and an employment situation that discriminated against those with dots on their noses instead of stripes. The rights items dealt with minority rights and freedom of the press.

The elementary school children did indeed recognize injustice and often came up with interesting solutions to problems. For example, all but two children believed that teachers should earn as much as janitors. The holdouts said teachers should make less because they stay in one room or because cleaning toilets is more disgusting and therefore deserves higher wages. Children were especially responsive to the economic inequality items. All but one thought that not giving a job to a qualified applicant who had different physical characteristics (a dotted rather than a striped nose) was unfair. The majority recommended giving the job to the one from the discriminated-against minority.

Overall, the types of rules the children believed a society should abide by were quite sensible. Almost all the children recognized the need for equitable sharing of resources and work and for prohibitions against aggression. How children come to understand these concepts and how this understanding affects their behavior are just two of the questions that are examined in the field of moral development.

PREVIEW

Moral development is one of the oldest topics of interest to those who are curious about human nature. In prescientific periods, philosophers and theologians debated children's moral status at birth, which they believed had implications for how children should be reared. Today, most people have strong opinions not only about moral and immoral behavior but also about how moral behavior should be fostered in children. We will begin our coverage of moral development by exploring its main domains and then examine some important contexts that influence moral development. We will conclude by discussing children's prosocial and antisocial behavior.

1 DOMAINS OF MORAL DEVELOPMENT

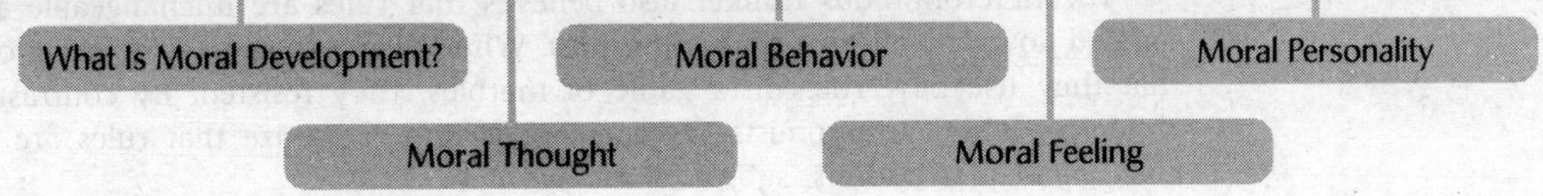

Just what is moral development, and what are its main domains?

What Is Moral Development?

Moral development involves changes in thoughts, feelings, and behaviors regarding standards of right and wrong. Moral development has an *intrapersonal* dimension, which regulates a person's activities when she or he is not engaged in social interaction, and an *interpersonal* dimension, which regulates social interactions and arbitrates conflict (Gibbs, 2003; Power, 2004; Walker & Pitts, 1998). To understand moral development, we need to consider four basic questions:

First, how do individuals *reason* or *think* about moral decisions?
Second, how do individuals actually *behave* in moral circumstances?
Third, how do individuals *feel* about moral matters?
Fourth, what characterizes an individual's moral *personality?*

As we consider these four domains in the following sections, keep in mind that thoughts, behaviors, feelings, and personality often are interrelated. For example, if the focus is on an individual's behavior, it is still important to evaluate the person's reasoning. Also, emotions can distort moral reasoning. And moral personality encompasses thoughts, behavior, and feeling.

Moral Thought

How do individuals think about what is right and wrong? Can children evaluate moral questions in the same way that adults can? Piaget had some thoughts about these questions. So did Lawrence Kohlberg.

Piaget's Theory Interest in how children think about moral issues was stimulated by Piaget (1932), who extensively observed and interviewed children from the ages of 4 through 12. Piaget watched children play marbles to learn how they used and thought about the game's rules. He also asked children about ethical issues—theft, lies, punishment, and justice, for example. Piaget concluded that children go through two distinct stages in how they think about morality.

- From 4 to 7 years of age, children display **heteronomous morality,** the first stage of moral development in Piaget's theory. Children think of justice and rules as unchangeable properties of the world, removed from the control of people.
- From 7 to 10 years of age, children are in a transition showing some features of the first stage of moral reasoning and some stages of the second stage, autonomous morality.
- From about 10 years of age and older, children show **autonomous morality.** They become aware that rules and laws are created by people, and in judging an action, they consider the actor's intentions as well as the consequences.

Because young children are heteronomous moralists, they judge the rightness or goodness of behavior by considering its consequences, not the intentions of the actor. For example, to the heteronomous moralist, breaking 12 cups accidentally is

moral development Changes in thoughts, feelings, and behaviors regarding standards of right and wrong.

heteronomous morality The first stage of moral development in Piaget's theory, occurring at 4 to 7 years of age. Justice and rules are conceived of as unchangeable properties of the world, removed from the control of people.

autonomous morality The second stage of moral development in Piaget's theory, displayed by older children (about 10 years of age and older). The child becomes aware that rules and laws are created by people and that, in judging an action, one should consider the actor's intentions as well as the consequences.

worse than breaking 1 cup intentionally. As children develop into moral autonomists, intentions assume paramount importance.

The heteronomous thinker also believes that rules are unchangeable and are handed down by all-powerful authorities. When Piaget suggested to young children that they use new rules in a game of marbles, they resisted. By contrast, older children—moral autonomists—accept change and recognize that rules are merely convenient conventions, subject to change.

Exploring Moral Development

The heteronomous thinker also believes in **immanent justice,** *the concept that if a rule is broken, punishment will be meted out immediately.* The young child believes that a violation is connected automatically to its punishment. Thus, young children often look around worriedly after doing something wrong, expecting inevitable punishment. Immanent justice also implies that if something unfortunate happens to someone, the person must have transgressed earlier. Older children, who are moral autonomists, recognize that punishment occurs only if someone witnesses the wrongdoing and that, even then, punishment is not inevitable.

How do these changes in moral reasoning occur? Piaget argued that, as children develop, they become more sophisticated in thinking about social matters, especially about the possibilities and conditions of cooperation. Piaget believed that this social understanding comes about through the mutual give-and-take of peer relations. In the peer group, where others have power and status similar to the child's, plans are negotiated and coordinated, and disagreements are reasoned about and eventually settled. Parent-child relations, in which parents have the power and children do not, are less likely to advance moral reasoning, because rules are often handed down in an authoritarian way.

Kohlberg's Theory

Like Piaget, Lawrence Kohlberg (1958, 1976, 1986) stressed that moral reasoning unfolds in stages. The stages, Kohlberg theorized, are universal. Kohlberg arrived at his view after 20 years of using a unique interview with children. In the interview, children are presented with a series of stories in which characters face moral dilemmas. The following is the most popular Kohlberg dilemma:

> In Europe a woman was near death from a special kind of cancer. There was one drug that the doctors thought might save her. It was a form of radium that a druggist in the same town had recently discovered. The drug was expensive to make, but the druggist was charging ten times what the drug cost him to make. He paid $200 for the radium and charged $2,000 for a small dose of the drug. The sick woman's husband, Heinz, went to everyone he knew to borrow the money, but he could only get together $1,000 which is half of what it cost. He told the druggist that his wife was dying and asked him to sell it cheaper or let him pay later. But the druggist said, "No, I discovered the drug, and I am going to make money from it." So Heinz got desperate and broke into the man's store to steal the drug for his wife. (Kohlberg, 1969, p. 379)

Lawrence Kohlberg the architect of a provocative cognitive developmental theory of moral development. *What is the nature of his theory?*

This story is 1 of 11 that Kohlberg devised to investigate the nature of moral thought. After reading the story, the interviewee answers a series of questions about the moral dilemma. Should Heinz have stolen the drug? Was stealing it right or wrong? Why? Is it a husband's duty to steal the drug for his wife if he can get it no other way? Would a good husband steal? Did the druggist have the right to charge that much when there was no law setting a limit on the price? Why or why not?

immanent justice Piaget's concept that if a rule is broken, punishment will be meted out immediately.

preconventional reasoning The lowest level in Kohlberg's theory of moral development. The individual's moral reasoning is controlled primarily by external rewards and punishment.

The Kohlberg Stages Based on the answers interviewees gave for this and other moral dilemmas, Kohlberg described three levels of moral thinking, each of which is characterized by two stages (see figure 14.1).

Preconventional reasoning is the lowest level of moral reasoning, said Kohlberg. At this level, good and bad are interpreted in terms of external rewards and punishments.

LEVEL 1 Preconventional Level No Internalization	LEVEL 2 Conventional Level Intermediate Internalization	LEVEL 3 Postconventional Level Full Internalization
Stage 1 Heteronomous Morality *Children obey because adults tell them to obey. People base their moral decisions on fear of punishment.*	**Stage 3** Mutual Interpersonal Expectations, Relationships, and Interpersonal Conformity *Individuals value trust, caring, and loyalty to others as a basis for moral judgments.*	**Stage 5** Social Contract or Utility and Individual Rights *Individuals reason that values, rights, and principles undergird or transcend the law.*
Stage 2 Individualism, Purpose, and Exchange *Individuals pursue their own interests but let others do the same. What is right involves equal exchange.*	**Stage 4** Social Systems Morality *Moral judgments are based on understanding of the social order, law, justice, and duty.*	**Stage 6** Universal Ethical Principles *The person has developed moral judgments that are based on universal human rights. When faced with a dilemma between law and conscience, a personal, individualized conscience is followed.*

FIGURE 14.1 Kohlberg's Three Levels and Six Stages of Moral Development

- *Stage 1.* **Heteronomous morality** is the first stage in preconventional reasoning. At this stage, moral thinking is tied to punishment. For example, children think that they must obey because they fear punishment for disobedience.
- *Stage 2.* **Individualism, instrumental purpose, and exchange** is the second stage of preconventional reasoning. At this stage, individuals reason that pursuing their own interests is the right thing to do but they let others do the same. Thus, they think that what is right involves an equal exchange. They reason that if they are nice to others, others will be nice to them in return.

Conventional reasoning is the second, or intermediate, level in Kohlberg's theory of moral development. At this level, individuals apply certain standards, but they are the standards set by others, such as parents or the government.

- *Stage 3.* **Mutual interpersonal expectations, relationships, and interpersonal conformity** is Kohlberg's third stage of moral development. At this stage, individuals value trust, caring, and loyalty to others as a basis of moral judgments. Children and adolescents often adopt their parents' moral standards at this stage, seeking to be thought of by their parents as a "good girl" or a "good boy."
- *Stage 4.* **Social systems morality** is the fourth stage in Kohlberg's theory of moral development. At this stage, moral judgments are based on understanding the social order, law, justice, and duty. For example, adolescents may reason that in order for a community to work effectively, it needs to be protected by laws that are adhered to by its members.

Postconventional reasoning is the highest level in Kohlberg's theory of moral development. At this level, the individual recognizes alternative moral courses, explores the options, and then decides on a personal moral code.

- *Stage 5.* **Social contract or utility and individual rights** is the fifth Kohlberg stage. At this stage, individuals reason that values, rights, and principles undergird or transcend the law. A person evaluates the validity of actual laws, and social systems can be examined in terms of the degree to which they preserve and protect fundamental human rights and values.

individualism, instrumental purpose, and exchange The second Kohlberg stage of moral development. At this stage, individuals pursue their own interests but also let others do the same.

conventional reasoning The second, or intermediate, level in Kohlberg's theory of moral development. At this level, individuals abide by certain standards but they are the standards of others such as parents or the laws of society.

mutual interpersonal expectations, relationships, and interpersonal conformity Kohlberg's third stage of moral development. At this stage, individuals value trust, caring, and loyalty to others as a basis of moral judgments.

social systems morality The fourth stage in Kohlberg's theory of moral development. Moral judgments are based on understanding the social order, law, justice, and duty.

postconventional reasoning The highest level in Kohlberg's theory of moral development. At this level, morality is completely internalized and not based on others' standards.

social contract or utility and individual rights The fifth Kohlberg stage. At this stage, individuals reason that values, rights, and principles undergird or transcend the law.

Stage Description	Examples of Moral Reasoning That Support Heinz's Theft of the Drug	Examples of Moral Reasoning That Indicate That Heinz Should Not Steal the Drug
Preconventional reasoning		
Stage 1: Heteronomous morality	Heinz should not let his wife die; if he does, he will be in big trouble.	Heinz might get caught and sent to jail.
Stage 2: Individualism, purpose, and exchange	If Heinz gets caught, he could give the drug back and maybe they would not give him a long jail sentence.	The druggist is a businessman and needs to make money.
Conventional reasoning		
Stage 3: Mutual interpersonal expectations, relationships, and interpersonal conformity	Heinz was only doing something that a good husband would do; it shows how much he loves his wife.	If his wife dies, he can't be blamed for it; it is the druggist's fault. The druggist is the selfish one.
Stage 4: Social systems morality	It isn't morally wrong for Heinz to steal the drug in this case because the law is not designed to take into account every particular case or anticipate every circumstance.	Heinz should obey the law because laws serve to protect the productive and orderly functioning of society.
Postconventional reasoning		
Stage 5: Social contract or utility and individual rights	Heinz was justified in stealing the drug because a human life was at stake and that transcends any right the druggist had to the drug.	It is important to obey the law because laws represent a necessary structure of common agreement if individuals are to live together in society.
Stage 6: Universal ethical principles	Human life is sacred because of the universal principle of respect for the individual and it takes precedence over other values.	Heinz needs to decide whether or not to consider the other people who need the drug as badly as his wife does. He ought not to act based on his particular feelings for his wife, but consider the value of all the lives involved.

FIGURE 14.2 Moral Reasoning at Kohlberg's Stages in Response to the "Heinz and the Druggist" Story

- *Stage 6.* **Universal ethical principles** is the sixth and highest stage in Kohlberg's theory of moral development. At this stage, the person has developed a moral standard based on universal human rights. When faced with a conflict between law and conscience, the person reasons that conscience should be followed, even though the decision might bring risk.

Figure 14.2 provides examples of how people at each of these stages might respond to the Heinz dilemma.

Kohlberg believed that these levels and stages occur in a sequence and are age related. Before age 9, most children use level 1, preconventional reasoning, when they consider moral choices. By early adolescence, they reason in more conventional ways. Most adolescents reason at stage 3, with some signs of stages 2 and 4. By early adulthood, a small number of individuals reason in postconventional ways.

What evidence supports this description of development? In a 20-year longitudinal investigation, the uses of stages 1 and 2 decreased (Colby & others, 1983) (see figure 14.3). Stage 4, which did not appear at all in the moral reasoning of 10-year-olds, was reflected in the moral thinking of 62 percent of the 36-year-olds. Stage 5 did not appear until age 20 to 22 and never characterized more than 10 percent of the individuals.

Thus, the moral stages appeared somewhat later than Kohlberg initially envisioned, and reasoning at the higher stages, especially stage 6, was rare. Although stage 6 has been removed from the Kohlberg moral judgment scoring manual, it still is considered to be theoretically important in the Kohlberg scheme of moral development.

universal ethical principles The sixth and highest stage in Kohlberg's theory of moral development. Individuals develop a moral standard based on universal human rights.

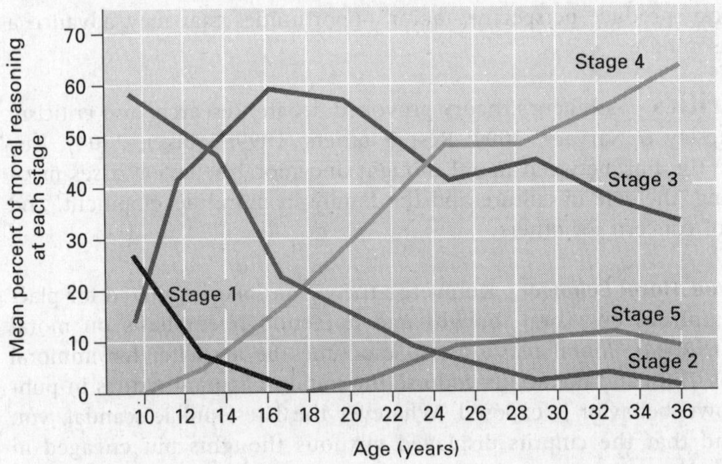

FIGURE 14.3 Age and the Percentage of Individuals at Each Kohlberg Stage

Influences on the Kohlberg Stages What factors influence movement through Kohlberg's stages? Although moral reasoning at each stage presupposes a certain level of cognitive development, Kohlberg argued that advances in children's cognitive development did not ensure development of moral reasoning. Instead, moral reasoning also reflects children's experiences in dealing with moral questions and moral conflict.

Several investigators have tried to advance individuals' levels of moral development by having a model present arguments that reflect moral thinking one stage above the individuals' established levels. This approach applies the concepts of equilibrium and conflict that Piaget used to explain cognitive development. By presenting arguments slightly beyond the children's level of moral reasoning, the researchers created a disequilibrium that motivated the children to restructure their moral thought. The upshot of studies using this approach is that virtually any plus-stage discussion, for any length of time, seems to promote more advanced moral reasoning (Walker, 1982).

Kohlberg believed that peer interaction is a critical part of the social stimulation that challenges children to change their moral reasoning. Whereas adults characteristically impose rules and regulations on children, the give-and-take among peers gives children an opportunity to take the perspective of another person and to generate rules democratically. Kohlberg stressed that, in principle, encounters

Both Piaget and Kohlberg believed that peer relations are a critical part of the social stimulation that challenges children to advance their moral reasoning. The mutual give-and-take of peer relations provides children with role-taking opportunities that give them a sense that rules are generated democratically.

with any peers can produce perspective-taking opportunities that may advance a child's moral reasoning.

Kohlberg's Theory of Moral Development
Kohlberg's Moral Dilemmas
Kohlberg's Moral Stages

Kohlberg's Critics Kohlberg's theory provoked debate, research, and criticism (Gibbs, 2003; Lapsley & Narvaez, 2004; Rest & others, 1999; Walker, 2004). Key criticisms involve the link between moral thought and moral behavior, assessment of moral reasoning, the role of culture and the family in moral development, and the significance of concern for others.

Moral Thought and Moral Behavior Kohlberg's theory has been criticized for placing too much emphasis on moral thought and not enough emphasis on moral behavior (Walker, 2004). Moral reasons can sometimes be a shelter for immoral behavior. Corrupt CEOs and politicians endorse the loftiest of moral virtues in public before their own behavior is exposed. Whatever the latest public scandal, you will probably find that the culprits displayed virtuous thoughts but engaged in immoral behavior. No one wants a nation of cheaters and thieves who can reason at the postconventional level. The cheaters and thieves may know what is right yet still do what is wrong. Heinous actions can be cloaked in a mantle of moral virtue.

The mantle of virtue is not necessarily a ruse; it is often taken on sincerely. Social cognitive theorist Albert Bandura (1999, 2002) argues that people usually do not engage in harmful conduct until they have justified the morality of their actions to themselves. Immoral conduct is made personally and socially acceptable by portraying it as serving socially worthy or moral purposes or even as doing God's will. Bandura provides the examples of Islamic extremists who mount jihad (holy war) against what they see as a tyrannical, decadent people seeking to enslave the Islamic world and antiabortion activists who bomb abortion clinics or murder doctors in order to discourage abortions.

Assessment of Moral Reasoning Some developmentalists fault the quality of Kohlberg's research and believe that more attention should be paid to the way moral reasoning is assessed. For example, James Rest (1986; Rest & others, 1999) argued that alternative methods should be used to collect information about moral thinking. Rest also said that Kohlberg's stories are extremely difficult to score. To help remedy this problem, Rest developed his own measure of moral development, called the Defining Issues Test (DIT).

The DIT attempts to determine which moral issues individuals feel are more crucial in a given situation. It presents a series of dilemmas and (unlike Kohlberg's procedure) a list of definitions of the major issues involved. In the dilemma of Heinz and the druggist, for example, individuals might be asked whether a community's laws should be upheld or whether Heinz should be willing to risk being injured or caught as a burglar. They might also be asked to list the most important values that govern human interaction. They are given six stories and asked to rate the importance of each issue involved in deciding what ought to be done. Then they are asked to list what they believe are the four most important issues. Rest argued that this method provides a more valid and reliable way to assess moral thinking than Kohlberg's method (Rest & others, 1999).

The dilemmas that Kohlberg used to assess moral reasoning have also been criticized. Researchers have found that Kohlberg's dilemmas do not match the moral dilemmas many children and adults face in their everyday lives (Walker, de Vries, & Trevethan, 1987). Most of Kohlberg's stories focus on the family and authority. However, when one researcher invited adolescents to write stories about their own moral dilemmas, the adolescents generated dilemmas that were broader in scope, focusing on friends, acquaintances, and other issues, as well as family and authority (Yussen, 1977). The adolescents' moral dilemmas also were analyzed in terms of their content. As shown in figure 14.4, the moral issues that concerned adolescents most involved interpersonal relationships.

Culture and Moral Reasoning Kohlberg emphasized that his stages of moral reasoning are universal, but some critics claim his theory is culturally biased (Banks, 1993; Miller, 1995). Both Kohlberg and his critics may be partially correct.

One review of 45 studies in 27 cultures around the world, mostly non-European, provided support for the universality of Kohlberg's first four stages (Snarey, 1987). Individuals in diverse cultures developed through these four stages in sequence as Kohlberg predicted. Stages 5 and 6, however, were not found in all cultures. Furthermore, this review found that Kohlberg's scoring system does not recognize the higher-level moral reasoning of certain cultures and thus that moral reasoning is more culture-specific than Kohlberg envisioned (Snarey, 1987).

In particular, researchers had heard moral judgments based on the principles of communal equity and collective happiness in Israel, the unity and sacredness of all life forms in India, and collective moral responsibility in New Guinea (Snarey, 1987). These examples of moral reasoning would not be scored at the highest level in Kohlberg's system because they are not based on principles of justice. Similar results occurred in a study that assessed the moral development of 20 adolescent male Buddhist monks in Nepal (Huebner & Garrod, 1993). Justice, a basic theme in Kohlberg's theory, was not of paramount importance in the monks' moral views, and their concerns about the prevention of suffering and the role of compassion are not captured by Kohlberg's theory.

In sum, although Kohlberg's approach does encompass much of the moral reasoning voiced in various cultures around the world, his approach misses or misconstrues some important moral concepts in particular cultures (Gibbs, 2003; Lapsley & Narvaez, 2004; Walker, 2004).

Story Subject	Grade 7	Grade 9	Grade 12
	Percentage		
Alcohol	2	0	5
Civil rights	0	6	7
Drugs	7	10	5
Interpersonal relations	38	24	35
Physical saftey	22	8	3
Sexual relations	2	20	10
Smoking	7	2	0
Stealing	9	2	0
Working	2	2	15
Other	11	26	20

FIGURE 14.4 Actual Moral Dilemmas Generated by Adolescents

This 14-year-old boy in Nepal is thought to be the sixth-holiest Buddhist in the world. *How might his moral reasoning be different than Kohlberg's theory would predict?*

Families and Moral Development Kohlberg believed that family processes are essentially unimportant in children's moral development. As noted earlier, he argued that parent-child relationships usually provide children with little opportunity for give-and-take or perspective taking. Rather, Kohlberg said that such opportunities are more likely to be provided by children's peer relations (Brabeck, 2000).

Did Kohlberg underestimate the contribution of family relationships to moral development? A number of developmentalists emphasize that *inductive discipline*, which uses reasoning and focuses children's attention on the consequences of their actions for others, positively influences moral development (Hoffman, 1970). They also stress that parents' moral values influence children's developing moral thoughts (Gibbs, 1993). Nonetheless, most developmentalists agree with Kohlberg and Piaget, that peers too play an important role in the development of moral reasoning.

Gender and the Care Perspective Perhaps the most publicized criticism of Kohlberg's theory has come from Carol Gilligan (1982, 1992, 1996; Gilligan & others, 2003), who argues that Kohlberg's theory reflects a gender bias. According to Gilligan, Kohlberg's theory is based on a male norm that puts abstract principles above relationships and concern for others and sees the individual as standing alone and independently making moral decisions. It puts justice at the heart of morality. In contrast to Kohlberg's **justice perspective,** Gilligan argues for a **care perspective,** which is a moral perspective that views people in terms of their connectedness with others and emphasizes interpersonal communication, relationships with others, and concern for others. According to Gilligan, Kohlberg greatly underplayed the care perspective, perhaps because he was a male, because most of his research was with males rather than females, and because he used male responses as a model for his theory.

In extensive interviews with girls from 6 to 18 years of age, Gilligan and her colleagues found that girls consistently interpret moral dilemmas in terms of human

justice perspective A moral perspective that focuses on the rights of the individual; individuals independently make moral decisions.

care perspective The moral perspective of Carol Gilligan that views people in terms of their connectedness with others and emphasizes interpersonal communication, relationships with others, and concern for others.

Many girls seem to fear, most of all, being alone—without friends, family, or relationships.

—Carol Gilligan
Contemporary Psychologist, Harvard University

Carol Gilligan (*center*) is shown with some of the students she has interviewed about the importance of relationships in a female's development. *What is Gilligan's view of moral development?*

relationships and base these interpretations on listening and watching other people (Gilligan, 1992, 1996; Gilligan & others, 2003). However, a meta-analysis (a statistical analysis that combines the results of many different studies) casts doubt on Gilligan's claim of substantial gender differences in moral judgment (Jaffee & Hyde, 2000). Overall, this analysis found only a small gender difference in care-based reasoning, and the difference was greater in adolescence than childhood. When differences in moral reasoning occurred, they were better explained by the nature of the dilemma than by gender. For example, both males and females tended to use care reasoning to deal with interpersonal dilemmas and justice reasoning to handle societal dilemmas.

Along with this lack of support for gender differences in moral reasoning, however, other research does find differences in how boys and girls tend to interpret situations (Eisenberg & Morris, 2004). In support of this idea, one recent study found that females rated prosocial dilemmas (those emphasizing altruism and helping) as more significant than males did (Wark & Krebs, 2000). Another recent study revealed that young adolescent girls used more care-based reasoning about dating dilemmas than boys did (Weisz & Black, 2002).

Social Conventional Reasoning Some theorists and researchers argue that it is important to distinguish between moral reasoning and social conventional reasoning, something they believe Kohlberg did not adequately do (Smetana & Turiel, 2003; Turiel, 1998, 2003, 2006; Lapsley, 1996, 2005). **Social conventional reasoning** focuses on thoughts about social consensus and convention. In contrast, moral reasoning emphasizes ethical issues. Conventional rules are created to control behavioral irregularities and maintain the social system. Conventional rules are arbitrary and subject to individual judgment. For example, using a fork and spoon at meals is a social conventional rule, as is raising one's hand in class before speaking.

In contrast, moral rules are not arbitrary and determined by whim. They also are not created by social consensus. Rather, moral rules are obligatory, widely accepted, and somewhat impersonal (Turiel, 1998). Thus, rules pertaining to lying, cheating, stealing, and physically harming another person are moral rules because violation of these rules affronts ethical standards that exist apart from social consensus and convention. In sum, moral judgments involve concepts of justice, whereas social conventional judgments are concepts of social organization.

Recently, a distinction has also been made between moral and conventional issues, which are viewed as legitimately subject to adult social regulation, and personal issues, which are more likely subject to the child's or adolescent's independent decision making and personal discretion (Smetana, 2005). Personal issues include control over one's body, privacy, and choice of friends and activities.

In a Different Voice
Exploring Girls' Voices

Moral Behavior

The children discussed at the opening of this chapter who "visited" the Planet Pax demonstrated that they could understand many moral concepts, but moral understanding does not always translate into moral behavior. What determines how they would actually behave? What basic processes are responsible for moral behavior?

Basic Processes The processes of reinforcement, punishment, and imitation have been invoked to explain how individuals learn certain responses and why their responses differ from one another. When individuals are reinforced for behavior that is consistent with laws and social conventions, they are likely to repeat that behavior. When provided with models who behave morally, individuals are likely to adopt their actions. Finally, when individuals are punished for immoral behaviors, those behaviors can be eliminated, but at the expense of sanctioning punishment by its very use and of causing emotional side effects for the individual.

social conventional reasoning Thoughts about social consensus and convention, as opposed to moral reasoning that stresses ethical issues.

These general conclusions come with some important qualifiers. The effectiveness of reward and punishment depends on the consistency and timing with which they are administered. The effectiveness of modeling depends on the characteristics of the model and the cognitive skills of the observer.

Furthermore, behavior is situationally dependent. People learn that certain behaviors are reinforced in particular situations but not others, and they behave accordingly. Thus, the behavioral approach predicts that individuals do not consistently display moral behavior in different situations.

How consistent is moral behavior? In a classic investigation of moral behavior, one of the most extensive ever conducted, Hugh Hartshorne and Mark May (1928–1930) observed the moral responses of 11,000 children who were given the opportunity to lie, cheat, and steal in a variety of circumstances—at home, at school, at social events, and in athletics. A completely honest or a completely dishonest child was difficult to find. Situation-specific behavior was the rule. Children were more likely to cheat when their friends put pressure on them to do so and when the chance of being caught was slim. However, other analyses suggest that although moral behavior is influenced by situational determinants, some children are more likely than others to cheat, lie, and steal (Burton, 1984). Reinforcement, punishment, imitation, and the situation only partially account for whether children behave morally or not.

Resistance to Temptation and Self-Control When pressures mount for individuals to cheat, lie, or steal, it is important to ask whether they have developed the ability to resist temptation and to exercise self-control (Bandura, 1991; Mischel, 1986). Walter Mischel (2004) argues that self-control is strongly influenced by cognitive factors. Researchers have shown that children can instruct themselves to be more patient and, in the process, show more self-control. In one investigation, preschool children were asked to perform a very dull task (Mischel & Patterson, 1976). Close by was a very enticing talking mechanical clown that tried to persuade the children to play with it. The children who had been trained to say to themselves, "I'm not going to look at Mr. Clown when Mr. Clown says to look at him" were more likely to control their behavior and continue working on the dull task than were children who were not given the self-instructional strategy.

There has been considerable interest in the effects of punishment on children's ability to resist temptation (Parke, 1972, 1977). For the most part, offering children cognitive rationales enhances most forms of punishment, such as reasons why a child should not play with a forbidden toy. Cognitive rationales are more effective in getting children to resist temptation over a period of time than punishments that do not use reasoning, such as placing children in their rooms without explaining how the children's actions affected other people.

Social Cognitive Theory The role of cognitive factors in resistance to temptation and self-control illustrates ways in which cognitions mediate the link between environmental experiences and moral behavior. The relationships between these three elements—environment, cognition, and behavior—are highlighted by social cognitive theorists.

The **social cognitive theory of morality** emphasizes a distinction between an individual's moral competence (the ability to perform moral behaviors) and moral performance (performing those behaviors in specific situations) (Mischel & Mischel, 1975). *Moral competencies* include what individuals are capable of doing, what they know, their skills, their awareness of moral rules and regulations, and their cognitive ability to construct behaviors. Moral competence is the outgrowth of cognitive-sensory processes. *Moral performance,* or behavior, however, is determined by motivation and the rewards and incentives to act in a specific moral way.

social cognitive theory of morality The theory that distinguishes between moral competence—the ability to produce moral behaviors—and moral performance—those behaviors in specific situations.

Albert Bandura (1991, 2002, 2004) also believes that moral development is best understood by considering a combination of social and cognitive factors, especially those involving self-control. He proposes that in developing a "moral self, individuals adopt standards of right and wrong that serve as guides and deterrents for conduct. In this self-regulatory process, people monitor their conduct and the conditions under which it occurs, judge it in relation to moral standards, and regulate their actions by the consequences they apply to themselves. They do things that provide them satisfaction and a sense of self-worth. They refrain from behaving in ways that violate their moral standards because such conduct will bring self-condemnation. Self-sanctions keep conduct in line with internal standards" (Bandura, 2002, p. 102). Thus, in Bandura's view, self-regulation rather than abstract reasoning is the key to positive moral development.

Moral Feeling

Think about when you do something you sense is wrong. Does it affect you emotionally? Maybe you get a twinge of guilt. And when you give someone a gift, you might feel joy. What role do emotions play in moral development, and how do these emotions develop?

Psychoanalytic Theory According to Sigmund Freud, guilt and the desire to avoid feeling guilty are the foundation of moral behavior. In Freud's theory, as we discussed in chapter 1, the *superego* is the moral branch of personality. The superego consists of two main components, the ego ideal and conscience. The **ego ideal** rewards the child by conveying a sense of pride and personal value when the child acts according to ideal standards approved by the parents. The **conscience** punishes the child for behaviors disapproved by the parents by making the child feel guilty and worthless.

How do the superego and hence guilt develop? According to Freud, children fear losing their parents' love and being punished for their unacceptable sexual wishes toward the opposite-sex parent. To reduce anxiety, avoid punishment, and maintain parental affection, children identify with the same-sex parent. Through this identification, children *internalize* the parent's standards of right and wrong, which reflect societal prohibitions, and hence children develop the superego. In addition, children turn inward the hostility that was previously aimed externally at the same-sex parent. This inwardly directed hostility is then experienced self-punitively (and unconsciously) as guilt.

In short, in the psychoanalytic account of moral development, children conform to societal standards to avoid guilt. In this way, self-control replaces parental control.

Freud's claims regarding the formation of the ego ideal and conscience cannot be verified. However, researchers can examine the extent to which children feel guilty when they misbehave. In one recent study, 106 preschool children were observed in laboratory situations in which they were led to believe that they had damaged valuable objects (Kochanska & others, 2002). In these mishaps, the behavioral indicators of guilt that were coded by observers included avoiding gaze (looking away or down), body tension (squirming, backing away, hanging head down, covering face with hands), and distress (looking uncomfortable, crying). Girls expressed more guilt than boys did. Children with a more fearful temperament expressed more guilt. Children of mothers who used power-oriented discipline (such as spanking, slapping, and yelling) displayed less guilt.

As children develop socially and cognitively, the triggers for guilt change. In one study of fifth-, eighth-, and eleventh-graders, parents were the individuals most likely to evoke guilt (Williams & Bybee, 1994). With development, guilt evoked by family members was less prevalent, but guilt engendered by girlfriends or boyfriends was more frequent. At the higher grade levels, the percentage of students reporting guilt about aggressive, externalizing behaviors declined, whereas those mentioning guilt over internal thoughts and inconsiderateness increased. Males were more likely to report guilt over externalizing behaviors, while females reported more guilt over violating norms of compassion and trust.

ego ideal The component of the superego that rewards the child by conveying a sense of pride and personal value when the child acts according to ideal standards approved by the parents.

conscience The component of the superego that punishes the child for behaviors disapproved of by parents by making the child feel guilty and worthless.

Empathy Positive feelings, such as empathy, contribute to the child's moral development. Feeling **empathy** means reacting to another's feelings with an emotional response that is similar to the other's feelings (Damon, 1988). To empathize is not just to sympathize; it is to put oneself in another's place emotionally.

What is moral is what you feel good after and what is immoral is what you feel bad after.

—Ernest Hemingway
American Author, 20th Century

Although empathy is an emotional state, it has a cognitive component—the ability to discern another's inner psychological states, or what we have previously called *perspective taking*. Infants have the capacity for some purely empathic responses, but for effective moral action, children must learn to identify a wide range of emotional states in others and to anticipate what kinds of action will improve another person's emotional state.

What are the milestones in children's development of empathy? According to an analysis by child developmentalist William Damon (1988), changes in empathy take place in early infancy, at 1 to 2 years of age, in early childhood, and at 10 to 12 years of age.

Global empathy is the young infant's empathic response in which clear boundaries between the feelings and needs of the self and those of another have not yet been established. For example, one 11-month-old infant fought off her own tears, sucked her thumb, and buried her head in her mother's lap after she had seen another child fall and hurt himself. Not all infants cry every time someone else is hurt, though. Many times, an infant will stare at another's pain with curiosity. Although global empathy is observed in some infants, it does not consistently characterize all infants' behavior.

When they are 1 to 2 years of age, infants may feel genuine concern for the distress of other people, but only when they reach early childhood can they respond appropriately to another person's distress. This ability depends on children's new awareness that people have different reactions to situations. By late childhood, they may begin to feel empathy for the unfortunate. To read further about Damon's description of the developmental changes in empathy from infancy through adolescence, see figure 14.5.

The Contemporary Perspective on the Role of Emotion in Moral Development We have seen that classical psychoanalytic theory emphasizes the power of unconscious guilt in moral development but that other theorists, such as Damon, emphasize the role of empathy. Today, many child developmentalists believe that both positive feelings—such as empathy, sympathy, admiration, and self-esteem—and negative feelings—such as anger, outrage, shame, and guilt—contribute to children's moral development (Damon, 1988; Eisenberg & Fabes, 1998; Roberts

empathy Reacting to another's feelings with an emotional response that is similar to the other's feelings.

Age Period	Nature of Empathy
Early infancy	Characterized by global empathy, the young infant's empathic response does not distinguish between feelings and needs of self and others.
1 to 2 years of age	Undifferentiated feelings of discomfort at another's distress grow into more genuine feelings of concern, but infants cannot translate realization of other's unhappy feelings into effective action.
Early childhood	Children become aware that every person's perspective is unique and that someone else may have a different reaction to a situation. This awareness allows the child to respond more appropriately to another person's distress.
10 to 12 years of age	Children develop an emergent orientation of empathy for people who live in unfortunate circumstances—the poor, the handicapped, and the socially outcast. In adolescence, this newfound sensitivity may give a humanitarian flavor to the individual's ideological and political views.

FIGURE 14.5 Damon's Description of Developmental Changes in Empathy

& Strayer, 1996). When strongly experienced, these emotions influence children to act in accord with standards of right and wrong.

Such emotions as empathy, shame, guilt, and anxiety over other people's violations of standards are present early in development and undergo developmental change throughout childhood and beyond (Damon, 1988). These emotions provide a natural base for children's acquisition of moral values, motivating them to pay close attention to moral events. However, moral emotions do not operate in a vacuum to build a child's moral awareness, and they are not sufficient in themselves to generate moral responses. They do not give the "substance" of moral regulation—the rules, values, and standards of behavior that children need to understand and act on. Moral emotions are inextricably interwoven with the cognitive and social aspects of children's development.

Moral Personality

So far we have examined three key dimensions of moral development: thoughts, behavior, and feelings. Recently, there has been a surge of interest in a fourth dimension: personality (Lapsley, 2005; Lapsley & Narvaez, 2006). Thoughts, behavior, and feelings can all be involved in an individual's moral personality. For many years, skepticism characterized the likelihood that a set of moral characteristics or traits could be discovered that would constitute a core of moral personality. Much of this skepticism stemmed from the results of Hartshorne & May's (1928–1930) classic study, and Mischel's (1968) social learning theory and research, which argued that situations trump traits when attempts are made to predict moral behavior. Mischel's (2004) subsequent research and theory and Bandura's (2004) social cognitive theory have emphasized the importance of "person" factors while still recognizing situational variation. Until recently, though, there has been little interest in studying what might comprise a moral personality. Three aspects of moral personality that have recently been emphasized are (1) moral identity, (2) moral character, and (3) moral exemplars.

Moral Identity A central aspect of the recent interest in the role of personality in moral development focuses on **moral identity.** Individuals have a moral identity when moral notions and commitments are central to one's life (Blasi, 1995, 2005). In this view, behaving in a manner that violates this moral commitment places the integrity of the self at risk (Lapsley & Narvaez, 2006).

Augusto Blasi (2005) recently argued that developing a moral identity and commitment is influenced by three important virtues: (1) willpower (self-control), (2) integrity, and (3) moral desire. *Willpower* involves strategies and metacognitive skills that involve analyzing problems, setting goals, focusing attention, delaying gratification, avoiding distractions, and resisting temptation. *Integrity* consists of a sense of responsibility that is present when individuals hold themselves accountable for the consequences of their actions. *Moral desire* is the motivation and intention to pursue a moral life. In Blasi's view, "willpower and integrity are neutral unless they are attached to moral desires" (Lapsley & Narvaez, 2006).

Moral Character Blasi's view (2005) has much in common with James Rest's (1995) view that moral character has not been adequately emphasized in moral development. In Rest's view, *moral character* involves having the strength of your convictions, persisting, and overcoming distractions and obstacles. If individuals don't have moral character, they may wilt under pressure or fatigue, fail to follow through, or become distracted and discouraged, and fail to behave morally. Moral character presupposes that the person has set moral goals and that achieving those goals involves the commitment to act in accord with those goals. Rest (1995), like Blasi (2005), also argues that motivation (desire) has not been adequately emphasized in moral development. In Rest's view, *moral motivation* involves prioritizing moral values over other personal values.

moral identity The aspect of personality that is present when individuals have moral notions and commitments that are central to their lives.

Lawrence Walker (2002; Walker & Pitts, 1998) has studied moral character by examining people's conceptions of moral excellence. Among the moral virtues people emphasize are "honesty, truthfulness, and trustworthiness, as well as those of care, compassion, thoughtfulness, and considerateness. Other salient traits revolve around virtues of dependability, loyalty, and conscientiousness" (Walker, 2002, p. 74). In Walker's perspective, these aspects of moral character provide a foundation for positive social relationships and functioning. He also agrees with Blasi that integrity is a key aspect of moral development.

Moral Exemplars **Moral exemplars** are people who have lived exemplary lives. Moral exemplars have a moral personality, identity, character, and set of virtues that reflect moral excellence and commitment.

In one study, three different exemplars of morality were examined—brave, caring, and just (Walker & Hennig, 2004). Different personality profiles emerged for the three exemplars. The brave exemplar was characterized by being dominant and extraverted, the caring exemplar by being nurturant and agreeable, and the just exemplar by being conscientious and open to experience. However, a number of traits characterized all three moral exemplars, considered by the researchers to reflect a possible core of moral functioning. This core included being honest and dependable.

Another recent study examined the personality of exemplary young adults to determine what characterized their moral excellence (Matsuba & Walker, 2004). Forty young adults were nominated by executive directors of a variety of social organizations (such as Big Brothers, AIDS society, and Ronald MacDonald House) as moral exemplars based on their extraordinary moral commitment to these social organizations. They were compared with 40 young adults matched in age, education, and other variables who were attending a university. The participants were given a personality test and questionnaires, and were interviewed regarding their faith and moral reasoning. The moral exemplars "were more agreeable, more advanced in their faith and moral reasoning development, further along in forming an adult identity, and more willing to enter into close relationships" (Matsuba & Walker, 2004, p. 413).

Review and Reflect • LEARNING GOAL 1

1 Discuss theory and research on the domains of moral development

Review
- What is moral development?
- What are Piaget's and Kohlberg's theories of moral development? How can Kohlberg's theory be evaluated?
- What is social conventional reasoning?
- What processes are involved in moral behavior? What is the social cognitive theory of moral development?
- How are moral feelings related to moral development?
- What characterizes moral personality?

Reflect
- What do you think about the following circumstances?
  –A man who had been sentenced to serve 10 years for selling a small amount of marijuana walked away from a prison camp after serving only 6 months of his sentence. Twenty-five years later he was caught. He is now in his fifties and is a model citizen. Should he be sent back to prison? Why or why not? At which Kohlberg stage should your response be placed?
  –A young woman who had been in a tragic accident is "brain dead" and has been kept on life support systems for four years without ever regaining consciousness. Should the life support systems be removed? Explain your response. At which Kohlberg stage should your response be placed?

moral exemplars People who have lived exemplary lives. They have a moral personality, identity, character, and set of virtues that reflect moral excellence and commitment.

2 CONTEXTS OF MORAL DEVELOPMENT

Parenting | Schools

So far, we have examined the four main domains of moral development—thoughts, behaviors, feelings, and personality. Next, we will explore important contexts that can influence moral development. We noted that both Piaget and Kohlberg believed that peer relations exert an important influence on moral development. What other contexts play a role in moral development? In particular, what are the roles of parents and schools?

Parenting

Both Piaget and Kohlberg held that parents do not provide unique or essential inputs to children's moral development. Parents, in their view, are responsible for providing role-taking opportunities and cognitive conflict, but peers play the primary role in moral development. Research, however, has revealed that parents as well as peers can contribute to children's moral maturity if they elicit children's opinions and check for understanding (Walker, Hennig, & Krettenauer, 2000).

In Ross Thompson's (2006; Thompson, McGinley & Meyer, 2005) view, young children are moral apprentices, striving to understand what is moral. They can be assisted in this quest by the "sensitive guidance of adult mentors in the home who provide lessons about morality in everyday experiences" (Thompson, McGinley, & Meyer, 2005). Among the most important aspects of the relationship between parents and children that contribute to children's moral development are relational quality, parental discipline, proactive strategies, and conversational dialogue.

Relational Quality Parent-child relationships introduce children to the mutual obligations of close relationships (Thompson, 2006; Thompson, McGinley, & Meyer, 2005). Parents' obligations include engaging in positive caregiving and guiding children to become competent human beings. Children's obligations include responding appropriately to parents' initiatives and maintaining a positive relationship with parents. Thus, warmth and responsibility in the mutual obligations of parent-child relationships are important foundations for the positive moral growth in the child.

In terms of relationship quality, secure attachment may play an important role in children's moral development. A secure attachment can place the child on a positive path for internalizing parents' socializing goals and family values (Waters & others, 1990). In one study, secure attachment in infancy was linked to early conscience development (Laible & Thompson, 2000). And in a recent longitudinal study, secure attachment at 14 months of age served as a precursor for a link between positive parenting and the child's conscience during early childhood (Kochanska & others, 2004).

Parental Discipline Historically, by far the most attention has been given to discipline. Parents may discipline children through love withdrawal, power assertion, and induction (Hoffman, 1970):

- **Love withdrawal** is a discipline technique in which a parent withholds attention or love from the child, as when the parent refuses to talk to the child or states a dislike for the child. For example, the parent might say, "I'm going to leave you if you do that again," or "I don't like you when you do that."

love withdrawal A discipline technique in which a parent withholds attention or love from the child.

- **Power assertion** is a discipline technique in which a parent attempts to gain control over the child or the child's resources. Examples include spanking, threatening, or removing privileges.
- **Induction** is the discipline technique in which a parent uses reason and explanation of the consequences for others of the child's actions. Examples of induction include, "Don't hit him. He was only trying to help" and "Why are you yelling at her? She didn't mean to trip you."

Both theory and empirical data support the conclusion that parents play an important role in children's moral development.

—Nancy Eisenberg
Contemporary Psychologist, Arizona State University

How are these techniques likely to affect moral development? Moral development theorist and researcher Martin Hoffman (1970) emphasizes that all of them produce arousal on the child's part, but to different extents. Love withdrawal and power assertion are likely to evoke a very high level of arousal, with love withdrawal generating considerable anxiety and power assertion considerable hostility. As a result, when a parent uses power assertion or love withdrawal, the child may be so aroused that even if the parent explains the consequences of the child's actions for others, the child might not pay attention. Also, power assertion presents parents as weak models of self-control—as individuals who cannot control their feelings. Accordingly, children may imitate this model of poor self-control when they face stressful circumstances.

In contrast to love withdrawal and power assertion, induction is more likely to produce only a moderate level of arousal in children, a level that permits children to pay attention to the cognitive rationale that parents offer for disciplining them. Furthermore, induction focuses the child's attention on the action's consequences for others, not on the child's own shortcomings. For these reasons, Hoffman (1988) believes that parents should use induction to encourage children's moral development.

In research contrasting these forms of discipline, findings vary according to children's developmental level and socioeconomic status, but generally induction is more positively related to moral development than is love withdrawal or power assertion. Induction works better with elementary-school-age children than with preschool children (Brody & Shaffer, 1982), and it works better with middle-SES than with lower-SES children (Hoffman, 1970). Older children are probably better able to understand the reasons given to them and are better at perspective taking. Some theorists believe that the internalization of society's moral standards is more likely among middle-SES than among lower-SES individuals, because internalization is more rewarding in those in the middle-SES culture (Kohn, 1977).

Proactive Strategies An important parenting strategy is to proactively avert potential misbehavior by children before it takes place (Thompson, McGinley, & Meyer, 2005). With younger children, being proactive means using diversion, such as distracting their attention or moving them to alternative activities. With older children, being proactive may involve talking with them about values that the parents deem important. Transmitting these values can help older children and adolescents to resist the temptations that inevitably emerge in such contexts as peer relations and the media that can be outside the scope of direct parental monitoring.

Conversational Dialogue Conversations related to moral development can benefit children whether they occur as part of a discipline encounter or outside the encounter in the everyday stream of parent-child interaction (Thompson, 2006; Thompson, McGinley, & Meyer, 2005). The conversations can be planned or spontaneous and can focus on topics such as past events (for example, a child's prior misbehavior or positive moral conduct), shared future events (for example, going somewhere that may involve a temptation and requires positive moral behavior), and immediate events (for example, talking with the child about a sibling's

power assertion A discipline technique in which a parent attempts to gain control over the child or the child's resources.

induction A discipline technique in which a parent uses reason and explanation of the consequences for others of the child's actions.

tantrums). Even when they are not intended to teach a moral lesson or explicitly encourage better moral judgment, such conversations can contribute to children's moral development.

Parenting Recommendations A recent review of research concluded that, in general, moral children tend to have parents who (Eisenberg & Valiente, 2002, p. 134)

- Are warm and supportive rather than punitive
- Use inductive discipline
- Provide opportunities for the children to learn about others' perspectives and feelings
- Involve children in family decision making and in the process of thinking about moral decisions . . .
- Model moral behaviors and thinking themselves, and provide opportunities for their children to do so . . .
- Provide information about what behaviors are expected and why
- Foster an internal rather than an external sense of morality

Parents who show this configuration of behaviors likely foster concern and caring about others in their children, and create a positive parent-child relationship.

In addition, parenting recommendations based on Ross Thompson's (2006; Thompson, McGinley, & Meyer, 2005) analysis of parent-child relations suggest that children's moral development is likely to benefit when there are mutual parent-child obligations involving warmth and responsibility, when parents use proactive strategies, and when parents engage children in conversational dialogue.

Schools

However parents treat their children at home, they may feel that they have little control over a great deal of their children's moral education. Children spend extensive time away from their parents at school. How do schools influence children's moral development?

www.mhhe.com/santrockcd11

Association for Moral Education
Moral Education in Japan

The Hidden Curriculum More than 60 years ago, educator John Dewey (1933) recognized that even when schools do not have specific programs in moral education, they provide moral education through a "hidden curriculum." The **hidden curriculum** is conveyed by the moral atmosphere, which is created by school and classroom rules, the moral orientation of teachers and school administrators, and text materials. The rules transmit attitudes about cheating, lying, stealing, and consideration of others. The teachers serve as models of ethical or unethical behavior. Text materials may also foster certain attitudes and values. One recent analysis revealed that middle school textbooks are far more likely to discuss an individual's rights than social responsibility (Simmons & Avery, in press).

Character Education Critics of U.S. public schools claim that the "hidden curriculum" is teaching moral relativism. Through books such as William Bennet's *The Book of Virtues* (1993) and William Damon's *Greater Expectations* (1995), these critics promote **character education,** which teaches students "moral literacy" to prevent them from engaging in immoral behavior. Proponents of character education argue that certain behaviors are wrong and that students should be taught that they are wrong throughout their education (Lapsley & Narvaez, 2006; Wales, 2004). Every school should have an explicit moral code that is clearly communicated to students. Any violations of the code should be met with sanctions (Bennett, 1993). Instruction in moral concepts can take the form of class discussions and role-playing or rewarding students for proper behavior.

hidden curriculum The pervasive moral atmosphere that characterizes schools.

character education A direct moral education approach that involves teaching students a basic moral literacy to prevent them from engaging in immoral behavior or doing harm to themselves or others.

Lawrence Walker (2002) argues that it is important for character education to involve more than a listing of moral virtues on a classroom wall. Instead, he emphasizes that children and adolescents need to participate in critical discussions of values; they need to discuss and reflect on how to incorporate virtues into their daily lives. Walker also advocates exposing children to moral exemplars worthy of emulating and getting them to participate in community service. The character education approach reflects the moral personality domain of moral development we discussed earlier in the chapter.

Cognitive Moral Education **Cognitive moral education** is a concept based on the belief that students should learn to value things like democracy and justice as their moral reasoning develops. Kohlberg's theory has been the basis for a number of cognitive moral education programs. In a typical program, high school students meet in a semester-long course to discuss a number of moral issues. The instructor acts as a facilitator rather than as a director of the class. The hope is that students will develop more advanced notions of such concepts as cooperation, trust, responsibility, and community.

Toward the end of his life, Kohlberg (1986) recognized that the moral atmosphere of the school is more important than he initially envisioned. For example, in one study, a semester-long moral education class based on Kohlberg's theory was successful in advancing moral thinking in three democratic schools but not in three authoritarian schools (Higgins, Power, & Kohlberg, 1983).

Values Clarification A third approach to providing moral education is **values clarification,** which means helping people to clarify what their lives are for and what is worth working for. Unlike character education, which tells students what their values should be, values clarification encourages students to define their own values and understand the values of others (Williams & others, 2003).

Advocates of values clarification say it is value-free. However, critics argue that the exercises undermine accepted values and fail to stress right behavior.

Service Learning Another approach to moral education—service learning—takes education out into the community (Flanagan, 2004). **Service learning** is a form of education that promotes social responsibility and service to the community. In service learning, students engage in activities such as tutoring, helping older adults, working in a hospital, assisting at a child-care center, or cleaning up a vacant lot to make a play area.

One goal of service learning is to help students to become less self-centered and more strongly motivated to help others (Pritchard & Whitehead, 2004; Waterman, 1997). One college student worked as a reading tutor for students from low-income backgrounds. She commented that until she did the tutoring she did not realize how many students had not experienced the same opportunities that she had.

Students who engage in service learning tend to share certain characteristics, such as being extraverted, having a high level of self-understanding, and showing a commitment to others (Eisenberg & Morris, 2004). Also, females are more likely to volunteer to engage in community service than males (Eisenberg & Morris, 2004).

A key feature of service learning is that it benefits both the student volunteers and the recipients of their help (Hamilton & Hamilton, 2004). Researchers have found that service learning benefits students in a number of ways:

- Their grades improve, they become more motivated, and they set more goals (Johnson & others, 1998; Search Institute, 1995).
- Their self-esteem improves (Hamburg, 1997; Johnson & others, 1998).
- They have an improved sense of being able to make a difference for others (Search Institute, 1995).
- They become less alienated (Calabrese & Schumer, 1986).
- They increasingly reflect on society's political organization and moral order (Yates, 1995).

More than just about anything else, 12-year-old Katie Bell (*at bottom*) wanted a playground in her New Jersey town. She knew that other kids also wanted one so she put together a group, which generated fund-raising ideas for the playground. They presented their ideas to the town council. Her group got more youth involved. They helped raise money by selling candy and sandwiches door-to-door. Katie says, "We learned to work as a community. This will be an important place for people to go and have picnics and make new friends." Katie's advice: "You won't get anywhere if you don't try."

cognitive moral education Education based on the belief that students should learn to value things like democracy and justice as their moral reasoning develops; Kohlberg's theory has been the basis for many of the cognitive moral education approaches.

values clarification Helping people clarify what their lives are for and what is worth working for. Students are encouraged to define their own values and understand others' values.

service learning A form of education that promotes social responsibility and service to the community.

Review and Reflect • LEARNING GOAL 2

2 Explain how parenting and schools influence moral development

Review

- How is parental discipline related to moral development? What are some effective parenting strategies for advancing children's moral development?
- What is the hidden curriculum?
- What are some contemporary approaches to moral education?

Reflect

- What type of discipline did your parents use with you? What effect do you think this has had on your moral development?

3 PROSOCIAL AND ANTISOCIAL BEHAVIOR

Prosocial Behavior | Antisocial Behavior

Service learning encourages positive moral behavior. This behavior is not just moral behavior but behavior that is intended to benefit other people, and psychologists call it *prosocial behavior* (Eisenberg & Morris, 2004). Of course, people have always engaged in antisocial behavior as well. In this section, we will take a closer look at prosocial and antisocial behavior and how they develop.

Prosocial Behavior

Caring about the welfare and rights of others, feeling concern and empathy for them, and acting in a way that benefits others are all components of prosocial behavior (Eisenberg, Fabes, & Spinrad, 2006). What motivates this behavior and how does it develop in children?

Altruism and Reciprocity The purest forms of prosocial behavior are motivated by **altruism,** an unselfish interest in helping another person (Eisenberg & Wang, 2003). Human acts of altruism are plentiful. Think of the hardworking laborer who places $5 in a Salvation Army kettle, the volunteers at homeless shelters, the person who donates a kidney so someone else can live; and the child who takes in a wounded cat and cares for it. Altruism is found throughout the human world. It is also taught by every widely practiced religion in the world—Christianity, Judaism, Islam, Baha'i, Hinduism, Buddhism. The circumstances most likely to evoke altruism are empathy for an individual in need or a close relationship between the benefactor and the recipient (Batson, 1989).

Some people, though, argue that true altruism does not exist because behind any action one can propose some benefit to the person performing the action so that it is not truly unselfish. Whether this is the case or not, many prosocial behaviors that appear altruistic are in fact motivated by the norm of *reciprocity,* which is the obligation to return a favor with a favor.

The notion of reciprocity pervades human interactions all over the world. Fund-raisers try to exploit the norm of reciprocity when they send free calendars or other knickknacks in the mail, hoping that you'll feel obligated to reciprocate with a donation to their cause. Individuals feel guilty when they do not reciprocate, and they may feel angry if someone else does not reciprocate. Reciprocity or

altruism An unselfish interest in helping another person.

altruism may motivate many important prosocial behaviors, including sharing (Piliavin, 2003).

Without civic morality communities perish; without personal morality their survival has no value.

—Bertrand Russell
English Philosopher, 20th Century

Sharing and Fairness William Damon (1988) has described a developmental sequence by which sharing develops in children. Most sharing during the first three years of life is done for nonempathic reasons. It occurs because the children are imitating others or because sharing allows them to enjoy the fun of social play. Then, at about 4 years of age, a combination of empathic awareness and adult encouragement produces a sense of obligation on the part of the child to share with others.

Most 4-year-olds are not selfless saints, however. Children believe they have an obligation to share but do not necessarily think they should be as generous to others as they are to themselves. Neither do their actions always support their beliefs, especially when they covet an object. What is important developmentally is that the child has developed a belief that sharing is an obligatory part of a social relationship and involves a question of right and wrong. These early ideas about sharing set the stage for giant strides that children make in the years that follow.

By the start of the elementary school years, children begin to express more complicated notions of what is fair. Throughout history varied definitions of fairness have been used as the basis for distributing goods and resolving conflicts. These definitions involve the principles of equality, merit, and benevolence:

- *Equality* means that everyone is treated the same.
- *Merit* means giving extra rewards for hard work, a talented performance, or other laudatory behavior.
- *Benevolence* means giving special consideration to individuals in a disadvantaged condition.

Equality is the first of these principles used regularly by elementary school children. It is common to hear 6-year-old children use the word *fair* as synonymous with *equal* or *same*. By the mid to late elementary school years, children also believe that equity means special treatment for those who deserve it—a belief that applies the principles of merit and benevolence.

Missing from the factors that guide children's sharing is one that many adults might expect to be the most influential: the motivation to obey adult authority figures. Surprisingly, a number of studies have shown that adult authority has only a small influence on children's sharing. For example, when Nancy Eisenberg (1982) asked children to explain their own spontaneous acts of sharing, they mainly gave empathic and pragmatic reasons. Not one of the children referred to the demands of adult authority.

Parental advice and prodding certainly foster standards of sharing, but the give-and-take of peer requests and arguments provide the most immediate stimulation of sharing. Parents can set examples that children carry with them when they interact and communicate with their peers, but parents are not present during all of their children's peer exchanges. The day-to-day construction of fairness standards is done by children in collaboration and negotiation with each other. Over the course of many years and thousands of encounters, children's understanding of such notions as equality, merit, benevolence, and compromise deepens. With this understanding comes a greater consistency and generosity in children's sharing (Damon, 1988).

Prosocial behavior occurs more often in adolescence than in childhood, although examples of caring for others and comforting someone in distress occur even during the preschool years (Eisenberg & Fabes, 1998; Eisenberg, Fabes, & Spinrad, 2006; Eisenberg & Morris, 2004). The Research in Child Development interlude on the next page focuses on a research study that examines the consistency and development of prosocial behavior.

RESEARCH IN CHILD DEVELOPMENT

The Consistency and Development of Prosocial Behavior

Nancy Eisenberg and her colleagues (1999) studied 32 individuals from the time they were 4 to 5 years of age to when they were in their early twenties. They were assessed on 11 occasions through a variety of procedures, including observations, interviews, parents' reports, and friends' reports. Observations of prosocial behavior in the preschool the children were attending focused on behaviors of sharing, helping, and offering comfort. In elementary school, the children were given an opportunity to anonymously donate eight nickels (given to them by the experimenter) to a charity for needy children. Their helping behavior also was assessed in such tasks as giving them an opportunity to help the experimenter pick up dropped paper clips. In the later elementary school years, adolescence, and in their early twenties, the individuals filled out a self-report scale of items that focused on altruism.

The results indicated that the observed prosocial behaviors in preschool (sharing, helping, and offering comfort) were related to the children's prosocial behavior in the elementary school years and in the early twenties. These findings support the view that prosocial behavior is rather stable from the early childhood years into at least the first part of early adulthood.

Antisocial Behavior

Most children and adolescents at one time or another act out or do things that are destructive or troublesome for themselves or others. If these behaviors occur often, psychiatrists diagnose them as conduct disorders. If these behaviors result in illegal acts by juveniles, society labels them *delinquents.* Both problems are much more common in males than females.

Conduct Disorder

Conduct disorder refers to age-inappropriate actions and attitudes that violate family expectations, society's norms, and the personal or property rights of others. Children with conduct problems show a wide range of rule-violating behaviors, from swearing and temper tantrums to severe vandalism, theft, and assault. Conduct disorder is much more common among boys than girls (Dodge, Coie, & Lynam, 2006).

Consider 4-year-old Andy, who threw his booster seat in his mother's face and thought it was funny. He was acting up even though he had already received one time-out for yelling and screaming at the table. Then he picked up a fork and threw it at his sister, barely missing her eye. Consider also 10-year-old Nick who, when he was only 2 years old, put two unopened cans of cat food on the stove and lit the burner. One of the cans exploded. Over the next 10 years, Nick killed several family pets, set fires, beat up classmates, stole money, and regularly terrorized his younger sister. Both of these children's behaviors suggest that they have a conduct disorder (Mash & Wolfe, 1999).

conduct disorder Age-inappropriate actions and attitudes that violate family expectations, society's norms, and the personal property rights of others.

As part of growing up, most children and youth break the rules from time to time—they fight, skip school, break curfew, steal, and so on. As many as 50 percent of the parents of 4- to 6-year-old children report that their children steal, lie, disobey, or destroy property at least some of the time (Achenbach, 1997). Most of these children show a decrease in antisocial behavior from 4 to 18 years of age, but adolescents who are referred to psychological clinics for therapy still show high rates of antisocial behavior (Achenbach, 1997).

It has been estimated that about 5 percent of children show serious conduct problems, like those of Nick. These children are often described as showing an *externalizing* or *undercontrolled* pattern of behavior. Children who show this pattern often are impulsive, overactive, and aggressive and engage in delinquent actions (Rappaport & Thomas, 2004).

Conduct problems in children are best explained by a confluence of causes, or risk factors, operating over time (Coie, 2004; Conduct Problems Prevention Research Group, 2004; Dodge & Pettit, 2003). These include possible genetic inheritance of a difficult temperament, ineffective parenting, and living in a neighborhood where violence is the norm.

Despite considerable efforts to help children with conduct problems, there is a lack of consensus on what works (Mash & Wolfe, 1999). A multisystem treatment is sometimes recommended, which is carried out with all family members, school personnel, juvenile justice staff, and other individuals in the child's life.

Office of Juvenile Justice and Delinquency Prevention
Justice Information Center
Preventing Crime

Juvenile Delinquency Closely linked with conduct disorder is **juvenile delinquency,** which refers to a broad range of behaviors, ranging from socially unacceptable behavior such as acting out in school to criminal acts such as burglary. For legal purposes, a distinction is made between index offenses and status offenses:

- **Index offenses** are criminal acts, whether they are committed by juveniles or adults. They include such acts as robbery, aggravated assault, rape, and homicide. Rates for property offenses are higher than for other types of offenses (such as toward persons, drug offenses, and public order offenses).
- **Status offenses,** such as running away, truancy, underage drinking, sexual promiscuity, and uncontrollability, are less serious acts. They are illegal only when they are performed by youth under a specified age.

States differ in the age used to classify individuals as juveniles or adults. Approximately three-fourths of the states have established age 18 as a maximum for defining juveniles. Two states use age 19 as the cutoff, seven states use age 17, and four states use age 16. Thus, running away from home at age 17 may be a status offense in some states but not others.

According to U.S. government statistics, 8 of 10 cases of juvenile delinquency involve males (Snyder & Sickmund, 1999). In the last two decades, however, delinquency among girls has been increasing at a higher rate than among boys (Kroneman, Loeber, & Hipwell, 2004; Snyder & Sickmund, 1999).

Delinquency rates among minority groups and youth with low socioeconomic status are especially high. However, these rates may be inflated by various types of bias; youth in minority and low-SES groups may be judged delinquent more readily than adolescents who are White or have middle socioeconomic status.

Should adolescents who commit a crime be tried as adults (Morreale, 2004; Steinberg & Cauffman, 2001)? In one study, trying adolescent offenders as adults increased rather than reduced their crime rate (Myers, 1999). The study evaluated more than 500 violent youth in Pennsylvania, which has adopted a "get tough" policy. Although these 500 offenders had been given harsher punishment than a comparison group retained in juvenile court, they were *more* likely to be rearrested—and rearrested more quickly—for new offenses once they were returned to the community. This suggests that the short-term gain in safety attained by prosecuting juveniles as adults might increase the number of criminal offenses over the long run.

juvenile delinquency Refers to a great variety of behaviors, ranging from unacceptable behavior to status offenses to criminal acts.

index offenses Criminal acts, whether they are committed by juveniles or adults. They include such acts as robbery, aggravated assault, rape, and homicide.

status offenses Less serious acts (than index offenses). Status offenses include truancy, underage drinking, sexual promiscuity, and uncontrollability. They are performed by youth under a specified age, which make them juvenile offenses.

Antecedents of Delinquency How do children grow up to be delinquents? One portrait of the paths they take comes from the Pittsburgh Youth Study, a longitudinal study of more than 1,500 inner-city boys. It found three pathways to delinquency (Loeber & Farrington, 2001; Loeber & others, 1998; Stouthamer-Loeber & others, 2002):

- *Authority conflict.* Youth on this pathway showed stubbornness prior to age 12, and then moved on to defiance and avoidance of authority.
- *Covert.* Minor covert acts such as lying were followed by property damage and moderately serious delinquency, then serious delinquency.
- *Overt.* Minor aggression was followed by fighting and violence.

The study found that by the eighth grade, many boys had been exhibiting problem behaviors for about six years before they appeared in court (Loeber & others, 1998).

Another recent study examined the developmental trajectories of childhood disruptive behaviors and adolescent delinquency (Broidy & others, 2003). For boys, early problem behavior involving aggression was linked with delinquency in adolescence. However, no connection between early aggression problems and later delinquency was found for girls.

Let's look at several factors that are related to delinquency. Erik Erikson (1968) believes that adolescents whose development has restricted their access to acceptable social roles or made them feel that they cannot measure up to the demands placed on them may choose a *negative identity*. Adolescents with a negative identity may find support for their delinquent image among peers, reinforcing the negative identity. For Erikson, delinquency is an attempt to establish an identity, although it is a negative identity.

Although delinquency is less exclusively a lower-SES phenomenon than it was in the past, some characteristics of lower-SES culture can promote delinquency. The norms of many low-SES peer groups and gangs are antisocial, opposing the goals and norms of society at large. Getting into and staying out of trouble are prominent features of life for some adolescents in low-income neighborhoods. Adolescents from low-income backgrounds may sense that they can gain attention and status by performing antisocial actions. Being "tough" and "masculine" are high-status traits for low-SES boys, and these traits are often measured by the adolescent's success in performing and getting away with delinquent acts. Adolescents in a community with a high crime rate observe many models who engage in criminal activities. These communities may be characterized by poverty, unemployment, and feelings of alienation toward higher-SES individuals (Richards & others, 2004; Sabol, Coulton, & Korbin, 2004; Swisher & Whitlock, 2004). Quality schooling, educational funding, and organized neighborhood activities may be lacking in these communities (Barton, 2004; Tolan, Gorman-Smith, & Henry, 2003).

Inadequate family support systems are also associated with delinquency (Bradshaw & Garbarino, 2004; Feldman & Weinberger, 1994). Parents of delinquents are less skilled in discouraging antisocial behavior and in encouraging skilled behavior than are parents of nondelinquents. Parental monitoring of adolescents is especially important in determining whether an adolescent becomes a delinquent (Patterson, DeBaryshe, & Ramsey, 1989). One recent longitudinal study found that the less parents knew about their adolescents' whereabouts, activities, and peers, the more likely they were to engage in delinquent behavior (Laird & others, 2003). A recent study revealed that father absence, assessed when youth were 14 to 17 years of age, was linked with a higher risk of incarceration in males, assessed at 15 to 30 years of age (Harper & McLanahan, 2004). Family discord and inconsistent and inappropriate discipline are also associated with delinquency.

An increasing number of studies have found that siblings can have a strong influence on delinquency (Bank, Burraston, & Snyder, 2004; Conger & Reuter,

1996). In one recent study, high levels of hostile relationships with a sibling and delinquency by an older sibling were linked with delinquency by the younger sibling in both brother and sister pairs (Slomkowski & others, 2001).

Peer relations also play an important role in delinquency (Dodge, Coie, & Lynam, 2006; Rubin, Bukowski, & Parker, 2006). Having delinquent peers increases the risk of becoming delinquent. One recent study found that the link between associating with delinquent peers and engaging in delinquency held for both boys and girls (Heinze, Toro, & Urberg, 2004).

Preventing Delinquency One program that seeks to prevent juvenile delinquency is called *Fast Track* (Conduct Problems Prevention Research Group, 2002, 2004; Dodge, 2001). Children who showed conduct problems at home and at kindergarten were identified. Then, during the elementary school years, the at-risk children and their families are given support and training in parenting, problem-solving and coping skills, peer relations, classroom atmosphere and curriculum, academic achievement, and home-school relations. Ten project interventionists work with the children, their families, and schools to increase the protective factors and decrease the risk factors in these areas. Thus far, comparisons with high-risk children who did not experience the intervention show that the intervention improved parenting practices and children's problem-solving and coping skills, peer relations, reading achievement, and behavior at home and school during the elementary school years (Dodge, Coie, & Lynam, 2006).

One individual whose goal is to reduce violence in adolescence and help at-risk adolescents cope more effectively with their lives is Rodney Hammond. To read about his work, see the Careers in Child Development insert.

Violence and Youth

Youth violence is a special concern in the United States today (U.S. Department of Health and Human Services, 2001). In one study, 17 percent of U.S. high school students reported carrying a gun or other weapon the past 30 days (National Center for Health Statistics, 2000). In this same study, a smaller percentage (7 percent) reported bringing a gun or other weapon onto school property.

The following factors often are present in at-risk youth and seem to propel them toward violent acts (Walker, 1998):

- Early involvement with drugs and alcohol
- Easy access to weapons, especially handguns
- Association with antisocial, deviant peer groups
- Pervasive exposure to violence in the media

CAREERS in CHILD DEVELOPMENT

Rodney Hammond
Health Psychologist

Rodney Hammond described his college experiences, "When I started as an undergraduate at the University of Illinois, Champaign-Urbana, I hadn't decided on my major. But to help finance my education, I took a part-time job in a child development research program sponsored by the psychology department. There, I observed inner-city children in settings designed to enhance their learning. I saw first-hand the contribution psychology can make, and I knew I wanted to be a psychologist" (American Psychological Association, 2003, p. 26).

Rodney Hammond went on to obtain a doctorate in school and community college with a focus on children's development. For a number of years, he trained clinical psychologists at Wright State University in Ohio and directed a program to reduce violence in ethnic minority youth. There, he and his associates taught at-risk youth how to use social skills to effectively manage conflict and to recognize situations that could lead to violence. Today, Rodney is Director of Violence Prevention at the Centers for Disease Control and Prevention in Atlanta. Rodney says that if you are interested in people and problem solving, psychology is a wonderful way to put these together.

Rodney Hammond, counseling an adolescent girl about the risks of adolescence and how to effectively cope with them.

Many at-risk youth also are easily provoked to rage: they react aggressively to real or imagined slights and act upon them, sometimes with tragic consequences. They might misjudge the motives and intentions of others because of hostility and agitation (Coie & Dodge, 1998). Consequently, they frequently engage in hostile confrontations with peers and teachers. It is not unusual to find anger-prone youth threatening bodily harm to others. The Caring for Children interlude offers some recommendations for reducing youth violence.

Caring for Children

Reducing Youth Violence

These are some of the Oregon Social Learning Center's recommendations for reducing youth violence (Walker, 1998):

- *Recommit to raising children safely and effectively.* This includes engaging in parenting practices that have been shown to produce healthy, well-adjusted children. Such practices include consistent, fair discipline that is not harsh or severely punitive, careful monitoring and supervision, positive family management techniques, involvement in the child's daily life, daily debriefings about the child's experiences, and teaching problem-solving strategies.
- *Make prevention a reality.* Too often lip service is given to prevention strategies but not enough is invested in them to make them effective.
- *Give more support to schools, which are struggling to educate a population that includes many at-risk children.*
- *Forge effective partnerships among families, schools, social service systems, churches, and other agencies to create the socializing experiences that will provide all youth with the opportunity to develop in positive ways.*

What are some of the reasons psychologists give to explain why youth like Eric Harris kill?

A few years ago a rash of murders was committed by adolescents, with the targets of their violence being classmates or school personnel. In April 1999, two students at Columbine High School (in Littleton, Colorado), Eric Harris (18) and Dylan Klebold (17), shot and killed 12 students and a teacher, and wounded 23 others. In 2001, 15-year-old Charles "Andy" Williams fired shots at Santee High School in Southern California that killed 2 classmates and injured 13 others. According to students at the school, Andy was a victim of bullying and had joked the previous weekend of his violent plans, but no one took him seriously after he said he was just kidding.

Is there any way to predict whether a youth will turn violent? It's a complex task, but psychologists have pieced together some clues (Cowley, 1998; Harter & Whitesell, 2001). Violent youth are overwhelmingly male, and many are driven by feelings of powerlessness. Violence seems to infuse these youth with a sense of power. They may clearly indicate their violent intentions but are not taken seriously. Psychologist James Garbarino (1999, 2001) notes that a lot of ignoring goes on in these situations. Harris and Klebold, for example, made a video for a class that depicted them walking down the halls and shooting other students. We often don't want to acknowledge what might be a very upsetting reality.

Garbarino (1999) has interviewed a number of young killers. He concludes that nobody really knows precisely why a tiny minority of youth kill, but the cause might be a lack of a spiritual center. In many of the young killers he interviewed, Garbarino found a spiritual or emotional emptiness that the youth filled by seeking meaning in the dark side of life.

Review and Reflect • LEARNING GOAL 3

3 Describe the development of prosocial and antisocial behavior

Review

- How is altruism defined? How does prosocial behavior develop?
- What is conduct disorder? What are key factors in the development of juvenile delinquency and youth violence?

Reflect

- As the head of a major government agency responsible for reducing delinquency in the United States, what programs would you try to implement?

REACH YOUR LEARNING GOALS

MORAL DEVELOPMENT

- **1 DOMAINS OF MORAL DEVELOPMENT**
  - What Is Moral Development?
  - Moral Thought
  - Moral Behavior
  - Moral Feeling
  - Moral Personality
- **2 CONTEXTS OF MORAL DEVELOPMENT**
  - Parenting
  - Schools
- **3 PROSOCIAL AND ANTISOCIAL BEHAVIOR**
  - Prosocial Behavior
  - Antisocial Behavior

SUMMARY

1 Discuss theory and research on the domains of moral development

- Moral development involves changes in thoughts, feelings, and behaviors regarding right and wrong. Moral development consists of intrapersonal and interpersonal dimensions.
- Piaget distinguished between the heteronomous morality of younger children and the autonomous morality of older children. Kohlberg developed a provocative theory of moral reasoning. He argued that reasoning develops through three levels—preconventional, conventional, and postconventional—and six stages (two at each level). Kohlberg believed that these stages were age-related. Influences on Kohlberg's stages include cognitive development, cognitive conflict and exposure to moral arguments, and peer relations and opportunities for perspective taking. Critics of Kohlberg's theory have noted that moral reasoning does not adequately predict moral behavior, that other methods should be used to assess moral reasoning, that Kohlberg's stages are not universal, that he underestimated the influence of family relationships on moral development, that his theory reflects a male bias and gives too little attention to the care perspective, and that it does not adequately distinguish between moral reasoning and social conventional reasoning.
- The processes of reinforcement, punishment, and imitation and the influence of the situation have been used to explain moral behavior, but they provide only a partial explanation. Cognitions can play a role in resistance to temptation and self-control. Social cognitive theory emphasizes a distinction between moral competence and moral performance.
- In Freud's theory, the moral branch of personality is the superego, which consists of the ego ideal and the conscience. According to Freud, guilt is the foundation of children's moral behavior. In the contemporary perspective, both positive and negative feelings contribute to moral development. Empathy is one of the positive feelings that influences children to act in accord with moral standards.
- Recently, there has been a surge of interest in studying moral personality. This interest has focused on moral identity, moral character, and moral exemplars. Blasi's view of moral identity emphasizes willpower (self-control), integrity, and moral desire. Moral character involves having the strength of your convictions, persisting, and overcoming distractions and obstacles. Moral character consists of having certain virtues, such as honesty, care, and conscientiousness. Moral exemplars are people who have lived exemplary lives.

2 Explain how parenting and schools influence moral development

- Warmth and responsibility in mutual obligations of parent-child relationships provide important foundations for the child's positive moral growth. Secure attachment appears to provide the basis for parents to influence a child's moral development in positive ways. Discipline techniques include love withdrawal, power assertion, and induction. Induction is most likely to be linked with positive moral development, at least in middle-SES children. An important parenting strategy is to proactively avert his behavior before it takes place. Parents may also contribute to children's moral development by providing opportunities for perspective taking and by modeling moral reasoning and behavior.
- The hidden curriculum, initially described by Dewey, is the moral atmosphere of a school, and it may influence children's moral development even when schools do not aim to do so. Contemporary approaches to moral education include character education, cognitive moral education, values clarification, and service learning.

3 Describe the development of prosocial and antisocial behavior

- Altruism, which is an unselfish interest in helping another person, or reciprocity often motivates prosocial behavior such as sharing. Damon described a sequence by which children develop their understanding of fairness and come to share more consistently. Peers play a key role in this development. Adolescents engage in prosocial behavior more than children, and girls engage in prosocial behavior more than boys.
- Conduct disorder involves age-inappropriate actions and attitudes that violate family expectations, society's norms, and the personal or property rights of others. The disorder is more common in boys than in girls. Juvenile delinquency involves a broad range of behaviors, from socially unacceptable behavior to status offenses to criminal behavior. In the Pittsburgh Youth Study, pathways to delinquency included conflict with authority, minor covert acts followed by property damage and more serious acts, and minor aggression followed by fighting and violence. Living in an urban, high-crime area, low parental monitoring, ineffective discipline, having an older sibling who is a delinquent, and associating with peers who are delinquents are also

linked with delinquency. Early involvement with drugs and violence, easy access to weapons, associations with antisocial peer groups, and pervasive exposure to violent content in the media are associated with violent youth. Recommendations for reducing youth violence include effective parenting, prevention, support for schools, and forging effective partnerships among families, schools, and communities.

KEY TERMS

moral development 423
heteronomous morality 423
autonomous morality 423
immanent justice 424
preconventional reasoning 424
individualism, instrumental purpose, and exchange 425
conventional reasoning 425
mutual interpersonal expectations, relationships, and interpersonal conformity 425
social systems morality 425
postconventional reasoning 425
social contract or utility and individual rights 425
universal ethical principles 426
justice perspective 429
care perspective 429
social conventional reasoning 430
social cognitive theory of morality 431
ego ideal 432
conscience 432
empathy 433
moral identity 434
moral exemplars 435
love withdrawal 436
power assertion 437
induction 437
hidden curriculum 438
character education 438
cognitive moral education 439
values clarification 439
service learning 439
altruism 440
conduct disorder 442
juvenile delinquency 443
index offenses 443
status offenses 443

KEY PEOPLE

Jean Piaget 423
Lawrence Kohlberg 424
Carol Gilligan 429
Hugh Hartshorne and Mark May 431
Walter Mischel 431
Albert Bandura 431
Sigmund Freud 432
Augusto Blasi 434
Ross Thompson 436
Martin Hoffman 437
John Dewey 438
William Damon 438
Nancy Eisenberg 441
James Garbarino 447

E-LEARNING TOOLS

To help you master the material in this chapter, visit the Online Learning Center for *Child Development,* eleventh edition (**www.mhhe.com/santrockcd11**), where you'll find these additional resources:

Taking It to the Net

1. Geraldine is giving a report on Kohlberg's theory of moral development. She is having a hard time thinking of an example of moral reasoning that would demonstrate each of Kohlberg's six stages of moral development. What examples would best demonstrate each of the six stages of moral development?
2. Kirk is planning to be a fifth-grade teacher. He is interested in the new approach to disciplining students that is designed to strengthen a child's character and impart moral values. How can Kirk begin to use this approach in the classroom?
3. Justin was having a heated discussion with his dad over the factors that may have contributed to a young boy's shooting and killing a schoolmate. Justin thinks that the boy may have witnessed, or been a victim of, violence in his home. His father says that if everyone who saw violence was violent we would all be locked up. How should Justin respond?

Nursing, Parenting, and Teaching Exercises

Build your decision-making skills by trying your hand at the scenarios on the Online Learning Center.

Video Clips

The Online Learning Center includes the following videos for this chapter:

- Juvenile Offenders
  Laurence Steinberg, Department of Psychology, Temple University, discusses juvenile offenders. Should they be held accountable? How should they be punished? He states that how society handles the prosecution of youth should be developmentally appropriate.

Section 5

SOCIAL CONTEXTS OF DEVELOPMENT

It is not enough for parents to understand children. They must also accord children the privilege of understanding them.

—MILTON SAPIRSTEIN
American Psychiatrist and Writer, 20th Century

Parents cradle children's lives, but children's growth is also shaped by successive choirs of siblings, peers, friends, and teachers. Children's small worlds widen as they discover new refuges and new people. In the end there are but two lasting bequests that parents can leave children: one being roots, the other wings. In this section, we will study four chapters: "Families" (chapter 15), "Peers" (chapter 16), "Schools and Achievement" (chapter 17), and "Culture" (chapter 18).

Chapter 15 FAMILIES

There's no vocabulary for love within a family, love that's lived in but not looked at, love within the light of which all else is seen, the love within which all other love finds speech. That love is silent.

—T. S. Eliot
American-Born English Poet, 20th Century

CHAPTER OUTLINE

FAMILY PROCESSES

Interactions in the Family System
Cognition and Emotion in Family Processes
The Developmental Construction of Relationships
Sociocultural and Historical Changes

PARENTING

The Parental Role
Adapting Parenting to Developmental Changes in the Child
Parenting Styles
Punishment
Child Maltreatment
Parenting Takes Time and Effort

FAMILIES AND ADOLESCENTS

Autonomy
Attachment
Parent-Adolescent Conflict

SIBLINGS

Sibling Relationships
Birth Order

THE CHANGING FAMILY IN A CHANGING SOCIAL WORLD

Working Parents
Children in Divorced Families
Stepfamilies
Gay Male and Lesbian Parents
Cultural, Ethnic, and Socioeconomic Variations in Families
Gender and Parenting

LEARNING GOALS

1 Discuss family processes

2 Explain how parenting is linked to children's development

3 Summarize the changes in families with adolescents

4 Identify how siblings influence children's development

5 Characterize the changing family in a changing social world

The Story of a Mother with Multiple Sclerosis

Shelley Peterman Schwarz (left) with her family

When Shelley Peterman Schwarz (2004) and her husband, David, had been married four years, they decided to have children. They had two children, Andrew and Jamie. When they were 3 and 5 years old, Shelley was diagnosed with multiple sclerosis. Two years later, she had to quit her job as a teacher of hearing-impaired children because of her worsening condition.

By the time the children were 7 and 9 years old, it was more difficult for Shelley to prepare meals for the family by herself, so David began taking over that responsibility. They also enlisted the children's help in preparing meals.

Despite her multiple sclerosis, Shelley participated in parenting classes and workshops at her children's school. She even initiated a "Mothers-of-10-Year-Olds" support group. But parenting with multiple sclerosis had its frustrations for Shelley. In her words,

> attending school functions, teacher's conferences, and athletic events often presented problems because the facilities weren't always easily wheelchair accessible. I felt guilty if I didn't at least "try" to attend. I didn't want my children to think I didn't care enough to try . . .
>
> When Jamie was 19 and Andrew was 17, I started to relax a little. I could see how capable and independent they were becoming. My having a disability hadn't ruined their lives. In fact, in some ways, they are better off because of it. They learned to trust themselves and to face personal challenges head-on. When the time came for them to leave the nest and head off to college, I knew they were ready.
>
> As for me, I now understand that having a disability wasn't the worst thing in the world that could happen to a parent. What would be a tragedy is letting your disability cripple your ability to stay in your children's lives. Parenting is so much more than driving car pools, attending gymnastic meets, or baking cookies for an open house. It's loving, caring, listening, guiding, and supporting your child. It's consoling a child crying because her friends thought her haircut was ugly. It's counseling a child worried because his 12-year-old friend is drinking. It's helping a child understand relationships and what it's like to "be in love." (Schwarz, 2004, p. 5)

PREVIEW

This chapter is about the many aspects of children's development in families. We will explore the best ways to parent children, relationships among siblings, and the changing family in a changing social world. Along the way, we will examine such topics as child maltreatment, working parents, children in divorced families, stepfamilies, and many others.

1 FAMILY PROCESSES

- Interactions in the Family System
- Cognition and Emotion in Family Processes
- The Developmental Construction of Relationships
- Sociocultural and Historical Changes

As we examine the family and other social contexts of development, keep in mind Urie Bronfenbrenner's (1995, 2000, 2004; Bronfenbrenner & Morris, 2006) ecological theory, which we discussed in chapter 2. Recall that Bronfenbrenner analyzes the social contexts of development in terms of five environmental systems:

- The microsystem or the setting in which the individual lives, such as a family, the world of peers, schools, work, and so on
- The mesosystem, which consists of links between microsystems, such as the connection between family processes and peer relations
- The exosystem, which consists of influences from another setting that the individual does not experience directly, such as how parents' experiences at work might affect their parenting at home
- The macrosystem or the culture in which the individual lives, such as a nation or an ethnic group
- The chronosystem or sociohistorical circumstances, such as the increase in the numbers of working mothers, divorced parents, and stepparent families in the United States in the last 30 to 40 years

Let's begin our examination of the family at the level of the microsystem.

Interactions in the Family System

Every family is a *system*—a complex whole made up of interrelated and interacting parts. The relationships never go in just one direction. For example, the interaction of mothers and their infants is sometimes symbolized as a dance in which successive actions of the partners are closely coordinated. This coordinated dance can assume the form of *mutual synchrony,* which means that each person's behavior depends on the partner's previous behavior. Or the interaction can be *reciprocal* in a precise sense, which means that the actions of the partners can be matched, as when one partner imitates the other or when there is mutual smiling (Cohn & Tronick, 1988).

One important example of early synchronized interaction is mutual gaze or eye contact (Fogel, Toda, & Kawai, 1988). In one investigation, the mother and infant engaged in a variety of behaviors while they looked at each other; by contrast, when they looked away from each other, the rate of such behaviors dropped considerably (Stern & others, 1977). In one investigation, synchrony in parent-child relationships was positively related to children's social competence (Harrist, 1993).

Another example of synchronization occurs in **scaffolding,** which means adjusting the level of guidance to fit the child's performance, as we discussed in chapter 7. The parent responds to the child's behavior with scaffolding, which in turn affects the child's behavior. Scaffolding can be used to support children's efforts at any age (Stringer & Neal, 1993). For example, in the game peekaboo, parents initially cover their babies, then remove the covering, and finally register "surprise" at the babies' reappearance. As infants become more skilled at peekaboo, infants gradually do some of the covering and uncovering. Parents try to time their actions in such a way that the infant takes turns with the parent.

Children, Youth, and Families Education and Research Network
Children, Youth, and Family Services

In addition to peekaboo, patty-cake and so-big are other caregiver games that exemplify scaffolding and turn-taking sequences. In one investigation, infants who had more extensive scaffolding experiences with their parents, especially in the form of turn-taking, were more likely to engage in turn-taking as they interacted with their peers (Vandell & Wilson, 1988).

The mutual influence that parents and children exert on each other goes beyond specific interactions in games such as peekaboo; it extends to the whole process of socialization. Socialization between parents and children is not a one-way process (Bugental & Grusec, 2006). Parents do socialize children, but socialization in families is reciprocal. **Reciprocal socialization** is socialization that is bidirectional; children socialize parents just as parents socialize children (Crouter & Booth, 2003; Karraker & Coleman, 2005; Patterson & Fisher, 2002).

scaffolding Parental behavior that supports children's efforts, allowing children to be more skillful than they would be if they relied only on their own abilities.

reciprocal socialization The process by which children socialize parents just as parents socialize them.

Of course, while parents are interacting with their children, they are also interacting with each other. To understand these interactions and relationships, it helps

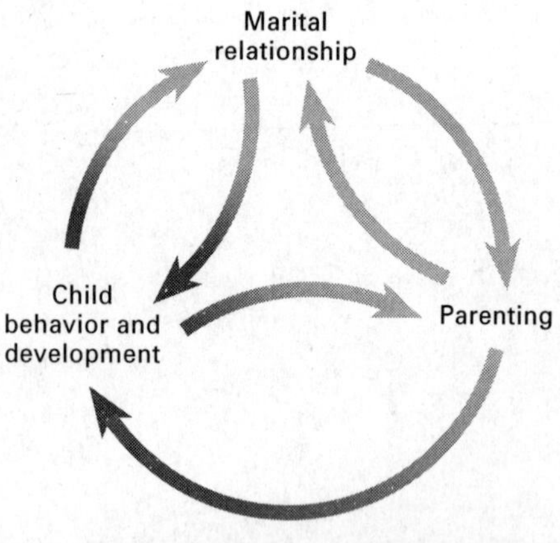

FIGURE 15.1 Interaction Between Children and Their Parents: Direct and Indirect Effects

to think of the family as a constellation of subsystems defined in terms of generation, gender, and role. Each family member is a participant in several subsystems—some *dyadic* (involving two people), some *polyadic* (involving more than two people). The father and child represent one dyadic subsystem, the mother and father another; the mother-father-child represent one polyadic subsystem, the mother and two siblings another.

These subsystems interact and influence one another (Cox & Paley, 2003). Thus, as figure 15.1 illustrates, marital relations, parenting, and infant/child behavior can have both direct and indirect effects on one another (Belsky, 1981). The link between marital relationships and parenting has recently received increased attention. The most consistent findings are that compared with unhappily married parents, happily married parents are more sensitive, responsive, warm, and affectionate toward their children (Grych, 2002).

Researchers have found that promoting marital satisfaction often leads to good parenting. The marital relationship provides an important support for parenting (Cummings & others, 2002; Fincham & Hall, 2005). When parents report more intimacy and better communication in their marriage, they are more affectionate to their children (Grych, 2002). Thus, marriage-enhancement programs may end up improving parenting and helping children. Programs that focus on parenting skills might also benefit from including attention to the participants' marriages.

Cognition and Emotion in Family Processes

Both cognition and emotion are increasingly thought to be central to understanding how family processes work (Parke, 2004; Parke & Buriel, 1998, 2006). The role of cognition in family socialization comes in many forms, including parents' cognitions, beliefs, and values about their parental role, as well as how parents perceive, organize, and understand their children's behaviors and beliefs. For example, one study found a link between mothers' beliefs and their preschool children's social problem-solving skills (Rubin, Mills, & Rose-Krasnor, 1989). Mothers who placed a higher value on such skills as making friends, sharing with others, and leading or influencing other children had children who were more assertive, prosocial, and competent problem solvers than mothers who valued these skills less.

Children's social competence is also linked to the emotional lives of their parents (Fitness & Duffield, 2004). For example, one study found that parents who expressed positive emotions had children who were high in social competence (Boyum & Parke, 1995). Through interaction with their parents, children learn to express their emotions in appropriate ways.

Researchers are also finding that parental support and acceptance of children's emotions is related to children's ability to manage their emotions in positive ways (Parke, 2004). Parental comforting of children when they experience negative emotion is linked with children's ability to more effectively control their anger (Eisenberg & Fabes, 1994). Also, parental motivation to discuss emotions with their children is related to children's awareness and understanding of others' emotions (Denham, Cook, & Zoller, 1992; Dunn & Brown, 1994). In one study, fathers' acceptance and assistance with children's sadness and anger at 5 years of age was linked with children's social competence with peers at 8 years of age (Gottman, Katz, & Hooven, 1997).

The Developmental Construction of Relationships

How far does parents' influence on children's social competence go? Does the relationship between the parents and the child determine the child's future relationships?

Developmentalists have shown an increased interest in understanding how we construct relationships as we grow up (Conger, Lorenz, & Wickrama, 2004; Cox & others, 2004). Psychoanalytic theorists have always been interested in how this process works in families. However, unlike classical psychoanalytic theory, current explanations of how relationships are constructed virtually abandon Freud's psychosexual stages and go beyond the first five years of life. Today's **developmental construction views** share the belief that as individuals grow up they acquire modes of relating to others. Some developmental construction views emphasize continuity and stability in how we relate to others; others emphasize discontinuity and change.

I looked on child rearing not only as a work of love and duty but as a profession that was fully as interesting and challenging as any honorable profession in the world and one that demanded the best that I could bring to it.

—Rose Kennedy
U.S. Public Figure and Philanthropist, 20th Century

The Continuity View The **continuity view** emphasizes the role that early parent-child relationships play in constructing a basic way of relating to people. These early parent-child relationships influence later points in development and all subsequent relationships (with peers, with friends, with teachers, and with romantic partners, for example) (Ainsworth, 1979; Bowlby, 1989; Carlson, Sroufe, & Egeland, 2004; Sroufe, 2002; Sroufe & others, 2005). In its extreme form, this view states that the basic components of social relationships are laid down and shaped by the security or insecurity of parent-infant attachment in the first year or two of the infant's life (remember our discussion of attachment in chapter 11).

Less extreme versions of the continuity view note that the quality of any relationship depends to some degree on the specific individual with whom the relationship is formed. Close relationships do not repeat themselves in an endless fashion over the course of the child's development. Nevertheless, in this view, close relationships with parents function as models or templates that are carried forward over time to influence the construction of new relationships. And the nature of earlier relationships often can be detected in later relationships, both with the same individuals and with others (Gjerde, Block, & Block, 1991). Thus, for example, parent-adolescent relationships do not depend only on what happens in the relationship during adolescence. Relationships with parents over the long course of childhood are carried forward to influence, at least to some degree, parent-adolescent relationships. And the long course of parent-child relationships also can be expected to influence to some degree the fabric of the adolescent's peer relationships, friendships, and dating relationships.

One investigation that supports the importance of continuity in development is the longitudinal study by Alan Sroufe and his colleagues (Sroufe, 2002; Sroufe, Egeland, & Carlson, 1999; Sroufe & others, 2005) that we discussed in chapter 11, "Emotional Development." Recall that attachment history and early care were linked with peer competence in adolescence, up to 15 years after the infant assessments. For most children, there was a cascading effect in which early family relationships provided the necessary support for effectively engaging in the peer world, which in turn provided the foundation for more extensive, complex peer relationships.

The Discontinuity View The **discontinuity view** emphasizes change and growth in relationships over time. As people grow up, they develop many different types of relationships—with parents, with peers, with teachers, and with romantic partners, for example. Each of these relationships is structurally different. With each new type of relationship, individuals encounter new modes of relating (Buhrmester & Furman, 1987; Piaget, 1932; Sullivan, 1953; Youniss, 1980). For example, Jean Piaget (1932) argued that parent-child relationships are strikingly different from children's peer relationships. Parent-child relationships, he said, are more likely to consist of parents' having unilateral authority over children. By contrast, peer relationships are more likely to consist of participants who relate to each other on a much more equal basis. In parent-child relationships, since parents have greater knowledge and authority, their children often must learn how to conform to rules and regulations laid down by parents. In this view, we usc the parental-child mode when relating to authority figures (such as with teachers and experts) and when we ourselves become authority figures (when we become parents, teachers, and experts).

In contrast, relationships with romantic partners, friends, and coworkers call on the mode of relating to others that is learned in relationships with peers. Because two peers possess relatively equal knowledge and authority (their relationship is

developmental construction views Views sharing the belief that as individuals grow up, they acquire modes of relating to others. There are two main variations of this view. One emphasizes continuity and stability in relationships throughout the life span; the other emphasizes discontinuity and changes in relationships throughout the life span.

continuity view A developmental view that emphasizes the role of early parent-child relationships in constructing a basic way of relating to people throughout the life span.

discontinuity view A developmental view that emphasizes change and growth in relationships over time.

reciprocal and symmetrical), children learn a democratic mode of relating that is based on mutual influence. With peers, children learn to formulate and assert their own opinions, appreciate the perspectives of peers, cooperatively negotiate solutions to disagreements, and evolve standards for conduct that are mutually acceptable. Because peer relationships are voluntary (rather than obligatory, as in the family), children and adolescents who fail to become skillful in the symmetrical, mutual, egalitarian, reciprocal mode of relating have difficulty being accepted by peers.

Evidence that relationships formed after infancy may influence other relationships was found in the longitudinal study conducted by Andrew Collins and his colleagues (Collins, Hennighausen, & Sroufe, 1998). The researchers assessed the quality of interaction in friendships by observing coordinated behaviors among children such as turn-taking, sharing, eye contact, and touching, and the duration of these behaviors. They found that the quality of friendship relationships during middle childhood was related to security with dating and to disclosure and intimacy with a dating partner, at age 16.

The discontinuity view does not deny that prior close relationships (such as with parents) are carried forward to influence later relationships, but it stresses that each new type of relationship that children and adolescents encounter (such as with peers, with friends, and with romantic partners) requires the construction of different and ever-more sophisticated modes of relating to others. In the change-and-growth view, each period of development uniquely contributes to the construction of knowledge about relationships; development across the life span is not solely determined by a sensitive or critical period during infancy.

Sociocultural and Historical Changes

Family development does not occur in a social vacuum. As Bronfenbrenner's concepts of the macrosystem and chronosystem indicate, sociocultural and historical influences affect family processes (Bronfenbrenner & Morris, 2006). Both great upheavals such as war, famine, or mass immigration and subtle transitions in ways of life may stimulate changes in families. One example is the effect on U.S. families of the Great Depression of the 1930s. During its height, the Depression produced economic deprivation,

One of the sociocultural and historical changes in children's lives in recent years is the increase in family moves. *How might these moves affect children's development?*

adult discontent, and depression about living conditions. It also increased marital conflict, inconsistent child rearing, and unhealthy lifestyles—heavy drinking, demoralized attitudes, and health disabilities—especially in fathers (Elder, 1980).

Subtle changes in a culture that have significant influences on the family were described by anthropologist Margaret Mead (1978). Such changes include the longevity of older adults, movement to urban and suburban areas, television, and a general dissatisfaction and restlessness.

In the early 20th century, the older people who survived were usually hearty and still closely linked to the family, often helping to maintain the family's existence. Today, older people live longer, which means that their middle-aged children are often pressed into a caretaking role for their parents, or the elderly parents may be placed in a nursing home. Older parents may have lost some of their socializing role in the family during the twentieth century as many of their children moved great distances away.

Many of these family moves were away from farms and small towns to urban and suburban settings. In the small towns and farms, individuals were surrounded by lifelong neighbors, relatives, and friends. Today, neighborhood and extended-family support systems are not nearly as prevalent. Families now move all over the country, often uprooting the child from a school and peer group he or she has known for a considerable length of time. And for many families, this type of move occurs every year or two, as one or both parents are transferred from job to job.

Television is one of the sociocultural and historical changes in children's lives. *How might heavy TV viewing influence children's development?*

The media and technology also play a major role in the changing family. Many children who watch television find that parents are too busy working to share this experience with them. Children increasingly experience a world that their parents are not a part of. Instead of participating in neighborhood peer groups, children come home after school and plop down in front of the television set or a computer screen. And television allows children and their families to see new ways of life. Lower-SES families can look into the family lives of middle-SES families by simply pushing a button.

Another change in families has been an increase in general dissatisfaction and restlessness. The result of such restlessness and the tendency to divorce and remarry has been a hodgepodge of family structures, with far greater numbers of single-parent and stepparent families than ever before in history. Later in the chapter, we discuss such aspects of the changing social world of the child and the family in greater detail.

Review and Reflect • LEARNING GOAL 1

1 Discuss family processes

Review

- How can the family be viewed as a system? What is reciprocal socialization?
- What roles do cognition and emotion play in family relationships?
- What are the two versions of the developmental construction of relationships?
- What are some sociocultural and historical changes that have influenced the family?

Reflect

- What do you predict will be some major changes in families by the end of the twenty-first century?

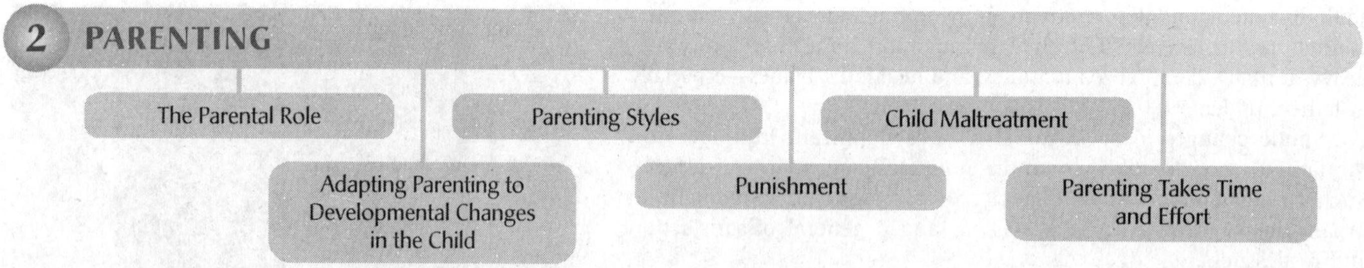

Parenting calls on a number of interpersonal skills and makes intense emotional demands, yet there is little in the way of formal education for this task. Most parents learn parenting practices from their own parents. Some of these practices they accept, some they discard. Husbands and wives may bring different views of parenting to the marriage.

Unfortunately, when parents' methods are passed on from one generation to the next, both desirable and undesirable practices are perpetuated. What have developmentalists learned about parenting? What is the parent's role in the child's development, and how do different parenting styles influence children's development?

CAREERS in CHILD DEVELOPMENT

Janis Keyser
Parent Educator

Janis Keyser is a parent educator and teaches in the Department of Early Childhood Education at Cabrillo College in California. In addition to teaching college classes and conducting parenting workshops, Janis also has co-authored a book with Laura Davis (1997), *Becoming the Parent You Want to Be: A Sourcebook of Strategies for the First Five Years.*

Janis also writes as an expert on the iVillage website (http://www.parentsplace.com). And she co-authors a nationally syndicated parenting column, "Growing Up, Growing Together." She is the mother of 3, stepmother of 5, grandmother of 12, and great-grandmother of 6.

Janis Keyser (*right*), conducting a session to help parents interact more effectively with their children.

The Parental Role

For many adults, the parental role is well planned and coordinated with other roles in life and is developed with the individual's economic situation in mind. For others, the discovery that they are about to become parents is a startling surprise. In either event, the prospective parents may have mixed emotions and romantic illusions about having a child.

The needs and expectations of parents have stimulated many myths about parenting, such as these (Okun & Rappaport, 1980):

- The birth of a child will save a failing marriage.
- As a possession or extension of the parent, the child will think, feel, and behave like the parents did in their childhood.
- Children will take care of parents in old age.
- Parents can expect respect and get obedience from their children.
- Having a child means that the parents will always have someone who loves them and is their best friend.
- Having a child gives the parents a "second chance" to achieve what they should have achieved.
- If parents learn the right techniques, they can mold their children into what they want.
- It's always the parents' fault when children fail.
- Mothers are naturally better parents than fathers.
- Parenting is an instinct and requires no training.

One career involving parenting is parent educator. To read about the work of one parent educator, see the Careers in Child Development insert.

What is a realistic view of the parents' role in their children's lives? One way to conceptualize the parental role is to think of parents as managers of children's lives.

In infancy, this might involve taking a child to a doctor and arranging for child care. In childhood, the managerial role might involve deciding on which preschool the child should attend, directing the child to wear clean clothes and put toys away, and structuring the child's after-school activities. In adolescence, the managerial role might include setting curfews and monitoring the adolescent's college and career interests. From infancy through adolescence, mothers are more likely than fathers to have a managerial role in parenting.

The managerial role is especially important in the child's socioemotional development. As managers, parents may regulate children's opportunities for social contact with peers, friends, and adults (Parke, 2004; Parke & Buriel, 1998). Parents play an important role in facilitating children's development by initiating contact between children and potential play partners. In one study, children of parents who arranged peer contacts had a larger number of playmates outside of their school than children of parents who were less active in managing these contacts (Ladd, LeSeiur, & Profilet, 1993).

Another important aspect of the managerial role is effective monitoring of the child. This is especially important as children move into the adolescent years. Monitoring includes supervising a child's choice of social settings, activities, and friends. As we saw in chapter 14, "Moral Development," a lack of adequate parental monitoring is related to juvenile delinquency more than any other parenting factor (Patterson & Stouthamer-Loeber, 1984).

Adapting Parenting to Developmental Changes in the Child

Children change as they grow from infancy to early childhood and on through middle and late childhood and adolescence. The 5-year-old and the 2-year-old have different needs and abilities. A competent parent adapts to the child's developmental changes (Maccoby, 1984).

In the first year, parent-child interaction moves from a heavy focus on routine caretaking—feeding, changing diapers, bathing, and soothing—to later include more noncaregiving activities, such as play and visual-vocal exchanges (Bornstein, 2002). During the child's second and third years, parents often handle disciplinary matters by physical manipulation: they carry the child away from a mischievous activity to the place they want the child to go to; they put fragile and dangerous objects out of reach; they sometimes spank. As the child grows older, however, parents increasingly turn to reasoning, moral exhortation, and giving or withholding special privileges. As children move toward the elementary school years, parents show them less physical affection.

Calvin and Hobbes **by Bill Watterson**

Parent-child interactions during early childhood focus on such matters as modesty, bedtime regularities, control of temper, fighting with siblings and peers, eating behavior and manners, autonomy in dressing, and attention seeking (Edwards & Liu, 2002). Although some of these issues—fighting and reaction to discipline, for example—are carried forward into the elementary school years, many new issues appear by the age of 7. These include whether children should be made to perform chores and, if so, whether they should be paid for them, how to help children learn to entertain themselves rather than relying on parents for everything, and how to monitor children's lives outside the family in school and peer settings.

As children move into the middle and late childhood years, parents spend considerably less time with them (Collins & Madsen, 2002). In one investigation, parents spent less than half as much time with their children aged 5 to 12 in caregiving, instruction, reading, talking, and playing as when the children were young (Hill & Stafford, 1980). This drop in parent-child interaction may be even more extensive in families with little parental education. Although parents spend less time with their children in middle and late childhood than in early childhood, parents continue to be extremely important socializing agents in their children's lives (Collins, Harris, & Susman, 1995). Children also must learn to relate to adults outside the family on a regular basis—adults who interact with the child much differently than parents do. During middle and late childhood, interactions with adults outside the family involve more formal control and achievement orientation.

Discipline during middle and late childhood is often easier for parents than it was during early childhood; it may also be easier than during adolescence. In middle and late childhood, children's cognitive development has matured to the point where it is possible for parents to reason with them about resisting deviation and controlling their behavior. By adolescence, children's reasoning has become more sophisticated, and they may be less likely to accept parental discipline. Adolescents also push more strongly for independence, which contributes to parenting difficulties (Steinberg & Silk, 2002). Parents of elementary school children use less physical discipline than do parents of preschool children. By contrast, parents of elementary school children are more likely to use deprivation of privileges, appeals directed at the child's self-esteem, comments designed to increase the child's sense of guilt, and statements indicating to the child that she is responsible for her actions.

During middle and late childhood, some control is transferred from parent to child, although the process is gradual and involves coregulation rather than control by either the child or the parent alone (Maccoby, 1984). The major shift to autonomy does not occur until about the age of 12 or later. During middle and late childhood, parents continue to exercise general supervision and exert control while children are allowed to engage in moment-to-moment self-regulation. This coregulation process is a transition period between the strong parental control of early childhood and the increased relinquishment of general supervision during adolescence.

During this coregulation, parents should

- monitor, guide, and support children at a distance;
- effectively use the times when they have direct contact with the child; and
- strengthen in their children the ability to monitor their own behavior, to adopt appropriate standards of conduct, to avoid hazardous risks, and to sense when parental support and contact are appropriate.

By adolescence, children's reasoning has become more sophisticated and they may be less likely to accept parental discipline. Adolescents also push for more independence, which contributes to parenting difficulties (Collins & Steinberg, 2006; Steinberg & Silk, 2002). A study by Reed Larson and Marsye Richards (1994) provided a portrait of the hour-by-hour emotional realities lived by families with adolescents. Differences between the fast-paced daily realities lived by each family member created considerable potential for misunderstanding and conflict. Because each family member was often attending to different priorities, needs, and stressors, their realities were often out of sync. Even when they wanted to share leisure activity, their interests were at odds. One father said that his wife liked to shop, his daughter liked to play video games, and he liked to stay home. Although the main theme of this work was the hazards of contemporary life, some families with adolescents were buoyant, and their lives were coordinated. Later in the chapter, we will discuss the adaptations needed to become a competent parent as children become adolescents.

Parenting Styles

Although the specific issues faced by parents change as a child grows up, at every age parents face choices about how much to respond to a child's needs, how much control to exert, and how to exert it. Parents want their children to grow into socially mature individuals, but they may feel frustrated in trying to discover the best way to accomplish this.

Advice from experts has varied over the years. In the 1930s, John Watson argued that parents are too affectionate with their children. In the 1950s, a distinction was made between physical and psychological discipline. Psychological discipline, especially reasoning, was emphasized as the best way to rear a child. Since the 1970s developmentalists have constructed more precise dimensions of competent parenting.

Baumrind's Styles Especially influential is the work of Diana Baumrind (1971). She believes parents should be neither punitive nor aloof. Rather, they should develop rules for their children and be affectionate with them. She has described four types of parenting styles:

- **Authoritarian parenting** is a restrictive, punitive style in which parents exhort the child to follow their directions and respect their work and effort. The authoritarian parent places firm limits and controls on the child and allows little verbal exchange. For example, an authoritarian parent might say, "You do it my way or else." Authoritarian parents also might spank the child frequently, enforce rules rigidly but not explain them, and show rage toward the child. Children of authoritarian parents are often unhappy, fearful, and anxious about comparing themselves with others, fail to initiate activity, and have weak communication skills. Sons of authoritarian parents may behave aggressively (Hart & others, 2003).
- **Authoritative parenting** encourages children to be independent but still places limits and controls on their actions. Extensive verbal give-and-take is allowed, and parents are warm and nurturant toward the child. An authoritative parent might put his arm around the child in a comforting way and say, "You know you should not have done that. Let's talk about how you can handle the situation better next time." Authoritative parents show pleasure and support in response to children's constructive behavior. They also expect mature, independent, and age-appropriate behavior by children. Children whose parents are authoritative are often cheerful, self-controlled and self-reliant, and achievement-oriented; they tend to maintain friendly relations with peers, cooperate with adults, and cope well with stress.
- **Neglectful parenting** is a style in which the parent is very uninvolved in the child's life. Children whose parents are neglectful develop the sense that other aspects of the parents' lives are more important than they are. These children tend to be socially incompetent. Many have poor self-control and don't handle independence well. They frequently have low self-esteem, are immature, and may be alienated from the family. In adolescence, they may show patterns of truancy and delinquency.

authoritarian parenting This is a restrictive, punitive style in which the parent exhorts the child to follow the parent's directions and to respect their work and effort. Firm limits and controls are placed on the child, and little verbal exchange is allowed. This style is associated with children's socially incompetent behavior.

authoritative parenting This style encourages children to be independent but still places limits and controls on their actions. Extensive verbal give-and-take is allowed, and parents are warm and nurturant toward the child. This style is associated with children's socially competent behavior.

neglectful parenting A style in which the parent is very uninvolved in the child's life. It is associated with children's social incompetence, especially a lack of self-control.

	Accepting, responsive	Rejecting, unresponsive
Demanding, controlling	Authoritative	Authoritarian
Undemanding, uncontrolling	Indulgent	Neglectful

FIGURE 15.2 Classification of Parenting Styles. The four types of parenting styles (authoritative, authoritarian, indulgent, and neglectful) involve the dimensions of acceptance and responsiveness on the one hand and demand and control on the other. For example, authoritative parenting involves being both accepting/responsive and demanding/controlling.

- **Indulgent parenting** is a style of parenting in which parents are highly involved with their children but place few demands or controls on them. Such parents let their children do what they want. The result is that the children never learn to control their own behavior and always expect to get their way. Some parents deliberately rear their children in this way because they believe the combination of warm involvement and few restraints will produce a creative, confident child. However, children whose parents are indulgent rarely learn respect for others and have difficulty controlling their behavior. They might be domineering, egocentric, noncompliant, and have difficulties in peer relations.

These four classifications of parenting involve combinations of acceptance and responsiveness on the one hand and demand and control on the other (Maccoby & Martin, 1983). How these dimensions combine to produce authoritarian, authoritative, neglectful, and indulgent parenting is shown in figure 15.2.

Why is authoritative parenting likely to be the most effective style? These reasons have been given (Hart, Newell, & Olsen, 2003; Steinberg & Silk, 2002):

1. Authoritative parents establish an appropriate balance between control and autonomy, giving children opportunities to develop independence while providing the standards, limits, and guidance that children need (Reuter & Conger, 1995).
2. Authoritative parents are more likely to engage children in verbal give-and-take and allow children to express their views (Kuczynski & Lollis, 2002). This type of family discussion is likely to help children to understand social relationships and what is required for being a socially competent person.
3. The warmth and parental involvement provided by authoritative parents make the child more receptive to parental influence (Sim, 2000).

Parenting Styles and Ethnicity Do the benefits of authoritative parenting transcend the boundaries of ethnicity, socioeconomic status, and household composition? Although occasional exceptions have been found, evidence linking authoritative parenting with competence on the part of the child occurs in research across a wide range of ethnic groups, social strata, cultures, and family structures (Steinberg & Silk, 2002).

Nonetheless, researchers have found that in some ethnic groups, aspects of the authoritarian style may be associated with more positive child outcomes than Baumrind predicts. Elements of the authoritarian style may take on different meanings and have different effects depending on the context.

For example, Asian American parents often continue aspects of traditional Asian child-rearing practices that have sometimes been described as authoritarian. The parents exert considerable control over their children's lives. However, Ruth Chao (2001, 2005; Chao & Tseng, 2002) argues that the style of parenting used by many Asian American parents is distinct from the domineering control of the authoritarian style. Instead, Chao argues that the control reflects the parents' concern and involvement in their children's lives and is best conceptualized as a type of training. The high academic achievement of Asian American children may be a consequence of their "training" parents (Stevenson & Zusho, 2002).

An emphasis on requiring respect and obedience is also associated with the authoritarian style, but in Latino child rearing this focus may be positive rather than punitive. Rather than suppressing the child's development, it may encourage the development of a different type of self. Latino child-rearing practices encourage the

indulgent parenting A style in which parents are highly involved with their children but place few demands or controls on them. This is associated with children's social incompetence, especially a lack of self-control.

development of a self and identity that is embedded in the family (Harwood & others, 2002). Furthermore, many Latino families have several generations living together and helping each other (Zinn & Wells, 2000). In these circumstances, emphasizing respect and obedience by children may be part of maintaining a harmonious home and important in the formation of the child's identity.

Even physical punishment, another characteristic of the authoritarian style, may have varying effects in different contexts. African American parents are more likely than non-Latino White parents to use physical punishment (Deater-Deckard & Dodge, 1997). However, the use of physical punishment has been linked with increased externalized problems (such as acting out and high levels of aggression) in non-Latino White families but not African American families. One explanation of this finding points to the need for African American parents to enforce rules in the dangerous environments in which they are more likely to live (Harrison-Hale, McLoyd, & Smedley, 2004). In this context, requiring obedience to parental authority may be an adaptive strategy to keep children from engaging in antisocial behavior that can have serious consequences for the victim or the perpetrator. As we see next, though, overall, the use of physical punishment in disciplining children raises many concerns.

Punishment

For centuries, corporal (physical) punishment, such as spanking, has been considered a necessary and even desirable method of disciplining children (Greven, 1991). Use of corporal punishment is legal in every state in America, and it is estimated that 70 to 90 percent of American parents have spanked their children (Straus, 1991). A recent national survey of U.S. parents with 3- and 4-year-old children found that 26 percent of parents reported spanking their children frequently and 67 percent of the parents reported yelling at their children frequently (Regalado & others, 2004). A recent cross-cultural comparison found that individuals in the United States and Canada were among those with the most favorable attitudes toward corporal punishment and were most likely to remember it being used by their parents (Curran & others, 2001).

Despite the widespread use of corporal punishment, there have been surprisingly few research studies on physical punishment, and those that have been conducted are correlational (Baumrind, Larzelere, & Cowan, 2002; Benjet & Kazdin, 2003; Kazdin & Benjet, 2003). Clearly, it would be highly unethical to randomly assign parents to either spank or not spank their children in an experimental study. Recall that cause and effect cannot be determined in a correlational study. In one correlational study, spanking by parents was linked with children's antisocial behavior, including cheating, telling lies, being mean to others, bullying, getting into fights, and being disobedient (Strauss, Sugarman, & Giles-Sims, 1997).

A recent research review concluded that corporal punishment by parents is associated with higher levels of immediate compliance and aggression by the children (Gershoff, 2002). The review also found that it is associated with lower levels of moral internalization and mental health (Gershoff, 2002). A longitudinal study found that spanking before age 2 was related to behavioral problems in middle and late childhood (Slade & Wissow, 2004). Some critics, though, argue that the research evidence is not yet sound enough to warrant a blanket injunction against corporal punishment, especially mild corporal punishment (Baumrind, Larzelere, & Cowan, 2002; Kazdin & Benjet, 2003).

What are some reasons for avoiding spanking or similar punishments? The reasons include:

- When adults punish a child by yelling, screaming, or spanking, they are presenting children with out-of-control models for handling stressful situations. Children may imitate this aggressive, out-of-control behavior (Sim & Ong, 2005).
- Punishment can instill fear, rage, or avoidance. For example, spanking the child may cause the child to avoid being around the parent and to fear the parent.

- Punishment tells children what not to do rather than what to do. Children should be given feedback, such as "Why don't you try this?"
- Punishment can be abusive. When parents discipline their children, they might not intend to be abusive but become so aroused when they are punishing the child that they become abusive (Ateah, 2005; Baumrind, Larzelere, & Cowan, 2002).

Because of reasons such as these, Sweden passed a law in 1979 forbidding parents to physically punish children (by spanking or slapping, for example). Since the law was enacted youth rates of delinquency, alcohol abuse, rape, and suicide have dropped in Sweden (Durrant, 2000). These improvements may have occurred for other reasons, such as changing attitudes and opportunities for youth. Nonetheless, the Swedish experience suggests that physical punishment of children may be unnecessary. Other countries that have passed antispanking laws include Finland (1984), Denmark (1986), Norway (1987), Austria (1989), Cyprus (1994), Latvia (1998), Croatia (1999), Germany (2000), and Israel (2000).

Most child psychologists recommend reasoning with the child, especially explaining the consequences of the child's actions for others, as the best way to handle children's misbehaviors. The time-out technique, in which the child is removed from a setting where the child experiences positive reinforcement, can also be effective. For example, when the child has misbehaved, a parent might take away TV viewing for a specified period of time.

Earlier in the chapter, we described the importance of viewing the family as a system. In this discussion, we indicated that researchers have been increasingly interested in possible links between marital relationships and parenting practices (Cox & others, 2004). To read about a recent family systems study involving marital conflict and the use of physical punishment, see the Research in Child Development interlude.

RESEARCH IN CHILD DEVELOPMENT

Marital Conflict, Individual Hostility, and the Use of Physical Punishment

A longitudinal study assessed couples across the transition to parenting to investigate possible links between marital conflict, individual adult hostility, and the use of physical punishment with young children (Kanoy & others, 2003). Before the birth of the first child, the level of marital conflict was observed in a marital problem-solving discussion; answers to questionnaires regarding individual characteristics were also obtained. Thus, these characteristics of the couples were not influenced by characteristics of the child. When the children were 2 and 5 years old, the couples were interviewed about the frequency and intensity of their physical punishment of the children. At both ages, the parents' level of marital conflict was again observed in a marital problem-solving discussion.

The researchers found that both hostility and marital conflict were linked with the use of physical punishment. Individuals with high rates of hostility on the prenatal measures used more frequent and more severe physical punishment with their children. The same was evident for marital conflict—when marital conflict was high, both mothers and fathers were more likely to use physical punishment in disciplining their young children.

If parents who have a greater likelihood of using physical punishment can be identified, these at-risk families could be encouraged to use alternative discipline practices before they get into a pattern of physically punishing their children. This might be accomplished in prenatal classes.

Child Maltreatment

Unfortunately, punishment sometimes leads to the abuse of infants and children (Sabol, Coulton, & Polousky, 2004). In 2002, approximately 896,000 U.S. children were found to be victims of child abuse (U.S. Department of Health and Human Services, 2003). Eighty-four percent of these children were abused by a parent or parents. Laws in many states now require doctors and teachers to report suspected cases of child abuse, yet many cases go unreported, especially those of battered infants.

Many people have difficulty understanding parents who abuse or neglect their children. Our response is often outrage and anger at the parent. This outrage focuses attention on parents as bad, sick, monstrous, sadistic individuals who cause their children to suffer. Experts on child abuse believe that this view is too simple and deflects attention away from the social context of the abuse and the parents' coping skills. It is important to recognize that child abuse is a diverse condition, that it is usually mild to moderate in severity, and that it is only partially caused by personality characteristics of the parent (Azar, 2002; Field, 2000). Most often, the abuser is not a raging, uncontrolled physical abuser but an overwhelmed single mother in poverty who neglects the child.

Whereas the public and many professionals use the term *child abuse* to refer to both abuse and neglect, developmentalists increasingly use the term *child maltreatment* (Cicchetti & Blender, 2004; Cicchetti & Toth, 2005, 2006). This term does not have quite the emotional impact of the term *abuse* and acknowledges that maltreatment includes diverse conditions.

www.mhhe.com/santrockcd11

National Clearinghouse on Child Abuse and Neglect
Child Abuse Prevention Network
International Aspects of Child Abuse

Types of Child Maltreatment

The four main types of child maltreatment are physical abuse, child neglect, sexual abuse, and emotional abuse (National Clearinghouse on Child Abuse and Neglect, 2002, 2004):

- *Physical abuse* is characterized by the infliction of physical injury as result of punching, beating, kicking, biting, burning, shaking, or otherwise harming a child. The parent or other person may not have intended to hurt the child; the injury may have resulted from excessive physical punishment (Hornor, 2005; Maguire & others, 2005).
- *Child neglect* is characterized by failure to provide for the child's basic needs (Dubowitz, Pitts, & Black, 2004; Golden, Samuels, & Southall, 2003). Neglect can be physical, educational, or emotional:
  —Physical neglect includes refusal of, or delay in, seeking health care; abandonment; expulsion from the home or refusal to allow a runaway to return home; and inadequate supervision.
  —Educational neglect involves the allowance of chronic truancy, failure to enroll a child of mandatory school age in school, and failure to attend to a special education need.
  —Emotional neglect includes such actions as marked inattention to the child's needs for affection; refusal of or failure to provide necessary psychological care; spouse abuse in the child's presence; and permission of drug or alcohol use by the child.
- *Sexual abuse* includes fondling a child's genitals, intercourse, incest, rape, sodomy, exhibitionism, and commercial exploitation through prostitution or the production of pornographic materials. Many experts believe that sexual abuse is the most underreported type of child maltreatment because of the secrecy or "conspiracy of silence" that so often characterizes sexual abuse cases (Hobbins, 2004; Jones & Worthington, 2005; London, Bruck, & Ceci, 2005).
- *Emotional abuse (psychological/verbal abuse/mental injury)* includes acts or omissions by parents or other caregivers that have caused, or could cause, serious

behavioral, cognitive, or emotional problems (Gelles & Cavanaugh, 2005). In some cases of emotional abuse that warrant intervention, the child's behavior and condition do not reveal that the child has been harmed. For example, parents or others may use unusual types of punishment, such as confining a child in a dark closet. Less severe acts, such as frequent belittling and rejection of the child, are often difficult to prove and make it difficult for child protective services to intervene.

Although any of these forms of child maltreatment may be found separately, they often occur in combination. Emotional abuse is almost always present when other forms are identified.

The Context of Abuse Researchers have found that no single factor causes child maltreatment (Cicchetti & Toth, 2005, 2006). A combination of factors, including the culture, family, and development, likely contribute to child maltreatment.

The extensive violence that takes place in American culture is reflected in the occurrence of violence in the family (Azar, 2002). A regular diet of violence appears on television screens, and parents often resort to power assertion as a disciplinary technique. In China, where physical punishment is rarely used to discipline children, the incidence of child abuse is reported to be very low.

Other aspects of the culture may be linked to abuse. In the United States, many abusing parents report that they do not have sufficient resources or help from others. This may be a realistic evaluation of the situation of many low-income families.

The family itself is obviously a key part of the context of abuse. The interactions of all family members need to be considered, regardless of who performs the violent acts against the child (Kim & Cicchetti, 2004; Margolin, 1994). For example, even though the father may be the one who physically abuses the child, contributions by the mother, the child, and siblings also should be evaluated.

The parents' personal history and beliefs have also been linked to abuse. Many parents who abuse their children come from families in which physical punishment was used. These parents view physical punishment as a legitimate way of controlling the child's behavior.

Were parents who abuse children abused by their own parents? About one-third of parents who were abused themselves when they were young abuse their own children (Cicchetti & Toth, 2005, 2006). Thus, some, but not a majority, of parents are locked into an intergenerational transmission of abuse (Dixon, Browne, & Hamilton-Giachritsis, 2005; Leifer & others, 2004). Mothers who break out of the intergenerational transmission of abuse often have at least one warm, caring adult in their background; have a close, positive marital relationship; and have received therapy (Egeland, Jacobvitz, & Sroufe, 1988).

Developmental Consequences of Abuse Among the developmental consequences of child maltreatment are poor emotion regulation, attachment problems, problems in peer relations, difficulty in adapting to school, and other psychological problems (Azar, 2002; Cicchetti & Toth, 2005, 2006). Maltreated infants may show excessive negative affect (such as irritability and crying), or they may display blunted positive affect (rarely smiling or laughing). When younger children are maltreated, they often show insecure attachment patterns in their social relationships later in development (Cicchetti & Toth, 2005, 2006). Maltreated children appear to be poorly equipped to develop successful peer relations. They tend to be overly aggressive with peers or avoid interacting with peers (Bolger & Patterson, 2001). Abused and neglected children are at risk for academic problems (Cicchetti & Toth, 2005).

Being physically abused has been linked with children's anxiety, personality problems, depression, suicide attempts, conduct disorder, and delinquency (Danielson & others, 2005; Malmgren & Meisel, 2004; Zielinski, Campa, & Eckenrode, 2003). Later, during the adult years, maltreated children often have difficulty in establishing and maintaining healthy intimate relationships (Colman & Widom, 2004). As adults, maltreated children also show increased violence toward other adults, dating partners, and marital partners, as well as increased substance abuse, anxiety, and depression (Sachs-Ericsson & others, 2005; Shea & others, 2005). In sum, maltreated children are at risk for developing a wide range of problems and disorders (Arias, 2004; Haugaard & Hazan, 2004).

An important strategy is to prevent child maltreatment (Cicchetti & Toth, 2005, 2006; Lyons, Henly, & Schuerman, 2005). In one recent study of maltreating mothers and their 1-year-olds, two treatments were effective in reducing child maltreatment: (1) home visitation that emphasized improved parenting, coping with stress, and increasing support for the mother, and (2) parent-infant psychotherapy that focused on improving maternal-infant attachment (Cicchetti, Toth, & Rogusch, 2005).

Parenting Takes Time and Effort

In today's society, there is an unfortunate theme that suggests that parenting can be done quickly and with little or no inconvenience (Sroufe, 2000). One example is the marketing of Mozart CDs with the promise that playing them will enrich infants' and young children's brains. Some parents might be thinking "I don't have enough time to spend with my children so I'll just play these intellectual CDs and then they won't need me as much." Judith Harris' book *The Nurture Assumption* (which states that heredity and peer relations are the key factors in children's development) fits into this theme that parents don't need to spend much time with their children. Why did Harris' book become so popular? To some degree, some people who don't spend much time with their children saw it as supporting their neglect and reducing their guilt.

One-minute bedtime stories also are now being marketed successfully for parents to read to their children (Walsh, 2000). Most of these are brief summaries of longer stories. There are one-minute bedtime bear books, puppy books, and so on. These parents know it is good for them to read with their children, but they don't want to spend a lot of time doing it.

What is wrong with these quick-fix approaches to parenting? Good parenting takes time and effort (Bradley & Corwyn, 2004; Powell, 2005). You can't do it in a minute here and a minute there. You can't do it with CDs. Of course, it's not just the quantity of time parents spend with children that is important for children's development—the quality of the parenting is clearly important.

Parents who do not spend enough time with their children or who have problems in child rearing can benefit from counseling and therapy. To read about the work of marriage and family counselor Darla Botkin, see the Careers in Child Development insert.

CAREERS in CHILD DEVELOPMENT

Darla Botkin
Marriage and Family Therapist

Darla Botkin is a marriage and family therapist who teaches, conducts research, and engages in therapy in the area of marriage and family therapy. She is on the faculty of the University of Kentucky. Darla obtained a bachelor's degree in elementary education with a concentration in special education and then went on to receive a master's degree in early childhood education. She spent the next six years working with children and their families in a variety of settings, including day care, elementary school, and Head Start. These experiences led Darla to recognize the interdependence of the developmental settings that children and their parents experience (such as home, school, and work). She returned to graduate school and obtained a Ph.D. in family studies from the University of Tennessee. She then became a faculty member in the Family Studies program at the University of Kentucky. Completing further coursework and clinical training in marriage and family therapy, she became licensed as a marriage and family therapist in the state of Kentucky and an Approved Supervisor with the American Association for Marriage and Family Therapy.

Darla's current interests include (1) working with young children in family therapy and (2) the use of play in clinical, educational, and business settings.

Darla Botkin (*left*), conducting a family therapy session.

Review and Reflect • LEARNING GOAL 2

2 Explain how parenting is linked to children's development

Review

- What are some dimensions of the parental role?
- How can parenting be adapted to the developmental changes in the child?
- What are the four main styles of parenting? How are they linked to children's development?
- How does punishment affect children?
- What are some factors involved in child maltreatment? What are the developmental outcomes of child maltreatment?
- How does effective parenting involve time and effort?

Reflect

- In our discussion of parenting, authoritative parenting was associated with children's social competence. In some cases, though, a child's parents differ in their parenting styles. Consider all four parenting styles–authoritarian, authoritative, neglectful, and indulgent–on the parts of the mother and father. A best case is when both parents are authoritative. What might be the effects on the child when one parent uses one style and the other parent uses a different style? Also, consider what style or styles of parenting your mother and father used in rearing you. What effects do you think their parenting style(s) had on your development?

3 FAMILIES AND ADOLESCENTS

Autonomy | Attachment | Parent-Adolescent Conflict

Shelley Schwarz, whose story we discussed in the opening to this chapter, offers this advice: "To a parent of teenagers, I have one statement: Pick your battles carefully! Teenagers desperately want more control in their lives, and one way or another they'll get it" (Schwarz, 2004). What roles do autonomy and attachment play in parent-adolescent relationships?

Autonomy

When I was a boy of 14, my father was so ignorant I could hardly stand to have the man around. But when I got to be 21, I was astonished at how much he had learnt in 7 years.

—Mark Twain
American Writer and Humorist, 19th Century

The adolescent's push for autonomy and responsibility puzzles and angers many parents. Parents see their teenager slipping from their grasp. They may have an urge to take stronger control as the adolescent seeks autonomy and responsibility. Heated emotional exchanges may ensue, with either side calling names, making threats, and doing whatever seems necessary to gain control. Parents may seem frustrated because they expect their teenager to heed their advice, to want to spend time with the family, and to grow up to do what is right. Most parents anticipate that their teenager will have some difficulty adjusting to the changes that adolescence brings, but few parents can imagine and predict just how strong an adolescent's desires will be to spend time with peers or how much adolescents will want to show that it is they—not their parents—who are responsible for their successes and failures.

Gender differences characterize autonomy-granting in adolescence with boys being given more independence than girls. In one recent study, this was especially true in U.S. families with a traditional gender-role orientation (Bumpus, Crouter, & McHale, 2001).

Cultural differences also characterize adolescent autonomy. In one study, U.S. adolescents sought autonomy earlier than Japanese adolescents (Rothbaum & others, 2000). In the transition to adulthood, Japanese youth are less likely to live outside the home than Americans are (Hendry, 1999).

The ability to attain autonomy and gain control over one's behavior in adolescence is acquired through appropriate adult reactions to the adolescent's desire for control. At the onset of adolescence, the average individual does not have the knowledge to make appropriate or mature decisions in all areas of life. As the adolescent pushes for autonomy, the wise adult relinquishes control in those areas in which the adolescent can make reasonable decisions but continues to guide the adolescent to make reasonable decisions in areas in which the adolescent's knowledge is more limited. Gradually, adolescents acquire the ability to make mature decisions on their own.

The continued involvement of parents may be important to how adolescents handle their increased autonomy. In the National Longitudinal Study on Adolescent Health, adolescents who did not eat dinner with a parent five or more days a week had dramatically higher rates of smoking, drinking, marijuana use, getting into fights, and early initiation of sexual activity (Council of Economic Advisors, 2000). In another recent study, parents who played an active role in monitoring and guiding their adolescents' development were more likely to have adolescents with positive peer relations and lower drug use than parents who had a less active role (Mounts, 2002).

Parents' and Adolescents' Expectations
Parenting Adolescents

Attachment

Despite their desire for autonomy, most adolescents continue to be attached to their parents. In the past several decades, developmentalists have applied the concepts of secure and insecure attachment, which we discussed in chapter 11, "Emotional Development," and related concepts, such as connectedness to parents, to adolescence (Allen & others, 2004). They argue that secure attachment to parents in adolescence may facilitate the adolescent's social competence and well-being, as reflected in such characteristics as self-esteem, emotional adjustment, and physical health (Egeland & Carlson, 2004; Allen & others, 2003). In the research of Joseph Allen and his colleagues (Allen & Hauser, 1994; Allen & others, 2003, 2004), securely attached adolescents had somewhat lower probabilities of engaging in problem behaviors.

Many studies that assess secure and insecure attachment in adolescence use the Adult Attachment Interview (AAI) (George, Main, & Kaplan, 1984). This measure examines an individual's memories of significant attachment relationships. Based on the responses to questions on the AAI, individuals are classified as having **secure-autonomous attachment,** which corresponds to secure attachment in infancy, or one of these three insecure categories:

- **Dismissing/avoidant attachment** is an insecure category in which individuals de-emphasize the importance of attachment. This category is associated with consistent experiences of the rejection of attachment needs by caregivers. One possible outcome of dismissing/avoidant attachment is that parents and adolescents may mutually distance themselves from each other, which lessens parents' influence. In one study, dismissing/avoidant attachment was related to violent and aggressive behavior by the adolescent.
- **Preoccupied/ambivalent attachment** is an insecure attachment category in which adolescents are hypertuned to attachment experiences. This is thought to occur mainly when parents are inconsistently available to the adolescent. The result may be a high degree of attachment-seeking behavior, mixed with angry feelings. Conflict between parents and adolescents in this type of attachment may be too great for healthy development.
- **Unresolved/disorganized attachment** is an insecure category in which the adolescent has an unusually high level of fear and is disoriented. This may result from such traumatic experiences as a parent's death or abuse by parents.

secure-autonomous attachment A positive attachment to parents in adolescents that corresponds to secure attachment in infancy.

dismissing/avoidant attachment An insecure attachment category in which individuals de-emphasize the importance of attachment. This category is associated with consistent experiences of rejection of attachment needs by caregivers.

preoccupied/ambivalent attachment An insecure attachment category in which adolescents are hypertuned to attachment experiences. This is thought to mainly occur because parents are inconsistently available to the adolescent.

unresolved/disorganized attachment An insecure category in which the adolescent has an unusually high level of fear and is disoriented. This may result from such traumatic experiences as a parent's death or abuse by parents.

Secure attachment, or connectedness to parents, promotes competent peer relations and positive, close relationships outside of the family (Cassidy, 1999). In one investigation that assessed attachment to parents and peers, adolescents who were securely attached to parents also were securely attached to peers; those who were insecurely attached to parents also were more likely to be insecurely attached to peers (Armsden & Greenberg, 1984). There are times when adolescents reject closeness, connection, and attachment to their parents as they assert their ability to make decisions and to develop an identity. But, for the most part, the worlds of parents and peers are coordinated and connected, not uncoordinated and disconnected.

Parent-Adolescent Conflict

Although attachment to parents remains strong during adolescence, the connectedness is not always smooth. Early adolescence is a time when conflict with parents escalates beyond childhood levels (Collins & Steinberg, 2006; Riesch & others, 2003). This increase may be due to a number of factors: the biological changes of puberty, cognitive changes involving increased idealism and logical reasoning, social changes focused on independence and identity, maturational changes in parents, and expectations that are violated by parents and adolescents. The adolescent compares her parents to an ideal standard and then criticizes their flaws. A 13-year-old girl tells her mother, "That is the tackiest-looking dress I have ever seen. Nobody would be caught dead wearing that." The adolescent demands logical explanations for comments and discipline. A 14-year-old boy tells his mother, "What do you mean I have to be home at 10 P.M. because it's the way we do things around here? Why do we do things around here that way? It doesn't make sense to me."

Many parents see their adolescent changing from a compliant child to someone who is noncompliant, oppositional, and resistant to parental standards. When this happens, parents tend to clamp down and put more pressure on the adolescent to conform to parental standards. Parents often expect their adolescents to become mature adults overnight, instead of understanding that the journey takes 10 to 15 years. Parents who recognize that this transition takes time handle their youth more competently and calmly than those who demand immediate conformity to adult standards. The opposite tactic—letting adolescents do as they please without supervision—is also unwise.

Conflict with parents increases in early adolescence. A high degree of conflict characterizes some parent-adolescent relationships. One estimate of the proportion of parents and adolescents who engage in prolonged, intense, repeated, unhealthy conflict is about one in five families (Montemayor, 1982). Although this figure represents a minority of adolescents, it indicates that 4 to 5 million American families encounter serious, highly stressful parent-adolescent conflict. And this prolonged, intense conflict is associated with a number of adolescent problems—movement out of the home, juvenile delinquency, school dropout, pregnancy and early marriage, membership in religious cults, and drug abuse (Brook & others, 1990).

Usually, though, conflict does not escalate to tumultuous proportions (Laursen & Collins, 2004; Collins & Steinberg, 2006; Holmbeck, 1996; Steinberg & Silk, 2002). Much of the conflict involves the everyday events of family life, such as keeping a bedroom clean, dressing neatly, getting home by a certain time, and not talking forever on the phone. The conflicts rarely involve major dilemmas, such as drugs and delinquency.

It is not unusual to hear parents of young adolescents ask, "Is it ever going to get better?" Things usually do get better as adolescents move from early to late adolescence. Conflict with parents often escalates during early adolescence, remains somewhat stable during the high school years, and then lessens as the adolescent reaches 17 to 20 years of age. Parent-adolescent relationships become more positive

www.mhhe.com/santrockd11

Families as Asset Builders
Prevention of Adolescent Problems
Reengaging Families with Adolescents

Old Model	New Model
Autonomy, detachment from parents; parent and peer worlds are isolated	Attachment and autonomy; parents are important support systems and attachment figures; adolescent-parent and adolescent-peer worlds have some important connections
Intense, stressful conflict throughout adolescence; parent-adolescent relationships are filled with storm and stress on virtually a daily basis	Moderate parent-adolescent conflict common and can serve a positive developmental function; conflict greater in early adolescence, especially during the apex of puberty

FIGURE 15.3 Old and New Models of Parent-Adolescent Relationships

if adolescents go away to college than if they stay at home and go to college (Sullivan & Sullivan, 1980).

The everyday conflicts that characterize parent-adolescent relationships may actually serve a positive developmental function. These minor disputes and negotiations facilitate the adolescent's transition from being dependent on parents to becoming an autonomous individual. For example, in one study, adolescents who expressed disagreement with their parents explored identity development more actively than did adolescents who did not express disagreement with their parents (Cooper & others, 1982).

One way for parents to cope with the adolescent's push for independence and identity is to recognize that adolescence is a 10- to 15-year transitional period in the journey to adulthood, rather than an overnight accomplishment. Recognizing that conflict and negotiation can serve a positive developmental function can tone down parental hostility, too. Understanding parent-adolescent conflict, though, is not simple (Conger & Ge, 1999).

In sum, the old model of parent-adolescent relationships suggested that as adolescents mature they detach themselves from parents and move into a world of autonomy apart from parents. The old model also suggested that parent-adolescent conflict is intense and stressful throughout adolescence. The new model emphasizes that parents serve as important attachment figures and support systems as adolescents explore a wider, more complex social world. The new model also emphasizes that, in most families, parent-adolescent conflict is moderate rather than severe and that the everyday negotiations and minor disputes are normal and can serve the positive developmental function of helping the adolescent make the transition from childhood dependency to adult independence (see figure 15.3).

Review and Reflect • LEARNING GOAL 3

3 Summarize the changes in families with adolescents

Review

- What role does autonomy play in parent-adolescent relationships?
- What role does attachment play in parent-adolescent relationships?
- How extensive is parent-adolescent conflict? How does parent-adolescent conflict affect adolescent development?

Reflect

- What was the nature of your relationship with your parents during middle school and high school? Has your relationship with your parents changed since then? Does it involve less conflict? What do you think are the most important characteristics of a competent parent of adolescents?

4 SIBLINGS

Sibling Relationships

Birth Order

So far our examination of families has taken us through the nature of family processes and many aspects of parenting. Next, we explore another important aspect of family life for many children—siblings. More than 80 percent of American children have one or more siblings (brothers or sisters). An anecdote recounted by Shelley Schwarz (2004) captures some of the many possibilities of sibling relationships:

> Jamie and Andy were fighting over wooden building blocks and began throwing them at each other. . . . the stress was depleting my strength and ability to cope. . . . I didn't know what to do so I sent them to their bedrooms while I took time to think.
>
> Then a curious thing happened. While still in their rooms, the kids began talking to each other. Jamie thought of a way they could solve the problem. Andy vetoed it. They continued talking back and forth until a settlement was reached, all without my saying a word!

Of course, many sibling interactions involve less civilized endings. Sandra describes to her mother what happened in a conflict with her sister:

> We had just come home from the ball game. I sat down on the sofa next to the light so I could read. Sally [the sister] said, "Get up, I was sitting there first. I just got up for a second to get a drink." I told her I was not going to get up and that I didn't see her name on the chair. I got mad and started pushing her. Her drink spilled all over her. Then she got really mad; she shoved me against the wall, hitting and clawing at me. I managed to grab a handful of hair.

Sibling Relationships

Any of you who have grown up with siblings probably have a rich memory of aggressive, hostile interchanges. But sibling relationships also have many pleasant, caring moments (Noller, 2005; Volling, 2002; Zukow-Goldring, 2002). Children's sibling relationships include helping, sharing, teaching, fighting, and playing. Children can act as emotional supports, rivals, and communication partners (Carlson, 1995).

High sibling conflict can be detrimental to adolescent development, especially when combined with ineffective parenting. A longitudinal study revealed that a combination of ineffective parenting (poor problem-solving skills, weak supervision skills, parent-adolescent conflict) and sibling conflict (hitting, fighting, stealing, cheating) at 10 to 12 years of age was linked to antisocial behavior and poor peer relations from 12 to 16 years of age (Bank, Burraston, & Snyder, 2004). Also, by virtue of having a sibling, children may be treated differently by their parents (Brody, 2004).

Is sibling interaction different from parent-child interaction? There is some evidence that it is. Observations indicate that children interact more positively and in more varied ways with their parents than with their siblings (Baskett & Johnson, 1982). Children also follow their parents' dictates more than those of their siblings, and they behave more negatively and punitively with their siblings than with their parents. In some instances, siblings may be stronger socializing influences on the child than parents are (Circirelli, 1994). Someone close in age to the child—such as a sibling—may be able to understand the child's problems and communicate more effectively than parents can. In dealing with peers, coping with difficult teachers, and discussing such taboo subjects as sex, siblings may have more influence than parents.

Is sibling interaction the same around the world? In industrialized societies, such as the United States, parents tend to delegate responsibility for younger siblings to older siblings primarily to give the parents freedom to pursue other activities. However, in nonindustrialized countries, such as Kenya, the older sibling's role as a caregiver to younger siblings has much more importance. In industrialized countries, the older sibling's caregiving role is often discretionary; in nonindustrialized countries, it is more obligatory (Circirelli, 1994).

Because there are so many possible sibling combinations, it is difficult to generalize about sibling influences. Among the factors to consider are the number of siblings, the ages of siblings, birth order, age spacing, and the sex of siblings (Teti, 2001). There is something unique about same-sex sibling relationships. Aggression and dominance occur more in same-sex sibling relationships than opposite-sex sibling relationships (Minnett, Vandell, & Santrock, 1983).

Temperamental traits ("easy" and "difficult," for example), as well as differential treatment of siblings by parents, influence how siblings get along (Stocker & Dunn, 1991). Siblings with "easy" temperaments who are treated in relatively equal ways by parents tend to get along with each other the best. By contrast, siblings with "difficult" temperaments, or whose parents have given one of them preferential treatment, get along the worst. Variations in sibling relationships are also linked to birth order, as we discuss in the following section.

Big sisters are the crab grass in the lawn of life.

—CHARLES SCHULZ, "PEANUTS"
American Cartoonist, 20th Century

Birth Order

Birth order is a special interest of sibling researchers. The oldest sibling is expected to exercise self-control and show responsibility in interacting with younger siblings. When the oldest sibling is jealous or hostile, parents often protect the younger sibling. The oldest sibling is more dominant, competent, and powerful than the younger siblings. The oldest sibling is also expected to assist and teach younger siblings. Indeed, researchers have shown that older siblings are both more antagonistic—hitting, kicking, and biting—and more nurturant toward their younger siblings than vice versa (Abramovitch & others, 1986).

The influence of birth order goes well beyond its link with sibling relationships. Indeed, many people are fascinated by links between birth order and personality characteristics and achievement. For example, firstborn children are more adult-oriented, helpful, conforming, anxious, and self-controlled than their siblings. Firstborns excel in academic and professional endeavors. Firstborns are overrepresented in *Who's Who* and Rhodes scholars, for example. They also have more guilt, anxiety, and difficulty in coping with stressful situations, as well as higher admission to child guidance clinics, than other children.

What accounts for such differences related to birth order? Proposed explanations usually point to variations in interactions with parents and siblings associated with being in a particular position in the family. This is especially true in the case of the firstborn child (Teti & others, 1993). The oldest child is the only one who does not have to share parental love and affection with other siblings—until another sibling comes along. An infant requires more attention than an older child; this means that the firstborn sibling now gets less attention than before the newborn arrived. Does this result in conflict between parents and the firstborn? In one research study, mothers became more negative, coercive, and restraining and played less with the firstborn following the birth of a second child (Dunn & Kendrick, 1982).

Even though a new infant requires more attention from parents than does an older child, parents and firstborns often maintain an especially intense relationship throughout the life span. Parents have higher expectations for firstborn children than for later-born children. They put more pressure on them for achievement and responsibility. They also interfere more with their activities (Rothbart, 1971). The extra attention that firstborns receive has been linked to firstborns' nurturant behavior (Stanhope & Corter, 1993). Parental demands and high standards established for firstborns have been associated with both their achievement and their difficulties, such as anxiety and guilt. Given the differences in family dynamics involved in birth

The one-child family is becoming much more common in China because of the strong motivation to limit the population growth in the People's Republic of China. The policy is still relatively new, and its effects on children have not been fully examined. *In general, though, what have researchers found the only child to be like?*

order, it is not surprising that firstborns and later-borns have different characteristics (Zajonc, 2001).

What is the only child like? The popular conception is that the only child is a "spoiled brat," with such undesirable characteristics as dependency, lack of self-control, and self-centered behavior. But researchers present a more positive portrayal of the only child. Only children often are achievement-oriented and display a desirable personality, especially in comparison with later-borns and children from large families (Falbo & Poston, 1993; Jiao, Ji, & Jing, 1996).

So far, our consideration of birth-order effects suggests that birth order might be a strong predictor of behavior. However, an increasing number of family researchers believe that birth order has been overdramatized and overemphasized. The critics argue that, when all of the factors that influence behavior are considered, birth order itself shows limited ability to predict behavior. Consider sibling relationships alone. They vary not only in birth order but also in number of siblings, age of siblings, age spacing of siblings, and sex of siblings.

Think about some of the other important factors in children's lives that influence their behavior beyond birth order. They include heredity, models of competency or incompetency that parents present to children on a daily basis, peer influences, school influences, socioeconomic factors, sociohistorical factors, and cultural variations. When someone says firstborns are always like this but last-borns are always like that, you now know that the person is making overly simplistic statements that do not adequately take into account the complexity of influences on a child's behavior.

Review and Reflect • **LEARNING GOAL 4**

4 Identify how siblings influence children's development

Review

- How can sibling relationships be characterized?
- What role does birth order play in children's development?

Reflect

- If you grew up with a sibling, you likely showed some jealousy of your sibling and vice versa. What can parents do to help children reduce their jealousy toward a sibling?

5 THE CHANGING FAMILY IN A CHANGING SOCIAL WORLD

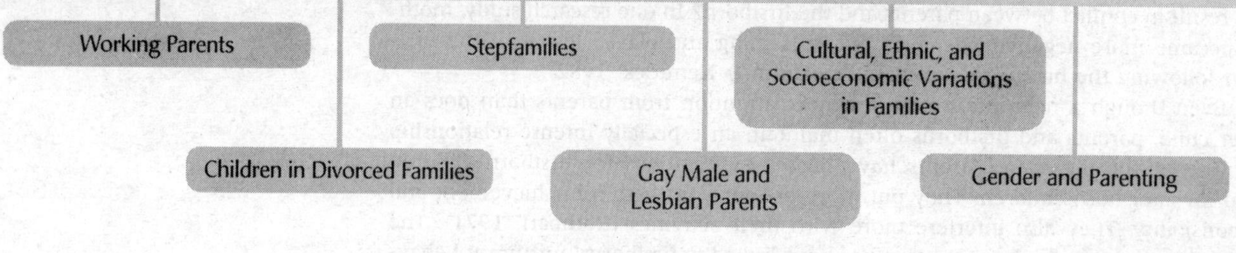

U.S. children are growing up in a greater variety of family contexts than ever before. As we discussed in chapter 11, "Emotional Development," the country's children are experiencing many sorts of caregiving—not only from stay-at-home mothers but also

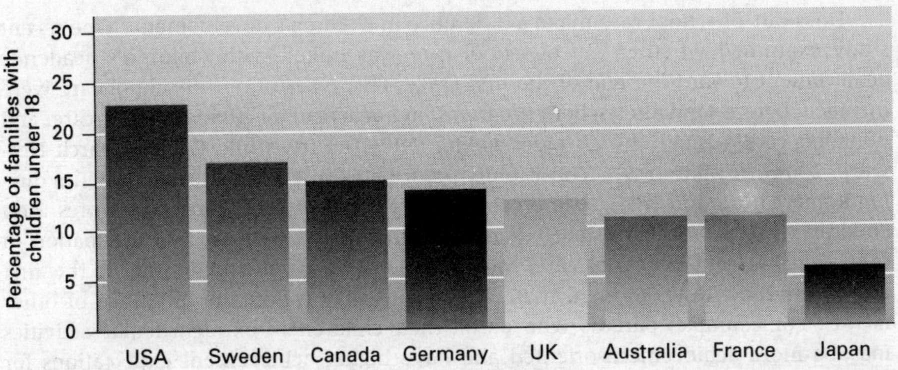

FIGURE 15.4 Single-Parent Families in Different Countries

from stay-at-home fathers, from different types of child-care programs, and from after-school programs. The structure of American families also varies. As shown in figure 15.4, the United States has a higher percentage of single-parent families than other countries with similar levels of economic and technological development. And many U.S. children are being raised in stepfamilies formed after a divorce and by gay male or lesbian parents. How are these and other variations in family life affecting children?

Working Parents

Many mothers spend the greatest part of their day away from their children, even their infants. More than one of every two U.S. mothers with a child under the age of 5 is in the labor force; more than two of every three with a child from 6 to 17 years of age is. And the increasing number of children growing up in single-parent families is staggering. Maternal employment is a part of modern life, but its effects are still debated.

Lois Hoffman (1989) described some possible influences of maternal employment on children's development. In her view, because household operations have become more efficient and family size has decreased in America, it is not certain that children today receive less attention when both parents work outside the home than children in the past whose mothers were not employed. Parents might spend less time than in the past keeping the house clean or pursuing hobbies. Time once split among several children might now be focused on just one or two. It also cannot be assumed that the child would benefit from the extra time and attention from a stay-at-home parent. Parenting does not always have a positive effect on the child. Parents may overinvest in their children, worrying excessively and discouraging the child's independence. The needs of the growing child require parents to give increasing independence to the child, which may be easier for parents whose jobs provide an additional source of identity and self-esteem.

A number of researchers have found no detrimental effects of maternal employment on children's development (Gottfried, Gottfried, & Bathurst, 2002; Hoffman & Youngblade, 1999). Work can produce positive and negative effects on parenting (Crouter & McHale, 2005). Work-related stress can spill over and harm parenting, but a sense of well-being produced by work can lead to more positive parenting.

However, when a child's mother works in the first year of life, it can have a negative effect on the child's later development (Belsky & Eggebeen, 1991; Hill & others, 2001). For example, a recent major longitudinal study found that the 3-year-old children of mothers who went to work before the children were 9 months old had poorer cognitive outcomes than 3-year-old children whose mothers had stayed at home with them in the first nine months of the child's life (Brooks-Gunn, Han, & Waldfogel, 2002). The negative effects of going to work during the child's first nine months were less pronounced when the mothers worked less than 30 hours a week, when the mothers were more responsive and comforting in their caregiving, and when the child care the children received outside the home was higher in quality.

Working Parents
Family and the Workplace

Does out-of-school care make a difference in children's development? One recent study examined whether out-of-school care was linked with children's academic achievement toward the end of the first grade. Five types of out-of-school care were included: before- and after-school programs, extracurricular activities, father care, and nonadult care—usually by an older sibling (NICHD Early Child Care Research Network, 2004). "Children who consistently participated in extracurricular activities during kindergarten and first grade obtained higher standardized math test scores than children who did not consistently participate in these activities. . . . Participation in other types of out-of-school care was not related to child functioning in the first grade" (p. 280). Note, though, that these results may reflect the influence of other factors. For example, parents who enroll their children in extracurricular activities may be more achievement-oriented and have higher achievement expectations for their children than parents who don't place their children in these activities.

The subset of children known as *latchkey children* deserves further scrutiny. These children are given the key to their home, take the key to school, and then use it to let themselves into the home while their parents are still at work. Latchkey children are largely unsupervised for two to four hours a day during each school week. During the summer months, they might be unsupervised for entire days, five days a week.

How do latchkey children handle the lack of limits and structure during the latchkey hours? In one study of more than 1,500 latchkey children, a slight majority had negative latchkey experiences (Long & Long, 1983). Without limits and parental supervision, latchkey children find their way into trouble more easily than other children, possibly stealing, vandalizing, or abusing a sibling. Ninety percent of the juvenile delinquents in Montgomery County, Maryland, are latchkey children. Joan Lipsitz (1983) called the lack of adult supervision of children in the after-school hours the "three-to-six-o'clock problem" because it was during this time that the Center for Early Adolescence in North Carolina, when Lipsitz was director, experienced a peak of referrals for clinical help.

Although latchkey children may be vulnerable to problems, their experiences vary enormously. Parents need to give special attention to the ways in which their latchkey children can be effectively monitored. Parental monitoring and authoritative parenting help the children cope more effectively with latchkey experiences, especially in resisting peer pressure (Galambos, 2004; Galambos & Maggs, 1989; Steinberg, 1986). In one study of children in the after-school hours, unsupervised peer contact, lack of neighborhood safety, and low monitoring were linked with externalizing problems such as acting out problems and delinquency (Pettit & others, 1999). In one recent study of 819 10- to 14-year-olds, out-of-home care, whether supervised or unsupervised, was linked to delinquency, drug and alcohol use, and school problems (Coley, Morris, & Hernandez, 2004).

After-school programs can make a difference in children's lives. One study compared elementary-school children who attended a formal after-school program that included academic, recreational, and remedial activities with children who had only informal adult supervision after school or were on their own (Posner & Vandell, 1994). Participation in the formal after-school program was associated with better academic achievement and social adjustment.

A recent study found that low-income parents were especially dissatisfied with the quality of options available in after-school programs (Wallace Foundation, 2004). Researchers and policymakers recommend that after-school programs have warm and supportive staff, a flexible and relaxed schedule, multiple activities, and opportunities for positive interactions with staff and peers (Vandell & Pierce, 2002).

Children in Divorced Families

Divorce rates changed rather dramatically in the United States and many countries around the world in the late twentieth century. The U.S. divorce rate increased dramatically in the 1960s and 1970s but has declined since the 1980s (Amato, 2005).

By comparison, the divorce rate in Japan increased in the 1990s (Ministry of Health, Education, and Welfare, 2002). However, the divorce rate in the United States is still much higher than in Japan and higher than most other countries as well. It is estimated that 40 percent of children born to married parents in the United States will experience their parents' divorce (Hetherington & Stanley-Hagan, 2002).

These are the questions that we will explore regarding the influence of divorce: Are children better adjusted in intact, never-divorced families than in divorced families? Should parents stay together for the sake of their children? How much do family processes matter in divorced families? What factors influence the child's vulnerability to social and psychological problems in a divorced family? What role does socioeconomic status play in the lives of children in divorced families?

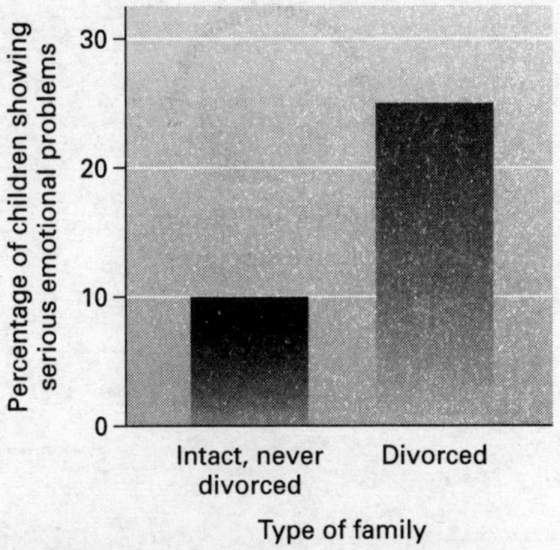

FIGURE 15.5 Divorce and Children's Emotional Problems. In Hetherington's research, 25 percent of children from divorced families showed serious emotional problems compared to only 10 percent of children from intact, never-divorced families. However, keep in mind that a substantial majority (75 percent) of the children from divorced families did not show serious emotional problems.

Are Children Better Adjusted in Intact, Never-Divorced Families Than in Divorced Families? Most researchers agree that children from divorced families show poorer adjustment than their counterparts in nondivorced families (Amato & Keith, 1991; Fine & Harvey, 2005; Harvey & Fine, 2004; Hetherington & Stanley-Hagan, 2002) (see figure 15.5). Those children who have experienced multiple divorces are at greater risk.

Children in divorced families are more likely than children in nondivorced families to have academic problems, to show externalized problems (such as acting out and delinquency) and internalized problems (such as anxiety and depression), to be less socially responsible, to have less competent intimate relationships, to drop out of school, to become sexually active at an early age, to take drugs, to associate with antisocial peers, and to have low self-esteem (Conger & Chao, 1996). Nonetheless, keep in mind that a majority of children in divorced families (about 75 percent) do not have significant adjustment problems (Buchanan, 2001). In a 20-year longitudinal study, a large majority of the young adults whose parents divorced when they were children were adapting and functioning effectively (Ahrons, 2004).

Should Parents Stay Together for the Sake of Their Children?

Whether parents should stay in an unhappy or conflict-filled marriage for the sake of their children is one of the most commonly asked questions about divorce (Hetherington, 1999, 2000). If a divorce reduces the stresses and disruptions associated with an unhappy marriage that erode children's well-being, then divorce can be advantageous. However, if the diminished resources associated with divorce are accompanied by inept parenting and sustained or increased conflict—not only between the divorced couple but also between the parents, children, and siblings—then the best choice for the children would be to continue the unhappy marriage (Hetherington & Stanley-Hagan, 2002). These are "ifs": parents cannot be certain ahead of time how the possibilities will play out. Note that marital conflict may have negative consequences for children in the context of either marriage or divorce (Cummings, Braungart-Rieker, & Du Rocher-Schudlich, 2003; Cummings & Davies, 2002; Hetherington & Kelly, 2002).

How Much Do Family Processes Matter in Divorced Families?

Family processes matter a lot (Emery & others, 2001; Fine, Ganong, & Demo, 2005; Hetherington & Stanley-Hagan, 2002; Kelly, 2001; Wallerstein & Johnson-Reitz, 2004). When divorced parents' relationship with each other is harmonious and when they use authoritative parenting, the adjustment of children improves (Hetherington, Bridges, & Insabella, 1998). A secure attachment also matters. One recent study found that experiencing a divorce in childhood was associated with insecure attachment in early adulthood (Brockmeyer, Treboux, & Crowell, 2005).

Responses to a divorce change over time. A number of researchers have shown that a disequilibrium, which includes diminished parenting skills, occurs in the year following the divorce. But by two years after the divorce, restabilization has occurred and parenting skills have improved (Hetherington, 1989).

www.mhhe.com/santrockcd11

Children and Divorce
Divorce Resources

About one-fourth to one-third of children in divorced families, compared with 10 percent in nondivorced families, become disengaged from their families, spending as little time as possible at home and in interaction with family members (Hetherington & Jodl, 1994). This disengagement is higher for boys than girls in divorced families. However, if there is a caring adult outside the home, such as a mentor, disengagement may be a positive solution to a disrupted, conflict-filled family.

What Factors Are Involved in the Child's Vulnerability in a Divorced Family? Among the factors involved in the child's vulnerability to emotional and social problems are the child's adjustment prior to the divorce as well as the child's personality, temperament, developmental status, and gender, and the custody situation (Hetherington & Stanley-Hagan, 2002). Children whose parents later divorce show poorer adjustment before the breakup (Amato & Booth, 1996). When antecedent levels of problem behaviors are controlled, differences found in the adjustment of children in divorced and nondivorced families decrease (Cherlin & others, 1991).

Personality and temperament play a role in children's adjustment in divorced families. Children who are socially mature and responsible, who show few behavioral problems, and who have an easy temperament are better able to cope with their parents' divorce. Children with a difficult temperament often have problems in coping with their parents' divorce (Hetherington & Stanley-Hagan, 2002).

Earlier studies reported gender differences in response to divorce, with divorce being more negative for boys than for girls in mother-custody families. However, more recent studies have shown that gender differences are less pronounced and consistent than was previously believed. Some of the inconsistency may be due to the increase in father custody, joint custody, and increased involvement of noncustodial fathers, especially in their sons' lives. One recent analysis of studies found that children in joint-custody families were better adjusted than children in sole-custody families (Bauserman, 2002). Some studies have shown that boys adjust better in father-custody families, girls in mother-custody families (Maccoby & Mnookin, 1992; Santrock & Warshak, 1979).

What Role Does Socioeconomic Status Play in the Lives of Children in Divorced Families? Custodial mothers experience the loss of about one-fourth to one-half of their predivorce income, in comparison with a loss of only one-tenth by custodial fathers (Emery, 1994). This income loss for divorced mothers is accompanied by increased workloads, high rates of job instability, and residential moves to less desirable neighborhoods with inferior schools.

In sum, many factors are involved in determining how divorce influences a child's development (Braver, Goodman, & Shapiro, 2005). To read about some strategies for helping children cope with the divorce of their parents, see the Caring for Children interlude.

CARING FOR CHILDREN

Communicating with Children About Divorce

Ellen Galinsky and Judy David (1988) developed a number of guidelines for communicating with children about divorce.

Explain the Separation

As soon as daily activities in the home make it obvious that one parent is leaving, tell the children. If possible, both parents should be present when children are told about the separation to come. The reasons for the separation are very difficult for young children to understand. No matter what parents tell children, children can find reasons to argue against the separation. A child may say something like, "If you don't love each other anymore, you need to start trying harder." One set of parents told their 4-year-old, "We both love you. We will both always love you and take care of you, but we aren't going to live in the same house anymore. Daddy is moving to an apartment near the stores where we shop." It is extremely important for parents to tell the children who will take care of them and to describe the specific arrangements for seeing the other parent.

Explain That the Separation Is Not the Child's Fault

Young children often believe their parents' separation or divorce is their own fault. Therefore, it is important to tell children that they are not the cause of the separation. Parents need to repeat this a number of times.

Explain That It May Take Time to Feel Better

It is helpful to tell young children that it's normal to not feel good about what is happening and that lots of other children feel this way when their parents become separated. It is also okay for divorced parents to share some of their emotions with children, by saying something like, "I'm having a hard time since the separation just like you, but I know it's going to get better after a while." Such statements are best kept brief and should not criticize the other parent.

Keep the Door Open for Further Discussion

Tell your children to come to you anytime they want to talk about the separation. It is healthy for children to express their pent-up emotions in discussions with their parents and to learn that the parents are willing to listen to their feelings and fears.

Provide as Much Continuity as Possible

The less children's worlds are disrupted by the separation, the easier their transition to a single-parent family will be. This means maintaining the rules already in place as much as possible. Children need parents who care enough to not only give them warmth and nurturance but also set reasonable limits. If the custodial parent has to move to a new home, it is important to preserve as much of what is familiar to the child as possible. In one family, the child helped arrange her new room exactly as it had been prior to the divorce. If children must leave friends behind, it is important for parents to help the children stay in touch by phone or by letter. Keeping the children busy and involved in the new setting can also keep their minds off stressful thoughts about the separation.

Provide Support for Your Children and Yourself

After a divorce or separation, parents are as important to children as before the divorce or separation. Divorced parents need to provide children with as much support as possible. Parents function best when other people are available to give them support as adults and as parents. Divorced parents can find people who provide practical help and with whom they can talk about their problems. One divorced parent commented, "I've made a mess of my life. I don't deserve anybody's help." Seeking out others for support and feedback about problems can make the transition to a single-parent family more bearable.

Stepfamilies

Not only has divorce become commonplace in the United States, so has getting remarried (Dunn & others, 2001). The number of remarriages involving children has grown steadily in recent years. Also, divorces occur at a 10 percent higher rate

How does living in a stepfamily influence a child's development?

in remarriages than in first marriages (Cherlin & Furstenberg, 1994). About half of all children whose parents divorce will have a stepparent within four years of the separation.

Remarried parents face some unique tasks. The couple must define and strengthen their marriage and at the same time renegotiate the biological parent-child relationships and establish stepparent-stepchild and stepsibling relationships (Ganong, Coleman, & Hans, 2005; Love & Murdock, 2004). The complex histories and multiple relationships make adjustment difficult in a stepfamily (Hetherington & Stanley-Hagan, 2002). Only one-third of stepfamily couples stay remarried.

In some cases, the stepfamily may have been preceded by the death of a spouse. However, by far the largest number of stepfamilies are preceded by divorce rather than death (Pasley & Moorefield, 2004). Three common types of stepfamily structure are (1) stepfather, (2) stepmother, and (3) blended or complex. In stepfather families, the mother typically had custody of the children and remarried, introducing a stepfather into her children's lives. In stepmother families, the father usually had custody and remarried, introducing a stepmother into his children's lives. In a blended or complex stepfamily, both parents bring children from previous marriages to live in the newly formed stepfamily.

Researchers have found that children often have better relationships with their custodial parents (mothers in stepfather families, fathers in stepmother families) than with stepparents (Santrock, Sitterle, & Warshak, 1988). Also, children in simple families (stepmother, stepfather) often show better adjustment than their counterparts in complex (blended) families (Anderson & others, 1999; Hetherington & Kelly, 2002).

www.mhhe.com/santrockcd11

Stepfamilies
Stepfamily Resources
Stepfamily Support

As in divorced families, children in stepfamilies show more adjustment problems than children in nondivorced families (Hetherington, Bridges, & Insabella, 1998; Hetherington & Kelly, 2002). The adjustment problems are similar to those found among children of divorced parents—academic problems and lower self-esteem, for example (Anderson & others, 1999). However, it is important to recognize that a majority of children in stepfamilies do not have problems. In one recent analysis, 25 percent of children from stepfamilies showed adjustment problems compared to 10 percent in intact, never-divorced families (Hetherington & Kelly, 2002; Hetherington & Stanley-Hagan, 2002).

Early adolescence is an especially difficult time for the formation of a stepfamily (Anderson & others, 1999). This may occur because becoming part of a stepfamily exacerbates normal adolescent concerns about identity, sexuality, and autonomy.

Gay Male and Lesbian Parents

Increasingly, gay male and lesbian couples are creating families that include children. Approximately 20 percent of lesbians and 10 percent of gay men are parents (Patterson, 2004). There may be more than 1 million gay and lesbian parents in the United States today.

Diversity Among Lesbian Mothers, Gay Fathers, and Their Children Gay male and lesbian parents may be single or they may have same-gender partners. Many lesbian mothers and gay fathers are noncustodial parents because they lost custody of their children to heterosexual spouses after a divorce.

Most children of gay and lesbian parents were born in a heterosexual relationship that ended in a divorce; in most cases, it was probably a relationship in which one or both parents only later identified themselves as gay male or lesbian. In other cases, lesbians and gay men became parents as a result of donor insemination and surrogates, or through adoption.

What are the research findings regarding the development and psychological well-being of children raised by gay male and lesbian couples?

Effects on Children of Having Lesbian Mothers and Gay Fathers

Parenthood among lesbians and gay men is controversial. Opponents claim that being raised by gay male or lesbian parents harms the child's development. But researchers have found few differences between children growing up with lesbian mothers or gay fathers and children growing up with heterosexual parents (Patterson, 2002, 2004; Wainright & Patterson, 2005). For example, children growing up in gay male or lesbian families are just as popular with their peers, and there are no differences in the adjustment and mental health of children living in these families when they are compared with children in heterosexual families (Hyde & DeLamater, 2005; Lambert, 2005). Also, the overwhelming majority of children growing up in a gay or lesbian family have a heterosexual orientation (Tasker & Golombok, 1997).

Cultural, Ethnic, and Socioeconomic Variations in Families

Parenting can be influenced by culture, ethnicity, and socioeconomic status. In Bronfenbrenner's theory, these influences are described as part of the macrosystem.

Cross-Cultural Studies Different cultures often give different answers to such basic questions as what the father's role in the family should be, what support systems are available to families, and how children should be disciplined (Harkness & Super, 2002). There are important cross-cultural variations in parenting (Whiting & Edwards, 1988). In some countries, authoritarian parenting is widespread. For example, in the Arab world, many families today are very authoritarian, dominated by the father's rule, and children are taught strict codes of conduct and family loyalty (Booth, 2002).

What type of parenting is most frequent? In one study of parenting behavior in 186 cultures around the world, the most common pattern was a warm and controlling style, one that was neither permissive nor restrictive (Rohner & Rohner, 1981). The investigators commented that the majority of cultures have discovered, over many centuries, a "truth" that only recently emerged in the Western world—namely, that children's healthy social development is most effectively promoted by love and at least some moderate parental control.

Family Diversity

Cultural change is coming to families in many countries around the world. There are trends toward greater family mobility, migration to urban areas, separation as some family members work in cities or countries far from their homes, smaller families, fewer extended-family households, and increases in maternal employment (Brown & Larson, 2002). These trends can change the resources that are available to children. For example, when several generations no longer live close by, children may lose support and guidance from grandparents, aunts, and uncles. Also, smaller families may produce more openness and communication between parents and children.

Ethnicity Families within different ethnic groups in the United States differ in their size, structure, composition, reliance on kinship networks, and levels of income and education (Coll & Pachter, 2002; Gonzales & others, 2004; Leyendecker & others, 2005; Parke, 2004; Parke & Buriel, 2006). Large and extended families are more

What are some characteristics of families within different ethnic groups?

common among minority groups than among the White majority. For example, 19 percent of Latino families have three or more children, compared with 14 percent of African American and 10 percent of White families. African American and Latino children interact more with grandparents, aunts, uncles, cousins, and more-distant relatives than do White children.

Single-parent families are more common among African Americans and Latinos than among White Americans (Weinraub, Horvath, & Gringlas, 2002). In comparison with two-parent households, single parents often have more limited resources of time, money, and energy (Gyamfi, Brooks-Gunn, & Jackson, 2001). Ethnic minority parents also are less educated and more likely to live in low-income circumstances than their White counterparts. Still, many impoverished ethnic minority families manage to find ways to raise competent children (Coll & Pachter, 2002).

Some aspects of home life can help protect ethnic minority children from injustice. The family can filter out destructive racist messages, and parents can present alternative frames of reference to those presented by the majority. For example, TV shows may tell the 10-year-old boy that he will grow up to be either a star athlete or a bum; his parents can show him that his life holds many possibilities other than these. The extended family also can serve as an important buffer to stress (McAdoo, 2002).

Of course, individual families vary, and how ethnic minority families deal with stress depends on many factors (Fuligni & Yoshikawa, 2004). Whether the parents are native-born or immigrants, how long the family has been in this country, their socioeconomic status, and their national origin all make a difference. The characteristics of the family's social context also influence its adaptation. What are the attitudes toward the family's ethnic group within its neighborhood or city? Can the family's children attend good schools? Are there community groups that welcome people from the family's ethnic group? Do members of the family's ethnic group form community groups of their own?

Socioeconomic Status In America and most Western cultures, differences have been found in child rearing among different socioeconomic-status (SES) groups (Hoff, Laursen, & Tardif, 2002, p. 246):

- "Lower-SES parents (1) are more concerned that their children conform to society's expectations, (2) create a home atmosphere in which it is clear that parents have authority over children,"(3) use physical punishment more in disciplining their children, and (4) are more directive and less conversational with their children.
- "Higher-SES parents (1) are more concerned with developing children's initiative" and delay of gratification, "(2) create a home atmosphere in which children are more nearly equal participants and in which rules are discussed as opposed to being laid down" in an authoritarian manner, (3) are less likely to use physical punishment, and (4) "are less directive and more conversational" with their children.

Parents in different socioeconomic groups also tend to think differently about education (Hoff, Laursen, & Tardif, 2002; Magnuson & Duncan, 2002). Middle- and upper-income parents more often think of education as something that should be mutually encouraged by parents and teachers. By contrast, low-income parents are more likely to view education as the teacher's job. Thus, increased school-family linkages especially can benefit students from low-income families.

Gender and Parenting

For U.S. families, perhaps the greatest change in the late twentieth century involved changing attitudes toward the roles of men and women. Gone were the assumptions that fathers should always be the breadwinners but also the decision makers for the family and that unless they were poor, mothers would stay at home, out of the paid labor force. U.S. society today is more open to the idea that mothers and fathers may define their roles in different ways.

The Mother's Role What do you think of when you hear the word *motherhood?* If you are like most people, you associate motherhood with a number of positive images (Barnard & Solchany, 2002). For example, you might associate motherhood with warmth, selflessness, dutifulness, and tolerance (Matlin, 2004). But the image of mothers in the United States is not linked with money, power, or achievement, and the role of being a mother has relatively low prestige in our society.

Stereotypes have associated motherhood with one type of power. When children don't succeed or develop problems, our society has had a tendency to attribute the lack of success or the development of problems to a single source—mothers. One of psychology's most important lessons is that behavior is multiply determined. So it is with children's development—when development goes awry, mothers are not the single cause of the problems.

The reality of motherhood today is that in many families the main responsibility for children—as well as for housework and other forms of "family work"—still falls on the mother's shoulders (Barnard & Martell, 1995). Not only do women do more family work than men, the family work most women do is unrelenting, repetitive, and routine. Much of it involves cleaning, cooking, child care, shopping, laundry, and straightening up. The family work most men do is infrequent, irregular, and nonroutine, often involving household repairs, taking out the garbage, and yard work. Women report that they often have to do several tasks at once, which helps to explain why they find domestic work less relaxing and more stressful than men do (Shaw, 1988).

Because family work is intertwined with love and embedded in family relations, it has complex and contradictory meanings (Villiani, 1997). Many women feel that family tasks are mindless but essential. They usually enjoy tending to the needs of their loved ones and keeping the family going, even if they do not find the activities themselves enjoyable and fulfilling. Family work is both positive and negative for women. They are unsupervised and rarely criticized, they plan and control their own work, and they have only their own standards to meet. However, women's family work is often worrisome, tiresome, menial, repetitive, isolating, unfinished, inescapable, and often unappreciated. It is not surprising that compared with women, men report that they are more satisfied with their marriage.

The Father's Role The father's role in U.S. families has undergone major changes (Day & Lamb, 2004; Lamb, 1997; Parke, 2002, 2004; Parke & Buriel, 2006). During the colonial period in America, fathers were primarily responsible for moral teaching. Fathers provided guidance and values, especially about religion. With the Industrial Revolution, the focus of the father's role changed to emphasize his position as the breadwinner for the family. By the end of World War II, another role for fathers emerged, that of being a gender-role model, especially for sons. Then, in the 1970s, the interest in the father as an active, caregiving parent emerged. Rather than being responsible only for the discipline and control of older children and for providing the family's economic base, the father was also evaluated in terms of his active, nurturing involvement with his children (Day & Lamb, 2004).

Can fathers take care of infants as competently as mothers can? Observations of fathers and their infants suggest that fathers have the ability to act sensitively and responsively with their infants (Parke, 1995, 2000, 2002, 2004). One recent study revealed the importance of fathers when mothers were depressed (Mezulis, Hyde, & Clark, 2004). In these families, a pattern of paternal warmth and involvement with infants was linked with fewer problem behaviors later in childhood.

Do fathers behave differently toward infants than mothers do? Maternal interactions usually center on child-care activities—feeding, changing diapers, bathing. Paternal interactions are more likely to include play. Fathers engage in more rough-and-tumble play. They bounce infants, throw them up in the air, tickle them, and so on (Lamb, 1986, 2000). Mothers do play with infants, but their play is less physical and arousing than that of fathers.

In one study, fathers were interviewed about their caregiving responsibilities when their children were 6, 15, 24, and 36 months of age (NICHD Early Child Care Research Network, 2000). A subset was videotaped during father-child play at 6 and 36 months. Caregiving activities (such as bathing, feeding, and dressing the child, and taking the child to day care) and sensitivity during play interactions (such as being responsive to the child's signals and needs, and expressing positive feelings) with their children were predicted by several factors. Fathers were more involved in caregiving when they worked fewer hours and mothers worked more hours, when fathers and mothers were younger, when mothers reported greater marital intimacy, and when the children were boys. Fathers who had less-traditional child-rearing beliefs and reported more marital intimacy were more sensitive during play.

Is the nature of parent-infant interaction different in families that adopt non-traditional gender roles? Michael Lamb and his colleagues (1982) studied Swedish families in which the fathers were the primary caregivers of their firstborn, 8-month-old infants and the mothers worked full-time. The researchers found that having fathers assume the primary caregiving role did not substantially alter the way they interacted with their infants.

Amount of Father Involvement How much time do children spend with fathers? Fathers' involvement with their children has increased in the United States in the last several decades. Research conducted in the 1970s suggested that fathers spent about one-third as much time with their children as mothers did. In the early 1990s, that figure jumped to approximately 43 percent.

More recently, a study with a nationally representative sample of more than 1,700 children up to 12 years of age found that fathers spent about 65 percent as much time with children as mothers did on weekdays and about 87 percent as much as mothers did on weekends (Yeung & others, 2001). The children spent an average of 2.5 hours a day with their fathers on weekdays and 6.2 hours a day on weekends (Yeung & others, 2001). For about half that time, fathers are directly engaged with their children—playing, eating, shopping, watching TV, or working together around the house. The rest of the time they are nearby or available to their children if needed. According to this study, mothers still shoulder the lion's share of parenting, especially on weekdays (see figure 15.6).

In the study just described, the entire sample was drawn from intact, nondivorced families (Yeung & others, 2001). Other studies that include mother-custody single-parent families often find that fathers spend less time with children. For example, a typical finding is that American fathers spend about an average of 45 minutes a day caring for children by themselves.

In sum, although U.S. fathers have increased the amount of time they spend with their children, it is still less time than mothers spend (Parke & Buriel, 2006; Pleck & Masciadrelli, 2004). This gender difference in parenting involvement occurs not only for non-Latino White parents, but also for Latino and African American parents (Yeung & others, 2001). And researchers have found that fathers in many other countries—such as Australia, Great Britain, France, and Japan—also spend less time with their children than mothers do (Zuzanek, 2000).

Impact of Fathering on Men Themselves Fathering has implications for men themselves (Parke, 2002). Marital satisfaction typically declines, especially among men,

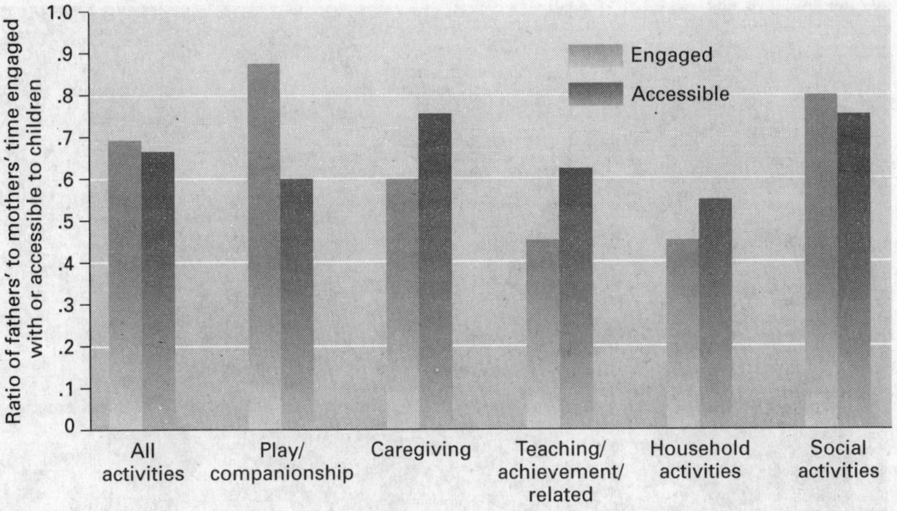

FIGURE 15.6 Ratio of Fathers' to Mothers' Time Engaged with or Accessible to Children on Weekdays. Note: A value of 1 indicates an equal contribution by mothers and fathers, value less than 1 a greater contribution by mothers. *Engaged* refers to doing an activity with the child. *Accessible* refers to the time a father is available to the child but not directly involved with him or her.

when a child is born (Belsky & Pensky, 1988). This decline may occur for a number of reasons, such as increased financial strain, physical demands of child care, restrictions of parenthood, and the emotional demands of new family responsibilities. Over time, however, involved fathering is associated with many positive characteristics. For example, a longitudinal study found that fatherhood was linked to men's ability to understand themselves, to understand others sympathetically, and to integrate their own feelings (Heath, 1977). Other researchers have found that involved fathering is related to being a good spouse, a good citizen, and participating in neighborhood and community activities (Snarey, 1993).

Influence of Fathering on Children's Development Fathering also makes a difference to children. One longitudinal study found that fathers' child-rearing involvement at age 5 was the strongest predictor of empathy for both men and women at 31 years of age (Koestner, Franz, & Weinberger, 1990). In further study, at age 41, men and women with better social relationships (marriage quality and extrafamilial ties such as friendships) had experienced more paternal warmth as children (Franz, McClelland, & Weinberger, 1991). Fathers who use an authoritative parenting style are likely to have children with fewer externalized problems (such as acting out or being highly aggressive) and internalized problems (such as anxiety or depression) than fathers who use other parenting styles (Marsiglio, 2004; Marsiglio & others, 2000).

Coparenting

A dramatic increase in research on **coparenting,** the amount of support parents provide for each other in raising their children, has occurred in the last two decades (Doherty & Beaton, 2004; McHale, Kuersten-Hogan, & Rao, 2004). The organizing theme of this research is that poor coordination, active undermining and disparagement of the other parent, lack of cooperation and warmth, and disconnection by one parenting partner—either alone or in combination with overinvolvement by the other—are conditions that place children at developmental risk (McHale & others, 2002; Van Egeren & Hawkins, 2004). By contrast, parental solidarity, cooperation, and warmth show clear ties to children's prosocial behavior and competence in peer relations. For example, in one study, 4-year-old children from families characterized by low levels of mutuality and support in coparenting were more likely than their classmates to show difficulties in social adjustment when observed on the playground (McHale, Johnson, & Sinclair, 1999).

coparenting The amount of support parents provide for each other in raising children.

What are some characteristics of coparenting?

When parents show cooperation, mutual respect, balanced communication, and attunement to each other's needs, this helps the child to develop positive attitudes toward both males and females (Biller, 1993; Tamis-LeMonda & Cabrera, 1999). It is much easier for working parents to cope with changing family circumstances when the mother and the father cooperate and equitably share child-rearing responsibilities. Mothers feel less stress and have more positive attitudes toward their husbands when the husband is a supportive partner.

Review and Reflect • LEARNING GOAL 5

5 Characterize the changing family in a changing social world

Review

- How are children influenced by working parents?
- How does divorce affect children's development?
- How does living in a stepfamily influence children's development?
- How do lesbian mothers and gay fathers influence children's development?
- How do culture, ethnicity, and socioeconomic status influence children's development in a family?
- What roles do mothers and fathers play in children's development? How does coparenting affect children's development?

Reflect

- Now that you have studied many aspects of families in this chapter, imagine that you have decided to write a book on some aspect of families. What specific aspect of families would you mainly focus on? What would be the title of your book? What would be the major theme of the book?

REACH YOUR LEARNING GOALS

FAMILIES

- **1 FAMILY PROCESSES**
  - Interactions in the Family System
  - The Developmental Construction of Relationships
  - Cognition and Emotion in Family Processes
  - Sociocultural and Historical Changes
- **2 PARENTING**
  - The Parental Role
  - Parenting Styles
  - Child Maltreatment
  - Adapting Parenting to Developmental Changes in the Child
  - Punishment
  - Parenting Takes Time and Effort
- **3 FAMILIES AND ADOLESCENTS**
  - Autonomy
  - Attachment
  - Parent-Adolescent Conflict
- **4 SIBLINGS**
  - Sibling Relationships
  - Birth Order
- **5 THE CHANGING FAMILY IN A CHANGING SOCIAL WORLD**
  - Working Parents
  - Stepfamilies
  - Cultural, Ethnic, and Socioeconomic Variations in Families
  - Children in Divorced Families
  - Gay Male and Lesbian Parents
  - Gender and Parenting

SUMMARY

1 Discuss family processes

- The family is a system of interacting individuals with different subsystems—some dyadic, some polyadic. The subsystems have both direct and indirect effects on one another. Positive marital relations can have a positive influence on parenting. Reciprocal socialization is the process by which children socialize parents just as parents socialize them.
- The role of cognition in family processes includes parents' cognitions, beliefs, and values about their parental role, as well as the way they perceive, organize, and understand their children's behaviors and beliefs. The role of emotion in family processes includes the regulation of emotion in children, the emotional development of children, and emotion in carrying out the parenting role.
- The developmental construction views share the belief that as individuals grow up they acquire modes of relating to others. There are two main variations within this view, one that emphasizes continuity and stability in relationships (the continuity view) and one that focuses on discontinuity and change in relationships (the discontinuity view).
- Changes in families may be due to great upheavals, such as war, or more subtle changes, such as television and the mobility of families.

2 Explain how parenting is linked to children's development

- For some, the parental role is well planned and coordinated. For others, it comes as a surprise. There are many myths about parenting, including the myth that the birth of a child will save a failing marriage. An increased trend is to conceptualize parents as managers of children's lives. Parents play important roles as managers of children's opportunities, in monitoring children's relationships, and as social initiators and arrangers.
- Parents need to adapt their parenting as children grow older, using less physical manipulation and more reasoning in the process. Parents spend less time in caregiving, instruction, reading, talking, and playing with children in middle childhood than earlier in the child's development. In middle and late childhood, control becomes more coregulatory.
- Authoritarian, authoritative, neglectful, and indulgent are the four main categories of parenting styles. Authoritative parenting is associated with socially competent child behavior more than the other styles. However, ethnic variations in parenting styles indicate that in African American and Asian American families, some aspects of control may benefit children. Latino parents often emphasize connectedness with the family and respect and obedience in their child rearing.
- There are a number of reasons not to use physical punishment in disciplining children, and in some countries physical punishment of children has been outlawed. Intense punishment presents the child with an out-of-control model. Punishment can instill fear, rage, or avoidance in children. Punishment tells children what not to do rather than what to do. Punishment can be abusive.
- Child maltreatment is a multifaceted problem. Understanding child maltreatment requires information about the cultural context and family influences. Child maltreatment places the child at risk for a number of developmental problems.
- In today's world, too many parents do not spend enough time in parenting. Competent parenting takes time and effort.

3 Summarize the changes in families with adolescents

- Many parents have a difficult time handling the adolescent's push for autonomy.
- Researchers classify relationships between parents and adolescents as secure-autonomous or insecure; they categorize insecure attachment into three different types. Secure attachment to parents increases the likelihood that the adolescent will be socially competent.
- Conflict with parents often increases in early adolescence, but this conflict is often moderate rather than severe. The increase in conflict probably serves the positive developmental functions of increasing adolescent autonomy and identity. A subset of adolescents experience high parent-adolescent conflict, and this is linked with negative outcomes for adolescents.

4 Identify how siblings influence children's development

- Siblings interact with each other in more negative and less varied ways than parents and children interact.
- Birth order is related in certain ways to child characteristics, but some critics believe it has been overestimated as a predictor of child behavior.

5 Characterize the changing family in a changing social world

- Most studies indicate that the mother's working outside the home generally does not have an adverse effect on children's development. However, in certain circumstances, negative effects of working mothers have been found, such as when mothers work more than 30 hours in the first year of the infant's life. Latchkey children raise special concern. Although the experiences of latchkey children vary, these children are vulnerable to problems. Parental monitoring and participation in structured activities with competent supervision are important influences on latchkey children's adjustment.

- Children in divorced families show more adjustment problems than their counterparts in nondivorced families. Whether parents should stay in an unhappy or conflicted marriage for the sake of the children is difficult to determine. Children show better adjustment in divorced families when parents' relationships with each other are harmonious and authoritative parenting is used. Factors to be considered in the adjustment of children in divorced families are adjustment prior to the divorce, personality and temperament, developmental status, gender, and custody. Income loss for divorced mothers may be linked with a number of stresses that can affect the child's adjustment.
- Like in divorced families, children in stepfamilies have more problems than their counterparts in nondivorced families. Restabilization often takes longer in stepfamilies than in divorced families. Children have better relationships with their biological parents than with their stepparents and show more problems in complex, blended families than simple ones. Early adolescence is an especially difficult time to experience the remarriage of parents.
- Approximately 20 percent of lesbians and 10 percent of gay men are parents. There is considerable diversity among lesbian mothers, gay fathers, and their children. Researchers have found few differences between children growing up in gay male or lesbian families and children growing up in heterosexual families.
- Cultures vary on a number of issues regarding families. African American and Latino children are more likely than White American children to live in single-parent families, larger families, and families with extended connections. Higher-income families are more likely to use discipline that promotes internalization; low-income families are more likely to use discipline that encourages externalization.
- Most people associate motherhood with a number of positive images, but the reality is that motherhood is accorded a relatively low status in our society. Over time, the father's role in the child's development has evolved from moral teacher to breadwinner to gender-role model to nurturant caregiver. Fathers are much less involved in child rearing than mothers are. Coparenting has positive effects on children's development. Father-mother cooperation and mutual respect help the child to develop positive attitudes toward both males and females.

KEY TERMS

scaffolding 457
reciprocal socialization 457
developmental construction views 459
continuity view 459
discontinuity view 459
authoritarian parenting 465
authoritative parenting 465
neglectful parenting 465
indulgent parenting 466
secure-autonomous attachment 473
dismissing/avoidant attachment 473
preoccupied/ambivalent attachment 473
unresolved/disorganized attachment 473
coparenting 489

KEY PEOPLE

Jean Piaget 459
Andrew Collins 460
Reed Larson and Marsye Richards 464
Diana Baumrind 465
Joseph Allen 473
Lois Hoffman 479
Joan Lipsitz 480
E. Mavis Hetherington 481

E-LEARNING TOOLS

To help you master the material in this chapter, visit the Online Learning Center for *Child Development*, eleventh edition (**www.mhhe.com/santrockcd11**), where you'll find these additional resources:

Taking It to the Net

1. Frieda is the middle child in a family with five siblings. She is interested in what sibling researchers have to say about the effect of birth order on sibling relationships. How does being a middle child contribute to the dynamics between Frieda and her brothers and sisters?
2. Mary and Peter are the parents of 13-year-old Cameron and 15-year-old Suzanne. They had heard that the adolescent years could be difficult, but they were not prepared for the constant conflicts and bickering. They don't feel that they are doing a very good job as parents. Are there some guidelines that will help them restore some peace and sanity to their family?
3. Bruce and Caitlin are planning to separate and divorce. Both are miserable, and the household is like an armed camp. They have three children, ages 6, 8, and 12. What should they tell the children and how and when should they do so?

Nursing, Parenting, and Teaching Exercises

Build your decision-making skills by trying your hand at the scenarios on the Online Learning Center.

Video Clips

The Online Learning Center includes the following videos for this chapter:

- Children and Divorce
  Robert Emery, Department of Psychology, University of Virginia, gives advice on how parents can help children cope with divorce.
- Children's Feelings About Work and Family
  A very cute clip in which two siblings discuss their feelings about their dad working. They say that their dad should spend more time with them instead of traveling (although they like when he brings them presents!). When asked about their mother they say, "she works for us!"
- Social Worker's View on Children's Abuse and Neglect
  An elementary school social worker describes the prevalence of abuse and neglect among children and how, unfortunately, it is difficult to identify until it is too late.
- Teen Pregnancy and Families
  Dr. Gunn describes the risk factors that are related to teen pregnancy. All involve the context in which these young girls are raised (for example, poverty, poor schools). She talks about the importance of understanding families of pregnant teens from a family systems approach.

Chapter 16 PEERS

You are troubled at seeing him spend his early years in doing nothing. What! Is it nothing to be happy? Is it nothing to skip, to play, to run about all day long? Never in his life will he be so busy as now.

—JEAN-JACQUES ROUSSEAU
Swiss-Born French Philosopher, 18th Century

CHAPTER OUTLINE

LEARNING GOALS

PEER RELATIONS

1 Discuss peer relations in childhood

Peer Group Functions
The Developmental Course of Peer Relations in Childhood
The Distinct but Coordinated Worlds of Parent-Child and Peer Relations
Social Cognition and Emotion
Peer Statuses
Bullying
The Role of Culture in Peer Relations

PLAY

2 Describe children's play

Play's Functions
Parten's Classic Study of Play
Types of Play

FRIENDSHIP

3 Explain friendship

Friendship's Functions
Similarity and Intimacy
Mixed-Age Friendships

ADOLESCENCE, PEERS, AND ROMANTIC RELATIONSHIPS

4 Characterize peer relations and romantic relationships in adolescence

Peer Pressure and Conformity
Cliques and Crowds
Adolescent Groups Versus Child Groups
Dating and Romantic Relationships

The Stories of Young Adolescent Girls' Friends and Relational Worlds

Lynn Brown and Carol Gilligan (1992) conducted in-depth interviews of one hundred 10- to 13-year-old girls who were making the transition to adolescence. They listened to what these girls were saying.

A number of the girls talked about how many girls say nice things to be polite but often don't really mean them. The girls know the benefits of being perceived as the perfect, happy girl. Judy spoke about her interest in romantic relationships. Although she and her girlfriends were only 13, they wanted to be romantic, and she talked about her lengthy private conversations with her girlfriends about boys. Noura said that she learned how very painful it is to be the person everyone doesn't like.

Cliques figured largely in these girls' lives. They provided emotional support for girls who were striving to be perfect but knew they were not. Victoria commented that some girls like her, who weren't very popular, nonetheless were accepted into a "club" with three other girls. Now when she was sad or depressed she could count on the "club" for support. Though they were "leftovers" and did not get into the most popular cliques, these four girls knew they were liked.

Through these interviews we see the girls' curiosity about the human world they lived in. They kept track of what was happening to their peers and friends. The girls spoke at length about the pleasure they derived from the intimacy and fun of human connection, about the potential for hurt in relationships, and about the importance of friends.

PREVIEW

This chapter is about peers, who clearly are very important in the lives of the adolescent girls just described. They also are very important in the lives of children. We begin this chapter by examining a number of ideas about children's peer relations, including their functions and variations. Then we turn to children's play and the roles of friends in children's development. We conclude by discussing peer and romantic relationships in adolescence.

1 PEER RELATIONS

- Peer Group Functions
- The Developmental Course of Peer Relations in Childhood
- The Distinct but Coordinated Worlds of Parent-Child and Peer Relations
- Social Cognition and Emotion
- Peer Statuses
- Bullying
- The Role of Culture in Peer Relations

As children grow up, they spend increasing amounts of time with their peers. What is the function of a child's peer group?

Peer Group Functions

peers Children of about the same age or maturity level.

Peers are children of about the same age or maturity level. They fill a unique role in the child's development. One of their most important functions is to provide a source of information and comparison about the world outside the family. Children receive feedback about their abilities from their peer group. They evaluate what they do in terms of whether it is better than, as good as, or worse than what other children do. It is hard to do this at home because siblings are usually older or younger.

Beyond the information they provide, peer interactions also fill socioemotional needs. Anna Freud (Freud & Dann, 1951) studied six children from different families who banded together after their parents were killed in World War II. Intensive peer attachment was observed; the children formed a tightly knit group, dependent on one another and aloof with outsiders. Even though deprived of parental care, they became neither delinquent nor psychotic.

Good peer relations may be necessary for normal socioemotional development. When peer monkeys who have been reared together are separated, they become depressed and regress socially (Suomi, Harlow, & Domek, 1970). Withdrawn children who are rejected by peers or victimized and feeling lonely are at risk for depression. Children who are aggressive with their peers are at risk for developing a number of problems, including delinquency and dropping out of school (Bukowski & Adams, 2005; Coie, 2004; Ladd, 2006; Masten, 2005).

Both Jean Piaget (1932) and Harry Stack Sullivan (1953) provided explanations of the role of peers in socioemotional development. They stressed that it is through peer interaction that children and adolescents learn how to interact in symmetrical, reciprocal relationships. As we discussed in chapter 15, because parents have greater knowledge and authority than children, parent-child interactions often teach children how to conform to rules and regulations. In contrast, peer relations are more likely to occur on an equal basis. With peers, children learn to formulate and assert their opinions, appreciate the perspective of peers, cooperatively negotiate solutions to disagreements, and evolve standards of conduct that are mutually acceptable. They also learn to be keen observers of peers' interests and perspectives in order to smoothly integrate themselves into ongoing peer activities.

What are some important functions of peers in children's development?

In addition, Sullivan argued that adolescents learn to be skilled and sensitive partners in intimate relationships by forging close friendships with selected peers. These intimacy skills are carried forward to help form the foundation of later romantic and marital relationships, according to Sullivan.

We discussed yet another function of peers in chapter 14: according to Piaget and Lawrence Kohlberg, through the give-and-take of peer relations, children develop their social understanding and moral reasoning. Children explore the principles of fairness and justice by working through disagreements with peers.

Of course, peer relations can be negative as well as positive (Bukowski & Adams, 2005; Kupersmidt & DeRosier, 2004). Being rejected or overlooked by peers leads some children to feel lonely or hostile. Further, such rejection and neglect by peers are related to an individual's subsequent mental health and criminal problems (Bukowski & Adams, 2005; Dodge, Coie, & Lynam, 2006; Masten, 2005). Some theorists have also described the children's peer culture as a corrupt influence that undermines parental values and control. Peers can introduce adolescents to alcohol, drugs, delinquency, and other forms of behavior that adults view as maladaptive.

As you read about peers, also keep in mind that findings about the influence of peers vary according to the way peer experience is measured, the outcomes specified, and the developmental trajectories traversed (Hartup & Laursen, 1999). "Peers" and "peer group" are global concepts. A "peer group" of an adolescent might refer to a neighborhood crowd, reference crowd, church crowd, sports team, friendship group, and friend (Brown, 1999). The influence of peers or peer groups depends on their specific setting or context.

The Developmental Course of Peer Relations in Childhood

Some researchers argue that the quality of peer interaction in infancy provides valuable information about socioemotional development (Vandell, 1985). For example, in one investigation, positive affect in infant peer relations was related to easy access to peer play groups and to peer popularity in early childhood (Howes, 1985). As increasing numbers of children attend child care, peer interaction in infancy takes on a more important developmental role.

Around the age of 3, children already prefer to spend time with same-sex rather than opposite-sex playmates, and this preference increases in early childhood. During these same years the frequency of peer interaction, both positive and negative, picks up considerably (Hartup, 1983). Although aggressive interaction and rough-and-tumble play increase, the proportion of aggressive exchanges, compared to friendly exchanges, decreases. Many preschool children spend considerable time in peer interaction just conversing with playmates about such matters as "negotiating roles and rules in play, arguing, and agreeing" (Rubin, Bukowski, & Parker, 2006).

As children enter the elementary school years, reciprocity becomes especially important in peer interchanges. Children play games, function in groups, and cultivate friendships. Until about 12 years of age, their preference for same-sex groups increases. The amount of time children spend in peer interaction also rises during middle and late childhood and adolescence. Researchers estimate that the percentage of time spent in social interaction with peers increases from approximately 10 percent at 2 years of age to more than 30 percent in middle and late childhood (Rubin, Bukowski, & Parker, 2006). In one early study, children interacted with peers 10 percent of their day at age 2, 20 percent at age 4, and more than 40 percent between the ages of 7 and 11. A typical school day included 299 episodes with peers (Barker & Wright, 1951). Other changes in peer relations as children move through middle and late childhood involve an increase in the size of their peer group and peer interaction that is less closely supervised by adults (Rubin, Bukowski, & Parker, 2006).

These many interactions take varied forms—cooperative and competitive, boisterous and quiet, joyous and humiliating. There is increasing evidence that gender plays an important role in these interactions (Ruble, Martin, & Berenbaum, 2006; Sebanc & others, 2003; Underwood, 2004). Gender influences not only the composition of children's groups but also their size and interactions within them (Maccoby, 1998, 2002). From about 5 years of age onward, boys tend to associate in large clusters more than girls do; girls are more likely than boys to play in groups of two or three. As discussed in chapter 13, "Gender," boys' groups and girls' groups also tend to favor certain types of activities. Boys' groups are more likely to engage in rough-and-tumble play, competition, conflict, ego displays, risk taking, and dominance seeking. By contrast, girls' groups are more likely to engage in collaborative discourse (Leman, Ahmed, & Ozarow, 2005). Let's now examine these factors that may influence children's relations with peers: parents, social cognition, and emotion.

The Distinct but Coordinated Worlds of Parent-Child and Peer Relations

Parents may influence their children's peer relations in many ways, both direct and indirect. For one thing, they may coach their children in ways of relating to peers (Ladd & Pettit, 2002). In one investigation, parents indicated that they recommended specific strategies to their children regarding peer relations (Rubin & Sloman, 1984). For example, parents told their children how to mediate disputes or how to become less shy with others. They also encouraged them to be tolerant and to resist peer pressure.

Parents also influence their children's peer relations by how they manage their children's lives and their opportunities for interacting with peers, which we discussed in chapter 15 (Collins & Steinberg, 2006). One study found that parents who frequently initiated peer contacts for their preschool children had children who were more accepted by their peers and had higher levels of prosocial behavior (Ladd & Hart, 1992). Furthermore, basic lifestyle decisions by parents—their choices of neighborhoods, churches, schools, and their own friends—largely determine the pool from which their children select possible friends (Cooper & Ayers-Lopez, 1985). For example, the chosen schools can lead to particular academic and extracurricular activities, which in turn affect which students their children meet, their purpose in interacting, and eventually which children become their friends. The chosen schools may also have policies that influence children's peer relations. For example, classrooms in which teachers encourage cooperative peer interchanges tend to have fewer isolated children.

Parents may also influence their children's peer relations in deeper, more subtle ways (Rubin, Bukowski, & Parker, 2006). A number of theorists and researchers argue that parent-child relationships serve as emotional bases for exploring and enjoying peer relations (Carlson, Sroufe, & Egeland, 2004; Sroufe & others, 2005). In one study, the parent-child relationship history of each peer helped to predict the nature of peer interaction (Olweus, 1980) (see figure 16.1). Some boys were highly aggressive ("bullies") and other boys were the recipients of aggression ("whipping boys") throughout their preschool years. The bullies and the whipping boys had distinctive relationship histories. The bullies' parents frequently rejected them, were authoritarian, and were permissive about their sons' aggression, and the bullies' families were characterized by discord. By contrast, the whipping boys' parents were anxious and overprotective, taking special care to have their sons avoid aggression. The well-adjusted boys in the study were much less likely to be involved in aggressive peer interchanges than were the bullies and the recipients of aggression. Their parents did not sanction aggression, and their responsive involvement with their sons promoted the development of self-assertion rather than aggression or wimpish behavior.

Do these results indicate that children's peer relations are wedded to parent-child relationships (Hartup & Laursen, 1999)? Recall our discussion of the continuity and discontinuity views of the developmental construction of relationships in chapter 15. Although parent-child relationships influence children's subsequent peer

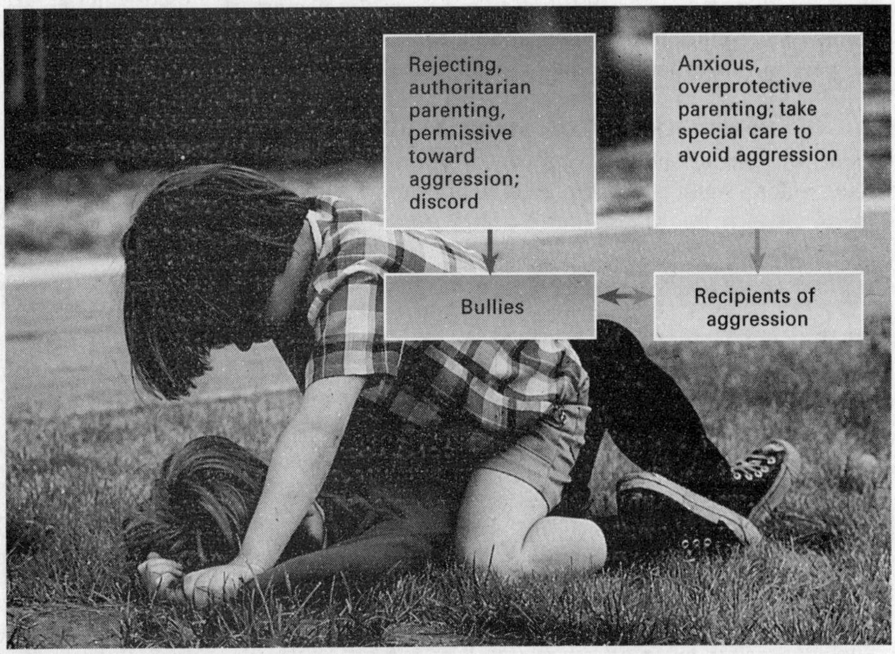

FIGURE 16.1 Peer Aggression and Parent-Child Relationship Histories. Children's peer behavior is influenced by their parent-child relationship histories.

relations, children also learn other modes of relating through their relationships with peers, as our discussion of Piaget and Sullivan indicated.

In sum, parent-child and peer worlds are coordinated and connected (Ladd & Pettit, 2002; Maccoby, 1996). However, they also are distinct. Rough-and-tumble play occurs mainly with other children, not in parent-child interaction. And, in times of stress, children often turn to parents, not peers, for support. In parent-child relationships, children learn how to relate to authority figures. With their peers, children are likely to interact on a much more equal basis and to learn a mode of relating based on mutual influence.

Social Cognition and Emotion

www.mhhe.com/santrockcd11

Social Cognition
Reducing Bullying

Mariana expects all her playmates to let her play with their toys whenever she asks. When Josh isn't picked for a team on the playground, he thinks his friends have turned against him. These are examples of social cognitions, which involve thoughts about social matters (Lewis & Carpendale, 2004). How might children's social cognitions contribute to their peer relations? Three possibilities are through their perspective-taking ability, social information-processing skills, and social knowledge.

Perspective Taking As children enter the elementary school years, both their peer interaction and their perspective-taking ability increase. As we discussed in chapter 14, "Moral Development," **perspective taking** involves taking another's point of view. Researchers have documented a link between perspective-taking skills and the quality of peer relations, especially in the elementary school years (LeMare & Rubin, 1987).

Perspective taking is important in part because it helps children communicate effectively. In one investigation, the communication exchanges among peers at kindergarten, first-, third-, and fifth-grade levels were evaluated (Krauss & Glucksberg, 1969). Children were asked to instruct a peer in how to stack a set of blocks. The peer sat behind a screen with blocks similar to those the other child was stacking (see figure 16.2). The kindergarten children made numerous errors in telling the peer how to duplicate the novel block stack. The older children, especially the fifth-graders, were much more efficient in communicating to a peer how to stack the blocks. They were far superior at perspective taking and figuring out how to talk to a peer so that the peer could understand them. In elementary school, children also become more efficient at understanding complex messages, so the listening skills of the peer in this experiment probably helped the communicating peer as well.

perspective taking The ability to assume another person's perspective and understand his or her thoughts and feelings.

Social Information-Processing Skills How children process information about peer relationships also influences those relationships (Dodge, Coie, & Lynam, 2006; Gifford-Smith & Rabiner, 2004). For example, suppose Andrew accidentally trips

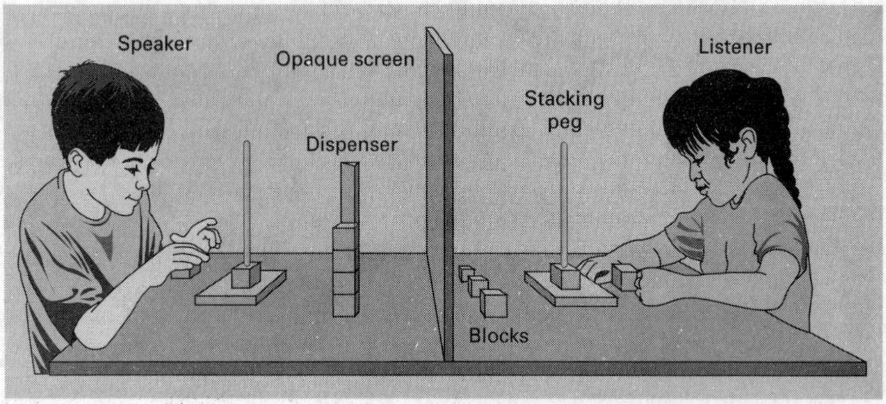

FIGURE 16.2 The Development of Communication Skills. This is an experimental arrangement of speaker and listener in the investigation of the development of communication skills.

and knocks Alex's soft drink out of his hand. Alex misinterprets the encounter as hostile, which leads him to retaliate aggressively against Andrew. Through repeated encounters of this kind, other peers come to perceive Alex as habitually acting inappropriately.

Peer relations researcher Kenneth Dodge (1993) argues that children go through five steps in processing information about their social world: decoding social cues, interpreting, searching for a response, selecting an optimal response, and enacting it. Dodge has found that aggressive boys are more likely to perceive another child's actions as hostile when the child's intention is ambiguous, and when aggressive boys search for clues to determine a peer's intention, they respond more rapidly, less efficiently, and less reflectively than nonaggressive children.

Social Knowledge Children's ability to get along with peers also depends on social knowledge. Children need to know what goals to pursue when situations are ambiguous, how to initiate and maintain a social bond, and what scripts to follow in order to make friends. For example, as part of the script for getting friends, it helps to know that saying nice things, regardless of what the peer does or says, will make the peer like the child more.

The social cognitive perspective views children who are maladjusted as lacking social cognitive skills to interact effectively with others (Rabiner & others, 1991). One investigation identified boys with and without peer adjustment difficulties and assessed their social cognitive skills (Asarnow & Callan, 1985). Boys without peer adjustment problems generated more alternative solutions to problems, proposed more assertive and mature solutions, gave less-intense aggressive solutions, showed more adaptive planning, and evaluated physically aggressive responses less positively than did the boys with peer adjustment problems.

Emotion Not only does cognition play an important role in peer relations, so does emotion. For example, the ability to regulate emotion is linked to successful peer relations (Orobio de Castro & others, 2005; Rubin, Bukowski, & Parker, 2006; Underwood, 2003; Underwood & Hurley, 1997). Moody and emotionally negative individuals experience greater rejection by peers, whereas emotionally positive individuals are more popular (Saarni, 1999). Children who have effective self-regulatory skills can modulate their emotional expressiveness in contexts that evoke intense emotions, as when a peer says something negative (Orobio de Castro & others, 2005). In one study, rejected children were more likely than popular children to use negative gestures in a provoking situation (Underwood & Hurley, 1997).

A recent study focused on the emotional aspects of social information processing in aggressive boys (Orobio de Castro & others, 2005). Highly aggressive boys and a control group of less-aggressive boys listened to vignettes involving provocations involving peers. The highly aggressive boys expressed less guilt, attributed more hostile intent, and generated less adaptive emotion-regulation strategies than the comparison group of boys.

Peer Statuses

Which children are likely to be popular with their peers and which ones are disliked? Developmentalists address this and similar questions by examining *sociometric status,* a term that describes the extent to which children are liked or disliked by their peer group (Cillessen & Mayeux, 2004; Rubin, Bukowski, & Parker, 2006). Sociometric status is typically assessed by asking children to rate how much they like or dislike each of their classmates. Or it may be assessed by asking children to nominate the children they like the most and those they like the least.

Developmentalists have distinguished five peer statuses (Wentzel & Asher, 1995):

- **Popular children** are frequently nominated as a best friend and are rarely disliked by their peers.
- **Average children** receive an average number of both positive and negative nominations from their peers.

popular children Children who are frequently nominated as a best friend and are rarely disliked by their peers.

average children Children who receive an average number of both positive and negative nominations from their peers.

- **Neglected children** are infrequently nominated as a best friend but are not disliked by their peers.
- **Rejected children** are infrequently nominated as someone's best friend and are actively disliked by their peers.
- **Controversial children** are frequently nominated both as someone's best friend and as being disliked.

Popular children have a number of social skills that contribute to their being well liked. Researchers have found that popular children give out reinforcements, listen carefully, maintain open lines of communication with peers, are happy, control their negative emotions, act like themselves, show enthusiasm and concern for others, and are self-confident without being conceited (Hartup, 1983; Rubin, Bukowski, & Parker, 2006).

Neglected children engage in low rates of interaction with their peers and are often described as shy by peers. Rejected children often have more serious adjustment problems than those who are neglected (Coie, 2004; Hay, Payne, & Chadwick, 2004; Parker & Asher, 1987; Rubin, Bukowski, & Parker, 2006; Sandstrom & Zakriski, 2004). One recent study found that in kindergarten, children who were rejected by their peers were less likely to engage in classroom participation, more likely to express a desire to avoid school, and more likely to report being lonely than children who were accepted by their peers (Buhs & Ladd, 2001).

Peer Rejection and Aggression The combination of being rejected by peers and being aggressive forecasts problems (Ladd, 2006; Rubin, Bukowski, & Parker, 2006). One study evaluated 112 fifth-grade boys over a period of seven years until the end of high school (Kupersmidt & Coie, 1990). The best predictor of whether rejected children would engage in delinquent behavior or drop out of school later during adolescence was aggression toward peers in elementary school. Another recent study found that when third-grade boys were highly aggressive and rejected by their peers, they showed markedly higher levels of delinquency as adolescents and young adults than other boys (Miller-Johnson, Coie, & Malone, 2003).

A recent analysis by John Coie (2004, pp. 252–253) provided three reasons why aggressive peer-rejected boys have problems in social relationships:

- First, the rejected, aggressive boys are more impulsive and have problems sustaining attention. As a result, they are more likely to be disruptive of ongoing activities in the classroom and in focused group play.
- Second, rejected, aggressive boys are more emotionally reactive. They are aroused to anger more easily and probably have more difficulty calming down once aroused. Because of this they are more prone to become angry at peers and attack them verbally and physically . . .
- Third, rejected children have fewer social skills in making friends and maintaining positive relationships with peers.

Peer rejection contributes to subsequent problems of adaptation, including antisocial behavior.

—John Coie
Contemporary Psychologist, Duke University

Not all rejected children are aggressive (Dodge, Coie, & Lynam, 2006; Haselager & others, 2002; Hymel, McDougall, & Renshaw, 2004). Although aggression and its related characteristics of impulsiveness and disruptiveness underlie rejection about half the time, approximately 10 to 20 percent of rejected children are shy.

Social Skills Training Programs How can neglected children and rejected children be trained to interact more effectively with their peers? The goal of many training programs for neglected children is to help them attract attention from their peers in positive ways and to hold their attention by asking questions, by listening in a warm and friendly way, and by saying things about themselves that relate to the peers' interests. They also are taught to enter groups more effectively.

neglected children Children who are infrequently nominated as a best friend but are not disliked by their peers.

rejected children Children who are infrequently nominated as a best friend and are actively disliked by their peers.

controversial children Children who are frequently nominated both as someone's best friend and as being disliked.

For rejected children, training programs may teach how to more accurately assess whether the intentions of their peers are negative. Rejected children also may be asked to engage in role-playing or to discuss hypothetical situations involving negative encounters with peers, such as when a peer cuts into line ahead of them. In some programs, children are shown videotapes of appropriate peer interaction; then they are asked to comment on them and to draw lessons from what they have seen (Ladd, Buhs, & Troop, 2004).

One recent social-skills intervention program was successful in increasing social acceptance and self-esteem and decreasing depression and anxiety in peer-rejected children (DeRosier & Marcus, 2005). Students participated in the program once a week (50 to 60 minutes) for eight weeks. The program included instruction in how to manage emotions, how to improve prosocial skills, how to become better communicators, and how to compromise and negotiate.

Despite the positive outcomes of some programs that attempt to improve the social skills of adolescents, researchers have often found it difficult to improve the social skills of adolescents who are actively disliked and rejected. Many of these adolescents are rejected because they are aggressive or impulsive and lack the self-control to keep these behaviors in check. Still, some intervention programs have been successful in reducing the aggressive and impulsive behaviors of these adolescents (Ladd, Buhs, & Troop, 2004).

Social-skills training programs have generally been more successful with children 10 years of age or younger than with adolescents (Malik & Furman, 1993). Peer reputations become more fixed as cliques and peer groups become more salient in adolescence. Once an adolescent gains a negative reputation among peers as being "mean," "weird," or a "loner," the peer group's attitude is often slow to change, even after the adolescent's problem behavior has been corrected. Thus, researchers have found that skills interventions may need to be supplemented by efforts to change the minds of peers. One such intervention strategy involves cooperative group training (Slavin, Hurley, & Chamberlin, 2003). In this approach, children or adolescents work toward a common goal that holds promise for changing reputations. Most cooperative group programs have been conducted in academic settings, but other contexts might be used. For example, participation in cooperative games and sports increases sharing and feelings of happiness. And some video games require cooperative efforts by the players.

Bullying

Significant numbers of students are victimized by bullies (DeRosier & Marcus, 2005; Espelage & Swearer, 2004; Hanish & Guerra, 2004). In one recent national survey of more than 15,000 sixth- through tenth-grade students, nearly 1 of every 3 students said that they had experienced occasional or frequent involvement as a victim or perpetrator in bullying (Nansel & others, 2001). In this study, bullying was defined as verbal or physical behavior intended to disturb someone less powerful. As shown in figure 16.3, being belittled about looks or speech was the most frequent type of bullying.

Who is likely to be bullied? In the study just described, boys and younger middle school students were most likely to be affected (Nansel & others, 2001). Children who said they were bullied reported more loneliness and difficulty in making friends, while those who did the bullying were more likely to have low grades and to smoke and drink alcohol. Researchers have found that anxious, socially withdrawn, and aggressive children are often the victims of bullying (Hanish & Guerra, 2004). Anxious and socially withdrawn children may be victimized because they are nonthreatening and unlikely to retaliate if bullied while aggressive children may be the targets of bullying because their behavior is irritating to bullies (Rubin, Bukowski, & Parker, 2006).

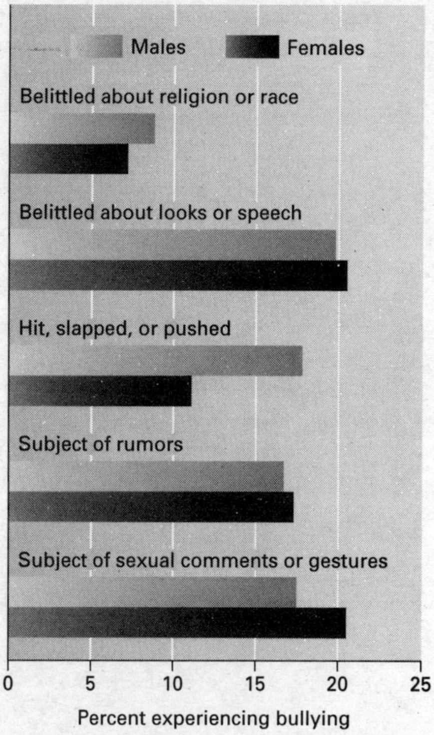

FIGURE 16.3 Bullying Behaviors Among U.S. Youth. This graph shows the type of bullying most often experienced by U.S. youth (Nansel & others, 2001). The percentages reflect the extent to which bullied students said that they had experienced a particular type of bullying. In terms of gender, note that when they were bullied, boys were more likely to be hit, slapped, or pushed than girls were.

What are the outcomes of bullying? A recent study of 9- to 12-year-old children in the Netherlands found that the victims of bullies had a much higher incidence of headaches, sleeping problems, abdominal pain, feeling tired, and depression than children not involved in bullying behavior (Fekkes, Pijpers, & Verloove-Vanhorick, 2004). A study of U.S. sixth grade students examined three groups: bullies, victims, and those who were both bullies and victims (Juvonen, Graham, & Schuster, 2003). Bully-victims were the most troubled group, displaying the highest level of conduct, school, and relationship problems. Despite increased conduct problems, bullies enjoyed the highest standing of the three groups among their classmates. To read further about bullying, see the Research in Child Development interlude.

Research in Child Development

Aggressive Victims, Passive Victims, and Bullies

One recent study examined the extent to which aggressive victims (who provoke their peers and respond to threats or attacks with reactive aggression), passive victims (who submit to aggressors' demands), and bullies (who aggress against peers but are rarely attacked in return) showed different developmental pathways (Hanish & Guerra, 2004). The children were assessed initially in the fourth grade and then again in the sixth grade.

Peer sociometric ratings were used to identify aggressive victim, passive victim, bully, uninvolved, and average children. Each child received a booklet containing randomized lists (separated by gender) of the names of all children in the class. The children were asked to mark all peers' names that were applicable to certain questions, which included items that assessed aggression (for example, "Who starts a fight over nothing?") and victimization (for example, "Who are the children who are getting picked on?").

The results indicated that "aggressive victims became less prevalent and passive victims and bullies became more prevalent with age. Although it was common for aggressive victims and bullies to move from one group to the other across time, there was little overlap with the passive victim group" (p. 17).

To reduce bullying, schools can do the following (Cohn & Canter, 2003; Limber, 1997, 2004):

- Get older peers to serve as monitors for bullying and intervene when they see it taking place.
- Develop schoolwide rules and sanctions against bullying and post them throughout the school.
- Form friendship groups for adolescents who are regularly bullied by peers.
- Incorporate the message of the antibullying program into places of worship, school, and other contexts where adolescents are involved in community activities.
- Encourage parents to reinforce their children's positive behaviors and model appropriate interpersonal interactions.
- Identify bullies and victims early and use social-skills training to improve their behavior.

Parents can take the following steps to reduce bullying (Cohn & Canter, 2003):

- Contact the school's psychologist, counselor, or social worker and ask for help with their child's bullying or victimization.
- Become involved in school programs to counteract bullying.
- Reinforce their children's positive behaviors and model interactions that do not include bullying or aggression.

The Role of Culture in Peer Relations

Peer relations can be influenced by the cultural context in which the child lives (Bergeron & Schneider, 2005; Rubin, Bukowski, & Parker, 2006). In many schools, peer groups are strongly segregated according to socioeconomic status and ethnicity. In schools with large numbers of middle- and lower-SES students, middle-SES students often assume the leadership roles in formal organizations, such as student council, the honor society, fraternity-sorority groups, and so on. Athletic teams are one type of adolescent group in which African American adolescents and adolescents from low-income families have been able to gain parity or even surpass adolescents from middle- and upper-SES families in achieving status.

For many ethnic minority youth, especially immigrants, peers from their own ethnic group provide a crucial sense of brotherhood or sisterhood within the majority culture. Peer groups may form to oppose those of the majority group and to provide adaptive supports that reduce feelings of isolation.

Peer relations also may vary cross-culturally. In some countries, adults restrict children's access to peers. For example, in many areas of rural India and in Arab countries, opportunities for peer relations are severely restricted, especially for girls (Brown & Larson, 2002). If girls attend school in these regions of the world, it is usually in sex-segregated schools. In these countries, interaction with the other sex or opportunities for romantic relationships are restricted (Booth, 2002).

In many countries and regions, though, peers play more prominent roles in children's lives (Brown & Larson, 2002). For example, in sub-Saharan Africa, the peer group is a pervasive aspect of children's lives (Nsamenang, 2002); similar results have been observed throughout Europe and North America (Arnett, 2002).

In some cultures, children are placed in peer groups for much greater lengths of time at an earlier age than they are in the United States. For example, in the Murian culture of eastern India, both male and female children live in a dormitory from the age of 6 until they get married (Barnouw, 1975). The dormitory is a religious haven where members are devoted to work and spiritual harmony. Children work for their parents, and the parents arrange the children's marriages.

Muslim school in Middle East with boys only

Asian Indian adolescents in a marriage ceremony

Street youth in Rio De Janeiro

The children continue to live in the dormitory through adolescence, until they marry.

In some cultural settings, peers even assume responsibilities usually assumed by parents. For example, street youth in South America rely on networks of peers to help them negotiate survival in urban environments (Welti, 2002).

Review and Reflect • LEARNING GOAL 1

1 Discuss peer relations in childhood

Review

- What are the functions of peer groups?
- What is the developmental course of peer relations in childhood?
- How are the worlds of parents and peers distinct but coordinated?
- How is social cognition involved in peer relations? How is emotion involved in peer relations?
- How are peer statuses related to development?
- What is the nature of bullying?
- How are peer relations influenced by culture?

Reflect

- Think back to your middle school/junior high and high school years. What was your relationship with your parents like? Were you securely attached or insecurely attached to them? How do you think your relationship with your parents affected your friendship and peer relations?

2 PLAY

Play's Functions | Parten's Classic Study of Play | Types of Play

Much of the time when children, especially young children, are interacting with their peers, they are playing. **Play** is a pleasurable activity that is engaged in for its own sake, and social play is just one type of play.

Play's Functions

Many of the key theorists discussed in early chapters have written about the functions of play in the child's development. According to Freud and Erikson, play helps the child master anxieties and conflicts. Because tensions are relieved in play, the child can cope with life's problems. Play permits the child to work off excess physical energy and to release pent-up emotions, which increases the child's ability to cope with problems. In part, these functions of play inspired the development of **play therapy,** in which therapists use play to allow children to work off frustrations and to provide an opportunity for analyzing children's conflicts and ways of coping. Children may feel less threatened and be more likely to express their true feelings in the context of play.

Piaget (1962) saw that play is both an activity constrained by a child's cognitive development and a medium that advances cognitive development. Play permits children to practice their competencies and skills in a relaxed, pleasurable way. Piaget believed that cognitive structures need to be exercised, and play provides the perfect setting for this exercise. For example, children who have just learned to add or multiply begin to play with numbers in different ways as they perfect these operations, laughing as they do so.

play A pleasurable activity that is engaged in for its own sake.

play therapy Therapy that allows the child to work off frustrations and is a medium through which the therapist can analyze the child's conflicts and ways of coping with them. Children may feel less threatened and be more likely to express their true feelings in the context of play.

Vygotsky (1962) also believed that play is an excellent setting for cognitive development. He was especially interested in the symbolic and make-believe aspects of play, as when a child rides a stick as if it were a horse. For young children, the imaginary situation is real. Parents should encourage such imaginary play because it advances the child's cognitive development, especially creative thought.

www.mhhe.com/santrockcd11

Play

Daniel Berlyne (1960) described play as exciting and pleasurable in itself because it satisfies the exploratory drive each of us possesses. This drive involves curiosity and a desire for information about something new or unusual. Play is a means whereby children can safely explore and seek out new information—something they might not otherwise do. Play encourages this exploratory behavior by offering children the possibilities of novelty, complexity, uncertainty, surprise, and incongruity.

Play also teaches children about gender roles. One study found that over the course of six months, the more time boys spent playing with other boys, their activity level, rough-and-tumble play, and sex-typed choices of toys and games increased, and the less time they spent near adults (Martin & Fabes, 2001). By contrast, the more time girls spent playing with girls, the lower was their aggression and activity level, the higher their choices of girl-type play and activities, and the more time they spent near adults.

In short, theorists and researchers paint a convincing portrait of the importance of play to development. Play is essential to a young child's health. Play releases tension, advances cognitive development, and increases exploration. Play also increases affiliation with peers; it raises the probability that children will interact and converse with each other. During this interaction, children practice the roles that they will assume later in life.

Parten's Classic Study of Play

Many years ago, Mildred Parten (1932) developed an elaborate classification of children's play. Based on observations of children in free play at nursery school, Parten proposed the following types of play:

- **Unoccupied play** is not play as it is commonly understood. The child may stand in one spot or perform random movements that do not seem to have a goal. In most nursery schools, unoccupied play is less frequent than other forms of play.
- **Solitary play** happens when the child plays alone and independently of others. The child seems engrossed in the activity and does not care much about anything else that is happening. Two- and 3-year-olds engage more frequently in solitary play than older preschoolers do.
- **Onlooker play** takes place when the child watches other children play. The child may talk with other children and ask questions but does not enter into their play behavior. The child's active interest in other children's play distinguishes onlooker play from unoccupied play.
- **Parallel play** occurs when the child plays separately from others but with toys like those the others are using or in a manner that mimics their play. The older children are, the less frequently they engage in this type of play. However, even older preschool children engage in parallel play quite often.
- **Associative play** involves social interaction with little or no organization. In this type of play, children seem to be more interested in each other than in the tasks they are performing. Borrowing or lending toys and following or leading one another in line are examples of associative play.
- **Cooperative play** consists of social interaction in a group with a sense of group identity and organized activity. Children's formal games, competitions aimed at winning, and groups formed by a teacher for doing things together are examples of cooperative play. Cooperative play is the prototype for the games of middle childhood. Little cooperative play is seen in the preschool years.

unoccupied play Play in which the child is not engaging in play as it is commonly understood and might stand in one spot, look around the room, or perform random movements that do not seem to have a goal.

solitary play Play in which the child plays alone and independently of others.

onlooker play Play in which the child watches other children play.

parallel play Play in which the child plays separately from others, but with toys like those the others are using or in a manner that mimics their play.

associative play Play that involves social interaction with little or no organization.

cooperative play Play that involves social interaction in a group with a sense of group identity and organized activity.

Mildred Parten classified play into six categories. *Which of her categories are reflected in the behavior of the children pictured?*

Types of Play

Parten's categories represent one way of thinking about the different types of play, but they omit some types of play that are important in children's development. Whereas Parten's categories emphasize the role of play in the child's social world, the contemporary perspective on play emphasizes both the cognitive and the social aspects of play. Among the most widely studied types of children's play today are sensorimotor and practice play, pretense/symbolic play, social play, constructive play, and games (Bergen, 1988).

Sensorimotor and Practice Play **Sensorimotor play** is behavior by infants to derive pleasure from exercising their sensorimotor schemes. The development of sensorimotor play follows Piaget's description of sensorimotor thought, which we discussed in chapter 7. Infants initially engage in exploratory and playful visual and motor transactions in the second quarter of the first year of life. At 9 months of age, infants begin to select novel objects for exploration and play, especially those that are responsive, such as toys that make noise or bounce. At 12 months of age, infants enjoy making things work and exploring cause and effect.

Practice play involves the repetition of behavior when new skills are being learned or when physical or mental mastery and coordination of skills are required for games or sports. Sensorimotor play, which often involves practice play, is primarily confined to infancy, while practice play can be engaged in throughout life. During the preschool years, children often engage in play that involves practicing various skills. Although practice play declines in the elementary school years, practice play activities such as running, jumping, sliding, twirling, and throwing balls or other objects are frequently observed on the playgrounds at elementary schools.

sensorimotor play Behavior engaged in by infants to derive pleasure from exercising their existing sensorimotor schemas.

practice play Play that involves repetition of behavior when new skills are being learned or when physical or mental mastery and coordination of skills are required for games or sports. Sensorimotor play, which often involves practice play, is primarily confined to infancy, while practice play can be engaged in throughout life.

Pretense/Symbolic Play

Pretense/symbolic play occurs when the child transforms the physical environment into a symbol. Between 9 and 30 months of age, children increase their use of objects in symbolic play. They learn to transform objects—substituting them for other objects and acting toward them as if they were these other objects. For example, a preschool child treats a table as if it were a car and says, "I'm fixing the car," as he grabs a leg of the table.

Many experts on play consider the preschool years the "golden age" of symbolic/pretense play that is dramatic or sociodramatic in nature (Fein, 1986; Rubin, Bukowski, & Parker, 2006). This type of make-believe play often appears at about 18 months of age and reaches a peak at 4 to 5 years of age, then gradually declines.

A preschool "superhero" at play.

Social Play

Social play is play that involves interaction with peers. Parten's categories, described earlier, are oriented toward social play. Social play with peers increases dramatically during the preschool years.

Constructive Play

Constructive play combines sensorimotor/practice play with symbolic representation of ideas. Constructive play occurs when children engage in the self-regulated creation of a product or a solution. Constructive play increases in the preschool years as symbolic play increases and sensorimotor play decreases. In the preschool years, some practice play is replaced by constructive play. For example, instead of moving their fingers around and around in finger paint (practice play), children are more likely to draw the outline of a house or a person in the paint (constructive play). Constructive play is also a frequent form of play in the elementary school years, both in and out of the classroom. Constructive play is one of the few playlike activities allowed in work-centered classrooms. For example, if children create a play about a social studies topic, they are engaging in constructive play.

And that park grew up with me; that small world widened as I learned its secret boundaries, as I discovered new refuges in its woods and jungles: hidden homes and lairs for the multitudes of imagination, for cowboys . . . and Devon-facing seashore, hoping for gold watches or the skull of a sheep or a message in a bottle to be washed up with the tide.

—Dylan Thomas
Welsh Poet, 20th Century

Games

Games are activities that are engaged in for pleasure and have rules. Often they involve competition with one or more individuals. Preschool children may begin to participate in social game play that involves simple rules of reciprocity and turn-taking. However, games take on a much stronger role in the lives of elementary school children. In one study, the highest incidence of game playing occurred between 10 and 12 years of age (Eiferman, 1971). After age 12, games decline in popularity (Bergen, 1988).

In sum, play ranges from an infant's simple exercise of a new sensorimotor talent to a preschool child's riding a tricycle to an older child's participation in organized games. It is also important to note that children's play can involve a combination of the play categories we have described. For example, social play can be sensorimotor (rough-and-tumble), symbolic, or constructive.

Review and Reflect • LEARNING GOAL 2

2 Describe children's play

Review

- What are the functions of play?
- How would you describe Parten's classic study of play?
- What are the different types of play?

Reflect

- Do you think most young children's lives today are too structured? Do young children have too little time to play? Explain.

pretense/symbolic play Play that occurs when a child transforms the physical environment into a symbol.

social play Play that involves social interactions with peers.

constructive play Play that combines sensorimotor/practice repetitive activity with symbolic representation of ideas. Constructive play occurs when children engage in self-regulated creation or construction of a product or a problem solution.

games Activities engaged in for pleasure that include rules and often competition with one or more individuals.

3 FRIENDSHIP

Friendship's Functions | Similarity and Intimacy | Mixed-Age Friendships

Children play with varying acquaintances. They interact with some children they barely know, and with others they know well, for hours every day. It is to the latter type—friends—that we now turn.

Friendship's Functions

Friendships serve six functions (Gottman & Parker, 1987):

1. *Companionship*. Friendship provides children with a familiar partner, someone who is willing to spend time with them and join in collaborative activities.
2. *Stimulation*. Friendship provides children with interesting information, excitement, and amusement.
3. *Physical support*. Friendship provides resources and assistance.
4. *Ego support*. Friendship provides the expectation of support, encouragement, and feedback that helps children to maintain an impression of themselves as competent, attractive, and worthwhile individuals.
5. *Social comparison*. Friendship provides information about where children stand vis-à-vis others and whether children are doing okay.
6. *Intimacy/affection*. Friendship provides children with a warm, close, trusting relationship with another individual, a relationship that involves self-disclosure.

Of course, the quality of friendship varies. Some friendships are deeply intimate and long-lasting, others more shallow and short-lived. Some friendships run smoothly; others can be conflicted (Parker & others, 2004; Rubin, Bukowski, & Parker, 2006). One recent study focused on conflict with parents and friends (Adams & Laursen, 2001). Parent-adolescent conflicts were more likely to be characterized by a combination of daily hassle topics, neutral or angry affect afterward, power-assertive outcomes, and win-lose outcomes. Conflicts between friends were more likely to involve a combination of relationship topics, friendly affect afterward, disengaged resolutions, and equal or no outcomes.

What are the main functions of friendship?

The importance of friendship was recently underscored in a two-year longitudinal study (Wentzel, Barry, & Caldwell, 2004). Sixth-grade students who did not have a friend engaged in less prosocial behavior (cooperation, sharing, helping others), had lower grades, and were more emotionally distressed (depression, low well-being) than their counterparts who had one or more friends. Two years later, in the eighth grade, the students who did not have a friend in the sixth grade were still more emotionally distressed. Why are friendships so significant?

Harry Stack Sullivan (1953) was the most influential theorist to discuss the importance of friendships. In contrast to other psychoanalytic theorists' narrow emphasis on the importance of parent-child relationships, Sullivan contended that friends also play important roles in shaping children's and adolescents' well-being and development.

According to Sullivan, all people have a number of basic social needs, including the need for tenderness (secure attachment), playful companionship, social acceptance, intimacy, and sexual relations. Whether or not these needs are fulfilled largely determines our emotional well-being. For example, if the need for playful companionship goes unmet, then we become bored and depressed; if the need for social acceptance is not met, we suffer a lowered sense of self-worth. Sullivan stressed that the need for intimacy intensifies during early adolescence, motivating teenagers to seek out close friends.

Research findings support many of Sullivan's ideas. For example, adolescents report disclosing intimate and personal information to their friends more often than do younger children (Buhrmester, 1990; Buhrmester & Furman, 1987) (see figure 16.4). Adolescents also say they depend more on friends than on parents to satisfy their needs for companionship, reassurance of worth, and intimacy (Furman & Buhrmester, 1992). In one study, daily interviews with 13- to 16-year-old adolescents over a five-day period were conducted to find out how much time they spent engaged in meaningful interactions with friends and parents (Buhrmester & Carbery, 1992). Adolescents spent an average of 103 minutes per day in meaningful interactions with friends, compared with just 28 minutes per day with parents. In addition, the quality of friendship is more strongly linked to feelings of well-being during adolescence than during childhood. Teenagers with superficial friendships, or no close friendships at all, report feeling lonelier and more depressed, and they have a lower sense of self-esteem than do teenagers with intimate friendships (Yin, Buhrmester, & Hibbard, 1996). In another study, friendship in early adolescence was a significant predictor of self-worth in early adulthood (Bagwell, Newcomb, & Bukowski, 1994).

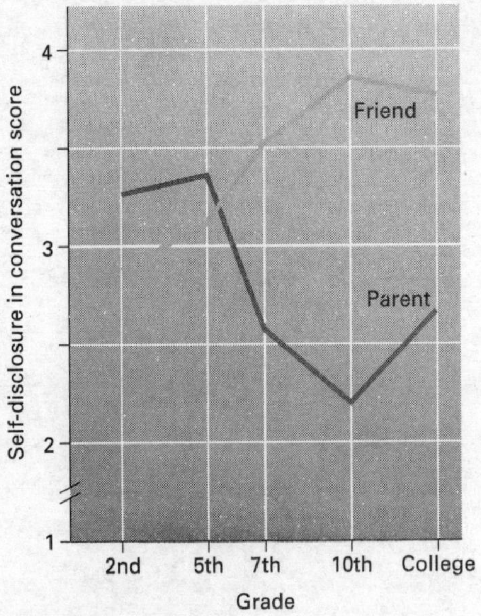

FIGURE 16.4 Developmental Changes in Self-Disclosing Conversations. Self-disclosing conversations with friends increased dramatically in adolescence while declining in an equally dramatic fashion with parents. However, self-disclosing conversations with parents began to pick up somewhat during the college years. The measure of self-disclosure involved a 5-point rating scale completed by the children and youth with a higher score representing greater self-disclosure. The data shown represent the means for each age group.

Friendship relationships are often important sources of support (Berndt, 1999). Sullivan described how adolescent friends support one another's sense of personal worth. When close friends disclose their mutual insecurities and fears about themselves, they discover that they are not "abnormal" and that they have nothing to be ashamed of. Friends also act as important confidants who help children and adolescents work through upsetting problems (such as difficulties with parents or the breakup of romance) by providing both emotional support and informational advice. Friends can also protect "at-risk" adolescents from victimization by peers (Bukowski, Sippola, & Boivin, 1995). In addition, friends can become active partners in building a sense of identity. During countless hours of conversation, friends act as sounding boards as teenagers explore issues ranging from future plans to stances on religious and moral issues.

Willard Hartup (1996, 2000), who has studied peer relations across four decades, has concluded that children often use friends as cognitive and social resources on a regular basis. Hartup also commented that normative transitions, such as moving from elementary to middle school, are negotiated more competently by children who have friends than by those who don't.

The quality of friendship is also important to consider (Rubin, Bukowski, & Parker, 2006). Supportive friendships between socially skilled individuals are developmentally advantageous, whereas coercive and conflict-ridden friendships are not (Hartup & Abecassis, 2004). The friend's character, interests, and attitudes also matter (Brown, 2004). For example, researchers have found that delinquent adolescents often have delinquent friends, and they reinforce each other's delinquent behavior (Dishion, Andrews, & Crosby, 1995). Other research has indicated that nonsmoking adolescents who become friends with smoking adolescents are more likely to start smoking themselves (Urberg, 1992). By the same token, having friends who are into school, sports, or religion is likely to have a positive influence on the adolescent. Friendship and its developmental significance can vary from one child to another. Children's characteristics such as temperament ("easy" versus "difficult" for example) and aggressive tendencies influence the nature of their friendships. One recent study found that the quality of friendships was more positive when friends engaged in prosocial behavior and more negative when they engaged in aggressive behavior (Cillessen & others, 2005). Being able to forgive also is important in maintaining friendships (Rose & Asher, 1999).

To read about appropriate and inappropriate strategies for making friends, see the Caring for Children interlude on the next page.

CARING FOR CHILDREN

Appropriate and Inappropriate Strategies for Making Friends

Here are some strategies that adults can recommend to children and adolescents for making friends (Wentzel, 1997):

- *Initiate interaction.* Learn about a friend: ask for his or her name, age, favorite activities. Use these prosocial overtures: introduce yourself, start a conversation, and invite him or her to do things.
- *Be nice.* Show kindness, be considerate, and compliment the other person.
- *Engage in prosocial behavior.* Be honest and trustworthy: tell the truth, keep promises. Be generous, share, and be cooperative.
- *Show respect for yourself and others.* Have good manners, be polite and courteous, and listen to what others have to say. Have a positive attitude and personality.
- *Provide social support.* Show you care.

And here are some inappropriate strategies for making friends that adults can recommend that children and adolescents avoid using (Wentzel, 1997):

- *Be psychologically aggressive.* Show disrespect and have bad manners. Use others, be uncooperative, don't share, ignore others, gossip, and spread rumors.
- *Present yourself negatively.* Be self-centered, snobby, conceited, and jealous; show off, care only about yourself. Be mean, have a bad attitude, be angry, throw temper tantrums, and start trouble.
- *Behave antisocially.* Be physically aggressive, yell at others, pick on them, make fun of them, be dishonest, tell secrets, and break promises.

Similarity and Intimacy

What characteristics do children and adolescents look for in their friends? The answers change somewhat as children grow up but one characteristic of friends is found throughout the childhood and adolescent years: friends are generally similar—in terms of age, sex, ethnicity, and many other factors. Friends often have similar attitudes toward school, similar educational aspirations, and closely aligned achievement orientations. Friends like the same music, wear the same kind of clothes, and prefer the same leisure activities (Berndt, 1982). Differences may lead to conflicts that weaken the friendship. For example, if two friends have differing attitudes toward school, one may repeatedly want to play basketball or go to the mall while the other insists on completing homework, and the two may drift apart.

Priorities change as the child reaches adolescence (Collins & Steinberg, 2006). The most consistent finding in the last two decades of research on adolescent friendships is that intimacy is an important feature of friendship (Berndt & Perry, 1990; Bukowski, Newcomb, & Hoza, 1987). In most research studies, **intimacy in friendship** is defined narrowly as self-disclosure or sharing of private thoughts; private or personal knowledge about a friend has been used as an index of intimacy (Selman, 1980; Sullivan, 1953). When young adolescents are asked what they want from a friend or how they can tell someone is their best friend, they frequently say that a best friend will share problems with them, understand them, and listen when they talk about their own thoughts or feelings. When young children talk about their friendships, they rarely comment about intimate self-disclosure or mutual

intimacy in friendship Self-disclosure or the sharing of private thoughts.

understanding. In one investigation, friendship intimacy was more prominent in 13- to 16-year-olds than in 10- to 13-year-olds (Buhrmester, 1990).

Are the friendships of adolescent girls more intimate than the friendships of adolescent boys? When asked to describe their best friends, girls refer to intimate conversations and faithfulness more than boys do (Collins & Steinberg, 2006; Ruble, Martin, & Berenbaum, 2006). For example, girls are more likely to describe their best friend as "sensitive just like me" or "trustworthy just like me" (Duck, 1975). When conflict is present, girls place a higher priority on relationship goals such as being patient until the relationship improves, while boys are more likely to seek control over a friend (Rose & Asher, 1999; Ruble, Martin, & Berenbaum, 2006). While girls' friendships in adolescence are more likely to focus on intimacy, boys' friendships tend to emphasize power and excitement (Rose, 2002; Ruble, Martin, & Berenbaum, 2006). Boys may discourage one another from openly disclosing their problems because self-disclosure is not masculine (Maccoby, 1996). Boys make themselves vulnerable to being called "wimps" if they can't handle their own problems and insecurities. These gender differences are generally assumed to reflect a greater orientation toward interpersonal relationships among girls than boys.

Mixed-Age Friendships

Although most adolescents develop friendships with individuals who are close to their own age, some adolescents become best friends with younger or older individuals. A common fear, especially among parents, is that adolescents who have older friends will be encouraged to engage in delinquent behavior or early sexual behavior. Researchers have found that adolescents who interact with older youths do engage in these behaviors more frequently, but it is not known whether the older youths guide younger adolescents toward deviant behavior or whether the younger adolescents were already prone to deviant behavior before they developed the friendship with the older youths (Billy, Rodgers, & Udry, 1984).

In a longitudinal study of eighth-grade girls, early-maturing girls developed friendships with girls who were chronologically older but biologically similar to them (Magnusson, 1988). Because of their associations with older friends, the early-maturing girls were more likely than their peers to engage in a number of deviant behaviors, such as being truant from school, getting drunk, and stealing. Also, as adults (26 years of age), the early-maturing girls were more likely to have had a child and were less likely to be vocationally and educationally oriented than their later-maturing counterparts. Thus, parents do seem to have reason to be concerned when their adolescents become close friends with individuals who are considerably older than they are.

Review and Reflect • LEARNING GOAL 3

3 Explain friendship

Review

- What are six functions of friendship? What is Sullivan's view of friendship?
- What role do similarity and intimacy play in friendship?
- What is the developmental outcome of mixed-age friendship?

Reflect

- Examine the list of six functions of friendships at the beginning of this section. Rank order the six functions from most (1) to least (6) important as you were growing up.

4 ADOLESCENCE, PEERS, AND ROMANTIC RELATIONSHIPS

- Peer Pressure and Conformity
- Adolescent Groups Versus Child Groups
- Cliques and Crowds
- Dating and Romantic Relationships

Peer relations play powerful roles in the lives of adolescents. When you think back to your adolescent years, many of your most enjoyable moments probably were spent with peers—on the telephone, in school activities, in the neighborhood, at dances, or just hanging out. Peer relations undergo important changes in adolescence. In childhood, the focus of peer relations is on being liked by classmates and being included in games or lunchroom conversations. Being overlooked or, worse yet, being rejected can have damaging effects on children's development that sometimes are carried forward to adolescence. Beginning in early adolescence, teenagers typically prefer to have a smaller number of friendships that are more intense and intimate than those of young children. Cliques are formed and shape the social lives of adolescents as they begin to "hang out" together. Dating and romantic relationships become important in the social lives of most older adolescents.

Peer Pressure and Conformity

Consider this statement made by an adolescent girl:

> Peer pressure is extremely influential in my life. I have never had very many friends, and I spend quite a bit of time alone. The friends I have are older. . . . The closest friend I have had is a lot like me in that we are both sad and depressed a lot. I began to act even more depressed than before when I was with her. I would call her up and try to act even more depressed than I was because that is what I thought she liked. In that relationship, I felt pressure to be like her.

Conformity to peer pressure in adolescence can be positive or negative. Teenagers engage in all sorts of negative conformity behavior—for instance, they use seedy language, steal, vandalize, and make fun of parents and teachers. However, a great deal of peer conformity, such as dressing like one's friends and wanting to spend huge chunks of time with members of a clique, is not negative and reflects the desire to be involved in the peer world.

During adolescence, especially early adolescence, we conformed more to peer standards than we did in childhood. Investigators have found that, around the eighth and ninth grades, conformity to peers—especially to their antisocial standards—peaks (Berndt, 1979; Leventhal, 1994). At this point in development, an adolescent is most likely to go along with a peer to steal hubcaps off a car, draw graffiti on a wall, or steal cosmetics from a store counter.

Cliques and Crowds

Cliques and crowds assume more important roles in the lives of adolescents than children (Brown, 2003, 2004). **Cliques** are small groups that range from 2 to about 12 individuals and average about 5 to 6 individuals. The clique members are usually of the same sex and about the same age. Cliques can form because adolescents engage in similar activities, such as being in a club or on a sports team. Some cliques also form because of friendship. Several adolescents may form a clique because they have spent time with each other and enjoy each other's company. Not necessarily friends, they often develop a friendship if they stay in the

cliques Small groups that range from 2 to about 12 individuals and average about 5 to 6 individuals. Cliques can form because of friendship or because individuals engage in similar activities, and members usually are of the same sex and about the same age.

clique. What do adolescents do in cliques? They share ideas, hang out together, and often develop an in-group identity in which they believe that their clique is better than other cliques.

Crowds are a larger group structure than cliques. Adolescents are usually members of a crowd based on reputation and may or may not spend much time together. Crowds are less personal than cliques. Many crowds are defined by the activities adolescents engage in (such as "jocks," who are good at sports, or "druggies," who take drugs). Reputation-based crowds often appear for the first time in early adolescence and usually become less prominent in late adolescence (Collins & Steinberg, 2006).

I didn't belong as a kid, and that always bothered me. If only I'd known that one day my differentness would be an asset, then my early life would have been much easier.

—Bette Midler
Contemporary American Actress

In one study, crowd membership was associated with adolescent self-esteem (Brown & Lohr, 1987). The crowds included jocks (athletically oriented), populars (well-known students who led social activities), normals (middle-of-the-road students who made up the masses), druggies or toughs (known for illicit drug use or other delinquent activities), and nobodies (low in social skills or intellectual abilities). The self-esteem of the jocks and the populars was highest, whereas that of the nobodies was lowest. One group of adolescents not in a crowd had self-esteem equivalent to that of the jocks and the populars; this group was the independents, who indicated that crowd membership was not important to them. Keep in mind that these data are correlational; self-esteem could increase an adolescent's probability of becoming a crowd member, just as crowd membership could increase the adolescent's self-esteem.

www.mhhe.com/santrockcd11
Adolescent Peer Relationships

Adolescent Groups Versus Child Groups

Adolescent groups differ from child groups in at least three important ways. First, during the adolescent years, groups tend to include a broader array of members than they did during childhood. The members of child groups often are friends nor neighborhood acquaintances; in contrast, many adolescent groups include members who are neither friends nor neighborhood acquaintances. Try to recall the student council, honor society, or football team at your junior high school. If you were a member of any of these organizations, you probably remember that they were made up of many people you had not met before and that they were a more heterogeneous group than your childhood peer groups. For example, peer groups in adolescence are more likely to have a mixture of individuals from different ethnic groups than are peer groups in childhood.

Second, in adolescent peer groups, rules and regulations are usually defined more precisely than in children's peer groups. Childhood groups are usually not as formalized as many adolescent groups. For example, captains or leaders are often formally elected or appointed in adolescent peer groups.

Third, during adolescence mixed-sex participation in groups increases (Collins & Steinberg, 2006). Dexter Dunphy (1963) documented this increase in mixed-sex groups in a well-known observational study. Figure 16.5 outlines his view of how these mixed-sex groups develop. In late childhood, boys and girls participate in small, same-sex cliques. As they move into the early adolescent years, the same-sex cliques begin to interact with each other. Gradually, the leaders and high-status members form further cliques based on mixed-sex relationships. Eventually, the newly created mixed-sex cliques replace the same-sex cliques. The mixed-sex cliques interact with each other in large crowd activities, too—at dances and athletic events, for example. In late adolescence, the crowd begins to dissolve as couples develop more-serious relationships and make long-range plans that may include engagement and marriage.

crowds The crowd is a larger group structure than a clique. Adolescents usually are members of a crowd based on reputation and may or may not spend much time together. Many crowds are defined by the activities adolescents engage in.

Dating and Romantic Relationships

Though many adolescent boys and girls have social interchanges through formal and informal peer groups, it is through dating that more serious contacts between the

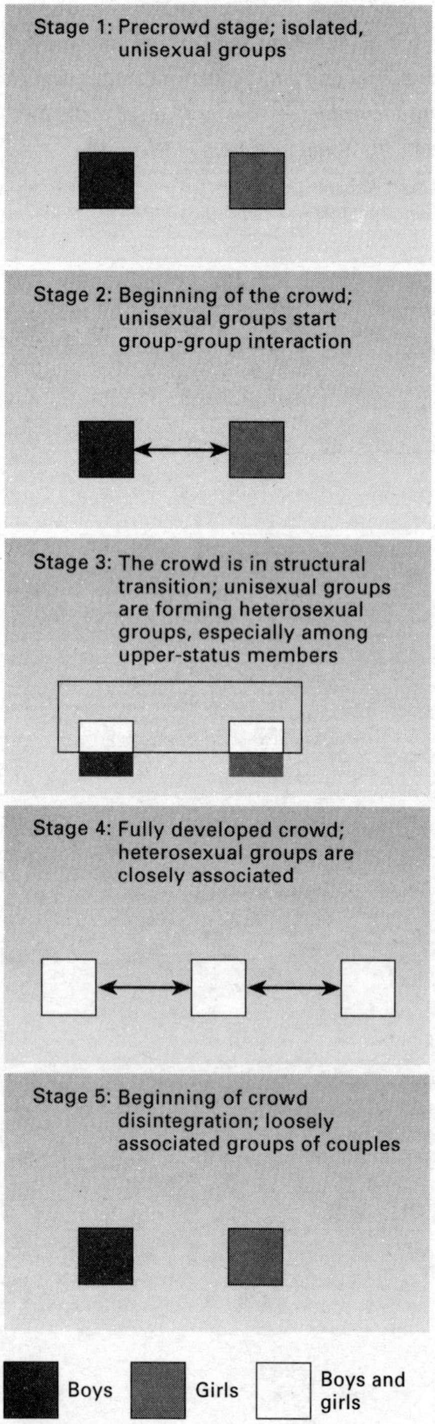

FIGURE 16.5 Dunphy's Progression of Peer Group Relations in Adolescence

sexes occur (Bouchey & Furman, 2003; Carver, Joyner, & Udry, 2003; Collins & Steinberg, 2006). One recent study of 14- to 19-year-olds found that adolescents who were not involved in a romantic relationship had more social anxiety than their counterparts who were dating or romantically involved (La Greca & Harrison, 2005).

Adolescents spend considerable time either dating or thinking about dating. Dating has gone far beyond its original courtship function to become a form of recreation, a source of status and achievement, and a setting for learning about close relationships. One function of dating, though, continues to be mate selection.

Heterosexual Romantic Relationships A number of developmental changes characterize heterosexual dating. In their early exploration of romantic relationships, today's adolescents often find comfort in numbers and begin hanging out together in heterosexual groups. Sometimes they just hang out at someone's house or get organized enough to get someone to drive them to a mall or a movie (Peterson, 1997).

Research by Jennifer Connolly and her colleagues (Connolly, Furman, & Konarksi, 1995, 2000; Connolly & Goldberg, 1999; Connolly & others, 2004; Connolly & Stevens, 1999) documents the role of peers in the emergence of romantic involvement in adolescence. A recent study confirmed that young adolescents increase their participation in mixed-gender peer groups (Connolly & others, 2004). This participation was "not explicitly focused on dating but rather brought boys and girls together in settings in which heterosocial interaction might occur but is not obligatory. . . . We speculate that mixed-gender groups are important because they are easily available to young adolescents who can take part at their own comfort level" (p. 201). In one study, adolescents who were part of mixed-sex peer groups moved more readily into romantic relationships than their counterparts whose mixed-sex peer groups were more limited (Connolly, Furman, & Konarksi, 2000).

The Internet has created another possibility: cyberrdating (Thomas, 1998). One 10-year-old girl posted this ad on the Net:

> Hi! I'm looking for a Cyber Boyfriend! I'm 10. I have brown hair and brown eyes. I love swimming, playing basketball, and think kittens are adorable!!!

Adolescents should be cautioned about the potential hazards of not knowing who is on the other end of the computer connection. Cyberdating is especially becoming popular among middle school students. By the time they reach high school and are able to drive, adolescents usually prefer real-life dating.

Over the course of adolescence the percentage of boys and girls who are engaged in a sustained romantic involvement increases (Collins & Steinberg, 2006). In one recent study, by the sixth grade 40 percent of the individuals had announced that "I like someone" (Buhrmester, 2001) (see figure 16.6). However, it was not until the tenth grade that 50 percent of the adolescents had a sustained romantic relationship that lasted two months or longer. By their senior year, 25 percent still had not engaged in this type of sustained romantic relationship. Early romantic involvement by the girls in this study was linked with lower grades, less active participation in class discussion, and school-related problems. "Going with" someone at a young age is associated with adolescent pregnancy and problems at home and school (Downey & Bonica, 1997). A rather large portion of adolescents in dating relationships say that their relationships have persisted 11 months or longer: 20 percent of adolescents 14 or younger, 35 percent of 15- to 16-year-olds, and almost 60 percent of 17- and 18-year-olds (Carver, Joyner, & Udry, 2003).

The motivation for romantic relationships also changes during adolescence. In their early romantic relationships, many adolescents are not motivated to fulfill attachment or even sexual needs. Rather, early romantic relationships serve as a context for adolescents to explore how attractive they are, how they should romantically

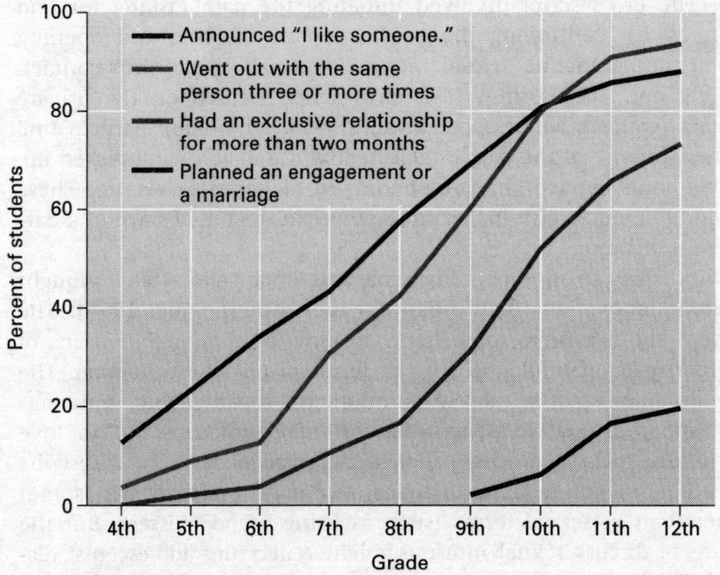

FIGURE 16.6 Age of Onset of Heterosexual Romantic Activity. In this study, announcing that "I like someone" occurred earliest, followed by going out with the same person three or more times, having an exclusive relationship for over two months, and finally planning an engagement or marriage (which characterized only a very small percentage of participants by the twelfth grade) (Buhrmester, 2001).

interact with someone, and how all of this looks to the peer group (Brown, 2003). Only after adolescents acquire some basic competencies in interacting with romantic partners does the fulfillment of attachment and sexual needs become central functions of these relationships (Furman & Wehner, 1999).

Romantic Relationships in Sexual Minority Youth

Most research on romantic relationships in adolescence has focused on heterosexual relationships. Recently, researchers have begun to study romantic relationships in gay male, lesbian, and bisexual youth (Diamond & Savin-Williams, 2003; Savin-Williams & Diamond, 2004).

The average age of the initial same-sex activity for females ranges from 14 to 18 years of age and for males from 13 to 15 (Savin-Williams & Diamond, 2004). The most common initial same-sex partner is a close friend. More lesbian adolescent girls than gay adolescent boys have heterosexual encounters before having same-sex activity; gay adolescent boys are more likely to show the opposite sequence (Savin-Williams & Diamond, 2004).

Most sexual minority youth have same-sex sexual experience, but relatively few have same-sex romantic relationships because of limited opportunities and the social disapproval such relationships may generate from families or heterosexual peers (Diamond, 2003). The importance of romance to sexual minority youth was underscored in a study that found that they rated the breakup of a current romance as their second most stressful problem, second only to disclosure of their sexual orientation to their parents (D'Augelli, 1991).

The romantic possibilities of sexual minority youth are complex (Diamond, 2003; Savin-Williams & Diamond, 2004). To adequately address the relational interests of sexual minority youth, we can't simply generalize from heterosexual youth and simply switch the labels. Instead, the full range of variation in sexual minority youths' sexual desires and romantic relationships for same- and other-sex partners needs to be considered.

Dating Scripts

Dating scripts are the cognitive models that guide individuals' dating interactions. In one study, first dates were highly scripted along gender lines (Rose & Frieze, 1993). The boys followed a proactive dating script, the girls a reactive

dating scripts The cognitive models that adolescents and adults use to guide and evaluate dating interactions.

What are some examples of dating scripts in adolescence?

one. The boy's script involved initiating the date (asking for and planning it), controlling the public domain (driving and opening doors), and initiating sexual interaction (making physical contact, making out, and kissing). The girl's script focused on the private domain (concern about appearance, enjoying the date), participating in the structure of the date established by the male (being picked up, having doors opened), and responding to his sexual overtures. These gender differences give males more power in the initial stage of a dating relationship.

According to another study, male and female adolescents brought different motivations to the dating experience (Feiring, 1996). The 15-year-old girls were more likely to describe romance in terms of interpersonal qualities, the boys in terms of physical attraction. The young adolescents frequently mentioned companionship, intimacy, and support as positive aspects of romantic relationships, but not love and security. Also, the young adolescents were more likely to describe physical attraction in terms of appearance (cute, pretty, or handsome) rather than in sexual terms (such as being a good kisser). But the failure to discuss sexual interests might reflect the adolescents' discomfort in talking about such personal feelings with an unfamiliar adult.

Emotion and Romantic Relationships The strong emotions of romantic relationships can thrust adolescents into a world in which things are turned upside down and ordinary reality recedes from view (Larson, Clore, & Wood, 1999). One 14-year-old reports that he is so in love he can't think about anything else. A 15-year-old girl is enraged by the betrayal of her boyfriend. She is obsessed with ways to get back at him. The daily fluctuations in the emotions of romantic relationships can make the world seem almost surreal.

Although the strong emotions of romance can have disruptive effects on adolescents, they also provide a source for possible mastery and growth. Learning to manage these strong emotions can give adolescents a sense of competence.

Many of an adolescent's emotional experiences involve romantic relationships (Collins, 2002). In one study of ninth- to twelfth-graders, girls gave real and fantasized heterosexual relationships as the explanation for more than one-third of their strong emotions, and boys gave this reason for 25 percent of their strong emotions (Wilson-Shockley, 1995). Strong emotions were attached far less to school (13 percent), family (9 percent), and same-sex peer relations (8 percent). The majority of the emotions tied to romantic relationships were reported as positive, but a substantial minority (42 percent) were reported as negative, including feelings of anxiety, anger, jealousy, and depression. The most common trigger of the first episode of major depression in adolescence is a romantic breakup.

www.mhhe.com/santrockcd11

Exploring Dating
Teen Chat

Sociocultural Contexts and Dating The sociocultural context exerts a powerful influence on adolescent dating patterns and on mate selection (Booth, 2002; Stevenson & Zusho, 2002). Values and religious beliefs of people in various cultures often dictate the age at which dating begins, how much freedom in dating is allowed, whether dates must be chaperoned by adults or parents, and the roles of males and females in dating. In the Arab world, Asian countries, and South America, adults are typically highly restrictive of adolescent girls' romantic relationships.

Many immigrants to the United States have brought restrictive standards with them. For example, in the United States, Latino and Asian American cultures have more conservative standards regarding adolescent dating than the Anglo-American culture.

Dating can be a source of cultural conflict for many adolescents whose families have come from cultures in which dating begins at a late age, little freedom in dating is allowed, dates are chaperoned, and dating by adolescent girls is especially restricted. In one recent study, Latino young adults living in the midwestern region of the United States reflected on their socialization for dating and sexuality (Raffaelli & Ontai, 2001). Because U.S.-style dating was viewed as a violation of traditional courtship styles by most of their parents, the parents placed strict boundaries on their romantic involvement. As a result, many of the Latinos described their adolescent dating experiences as filled with tension and conflict. The average age at which the girls began dating was 15.7 years; early dating experiences usually occurred without parental knowledge or permission. Over half of the girls engaged in "sneak dating."

Review and Reflect • LEARNING GOAL 4

4 Characterize peer relations and romantic relationships in adolescence

Review

- What is peer pressure and conformity like in adolescence?
- How are cliques and crowds involved in adolescent development?
- How do adolescents' groups differ from children's groups?
- What is the nature of adolescent dating and romantic relationships?

Reflect

- What were your peer relationships like during adolescence? What peer groups were you involved in? How did they influence your development? What were your dating and romantic relationships like in adolescence? If you could change anything about the way you experienced peer relations in adolescence, what would it be?

REACH YOUR LEARNING GOALS

PEERS

1 PEER RELATIONS

- Peer Group Functions
- The Distinct but Coordinated Worlds of Parent-Child and Peer Relations
- Peer Statuses
- The Role of Culture in Peer Relations
- The Developmental Course of Peer Relations in Childhood
- Social Cognition and Emotion
- Bullying

2 PLAY

- Play's Functions
- Parten's Classic Study of Play
- Types of Play

3 FRIENDSHIP

- Friendship's Functions
- Similarity and Intimacy
- Mixed-Age Friendships

4 ADOLESCENCE, PEERS, AND ROMANTIC RELATIONSHIPS

- Peer Pressure and Conformity
- Adolescent Groups Versus Child Groups
- Cliques and Crowds
- Dating and Romantic Relationships

SUMMARY

1 Discuss peer relations in childhood

- Peers are individuals who are at about the same age or maturity level. Peers provide a means of social comparison and a source of information about the world outside the family. Good peer relations may be necessary for normal social development. The inability to "plug in" to a social network is associated with a number of problems. Peer relations can be both positive and negative. Piaget and Sullivan stressed that peer relations provide the context for learning the symmetrical reciprocity mode of relationships. Peer relations vary according to the way peer experience is measured, the outcomes specified, and the developmental trajectories traversed.
- Some researchers believe that the quality of social interaction with peers in infancy provides valuable information about socioemotional development. As increasing numbers of infants have attended child care, infant peer relations have increased. The frequency of peer interaction, both positive and negative, increases in the preschool years. Children spend even more time with peers in the elementary and secondary school years, and their preference for same-sex groups increases. Boys' groups are larger than girls', and they participate in more organized games than girls. Girls engage in more collaborative discourse in peer groups than girls.
- Healthy family relations usually promote healthy peer relations. Parents can model or coach their children in ways of relating to peers. Parents' choices of neighborhoods, churches, schools, and their own friends influence the pool from which their children might select possible friends. Rough-and-tumble play occurs mainly in peer relations rather than in parent-child relations. In times of stress, children usually turn to parents rather than peers. Peer relations have a more equal basis than parent-child relations.
- Perspective taking, social information-processing skills, and social knowledge are important dimensions of social cognition in peer relations. Self-regulation of emotion is associated with positive peer relations.
- Popular children are frequently nominated as a best friend and are rarely disliked by their peers. Average children receive an average number of both positive and negative nominations from their peers. Neglected children are infrequently nominated as a best friend but are not disliked by their peers. Rejected children are infrequently nominated as a best friend and are disliked by their peers. Rejected children often have more serious adjustment problems than neglected children. Controversial children are frequently nominated both as one's best friend and as being disliked by peers.
- Significant numbers of students are bullied, and this can result in problems for the victim.
- The child's and adolescent's peer relations can be influenced by culture. Variations in peer relations have been found across socioeconomic groups, ethnic groups, and nations.

2 Describe children's play

- The functions of play include affiliation with peers, tension release, advances in cognitive development, and exploration.
- Parten examined these categories of social play: unoccupied, solitary, onlooker, parallel, associative, and cooperative.
- The contemporary perspective emphasizes both social and cognitive aspects of play. The most widely studied types of play include sensorimotor and practice play, pretense/symbolic play, social play, constructive play, and games.

3 Explain friendship

- The functions of friendship include companionship, stimulation, physical support, ego support, social comparison, and intimacy/affection. Sullivan argued that there is a dramatic increase in the psychological importance and intimacy of close friends in adolescence. Research findings support his view.
- Similarity and intimacy are two of the most common characteristics of friendships. Friends often have similar attitudes toward school, similar educational aspirations, and so on. Intimacy in friendship is much more common in adolescents than children.
- Children and adolescents who become friends with older individuals engage in more deviant behaviors than their counterparts with same-age friends. Early-maturing girls are more likely than late-maturing girls to have older friends, which can contribute to their problem behaviors.

4 Characterize peer relations and romantic relationships in adolescence

- The pressure to conform to peers is strong during adolescence, especially in eighth and ninth grade.
- Cliques and crowds assume more importance in the lives of adolescents than children. Membership in certain crowds—especially jocks and populars—is associated with increased self-esteem. Independents also show high self-esteem.

- Children's groups are less formal, less heterogeneous, and less heterosexual than adolescents' groups.
- Dating takes on added importance in adolescence, and it can have many functions. Younger adolescents often begin to hang out together in heterosexual groups. A special concern is early dating, which is linked with developmental problems. Male dating scripts are proactive, those of females reactive. Many sexual minority youth have same-sex sexual experience but relatively few have same-sex romantic relationships. Emotions are heavily involved in adolescent dating and romantic relationships. Culture can exert a powerful influence on adolescent dating.

KEY TERMS

peers 498
perspective taking 502
popular children 503
average children 503
neglected children 504
rejected children 504
controversial children 504
play 508
play therapy 508
unoccupied play 509
solitary play 509
onlooker play 509
parallel play 509
associative play 509
cooperative play 509
sensorimotor play 510
practice play 510
pretense/symbolic play 511
social play 511
constructive play 511
games 511
intimacy in friendship 514
cliques 516
crowds 517
dating scripts 519

KEY PEOPLE

Anna Freud 499
Kenneth Dodge 503
Erik Erikson 508
Sigmund Freud 508
Jean Piaget 508
Lev Vygotsky 509
Daniel Berlyne 509
Mildred Parten 509
Harry Stack Sullivan 512
Willard Hartup 513
Dexter Dunphy 517
Jennifer Connolly 518

E-LEARNING TOOLS

To help you master the material in this chapter, visit the Online Learning Center for *Child Development*, eleventh edition (**www.mhhe.com/santrockcd11**), where you'll find these additional resources:

Taking It to the Net

1. Barbara is going to lead a discussion in her child development class about peer relationships and friendships in early childhood. What should Barbara tell the class about how peer relationships develop between the ages of 3 and 6 years?
2. Darla, 13, has been living in foster homes since she was 4. As a result of being abandoned by her parents and moved from foster home to foster home, she doesn't trust anyone. She is in counseling to help her adjust to her latest home and new middle school. Her therapist brings up the importance of making and having friends, a concept alien to Darla. Why does Darla need to learn to have friends and to be one?
3. Kristin is getting intense pressure from her friends at school to go out and drink with them. She wants to spend time with them, but has no interest in drinking. Since she can't turn to her friends to help her, she hopes her mother can give her some pointers for dealing with this pressure. How can Kristin's mother help?

Nursing, Parenting, and Teaching Exercises

Build your decision-making skills by trying your hand at the scenarios on the Online Learning Center.

Video Clips

The Online Learning Center includes the following videos for this chapter:

- Describing Friends at Age 5
  Tara states that she has two special friends. She explains that these friends are special because they play together.
- Describing Friendships at Age 8
  In this clip a boy describes his two best friends and what they like to do together. When asked if he has any girl friends, he quickly responds, "no." But then he adds that his sisters are his friends.
- 15 Year Old Girls' Relationships with Boys
  In this clip we hear three high school students talk about how their relationships with boys have changed since middle school. They discuss how boys are more mature in high school and are often easier to talk to than girls.
- Talking about Cliques at Age 15
  Three high school girls describe the cliques in their school and what makes someone popular. They describe physical appearance as important but personality too.

Chapter 17 SCHOOLS AND ACHIEVEMENT

The whole art of teaching is the art of awakening the natural curiosity of young minds.

—ANATOLE FRANCE
French Novelist, 20th Century

CHAPTER OUTLINE

EXPLORING CHILDREN'S SCHOOLING

Contemporary Approaches to Student Learning and Assessment
Early Childhood Education
Elementary School
Educating Adolescents

SOCIOECONOMIC STATUS AND ETHNICITY IN SCHOOLS

Socioeconomic Status
Ethnicity in Schools

CHILDREN WITH DISABILITIES

Learning Disabilities
Attention Deficit Hyperactivity Disorder
Educational Issues

ACHIEVEMENT

Extrinsic and Intrinsic Motivation
Mastery Motivation
Attribution
Self-Efficacy
Goal-Setting, Planning, and Self-Monitoring
Ethnicity and Culture

LEARNING GOALS

1. Discuss approaches to schooling and development
2. Describe the roles of socioeconomic status and ethnicity in schools
3. Characterize children with disabilities and their schooling
4. Explain the development of achievement in children

The Story of Reggio Emilia's Children

A Reggio Emilia classroom in which young children explore topics that interest them.

The Reggio Emilia approach is an educational program for young children that was developed in the northern Italian city of Reggio Emilia. Children of single parents and children with disabilities have priority in admission; other children are admitted according to a scale of needs. Parents pay on a sliding scale based on income.

The children are encouraged to learn by investigating and exploring topics that interest them. A wide range of stimulating media and materials is available for children to use as they learn—music, movement, drawing, painting, sculpting, collages, puppets and disguises, and photography, for example. In this program, children often explore topics in a group, which fosters a sense of community, respect for diversity, and a collaborative approach to problem solving. Two coteachers are present to serve as guides for children. The Reggio Emilia teachers consider a project as an adventure, which can start from an adult's suggestion, from a child's idea, or from an event, such as a snowfall or something else unexpected. Every project is based on what the children say and do. The teachers allow children enough time to think and craft a project.

At the core of the Reggio Emilia approach is the image of children who are competent and have rights, especially the right to outstanding care and education (Bredekamp, 1993). Parent participation is considered essential, and cooperation is a major theme in the schools. Many early childhood education experts believe the Reggio Emilia approach provides a supportive, stimulating context in which children are motivated to explore their world in a competent and confident manner (Firlik, 1996; Stegelin, 2003).

PREVIEW

This chapter is about becoming educated and achieving. We will explore such topics as contemporary approaches to student learning, school transitions, the roles that socioeconomic status and ethnicity play in schools, educational issues involving children with disabilities, and becoming motivated to achieve goals.

1 EXPLORING CHILDREN'S SCHOOLING

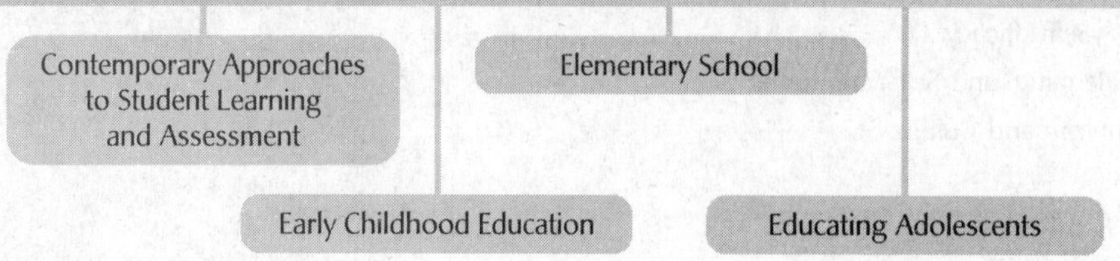

We have discussed many aspects of schools throughout this book but especially in section 3, "Cognition and Language." Recall our coverage of applications of Piaget's and Vygotsky's theories to education in chapter 7, strategies for encouraging children's critical thinking in schools in chapter 8, applications of Gardner's and Sternberg's theories of intelligence to education in chapter 9, and bilingual education in chapter 10. Here we take a closer look at contemporary approaches to student learning in U.S. schools and at how schooling varies from early childhood education through high school.

Contemporary Approaches to Student Learning and Assessment

Controversy swirls about the best way to teach children and how to hold schools and teachers accountable for whether children are learning.

Direct Instruction and Constructivist Approaches Many people believe that schools should use a **direct instruction approach,** a teacher-centered approach that emphasizes teacher direction and control, mastery of academic skills by children, high expectations for students, and maximum time spent on learning tasks. In the 1990s, interest in school reform focused on constructivist approaches, which comes in two forms, cognitive and social (Santrock, 2006).

Cognitive constructivist approaches emphasize the child's active, cognitive construction of knowledge and understanding. The teacher's role is to provide support for students to explore their world and develop understanding. Piaget's theory, which we discussed in chapter 6, is the main developmental theory that is linked with cognitive constructivist approaches. **Social constructivist approaches** focus on the importance of collaborating with others to produce knowledge and understanding (John-Steiner & Mahn, 2003). The implication is that teachers should create many opportunities for students to learn with the teacher and with peers in coconstructing understanding (Blumenfeld, Krajik, & Kempler, 2006). Vygotsky's theory, which we also discussed in chapter 6, is the main developmental theory that has served as the foundation for social constructivist approaches.

In short, constructivist approaches place the learner, not the teacher, at the center of the education process; the Reggio Emilia approach, which was described in the opening of the chapter, is one example. Constructivist approaches apply *learner-centered principles* (McCombs, 2003). Figure 17.1 summarizes 14 learner-centered principles. These principles were constructed by a prestigious group of scientists and educators from a wide range of disciplines and published by the American Psychological Association in *Learner-Centered Principles: A Framework for School Reform and Redesign* (Learner-Centered Principles Work Group, 1997).

Advocates of the cognitive and social constructivist and learner-centered approaches argue that the direct instruction approach turns children into passive learners and does not adequately challenge them to think in critical and creative ways (Duffy & Kirkley, 2004). The direct instruction enthusiasts say that the constructivist approaches do not give enough attention to the content of a discipline, such as history or science. They also believe that the constructivist approaches are too relativistic and vague.

Accountability Since the 1990s the U.S. public and governments at every level have demanded increased accountability from schools. One result was the spread of state-mandated tests to measure just what students had or had not learned (Hambleton, 2002; Thomas, 2005; Whithause, 2005). Many states identified objectives for students in their state and created tests to measure whether students were meeting those objectives (Cizek, 2005). This approach became national policy in 2002 when the No Child Left Behind (NCLB) legislation was signed into law.

Advocates argue that statewide standardized testing will have a number of positive effects. These include improved student performance; more time teaching the subjects that are tested; high expectations for all students; identification of poorly performing schools, teachers, and administrators; and improved confidence in schools as test scores increase.

Most educators support high expectations and high standards for students (Revelle, 2004). At issue, however, is whether the tests and procedures mandated by NCLB are the best ones for achieving high standards. Critics argue that the NCLB legislation will do more harm than good (Ambrosio, 2004; Fair Test, 2004; Neill, 2003). One criticism stresses that using a single test as the sole indicator of

www.mhhe.com/santrockcd11

National Education Research Centers
Pathways to School Improvement
APA's Learner-Centered Psychological Principles

direct instruction approach A teacher-centered approach characterized by teacher direction and control, mastery of academic material, high expectations for students' progress, and maximum time spent on learning tasks.

cognitive constructivist approaches An approach that emphasizes the child's active, cognitive construction of knowledge and understanding; Piaget's theory is an example of this approach.

social constructivist approaches An approach that focuses on collaboration with others to produce knowledge and understanding; Vygotsky's theory is an example of this approach.

FIGURE 17.1 Learner-Centered Psychological Principles

Cognitive and Metacognitive Factors

1. Nature of the Learning Process
   The learning of complex subject matter is most effective when it is an intentional process of constructing meaning and experience.
2. Goals of the Learning Process
   Successful learners, over time and with support and instructional guidance, can create meaningful, coherent representations of knowledge.
3. Construction of Knowledge
   Successful learners can link new information with existing knowledge in meaningful ways.
4. Strategic Thinking
   Successful learners can create a repertoire of thinking and reasoning strategies to achieve complex goals.
5. Thinking About Thinking
   Higher order strategies for selecting and monitoring mental operations facilitate creative and critical thinking.
6. Context of Learning
   Learning is influenced by environmental factors, including culture, technology, and instructional practices.

Motivational and Instructional Factors

7. Motivational and Emotional Influences on Learning
   What and how much is learned is influenced by the learner's motivation. Motivation to learn, in turn, is influenced by the learner's emotional states, beliefs, interests, goals, and habits of thinking.
8. Intrinsic Motivation to Learn
   The learner's creativity, higher order thinking, and natural curiosity all contribute to motivation to learn. Intrinsic (internal, self-generated) motivation is stimulated by tasks of optimal novelty and difficulty, tasks that are relevant to personal interests, and when learners are provided personal choice and control.
9. Effects of Motivation on Effort
   Acquiring complex knowledge and skills requires extended learner effort and guided practice. Without learners' motivation to learn, the willingness to exert this effort is unlikely without coercion.

Developmental and Social Factors

10. Developmental Influences on Learning
    As individuals develop, there are different opportunities and constraints for learning. Learning is most effective when development within and across physical, cognitive, and socioemotional domains is taken into account.
11. Social Influences on Learning
    Learning is influenced by social interactions, interpersonal relations, and communication with others.

Individual Difference Factors

12. Individual Differences in Learning
    Learners have different strategies, approaches, and capabilities for learning that are a function of prior experience and heredity.
13. Learning and Diversity
    Learning is most effective when differences in learners' linguistic, cultural, and social backgrounds are considered.
14. Standards and Assessment
    Setting appropriately high and challenging standards and assessing the learner as well as learning progress are integral aspects of the learning experience.

students' progress and competence presents a very narrow view of students' skills. This criticism is similar to the one leveled at IQ tests, which we described in chapter 9. To assess student progress and achievement, many psychologists and educators emphasize that a number of measures should be used, including tests, quizzes, projects, portfolios, classroom observations, and so on. Also, the tests used as part of NCLB don't measure creativity, motivation, persistence, flexible thinking, and social skills (Droege, 2004). Critics point out that teachers end up spending far too much class time "teaching to the test" by drilling students and having them memorize isolated facts at the expense of teaching that focuses on thinking skills, which students need for success in life (Crocker, 2005). Despite such criticisms, most U.S. schools are making accommodations to meet the requirements of NCLB.

Early Childhood Education

There are many variations in early childhood education—the way young children about 3 to 5 years of age are educated (Brewer, 2004; Goelman & others, 2003; Hyson, Copple, & Jones, 2006). In the story that opened this chapter, you read about the Reggio Emilia program in northern Italy, a promising strategy that is receiving increased attention. Other strategies include the child-centered kindergarten, the Montessori approach, and early childhood education programs designed for children who are disadvantaged.

www.mhhe.com/santrockcd11

Early Childhood Education
Reggio Emilia

The Child-Centered Kindergarten In the 1840s, Friedrich Froebel's concern for quality education for young children led to the founding of the kindergarten—literally, "a garden for children." The founder of the kindergarten understood that, like growing plants, children require careful nurturing. Unfortunately, too many of today's kindergartens have forgotten the importance of careful nurturing (Krogh & Slentz, 2001).

Nurturing is still key in the **child-centered kindergarten.** It emphasizes the education of the whole child and concern for his or her physical, cognitive, and socioemotional development. Instruction is organized around the child's needs, interests, and learning styles. Emphasis is on the process of learning, rather than what is learned (White & Coleman, 2000). The child-centered kindergarten honors three principles: (1) each child follows a unique developmental pattern; (2) young children learn best through firsthand experiences with people and materials; and (3) play is extremely important in the child's total development.

Experimenting, exploring, discovering, trying out, restructuring, speaking, and *listening* are frequent activities in excellent kindergarten programs. Such programs are closely attuned to the developmental status of 4- and 5-year-old children (Goelman & others, 2003).

The Montessori Approach Montessori schools are patterned after the educational philosophy of Maria Montessori (1870–1952), an Italian physician-turned-educator, who crafted a revolutionary approach to young children's education at the beginning of the twentieth century (Wentworth, 1999). Her work began in Rome with a group of children who were mentally retarded. She was successful in teaching them to read, write, and pass examinations designed for normal children. Some time later, she turned her attention to poor children from the slums of Rome and had similar success in teaching them. Her approach has since been adopted extensively in private nursery schools in the United States.

The **Montessori approach** is a philosophy of education in which children are given considerable freedom and spontaneity in choosing activities. They are allowed to move from one activity to another as they desire. The teacher acts as a facilitator rather than a director of learning. The teacher shows the child how to perform intellectual activities, demonstrates interesting ways to explore curriculum materials, and offers help when the child requests it.

Some developmentalists favor the Montessori approach, but others believe that it neglects children's social development (Chattin-McNichols, 1992). For example, while Montessori fosters independence and the development of cognitive skills, it de-emphasizes verbal interaction between the teacher and child and peer interaction. Montessori's critics also argue that it restricts imaginative play and that its

child-centered kindergarten Education that involves the whole child by considering both the child's physical, cognitive, and social development and the child's needs, interests, and learning styles.

Montessori approach An educational philosophy in which children are given considerable freedom and spontaneity in choosing activities and are allowed to move from one activity to another as they desire.

CAREERS in CHILD DEVELOPMENT

Yolanda Garcia
Director of Children's Services/Head Start

Yolanda Garcia has worked in the field of early childhood education and family support for three decades. She has been the Director of the Children's Services Department for the Santa Clara, California, County Office of Education since 1980. As director, she is responsible for managing child development programs for 2,500 3- to 5-year-old children in 127 classrooms. Her training includes two master's degrees, one in public policy and child welfare from the University of Chicago and another in educational administration from San Jose State University.

Yolanda has served on many national advisory committees that have resulted in improvements in the staffing of Head Start programs. Most notably, she served on the Head Start Quality Committee that recommended the development of Early Head Start and revised performance standards for Head Start programs. Yolanda currently is a member of the American Academy of Science Committee on the Integration of Science and Early Childhood Education.

Yolanda Garcia, Director of Children's Services/Head Start, working with some Head Start children in Santa Clara, California.

heavy reliance on self-corrective materials may not adequately allow for creativity and learning-style flexibility.

Education for Young Children Who Are Disadvantaged For many years, children from low-income families did not receive any education before they entered the first grade. In the 1960s, an effort was made to try to break the cycle of poverty and poor education for young children in the United States through compensatory education. **Project Head Start** is a compensatory program designed to provide children from low-income families the opportunity to acquire the skills and experiences important for success in school. Project Head Start began in the summer of 1965, funded by the Economic Opportunity Act, and it continues to serve disadvantaged children today.

Head Start programs are not all created equal. One estimate is that 40 percent of the 1,400 Head Start programs are of questionable quality (Zigler & Styfco, 1994). More attention needs to be given to developing consistently high-quality Head Start programs (Bronfenbrenner, 1995). One individual who is strongly motivated to make Head Start a valuable learning experience for young children from disadvantaged backgrounds is Yolanda Garcia. To read about her work, see the Careers in Child Development insert.

Evaluations support the positive influence of quality early childhood programs on both the cognitive and social worlds of disadvantaged young children (Anderson & others, 2003; Barnett & Hustedt, 2005; Reynolds, 1999). One high-quality early childhood education program (although not a Head Start program) is the Perry Preschool program in Ypsilanti, Michigan, a two-year preschool program that includes weekly home visits from program personnel. In an analysis of the long-term effects of the program, young adults who had been in the Perry Preschool program were compared with a control group of young adults from the same background who did not receive the enriched early childhood education (Weikart, 1993). Those who had been in the Perry Preschool program had higher high school graduation rates and more were in the workforce; fewer needed welfare; and they had lower crime rates and fewer teen pregnancies.

Another longitudinal investigation of early childhood education pooled the data from 11 different studies of early education that focused on children ranging in age from 9 to 19 years (Lazar, Darlington, & others, 1982). The early education models varied substantially, but all were carefully planned and executed by experts in early childhood education. Outcome measures included indicators of school competence (such as special education and grade retention), abilities (as measured by standardized intelligence and achievement tests), attitudes and values, and impact on the family. The results indicated substantial benefits of competent preschool education for low-income children on all four dimensions investigated. In sum, ample evidence indicates that well-designed and well-implemented early childhood education programs are successful with low-income children.

One change currently being considered by the U.S. Congress is to infuse Head Start programs with a stronger academic focus. Although early childhood experts clearly hope that the overall quality of Head Start programs will improve, some worry that the emphasis on academic skills will come at the expense of reduced health services and decreased emphasis on socioemotional skills.

www.mhhe.com/santrockcd11

Head Start Resources
Poverty and Learning

Developmentally Appropriate and Inappropriate Education

A growing number of educators and psychologists believe that preschool and young elementary school children learn best through active, hands-on teaching methods such as games and dramatic play. They know that children develop at varying rates and that schools need to allow for these individual differences (Golbeck, 2001; Henninger, 1999; Jalongo & Isenberg, 2000). They also believe that schools should focus on improving children's social development, as well as their cognitive development. Educators refer to this type of schooling as **developmentally appropriate practice;** it is based on knowledge of the typical development of children within an age span (age appropriateness) as well as the uniqueness of the child (individual appropriateness). In contrast, developmentally inappropriate practice for young children relies on abstract paper-and-pencil activities presented to large groups. The Reggio Emilia approach, described in the opening of the chapter, reflects developmentally appropriate practice.

A comprehensive document regarding developmentally appropriate practice in early childhood programs is the position statement by the National Association for the Education of Young Children (NAEYC) (Bredekamp, 1987, 1997; NAEYC, 1986). Figure 17.2 presents some of the NAEYC's descriptions of developmentally appropriate practice.

One recent study compared 182 children from five developmentally appropriate kindergarten classrooms (with hands-on activities and an integrated curriculum tailored to the age group, culture, and individual learning styles) and five developmentally inappropriate kindergarten classrooms (which had an academic, direct instruction emphasis with extensive use of workbooks/worksheets, seatwork, and rote drill/practice activities) in a Louisiana school system (Hart & others, 2003). Children from the two types of classrooms did not differ in prekindergarten readiness, and the classrooms were balanced in terms of sex and socioeconomic status. Teacher ratings of the children's behavior and scores on the California Achievement Test were obtained through the third grade. Children who were in developmentally appropriate classrooms were more advanced in vocabulary, math application, and math computation.

In another recent study, the academic achievement of mostly African American and Latino children who were attending Head Start was assessed in terms of whether they were in schools emphasizing developmentally appropriate or inappropriate practices (Huffman & Speer, 2000). The young children in the developmentally appropriate classrooms were more advanced in letter/word identification and showed better performance in applying problems over time.

Currently there is controversy about what the curriculum of U.S. early childhood education should be (Cress, 2004). On one side are those who advocate a child-centered, constructivist approach much like that emphasized by the NAEYC along the lines of developmentally appropriate practice. On the other side are those who advocate an academic, direct instruction approach.

In reality, many high-quality early childhood education programs include both academic and constructivist approaches. Many education experts like Lilian Katz (1999), though, worry about academic approaches that place too much pressure on young children to achieve and don't provide any opportunities to actively construct

Project Head Start Compensatory education designed to provide children from low-income families the opportunity to acquire the skills and experiences important for school success.

developmentally appropriate practice Education that focuses on the typical developmental patterns of children (age appropriateness) and the uniqueness of each child (individual appropriateness). Such practice contrasts with developmentally inappropriate practice, which ignores the concrete, hands-on approach to learning. Direct teaching largely through abstract paper-and-pencil activities presented to large groups of young children is believed to be developmentally inappropriate.

Component	Appropriate Practice	Inappropriate Practice
Curriculum goals	Experiences are provided in all developmental areas—physical, cognitive, social, and emotional.	Experiences are narrowly focused on cognitive development without recognition that all areas of the child's development are interrelated.
	Individual differences are expected, accepted, and used to design appropriate activities.	Children are evaluated only against group norms, and all are expected to perform the same tasks and achieve the same narrowly defined skills.
	Interactions and activities are designed to develop children's self-esteem and positive feelings toward learning.	Children's worth is measured by how well they conform to rigid expectations and perform on standardized tests.
Teaching strategies	Teachers prepare the environment for children to learn through active exploration and interaction with adults, other children, and materials.	Teachers use highly structured, teacher-directed lessons almost exclusively.
	Children select many of their own activities from among a variety the teacher prepares.	The teacher directs all activity, deciding what children will do and when.
	Children are expected to be mentally and physically active.	Children are expected to sit down, be quiet, and listen or do paper-and-pencil tasks for long periods of time. A major portion of time is spent passively sitting, watching, and listening.
Guidance of socioemotional development	Teachers enhance children's self-control by using positive guidance techniques, such as modeling and encouraging expected behavior, redirecting children to a more acceptable activity, and setting clear limits.	Teachers spend considerable time enforcing rules, punishing unacceptable behavior, demeaning children who misbehave, making children sit and be quiet, and refereeing disagreements.
	Children are provided many opportunities to develop social skills, such as cooperating, helping, negotiating, and talking with the person involved to solve interpersonal problems.	Children work individually at desks and tables most of the time and listen to the teacher's directions to the whole group.

FIGURE 17.2 NAEYC Recommendations for Developmentally Appropriate and Inappropriate Education

What is the curriculum controversy in early childhood education?

knowledge. Competent early childhood programs also should focus on cognitive development *and* socioemotional development, not exclusively on cognitive development (Anderson & others, 2003; Jacobson, 2004; Kagan & Scott-Little, 2004; NAEYC, 2002).

Early childhood education should encourage adequate preparation for learning, varied learning activities, trusting relationships between adults and children, and increased parental involvement (Hildebrand, Phenice, & Hines, 2000). Too many young children go to substandard early childhood programs. According to a report by the Carnegie Corporation (1996), four out of five early childhood programs did not meet quality standards.

Elementary School

For many children, entering the first grade signals a change from being a "home-child" to being a "school-child"—a situation that brings new roles and obligations. Children take up the new role of being a student, interact, develop new relationships, adopt new reference groups, and develop new standards by which to judge themselves. School provides children with a rich source of new ideas to shape their sense of self.

Evidence is mounting that early schooling proceeds mainly on the basis of negative feedback. Children's self-esteem in the latter part of elementary school is lower than it is in the earlier part, and older children rate themselves as less smart, less good, and less hardworking than do younger ones (Blumenfeld & others, 1981; Eccles & Wigfield, 2002).

Elementary teachers often feel pressured to "cover the curriculum." Frequently, teachers do so by tightly scheduling discrete time segments for each subject. This approach ignores the fact that children often do not need to distinguish learning by subject area. For example, they advance their knowledge of reading and writing when they work on social studies projects; they learn mathematical concepts through music and physical education (Katz & Chard, 1989). Thus, to facilitate leaning, the classroom might include a publishing center, complete with materials for writing, illustrating, typing, and binding student-made books; a science area, with animals and plants for observation and books to study; and other similar areas. Classrooms should also provide opportunities for spontaneous play,

As children make the transition to elementary school, they interact and develop relationships with new and significant others. School provides them with a rich source of new ideas to shape their sense of self.

recognizing that elementary school children continue to learn in all areas through unstructured play.

Many contemporary education experts believe children should be active, constructivist learners and taught through concrete, hands-on experience (Bonk & Cunningham, 1999). Let's examine an elementary school classroom based on these principles (Katz & Chard, 1989). The children were investigating a school bus. They wrote to the district's school superintendent and asked if they could have a bus parked at their school for a few days. They studied the bus, discovered the functions of its parts, and discussed traffic rules. Then, in the classroom, they built their own bus out of cardboard. The children had fun, but they also practiced writing, problem solving, and even some arithmetic. When the class had their parents' night, the teacher was ready with reports on how each child was doing. However, all that the parents wanted to see was the bus because their children had been talking about it at home for weeks.

Educating Adolescents

Adolescents present special challenges to U.S. schools. To understand the challenges, let's explore what the transition to middle/junior high school is like and the nature of effective schools for young adolescents.

www.mhhe.com/santrockcd11

Elementary Education

The Transition to Middle or Junior High School Junior high schools were established in the United States in the 1920s and 1930s because of the physical, cognitive, and social changes that characterize early adolescence, as well as the need for more schools for the growing student population. Old high schools became junior high schools, and new regional high schools were built. In most systems, the ninth grade remained a part of the high school in content, although physically separated from it in a 6-3-3 system. Gradually, the ninth grade was restored to the high school, as many school systems developed middle schools that include the seventh and eighth grades, or sixth, seventh, and eighth grades. The creation of middle schools was influenced by the earlier onset of puberty in recent decades.

The transition from elementary school to middle school has several benefits for students. In middle school, they are more likely to feel grown up, have more subjects from which to select, and have more opportunities to spend time with peers and to locate compatible friends. They enjoy increased independence from direct parental monitoring, and they may be more challenged intellectually by academic work.

Despite these potential benefits, the first year of middle or junior high school is difficult for many students (Collins & Steinberg, 2006; Hawkins & Berndt, 1985). For example, in one study of the transition from sixth grade in an elementary school to the seventh grade in a junior high school, adolescents' perceptions of the quality of their school life plunged in the seventh grade (Hirsch & Rapkin, 1987). In the seventh grade, the students were less satisfied with school, were less committed to school, and liked their teachers less. The drop in school satisfaction occurred regardless of how academically successful the students were.

In short, the transition to middle school or junior high school can be stressful (Eccles, 2004; Seidman, 2000; Wigfield & others, 2006). Why? The transition takes place at a time when many changes—in the individual, in the family, and in school—are occurring simultaneously. These changes include puberty and related concerns about body image; the emergence of at least some aspects of formal operational thought, including accompanying changes in social cognition; increased responsibility; and decreased dependency on parents. Changes in the school include a switch to a larger, more impersonal classroom; to having many teachers; to having a larger, more heterogeneous set of peers; and to an increased focus on achievement and performance. Also, when students make the transition to middle or junior

The transition from elementary to middle or junior high school occurs at the same time as a number of other developmental changes. *What are some of these other developmental changes?*

high school, they experience the **top-dog phenomenon,** the circumstance of moving from the top position (being the oldest, biggest, and most powerful students in elementary school) to the lowest position (being the youngest, smallest, and least powerful in middle or junior high school).

Effective Schools for Young Adolescents Some critics of today's junior high and middle schools argue that they have become watered-down versions of high schools. Instead of offering curricular and extracurricular activities geared to the biological and psychological development of young adolescents, say the critics, middle and junior high schools mimic the curricular and extracurricular schedules of high schools.

In a 1989 report, *Turning Points: Preparing American Youth for the 21st Century,* the Carnegie Foundation concluded that most young adolescents in the United States attend massive, impersonal schools; learn from seemingly irrelevant curricula; trust few adults in school; and lack access to health care and counseling. The Carnegie Foundation (1989) report recommended the following:

- Develop smaller "communities" or "houses" to lessen the impersonal nature of large middle schools.
- Lower student-to-counselor ratios from several-hundred-to-1 to 10-to-1.
- Involve parents and community leaders in schools.
- Develop curricula that produce students who are literate, understand the sciences, and have a sense of health, ethics, and citizenship.
- Have teachers team teach in more flexibly designed curriculum blocks that integrate several disciplines, instead of presenting students with disconnected, rigidly separated 50-minute segments.
- Boost students' health and fitness with more in-school programs, and help students who need public health care to get it.

In *Turning Points 2000,* there was continued emphasis on the earlier *Turning Points* recommendations (Jackson & Davis, 2000). Some of the new emphases in the 2000 recommendations focused on teaching a curriculum grounded in rigorous academic standards, using instructional methods designed to prepare all students to achieve higher standards, provide a safe and healthy school environment, and involve parents and communities in supporting student learning and healthy development. In sum,

www.mhhe.com/santrockcd11

Schools for Adolescents
National Center for Education Statistics
United States Department of Education
Middle Schools

top-dog phenomenon The circumstance of moving from the top position in elementary school to the lowest position in middle or junior high school.

FIGURE 17.3 Trends in High School Dropout Rates. From 1972 through 2001, the school dropout rate for Latinos remained very high (27 percent of 16- to 24-year-olds in 2001). The African American dropout rate was still higher (10.9 percent) than the White non-Latino rate (7.3 percent) in 2001. The overall dropout rate declined considerably from the 1940s through the 1960s but has declined only slightly since 1972.

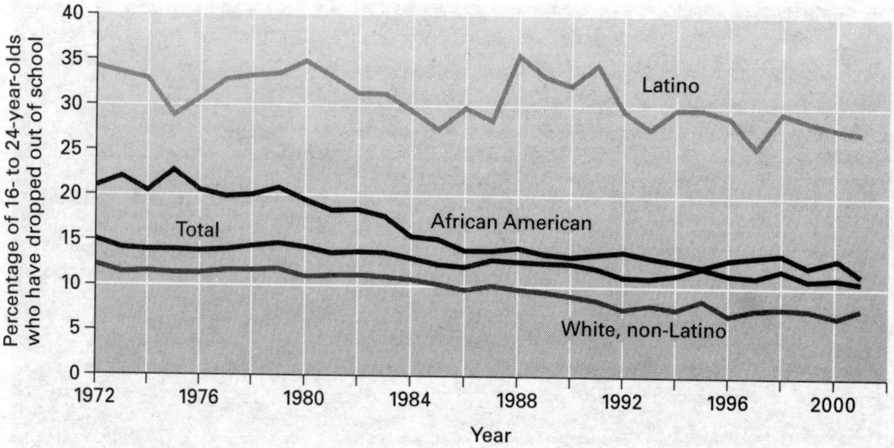

middle schools throughout the nation need a major redesign if they are to be effective in educating adolescents for becoming competent adults in the twenty-first century.

High School Just as there are concerns about U.S. middle school education, so are there concerns about U.S. high school education (Dornbusch & Kaufman, 2001; Hemmings, 2004). Many students graduate from high school with inadequate reading, writing, and mathematical skills, including many who go on to college and must enroll in remediation classes there. Other students drop out of high school and do not have skills that will allow them to advance in the work world.

In the last half of the twentieth century, high school dropout rates declined overall (National Center for Educational Statistics, 2001). For example, in the 1940s, more than half of U.S. 15- to 24-year-olds had dropped out of school; in 2001, this figure had decreased to only 10.7 percent. Figure 17.3 shows the trends in high school dropout rates from 1972 through 2001. Notice that the dropout rate of Latino adolescents remains high (27 percent of 16- to 24-year-old Latino adolescents had dropped out of school in 2001). Although adequate statistics on Native American youth have not been obtained, some estimates indicate that they likely have the highest dropout rate in the United States, with only about 50 to 70 percent completing their high school education.

Gender differences characterize U.S. dropout rates, with males more likely to drop out than females (12.2 versus 9.3 percent). The gender gap in dropout rates is especially large for Latino adolescents (31.6 versus 22.1 percent) and African American adolescents (13.0 versus 9.0 percent) (data for 2001).

Students drop out of schools for many reasons (Anguiano, 2004; Christenson & Thurlow, 2004). In one study, almost 50 percent of the dropouts cited school-related reasons for leaving school, such as not liking school or being expelled or suspended (Rumberger, 1995). Twenty percent of the dropouts (but 40 percent of the Latino students) cited economic reasons for leaving school. One-third of the female students dropped out for personal reasons, such as pregnancy or marriage.

A recent review of school-based dropout programs found that the most effective programs provided early reading programs, tutoring, counseling, and mentoring (Lehr & others, 2003). They also emphasized the importance of creating caring environments and relationships, and they offered community-service opportunities.

These adolescents participate in the "I Have a Dream" (IHAD) Program, a comprehensive, long-term dropout prevention program that has been very successful.

"I Have a Dream" (IHAD) is an innovative comprehensive, long-term dropout prevention program administered by the National "I Have a Dream" Foundation in New York. Since the National IHAD Foundation was created in 1986 it has grown to number over 180 projects in 64 cities and 27 states, serving more than 12,000 children ("I Have a Dream" Foundation, 2005). Local IHAD projects around the country "adopt" entire grades (usually the third or fourth) from public elementary schools, or corresponding age cohorts from public housing developments. These children—"Dreamers"—are then provided with a program of academic, social, cultural, and recreational activities throughout their elementary, middle school, and high school years. An important part of this program is that it is personal rather than institutional: IHAD sponsors and staff develop close long-term relationships with the children. When participants complete high school, IHAD provides the tuition assistance necessary for them to attend a state or local college or vocational school.

The IHAD Program was created in 1981, when philanthropist Eugene Lang made an impromptu offer of college tuition to a class of graduating sixth-graders at P.S. 121 in East Harlem. Statistically, 75 percent of the students should have dropped out of school; instead, 90 percent graduated and 60 percent went on to college. Other evaluations of IHAD programs have found dramatic improvements in grades, test scores, and school attendance, as well as a reduction of behavioral problems among Dreamers. For example, in Portland, Oregon, twice as many Dreamers as control group students had reached a math standard, and the Dreamers were less likely to be referred to the juvenile justice system (Davis, Hyatt, & Arrasmith, 1998).

Review and Reflect • LEARNING GOAL 1

1 Discuss approaches to schooling and development

Review

- What are some contemporary approaches to student learning?
- What are some variations in early childhood education?
- What are some characteristics of elementary education?
- How are U.S. adolescents educated, and what are the challenges in educating adolescents?

Reflect

- How would you characterize the approach of the schools that you attended as a child and as an adolescent? Do you think your schools were effective? Explain.

2 SOCIOECONOMIC STATUS AND ETHNICITY IN SCHOOLS

Socioeconomic Status | Ethnicity in Schools

Children from low-income, ethnic minority backgrounds have more difficulties in school than do their middle-socioeconomic-status, White counterparts. Why? Critics argue that schools are not doing a good job of educating low-income or ethnic minority students (Scott-Jones, 1995; Spencer, 2006). Let's further explore the roles of socioeconomic status and ethnicity in schools.

Socioeconomic Status

Many children in poverty face problems that present barriers to their learning (Books, 2004; Cooter, 2004; Parke & Buriel, 2006). They might have parents who don't set high educational standards for them, who are incapable of reading to them, and who don't have enough money to pay for educational materials and experiences, such as books and trips to zoos and museums. They might be malnourished and live in areas where crime and violence are a way of life.

In his book *Savage Inequalities,* Jonathan Kozol (1991) vividly portrayed the problems that children of poverty face in their neighborhood and at school. *What are some of these problems?*

Interview with Jonathan Kozol
Exploring Multicultural Education
Multicultural Education Resources
The Comer School Development Program

Compared with schools in higher income areas, schools in low-income areas are more likely to have more students with low achievement test scores, low graduation rates, and small percentages of students going to college; they are more likely to have young teachers with less experience; and they are more likely to encourage rote learning (Spring, 2005). Too few schools in low-income neighborhoods provide students with environments that are conducive to learning (Tozer, Senese, & Violas, 2005). Many of the schools' buildings and classrooms are old and crumbling.

Ethnicity in Schools

More than one-third of all African American and almost one-third of all Latino students attend schools in the 47 largest city school districts in the United States, compared with only 5 percent of all White and 22 percent of all Asian American students. Many of these inner-city schools are still segregated, are grossly underfunded, and do not provide adequate opportunities for children to learn effectively. Thus, the effects of SES and the effects of ethnicity are often intertwined.

Even outside of inner-city schools, school segregation is still a factor in U.S. education. Almost one-third of all African American and Latino students attend schools in which 90 percent or more of the students are from minority groups (Banks, 2002, 2003, 2006).

The school experiences of students from different ethnic groups vary considerably (Spring, 2005, 2006; Padilla, 2005; Pang, 2005; Pedraza & Rivera, 2005; Powell & Caseau, 2004). African American and Latino students are much less likely than non-Latino White or Asian American students to be enrolled in academic, college preparatory programs and are much more likely to be enrolled in remedial and special education programs. Asian American students are far more likely than other ethnic minority groups to take advanced math and science courses in high school. African American students are twice as likely as Latinos, Native Americans, or Whites to be suspended from school.

Some experts say that a form of institutional racism permeates many American schools by which teachers accept a low level of performance from children of color (Ogbu & Stern, 2001; Spencer, 1990). American anthropologist John Ogbu (1989) proposed that ethnic minority students are placed in a position of subordination and exploitation in the American educational system. He believes that students of color, especially African Americans and Latinos, have inferior educational opportunities, are exposed to teachers and school administrators who have low academic expectations for them, and encounter negative stereotypes (Ogbu & Stern, 2001). In one study of middle schools in predominantly Latino areas of Miami, Latino and White teachers rated African American students as having more behavioral problems than African American teachers rated the same students as having (Zimmerman & others, 1995).

Following are some strategies for improving relationships among ethnically diverse students (Santrock, 2006).

- *Turn the class into a jigsaw classroom.* When Eliot Aronson was a professor at the University of Texas at Austin, the school system contacted him for ideas on how to reduce the increasing racial tension in classrooms. Aronson (1986) developed the concept of "jigsaw classroom," in which students from different cultural backgrounds are placed in a cooperative group in which they have to construct different parts of a project to reach a common goal. Aronson used the term *jigsaw* because he saw the technique as much like a group of students cooperating to put different pieces together to complete a jigsaw puzzle. How might this work? Team sports, drama productions, and music performances are examples of contexts in which students cooperatively participate to reach a common goal.
- *Use technology to foster cooperation with students from around the world.*
- *Encourage students to have positive personal contact with diverse other students.* Contact alone does not do the job of improving relationships with diverse others.

For example, busing ethnic minority students to predominantly White schools, or vice versa, has not reduced prejudice or improved interethnic relations (Minuchin & Shapiro, 1983). What matters is what happens after children get to school. Especially beneficial in improving interethnic relations is sharing one's worries, successes, failures, coping strategies, interests, and other personal information with people of other ethnicities. When this happens, people are seen more as individuals than as a homogeneous cultural group.

- *Encourage students to engage in perspective taking.* Exercises and activities that help students see others' perspectives can improve interethnic relations (Pederson, 2004). This helps students "step into the shoes" of peers who are culturally different and feel what it is like to be treated in fair or unfair ways.
- *Help students think critically and be emotionally intelligent when cultural issues are involved.* Students who learn to think critically and deeply about interethnic relations are likely to decrease their prejudice. Becoming more emotionally intelligent includes understanding the causes of one's feelings, managing anger, listening to what others are saying, and being motivated to share and cooperate.
- *Reduce bias.* Teachers can reduce bias by displaying images of children from diverse ethnic and cultural groups, selecting play materials and classroom activities that encourage cultural understanding, helping students resist stereotyping, and working with parents.
- *View the school and community as a team to help support teaching efforts.* James Comer (1988; Comer & others, 1996) believes that a community, team approach is the best way to educate children. Three important aspects of the Comer Project for Change are (1) a governance and management team that develops a comprehensive school plan, assessment strategy, and staff development plan; (2) a mental health or school support team; and (3) a parent's program. Comer believes that the entire school community should have a cooperative rather than an adversarial attitude. The Comer program is currently operating in more than 600 schools in 26 states. To read further about James Comer's work, see the Careers in Child Development insert.
- *Be a competent cultural mediator.* Teachers can play a powerful role as cultural mediators by being sensitive to racist content in materials and classroom interactions, learning more about different ethnic groups, being sensitive to children's ethnic attitudes, viewing students of color positively, and thinking of positive ways to get parents of color more involved as partners with teachers in educating children (Jones & Fuller, 2003).

CAREERS in CHILD DEVELOPMENT

James Comer
Child Psychiatrist

James Comer grew up in a low-income neighborhood in East Chicago, Indiana, and credits his parents with leaving no doubt about the importance of education. He obtained a BA degree from Indiana University. He went on to obtain a medical degree from Howard University College of Medicine, a Master of Public Health degree from the University of Michigan School of Public Health, and psychiatry training at the Yale University School of Medicine's Child Study Center. He currently is the Maurice Falk Professor of Child Psychiatry at the Yale University Child Study Center and an associate dean at the Yale University Medical School. During his years at Yale, James has concentrated his career on promoting a focus on child development as a way of improving schools. His efforts in support of healthy development of young people are known internationally.

Comer, perhaps, is best known for the founding of the School Development Program in 1968, which promotes the collaboration of parents, educators, and community to improve social, emotional, and academic outcomes for children. His concept of teamwork is currently improving the educational environment in more than 500 schools throughout America.

James Comer (*left*) is shown with some of the inner-city African American children who attend a school that became a better learning environment because of Comer's intervention. Comer is convinced that a strong, familylike atmosphere is a key to improving the quality of inner-city schools.

Review and Reflect • LEARNING GOAL 2

2 Describe the roles of socioeconomic status and ethnicity in schools

Review

- How do socioeconomic status and poverty influence children's schooling?
- How is ethnicity involved in children's schooling?

Reflect

- In the context of education, are ethnic differences always negative? Come up with some differences that might be positive in U.S. classrooms.

3 CHILDREN WITH DISABILITIES

Learning Disabilities | Attention Deficit Hyperactivity Disorder | Educational Issues

Prejudice and discrimination may be barriers to learning not only for children from less-favored socioeconomic and ethnic backgrounds but also for children with a disability. Approximately 10 percent of all children in the United States receive special education or related services for a disability. As figure 17.4 shows, a little more than half of these children have a learning disability (U.S. Department of Education, 2000). Substantial percentages of children also have speech or language impairments (19.4 percent of those with disabilities who received special services), mental retardation (11 percent), and serious emotional disturbance (8.4 percent).

Learning Disabilities

Bobby's second-grade teacher complains that his spelling is awful. Eight-year-old Tim says reading is really hard for him, and a lot of times the words don't make

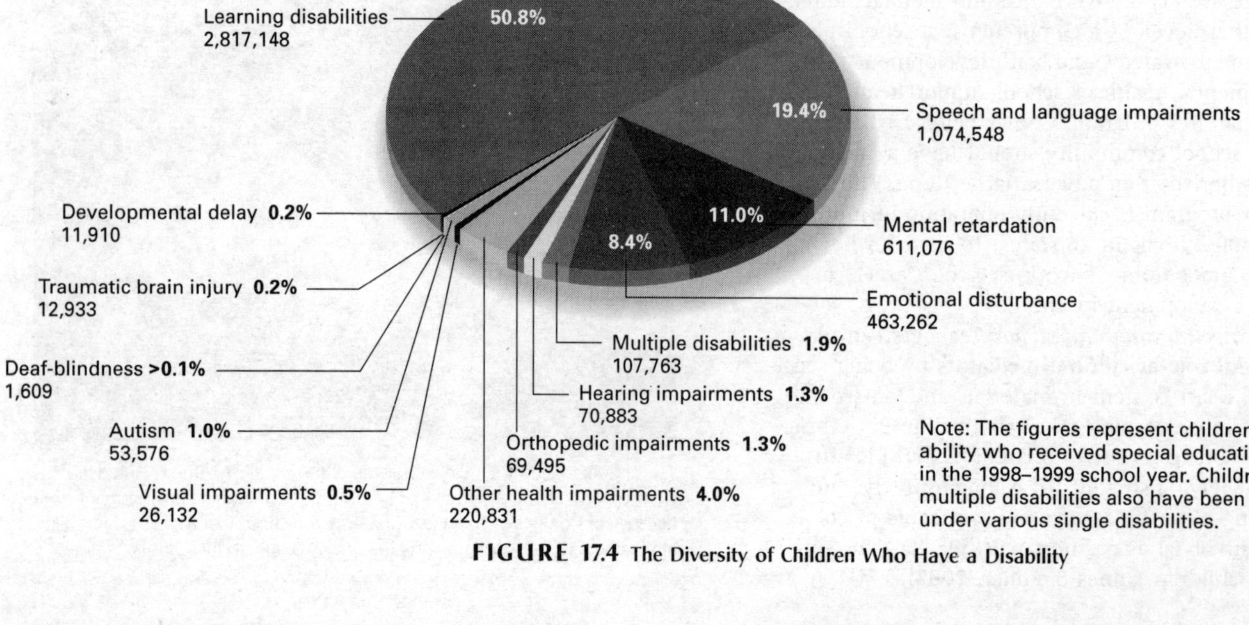

Note: The figures represent children with a disability who received special education services in the 1998–1999 school year. Children with multiple disabilities also have been counted under various single disabilities.

FIGURE 17.4 The Diversity of Children Who Have a Disability much sense. Alisha has good oral language skills but has considerable difficulty in computing correct answers to arithmetic problems. Each of these students has a learning disability.

Characteristics After examining the research on learning disabilities, leading expert Linda Siegel (2003) recently concluded that a diagnosis of a **learning disability** should be given only when the child (1) has a minimum IQ level, (2) has a significant difficulty in a school-related area (especially reading or mathematics), and (3) does not display certain severe emotional disorders, or experiences difficulties as a result of using English as a second language, or have sensory disabilities, or specific neurological deficits.

About three times as many boys as girls are classified as having a learning disability (U.S. Department of Education, 2000). Among the explanations for this gender difference are a greater biological vulnerability among boys and *referral bias* (that is, boys are more likely to be referred by teachers for treatment because of their behavior) (Liederman & others, 2005).

About 5 percent of all school-age children in the United States receive special education or related services because of a learning disability. In the federal classification of children receiving special education and related services, attention deficit hyperactivity disorder (ADHD) is included in the learning disabilities category. Because of the significant interest in ADHD today, we will discuss it by itself following learning disabilities.

In the past two decades, the percentage of children classified as having a learning disability has increased substantially—from less than 30 percent of all children receiving special education and related services in 1977 to a little more than 50 percent today. Some experts say that the dramatic increase reflects poor diagnostic practices and overidentification. They believe that teachers sometimes are too quick to label children with the slightest learning problem as having a learning disability, instead of recognizing that the problem may rest in their ineffective teaching. Other experts say the increase in children being labeled with a "learning disability" is justified (Hallahan & Kauffmann, 2006).

Identification Diagnosing whether a child has a learning disability is often a difficult task (Berninger, 2006). One identification procedure requires a significant discrepancy between actual achievement and expected achievement, the latter being estimated by an individually administered intelligence test. However, many educators question the adequacy of this approach (Francis & others, 2005). Another identification strategy that has recently been proposed is *response-to-intervention* or *response-to-treatment,* which involves students not learning effectively in response to effective instruction (Fuchs & others, 2003). However, whether this approach can be effectively implemented is still being debated (Kavale, Holdnack, & Mostert, 2005).

Initial identification of a possible learning disability is usually made by the classroom teacher. If a learning disability is suspected, the teacher calls on specialists. An interdisciplinary team of professionals is best suited to verify whether a student has a learning disability. Individual psychological evaluations (of intelligence) and educational assessments (such as current level of achievement) are required (Mercer & Pullen, 2005; Overton, 2000). In addition, tests of visual-motor skills, language, and memory may be used.

Dyslexia The most common problem that characterizes children with a learning disability involves reading (Moats, 2004; Pugh & others, 2005; Vaughn & others, 2005). Such children especially show problems with phonological skills, which involve being able to understand how sounds and letters match up to make words (Savage & others, 2005). **Dyslexia** is a category that is reserved for individuals who have a severe impairment in their ability to read and spell (Ramus, 2004; Spafford & Grosser, 2005).

learning disability Includes three components: (1) a minimum IQ level, (2) a significant difficulty in a school-related area (especially reading or mathematics), and (3) exclusion of only severe emotional disorders, second-language background, sensory disabilities, and/or specific neurological deficits.

dyslexia A category of learning disabilities involving a severe impairment in the ability to read and spell.

Children with a learning disability often have difficulties in handwriting, spelling, or composition. Their writing may be extremely slow, their writing products may be virtually illegible, and they may make numerous spelling errors because of their inability to match up sounds and letters.

Causes and Intervention Strategies The precise causes of learning disabilities have not yet been determined. However, some possible causes have been proposed. Learning disabilities tend to run in families with one parent having a disability such as dyslexia, although the specific genetic transmission of learning disabilities has not been discovered (McCrory & others, 2005; Monuteaux & others, 2005). Researchers also use brain imaging techniques, such as magnetic resonance imaging, to reveal any regions of the brain that might be involved in learning disabilities (Berninger, 2006; Vinckenbosch, Robichon, & Eliez, 2005). This research has indicated that it is unlikely learning disabilities reside in a single, specific brain location and more likely are due to problems in integrating information from multiple brain regions or subtle difficulties in brain structures and functions (National Institute of Mental Health, 1993). Another possibility is that some learning disabilities are caused by problems during prenatal development or delivery. A number of studies have found that learning disabilities are more prevalent in low birth weight infants (Litt & others, 2005).

Many interventions have focused on improving the child's reading ability (Alexander & Slinger-Constant, 2004; Berninger, 2006). For example, in one study, instruction in phonological awareness at the kindergarten level had positive effects on reading development when the children reached the first grade (Blachman & others, 1994).

Unfortunately, not all children who have a learning disability that involves reading problems have the benefit of appropriate early intervention. Most children whose reading disability is not diagnosed until the third grade or later and who receive standard interventions fail to show noticeable improvement (Lyon, 1996). However, intensive instruction over a period of time by a competent teacher can remediate the deficient reading skills of many children (Bost & Vaughn, 2002).

Children with severe phonological deficits that lead to poor decoding and word recognition skills respond to intervention more slowly than do children with mild to moderate reading problems (Torgesen, 1999). Also, the success of even the best-designed reading intervention depends on the training and skills of the teacher.

attention deficit hyperactivity disorder (ADHD) A disability in which children consistently show one or more of the following characteristics: (1) inattention, (2) hyperactivity, and (3) impulsivity.

Improving outcomes for children with a learning disability is a challenging task and generally has required intensive intervention for even modest improvement in outcomes (Berninger, 2006; Hallahan & Kauffman, 2006). However, no model program has proven to be effective for all children with learning disabilities (Terman & others, 1996).

Many children with ADHD show impulsive behavior, such as this child who is jumping out of his seat and throwing a paper airplane at other children. *How would you handle this situation if you were a teacher and this were to happen in your classroom?*

Attention Deficit Hyperactivity Disorder

Matthew has attention deficit hyperactivity disorder, and the outward signs are fairly typical. He has trouble attending to the teacher's instructions and is easily distracted. He can't sit still for more than a few minutes at a time, and his handwriting is messy. His mother describes him as very fidgety.

Characteristics **Attention deficit hyperactivity disorder (ADHD)** is a disability in which children consistently show one or more of these characteristics over a period of time: (1) inattention, (2) hyperactivity, and (3) impulsivity. Children who are inattentive have difficulty focusing on any one thing and may get bored with a task after only a few minutes. Children who are hyperactive show high levels of physical activity, almost always seeming to be in motion. Children who are impulsive have difficulty curbing their reactions and don't do a good job of thinking before they act. Depending on the characteristics that children with ADHD display, they can be diagnosed as (1) ADHD with predominantly inattention, (2) ADHD with predominantly hyperactivity/impulsivity, or (3) ADHD with both inattention and hyperactivity/impulsivity.

Diagnosis and Developmental Status The number of children diagnosed and treated for ADHD has increased substantially, by some estimates doubling in the 1990s (Stein, 2004). The disorder occurs as much as four to nine times more in boys than in girls. There is controversy about the increased diagnosis of ADHD (Terman & others, 1996), however. Some experts attribute the increase mainly to heightened awareness of the disorder. Others are concerned that many children are being diagnosed without undergoing extensive professional evaluation based on input from multiple sources.

Signs of ADHD may be present in the preschool years. Parents and preschool or kindergarten teachers may notice that the child has an extremely high activity level and a limited attention span. They may say the child is "always on the go," "can't sit still even for a second," or "never seems to listen." Many children with ADHD are difficult to discipline, have a low tolerance for frustration, and have problems in peer relations. Other common characteristics of children with ADHD include general immaturity and clumsiness.

Although signs of ADHD are often present in the preschool years, their classification often doesn't take place until the elementary school years (Foy & Earls, 2005; Stein & Perrin, 2003). The increased academic and social demands of formal schooling, as well as stricter standards for behavioral control, often illuminate the problems of the child with ADHD. Elementary school teachers typically report that this type of child has difficulty in working independently, completing seatwork, and organizing work. Restlessness and distractibility also are often noted. These problems are more likely to be observed in repetitive or taxing tasks, or tasks the child perceives to be boring (such as completing worksheets or doing homework).

It used to be thought that ADHD decreased in adolescence, but now it is believed that this often is not the case. Estimates suggest that ADHD decreases in only about one-third of adolescents. Increasingly, it is being recognized that these problems may continue into adulthood (Dige & Wik, 2005; Wilens & Dodson, 2004).

Causes and Treatment Definitive causes of ADHD have not been found. However, a number of causes have been proposed, such as low levels of certain neurotransmitters (chemical messengers in the brain), prenatal and postnatal abnormalities, and environmental toxins, such as lead (Biderman & Faraone, 2003). Thirty to 50 percent of children with ADHD have a sibling or parent who has the disorder (Heiser & others, 2004; Voeller, 2004).

Many experts recommend a combination of academic, behavioral, and medical interventions to help students with ADHD learn and adapt more effectively (Voeller, 2004). This intervention requires cooperation and effort on the part of the parents of students with ADHD, teachers, administrators, special educators, school psychologists, and health-care professionals (Whalen, 2001; Zentall, 2006).

About 85 to 90 percent of children with ADHD are taking stimulant medication such as Ritalin or Adderall (which has fewer side effects than Ritalin) to control their behavior (Denny, 2001; Fone & Nutt, 2005). Ritalin and Adderall are stimulants, and for most individuals, they speed up the nervous system and behavior (Raphaelson, 2004; Rowe, 2005). However, in many children with ADHD, the drug speeds up underactive areas of the prefrontal cortex that control attention, impulsivity, and planning. This enhanced ability to focus their attention results in what *appears* to be a "slowing down" of behavior in these children (Reeves & Schweitzer, 2004). Researchers have found that a combination of medication (such as Ritalin) and behavior management improves the behavior of children with ADHD better than medication alone or behavior management alone (Chronis & others, 2004; Steer, 2005; Swanson & Volkow,

2002). Some critics argue that many physicians are too quick to prescribe stimulants for children with milder forms of ADHD (Marcovitch, 2004; Zakriski & others, 2005).

Educational Issues

The legal requirement that U.S. schools serve all children with a disability is fairly recent. Until laws were passed in the 1970s that mandated services for children with disabilities, most public schools either refused to enroll them or inadequately served them. In 1975, *Public Law 94-142*, the Education for All Handicapped Children Act, required that all students with disabilities be given a free, appropriate public education.

In 1990, Public Law 94-142 was recast as the *Individuals with Disabilities Education Act (IDEA)*. IDEA was amended in 1997 and then reauthorized in 2004 and renamed the Individuals with Disabilities Education Improvement Act. IDEA spells out broad mandates for services to all children with disabilities (Friend, 2006; Hallahan & Kauffman, 2006; Hardman, Drew, & Egan, 2006; Smith, 2006). These include evaluation and eligibility determination, appropriate education and an individualized education plan (IEP), and education in the least restrictive environment (LRE).

A major aspect of the 2004 reauthorization of IDEA involved aligning it with the government's No Child Left Behind (NCLB) legislation that was designed to improve the educational achievement of all students, including those with disabilities. Both IDEA and NCLB mandate that most students with disabilities be included in general assessments of educational progress. This alignment includes requiring most students with disabilities "to take standard tests of academic achievement and to achieve at a level equal to that of students without disabilities. Whether this expectation is reasonable is an open question" (Hallahan & Kauffman, 2006, pp. 28–29). Alternate assessments for students with disabilities and funding to help states improve instruction, assessment, and accountability for educating students with disabilities are included in the 2004 reauthorization of IDEA.

Increasingly, children with disabilities are being taught in the regular classroom, as is this child with mild mental retardation.

An **individualized education plan (IEP)** is a written statement that spells out a program that is specifically tailored for the student with a disability. In general, the IEP should be (1) related to the child's learning capacity, (2) specifically constructed to meet the child's individual needs and not merely a copy of what is offered to other children, and (3) designed to provide educational benefits.

The **least restrictive environment (LRE)** is a setting that is as similar as possible to the one in which children who do not have a disability are educated. This provision of the IDEA has given a legal basis to efforts to educate children with a disability in the regular classroom (Dettmer, Dyck, & Thurston, 2002). The term **inclusion** describes educating a child with special education needs full-time in the regular classroom (Choate, 2004; Friend, 2006; Lewis & Doorlag, 2006).

Many legal changes regarding children with disabilities have been extremely positive (Heward, 2006). Compared with several decades ago, far more children today are receiving competent, specialized services. For many children, inclusion in the regular classroom, with modifications or supplemental services, is appropriate (Smith & others, 2006; Wood, 2006). However, some leading experts on special education argue that the effort to use inclusion to educate children with disabilities has become too extreme in some cases. For example, James Kauffman and his colleagues (Kauffman & Hallahan, 2005; Kaufmann, McGee, & Brigham, 2004) state that inclusion too often has meant making accommodations in the regular classroom that do not always benefit children with disabilities. They advocate a more individualized approach that does not always involve full inclusion but offers options such as special education outside the regular classroom. Kauffman and his colleagues (2004, p. 620) acknowledge that children with disabilities "*do* need the services of specially trained professionals to achieve their full potential. They *do* sometimes need altered curricula

individualized education plan (IEP) A written statement that spells out a program tailored to a child with a disability. The plan should be (1) related to the child's learning capacity, (2) specially constructed to meet the child's individual needs and not merely a copy of what is offered to other children, and (3) designed to provide educational benefits.

least restrictive environment (LRE) The concept that a child with a disability must be educated in a setting that is as similar as possible to the one in which children who do not have a disability are educated.

inclusion Educating a child with special education needs full-time in the regular classroom.

or adaptations to make their learning possible." However, "we sell students with disabilities short when we pretend that they are not different from typical students. We make the same error when we pretend that they must *not* be expected to put forth extra effort if they are to learn to do some things—or learn to do something in a different way." Like general education, an important aspect of special education should be to challenge students with disabilities "to become all they can be."

www.mhhe.com/santrockcd11

Education of Children Who Are Exceptional
Inclusion
The Council for Exceptional Children
Legal Issues and Disabilities

Review and Reflect • LEARNING GOAL 3

3 Characterize children with disabilities and their schooling

Review

- Who are children with disabilities, and what characterizes children with learning disabilities?
- How would you describe children with attention deficit hyperactivity disorder? What kind of treatment are they typically given?
- What are some issues in educating children with disabilities?

Reflect

- Think back to your own schooling and how children with learning disabilities or ADHD either were or were not diagnosed. Were you aware of such individuals in your classes? Were they helped by specialists? You may know one or more individuals with a learning disability or ADHD. Ask them about their educational experiences and whether they believe schools could have done a better job of helping them.

4 ACHIEVEMENT

Extrinsic and Intrinsic Motivation | Attribution | Goal-Setting, Planning, and Self-Monitoring

Mastery Motivation | Self-Efficacy | Ethnicity and Culture

In any classroom, whoever the teacher is and whatever approach is used, some children achieve more than others. Why? The reasons for variations in achievement include the motivation, goals, and other characteristics of the child as well as sociocultural contexts.

Extrinsic and Intrinsic Motivation

Are you reading this paragraph because you want to learn about achievement or because you want to obtain a good grade or both? Your answer points to two basic types of motivation that influence achievement: extrinsic and intrinsic motivation. The behavioral perspective emphasizes the importance of extrinsic motivation. **Extrinsic motivation** involves doing something to obtain something else (the activity is a means to an end). Extrinsic motivation is often influenced by external incentives such as rewards and punishments. For example, a student may study for a test in order to obtain a good grade.

Whereas the behavioral perspective emphasizes extrinsic motivation, the cognitive perspective stresses the importance of intrinsic motivation. **Intrinsic motivation** involves the internal motivation to do something for its own sake (the activity is an end in itself). For example, a student may study for a test because he or she enjoys the content of the course.

extrinsic motivation Response to external incentives such as rewards and punishments.

intrinsic motivation Internal motivational factors such as self-determination, curiosity, challenge, and effort.

Intrinsic and extrinsic motivation are not simply two sides of one coin; they do not have the same effects. Current evidence indicates that teachers should aim to establish a classroom climate in which students are intrinsically motivated to learn (Alderman, 2004; Blumenfeld, Krajik, & Kempler, 2006; Eccles, 2004; Wigfield & Eccles, 2002; Wigfield & others, 2006).

Self-Determination and Choice Granting students some autonomy is one way to encourage internal motivation. Students' internal motivation and intrinsic interest in school tasks increase when they have opportunities to make choices and take responsibility for their learning (Stipek, 1996, 2002). For example, in one study, high school science students who were encouraged to organize their own experiments demonstrated more care and interest in the laboratory than did their counterparts who had to follow detailed instructions and directions (Rainey, 1965). In another study, those students who were given some choice of activities and when to do them, and were encouraged to take personal responsibility for their behavior, had higher achievement gains and were more likely to graduate from high school than a control group (deCharms, 1984).

Extrinsic Rewards and Internal Motivation The desire for autonomy has another result: students want to believe that they are doing something because of their own will, not because of external rewards (Deci, Koestner, & Ryan, 2001; Deci & Ryan, 1994). In some situations, rewards can actually undermine learning. For example, in one study, students who had a strong interest in art spent more time drawing when they did not expect a reward than did their counterparts who also had a strong interest in art but knew they would be rewarded (Lepper, Greene, & Nisbett, 1973). Other researchers have found similar effects (Morgan, 1984).

However, classroom rewards can be useful (Cameron, 2001). Rewards can (1) act as an incentive to engage in tasks, in which case the goal is to control the student's behavior, and (2) convey information about mastery (Bandura, 1982; Deci, 1975). Rewards used as incentives lead to perceptions that the student's behavior was caused by the external reward and not by the student's own motivation. In contrast, when rewards convey information about mastery, they can enhance students' feelings of competence (Schunk, 2004).

To understand the difference between using rewards to control students' behavior and using them to provide information about mastery, consider this example (Schunk, 2004). A teacher puts a reward system in place in which the more work

CALVIN AND HOBBES Copyright © Watterson. Distributed by UNIVERSAL PRESS SYNDICATE. Reprinted with permission. All rights reserved.

students accomplish, the more points they will earn. The points can be exchanged for privileges, but the points also provide the students with information about their capabilities. That is, the more points students earn, the more work they have accomplished. As they accumulate points, students are more likely to feel competent. In contrast, suppose the points were awarded simply for spending time on a task. Because the points don't convey anything about capabilities, students are likely to perceive that the rewards control their behavior.

Thus, rewards that convey information about students' mastery can increase intrinsic motivation by increasing their sense of competence. However, criticism that carries information that students are incompetent can undermine intrinsic motivation, especially if students doubt their ability to become competent (Stipek, 2002).

The reward of a thing well done is to have done it.

—RALPH WALDO EMERSON
American Poet and Essayist, 19th Century

Developmental Shifts in Intrinsic and Extrinsic Motivation As students move from the early elementary school years to the high school years, intrinsic motivation tends to drop (Harter, 1996). In one study, the biggest drop in intrinsic motivation and largest increase in extrinsic motivation occurred between the sixth and seventh grade (Harter, 1981). In another study, as students moved from the sixth to the eighth grade, they increasingly said that school is boring and irrelevant (Harter, 1996). In this study, students who were intrinsically motivated were doing much better academically than those who were extrinsically motivated.

Why the shift toward extrinsic motivation as children move to higher grades? One explanation is that grading practices reinforce external motivation. That is, as students get older, they lock into the increasing emphasis on grades and their internal motivation drops.

Other characteristics of schools may contribute to the change in motivation (Collins & Steinberg, 2006). Jacquelynne Eccles and her colleagues (Eccles, 2004; Eccles & Midgley, 1989; Wigfield & Eccles, 2002; Wigfield & others, 2006) identified some specific changes in the school context that help to explain the decline in intrinsic motivation. Middle and junior high schools are more impersonal, more formal, more evaluative, and more competitive than elementary schools. Students compare themselves more with other students because they are increasingly graded in terms of their relative performance on assignments and standardized tests, which encourages extrinsic rather than intrinsic motivation.

Can teachers make a difference in determining whether students maintain their motivation to learn? That is the subject of the Caring for Children interlude.

www.mhhe.com/santrockcd11

Motivation and Achievement
Intrinsic Motivation

CARING FOR CHILDREN

Teachers Who Care

Researchers have found that students who feel they have supportive, caring teachers are more strongly motivated to engage in academic work than students with unsupportive, uncaring teachers (McCombs, 2001; Ryan & Deci, 2000). One researcher examined students' views of the qualities of good relationships with a teacher by asking middle school students questions such as how they knew a teacher cared about them (Wentzel, 1997). As shown in figure 17.5, attentiveness to the students as human beings was important to the students. Interestingly, students also considered teachers' instructional behaviors in evaluating how much their teachers cared about them. The students said that teachers convey that they care about their students when they make serious efforts to promote learning and have appropriately high standards.

Nel Noddings (1992, 1998, 2001) believes that students are most likely to develop into competent human beings when they feel cared for. This requires teachers to get to know students fairly well. She believes that this is difficult in large

(continued on next page)

	Teachers Who Care	Teachers Who Do *Not* Care
Teaching behaviors	Makes an effort to make class interesting, teaches in a special way	Teaches in a boring way, gets off-task, teaches while students aren't paying attention
Communication style	Talks to me, pays attention, asks questions, listens	Ignores, interrupts, screams, yells
Equitable treatment and respect	Is honest and fair, keeps promises, trusts me, tells the truth	Embarrasses, insults
Concern about individuals	Asks what's wrong, talks to me about my problems, acts as a friend, asks when I need help, takes time to make sure I understand, calls on me	Forgets my name, does nothing when I do something wrong, doesn't explain things or answer questions, doesn't try to help me

FIGURE 17.5 Students' Descriptions of Teachers Who Care

schools with large numbers of students in each class. She would have teachers remain with the same students for two to three years (voluntarily on the part of the teacher and the pupil) so that teachers would be better positioned to attend to the interests and capacities of each student (Thornton, 2001).

Mastery Motivation

www.mhhe.com/santrockcd11
Mastery Motivation

The increasingly competitive, impersonal atmosphere of middle schools obviously does not discourage all students. To some, these characteristics represent a challenge. Researchers have found that how students typically respond to challenges has a lot to do with how much they achieve (Brophy, 2004). Carol Dweck and her colleagues (Dweck & Elliott, 1983; Dweck & Leggett, 1988; Dweck, Mangels, & Good, 2004) have found that children show two distinct responses to difficult or challenging circumstances: a mastery orientation or a helpless orientation.

Children with a **mastery orientation** focus on the task rather than on their ability, have positive affect (suggesting they enjoy the challenge), and generate solution-oriented strategies that improve their performance. Mastery-oriented students often instruct themselves to pay attention, to think carefully, and to remember strategies that worked for them in the past (Anderman, Maehr, & Midgley, 1996). One recent study of elementary school students found that a higher level of mastery motivation was linked to higher math and reading grades (Broussard, 2004).

In contrast, children with a **helpless orientation** focus on their inadequacies, often attribute their difficulty to a lack of ability, and display negative affect (including boredom and anxiety). This orientation undermines their performance.

A mastery orientation can also be contrasted with a **performance orientation**, which involves being concerned with the outcome rather than the process. For performance-oriented students, winning is what matters. For mastery-oriented students, what matters is the sense that they are effectively interacting with their environment. Mastery-oriented students do like to win, but developing their skills is more important.

mastery orientation An orientation in which one is task-oriented and, instead of focusing on one's ability, is concerned with learning strategies.

helpless orientation An orientation in which one seems trapped by the experience of difficulty and attributes one's difficulty to a lack of ability.

performance orientation An orientation in which one focuses on achievement outcomes; winning is what matters most, and happiness is thought to result from winning.

attributions Attributions are explanations people give for behavior; one way to classify these explanations is whether they are internal or external.

Attribution

What determines whether students develop a mastery or a helpless orientation? Based on her research, Dweck has emphasized the importance of whether they believe that their performance depends on their effort or on some fixed ability, some unchangeable "amount" of intelligence. If they believe that their performance reflects an unchangeable intelligence, Dweck argues, they are not likely to have a mastery orientation. What students believe about the causes of their success or failure influences their motivation and ultimately their performance.

Another way to view this relationship is in terms of **attributions,** which are the explanations people give for behavior. The reasons individuals behave the way they do can be classified in a number of ways, but one basic distinction stands out above all others—the distinction between internal causes, such as the actor's personality traits or motives, and external causes, which are environmental, situational factors such as rewards or task difficulty (Heider, 1958). If students do not do well on a test, do they attribute it to the teacher making the test too difficult (external cause) or to their not studying hard enough (internal cause)?

Attributing success or failure to effort encourages achievement (Alderman, 2004). Unlike many causes of success, effort is under a person's control and amenable to change (Brophy, 2004). The importance of effort in achievement is recognized even by children. In one study, third- to sixth-grade students felt that effort was the most effective strategy for good school performance (Skinner, Wellborn, & Connell, 1990).

Self-Efficacy

Another way of analyzing differences in motivation and achievement emphasizes an individual's **self-efficacy,** the belief that one can master a situation and produce favorable outcomes. Albert Bandura (1997, 2001, 2004), whose social cognitive theory we described in chapter 1, believes that self-efficacy is a critical factor in whether or not students achieve. Self-efficacy is the belief that "I can"; helplessness is the belief that "I cannot" (Bandura & Locke, 2003; Maddux, 2002; Stipek, 2002). Students with high self-efficacy endorse such statements as "I know that I will be able to learn the material in this class" and "I expect to be able to do well at this activity."

Exploring Self-Efficacy
Self-Efficacy Resources

Dale Schunk (1991, 2004) has applied the concept of self-efficacy to many aspects of students' achievement. In his view, self-efficacy influences a student's choice of activities. Students with low self-efficacy for learning may avoid many learning tasks, especially those that are challenging. By contrast, high self-efficacy counterparts eagerly work at learning tasks (Schunk & Zimmerman, 2003; Zimmerman & Schunk, 2004). Students with high self-efficacy are more likely to expend effort and persist longer at a learning task than students with low self-efficacy.

Goal-Setting, Planning, and Self-Monitoring

Self-efficacy and achievement improve when individuals set goals that are specific, proximal, and challenging (Bandura, 2001, 2004; Schunk, 2004). A nonspecific, fuzzy goal is "I want to be successful." A more concrete, specific goal is "I want to make the honor roll by the end of the semester."

Students can set both long-term (distal) and short-term (proximal) goals. It is okay for individuals to set some long-term goals, such as "I want to graduate from high school" or "I want to go to college," but they also need to create short-term goals, which are steps along the way. "Getting an A on the next math test" is an example of a short-term, proximal goal. So is "Doing all of my homework by 4 P.M. Sunday."

Another good strategy is for individuals to set challenging goals. A challenging goal is a commitment to self-improvement. Strong interest and involvement in activities are sparked by challenges. Goals that are easy to reach generate little interest or effort. However, goals should be optimally matched to the individual's skill level. If goals are unrealistically high, the result will be repeated failures that lower the individual's self-efficacy.

It is not enough just to set goals. In order to achieve, it also is important to plan how to reach those goals. Being a good planner means managing time effectively, setting priorities, and being organized.

Individuals should not only plan their next week's activities but also monitor how well they are sticking to their plan. Once engaged in a task, they need to monitor their progress, judge how well they are doing on the task, and evaluate the outcomes to regulate what they do in the future (Eccles, Wigfield, & Schiefele, 1998). High-achieving children are often self-regulatory learners (Schunk & Zimmerman, 2003;

self-efficacy The belief that one can master a situation and produce favorable outcomes.

Zimmerman & Schunk, 2004). For example, high-achieving children monitor their learning and systematically evaluate their progress toward a goal more than low-achieving students do. Encouraging children to monitor their learning conveys the message that they are responsible for their own behavior and that learning requires their active, dedicated participation.

In sum, we have seen that a number of internal factors influence children's achievement. Especially important are intrinsic motivation, a mastery orientation, and goal-setting, planning, and self-regulation (Linnenbrink & Pintrich, 2004; Pintrich, 2003; Zimmerman & Schunk, 2004). Students are more motivated to learn when they are given choices, receive rewards that have informational value but are not used for control, and become absorbed in challenges that match their skills.

Ethnicity and Culture

How do ethnicity and culture influence children's achievement? Of course, diversity exists within every group in terms of achievement. But Americans have been especially concerned about two questions related to ethnicity and culture. First, does their ethnicity deter ethnic minority children from high achievement in school? And second, is there something about American culture that accounts for the poor performance of U.S. children in math and science?

Ethnicity Analyzing the effects of ethnicity in the United States is complicated by the fact that a disproportionate number of ethnic minorities have low socioeconomic status. Disentangling the effects of SES and ethnicity can be difficult, and many investigations overlook the socioeconomic status of ethnic minority students. In many instances, when ethnicity *and* socioeconomic status are investigated, socioeconomic status predicts achievement better than ethnicity does. Students from middle- and upper-income families fare better than their counterparts from low-income backgrounds in a host of achievement situations—for example, expectations for success, achievement aspirations, and recognition of the importance of effort (Gibbs, 1989).

Negative stereotypes and discrimination present special challenges for many ethnic minority students. Despite these barriers, in her research, Sandra Graham (1986, 1990) has been struck by how consistently middle-income African American students, like their White middle-income counterparts, have high achievement expectations and understand that failure is usually due to a lack of effort.

Many ethnic minority students living in poverty must also deal with conflict between the values of their neighborhood and those of the majority culture, a lack of high-achieving role models, and as we discussed earlier, poor schools (McLoyd, 2000). Even students who are motivated to learn and achieve may find it difficult to perform effectively in such contexts.

Cross-Cultural Comparisons In the past decade, the poor performance of American children in math and science has become well publicized. For example, in one cross-national comparison of the math and science achievement of 9- to 13-year-old students, the United States finished 13th (out of 15) in science and 15th (out of 16) in math achievement (Educational Testing Service, 1992). In this study, Korean and Taiwanese students placed first and second, respectively. Critics of cross-national comparisons argue that, in many comparisons, virtually all U.S. children are being compared with a "select" group of children from other countries; therefore, they conclude, it is no wonder that American students don't fare so well. That criticism holds for some international comparisons. However, when the top 25 percent of students in different countries were compared, U.S. students moved up some, but not a lot (Mullis & others, 1998). In the Research in Child Development interlude, you can read about Harold Stevenson's efforts to find out why American students fare so poorly in mathematics.

RESEARCH IN CHILD DEVELOPMENT

Cross-Cultural Comparisons in Learning Math and Math Instruction

The University of Michigan's Harold Stevenson has been conducting research on children's learning for five decades. His current research explores reasons for the poor performance of American students. Stevenson and his colleagues (Stevenson, 1995, 2000; Stevenson, Hofer, & Randel, 1999; Stevenson & others, 1990; Stevenson & Zusho, 2002) have completed five cross-cultural comparisons of students in the United States, China, Taiwan, and Japan. In these studies, Asian students consistently outperform American students in mathematics. And, the longer the students are in school, the wider the gap becomes between Asian and American students—the lowest difference is in the first grade, the highest in the eleventh grade (the highest grade studied).

Asian grade schools intersperse studying with frequent periods of activities. This approach helps children maintain their attention and likely makes learning more enjoyable. Shown here are Japanese fourth-graders making wearable masks.

To learn more about the reasons for these large cross-cultural differences, Stevenson and his colleagues spent thousands of hours observing in classrooms, as well as interviewing and surveying teachers, students, and parents. They found that the Asian teachers spent more of their time teaching math than did the American teachers. For example, more than one-fourth of total classroom time in the first grade was spent on math instruction in Japan, compared with only one-tenth of the time in the U.S. first-grade classrooms. Also, the Asian students were in school an average of 240 days a year, compared with 178 days in the United States.

In addition, differences were found between the Asian and American parents. The American parents had much lower expectations for their children's education and achievement than did the Asian parents. Also, the American parents were more likely to believe that their children's math achievement was due to innate ability; the Asian parents were more likely to say that their children's math achievement was the consequence of effort and training (see figure 17.6). The Asian students were more likely to do math homework than were the American students, and the Asian parents were far more likely to help their children with their math homework than were the American parents (Chen & Stevenson, 1989).

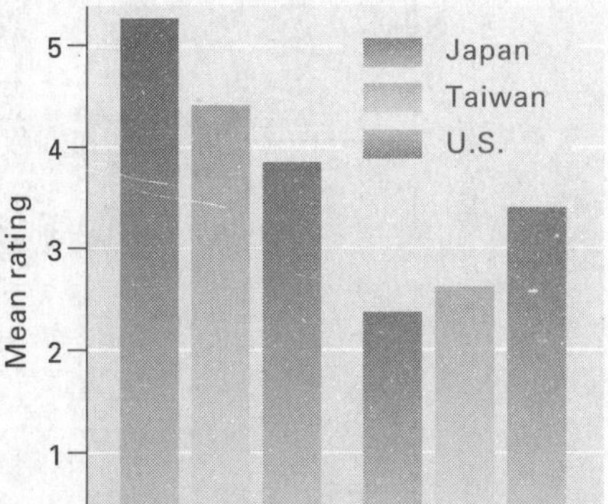

FIGURE 17.6 Mothers' Beliefs About the Factors Responsible for Children's Math Achievement in Three Countries. In one study, mothers in Japan and Taiwan were more likely to believe that their children's math achievement was due to effort rather than innate ability, while U.S. mothers were more likely to believe their children's math achievement was due to innate ability (Stevenson, Lee, & Stigler, 1986). If parents believe that their children's math achievement is due to innate ability and their children are not doing well in math, the implication is that they are less likely to think their children will benefit from putting forth more effort.

Review and Reflect • LEARNING GOAL 4

4 Explain the development of achievement in children

Review
- What are intrinsic and extrinsic motivation? How are they related to achievement?
- How are mastery, helpless, and performance orientations linked with achievement?
- What is attribution and how is it linked with achievement?
- What is self-efficacy and how is it related to achievement?
- Why are goal-setting, planning, and monitoring important in achievement?
- How do cultural, ethnic, and socioeconomic variations influence achievement?

Reflect
- Think about several of your own past schoolmates who showed low motivation in school. Why do you think they behaved that way? What teaching strategies may have helped them?

REACH YOUR LEARNING GOALS

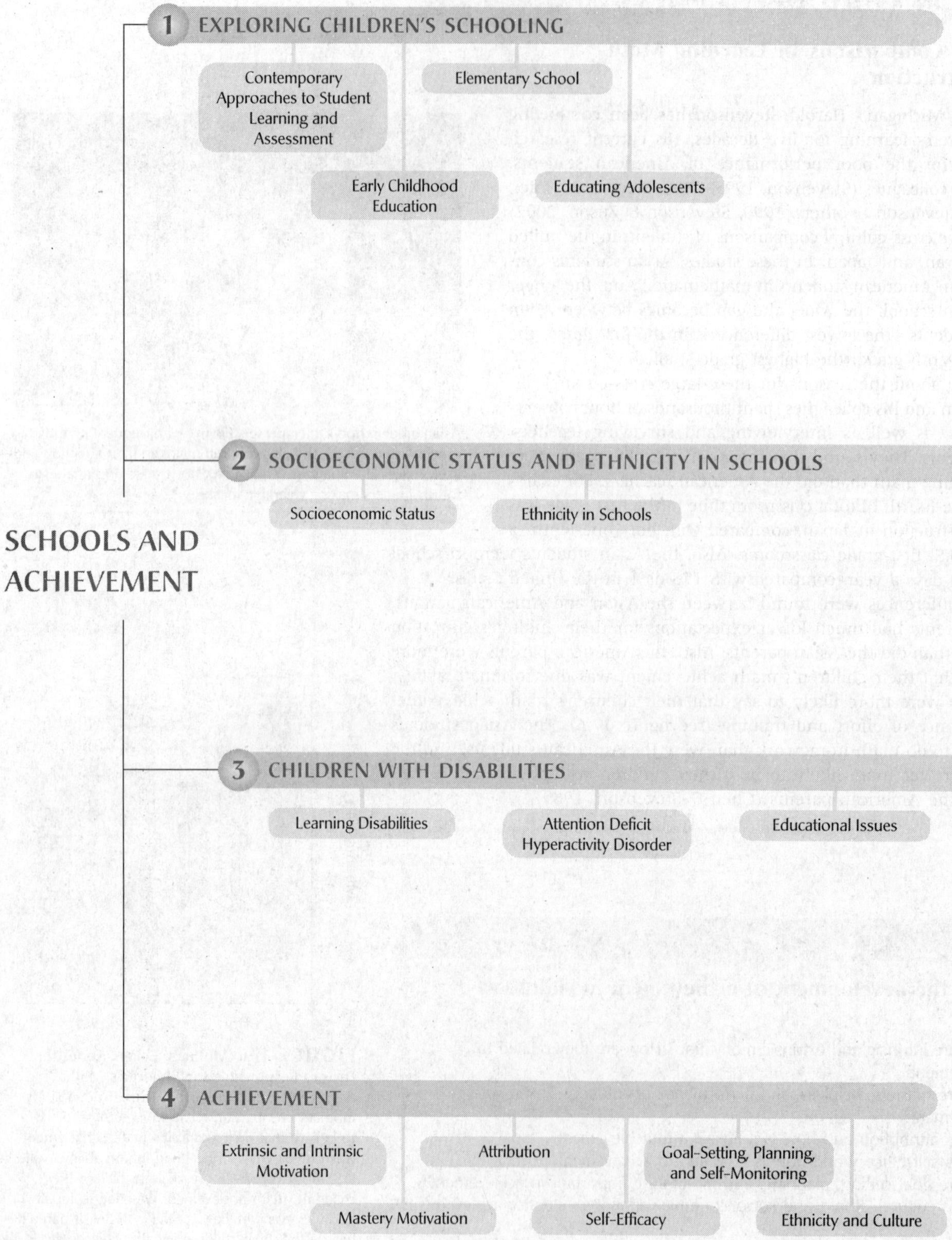

SUMMARY

1 Discuss approaches to schooling and development

- Contemporary approaches to student learning include direct instruction, cognitive constructivist, and social constructivist. A number of learner-centered principles with a constructivist theme have been advocated by a team of experts convened by the American Psychological Association. Demands that schools and teachers be held accountable for students' performance have produced extensive state-mandated tests, which have both strengths and weaknesses and are controversial. The most visible example of increased state-mandated testing is the No Child Left Behind federal legislation.
- Early childhood education has many variations, but developmentally appropriate education is an important theme. Compensatory education has tried to break through the poverty cycle with programs like Project Head Start. Long-term studies reveal that model preschool programs have positive effects on children's development.
- A special concern is that early elementary school education proceeds too much on the basis of negative feedback to children.
- The transition from elementary school to middle or junior high school can be stressful. A number of criticisms of middle school education have been presented. School dropout rates for Native American and Latino adolescents remain high.

2 Describe the roles of socioeconomic status and ethnicity in schools

- Children in poverty face problems at home and at school that present barriers to their learning. Schools in low-income neighborhoods often have fewer resources, have less experienced teachers, and are more likely to encourage rote learning rather than thinking skills.
- The school experiences of students from different ethnic groups vary considerably. It is important for teachers to have positive expectations for students of color. Comer believes a community, team approach is the best way to educate children. Aronson created the jigsaw classroom to reduce racial tension.

3 Characterize children with disabilities and their schooling

- An estimated 10 percent of U.S. children receive special services because they have a disability. Slightly more than 50 percent of these children are classified as having a learning disability. Children have a learning disability if they have (1) a minimum IQ level and (2) a significant difficulty in a school-related area that is not due to certain severe emotional disorders, second-language background, sensory disabilities, or specific neurological deficits. Diagnosing whether a child has a learning disability is difficult. Dyslexia is a category of learning disabilities that involves a severe impairment in the ability to read and spell. Various causes of learning disabilities have been proposed. Interventions with children who have a learning disability often focus on improving reading skills.
- Attention deficit hyperactivity disorder (ADHD) is a disability in which individuals consistently show problems in one or more of these areas: (1) inattention, (2) hyperactivity, and (3) impulsivity. ADHD has been increasingly diagnosed.
- Federal laws in the United States require that children with a disability receive a free, appropriate education and are provided adequate services. Students with a disability must be given an individualized education plan and be educated in the least restrictive environment. The 2004 version of the Individuals with Disabilities Act (IDEA) especially focuses on its alignment with No Child Left Behind legislation, which has raised questions about whether students with disabilities can be expected to meet the same general education standards and achievement as students without disabilities.

4 Explain the development of achievement in children

- Extrinsic motivation involves doing something to obtain something else (a means to an end). Intrinsic motivation involves the internal motivation to do something for its own sake (an end in itself). Overall, most experts recommend that teachers create a classroom climate in which students are intrinsically motivated to learn. Giving students some choice and providing opportunities for personal responsibility increase intrinsic motivation. When rewards are used, they should convey information about task mastery rather than provide external control. Researchers have found that as students move from the early elementary school years to high school, their intrinsic motivation declines, especially during the middle school years.
- A mastery orientation focuses on the task rather than ability, involves positive affect, and includes solution-oriented strategies. A helpless orientation focuses on personal inadequacies, attributing difficulty to lack of ability. Negative affect (boredom, anxiety, for example)

also is present. A performance orientation involves being concerned with the achievement outcome rather than the achievement process. Mastery orientation is the preferred achievement orientation.

- Attributions may focus on internal causes or external causes. Attributing results to effort fosters achievement.
- Self-efficacy is the belief that one can master a situation and produce positive outcomes. Bandura believes that self-efficacy is a critical factor in whether students will achieve. Schunk argues that self-efficacy influences a student's choice of tasks, with low-efficacy students avoiding many learning tasks.
- Setting specific, proximal (short-term), and challenging goals benefits students' self-efficacy and achievement. Being a good planner means managing time effectively, setting priorities, and being organized. Self-monitoring is a key aspect of self-regulation and benefits student learning.
- In most investigations, socioeconomic status predicts achievement better than ethnicity does. U.S. children do more poorly on math and science achievement tests than children in Asian countries such as China, Taiwan, and Japan. Their poor performance has been linked to characteristics of U.S. schools and parents.

KEY TERMS

direct instruction approach 529
cognitive constructivist approaches 529
social constructivist approaches 529
child-centered kindergarten 531
Montessori approach 531
Project Head Start 533
developmentally appropriate practice 533
top-dog phenomenon 537
learning disability 543
dyslexia 543
attention deficit hyperactivity disorder (ADHD) 544
individualized education plan (IEP) 546
least restrictive environment (LRE) 546
inclusion 546
extrinsic motivation 547
intrinsic motivation 547
mastery orientation 550
helpless orientation 550
performance orientation 550
attributions 550
self-efficacy 551

KEY PEOPLE

Friedrich Froebel 531
Maria Montessori 531
John Ogbu 540
Eliot Aronson 540
James Comer 541
Nel Noddings 549
Carol Dweck 550
Albert Bandura 551
Dale Schunk 551
Harold Stevenson 553

E-LEARNING TOOLS

To help you master the material in this chapter, visit the Online Learning Center for *Child Development,* eleventh edition (**www.mhhe.com/santrockcd11**), where you'll find these additional resources:

Taking It to the Net

1. Mark is going to teach high school mathematics. He has read that parents' involvement in their children's education is virtually nonexistent by the time their kids reach high school. What can Mark do as a teacher to encourage parental involvement?
2. Eight-year-old Grace has just been diagnosed with dyslexia. Her parents do not know what causes the disorder or how to help her. What causes dyslexia? And what can be done to help Grace?
3. Karen is on a school board committee studying how the transition to middle school may decrease student motivation and lead to social and academic problems that may continue into high school. She wants to present an overview of the psychological research on this issue. What have psychologists found to be the negative effects that middle schools have on achievement and motivation?

Nursing, Parenting, and Teaching Exercises

Build your decision-making skills by trying your hand at the scenarios on the Online Learning Center.

Video Clips

The Online Learning Center includes the following videos for this chapter:

- Philosophy of Preschool Teaching
  A head teacher of a 4-year-old classroom describes her "whole child" philosophy to teaching young children.
- Schools and Public Policy
  Dr. Eccles describes how her research on gender and school transitions has influenced public policy.
- Non-College-Bound Adolescents
  A discussion of the unique problems faced by non-college bound adolescents.
- Sex Differences and School
  Why are there achievement differences between boys and girls? The research is unclear, according to Dr. Eccles. She states most likely it is a two-way interaction between biological and cultural factors.

Chapter 18 CULTURE

Our most basic common link is that we all inhabit this planet. We all breathe the same air. We all cherish our children's future.

—JOHN F. KENNEDY
United States President, 20th Century

CHAPTER OUTLINE

CULTURE AND CHILDREN'S DEVELOPMENT

The Relevance of Culture to the Study of Children

Cross-Cultural Comparisons

SOCIOECONOMIC STATUS AND POVERTY

What Is Socioeconomic Status?

Socioeconomic Variations in Families, Neighborhoods, and Schools

Poverty

ETHNICITY

Immigration

Ethnicity and Socioeconomic Status

Differences and Diversity

Prejudice, Discrimination, and Bias

Assimilation and Pluralism

The United States and Canada: Nations with Many Cultures

TECHNOLOGY

Media Use

Television

Computers and the Internet

LEARNING GOALS

1 Discuss the role of culture in children's development

2 Describe how socioeconomic status and poverty impact children's lives

3 Explain how ethnicity is linked to children's development

4 Summarize the influence of technology on children's development

The Stories of Sonya's and Michael's Cultural Conflicts

A 16-year-old Japanese American girl (we will call her "Sonya") was upset over her family's reaction to her White American boyfriend. "Her parents refused to meet him and on several occasions threatened to disown her" (Sue & Morishima, 1982, p.142). Her older brothers also reacted angrily to Sonya's dating a White American, warning that they were going to beat him up. Her parents were also disturbed that Sonya's grades, above average in middle school, were beginning to drop.

Generational issues contributed to the conflict between Sonya and her family (Nagata, 1989). Her parents had experienced strong sanctions against dating Whites when they were growing up and were legally prevented from marrying anyone but a Japanese. As Sonya's older brothers were growing up, they valued ethnic pride and solidarity. The brothers saw her dating a White as "selling out" her own ethnic group. Sonya and the other members of her family obviously had different cultural values.

Michael, a 17-year-old Chinese American high school student, was referred to a therapist by the school counselor because he was depressed and had suicidal tendencies (Huang & Ying, 1989). Michael was failing several classes and frequently was absent from school. Michael's parents, successful professionals, expected Michael to excel in school and go on to become a doctor. They were angered by Michael's school failures, especially since he was the firstborn son, who in Chinese families is expected to achieve the highest standards.

The therapist encouraged the parents to put less academic pressure on Michael and to have more realistic expectations for Michael (who had no interest in becoming a doctor). Michael's school attendance changed and his parents noticed his improved attitude toward school. Michael's case illustrates how expectations that Asian American youth will be "whiz kids" can become destructive.

PREVIEW

Culture had a strong influence on the conflict Sonya and Michael experienced in their families and on their behavior outside of the family—in Sonya's case, dating; in Michael's case, school. Of course, a family's cultural background does not always produce conflict between children and other family members, but these two cases underscore the importance of culture in children's development. In this chapter, we will explore many aspects of culture, including cross-cultural comparisons of children's development, the harmful effects of poverty, the role of ethnicity, and the benefits and dangers that technology can bring to children's lives.

1 CULTURE AND CHILDREN'S DEVELOPMENT

The Relevance of Culture to the Study of Children

Cross-Cultural Comparisons

culture The behavior, patterns, beliefs, and all other products of a particular group of people that are passed on from generation to generation.

In chapter 1, we defined **culture** as the behavior, patterns, beliefs, and all other products of a particular group of people that are passed on from generation to generation. The products result from the interaction between groups of people and their environment over many years. Here we examine the role of culture in children's development.

The Relevance of Culture to the Study of Children

Culture includes many components and can be analyzed in many ways (Berry, 2000; Cole, 2006; Matsumoto, 2004; Shweder & others, 2006). Cross-cultural expert Richard Brislin (1993) described a number of characteristics of culture:

- Culture is made up of ideals, values, and assumptions about life that guide people's behavior.
- Culture consists of those aspects of the environment that people make.
- Culture is transmitted from generation to generation, with the responsibility for the transmission resting on the shoulders of parents, teachers, and community leaders.
- Culture's influence becomes noticed the most in well-meaning clashes between people from very different cultural backgrounds.
- Despite compromises, cultural values still remain.
- When their cultural values are violated or their cultural expectations are ignored, people react emotionally.
- It is not unusual for people to accept a cultural value at one point in their lives and reject it at another point. For example, rebellious adolescents and young adults might accept a culture's values and expectations after having children of their own.

Despite all the differences among cultures, research by American psychologist Donald Campbell and his colleagues (Brewer & Campbell, 1976; Campbell & LeVine, 1968) revealed that people in all cultures tend to

- believe that what happens in their culture is "natural" and "correct" and that what happens in other cultures is "unnatural" and "incorrect."
- perceive their cultural customs as universally valid; that is, they believe that "what is good for us is good for everyone."
- behave in ways that favor their cultural group.
- feel hostile toward other cultural groups.

In other words, people in all cultures tend to be *ethnocentric;* favoring their own group over others.

Ethnocentrism has also influenced scientists and scholars. Many of the assumptions in fields like psychology were developed in Western cultures (Triandis, 2001). More specifically, the study of children emerged in the context of Western industrialized society, with the practical needs and social norms of this culture dominating thinking about child development. Consequently, the development of children in Western cultures evolved as the norm for all children, regardless of economic and cultural circumstances. Overgeneralizations about the universal aspects of children were made based on data and experience in a single culture—the middle-socioeconomic-status culture of the United States (Havighurst, 1976). For the most part, the study of child development has been ethnocentric and has emphasized American values, especially the values of middle-socioeconomic-status White males (Matsumoto, 2004).

One example of overgeneralizations based on Western culture was the belief that adolescents everywhere went through a period of "storm and stress" characterized by self-doubt and conflict. However, when anthropologist Margarent Mead (1928) visited the island of Samoa early in the twentieth century, she found that Samoan adolescents were not experiencing such stress. Mead concluded that the basic nature of adolescence depends not on biology but on sociocultural factors. She argued that cultures promote a relatively stress-free adolescence when, like

The Web of Culture
Global Internet Communication
The Global Lab Project
Worldwide Classroom
Cross-Cultural Comparisons

Samoan culture, they provide a smooth, gradual transition from childhood to adulthood and allow adolescents to observe sexual relations, see babies born, regard death as natural, do important work, engage in sex play, and know clearly what their adult roles will be. However, in cultures like the United States, in which children are considered very different from adults and where adolescence is not characterized by the aforementioned experiences, adolescence is more likely to be stressful.

More than half a century after Mead's Samoan findings, her work was criticized as being biased and error-prone (Freeman, 1983). Current critics hold that Samoan adolescence is more stressful than Mead observed, and that delinquency appears among Samoan adolescents just as it does among Western adolescents. In the current controversy over Mead's findings, some researchers have defended Mead's work (Holmes, 1987).

As the debate about Samoan adolescents illustrates, interpreting other cultures and reaching consensus about issues across the divide of cultures can be extremely difficult. But the future will bring extensive contact between people from varied cultural and ethnic backgrounds (Matsumoto, 2004). If the study of child development is to be a relevant discipline in the twenty-first century, increased attention will need to be given to culture and ethnicity. Global interdependence is no longer a matter of belief or choice. It is an inescapable reality. Children and their parents are not just citizens of the United States, or Canada, or another country. They are citizens of the world—a world that, through advances in transportation and technology, has become increasingly interactive. By better understanding the behavior and values of cultures around the world, we may be able to interact more effectively with each other and make this planet a more hospitable, peaceful place in which to live (Matsumoto, 2004).

Cross-cultural studies involve the comparison of a culture with one or more other cultures. Shown here is a 14-year-old !Kung girl who has added flowers to her beadwork during the brief rainy season in the Kalahari desert in Botswana, Africa. Delinquency and violence occur much less frequently in the peaceful !Kung culture than in most other cultures around the world.

Cross-Cultural Comparisons

Cross-cultural studies, which involve the comparison of a culture with one or more other cultures, provide helpful information about other cultures and the role of culture in children's development. This comparison provides information about the degree to which children's development is similar, or universal, across cultures, or the degree to which it is culture-specific (Cole, 2006; Greenfield, Suzuki, & Rothstein-Fisch, 2006). In terms of gender, for example, the experiences of male and female children and adolescents continue to be worlds apart in some cultures (Larson & Wilson, 2004). In many countries, males have far greater access to educational opportunities, more freedom to pursue a variety of careers, and fewer restrictions on sexual activity than females (UNICEF, 2005).

Individualism and Collectivism In cross-cultural research, the search for basic traits has focused on the dichotomy between individualism and collectivism (Hofstede, 1980; Triandis, 1994, 2001):

- **Individualism** involves giving priority to personal goals rather than to group goals; it emphasizes values that serve the self, such as feeling good, personal distinction and achievement, and independence.
- **Collectivism** emphasizes values that serve the group by subordinating personal goals to preserve group integrity, interdependence of the members, and harmonious relationships.

Figure 18.1 summarizes some of the main characteristics of individualistic and collectivistic cultures. Many Western cultures, such as the United States, Canada, Great Britain, and the Netherlands, are described as individualistic; many Eastern cultures, such as China, Japan, India, and Thailand, are described as collectivistic. So is Mexican culture.

cross-cultural studies Studies that compare a culture with one or more other cultures. Such studies provide information about the degree to which children's development is similar, or universal, across cultures or about the degree to which it is culture-specific.

individualism Giving priority to personal goals rather than to group goals; emphasizing values that serve the self, such as feeling good, personal distinction and achievement, and independence.

collectivism Emphasizing values that serve the group by subordinating personal goals to preserve group integrity, interdependence of members, and harmonious relationships.

Many of psychology's basic tenets have been developed in individualistic cultures like the United States. Consider the flurry of self-terms in psychology that have an individualistic focus: for example, self-actualization, self-awareness, self-efficacy, self-reinforcement, self-criticism, self-serving, selfishness, and self-doubt (Lonner, 1988).

Researchers have found that self-conceptions are related to culture. In one study, American and Chinese college students completed 20 sentences beginning with "I am ______" (Trafimow, Triandis, & Goto, 1991). As indicated in figure 18.2, the American college students were much more likely to describe themselves with personal traits ("I am assertive"), while the Chinese students were more likely to identify themselves by their group affiliations ("I am a member of the math club").

Human beings have always lived in groups, whether large or small, and have always needed one another for survival. Critics of the Western notion of psychology argue that the Western emphasis on individualism may undermine our basic species need for relatedness (Kagitcibasi, 1988, 1995). Some social scientists believe that many problems in Western cultures are intensified by their emphasis on individualism. Compared with collectivist cultures, individualistic cultures have higher rates of suicide, drug abuse, crime, teenage pregnancy, divorce, child abuse, and mental disorders. Regardless of their cultural background, people need both a positive sense of self and connectedness to others to develop fully as human beings.

Individualistic	Collectivistic
Focuses on individual	Focuses on groups
Self is determined by personal traits independent of groups; self is stable across contexts	Self is defined by in-group terms; self can change with context
Private self is more important	Public self is most important
Personal achievement, competition, power are important	Achievement is for the benefit of the in-group; cooperation is stressed
Cognitive dissonance is frequent	Cognitive dissonance is infrequent
Emotions (such as anger) are self-focused	Emotions (such as anger) are often relationship based
People who are the most liked are self-assured	People who are the most liked are modest, self-effacing
Values: pleasure, achievement, competition, freedom	Values: security, obedience, in-group harmony, personalized relationships
Many casual relationships	*Few close* relationships
Save own face	Save own and other's face
Independent behaviors: swimming, sleeping alone in room, privacy	Interdependent behaviors: co-bathing, co-sleeping
Relatively rare mother-child physical contact	Frequent mother-child physical contact (such as hugging, holding)

FIGURE 18.1 Characteristics of Individualistic and Collectivistic Cultures

Use of Time by Adolescents Cross-cultural studies illuminate not only broad cultural themes such as individualism and collectivism but also very specific differences in everyday life that influence development. For example, do adolescents around the world spend their time in ways similar to U.S. adolescents? Reed Larson and Suman Verma (Larson, 2001; Larson & Verma, 1999) examined how adolescents spend their time in work, play, and developmental activities such as school. They found that U.S. adolescents spent more time in paid work than their counterparts in most developed countries. Adolescent males in developing countries often spent more time in paid work than adolescent females, who spent more time in unpaid household labor.

Figure 18.3 summarizes the average daily time use by adolescents in different regions of the world (Larson & Verma, 1999). U.S. adolescents spent about 60 percent as much time on schoolwork as East Asian adolescents did, mainly because U.S. adolescents did less homework.

What U.S. adolescents had more of than adolescents in other industrialized countries was discretionary time. About 40 to 50 percent of U.S. adolescents' waking hours (not counting summer vacations) was spent in discretionary activities, compared with 25 to 35 percent in East Asia and 35 to 45 percent in Europe. Whether this additional discretionary time is a liability or an asset for U.S. adolescents, of course, depends on how they use it.

The largest amounts of U.S. adolescents' free time were spent using the media and engaging in unstructured leisure activities, often with friends. (We will further explore adolescents' media use later in the chapter.) U.S. adolescents spent more time in voluntary structured activities—such as sports, hobbies, and organizations—than did East Asian adolescents.

According to Reed Larson (2001), U.S. adolescents may have too much unstructured time for optimal development. When adolescents are allowed to choose what

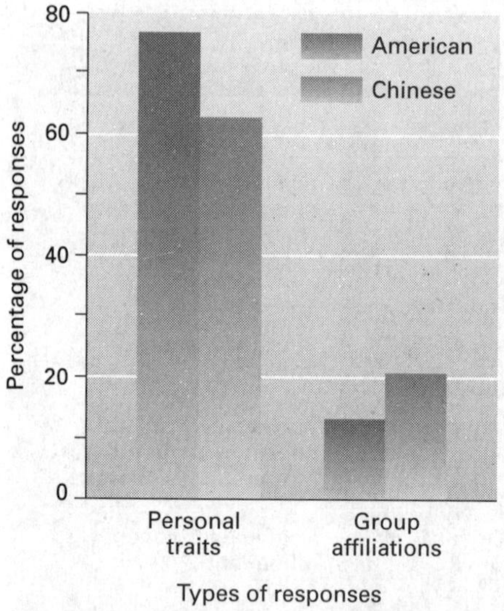

FIGURE 18.2 American and Chinese Self-Conceptions. College students from the United States and China completed 20 "I am ______" sentences. Both groups filled in personal traits more than group affiliations. However, the U.S. college students more often filled in the blank with personal traits, the Chinese with group affiliations.

they do with their time, they typically engage in unchallenging activities such as hanging out and watching TV. Although relaxation and social interaction are important aspects of adolescence, it seems unlikely that spending large numbers of hours per week in unchallenging activities fosters development. Structured voluntary activities may provide more promise for adolescent development than unstructured time, especially if adults give responsibility to adolescents, challenge them, and provide competent guidance in these activities (Larson, 2001; Larson & Seepersad, 2003).

Rites of Passage **Rites of passage** are ceremonies or rituals that mark an individual's transition from one status to another, especially into adulthood. Some societies have elaborate rites of passage that signal the adolescent's transition to adulthood; others do not (Kottak, 2002). In many premodern cultures, rites of passage are the avenue through which adolescents gain access to sacred adult practices, knowledge, and sexuality (Sommer, 1978). These rites often involve dramatic practices intended to facilitate the adolescent's separation from the immediate family, especially the mother. The transformation usually is characterized by some form of ritual death and rebirth, or by means of contact with the spiritual world. Bonds are forged between the adolescent and the adult instructors through shared rituals, hazards, and secrets to allow the adolescent to enter the adult world. This kind of ritual provides a forceful break with childhood and entry into the adult world at a time when the adolescent is perceived to be ready for the change.

Africa, especially sub-Saharan Africa, has been the location of many rites of passage for adolescents. Under the influence of Western culture, many of the rites are disappearing today. Americans do not have formal rites of passage that mark the transition from adolescence to adulthood. Some religious and social groups have initiation ceremonies that indicate an advance in maturity; the Jewish bar mitzvah, the Catholic confirmation, and social debuts are examples. But school graduation ceremonies come the closest to being culturewide rites of passage in the United States. The high school graduation ceremony has become nearly universal for middle-SES adolescents and increasing numbers of adolescents from low-income backgrounds (Fasick, 1994). Nonetheless, high school graduation does not result in universal changes—many high school graduates continue to live with their parents, to be economically dependent on them, and to be undecided about career and lifestyle matters.

rites of passage Ceremonies that mark an individual's transition from one status to another, especially into adulthood.

Activity	Nonindustrial, unschooled populations	Postindustrial, schooled populations: United States	Europe	East Asia
Household labor	5 to 9 hours	20 to 40 minutes	20 to 40 minutes	10 to 20 minutes
Paid labor	0.5 to 8 hours	40 to 60 minutes	10 to 20 minutes	0 to 10 minutes
Schoolwork	—	3.0 to 4.5 hours	4.0 to 5.5 hours	5.5 to 7.5 hours
Total work time	6 to 9 hours	4 to 6 hours	4.5 to 6.5 hours	6 to 8 hours
TV viewing	*insufficient data*	1.5 to 2.5 hours	1.5 to 2.5 hours	1.5 to 2.5 hours
Talking	*insufficient data*	2 to 3 hours	*insufficient data*	45 to 60 minutes
Sports	*insufficient data*	30 to 60 minutes	20 to 80 minutes	0 to 20 minutes
Structured voluntary activities	*insufficient data*	10 to 20 minutes	1.0 to 20 minutes	0 to 10 minutes
Total free time	4 to 7 hours	6.5 to 8.0 hours	5.5 to 7.5 hours	4.0 to 5.5 hours

Note. The estimates in the table are averaged across a 7-day week, including weekdays and weekends. Time spent in maintenance activities like eating, personal care, and sleeping is not included. The data for nonindustrial, unschooled populations come primarily from rural peasant populations in developing countries.

FIGURE 18.3 Average Daily Time Use of Adolescents in Different Regions of the World

The absence of clear-cut rites of passage in the United States makes the attainment of adult status ambiguous. Many individuals are unsure whether they have reached adult status. In Texas, the age for beginning employment is 15, but many younger adolescents and even children are employed, especially Mexican immigrants. The age for driving is 16, but when emergency need is demonstrated, a driver's license can be obtained at age 15. Even at age 16, some parents might not allow their son or daughter to obtain a driver's license, believing that 16-year-olds are too young for this responsibility. The age for voting is 18, and the age for drinking has recently been raised to 21. Exactly when adolescents become adults has not been clearly delineated in the United States.

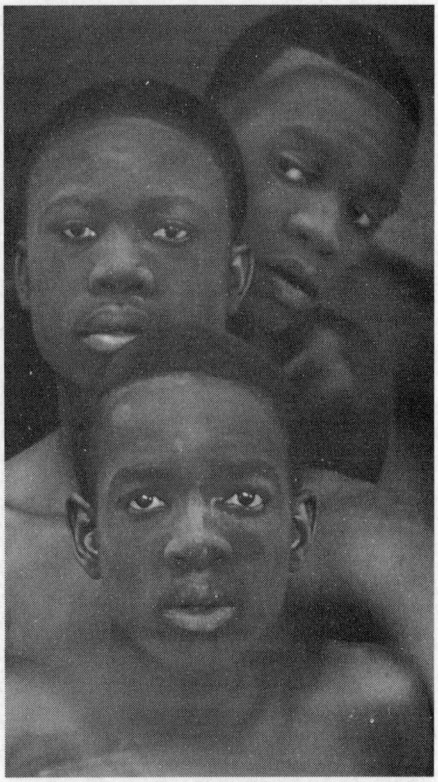

These Congolese Koto boys painted their faces as part of a rite of passage to adulthood. *What kinds of rites of passage do American adolescents have?*

Review and Reflect • **LEARNING GOAL 1**

1 Discuss the role of culture in children's development

Review
- What is the relevance of culture to the study of children?
- What are cross-cultural comparisons? Describe cross-cultural comparisons in a number of areas of children's and adolescents' development.

Reflect
- What was the achievement orientation in your family as you grew up? How did the cultural background of your parents influence this orientation?

2 SOCIOECONOMIC STATUS AND POVERTY

What Is Socioeconomic Status? | Socioeconomic Variations in Families, Neighborhoods, and Schools | Poverty

Many subcultures exist within countries. For example, Sonya's family, discussed in the opening of the chapter, had beliefs and patterns different from Michael's family. Some but not all subcultures are tied to ethnicity or socioeconomic characteristics or both. For example, the values and attitudes of children growing up in an urban ghetto or rural Appalachia may differ from those of children growing up in a wealthy suburb. In any event, children growing up in these different contexts are likely to have different socioeconomic statuses, and this inequality may influence their development.

What Is Socioeconomic Status?

In chapter 1, we defined **socioeconomic status (SES)** as the grouping of people with similar occupational, educational, and economic characteristics. Socioeconomic status implies certain inequalities. Generally, members of a society have (1) occupations that vary in prestige, and some individuals have more access than others to higher-status occupations; (2) different levels of educational attainment, and some individuals have more access than others to better education; (3) different economic resources; and (4) different levels of power to influence a community's institutions.

socioeconomic status (SES) A grouping of people with similar occupational, educational, and economic characteristics.

These differences in the ability to control resources and to participate in society's rewards produce unequal opportunities.

The number of significantly different socioeconomic statuses depends on the community's size and complexity. Most research on socioeconomic status delineates two categories, low and middle, but some research delineates as many as six categories. Sometimes low socioeconomic status is described as low-income, working class, or blue collar; sometimes the middle category is described as middle-income, managerial, or white collar. Examples of low-SES occupations are factory worker, manual laborer, welfare recipient, and maintenance worker. Examples of middle-SES occupations include skilled worker, manager, and professional (doctor, lawyer, teacher, accountant, and so on).

Socioeconomic Variations in Families, Neighborhoods, and Schools

The families, neighborhoods, and schools of children have socioeconomic characteristics. Some children have parents who have a great deal of money and who work in prestigious occupations. These children live in attractive houses and neighborhoods and attend schools where the students come primarily from middle- and upper-SES backgrounds. Other children have parents who do not have very much money and who work in less prestigious occupations. These children do not live in very attractive houses and neighborhoods, and they attend schools where the students come mainly from lower-SES backgrounds.

Such variations in neighborhood and schools can influence children's adjustment and development (Blyth, 2000; Collins & Steinberg, 2006; Leventhal & Brooks-Gunn, 2003, 2004). Schools in low-income areas not only have fewer resources than those in higher-income areas but also tend to have more students with lower achievement test scores, lower rates of graduation, and smaller percentages of students going to college (Garbarino & Asp, 1981; Wigfield & others, 2006).

Socioeconomic differences also characterize family life. For example, in chapter 15, "Families," we described socioeconomic differences in child rearing (Hoff, Laursen, & Tardif, 2002). Recall that lower-SES parents are more concerned that their children conform to society's expectations, have an authoritarian parenting style, use physical punishment more in disciplining their children, and are more directive and less conversational with their children. By contrast, higher-SES parents tend to be more concerned with developing children's initiative, create a home atmosphere in which children are more nearly equal participants, are less likely to use physical punishment, and are less directive and more conversational with their children.

SES differences also influence children's intellectual orientation (Chapman, 2003). Although variations exist, one study found that students from low-SES families read less and watched television—which is primarily a visual medium—more than their middle-SES counterparts (Erlick & Starry, 1973). This pattern among low-SES students does not encourage the development of intellectual skills, such as reading and writing, that promote academic success.

Like their parents, children from low-SES backgrounds are at high risk for experiencing mental health problems (McLoyd, 1998, 2000). Problems such as depression, low self-confidence, peer conflict, and juvenile delinquency are more prevalent among children living in low-SES families than among economically advantaged children (Gibbs & Huang, 1989).

Of course, children from low-SES backgrounds vary considerably in intellectual and psychological functioning. For example, a sizable portion of children from low-SES backgrounds perform well in school; some perform better than many middle-SES students. One recent study found that when low-income parents had high educational aspirations it was linked to more positive educational outcomes in youth (Schoon, Parsons, & Sacker, 2004). When children from low-SES backgrounds are achieving well in school, it is not unusual to find a parent or parents making special sacrifices to provide the living conditions and support that contribute to school success.

Poverty

When sixth-graders in a poverty-stricken area of St. Louis were asked to describe a perfect day, one boy said he would erase the world, then he would sit and think (Children's Defense Fund, 1992). Asked if he wouldn't rather go outside and play, the boy responded, "Are you kidding, out there?"

The world is a dangerous and unwelcoming place for too many of America's youth, especially those whose families, neighborhoods, and schools are low-income (Edelman, 1997; Swisher & Whitlock, 2003). Some children are resilient and cope with the challenges of poverty without any major setbacks, but too many struggle unsuccessfully (Magnuson & Duncan, 2002; Spencer, 2006). Each child of poverty who reaches adulthood unhealthy, unskilled, or alienated keeps our nation from being as competent and productive as it can be (Children's Defense Fund, 1992).

In 2003, 17.6 percent of U.S. children were living in families below the poverty line, a slight increase from 2001 (16.2 percent) but down from a peak of 22.7 percent in 1993 (U.S. Bureau of the Census, 2004). The current poverty rate for U.S. children is still much higher than the rates in other industrialized nations. For example, Canada has a child poverty rate of 9 percent and Sweden has a rate of 2 percent.

Poverty in the United States follows ethnic lines. Half of African American and one-third of Latino children live in poverty. Compared with White children, ethnic minority children are more likely to experience persistent poverty over many years and live in isolated poor neighborhoods where social supports are minimal and threats to positive development abundant (Jarrett, 1995) (see figure 18.4).

Why is poverty among American children so high? Three reasons are apparent (Huston, McLoyd, & Coll, 1994): (1) economic changes have eliminated many blue-collar jobs that paid reasonably well, (2) the percentage of children living in single-parent families headed by the mother has increased, and (3) reduced government benefits.

Psychological Ramifications of Poverty Living in poverty has many psychological effects on both adults and children (Stevens, 2005). First, the poor are often powerless. In occupations, they rarely are the decision makers. Rules are handed down to them in an authoritarian manner. Second, the poor are often vulnerable to disaster. They are not likely to be given notice before they are laid off from work and usually do not have financial resources to fall back on when problems arise. Third, their range of alternatives is often restricted. Only a limited number of jobs are open to them. Even when alternatives are available, the poor might not know about them or be prepared to make a wise decision, because of inadequate education and inability to read well. Fourth, being poor means having less prestige. This lack of prestige is transmitted to children early in their lives. The child in poverty observes that many other children wear nicer clothes and live in more attractive houses.

Although positive times occur in the lives of children growing up in poverty, many of their negative experiences are worse than those of their middle-SES counterparts (Richards & others, 1994). These adversities involve physical punishment and lack of structure at home, violence in the neighborhood, and domestic violence in their buildings. A recent review concluded that compared with their economically more advantaged counterparts, poor children experience widespread environmental inequities that include (Evans, 2004, p. 77) the following:

- Exposure "to more family turmoil, violence, separation from their families, instability, and chaotic households" (Emery & Laumann-Billings, 1998)

www.mhhe.com/santrockcd11

Children, Youth, and Poverty
Poverty in Canada
Research on Poverty

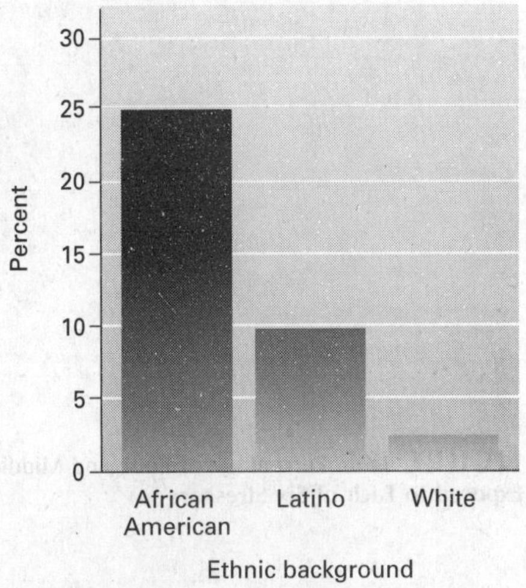

Note: A distressed neighborhood is defined by high levels (at least one standard deviation above the mean) of (1) poverty; (2) female-headed families; (3) high school dropouts; (4) unemployment; and (5) reliance on welfare.

FIGURE 18.4 Percentages of Youth Under 18 Who Are Living in Distressed Neighborhoods

- "Less social support, and their parents are less responsive and more authoritarian" (Bo, 1994; Cochran & others, 1990)
- "Read to relatively infrequently, watch more TV, and have less access to books and computers" (Bradley & others, 2001; Hart & Risley, 1995)
- Schools and child care facilities that are inferior and parents who "are less involved in their children's school activities" (Benveniste, Carnoy, & Rothstein, 2003; U.S. Department of Health and Human Services, 1999)
- Air and water that are more polluted and homes that "are more crowded, more noisy, and of lower quality" (Myers, Baer, & Choi, 1996)
- More dangerous and physically deteriorating neighborhoods with less adequate municipal services (Brody & others, 2001; Sampson, Raudenbush, & Earls, 1997)

To read further about the risks that children living in poverty face, see the Research in Child Development interlude.

RESEARCH IN CHILD DEVELOPMENT

Multiple Risks of Children Living in Poverty

One recent study explored multiple risks in the lives of children from poverty and middle-income backgrounds (Evans & English, 2002). Six multiple risks were examined in 287 8- to 10-year-old non-Latino White children living in rural areas of upstate New York: family turmoil, child separation (a close family member being away from home often), exposure to violence, crowding, noise level, and housing quality. Family turmoil, child separation, and exposure to violence were assessed by maternal reports of the life events their children had experienced. Crowding was determined by the number of people per room, and noise level was measured by the decibel level in the home. Housing quality (based on structural quality, cleanliness, clutter, resources for children, safety hazards, and climatic conditions) was rated by observers who visited the homes. Each of the six factors was defined as presenting a risk or no risk. Thus, the multiple stressor exposure for children could range from 0 to 6. Families were defined as poor if the household lived at or below the federally defined poverty line.

Children in poor families experienced greater risks than their middle-income counterparts. As shown in figure 18.5, a higher percentage of children in poor families were exposed to each of the six risk factors (family turmoil, child separation, exposure to violence, crowding, noise level, and poor quality of housing).

Were there differences in the children's adjustment that might reflect these differences in exposure to risk factors? The researchers assessed the children's levels of psychological stress through reports by the children and their mothers. Problems in self-regulation of behavior were determined by whether children chose immediate

FIGURE 18.5 Percentage of Poor and Middle-Income Children Exposed to Each of Six Stressors

Risk factor (stressor)	Poor children exposed (%)	Middle-income children exposed (%)
Family turmoil	45	12
Child separation	45	14
Exposure to violence	73	49
Crowding	16	7
Excessive noise	32	21
Poor housing quality	24	3

rather than delayed gratification on a task. Resting blood pressure and overnight neuroendocrine hormones were measured to indicate children's levels of psychophysiological stress.

The researchers found that compared with children from middle-income backgrounds, poor children had higher levels of psychological stress, more problems in self-regulation of behavior, and elevated psychophysiological stress. Analysis indicated that cumulative exposure to stressors may contribute to difficulties in socioemotional development for children living in poverty.

When poverty is persistent and long-standing, it can have especially damaging effects on children (Evans, 2004). In one study, the longer children lived in families with income below the poverty line, the lower was the quality of their home environments (Garrett, Ng'andu, & Ferron, 1994). Also in this study, improvements in family income had their strongest effects on the home environments of chronically poor children. In another study, children in families experiencing both persistent and occasional poverty had lower IQs and more internalized behavior problems than never-poor children, but persistent poverty had a much stronger negative effect on these outcomes than occasional poverty did (Duncan, Brooks-Gunn, & Klebanov, 1994). Further, one recent study of more than 30,000 individuals from birth into the adult years found that the greater risk for developmental outcomes took place with persistent and accumulating socioeconomic disadvantage throughout childhood and adolescence (Schoon & others, 2002).

A special concern is the high percentage of single mothers in poverty, more than one-third of whom are in poverty, compared with only 10 percent of single fathers. Vonnie McLoyd (1998) concludes that because poor, single mothers are more distressed than their middle-SES counterparts are, they often show low support, nurturance, and involvement with their children. Among the reasons for the high poverty rate of single mothers are women's low pay, infrequent awarding of alimony payments, and poorly enforced child support by fathers.

One recent study documented the importance of family processes in elementary school children's social adjustment in low-income families (Mistry & others, 2002). Lower levels of economic well-being and elevated perceptions of economic pressure were linked with parenting behavior. Parents who were distressed by their economic situation reported feeling less effective and capable in disciplining their children and were observed to be less affectionate in parent-child interactions. In turn, less optimal parenting predicted lower teacher ratings of children's positive social behavior and higher ratings of behavior problems.

Countering Poverty's Effects Some recent studies show that benefits provided to parents may have important effects on children as well. One study showed that work-based antipoverty programs for parents were linked to enhanced school performance and social behavior of children (Huston & others, 2001). In this study, wage supplements sufficient to raise family income above the poverty threshold and subsidies for child care and health insurance were given to adults who worked full-time. Positive effects were found for boys' academic achievement, classroom behavior skills, problem behaviors, and educational and occupational aspirations. The effects were more positive for boys than girls, perhaps because boys have more behavioral and school-related problems to begin with.

One recent trend in antipoverty programs is to conduct two-generation interventions (McLoyd, 1998). That is, the programs provide both services for children (such as educational day care or preschool education) and services for parents (such as adult education, literacy training, and job-skill training). Evaluations suggest that two-generation programs have more positive effects on parents than they do on children (St. Pierre, Layzer, & Barnes, 1996). Also, when the two-generation programs do show benefits for children, these are more likely to be health benefits than

What happens to a dream deferred?
Does it dry up
Like a raisin in the sun?

—Langston Hughes
American Poet and Author, 20th Century

cognitive gains. To read about a program that benefited youth living in poverty, see the Caring for Children interlude.

Caring for Children

The Quantum Opportunities Program

A downward trajectory is not inevitable for youth living in poverty (Carnegie Council on Adolescent Development, 1995). One potential positive path for such youth is to become involved with a caring mentor. The Quantum Opportunities Program, funded by the Ford Foundation, was a four-year, year-round mentoring effort. The students were entering the ninth grade at a high school with high rates of poverty, were minorities, and came from families that received public assistance. Each day for four years, mentors provided sustained support, guidance, and concrete assistance to their students.

The Quantum program required students to participate in (1) academic-related activities outside school hours, including reading, writing, math, science, social studies, peer tutoring, and computer skills training; (2) community service projects, including tutoring elementary school students, cleaning up the neighborhood, and volunteering in hospitals, nursing homes, and libraries; and (3) cultural enrichment and personal development activities, including life skills training and college and job planning. In exchange for their commitment to the program, students were offered financial incentives that encouraged participation, completion, and long-range planning. A stipend of $1.33 was given to students for each hour they participated in these activities. For every 100 hours of education, service, or development activities, students received a bonus of $100. The average cost per participant was $10,600 for the four years, which was one-half the cost of one year in prison at the time the program was conducted.

An evaluation of the Quantum project compared the mentored students with a nonmentored control group. Sixty-three percent of the mentored students graduated from high school but only 42 percent of the control group did; 42 percent of the mentored students were enrolled in college, but only 16 percent of the control group was at the time of the assessment. Furthermore, control-group students were twice as likely as the mentored students to receive food stamps or welfare, and they had more arrests. This type of program has the potential to overcome the intergenerational transmission of poverty and its negative outcomes.

Review and Reflect • LEARNING GOAL 2

2 Describe how socioeconomic status and poverty impact children's lives

Review

- What is socioeconomic status?
- What are some socioeconomic variations in families, neighborhoods, and schools?
- What characterizes children living in poverty?

Reflect

- What would you label the socioeconomic status of your family as you grew up? How do you think the SES status of your family influenced your development?

3 ETHNICITY

- Immigration
- Ethnicity and Socioeconomic Status
- Differences and Diversity
- Prejudice, Discrimination, and Bias
- Assimilation and Pluralism
- The United States and Canada: Nations with Many Cultures

Nowhere are cultural changes in the United States more dramatic than in the increasing ethnic diversity of America's children. Recall from chapter 1 that **ethnicity** refers to characteristics rooted in cultural heritage, including nationality, race, religion, and language. Ninety-three languages are spoken in Los Angeles alone! With increased diversity have come conflict and concerns about the future.

Immigration

Relatively high rates of immigration are contributing to the growth in the proportion of ethnic minorities in the U.S. population (Cushner, 2006; Cushner, McClelland, & Safford, 2006; McLoyd, 2000, 2005; Padilla & Perez, 2003; Phinney, 2003). Immigrants often experience stressors uncommon to or less prominent among longtime residents, such as language barriers, dislocations and separations from support networks, a dual struggle to preserve identity and to acculturate, and changes in SES status (Cushner, 2003; McLoyd, 2005; Suarez-Orozco, 2002).

Earlier in the chapter, we described the differences in individualist (emphasis on personal goals and the self) and collectivist (emphasis on the group and relationships) cultures. Many of the families that have immigrated in recent decades to the United States, such as Mexican Americans and Asian Americans, come from collectivist cultures in which family obligation and duty to one's family is strong (Fuligni & Hardway, 2004; Fuligni & Witkow, 2004). This family obligation and duty may take the form of assisting parents in their occupations and contributing to the family's welfare (Parke & Buriel, 2006). This often occurs in service and manual labor jobs, such as those in construction, gardening, cleaning, and restaurants.

As Sonya's story at the opening of the chapter illustrated, immigrants and their children may be at different stages of adapting to the majority culture, which can produce conflict over cultural values (Roosa & others, 2002; Samaniego & Gonzales, 1999). The children of immigrants may learn attitudes in U.S. schools that challenge the authority patterns in the home (Brislin, 1993). One individual who is deeply concerned about immigrant youth and conducts research to learn more about ways to help them cope with life in America is Carola Suarez-Orozco. To read about her work, see the Careers in Child Development insert.

CAREERS in CHILD DEVELOPMENT

Carola Suarez-Orozco
Lecturer, Researcher, and Codirector of Immigration Projects

Carola Suarez-Orozco is a researcher and lecturer in the Human Development and Psychology area at Harvard University. She also is codirector of the Harvard Immigration Projects. She obtained her undergraduate degree (development studies) and graduate (clinical psychology) degrees from the University of California at Berkeley.

Carola has worked both in clinical and public school settings in California and Massachusetts. She currently is codirecting a five-year longitudinal study of immigrant adolescents' (coming from Central America, China, and the Dominican Republic) adaptation to schools and society. One of the courses she teaches at Harvard is on the psychology of immigrant youth. She especially believes that more research needs to be conducted on the intersection of cultural and psychological factors in the adaptation of immigrant and ethnic minority youth.

Carola Suarez-Orozco, with her husband, Marcelo, who also studies the adaptation of immigrants.

ethnicity A dimension of culture based on cultural heritage, nationality, race, religion, and language.

Ethnicity and Socioeconomic Status

As we indicated in chapter 17, much of the research on ethnic minority children has failed to tease apart the influences of ethnicity and socioeconomic status (SES). Ethnicity and SES can interact in ways that exaggerate the negative influence of ethnicity because ethnic minority individuals are overrepresented in the lower socioeconomic levels of American society (Coll & Pachter, 2002; Spencer & Dornbusch, 1990). Ethnicity has often defined who will enjoy the privileges of citizenship and to what degree and in what ways. In many instances, an individual's ethnic background has determined whether the individual will be alienated or disadvantaged.

Too often researchers have given ethnic explanations of child development that were largely based on socioeconomic status rather than on ethnicity. For example, decades of research on group differences in self-esteem failed to consider the socioeconomic status of African American and White American children (Hare & Castenell, 1985). When the self-esteem of African American children from low-income backgrounds is compared with that of White American children from middle-class backgrounds, the differences are often large but not informative because of the confounding of ethnicity and SES (Scott-Jones, 1995).

Even ethnic minority children from middle-SES backgrounds do not entirely escape the problems of minority status (Banks, 2006; Harwood & others, 2002; McAdoo, 2002; Spencer & Dornbusch, 1990). Middle-SES ethnic minority children still encounter much of the prejudice, discrimination, and bias associated with being a member of an ethnic minority group.

Although not all ethnic minority families are poor, poverty contributes to the stressful life experiences of many ethnic minority children (Coll & Pachter, 2002; Parke & Buriel, 2006; Stevens, 2005). Vonnie McLoyd (1990) concluded that ethnic minority children experience a disproportionate share of the adverse effects of poverty and unemployment in America today. Thus, many ethnic minority children experience a double disadvantage: (1) prejudice, discrimination, and bias because of their ethnic minority status; and (2) the stressful effects of poverty.

www.mhhe.com/santrockcd11

Migration and Ethnic Relations
Immigration: Journals and Newsletters
Immigration and Ethnicity: Research Centers
Immigrant Families

Differences and Diversity

Historical, economic, and social experiences produce differences between various ethnic minority groups, and between ethnic minority groups and the majority White group (Diaz, Pelletier, & Provenzo, 2006; Halonen & Santrock, 1999). Individuals living in a particular ethnic or cultural group adapt to the values, attitudes, and stresses of that culture. Recognizing and respecting these differences is an important aspect of getting along with others in a diverse, multicultural world. Children, like all of us, need to take the perspective of individuals from ethnic and cultural groups that are different from their own and think, "If I were in their shoes, what kind of experiences might I have had?" "How would I feel if I were a member of their ethnic or cultural group?" "How would I think and behave if I had grown up in their world?" Such perspective taking often increases empathy and understanding of individuals from ethnic and cultural groups different from one's own.

For too long, differences between any ethnic minority group and Whites were conceptualized as deficits or inferior characteristics on the part of the ethnic minority group. Indeed, research on ethnic minority groups often focused only on a group's negative, stressful aspects. For example, research on African American adolescent girls invariably examined such topics as poverty, unwed mothers, and dropping out of school; research on the psychological strengths of African American adolescent girls was sorely needed. The self-esteem, achievement, motivation, and self-control of children from different ethnic minority groups deserve considerable study.

The current, long-overdue emphasis of research on ethnic groups underscores the strengths of various minority groups (Quintana, 2004). For example, the extended-family support system that characterizes many ethnic minority groups is now recognized as an important factor in coping. And researchers are finding that African American males are better than Anglo-American males at detecting and using nonverbal cues such as body language in communication, at communicating with people from different cultures, and at solving unexpected problems (Evans & Whitfield, 1988).

As we noted in chapter 1, there is considerable diversity within each ethnic group (Banks, 2003, 2006; Cushner, 2006; Cuéllar, Siles, & Bracamontes, 2004). Ethnic minority groups have different social, historical, and economic backgrounds (Spring, 2006; Stevenson, 1998). For example, Mexican, Cuban, and Puerto Rican immigrants are Latinos, but they had different reasons for migrating, came from varying socioeconomic backgrounds in their native countries, and experience different rates and types of employment in the United States (Coll & others, 1995). The U.S. federal government now recognizes the existence of 511 different Native American tribes, each having a unique ancestral background with differing values and characteristics. Asian Americans include the Chinese, Japanese, Filipinos, Koreans, and Southeast Asians, each group having a distinct ancestry and language. The diversity of Asian Americans is reflected in their educational attainment: some achieve a high level of education; many others have little education. For example, 90 percent of Korean American males graduate from high school, but only 71 percent of Vietnamese American males do.

Jason Leonard, age 15: "I want America to know that most of us black teens are not troubled people from broken homes and headed to jail. . . . In my relationships with my parents, we show respect for each other and we have values in our house. We have traditions we celebrate together, including Christmas and Kwanzaa."

Diversity also exists within each of these groups (Parke & Buriel, 2006). No group is homogeneous. Sometimes, well-meaning individuals fail to recognize the diversity within an ethnic group (Sue, 1990). For example, a sixth-grade teacher had two Mexican American adolescents in her class. She asked them to be prepared to demonstrate to the class on the following Monday how they danced at home. The first boy got up in front of the class and began dancing in a typical American fashion. The teacher said, "No, I want you to dance like you and your family do at home, like you do when you have Mexican American celebrations." The boy informed the teacher that his family did not dance that way. The second boy demonstrated a Mexican folk dance to the class. Failing to recognize diversity within ethnic groups reinforces stereotypes and encourages prejudice.

Prejudice, Discrimination, and Bias

Prejudice is an unjustified negative attitude toward an individual because of the individual's membership in a group. The group toward which the prejudice is directed can be made up of people of a particular ethnic group, sex, age, religion, or other detectable difference. Our concern here is prejudice against ethnic minority groups.

Many ethnic minority individuals continue to experience persistent forms of prejudice, discrimination, and bias (Banks, 2006; Scott, 2003; Sue, 1990). Ethnic minority adolescents are taught in schools that often have a middle-SES, White bias and in classroom contexts that are not adapted to ethnic minority adolescents' learning styles. They are assessed by tests that are often culturally biased and are evaluated by teachers whose appreciation of their abilities may be hindered by negative stereotypes about ethnic minorities (Spencer & Dornbusch, 1990). Discrimination and prejudice continue to be present in the media, interpersonal interactions, and daily conversations (Aboud, Mendelson, & Purdy, 2003). Crimes, strangeness, poverty, mistakes, and deterioration are often mistakenly attributed to ethnic minority individuals or foreigners.

For several reasons, the "browning" of Americans portends heightened racial/ethnic prejudice and conflict, or at least sharper racial and ethnic cleavages (McLoyd, 1998). First, it is occurring against a backdrop of long-standing White privilege and an ingrained sense of entitlement and superiority among non-Latino Whites. Second, the youth of today's immigrants are less likely than their

prejudice An unjustified negative attitude toward an individual because of her or his membership in a group.

counterparts in the early twentieth century to believe that they must reject the values and ways of their parents' homeland to succeed in American society. Many espouse economic, but not cultural, assimilation into mainstream society. Ethnic minority individuals increasingly refuse to become part of a homogeneous melting pot, instead requesting that schools, employers, and governments honor many of their cultural customs. Third, today's immigrants often settle in inner-city neighborhoods where assimilation often means joining a world that is antagonistic to the American mainstream because of its experience of racism and economic barriers.

Progress has been made in ethnic minority relations, but discrimination and prejudice still exist, and equality has not been achieved (Banks, 2006). Much remains to be accomplished.

Assimilation and Pluralism

Ethnic Minority Families
African Americans
Latinos and Native Americans
Asian Americans
Prejudice

Assimilation refers to the absorption of ethnic minority groups into the dominant group. This often means the loss of some or virtually all of the behavior and values that set the ethnic minority group apart from the dominant culture. In the United States those who favor assimilation usually advocate that ethnic minority groups should become more American. By contrast, **pluralism** refers to the coexistence of distinct ethnic and cultural groups in the same society. Individuals who advocate pluralism usually advocate that cultural differences should be maintained and appreciated (Leong, 2000).

For many years, assimilation was thought to be the best course for American society because the mainstream was believed to be superior in many ways. Today, the notion of intrinsic superiority has been discredited and assimilation is often advocated instead for practical and functional reasons. For example, advocates of assimilation say that educational programs for immigrant children (Mexican, Chinese, and so on) should stress the learning of English as early as possible, rather than bilingual education, because using a language other than English may be a handicap. By contrast, the advocates of pluralism argue that an English-only approach reasserts the mainstream-is-right-and-best belief. Thus, responses to the issue of bilingual education involve a clash of values.

Prejudice is the reason of fools.

—VOLTAIRE
French Philosopher, 18th Century

As Stanley Sue (1990) asks, how can one argue against the development of functional skills and, to some degree, Americanization? Similarly, how can one doubt that pluralism, diversity, and respect for different cultures are valid? Sue thinks that advocates of assimilation often overlook the fact that a consensus may be lacking on what constitutes functional skills or that a particular context may alter what skills are useful. For example, with an increasing immigrant population, the ability to speak Spanish or Japanese may be an asset, as is the ability to interact productively with diverse ethnic groups.

Sue proposes that one way to resolve value conflicts about sociocultural issues is to redefine them and think about them in innovative ways. For example, in the assimilation/pluralism conflict, rather than assuming that assimilation is necessary for the development of functional skills, we could focus on the fluctuating criteria of what skills are considered functional or the possibility that developing functional skills does not prevent the existence of pluralism.

The United States and Canada: Nations with Many Cultures

The United States has been and continues to be a great receiver of ethnic groups. It has embraced new ingredients from many cultures. The cultures often collide and cross-pollinate, mixing their ideologies and identities. Some of the culture of origin is retained, some of it is lost, some of it is mixed with the American culture (Chun, Organista, & Marin, 2003; Ramirez, 2004).

Other nations have also experienced the immigration of varied ethnic groups. Possibly we can learn more about the potential benefits, problems, and varied responses by examining their experiences. Canada is a prominent example. Canada

assimilation The absorption of ethnic minority groups into the dominant group, which often means the loss of some or virtually all of the behavior and values of the ethnic minority group.

pluralism The coexistence of distinct ethnic and cultural groups in the same society.

comprises a mixture of cultures that are loosely organized along the lines of economic power. The Canadian cultures include these (Siegel & Wiener, 1993):

- Native peoples, or First Nations, who were Canada's original inhabitants
- Descendants of French settlers who came to Canada during the seventeenth and eighteenth centuries
- Descendants of British settlers who came to Canada during and after the seventeenth century, or from the United States after the American Revolution in the latter part of the eighteenth century
- Descendants of immigrants from Asia, mainly China, who settled on the west coast of Canada in the latter part of the nineteenth and early twentieth centuries
- Descendants of nineteenth-century immigrants from various European countries, who came to central Canada and the prairie provinces
- Twentieth-century and current immigrants from countries in economic and political turmoil (in Latin America, the Caribbean, Asia, Africa, the Indian subcontinent, the former Soviet Union, and the Middle East), who have settled in many parts of Canada

Canada has two official languages—English and French. Primarily French-speaking individuals reside mainly in the province of Quebec; primarily English-speaking individuals reside mainly in other Canadian provinces. In addition to its English- and French-speaking populations, Canada has a large multicultural community. In three large Canadian cities—Toronto, Montreal, and Vancouver—more than 50 percent of the children and adolescents come from homes in which neither English nor French is the native language (Siegel & Wiener, 1993).

Review and Reflect • LEARNING GOAL 3

3 Explain how ethnicity is linked to children's development

Review

- How does immigration influence children's development?
- How are ethnicity and socioeconomic status related?
- What is important to know about differences and diversity?
- How are prejudice, discrimination, and bias involved in children's development?
- What are assimilation and pluralism? How have attitudes toward each changed in recent years?
- How are the United States and Canada nations of blended cultures?

Reflect

- No matter how well intentioned children are, their life circumstances likely have given them some prejudices. If they don't have prejudices toward people with different cultural and ethnic backgrounds, other kinds of people may bring out prejudices in them. For example, prejudices can be developed about people who have certain religious or political conventions, people who are unattractive or too attractive, people with a disability, and people in a nearby town. As a parent or teacher, how would you attempt to reduce children's prejudices?

4 TECHNOLOGY

- Media Use
- Television
- Computers and the Internet

Earlier in the chapter, we saw that children in low-socioeconomic circumstances watch TV more and read less than their middle-socioeconomic-status counterparts. Few cultural changes have affected children's lives in the twentieth century more than technology, including the introduction of television into children's lives. These changes are likely to continue throughout the twenty-first century. We will begin our exploration of technology's influence on children's development by focusing on children's and adolescents' use of different media, then focus on television, and conclude by discussing computers and the Internet.

Media Use

If the amount of time spent in an activity is any indication of its importance, then there is no doubt that the mass media play important roles in the lives of U.S. children and adolescents (Calvert, 2004; Comstock & Scharrer, 2006; Houston, 2004). A recent national study that surveyed more than 2,000 children and adolescents from 8 through 18 years of age confirmed that they use media heavily (Rideout, Roberts, & Foehr, 2005). The average child and adolescent in the study spent more than 44 hours a week with electronic media. The nearly 6½ hours a day using media compares with approximately 2¼ hours spent with parents, about 1½ hours in physical activity, and 50 minutes in homework. As shown in figure 18.6, the children and adolescents spent the most time watching TV (almost 4 hours a day) and listening to the radio and CDs, tapes or MP players (about 1¾ hours a day).

Media use by children and adolescents varies greatly not only with age but also with gender, ethnicity, socioeconomic status, and intelligence. For example, a national survey found that 8- to 18-year-old boys spent more time watching television than girls do but that girls spent considerably more time listening to music (Roberts & Foehr, 2003). Boys use computers and video games more than girls do (Roberts & others, 1999). African American and Latino children and adolescents spend significantly more time using media—especially television—than non-Latino White children do (Roberts, Henriksen, & Foehr, 2004; Roberts & others, 1999). Media exposure among African American 8- to 18-year-olds averages just over 9 hours daily, among Latino youth more than 8 hours, and among non-Latino White youth about 7 hours (Roberts, Henriksen, & Foehr, 2004).

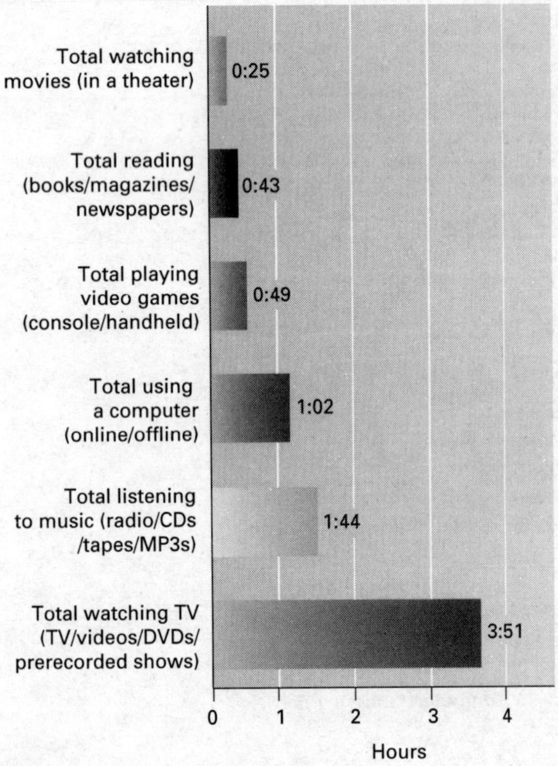

FIGURE 18.6 Hours Per Day Spent by U.S. 8- to 18-year-olds Using Various Media

Television

Few developments during the second half of the twentieth century had a greater impact on children than television (Murray, 2000). Many children spend more time in front of the television set than they do with their parents. Although it is only one of the many mass media that affect children's behavior, television is the most influential. The persuasive capabilities of television are staggering (Kotler, Wright, & Huston, 2001). The 20,000 hours of television watched by the time the average American adolescent graduates from high school are greater than the number of hours spent in the classroom.

Television's Many Roles Television has been called many things, not all of them good. Depending on one's point of view, it may be a "window on the world," the "one-eyed monster," or the "boob tube."

Television can have a positive influence on children's development by increasing their information about the world beyond their immediate environment and by providing models of prosocial behavior (Clifford, Gunter, & McAleer, 1995). *Sesame Street* demonstrates that education and entertainment can work well together (Cole, Richman, & Brown, 2001). Through *Sesame Street,* children experience a world of learning that is both exciting and entertaining. *Sesame Street* also follows the principle that teaching can be accomplished both directly and indirectly. Rather than merely telling children, "You should cooperate with others," TV can *show* children so that they can figure out what it means to be cooperative and what the advantages are.

"Mrs. Horton, could you stop by school today?"

Television also has many potential negative effects. Television has been attacked as one reason for low scores on national achievement tests in reading and mathematics. Television, it is claimed, attracts children away from books and schoolwork. In one study, children who read printed materials, such as books, watched television less than those who did not read (Huston, Seigle, & Bremer, 1983). Furthermore, critics argue that television trains children to become passive learners.

Television also is said to deceive; that is, it teaches children that problems are resolved easily and that everything always comes out right in the end. For example, TV detectives usually take only 30 to 60 minutes to sort through a complex array of clues to reveal a killer—and they always find the killer. Violence is a way of life on many shows. On TV it is all right for police to use violence and to break moral codes in their fight against evildoers. The lasting results of violence are rarely brought home to the viewer. A person who is injured on TV suffers for only a few seconds; in real life, the person might need months or years to recover, or might not recover at all. Yet one out of every two first-grade children says that the adults on television are like adults in real life (Lyle & Hoffman, 1972). In short, television can have a negative influence on children's development by taking them away from their homework, making them passive learners, teaching them stereotypes, providing them with violent models of aggression, and presenting them with unrealistic views of the world (Wilson, 2003).

Television, Violent Video Games, and Aggression A hostile motorcycle gang terrorizes a neighborhood and kidnaps a well-known rock singer. A former boyfriend of the singer then tries to rescue her. He sneaks up on the gang and shoots six of them, one at a time. Some of the gunfire causes the motorcycles to blow up. The scene ends with the former boyfriend rescuing the tied-up singer.

This example of violence on television contains numerous features that encourage aggression in adolescents. The ex-boyfriend is young and good-looking, a rugged hero. His attack on the gang is shown as justifiable: after all, the gang members are ruthless and uncontrollable and have kidnapped an innocent woman. The "hero" is never punished or disciplined, even though it appears that he has taken the law into his own hands. Serving as the ultimate reward, the young woman proclaims her love for him after he rescues her. And despite the extensive violence, no one is shown as being seriously hurt. The focus quickly shifts away from gang members after they have been shot, and viewers do not see anyone die or suffer.

What role does televised violence like this play in aggression among children and adolescents? Does television merely stimulate a child to go out and buy a Star Wars ray gun, or can it trigger an attack on a playmate? When children grow up, can television violence increase the likelihood that they will violently attack someone?

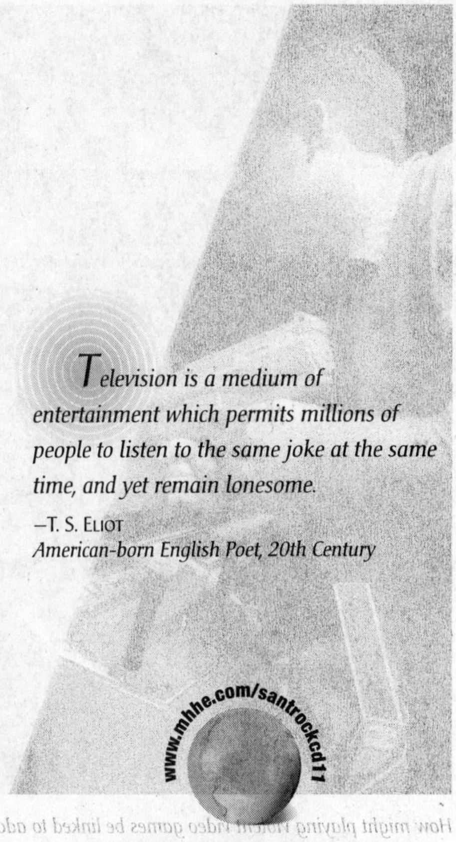

Television is a medium of entertainment which permits millions of people to listen to the same joke at the same time, and yet remain lonesome.

—T. S. Eliot
American-born English Poet, 20th Century

Children's Television Workshop

In one longitudinal investigation, the amount of violence viewed on television at age 8 was significantly related to the seriousness of criminal acts performed as an adult (Huesmann, 1986). In another investigation, long-term exposure to television violence was significantly related to the likelihood of aggression in 1,565 boys 12 to 17 years old (Belson, 1978). Boys who watched the most aggression on television were the most likely to commit a violent crime, swear, be aggressive in sports, threaten violence toward another boy, write slogans on walls, or break windows. These investigations are correlational, so we can conclude from them not that television violence causes children to be more aggressive, but only that watching television violence is associated with aggressive behavior.

In one experiment, children were randomly assigned to one of two groups: one group watched television shows taken directly from violent Saturday-morning cartoons on 11 different days; the second group watched television cartoon shows with all of the violence removed (Steur, Applefield, & Smith, 1971). The children were

www.mhhe.com/santrockcd11

Exploring Television Violence
Children, Youth, Media, and Violence
Culture and TV Violence

then observed during play at their preschool. The preschool children who saw the TV cartoon shows with violence kicked, choked, and pushed their playmates more than the preschool children who watched nonviolent TV cartoon shows did. Because children were randomly assigned to the two conditions (TV cartoons with violence versus with no violence), we can conclude that exposure to TV violence caused the increased aggression in children in this investigation.

Some critics have argued that research results do not warrant the conclusion that TV violence causes aggression (Freedman, 1984). However, many experts insist that TV violence can cause aggressive or antisocial behavior in children (Anderson & Bushman, 2001; Bushman & Huesmann, 2001; Comstock & Scharrer, 2006; Perse, 2001). Of course, television violence is not the only cause of aggression. There is no one cause of any social behavior. Aggression, like all other social behaviors, has multiple determinants (Donnerstein, 2001). The link between TV violence and aggression in children is influenced by children's aggressive tendencies and by their attitudes toward violence and their exposure to it.

One recent study implemented a yearlong intervention with the goal of reducing the harmful effects of violent TV on children's behavior (Rosenkoetter & others, 2004). The classroom-based intervention consisted of 31 brief lessons with first- through third-grade children that focused on the many ways that television distorts violence. The intervention reduced the frequency that children watched violent TV and decreased their identification with violent TV characters.

Violent video games, especially those that are highly realistic, also raise concerns about their effects on children and adolescents. One difference between television and violent video games is that the games can engage children and adolescents so intensely that they experience an altered state of consciousness in "which rational thought is suspended and highly arousing aggressive scripts are increasingly likely to be learned" (Roberts, Henriksen, & Foehr, 2004, p. 498). Another difference involves the direct rewards ("winning points") that game players receive for their behavior. Correlational studies indicate that children and adolescents who extensively play violent electronic games are more aggressive and more likely to engage in delinquent acts than their counterparts who spend less time playing the games or do not play them at all (Anderson & Bushman, 2001; Anderson & Dill, 2000; Cohen, 1995).

How might playing violent video games be linked to adolescent aggression?

Prosocial Behavior Television also can teach children that it is better to behave in positive, prosocial ways than in negative, antisocial ways (Dorr, Rabin, & Irlen, 2002; Wilson, 2001). Aimee Leifer (1973) demonstrated that television is associated with prosocial behavior in young children. She selected a number of episodes from the television show *Sesame Street* that reflected positive social interchanges. She was especially interested in situations that taught children how to use their social skills. For example, in one interchange, two men were fighting over the amount of space available to them. They gradually began to cooperate and to share the space. Children who watched these episodes copied these behaviors, and in later social situations they applied the prosocial lessons they had learned.

Television and Sex Many adolescents, not unlike many adults, like to watch television programs with sexual content. In one study, the four TV programs preferred most by adolescents were the ones with the highest percentage of interactions containing sexual messages (Ward, 1995). In recent years, sexual content on television has increased and become more explicit. The most consistent messages from that content are that sexual behaviors usually occur between unmarried couples, that contraception is rarely discussed, and that unwanted pregnancies and sexually transmitted infections are rare (Greenberg & others, 1986).

What effects, if any, do these sexual messages have? One experiment found that 13- to 14-year-old boys and girls who watched 15 hours of prime-time TV shows that included sexual relations between unmarried partners rated sexual indiscretions as less objectionable than their counterparts who viewed sexual relations between married partners or saw nonsexual relationships (Bryant & Rockwell, 1994). Researchers also have shown that exposure to sexual content is related to more permissive attitudes about premarital and recreational sex (Ward, 2002).

These studies, along with a number of others, lead to the conclusion that television teaches children and adolescents about sex (Bence, 1991; Caruthers & Ward, 2002; Ward, Gorvine, & Cytron, 2002). Watching sexual portrayals on television can influence adolescents' sexual attitudes and behavior. Nonetheless, as with televised aggression, whether sex on television in fact influences an adolescent's behavior depends on a number of factors, including the adolescent's needs, interests, concerns, and maturity (Strasburger & Donnerstein, 1999).

The information that adolescents receive about sex from television raises special concerns because they may lack other sources of accurate information. Parents and teachers usually don't feel comfortable discussing sex with adolescents (Roberts, 1993). Peers do talk about sex but often perpetuate misinformation. According to one recent national survey of 15- to 17-year-olds in the United States, television does sometimes provide helpful information about sex (Kaiser Family Foundation, 2002b). Many adolescents in this survey said that they have learned something positive from sexual scenes on TV, such as how to say no in a sexual situation that makes them uncomfortable (60 percent) and how to talk with a partner about safer sex (43 percent).

Television and Cognitive Development Several important cognitive shifts take place between early childhood and middle and late childhood, and these shifts influence the effects of television (Wilson, 2001). Children bring varied cognitive skills and abilities to their television viewing (Rabin & Dorr, 1995). Preschool children often focus on the most striking perceptual features of a TV program and are likely to have difficulty in distinguishing reality from fantasy in the portrayals. As children enter elementary school, they are better able to link scenes together and draw causal conclusions from narratives. Judgments about what is reality and what is fantasy also become more accurate as children grow up.

How does television influence children's creativity and mental ability? In general, television has not been shown to influence children's creativity but is negative related to their mental ability (Comstock & Scharrer, 2006). Exposure to aural and printed media does more than television to enhance children's verbal skills, especially their expressive language (Beagles-Roos & Gat, 1983; Williams, 1986).

The more children watch TV the lower their school achievement is (Comstock & Scharrer, 2006). Why might TV watching be negatively linked to children's achievement? Three possibilities involve interference, displacement, and self-defeating tastes/preferences (Comstock & Scharrer, 2006). In terms of interference, having a television on while doing homework can distract children while they are doing cognitive tasks, such as homework. In terms of displacement, television can take away time and attention from engaging in achievement-related tasks, such as homework, reading, writing, and mathematics. Researchers have found that children's reading achievement is negatively linked with the amount of time they watch TV (Comstock & Scharrer, 2006). In terms of self-defeating tastes and preferences, television attracts children to entertainment, sports, commercials, and other activities that capture their interest more than school achievement. Children who are heavy TV watchers tend to view books as dull and boring (Comstock & Scharrer, 2006).

However, some types of television content—such as educational programming for young children—may enhance achievement. You might recall from chapter 1 the description of a longitudinal study in which viewing educational programs, such as *Sesame Street* and *Mr. Roger's Neighborhood,* as preschoolers was related to a number of positive outcomes through high school, including higher grades, reading more books, and enhanced creativity (Anderson & others, 2001). Newer technologies, especially interactive television, hold promise for motivating children to learn and become more exploratory in solving problems (Singer, 1993).

Computers and the Internet

Culture involves change, and nowhere is that change greater than in the technological revolution today's children are experiencing with increased use of computers and the Internet. Society still relies on some basic nontechnological competencies: for example, good communication skills, positive attitudes, and the ability to solve problems and to think deeply and creatively. But how people pursue these competencies is changing in ways and at a speed that few people had to cope with in previous eras (Bissell, Manring, & Rowland, 1999). People are using computers to communicate today the way they used to use pens, postage stamps, and telephones. For children to be adequately prepared for tomorrow's jobs, technology needs to become an integral part of their lives (Sharp, 1999).

The Internet The Internet is the core of computer-mediated communication. The Internet connects thousands of computer networks, providing an incredible array of information (Donnerstein, 2002). In many cases, the Internet has more current, up-to-date information than books.

Children and adolescents throughout the world are increasingly using the Internet, although use in different countries and socioecomomic groups varies considerably (Anderson, 2002). Between 1998 and 2001, the percentage of U.S. 14- to 17-year-olds using the Internet increased from 51 percent to 75 percent and the percentage of U.S. 10- to 13-year-olds increased from 39 percent to 65 percent (Kaiser Family Foundation, 2001). Only 5 percent of U.S. adolescents say they learned how to use the Internet at school; 40 percent said they taught themselves; others learned from their parents, friends, or siblings (Kaiser Family Foundation, 2001). Almost 50 percent of U.S. adolescents go online every day (Kaiser Family Foundation, 2001). Among 15- to 17-year-olds, one-third use the Internet for 6 hours a week or more, 24 percent use it for 3 to 5 hours a week, and 20 percent use it for 1 hour a week or less (Woodard, 2000).

What do adolescents do when they are online? As shown in figure 18.7, e-mail is the Internet activity they engage in most frequently, and more than 40 percent of the adolescents who go online connect with a chat room (Kaiser Family Foundation, 2001).

E-mail	83%
Search engine	78
Music sites	59
General research	58
Games	51
TV/movie sites	43
Chat room	42
Own Web page	38
Sports sites	35

FIGURE 18.7 Percentage of U.S. 15- to 17-Year-Olds Engaging in Different Online Activities. Note: Study conducted by telephone in fall 2001, with a national random sample of 398 15- to 17-year-olds.

With as many as 11 million American adolescents now online, more and more of adolescent life is taking place in a landscape that is inaccessible to many parents. Many adolescents have a computer in their bedroom, and most parents don't have any idea what information their adolescents are obtaining online.

In one study, about half of parents said that being online is a more positive activity for adolescents than watching TV (Tarpley, 2001). However, an analysis of Internet content suggests that parents might be wise to be more concerned about their adolescents' online activities (Donnerstein, 2002, p. 307):

- Of the 1,000 most-visited sites, 10 percent are adult sex oriented.
- Forty-four percent of adolescents have seen an adult site.
- Twenty-five percent have visited a site that promotes hate groups.
- Twelve percent have found a site where they can receive information about how to buy a gun.

In sum, the Internet holds a great deal of potential for increasing educational opportunities, but it also has limitations and dangers. Parents need to monitor and regulate their children's and adolescents' use of the Internet. Some psychologists recommend putting the computer in the family room, where adults and their children have more opportunities to discuss the information found online. Every Web browser records what sites users visit. With just elementary computer know-how, parents can monitor their children's and adolescents' computer activities.

Technology and Education Technology has been a part of schooling for many decades, but in the past the technologies used were rather simple and changed slowly. The pace of technological change has quickened dramatically in recent years. In 1983 there were fewer than 50,000 computers in America's schools. In 2002, there were more than 6 million! Hardly a school in America today is without at least one computer. Nearly every week, a school board approves the purchase of 10 to 20 computers for improving students' writing skills, another school board approves a high school's use of Channel One (a 10-minute daily recap of news that has become controversial because it also includes 2 minutes of advertising), and another sets aside funds for a telecomputing network that connects classrooms within a school and with different schools.

Will the increased use of computers in homes and schools widen the learning gap between rich and poor and between different ethnic groups (Kaiser Family Foundation, 2002a)? One national survey found that children and adolescents who go to school in lower-income communities spend more time with most types of media than their counterparts in wealthier neighborhoods, but were significantly less likely to use computers (Roberts & others, 1999) (see figure 18.8). There are gaps in computer availability across ethnic groups as well. A recent study found that while 80 percent of non-Latino White adolescents have Internet access at home, only 67 percent of Latinos and 61 percent of African Americans do (Rideout, Roberts, & Foehr, 2005).

It is important to keep in mind that technology itself does not improve a child's ability to learn. A number of elements are needed to create environments that adequately support students' learning. These include vision and support from educational leaders, educators who are skilled in the use of technology for learning, access to contemporary technologies, and an emphasis on the child as an active, constructivist learner (International Society for Technology in Education, 2001).

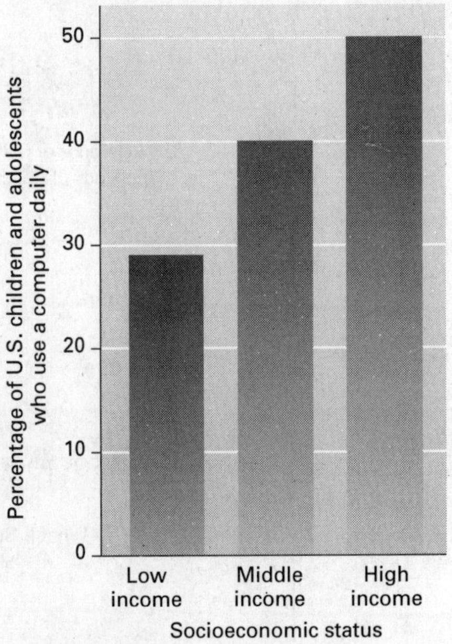

FIGURE 18.8 Daily Computer Use by Children and Adolescents in Different Socioeconomic Groups

Technology and Education
Internet Pals

Review and Reflect LEARNING GOAL 4

4 Summarize the influence of technology on children's development

Review

- What role do mass media play in the lives of children and adolescents?
- How does television influence children's development?
- What roles do computers and the Internet play in children's development?

Reflect

- How much television did you watch as a child? What effect do you believe it has had on your development?

REACH YOUR LEARNING GOALS

CULTURE

- **1 CULTURE AND CHILDREN'S DEVELOPMENT**
  - The Relevance of Culture to the Study of Children
  - Cross-Cultural Comparisons
- **2 SOCIOECONOMIC STATUS AND POVERTY**
  - What Is Socioeconomic Status?
  - Socioeconomic Variations in Families, Neighborhoods, and Schools
  - Poverty
- **3 ETHNICITY**
  - Immigration
  - Differences and Diversity
  - Assimilation and Pluralism
  - Ethnicity and Socioeconomic Status
  - Prejudice, Discrimination, and Bias
  - The United States and Canada: Nations with Many Cultures
- **4 TECHNOLOGY**
  - Media Use
  - Television
  - Computers and the Internet

SUMMARY

1 Discuss the role of culture in children's development

- Culture refers to the behavior patterns, beliefs, and all other products of a particular group of people that are passed on from generation to generation. If the study of children is to be a relevant discipline in the twenty-first century, there will have to be increased attention to culture.
- Cross-cultural comparisons compare one culture with one or more other cultures, which provides information about the degree to which characteristics are universal or culture-specific. The social contexts in which children develop—gender, family, and school—display important differences from one culture to another. Cross-cultural comparisons indicate that children raised in individualistic cultures are taught different values and conceptions of the self than those raised in collectivistic cultures. Cross-cultural comparisons of how adolescents spend their time and of rites of passage provide other examples of the influence of culture on development.

2 Describe how socioeconomic status and poverty impact children's lives

- Socioeconomic status (SES) is the grouping of people with similar occupational, educational, and economic characteristics. SES implies inequalities.
- The families, neighborhoods, and schools of children have SES characteristics that are related to the child's development. Parents from low-SES families are more likely to value conformity and to use physical punishment than their middle-SES counterparts.
- Poverty is defined by economic hardship. The poor often face not only economic hardship but also social and psychological difficulties. When poverty is persistent and long lasting, it especially has adverse effects on children's development.

3 Explain how ethnicity is linked to children's development

- Ethnicity is based on cultural heritage, nationality characteristics, race, religion, and language. The immigration of families to the United States brings about a number of challenges for helping children adapt to their new culture. Parents and children may be at different stages of acculturation.
- Too often researchers have not teased apart the influence of ethnic and socioeconomic status when studying ethnic minority children. Although not all ethnic minority families are poor, poverty contributes to the stress of many ethnic minority families and to differences between ethnic minority groups and the White majority.
- Recognizing differences in ethnicity is an important aspect of getting along with others in a diverse, multicultural world. Too often differences have been described as deficits on the part of ethnic minority individuals. Ethnic minority groups are not homogeneous. Failure to recognize this diversity results in stereotyping.
- Prejudice is an unjustified negative attitude toward an individual because of the individual's membership in a group. Despite progress in the treatment of minority groups, children who are members of these groups still often face prejudice and discrimination.
- For many years, assimilation (the absorption of ethnic groups into the dominant group, which often means the loss of some or virtually all of the behavior patterns and values of the minority groups' cultures) was thought to be the best course for American society, but pluralism (the coexistence of distinct ethnic and cultural groups in the same society) is increasingly being advocated.
- The United States and Canada have been, and continue to be, great receivers of ethnic immigrants. This has resulted in the United States and Canada being nations with many cultures.

4 Summarize the influence of technology on children's development

- There are large individual variations in media use by children and adolescents, but the average U.S. 8- to 18-year-old spends almost 6½ hours using electronic media, with the most hours spent watching television (almost 4 hours per day). However, children and adolescents are rapidly increasing the time they spend online.
- Although television can have a negative influence on children's development by taking them away from homework, making them passive learners, teaching them stereotypes, providing violent models, and presenting them with unrealistic views of the world, television also can have positive influences by presenting motivating educational programs, increasing children's information beyond their immediate environment, and providing models of prosocial behavior. TV violence is not the only cause of children's aggression, but most experts agree that it can induce aggression and antisocial behavior. There also is concern about children playing violent video games. Prosocial behavior on TV

is associated with increased positive behavior by children. A special concern is the way sex is portrayed on television and the influence this can have on adolescents' sexual attitudes and behaviors. Children's cognitive skills and abilities influence their TV viewing experiences. TV viewing is negatively related to children's mental ability and achievement.

- Today's children are experiencing a technological revolution through the dramatic increase in the use of computers and the Internet. The Internet is the core of computer-mediated communication, and it is worldwide. A special concern is the difficulty parents have monitoring the information their children are accessing. Another concern is whether increased use of technology will widen the learning gap between rich and poor, and between different ethnic groups. Keep in mind that technology alone does not improve children's learning. A combination of other factors such as an emphasis on active, constructivist learning also is required.

KEY TERMS

culture 560
cross-cultural studies 562
individualism 562
collectivism 562
rites of passage 564
socioeconomic status (SES) 565
ethnicity 571
prejudice 573
assimilation 574
pluralism 574

KEY PEOPLE

Donald Campbell 561
Margaret Mead 561
Reed Larson and Suman Verma 563
Vonnie McLoyd 569
Stanley Sue 574
Aimee Leifer 578

E-LEARNING TOOLS

To help you master the material in this chapter, visit the Online Learning Center for *Child Development*, eleventh edition (**www.mhhe.com/santrockcd11**), where you'll find these additional resources:

Taking It to the Net

1. Jeremy is attending college in California, where he is majoring in political science. For his senior thesis he is required to choose an area of social policy and develop a legislative agenda. Based upon recent news reports about the increasing number of low- and middle-income wage earners who don't make enough money for decent housing, food, and health care for their children, he decides to make the needs of these children his priority. What types of programs should he propose for the children of these families?
2. Mrs. Bernstein thinks that she ought to involve her fourth-grade students in a dialogue about racism and prejudice, since there are several ethnic groups represented in her class. But a colleague warned her that talking to kids about racism could backfire and actually cause prejudice. What are the possible reactions of students to a discussion of racism?
3. Denise has heard about the "digital divide," the concept that ethnic minorities and economically deprived populations are not participating in the Internet explosion. Since Denise is about to begin teaching third grade in an inner-city school, she wonders if the school will be as well equipped technologically as a school in a better neighborhood. What are the facts?

Nursing, Parenting, and Teaching Exercises

Build your decision-making skills by trying your hand at the scenarios on the Online Learning Center.

Video Clips

The Online Learning Center includes the following videos for this chapter:

- Ethnic and Racial Identity in Adolescence
  Two African American girls discuss candidly their feelings about being Black. One describes being Black as being a mixture of many cultures. The other says it's hard to be African American because there is no distinct culture for Blacks.
- Talking About Ethnic Identity in Adolescence
  They view the diversity among them, as well as among their peers, very positively. They admit that they are different from one another because of their ethnic backgrounds but they each benefit from one another because of these differences.
- Impact of Media on Children
  Sandra Calvert, Department of Psychology, Georgetown University, defines the three ways in which the media impact children. She also describes what children report learning from television and movies.

GLOSSARY

A

A$\bar{B}$ error The Piagetian object-permanence concept in which an infant progressing into substage 4 makes frequent mistakes, selecting the familiar hiding place (A) rather than the new hiding place (B).

accommodation (culture) Occurs when children adjust their knowledge to fit new information and experience.

accommodation Piagetian concept of adjusting schemes to fit new information and experiences.

active (niche-picking) genotype-environment correlations Correlations that exist when children seek out environments they find compatible and stimulating.

adolescence The developmental period of transition from childhood to early adulthood, entered at approximately 10 to 12 years of age and ending at 18 to 22 years of age.

adolescent egocentrism The heightened self-consciousness of adolescents, which is reflected in adolescents' beliefs that others are as interested in them as they are in themselves, and in adolescents' sense of personal uniqueness and invincibility.

adoption study A study in which investigators seek to discover whether, in behavior and psychological characteristics, adopted children are more like their adoptive parents, who provided a home environment, or more like their biological parents, who contributed their heredity. Another form of the adoption study is to compare adoptive and biological siblings.

affordances Opportunities for interaction offered by objects that are necessary to perform activities.

altruism An unselfish interest in helping another person.

amnion The life-support system that is a bag or envelope that contains a clear fluid in which the developing embryo floats.

androgens The main class of male sex hormones.

androgyny The presence of masculine and feminine characteristics in the same person.

anger cry A cry similar to the basic cry but with more excess air forced through the vocal cords (associated with exasperation or rage).

animism A facet of preoperational thought, the belief that inanimate objects have "lifelike" qualities and are capable of action.

anorexia nervosa An eating disorder that involves the relentless pursuit of thinness through starvation.

Apgar Scale A widely used method to assess the health of newborns at one and five minutes after birth. The Apgar Scale evaluates infants' heart rate, respiratory effort, muscle tone, body color, and reflex irritability.

aphasia A loss or impairment of language ability caused by brain damage.

assimilation (Piaget) Occurs when children incorporate new information into their existing knowledge (schemes).

assimilation (culture) The absorption of ethnic minority groups into the dominant group, which often means the loss of some or virtually all of the behavior and values of the ethnic minority group.

associative play Play that involves social interaction with little or no organization.

attachment A close emotional bond between two people.

attention Concentrating and focusing mental resources.

attention deficit hyperactivity disorder (ADHD) A disability in which children consistently show one or more of the following characteristics: (1) inattention, (2) hyperactivity, and (3) impulsivity.

attributions Attributions are explanations people give for behavior; one way to classify these explanations is whether they are internal or external.

authoritarian parenting This is a restrictive, punitive style in which the parent exhorts the child to follow the parent's directions and to respect their work and effort. Firm limits and controls are placed on the child, and little verbal exchange is allowed. This style is associated with children's socially incompetent behavior.

authoritative parenting This style encourages children to be independent but still places limits and controls on their actions. Extensive verbal give-and-take is allowed, and parents are warm and nurturant toward the child. This style is associated with children's socially competent behavior.

automaticity The ability to process information with little or no effort.

autonomous morality The second stage of moral development in Piaget's theory, displayed by older children (about 10 years of age and older). The child becomes aware that rules and laws are created by people and that, in judging an action, one should consider the actor's intentions as well as the consequences.

average children Children who receive an average number of both positive and negative nominations from their peers.

B

basal metabolism rate (BMR) The minimum amount of energy an individual uses in a resting state.

basic cry A rhythmic pattern usually consisting of a cry, a briefer silence, a shorter inspiratory whistle that is higher pitched than the main cry, and then a brief rest before the next cry.

basic-skills-and-phonics approach An approach that emphasizes that reading instruction should teach phonics and its basic rules for translating written symbols into sounds.

Bayley Scales of Infant Development Developed by Nancy Bayley, these scales are widely used in assessing infant development. The current version has three parts: a Mental Scale, a Motor Scale, and the Infant Behavior Profile.

behavior genetics The field that seeks to discover the influence of heredity and environment on individual differences in human traits and development.

biological processes Changes in an individual's body.

blastocyst The inner layer of cells that develops during the germinal period. These cells later develop into the embryo.

bonding The formation of a close connection, especially a physical bond between parents and their newborn in the period shortly after birth.

brainstorming A technique in which children are encouraged to come up with creative ideas in a group, play off one another's ideas, and say practically whatever comes to mind.

Brazelton Neonatal Behavioral Assessment Scale (NBAS) A test given several days after birth to assess newborns' neurological development, reflexes, and reactions to people.

breech position The baby's position in the uterus that causes the buttocks to be the first part to emerge from the vagina.

Broca's area An area of the brain's left frontal lobe that directs the muscle movements involved in speech production.

bulimia nervosa An eating disorder that involves a binge-and-purge sequence on a regular basis.

C

care perspective The moral perspective of Carol Gilligan that views people in terms of their connectedness with others and emphasizes interpersonal communication, relationships with others, and concern for others.

case study An in-depth look at a single individual.

centration The focusing of attention on one characteristic to the exclusion of all others.

cephalocaudal pattern The sequence in which the greatest growth occurs at the top—the head—with physical growth in size, weight, and feature differentiation gradually working from top to bottom.

character education A direct moral education approach that involves teaching students a basic moral literacy to prevent them from engaging in immoral behavior or doing harm to themselves or others.

child-centered kindergarten Education that involves the whole child by considering both the child's physical, cognitive, and social development and the child's needs, interests, and learning styles.

child-directed speech Language spoken in a higher pitch than normal with simple words and sentences.

chromosomes Threadlike structures that come in 23 pairs, one member of each pair coming from each parent. Chromosomes contain the genetic substance DNA.

cliques Small groups that range from 2 to about 12 individuals and average about 5 to 6 individuals. Cliques can form because of friendship or because individuals engage in similar activities, and members usually are of the same sex and about the same age.

cognitive appraisal Lazarus' term for children's interpretations of events in their lives that are harmful, threatening, or challenging, and their determination of whether they have the resources to effectively cope with the event.

cognitive constructivist approaches An approach that emphasizes the child's active, cognitive construction of knowledge and understanding; Piaget's theory is an example of this approach.

cognitive developmental theory of gender In this view, children's gender typing occurs after they have developed a concept of gender. Once they begin to consistently conceive of themselves as male or female, children often organize their world on the basis of gender.

cognitive moral education Education based on the belief that students should learn to value things like democracy and justice as their moral reasoning develops; Kohlberg's theory has been the basis for many of the cognitive moral education approaches.

cognitive processes Changes in an individual's thought, intelligence, and language.

collectivism Emphasizing values that serve the group by subordinating personal goals to preserve group integrity, interdependence of members, and harmonious relationships.

commitment The part of identity development in which adolescents show a personal investment in what they are going to do.

concepts Categories that group objects, events, and characteristics on the basis of common properties.

concrete operational stage Piaget's third stage, which lasts from approximately 7 to 11 years of age; children can perform operations, and logical reasoning replaces intuitive reasoning as long as the reasoning can be applied to specific, concrete examples.

conduct disorder Age-inappropriate actions and attitudes that violate family expectations, society's norms, and the personal property rights of others.

connectedness An important element in adolescent identity development. It consists of two dimensions: mutuality, sensitivity to and respect for others' views; and permeability, openness to others' views.

conscience The component of the superego that punishes the child for behaviors disapproved of by parents by making the child feel guilty and worthless.

conservation The idea that an amount stays the same regardless of how its container changes.

constructive play Play that combines sensorimotor/practice repetitive activity with symbolic representation of ideas. Constructive play occurs when children engage in self-regulated creation or construction of a product or a problem solution.

continuity view A developmental view that emphasizes the role of early parent-child relationships in constructing a basic way of relating to people throughout the life span.

continuity-discontinuity issue The issue regarding the extent to which development involves gradual, cumulative change (continuity) or distinct stages (discontinuity).

controversial children Children who are frequently nominated both as someone's best friend and as being disliked.

conventional reasoning The second, or intermediate, level in Kohlberg's theory of moral development. At this level, individuals abide by certain standards but they are the standards of others such as parents or the laws of society.

convergent thinking Thinking that produces one correct answer; characteristic of the kind of thinking required on conventional intelligence tests.

cooperative play Play that involves social interaction in a group with a sense of group identity and organized activity.

coparenting The amount of support parents provide for each other in raising children.

correlation coefficient A number based on a statistical analysis that is used to describe the degree of association between two variables.

correlational research The goal is to describe the strength of the relation between two or more events or characteristics.

creativity The ability to think in novel and unusual ways and come up with unique solutions to problems.

crisis A period of identity development during which the adolescent is choosing among meaningful alternatives.

critical thinking Thinking reflectively and productively, and evaluating the evidence.

cross-cultural studies Studies that compare a culture with one or more other cultures. Such studies provide information about the degree to which children's development is similar, or universal, across cultures or about the degree to which it is culture-specific.

cross-sectional approach A research strategy in which individuals of different ages are compared at one time.

crowds The crowd is a larger group structure than a clique. Adolescents usually are members of a crowd based on reputation and may or may not spend much time together. Many crowds are defined by the activities adolescents engage in.

culture The behavior patterns, beliefs, and all other products of a group that are passed on from generation to generation.

culture-fair tests Intelligence tests that are intended to not be culturally biased.

D

dating scripts The cognitive models that adolescents and adults use to guide and evaluate dating interactions.

descriptive research This type of research aims to observe and record behavior.

development The pattern of change that begins at conception and continues through the life span.

developmental construction views Views sharing the belief that as individuals grow up, they acquire modes of relating to others. There are two main variations of this view. One emphasizes continuity and stability in relationships throughout the life span; the other emphasizes discontinuity and changes in relationships throughout the life span.

developmental quotient (DQ) An overall developmental score that combines subscores on motor, language, adaptive, and personal-social domains in the Gesell assessment of infants.

developmentally appropriate practice Education that focuses on the typical developmental patterns of children (age appropriateness) and the uniqueness of each child (individual appropriateness). Such practice contrasts with developmentally inappropriate practice, which ignores the concrete, hands-on approach to learning. Direct teaching largely through abstract paper-and-pencil activities presented to large groups of young children is believed to be developmentally inappropriate.

dialect A variety of language that is distinguished by its vocabulary, grammar, or pronunciation.

difficult child A temperament style in which the child tends to react negatively and cry frequently, engages in irregular daily routines, and is slow to accept new experiences.

direct instruction approach A teacher-centered approach characterized by teacher direction and control, mastery of academic material, high expectations for students' progress, and maximum time spent on learning tasks.

discontinuity view A developmental view that emphasizes change and growth in relationships over time.

dishabituation The recovery of a habituated response after a change in stimulation.

dismissing/avoidant attachment An insecure attachment category in which individuals de-emphasize the importance of attachment. This category is associated with consistent experiences of rejection of attachment needs by caregivers.

divergent thinking Thinking that produces many answers to the same question; characteristic of creativity.

divided attention Concentrating on more than one activity at a time.

DNA A complex molecule that contains genetic information.

doula A caregiver who provides continuous physical, emotional, and educational support for the mother before, during, and after childbirth.

Down syndrome A chromosomally transmitted form of mental retardation, caused by the presence of an extra copy of chromosome 21.

dynamic systems theory A theory, proposed by Esther Thelen, that seeks to explain how motor behaviors are assembled for perceiving and acting.

dyslexia A category of learning disabilities involving a severe impairment in the ability to read and spell.

E

early childhood The developmental period that extends from the end of infancy to about 5 to 6 years of age, sometimes called the preschool years.

early-later experience issue The issue of the degree to which early experiences (especially infancy) or later experiences are the key determinants of the child's development.

easy child A temperament style in which the child is generally in a positive mood, quickly establishes regular routines, and adapts easily to new experiences.

eclectic theoretical orientation An orientation that does not follow any one theoretical approach, but rather, selects from each theory whatever is considered the best in it.

ecological theory Bronfenbrenner's environmental systems theory that focuses on five environmental systems: microsystem, mesosystem, exosystem, macrosystem, and chronosystem.

ecological view The view, proposed by the Gibsons, that people directly perceive information in the world around them. Perception brings people in contact with the environment in order to interact with it and adapt to it.

ego ideal The component of the superego that rewards the child by conveying a sense of pride and personal value when the child acts according to ideal standards approved by the parents.

egocentrism An important feature of preoperational thought, the inability to distinguish between one's own and someone else's perspective.

embryonic period The period of prenatal development that occurs two to eight weeks after conception. During the embryonic period, the rate of cell differentiation intensifies, support systems for the cells form, and organs appear.

emotion Feeling, or affect, that occurs when a person is in a state or interaction that is important to him or her. Emotion is characterized by behavior that reflects (expresses) the pleasantness or unpleasantness of the state he or she is in, or the transaction he or she is experiencing.

emotional intelligence The ability to perceive and express emotions accurately and adaptively, to understand emotion and emotional knowledge, to use feelings to facilitate thought, and to manage emotions in oneself and others.

empathy Reacting to another's feelings with an emotional response that is similar to the other's feelings.

encoding The mechanism by which information gets into memory.

epigenetic view Emphasizes that development is the result of an ongoing, bidirectional interchange between heredity and environment.

equilibration A mechanism that Piaget proposed to explain how children shift from one stage of thought to the next. The shift occurs as children experience cognitive conflict or disequilibrium in trying to understand the world. Eventually, they resolve the conflict and reach a balance or equilibrium of thought.

Erikson's theory Includes eight stages of human development. Each stage consists of a unique developmental task that confronts individuals with a crisis that must be faced.

estrogens The main class of female sex hormones.

ethnic gloss A superficial way of using an ethnic label, such as African American or Latino, that portrays an ethnic group as being more homogeneous than it really is.

ethnic identity A sense of membership in an ethnic group, based on shared language, religion, customs, values, history, and race.

ethnicity A dimension of culture based on cultural heritage, nationality, race, religion, and language.

ethological theory Stresses that behavior is strongly influenced by biology, is tied to evolution, and is characterized by critical or sensitive periods.

evocative genotype-environment correlations Correlations that exist when the child's genotype elicits certain types of physical and social environments.

evolutionary psychology Emphasizes the importance of adaptation, reproduction, and "survival of the fittest" in shaping behavior.

expanding Restating, in a linguistically sophisticated form, what a child has said.

experiment A carefully regulated procedure in which one or more of the factors believed to influence the behavior being studied is manipulated and all other factors are held constant.

experimental research Research involving experiments that permit the determination of cause.

explicit memory Conscious memory of facts and experiences.

extrinsic motivation Response to external incentives such as rewards and punishments.

F

factor analysis A statistical procedure that correlates test scores to identify underlying clusters, or factors.

fertilization A stage in reproduction whereby an egg and a sperm fuse to create a single cell, called a zygote.

fetal alcohol syndrome (FAS) A cluster of abnormalities that appears in the offspring of mothers who drink alcohol heavily during pregnancy.

fetal period The prenatal period of development that begins two months after conception and lasts for seven months, on the average.

fine motor skills Motor skills that involve more finely tuned movements, such as finger dexterity.

formal operational stage Piaget's fourth and final stage, which occurs between the ages of 11 and 15; individuals move beyond concrete experiences and think in more abstract and logical ways.

fragile X syndrome A genetic disorder involving an abnormality in the X chromosome, which becomes constricted and, often, breaks.

fuzzy trace theory States that memory is best understood by considering two types of memory representations: (1) verbatim memory trace and (2) gist. In this theory, older children's better memory is attributed to the fuzzy traces created by extracting the gist of information.

G

games Activities engaged in for pleasure that include rules and often competition with one or more individuals.

gender The psychological and sociocultural dimensions of being male or female.

gender identity The sense of being female or male, which most children acquire by the time they are 3 years old.

gender role A set of expectations that prescribes how females and males should think, act, and feel.

gender schema theory According to this theory, an individual's attention and behavior are guided by an internal motivation to conform to gender-based sociocultural standards and stereotypes.

gender stereotypes Broad categories that reflect impressions and beliefs about what behavior is appropriate for females and males.

genes Units of hereditary information composed of DNA. Genes direct cells to reproduce themselves and manufacture the proteins that maintain life.

genetic epistemology The study of how children's knowledge changes over the course of their development.

genotype A person's genetic heritage; the actual genetic material.

germinal period The period of prenatal development that takes place in the first two weeks after conception. It includes the creation of the zygote, continued cell division, and the attachment of the zygote to the uterine wall.

gifted Having high intelligence (an IQ of 130 or higher) or superior talent for something.

goodness of fit Refers to the match between a child's temperament and the environmental demands the child must cope with.

grasping reflex A neonatal reflex that occurs when something touches the infant's palms. The infant responds by grasping tightly.

gross motor skills Motor skills that involve large-muscle activities, such as walking.

growth hormone deficiency The absence or deficiency of growth hormone produced by the pituitary gland to stimulate the body to grow.

H

habituation Decreased responsiveness to a stimulus after repeated presentations of the stimulus.

helpless orientation An orientation in which one seems trapped by the experience of difficulty and attributes one's difficulty to a lack of ability.

heritability The fraction of the variance in a population that is attributed to genetics.

heteronomous morality The first stage of moral development in Piaget's theory, occurring at 4 to 7 years of age. Justice and rules are conceived of as unchangeable properties of the world, removed from the control of people.

hidden curriculum The pervasive moral atmosphere that characterizes schools.

horizontal décalage Piaget's concept that similar abilities do not appear at the same time within a stage of development.

hormones Powerful chemical substances secreted by the endocrine glands and carried through the body by the bloodstream.

hypothesis *(plural hypotheses)* Specific assumptions and predictions that can be tested to determine their accuracy.

hypothetical-deductive reasoning Piaget's formal operational concept that adolescents have the cognitive ability to develop hypotheses about ways to solve problems and can systematically deduce which is the best path to follow in solving the problem.

I

identity achievement Marcia's term for an adolescent's having undergone a crisis and made a commitment.

identity diffusion Marcia's term for the state adolescents are in when they have not yet experienced a crisis (that is, they have not yet explored meaningful alternatives) or made any commitments.

identity foreclosure Marcia's term for the state adolescents are in when they have made a commitment but have not experienced a crisis.

identity moratorium Marcia's term for the state adolescents are in when they are in the midst of a crisis, but whose commitments either are absent or are only vaguely defined.

identity versus identity confusion Erikson's fifth developmental stage, which individuals experience during the adolescent years. At this time, adolescents examine who they are, what they are all about, and where they are going in life.

imaginary audience The aspect of adolescent egocentrism that involves attention-getting behavior motivated by a desire to be noticed, visible, and "onstage."

immanent justice Piaget's concept that if a rule is broken, punishment will be meted out immediately.

implicit memory Memory without conscious recollection; memory of skills and routine procedures that are performed automatically.

inclusion Educating a child with special education needs full-time in the regular classroom.

index offenses Criminal acts, whether they are committed by juveniles or adults. They include such acts as robbery, aggravated assault, rape, and homicide.

individualism Giving priority to personal goals rather than to group goals; emphasizing values that serve the self, such as feeling good, personal distinction and achievement, and independence.

individualism, instrumental purpose, and exchange The second Kohlberg stage of moral development. At this stage, individuals pursue their own interests but also let others do the same.

individuality An important element in adolescent identity development. It consists or two dimensions: self-assertion, the ability to have and communicate a point of view; and separateness, the use of communication patterns to express how one is different from others.

individualized education plan (IEP) A written statement that spells out a program tailored to a child with a disability. The plan should be (1) related to the child's learning capacity, (2) specially constructed to meet the child's individual needs and not merely a copy of what is offered to other children, and (3) designed to provide 1educational benefits.

induction A discipline technique in which a parent uses reason and explanation of the consequences for others of the child's actions.

indulgent parenting A style in which parents are highly involved with their children but place few demands or controls on them. This is associated with children's social incompetence, especially a lack of self-control.

infancy The developmental period that extends from birth to about 18 to 24 months.

infinite generativity The ability to produce an endless number of meaningful sentences using a finite set of words and rules.

information-processing approach An approach that focuses on the ways children process information about their world—how they manipulate information, monitor it, and create strategies to deal with it.

information-processing theory A theory that emphasizes that individuals manipulate information, monitor it, and strategize about it. The processes of memory and thinking are central.

innate goodness view The idea, presented by Swiss-born philosopher Jean-Jacques Rousseau, that children are inherently good.

insecure avoidant babies Babies who show insecurity by avoiding the mother.

insecure disorganized babies Babies who show insecurity by being disorganized and disoriented.

insecure resistant babies Babies who might cling to the caregiver, then resist her by fighting against the closeness, perhaps by kicking or pushing away.

intelligence Thinking skills and the ability to adapt to and learn from life's everyday experiences.

intelligence quotient (IQ) An individual's mental age divided by chronological age multiplied by 100; devised in 1912 by William Stern.

intermodal perception The ability to relate and integrate information about two or more sensory modalities, such as vision and hearing.

intimacy in friendship Self-disclosure or the sharing of private thoughts.

intrinsic motivation Internal motivational factors such as self-determination, curiosity, challenge, and effort.

intuitive thought substage The second substage of preoperational thought, occurring between approximately 4 and 7 years of age. Children begin to use primitive reasoning and want to know the answers to all sorts of questions.

J

justice perspective A moral perspective that focuses on the rights of the individual; individuals independently make moral decisions.

juvenile delinquency Refers to a great variety of behaviors, ranging from unacceptable behavior to status offenses to criminal acts.

K

kangaroo care A way of holding a preterm infant so that there is skin-to-skin contact.

Klinefelter syndrome A chromosomal disorder in which males have an extra X chromosome, making them XXY instead of XY.

kwashiorkor A condition caused by a deficiency in protein in which the child's abdomen and feet become swollen with water.

L

labeling Identifying the names of objects.

laboratory A controlled setting in which many of the complex factors of the "real world" are removed.

language A form of communication, whether spoken, written, or signed, that is based on a system of symbols.

language acquisition device (LAD) Chomsky's term that describes a biological endowment that enables the child to detect the features and rules of language, including phonology, syntax, and semantics.

lateralization Specialization of functions in one hemisphere of the cerebral cortex or the other.

learning disability Includes three components: (1) a minimum IQ level, (2) a significant difficulty in a school-related area (especially reading or mathematics), and (3) exclusion of only severe emotional disorders, second-language background, sensory disabilities, and/or specific neurological deficits.

least restrictive environment (LRE) The concept that a child with a disability must be educated in a setting that is as similar as possible to the one in which children who do not have a disability are educated.

longitudinal approach A research strategy in which the same individuals are studied over a period of time, usually several years or more.

long-term memory A relatively permanent and unlimited type of memory.

love withdrawal A discipline technique in which a parent withholds attention or love from the child.

low birth weight infants An infant that weighs less than 5½ pounds at birth.

M

marasmus A wasting away of body tissues in the infant's first year, caused by severe protein-calorie deficiency.

mastery orientation An orientation in which one is task-oriented and, instead of focusing on one's ability, is concerned with learning strategies.

meiosis A specialized form of cell division that occurs to form eggs and sperm (or gametes).

memory Retention of information over time.

menarche A girl's first menstrual period.

mental age (MA) An individual's level of mental development relative to others.

mental retardation A condition of limited mental ability in which the individual (1) has a low IQ, usually below 70 on a traditional intelligence test, (2) has difficulty adapting to everyday life, and (3) has an onset of these characteristics by age 18.

metacognition Cognition about cognition, or "knowing about knowing."

metalinguistic awareness Knowledge of language

metamemory Knowledge about memory.

metaphor An implied comparison between two unlike things.

middle and late childhood The developmental period that extends from about 6 to 11 years of age, sometimes called the elementary school years.

mitosis Cellular reproduction in which the cell's nucleus duplicates itself with two new cells being formed, each containing the same DNA as the parent cell, arranged in the same 23 pairs of chromosomes.

Montessori approach An educational philosophy in which children are given considerable freedom and spontaneity in choosing activities and are allowed to move from one activity to another as they desire.

moral development Changes in thoughts, feelings, and behaviors regarding standards of right and wrong.

moral exemplars People who have lived exemplary lives. They have a moral personality, identity, character, and set of virtues that reflect moral excellence and commitment.

moral identity The aspect of personality that is present when individuals have moral notions and commitments that are central to their lives.

Moro reflex A neonatal startle response that occurs in reaction to a sudden, intense noise or movement. When startled, the newborn arches its back, throws its head back, and flings out its arms and legs. Then the newborn rapidly closes its arms and legs to the center of the body.

morphology Units of meaning involved in word formation.

multiple-factor theory L. L. Thurstone's theory that intelligence consists of seven primary mental abilities: verbal comprehension, number ability, word fluency, spatial visualization, associative memory, reasoning, and perceptual speed.

mutual interpersonal expectations, relationships, and interpersonal conformity Kohlberg's third stage of moral development. At this stage, individuals value trust, caring, and loyalty to others as a basis of moral judgments.

N

natural childbirth Developed in 1914 by Dick-Read, this method attempts to reduce the mother's pain by decreasing her fear through education about childbirth and relaxation techniques during delivery.

naturalistic observation Observing behavior in real-world settings.

nature-nurture issue Nature refers to an organism's biological inheritance, nurture to environmental influences. The "nature" proponents claim biological inheritance is the most important influence on development; the "nurture" proponents claim that environmental experiences are the most important.

neglected children Children who are infrequently nominated as a best friend but are not disliked by their peers.

neglectful parenting A style in which the parent is very uninvolved in the child's life. It is associated with children's social incompetence, especially a lack of self-control.

Neonatal Intensive Care Unit Network Neurobehavioral Scale (NNNS) An "offspring" of the NBAS, the NNNS provides a more comprehensive analysis of the newborn's behavior, neurological and stress responses, and regulatory capacities.

neo-Piagetians Developmentalists who have elaborated on Piaget's theory, believing that children's cognitive development is more specific in many respects than he thought.

neurons Nerve cells that handle information processing at the cellular level.

nonshared environmental experiences The child's own unique experiences, both within the family and outside the family, that are not shared by another sibling. Thus, experiences occurring within the family can be part of the "nonshared environment."

normal distribution A symmetrical distribution with a majority of the cases falling in the middle of the possible range of scores and few scores appearing toward the extremes of the range.

O

object permanence The Piagetian term for one of an infant's most important accomplishments: understanding that objects and events continue to exist even when they cannot directly be seen, heard, or touched.

onlooker play Play in which the child watches other children play.

operations Internalized sets of actions that allow children to do mentally what before they had done physically. Operations also are reversible mental actions.

organization Piaget's concept of grouping isolated behaviors into a higher-order, more smoothly functioning cognitive system; the grouping or arranging of items into categories.

organogenesis Organ formation that takes place during the first two months of prenatal development.

original sin view Advocated during the Middle Ages, the belief that children were born into the world as evil beings and were basically bad.

P

pain cry A sudden appearance of loud crying without preliminary moaning and a long initial cry followed by an extended period of breath holding.

parallel play Play in which the child plays separately from others, but with toys like those the others are using or in a manner that mimics their play.

passive genotype-environment correlations Correlations that exist when the natural parents, who are genetically related to the child, provide a rearing environment for the child.

peers Children of about the same age or maturity level.

perception The interpretation of sensation.

performance orientation An orientation in which one focuses on achievement outcomes; winning is what matters most, and happiness is thought to result from winning.

personal fable The part of adolescent egocentrism that involves an adolescent's sense of uniqueness and invincibility.

perspective taking The ability to assume another person's perspective and understand his or her thoughts and feelings.

phenotype The way an individual's genotype is expressed in observed and measurable characteristics.

phenylketonuria (PKU) A genetic disorder in which an individual cannot properly metabolize an amino acid. PKU is now easily detected but, if left untreated, results in mental retardation and hyperactivity.

phonology The sound system of the language, including the sounds that are used and how they may be combined.

Piaget's theory States that children actively construct their understanding of the world and go through four stages of cognitive development.

placenta A life-support system that consists of a disk-shaped group of tissues in which small blood vessels from the mother and offspring intertwine.

play A pleasurable activity that is engaged in for its own sake.

play therapy Therapy that allows the child to work off frustrations and is a medium through which the therapist can analyze the child's conflicts and ways of coping with them. Children may feel less threatened and be more likely to express their true feelings in the context of play.

pluralism The coexistence of distinct ethnic and cultural groups in the same society.

popular children Children who are frequently nominated as a best friend and are rarely disliked by their peers.

possible self What an individual might become, what the person would like to become, and what the person is afraid of becoming.

postconventional reasoning The highest level in Kohlberg's theory of moral development. At this level, morality is completely internalized and not based on others' standards.

postpartum depression Characteristic of women who have such strong feelings of sadness, anxiety, or despair that they have trouble coping with daily tasks in the postpartum period.

postpartum period The period after childbirth when the mother adjusts, both physically and psychologically, to the process of childbirth. This period lasts for about six weeks or until her body has completed its adjustment and returned to a near prepregnant state.

power assertion A discipline technique in which a parent attempts to gain control over the child or the child's resources.

practice play Play that involves repetition of behavior when new skills are being learned or when physical or mental mastery and coordination of skills are required for games or sports. Sensorimotor play, which often involves practice play, is primarily confined to infancy, while practice play can be engaged in throughout life.

pragmatics The appropriate use of language in context.

preconventional reasoning The lowest level in Kohlberg's theory of moral development. The individual's moral reasoning is controlled primarily by external rewards and punishment.

prejudice An unjustified negative attitude toward an individual because of her or his membership in a group.

prenatal period The time from conception to birth.

preoccupied/ambivalent attachment An insecure attachment category in which adolescents are hypertuned to attachment experiences. This is thought to mainly occur because parents are inconsistently available to the adolescent.

preoperational stage The second Piagetian developmental stage, which lasts from about 2 to 7 years of age; children begin to represent the world with words, images, and drawings.

prepared childbirth Developed by French obstetrician Ferdinand Lamaze, this childbirth strategy is similar to natural childbirth but includes a special breathing technique to control pushing in the final stages of labor and a more detailed anatomy and physiology course.

pretense/symbolic play Play that occurs when a child transforms the physical environment into a symbol.

preterm infants Those born three weeks or more before the pregnancy has reached its full term.

primary appraisal Individuals interpret whether an event involves harm or loss that has already occurred, a threat that involves some future danger, or a challenge to be overcome.

primary emotions Emotions that are present in humans and animals, including surprise, interest, joy, anger, sadness, fear, and disgust, that appear in the first six months of life.

Project Head Start Compensatory education designed to provide children from low-income families the opportunity to acquire the skills and experiences important for school success.

proximodistal pattern The sequence in which growth starts at the center of the body and moves toward the extremities.

psychoanalytic theory Describes development as primarily unconscious and heavily colored by emotion. Behavior is merely a surface characteristic, and the symbolic workings of the mind have to be analyzed to understand behavior. Early experiences with parents are emphasized.

psychoanalytic theory of gender A theory that stems from Freud's view that preschool children develop a sexual attraction to the opposite-sex parent, then at 5 to 6 years of age renounce the attraction because of anxious feelings, subsequently identifying with the same-sex parent and unconsciously adopting the same-sex parent's characteristics.

psychosocial moratorium Erikson's term for the gap between childhood security and adult autonomy that adolescents experience as part of their identity exploration.

puberty A period of rapid physical maturation involving hormonal and bodily changes that take place in early adolescence.

R

rapport talk The language of conversation and a way of establishing connections and negotiating relationships; more characteristic of females than of males.

recasting Rephrasing a statement that a child has said, perhaps turning it into a question.

reciprocal socialization The process by which children socialize parents just as parents socialize them.

reciprocal teaching Individuals take turns leading small-group discussions.

reflexive smile A smile that does not occur in response to external stimuli. It happens during the month after birth, usually during irregular patterns of sleep, not when the infant is in an alert state.

rejected children Children who are infrequently nominated as a best friend and are actively disliked by their peers.

report talk Talk that conveys information; more characteristic of males than females.

rites of passage Ceremonies that mark an individual's transition from one status to another, especially into adulthood.

rooting reflex A newborn's built-in reaction that occurs when the infant's cheek is stroked or the side of the mouth is touched. In response, the infant turns its head toward the side that was touched, in an apparent effort to find something to suck.

S

satire The use of irony, derision, or wit to expose folly or wickedness.

scaffolding (cognitive development) Vygotsky used this term to describe the changing support over the course of a teaching session, with the more skilled person adjusting guidance to fit the child's current performance level.

scaffolding (parenting) Parental behavior that supports children's efforts, allowing children to be more skillful than they would be if they relied only on their own abilities.

schema theory States that when people reconstruct information, they fit it into information that already exists in their mind.

schemas Mental frameworks that organize concepts and information.

schemes In Piaget's theory, actions or mental representations that organize knowledge.

scientific method An approach that can be used to obtain accurate information. It includes these steps: (1) conceptualize the problem, (2) collect data, (3) draw conclusions, and (4) revise research conclusions and theory.

secondary appraisal Individuals evaluate their resources and determine how effectively they can cope with the event.

secure-autonomous attachment A positive attachment to parents in adolescents that corresponds to secure attachment in infancy.

securely attached babies The infant uses the caregiver as a secure base from which to explore the environment.

selective attention Focusing on a specific aspect of experience that is relevant while ignoring others that are irrelevant.

self-concept Domain-specific self-evaluations.

self-conscious emotions Emotions that require cognition, especially consciousness; they include empathy, jealousy, and embarrassment, which first appear at about 1½ to 2 years and pride, shame, and guilt, which first appear at about 2½ years of age.

self-efficacy The belief that one can master a situation and produce favorable outcomes.

self-esteem The global evaluative dimension of the self; also called self-worth or self-image.

self-regulatory learning Generating and monitoring thoughts, feelings, and behaviors to reach a goal.

self-understanding A child's cognitive representation of the self; the substance and content of a child's self-conceptions.

semantics The meanings of words and sentences.

sensation Reaction that occurs when information contacts sensory receptors—the eyes, ears, tongue, nostrils, and skin.

sensorimotor play Behavior engaged in by infants to derive pleasure from exercising their existing sensorimotor schemas.

sensorimotor stage The first of Piaget's stages, which lasts from birth to about 2 years of age; infants construct an understanding of the world by coordinating sensory experiences (such as seeing and hearing) with motoric actions.

separation protest Occurs when infants experience a fear of being separated from a caregiver, which results in crying when the caregiver leaves.

seriation The concrete operation that involves ordering stimuli along a quantitative dimension (such as length).

service learning A form of education that promotes social responsibility and service to the community.

shape constancy Recognition that an object remains the same even though its orientation to us changes.

shared environmental experiences Siblings' common environmental experiences, such as their parents' personalities and intellectual orientation, the family's socioeconomic status, and the neighborhood in which they live.

short-term memory Retention of information for up to 15 to 30 seconds, assuming there is no rehearsal of the information. Using rehearsal, individuals can keep the information in short-term memory longer.

sickle-cell anemia A genetic disorder that affects the red blood cells and occurs most often in people of African descent.

size constancy Recognition that an object remains the same even though the retinal image of the object changes.

slow-to-warm-up child A temperament style in which the child has low activity level, is somewhat negative, shows low adaptability, and displays a low intensity of mood.

small for date infants Also called small for gestational age infants, these infants' birth weights are below normal when the length of pregnancy is considered. Small for date infants may be preterm or full term.

social cognitive theory The view of psychologists who emphasize that behavior, environment, and cognition are the key factors in development.

social cognitive theory of gender This theory emphasizes that children's gender development occurs through observation and imitation of gender behavior, and through rewards and punishments they experience for gender-appropriate and -inappropriate behavior.

social cognitive theory of morality The theory that distinguishes between moral competence—the ability to produce moral behaviors—and moral performance•those behaviors in specific situations.

social constructivist approach An emphasis on the social contexts of learning and the construction of knowledge through social interaction. Vygotsky's theory reflects this approach.

social contract or utility and individual rights The fifth Kohlberg stage. At this stage, individuals reason that values, rights, and principles undergird or transcend the law.

social conventional reasoning Thoughts about social consensus and convention, as opposed to moral reasoning that stresses ethical issues.

social play Play that involves social interactions with peers.

social policy A government's course of action designed to promote the welfare of its citizens.

social referencing "Reading" emotional cues in others to help determine how to act in a particular situation.

social smile A smile in response to an external stimulus, which, early in development, typically is a face.

social systems morality The fourth stage in Kohlberg's theory of moral development. Moral judgments are based on understanding the social order, law, justice, and duty.

socioeconomic status (SES) A grouping of people with similar occupational, educational, and economic characteristics.

socioemotional processes Changes in an individual's relationships with other people, emotions, and personality.

solitary play Play in which the child plays alone and independently of others.

spermarche A boy's first ejaculation of semen.

standardized test A test with uniform procedures for administration and scoring. Many standardized tests allow a person's performance to be compared with the performance of other individuals.

status offenses Less serious acts (than index offenses). Status offenses include truancy, underage drinking, sexual promiscuity, and uncontrollability. They are performed by youth under a specified age, which make them juvenile offenses.

Strange Situation Ainsworth's observational measure of infant attachment to a caregiver that requires the infant to move through a series of introductions, separations, and reunions with the caregiver and an adult stranger in a prescribed order.

stranger anxiety An infant's fear of and wariness toward strangers; it tends to appear in the second half of the first year of life.

strategy construction Discovering a new procedure for processing information.

stress The response of individuals to the circumstances and events (called stressors) that threaten and tax their coping abilities.

sucking reflex A newborn's built-in reaction of automatically sucking an object placed in its mouth. The sucking reflex enables the infant to get nourishment before it has associated a nipple with food.

sudden infant death syndrome (SIDS) A condition that occurs when an infant stops breathing, usually during the night, and suddenly dies without an apparent cause.

sustained attention The state of readiness to detect and respond to small changes occurring at random times in the environment; also called vigilance.

symbolic function substage The first substage of preoperational thought, occurring roughly between the ages of 2 and 4. In this substage, the young child gains the ability to represent mentally an object that is not present.

syntax The ways words are combined to form acceptable phrases and sentences.

T

tabula rasa view The idea, proposed by John Locke, that children are like a "blank tablet."

telegraphic speech The use of short and precise words without grammatical markers such as articles, auxiliary verbs, and other connectives.

temperament An individual's behavioral style and characteristic emotional response.

teratogen From the Greek word *tera*, meaning "monster." Any agent that causes a birth defect. The field of study that investigates the causes of birth defects is called teratology.

theory An interrelated, coherent set of ideas that helps to explain and to make predictions.

theory of mind Thoughts about how mental processes work, such as a child's becoming aware that the mind exists and understanding cognitive connections to the physical world.

thinking Manipulating and transforming information in memory, usually to form concepts, reason, think critically, and solve problems.

top-dog phenomenon The circumstance of moving from the top position in elementary school to the lowest position in middle or junior high school.

transitivity If a relation holds between a first object and a second object, and holds between the second object and a third object, then it holds between the first object and the third object. Piaget believed that an understanding of transitivity is characteristic of concrete operational thought.

triarchic theory of intelligence Sternberg's theory that intelligence consists of compontential intelligence, experiential intelligence, and contextual intelligence.

trophoblast The outer layer of cells that develops in the germinal period. These cells provide nutrition and support for the embryo.

Turner syndrome A chromosome disorder in females in which either an X chromosome is missing, making the person XO instead of XX, or the second X chromosome is partially deleted.

twin study A study in which the behavioral similarity of identical twins is compared with the behavioral similarity of fraternal twins.

two-factor theory Spearman's theory that individuals have both general intelligence, which he called *g*, and a number of specific intelligences, referred to as *s*.

U

umbilical cord A life-support system containing two arteries and one vein that connects the baby to the placenta.

universal ethical principles The sixth and highest stage in Kohlberg's theory of moral development. Individuals develop a moral standard based on universal human rights.

unoccupied play Play in which the child is not engaging in play as it is commonly understood and might stand in one spot, look around the room, or perform random movements that do not seem to have a goal.

unresolved/disorganized attachment An insecure category in which the adolescent has an unusually high level of fear and is disoriented. This may result from such traumatic experiences as a parent's death or abuse by parents.

V

values clarification Helping people clarify what their lives are for and what is worth working for. Students are encouraged to define their own values and understand others' values.

visual preference method A method developed by Fantz to determine whether infants can distinguish one stimulus from another by measuring the length of time they attend to different stimuli.

Vygotsky's theory A sociocultural cognitive theory that emphasizes how culture and social interaction guide cognitive development.

W

Wernicke's area An area of the brain's left hemisphere that is involved in language comprehension.

whole-language approach An approach that stresses that reading instruction should parallel children's natural language learning. Reading materials should be whole and meaningful.

working memory A mental "workbench" where individuals manipulate and assemble information when making decisions, solving problems, and comprehending written and spoken language.

X

XYY syndrome A chromosomal disorder in which males have an extra Y chromosome.

Z

zone of proximal development (ZPD) Vygotsky's term for tasks too difficult for children to master alone but that can be mastered with assistance.

zygote A single cell formed through fertilization.

REFERENCES

Aboud, F.E., Mendelson, M.J., & Purdy, K.T. (2003). Cross-race peer relations and friendship quality. *International Journal of Behavioral Development, 27,* 165–173.

Aboud, F.E., & Skerry, S. (1983). Self and ethnic concepts in relation to ethnic constancy. *Canadian Journal of Behavioral Science, 15,* 3–34.

Abramovitch, R., Corter, C., Pepler, D.J., & Stanhope, L. (1986). Sibling and peer interaction: A final follow-up and comparison. *Child Development, 47,* 217–229.

Abramson, L.Y., Metalsky, G.I., & Alloy, L.B. (1989). Hopelessness depression: A theory-based subtype of depression. *Psychological Bulletin, 96,* 358–372.

Abruscato, J. (2004). *Teaching children science* (2nd ed.). Boston: Allyn & Bacon.

Achenbach, T.M. (1997). What is normal? What is abnormal? Developmental perspectives on behavioral and emotional problems. In S.S. Luthar, J.A. Burack, D. Cicchetti, & J.R. Weisz (Eds.), *Developmental psychopathology: Perspectives on adjustment, risk, and disorder.* New York: Cambridge University Press.

Acredolo, L.P., & Hake, J.L. (1982). Infant perception. In B.B. Wolman (Ed.), *Handbook of developmental psychology.* Englewood Cliffs, NJ: Prentice Hall.

Adams, G.R., Gulotta, T.P., & Montemayor, R. (Eds.). (1992). *Adolescent identity formation.* Newbury Park, CA: Sage.

Adams, R., & Laursen, B. (2001). The organization and dynamics of adolescent conflict with parents and friends. *Journal of Marriage and the Family, 63,* 97–110.

Adams, R.J. (1989). Newborns' discrimination among mid- and long-wavelength stimuli. *Journal of Experimental Child Psychology, 47,* 130–141.

Adamson, H.D. (2004). *Language minority students in America.* Mahwah, NJ: Erlbaum.

Addis, A., Magrini, N., & Mastroiacovo, P. (2001). Drug use during pregnancy. *Lancet, 357,* 800.

Adickes, M.S., & Stuart, M.J. (2004). Youth football injuries. *Sports Medicine, 34,* 201–207.

Adler, T. (1991, January). Seeing double? Controversial twins study is widely reported, debated. *APA Monitor, 22,* 1, 8.

Adolph, K.E. (1997). Learning in the development of infant locomotion. *Monographs of the Society for Research in Child Development, 62* (3, Serial No. 251).

Adolph, K.E. (2005). Learning to learn in the development of action. In J.J. Rieser, J.J. Lockman, & C.E. Nelson (Eds.), *Action as an organizer of learning and development.* Mahwah, NJ: Erlbaum.

Adolph, K.E., & Avolio, A.M. (2000). Walking infants adapt locomotion to changing body dimensions. *Journal of Experimental Psychology: Human Perception and Performance, 26,* 1148–1166.

Adolph, K.E., & Berger, S.E. (2005). Physical and motor development. In M.H. Bornstein & M.E. Lamb (Eds.), *Developmental psychology* (5th ed.). Mahwah, NJ: Erlbaum.

Adolph, K.E., & Berger, S.E. (2006). Motor development. In W. Damon & R. Lerner (Eds.), *Handbook of child psychology* (6th ed.). New York: Wiley.

Adolph, K.E., Vereijken, B., & Shrout, P.E. (2003). What changes in infant walking and why. *Child Development, 74,* 475–497.

Agras, W.S., & others. (2004). Report of the National Institutes of Health workshop on overcoming barriers to treatment research in anorexia nervosa. *International Journal of Eating Disorders, 35,* 509–521.

Aguiat, A., & Baillargeon, R. (2002). Developments in young infants' reasoning about occluded objects. *Cognitive Psychology, 45,* 267–336.

Ahluwalia, I.B., Tessaro, I., Grumer-Strawn, L.M., MacGowan, C., & Benton-Davis, S. (2000). Georgia's breast-feeding promotion program for low-income women. *Pediatrics, 105,* E-85–E-87.

Ahrons, C. (2004). *We're still family.* New York: HarperCollins.

Aiken, L.R. (2003). *Psychological testing and assessment* (11th ed.). Boston: Allyn & Bacon.

Ainsworth, M.D.S. (1979). Infant-mother attachment. *American Psychologist, 34,* 932–937.

Alderman, M.K. (2004). *Motivation and achievement.* Mahwah, NJ: Erlbaum.

Alegre, M., & Welsch, D. (2003). *Maxine Hong Kingston after the fire.* www.powers.com/authors.

Alexander, A.W., & Slinger-Constant, A.M. (2004). Current status of treatments for dyslexia. *Journal of Child Neurology, 19,* 544–558.

Alexander, G.R., Kogan, M.D., & Nabukera, S. (2002). Racial differences in prenatal care use in the United States: Are disparities increasing? *American Journal of Public Health, 92,* 1970–1975.

Alexander, P.A. (2006). *Psychology in learning and instruction.* Upper Saddle River, NJ; Prentice Hall.

Alexander, R.T., & Radisch, D. (2005). Sudden infant death syndrome risk factors with regards to sleep position, sleep surface, and co-sleeping. *Journal of Forensic Science, 50,* 147–151.

Alfirevic, Z., & Neilson, J.P. (2004). Antenatal screening for Down syndrome. *British Medical Journal, 329,* 811–812.

Aliyu, M.H., Salihu, H.M., Blankson, M.L., Alexander, G.R., & Keith, L. (2004). Risks in triplet pregnancy: Advanced maternal age, premature rupture of membranes, and risk of mortality. *Journal of Reproductive Medicine, 49,* 721–726.

Allen, J.P., & Hauser, S.T. (1994, February). *Adolescent-family interactions as predictors of qualities of parental, peer, and romantic relationships at age 25.* Paper presented at the meeting of the Society for Research on Adolescence, San Diego.

Allen, J.P., McElhaney, K.B., Kuperminc, G.P., & Jodl, K.M. (2004). Stability and change in attachment security across adolescence. *Child Development, 75,* 1792–1805.

Allen, J.P., McElhaney, K.B., Land, D.J., Kumperminc, G.P., Moore, C.W., O'Beirne-Kelly, H., & Kilmer, S.L. (2003). A secure base in adolescence: Markers of attachment security in the mother-adolescent relationship. *Child Development, 74,* 292–307.

Allen, M., Brown, P., & Finlay, B. (1992). *Helping children by strengthening families.* Washington, DC: Children's Defense Fund.

Allen, R., McGeorge, P., Pearson, D., & Milne, A.B. (2004). Attention and expertise in multiple target tracking. *Applied Cognitive Psychology, 18,* 337–347.

Alvarez, M. (2004). Caregiving and early infant crying in a Danish community. *Journal of Developmental and Behavioral Pediatrics, 25,* 91–98.

Amabile, T.M. (1993). Commentary. In D. Goleman, P. Kaufman, & M. Ray. *The creative spirit.* New York: Plume.

Amabile, T.M., & Hennesey, B.A. (1992). The motivation for creativity in children. In A.K. Boggiano & T.S. Pittman (Eds.), *Achievement and motivation.* New York: Cambridge University Press.

Amato, P. (2005). Historical trends in divorce and dissolution. In M.A. Fine & J.H. Harvey (Eds.), *Handbook of divorce and relationship dissolution.* Mahwah, NJ: Erlbaum.

Amato, P.R., & Booth, A. (1996). A prospective study of divorce and parent-child relationships. *Journal of Marriage and the Family, 58,* 356–365.

Amato, P.R., & Keith, B. (1991). Parental divorce and the well-being of children: A meta-analysis. *Psychological Bulletin, 110,* 26–46.

Ambrosio, J. (2004). No Child Left Behind. *Phi Delta Kappan, 85,* 709–711.

American Academy of Pediatrics. (2000). Suicide and suicide attempts in adolescence. *Pediatrics, 105,* 871–874.

American Academy of Pediatrics. (2001). Health care supervision for children with Williams syndrome. *Pediatrics, 107,* 1192–1204.

American Academy of Pediatrics (AAP) Committee on Drugs. (1994). The transfer of drugs and other chemicals into human milk. *Pediatrics, 93,* 137–150.

American Academy of Pediatrics Task Force on Infant Positioning and SIDS. (2000). Changing concepts of sudden infant death syndrome. *Pediatrics, 105,* 650–656.

American Academy of Pediatrics (AAP) Work Group on Breastfeeding. (1997). Breastfeeding and the use of human milk. *Pediatrics, 100,* 1035–1039.

American Association on Mental Retardation, Ad Hoc Committee on Terminology and Classification. (1992). *Mental retardation* (9th ed.). Washington, DC: Author.

American Psychological Association. (2003). *Psychology: Scientific problem solvers.* Washington, DC: American Psychological Association.

Amisola, R.V., & Jacobson, M.S. (2003). Physical activity, exercise, and sedentary activity: Relationship to the causes and treatment of obesity. *Adolescent Medicine, 14,* 23–35.

Amsterdam, B.K. (1968). *Mirror behavior in children under two years of age.* Unpublished doctoral dissertation, University of North Carolina, Chapel Hill.

Anastasi, A., & Urbina, S. (1996). *Psychological testing* (7th ed.). Upper Saddle River, NJ: Prentice Hall.

Anderman, E.M., Maehr, M.L., & Midgley, C. (1996). *Declining motivation after the transition to middle school: Schools can make a difference.* Unpublished manuscript, University of Kentucky, Lexington.

Anderson, C.A., & Bushman, B.J. (2001). Effects of violent video games on aggressive behavior, aggressive cognition, aggressive affect, physiological arousal, and prosocial behavior: A meta-analytic review of the scientific literature. *Psychological Science, 12,* 353–359.

Anderson, C.A., & Dill, K.E. (2000). Video games and aggressive thoughts, feelings, and behavior in the laboratory and in life. *Journal of Personality and Social Psychology, 78,* 772–790.

Anderson, D.R., Huston, A.C., Schmitt, K., Linebarger, D.L., & Wright, J.C. (2001). Early childhood viewing and adolescent behavior: The recontact study. *Monographs of the Society for Research in Child Development, 66* (1, Serial No. 264).

Anderson, D.R., Lorch, E.P., Field, D.E., Collins, P.A., & Nathan, J.G. (1986). Television viewing at home: Age trends in visual attention and time with TV. *Child Development, 57,* 1024–1033.

Anderson, E., Greene, S.M., Hetherington, E.M., & Clingempeel, W.G. (1999). The dynamics of parental remarriage. In E.M. Hetherington (Ed.), *Coping with divorce, single parenting, and remarriage.* Mahwah, NJ: Erlbaum.

Anderson, L.M., Shinn, C., Fullilove, M.T., Serimshaw, S.C., Fielding, J.E., Normand, J., & Carande-Kulis, V.G. (2003). The effectiveness of early childhood development programs: A systematic review. *American Journal of Preventive Medicine, 24* (Suppl. 3), 32–46.

Anderson, R.E. (2002). Youth and information technology. In J.T. Mortimer & R.W. Larson (Eds.), *The changing adolescent experience.* New York: Cambridge University Press.

Anderson, S.E., Dallal, G.E., & Must, A. (2003). Relative weight and race influence average age at menarche: Results from two nationally representative surveys of U.S. girls studied 25 years apart. *Pediatrics, 111,* 844–850.

Angold, A., Costello, E.J., & Worthman, C.M. (1999). Puberty and depression: The roles of age, pubertal status and pubertal timing. *Psychological Medicine, 28,* 51–61.

Anguiano, R.P.V. (2004). Families and schools: The effect of parental involvement on high school completion. *Journal of Family Issues, 25,* 61–85.

Appelman, Z., & Furman, B. (2005). Invasive genetic diagnosis in multiple pregnancies. *Obstetrics and Gynecological Clinics of North America, 32,* 97–103.

Ara, I., Vicente-Rodriguez, G., Jimenez-Ramirez, J., Dorado, C., Serrano-Sanchez, J.A., & Calbet, J.A. (2004). Regular participation in sports is associated with enhanced physical fitness and lower body mass in prepubertal boys. *International Journal of Obesity and Related Metabolic Disorders, 28,* 1585–1593.

Archer, S.L. (1989). The status of identity: Reflections on the need for intervention. *Journal of Adolescence, 12,* 345–359.

Archer, S.L. (Ed.). (1994). *Intervention for adolescent identity development.* Newbury Park, CA: Sage.

Archer, S.L., & Waterman, A.S. (1994). Adolescent identity development: Contextual perspectives. In C.B. Fisher & R.M. Lerner (Eds.), *Applied developmental psychology.* New York: McGraw-Hill.

Archibald, A.B., Graber, J.A., & Brooks-Gunn, J. (1999). Associations among parent-adolescent relationships, pubertal growth, dieting, and body image in young adolescent girls: A short-term longitudinal study. *Journal of Research on Adolescence, 9,* 395–415.

Archibald, A.B., Graber, J.A., & Brooks-Gunn, J. (2003). Pubertal processes and physical growth in adolescence. In G. Adams & M. Berzonsky (Eds.), *Blackwell handbook of adolescence.* Malden, MA: Blackwell.

Archibald, S.L., Fennema-Notetine, C., Gamst, A., Riley, E.P., Mattson, S.N., & Jernigan, T.L. (2001). Brain dysmorphology in individuals with severe prenatal alcohol exposure. *Developmental Medicine and Child Neurology, 43,* 148–154.

Arehart, D.M., & Smith, P.H. (1990). Identity in adolescence: Influences on dysfunction and psychosocial task issues. *Journal of Youth and Adolescence, 19,* 63–72.

Arendt, R., Angelopoulos, J., Salvator, A., & Singer, L. (1999). Motor development of cocaine-exposed children at age two years. *Pediatrics, 103,* 86–92.

Arias, I. (2004). The legacy of child maltreatment: Long-term health consequences for women. *Journal of Women's Health, 13,* 468–473.

Ariceli, G., Castro, J., Cesena, J., & Toro, J. (2005). Anorexia nervosa in male adolescents: Body image, eating attitudes, and psychological traits. *Journal of Adolescent Health, 36,* 221–226.

Ariès, P. (1962). *Centuries of childhood* (R. Baldrick, Trans.). New York: Knopf.

Armsden, G., & Greenberg, M.T. (1984). *The inventory of parent and peer attachment: Individual differences and their relationship to psychological well-being in adolescence.* Unpublished manuscript, University of Washington.

Armstrong, J., Boada, M., Rey, M.J., Vidal, N., & Ferrer, I. (2004). Familial Alzheimer disease associated with A713T mutation in APP. *Neuroscience Letters, 370,* 241–243.

Arndt, J., & Goldenberg, J.L. (2002). From threat to sweat: The role of physiological arousal in the motivation to maintain self-esteem. In A. Tesser, D.A. Stapel, & J.V. Wood (Eds.), *Self and motivation: Emerging psychological perspectives.* Washington, DC: American Psychological Association.

Arnett, J. (1990). Contraceptive use, sensation seeking, and adolescent egocentrism. *Journal of Youth and Adolescence, 19,* 171–180.

Arnett, J. (2002). Adolescents in Western countries in the 21st century: Vast opportunities—for all? In B.B. Brown, R.W. Larson, & T.S. Saraswathi (Eds.), *The world's youth.* New York: Cambridge University Press.

Aronson, E. (1986, August). *Teaching students things they think they already know about: The case of prejudice and desegregation.* Paper presented at the meeting of the American Psychological Association, Washington, DC.

Aronson, J. (2002). Stereotype threat: Contending and coping with unnerving expectations. *Improving academic achievement.* San Diego: Academic Press.

Aronson, J., Fried, C.B., & Good, C. (2002). Reducing the effects of stereotype threat on African American college students by shaping theories of intelligence. *Journal of Experimental Social Psychology, 38,* 113–125.

Aronson, J., Lustina, M.J., Good, C., Keough, K., Steele, C.M., & Brown, J. (1999). When white men can't do math: Necessary and sufficient factors in stereotype threat. *Journal of Experimental Social Psychology, 35,* 29–46.

Arshad, S.H. (2001). Food allergen avoidance in primary prevention of food allergy. *Allergy, 56,* 113–116.

Asarnow, J.R., & Callan, J.W. (1985). Boys with peer adjustment problems: Social cognitive processes. *Journal of Consulting and Clinical Psychology, 53,* 80–87.

Ashdown-Lambert, J.R. (2005). A review of low birth weight: Predictors, precursors, and morbidity outcomes. *Journal of Research in Society and Health, 125,* 76–83.

Asher, J., & Garcia, R. (1969). The optimal age to learn a foreign language. *Modern Language Journal, 53,* 334–341.

Ashmead, D.H., Wall, R.S., Ebinger, K.A., Hill, M.-M., Yang, X., & Eaton, S. (1998). Spatial hearing in children with visual disabilities. *Perception, 27,* 105–122.

Aslin, R.N. (1987). Visual and auditory development in infancy. In J. Osofsky (Ed.), *Handbook of infant development* (2nd ed.). New York: Wiley.

Aslin, R.N., Jusczyk, P.W., & Pisoni, D.B. (1998). Speech and auditory processing during infancy: Constraints on and precursors to language. In W. Damon (Ed.), *Handbook of child psychology* (5th ed., Vol. 2). New York: Wiley.

Ateah, C.A. (2005). Maternal use of physical punishment in response to child misbehavior: Implications for child abuse prevention. *Child Abuse and Neglect, 29,* 169–185.

Atkinson, A.P., & Wheeler, M. (2004). The grain of domains: The evolutionary-psychological case against domain-general cognition. *Mind and Language, 19,* 147–176.

Attie, I., & Brooks-Gunn, J. (1989). Development of eating problems in adolescent girls: A longitudinal study. *Developmental Psychology, 25,* 70–79.

Austin, A.A., & Chorpita, B.F. (2004). Temperament, anxiety, and depression: Comparisons across five ethnic groups of children. *Journal of Clinical Child and Adolescent Psychology, 33,* 216–226.

Azar, S.T. (2002). Parenting and child maltreatment. In M.H. Bornstein (Ed.), *Handbook of parenting* (2nd ed., Vol. 4). Mahwah, NJ: Erlbaum.

Babbie, E.R. (2005). *The basics of social research* (3rd ed.). Belmont, CA: Wadsworth.

Bacak, S.J., Baptiste-Roberts, K., Amon, E., Ireland, B., & Leet, T. (2005). Risk factors for neonatal mortality among extremely-low-birth-weight infants. *American Journal of Obstetrics and Gynecology, 192,* 862–867.

Baddeley, A. (1990). *Human memory: Theory and practice.* Boston: Allyn & Bacon.

Baddeley, A. (1998). *Human memory* (rev. ed). Boston: Allyn & Bacon.

Baddeley, A. (2001). *Is working memory still working?* Paper presented at the meeting of the American Psychological Association, San Francisco.

Bagwell, C.L., Newcomb, A.F., & Bukowski, W.M. (1994, February). *Early adolescent friendship as a predictor of adult adjustment: A twelve year follow-up investigation.* Paper presented at the biennial meeting of the Society for Research on Adolescence, San Diego.

Bahrampour, T. (2005, February 8). The pied piper of preschool. *Washington Post,* p. 801.

Bailey, B., Delaney-Black, V., Covington, C.Y., Ager J., Janisse, J., Hannigan, J.H., & Sokol, R.J. (2004). Prenatal exposure to binge drinking and cognitive and behavioral outcomes at age 7 years. *American Journal of Obstetrics and Gynecology, 191,* 1037–1043.

Bailey, B., Forget, S., & Koren, G. (2002). Pregnancy outcome of women who failed appointments at a teratogen information service clinic. *Reproductive Toxicology, 16,* 77–80.

Bailey, L.B., & Berry, R.J. (2005). Folic acid supplementation and the occurrence of congenital heart defects, orofacial clefts, multiple births, and miscarriage. *American Journal of Clinical Nutrition, 81,* 1213S–1217S.

Baillargeon, R. (1995). The object concept revisited: New directions in the investigation of infants' physical knowledge. In C.E. Granrud (Ed.), *Visual perception and cognition in infancy.* Hillsdale, NJ: Erlbaum.

Baillargeon, R. (2002). The acquisition of physical knowledge in infancy: A summary in eight lessons. In U. Goswami (Ed.), *Blackwell handbook of childhood cognitive development.* Malden, MA: Blackwell.

Baillargeon, R. (2004). Infants' physical world. *Current Directions in Psychological Science, 13,* 89–94.

Baillargeon, R., & DeVoe, J. (1991). Object permanence in young children: Further evidence. *Child Development, 62,* 1227–1246.

Baird, A.A., Gruber, S.A., Cohen, B.M., Renshaw, R.J., & Yureglum-Todd, D.A. (1999). MRI of the amygdala in children and adolescents. *American Academy of Child and Adolescent Psychiatry, 38,* 195–199.

Bakeman, R., & Brown, J.V. (1980). Early interaction: Consequences for social and mental development at three years. *Child Development, 51,* 437–447.

Balk, D., & Corr, C. (2001). Bereavement during adolescence: A review of research. In M. Stroebe, R.O. Hansson, W. Stroebe, & H. Schut (Eds.), *Handbook of bereavement research.* Washington, DC: American Psychological Association.

Baltes, P.B. (2003). On the incomplete architecture of human ontogeny: Selection, optimization, and compensation as foundation of developmental theory. In U.M. Staudinger & U. Lindenberger (Eds.), *Understanding human development.* Boston: Kluwer.

Baltes, P.B., Lindenberger, U., & Staudinger, U. (2006). Life span theory in developmental psychology. In W. Damon & R. Lerner (Eds.), *Handbook of child psychology* (6th ed.). New York: Wiley.

Bandura, A. (1982). Self-efficacy mechanism in human agency. *American Psychologist, 37,* 122–147.

Bandura, A. (1986). *Social foundations of thought and action: A social cognitive theory.* Englewood Cliffs, NJ: Prentice Hall.

Bandura, A. (1991). Social cognitive theory of moral thought and action. In W.M. Kurtines & J.L. Gewirtz (Eds.), *Handbook of moral behavior and development* (Vol. 1). Hillsdale, NJ: Erlbaum.

Bandura, A. (1997). *Self-efficacy.* New York: W.H. Freeman.

Bandura, A. (1998, August). *Swimming against the mainstream: Accentuating the positive aspects of humanity.* Paper presented at the meeting of the American Psychological Association, San Francisco.

Bandura, A. (1999). Moral disengagement in the perpetuation of inhumanities. *Personality and Social Psychology Review, 3,* 193–209.

Bandura, A. (2000). Social cognitive theory. In A. Kazdin (Ed.), *Encyclopedia of psychology.* Washington, DC, & New York: American Psychological Association and Oxford University Press.

Bandura, A. (2001). Social cognitive theory. *Annual Review of Psychology, 52.* Palo Alto, CA: Annual Reviews.

Bandura, A. (2002). Selective moral disengagement in the exercise of moral agency. *Journal of Moral Education, 31,* 101–119.

Bandura, A. (2004, May). *Toward a psychology of human agency.* Paper presented at the meeting of the American Psychological Society, Chicago.

Bandura, A., & Locke, E.A. (2003). Negative self-efficacy and goals revisited. *Journal of Applied Psychology, 88,* 87–99.

Bank, L., Burraston, B., & Snyder, J. (2004). Sibling conflict and ineffective parenting as predictors of adolescent boys' antisocial behavior and peer difficulties: Additive and interactional effects. *Journal of Research on Adolescence, 14,* 99–125.

Banks, E.C. (1993, March). *Moral education curriculum in a multicultural context: The Malaysian primary curriculum.* Paper presented at the biennial meeting of the Society for Research in Child Development, New Orleans.

Banks, J.A. (2002). *Introduction to multicultural education* (3rd ed.). Boston: Allyn & Bacon.

Banks, J.A. (2003). *Teaching strategies for ethnic studies* (7th ed.). Boston: Allyn & Bacon.

Banks, J.A. (2006). *Cultural diversity and education* (5th ed.). Boston: Allyn & Bacon.

Banks, M.S. (2005). The benefits and costs of combining information between and within the senses. In J.J. Rieser, J.J. Lockman, & C.A. Nelson (Eds.), *Action as an organizer of learning and development.* Mahwah, NJ: Erlbaum.

Banks, M.S., & Salapatek, P. (1983). Infant visual perception. In P.H. Mussen (Ed.), *Handbook of child psychology* (4th ed., Vol. 2). New York: Wiley.

Baquet, G., van Praagh, E., & Berthoin, S. (2004). Endurance training and aerobic fitness in young people. *Sports Medicine, 33,* 1127–1143.

Barker, R., & Wright, H.F. (1951). *One boy's day.* New York: Harper & Row.

Barnard, K.E., & Martell, L.K. (1995). Mothering. In M.H. Bornstein (Ed.), *Handbook of parenting* (Vol. 3). Hillsdale, NJ: Erlbaum.

Barnard, K.E., & Solchany, J.E. (2002). Mothering. In M.H. Bornstein (Ed.), *Handbook of parenting* (2nd ed., Vol. 3), Mahwah, NJ: Erlbaum.

Barnett, D., Ganiban, J., & Cichetti, D. (1999). Maltreatment, negative expressivity, and the development of type D attachments from 12 to 24 months of age. In J.I. Vondra & D. Barnett (Eds.), *Monograph of the Society for Research in Child Development, 64* (3, Serial No. 258), 97–118.

Barnett, W.S., & Hustedt, J.T. (2005). Head Start's lasting benefits. *Infants and Young Children, 18,* 16–24.

Barnouw, V. (1975). *An introduction to anthropology: Vol. 2. Ethnology.* Homewood, IL: Dorsey Press.

Baron, N.S. (1992). *Growing up with language.* Reading, MA: Addison-Wesley.

Barr, H.M., & Streissguth, A.P. (2001). Identifying maternal self-reported alcohol use associated with fetal alcohol disorders. *Alcoholism: Clinical and Experimental Research, 25,* 283–287.

Barrett, D.E., Radke-Yarrow, M., & Klein, R.E. (1982). Chronic malnutrition and child behavior: Effects of calorie supplementation on social and emotional functioning at school age. *Developmental Psychology, 18,* 541–556.

Barton, W.H. (2004). Bridging juvenile justice and positive youth development. In S.F. Hamilton & M.A. Hamilton (Eds.), *The youth development handbook.* Thousand Oaks, CA: Sage.

Baskett, L.M., & Johnson, S.M. (1982). The young child's interaction with parents versus siblings. *Child Development, 53,* 643–650.

Bassett, K., Lee, P.M., Green, C.J., Mitchell, L., & Kazanjian, A. (2004). Improving population health or the population itself? Health technology assessment and our genetic future. *International Journal of Technology Assessment in Health Care, 20,* 106–114.

Bates, A.S., Fitzgerald, J.F., Dittus, R.S., & Wollinsky, F.D. (1994). Risk factors for underimmunization in poor urban infants. *Journal of the American Medical Association, 272,* 1105–1109.

Batson, C.D. (1989). Personal values, moral principles, and the three path model of prosocial motivation. In N. Eisenberg & J. Reykowski (Eds.), *Social and moral values.* Hillsdale, NJ: Erlbaum.

Bauer, P.J. (2002). Long-term recall memory: Behavioral and neuro-developmental changes in the first 2 years of life. *Current Directions in Psychological Science, 11,* 137–141.

Bauer, P.J. (2004). Getting explicit memory off the ground: Steps toward construction of a neuro-developmental account of changes in the first two years of life. *Developmental Review, 24,* 347–373.

Bauer, P.J. (2005). Developments in declarative memory. *Psychological Science, 16,* 41–47.

Bauer, P.J. (2006). Event memory. In W. Damon & R. Lerner (Eds.), *Handbook of child psychology* (6th ed.). New York: Wiley.

Bauer, P.J., Wenner, J.A., Dropik, P.L., & Wewerka, S.S. (2000). Parameters of remembering and forgetting in the transition from infancy to early childhood. *Monographs of the Society for Research in Child Development, 65* (4, Serial No. 263).

Bauer, P.J., Wiebe, S.A., Carver, L.J., Waters, J.M., & Nelson, C.A. (2003). Developments in long-term explicit memory late in the first year of life: Behavioral and electrophysiological indices. *Psychological Science, 14,* 629–635.

Baumeister, R.F., Campbell, J.D., Krueger, J.I., & Vohs, K.D. (2003). Does high self-esteem cause better performance, interpersonal success, happiness, or healthier lifestyles? *Psychological Science in the Public Interest, 4,* 11–44.

Baumrind, D. (1971). Current patterns of parental authority. *Developmental Psychology Monographs, 4* (1, Pt. 2).

Baumrind, D. (1999, November). Unpublished review of J.W. Santrock's *Child development* (9th ed.). New York: McGraw-Hill.

Baumrind, D., Larzelere, R.E., & Cowan, P.A. (2002). Ordinary physical punishment: Is it harmful? Comment on Gershoff. *Psychological Bulletin, 128,* 590–595.

Bauserman, R. (2002). Child adjustment in joint-custody versus sole-custody arrangements: A meta-analytic review. *Journal of Family Psychology, 16,* 91–102.

Bavelier, D., & Neville, H.J. (2002). Cross-modal plasticity: Where and how? *Nature Reviews: Neuroscience, 3,* 443–452.

Bayley, N. (1943). Mental growth during the first three years. In R.G. Barker, J.S. Kounin, & H.F. Wright (Eds.), *Child behavior and development.* New York: McGraw-Hill.

Bayley, N. (1969). *Manual for the Bayley Scales of Infant Development.* New York: Psychological Corporation.

Beachy, J.M. (2003). Premature infant massage in the NICU. *Neonatal Network, 22,* 39–45.

Beagles-Roos, J., & Gat, I. (1983). Specific impact of radio and television on children's story comprehension. *Journal of Educational Psychology, 75,* 128–137.

Beal, C.R. (1994). *Boys and girls: The development of gender roles.* New York: McGraw-Hill.

Beardslee, W. (2002). *Out of the darkened room.* Boston: Little, Brown.

Bearison, D.J., & Dorval, B. (2002). *Collaborative cognition.* Wesport, CT: Ablex.

Beaudet, A.L. (2004). Complex imprinting. *Nature Genetics, 36,* 793–795.

Bechtold, A.G., Bushnell, E.W., & Salapatek, P. (1979, April). *Infants' visual localization of visual and auditory targets.* Paper presented at the meeting of the Society for Research in Child Development, San Francisco.

Beck, A.T. (1973). *The diagnosis and management of depression.* Philadelphia: University of Pennsylvania Press.

Beck, C.T. (2002). Theoretical perspectives of postpartum depression and their treatment implications. *American Journal of Maternal/Child Nursing, 27,* 282–287.

Becker-Blease, K.A., Deater-Deckard, K., Eley, T., Freyd, J.J., Stevenson, J., & Plomin, R. (2004). A genetic analysis of individual differences in dissociative behaviors in childhood and adolescence. *Journal of Child Psychology and Psychiatry, 45,* 522–532.

Begley, S. (1997). How to build a baby's brain. *Newsweek Special Issue.* Spring/Summer, 28–32.

Beins, B. (2004). *Research methods.* Boston: Allyn & Bacon.

Bell, A.C., & Swinburn, B.A. (2004). What are the key food groups to target for preventing obesity and improving nutrition in schools? *European Journal of Clinical Nutrition, 58,* 258–263.

Bell, M.A., & Fox, N.A. (1992). The relations between frontal brain electrical activity and cognitive development during infancy. *Child Development, 63,* 1142–1163.

Bell, S.M., & Ainsworth, M.D.S. (1972). Infant crying and maternal responsiveness. *Child Development, 43,* 1171–1190.

Bellinger, D. (2005). Teratogen update: Lead and pregnancy. *Birth Defects Research, 73,* 409–420.

Bellinger, D., Leviton, A., Waternaux, C., Needleman, H., & Rabinowitz, M. (1987). Longitudinal analysis of prenatal and postnatal lead exposure and early cognitive development. *New England Journal of Medicine, 316,* 1037–1043.

Bellugi, U., & George, M. (Eds.). (2001). *Journey from cognition to brain to gene: Perspectives from Williams syndrome.* Cambridge, MA: MIT Press.

Bellugi, U., & Wang, P.P. (1996). Williams syndrome: From brain to cognition. *Encyclopedia of neuroscience*. Amsterdam: Elsevier.

Belsky, J. (1981). Early human experience: A family perspective. *Developmental Psychology, 17,* 3–23.

Belsky, J., & Eggebeen, D. (1991). Early and extensive maternal employment/child care and 4–6-year-olds socioemotional development: Children of the National Longitudinal Survey of Youth. *Journal of Marriage and the Family, 53,* 1083–1099.

Belsky, J., & Pensky, E. (1988). Marital change across the transition to parenthood. In R. Palkowitz & M.B. Sussman (Eds.), *Transitions to parenthood*. New York: Haworth.

Belson, W. (1978). *Television violence and the adolescent boy*. London: Saxon House.

Bem, S.L. (1977). On the utility of alternative procedures for assessing psychological androgyny. *Journal of Consulting and Clinical Psychology, 45,* 196–205.

Bence, P. (1991). Television, adolescents and development. In R.M. Lerner, A.C. Petersen, & J. Brooks-Gunn (Eds.), *Encyclopedia of adolescence* (Vol. 2). New York: Garland.

Bendersky, M., & Sullivan, M.W. (2002). Basic methods in infant research. In A. Slater & M. Lewis (Eds.), *Infant development*. New York: Oxford University Press.

Benfey, P. (2005). *Essentials of genomics*. Upper Saddle River, NJ: Prentice Hall.

Benjet, C., & Kazdin, A.E. (2003). Spanking children: The controversies, findings, and new directions. *Clinical Psychology Review, 23,* 197–224.

Benn, P.A., Fang, M., & Egan, J.F. (2005). Trends in the use of second trimester maternal serum screening from 1991 to 2003. *Genetics in Medicine, 7,* 328–331.

Bennett, W. (1993). *The book of virtues*. New York: Simon & Schuster.

Benson, E. (2003, February). Intelligence across cultures. *Monitor on Psychology, 34* (2), 56–58.

Benson, P.L., Scales, P.C., Hamilton, S.F., & Sesma, A. (2006). Positive youth development. In W. Damon & R. Lerner (Eds.), *Handbook of child psychology* (6th ed.). New York: Wiley.

Benveniste, L., Carnoy, M., & Rothstein, R. (2003). *All else equal*. New York: Routledge-Farmer.

Benz, E.J. (2004). Genotypes and phenotypes—another lesson from the Hemoglobinpathies. *New England Journal of Medicine, 351,* 1532–1538.

Berenbaum, S.A., & Bailey, J.M. (2003). Effects on gender identity of prenatal androgens and genital appearance: Evidence from girls with congenital adrenal hyperplasia. *Journal of Clinical Endocrinology and Metabolism, 88,* 1102–1106.

Bergen, D. (1988). Stages of play development. In D. Bergen (Ed.), *Play as a medium for learning and development*. Portsmouth, NH: Heinemann.

Bergeron, N., & Schneider, B.H. (2005). Explaining cross-national differences in peer-directed aggression: A quantitative analysis. *Aggressive Behavior, 31,* 116–137.

Berk, L.E. (1994). Why children talk to themselves. *Scientific American, 271* (5), 78–83.

Berk, L.E., & Spuhl, S.T. (1995). Maternal interaction, private speech, and task performance in preschool children. *Early Childhood Research Quarterly, 10,* 145–169.

Berko, J. (1958). The child's learning of English morphology. *Word, 14,* 150–177.

Berko Gleason, J. (2004). Unpublished review of Santrock *Life-span development* (10th ed.). New York: McGraw-Hill.

Berko Gleason, J. (2005). The development of language: An overview and a preview. In J. Berko Gleason (Ed.), *The development of language* (6th ed.). Boston: Allyn & Bacon.

Berkowitz, C.D. (2004). Cosleeping: Benefits, risks, and cautions. *Advances in Pediatrics, 51,* 329–349.

Berlin, L., & Cassidy, J. (2000). Understanding parenting: Contributions of attachment theory and research. In J.D. Osofsky & H.E. Fitzgerald (Eds.), *WAIMH handbook of infant mental health* (Vol. 3). New York: Wiley.

Berlyne, D.E. (1960). *Conflict, arousal, and curiosity*. New York: McGraw-Hill.

Berndt, T.J. (1979). Developmental changes in conformity to peers and parents. *Developmental Psychology, 15,* 608–616.

Berndt, T.J. (1982). The features and effects of friendships in early adolescence. *Child Development, 53,* 1447–1460.

Berndt, T.J. (1999). Friends' influence on children's adjustment. In W.A. Collins & B. Laursen (Eds.), *Relationships as developmental contexts*. Mahwah, NJ: Erlbaum.

Berndt, T.J., & Perry, T.B. (1990). Distinctive features and effects of early adolescent friendships. In R. Montemayor (Ed.), *Advances in adolescent research*. Greenwich, CT: JAI Press.

Berninger, V.W. (2006). Learning disabilities. In W. Damon & R. Lerner (Eds.), *Handbook of child psychology* (6th ed.). New York: Wiley.

Berninger, V.W., Dunn, A., Shin-Ju, C.L., & Shimada, S. (2004). School evolution: Scientist-practitioner educators creating optimal learning environments for all students. *Journal of Learning Disabilities, 37,* 500–508.

Bernstein, J. (2004). The low-wage labor market: Trends and policy implications. In A.C. Crouter & A. Booth (Eds.), *Work-family challenges for low-income families and their children*. Mahwah, NJ: Erlbaum.

Berry, J. (2000). Cultural foundations of human behavior. In A. Kazdin (Ed.), *Encyclopedia of psychology*. Washington, DC, and New York: American Psychological Association and Oxford University Press.

Bertenthal, B. (2005). Theories, methods, and models: Discussion of the chapters by Newcombe, Thelen, & Whitmeyer. In J.J. Rieser, J.J. Lockman, & C.A. Nelson (Eds.), *Action as an organizer of learning and development*. Mahwah, NJ: Erlbaum.

Best, D. (2001). Cross-cultural gender roles. In J. Worell (Ed.), *Encyclopedia of women and gender*. San Diego: Academic Press.

Best, J.W., & Kahn, J.V. (2006). *Research in education* (10th ed.). Boston: Allyn & Bacon.

Bhutta, Z.A., Darmstadt, G.L., Hasan, B.S., & Haws, R.A. (2005). Community-based interventions for improving perinatal and neonatal health outcomes in developing countries: A review of the evidence. *Pediatrics, 115,* 519–616.

Bialystok, E. (1997). Effects of bilingualism and biliteracy on children's emerging concepts of print. *Developmental Psychology, 33,* 429–440.

Bialystok, E. (1999). Cognitive complexity and attentional control in the bilingual mind. *Child Development, 70,* 537–544.

Bialystok, E. (2001). Metalinguistic aspects of bilingual processing. *Annual Review of Applied Linguistics, 21,* 169–181.

Biderman, J., & Faraone, S.V. (2003). Current concepts on the neurobiology of attention-deficit/hyperactivity disorder. *Journal of Attention Disorders, 6* (Suppl. 1), S7–S16.

Biller, H.B. (1993). *Fathers and families: Paternal factors in child development*. Westport, CT: Auburn House.

Billman, J. (2003). *Observation and participation in early childhood settings: A practicum guide* (2nd ed.). Boston: Allyn & Bacon.

Billy, J.O.G., Rodgers, J.L., & Udry, J.R. (1984). Adolescent sexual behavior and friendship choice. *Social Forces, 62,* 653–678.

Birney, D.P., Citron-Pusty, J.H., Lutz, D.J., & Sternberg, R.J. (2005). The development of cognitive and intellectual abilities. In M.H. Bornstein & M.E. Lamb (Eds.), *Developmental psychology* (5th ed.). Mahwah, NJ: Erlbaum.

Bishop, K.M., & Wahlsten, D. (1997). Sex differences in the human corpus callosum: Myth or reality? *Neuroscience and Biobehavioral Reviews, 21,* 581–601.

Bissell, J., Manring, A., & Rowland, V. (1999). *Cybereducator*. New York: McGraw-Hill.

Bjorklund, D. (2005). *Children's thinking* (4th ed.). Belmont, CA: Wadsworth.

Bjorklund, D.F., & Pellegrini, A.D. (2002). *The origins of human nature*. New York: Oxford University Press.

Bjorklund, D.F., & Rosenbaum, K. (2000). Middle childhood: Cognitive development. In A. Kazdin (Ed.), *Encyclopedia of psychology*. Washington, DC, & New York: American Psychological Association and Oxford University Press.

Blaasaas, K.G., Tynes, T., & Lie, R.T. (2004). Risk of selected birth defects by maternal residence close to power lines during pregnancy. *Occupational and Environmental Medicine, 61,* 174–176.

Blachman, B.A., Ball, E., Black, R., & Tangel, D. (1994). Kindergarten teachers develop phoneme awareness in low-income inner-city classrooms: Does it make a difference? In B.A. Blachman (Ed.), *Reading and writing.* Mahwah, NJ: Erlbaum.

Black, M., & Matula, K. (1999). *Essentials of Bayley Scales of Infant Development II: Assessment.* New York: John Wiley.

Black, M.M., Baqui, A.H., Zaman, K., Persson, L.A., El Arifeen, S., Le, K., McNary, S.W., Parveen, M., & Black, R.E. (2003, April). *Iron and zinc supplementation promote motor development and exploratory behavior in Bangladesh infants.* Paper presented at the meeting of the Society for Research in Child Development, Tampa.

Black, M.M., & others. (2004). Special Supplemental Nutrition Program for Women, Infants, and Children participation and infants' growth and health: A multisite surveillance study. *Pediatrics, 114,* 169–176.

Blair, C., Gamson, D., Thorne, S., & Baker, D. (2005). Rising mean IQ: Cognitive demand of mathematics education for young children, population exposure to formal schooling, and the neurobiology of the prefrontal cortex. *Intelligence, 33,* 93–106.

Blair, J.M., Hanson, D.L., Jones, H., & Dworkin, M.S. (2004). Trends in pregnancy rates among women with human immunodeficiency virus. *Obstetrics and Gynecology, 103,* 663–668.

Blakemore, J.E.O., Berenbaum, S.A., & Liben, L.S. (2005). *Gender development.* Mahwah, NJ: Erlbaum, in preparation.

Blasi, A. (1988). Identity and the development of the self. In D. Lapsley & F.C. Power (Eds.), *Self, ego, and identity: Integrative approaches.* New York: Springer-Verlag.

Blasi, A. (1995). Moral understanding and the moral personality: The process of moral integration. In W. Kurtines & J.L. Gewirtz (Eds.), *Moral development: An introduction.* Boston: Allyn & Bacon.

Blasi, A. (2005). Moral character: A psychological approach. In D.K. Lapsley & F.C. Power (Eds.), *Character psychology and character education.* Notre Dame, IN: University of Notre Dame Press.

Blatt, S.J. (2004). *Experiences of depression.* Washington, DC: American Psychological Association.

Bloch, M., Rotenberg, N., Koren, D., & Klein, E. (2005). Risk factors associated with the development of postpartum mood disorders. *Journal of Affective Disorders, in press.*

Block, J. (1993). Studying personality the long way. In D. Funder, R.D. Parke, C. Tomlinson-Keasey, & K. Widaman (Ed.), *Studying lives through time.* Washington, DC: American Psychological Association.

Block, J.H., & Block, J. (1980). The role of ego-control and ego-resiliency in the organization of behavior. In W.A. Collins (Ed.), *Minnesota symposium on child psychology* (Vol. 13). Minneapolis: University of Minnesota Press.

Bloom, B. (1985). *Developing talent in young people.* New York: Ballantine.

Bloom, K.C., Bednarzyk, M.S., Devitt, D.L., Renault, R.A., Teaman, V., & Van Loock, D.M. (2004). Barriers to prenatal care for homeless pregnant women. *Journal of Obstetrics, Gynecologic, and Neonatal Nursing, 33,* 428–435.

Bloom, L. (1998). Language acquisition in its developmental context. In W. Damon (Ed.), *Handbook of child psychology* (5th ed., Vol. 2). New York: Wiley.

Bloom, L., Lifter, K., & Broughton, J. (1985). The convergence of early cognition and language in the second year of life: Problems in conceptualization and measurement. In M. Barrett (Ed.), *Single word speech.* London: Wiley.

Bloom, P. (2002). *How children learn the meaning of words.* Cambridge, MA: MIT Press.

Blumenfeld, P., Krajcik, J., & Kempler, T. (2006). Motivation in the classroom. In W. Damon & R. Lerner (Eds.), *Handbook of child psychology* (6th ed.). New York: Wiley.

Blumenfeld, P., Modell, J., Bartko, T., Secada, W., Fredricks, J., Friedel, J., & Paris, A. (2005). School engagement of inner city students during middle childhood. In C.R. Cooper, C.T. Garcia Coll, W.T. Bartko, H.M. Davis, & C. Chatman (Eds.), *Developmental pathways through middle childhood.* Mahwah, NJ: Erlbaum.

Blumenfeld, P.C., Pintrich, P.R., Wessles, K., & Meece, J. (1981, April). *Age and sex differences in the impact of classroom experiences on self-perceptions.* Paper presented at the biennial meeting of the Society for Research in Child Development, Boston.

Blyth, D.A. (2000). Community approaches to improving outcomes for urban children, youth, and families. In A. Booth & A.C. Crouter (Eds.), *Does it take a village?* Mahwah, NJ: Erlbaum.

Bo, I. (1994). The sociocultural environment as a source of support. In F. Nestmann & K. Hurrelmann (Eds.), *Social networks and social support in childhood and adolescence.* New York: Walter de Gruyter.

Bohlin, G., & Hagekull, B. (1993). Stranger wariness and sociability in the early years. *Infant Behavior and Development, 16,* 53–67.

Bolger, K.E., & Patterson, C.J. (2001). Developmental pathways from child maltreatment to peer rejection. *Child Development, 72,* 549–568.

Bonari, L., Bennett, H., Einarson, A., & Koren, G. (2004). Risk of untreated depression during pregnancy. *Journal of Family Health Care, 13,* 144–145.

Bonk, C.J., & Cunningham, D.J. (1999). Searching for learner-centered, constructivist, and sociocultural components of collaborative educational learning tools. In C.J. Bonk & K.S. King (Eds.), *Electronic collaborators.* Mahwah, NJ: Erlbaum.

Books, S. (2004). *Poverty and schooling in the U.S.* Mahwah, NJ: Erlbaum.

Bookstein, F.L., Streissguth A.P., Sampson, P.D., Connor, P.D., & Barr, H.M. (2002). Corpus callosum shape and neuropsychological deficits in adult males with heavy fetal alcohol exposure. *Neuroimage, 15,* 233–251.

Booth, A., Johnson, D.R., Granger, D.A., Crouter, A.C., & McHale, S. (2003). Testosterone and child and adolescent adjustment: The moderating role of parent-child relationships. *Developmental Psychology, 39,* 85–98.

Booth, M. (2002). Arab adolescents facing the future: Enduring ideals and pressures to change. In B.B. Brown, R.W. Larson, & T.S. Saraswathi (Eds.), *The world's youth.* New York: Cambridge University Press.

Bornstein, M.H. (2002). Parenting infants. In M.H. Bornstein (Ed.), *Handbook of parenting* (2nd ed., Vol. 1). Mahwah, NJ: Erlbaum.

Bornstein, M.H. (2006). Parenting science and practice. In W. Damon & R. Lerner (Eds.), *Handbook of child psychology* (6th ed.). New York: Wiley.

Bornstein, M.H., Arterberry, M.E., & Mash, C. (2005). Perceptual development. In M.H. Bornstein & M.E. Lamb (Eds.), *Developmental psychology* (5th ed.). Mahwah, NJ: Erlbaum.

Bornstein, M.H., & Sigman, M.D. (1986). Continuity in mental development from infancy. *Child Development, 57,* 251–274.

Borowsky, L.W., Ireland, M., & Resnick, M.D. (2001). Adolescent suicide attempts: Risks and protectors. *Pediatrics, 107,* 485–493.

Bost, C.S., & Vaughn, S. (2002). *Strategies for teaching students with learning and behavioral problems* (5th ed.). Boston: Allyn & Bacon.

Bouchard, T.J. (1995, August). *Heritability of intelligence.* Paper presented at the meeting of the American Psychological Association, New York, NY.

Bouchard, T.J. (2004). Genetic influence on human psychological traits. *Current Directions in Psychological Science, 13,* 148–151.

Bouchard, T.J., Lykken, D.T., McGue, M., Segal, N.L., & Tellegen, A. (1990). Source of human psychological differences. The Minnesota Study of Twins Reared Apart. *Science, 250,* 223–228.

Bouchey, H.A., & Furman, W. (2003). Dating and romantic relationships in adolescence. In G. Adams & M. Berzonsky (Eds.), *Blackwell handbook of adolescence.* Malden, MA: Blackwell.

Boukydis, C.F.Z., Bigsby, R., & Lester, B.M. (2004). Clinical use of the Neonatal Intensive Care Unit Network Neurobehavioral Scale. *Pediatrics, 113* (Supplement), S679–S689.

Bower, B. (1985). The left hand of math and verbal talent. *Science News, 127,* 263.

Bower, T.G.R. (1966). Slant perception and shape constancy in infants. *Science, 151,* 832–834.

Bower, T.G.R. (2002). Space and objects. In A. Slater & M. Lewis (Eds.), *Introduction to infant development.* New York: Oxford University Press.

Bowlby, J. (1969). *Attachment and loss* (Vol. 1). London: Hogarth Press.

Bowlby, J. (1989). *Secure and insecure attachment.* New York: Basic Books.

Bowles, T. (1999). Focusing on time orientation to explain adolescent self concept and academic achievement: Part II. Testing a model. *Journal of Applied Health Behaviour, 1,* 1–8.

Boyer, K., & Diamond, A. (1992). Development of memory for temporal order in infants and young children. In A. Diamond (Ed.), *Development and neural bases of higher cognitive function.* New York: New York Academy of Sciences.

Boyle, J., & Cropley, M. (2004). Children's sleep: Problems and solutions. *Journal of Family Health Care, 14,* 61–63.

Boyum, L., & Parke, R.D. (1995). Family emotional expressiveness and children's social competence. *Journal of Marriage and the Family, 57,* 593–608.

Brabeck, M.M. (2000). Kohlberg, Lawrence. In A. Kazdin (Ed.), *Encyclopedia of psychology.* Washington, DC, and New York: American Psychological Association and Oxford University Press.

Brabeck, M.M., & Shore, E.L. (2003). Gender differences in intellectual and moral development. In J. Demick & C. Andreoletti (Eds.), *Handbook of adult development.* New York: Kluwer.

Bracey, J.R., Bamaca, M.Y., & Umana-Taylor, A.J. (2004). Examining ethnic identity among biracial and monoracial adolescents. *Journal of Youth and Adolescence, 33,* 123–132.

Bracken, M.B., Eskenazi, B., Sachse, K., McSharry, J., Hellenbrand, K., & Leo-Summers, L. (1990). Association of cocaine use with sperm concentration, motility, and morphology. *Fertility and Sterility, 53,* 315–322.

Bradley, R.H., & Corwyn, R.F. (2004). "Family process" investments that matter for child well-being. In A. Kalil & T. DeLeire (Eds.), *Family investments in children's potential.* Mahwah, NJ: Erlbaum.

Bradley, R.H., Corwyn, R.F., McAdoo, H.P., & Coll. C.G. (2001). The home environments of children in the United States Part I: Variations by age, ethnicity, and poverty status. *Child Development, 72,* 1844–1867.

Bradshaw, C.P., & Garbarino, J. (2004). Using and building family strengths to promote youth development. In S.F. Hamilton & M.A. Hamilton (Eds.), *The youth development handbook.* Thousand Oaks, CA: Sage.

Brainerd, C.J., & Gordon, L.L. (1994). Development of verbatim and gist memory for numbers. *Developmental Psychology, 30,* 163–177.

Brainerd, C.J., & Reyna, V.F. (2004). Fuzzy-trace theory and memory development. *Developmental Review, 24,* 396–439.

Braver, S., Goodman, M., & Shapiro, J. (2005). The consequences of divorce for parents. In M.A. Fine & J.H. Harvey (Eds.), *Handbook of divorce and relationship dissolution.* Mahwah, NJ: Erlbaum.

Brazelton, T.B. (1956). Sucking in infancy. *Pediatrics, 17,* 400–404.

Brazelton, T.B. (2004). Preface: The Neonatal Intensive Care Unit Network Neurobehavioral Scale. *Pediatrics, 113* (Supplement), S632–S633.

Bredekamp, S. (1987). *Developmentally appropriate practice in early childhood programs serving children from birth through age 8.* Washington, DC: National Association for the Education of Young Children.

Bredekamp, S. (1993). Reflections on Reggio Emilia. *Young Children, 49,* 13–16.

Bredekamp, S. (1997). NAEYC issues revised position statement on developmentally appropriate practice in early childhood programs. *Young Children, 52,* 34–40.

Bremner, J.G. (2004). Cognitive development: Knowledge of the physical world. In J.G. Bremner & A. Fogel (Eds.), *Blackwell handbook of infant development.* Malden, MA: Blackwell.

Brenner, R.A., Trumble, A.C., Smith, G.S., Kessler, E.P., & Overpeck, M.D. (2001). Where children drown, 1995. *Pediatrics, 108,* 85–89.

Brent, R.L. (2004). Environmental causes of human congenital malformations. *Pediatrics, 113* (Supplement 4), 957–968.

Brent, R.L., & Fawcett, L.B. (2000, May). *Environmental causes of human birth defects: What have we learned about the mechanism, nature, and etiology of congenital malformations in the past 50 years?* Paper presented at the joint meetings of the Pediatric Academic Societies and the American Academy of Pediatrics, Boston.

Bretherton, I., Stolberg, U., & Kreye, M. (1981). Engaging strangers in proximal interaction: Infants' social initiative. *Developmental Psychology, 17,* 746–755.

Brewer, J.A. (2004). *Introduction to early childhood education.* Boston: Allyn & Bacon.

Brewer, M.B., & Campbell, D.T. (1976). *Ethnocentrism and intergroup attitudes.* New York: Wiley.

Bridges, L.J. (2003). Coping as an element of developmental well-being. In M.H. Bornstein, L. Davidson, C.L.M. Keyes, & K.A. Moore (Eds.), *Well-being.* Mahwah, NJ: Erlbaum.

Bril, B. (1999). Dires sur l'enfant selon les cultures. Etat des lieux et perspectives. In B. Bril, P.R. Dasen, C. Sabatier, & B. Krewer (Eds.), *Propos sur l'enfant et l'adolescent. Quels enfants pour quelles cultures?* Paris: L'Harmattan.

Brislin, R. (1993). *Understanding culture's influence on behavior.* Fort Worth, TX: Harcourt Brace.

Brockmeyer, S., Treboux, D., & Crowell, J.A. (2005, April). *Parental divorce and adult children's attachment status and marital relationships.* Paper presented at the meeting of the Society for Research in Child Development, Atlanta.

Brody, G. (2004). Siblings' direct and indirect contributions to child development. *Current Directions in Psychological Science, 13,* 124–126.

Brody, G.H., Ge, X., Conger, R.D., Gibbons, F., Murry, V., Gerrard, M., & Simons, R. (2001). The influence of neighborhood disadvantage, collective socialization, and parenting on African American children's affiliation with deviant peers. *Child Development, 72,* 1231–1246.

Brody, G.H., & Shaffer, D.R. (1982). Contributions of parents and peers to children's moral socialization. *Developmental Review, 2,* 31–75.

Brody, J.E. (1994, April 6). The value of breast milk. *New York Times,* p. C11.

Brody, N. (2000). Intelligence. In A. Kazdin (Ed.), *Encyclopedia of psychology.* Washington, DC, & New York: American Psychological Association and Oxford University Press.

Brodzinsky, D.M., Lang, R., & Smith, D.W. (1995). Parenting adopted children. In M.H. Bornstein (Ed.), *Handbook of parenting* (Vol. 3). Hillsdale, NJ: Erlbaum.

Brodzinsky, D.M., & Pinderhughes, E. (2002). Parenting and child development in adoptive families. In M.H. Bornstein (Ed.), *Handbook of parenting* (Vol. 1). Mahwah, NJ: Erlbaum.

Brodzinsky, D.M., Schechter, D.E., Braff, A.M., & Singer, L.M. (1984). Psychological and academic adjustment in adopted children. *Journal of Consulting and Clinical Psychology, 52,* 582–590.

Broidy, L.M., Nagin, D.S., Tremblay, R.E., Bates, J.E., Dodge, K.A., Fegusson, D., Horwood, J.L., Loeber, R., Laird, R., Lynam, D.R., Moffitt, T.E., Pettit, G.S., & Vitaro, F. (2003). Developmental trajectories of childhood disruptive behaviors and adolescent delinquency: A six-site, cross-national study. *Developmental Psychology, 39,* 222–245.

Brom, B. (2005). *NutritionNow* (4th ed.). Belmont CA: Wadsworth.

Bronfenbrenner, U. (1986). Ecology of the family as a context for human development: Research perspectives. *Developmental Psychology, 22,* 723–742.

Bronfenbrenner, U. (1995). Developmental ecology through space and time: A future perspective. In P. Moen, G.H. Elder, & K. Lüscher (Eds.), *Examining lives in context.* Washington, DC: American Psychological Association.

Bronfenbrenner, U. (1995, March). *The role research has played in Head Start.* Paper presented at the meeting of the Society for Research in Child Development, Indianapolis.

Bronfenbrenner, U. (2000). Ecological theory. In A. Kazdin (Ed.), *Encyclopedia of psychology.* Washington, DC, & New York: American Psychological Association and Oxford University Press.

Bronfenbrenner, U. (2004). *Making human beings human.* Thousand Oaks, CA: Sage.

Bronfenbrenner, U., & Morris, P. (1998). The ecology of developmental processes. In W. Damon (Ed.), *Handbook of child psychology* (5th ed., Vol. 1). New York: Wiley.

Bronfenbrenner, U., & Morris, P.A. (2006). The ecology of developmental processes. In W. Damon & R. Lerner (Eds.), *Handbook of child psychology* (6th ed.). New York: Wiley.

Brook, J.S., Brook, D.W., Gordon, A.S., Whiteman, M., & Cohen, P. (1990). The psychological etiology of adolescent drug use: A family interactional approach. *Genetic, Social, and General Psychology Monographs, 116,* 110–267.

Brooker, R.J. (2005). *Genetics* (2nd ed.). New York: McGraw-Hill.

Brooks, J.G., & Brooks, M.G. (1993). *The case for constructivist classrooms.* Alexandria, VA: Association for Supervision and Curriculum.

Brooks, J.G., & Brooks, M.G. (2001). *The case for constructivist classrooms* (2nd ed.). Upper Saddle River, NJ: Prentice Hall.

Brooks-Gunn, J. (2003). Do you believe in magic?: What we can expect from early childhood programs. *Social Policy Report, Society for Research in Child Development, 27* (1), 1–13.

Brooks-Gunn, J., Currie, J., Emde, R.E., & Zigler, E. (2003). Do you believe in magic? What we can expect from early childhood intervention programs. *SRCD Social Policy Report, 17* (1), 3–15.

Brooks-Gunn, J., Han, W.J., & Waldfogel, J. (2002). Maternal employment and child cognitive outcomes in the first three years of life: The NICHD Study of Early Child Care. *Child Development, 73,* 1052–1072.

Brooks-Gunn, J., Leventhal, T., & Duncan, G. (2000). Why poverty matters for young children: Implications for policy. In J. Osofsky & H.E. Fitzgerald (Eds.), *WAIMH handbook of infant mental health* (Vol. 3). New York: Wiley.

Brooks-Gunn, J., & Matthews, W.S. (1979). *He and she: How children develop their sex role identity.* Englewood Cliffs, NJ: Prentice Hall.

Brooks-Gunn, J., & Paikoff, R. (1993). "Sex is a gamble, kissing is a game": Adolescent sexuality, contraception, and sexuality. In S.P. Millstein, A.C. Petersen, & E.O. Nightingale (Eds.), *Promoting the health behavior of adolescents.* New York: Oxford University Press.

Brooks-Gunn, J., & Warren, M.P. (1989). The psychological significance of secondary sexual characteristics in 9- to 11-year-old girls. *Child Development, 59,* 161–169.

Brophy, J. (2004). *Motivating students to learn* (2nd ed.). Mahwah, NJ: Erlbaum.

Broughton, J.M. (1978). Development of concepts of self, mind, reality, and knowledge. In W. Damon (Ed.), *Social cognition.* San Francisco: Jossey-Bass.

Broussard, S.C. (2004). The relationship between classroom motivation and academic achievement in elementary-school-aged children. *Family and Consumer Sciences Research Journal, 33,* 106–120.

Brown, A.L. (1990). Domain-specific principles affect learning and transfer in children. *Cognitive Science, 14,* 107–133.

Brown, A.L. (1997). Transforming schools into communities of learners. *American Psychologist, 52,* 399–409.

Brown, A.L. (1998, April). *Reciprocal teaching.* Paper presented at the meeting of the American Educational Research Association, San Diego.

Brown, A.L., & Campione, J.C. (1996). Psychological learning theory and the design of innovative environments. In L. Schauble, & R. Glaser (Eds.), *Contributions of instructional innovation to understanding learning.* Mahwah, NJ: Erlbaum.

Brown, A.L., & Day, J.D. (1983). Macrorules for summarizing texts: The development of expertise. *Journal of Verbal Learning and Verbal Behavior, 22,* 1–14.

Brown, A.L., Kane, M.J., & Echols, K. (1986). Young children's mental models determine analogical transfer across problems with a common goal structure. *Cognitive Development, 1,* 103–122.

Brown, B.B. (1999). Measuring the peer environment of American adolescents. In S.L. Friedman & T.D. Wachs (Eds.), *Measuring environment across the life span.* Washington, DC: American Psychological Association.

Brown, B.B. (2003). Crowds, cliques, & friendships. In G. Adams & M. Berzonsky (Eds.), *Blackwell hanbook of adolescence.* Malden, MA: Blackwell.

Brown, B.B. (2004). Adolescents' relationships with peers. In R. Lerner & L. Steinberg (Eds.), *Handbook of adolescent psychology* (2nd ed.). New York: Wiley.

Brown, B.B., & Larson, R.W. (2002). The kaleidoscope of adolescence: Experiences of the world's youth at the beginning of the 21st century. In B.B. Brown, R.W. Larson, & T.S. Saraswathi (Eds.), *The world's youth.* New York: Cambridge University Press.

Brown, B.B., & Lohr, M.J. (1987). Peer-group affiliation and adolescent self-esteem: An integration of ego-identity and symbolic-interaction theories. *Journal of Personality and Social Psychology, 52,* 47–55.

Brown, J.D., & Siegel, J.D. (1988). Exercise as a buffer of life stress: A prospective study of adolescent health. *Health Psychology, 7,* 341–353.

Brown, L.M., & Gilligan, C. (1992). *Meeting at the crossroads: Women's and girls' development.* Cambridge, MA: Harvard University Press.

Brown, R. (1973). *A first language: The early stages.* Cambridge, MA: Harvard University Press.

Brownlee, S. (1998, June 15). Baby talk. *U.S. News & World Report,* 48–54.

Bruce. J.M., Olen, K., & Jensen, S.J. (1999, April). *The role of emotion and regulation in social competence.* Paper presented at the meeting of the Society for Research in Child Development, Albuquerque, NM.

Bruck, M., & Ceci, S.J. (1999). The suggestibility of children's memory. *Annual Review of Psychology, 50,* 419–439.

Bruck, M., & Ceci, S.J. (2004). Forensic developmental psychology. *Current Directions in Psychological Science, 13,* 229–232.

Bruck, M., Ceci, S.J., & Hembrooke, H. (1998). Reliability and credibility of young children's reports: From research to policy and practice. *American Psychologist, 53* (2), 136–151.

Bruck, M., & Melnyk, L. (2004). Individual differences in children's suggestibility: A review and a synthesis. *Applied Cognitive Psychology, 18,* 947–996.

Brumm, V.L., Azen, C., Moats, R.A., Stern, A.M., Broomand, C., Nelson, M.D., & Koch, R. (2004). Neuropsychological outcome of subjects participating in mild phenylketonuria mutations. *Journal of Inherited Metabolic Disease, 27,* 549–566.

Bruner, J.S. (1983). *Child talk.* New York: W.W. Norton.

Bruner, J.S. (1996). *The culture of education.* Cambridge, MA: Harvard University Press.

Bryant, A., & LaFromboise, T.D. (2005). The racial identity and cultural orientation of Lumbee American Indian high school students. *Cultural Diversity and Ethnic Minority Psychology, 11,* 82–89.

Bryant, J., & Rockwell, S.C. (1994). Effects of massive exposure to sexually oriented prime-time television programming on adolescents' moral judgment. In D. Zillman, J. Bryant, & A.C. Huston (Eds.), *Media, children, and the family: Social scientific, psychodynamic, and clinical perspectives.* Hillsdale, NJ: Erlbaum.

Bryant, J.B. (2005). Language in social contexts: Communicative competence in the preschool years. In J. Berko Gleason (Ed.), *The development of language* (6th ed.). Boston: Allyn & Bacon.

Buchanan, C.M. (2001, August). *Understanding the variability in children's adjustment after divorce.* Paper presented at the meeting of the American Psychological Association, San Francisco.

Bugental, D.B., & Grusec, J.E. (2006). Socialization processes. In W. Damon & R. Lerner (Eds.), *Handbook of child psychology* (6th ed.). New York: Wiley.

Buhrmester, D. (1990). Friendship, interpersonal competence, and adjustment in preadolescence and adolescence. *Child Development, 61,* 1101–1111.

Buhrmester, D. (2001, April). *Romantic development: Does age at which romantic involvement starts matter?* Paper presented at the meeting of the Society for Research in Child Development, Minneapolis.

Buhrmester, D., & Carbery, J. (1992, March). *Daily patterns of self-disclosure and adolescent adjustment.* Paper presented at the biennial meeting of the Society for Research on Adolescence, Washington, DC.

Buhrmester, D., & Furman, W. (1987). The development of companionship and intimacy. *Child Development, 58,* 1101–1113.

Buhs, E.S., & Ladd, G.W. (2001). Peer rejection as an antecedent of young children's school adjustment: An examination of mediating processes. *Developmental Psychology, 37,* 550–560.

Bukowski, W.M., & Adams, R. (2005). Peer relationships and psychopathology. *Journal of Clinical Child and Adolescent Psychology, 34,* 3–10.

Bukowski, W.M., Newcomb, A.F., & Hoza, B. (1987). Friendship conceptions among early adolescents: A longitudinal study of stability and change. *Journal of Early Adolescence, 7,* 143–152.

Bukowski, W.M., Sippola, L.K., & Boivin, M. (1995, March). *Friendship protects "at risk" children from victimization by peers.* Paper presented at the meeting of the Society for Research in Child Development, Indianapolis.

Bumpus, M.F., Crouter, A.C., & McHale, S.M. (2001). Parental autonomy granting during adolescence: Exploring gender differences in context. *Developmental Psychology, 37,* 161–173.

Burden, M.J., Jacobson, S.W., Sokol, R.J., & Jacobson, J.L. (2005). Effects of prenatal alcohol exposure on attention and working memory at 7.5 years of age. *Alcoholism: Clinical and Experimental Research, 29,* 443–452.

Burke, V., Beilin, L.J., Dunbar, D., & Kevan, M. (2004). Associations between blood pressure and overweight defined by new standards for body mass index in childhood. *Preventive Medicine, 38,* 558–564.

Burton, R.V. (1984). A paradox in theories and research in moral development. In W.M. Kurtines & J.L. Gewirtz (Eds.), *Morality, moral behavior, and moral development.* New York: Wiley.

Bushman, B.J., & Huesmann, L.R. (2001). Effects of televised violence on aggression. In D. Singer & J. Singer (Eds.), *Handbook of children and the media.* Thousand Oaks, CA: Sage.

Buss, D.M. (1995). Psychological sex differences: Origins through sexual selection. *American Psychologist, 50,* 164–168.

Buss, D.M. (2000). Evolutionary psychology. In A. Kazdin (Ed.), *Encyclopedia of psychology.* Washington, DC, & New York: American Psychological Association and Oxford University Press.

Buss, D.M. (2004). *Evolutionary psychology* (2nd ed.). Boston: Allyn & Bacon.

Buss, D.M., & Schmitt, D.P. (1993). Sexual strategies theory: An evolutionary perspective on human mating. *Psychological Review, 100,* 204–232.

Bussey, K., & Bandura A. (1999). Social cognitive theory of gender development and differentiation. *Psychological Review, 106,* 676–713.

Byrnes, J.P. (1997). *The nature and development of decision making.* Mahwah, NJ: Erlbaum.

Byrnes, J.P. (2001). *Minds, brains, and learning.* New York: Guilford.

Byrnes, J.P. (2003). Cognitive development during adolescence. In G. Adams & M. Berzonsky (Eds.), *Blackwell handbook of adolescence.* Malden, MA: Blackwell.

Byrnes, J.P. (2005). The development of regulated decision making. In J.E. Jacobs & P.A. Klaczynski (Eds.), *The development of judgment and decision making in children and adolescents.* Mahwah, NJ: Erlbaum.

Caballero, B. (2004). Obesity prevention in children: Opportunities and challenges. *International Journal of Obesity and Related Metabolic Disorders, 28* (Supplement 3), S90–S95.

Cairns, R.B. (1983). The emergence of developmental psychology. In P.H. Mussen (Ed.), *Handbook of child psychology* (4th ed., Vol.1). New York: Wiley.

Cairns, R.B. (1998). The making of developmental psychology.

Cairns, R.B. (2006). The making of developmental psychology. In W. Damon & R. Lerner (Eds.), *Handbook of child psychology* (6th ed.). New York: Wiley.

Calabrese, R.L., & Schumer, H. (1986). The effects of service activities on adolescent alienation. *Adolescence, 21,* 675–687.

Caley, L.M., Kramer, C., & Robinson, L.K. (2005). Fetal alcohol spectrum disorder. *Journal of School Nursing, 21,* 139–146.

Callaghan, W.M., & Berg, C.J. (2004). Pregnancy-related mortality among women aged 35 years and older, United States 1991–1997. *Obstetrics and Gynecology, 102,* 1015–1021.

Callan, J.E. (2001). Gender development: Psychoanalytic perspectives. In J. Worell (Ed.), *Encyclopedia of women and gender.* San Diego: Academic Press.

Callas, P.W., Flynn, B.S., & Worden, J.K. (2004). Potentially modifiable psychosocial factors associated with alcohol use during early adolescence. *Addictive Behavior, 29,* 1503–1515.

Calvert, S. (1999). *Children's journeys through the information age.* New York: McGraw-Hill.

Calvert, S. (2004). Changing media: Fast forward to the information age. *Society for Research in Child Development Policy Report, 28* (4), 14.

Camaioni, L. (2004). Early language. In J.G. Bremner & A. Fogel (Eds.), *Blackwell handbook of infant development.* Malden, MA: Blackwell.

Cameron, J. (2001). Negative effects of reward on intrinsic motivation—a limited phenomenon. *Review of Educational Research, 71,* 29–42.

Camilleri, B. (2005). Dynamic assessment and intervention: Improving children's narrative abilities. *International Journal of Language & Communication Disorders, 40,* 240–242.

Campbell, C.Y. (1988, August 24). Group raps depiction of teenagers. *Boston Globe,* p. 44.

Campbell, D.T., & LeVine, R.A. (1968). Ethnocentrism and intergroup relations. In R. Abelson & others (Eds.), *Theories and cognitive consistency: A sourcebook.* Chicago: Rand-McNally.

Campbell, F.A., Pungello, E.P., Miller-Johnson, S., Burchinal, M., & Ramey, C.T. (2001). The development of cognitive and academic abilities: Growth curves from an early childhood educational experiment. *Developmental Psychology, 37,* 231–243.

Campbell, L., Campbell, B., & Dickinson, D. (2004). *Teaching and learning through multiple intelligences* (3rd ed.). Boston: Allyn & Bacon.

Campos, J.J. (1994, spring). The new functionalism in emotions. *SRCD Newsletter,* pp. 1, 7, 9–11, 14.

Campos, J.J. (2001, April). *Emotion in emotional development: Problems and prospects.* Paper presented at the meeting of the Society for Research in Child Development Minneapolis.

Campos, J.J. (2004). Unpublished review of Santrock, J.W., *Life-span development* (10th ed.). New York: McGraw-Hill.

Campos, J.J., Langer, A., & Krowitz, A. (1970). Cardiac responses on the visual cliff in prelocomotor human infants. *Science, 170,* 196–197.

Canfield, R.L., & Haith, M.M. (1991). Young infants' visual expectations for symmetric and asymmetric stimulus sequences. *Developmental Psychology, 27,* 198–208.

Canterino, J.C., Ananth, C.V., Smulian, J., Harrigan, J.T., & Vintzileos, A.M. (2004). Maternal age and risk of fetal death in Singleton gestations: United States, 1995–2000. *Obstetrics and Gynecology Survey, 59,* 649–650.

Caplan, P.J., & Caplan, J.B. (1999). *Thinking critically about research on sex and gender* (2nd ed.). New York: HarperCollins.

Carbonell, O.A., Alzte, G., Bustamante, M.R., & Quiceno, J. (2002). Maternal caregiving and infant security in two cultures. *Developmental Psychology, 38,* 67–78.

Carbonne, B., Tsatsaris, V., & Goffinet, F. (2001). The new tocolytics. *Gynecology, Obstetrics, and Fertility, 29,* 316–319.

Cardelle-Elawar, M. (1992). Effects of teaching metacognitive skills to students with low mathematics ability. *Teaching and Teacher Education, 8* (2), 109–121.

Carey, S. (1997). The child as word learner. In M. Halle, J. Bresman, & G. Miller (Eds.), *Linguistic theory and psychological reality.* Cambridge, MA: MIT Press.

Carlson, C., Cooper, C., & Hsu, J. (1990, March). *Predicting school achievement in early adolescence: The role of family process.* Paper presented at the meeting of the Society for Research in Adolescence, Atlanta.

Carlson, E.A., Sroufe, L.A., & Egeland, B. (2004). The construction of experience: A longitudinal study of representation and behavior. *Child Development, 75,* 66–83.

Carlson, K.S. (1995, March). *Attachment in sibling relationships during adolescence: Links to other familial and peer relationships.* Paper presented at the meeting of the Society for Research in Child Development, Indianapolis.

Carlson, S.M. (2003). Commentary. Executive function in context: Development, measurement, theory, and experience. *Monographs of the Society for Research in Child Development, 68* (3, Serial No. 274).

Carmichael, S.L., Shaw, G.M., & Nelson, V. (2002). Timing of prenatal care initiation and risk of congenital malformations. *Teratology, 66,* 326–330.

Carnegie Corporation. (1996). *Report on education for children 3–10 years of age.* New York: Carnegie Foundation.

Carnegie Council on Adolescent Development. (1995). *Great transitions.* New York: Carnegie Foundation.

Carnegie Foundation. (1989). *Turning points: Preparing American youth for the 21st century.* New York: Author.

Carpendale, J.I., & Chandler, M.J. (1996). On the distinction between false belief understanding and subscribing to an interpretive theory of mind. *Child Development, 67,* 1686–1706.

Carroll, J. (1993). *Human cognitive abilities.* Cambridge: Cambridge University Press.

Carskadon, M.A. (2004a). Sleep difficulties in young people. *Archives of Pediatric and Adolescent Health, 158,* 597–598.

Carskadon, M.A. (Ed.). (2004b). *Adolescent sleep patterns.* New York: Cambridge University Press.

Carskadon, M.A. (2005). Sleep and circadian rhythms in children and adolescents: Relevance for athletic performance of young people. *Clinical Sports Medicine, 24,* 319–328.

Carskadon, M.A., Acebo, C., & Jenni, O.G. (2004). Regulation of adolescent sleep: Implications for behavior. *Annals of the New York Academy of Science, 102,* 276–291.

Carskadon, M.A., Acebo, C., & Seifer, R. (2001). Extended nights, sleep loss, and recovery sleep in adolescents. *Archives of Italian Biology, 139,* 301–312.

Carter-Saltzman, L. (1980). Biological and sociocultural effects on handedness: Comparison between biological and adoptive families. *Science, 209,* 1263–1265.

Caruthers, A.S., & Ward, L.M. (2002, April). *Mixed messages: The divergent nature of sexual communication received from parents, peers, and the media.* Paper presented at the meeting of the Society for Research on Adolescence, New Orleans.

Carver, K., Joyner, K., & Udry, J.R. (2003). National estimates of romantic relationships. In P. Florsheim (Ed.), *Adolescent romantic relations and sexual behavior: Theory, research, and practical implications.* Mahwah, NJ: Erlbaum.

Carver, L.J., & Bauer, P.J. (2001). The dawning of a past: The emergence of long-term explicit memory in infancy. *Journal of Experimental Psychology: General, 130* (4), 726–745.

Cary, P. (2004). Fixing kids' sports. *U.S. News & World Report, 136,* 44–48, 50, 52–53.

Case, R. (1987). Neo-Piagetian theory: Retrospect and prospect. *International Journal of Psychology, 22,* 773–791.

Case, R. (1999). Conceptual development in the child and the field: A personal view of the Piagetian legacy. In E.K. Skolnick, K. Nelson, S.A. Gelman, & P.H. Miller (Eds.), *Conceptual development.* Mahwah, NJ: Erlbaum.

Case, R., Kurland, D.M., & Goldberg, J. (1982). Operational efficiency and the growth of short-term memory span. *Journal of Experimental Child Psychology, 33,* 386–404.

Case, R., & Mueller, M.P. (2001). Differentiation, integration, and covariance mapping as fundamental processes in cognitive and neurological growth. In J.L. McClelland & R.S. Siegler (Eds.), *Mechanisms of cognitive development.* Mahwah, NJ: Erlbaum.

Casey, B.J., Durston, S., & Fossella, J.A. (2001). Evidence for a mechanistic model of cognitive control. *Clinical Neuroscience Research, 1,* 267–282.

Caspi, A. (1998). Personality development across the life course. In W. Damon (Ed.), *Handbook of child psychology* (Vol. 3). New York: Wiley.

Caspi, A. (2006). Personality development. In W. Damon & R. Lerner (Eds.), *Handbook of child psychology* (6th ed.). New York: Wiley.

Cassidy, J. (1999). The nature of the child's ties. In J. Cassidy & P. Shaver (Eds.), *Handbook of attachment.* New York: Guilford.

Cauffman, B.E. (1994, February). *The effects of puberty, dating, and sexual involvement on dieting and disordered eating in young adolescent girls.* Paper presented at the meeting of the Society for Research on Adolescence, San Diego.

Caulfield, R.A. (2001). *Infants and toddlers.* Upper Saddle River, NJ: Prentice Hall.

Cave, R.K. (2002, August). *Early adolescent language: A content analysis of child development and educational psychology textbooks.* Unpublished doctoral dissertation, University of Nevada-Reno, Reno, NV.

Ceci, S.J. (2000). Bronfenbrenner, Urie. In A. Kazdin (Ed.), *Encyclopedia of psychology.* Washington, DC, & New York: American Psychological Association and Oxford University Press.

Ceci, S.J., & Bruck, M. (1993). The suggestibility of the child witness: A historical review and synthesis. *Psychological Bulletin, 113,* 403–439.

Ceci, S.J., & Gilstrap, L.L. (2000). Determinants of intelligence: Schooling and intelligence. In A. Kazdin (Ed.), *Encyclopedia of Psychology.* Washington, DC, & New York: American Psychological Association and Oxford University Press.

Celi, F., Bini, V., Papi, F., Contessa, G., Santilli, E., & Falorni, A. (2004). Leptin serum levels are involved in the relapse after weight excess reduction in obese children and adolescents. *Diabetes Nutrition and Metabolism, 16,* 306–311.

Centers for Disease Control and Prevention. (2000). *Reproductive health.* Atlanta: Author.

Cerel, J., & Roberts, T.A. (2005). Suicidal behavior in the family and adolescent risk behavior, *Journal of Adolescent Health, 36,* e8–e14.

Chall, J.S. (1979). The great debate: Ten years later with a modest proposal for reading stages. In L.B. Resnick & P.A. Weaver (Eds.), *Theory and practice of early reading.* Hillsdale, NJ: Erlbaum.

Chan, A., Keane, R.J., & Robinson, J.S. (2001). The contribution of maternal smoking to preterm birth, small for gestational age, and low birth weight among Aboriginal and non-Aboriginal births in South Australia. *Medical Journal of Australia, 174,* 389–393.

Chan, W.S. (1963). *A source book in Chinese philosophy.* Princeton, NJ: Princeton University Press.

Chan-Yeung, M., & Dimich-Ward, H. (2003). Respiratory health effects of exposure to environmental tobacco smoke. *Respirology, 8,* 131–139.

Chang, S.C., O'Brien, K.O., Nathanson, M.S., Mancini, J., & Witter, F.R. (2003). Characteristics and risk factors for adverse birth outcomes in pregnant black adolescents. *Journal of Obstetrics and Gynecology Canada, 25,* 751–759.

Channon, S., German, E., Cassina, C., & Lee, P. (2004). Executive functioning, memory, and learning in phenylketonuria. *Neuropsychology, 18,* 613–620.

Chao, R. (2001). Extending research on the consequences of parenting style for Chinese Americans and European Americans. *Child Development, 72,* 1832–1843.

Chao, R., & Tseng, V. (2002). Parenting of Asians. In M.H. Bornstein, *Handbook of parenting* (2nd ed., Vol. 4). Mahwah, NJ: Erlbaum.

Chao, R.K. (2005, April). *The importance of* Guan *in describing control of immigrant Chinese.* Paper presented at the meeting of the Society for Research in Child Development, Atlanta.

Chapman, M.V. (2003). Poverty level and school performance: Using contextual and self-report measures to inform intervention. *Children and Schools, 25,* 5–17.

Chase-Lansdale, P.L., Coley, R.L., & Grining, C.P.L. (2001, April). *Low-income families and child care.* Paper presented at the meeting of the Society for Research in Child Development, Minneapolis.

Chattin-McNichols, J. (1992). *The Montessori controversy*. Albany, NY: Delmar.

Chauhuri, J.H., & Williams, P.H. (1999, April). *The contribution of infant temperament and parent emotional availability to toddler attachment.* Paper presented at the meeting of the Society for Research in Child Development, Albuquerque.

Chauma, C.M., Auda, B.M., & Kyari, O. (2004). Prevention of mother-to-child transmission of HIV at Maiduguri, Nigeria. *Journal of Obstetrics and Gynecology, 24,* 266–269.

Chavkin, W. (2001). Cocaine and pregnancy—time to look at the evidence. *Journal of the American Medical Association, 285,* 1626–1628.

Chen, C., & Stevenson, H.W. (1989). Homework: A cross-cultural examination. *Child Development, 60,* 551–561.

Chen, F.S., Diaz, V.A., Loebenberg, M., & Rosen, J.E. (2005). Shoulder and elbow injuries in the skeletally immature athlete. *Journal of the American Academy of Orthopedic Surgery, 13,* 172–185.

Chen, I.G., Durbin, D.R., Elliott, M.R., Kallan, M.J., & Winston, F.K. (2005). Trip characteristics of vehicle crashes involving child passengers. *Injury Prevention, 11,* 219–224.

Chen, X., Hastings, P.D., Rubin, K.H., Chen, H., Cen, G., & Stewart, S.L. (1998). Childrearing attitudes and behavioral inhibition in Chinese and Canadian toddlers: A cross-cultural study. *Developmental Psychology, 34,* 677–686.

Cherlin, A.J., & Furstenberg, F.F. (1994). Stepfamilies in the United States: A reconsideration. In J. Blake & J. Hagen (Eds.), *Annual review of sociology.* Palo Alto, CA: Annual Reviews.

Cherlin, A.J., Furstenberg, F.F., Chase-Lansdale, P.L., Kiernan, K.E., Robins, P.K., Morrison, D.R., & Teitler, J.O. (1991). Longitudinal studies of effects of divorce in children in Great Britain and the United States. *Science, 252,* 1386–1389.

Chernausek, S.D. (2004). Growth hormone treatment of short children born small for gestational age: A U.S. perspective. *Hormone Research, 62* (Supplement 3), S124–S127.

Chess, S., & Thomas, A. (1977). Temperamental individuality from childhood to adolescence. *Journal of Child Psychiatry, 16,* 218–226.

Chi, M.T. (1978). Knowledge structures and memory development. In R.S. Siegler (Ed.), *Children's thinking: What develops?* Hillsdale, NJ: Erlbaum.

Chiappe, D., & MacDonald, K. (2005). The evolution of domain-general mechanisms in intelligence and learning. *Journal of General Psychology, 132,* 5–40.

Children's Defense Fund. (1992). *The state of America's children, 1992.* Washington, DC: Author.

Chiurazzi, P., Neri, G., & Oostra, B.A. (2003). Understanding the biological underpinnings of fragile X syndrome. *Current Opinions in Pediatrics, 15,* 559–566.

Choate, J.S. (2004). *Successful inclusive teaching* (4th ed.). Boston: Allyn & Bacon.

Choi, N. (2004). Sex role group differences in specific, academic, and general self-efficacy. *Journal of Psychology, 138,* 149–159.

Chomsky, N. (1957). *Syntactic structures.* The Hague Mouton.

Christensen, L.B. (2004). *Experimental methodology* (9th ed.). Boston: Allyn & Bacon.

Christenson, S.L., & Thurlow, M.L. (2004). School dropouts: Prevention considerations, interventions, and challenges. *Current Directions in Psychological Science, 13,* 36–39.

Christian, K., Bachnan, H.J., & Morrison, F.J. (2001). Schooling and cognitive development. In R.J. Sternberg & E.L. Grigorenko (Eds.), *Environmental effects on cognitive development.* Mahwah, NJ: Erlbaum.

Chronis, A.M., Chacko, A., Fabiano, G.A., Wymbs, B.T., & Pelham, W.E. (2004). Enhancements to the behavioral parent training paradigm for families of children with ADHD: Review and future directions. *Clinical Child and Family Psychology Review, 7,* 1–27.

Chun, K.M., Organista, P.B., & Marín, G. (Eds.). (2003). *Acculturation.* Washington, DC: American Psychological Association.

Cicchetti, D. (2001). How a child builds a brain. In W.W. Hartup & R.A. Weinberg (Eds.), *Child psychology in retrospect and prospect.* Mahwah, NJ: Erlbaum.

Cicchetti, D., & Blender, J.A. (2004, December 14). A multiple-levels-of-analysis approach to the study of developmental processes in maltreated children. *Proceedings of the National Academy of Science USA, 101,* 17325–17326.

Cicchetti, D., & Toth, S.L. (2005). Child maltreatment. *Annual Review of Clinical Psychology, 1.* Palo Alto, CA: Annual Reviews.

Cicchetti, D., & Toth, S.L. (2006). A developmental psychopathology perspective on preventive interventions with high risk children and their families. In W. Damon & R. Lerner (Eds.), *Handbook of child psychology* (6th ed.). New York: Wiley.

Cicchetti, D., Toth, S.L., & Rogusch, F.A. (2005). *A prevention program for child maltreatment.* Unpublished manuscript, University of Rochester, Rochester, NY.

Cillessen, A.H.N., Lu Jang, X., West, T.V., & Laszkowski, D.K. (2005). Predictors of dyadic friendship quality in adolescence. *International Journal of Behavioral Development, 29,* 165–172.

Cillessen, A.H.N., & Mayeux, L. (2004). Sociometric status and peer group behavior: Previous findings and current directions. In J.B. Kupersmidt & K.A. Dodge (Eds.), *Children's peer relations: From development to intervention.* Washington, DC: American Psychological Association.

Circirelli, V.G. (1994). Sibling relationships in cross-cultural perspective. *Journal of Marriage and Family, 56,* 7–20.

Cizek, G.J. (2005). High-stakes testing. In R.P. Phelps (Ed.), *Defending standardized testing.* Mahwah, NJ: Erlbaum.

Clark, E. (2000). Language acquisition. In A. Kazdin (Ed.), *Encyclopedia of psychology.* Washington, DC, & New York: American Psychological Association and Oxford University Press.

Clark, R.D., & Hatfield, E. (1989). Gender differences in receptivity to sexual offers. *Journal of Psychology and Human Sexuality, 2,* 39–55.

Clarke-Stewart, K.A., Malloy, L.C., & Allhusen, V.D. (2004). Verbal ability, self-control, and close relationships with parents protect children against misleading statements. *Applied Cognitive Psychology, 18,* 1037–1058.

Clay, E.C., & Seehusen, D.A. (2004). A review of postpartum depression for the primary care physician. *Southern Medical Journal, 97,* 157–162.

Cleary-Goldman, J., & others. (2005). Impact of maternal age on obstetric outcome. *Obstetrics and Gynecology, 105,* 983–990.

Cleves, M.A., Hobbs, C.A., Collins, H.B., Andrews, N., Smith, L.N., & Robbins, J.N. (2004). Folic acid use by women receiving gynecologic care. *Obstetrics and Gynecology, 103,* 746–753.

Clifford, B.R., Gunter, B., & McAleer, J.L. (1995). *Television and children.* Hillsdale, NJ: Erlbaum.

Clifton, R.K., Morrongiello, B.A., Kulig, J.W., & Dowd, J.M. (1981). Developmental changes in auditory localization in infancy. In R.N. Aslin, J.R. Alberts, & M.R. Petersen (Eds.), *Development of perception* (Vol. 1). Orlando, FL: Academic Press.

Clifton, R.K., Muir, D.W., Ashmead, D.H., & Clarkson, M.G. (1993). Is visually guided reaching in early infancy a myth? *Child Development, 64,* 1099–1110.

Clinton Smith, J. (2004). The current epidemic of childhood obesity and its implications for future coronary heart disease. *Pediatric Clinics of North America, 51,* 1679–1695.

Cnattingius, S., Bergström, R., Lipworth, L., & Kramer, M.S. (1998). Prepregnancy weight and the risk of adverse pregnancy outcomes. *New England Journal of Medicine, 338,* 147–152.

Cnattingius, S., Signorello, L.B., Anneren, G., Classon, B., Ekbom, A., Ljunger, E., Blot, W.J., McLaughlin, J.K., Petersson, G., Rane, A., & Granath, F. (2000). Caffeine intake and the risk of first-trimester spontaneous abortion. *New England Journal of Medicine, 343,* 1839–1845.

Cochran, M., Larner, M., Riley, D., Gunnarson, L., & Henderson, C. (1990). *Extending families: The social networks of parents and their children.* New York: Cambridge University Press.

Cohen, G.J. (2000). *American Academy of Pediatrics guide to your child's sleep: Birth through adolescence.* New York: Villard Books.

Cohen, G.L., & Sherman, D.K. (2005). Stereotype threat and the social and scientific contexts of the race achievement gap. *American Psychologist, 60,* 270–271.

Cohen, L.B. (1995). Violent video games: Aggression, arousal, and desensitization in young adolescent boys. Doctoral dissertation, University of Southern California, 1995. *Dissertation Abstracts International, 57* (2-B), 1463. (University Microfilms No. 9616947)

Cohen, L.B., & Cashon, C.H. (2006). Infant cognition. In W. Damon & R. Lerner (Eds.), *Handbook of child psychology* (6th ed.). New York: Wiley.

Cohn, A., & Canter, A. (2003). *Bullying: Facts for schools and parents.* Washington, DC: National Association of School Psychologists Center.

Cohn, J.F., & Tronick, E.Z. (1988). Mother-infant face-to-face interaction. Influence is bidirectional and unrelated to periodic cycles in either partner's behavior. *Developmental Psychology, 24,* 396–397.

Coie, J.D. (2004). The impact of negative social experiences on the development of antisocial behavior. In J.B. Kupersmidt & K.A. Dodge (Eds.), *Children's peer relations: From development to intervention.* Washington, DC: American Psychological Association.

Coie, J.D., & Dodge, K.A. (1998). Aggression and antisocial behavior, In W. Damon (Ed.), *Handbook of child psychology* (5th ed., Vol. 3). New York: Wiley.

Colangelo, N.C., Assouline, S.G., & Gross, M.U.M. (2004). *A nation deceived: How schools hold back America's brightest students.* Available on the Internet at http://nationdeceived.org/

Colapinto, J. (2000). *As nature made him.* New York: Simon & Schuster.

Colby, A., Kohlberg, L., Gibbs, J., & Lieberman, M. (1983). A longitudinal study of moral judgment. *Monographs of the Society for Research in Child Development, 48* (21, Serial No. 201).

Cole, C.F., Richman, B.A., & Brown, S.K. (2001). The world of *Sesame Street* research. In S.M. Fisch & R.T. Truglio (Eds.), *"G" is for growing: Thirty years of research on children and* Sesame Street. Mahwah, NJ: Erlbaum.

Cole, M. (2005). Culture in development. In M.H. Bornstein & M.E. Lamb (Eds.), *Developmental science* (5th ed.). Mahwah, NJ: Erlbaum.

Cole, M. (2006). Culture and cognitive development in phylogenetic, historical, and ontogenetic perspective. In W. Damon & R. Lerner (Eds.), *Handbook of child psychology* (6th ed.). New York: Wiley.

Coles, R. (1970). *Erik H. Erikson: The growth of his work.* Boston: Little, Brown.

Coley, R. (2001). *Differences in the gender gap: Comparisons across racial/ethnic groups in the United States.* Princeton, NJ: Educational Testing Service.

Coley, R.L., Morris, J.E., & Hernandez, D. (2004). Out-of-school care and problem behavior trajectories among low-income adolescents: Individual, family, and neighborhood characteristics as added risks. *Child Development, 75,* 948–965.

Coll, C.G., Bearer, E.L., & Lerner, R.M. (Eds.). (2004). *Nature and nurture.* Mahwah, NJ: Erlbaum.

Coll, C.G., & Pachter, L.M. (2002). Ethnic and minority parenting. In M.H. Bornstein (Ed.), *Handbook of parenting* (2nd ed., Vol. 4). Mahwah, NJ: Erlbaum.

Coll, C.T.G., Erkut, S., Alarcon, O., Garcia, H.A.V., & Tropp, L. (1995, March). *Puerto Rican adolescents and families: Lessons in construct and instrument development.* Paper presented at the meeting of the Society for Research in Child Development, Indianapolis.

Collins, W.A. (2002, April). *More than myth: The developmental significance of romantic relationships during adolescence.* Paper presented at the meeting of the Society for Research in Adolescence, New Orleans.

Collins, W.A., Harris, M., & Susman, A. (1995). Parenting during middle childhood. In M.H. Bornstein (Ed.), *Handbook of parenting* (Vol. 1). Hillsdale, NJ: Erlbaum.

Collins, W.A., Hennighausen, K.H., & Sroufe, L.A. (1998, June). *Developmental precursors of intimacy in romantic relationships: A longitudinal analysis.* Paper presented at the International Conference on Personal Relationships, Saratoga Springs, NY.

Collins, W.A., Maccoby, E.E., Steinberg, L., Hetherington, E.M., & Bornstein, M.H. (2000). Contemporary research on parenting: The case for nature and nurture. *American Psychologist, 55,* 218–232.

Collins, W.A., Maccoby, E.E., Steinberg, L., Hetherington, E.M., & Bornstein, M.H. (2001). Toward nature WITH nurture. *American Psychologist, 56,* 171–173.

Collins, W.A., & Madsen, S.D. (2002). Parenting during middle childhood. In M.H. Bornstein (Ed.), *Handbook of parenting* (2nd ed., Vol. 1). Mahwah, NJ: Erlbaum.

Collins, W.A., & Steinberg, L. (2006). Adolescent development in interpersonal context. In W. Damon & R. Lerner (Eds.), *Handbook of child psychology* (6th ed.). New York: Wiley.

Colman, R.A., & Widom, C.S. (2004). Childhood abuse and neglect and adult intimate relationships: A prospective study. *Child Abuse and Neglect, 28,* 1133–1151.

Comer, J.P. (1988). Educating poor minority children. *Scientific American, 259,* 42–48.

Comer, J.P., Haynes, N.M., Joyner, E.T., & Ben-Avie, M. (1996). *Rallying the whole village: The Comer process for reforming urban education.* New York: Teachers College Press.

Committee on Drugs. (2000). Use of psychoactive medication during pregnancy and possible effects on the fetus and newborn. *Pediatrics, 105,* 880–887.

Committee on Fetus and Newborn. (2000). Prevention and management of pain and stress in the newborn. *Pediatrics, 105,* 454–461.

Commoner, B. (2002). Unraveling the DNA myth: The spurious foundation of genetic engineering. *Harper's Magazine, 304,* 39–47.

Compas, B.E. (2004). Processes of risk and resilience during adolescence: Linking contexts and individuals. In R. Lerner & L. Steinberg (Eds.), *Handbook of adolescent psychology.* New York: Wiley.

Compas, B.E., Connor-Smith, J.K., Saltzman, H., Thomsen, A.H., & Wadsworth, M.E. (2001). Coping with stress during childhood and adolescence. *Psychological Bulletin, 127,* 87–127.

Compas, B.E., & Grant, K.E. (1993, March). *Stress and adolescent depressive symptoms: Underlying mechanisms and processes.* Paper presented at the biennial meeting of the Society for Research in Child Development, New Orleans.

Comstock, G., & Scharrer, E. (2006). Media and popular culture. In W. Damon & R. Lerner (Eds.), *Handbook of child psychology* (6th ed.). New York: Wiley.

Condry, K.F., Smith, W.C., & Spelke, E.S. (2001). Development of perceptual organization. In F. Lacerda, C. von Hofsten, & M. Heimann (Eds.), *Emerging cognitive abilities in infancy.* Mahwah, NJ: Erlbaum.

Conduct Problems Prevention Research Group. (2002). Evaluation of the first 3 years of the Fast Track prevention trial with children at high risk for adolescent conduct problems. *Journal of Abnormal Child Psychology, 30,* 19–35.

Conduct Problems Prevention Research Group. (2004). The Fast Track experiment: Translating the developmental model into a preventive design. In J.B. Kupersmidt & K.A. Dodge (Eds.), *Children's peer relations: From development to intervention.* Washington, DC: American Psychological Association.

Conger, R., & Reuter, M. (1996). Siblings, parents, and peers: A longitudinal study of social influences in adolescent risk for alcohol use and abuse. In G.H. Brody (Ed.), *Sibling relationships: Their causes and consequences.* Norwood, NJ: Ablex.

Conger, R.D., & Chao, W. (1996). Adolescent depressed mood. In R.L. Simons (Ed.), *Understanding differences between divorced and intact families: Stress, interaction, and child outcome.* Thousand Oaks, CA: Sage.

Conger, R.D., & Ge, X. (1999). Conflict and cohesion in parent-adolescent relations: Changes in emotional expression. In M.J. Cox & J. Brooks-Gunn (Eds.), *Conflict and cohesion in families.* Mahwah, NJ: Erlbaum.

Conger, R.D., Lorenz, F.O., & Wickrama, K.A.S. (2004). Changing families in changing times. In R.D. Conger, F.O. Lorenz, & K.A.S. Wickrama (Eds.), *Continuity and change in family relations.* Mahwah, NJ: Erlbaum.

Connolly, J., Craig, W., Goldberg, A., & Pepler, D. (2004). Mixed-gender groups, dating, and romantic relationships in early adolescence. *Journal of Research on Adolescence, 14,* 185–207.

Connolly, J., Furman, W., & Konarski, R. (1995, April). *The role of social networks in the emergence of romantic relationships in adolescence.* Paper presented at the meeting of the Society for Research in Child Development, Indianapolis.

Connolly, J., Furman, W., & Konarski, R. (2000). The role of peers in the emergence of heterosexual romantic relationships in adolescence. *Child Development, 71,* 1395–1408.

Connolly, J., & Goldberg, A. (1999). Romantic relationships in adolescence: The role of friends and peers in their emergence and development. In W. Furman, B.B. Brown, & C. Feiring (Eds.), *The development of romantic relationships in adolescence.* New York: Cambridge University Press.

Connolly, J., & Stevens, V. (1999, April). *Best friends, cliques, and young adolescents' romantic involvement.* Paper presented at the meeting of the Society for Research in Child Development, Albuquerque.

Cook, M., & Birch, R. (1984). Infant perception of the shapes of tilted plane forms. *Infant Behavior and Development, 7,* 389–402.

Cooper, C.R., & Ayers-Lopez, S. (1985). Family and peer systems in early adolescence: New models of the role of relationships in development. *Journal of Early Adolescence, 5,* 9–22.

Cooper, C.R., Cooper, R.G., Azmitia, M., Chavira, G., & Gullatt, Y. (2002). Bridging multiple worlds: How African American and Latino youth in academic outreach programs navigate math pathways to college. *Applied Developmental Science, 6,* 73–87.

Cooper, C.R., Garcia Coll, C.T., Bartko, W.T., Davis, H.M., & Chatman, C. (Eds.). (2005). *Developmental pathways through middle childhood.* Mahwah, NJ: Erlbaum.

Cooper, C.R., & Grotevant, H.D. (1989, April). *Individuality and connectedness in the family and adolescent's self and relational competence.* Paper presented at the meeting of the Society for Research in Child Development, Kansas City.

Cooper, C.R., Grotevant, H.D., Moore, M.S., & Condon, S.M. (1982, August). *Family support and conflict: Both foster adolescent identity and role taking.* Paper presented at the meeting of the American Psychological Association, Washington, DC.

Coopersmith, S. (1967). *The antecedents of self-esteem.* San Francisco: W.H. Freeman.

Cooter, R.B. (Ed.). (2004). *Perspectives on rescuing urban literacy education.* Mahwah, NJ: Erlbaum.

Corrigan, R. (1981). The effects of task and practice on search for invisibly displaced objects. *Developmental Review, 1,* 1–17.

Corsini, R.J. (1999). *The dictionary of psychology.* Philadelphia: Brunner/Mazel.

Cortesi, F., Giannotti, F., Sebastiani, T., & Vagnoni, C. (2004). Cosleeping and sleep behavior in Italian school-aged children. *Journal of Developmental and Behavioral Pediatrics, 25,* 28–33.

Cosmides, L., Tooby, J., Cronin, H., & Curry, O. (Eds.). (2003). *What is evolutionary psychology? Explaining the new science of the mind.* New Haven, CT: Yale University Press.

Cote, J.E., & Levine, C. (1988). On critiquing the identity crisis paradigm: A rejoinder to Waterman. *Developmental Review, 8,* 209–218.

Council of Economic Advisors. (2000). *Teens and their parents in the 21st century: An examination of trends in teen behavior and the role of parent involvement.* Washington, DC: Author.

Courage, M.L., Howe, M.L., & Squires, S.E. (2004). Individual differences in 3.5 month olds' visual attention: What do they predict at 1 year? *Infant Behavior and Development, 127,* 19–30.

Cowan, C.P., & Cowan, P.A. (2000). *When partners become parents.* Mahwah, NJ: Erlbaum.

Cowan, P.A., Cowan, C.P., Ablow, J.C., Johnson, V.K., & Measelle, J.R. (Eds.). (2005). *The family context in children's adaptation to elementary school.* Mahwah, NJ: Erlbaum.

Cowley, G. (1998, April 6). Why children turn violent. *Newsweek,* 24–25.

Cox, B.J., Enns, M.W., & Clara, I.P. (2004). Psychological dimensions associated with suicidal ideation and attempts in the National Comorbidity Study. *Suicide and Life-Threatening Behavior, 34,* 209–219.

Cox, J.L., Holden, J.M., & Sagovsky, R. (1987). Detection of postnatal depression: Development of the 10-items Edinburgh Postnatal Depression Scale. *British Journal of Psychiatry, 150,* 782–786.

Cox, M.J., Burchinal, M., Taylor, L.C., Frosch, B., Goldman, B., & Kanoy, K. (2004). The transition to parenting: Continuity and change in early parenting behavior and attitudes. In R.D. Conger, F.O. Lorenz, & K.A.S. Wickrama (Eds.), *Continuity and change in family relations.* Mahwah, NJ: Erlbaum.

Cox, M.J., & Paley, B. (2003). Understanding families as systems. *Current Directions in Psychological Science, 12,* 193–196.

Crane, D.R., & Marshall, E.S. (Eds.). (2005). *Handbook of families and health.* Thousand Oaks, CA: Sage.

Crawford, M., & Unger, R. (2004). *The psychology of women* (3rd ed.). New York: McGraw-Hill.

Cress, S.W. (2004). Assessing standards in the "real" kindergarten classroom. *Early Childhood Education Journal, 32,* 95–99.

Crick, N.R. (2005, April). *Gender and psychopathology.* Paper presented at the meeting of the Society for Research in Child Development, Atlanta.

Crockenberg, S.B. (1986). Are temperamental differences in babies associated with predictable differences in caregiving? In J.V. Lerner & R.M. Lerner (Eds.), *Temperament and social interaction during infancy and childhood.* San Francisco: Jossey-Bass.

Crocker, L. (2005). Teaching FOR the test. In R.P. Phelps (Ed.), *Defending standardized testing.* Mahwah, NJ: Erlbaum.

Cromer, R. (1987). Receptive language in the mentally retarded: Processes and diagnostic distinctions. In R. Schiefelbusch & L. Lloyd (Eds.), *Language perspectives: Acquisition, retardation, and intervention.* Baltimore: University Park Press.

Crossman, A.M., Scullin, M.H., & Melnyk, L. (2004). Individual and developmental differences in suggestibility. *Applied Cognitive Psychology, 18,* 941–945.

Crouter, A.C., & Booth, A. (Eds.). (2003). *Children's influence on family dynamics.* Mahwah, NJ: Erlbaum.

Crouter, A.C., & Booth, A. (Eds.). (2004). *Work-family challenges for low-income parents and their children.* Mahwah, NJ: Erlbaum.

Crouter, A.C., & McHale, S. (2005). The long arm of the job revisited: Parenting in dual-earner families. In T. Luster & L. Okagaki (Eds.), *Parenting: An ecological perspective* (2nd ed.). Mahwah, NJ: Erlbaum.

Crowley, K., Callahan, M.A., Tenenbaum, H.R., & Allen, E. (2001). Parents explain more to boys than to girls during shared scientific thinking. *Psychological Science, 12,* 258–261.

Cruz, O.L., Kasse, C.A., & Leonhart, F.D. (2003). Efficacy of surgical treatment of chronic otitis media. *Otolaryngology, Head, and Neck Surgery, 128,* 263–266.

Csikszentmihalyi, M. (1996). *Creativity.* New York: HarperCollins.

Cuéllar, I., Siles, R.I., & Bracamontes, E. (2004). Acculturation: A psychological construct of continuing relevance for Chicana/o psychology. In R.J. Velasquez, B.W. McNeil, & L.M. Arellano (Eds.), *The handbook of Chicano psychology and mental health.* Mahwah, NJ: Erlbaum.

Cullen, K. (2001). *Context and eating behavior in children.* Unpublished research, Children's Nutrition Research Center, Baylor School of Medicine, Houston.

Cullen, M.J., Hardison, C.M., & Sackett, P.R. (2004). Using SAT-grade and ability-job job performance relationships to test predictions derived from stereotype threat theory. *Journal of Applied Psychology, 89,* 220–230.

Cummings, E.M. (1987). Coping with background anger in early childhood. *Child Development, 58,* 976–984.

Cummings, E.M., Braungart-Rieker, J.M., & Du Rocher-Schudlich, T. (2003). Emotion and personality development. In I.B. Weiner (Ed.), *Handbook of psychology* (Vol. 6). New York: Wiley.

Cummings, E.M., & Davies, P.T. (2002). Effects of marital conflict on children: Recent advances and emerging themes in process-oriented research. *Journal of Child Psychology and Psychiatry, 43,* 31–63.

Cummings, E.M., Goeke-Morey, M.C., Papp, L.M., & Dukewich, T.L. (2002). Children's responses to mothers' and fathers' emotionality and tactics in marital conflict in the home. *Journal of Family Psychology, 16,* 478–492.

Cummings, M. (2006). *Human heredity* (7th ed.). Pacific Grove, CA: Brooks Cole.

Cunningham, P.M. (2005). *Phonics they use* (4th ed.). Boston: Allyn & Bacon.

Curley, J.P., Barton, S., Surani, A., & Keverne, E.B. (2004). Coadaptation of mother and infant regulated by a paternally expressed imprinted gene. *Proceedings of the Royal Society of London: Biological Sciences, 27,* 1303–1309.

Curran, K., DuCette, J., Eisenstein, J., & Hyman, I.A. (2001, August). *Statistical analysis of the cross-cultural data: The third year.* Paper presented at the meeting of the American Psychological Association, San Francisco, CA.

Curtiss, S. (1977). *Genie.* New York: Academic Press.

Cushner, K.H. (2003). *Human diversity in action: Developing multicultural competencies for the classroom* (2nd ed.). New York: McGraw-Hill.

Cushner, K.H. (2006). *Human diversity in action* (3rd ed.). New York: McGraw-Hill.

Cushner, K.H., McClelland, A., & Safford, P. (2006). *Human diversity in action: An integrative approach* (5th ed.). New York: McGraw-Hill.

D'Angelo, B., & Wierzbicki, M. (2003). Relations of daily hassles with both anxious and depressed mood in students. *Psychological Reports, 92,* 416–418.

D'Augelli, A.R. (1991). Gay men in college: Identity processes and adaptations. *Journal of College Student Development, 32,* 140–146.

Dabbs, J.M., Jr., Frady, R.I., Carr, T.S., & Besch, M.F. (1987). Saliva, testosterone, and criminal violence in young adult prison inmates. *Psychosomatic Medicine, 49,* 174–182.

Dabbs, J.M., Jr., & Morris, R. (1990). Testosterone, social class, and antisocial behavior in a sample of 4,462 men. *Psychological Science, 1,* 209–211.

Dahl, R.E. (2004). Adolescent brain development: A period of vulnerabilities and opportunities. *Annals of the New York Academy of Sciences, 1021,* 1–22.

Dale, P., & Goodman, J. (2004). Commonality and differences in vocabulary growth. In M. Tomasello & D.I. Slobin (Eds.), *Beyond nature-nurture.* Mahwah, NJ: Erlbaum.

Daley, T.C., Whaley, S.E., Sigman, M.D., Espinosa, M.P., & Neumann, C. (2003). IQ on the rise: The Flynn effect in rural Kenyan children. *Psychological Science, 14,* 215–219.

Damon, W. (1988). *The moral child.* New York: Free Press.

Damon, W. (1995). *Greater expectations.* New York: Free Press.

Damon, W., & Hart, D. (1988). *Self-understanding in childhood and adolescence.* New York: Cambridge University Press.

Danielson, C.K., De Arellano, M.A., Kilpatrick, D.G., Saunders, B.E., & Resnick, H.S. (2005). Child maltreatment in depressed adolescents: Differences in symptomatology based on history of abuse. *Child Maltreatment, 10,* 37–48.

Darwin, C. (1859). *On the origin of species.* London: John Murray.

Darwin, C. (1965). *The expression of the emotions in man and animals.* Chicago: University of Chicago Press. (Original work published 1872)

Dasen, P.R. (1977). Are cognitive processes universal? A contribution to cross-cultural Piagetian psychology. In N. Warran (Ed.), *Studies in cross-cultural psychology* (Vol. 1). London: Academic Press.

Dattilio, F.M. (Ed.). (2001). *Case studies in couple and family therapy.* New York: Guilford.

Davey, M., Goettler Eaker, D., Stone Fish, L., & Klock, K. (2003). Ethnic identity in an American white minority group, *Identity, 3,* 143–158.

Davidson, D. (1996). The effects of decision characteristics on children's selective search of predecisional information. *Acta Psychologia, 92,* 263–281.

Davidson, J., & Davidson, B. (2004). *Genius denied: How to stop wasting our brightest young minds.* New York: Simon & Schuster.

Davies, J., & Brember, I. (1999). Reading and mathematics attainments and self-esteem in years 2 and 6—an eight-year cross-sectional study. *Educational Studies, 25,* 145–157.

Davis, A.E., Hyatt, G., & Arrasmith, D. (1998, February). "I Have a Dream" program. *Class One Evaluation Report.* Portland, OR: Northwest Regional Education Laboratory.

Davis, B.E., Moon, R.Y., Sachs, H.C., & Ottolini, M.C. (1998). Effects of sleep position on infant motor development. *Pediatrics, 102,* 1135–1140.

Davis, L., & Keyser, J. (1997). *Becoming the parent you want to be.* New York: Broadway Books.

Daws, D. (2000). *Through the night.* San Francisco: Free Association Books.

Day, N.L., Leech, S.L., Richardson, G.A., Cornelius, M.D., Robles, N., & Larkby, C. (2002). Prenatal alcohol exposure predicts continued deficits in offspring size at 14 years of age. *Alcohol: Clinical and Experimental Research, 26,* 1584–1591.

Day, R.D., & Lamb, M.E. (Eds.). (2004). *Conceptualizing and measuring father involvement.* Mahwah, NJ: Erlbaum.

Day, R.H., & McKenzie, B.E. (1973). Perceptual shape contancy in early infancy. *Perception, 2,* 315–320.

Day-Stirk, F. (2005). The big push for normal birth. *RCM Midwives, 8,* 18–20.

de Bellis, M.D., Keshavan, M.S., Beers, S.R., Hall, J., Frustaci, K., Masalehdan, A., & Boring, N.J. (2001). Sex differences in brain maturation during childhood and adolescence. *Cerebral Cortex, 11,* 552–557.

de la Rochebrochard, E., & Thonneau, P. (2002). Paternal age and maternal age are risk factors for miscarriage: Results of a multicentre European study. *Human Reproduction, 17,* 1649–1656.

de Villiers, J.G., & de Villiers, P.A. (1999). Language development. In M.H. Bornstein & M.E. Lamb (Eds.), *Developmental psychology: An advanced textbook* (4th ed.). Mahwah, NJ: Erlbaum.

de Vries, P. (2005). Lessons from home: Scaffolding vocal improvisation and song acquisition in a 2-year-old. *Early Childhood Education Journal, 32,* 307–312.

De, D. (2005). Sickle cell anemia. *British Journal of Nursing, 14,* 447–450.

Deater-Deckard, K., & Dodge, K. (1997). Externalizing behavior problems and discipline revisited: Non-linear effects and variation by culture, context and gender. *Psychological Inquiry, 8,* 161–175.

DeCasper, A.J., & Spence, M.J. (1986). Prenatal maternal speech influences newborn's perception of speech sounds. *Infant Behavior & Development, 9,* 133–150.

Decca, L., Daldoss, C., Fratelli, N., Lojacono, A., Slompo, M., Stegher, C., Valcamonico, A., & Frusca, T. (2004). Labor course and delivery in epidural amnesia: A case-control study. *Journal of Maternal-Fetal and Neonatal Medicine, 16,* 115–118.

deCharms, R. (1984). Motivation enhancement in educational settings. In R. Ames & C. Ames (Eds.), *Research on motivation in education* (Vol. 1). Orlando: Academic Press.

Deci, E. (1975). *Intrinsic motivation*. New York: Plenum Press.

Deci, E., & Ryan, R. (1994). Promoting self-determined education. *Scandinavian Journal of Educational Research, 38*, 3–14.

Deci, E.L., Koestner, R., & Ryan, R.M. (2001). Extrinsic rewards and intrinsic motivation in education: Reconsidered once again. *Review of Educational Research, 71*, 1–28.

DeLoache, J.S. (1989). The development of representation in young children. In H.W. Reese (Ed.), *Advances in child development and behavior*. New York: Academic Press.

DeLoache, J.S. (2001). The symbol–mindedness of young children. In W.W. Hartup & R.A. Weinberg (Eds.), *Child psychology in retrospect and prospect*. Mahwah, NJ: Erlbaum.

DeLoache, J.S. (2004). Early development of the understanding and use of symbolic artifacts. In U. Goswami (Ed.), *Blackwell handbook of childhood cognitive development*. Malden, MA: Blackwell.

DeLoache, J.S., Miller, K.F., & Pierroutsakos, S.L. (1998). Reasoning and problem solving. In D. Kuhn & R.S. Siegler (Eds.), *Handbook of child psychology* (5th ed., Vol. 2). New York: Wiley.

Demetriou, A. (2001, April). *Towards a comprehensive theory of intellectual development: Integrating psychometric and post–Piagetian theories*. Paper presented at the meeting of the Society for Research in Child Development, Minneapolis.

Demetriou, A., Christou, C., Spanoudis, G., & Platsidou, M. (2002). The development of mental processing: Efficiency, working memory, and thinking. *Monographs of the Society for Research in Child Development, 67* (1, Serial No. 268).

Demonet, J.F., Thierry, G., & Cardebat, D. (2005). Renewal of the neurophysiology of language: Functional neuroimaging. *Physiological Reviews, 85*, 49–95.

Demorest, R.A., & Landry, G.L. (2003). Prevention of pediatric sports injuries. *Current Sports Medicine Reports, 2*, 337–343.

Demorest, R.A., & Landry, G.L. (2004). Training issues in elite young athletes. *Current Sports Medicine Reports, 3*, 167–172.

Dempster, F.N. (1981). Memory span: Sources of individual and developmental differences. *Psychological Bulletin, 80*, 63–100.

Denham, S.A. (1998). *Emotional development in young children*. New York: Guilford.

Denham, S.A., Blair, K.A., DeMulder, E., Levitas, J., Sawyer, K., Averbach-Major, S., & Queenan, P. (2003). Preschool emotional competence: Pathway to social competence? *Child Development, 74*, 238–256.

Denham, S.A., Cook, M., & Zoller, D. (1992). Maternal emotional responsiveness to toddlers' social-emotional functioning. *Journal of Child Psychology and Psychiatry, 34*, 715–728.

Denmark, F.L. (2004). Looking ahead: Concluding remarks. *Sex Roles, 51*, 367–369.

Denmark, F.L., Russo, N.F., Frieze, I.H., & Eschuzur, J. (1988). Guidelines for avoiding sexism in psychological research: A report of the ad hoc committee on nonsexist research. *American Psychologist, 43*, 582–585.

Dennis, C.L. (2004). Can we identify mothers at risk for postpartum depression in the immediate postpartum period using the Edinburgh Postnatal Depression Scale? *Journal of Affective Disorders, 78*, 163–169.

Denny, C.B. (2001). Stimulant effects in attention deficit hyperactivity disorder. *Journal of Clinical Child Psychology, 30*, 98–109.

Denschlag, D., Tempfer, C., Kunze, M., Wolff, G., & Keck, C. (2004). Assisted reproductive techniques in patients with Klinefelter syndrome: A critical review. *Fertility and Sterility, 82*, 775–779.

DeRosier, M.E., & Marcus, S.R. (2005). Building friendships and combating bullying: Effectiveness of S.S.GRIN at one-year follow-up. *Journal of Clinical Child and Adolescent Psychology, 34*, 140–150.

Dettmer, P., Dyck, N., & Thurston, L.P. (2002). *Consultation, collaboration, and teamwork for students with special needs* (4th ed.). Boston: Allyn & Bacon.

Dewey, J. (1933). *How we think*. Lexington, MA: D.C. Heath.

Dewey, K.G. (2003). Is breastfeeding protective against childhood obesity? *Journal of Human Lactation, 19*, 9–18.

DeZolt, D.M., & Hull, S.H. (2001). Classroom and school climate. In J. Worell (Ed.), *Encyclopedia of women and gender*. San Diego: Academic Press.

Diamond, A.D. (1985). Development of the ability to use recall to guide action, as indicated by infants' performance on AB. *Child Development, 56*, 868–883.

Diamond, A.D. (2001). A model system for studying the role of dopamine in the prefrontal cortex during early development in humans: Early and continuously treated phenylketonuria. In C. Nelson & M. Luciana (Eds.), *Handbook of developmental cognitive neuroscience*. Cambridge, MA: MIT Press.

Diamond, L. (2003). Love matters: Romantic relations among sexual minority youth. In P. Florsheim (Ed.), *Adolescent romantic relations and sexual behavior*. Mahwah, NJ: Erlbaum.

Diamond, L., & Savin-Williams, R.C. (2003). The intimate relationships of sexual-minority youths. In G. Adams & M. Berzonsky (Eds.), *Blackwell handbook of adolescence*. Malden, MA: Blackwell.

Diamond, M., & Sigmundson, H.K. (1997). Sex reassignment at birth: Long-term review and clinical implications. *Archives of Pediatric and Adolescent Medicine, 151*, 298–304.

Diaz, C.F., Pelletier, C.M., & Provenzo, E.F. (2006). *Touch the future... teach!* Boston: Allyn & Bacon.

Diaz-Rico, L. (2004). *Teaching English learners*. Boston: Allyn & Bacon.

Dick, F., Dronkers, N.F., Pizzamiglio, L., Saygin, A.P., Small, S.L., & Wilson, S. (2004). *Languge and the brain*. Mahwah, NJ: Erlbaum.

Dickerscheid, J.D., Schwarz, P.M., Noir, S., & El-Taliawy, T. (1988). Gender concept development of preschool-aged children in the United States and Egypt. *Sex Roles, 18*, 669–677.

Diener, E., & Diener, M. (1995). Cross-cultural correlates of life satisfaction and self-esteem. *Journal of Personality and Social Psychology, 68*, 653–663.

Dietz, W.H., & Robinson, T.N. (2005). Clinical practice: Overweight children and adolescents. *New England Journal of Medicine, 352*, 2100–2109.

Dige, N., & Wik, G. (2005). Adult attention deficit hyperactivity disorder identified by neuropsychological testing. *International Journal of Neuroscience, 115*, 169–173.

DiGiorgio, L.F. (2005). Promoting breastfeeding to mothers in the Special Supplemental Nutrition Program for Women, Infants, and Children. *Journal of the American Diet Association, 105*, 716–717.

DiLalla, L.F. (2000). Development of intelligence: Current research and theories. *Journal of School Psychology, 38*, 3–8.

Dishion, T.J., Andrews, D.W., & Crosby, L. (1995). Antisocial boys and their friends in early adolescence: Relationship characteristics, quality, and interactional process. *Child Development, 66*, 139–151.

Dixon, L., Browne, K., & Hamilton-Giachritsis, C. (2005). Risk factors of parents abused as children: A mediational analysis of the intergenerational continuity of child maltreatment (Part I). *Journal of Child Psychology and Psychiatry and Allied Disciplines, 46*, 47–57.

Dodd, V.L. (2005). Implications of kangaroo care for growth and development in preterm infants. *Journal of Obstetrical, Gynecologic, and Neonatal Nursing, 34*, 218–222.

Dodge, K.A. (1993). Social cognitive mechanisms in the development of conduct disorder and depression. *Annual Review of Psychology, 44*, 559–584.

Dodge, K.A. (2001). The science of youth violence prevention: Progressing from developmental psychopathology to efficacy to effectiveness in public policy. *American Journal of Preventive Medicine, 20*, 63–70.

Dodge, K.A., Coie, J.D., & Lynam, D.R. (2006). Aggression and antisocial behavior in youth. In W. Damon & R. Lerner (Eds.), *Handbook of child psychology* (6th ed.). New York: Wiley.

Dodge, K.A., & Pettit, G.S. (2003). A biopsychosocial model of the development of chronic conduct problems in adolescence. *Developmental Psychology, 39,* 349–371.

Doherty, W.J., & Beaton, J.M. (2004). Mothers and fathers parenting together. In A.L. Vangelisti (Ed.), *Handbook of family communication.* Mahwah, NJ: Erlbaum.

Dolcini, M.M., Coh, L.D., Adler, N.E., Millstein, S.G., Irwin, C.E., Kegeles, S.M., & Stone, G.C. (1989). Adolescent egocentrism and feelings of invulnerability: Are they related? *Journal of Early Adolescence, 9,* 409–418.

Donnerstein, E. (2001). Media violence. In J. Worell (Ed.), *Encyclopedia of gender and women.* San Diego: Academic Press.

Donnerstein, E. (2002). The Internet. In V.C. Strasburger & B.J. Wilson, *Children, adolescents, and the media.* Newbury Park, CA: Sage.

Donovan, C.A., & Smolkin, L.B. (2002). Children's genre knowledge: An examination of K–5 student's performance on multiple tasks providing different levels of scaffolding. *Reading Research Quarterly, 37,* 428–465.

Dorn, L.D., Williamson, D.E., & Ryan, N.D. (2002, April). *Maturational hormone differences in adolescents with depression and risk for depression.* Paper presented at the meeting of the Society for Research on Adolescence, New Orleans.

Dornbusch, S., & Kaufman, J. (2001). The social structure of the U.S. high school. In T. Urdan & F. Pajares (Eds.), *Adolescence and education.* Greenwich, CT: IAP.

Dorr, A., Rabin, B.E., & Irlen, S. (2002). Parents, children, and the media. In M.H. Bornstein (Ed.), *Handbook of parenting* (2nd ed., Vol. 5). Mahwah, NJ: Erlbaum.

Downey, G., & Bonica, C.A. (1997, April). *Characteristics of early adolescent dating relationships.* Paper presented at the meeting of the Society for Research in Child Development, Washington, DC.

Downey, G., & Coyne, J.C. (1990). Children of depressed parents: An integrative review. *Psychological Bulletin, 108,* 50–76.

Doyle, T.F., Bellugi, U., Korenberg, J.R., & Graham, J. (2004). "Everybody in the world is my friend" hypersociability in young children with Williams syndrome. *American Journal of Medical Genetics, 214A,* 263–273.

Drake, A.J., & Walker, B.R. (2004). The intergenerational effects of fetal programming: Non-genomic mechanisms for the inheritance of low birth weight and cardiovascular risk. *Journal of Endocrinology, 180,* 1–16.

Drewnowski, A., & Spector, S.E. (2004). Poverty and obesity: The role of energy density and energy costs. *American Journal of Clinical Nutrition, 79,* 6–16.

Driesen, N.R., & Raz, N. (1995). The influence of sex, age, and handedness on corpus callosum morphology: A meta-analysis. *Psychobiology, 23,* 240–247.

Droege, K.L. (2004). Turning accountability on its head. *Phi Delta Kappan, 85,* 610–612.

Drongowski, R.A., Lee, D., Reynolds, P.I., Malviya, S., Harmon, C.S., Geiger, J., Lelli, J.L., & Coran, A.G. (2003). Increased respiratory symptoms following surgery in children exposed to environmental tobacco smoke. *Pediatric Anesthesiology, 13,* 304–310.

DuBois, D.L., & Karcher, M.J. (Eds.). (2005). *Handbook of youth mentoring.* Thousand Oaks, CA: Sage.

Dubowitz, H., Pitts, S.C., & Black, M.M. (2004). Measurement of three subtypes of child neglect. *Child Maltreatment, 9,* 344–356.

Duck, S.W. (1975). Personality similarity and friendship choices by adolescents. *European Journal of Social Psychology, 5,* 351–365.

Duffy, T.M., & Kirkley, J.R. (Eds.). (2004). *Learner-centered theory and practice in distance education.* Mahwah, NJ: Erlbaum.

Duggan, A., Fuddy, L., Burrell, L., Higman, S.M., McFarlane, E., Windham, A., & Sia, C. (2004). Randomized trial of statewide home visiting program to prevent child abuse: Impact in reducing parental risk factors. *Child Abuse & Neglect, 28,* 623–643.

Duncan, G.J., Brooks-Gunn, J., & Klebanov, P.K. (1994). Economic deprivation and early childhood development. *Child Development, 65.* 296–318.

Dunkel, C., & Kerpelman, J. (Eds.). (2004). *Possible selves: Theory, research, and application.* Huntington, NY: Nova.

Dunkel-Schetter, C. (1998). Maternal stress and preterm delivery. *Prenatal and Neonatal Medicine, 3,* 39–42.

Dunkel-Schetter, C., Gurang, R.A.R., Lobel, M., & Wadhwa, P.D. (2001). Stress processes in pregnancy and birth. In A. Baum, T.A. Revenson, & J.E. Singer (Eds.), *Handbook of health psychology.* Mahwah, NJ: Erlbaum.

Dunn, J., & Brown, J. (1994). Affect expression in the family, children's understanding of emotions, and their interactions with others. *Merrill-Palmer Quarterly, 40,* 120–137.

Dunn, J., Davies, L.C., O'Connor, T.G., & Sturgess, W. (2001). Family lives and friendships: The perspectives of children in step-, single-parent, and nonstep families. *Journal of Family Psychology, 15,* 272–287.

Dunn, J., & Kendrick, C. (1982). *Siblings.* Cambridge, MA: Harvard University Press.

Dunphy, D.C. (1963). The social structure of urban adolescent peer groups. *Society, 26,* 230–246.

Dunson, D.B., Baird, D.D., & Columbo, B. (2004). Increased fertility with age in men and women. *Obstetrics and Gynecology, 103,* 51–56.

Durkin, D. (2004). *Teaching them to read* (6th ed.). Boston: Allyn & Bacon.

Durkin, K. (1985). Television and sex-role acquisition: 1. Content. *British Journal of Social Psychology, 24,* 101–113.

Durodola, A., Kuti, O., Orji, E.O., & Ogunniyi, S.O. (2005). Rate of increase in oxytocin dose on the outcome of labor induction. *International Journal of Gynecology and Obstetrics, in press.*

Durrant, J.E. (2000). Trends in youth crime and well-being since the abolition of corporal punishment in Sweden. *Youth and Society, 3,* 437–455.

Durrant, R., & Ellis, B. (2003). Evolutionary psychology. In I.B. Weiner (Ed.), *Handbook of psychology* (Vol. III). New York: Wiley.

Dusek, J.B., & McIntyre, J.G. (2003). Self-concept and self-esteem development. In G. Adams & M. Berzonsky (Eds.), *Blackwell handbook of adolescence.* Malden, MA: Blackwell.

Dweck, C., & Elliott, E. (1983). Achievement motivation. In P. Mussen (Ed.), *Handbook of child psychology* (4th ed., Vol. 4). New York: Wiley.

Dweck, C., & Leggett, E. (1988). A social cognitive approach to motivation and personality. *Psychological Review, 95,* 256–273.

Dweck, C.S., Mangels, J.A., & Good, C. (2004). Motivational effects on attention, cognition, and performance. In D.Y. Dai & R.J. Sternberg (Eds.), *Motivation, emotion, and cognition.* Mahwah, NJ: Erlbaum.

Eagle, M. (2000). Psychoanalytic theory: History of the field. In A. Kazdin (Ed.), *Encyclopedia of psychology.* Washington, DC, & New York: American Psychological Association and Oxford University Press.

Eagly, A.H. (2000). Gender roles. In A. Kazdin (Ed.), *Encyclopedia of psychology.* Washington, DC, & New York: American Psychological Association and Oxford University Press.

Eagly, A.H. (2001). Social role theory of sex differences and similarities. In J. Worell (Ed.), *Encyclopedia of women and gender.* San Diego: Academic Press.

Eagly, A.H., & Crowley, M. (1986). Gender and helping behavior: A meta-analytic review of the social psychological literature. *Psychological Bulletin, 100,* 283–308.

Eagly, A.H., & Diekman, A.B. (2003). The malleability of sex differences in response to social roles. In L.G. Aspinwall & V.M. Staudinger (Eds.), A *psychology of human strengths.* Washington, DC: American Psychological Association.

Eagly, A.H., & Steffen, V.J. (1986). Gender and aggressive behavior: A meta-analytic review of the social psychological literature. *Psychological Bulletin, 100,* 309–330.

Eaves, L., Silberg, J., Foley, D., Bulik, C., Maes, H., Erkanli, A., Angold, A., Costello, E.J., & Worthman, C. (2004). Genetic and environmental influences on the relative timing of pubertal change. *Twin Research, 7,* 471–481.

Eaves, L.J., & Silberg, J.L. (2003). Modulation of gene expression by genetic and environmental heterogeneity in timing of developmental milestones. *Behavior Genetics, 33,* 1–6.

Eccles, J. (2004). Schools, academic motivation, and stage-environment fit. In R. Lerner & L. Steinberg (Eds.), *Handbook of adolescent psychology* (2nd ed.). New York: Wiley.

Eccles, J., Wigfield, A., & Byrnes, J. (2003). Cognitive development in adolescence. In I.B. Weiner (Ed.), *Handbook of psychology* (Vol. 6). New York: Wiley.

Eccles, J.S., & Midgley, C. (1989). Stage-environment fit: Developmentally appropriate classrooms for young adolescents. In C. Ames & R. Ames (Eds.), *Research on motivation in education* (Vol. 3). Orlando: Academic Press.

Eccles, J.S., & Roeser, R.W. (2005). School and community influences on human development. In M.H. Bornstein & M.E. Lamb (Eds.), *Developmental psychology* (5th ed.). Mahwah, NJ: Erlbaum.

Eccles, J.S., & Wigfield, A. (2002). Motivational beliefs, values, and goals. *Annual Review of Psychology* (Vol. 53). Palo Alto, CA: Annual Reviews.

Eccles, J.S., Wigfield, A., & Schiefele, U. (1998). Motivation to succeed. In W. Damon. (Ed.), *Handbook of child psychology* (5th ed., Vol. 3). New York: Wiley.

Edelman, M.W. (1995). *The state of America's children.* Washington, DC: The Children's Defense Fund.

Edelman, M.W. (1997, April). *Children, families, and social policy.* Paper presented at the meeting of the Society for Research in Child Development, Washington, DC.

Educational Testing Service. (1992, February). *Cross-national comparison of 9–13 year olds' science and math achievement.* Princeton, NJ: Educational Testing Service.

Edwards, C.P., & Liu, W. (2002). Parenting toddlers. In M.H. Bornstein (Ed.), *Handbook of parenting* (2nd ed., Vol. 1). Mahwah, NJ: Erlbaum.

Edwards, R., & Hamilton, M.A. (2004). You need to understand my gender role: An empirical test of Tannen's model of gender and communication. *Sex Roles, 50,* 491–504.

Egan, J.F., Benn, P.A., Zelop, C.M., Bolnick, A., Gianferrari, E., & Borgida, A.F. (2004). Down syndrome births in the United States from 1989 to 2001. *American Journal of Obstetrics and Gynecology, 191,* 1044–1048.

Egeland, B., & Carlson, B. (2004). Attachment and psychopathology. In L. Atkinson & S. Goldberg (Eds.), *Attachment issues in psychopathology and intervention.* Mahwah, NJ: Erlbaum.

Egeland, B., Jacobvitz, D., & Sroufe, L.A. (1988). Breaking the cycle of abuse. *New Directions for Child Development, 11,* 77–92.

Ehrhardt, A.A. (1987). A transactional perspective on the development of gender differences. In J.M. Reinisch, L.A. Rosenblum, & S.A. Sanders (Eds.), *Masculinity/femininity: Basic perspectives.* New York: Oxford University Press.

Eidelman, A.I., & Feldman, R. (2004). Positive effect of human milk on neurobehavioral and cognitive development of premature infants. *Advances in Experimental Medicine and Biology, 554,* 359–364.

Eiferman, R.R. (1971). Social play in childhood. In R. Herron & B. Sutton-Smith (Eds.), *Child's play.* New York: Wiley.

Eiger, M.S., & Olds, S.W. (1999). *The complete book of breastfeeding* (3rd ed.). New York: Bantam.

Eisenberg, N. (Ed.). (1982). *The development of prosocial behavior.* New York: Wiley.

Eisenberg, N. (1998). Introduction. In N. Eisenberg (Ed.), *Handbook of child psychology* (5th ed., Vol 3). New York: Wiley.

Eisenberg, N. (2001). Emotion-related regulation and its relation to quality of social functioning. In W.W. Hartup & R.A. Weinberg (Eds.), *Child psychology in retrospect and prospect.* Mahwah, NJ: Erlbaum.

Eisenberg, N., & Fabes, R.A. (1994). Emotional regulation and the development of social competence. In M. Clark (Ed.), *Review of personality and social psychology.* Newbury Park, CA: Sage.

Eisenberg, N., & Fabes, R.A. (1998). Prosocial development. In N. Eisenberg (Ed.), *Handbook of child psychology* (5th ed., Vol. 3). New York: Wiley.

Eisenberg, N., Fabes, R.A., & Spinrad, T.L. (2006). Prosocial development. In W. Damon & R. Lerner (Eds.), *Handbook of child psychology* (6th ed.). New York: Wiley.

Eisenberg, N., Gutherie, I.K., Murphy, B.C., Shepard, S.A., Cumberland, A., & Carlo, G. (1999). Consistency and development of prosocial dispositions: A longitudinal study. *Child Development, 70,* 1360–1372.

Eisenberg, N., Gutherie, I.K., Fabes, R.A., Shepard, S., Losoya, S., Murphy, B.C., & others. (2000). Prediction of elementary school children's externalizing problem behaviors from attentional and behavioral regulation and negative emotionality. *Child Development, 71,* 1367–1382.

Eisenberg, N., Martin, C.L., & Fabes, R.A. (1996). Gender development and gender effects. In D.C. Berliner & R.C. Calfee (Eds.), *Handbook of educational psychology.* New York: Macmillan.

Eisenberg, N., & Morris, A.S. (2004). Moral cognitions and prosocial responding in adolescence. In R. Lerner & L. Steinberg (Eds.), *Handbook of adolescent psychology.* New York: Wiley.

Eisenberg, N., Spinrad, T.L., & Smith, C.L. (2004). Emotion-related regulation: Its conceptualization, relations to social functioning, and socialization. In P. Philippot & R.S. Feldman (Eds.), *The regulation of emotion.* Mahwah, NJ: Erlbaum.

Eisenberg, N., & Valiente, C. (2002). Parenting and children's prosocial and moral development. In M.H. Bornstein (Ed.), *Handbook of parenting* (2nd ed.). Mahwah, NJ: Erlbaum.

Eisenberg, N., & Wang, V.O. (2003). Toward a positive psychology: Social developmental and cultural contributions. In L.G. Aspinwall & U.M. Staudinger (Eds.), *A psychology of human strengths.* Washington, DC: American Psychological Association.

Eisinger, F., & Burke, W. (2003). Breast cancer and breastfeeding. *Lancet, 361,* 176–177.

Eitle, D. (2005). The moderating effects of peer substance abuse on the family structure-adolescent substance use association: Quantity versus quality of parenting. *Addictive Behaviors, 30,* 963–980.

Ekwo, E.P., & Morwad, A. (2000). Maternal age and preterm births in a black population. *Pediatric Perinatal Epidemiology, 2,* 145–151.

Elder, G.H. (1980). Adolescence in historical perspective. In J. Adelson (Ed.), *Handbook of adolescent psychology.* New York: Wiley.

Elder, G.H., & Shanahan, M.J. (2006). The life course and human development. In W. Damon & R. Lerner (Eds.), *Handbook of child psychology* (6th ed.). New York: Wiley.

Eliakim, A., Frieland, O., Kowen, G., Wolach, B., & Nemet, D. (2004). Parental obesity and higher pre-intervention BMI reduce the likelihood of a multidisciplinary childhood obesity program to succeed—a clinical observation. *Journal of Pediatric Endocrinology and Metabolism, 17,* 1055–1071.

Elkind, D. (1976). *Child development and education: A Piagetian perspective.* New York: Oxford University Press.

Elkind, D. (1978). Understanding the young adolescent. *Adolescence, 13,* 127–134.

Elkind, D. (2004). Vygotsky's educational theory in cultural context. *Bulletin of the Menninger Clinic, 68,* 352–353.

Ely, R. (2005). Language and literacy in the school years. In J. Berko Gleason (Ed.), *The development of language* (6th ed.). Boston: Allyn & Bacon.

Emde, R.N., Gaensbauer, T.G., & Harmon, R.J. (1976). Emotional expression in infancy: A biobehavioral study. *Psychological Issues: Monograph Series, 10* (37).

Emery, C.A. (2003). Risk factors for injury in child and adolescent sport: A systematic review of the literature. *Clinical Journal of Sport Medicine, 13,* 256–268.

Emery, R.E. (1994). *Renegotiating family relationships.* New York: Guilford Press.

Emery, R.E., & Laumann-Billings, L. (1998). An overview of the nature, causes, and consequences of abusive family relationships. *American Psychologist, 53,* 121–135.

Emery, R.E., Laumann-Billings, L., Waldron, M.C., Sbarra, D.A., & Dillon, P. (2001). Child custody mediation and litigation: Custody, contact, and coparenting 12 years after initial dispute resolution. *Journal of Consulting and Clinical Psychology, 69,* 323–332.

Engels, R.C., Vermulst, A.A., Dubas, J.S., Bot, S.M., & Gerris, J. (2005). Long-term effects of family functioning and child characteristics on problem drinking in young adulthood. *European Addiction Research, 11,* 32–37.

England, L.J., Kendrick, J.S., Gargiullo, P.M., Zhniser, S.C., & Hannon, W.H. (2001). Measures of maternal tobacco exposure and infant birth weight at term. *American Journal of Epidemiology, 153,* 954–960.

Engler, A.J., Ludington-Hoe, S.M., Cusson, R.M., Adams, R., Bahnsen, M., Brumbaugh, E., Coates, P., Grief, J., McHargue, L., Ryan, D.L., Settle, M., & Williams, D. (2002). Kangaroo care: National survey of practice, knowledge, barriers, and perceptions. *American Journal of Maternal/Child Nursing, 27,* 146–153.

Enoch, M.A., & Goldman, D. (2002). Problem drinking and alcoholism: Diagnosis and treatment. *American Family Physician, 65,* 441–448.

Enright, R.D., Lapsley, D.K., Dricas, A.S., & Fehr, L.A. (1980). Parental influence on the development of adolescent autonomy and identity. *Journal of Youth and Adolescence, 9,* 529–546.

Epstein, J.L. (2001). *School, family, and community partnerships.* Boulder, CO: Westview Press.

Epstein, J.L., Sanders, M.G., Salinas, K.C., Simon, B.S., Jansorn, N.R., & Van Voorhis, F.L. (2002). *School, family, and community partnerships* (2nd ed.). Thousand Oaks, CA: Corwin Press.

Ericsson, K.A. (Ed.). (1996). *The road to excellence.* Mahwah, NJ: Erlbaum.

Ericsson, K.A., Krampe, R., & Tesch-Romer, C. (1993). The role of deliberate practice in the acquisition of expert performance. *Psychological Review, 100,* 363–406.

Erikson, E.H. (1950). *Childhood and society.* New York: W.W. Norton.

Erikson, E.H. (1962). *Young man Luther.* New York: W.W. Norton.

Erikson, E.H. (1968). *Identity: Youth and crisis.* New York: W.W. Norton.

Erikson, E.H. (1969). *Gandhi's truth.* New York: W.W. Norton.

Erikson, E.H. (2000). In A. Kazdin (Ed.), *Encyclopedia of psychology.* Washington, DC, & New York: American Psychological Association and Oxford University Press.

Erlick, A.C., & Starry, A.R. (1973, June). *Sources of information for career decisions.* Report of Poll No. 98, Purdue Opinion Panel.

Eskenazi, B., Stapleton, A.L., Kharrazi, M., & Chee, W.Y. (1999). Associations between maternal decaffeinated and caffeinated coffee consumption and fetal growth and gestational duration. *Epidemiology, 10,* 242–249.

Espelage, D.L., & Swearer, S.M. (Eds.). (2004). *Bullying in American schools.* Mahwah, NJ: Erlbaum.

Etaugh, C., & Bridges, J.S. (2004). *Psychology of women: A life-span perspective* (2nd ed.). Boston: Allyn & Bacon.

Etzel, R. (1988, October). *Children of smokers.* Paper presented at the meeting of the American Academy of Pediatrics, New Orleans.

Evans, B.J., & Whitfield, J.R. (Eds.). (1988). *Black males in the United States: An annotated bibliography from 1967 to 1987.* Washington, DC: American Psychological Association.

Evans, G.W. (2004). The environment of childhood poverty. *American Psychologist, 59,* 77–92.

Evans, G.W., & English, K. (2002). The environment of poverty: Multiple stressor exposure, psychophysiological stress, and socioemotional adjustment. *Child Development, 73,* 1238–1248.

Evans, M.I., Lluba, E., Landsberger, E.J., O'Brien, J.E., & Harrison, H.H. (2004). Impact of folic acid fortification in the United States: Markedly diminished high maternal serum alpha-fetoprotein values. *Obstetrics and Gynecology, 103,* 474–479.

Fabes, R.A., Eisenberg, N., Jones, S., Smith, M., Gutherie, I., Poulin, R., Shepard, S., & Friedman, J. (1999). Regulation, emotionality, and preschoolers' socially competent peer interactions. *Child Development, 70,* 432–442.

Fabes, R.A., Hanish, L.D., & Martin, C.L. (2003). Children at play: The role of peers in understanding the effects of child care. *Child Development, 74,* 1039–1043.

Fagan, J.F. (1992). Intelligence: A theoretical viewpoint. *Current Directions in Psychological Science, 1,* 82–86.

Fagot, B.J., Rodgers, C.S., & Leinbach, M.D. (2000). Theories of gender socialization. In T. Eckes & H.M. Trautner (Eds.), *The developmental social psychology of gender.* Mahwah, NJ: Erlbaum.

Fair Test. (2004). "No child left behind" after two years: A track record of failure. Retrieved online at http://www.fairtest.org.

Falbo, T., & Poston, D.L. (1993). The academic, personality, and physical outcomes of only children in China. *Child Development, 64,* 18–35.

Fang, J., Madhaven, S., & Alderman, M.H. (1999). Low birth weight: Race and maternal nativity—Impact of community income. *Pediatrics, 103,* e5.

Fantz, R.L. (1963). Pattern vision in newborn infants. *Science, 140,* 296–297.

Fasick, F.A. (1994). On the "invention" of adolescence. *Journal of Early Adolescence, 14,* 6–23.

Federal Interagency Forum on Child and Family Statistics. (2002). *Key national indicators of well-being.* Washington, DC: U.S. Government Printing Office.

Federenko, I.S., & Wadhwa, P.D. (2004). Women's mental health during pregnancy influences fetal and infant developmental and health outcomes. *CNS Spectrum, 9,* 198–206.

Fein, G.G. (1986). Pretend play. In D. Görlitz & J.F. Wohlwill (Eds.), *Curiosity, imagination, and play.* Hillsdale, NJ: Erlbaum.

Feinberg, M., & Hetherington, E.M. (2001). Differential parenting as a within-family variable. *Journal of Family Psychology, 15,* 22–37.

Feiring, C. (1996). Concepts of romance in 15-year-old adolescents. *Journal of Research on Adolescence, 6,* 181–200.

Fekkes, M., Pijpers, F.I., & Verloove-Vanhorick, S.P. (2004). Bullying behavior and associations with psychosomatic complaints and depression in victims. *Journal of Pediatrics, 144,* 17–22.

Feldhusen, J. (1999). Giftedness and creativity. In M.A. Runco & S. Prtizker (Eds.), *Encyclopedia of creativity.* San Diego: Academic Press.

Feldman, D.H. (1997, August). *Hitting middle C: Toward a more comprehensive domain for creativity research.* Paper presented at the meeting of the American Psychological Association, Chicago.

Feldman, R., Weller, A., Sirota, L., & Eidelman, A.I. (2002). Skin-to-skin contact (kangaroo care) promotes self-regulation in premature infants: Sleep-wake cyclicity, arousal modulation, and sustained exploration. *Developmental Psychology, 38,* 194–207.

Feldman, R., Weller, A., Sirota, L., & Eidelman, A.I. (2003). Testing a family intervention hypothesis: The contribution of mother-infant skin-to-skin (kangaroo care) to family interaction, proximity, and touch. *Journal of Family Psychology, 17,* 94–107.

Feldman, S.S., & Weinberger, D.A. (1994). Self-restraint as a mediator of family influences on boys' delinquent behavior: A longitudinal study. *Child Development, 65,* 195–211.

Felkner, M., Suarez, L., Hendricks, K., & Larsen, R. (2005). Implementation and outcomes of recommended folic acid supplementation in Mexican-American women with prior neural tube defect-affected pregnancies. *Preventive Medicine, 40,* 867–871.

Fenzel, L.M. (1994, February). *A prospective study of the effects of chronic strains on early adolescent self-worth and school adjustment.* Paper presented at the meeting of the Society for Research on Adolescence, San Diego.

Ferber, S.G., & Makhoul, J.R. (2004). The effect of skin-to-skin (kangaroo) care shortly after birth on the neurobehavioral responses of the term newborn. *Pediatrics, 113,* 858–865.

Ferguson, D.M., Harwood, L.J., & Beautrais, A.L. (1999). Is sexual orientation related to mental health problems and suicidality in young people? *Archives of General Psychiatry, 56,* 876–880.

Ferguson, D.M., Harwood, L.J., & Shannon, F.T. (1987). Breastfeeding and subsequent social adjustment in 6- to 8-year-old children. *Journal of Child Psychology and Psychiatry, 28,* 378–386.

Fernald, A. (2004). Hearing, listening, and understanding: Auditory development in infancy. In J.G. Bremner & A. Fogel (Eds.), *Blackwell handbook of infancy*. Malden, MA: Blackwell.

Fernandez, O., Sabharwal, M., Smiley, T., Pastuszak, A., Koren, G., & Einarson, T. (1998). Moderate to heavy caffeine consumption during pregnancy and relationship to spontaneous abortion and abnormal fetal growth: A meta-analysis. *Reproductive Toxicology, 12,* 435–444.

Fidalgo, Z., & Pereira, F. (2005). Sociocultural differences and the adjustment of mothers' speech to their children's cognitive and language comprehension skills. *Learning & Instruction, 15,* 1–21.

Field, A.E., Cambargo, C.A., Taylor, C.B., Berkey, C.S., Roberts, S.B., & Colditz, G.A. (2001). Peer, parent, and media influences on the development of weight concerns and frequent dieting among preadolescent and adolescent girls and boys. *Pediatrics, 107,* 54–60.

Field, T.M. (1998). Massage therapy effects. *American Psychologist, 53,* 1270–1281.

Field, T.M. (2000). Child abuse. In A. Kazdin (Ed.), *Encyclopedia of psychology.* Washington, DC, & New York: American Psychological Association and Oxford University Press.

Field, T.M. (2001). Massage therapy facilitates weight gain in preterm infants. *Current Directions in Psychological Science, 10,* 51–54.

Field, T.M. (2002). Infants' need for touch. *Human Development, 45,* 100–103.

Field, T.M. (2003). Stimulation of preterm infants. *Pediatrics in Review, 24,* 4–11.

Field, T.M., Grizzle, N., Scafidi, F., & Schanberg, S. (1996). Massage and relaxation therapies' effects on depressed adolescent mothers. *Adolescence, 31,* 903–911.

Field, T.M., Hernandez-Reif, M., Diego, M., Feijo, L., Vera, Y., & Gil, K. (2004). Massage therapy by parents improves early growth and development. *Infant Behavior & Development, 27,* 435–442.

Field, T.M., Hernandez-Reif, M., & Freedman, J. (2004, Fall). Stimulation programs for preterm infants. *SRCD Social Policy Reports, 28* (1), 1–20.

Field, T.M., Hernandez-Reif, M., Seligman, S., Krasnegor, J., & Sunshine, W. (1997). Juvenile rheumatoid arthritis: Benefits from massage therapy. *Journal of Pediatric Psychology, 22,* 607–617.

Field, T.M., Hernandez-Reif, M., Taylor, S., Quintino, O., & Burman, I. (1997). Labor pain is reduced by massage therapy. *Journal of Psychosomatic Obstetrics and Gynecology, 18,* 286–291.

Field, T.M., Lasko, D., Mundy, P., Henteleff, T., Kabat, S., Talpins, S., & Dowling, M. (1997). Brief report: Autistic children's attentiveness and responsivity improve after touch therapy. *Journal of Autism and Developmental Disorders, 27,* 333–338.

Field, T.M., Quintino, O., Hernandez-Reif, M., & Koslosky, G. (1998). Adolescents with attention deficit hyperactivity disorder benefit from massage therapy. *Adolescence, 33,* 103–108.

Field, T.M., Schanberg, S.M., Scafidi, F., Bauer, C.R., Vega-Lahr, N., Garcia, R., Nystrom, J., & Kuhn, C.M. (1986). Tactile/kinesthetic stimulation effects on preterm neonates. *Pediatrics, 77,* 654–658.

Filkins, K., & Koos, B.J. (2005). Ultrasound and fetal diagnosis. *Current Opinions in Obstetrics and Gynecology, 17,* 185–195.

Fincham, F.D., & Hall, J.H. (2005). Parenting and the marital relationship. In T. Luster & L. Okagaki (Eds.), *Parenting* (2nd ed.). Mahwah, NJ: Erlbaum.

Fine, M.A., Ganong, L.H., & Demo, D.H. (2005). Divorce as a family stressor. In P.C. McKenry & S.J. Price (Eds.), *Families and change* (3rd ed.). Thousand Oaks, CA: Sage.

Fine, M.A., & Harvey, J.H. (2005). Divorce and relationship dissolution in the United States. In M.A. Fine & J.H. Harvey (Eds.), *Handbook of divorce and relationship dissolution.* Mahwah, NJ: Erlbaum.

Firlik, R. (1996). Can we adapt the philosophies and practices of Reggio Emilia, Italy, for use in American schools? *Young Children, 51,* 217–220.

Fischer, K.W., & Bidell, T.R. (1998). Dynamic development of psychological structures in action and thought. In W. Damon (Ed.), *Handbook of child psychology* (Vol. 1). New York: Wiley.

Fischer, K.W., & Bidell, T.R. (2006). Dynamic development of action and thought. In W. Damon & R. Lerner (Eds.), *Handbook of child psychology* (6th ed.). New York: Wiley.

Fischer, K.W., & Lazerson, A. (1984). *Human development.* San Francisco: W.H. Freeman.

Fish, M. (2004). Attachment in infancy and preschool in low socioeconomic status rural Appalachian children: Stability and change and relations to preschool and kindergarten competence. *Developmental Psychopathology, 16,* 293–312.

Fitness, J., & Duffield, J. (2004). Emotion and communication in families. In A.L. Vangelisti (Ed.), *Handbook of family communication.* Mahwah, NJ: Erlbaum.

Fitzgerald, E.F., Hwang, S.A., Lannguth, K., Cayo, M., Yang, B.Z., Bush, S., Worswick, P., & Lauzon, T. (2004). Fish consumption and other environmental exposures and their associations with serum PCB concentrations among Mohawk women at Akwesasne. *Environmental Research, 94,* 160–170.

Fivush, R. (1993). Developmental perspectives on autobiographical recall. In G.S. Goodman & B. Bottoms (Eds.), *Child victims and child witnesses: Understanding and improving testimony.* New York: Guilford.

Flanagan, C. (2004). Volunteerism. In R. Lerner & L. Steinberg (Eds.), *Handbook of adolescent psychology.* New York: Wiley.

Flavell, J.H. (1999). Cognitive development. *Annual Review of Psychology, 50.* Palo Alto, CA: Annual Reviews.

Flavell, J.H. (2004). Theory-of-mind development: Retrospect and prospect. *Merrill-Palmer Quarterly, 50,* 274–290.

Flavell, J.H, Friedrichs, A., & Hoyt, J. (1970). Developmental changes in memorization processes. *Cognitive Psychology, 1,* 324–340.

Flavell, J.H., Green, F.L., & Flavell, E.R. (1995). Young children's knowledge about thinking. *Monographs of the Society for Research in Child Development, 60* (1, Serial No. 243).

Flavell, J.H., Miller, P.H., & Miller, S.A. (2002). *Cognitive development* (4th ed.). Upper Saddle River, NJ: Prentice Hall.

Flegal, K.M., Ogden, C.L., & Carroll, M.D. (2004). Prevalence and trends in Mexican-American adults and children. *Nutrition Review, 62,* S144–S148.

Fletcher, A.C., Steinberg, L., & Williams-Wheeler, M. (2004). Parental influences on problem behavior: Revisiting Stattin and Kerr. *Child Development, 75,* 781–796.

Flick, L., White, D.K., Vemulapalli, C., Stulac, B.B., & Kemp, J.S. (2001). Sleep position and the use of soft bedding during bed sharing among African American infants at increased risk for sudden infant death syndrome. *Journal of Pediatrics, 138,* 338–343.

Flohr, J.W., Atkins, D.H., Bower, T.G.R., & Aldridge, M.A. (2001, April). *Infant music preferences.* Paper presented at the meeting of the Society for Research in Child Development, Minneapolis.

Flores, D.L., & Hendrick, V.C. (2002). Etiology and treatment of postpartum depression. *Current Psychiatry Reports, 4,* 461–466.

Flores, G., Abreu, M., & Tomany-Korman, S.C. (2005). Limited English proficiency, primary language at home, and disparities in children's health care: How language barriers are measured matters. *Public Health Reports, 120,* 418–420.

Flynn, J.R. (1999). Searching for justice: The discovery of IQ gains over time. *American Psychologist, 54,* 5–20.

Foege, W. (2000). The power of immunization. *The progress of nations.* New York: UNICEF.

Fogel, A. (2001). *Infancy* (4th ed.). Belmont, CA: Wadsworth.

Fogel, A., Toda, S., & Kawai, M. (1988). Mother-infant face-to-face interaction in Japan and the United States: A laboratory comparison using 3-month-old infants. *Developmental Psychology, 24,* 398–406.

Folkman, S., & Moskowitz, J.T. (2004). Coping: Pitfalls and promises. *Annual Review of Psychology, 55.* Palo Alto, CA: Annual Reviews.

Fone, K.C., & Nutt, D.J. (2005). Stimulants: Use and abuse in the treatment of attention deficit hyperactivity disorder. *Current Opinions in Pharmacology, 5,* 87–93.

Fowler-Brown, A., & Kahwati, L.C. (2004). Prevention and treatment of overweight in children and adolescents. *American Family Physician, 69,* 2591–2598.

Fox, B., & Hull, M. (2002). *Phonics for the teacher of reading* (8th ed.). Upper Saddle River, NJ: Merrill.

Fox, M.K., Pac, S., Devaney, B., & Jankowski, L. (2004). Feeding infants and toddlers study: What foods are infants and toddlers eating? *Journal of the American Diet Association, 104,* 22–30.

Fox, N.A., Henderson, H.A., Marshall, P.J., Nichols, K.E., & Ghera, M.M. (2004). Behavioral inhibition: Linking biology and behavior within a developmental framework. *Annual Review of Psychology, 55.* Palo Alto, CA: Annual Reviews.

Fox, P.G., Burns, K.R., Popovich, J.M., Belknap, R.A., & Frank-Stromberg, M. (2004). Southeast Asia refugee children: Self-esteem as a predictor of depression and scholastic achievement in the U.S. *International Journal of Nursing Research, 9,* 1063–1072.

Foy, J.M., & Earls, M.F. (2005). A process for developing community consensus regarding the diagnosis and management of attention deficit hyperactivity disorder. *Pediatrics, 115,* e97–e104.

Fraenkel, J.R., & Wallen, N.E. (2006). *How to design and evaluate research in education* (6th ed.). New York: McGraw-Hill.

Fraga, C.G., Motchnik, P.A., Shigenaga, M.K., Helbock, H.J., Jacob, R.A., & Ames, B.N. (1991). Ascorbic acid protects against endogenous oxidative DNA damage in human sperm. *Proceedings of the National Academy of Sciences of the United States, 88,* 11003–11006.

Fraiberg, S. (1959). *The magic years.* New York: Scribner's.

Francis, D.J., Fletcher, J.M., Stuebing, K.K., Lyon, G.R., Shaywitz, B.A., & Shaywitz, S.E. (2005). Psychometric approaches to the identification of LD: IQ and achievement scores are not sufficient. *Journal of Learning Disabilities, 38,* 98–108.

Francis, J., Fraser, G., & Marcia, J.E. (1989). *Cognitive and experimental factors in moratorium-achievement (MAMA) cycles.* Unpublished manuscript, Department of Psychology, Simon Fraser University, Burnaby, British Columbia.

Franz, C.E. (1996). The implications of preschool tempo and motoric activity level for personality decades later. Reported in Caspi, A. (1998). Personality development across the life course. In W. Damon (Ed.), *Handbook of child psychology* (Vol 3). New York: Wiley, p. 337.

Franz, C.E., McClelland, D., & Weinberger, J. (1991). Childhood antecedents of conventional social accomplishment in midlife adults: A 26-year prospective study. *Journal of Personality and Social Psychology, 58,* 709–717.

Fraser, S. (Ed.). (1995). *The bell curve wars: Race, intelligence, and the future of America.* New York: Basic Books.

Frede, E.C. (1995). The role of program quality in producing early childhood program benefits. *The Future of Children, 5* (3), 115–132.

Frederikse, M., Lu, A., Aylward, E., Barta, P., Sharma, T., & Pearlson, G. (2000). Sex differences in inferior lobule volume in schizophrenia. *American Journal of Psychiatry, 157,* 422–427.

Fredrickson, D.D. (1993). Breastfeeding research priorities, opportunities, and study criteria: What we learned from the smoking trial. *Journal of Human Lactation, 3,* 147–150.

Fredrikson, K., Rhodes, J., Reddy, R., & Way, N. (2004). Sleepless in Chicago: Tracking the effects of sleep loss during middle school years. *Child Development, 75,* 84–95.

Freedman, J.L. (1984). Effects of television violence on aggressiveness. *Psychological Bulletin, 96,* 227–246.

Freeman, D. (1983). *Margaret Mead and Samoa.* Cambridge, MA: Harvard University Press.

Freeman, K.E., & Gehl, K.S. (1995, March). *Beginnings, middles, and ends: 24-month-olds' understanding of analogy.* Paper presented at the meeting of the Society for Research in Child Development, Indianapolis.

Freud, A., & Dann, S. (1951). Instinctual anxiety during puberty. In A. Freud (Ed.), *The ego and its mechanisms of defense.* New York: International Universities Press.

Freud, S. (1917). *A general introduction to psychoanalysis.* New York: Washington Square Press.

Frias, J.L., & Davenport, M.L. (2003). Health supervision for children with Turner Syndrome. *Pediatrics, 111,* 692–702.

Fridrich, A.H., & Flannery, D.J. (1995). The effects of ethnicity and acculturation on early adolescent delinquency. *Journal of Child & Family Studies, 4,* 69–87.

Fried, P.A., & Watkinson, B. (1990). 36- and 48-month neurobehavioral follow-up of children prenatally exposed to marijuana, cigarettes, and alcohol. *Developmental and Behavioral Pediatrics, 11,* 49–58.

Friedman, N.J., & Zeiger, R.S. (2005). The role of breast-feeding in the development of allergies and asthma. *Journal of Allergy and Clinical Immunology, 115,* 1238–1248.

Friend, M. (2006). *Special education (IDEA 2004 Update Ed.).* Boston: Allyn & Bacon.

Friesch, R.E. (1984). Body fat, puberty and fertility. *Biological Review, 59,* 161–188.

Frye, D. (1999). Development of intention: The relation of executive function to theory of mind. In P.D. Zelazo, J.W. Astington, & D.R. Olson (Eds.), *Developing theories of intention: Social understanding and self-control.* Mahwah, NJ: Erlbaum.

Frye, D. (2004). Unpublished review of Santrock, J.W. *Child development* (11th ed.). New York: McGraw-Hill.

Frye, D., Zelazo, P.D., Brooks, P.J., & Samuels, M.C. (1996). Inference and action in early causal reasoning. *Developmental Psychology, 32,* 120–131.

Fuchs, D., Mock, D., Morgan, P.L., & Young, C.L. (2003). Responsiveness-to-intervention: Definitions, evidence, and implications for the learning disabilities construct. *Learning Disabilities Research & Practice, 18,* 157–171.

Fuligni, A.J., & Hardway, C. (2004). Preparing diverse adolescents for the transition to adulthood. *Future of Children, 14,* 99–119.

Fuligni, A.J., & Witkow, M. (2004). The postsecondary educational progress of youth from immigrant families. *Journal of Research on Adolescence, 14,* 159–183.

Fuligni, A.J., & Yoshikawa, H. (2004). Investments in children among immigrant families. In A. Kalil & T. DeLeire (Eds.), *Family investments in children's potential.* Mahwah, NJ: Erlbaum.

Furman, W., & Buhrmester, D. (1992). Age and sex differences in perceptions of networks of personal relationships. *Child Development, 63,* 103–115.

Furman, W., & Wehner, E.A. (1999). Adolescent romantic relationships: A developmental perspective. In S. Shulman & W.A. Collins (Eds.), *New directions for child development: Adolescent romantic relationships.* San Francisco: Jossey-Bass.

Furth, H.G. (1973). *Deafness and learning: A psychosocial approach.* Belmont, CA: Wadsworth.

Furth, H.G., & Wachs, H. (1975). *Thinking goes to school.* New York: Oxford University Press.

Fussell, E., & Greene, M.E. (2002). Demographic trends affecting youth around the world. In B.B. Brown, R.W. Larson, & T.S. Saraswathi (Eds.), *The world's youth.* New York: Cambridge University Press.

Gadpaille, W.J. (1996). *Adolescent suicide.* Washington, DC: American Psychological Association.

Gaillard, W.D., Balsamo, L., Xu, B., McKinney, C., Papero, P.H., Weinstein, S., Conry, J., Pearl, P.L., Sachs, B., Sato, S., Vezina, L.G., Frattali, F.C., & Theodore, W.H. (2004). fMRI language task panel improves determination of language dominance. *Neurology, 63,* 1403–1408.

Galambos, N.L. (2004). Gender and gender role development in adolescence. In R. Lerner & L. Steinberg (Eds.), *Handbook of adolescence* (2nd ed.). New York: Wiley.

Galambos, N.L., & Maggs, J.L. (1989, April). *The afterschool ecology of young adolescents and self-reported behavior.* Paper presented at the biennial meeting of the Society for Research in Child Development, Kansas City.

Gale, C.R., & Martin, C.N. (2004). Birth weight and later risk of depression in a national cohort. *British Journal of Psychiatry, 184,* 28–33.

Galinsky, E., & David, J. (1988). *The preschool years: Family strategies that work—from experts and parents.* New York: Times Books.

Gall, J.P., Gall, M.D., & Borg, W.R. (2005). *Applying educational research* (5th ed.). Boston: Allyn & Bacon.

Galloway, J.C., & Thelen, E. (2004). Feet first: Object exploration in young infants. *Infant Behavior & Development, 27,* 107–112.

Galotti, K.M., & Kozberg, S.F. (1996). Adolescents' experience of a life-framing decision. *Journal of Youth and Adolescence, 25,* 3–16.

Gandrud, L.M., & Wilson, D.M. (2004). Is growth hormone stimulation testing in children still appropriate? *Growth Hormone IGF Research, 14,* 185–194.

Ganong, L., Coleman, M., & Hans, J. (2005). Divorce as prelude to stepfamily living and the consequences of re-divorce. In M.A. Fine & J.H. Harvey (Eds.), *Handbook of divorce and relationship dissolution.* Mahwah, NJ: Erlbaum.

Gao, Y., Elliott, M.E., & Waters, E. (1999, April). *Maternal attachment representations and support for three-year-olds' secure base behavior.* Paper presented at the meeting of the Society for Research in Child Development, Albuquerque.

Garbarino, J. (1999). *Lost boys: Why our sons turn violent and how we can save them.* New York: Free Press.

Garbarino, J. (2001). Violent children. *Archives of Pediatrics & Adolescent Medicine, 155,* 1–2.

Garbarino, J., & Asp, C.E. (1981). *Successful schools and competent students.* Lexington, MA: Lexington Books.

Garbarino, J., Bradshaw, C.P., & Kostelny, K. (2005). Neighborhood and community influences on parenting. In T. Luster & L. Okagaki (Eds.), *Parenting: An ecological perspective* (2nd ed.). Mahwah, NJ: Erlbaum.

Garcia Coll, C.T., Szalacha, L.A., & Palacios, N. (2005). Children of Dominican, Portuguese, and Cambodian immigrant families: Academic attitudes and pathways during middle childhood. In C.R. Cooper, C.T. Garcia Coll, W.T. Bartko, H.M. Davis, & C. Chatman (Eds.), *Developmental pathways through middle childhood.* Mahwah, NJ: Erlbaum.

Garcia, E., & Willis, A.I. (2001). Framework for understanding multicultural literacies. In P.R. Schmidt & P.B. Mosenthal (Eds.), *Reconceptualizing literacy in the new age of multiculturalism and pluralism.* Greenwich, CT: IAP.

Garcia, L., Hart, D., & Johnson-Ray, R. (1998). What do children and adolescents think about themselves? A developmental account of self-concept development. In S. Hala (Ed.), *The development of social cognition.* London: University College of London Press.

Garcia-Alba, C. (2004). Anorexia and depression. *Spanish Journal of Psychology, 7,* 40–52.

Gard, J.W., Alexander, J.M., Bawdon, R.E., & Albrecht, J.T. (2002). Oxytocin preparation stability in several common intravenous solutions. *American Journal of Obstetrics and Gynecology, 186,* 496–498.

Gardner, H. (1983). *Frames of mind.* New York: Basic Books.

Gardner, H. (1993). *Multiple intelligences.* New York: Basic Books.

Gardner, H. (2001, March 13). *An education for the future.* Paper presented to the Royal Symposium, Amsterdam.

Gardner, H. (2002). The pursuit of excellence through education. In M. Ferrari (Ed.), *Learning from extraordinary minds.* Mahwah, NJ: Erlbaum.

Gardner, H., Feldman, D.H., & Krechevsky, M. (Eds.). (1998). *Project Spectrum.* New York: Teachers College Press.

Garmezy, N. (1993). Children in poverty: Resilience despite risk. *Psychiatry, 56,* 127–136.

Garrett, P., Ng'andu, N., & Ferron, J. (1994). Poverty experiences of young children and the quality of their home environments. *Child Development, 65,* 331–345.

Garton, A.F. (2004). *Exploring cognitive development: The child as a problem solver.* Malden, MA: Blackwell.

Gaylor, A.S., & Condren, M.E. (2004). Type 2 diabetes mellitus in the pediatric population. *Pharmacotherapy, 24,* 871–888.

Gazzaniga, M.J., Ivry, R.B., & Mangun, G.R. (2002). *Cognitive neuroscience* (2nd ed.). New York: W.W. Norton.

Gelfand, D.M., Teti, D.M., & Fox, C.E.R. (1992). Sources of parenting stress for depressed and nondepressed mothers of infants. *Journal of Clinical Child Psychology, 21,* 262–272.

Gelles, R.J., & Cavanaugh, M.M. (2005). Violence, abuse, and neglect in families and intimate relationships. In P.C. McKenry & S.J. Price (Eds.), *Families and change* (3rd ed.). Thousand Oaks, CA: Sage.

Gelman, R. (1969). Conservation acquisition: A problem of learning to attend to relevant attributes. *Journal of Experimental Child Psychology, 7,* 67–87.

Gelman, R., & Williams, E.M. (1998). Enabling constraints for cognitive development and learning. In W. Damon (Ed.), *Handbook of child psychology* (5th ed., Vol. 4). New York: Wiley.

Gelman, S.A., & Opfer, J.E. (2004). Development of the animate-inanimate distinction. In U. Goswami (Ed.), *Blackwell handbook of childhood cognitive development.* Malden, MA: Blackwell.

Gelman, S.A., Taylor, M.G., & Nguyen, S.P. (2004). Mother-child conversations about gender. *Monographs of the Society for Research in Child Development, 69* (1, Serial No. 275).

Gennetian, L.A., & Miller, C. (2002). Children and welfare reform: A view from an experimental welfare reform program in Minnesota. *Child Development, 73,* 601–620.

George, C., Main, M., & Kaplan, N. (1984). *Attachment interview with adults.* Unpublished manuscript, University of California, Berkeley.

Gerrard, J.A., & Chudasama, G. (2003). Screening to reduce HIV transmission from mother to baby. *Nursing Times, 99,* 44–45.

Gershoff, E.T. (2002). Corporal punishment by parents and associated child behaviors and experiences: A meta-analysis and theoretical review. *Psychological Bulletin, 128,* 539–579.

Geschwind, N., & Behan, P.O. (1984). Laterality, hormones, and immunity. In N. Geschwind & A.M. Galaburda (Eds.), *Cerebral dominance: The biological foundations.* Cambridge, MA: Harvard University Press.

Gesell, A. (1934). *An atlas of infant behavior.* New Haven, CT: Yale University Press.

Gesell, A.L. (1928). *Infancy and human growth.* New York: Macmillan.

Gesell, A.L. (1934). *Infancy and human growth.* New York: Macmillan.

Gewirtz, J. (1977). Maternal responding and the conditioning of infant crying: Directions of influence within the attachment-acquisition process. In B.C. Etzel, J.M. LeBlanc, & D.M. Baer (Eds.), *New developments in behavioral research.* Hillsdale, NJ: Erlbaum.

Ghetti, S., & Alexander, K.W. (2004). "If it happened, I would remember it"; Strategic use of event memorability in the rejection of false autobiographical events. *Child Development, 75,* 542–561.

Ghosh, S., & Shah, D. (2004). Nutritional problems in urban slum children. *Indian Pediatrics, 41,* 682–696.

Giavecchio, L. (2001, April). *Sustained attention and receptive language in preschool Head Start story time.* Paper presented at the meeting of the Society for Research in Child Development, Minneapolis.

Gibbons, J.L. (2000). Gender development in cross-cultural perspective. In T. Eckes & H.M. Trautner (Eds.), *The developmental social psychology of gender.* Mahwah, NJ: Erlbaum.

Gibbs, J.C. (1993, March). *Inductive discipline's contribution to moral motivation.* Paper presented at the biennial meeting of the Society for Research in Child Development, New Orleans.

Gibbs, J.C. (2003). *Moral development & reality.* Thousand Oaks, CA: Sage.

Gibbs, J.T. (1989). Black American adolescents. In J.T. Gibbs & L.N. Huang (Eds.), *Children of color*. San Francisco: Jossey-Bass.

Gibbs, J.T., & Huang, L.N. (1989). A conceptual framework for assessing and treating minority youth. In J.T. Gibbs & L.N. Huang (Eds.), *Children of color.* San Francisco: Jossey-Bass.

Gibson, E.J. (1969). *Principles of perceptual learning and development.* New York: Appleton-Century-Crofts.

Gibson, E.J. (1989). Exploratory behavior in the development of perceiving, acting, and the acquiring of knowledge. *Annual Review of Psychology, 39.* Palo Alto, CA: Annual Reviews.

Gibson, E.J. (2001). *Perceiving the affordances.* Mahwah, NJ: Erlbaum.

Gibson, E.J., Riccio, G., Schmuckler, M.A., Stoffregen, T.A., Rosenberg, D., & Taormina, J. (1987). Detection of the traversability of surfaces by crawling and walking infants. *Journal of Experimental Psychology: Human Perception and Performance, 13,* 533–544.

Gibson, E.J., & Walk, R.D. (1960). The "visual cliff." *Scientific American, 202,* 64–71.

Gibson, J.H., Harries, M., Mitchell, A., Godfrey, R., Lunt, M., & Reeve, J. (2000). Derminants of bone density and prevalence of osteopenia among female runners in their second to seventh decades of age. *Bone, 26,* 591–598.

Gibson, J.J. (1966). *The senses considered as perceptual systems.* Boston: Houghton Mifflin.

Gibson, J.J. (1979). *The ecological approach to visual perception.* Boston: Houghton Mifflin.

Giedd, J., Jeffries, N., Blumenthal, J., Castellanos, F., Vatiuzis, A., Fernandez, T., Hamburger, S., Liu, H., Nelson, J., Bedwell, J., Tran, L., Lenane, M., Nicolson, R., & Rapoport, J. (1999). Childhood-onset schizophrenia: Progressive brain changes during adolescence. *Biological Psychiatry, 46,* 892–898.

Gifford-Smith, M.E., & Rabiner, D.L. (2004). The relation between social information processing and children's adjustment. In J.B. Kupersmidt & K.A. Dodge (Eds.), *Children's peer relations: From development to intervention.* Washington, DC: American Psychological Association.

Gilligan, C. (1982). *In a different voice.* Cambridge, MA: Harvard University Press.

Gilligan, C. (1992, May). *Joining the resistance: Girls' development in adolescence.* Paper presented at the symposium on development and vulnerability in close relationships, Montreal, Quebec.

Gilligan, C. (1996). The centrality of relationships in psychological development: A puzzle, some evidence, and a theory. In G.G. Noam & K.W. Fischer (Eds.), *Development and vulnerability in close relationships.* Hillsdale, NJ: Erlbaum.

Gilligan, C., Spencer, R., Weinberg, M.K., & Bertsch, T. (2003). On the listening guide: A voice-centered relational model. In P.M. Carnic & J.E. Rhodes (Eds.), *Qualitative research in psychology.* Washington, DC: American Psychological Association.

Gilstrap, L.L., & Ceci, S.J. (2005). Reconceptualizing children's suggestibility: Bidirectional and temporal properties. *Child Development, 76,* 40–53.

Gjerde, P.F., Block, J., & Block, J.H. (1991). The preschool family context of 18-year-olds with depressive symptoms: A prospective study. *Journal of Research on Adolescence, 1,* 63–92.

Glantz, J.C. (2005). Elective induction vs. spontaneous labor associations and outcomes. *Journal of Reproductive Medicine, 50,* 235–240.

Godding, V., Bonnier, C., Fiasse, L., Michel, M., Longueville, E., Lebecque, P., Robert, A., & Galanti, L. (2004). Does in utero exposure to heavy maternal smoking induce nicotine withdrawal symptoms in neonates? *Pediatric Research, 55,* 645–651.

Goelman, H., Anderson, C.J., Anderson, J., Gouzaousasis, P., Kendrick, M., Kindel, A.M., Porath, M., & Koh, J. (2003). Early childhood education. In I.B. Weiner (Ed.), *Handbook of psychology* (Vol. 7). New York: Wiley.

Golbeck, S.L. (Ed.). (2001). *Psychological perspectives on early childhood education.* Mahwah, NJ: Erlbaum.

Golden, M.H., Samuels, M.P., & Southall, D.P. (2003). How to distinguish between neglect and deprivational abuse. *Archives of Diseases in Childhood, 88,* 105–107.

Goldin-Meadow, S. (2000). Language: Language development, syntax, and communication. In A. Kazdin (Ed.), *Encyclopedia of psychology.* Washington, DC, & New York: American Psychological Association and Oxford University Press.

Goldsmith, H.H. (2002). Genetics of emotional development. In R.J. Davidson, K.R. Scherer, & H.H. Goldsmith (Eds.), *Handbook of affective sciences.* New York: Oxford University Press.

Goldsmith, H.H., & Davidson, R.J. (2004). Disambiguating the components of emotion regulation. *Child Development, 75,* 361–365.

Goldstein, J.M., Seidman, L.J., Horton, N.J., Makris, N., Kennedy, D.N., Caviness, V.S., Faraone, S.V., & Tsuang, M.T. (2001). Normal sexual dimorphism of the adult human brain assessed by in vivo magnetic resonance imaging. *Cerebral Cortex, 11,* 490–497.

Goldwater, P.N. (2001). SIDS: More facts and controversies. *Medical Journal of Australia, 174,* 302–304.

Goleman, D. (1995). *Emotional intelligence.* New York: Basic Books.

Golombok, S., MacCallum, F., & Goodman, E. (2001). The "test-tube" generation: Parent-child relationships and the psychological well-being of in vitro fertilization children at adolescence. *Child Development, 72,* 599–608.

Gonzales, N.A., Knight, G.P., Birman, D., & Sirolli, A.A. (2004). Acculturation and enculturation among Latino youths. In K.L. Maton, C.J. Schellenbach, & A.L. Solarz (Eds.), *Investing in children, families, and communities.* Washington, DC: American Psychological Association.

Gonzalez-del Angel, A.A., Vidal, S., Saldan, Y., del Castillo, V., Angel, M., Macias, M., Luna, P., & Orozco, L. (2000). Molecular diagnosis of the fragile X and FRAXE syndromes in patients with mental retardation of unknown cause in Mexico. *Annals of Genetics, 43,* 29–34.

Good, C., Aronson, J., & Inzlicht, M. (2003). Improving adolescents' standardized test performance: An intervention to reduce the effects of stereotype threat. *Journal of Applied Developmental Psychology, 24,* 645–662.

Goodman, G.S. (2000). *101 things parents should know before volunteering to coach their kids' sport teams.* New York: Contemporary Books.

Goodman, G.S., Batterman-Faunce, J.M., & Kenney, R. (1992). Optimizing children's testimony: Research and social policy issues concerning allegations of child sexual abuse. In D. Cicchetti & S. Toth (Eds.), *Child abuse, child development and social policy.* Norwood, NJ: Ablex.

Goodman, J.H. (2004). Paternal postpartum depression: Its relationship to maternal postpartum depression, and implications for family health. *Journal of Advanced Nursing, 45,* 26–35.

Goos, M. (2004). Learning mathematics in a classroom community of inquiry. *Journal for Research in Mathematics Education, 35,* 258–291.

Gopnik, A., & Meltzoff, A. (1997). *Words, thoughts, and theories.* Cambridge, MA: MIT Press.

Gotesdam, K.G., & Agras, W.S. (1995). General population-based epidemiological survey of eating disorders in Norway. *International Journal of Eating Disorders, 18,* 119–126.

Gottfried, A.E., Gottfried, A.W., & Bathurst, K. (2002). Maternal and dual-earner employment status and parenting. In M.H. Bornstein (Ed.), *Handbook of parenting* (2nd ed., Vol. 2.) Mahwah, NJ: Erlbaum.

Gottlieb, G. (1998). Normally occurring environmental and behavioral influences on gene activity: From central dogma to probabilistic epigenesis. *Psychological Review, 105,* 792–802.

Gottlieb, G. (2003). *Developmental behavior genetics and the statistical concept of interaction.* Unpublished manuscript, Department of Psychology, University of North Carolina, Chapel Hill.

Gottlieb, G. (2004). Normally occurring environmental and behavioral influences on gene activity. In C.G. Coll, E.L. Bearer, & R.M. Lerner (Eds.), *Nature and nurture.* Mahwah, NJ: Erlbaum.

Gottlieb, G., & Blair, C. (2004). How early experience matters in intellectual development in the case of poverty. *Prevention Science, 5,* 245–252.

Gottlieb, G., Wahlsten, D., & Lickliter, R. (1998). The significance of biology for human development: A developmental psychobiological systems view. In W. Damon (Ed.), *Handbook of child psychology* (5th ed., Vol. 1). New York: Wiley.

Gottlieb, G., Wahlsten, D., & Lickliter, R. (2006). The significance of biology for human development: A developmental psychobiological systems view. In W. Damon & R. Lerner (Eds.), *Handbook of child psychology* (6th ed.). New York: Wiley.

Gottman, J.M., & DeClaire, J. (1997). *The heart of parenting: Raising an emotionally intelligent child.* New York: Simon & Schuster.

Gottman, J.M., Katz, L.F., & Hooven, C. (1997). *Meta-emotion: How families communicate.* Mahwah, NJ: Erlbaum.

Gottman, J.M., & Parker, J.G. (Eds.). (1987). *Conversations of friends.* New York: Cambridge University Press.

Gould, S.J. (1981). *The mismeasure of man.* New York: W.W. Norton.

Graber, J.A. (2004). Internalizing problems during adolescence. In R. Lerner & L. Steinberg (Eds.), *Handbook of adolescent psychology.* New York: Wiley.

Graber, J.A., & Brooks-Gunn, J. (2001). *Co-occurring eating and depressive problems: An 8-year study of adolescent girls.* Unpublished manuscript, Center for Children and Families, Columbia University.

Graber, J.A., & Brooks-Gunn, J. (2002). Adolescent girls' sexual development. In G.M. Wingood & R.J. DiClemente (Eds.), *Handbook of sexual and reproductive health.* New York: Plenum.

Graber, J.A., Seeley, J.R., Brooks-Gunn, J., & Lewinsohn, P.M. (2004). Is pubertal timing associated with psychopathology in young adulthood? *Journal of the American Academy of Child and Adolescent Psychiatry, 43,* 718–726.

Grady, M.A., & Bloom, K.C. (2004). Pregnancy outcomes of adolescents enrolled in a Centering Pregnancy program. *Journal of Midwifery and Women's Health, 49,* 412–420.

Graham, S. (1986, August). *Can attribution theory tell us something about motivation in blacks?* Paper presented at the meeting of the American Psychological Association, Washington, DC.

Graham, S. (1990). Motivation in Afro-Americans. In G.L. Berry & J.K. Asamen (Eds.), *Black students: Psychosocial issues and academic achievement.* Newbury Park, CA: Sage.

Graham, S. (1992). Most of the subjects were white and middle class. *American Psychologist, 47,* 629–637.

Graham, S. (1997). Executive control in the revising of students with learning and writing difficulties. *Journal of Educational Psychology, 89,* 223–234.

Graham, S. (2005, February 16). Commentary in *USA Today,* p. 2D.

Grant, J.P. (1993). *The state of the world's children.* New York: Oxford University Press.

Grant, J.P. (1996). *State of the world's children.* New York: UNICEF and Oxford University Press.

Grant, J.P. (1997). *The state of the world's children.* New York: UNICEF and Oxford University Press.

Grasemann, C., Wessels, H.T., Knauer-Fischer, S., Richter-Unruh, A., & Hauffa, B.P. (2004). Increase of serum leptin after short-term pulsatile GnRH administration in children with delayed puberty. *European Journal of Endocrinology, 150,* 691–698.

Graven, S.N. (2004). Early neurosensory visual development of the fetus and newborn. *Clinical Perinatology, 31,* 199–216.

Graves, M.F., Juel, C., & Graves, B.B. (2004). *Teaching reading in the 21st century.* Boston: Allyn & Bacon.

Gray, J. (1992). *Men are from Mars, women are from Venus.* New York: HarperCollins.

Gray, P., & Feldman, J. (2004). Playing in the zone of proximal development: Qualities of self-directed age-mixing between adolescents and young children at a democratic school. *American Journal of Education, 110,* 108–143.

Graziano, A.M., & Raulin, M.L. (2004). *Research methods* (5th ed.). Boston: Allyn & Bacon.

Greenberg, B.S., Stanley, C., Siemicki, M., Heeter, C., Soderman, A., & Linsangan, R. (1986). *Sex content on soaps and prime-time television series most viewed by adolescents.* Project CAST Report #2. East Lansing: Michigan State Department of Telecommunication.

Greenfield, P.M. (1966). On culture and conservation. In J.S. Bruner, R.P. Oliver, & P.M. Greenfield (Eds.), *Studies in cognitive growth.* New York: Wiley.

Greenfield, P.M. (2000). Culture and development. In A. Kazdin (Ed.), *Encyclopedia of psychology.* Washington, DC, & New York: American Psychological Association and Oxford University Press.

Greenfield, P.M. (2003, February). Commentary. *Monitor on Psychology, 34* (2), 58.

Greenfield, P.M., Keller, H., Fuligni, A., & Maynard, A. (2003). Cultural pathways through universal development. *Annual Review of Psychology, 54,* 461–490.

Greenfield, P.M., Suzuki, L.K., & Rothstein-Fisch, C. (2006). Cultural pathways through human development. In W. Damon & R. Lerner (Eds.), *Handbook of child psychology* (6th ed.). New York: Wiley.

Greenough, W.T. (1997, April 21). Commentary in article, "Politics of biology." *U.S. News & World Report,* p. 79.

Greenough, W.T. (1999, April). *Experience, brain development, and links to mental retardation.* Paper presented at the meeting of the Society for Research in Child Development, Albuquerque.

Greenough, W.T. (2000). Brain development. In A. Kazdin (Ed.), *Encyclopedia of psychology.* Washington, DC, & New York: American Psychological Association and Oxford University Press.

Greenough, W.T. (2001, April). *Nature and nurture in the brain development process.* Paper presented at the meeting of the Society for Research in Child Development, Minneapolis.

Greenough, W.T., Klintsova, A.Y., Irvan, S.A., Galvez, R., Bates, K.E., & Weiler, I.J. (2001). Synaptic regulation of protein synthesis and the fragile X protein. *Proceedings of the National Academy of Science, USA, 98,* 7101–7106.

Gregory, R.L. (2004). *Psychological testing* (4th ed.). Boston: Allyn & Bacon.

Greven, P. (1991). *Spare the child: The religious roots of punishment and the psychological impact of physical abuse.* New York: Knopf.

Grigorenko, E. (2000). Heritability and intelligence. In R.J. Sternberg (Ed.), *Handbook of intelligence.* New York: Cambridge University Press.

Grigorenko, E.L. (2001). The invisible danger: The impact of ionizing radiation on cognitive development and functioning. In R.J. Sternberg & E.L. Grigorenko (Eds.), *Environmental effects on cognitive abilities.* Mahwah: NJ: Erlbaum.

Grigorenko, E.L., Geissler, P., Prince, R., Okatcha, F., Nokes, C., Kenney, D.A., Bundy, D.A., & Sternberg, R.J. (2001). The organization of Luo conceptions of intelligence: A study of implicit theories in a Kenyan village. *International Journal of Behavioral Development, 25,* 367–378.

Grigoriadis, S., & Kennedy, S.H. (2002). Role of estrogen in the treatment of depression. *American Journal of Therapy, 9,* 503–509.

Grimes, B., & Mattimore, K. (1989, April). *The effects of stress and exercise on identity formation in adolescence.* Paper presented at the biennial meeting at the Society for Research in Child Development, Kansas City.

Grodzinsky, Y. (2001). The neurology of syntax: Language use without Broca's area. *Behavior and Brain Sciences, 23,* 1–21.

Grolnick, W.S., Bridges, L.J., & Connell, J.P. (1996). Emotion regulation in two-year-olds: Strategies and emotional expression in four contexts. *Child Development, 67,* 928–941.

Gross, R.T. (1984). Patterns of maturation: Their effects on behavior and development. In M.D. Levine & P. Satz (Eds.), *Middle childhood: Development and dysfunction.* Baltimore: University Park Press.

Grossmann, K., Grossmann, K.E., Spangler, G., Suess, G., & Unzner, L. (1985). Maternal sensitivity and newborns' orientation responses as related to quality of attachment in northern Germany. In I. Bretherton & E. Waters (Eds.), Growing points of attachment theory and research. *Monographs of the Society for Research in Child Development, 50* (1–2, Serial No. 209).

Grotevant, H.D., & Cooper, C.R. (1985). Patterns of interaction in family relationships and the development of identity exploration in adolescence. *Child Development, 56,* 415–428.

Grotevant, H.D., & Cooper, C.R. (1998). Individuality and connectedness in adolescent development: Review and prospects for research on identity, relationships, and context. In E. Skoe & A. von der Lippe (Eds.), *Personality development in adolescence: A cross-national and life-span perspective.* London: Routledge.

Grotevant, H.D., & McRoy, R.G. (1990). Adopted adolescents in residential treatment: The role of the family. In D.M. Brodzinsky & M.D. Schechter (Eds.), *The psychology of adoption.* New York: Oxford University Press.

Grummer-Strawn, L.M., & Mei, Z. (2004). Does breastfeeding protect against pediatric overweight? Analysis of longitudinal data from the Centers for Disease Control and Prevention pediatric nutrition surveillance system. *Pediatrics, 113,* E81–E86.

Grych, J.H. (2002). Marital relationships and parenting. In M.H. Bornstein (Ed.), *Handbook of parenting* (2nd ed., Vol. 4). Mahwah, NJ: Erlbaum.

Guilford, J.P. (1967). *The structure of intellect.* New York: McGraw-Hill.

Gunnar, M.R. (2000). Early adversity and the development of stress reactivity and regulation. In C.A. Nelson (Ed.), *The effects of early adversity on neurobehavioral development. The Minnesota Symposia on Child Psychology* (Vol. 31). Mahwah, NJ: Erlbaum.

Gunnar, M.R., & Davis, E.P. (2003). Stress and emotion in early childhood. In I.B. Weiner (Ed.), *Handbook of psychology* (Vol. 6). New York: Wiley.

Gunnar, M.R., Malone, S., & Fisch, R.O. (1987). The psychobiology of stress and coping in the human neonate: Studies of the adrenocortical activity in response to stress in the first week of life. In T. Field, P. McCabe, & N. Scheiderman (Eds.), *Stress and coping.* Hillsdale, NJ: Erlbaum.

Guo, S.S., Wu, W., Chumlea, W.C., & Roche, A.F. (2002). Predicting overweight and obesity in adulthood from body mass index values in childhood and adolescence. *American Journal of Clinical Nutrition, 76,* 653–658.

Gur, R.C., Mozley, L.H., Mozley, P.D., Resnick, S.M., Karp, J.S., Alavi, A., Arnold, S.E., & Gur, R.E. (1995). Sex differences in regional cerebral glucose metabolism during a resting state. *Science, 267,* 528–531.

Gurwitch, R.H., Silovsky, J.F., Schultz, S., Kees, M., & Burlingame, B.A. (2001). Reactions and guidelines for children following trauma/disaster. *APA Online.* Washington, DC: American Psychological Association.

Guttentag, M., & Bray, H. (1976). *Undoing sex stereotypes: Research and resources for educators.* New York: McGraw-Hill.

Gyamfi, P., Brooks-Gunn, J., & Jackson, A.P. (2001). Associations between employment and financial and parental stress in low-income single Black mothers. In M.C. Lennon (Ed.), *Welfare, work, and well-being.* New York: Haworth Press.

Hahn, C.S., & DiPietro, J.A. (2001). In vitro fertilization and the family: Quality of parenting, family functioning, and child psychosocial adjustment. *Developmental Psychology, 37,* 37–48.

Hahn, W.K. (1987). Cerebral lateralization of function: From infancy through childhood. *Psychological Bulletin, 101,* 376–392.

Haig, D. (2003). Behavioral genetics: Family matters. *Nature, 421,* 491–492.

Haith, M.M., & Benson, J.B. (1998). Infant cognition. In W. Damon (Ed.), *Handbook of child psychology* (5th ed., Vol. 2). New York: Wiley.

Haith, M.M., Hazen, C., & Goodman, G.S. (1988). Expectation and anticipation of dynamic visual events by 3.5-month-old babies. *Child Development, 59,* 467–479.

Hakuta, K. (2000). Bilingualism. In A. Kazdin (Ed.), *Encyclopedia of psychology.* Washington, DC, and New York: American Psychological Association and Oxford University Press.

Hakuta, K. (2001, April 5). *Key policy milestones and directions in the education of English language learners.* Paper prepared for the Rockefeller Foundation Symposium, Leveraging change: An emerging framework for educational equity, Washington, DC.

Hakuta, K., Bialystok, E., & Wiley, E. (2003). Critical evidence: A test of the critical-period hypothesis for second-language acquisition. *Psychological Science, 14,* 31–38.

Hakuta, K., Butler, Y.G., & Witt, D. (2000). *How long does it take English learners to attain proficiency?* Berkeley, CA: The University of California Linguistic Minority Research Institute Policy Report 2000–1.

Hale, S. (1990). A global developmental trend in cognitive processing speed. *Child Development, 61,* 653–663.

Hales, D. (2006). *Personal health and wellness* (4th ed.). Belmont, CA: Wadsworth.

Haley, M.H., & Austin, T.Y. (2004). *Content-based second language teaching and learning.* Boston: Allyn & Bacon.

Halford, G.S. (2004). Information processing models of cognitive development. In U. Goswami (Ed.), *Blackwell handbook of childhood cognitive development.* Malden, MA: Blackwell.

Hall, C.M., Jones, J.A., Meyer-Bahlburg, H.F., Dolezal, C., Coleman, M., Foster, P., Price, D.A., & Clayton, P.E. (2004). Behavioral and physical masculinization are related to genotype in girls with congenital adrenal hyperplasia. *Journal of Clinical Endocrinology and Metabolism, 89,* 419–424.

Hall, G.S. (1904). *Adolescence* (Vols. 1 & 2). Englewood Cliffs, NJ: Prentice Hall.

Hall, J. (2005). Postnatal emotional wellbeing. *Practicing Midwife, 8,* 35–40.

Hallahan, D.P., & Kauffmann, J.M. (2006). *Exceptional learners* (10th ed.). Boston: Allyn & Bacon.

Hallemans, A., Aerts, P., Otten, B., De Deyn, P.P., & De Clercq, D. (2004). Mechanical energy in toddler gait: A trade-off between economy and stability. *Journal of Experimental Biology, 207,* 2417–2431.

Hallfors, D.D., Waller, M.W., Ford, C.A., Halpern, C.T., Brodish, P.H., & Iritani, B. (2004). Adolescent depression and suicide risk: Association with sex and drug behavior. *American Journal of Preventive Medicine, 27,* 224–231.

Halonen, J.A., & Santrock, J.W. (1999). *Psychology: Contexts and applications* (3rd ed.). New York: McGraw-Hill.

Halpern, D. (2001). Sex difference research: Cognitive abilities. In J. Worell (Ed.), *Encyclopedia of women and gender.* San Diego: Academic Press.

Hambleton, R.K. (2002). How can we make NAEP and state test score reporting scales and reports more understandable? In R.W. Lissitz & W.D. Schafer (Eds.), *Assessment in educational reform: Both means and ends.* Boston: Allyn & Bacon.

Hamburg, D.A. (1997). Meeting the essential requirements for healthy adolescent development in a transforming world. In R. Takanishi & D. Hamburg (Eds.), *Preparing adolescents for the 21st century.* New York: Cambridge University Press.

Hamilton, M.A., & Hamilton, S.F. (2004). Designing work and service for learning. In S.F. Hamilton & M.A. Hamilton (Eds.), *The youth development handbook.* Thousand Oaks, CA: Sage.

Hamilton, M.C. (1991). *Preference for sons or daughters and the sex role characteristics of potential parents.* Paper presented at the meeting of the Association for Women in Psychology, Hartford, CT.

Hamilton, S.F., & Hamilton, M.A. (2004). Contexts for mentoring: Adolescent-adult relationships in workplaces and communities. In R. Lerner & L. Steinberg (Eds.), *Handbook of adolescent psychology* (2nd ed.). New York: Wiley.

Hanish, L.D., & Guerra, N.G. (2004). Aggressive victims, passive victims, and bullies: Developmental continuity or developmental change? *Merrill-Palmer Quarterly, 50,* 17–38.

Hannah, W.J. (2005). Avoiding asphyxia during vaginal breech delivery. *British Journal of Gynecology, 112,* 846.

Hansen, M., Janssen, I., Schiff, A., Zee, P.C., & Dubocovich, M.L. (2005). The impact of school daily schedule on adolescent sleep. *Pediatrics, 115,* 1555–1561.

Hansford, B.C., & Hattie, J.A. (1982). The relationship between self and achievement/performance measures. *Review of Educational Research, 52,* 123–142.

Hanson, L.A., & Korotkova, A. (2002). The role of breastfeeding in prevention of neonatal infection. *Seminars in Neonatology, 7,* 257–281.

Harding, B., Risdon, R.A., & Krous, H.F. (2004). Shaken baby syndrome. *British Medical Journal, 328,* 719–720.

Hardman, M.L., Drew, C.J., & Egan, M.W. (2006). *Human exceptionality* (8th ed. Update). Boston: Allyn & Bacon.

Hare, B.R., & Castenell, L.A. (1985). No place to run, no place to hide: Comparative status and future prospects of Black boys. In M.B. Spencer, G.K. Brookins, & W.R. Allen (Eds.), *Beginnings: The social and affective development of Black children.* Hillsdale, NJ: Erlbaum.

Hargrove, K. (2005). What makes a "good" teacher "great"? *Gifted Child Today, 28,* 30–31.

Hariri, A.R., Mahay, V.S., Tessitore, A., Kolachana, B., Fera. F., Goldman. D., Egan, M.F., & Weinberger, D.R. (2002). Serotonin transporter genetic variation and the response of the human amygdala. *Science, 297,* 400–403.

Harkness, S., & Super, C.M. (1995). Culture and parenting. In M.H. Bornstein (Ed.), *Handbook of parenting* (Vol. 3). Hillsdale, NJ: Erlbaum.

Harkness, S., & Super, C.M. (2002). Culture and parenting. In M.H. Bornstein (Ed.), *Handbook of parenting* (2nd ed., Vol. 2). Mahwah, NJ: Erlbaum.

Harlow, H.F. (1958). The nature of love. *American Psychologist, 13,* 673–685.

Harper, C.C., & McLanahan, S.S. (2004). Father absence and youth incarceration. *Journal of Research on Adolescence, 14,* 369–397.

Harris, G., Thomas, A., & Booth, D.A. (1990). Development of salt taste in infancy. *Developmental Psychology, 26,* 534–538.

Harris, J.B. (1998). *The nurture assumption: Why children turn out the way they do: Parents matter less than you think and peers matter more.* New York: Free Press.

Harris, L. (1997). *A national poll of children and exercise.* Washington, DC: Lou Harris & Associates.

Harris, P.L. (2006). Social cognition. In W. Damon & R. Lerner (Eds.), *Handbook of child psychology* (6th ed.). New York: Wiley.

Harrison-Hale, A.O., McLoyd, V.C., & Smedley, B. (2004). Racial and ethnic status: Risk and protective processes among African-American families. In K.L. Maton, C.J. Schellenbach, B.J. Leadbetter, & A.L. Solarz (Eds.), *Investing in children, families, and communities.* Washington, DC: American Psychological Association.

Harrist, A.W. (1993, March). *Family interaction styles as predictors of children's competence: The role of synchrony and nonsynchrony.* Paper presented at the biennial meeting of the Society for Research in Child Development, New Orleans.

Hart, B., & Risley, T.R. (1995). *Meaningful differences.* Baltimore, MD: Paul Brookes.

Hart, C., Yang, C., Charlesworth, R., & Burts, D.C. (2003). *Kindergarten teaching practices: Associations with later child academic and social/emotional adjustment to school.* Paper presented at the meeting of the Society for Research in Child Development, Tampa.

Hart, C.H., Newell, L.D., & Olsen, S.F. (2003). Parenting skills and social-communicative competence in childhood. In J.O. Greene & B.R. Burleson (Eds.), *Handbook of communication and social interaction skill.* Mahwah, NJ: Erlbaum.

Hart, D., Burock, D., London, B., & Atkins, R. (2003). Prosocial development, antisocial development, and moral development. In A.M. Slater & G. Bremner (Eds.), *An introduction to developmental psychology.* Malden, MA: Blackwell.

Hart, D., & Karmel, M.P. (1996). Self-awareness and self-knowledge in humans, great apes, and monkeys. In A. Russon, K. Bard, & S. Parker (Eds.), *Reaching into thought.* New York: Cambridge University Press.

Harter, S. (1981). A new self-report scale of intrinsic versus extrinsic orientation in the classroom: Motivational and informational components. *Developmental Psychology, 17,* 300–312.

Harter, S. (1985). *Self-Perception Profile for Children.* Denver: University of Denver, Department of Psychology.

Harter, S. (1989). *Self-Perception Profile for Adolescents.* Denver: University of Denver, Department of Psychology.

Harter, S. (1990). Self and identity development. In S.S. Feldman & G.R. Elliott (Eds.), *At the threshold: The developing adolescent.* Cambridge, MA: Harvard University Press.

Harter, S. (1996). Teacher and classmate influences on scholastic motivation, self-esteem, and level of voice in adolescents. In J. Juvonen & K.R. Wentzel (Eds.), *Social motivation.* New York: Cambridge University Press.

Harter, S. (1998). The development of self-representations. In W. Damon (Ed.), *Handbook of child psychology* (5th ed., Vol. 3). New York: Wiley.

Harter, S. (1999). *The construction of the self.* New York: Guilford.

Harter, S. (2002). Unpublished review of Santrock, J.W. *Child development* (10th ed.). New York: McGraw-Hill.

Harter, S., & Marold, D.B. (1992). Psychosocial risk factors contributing to adolescent suicide ideation. In G. Noam & S. Borst (Eds.), *Child and adolescent suicide.* San Francisco: Jossey-Bass.

Harter, S., & Whitesell, N. (2001, April). *What we have learned from Columbine: The impact of self-esteem on suicidal and violent ideation among adolescents.* Paper presented at the meeting of the Society for Research in Child Development, Minneapolis.

Hartmann, D.P., & Pelzel, K.E. (2005). Design, measurement, and analysis in developmental research. In M.H. Bornstein & M.E. Lamb (Eds.), *Developmental psychology* (5th ed.). Mahwah, NJ: Erlbaum.

Hartshorne, H., & May, M.S. (1928–1930). *Moral studies in the nature of character: Studies in deceit* (Vol. 1); *Studies in self-control* (Vol. 2); *Studies in the organization of character* (Vol. 3). New York: Macmillan.

Hartup, W.W. (1983). The peer system. In P.H. Mussen (Ed.), *Handbook of child psychology* (4th ed., Vol. 4). New York: Wiley.

Hartup, W.W. (1996). The company they keep: Friendships and their development significance. *Child Development, 67,* 1–13.

Hartup, W.W. (1999, April). *Peer relations and the growth of the individual child.* Paper presented at the meeting of the Society for Research in Child Development, Albuquerque.

Hartup, W.W. (2000). Middle childhood: Socialization and social context. In A. Kazdin (Ed.), *Encyclopedia of psychology.* Washington, DC, & New York: American Psychological Association and Oxford University Press.

Hartup, W.W., & Abecassis, M. (2004). Friends and enemies. In P.K. Smith & C.H. Hart (Eds.), *Blackwell handbook of childhood social development.* Malden, MA: Blackwell.

Hartup, W.W., & Laursen, B. (1999). Relationships as developmental contexts: Retrospective themes and contemporary issues. In W. Andrew Collins & B. Laursen (Eds.), *Relationships as developmental contexts.* Mahwah, NJ: Erlbaum.

Hartwell, L., Hood, L., Goldberg, M.L., Silver, L.M., Veres, R.C., & Reynolds, A. (2004). *Genetics* (2nd ed.). New York: McGraw-Hill.

Harty-Golder, B. (2005). The plus and minus sides of Rh transfusions. *Medical Laboratory Observer, 37,* 36.

Harvey, J.H., & Fine, M.A. (2004). *Children of divorce.* Mahwah, NJ: Erlbaum.

Harwood, R., Leyendecker, B., Carlson, V., Asencio, M., & Miller, A. (2002). Parenting among Latino families in the U.S. In M.H. Bornstein (Ed.), *Handbook of parenting* (2nd ed.). Mahwah, NJ: Erlbaum.

Haselager, G.J.T., Cillessen, A.H.N., Van Lieshout, C.F.M., Riksen-Walraen, J.M.A., & Hartup, W.W. (2002). Heterogeneity among peer-rejected boys across middle childhood: Developmental pathways of social behavior. *Developmental Psychology, 38,* 446–456.

Hauck, F.R., Moore, C.M., Herman, S.M., Donovan, M., Kalelkar, M., Christoffel, K.K., Hoffman, H.J., & Rowley, D. (2002). The contribution of prone sleeping position to the racial disparity in sudden infant death syndrome: The Chicago Infant Mortality Study. *Pediatrics, 110,* 772–780.

Haugaard, J.J., & Hazan, C. (2004). Adoption as a natural experiment. *Developmental Psychopathology, 15,* 909–926.

Haugaard, J.J., & Hazan, C. (2004). Recognizing and treating uncommon behavioral and emotional disorders in children and adolescents who have been severely maltreated: Reactive attachment disorder. *Child Maltreatment, 9,* 154–160.

Hauser, S.T., & Bowlds, M.K. (1990). Stress, coping, and adaptation. In S.S. Feldman & G.R. Elliott (Eds.), *At the threshold: The developing adolescent.* Cambridge, MA: Harvard University Press.

Hauser, S.T., Powers, S.I., Noam, G.G., Jacobson, A.M., Weisse, B., & Follansbee, D.J. (1984). Familial contexts of adolescent ego development. *Child Development, 55,* 195–213.

Havighurst, R.J. (1976). A cross-cultural view. In J.F. Adams (Ed.), *Understanding adolescence.* Boston: Allyn & Bacon.

Havighurst, S.S., Harley, A., & Prior, M. (2004). Building preschool children's emotional competence. *Early Education and Development, 15,* 423–447.

Hawkins, J.A., & Berndt, T.J. (1985, April). *Adjustment following the transition to junior high school.* Paper presented at the biennial meeting of the Society for Research in Child Development, Toronto.

Hay, D.F., Payne, A., & Chadwick, A. (2004). Peer relations in childhood. *Journal of Child Psychology and Psychiatry, 45,* 84–108.

Hayne, H. (2004). Infant memory development: Implications for infantile amnesia. *Developmental Review, 24,* 33–73.

Hayslip, B., & Hansson, R. (2003). Death awareness and adjustment across the life span. In C.D. Bryant (Ed.), *Handbook of death and dying.* Thousand Oaks, CA: Sage.

Health Management Resources. (2001). *Child health and fitness.* Boston: Author.

Heath, D.H. (1977). Some possible effects of occupation on the maturing professional man. *Journal of Vocational Behavior, 11,* 263–281.

Heath, S.B., & McLaughlin, M.W. (Eds.). (1993). *Identity and inner-city youth.* New York: Teacher College Press.

Hedley, A.A., Ogden, C.L., Johnson, C.L., Carroll, M.D., Curtin, L.R., & Flegal, K.M. (2004). Prevalence of overweight and obesity among U.S. children, adolescents, and adults, 1999–2002. *Journal of the American Medical Association, 29,* 2847–2850.

Heider, F. (1958). *The psychology of interpersonal relations.* New York: Wiley.

Heinze, H.J., Toro, P.A., & Urberg, K.A. (2004). Antisocial behavior and affiliation with deviant peers. *Journal of Clinical Child and Adolescent Psychology, 33,* 336–346.

Heiser, P., Friedel, S., Dempfile, A., Kongrad, K., Smidt, J., Grabarkiewicz, J., Herpertz-Dahlann, B., Remschmidt, H., & Hebebrand, J. (2004). Molecular genetic aspects of attention deficit/hyperactivity disorder. *Neuroscience and Biobehavioral Reviews, 28,* 625–641.

Helms, J.E. (2005). Stereotype threat might explain the black-white test-score difference. *American Psychologist, 60,* 269–270.

Hemmings, A. (2004). *Coming of age in U.S. high schools.* Mahwah, NJ: Erlbaum.

Henderson, A.T., & Mapp, K.L. (2002). *A new wave of evidence: The impact of school, family, and community connections on academic achievement.* Austin, TX: National Center for Family and Community Connections with Schools.

Henderson, P., Martines, J., & de Zoysa, I. (2004). Mortality associated with reasons for not breast feeding. *AIDS, 18,* 361–362.

Hendry, J. (1999). *Social anthropology.* New York: Macmillan.

Henninger, M.L. (1999). *Teaching young children.* Columbus, OH: Merrill.

Henriksen, T.B., Hjollund, N.H., Jensen, T.K., Bonde, J.P., Andersson, A.M., Kolstad, H., Ernst, E., Giwereman, A., Skakkebaek, N.E., & Olsen, J. (2004). Alcohol consumption at the time of conception and spontaneous abortion. *American Journal of Epidemiology, 160,* 661–667.

Hepper, P.G., Shahidullah, S., & White, R. (1990). Origins of fetal handedness. *Nature, 347,* 431.

Herbst, M.A., Mercer, B.M., Beasley, D., Meyer, N., & Carr, T. (2003). Relationship of prenatal care and perinatal morbidity in low-birth-weight infants. *American Journal of Obstetrics and Gynecology, 189,* 930–933.

Herman-Giddens, M.E., Slora, E.J., Wasserman, R.C., Bourdony, C.J., Bhapkar, M.V., Koch, G.G., & Hasemeier, C. (1997). Secondary sexual characteristics and menses in young girls seen in office practice: A study from the Pediatric Research in Office Settings Network. *Pediatrics, 99,* 505–512.

Herrera, S.G., & Murray, K.G. (2005). *Mastering ESL and bilingual methods.* Boston: Allyn & Bacon.

Herrill, R., Goldberg, J., True, W.R., Ramakrishnan, V., Lyons, M., Eisen, S., & Tsuang, M.T. (1999). Sexual orientation and suicidality: A co-twin control study in adult men. *Archives of General Psychiatry, 56,* 867–874.

Herrnstein, R.J., & Murray, C. (1994). *The bell curve: Intelligence and class structure in American life.* New York: Macmillan.

Hetherington, E.M. (1989). Coping with family transitions: Winners, losers, and survivors. *Child Development, 60,* 1–14.

Hetherington, E.M. (1993). An overview of the Virginia Longitudinal Study of Divorce and Remarriage with a focus on early adolescence. *Journal of Family Psychology, 7,* 39–56.

Hetherington, E.M. (1999). Social capital and the development of youth from non-divorced, divorced, and remarried families. In W.A. Collas & B. Laursen (Eds.), *Relationships as developmental contexts.* Mahwah, NJ: Erlbaum.

Hetherington, E.M. (2000). Divorce. In A. Kazdin (Ed.), *Encyclopedia of psychology.* Washington, DC, & New York: American Psychological Association and Oxford University Press.

Hetherington, E.M., Bridges, M., & Insabella, G.M. (1998). What matters? What does not? Five perspectives on the association between marital transitions and children's adjustment. *American Psychologist, 53,* 167–184.

Hetherington, E.M., & Jodl, K.M. (1994). Stepfamilies as settings for child development. In A. Booth & J. Dunn (Eds.), *Stepfamilies: Who benefits? Who does not?* Hillsdale, NJ: Erlbaum.

Hetherington, E.M., & Kelly, J. (2002). *For better or for worse: Divorce reconsidered.* New York: Norton.

Hetherington, E.M., Reiss, D., & Plomin, R. (Eds.). (1994). *Separate social worlds of siblings: The impact of nonshared environment on development.* Hillsdale, NJ: Erlbaum.

Hetherington, E.M., & Stanley-Hagan, M. (2002). Parenting in divorced and remarried families. In M.H. Bornstein (Ed.), *Handbook of parenting* (2nd ed., Vol. 3). Mahwah, NJ: Erlbaum.

Heussler, H.S. (2005). Common causes of sleep disruption and daytime sleepiness: Childhood sleep disorders II. *Medical Journal of Australia, 182,* 482–489.

Heuwinkel, M.K. (1996). New ways of learning: 5 new ways of teaching. *Childhood Education, 72,* 27–31.

Heward, W.L. (2006). *Exceptional children* (8th ed.). Upper Saddle River, NJ: Prentice Hall.

Higgins, A., Power, C., & Kohlberg, L. (1983, April). *Moral atmosphere and moral judgment.* Paper presented at the biennial meeting of the Society for Research in Child Development, Detroit.

Hildebrand, V., Phenice, A., & Hines, R.P. (2000). *Knowing and serving diverse families.* Columbus, OH: Merrill.

Hill, C.R., & Stafford, F.P. (1980). Parental care of children: Time diary estimate of quantity, predictability, and variety. *Journal of Human Resources, 15,* 219–239.

Hill, J., Waldfogel, J., Brooks-Gunn, J., & Han, W. (2001, November). *Towards a better estimate of causal links in child policy: The case of maternal employment and child outcomes.* Paper presented at the Association for Public Policy Analysis and Management Fall Research Conference, Washington, DC.

Hinde, R.A. (1992). Developmental psychology in the context of other behavioral sciences. *Developmental Psychology, 28,* 1018–1029.

Hintz, S.R., Kendrick, D.E., Vohr, B.R., Poole, W.K., Higgins, R.D., and the National Institute of Child Health and Human Development Neonatal Research Network. (2005). Changes in neurodevelopmental outcomes at 18 to 22 months' corrected age among infants of less than 25 weeks' gestational age born in 1993–1999. *Pediatrics, 115,* 1645–1651.

Hipwell, A.E., Murray, L., Ducournau, P., & Stein, A. (2005). The effects of maternal depression and parental conflict on children's peer play. *Child Care, Health, and Development, 31,* 11–23.

Hirsch, B.J., & Rapkin, B.D. (1987). The transition to junior high school: A longitudinal study of self-esteem, psychological symptomatology, school life, and social support. *Child Development, 58,* 1235–1243.

Hirsh, R. (2004). *Early childhood curriculum: Incorporating multiple intelligences, developmentally appropriate practices, and play.* Boston: Allyn & Bacon.

Hiscock, H., & Jordan, B. (2004). Problem crying in infancy. *Medical Journal of Australia, 181,* 507–512.

Hobbins, D. (2004). Survivors of childhood sexual abuse: Implications for perinatal nursing care. *Journal of Obstetric, Gynecologic, and Neonatal Nursing, 33,* 485–497.

Hobel, C.J., Dunkel-Schetter, C., Roesch, S.C., Castro, L.C., & Arora, C.P. (1999). Maternal plasma corticotrophin-releasing hormone associated with stress at 20 weeks' gestation in pregnancies ending in preterm delivery. *American Journal of Obstetrics and Gynecology, 180,* S257–S263.

Hobson, A. (2000). Dreams. In A. Kazdin (Ed.), *Encyclopedia of psychology.* Washington, DC, New York: American Psychological Association and Oxford University Press.

Hoeger, W.W.K., & Hoeger, S.A. (2006). *Principles and labs for fitness and wellness* (8th ed.). Belmont, CA: Wadsworth.

Hoff, E., Laursen, B., & Tardif, T. (2002). Socioeconomic status and parenting. In M.H. Bornstein (Ed.), *Handbook of parenting* (2nd ed.). Mahwah, NJ: Erlbaum.

Hoffman, L.W. (1989). Effects of maternal employment in the two-parent family. *American Psychologist, 44,* 283–292.

Hoffman, L.W., & Youngblade, L.M. (1999). *Mothers at work: Effects on children's well-being.* New York: Cambridge.

Hoffman, M.L. (1970). Moral development. In P.H. Mussen (Ed.), *Manual of child psychology* (3rd ed., Vol. 2). New York: Wiley.

Hoffman, M.L. (1988). Moral development. In M.H. Bornstein & E. Lamb (Eds.), *Developmental psychology: An advanced textbook* (2nd ed.). Hillsdale, NJ: Erlbaum.

Hofstede, G. (1980). *Culture's consequences: International differences in work-related values.* Newbury Park, CA: Sage.

Hogan, D.M., & Tudge, J. (1999). Implications of Vygotsky's theory for peer learning. In A.M. O'Donnell & A. King (Eds.), *Cognitive perspectives on peer learning.* Mahwah, NJ: Erlbaum.

Holcomb, S.S. (2004). Obesity in children and adolescents: Guidelines for prevention and management. *Nurse Practitioner, 29,* 14–15.

Holding, S. (2002). Current state of screening for Down syndrome. *Annals of Clinical Biochemistry, 39,* 1–11.

Hollich, G., Newman, R.S., & Jusczyk, P.W. (2005). Infants' use of synchronized visual information to separate streams of speech. *Child Development, 76,* 598–613.

Hollier, L.M., Harstad, T.W., Sanchez, P.J., Twickler, D.M., & Wendel, G.D. (2001). Fetal syphilis: Clinical and laboratory characteristics. *Obstetrics and Gynecology, 97,* 947–953.

Hollon, S.D. (2006). Cognitive therapy in the treatment and prevention of depression. In T.E. Joiner, J.S. Brown, & J. Kistner (Eds.), *The interpersonal, cognitive, and social nature of depression.* Mahwah, NJ: Erlbaum.

Holmbeck, G.N. (1996). A model of family relational transformations during the transition to adolescence: Parent-adolescent conflict and adaptation. In J.A. Graber, J. Brooks-Gunn, & A.C. Petersen (Eds.), *Transitions through adolescence.* Hillsdale, NJ: Erlbaum.

Holmes, L.D. (1987). *Quest for the real Samoa: The Mead-Freeman controversy and beyond.* South Hadley, MA: Bergin & Garvey.

Holmes, R.M., & Holmes, S.T. (2005). *Suicide.* Thousand Oaks, CA: Sage.

Holtzen, D.W. (2000). Handedness and professional tennis. *International Journal of Neuroscience, 105,* 101–119.

Honzik, M.P., MacFarlane, I.W., & Allen, L. (1948). The stability of mental test performance between two and eighteen years. *Journal of Experimental Education, 17,* 309–324.

Hopkins, B. (1991). Facilitating early motor development: An intracultural study of West Indian mothers and their infants living in Britain. In J.K. Nugent, B.M. Lester, & T.B. Brazelton (Eds.), *The cultural context of infancy: Vol. 2. Multicultural and interdisciplinary approaches to parent-infant relations.* Norwood, NJ: Ablex.

Hopkins, B., & Westra, T. (1988). Maternal handling and motor development: An intracultural study. *Genetic Psychology Monographs, 14,* 377–420.

Hopkins, B., & Westra, T. (1990). Motor development, maternal expectations, and the role of handling. *Infant Behavior and Development, 13,* 117–122.

Hoppu, U., Kalliomaki, M., Laiho, K., & Isolauri, E. (2001). Breast milk—immunomodulatory signals against allergenic diseases. *Allergy, 56,* 23–26.

Horne, R.S., Franco, P., Adamson, T.M., Groswasser, J., & Kahn, A. (2002). Effects of body position on sleep and arousal characteristics in infants. *Early Human Development, 69,* 25–33.

Horne, R.S., Franco, P., Adamson, T.M., Groswasser, J., & Kahn, A. (2004). Influences of maternal cigarette smoking on infant arousability. *Early Human Development, 79,* 49–58.

Horne, R.S., Parslow, P.M., & Harding, R. (2004). Respiratory control and arousal in sleeping infants. *Pediatric Respiratory Reviews, 5,* 190–198.

Hornor, G. (2005). Physical abuse: Recognition and reporting. *Journal of Pediatric Health Care, 19,* 4–11.

Horowitz, F.D., & O'Brien, M. (1989). In the interest of the nation: A reflective essay on the state of knowledge and the challenges before us. *American Psychologist, 44,* 441–445.

Horowitz, J.A., & Goodman, J.H. (2005). Identifying and treating postpartum depression. *Journal of Obstetrics, Gynecology, and Neonatal Nursing, 34,* 264–273.

Horst, J.S., Oakes, L.M., & Madole, K.L. (2005). What does it look like and what can it do? Category structure influences how infants categorize. *Child Development, 76,* 614–631.

Horton, D.M. (2001). The disappearing bell curve. *Journal of Secondary Gifted Education, 12,* 185–188.

Host, A., & Halken, S. (2005). Primary prevention of food allergy in infants who are at risk. *Current Opinions in Allergy and Clinical Immunology, 5,* 255–259.

Houston, A. (2004). In new media as in old, content matters most. *Society for Research in Child Development Policy Report, 28* (4), 4–11.

Howard, R.W. (2001). Searching the real world for signs of rising population intelligence. *Personality & Individual Differences, 30,* 1039–1058.

Howe, M.J.A., Davidson, J.W., Moore, D.G., & Sloboda, J.A. (1995). Are there early childhood signs of musical ability? *Psychology of Music, 23,* 162–176.

Howell, K.K., Lynch, M.E., Platzman, K.A., Smith, G.H., & Coles, C.D. (2005, in press). Prenatal alcohol exposure and ability, academic achievement, and school functioning in adolescence: A longitudinal follow-up. *Journal of Pediatric Psychology.*

Howes, C. (1985, April). *Predicting preschool sociometric status from toddler peer interaction.* Paper presented at the meeting of the Society for Research in Child Development, Toronto.

Hoyle, R.H., & Judd, C.M. (2002). *Research methods in social psychology* (7th ed.). Belmont, CA: Wadsworth.

Hsu, H-C. (2004). Antecedents and consequences of separation anxiety in first-time mothers: Infant, mother, and social-contextual characteristics. *Infant Behavior & Development, 27,* 113–133.

Huang, C.M., Tung, W.S., Kuo, L.L., & Ying-Ju, C. (2004). Comparison of pain responses of premature infants to the heelstick between containment and swaddling. *Journal of Nursing Research, 12,* 31–40.

Huang, L.N., & Ying, Y. (1989). Chinese American children and adolescents, In J.T. Gibbs & L.N. Huang (Eds.), *Children of color.* San Francisco: Jossey-Bass.

Hubbard, J.A. (2001). Emotion expression processes in children's peer interaction: The role of peer rejection, aggression, and gender. *Child Development, 72,* 1426–1438.

Hudson, L.M., Forman, E.R., & Brion-Meisels, S. (1982). Role-taking as a predictor of prosocial behavior in cross-age tutors. *Child Development, 53,* 1320–1329.

Huebner, A.M., & Garrod, A.C. (1993). Moral reasoning among Tibetan monks: A study of Buddhist adolescents and young adults in Nepal. *Journal of Cross-Cultural Psychology, 24,* 167–185.

Huesmann, L.R. (1986). Psychological processes promoting the relation between exposure to media violence and aggressive behavior by the viewer. *Journal of Social Issues, 42,* 125–139.

Huffman, L.R., & Speer, P.W. (2000). Academic performance among at-risk children: The role of developmentally appropriate practices. *Early Childhood Research Quarterly, 15,* 167–184.

Hulse, G.K., O'Neill, G., Pereira, C., & Brewer, C. (2001). Obstetric and neonatal outcomes associated with maternal naltrexone exposure. *Australian and New Zealand Journal of Obstetrics and Gynecology, 41,* 424–428.

Hunt, E. (1995). *Will we be smart enough? A cognitive analysis of the coming work force.* New York: Russell Sage.

Hurt, H., Brodsky, N.L., Roth, H., Malmud, F., & Giannetta, J.M. (2005). School performance of children with gestational cocaine exposure. *Neurotoxicology and Teratology, 27,* 203–211.

Huston, A.C. (1983). Sex-typing. In P.H. Mussen (Ed.), *Handbook of child psychology* (4th ed., Vol. 4). New York: Wiley.

Huston, A.C., Duncan, G.J., Grander, R., Bos, J., McLoyd, V., Mistry, R., Crosby, D., Gibson, C., Magnuson, K., Romich, J., & Ventura, A. (2001). Work-based antipoverty programs for parents can enhance the school performance and social behavior of children. *Child Development, 72,* 318–336.

Huston, A.C., McLoyd, V.C., & Coll, C.G. (1994). Children and poverty: Issues in contemporary research. *Child Development, 65,* 275–282.

Huston, A.C., Siegle, J., & Bremer, M. (1983, April). *Family environment television use by preschool children.* Paper presented at the biennial meeting of the Society for Research in Child Development, Detroit.

Huttenlocher, J., & Cymerman, E. (1999). Unpublished data on speech syntax. Chicago: University of Chicago.

Huttenlocher, J., Haight, W., Bruk, A., Seltzer, M., & Lyons, T. (1991). Early vocabulary growth: Relation to language input and gender. *Developmental Psychology, 27,* 236–248.

Huttenlocher, J., Levine, S., & Vevea, J. (1998). Environmental input and cognitive growth: A study using time-period comparisons. *Child Development, 69,* 1012–1029.

Huttenlocher, P.R., & Dabholkar, A.S. (1997). Regional differences in synaptogenesis in human cerebral cortex. *Journal of Comparative Neurology, 37* (2), 167–178.

Hwang, S.J., Ji, E.H., Kim, Y.M., Shinn, Y., Cheon, Y.H., & Rhyu, I.J. (2004). Gender differences in the corpus collosum of neonates. *Neuroreport, 29,* 1029–1032.

Hyde, A., & Roche-Reid, B. (2004). Midwifery practice and the crisis of modernity. *Social Science Medicine, 58,* 2613–2623.

Hyde, J.S. (1986). Gender differences in aggression. In J.S. Hyde & M.C. Linn (Eds.), *The psychology of gender: Advances through meta-analysis.* Baltimore: Johns Hopkins University Press.

Hyde, J.S. (1993). Meta-analysis and the psychology of women. In F.L. Denmark & M.A. Paludi (Eds.), *Handbook on the psychology of women.* Westport, CT: Greenwood.

Hyde, J.S. (2005). *Half the human experience* (5th ed.). Boston: Houghton Mifflin.

Hyde, J.S. (2005 in press). The gender similarities hypothesis. *American Psychologist.*

Hyde, J.S., & DeLamater, J. (2005). *Human sexuality* (8th ed., revised). New York: McGraw-Hill.

Hyde, J.S., & Mezulis, A.H. (2001). Gender difference research: Issues and critique. In J. Worell (Ed.), *Encyclopedia of women and gender.* San Diego: Academic Press.

Hyman, E.E., & Loftus, E.F. (2001). In M.L. Eisen, J.A. Quas, & G.S. Goodman (Eds.), *Memory and suggestibility in the forensic interview.* Mahwah, NJ: Erlbaum.

Hymel, S., McDougall, P., & Renshaw, P. (2004). Peer acceptance/rejection. In P.K. Smith & C.H. Hart (Eds.), *Blackwell handbook of childhood social development.* Malden, MA: Blackwell.

Hyson, M.C., Copple, C., & Jones, J. (2006). Early childhood development and education. In W. Damon & R. Lerner (Eds.), *Handbook of child psychology* (6th ed.). New York: Wiley.

"I Have a Dream" Foundation. (2005). *About us.* Available on the Internet at http://www.ihad.org.

Iannucci, L. (2000). *Birth defects.* New York: Enslow.

Ingersoll, E.W., & Thoman, E.B. (1999). Sleep/wake states of preterm infants: Stability, developmental change, diurnal variation, and relation with caregiving activity. *Child Development, 170,* 1–10.

Insel, P.M., & Roth, W.T. (2006). *Core concepts in health* (10th ed.). New York: McGraw-Hill.

International Human Genome Sequencing Consortium. (2004). Finishing the euchromatic sequence of the human genome. *Nature, 431,* 931–945.

International Society for Technology in Education. (2001). *National educational technology standards for teachers—preparing teachers to use technology.* Eugene, OR: Author.

Irwin, S.A., Christman, C.A., Grossman, A.W., Galvez, R., Kim, S.H., DeGrush, B.J., Weiler, I.J., & Greenough, W.T. (2005). Fragile X mental retardation protein levels increase following complex environment exposure in rat brain regions undergoing active synaptogenesis. *Neurobiology, Learning, and Memory, 83,* 180–187.

Isquith, P.K., Gioia, G.A., & Espy, K.A. (2004). Executive function in preschool children: Examination through everyday behavior. *Developmental Neuropsychology, 26,* 403–422.

Issacs, C.E. (2005). Human milk inactivates pathogens individually, additively, and synergistically. *Journal of Nutrition, 135,* 1286–1288.

Ivanenko, A., Crabtree, V.M., & Gozal, D. (2004). Sleep in children with psychiatric disorders. *Pediatric Clinics of North America, 51,* 51–68.

Iverson, P., & Kuhl, P.K. (1996). Influences of phonetic identification and category goodness on American listeners' perceptions of /r/ and /l/. *Journal of the Acoustical Society of America, 99,* 1130–1140.

Iverson, P., Kuhl, P.K., Akahane-Yamada, R., Diesch, E., Tohkura, Y., Ketterman, A., & Siebert, C. (2003). A perceptual interference account of acquisition difficulties in non-native phonemes. *Cognition, 87,* B47–B57.

Jackson, A.W., & Davis, G.A. (2000). *Turning Points 2000.* New York: Teachers College Press.

Jacobs, J.E., & Klaczynski, P.A. (2002). The development of judgment and decision making during childhood and adolescence. *Current Directions in Psychological Science, 11,* 145–149.

Jacobs, J.E., & Potenza, M. (1990, March). *The use of decision-making strategies in late adolescence.* Paper presented at the meeting of the Society for Research in Adolescence, Atlanta.

Jacobson, J.L., & Jacobson, S.W. (2002). Association of prenatal exposure to an environmental contaminant with intellectual function in childhood. *Journal of Toxicology—Clinical Toxicology, 40,* 467–475.

Jacobson, J.L., & Jacobson, S.W. (2003). Prenatal exposure to polychlorinated biphenyls and attention at school age. *Journal of Pediatrics, 143,* 780–788.

Jacobson, J.L., Jacobson, S.W., Fein, G.G., Schwart, P.M., & Dowler, J. (1984). Prenatal exposure to an environmental toxin: A test of the multiple-effects model. *Developmental Psychology, 29,* 523–532.

Jacobson, L. (2004). Pre-K standards said to slight social, emotional skills. *Education Week, 23* (42), 13–14.

Jaffee, S., & Hyde, J.S. (2000). Gender differences in moral orientation: A meta-analysis. *Psychological Bulletin, 126,* 703–726.

Jahromi, L.B., Putnam, S.P., & Stifter, C.A. (2004). Maternal regulation of infant reactivity from 2 to 6 months. *Developmental Psychology, 40,* 477–487.

Jain, A.E., & Lacy, T. (2005). Psychotropic drugs in pregnancy and lactation. *Journal of Psychiatric Practice, 11,* 177–191.

Jalongo, M.R., & Isenberg, J.P. (2000). *Exploring your role: A practitioner introduction to early childhood education.* Columbus, OH: Merrill.

James, D.C., & Dobson, B. (2005). Position of the American Dietetic Association: Promoting and supporting breastfeeding. *Journal of the American Dietetic Association, 105,* 810–818.

James, W. (1890/1950). *The principles of psychology.* New York: Dover.

Janicki, M. (2004). Beyond sociobiology: A kinder and gentler evolutionary view of human nature. In C.B. Crawford & C.A. Salmon (Eds.), *Evolutionary psychology, public policy, and personal decisions.* Mahwah, NJ: Erlbaum.

Janssen, I., Craig, W.M., Boyce, W.F., & Picikett, W. (2004). Associations between overweight and obesity with bullying behaviors in school-aged children. *Pediatrics, 113,* 1187–1194.

Janssen, I., Katzmarzyk, P.T., Boyce, W.F., Vereecken, C., Mulvihill, C., Roberts, C., Currie, C., & Pickett, W. (2005). Comparison of overweight and obesity prevalence in school-aged youth from 34 countries and their relationships with physical activity and dietary patterns. *Obesity Research, 6,* 123–132.

Jarrett, R.L. (1995). Growing up poor: The family experiences of socially mobile youth in low-income African-American neighborhoods. *Journal of Adolescent Research, 10,* 111–135.

Jencks, C. (1979). *Who gets ahead? The determinants of economic success in America.* New York: Basic Books.

Jenkins, J.M., & Astington, J.W. (1996). Cognitive factors and family structure associated with theory of mind development in young children. *Developmental Psychology, 32,* 70–78.

Jenkins, T.M., Sciscione, A.C., Wapner, R.J., & Sarton, G.E. (2004). Training in chorionic villus sampling: Limited experience of U.S. fellows. *American Journal of Obstetrics and Gynecology, 191,* 1288–1290.

Jenni, O.G., & O'Connor, B.B. (2005). Chlidren's sleep: An interplay between culture and sleep. *Pediatrics, 115,* 204–216.

Jensen, A.R. (1969). How much can we boost IQ and scholastic achievement? *Harvard Educational Review, 39,* 1–123.

Ji, B.T., Shu, X.O., Linet, M.S., Zheng, W., Wacholde, S., Gao, Y.T., Ying, D.M., & Jin, F. (1997). Paternal cigarette smoking and the risk of childhood cancer among offspring of nonsmoking mothers. *Journal of the National Cancer Institute, 89,* 238–244.

Jiao, S., Ji, G., & Jing, Q. (1996). Cognitive development of Chinese urban only children and children with siblings. *Child Development, 67,* 387–395.

Jimenez, V., Herniquez, M., Llanos, P., & Riquelme, G. (2004). Isolation and purification of human placental plasma membranes from normal and pre-eclamptic pregnancies: A comparative study. *Placenta, 25,* 422–437.

John-Steiner, V., & Mahn, H. (2003). Sociocultural contexts for teaching and learning. In I.B. Weiner (Ed.), *Handbook of psychology* (Vol. 7). New York: Wiley.

Johnson, A.N. (2005). Kangaroo holding beyond the NICU. *Pediatric Nursing, 31,* 53–56.

Johnson, G.B. (2006). *The living world* (4th ed.). New York: McGraw-Hill.

Johnson, J.S., & Newport, E.L. (1991). Critical period effects on universal properties of language: The status of subjacency in the acquisition of a second language. *Cognition, 39,* 215–258.

Johnson, M.H. (2001). Functional brain development during infancy. In A. Fogel & G. Bremner (Eds.), *Blackwell handbook of infant development.* London: Blackwell.

Johnson, M.H. (2005). Developmental neuroscience, psychopathology, and genetics. In M.H. Bornstein & M.E. Lamb (Eds.), *Developmental science.* Mahwah NJ: Erlbaum.

Johnson, M.K., Beebe, T., Mortimer, J.T., & Snyder, M. (1998). Volunteerism in adolescence: A process perspective. *Journal of Research on Adolescence, 8,* 309–332.

Johnson, V.K. (2005). Family process and family structure in children's adaptation to school. In P.A. Cowan, C.P. Cowan, J.C. Ablow, V.K. Johnson, & J.R. Measelle (Eds.), *The family context in children's adaptation to school.* Mahwah, NJ: Erlbaum.

Johnson, W., Bouchard, T.J., Krueger, R.F., McGue, M., & Gottesman, I.I. (2004). Just one *g*: Consistent results from three test batteries. *Intelligence, 32,* 95–107.

Johnston, L.D., O'Malley, P.M., & Bachman, J.G. (2003). *Monitoring the Future national results on adolescent drug use: Overview of key findings, 2002.* Bethesda, MD: National Institute on Drug Abuse.

Johnston, L.D., O'Malley, P.M., Bachman, J.G., & Schulenberg, J.E. (2005). *Monitoring the Future national results on adolescent drug use: Overview of key findings, 2004.* Bethesda, MD: National Institute on Drug Abuse.

Jones, G., Riley, M., & Dwyer, T. (2000). Breastfeeding early in life and bone mass in pepubertal children: A longitudinal study. *Osteoporosis International, 11,* 146–152.

Jones, J.G., & Worthington, T. (2005). Management of sexually abused children by non-forensic sexual abuse examiners. *Journal of the Arkansas Medical Society, 101,* 224–226.

Jones, M.C. (1965). Psychological correlates of somatic development. *Child Development, 36,* 899–911.

Jones, T.G., & Fuller, M.L. (2003). *Teaching Hispanic children.* Boston: Allyn & Bacon.

Jordan, A. (2004). The role of the media in children's development: An ecological perspective. *Journal of Developmental and Behavioral Pediatrics, 25,* 196–206.

Jorm, A.F., Anstey, K.J., Christensen, H., & Rodgers, B. (2004). Gender differences in cognitive abilities: The mediating role of health state and health habits. *Intelligence, 32,* 7–23.

Joseph, C.L.M. (1989). Identification of factors associated with delayed antenatal care. *Journal of the American Medical Association, 81,* 57–63.

Jusczyk, P.W. (2000). *The discovery of spoken language.* Cambridge, MA: MIT Press.

Jusczyk, P.W. (2002). Language development: From speech perception to words. In A. Slater & M. Lewis (Eds.), *Introduction to infant development.* New York: Oxford University Press.

Jusczyk, P.W., & Hohne, E.A. (1997). Infants' memory for spoken words. *Science, 277,* 1984–1986.

Juvonen, J., Graham, S., & Schuster, M.A. (2003). Bullying among young adolescents. *Pediatrics, 112,* 1231–1237.

Kagan, J. (1987). Perspectives on infancy. In J.D. Osofsky (Ed.), *Handbook on infant development* (2nd ed.). New York: Wiley.

Kagan, J. (1992). Yesterday's promises, tomorrow's promises. *Developmental Psychology, 28,* 990–997.

Kagan, J. (1997). Temperament and the reactions to unfamiliarity. *Child Development, 68,* 139–143.

Kagan, J. (2000). Temperament. In A. Kazdin (Ed.), *Encyclopedia of psychology.* Washington, DC, & New York: American Psychological Association and Oxford University Press.

Kagan, J. (2002). Behavioral inhibition as a temperamental category. In R.J. Davidson, K.R. Scherer, & H.H. Goldsmith (Eds.), *Handbook of affective sciences.* New York: Oxford University Press.

Kagan, J. (2003). Biology, context, and development. *Annual Review of Psychology, 54.* Palo Alto, CA: Annual Reviews.

Kagan, J., & Fox, N. (2006). Biology, culture, and temperamental biases. In W. Damon & R. Lerner (Eds.), *Handbook of child psychology* (6th ed.). New York: Wiley.

Kagan, J., & Herschkowitz, N. (2005). *A young mind in a growing brain.* Mahwah, NJ: Erlbaum.

Kagan, J., Kearsley, R.B., & Zelazo, P.R. (1978). *Infancy: Its place in human development.* Cambridge, MA: Harvard University Press.

Kagan, J., & Snidman, N. (1991). Infant predictors of inhibited and uninhibited behavioral profiles. *Psychological Science, 2,* 40–44.

Kagan, S.L., & Scott-Little, C. (2004). Early learning standards. *Phi Delta Kappan, 82,* 388–395.

Kagitcibasi, C. (1988). Diversity of socialization and social change. In P.R. Dasen, J.W. Berry, & N. Sartorious (Eds.), *Health and cross-cultural psychology: Toward applications.* Newbury Park, CA: Sage.

Kagitcibasi, C. (1995). Is psychology relevant to global human development issues? Experience from Turkey. *American Psychologist, 50,* 293–300.

Kahn, A., Gorswasser, J., Franco, P., Scaillet, S., Sawaguchi, T., Kelmanson, I., & Dan, B. (2004). Sudden infant deaths: Stress, arousal, and SIDS. *Pathophysiology, 10,* 241–252.

Kail, R. (1988). Reply to Stigler, Nusbaum, and Chalip. *Child Development, 59,* 1154–1157.

Kail, R. (2000). Speed of information processing: Developmental change and links to intelligence. *Journal of School Psychology, 38,* 51–62.

Kaiser Family Foundation. (2001). *Generation Rx.com: How young people use the Internet for health information.* Menlo Park, CA: Henry J. Kaiser Family Foundation.

Kaiser Family Foundation. (2002a). *Key facts: Teens online.* Menlo, CA: Kaiser Family Foundation.

Kaiser Family Foundation. (2002b). *Teens say sex on TV influences behavior of peers.* Menlo Park, CA: Henry J. Kaiser Family Foundation.

Kalant, H. (2004). Adverse effects of cannabis on health: An update of the literature since 1996. *Progress in Neuropsychopharmacology and Biological Psychiatry, 28,* 849–863.

Kallen, B. (2004). Neonate characteristics after maternal use of antidepressants in late pregnancy. *Archives of Pediatric and Adolescent Medicine, 158,* 312–316.

Kamii, C. (1985). *Young children reinvent arithmetic: Implications of Piaget's theory.* New York: Teachers College Press.

Kamii, C. (1989). *Young children continue to reinvent arithmetic.* New York: Teachers College Press.

Kammerman, S.B. (1989). Child care, women, work, and the family: An international overview of child-care services and related policies. In J.S. Lande, S. Scarr, & N. Gunzenhauser (Eds.), *Caring for children: Challenge to America.* Hillsdale, NJ: Erlbaum.

Kammerman, S.B. (2000a). Parental leave policies. *Social Policy Report of the Society for Research in Child Development, 14* (2), 1–15.

Kammerman, S.B. (2000b). From maternity to paternity child leave policies. *Journal of the Medical Women's Association, 55,* 98–99.

Kanaya, T., Scullin, M.H., & Ceci, S.J. (2003). The Flynn effect and U.S. policies: The impact of rising IQ scores on American society via mental retardation diagnoses. *American Psychologist, 58,* 778–790.

Kanoy, K., Ulku-Steiner, B., Cox, M., & Burchinal, M. (2003). Marital relationship and individual psychological characteristics that predict physical punishment of children. *Journal of Family Psychology, 17,* 20–28.

Kantowitz, B.H., Roediger, H.L., & Elmes, D.G. (2005). *Experimental psychology* (8th ed.). Belmont, CA: Wadsworth.

Kaplow, J.B., Curran, P.J., Dodge, K.A., & The Conduct Problems Prevention Research Group. (2002). Child, parent, and peer predictors of early-onset substance use: A multisite longitudinal study. *Journal of Abnormal Child Psychology, 30,* 199–216.

Karp, H. (2002). *The happiest baby on the block.* New York: Bantam.

Karraker, K.H., & Coleman, P.K. (2005). The effects of child characteristics on parenting. In T. Luster & L. Okagaki (Eds.), *Parenting* (2nd ed.). Mahwah, NJ: Erlbaum.

Kastenbaum, R. (2004). *Death, society, and the human experience* (8th ed.). Boston: Allyn & Bacon.

Katz, L. (1999). Curriculum disputes in early childhood education. *ERIC Clearinghouse on Elementary and Early Childhood Education,* Document EDO-PS-99-13.

Katz, L., & Chard, S. (1989). *Engaging the minds of young children: The project approach.* Norwood, NJ: Ablex.

Katz, L.F. (1999, April). *Toward a family-based hypervigilance model of childhood aggression: The role of the mother's and the father's meta-emotion philosophy.* Paper presented at the meeting of the Society for Research in Child Development, Albuquerque.

Katz, P.A. (1987, August). *Children and social issues.* Paper presented at the meeting of the American Psychological Association, New York.

Katz, P.A. (2004). Introduction to special issue. *Sex Roles, 51,* 257–261.

Kauffman, J.M., & Hallahan, D.P. (2005). *Special education: What it is and why we need it.* Boston: Allyn & Bacon.

Kauffman, J.M., McGee, K., & Brigham, M. (2004). Enabling or disabling? Observations on changes in special education. *Phi Delta Kappan, 85,* 613–620.

Kaugers, A.S., Russ, S.W., & Singer, L.T. (2000, May). *Self-regulation among cocaine-exposed four-year-old children.* Paper presented at the joint meetings of the Pediatric Academic Societies and the American Academy of Pediatrics, Boston.

Kavsek, M. (2004). Predicting IQ from infant visual habituation and dishabituation: A meta-analysis. *Journal of Applied Developmental Psychology, 25,* 369–393.

Kavale, K.A., Holdnack, J.A., & Mostert, M.P. (2005). Responsivenes to intervention and the identification of specific learning disability: A critique and alternative proposal. *Learning Disability Quarterly, 28,* 2–16.

Kazdin, A.E., & Benjet, C. (2003). Spanking children: Evidence and issues. *Current Directions in Psychological Science, 12,* 99–103.

Keating, D.P. (1990). Adolescent thinking. In S.S. Feldman & G.R. Elliott (Eds.), *At the threshold: The developing adolescent.* Cambridge, MA: Harvard University Press.

Keating, D.P. (2004). Cognitive and brain development. In R. Lerner & L. Steinberg (Eds.), *Handbook of adolescent psychology* (2nd ed.). New York: Wiley.

Keel, P.K., Mitchell, J.E., Miller, K.B., Davis, T.L., & Crowe, S.J. (1999). Long-term outcome of bulimia nervosa. *Archives of General Psychiatry, 56,* 63–69.

Keen, R. (2005). Using perceptual representations to guide reaching and looking. In J.J. Reiser, J.J. Lockman, & C.A. Nelson (Eds.), *The role of action in learning and development.* Mahwah, NJ: Erlbaum.

Keil, F. (2006). Cognitive science and cognitive development. In W. Damon & R. Lerner (Eds.), *Handbook of child psychology* (6th ed.). New York: Wiley.

Keller, A., Ford, L., & Meacham, J. (1978). Dimensions of self-concept in preschool children. *Developmental Psychology, 14,* 483–489.

Keller, M. (2004). Self in social relationship. In D. Lapsley & D. Narvaez (Eds.), *Moral development, self, and identity.* Mahwah, NJ: Erlbaum.

Kellinghaus, C., & Luders, H.O. (2004). Frontal lobe epilepsy. *Epileptic Disorders, 6,* 223–229.

Kellman, P.J., & Arterberry, M.E. (2006). Infant visual perception. In W. Damon & R. Lerner (Eds.), *Handbook of child psychology* (6th ed.). New York: Wiley.

Kellman, P.J., & Banks, M.S. (1998). Infant visual perception. In W. Damon (Ed.), *Handbook of child psychology* (5th ed., Vol. 2). New York: Wiley.

Kelly, J.B. (2001). Legal and educational interventions for families in residence and contact disputes. *Australian Journal of Family Law, 15,* 92–113.

Kennedy, H.P., Beck, C.T., & Driscoll, J.W. (2002). A light in the fog: Caring for women with postpartum depression. *Journal of Midwifery & Women's Health, 47,* 318–330.

Kennell, J.H., & McGrath, S.K. (1999). Commentary: Practical and humanistic lessons from the third world for perinatal caregivers everywhere. *Birth, 26,* 9–10.

Kenrick, D.T., Li, N.P., & Butner, J. (2003). Dynamical evolutionary psychology: Individual decision rules and emergent social norms. *Psychological Review, 110,* 3–28.

Kerr, M. (2001). Culture as a context for temperament. In T.D. Wachs & G.A. Kohnstamm (Eds.), *Temperament in context.* Mahwah, NJ: Erlbaum.

Kessen, W., Haith, M.M., & Salapatek, P. (1970). Human infancy. In P.H. Mussen (Ed.), *Manual of child psychology* (3rd ed., Vol. 1). New York: Wiley.

Khedr, E.M., Hamed, E., Said, A., & Basahi, J. (2002). Handedness and language cerebral lateralization. *European Journal of Applied Physiology, 87,* 469–473.

Kiarie, J.N., Richardson, B.A., MboriNgacha, B., Nduati, R.W., & John-Stewart, T.M. (2004). Infant feeding practices of women in perinatal HIV-1 prevention study in Nairobi, Kenya. *Journal of Acquired Immune Deficiency Syndrome, 35,* 75–81.

Kilbride, H.W., Thorstad, K., & Daily, D.K. (2004). Preschool outcome of less than 801-gram preterm infants compared with full-term siblings. *Pediatrics, 113,* 742–747.

Kim, J., & Cicchetti, D. (2004). A longitudinal study of child maltreatment, mother-child relationship quality and maladjustment: The role of self-esteem and social competence. *Journal of Abnormal Child Psychology, 32,* 341–354.

Kimm, S.Y., Barton, B.A., Obarzanek, E., McMahon, R.P., Kronsberg, S.S., Waclawiw, M.A., Morrison, J.A., Schreiber, G.G., Sabry, Z.I., & Daniels, S.R. (2002). Obesity development during adolescence in a biracial cohort: The NHLBI Growth and Health Study. *Pediatrics, 110,* E54.

Kimm, S.Y., & Obarzanek, E. (2002). Childhood obesity: A new pandemic of the new millennium. *Pediatrics, 110,* 1003–1007.

Kimura, D. (2000). *Sex and cognition.* Cambridge, MA: MIT Press.

Kinginger, C. (2002). Defining the zone of proximal development in U.S. foreign language education. *Applied Linguistics, 23,* 240–261.

Kingston, M.K. (1976). *The woman warrior: Memoirs of a girlhood among ghosts.* New York: Vintage Books.

Kingston, M.K. (1980). *China men.* New York: Knopf.

Kirkham, C., Harris, S., & Grzybowski, S. (2005). Evidence-based prenatal care II: Third-trimester care and prevention of infectious diseases. *American Family Physician, 71,* 1555–1560.

Kisilevsky, B.S. (1995). The influence stimulus and subject variables on human fetal responses to sound and vibration. In J-P Lecaunet, W.P. Fifer, M.A. Krasnegor, & W.P. Smotherman (Eds.), *Fetal development.* Hillsdale, NJ: Erlbaum.

Kisilevsky, B.S., Hains, S.M., Jacquet, A.Y., Granier-Deferre, C., & Lecanuet, J.P. (2004). Maturation of fetal responses to music. *Developmental Science, 7,* 550–559.

Kite, M. (2001). Gender stereotypes. In J. Worell (Ed.), *Encyclopedia of women and gender.* San Diego: Academic Press.

Klaczynski, P.A., & Narasimham, G. (1998). Development of scientific reasoning biases: Cognitive versus ego-protective explanations. *Developmental Psychology, 34,* 175–187.

Klaus, M., & Kennell, J.H. (1976). *Maternal-infant bonding.* St. Louis: Mosby.

Klaus, M.H., Kennell, J.H., & Klaus, P.H. (1993). *Mothering the mother.* Reading, MA: Addison-Wesley.

Klesges, L.M., Johnson, K.C., Ward, K.D., & Barnard, M. (2001). Smoking cessation in pregnant women. *Obstetrics and Gynecological Clinics of North America, 28,* 269–282.

Kling, K.C., Hyde, J.S., Showers, C.J., & Buswell, B.N. (1999). Gender differences in self-esteem: A meta-analysis. *Psychological Bulletin, 125,* 470–500.

Klonoff-Cohen, H.S., & Natarajan, L. (2004). The effect of advancing paternal age on pregnancy and live birth rates in couples undergoing in vitro fertilization or gamete intrafallopian transfer. *American Journal of Obstetrics and Gynecology, 191,* 507–514.

Klug, W.S., & Cummings, M.R. (2005). *Essentials of genetics* (5th ed.). Upper Saddle River, NJ: Prentice Hall.

Klug, W.S., Cummings, M.R., & Spencer, C. (2006). *Concepts of genetics* (8th ed.). Upper Saddle River, NJ: Prentice Hall.

Knafo, A., Iervolino, A.C., & Plomin, R. (2005). Masculine girls and feminine boys: Genetic and environmental contributions to atypical gender development in early childhood. *Journal of Personality and Social Psychology, 88,* 400–412.

Knecht, S., Drager, B., Deppe, M., Bobe, L., Lohmann, H., Floel, A., Ringelstein, E.B., & Henningsen, H. (2000). Handedness and hemispheric language dominance in healthy humans. *Brain, 135,* 2512–2518.

Kobayashi, K., Tajima, M., Toishi, S., Fujimori, K., Suzuki, Y., & Udagama, H. (2005). Fetal growth restriction associated with measles virus infection during pregnancy. *Journal of Perinatal Medicine, 33,* 67–68.

Kochanska, G., Aksan, N., Knaack, A., & Rhines, H.M. (2004). Maternal parenting and children's conscience: Early security as a moderator. *Child Development, 75,* 1229–1242.

Kochanska, G., Gross, J.N., Lin, M., & Nichols, K.E. (2002). Guilt in young children: Development, determinants, and relations with a broader set of standards. *Child Development, 73,* 461–482.

Koestner, R., Franz, C., & Weinberger, J. (1990). The family origins of empathic concern: A 26-year longitudinal study. *Journal of Personality and Social Psychology, 58,* 709–717.

Kohlberg, L. (1958). *The development of modes of moral thinking and choice in the years 10 to 16.* Unpublished doctoral dissertation, University of Chicago.

Kohlberg, L. (1966). A cognitive-developmental analysis of children's sex-role concepts and attitudes. In E.E. Maccoby (Ed.), *The development of sex differences.* Palo Alto, CA: Stanford University Press.

Kohlberg, L. (1969). Stage and sequence: The cognitive-developmental approach to socialization. In D.A. Goslin (Ed.), *Handbook of socialization theory and research.* Chicago: Rand McNally.

Kohlberg, L. (1976). Moral stages and moralization: The cognitive-developmental approach. In T. Lickona (Ed.), *Moral development and behavior.* New York: Holt, Rinehart & Winston.

Kohlberg, L. (1986). A current statement on some theoretical issues. In S. Modgil & C. Modgil (Eds.), *Lawrence Kohlberg.* Philadelphia: Falmer.

Kohn, M.L. (1977). *Class and conformity: A study in values* (2nd ed.). Chicago: University of Chicago Press.

Kopp, C.B., & Neufeld, S.J. (2002). Emotional development in infancy. In R. Davidson & K. Scherer (Eds.), *Handbook of affective sciences.* New York: Oxford University Press.

Koppelman, K. (2005). *Understanding human differences.* Upper Saddle River, NJ: Prentice Hall.

Kornhaber, M., Fierros, E., & Veenema, S. (2005). *Multiple intelligences: Best ideas from research and practice.* Boston: Allyn & Bacon.

Kortenhaus, C.M., & Demarest, J. (1993). Gender role stereotyping in children's literature: An update. *Sex Roles, 28,* 219–230.

Kotler, J.A., Wright, J.C., & Huston, A.C. (2001). Television use in families with children. In J. Bryant & J.A. Bryant (Eds.), *Television and the American Family.* Mahwah, NJ: Erlbaum.

Kotovsky, L., & Baillargeon, R. (1994). Calibration-based reasoning about collision events in 11-month-old infants. *Cognition, 51,* 107–129.

Kottak, C.P. (2002). *Cultural anthropology* (9th ed.). New York: McGraw-Hill.

Kozol, J. (1991). *Savage inequalities.* New York: Crown.

Kozulin, A. (2000). Vygotsky. In A. Kazdin (Ed.), *Encyclopedia of psychology.* Washington, DC, & New York: American Psychological Association and Oxford University Press.

Kramer, M. (2003). Commentary: Breast-feeding and child health, growth, and survival. *International Journal of Epidemiology, 32,* 96–98.

Krauss, R.A., & Glucksberg, S. (1969). The development of communication: Competence as a function of age. *Child Development, 40,* 255–266.

Kretuzer, L.C., Leonard, C., & Flavell, J.H. (1975). An interview study of children's knowledge about memory. *Monographs of the Society for Research in Child Development, 40* (1, Serial No. 159).

Krimel, L.S., & Goldman-Rakic, P.S. (2001). Prefrontal microcircuits. *Journal of Neuroscience, 21,* 3788–3796.

Kroger, J. (2003). Identity development during adolescence. In G. Adams & M. Berzonsky (Eds.), *Blackwell handbook of adolescence.* Malden, MA: Blackwell.

Krogh, D. (2005). *Biology* (3rd ed.). Upper Saddle River, NJ: Prentice Hall.

Krogh, K.L., & Slentz, S.L. (2001). *Teaching young children.* Mahwah, NJ: Erlbaum.

Kroneman, L., Loeber, R., & Hipwell, A.E. (2004). Is neighborhood context differently related to externalizing problems and delinquency for girls compared with boys? *Clinical Child and Family Psychology Review, 7,* 109–122.

Kuczynski, L., & Lollis, S. (2002). Four foundations for a dynamic model of parenting. In J.R.M. Gerris (Ed.), *Dynamics of parenting.* Mahwah, NJ: Erlbaum.

Kuebli, J. (1994, March). Young children's understanding of everyday emotions. *Young Children,* pp. 36–48.

Kuhl, P.K. (1993). Infant speech perception: A window on psycholinguistic development. *International Journal of Psycholinguistics, 9,* 33–56.

Kuhl, P.K. (2000). A new view of language acquisition. *Proceedings of the National Academy of Science, 97* (22), 11850–11857.

Kuhn, D. (1998). Afterward to Volume 2: Cognition, perception, and language. In W. Damon (Ed.), *Handbook of child psychology* (5th ed., Vol. 2). New York: Wiley.

Kuhn, D. (2000). Adolescence: Adolescent thought processes. In A. Kazdin (Ed.), *Encyclopedia of psychology.* Washington, DC, & New York: American Psychological Association and Oxford University Press.

Kuhn, D., Amsel, E., & O'Laughlin, M. (1988). *The development of scientific thinking skills.* Orlando, FL: Academic Press.

Kuhn, D., & Franklin, S. (2006). The second decade: What develops (and how). In W. Damon & R. Lerner (Eds.), *Handbook of child psychology* (6th ed.). New York: Wiley.

Kuhn, D., & Pease, M. (in press). Do children and adults learn differently? *Journal of Cognition and Development.*

Kuhn, D., Schauble, L., & Garcia-Mila, M. (1992). Cross-domain development of scientific reasoning. *Cognition and Instruction, 9,* 285–327.

Kuiper, R.A., & Pesut, D.J. (2004). Promoting cognitive and metacognitive reflective reasoning skills in nursing practice: Self-regulated learning theory. *Journal of Advanced Nursing, 45,* 381–391.

Kulczewski, P. (2005). Vygotsky and the three bears. *Teaching children mathematics, 11,* 246–248.

Kumari, A.S. (2001). Pregnancy outcome in women with morbid obesity. *International Journal of Gynecology and Obstetrics, 73,* 101–107.

Kuo, P.H., Lin, C.C., Yang, H.J., Soong, W.T., & Chen, W.J. (2004). A twin study of competence and behavioral/emotional problems among adolescents in Taiwan. *Behavior Genetics, 34,* 63–74.

Kupersmidt, J.B., & Coie, J.D. (1990). Preadolescent peer status, aggression, and school adjustment as predictors of externalizing problems in adolescence. *Child Development, 61,* 1350–1363.

Kupersmidt, J.B., & DeRosier, M.E. (2004). How peer problems lead to negative outcomes: An integrative mediational model. In J.B. Kupersmidt & K.A. Dodge (Eds.), *Children's peer relations: From development to intervention.* Washington, DC: American Psychological Association.

Kurdek, L.A., & Krile, D. (1982). A developmental analysis of the relation between peer acceptance and both interpersonal understanding and perceived social self-competence. *Child Development, 53,* 1485–1491.

Kwak, H.K., Kim, M., Cho, B.H., & Ham, Y.M. (1999, April). *The relationship between children's temperament, maternal control strategies, and children's compliance.* Paper presented at the meeting of the Society for Research in Child Development, Albuquerque.

Kwan, M.L., Buffler, P.A., Abrams, B., & Kiley, V.A. (2004). Breastfeeding and the risk of childhood leukemia: A meta-analysis. *Public Health Reports, 119,* 521–535.

La Greca, A.M., & Harrison, H.M. (2005). Adolescent peer relations, friendships, and romantic relationships: Do they predict anxiety and depression? *Journal of Clinical Child & Adolescent Psychology, 34,* 49–61.

Lachlan, R.F., & Feldman, M.W. (2003). Evolution of cultural communication systems. *Journal of Evolutionary Biology, 16,* 1084–1095.

Ladd, G.W. (2006). *Peer relationships and social competence of children and adolescents.* New Haven, CT: Yale University Press.

Ladd, G.W., Buhs, E., & Troop, W. (2004). School adjustment and social skills training. In P.K. Smith & C.H. Hart (Eds.), *Blackwell handbook of childhood social development.* Malden, MA: Blackwell.

Ladd, G.W., & Hart, C.H. (1992). Creating informal play opportunities: Are parents' and preschoolers' initiations related to children's competence with peers? *Cognitive Psychology, 28,* 1179–1187.

Ladd, G.W., LeSeiur, K., & Profilet, S.M. (1993). Direct parental influences on young children's peer relations. In S. Duck (Ed.), *Learning about relationships* (Vol. 2). London: Sage.

Ladd, G.W., & Pettit, G.S. (2002). Parenting and development of children's peer relationships. In M. Bornstein (Ed.), *Handbook of parenting* (2nd ed.). Mahwah, NJ: Erlbaum.

Laditka, S.B., Laditka, J.N., Bennett, K.J., & Probst, J.C. (2005). Delivery complications associated with prenatal care access for Medicaid-insured mothers in rural and urban hospitals. *Journal of Rural Health, 21,* 158–166.

Laible, D.J., & Thompson, R.A. (2000). Mother-child discourse, attachment security, shared positive affect, and early conscience development. *Child Development, 71,* 1424–1440.

Laird, R.D., Pettit, G.S., Bates, J.E., & Dodge, K.A. (2003). Parents' monitoring-relevant knowledge and adolescents' delinquent behavior: Evidence of correlated developmental changes and reciprocal influences. *Child Development, 74,* 752–768.

Lamb, M.E. (1986). *The father's role: Applied perspectives.* New York: Wiley.

Lamb, M.E. (1994). Infant care practices and the application of knowledge. In C.B. Fisher & R.M. Lerner (Eds.), *Applied developmental psychology.* New York: McGraw-Hill.

Lamb, M.E. (1997), Fatherhood then and now. In A. Booth & A.C. Crouter (Eds.), *Men in families.* Mahwah, NJ: Erlbaum.

Lamb, M.E. (2000). The history of research on father involvement: An overview. *Marriage and Family Review, 29,* 23–42.

Lamb, M.E. (2005). Attachments, social networks, and developmental contexts. *Human Development, 48,* 108–112.

Lamb, M.E., & Ahnert, L. (2006). Nonparental care. In W. Damon & R. Lerner (Eds.), *Handbook of child psychology* (6th ed.). New York: Wiley.

Lamb, M.E., Bornstein, M.H., & Teti, D.M. (2002). *Development in infancy* (4th ed.). Mahwah, NJ: Erlbaum.

Lamb, M.E., Frodi, A.M., Hwant, C.P., Frodi, M., & Steinberg, J. (1982). Mother- and father-infant interaction involving play and holding in traditional and nontraditional Swedish families. *Developmental Psychology, 18,* 215–221.

Lamb, M.E., & Lewis, C. (2005). The role of parent-child relationships in child development. In M.H. Bornstein & M.E. Lamb (Eds.), *Developmental psychology* (5th ed.). Mahwah, NJ: Erlbaum.

Lamb, M.E., & Sternberg, K.J. (1992). Sociocultural perspectives in nonparental childcare. In M.E. Lamb, K.J. Sternberg, C. Hwang, & A.G. Broberg (Eds.), *Child care in context.* Hillsdale, NJ: Erlbaum.

Lamberg, L. (2005). Pediatric sleep medicine comes of age. *Journal of the American Medical Association, 293,* 2327–2329.

Lambert, S. (2005). Gay and lesbian families: What we know and where to go from here. *Family Journal, 13,* 43–51.

Lane, H. (1976). *The wild boy of Aveyron.* Cambridge, MA: Harvard University Press.

Lane, H.B., & Pullen, P.C. (2004). *Phonological awareness assessment and instruction.* Boston: Allyn & Bacon.

Lantz, P.M., Low, L.K., Varkey, S., & Watson, R.L. (2005). Doulas as childbirth professionals: Results from a national survey. *Womens Health Issues, 15,* 109–116.

Lapsley, D.K. (1996). *Moral psychology.* Boulder, CO: Westview Press.

Lapsley, D.K. (2005). Moral stage theory. In M. Killen & J. Smetana (Eds.), *Handbook of moral development.* Mahwah, NJ: Erlbaum.

Lapsley, D.K., & Narvaez, D. (Eds.). (2004). *Moral development, self, and identity.* Mahwah, NJ: Erlbaum.

Lapsley, D.K., & Narvaez, D. (2006). Character education. In W. Damon & R. Lerner (Eds.), *Handbook of child psychology* (6th ed.). New York: Wiley.

Lapsley, D.K., & Power, F.C. (Eds.). (1988). *Self, ego, and identity.* New York: Springer-Verlag.

Larson, R.W. (2001). How U.S. children and adolescents spend time: What it does (and doesn't) tell us about their development. *Current Directions in Psychological Science, 10,* 160–164.

Larson, R.W., Clore, G.L., & Wood, G.A. (1999). The emotions of romantic relationships. In W. Furman, B.B. Brown, & C. Feiring (Eds.), *The development of romantic relationships in adolescence.* New York: Cambridge University Press.

Larson, R.W., & Richards, M.H. (1994). *Divergent realities.* New York: Basic Books.

Larson, R.W., & Seepersad, S. (2003). Adolescents' leisure time in the U.S.: Partying, sports, and the American Experiment. In S. Verma & R. Larson (Eds.), *Examining adolescent leisure time across cultures.* San Francisco: Jossey-Bass.

Larson, R.W., & Verma, S. (1999). How children and adolescents spend time across the world: Work, play, and developmental opportunities. *Psychological Bulletin, 125,* 701–736.

Larson, R.W., & Wilson, S. (2004). Adolescence across place and time: Globalization and the changing pathways to adulthood. In R. Lerner & L. Steinberg (Eds.), *Handbook of adolescent psychology* (2nd ed.). New York: Wiley.

Laursen, B., & Collins, W.A. (2004). Parent-child communication during adolescence. In A.L. Vangelisti (Ed.), *Handbook of family communication.* Mahwah, NJ: Erlbaum.

Lazar, L., Darlington, R., & Collaborators. (1982). Lasting effects of early education: A report from the consortium for longitudinal studies. *Monographs of the Society for Research in Child Development, 47.*

Lazarus, R.S. (1996). *Psychological stress and the coping process.* New York: McGraw-Hill.

Lazarus, R.S., & Folkman, S. (1984). *Stress, appraisal and coping.* New York: Springer.

Le Vay, S. (1994). *The sexual brain.* Cambridge, MA: MIT Press.

Leach, P. (1990). *Your baby and child: From birth to age five.* New York: Knopf.

Leaper, C., & Bigler, R.S. (2004). Commentary: Gender language and sexist thought. *Monographs of the Society for Research in Child Development, 69* (1, Serial No. 275), 128–142.

Leaper, C., & Smith, T.E. (2004). A meta-analytic review of gender variations in children's language use: Talkativeness, affiliative speech, and assertive speech. *Developmental Psychology, 40,* 993–1027.

Learner-Centered Principles Work Group. (1997). *Learner-centered psychological principles: A framework for school redesign and reform.* Washington, DC: American Psychological Association.

Leary, M.R. (2004). *Introduction to behavioral research methods* (4th ed.). Boston: Allyn & Bacon.

LeDoux, J.E. (1996). *The emotional brain: The mysterious underpinnings of emotional life.* New York: Simon & Schuster.

LeDoux, J.E. (2000). Emotion circuits in the brain. *Annual Review of Neuroscience, 23,* 155–184.

Lee, J., & others. (2005). Maternal and infant characteristics associated with perinatal arterial stroke in the infant. *Obstetrical and Gynecological Survey, 60,* 430–431.

Lee, R.M. (2005). Resilience against discrimination: Ethnic identity and other-group orientation as protective factors for Korean Americans. *Journal of Counseling Psychology, 52,* 36–44.

Lehr, C.A., Hanson, A., Sinclair, M.F., & Christenson, S.L. (2003). Moving beyond dropout prevention towards school completion: An integrative review of data-based interventions. *School Psychology Review, 32,* 342–364.

Lehrer, R., & Schauble, L. (2006). Scientific thinking and scientific literacy. In W. Damon & R. Lerner (Eds.), *Handbook of child psychology* (6th ed.). New York: Wiley.

Lehtonen, L., & Martin, R.J. (2004). Ontongeny of sleep and awake states in relation to breathing in preterm infants. *Seminars in Neonatology, 9,* 229–238.

Leifer, A.D. (1973). *Television and the development of social behavior.* Paper presented at the meeting of the International Society for the Study of Behavioral Development, Ann Arbor, Michigan.

Leifer, M., Kilbane, T., Jacobsen, T., & Grossman, G. (2004). A three-generational study of transmission of risk for sexual abuse. *Journal of Clinical Child and Adolescent Psychology, 33,* 662–665.

Leman, P.J., Ahmed, S., & Ozarow, L. (2005). Gender, gender relations, and the social dynamics of children's conversations. *Developmental Psychology, 41,* 64–74.

LeMare, L.J., & Rubin, K.H. (1987). Perspective taking and peer interaction: Structural and developmental analyses. *Child Development, 58,* 306–315.

Lenders, C.M., McElrath, T.F., & Scholl, T.O. (2000). Nutrition in pregnancy. *Current Opinions in Pediatrics, 12,* 291–296.

Lenneberg, E. (1967). *The biological foundations of language.* New York: Wiley.

Lenoir, C.P., Mallet, E., & Calenda, E. (2000). Siblings of sudden infant death syndrome and near miss in about 30 families: Is there a genetic link? *Medical Hypotheses, 54,* 408–411.

Leong, F.T.L. (2000). Cultural pluralism. In A. Kazdin (Ed.), *Encyclopedia of psychology.* Washington, DC, and New York: American Psychological Association and Oxford University Press.

Lepper, M., Greene, D., & Nisbett, R. (1973). Undermining children's intrinsic interest with extrinsic rewards: A test of the overjustification hypothesis. *Journal of Personality and Social Psychology, 28,* 129–137.

Lerner, R. (2002). *Concepts and theories of human development* (3rd ed.). Mahwah, NJ: Erlbaum.

Lerner, R. (2006). Developmental science, developmental systems, and contemporary theories. In W. Damon & R. Lerner (Eds.), *Handbook of child psychology* (6th ed.). New York: Wiley.

Lessard, N., Pare, M., Lepore, F., & Lassonde, M. (1998). Early-blind human subjects localize sound sources better than sighted subjects. *Nature, 395,* 278–280.

Lessow-Hurley, J. (2005). *Foundations of dual language instruction* (4th ed.). Boston: Allyn & Bacon.

Lester, B.M. (2000). Unpublished review of J.W. Santrock's *Life-span development* (8th ed.). New York: McGraw-Hill.

Lester, B.M., Tronick, E.Z., & Brazelton, T.B. (2004). The Neonatal Intensive Care Unit Network Neurobehavioral Scale procedures. *Pediatrics, 113* (Supplement), S641–S667.

Lester, B.M., Tronick, E.Z., LaGasse, L., Seifer, R., Bauer, C.R., Shankaran, S., Bada, H.S., Wright, L.L., Smeriglio, V.L., Lu, J., Finnegan, L.P., & Maza, P.L. (2002). The maternal lifestyle study: Effects of substance exposure during pregnancy on neurodevelopmental outcome in 1-month-old infants. *Pediatrics, 110,* 1182–1192.

Levanen, S., & Hamdorf, D. (2001). Feeling vibrations: Enhanced tactile sensitivity in congenitally deaf humans. *Neuroscience Letters, 301,* 75–77.

Leventhal, A. (1994, February). *Peer conformity during adolescence: An integration of developmental, situational, and individual characteristics.* Paper presented at the meeting of the Society for Research on Adolescence, San Diego.

Leventhal, T., & Brooks-Gunn, J. (2003). Moving up: Neighborhood effects on children and families. In M.H. Bornstein & R.H. Bradley (Eds.), *Socioeconomics status, parenting, and child development.* Mahwah, NJ: Erlbaum.

Leventhal, T., & Brooks-Gunn, J. (2004). Diversity in developmental trajectories across adolescence: Neighborhood influences. In R. Lerner & L. Steinberg (Eds.), *Handbook of adolescent psychology* (2nd ed.). New York: Wiley.

Levy, G.D., Sadovsky, A.L., & Troseth, G.L. (2000). Aspects of young children's perceptions of gender-typed occupations. *Sex Roles, 42,* 993–1006.

Lewallen, L.P. (2004). Healthy behaviors and sources of health information among low-income pregnant women. *Public Health Nursing, 21,* 200–206.

Lewin, B. (2006). *Essential genes.* Upper Saddle River, NJ: Prentice Hall.

Lewis, C., & Carpendale, J. (2004). Social cognition. In P.K. Smith & C.H. Hart (Eds.), *Blackwell handbook of childhood social development.* Malden, MA: Blackwell.

Lewis, M. (1997). *Altering fate: Why the past does not predict the future.* New York: Guilford Press.

Lewis, M. (2002). Early emotional development. In A. Slater & M. Lewis (Eds.), *Infant development.* New York: Oxford University Press.

Lewis, M., & Brooks-Gunn, J. (1979). *Social cognition and the acquisition of the self.* New York: Plenum.

Lewis, M., & Ramsay, D.S. (1999). Effect of maternal soothing and infant stress response. *Child Development, 70,* 11–20.

Lewis, M., Sullivan, M.W., Sanger, C., & Weiss, M. (1989). Self-development and self-conscious emotions. *Child Development, 60,* 146–156.

Lewis, R. (2005). *Human genetics* (6th ed.). New York: McGraw-Hill.

Lewis, R. (2007). *Human genetics* (7th ed.). New York: McGraw-Hill.

Lewis, R.B., & Doorlag, D. (2006). *Teaching special students in general education classrooms* (7th ed.). Upper Saddle River, NJ: Prentice Hall.

Leyendecker, B., Harwood, R.L., Comparini, L., & Yalcinkaya, A. (2005). Socioeconomic status, ethnicity, and parenting. In T. Luster & L. Okagaki (Eds.), *Parenting.* Mahwah, NJ: Erlbaum.

Li, A.M., Chan, D., Wong, E., Yin, J., Nelson, E.A., & Fok, T.F. (2003). The effects of obesity on pulmonary function. *Archives of Diseases in Childhood, 88,* 361–363.

Li, H.J., Ji, C.Y., Wang, W., & Hu, Y.H. (2005). A twin study for serum leptin, soluble leptin receptor, and free insulin-like growth factor-1 in pubertal females. *Journal of Clinical Endocrinology and Metabolism, 90,* 3659–3664.

Li, R., Darling, N., Maurice, E., Barker, L., & Grummer-Strawn, M. (2005). Breastfeeding rates in the United States by characteristics of the child, mothers or family: The 2002 National Immunization Survey. *Pediatrics, 115,* e31–e37.

Liben, L.S. (1995). Psychology meets geography: Exploring the gender gap on the national geography bee. *Psychological Science Agenda, 8,* 8–9.

Liben, L.S., & Bigler, R.S. (2002). The developmental course of gender differentiation. *Monographs of the society for research in child development, 67* (2), 1–147.

Lickliter, R., & Bahrick, L.E. (2000). The development of infant intersensory perception: Advantages of a comparative convergent-operations approach. *Psychological Bulletin, 126,* 260–280.

Lidral, A.C., & Murray, J.C. (2005). Genetic approaches to identify disease genes for birth defects with cleft lip/palate as a model. *Birth Defects Research, 70,* 893–901.

Lie, E., & Newcombe, N. (1999). Elementary school children's explicit and implicit memory for faces of preschool classmates. *Developmental Psychology, 35,* 102–112.

Liederman, J., Kantrowitz, L., & Flannery, K. (2005). Male vulnerability to reading disability is not likely to be a myth: A call for new data. *Journal of Learning Disabilities, 38,* 109–129.

Limber, S.P. (1997). Preventing violence among school children. *Family Futures, 1,* 27–28.

Limber, S.P. (2004). Implementation of the Olweus Bullying Prevention Program in American schools: Lessons learned from the field. In D.L. Espelage & S.M. Swearer (Eds.), *Bullying in American Schools.* Mahwah, NJ: Erlbaum.

Lindberg, M.A., Keiffer, J., & Thomas, S.W. (2000). Eyewitness testimony for physical abuse as a function of personal experience, development, and focus of study. *Journal of Applied Developmental Psychology, 21,* 555–591.

Lindbohm, M. (1991). Effects of paternal occupational exposure in spontaneous abortions. *American Journal of Public Health, 121,* 1029–1033.

Linnenbrink, E.A., & Pintrich, P.R. (2004). Role of affect in cognitive processing in academic contexts. In D.Y. Dai & R.J. Sternberg (Eds.), *Motivation, emotion, and cognition.* Mahwah, NJ: Erlbaum.

Linver, M.R., Fuligni, A.S., Hernandez, M., & Brooks-Gunn, J. (2004). Poverty and child development: Promising interventions. In P. Allen-Meares & M.W. Fraser (Eds.), *Intervention with children and adolescents: An interdisciplinary perspective.* New York: Allyn & Bacon.

Liou, J.D., Chu, D.C., Cheng, P.J., Chang, S.D., Sun, C.F., Wu, Y.C., Liou, W.Y., & Chiu, D.T. (2004). Human chromosome 21-specific DNA markers are useful in prenatal detection of Down syndrome. *Annals of Clinical Laboratory Science, 34,* 319–323.

Lippa, R.A. (2002). *Gender, nature, and nurture.* Mahwah, NJ: Erlbaum.

Lippa, R.A. (2005). *Gender, nature, and nurture* (2nd ed.). Mahwah, NJ: Erlbaum.

Lipsitz, J. (1983, October). *Making it the hard way: Adolescents in the 1980s.* Testimony presented at the Crisis Intervention Task Force, House Select Committee on Children, Youth, and Families, Washington, DC.

Litovsky, R.Y., & Ashmead, D.H. (1997). Development of binaural and spatial hearing in infants and children. In R.H. Gilkey & T.R. Anderson (Eds.), *Binaural and spatial hearing in real and virtual environments.* Mahwah, NJ: Erlbaum.

Litt, J., Taylor, H.G., Klein, N., & Hack, M. (2005). Learning disabilities in children with very low birthweight: Prevalence, neuropsychological correlates, and educational interventions. *Journal of Learning Disabilities, 38,* 130–141.

Liu, J., Raine, A., Venables, P.H., Dalais, C., & Mednick, S.A. (2003). Malnutrition at age 3 years and lower cognitive ability at age 11 years: Independence from psychosocial adversity. *Archives of Pediatric and Adolescent Medicine, 157,* 593–600.

Livesly, W., & Bromley, D. (1973). *Person perception in childhood and adolescence.* New York: Wiley.

Lobel, M., Yali, A.M., Zhu, W., DeVincent, C.J., & Meyer, B.A. (2002). Beneficial associations between optimistic disposition and emotional distress in high-risk pregnancy. *Psychology and Health, 17,* 77–95.

Lock, A. (2004). Preverbal communication. In U. Goswami (Ed.), *Blackwell handbook of childhood cognitive development.* Malden, MA: Blackwell.

Lock, J., Walker, L.R., Rickert, V.I., & Katzman, D.K. (2005). Suicidality in adolescents being treated with antidepressant medications and the black box label: Position paper of the Society for Adolescent Medicine. *Journal of Adolescent Health, 36,* 92–93.

Lockman, J.J. (2000). A perception-action perspective on tool use development. *Child Development, 71,* 137–144.

Loeber, R., DeLamatre, M., Keenan, K., & Zhang, Q. (1998). A prospective replication of developmental pathways in disruptive and delinquent behavior. In R. Cairns, L. Bergman, & J. Kagan (Eds.), *Methods and models for studying the individual.* Thousand Oaks, CA: Sage.

Loeber, R., & Farrington, D.P. (Eds.). (2001). *Child delinquents: Development, intervention and service needs.* Thousand Oaks, CA: Sage.

Loftus, E.F. (2002). Memory faults and fixes. *Issues in Science and Technology, 28* (4), 41–50.

London, K., Bruck, M., & Ceci, S.J. (2005). Disclosure of child sexual abuse: What does the research tell us about the ways that children tell? *Psychology, Public Policy, and Law, 11,* 194–226.

Long, T., & Long, L. (1983). *Latchkey children.* New York: Penguin.

Lonner, W.J. (1988, October). *The introductory psychology text and cross-cultural psychology: A survey of cross-cultural psychologists.* Bellingham: Western Washington University, Center for Cross-cultural Research.

Loos, R.J., & Rankinen, T. (2005). Gene-diet interactions in body-weight changes. *Journal of the American Dietary Association, 105* (5, Pt 2), 29–34.

Lord, J., & Winell, J.J. (2004). Overuse injuries in pediatric athletes. *Current Opinions in Pediatrics, 16,* 47–50.

Lorenz, K.Z. (1965). *Evolution and the modification of behavior.* Chicago: University of Chicago Press.

Lott, B., & Maluso, D. (2001). Gender development: Social learning. In J. Worell (Ed.), *Encyclopedia of women and gender.* San Diego: Academic Press.

Love, K.M., & Murdock, T.B. (2004). Attachment to parents and psychological well-being: An examination of young adult college students in intact and stepfamilies. *Journal of Family Psychology, 18,* 600–608.

Loveland Cook, C.A., Flick, L.H., Homan, S.M., Campbell, C., McSweeney, M., & Gallagher, M.E. (2004). Posttraumatic stress disorder in pregnancy: Prevalence, risk factors, and treatment. *Obstetrics and Gynecology, 103,* 710–717.

Lowe, E.D., Weisner, T.S., & Geis, S. (2005). Child instability and the effort to sustain a daily routine: Evidence from the New Hope Ethnographic Study of Low-Income Families. In C.R. Cooper, C.T. Garcia Coll, W.T. Bartko, H.M. Davis, & C. Chatman (Eds.), *Developmental pathways through middle childhood.* Mahwah, NJ: Erlbaum.

Lowry, R., Galuska, D.A., Fulton, J.E., Burgeson, C.R., & Kann, L. (2005). Weight management goals and use of exercise for weight control among U.S. high school students, 1991–2001. *Journal of Adolescent Health, 36,* 320–326.

Lubinski, D. (2000). Measures of intelligence: Intelligence tests. In A. Kazdin (Ed.), *Encyclopedia of psychology.* Washington, DC, and New York: American Psychological Association and Oxford University Press.

Luciana, M., Sullivan, J., & Nelson, C.A. (2001). Associations between phenylalanine-to-tyrosine ratios and performance on tests of neuropsychological function in adolescents treated early and continuously for phenylketonuria.

Lucurto, C. (1990). The malleability of IQ as judged from adoption studies. *Intelligence, 14,* 275–292.

Luders, E., Narr, K.L., Thompson, P.M., Rex, D.E., Uancke, L., Steinmetz, H., & Toga, H.W. (2004). Gender differences in cortical complexity. *Nature Neuroscience, 7,* 799–800.

Ludington-Hoe, S., & Golant, S.K. (1993). *Kangaroo care: The best you can do to help your preterm baby.* New York: Bantam Doubleday.

Lumeng, J.C., Gannon, K., Cabral, H.J., Frank, D.A., & Zuckerman, B. (2003). Association between clinically meaningful behavior problems and overweight in children. *Pediatrics, 112,* 1138–1145.

Luo, Y., & Baillargeon, R. (2005). When the ordinary seems unexpected: Evidence for incremental physical knowledge in infants. *Cognition,* 95, 297–328.

Luria, A., & Herzog, E. (1985, April). *Gender segregation across and within settings.* Paper presented at the biennial meeting of the Society for Research in Child Development, Toronto.

Luster, T., & Okagaki, L. (Eds.). (2005). *Parenting: An ecological perspective* (2nd ed.). Mahwah, NJ: Erlbaum.

Lyle, J., & Hoffman, H.R. (1972). Children's use of television and other media. In E.A. Rubenstein, G.A. Comstock, & J.P. Murray (Eds.), *Television and social behavior* (Vol. 4). Washington, DC: U.S. Government Printing Office.

Lynn, R. (1996). Racial and ethnic differences in intelligence in the U.S. on the Differential Ability Scale. *Personality and Individual Differences, 26,* 271–273.

Lynn, R., Allik, J., Pullman, H., & Laidra, K. (2004). Sex differences on the progressive matrices among adolescents: Some data from Estonia. *Personality & Individual Differences, 36,* 1249–1255.

Lynn, R., & Irwing, P. (2004). Sex differences on the progressive matrices: A meta-analysis. *Intelligence, 32,* 481–498.

Lyon, G.R. (1996). Learning disabilities. *The Future of Children, 6* (1), 54–76.

Lyon, T.D., & Flavell, J.H. (1993). Young children's understanding of forgetting over time. *Child Development, 64,* 789–800.

Lyons, S.J., Henly, J.R., & Schuerman, J.R. (2005). Informal support in maltreating families: Its effects on parenting practices. *Children and Youth Services Review, 27,* 21–38.

Maccoby, E.E. (1984). Middle childhood in the context of the family. In W.A. Collins (Ed.), *Development during middle childhood.* Washington, DC: National Academy Press.

Maccoby, E.E. (1987, November). Interview with Elizabeth Hall: All in the family. *Psychology Today,* pp. 54–60.

Maccoby, E.E. (1996). Peer conflict and intrafamily conflict: Are there conceptual bridges? *Merrill-Palmer Quarterly, 42,* 165–176.

Maccoby, E.E. (1998). *The two sexes: Growing up apart, coming together.* Cambridge, MA: Harvard University Press.

Maccoby, E.E. (1999). The uniqueness of the parent-child relationship. In W.A. Collins & B. Laursen (Eds.), *Relationships as developmental contexts.* Mahwah, NJ: Erlbaum.

Maccoby, E.E. (2001, April). *Influencing policy through research.* Paper presented at the meeting of the Society for Research in Child Development, Minneapolis.

Maccoby, E.E. (2002). Gender and group process: A developmental perspective. *Current Directions in Psychological Science, 11,* 54–57.

Maccoby, E.E. (2002). Parenting effects. In J.G. Borkowski, S.L. Ramey, & M. Bristol-Power (Eds.), *Parenting and the child's world.* Mahwah, NJ: Erlbaum.

Maccoby, E.E., & Jacklin, C.N. (1974). *The psychology of sex differences.* Palo Alto, CA: Stanford University Press.

Maccoby, E.E., & Lewis, C.C. (2003). Less daycare or better daycare? *Child Development, 74,* 1069–1075.

Maccoby, E.E., & Martin, J.A. (1983). Socialization in the context of the family: Parent-child interaction. In P.H. Mussen (Ed.), *Handbook of child psychology* (4th ed., Vol. 4). New York: Wiley.

Maccoby, E.E., & Mnookin, R.H. (1992). *Dividing the child: Social and legal dilemmas of custody.* Cambridge, MA: Harvard University Press.

MacDorman, M.F., Minino, A.M., Strobino, D.M., & Guyer, B. (2002). Annual summary of vital statistics—2001. *Pediatrics, 110,* 1037–1052.

MacFarlane, J.A. (1975). Olfaction in the development of social preferences in the human neonate. In *Parent-infant interaction.* Ciba Foundation Symposium No. 33. Amsterdam: Elsevier.

MacGeorge, E.L. (2004). The myth of gender cultures: Similarities outweigh differences in men's and women's provisions of and responses to supportive communication. *Sex Roles, 50,* 143–175.

Maddux, J. (2002). The power of believing you can. In C.R. Snyder & S.J. Lopez (Eds.), *Handbook of positive psychology.* New York: Oxford University Press.

Mader, S.S. (2006). *Inquiry into life* (11th ed.). New York: McGraw-Hill.

Maeda, K. (1999). *The Self-Perception Profile for Children administered to a Japanese sample.* Unpublished data, Ibaraki Prefectural University of Health Sciences, Ibaraki, Japan.

Mael, F.A. (1998). Single-sex and coeducational schooling: Relationships to socioemotional and academic development. *Review of Educational Research, 68* (2), 101–129.

Maffulli, N., Baxter-Jones, A.D., & Grieve, A. (2005). Long term sport involvement and sport injury rate in elite athletes. *Archives of Disease in Childhood, 90,* 525–527.

Magnuson, K.A., & Duncan, G.J. (2002). Poverty and parenting. In M.H. Bornstein (Ed.), *Handbook of parenting* (2nd ed.). Mahwah, NJ: Erlbaum.

Magnusson, D. (1988). *Individual development from an interactional perspective: A longitudinal study.* Hillsdale, NJ: Erlbaum.

Maguire, S., Mann, M.K., Sibert, J., & Kemp, A. (2005). Are there patterns of bruising in childhood which are diagnostic or suggestive of abuse? A systematic review. *Archives of Diseases in Childhood, 90,* 182–186.

Mahoney, J.L., Larson, R.W., & Eccles, J.S. (Eds.). (2005). *Organized activities as contexts of development.* Mahwah, NJ: Erlbaum.

Main, M. (2000). Attachment theory. In A. Kazdin (Ed.), *Encyclopedia of psychology.* Washington, DC, & New York: American Psychological Association and Oxford University Press.

Makrides, M., Neumann, M., Simmer, K., Pater, J., & Gibson, R. (1995). Are long-chain polyunsaturated fatty acids essential nutrients in infancy? *Lancet, 345,* 1463–1468.

Malik, N.M., & Furman, W. (1993). Practitioner review: Problems in children's peer relations: What can the clinician do? *Journal of Child Psychology and Psychiatry 34,* 1303–1326.

Malmgren, K.W., & Meisel, S.M. (2004). Examining the link between child maltreatment and delinquency for youth with emotional and behavioral disorders. *Child Welfare, 83,* 175–188.

Mandel, D., Zimlichman, E., Mimouni, F.B., Grotto, I., & Kreiss, Y. (2005). Age at menarche and body mass index: A population study. *Journal of Pediatric Endocrinology and Metabolism, 17,* 1507–1510.

Mandler, J.M. (2000). Unpublished review of J.W. Santrock's *Life-span development* (8th ed.). New York: McGraw-Hill.

Mandler, J.M. (2003). Conceptual categorization. In D. Rakison & L.M. Oakes (Eds.), *Early category and concept development.* New York: Oxford University Press.

Mandler, J.M. (2004). *The foundations of mind.* New York: Oxford University Press.

Mandler, J.M. (2005). *Jean Mandler.* Available on the World Wide Web at: http://cogsci.ucsd._edu/~jean/.

Mandler, J.M., & McDonough, L. (1993). Concept formation in infancy. *Cognitive Development, 8,* 291–318.

Mandler, J.M., & McDonough, L. (1995). Long-term recall in infancy. *Journal of Experimental Child Psychology, 59,* 457–474.

Manis, F.R., Keating, D.P., & Morrison, F.J. (1980). Developmental differences in the allocation of processing capacity. *Journal of Experimental Child Psychology, 29,* 156–169.

Mannessier, L., Alie-Daram, S., Roubinet, F., & Brossard, Y. (2000). Prevention of fetal hemolytic disease: It is time to take action. *Transfusions in Clinical Biology, 7,* 527–532.

Many, J.E. (2002). An exhibition and analysis of verbal tapestries: Understanding how scaffolding is woven into the fabric of instructional conversations. *Reading Research Quarterly, 37,* 376–407.

Marchman, V. (2003). Review of Santrock, J.W. *Child development* (10th ed.). New York: McGraw-Hill.

Marcia, J.E. (1980). Ego identity development. In J. Adelson (Ed.), *Handbook of adolescent psychology.* New York: Wiley.

Marcia, J.E. (1987). The identity status approach to the study of ego identity development. In T. Honess & K. Yardley (Eds.), *Self and identity: Perspectives across the life-span,* London: Routledge & Kegan Paul.

Marcia, J.E. (1994). The empirical study of ego identity. In H.A. Bosma, T.L.G. Graafsma, H.D. Grotevant, & D.J. De Levita (Eds.), *Identity and development.* Newbury Park, CA: Sage.

Marcia, J.E. (1996). Unpublished review of J.W. Santrock's *Adolescence* (7th ed.). Dubuque, IA: Brown & Benchmark.

Marcia, J.E. (2002). Identity and psychosocial development in adulthood. *Identity, 2,* 7–28.

Marcovitch, H. (2004). Use of stimulants for attention deficit hyperactivity disorder: AGAINST. *British Medical Journal, 329,* 908–909.

Margolin, L. (1994). Child sexual abuse by uncles. *Child Abuse and Neglect, 18,* 215–224.

Marild, S., Hansson, S., Jodal, U., Oden, A., & Svedberg, K. (2004). Protective effect of breastfeeding against urinary tract infection. *Acta Paediatrica, 93,* 164–168.

Markus, H.R., & Kitayama, S. (1994). The cultural construction of self and emotion: Implications for social behavior. In S. Kitayama & H.R. Markus (Eds.), *Emotion and culture.* Washington, DC: American Psychological Association.

Markus, H.R., Mullally, P.R., & Kitayama, S. (1999). *Selfways: Diversity in modes of cultural participation.* Unpublished manuscript, Department of Psychology, University of Michigan.

Markus, H.R., & Nurius, P. (1986). Possible selves. *American Psychologist, 41,* 954–969.

Marshall, N.L. (2004). The quality of early child care and children's development. *Current Directions in Psychological Science, 13,* 165–168.

Marsiglio, W. (2004). Studying fathering trajectories. In R.D. Day & M.E. Lamb (Eds.), *Conceptualizing and measuring father involvement.* Mahwah, NJ: Erlbaum.

Marsiglio, W., Amato, P., Day, R.D., & Lamb, M.E. (2000). Scholarship on fatherhood in the 1990s and beyond. *Journal of Marriage and Family, 62,* 1173–1191.

Martin, C.L., & Dinella, L. (2001). Gender development: Gender schema theory. In J. Worell (Ed.), *Encyclopedia of women and gender.* San Diego: Academic Press.

Martin, C.L., & Fabes, R.A. (2001). The stability and consequences of young children's segregated social play. *Developmental Psychology, 37,* 431–446.

Martin, C.L., & Halverson, C.F. (1981). A schematic processing model of sex typing and stereotyping in children. *Child Development, 52,* 1119–1134.

Martin, C.L., Ruble, D.N., & Szkrybalo, J. (2002). Cognitive theories of early gender development. *Psychological Bulletin, 128,* 903–933.

Martin, D.W. (2004). *Doing psychology experiments* (6th ed.). Belmont, CA: Wadsworth.

Martin, R., Sexton, C., Franklin, T., & Gerlovich, J. (2005). *Teaching science for all children* (4th ed.). Boston: Allyn & Bacon.

Martinez-Pasarell, O., Nogues, C., Bosch, M., Egozcue, J., & Templado, C. (1999). Analysis of sex chromosome aneupolidy in sperm from fathers of Turner syndrome patients. *Human Genetics, 104,* 345–349.

Mash, E.J., & Wolfe, D.A. (1999). *Abnormal child psychology.* Belmont, CA: Wadsworth.

Mason, J.A., & Hermann, K.R. (1998). Universal infant hearing screening by automated auditory brainstem response measurement. *Pediatrics, 101,* 221–228.

Masten, A.S. (2001). Ordinary magic: Resilience processes in development. *American Psychologist, 56,* 227–238.

Masten, A.S. (2004). Regulatory processes, risk, and resilience in adolescent development. *Annals of the New York Academy of Science, 102,* 310–319.

Masten, A.S. (2005). Peer relationships and psychopathology in developmental perspective: Reflections on progress and promise. *Journal of Clinical Child and Adolescent Psychology, 34,* 87–92.

Masten, A.S., & Coatsworth, J.D. (1998). The development of competence in favorable and unfavorable environments. *American Psychologist, 53,* 205–220.

Matheny, A.P., & Phillips, K. (2001). Temperament and context: Correlates of home environment with temperament continuity and change. In T.D. Wachs & G.A. Kohnstamm (Eds.), *Temperament in context.* Mahwah, NJ: Erlbaum.

Mathews, T.J., Menacker, F., & MacDorman, M.F. (2003). Infant mortality statistics from the 2001 period linked birth/infant death data set. *National Vital Statistics Reports, 52,* 1–28.

Matias, A., Montenegro, N., & Blickstein, I. (2005). Down syndrome screening in multiple pregnancies. *Obstetrics and Gynecological Clinics of North America, 32,* 81–96.

Matlin, M.W. (2004). *The psychology of women* (5th ed.). Belmont, CA: Wadsworth.

Matsuba, M.K., & Walker, L.J. (2004). Extraordinary moral commitment: Young adults involved in social organizations. *Journal of Personality, 72,* 413–436.

Matsumoto, D. (2004). *Culture and psychology* (3rd ed.). Belmont, CA: Wadsworth.

Mattanah, J. (2005). Authoritative parenting and encouragement of children's autonomy. In P.A. Cowan, C.P. Cowan, J.C. Ablow, V.K. Johnson, & J.R. Measelle (Eds.), *The family context of parenting in children's adaptation to elementary school.* Mahwah, NJ: Erlbaum.

Matthews, G., Roberts, R.D., & Zeidner, M. (2004). Seven myths about emotional intelligence. *Psychological Inquiry, 15,* 179–196.

Maupin, R., Jr., Lyman, R., Fatsis, J., Prystowiski, E., Nguyen, A., Wright, C., Kissinger, P., & Miller, J., Jr. (2004). Characteristics of women who deliver with no prenatal care. *Journal of Maternal, Fetal, and Neonatal Medicine, 16,* 45–50.

Maurer, D., & Salapatek, P. (1976). Developmental changes in the scanning of faces by young infants. *Child Development, 47,* 523–527.

Mauro, V.P., Wood, I.C., Krushel, L., Crossin, K.L., & Edelman, G.M. (1994). Cell adhesion alters gene transcription in chicken embryo brain cells and mouse embryonal carcinoma cells. *Proceedings of the National Academy of Sciences USA, 91,* 2868–2872.

Maxson, S. (2003). Behavioral genetics. In I.B. Weiner (Ed.), *Encyclopedia of psychology* (Vol. 3). New York: Wiley.

May, F.B. (2006). *Teaching reading creatively: Reading and writing as communication* (7th ed.). Upper Saddle River, NJ: Prentice Hall.

Mayer, J.D., Salovey, P., & Caruso, D.R. (2002). *Mayer-Salovey-Caruso Emotional Intelligence Test (MSCEIT): User's Manual.* Toronto, Ontario, Canada: Multi-Health Systems.

Mayer, J.D., Salovey, P., & Caruso, D.R. (2004). Emotional intelligence: Theory, findings, and implications. *Psychological Inquiry, 15,* 197–215.

Mayer, R.E. (2003). *Learning and instruction.* Boston: Allyn & Bacon.

Mayer, R.E. (2004). Teaching of subject matter. *Annual Review of Psychology, 55.* Palo Alto, CA: Annual Reviews.

Mayes, L. (2003). Unpublished review of Santrock, J.W. *Topical life-span development* (2nd ed.). New York: McGraw-Hill.

Mayeux, R. (2005). Mapping the new frontier: Complex genetic disorders. *Journal of Clinical Investigations, 115,* 1404–1407.

Maynard, L.M., Galsuka, D.A., Blanck, H.M., & Serdula, M.K. (2003). Maternal perceptions of weight status of children. *Pediatrics, 111,* 1226–1231.

Mazza, J.J. (2005). Suicide. In S.W. Lee (Ed.), *Encyclopedia of school psychology.* Thousand Oaks, CA: Sage.

McAdoo, H.P. (2002). African American parenting. In M.H. Bornstein (Ed.), *Handbook of parenting* (2nd ed.). Mahwah, NJ: Erlbaum.

McCabe, M.P., & Ricciardelli, L.A. (2004). A longitudinal study of pubertal timing and extreme body change behaviors among adolescent boys and girls. *Adolescence, 39,* 145–166.

McCall, R.B., Applebaum, M.I., & Hogarty, P.S. (1973). Developmental changes in mental performance. *Monographs of the Society for Research in Child Development, 38* (Serial No. 150).

McCartney, K. (2003, July 16). Interview with Kathleen McCartney in A. Bucuvalas, "Child care and behavior." *HGSE News,* pp. 1–4. Cambridge, MA: Harvard Graduate School of Education.

McCarty, M.E., & Ashmead, D.H. (1999). Visual control of reaching and grasping in infants. *Developmental Psychology, 35,* 620–631.

McClearn, G.E. (2004). Nature and nurture: Interaction and coaction. *American Journal of Medical Genetics, 124B,* 124–130.

McCombs, B.L. (2001, April). *What do we know about learners and learning? The learner-centered framework.* Paper presented at the meeting of the American Educational Research Association, Seattle.

McCombs, B.L. (2003). Research to policy for guiding educational reform. In I.B. Weiner (Ed.), *Handbook of psychology* (Vol. 7). New York: Wiley.

McCormick, C.B. (2003). Metacognition and learning. In I.B. Weiner (Ed.), *Handbook of psychology* (Vol. 7). New York: Wiley.

McCormick, C.B., & Pressley, M. (1997). *Educational psychology.* New York: Longman.

McCoy, S.J., Beal, J.M., & Watson, G.H. (2003). Endocrine factors and postpartum depression. A selected review. *Journal of Reproductive Medicine, 48,* 402–408.

McCrory, E.J., Mechelli, A., Frith, U., & Price, C.J. (2005). More than words: A common neural basis for reading and naming deficits in developmental dyslexia. *Brain, 128,* 261–267.

McGee, L.M., & Richgels, D.J. (2004). *Literacy's beginnings* (4th ed.). Boston: Allyn & Bacon.

McGrath, S., Kennell, J., Suresh, M., Molse, K., & Hinkley, C. (1999, May). *Doula support vs. epidural analgesia: Impact on cesarean rates.* Paper presented at the meeting of the Society for Pediatric Research, San Francisco.

McGue, M., Bouchard, T.J., Iacono, W.G., & Lykken, D.T. (1993). Behavioral genetics of cognitive ability: A life-span perspective. In R. Plomin & G.E. McClearn (Eds.), *Nature, nurture, and psychology.* Washington, DC: American Psychological Association.

McHale, J., Johnson, D., & Sinclair, R. (1999). Family dynamics, preschoolers' family representations, and preschool peer relationships. *Early Education and Development, 10,* 373–401.

McHale, J., Khazan, I., Erera, P., Rotman, T., DeCourcey, W., & McConnell, M. (2002). Coparenting in diverse family systems. In M.H. Bornstein (Ed.), *Handbook of parenting* (2nd ed., Vol. 3). Mahwah, NJ: Erlbaum.

McHale, J.P., Kuersten-Hogan, R., & Rao, N. (2004). Growing points for coparenting theory and research. *Journal of Adult Development, 11,* 221–234.

McHale, J.P., Luretti, A., Talbot, J., & Pouquette, C. (2001). Retrospect and prospect in the psychological study of marital and couple relationships. In J.P. McHale & W.S. Grolnick (Eds.), *Retrospect and prospect in the psychological study of families.* Mahwah, NJ: Erlbaum.

McKee, J.K., Poirier, F.E., & McGraw, W.S. (2005). *Understanding human evolution* (5th ed.). Upper Saddle River, NJ: Prentice Hall.

McKenna, J.J., Mosko, S.S., & Richard, C.A. (1997). Bedsharing promotes breastfeeding. *Pediatrics, 100,* 214–219.

McLearn, K.T. (2004). Narrowing the income gaps in preventive care for young children: Families in healthy steps. *Journal of Urban Health, 81,* 556–567.

McLoyd, V. (1990). Minority children: An introduction to the special issue. *Child Development, 61,* 263–266.

McLoyd, V.C. (1998). Children in poverty. In I.E. Siegel & K.A. Renninger (Eds.), *Handbook of child psychology* (5th ed., Vol. 4). New York: Wiley.

McLoyd, V.C. (2000). Poverty. In A. Kazdin (Ed.), *Encyclopedia of psychology.* Washington, DC, & New York: American Psychological Association and Oxford University Press.

McLoyd, V.C. (2005). Pathways to academic achievement among children in immigrant families: A commentary. In C.R. Cooper, C.T. Garcia Coll, W.T. Bartko, H.M. Davis, & C. Chatman (Eds.), *Developmental pathways through middle childhood.* Mahwah, NJ: Erlbaum.

McMillan, J.H. (2004). *Educational research* (4th ed.). Boston: Allyn & Bacon.

McMillan, J.H., & Schumacher, S. (2006). *Research in education: Evidence based inquiry* (6th ed.). Boston: Allyn & Bacon.

McNamara, F., & Sullivan, C.E. (2000). Obstructive sleep apnea in infants. *Journal of Pediatrics, 136,* 318–323.

McVeigh, C.A., Baafi, M., & Williamson, M. (2002). Functional status after fatherhood: An Australian study. *Journal of Obstetrics, Gynecology, and Neonatal Nursing, 31,* 165–171.

Mead, M. (1928). *Coming of age in Samoa.* New York: Morrow.

Mead, M. (1978, Dec. 30–Jan. 5). The American family: An endangered species. *TV Guide,* pp. 21–24.

Mehler, J., Jusczyk, P.W., Lambertz, G., Halsted, N., Bertoncini, J., & Amiel-Tison, C. (1988). A precursor of language acquisition in young infants. *Cognition, 29,* 132–178.

Meijer, J., & Elshout, J.J. (2001). The predictive and discriminant validity of the zone of proximal development. *British Journal of Educational Psychology, 71,* 93–113.

Meis, P.J., & others. (2003). Prevention of recurrent preterm delivery by 17-alpha-hydroxyprogesterone caproate. *New England Journal of Medicine, 348,* 2379–2385.

Melgar-Quinonez, H.R., & Kaiser, L.L. (2004). Relationship of child-feeding practices to overweight in low-income Mexican-American preschool-aged children. *Journal of the American Dietetic Association, 104,* 1110–1119.

Meltzoff, A. (2004). Imitation as a mechanism of social cognition: Origins of empathy, theory of mind, and the representation of action. In U. Goswami (Ed.), *Blackwell handbook of childhood cognitive development.* Malden, MA: Blackwell.

Menn, L., & Stoel-Gammon, C. (2005). Phonological development: Learning sounds and sound patterns. In J. Berko Gleason (Ed.), *The development of language* (6th ed.). Boston: Allyn & Bacon.

Menyuk, P., Liebergott, J., & Schultz, M. (1995). *Early language development in full-term and premature infants.* Hillsdale, NJ: Erlbaum.

Mercer, C.D., & Pullen, P.C. (2005). *Students with learning disabilities* (6th ed.). Upper Saddle River, NJ: Prentice Hall.

Merchant, R.H., & Lala, M.M. (2005). Prevention of mother-to-child transmission of HIV—an overview. *Indian Journal of Medical Research, 121,* 489–501.

Meredith, N.V. (1978). Research between 1960 and 1970 on the standing height of young children in different parts of the world. In H.W. Reece & L.P. Lipsitt (Eds.), *Advances in child development and behavior* (Vol. 12). New York: Academic Press.

Merenda, P. (2004). Cross-cultural adaptation of educational and psychological testing. In R.K. Hambleton, P.F. Merenda, & C.D. Spielberger (Eds.), *Adapting educational and psychological tests for cross-cultural assessment.* Mahwah, NJ: Erlbaum.

Merrick, J., Aspler, S., & Schwartz, G. (2001). Should adults with phenylketonuria have diet treatment? *Mental Retardation, 39,* 215–217.

Merrick, J., Morad, M., Halperin, I., & Kandel, I. (2005). Physical fitness and adolescence. *International Journal of Adolescent Medicine, 17,* 89–91.

Mervis, C.B. (2003). Williams syndrome: 15 years of psychological research. *Developmental Neuropsychology, 23,* 1–12.

Mezulis, A.H., Hyde, J.S., & Clark, R. (2004). Father involvement mediates the effects of maternal depression during a child's infancy on child behavior problems in kindergarten. *Journal of Family Psychology, 18,* 575–588.

Mezzacappa, E. (2004). Alerting, orienting, and executive attention: Developmental properties and socioeconomic correlates in an epidemiological sample of young, urban children. *Child Development, 75,* 1373–1386.

Miceli Sopo, S., Zorzi, G., & Calvani, M. (2004). Should we screen every child with otitis media with effusion for allergic rhinitis? *Archives of Disease in Childhood, 89,* 287–288.

Michel, G.L. (1981). Right-handedness: A consequence of infant supine head-orientation preference? *Science, 212,* 685–687.

Miller, B.C., Fan, X., Christensen, M., Grotevant, H.D., & von Dulmen, M. (2000). Comparisons of adopted and nonadopted adolescents in a large, nationally representative sample. *Child Development, 71,* 1458–1473.

Miller, C.F., & Ruble, D.N. (2005). *Developmental changes in the accessibility of gender stereotypes.* Unpublished manuscript, Department of Psychology, New York: University.

Miller, G.A. (1981). *Language and speech.* New York: W.H. Freeman.

Miller, J.G. (1995, March). *Culture, context, and personal agency: The cultural grounding of self and morality.* Paper presented at the meeting of the Society for Research in Child Development, Indianapolis.

Miller-Johnson, S., Coie, J., & Malone, P.S. (2003, April). *Do aggression and peer rejection in childhood predict early adult outcomes?* Paper presented at the biennial meeting of the Society for Research in Child Development, Tampa, FL.

Miller-Jones, D. (1989). Culture and testing. *American Psychologist, 44,* 360–366.

Miller-Loncar, C., Lester, B.M., Seifer, R., Lagasse, L.L., Bauer, C.R., Shankaran, S., Bada, H.S., Wright, L.L., Smeriglio, V.L., Bigsby, R., & Liu, J. (2005, in press). Predictors of motor development in children prenatally exposed to cocaine. *Neurotoxicology and Teratology.*

Minczykowski, A., Gryczynska, M., Ziemnicka, K., Sowinksi, J., & Wysocki, H. (2005). The influence of growth hormone therapy on ultrasound myocardial tissue characterization in patients with childhood onset GH deficiency. *International Journal of Cardiology, 101,* 257–263.

Ministry of Health, Education, and Welfare. (2002). *Divorce trends in Japan.* Tokyo: Ministry of Health, Education, and Welfare.

Minnett, A.M., Vandell, D.L., & Santrock, J.W. (1983). The effects of sibling status on sibling interaction: Influence of birth order, age spacing, sex of the child, and sex of the sibling. *Child Development, 54,* 1064–1072.

Minns, R.A., & Busuttil, A. (2004). Patterns of presentation of the shaken baby syndrome: Four types of inflicted brain injury predominate. *British Medical Journal, 328,* 766.

Minuchin, P.O., & Shapiro, E.K. (1983). The school as a context for social development. In P.H. Mussen (Ed.), *Handbook of child psychology* (4th ed., Vol. 4). New York: Wiley.

Mirowsky, J. (2005). Age at first birth, health, and mortality. *Journal of Health and Social Behavior, 46,* 32–50.

Mischel, W. (1973). Toward a cognitive social learning reconceptualization of personality. *Psychological Review, 80,* 252–283.

Mischel, W. (1986). *Personality and assessment.* New York: Wiley.

Mischel, W. (1995, August). *Cognitive-affective theory of person-environment psychology.* Paper presented at the meeting of the American Psychological Association, New York City.

Mischel, W. (2004). Toward an integrative science of the person. *Annual Review of Psychology, 55.* Palo Alto, CA: Annual Reviews.

Mischel, W., & Mischel, H. (1975, April). *A cognitive social-learning analysis of moral development.* Paper presented at the meeting of the Society for Research in Child Development, Denver.

Mischel, W., & Patterson, C.J. (1976). Substantive and structural elements of effective plans for self-control. *Journal of Social and Personality Psychology, 34,* 942–950.

Mishell, D. (2000). *2000 Yearbook of obstetrics.* St. Louis: Mosby.

Misra, M., Miller, K., Almazan, C., Ramaswam, K., Aggarwal, A., Herzog, D.B., Newbauer, G., Breu, J., & Klibanski, A. (2004). Hormonal and body composition predictors of soluble leptin receptor, leptin, and free leptin index in adolescent girls with anorexia nervosa and controls and relation to insulin sensitivity. *Journal of Clinical Endocrinology and Metabolism, 89,* 3486–3495.

Mistry, J., & Rogoff, B. (1994). Remembering in cultural context. In W.J. Lonner & R. Malpass (Eds.), *Psychology and culture.* Boston: Allyn & Bacon.

Mistry, R.S., Vandewater, E.A., Huston, A.C., & McLoyd, V.C. (2002). Economic well-being and children's social adjustment: The role of family process in an ethnically diverse low-income sample. *Child Development, 73,* 935–951.

Mitchell, E.A., Stewart, A.W., Crampton, P., & Salmond, C. (2000). Deprivation and sudden infant death syndrome. *Social Science and Medicine, 51,* 147–150.

Mitchell, K.S., & Mazzeo, S.E. (2004). Binge eating and psychological distress in ethnically diverse college men and women. *Eating Behavior, 5,* 157–169.

Moats, L. (2004). Relevance of neuroscience to effective education for students with reading and other learning disabilities. *Journal of Child Neurology, 19,* 840–845.

Mohalla, B.K., Tucker, T.J., Besser, M.J., Williamson, C., Yeats, J., Smit, L., Anthony, J., & Puren, A. (2005). Investigation of HIV in amniotic fluid from HIV-infected pregnant women at full term. *Journal of Infectious Diseases, 192,* 488–491.

Mohan, R.M., Golding, S., & Paterson, D.J. (2001). Intermittent hypoxia improves atrial tolerance to subsequent anoxia and reduces stress protein expression. *Acta Physiology Scandinavia, 172,* 89–95.

Moise, K.J. (2005). Fetal RhD typing with free DNA I maternal plasma. *American Journal of Obstetrics and Gynecology, 192,* 663–665.

Molnar, D. (2004). The prevalence of the metabolic syndrome and type 2 diabetes mellitus in children and adolescents. *International Journal of Obesity and Related Metabolic Disorders, 28* (Supplement 3), S70–S74.

Monastirli, A., & others. (2005). Short stature, type E brachydactyly, gynecomastia, and cryptorchidism in a patient with 47, XYY/45, X/46, XY mosaicism. *American Journal of Medical Science, 329,* 208–210.

Montemayor, R. (1982). The relationship between parent-adolescent conflict and the amount of time adolescents spend with parents, peers, and alone. *Child Development, 53,* 1512–1519.

Monuteaux, M.C., Faraone, S.V., Herzig, K., Navsaria, N., & Biederman, J. (2005). ADHD and dyscalculia: Evidence for independent familial transmission. *Journal of Learning Disabilities, 38,* 86–93.

Moody, R. (2001). Adoption: Women must be helped to consider all options. *British Medical Journal, 323,* 867.

Moon, R.Y., Oden, R.P., & Grady, K.C. (2004). Back to sleep: An educational intervention with women, infants, and children program clients. *Pediatrics, 113,* 542–547.

Mooney, C.G. (2006). *Theories of childhood.* Upper Saddle River, NJ: Prentice Hall.

Moore, D. (2001). *The dependent gene.* New York: W.H. Freeman.

Moore, V.M., & Davies, M.J. (2005). Diet during pregnancy, neonatal outcomes, and later health. *Reproduction, Fertility, and Development, 17,* 341–348.

Moran, S., & Gardner, H. (2006). Extraordinary achievements. In W. Damon & R. Lerner (Eds.), *Handbook of child psychology* (6th ed.). New York: Wiley.

Morgan, J. (2005). Nutrition for toddlers: The foundation for good health—1. *Journal of Family Health Care, 15,* 56–59.

Morgan, M. (1984). Reward-induced decrements and increments in intrinsic motivation. *Review of Educational Research, 54,* 5–30.

Morreale, M.C. (2004). Executing juvenile offenders: A fundamental failure of society. *Journal of Adolescent Health, 35,* 341.

Morrison, G. (2006). *Teaching in America* (4th ed.). Boston: Allyn & Bacon.

Morrongiello, B.A., Fenwick, K.D., & Chance, G. (1990). Sound localization acuity in very young infants: An observer-based testing procedure. *Developmental Psychology, 26,* 75–84.

Morrow, A.L., & Rangel, J.M. (2004). Human milk protection against infectious diarrhea: Implications for prevention and clinical care. *Seminars in Pediatric Infectious Diseases, 15,* 221–228.

Morrow, C.E., Bandstra, E.S., Anthony, J.C., Ofir, A.Y., Xue, L., & Reyes, M.B. (2003). Influence of prenatal cocaine exposure on early language development: Longitudinal findings from four months to three years of age. *Journal of Developmental and Behavioral Pediatrics, 24,* 39–50.

Mounts, N.S. (2002). Parental management of adolescent peer relationships in context: The role of parenting style. *Journal of Family Psychology, 16,* 58–69.

Moya, J., Bearer, C.F., & Etzel, R.A. (2004). Children's behavior and physiology and how it affects exposure to environmental contaminants. *Pediatrics, 113* (Supplement 4), 996–1006.

Mozingo, J.N., Davis, M.W., Droppleman, P.G., & Merideth, A. (2000). "It wasn't working": Women's experiences with short-term breast feeding. *American Maternal Journal of Nursing, 25,* 120–126.

Mullick, S., Beksinksa, M., & Msomi, S. (2005). Treatment for syphilis in antenatal care. *Sexually Transmitted Infections, 81,* 220–222.

Mullis, I.V.S., Martin, M.O., Beaton, A.E., Gonzales, E.J., Kelly, D.L., & Smith, T.A. (1998). *Mathematics and science achievement in the final year of secondary school.* Chestnut Hill, MA: Boston College, TIMSS International Study Center.

Mumme, D.L., Fernald, A., & Herrera, C. (1996). Infant's responses to facial & emotional signals in a social referencing paradigm. *Child Development, 67,* 3219–3237.

Munakata, Y. (2006). Information processing approaches to development. In W. Damon & R. Lerner (Eds.), *Handbook of child psychology* (6th ed.). New York: Wiley.

Munroe, R.H., Himmin, H.S., & Munroe, R.L. (1984). Gender understanding and sex role preference in four cultures. *Developmental Psychology, 20,* 673–682.

Murphy, D.J., Fowlie, P.W., & McGuire, W. (2004). Obstetric issues and preterm birth. *British Medical Journal, 329,* 783–786.

Murray, C.S., Woodcock, A., Smillie, F.I., Cain, G., Kissen, P., & Castovie, A. (2004). Tobacco smoke exposure, wheeze, and atopy. *Pediatric Pulmonology, 37,* 492–498.

Murray, J.P. (2000). Media effects. In A. Kazdin (Ed.), *Encyclopedia of psychology.* Washington, DC, & New York: American Psychological Association and Oxford University Press.

Myers, B.J., Dawson, K.S., Britt, G.C., Lodder, D.E., Meloy, L.D., Saunders, M.K., Meadows, S.L., & Elswick, R.K. (2003). Prenatal cocaine exposure and infant performance on the Brazelton Neonatal Behavioral Assessment Scale. *Substance Use and Misuse, 38,* 2065–2096.

Myers, D., Baer, W., & Choi, S. (1996). The changing problem of overcrowded housing. *Journal of the American Planning Association, 62,* 66–84.

Myers, D.L. (1999). *Excluding violent youths from juvenile court: The effectiveness of legislative waiver.* Doctoral dissertation, University of Maryland, College Park.

Myerson, J., Rank, M.R., Raines, F.Q., & Schnitzler, M.A. (1998). Race and general cognitive ability: The myth of diminishing returns in education. *Psychological Science, 9,* 139–142.

NAEYC. (2002). *Early learning standards: Creating the conditions for success.* Washington, DC: National Association for the Education of Young Children.

Nagano, H., & Blumstein, S.E. (2004). Deficits in thematic integration processes in Broca's and Wernicke's aphasia. *Brain and Language, 88,* 96–107.

Nagata, D.K. (1989). Japanese American children and adolescents. In J.T. Gibbs & L.N. Huang (Eds.), *Children of color.* San Francisco: Jossey-Bass.

Nagy, Z., Westerberg, H., & Klingberg, T. (2004). Maturation of white matter is associated with the development of cognitive functions during childhood. *Journal of Cognitive Neuroscience, 16,* 1227–1233.

Nakai, K., & others. (2004). The Tohoku Study of Child Development: A cohort study of effects of perinatal exposure to methylmercury and environmentally persistent organic pollutants on neurobehavioral development in Japanese children. *Tohoku Journal of Experimental Medicine, 202,* 227–237.

Nansel, T.R., Overpeck, M., Pilla, R., Ruan, W., Simons-Morton, B., & Scheidt, P. (2001). Bullying behaviors among U.S. youth. *Journal of the American Medical Association, 285,* 2094–2100.

Narang, A., & Jain, N. (2001). Haemolytic disease of newborn. *Indian Journal of Pediatrics, 68,* 167–172.

Nash, S.G., McQueen, A., & Bray, J.H. (2005). Pathways to adolescent alcohol use: Family environment, peer influence, and parental expectations. *Journal of Adolescent Health, 37,* 19–28.

National Assessment of Educational Progress. (2000). *Reading achievement.* Washington, DC: National Center for Education Statistics.

National Association for the Education of Young Children. (1986). Position statement on developmentally appropriate practice in programs for 4- and 5-year olds. *Young Children 41,* 20–29.

National Center for Addiction and Substance Abuse. (2001). *2000 teen survey.* New York: National Center for Addiction and Substance Abuse, Columbia University.

National Center for Education Statistics. (2000). *The nation's report card.* Washington, DC: U.S. Department of Education.

National Center for Education Statistics. (2001). *Dropout rates in the United States.* Washington, DC: U.S. Department of Education.

National Center for Education Statistics. (2002). *Digest of education statistics.* Washington, DC: Author.

National Center for Health Statistics. (2000). *Health United States, 1999.* Atlanta: Centers for Disease Control and Prevention.

National Center for Health Statistics. (2002a). *Health United States, 2002.* Hyattsville, MD: Author.

National Center for Health Statistics. (2002b). Prevalence of overweight among children and adolescents: United States 1999–2000 (Table 71). *Health United States, 2002.* Atlanta, GA: Centers for Disease Control and Prevention.

National Center for Health Statistics. (2004). *Births.* Atlanta, GA: Centers for Disease Control and Prevention.

National Center for Health Statistics. (2004). *Health United States, 2004.* Hyattsville, MD: Author.

National Center for Health Statistics. (2004). *Health United States, 2004,* Bethesda, MD: U.S. Department of Health and Human Services.

National Clearinghouse on Child Abuse and Neglect. (2002). *What is child maltreatment?* Washington, DC: Administration for Children and Families.

National Clearinghouse on Child Abuse and Neglect. (2004). *What is child abuse and neglect?* Washington, DC: U.S. Department of Health and Human Services.

National Institute of Mental Health. (1993). *Learning disabilities* (NIH publication No. 93-3611). Bethesda, MD: Author.

National Reading Panel. (2000). *Teaching children to read.* Washington, DC: National Institute of Child Health and Human Development.

National Research Council. (1999). *How people learn.* Washington, DC: National Academy Press.

National Research Council. (1999). *Starting out right: A guide to promoting children's reading success.* Washington, DC: National Academy Press.

National Vital Statistics Reports. (2001). Deaths and death rates for the 10 leading causes of death in specified age groups. *National Vital Statistics Reports, 48* (11), Table 8.

Natsopoulos, D., Kiosseoglou, G., Xeroxmeritou, A., & Alevriadou, A. (1998). Do the hands talk on the mind's behalf? Differences in language between left- and right-handed children. *Brain and Language, 64,* 182–214.

Natsopoulos, D., Koutselini, M., Kiosseoglou, G., & Koundouris, F. (2002). Differences in language performance in variations of lateralization. *Brain and Language, 82,* 223–240.

Needham, A., Barrett, T., & Peterman, K. (2002). A pick-me-up for infants' exploratory skills: Early simulated experiences reaching for objects using "sticky mittens" enhances young infants' object exploration skills. *Infant Behavior & Development, 25,* 279–295.

Negalia, J.P., Friedman, D.L., Yasui, Y., Mertens, A., Hammond, S., Stoval, S., & Donaldson, M. (2001). Second malignant neoplasms in five-year survivors of childhood cancer. *Journal of the National Cancer Institute, 93,* 618–629.

Neill, M. (2003). Leaving children behind. *Phi Delta Kappan, 84,* 225–228.

Neisser, U. (2004). Memory development: New questions and old. *Developmental Review, 24,* 154–158.

Neisser, U., Boodoo, G., Bouchard, T.J., Boykin, A.W., Brody, N., Ceci, S.J., Halpern, D.F., Loehlin, J.C., Perloff, R.J., Sternberg, R., & Urbina, S. (1996). Intelligence: Knowns and unknowns. *American Psychologist, 51,* 77–101.

Nelson, C.A. (2000). Neural plasticity and human development: The role of early experience in sculpting memory systems. *Developmental Science, 3,* 115–130.

Nelson, C.A. (2001). The development and neural bases of face recognition. *Infant and Child Development, 10,* 3–18.

Nelson, C.A. (2003). Neural development and lifelong plasticity. In R.M. Lerner, F. Jacobs, & D. Wertlieb (Eds.), *Handbook of applied developmental science* (Vol. 1). Thousand Oaks, CA: Sage.

Nelson, C.A. (2005). Neurobehavioral development in the context of biocultural co-constructivism. In P.B. Baltes & P. Reuter-Lorenz (Eds.), *Brain, mind, and culture.* New York: Oxford University Press.

Nelson, C.A., Thomas, K.M., & de Haan, M. (2006). Neural bases of cognitive development. In W. Damon, R. Lerner, D. Kuhn, & R. Siegler (Eds.), *Handbook of child psychology* (6th ed., Vol. 2). New York: Wiley.

Nelson, K. (1999). Levels and modes of representation: Issues for the theory of conceptual change and development. In E.K. Skolnick, K. Nelson, S.A. Gelman, & P.H. Miller (Eds.), *Conceptual development.* Mahwah, NJ: Erlbaum.

Nelson, K. (2004). A welcome turn to meaning in infant development: Commentary on Mandler's *The foundation of the mind: Origins of conceptual thought. Developmental Science, 7,* 506–507.

Newcomb, M.D., & Bentler, P.M. (1988). Substance use and abuse among children and teenagers. *American Psychologist, 44,* 242–248.

Newcombe, N.S., Drummery, A.B., Fox, N.A., Lile, E., & Ottinger-Alberts, W. (2000). Remembering early childhood: How much, how, and why (or why not). *Current Directions in Psychological Science, 9,* 55–58.

Newcombe, N.S., & Fox, N. (1994). Infantile amnesia: Through a glass darkly. *Child Development, 65,* 31–40.

Newell, K., Scully, D.M., McDonald, P.V., & Baillargeon, R. (1989). Task constraints and infant grip configurations. *Developmental Psychobiology, 22,* 817–832.

Newman, D.L. (2005). Ego development and ethnic identity formation in rural American Indian adolescents. *Child Development, 76,* 734–746.

Newton, A.W., & Vandeven, A.M. (2005). Update on child maltreatment with a focus on shaken baby syndrome. *Current Opinions in Pediatrics, 17,* 246–251.

NICHD Early Child Care Research Network. (2000). Factors associated with fathers' caregiving activities and sensitivity with young children. *Developmental Psychology, 14,* 200–219.

NICHD Early Child Care Research Network. (2001). Nonmaternal care and family factors in early development: An overview of the NICHD study of Early Child Care. *Journal of Applied Developmental Psychology, 22,* 457–492.

NICHD Early Child Care Research Network. (2002). Structure → Process → Outcome: Direct and indirect effects of child care quality on young children's development. *Psychological Science, 13,* 199–206.

NICHD Early Child Care Research Network. (2003). Does amount of time spent in child care predict socioemotional adjustment during the transition to kindergarten? *Child Development, 74,* 976–1005.

NICHD Early Child Care Research Network. (2003). Do children's attention processes mediate the link between family predictors and school readiness. *Developmental Psychology, 39,* 581–593.

NICHD Early Child Care Research Network. (2004). Are child developmental outcomes related to before- and after-school care arrangement? *Child Development, 75,* 280–295.

NICHD Early Child Care Research Network. (2005). *Child care and development.* New York: Guilford.

Nielsen, S.J., Siega-Riz, A.M., & Popkin, B.M. (2002). Trends in energy intake in U.S. between 1977 and 1996: Similar shifts seen across age groups. *Obesity Research, 10,* 370–378.

Nisbett, R. (2003). *The geography of thought.* New York: Free Press.

Nocentini, U., Goulet, P., Roberts, P.M., & Joanette, Y. (2001). The effects of left- versus right-hemisphere lesions on the sensitivity to intra- and interconceptual semantic relationships. *Neuropsychologia, 39,* 443–451.

Noddings, N. (1992). *The challenge to care in schools.* New York: Teachers College Press.

Noddings, N. (1998). *Teaching for continuous learning.* Paper presented at the meeting of the American Educational Research Association, San Diego.

Noddings, N. (2001). The care tradition: Beyond "add women and stir." *Theory into Practice, 40,* 29–34.

Nolan, K., Schell, L.M., Stark, A.D., & Gomez, M.I. (2002). Longitudinal study of energy and nutrient intakes for infants from low-income, urban families. *Public Health Nutrition, 5,* 405–412.

Nolen-Hoeksema, S. (2004). *Abnormal psychology* (3rd ed.). New York: McGraw-Hill.

Nolen-Hoeksema, S. (2007). *Abnormal psychology* (4th ed.). New York: McGraw-Hill.

Noller, P. (2005). Sibling relationships in adolescence: Learning and growing together. *Personal Relationships, 12,* 1–22.

Norremolle, A., Hasholt, L., Petersen, C.B., Eiberg, H., Hasselbalch, S.G., Gideon, P., Nielson, J.E., & Sorensen, S.A. (2004). Mosaicism of the CAG repeat sequence in the Huntington disease gene in a pair of monozygotic twins. *American Journal of Medical Genetics, 130A,* 154–159.

Nottelmann, E.D., Susman, E.J., Blue, J.H., Inoff-Germain, G., Dorn, L.D., Loriaux, D.L., Cutler, G.B., & Chrousos, G.P. (1987). Gonadal and adrenal hormone correlates of adjustment in early adolescence. In R.M. Lerner & T.T. Foch (Eds.), *Biological-psychological interactions in early adolescence.* Hillsdale, NJ: Erlbaum.

Nsamenang, A.B. (2002). Adolescence in sub-Saharan Africa: An image constructed from Africa's triple heritage. In B.B. Brown, R.W. Larson, & T.S. Saraswathi (Eds.), *The world's youth*. New York: Cambridge University Press.

Nugent, K., & Brazelton, T.B. (2000). Preventive infant mental health: Uses of the Brazelton scale. In J.D. Osofsky & H.E. Fitzgerald (Eds.), *WAIMH Handbook of infant mental health* (Vol. 2). New York: Wiley.

O'Donnell, M.P., & Wood, M. (2004). *Becoming a reader* (3rd ed.). Boston: Allyn & Bacon.

O'Dowd, A. (2004). Why are midwife numbers in crisis? *Nursing Times, 100,* 12–13.

O'Leary, C. (2004). Fetal alcohol syndrome. *Journal of Pediatric Child Health, 40,* 2–7.

O'Neill, P. (2002). Acute otitis media. *Clinical Evidence, 8,* 251–261.

Oakes, L.M., Kannass, K.N., & Shaddy, D.J. (2002). Developmental changes in the endogenous control of attention: The role of target familiarity on infants' distraction latency. *Child Development, 73,* 1644–1655.

Oates, J., & Grayson, A. (2004). *Cognitive and language development in children*. Malden, MA: Blackwell.

Obler, L.K. (1993). Language beyond childhood. In J.B. Gleason (Ed.), *The development of language* (3rd ed.). New York: Macmillan.

Oehninger, S. (2001). Strategies for the infertile man. *Seminars in Reproductive Medicine, 19,* 231–238.

Ogbu, J. (1989, April). *Academic socialization of Black children: An innoculation against future failure?* Paper presented at the meeting of the Society for Research in Child Development, Kansas City.

Ogbu, J., & Stern, P. (2001). Caste status and intellectual ability. In R.J. Sternberg & E.L. Grigorenko (Eds.), *Environmental effects on cognitive abilities*. Mahwah, NJ: Erlbaum.

Ohgi, S., Akiyama, T., Arisawa, K., & Shigemori, K. (2004). Randomized controlled trial of swaddling versus massage in the management of excess crying in infants with cerebral injuries. *Archives of Disease in Childhood, 89,* 212–216.

Ohgi, S., Akiyama, T., & Fukuda, M. (2005). Neurobehavioral profile of low-birthweight infants with cystic periventricular leukomalacia. *Developmental Medicine and Child Neurology, 47,* 221–228.

Ohgi, S., Fukuda, M., Moriuchi, H., Kusumoto, T., Akiyama, T., Nugent, J.K., Brazelton, T.B., Arisawa, K., Takahashi, T., & Saitoh, H. (2002). Comparison of kangaroo care and standard care: Behavioral organization, development, and temperament in healthy, low birth weight infants through 1 year. *Journal of Perinatology, 22,* 374–379.

Okagaki, L. (2000). Determinants of intelligence: Socialization of intelligence. In A. Kazdin (Ed.), *Encyclopedia of psychology*. Washington, DC, & New York: American Psychological Association and Oxford University Press.

Okah, F.A., Cai, J., & Hoff, G.L. (2005). Term-gestation low birth weight and health-compromising behaviors during pregnancy. *Obstetrics and Gynecology, 105,* 543–550.

Okun, B.F., & Rappaport, L.J. (1980). *Working with families*. North Scituate, MA: Duxbury Press.

Olivardia, R., Pope, H.G., Mangweth, B., & Hudson, J.I. (1995). Eating disorders in college men. *American Journal of Psychiatry, 152,* 1279–1284.

Oltjenbruns, K. (2001). The developmental context of childhood grief. In M. Stroebe, R.O. Hansson, W. Stroebe, & H. Schut (Eds.), *Handbook of bereavement research*. Washington, DC: American Psychological Association.

Olweus, D. (1980). Bullying among schoolboys. In R. Barnen (Ed.), *Children and violence*. Stockholm: Acaemic Litteratur.

Onwuegbuzi, A.J., & Daley, C.E. (2001). Racial differences in IQ revisited: A synthesis of nearly a century of research. *Journal of Black Psychology, 27,* 209–220.

Orbanic, S. (2001). Understanding bulimia. *American Journal of Nursing, 101,* 35–41.

Ornstein, P.A., & Haden, C.A. (2001). False childhood memories and eyewitness suggestibility. In M.L. Eisen, J.A. Quas, & G.S. Goodman (Eds.), *Memory and suggestibility in the forensic interview*. Mahwah, NJ: Erlbaum.

Orobio de Castro, B., Merk, W., Koops, W., Veerman, J.W., & Bosch, J.D. (2005). Emotions in social information processing and their relations with reactive and proactive aggression in referred aggressive boys. *Journal of Clinical Child and Adolescent Psychology, 34,* 105–116.

Osborne, L., & Pober, B. (2001). Genetics of childhood disorders: XXVII. Genes and cognition in Williams syndrome. *Journal of the Academy of Child & Adolescent Psychiatry, 40,* 732–735.

Osvath, P., Voros, V., & Fekete, S. (2004). Life events and psychopathology in a group of suicide attempters. *Psychopathology, 37,* 36–40.

Ovando, C.J., Combs, M.C., & Collier, V.P. (2006). *Bilingual and ESL classrooms* (4th ed.). New York: McGraw-Hill.

Overton, T. (2000). *Assessment in special education* (3rd ed.). Upper Saddle River, NJ: Merrill.

Overton, W.F. (2004). Embodied development: Biology, person, and culture in a relational context. In C.G. Coll, E.L. Bearer, & R.M. Lerner (Eds.), *Nature and nurture*. Mahwah, NJ: Erlbaum.

Owens, J.A. (2005). Introduction: Culture and sleep in children. *Pediatrics, 115,* 201–203.

Oyserman, D., & Fryberg, S. (2004). The possible selves of diverse adolescents: Content and function across gender, race, and national origin. In C. Dunkel & J. Kerpelman (Eds.), *Possible selves: Theory, research, and application*. Huntington, NY: Nova.

Oyserman, D., Terry, K., & Bybee, D. (2002). A possible selves intervention to enhance school involvement. *Journal of Adolescence, 25,* 313–326.

Oztop, E., Bradley, N.S., & Arbib, M.A. (2004). Infant grasp learning: A computational model. *Experimental Brain Research, 158,* 480–503.

Pérez, B. (2004). Language, literacy, and biliteracy. In B. Pérez, T.L. McCarty, L.J. Watahomigie, M.E. Torres-Guzman, T. Dien, J. Chang, H.L. Smith, A. Davila de Silva, & A. Norlander (Eds.), *Sociocultural contexts of language and literacy*. Mahwah, NJ: Erlbuam.

Pérez, B., McCarty, T.L., Watahomigie, L.J., Torres-Guzman, M.E., Dien, T., Chang, J., Smith, H.L., Davila de Silva, A., & Norlander, A. (Eds.). (2004). *Sociocultural contexts of language and literacy*. Mahwah, NJ: Erlbaum.

Padilla, A.M., & Perez, W. (2003). Acculturation, social identity, and social cognition: A new perspective. *Hispanic Journal of Behavioral Science, 25,* 35–55.

Padilla, R.V. (2005). Latino/a education in the twenty-first century. In P. Pedraza & M. Rivera (Eds.), *Latino education*. Mahwah, NJ: Erlbaum.

Paludi, M.A. (2002). *Psychology of women* (2nd ed.). Upper Saddle River, NJ: Prentice Hall.

Pan, B. (2005). Semantic development: Learning the meaning of words. In J. Berko Gleason (Ed.), *The development of language* (6th ed.). Boston: Allyn & Bacon.

Pang, V.O. (2005). *Multicultural education* (2nd ed.). New York: McGraw-Hill.

Papp, C., & Papp, Z. (2003). Chorionic villus sampling and amniocentesis: What are the risks in current practice? *Current Opinions in Obstetrics and Gynecology, 15,* 159–165.

Parazzini, F., Chatenoud, L., Surace, M., Tozzi, L., Salerio, B., Bettoni, G., & Benzi, G. (2003). Moderate alcohol drinking and risk of preterm birth. *European Journal of Clinical Nutrition, 57,* 1345–1349.

Parke, R.D. (1972). Some effects of punishment on children's behavior. In W.W. Hartup (Ed.), *The young child* (Vol. 2). Washington, DC. National Association for the Education of Young Children.

Parke, R.D. (1977). Some effects of punishment on children's behavior—Revisited. In E.M. Hetherington & R.D. Parke (Eds.), *Readings in contemporary child psychology*. New York: McGraw-Hill.

Parke, R.D. (1995). Fathers and families. In M.H. Bornstein (Ed.), *Children and parenting* (Vol. 3). Hillsdale, NJ: Erlbaum.

Parke, R.D. (2000). Father involvement: A developmental psychology perspective. *Marriage and Family Review, 29,* 43–58.

Parke, R.D. (2001). Parenting in the new millennium. In J.P. McHale & W.S. Grolnick (Eds.), *Retrospect and prospect in the psychological study of families.* Mahwah, NJ: Erlbuam.

Parke, R.D. (2002). Fathering. In M.H. Bornstein (Ed.), *Handbook of parenting* (2nd ed.). Mahwah, NJ: Erlbaum.

Parke, R.D. (2004). Development in the family. *Annual Review of Psychology, 55,* Palo Alto, CA: Annual Reviews.

Parke, R.D., & Buriel, R. (1998). Socialization in the family. Ethnic and ecological perspectives. In W. Damon (Ed.), *Handbook of child psychology* (5th ed., Vol. 3). New York: Wiley.

Parke, R.D., & Buriel, R. (2006). Socialization in the family: Ethnic and ecological perspectives. In W. Damon & R. Lerner (Eds.), *Handbook of child psychology* (6th ed.). New York: Wiley.

Parke, R.D., & Clarke-Stewart, K.A. (2003). Developmental psychology. In I.B. Weiner (Ed.), *Handbook of psychology* (Vol. 1). New York: Wiley.

Parke, R.D., Dennis, J., Flyr, M.L., Leidy, M.S., & Schofield, T.J. (2005). Fathers: Cultural and ecological perspectives. In T. Luster & L. Okagaki (Eds.), *Parenting: An ecological perspective* (2nd ed.). Mahwah, NJ: Erlbaum.

Parke, R.D., Simpkins, S., McDowell, D., Kim, M., Killian, C., Dennis, J., Flyr, M.L., Wild, M., & Rah, Y. (2004). Family-peer influences: Relative contributions. In P. Smith & C. Hart (Eds.), *Blackwell handbook of social development.* Malden, MA: Blackwell.

Parker, J.G., & Asher, S.R. (1987). Peer relations and later personal adjustment: Are low accepted children at risk? *Psychological Bulletin, 102,* 357–389.

Parker, J.G., Walker, A.R., Low, C.M., & Gamm, B.K. (2004). Friendship jealousy in young adolescents: Individual differences and links to sex, self-esteem, aggression, and social adjustment. *Developmental Psychology, 41,* 235–250.

Parmar, R.C., Muranjan, M.N., & Swami, S. (2002). Trisomy 21 with XYY. *Indian Journal of Pediatrics, 11,* 979–981.

Parmet, S., Lynn, C., & Glass, R.M. (2004). Prenatal care. *Journal of the American Medical Association, 291,* 146.

Parten, M. (1932). Social play among preschool children. *Journal of Abnormal Social Psychology, 27,* 243–269.

Partnership for a Drug-Free America. (2005). *Partnership Attitude Tracking Study.* New York: Author.

Pascali-Bonaro, D. (2002). Pregnant and widowed on September 11: The birth community reaches out. *Birth, 29,* 62–64.

Pasch, L.A. (2001). Confronting fertility problems. In A. Baum, T.A. Revenson, & J.E. Singer (Eds.), *Handbook of health psychology.* Mahwah, NJ: Erlbaum.

Pasley, K., & Moorefield, B.S. (2004). Stepfamilies. In M. Coleman & L. Ganong (Eds.), *Handbook of contemporary families.* Thousand Oaks, CA: Sage.

Patterson, B., Ryan, J., & Dickey, J.H. (2004). The toxicology of mercury. *New England Journal of Medicine, 350,* 945–947.

Patterson, C.J. (2002). Lesbian and gay parenthood. In M.H. Bornstein (Ed.), *Handbook of parenting* (2nd ed., Vol. 3). Mahwah, NJ: Erlbaum.

Patterson, C.J. (2004). What differences does a civil union make? Changing pubic policies and the experiences of same-sex couples: Comment on Solomon, Rothblum, and Balsam (2004). *Journal of Family Psychology, 18,* 287–289.

Patterson, G.R., DeBaryshe, B.D., & Ramsey, E. (1989). A developmental perspective on antisocial behavior. *American Psychologist, 44,* 329–355.

Patterson, G.R., & Fisher, P.A. (2002). Recent developments in our understanding of parenting: Bidirectional effects, causal models, and the search for parsimony. In M.H. Bornstein (Ed.), *Handbook of parenting* (2nd ed., Vol. 5). Mahwah, NJ: Erlbaum.

Patterson, G.R., & Stouthamer-Loeber, M. (1984). The correlation of family management practices and delinquency. *Child Development, 55,* 1299–1307.

Pavlov, I.P. (1927). In G.V. Anrep (Trans.), *Conditioned reflexes.* London: Oxford University Press.

Payne, W.A., Hahn, D.B., & Maver, E.B. (2005). *Understanding your health* (8th ed.). New York: McGraw-Hill.

Pederson, D.R., & Moran, G. (1996). Expressions of the attachment relationship outside of the Strange Situation. *Child Development, 67,* 915–927.

Pederson, P.B. (2004). *110 experiences for multicultural learning.* Washington, DC: American Psychological Association.

Pedraza, P., & Rivera, M. (Eds.). (2005). *Latino education.* Mahwah, NJ: Erlbaum.

Pellizzer, C., Adler, S., Corvi, R., Hartung, T., & Bremer, S. (2004). Monitoring of teratogenic effects in vitro by analyzing a selected gene expression pattern. *Toxicology In Vitro, 18,* 325–335.

Peregoy, S., & Boyle, O. (2005). *Reading, writing, and learning in ESL* (4th ed.). Boston: Allyn & Bacon.

Perner, J., Stummer, S., Sprung, M., & Doherty, M. (2002). Theory of mind finds its Piagetian perspective: Why alternative naming comes with understanding belief. *Cognitive Development, 17,* 1451–1472.

Perse, E.M. (2001). *Media effects and society.* Mahwah, NJ: Erlbaum.

Persons, D.A., & Tisdale, J.F. (2004). Gene therapy for the hemoglobin disorders. *Seminars in Hematology, 41,* 279–286.

Peskin, H. (1967). Pubertal onset and ego functioning. *Journal of Abnormal Psychology, 72,* 1–15.

Petersen, A.C. (1979, January). Can puberty come any faster? *Psychology Today,* pp. 45–56.

Peterson, C.C., & Peterson, J.L. (1973). Preference for sex of offspring as a measure of change in sex attitudes. *Psychology, 10,* 3–5.

Peterson, K.S. (1997, September 3). In high school, dating is a world into itself. *USA Today,* pp. 1–2D.

Petrill, S.A. (2003). The development of intelligence: Behavioral genetic approaches. In R.J. Sternberg, J. Lautrey, & T.I. Lubert (Eds.), *Models of intelligence: International perspectives.* Washington, DC: American Psychological Association.

Petrill, S.A., & Deater-Deckard, K. (2004). The heritability of general cognitive ability: A within-family adoption design. *Intelligence, 32,* 403–409.

Pettit, G.S., Bates, J.E., Dodge, K.A., & Meece, D.W. (1999). The impact of after-school peer contact on early adolescent externalizing problems is moderated by parental monitoring, perceived neighborhood safety, and prior adjustment. *Child Development, 70,* 768–778.

Pettito, L.A., Kovelman, I., & Harasymowycz, U. (2003, April). *Bilingual language development: Does learning the new damage the old.* Paper presented at the meeting of the Society for Research in Child Development, Tampa.

Pfeffer, C.R. (1996). *Severe stress and mental disturbance in children.* Washington, DC: American Psychiatric Press.

Pfeifer, M., Goldsmith, H.H., Davidson, R.J., & Rickman, M. (2002). Continuity and change in inhibited and uninhibited children. *Child Development, 73,* 1474–1485.

Phinney, J.S. (1996). When we talk about American ethnic groups, what do we mean? *American Psychologist, 51,* 918–927.

Phinney, J.S. (2003). Ethnic identity and acculturation. In K.M. Chun, P.B. Organista, & G. Marin (Eds.), *Acculturation.* Washington, DC: American Psychological Associtation.

Phinney, J.S., & Alipuria, L.L. (1990). Ethnic identity in college students from four ethnic groups. *Journal of Adolescence, 13,* 171–183.

Piaget, J. (1932). *The moral judgment of the child.* New York: Harcourt race Jovanovich.

Piaget, J. (1952). Jean Piaget. In C.A. Murchison (Ed.), *A history of psychology in autobiography* (Vol. 4). Worcester, MA: Clark University Press.

Piaget, J. (1952). *The origins of intelligence in children.* (M. Cook, Trans.). New York: International Universities Press.

Piaget, J. (1954). *The construction of reality in the child.* New York: Basic Books.

Piaget, J. (1962). *Play, dreams, and imitation in childhood.* New York: W.W. Norton.

Piaget, J., & Inhelder, B. (1969). *The child's conception of space* (F.J. Langdon & J.L. Lunger, Trans.). New York: W.W. Norton.

Piata, R.C., Hurley, Hamre, B., & Stuhlman, M. (2003). Relationships between teachers and children. In I.B. Weiner (Ed.), *Handbook of psychology* (Vol. 7). New York: Wiley.

Pick, H.L. (1997). Review of Santrock *Child development* (8th ed.). New York: McGraw-Hill.

Pickrell, J., & Loftus, E.F. (2001). *Creating false memories.* Paper presented at the meeting of the American Psychological Society, Toronto.

Pietz, J., Peter, J., Graf, R., Rauterberg-Ruland, I., Rupp, A., Southheimer, D., & Linderkamp, O. (2004). Physical growth and neurodevelopmental outcome of nonhandicapped low-risk children born preterm. *Early Human Development, 79,* 131–143.

Pike, J.J., & Jennings, N.A. (2005). The effects of commercials on children's perceptions of gender appropriate toy use. *Sex Roles, 52,* 83–91.

Piliavin, J.A. (2003). Doing well by doing good: Benefits for the benefactor. In C.L.M. Keys & J. Haidt (Eds.), *Flourishing: Positive psychology and the life well-lived.* Washington, DC: American Psychological Association.

Pillow, D.R., Zautra, A.J., & Sandler, I. (1996). Major life events and minor stressors: Identifying mediational links in the stress process. *Journal of Personality and Social Psychology, 70,* 381–394.

Pinette, M.G., Wax, J., Blackstone, J., Crtin, A., & McCrann, D. (2004). Timing of early amniocentesis as a function of membrane fusion. *Journal of Clinical Ultrasound, 32,* 8–11.

Pinker, S. (1994). *The language instinct.* New York: William Morrow.

Pintrich, P.R. (2003). Motivation and classroom learning. In I.B. Weiner (Ed.), *Handbook of psychology* (Vol. 7). New York: Wiley.

Pintrich, P.R., & Maehr, M.L. (2004). *Motivating students, improving schools.* Mahwah, NJ: Erlbaum.

Pittman, K., Diversi, M., Irby, M., & Fabber, T. (2003). Social policy implications. In R. Larson, B. Brown, & J. Mortimer (Eds.), *Adolescents' preparation for the future: Perils and promises.* Malden, MA: Blackwell.

Piwoz, E.G., & Ross, J.S. (2005). Use of population-specific infant mortality rates to inform policy decisions regarding HIV and infant feeding. *Journal of Nutrition, 135,* 1113–1119.

Plackslin, S. (2000). *Mothering the new mother: Women's feelings and needs after childbirth—A support and resource guide.* New York: Newmarket Press.

Plant, T.M., & Barker-Gibb, M.L. (2004). Neurobiological mechanisms of puberty in higher primates. *Human Reproduction Update, 10,* 67–77.

Pleck, J.H. (1983). The theory of male sex role identity: Its rise and fall, 1936–present. In M. Levin (Ed.), *In the shadow of the past: Psychology portrays the sexes.* New York: Columbia University Press.

Pleck, J.H. (1995). The gender-role strain paradigm. In R.F. Levant & W.S. Pollack (Eds.), *A new psychology of men.* New York: Basic Books.

Pleck, J.H., & Masciadrelli, B.P. (2004). Paternal involvement: Levels, sources and consequences. In M.E. Lamb (Ed.), *The role of the father in child development.* New York: Wiley.

Plomin, R. (1993, March). *Human behavioral genetics and development: An overview and update.* Paper presented at the biennial meeting of the Society for Research in Child Development, New Orleans.

Plomin, R. (1999). Genetics and general cognitive ability. *Nature, 402* (Suppl.), C25–C29.

Plomin, R., Asbury, K., & Dunn, J. (2001). Why are children in the same family so different? Nonshared environment a decade later. *Canadian Journal of Psychiatry, 46,* 225–233.

Plomin, R., DeFries, J.C., Craig, I.W., & McGuffin, P. (Eds.). (2003). *Behavioral genetics in the postgenomic era.* APA Books: Washington, DC.

Plomin, R., Fulker, D.W., Corley, R., & DeFries, J.C. (1997). Nature, nurture, and cognitive development from 1 to 16 years: A parent-offspring adoption study. *Psychological Science, 8,* 442–447.

Plomin, R., Reiss, D., Hetherington, E.M., & Howe, G.W. (1994). Nature and nurture: Contributions to measures of the family environment. *Developmental Psychology, 30,* 32–43.

Poelmans, S.A. (Ed.). (2005). *Work and family.* Mahwah, NJ: Erlbaum.

Polivy, J., Herman, C.P., Mills, J., & Brock, H. (2003). Eating disorders in adolescence. In G. Adams & M. Berzonsky (Eds.), *Blackwell handbook of adolescence.* Malden, MA: Blackwell.

Pollack, W. (1999). *Real boys.* New York: Owl Books.

Pollitt, E.P., Gorman, K.S., Engle, P. L., Martocell, R., & Rivera, J. (1993). Early supplementary feeding and cognition. Monographs of the *Society for Research in Child Development, 58* (7, Serial No. 235).

Ponterotto, J.G., Casas, J.M., Suzuki, L.A., & Alexander, C.M. (Eds.). (2001). *Handbook of multicultural counseling.* Thousand Oaks, CA: Sage.

Poole, D.A., & Lindsay, D.S. (1995). Interviewing preschoolers: Effects of nonsuggestive techniques, parental coaching, and leading questions on reports of nonexperienced events. *Journal of Experimental Child Psychology, 60,* 129–154.

Poole, D.A., & Lindsay, D.S. (1996). *Effects of parents' suggestions, interviewing techniques, and age on young children's event reports.* Presented at the NATO Advanced Study Institute, Port de Bourgenay, France.

Porac, C., & Searleman, A. (2002). The effects of hand preference side and hand preference switch history on measures of psychological and physical well-being and cognitive performance in a sample of older adult right- and left-handers. *Neuropsychologia, 40,* 2074–2083.

Posner, J.K., & Vandell, D.L. (1994). Low-income children's after-school care: Are there benefits of after-school programs? *Child Development, 65,* 440–456.

Potvin, L., Champagne, F., & Laberge-Nadeau, C. (1988). Mandatory driver training and road safety: The Quebec experience. *American Journal of Public Health, 78,* 1206–1212.

Poulton, S., & Sexton, D. (1996). Feeding young children: Developmentally appropriate considerations for supplementing family care. *Childhood Education, 73,* 66–71.

Powell, D.R. (2005). Searching for what works in parenting interventions. In T. Luster & L. Okagaki (Eds.), *Parenting* (2nd ed.). Mahwah, NJ: Erlbaum.

Powell, D.R. (2006). Families and early childhood interventions. In W. Damon & R. Lerner (Eds.), *Handbook of child psychology* (6th ed.). New York: Wiley.

Powell, R.G., & Caseau, D. (2004). *Classroom communication and diversity.* Mahwah, NJ: Erlbaum.

Power, F.C. (2004). The moral self in community. In D.K. Lapsley & D. Narvaez (Eds.), *Moral development, self, and identity.* Mahwah, NJ: Erlbaum.

Pressley, M. (2003). Psychology of literacy and literacy instruction. In I.B. Weiner (Ed.), *Handbook of psychology* (Vol. 7). New York: Wiley.

Pressley, M., Cariligia-Bull, T., Deane, S., & Schneider, W. (1987). Short-term memory, verbal competence, and age as predictors of imagery instructional effectiveness. *Journal of Experimental Child Psychology, 43,* 194–211.

Pressley, M., & Hilden, K. (2005). Commentary on three important directions in comprehension assessment. In S.G. Paris & S.A. Stahl (Eds.), *Children's reading comprehension and assessment.* Mahwah, NJ: Erlbaum.

Pressley, M., & Hilden, K. (2006). Cognitive strategies. In W. Damon & R. Lerner (Eds.), *Handbook of child psychology* (6th ed.). New York: Wiley.

Pressley, M., Roehrig, A.D., Raphael, L., Dolezal, S., Bohn, C., Mohan, L., Wharton-McDonald, R., Bogner, K., & Hogna, K. (2003). Teaching processes in elementary and secondary education. In I.B. Weiner (Ed.), *Handbook of psychology* (Vol. 7). New York: Wiley.

Price, L.F. (2005). The biology of risk-taking. *Educational Leadership, 62* (No. 7), 22–26.

Pringle, P.J., Geary, M.P., Rodeck, C.H., Kingdom, J.C., Kayamba-Kays, S., & Hindmarsh, P.C. (2005). The influence of cigarette smoking on antenatal growth, birth size, and the insulin-like growth factor axis. *Journal of Clinical Endocrinology and Metabolism, 90,* 2556–2562.

Pritchard, F.F., & Whitehead, G.I. (2004). *Serve and learn.* Mahwah, NJ: Erlbaum.

Provenzo, E.F. (2002). *Teaching, learning, and schooling in American culture: A critical perspective.* Boston: Allyn & Bacon.

Pugh, K.R., Sandak, R., Frost, S.J., Moore, D., & Menci, W.E. (2005). Examining reading development and reading disability in English language learners: Potential contributions from functional neuroimaging. *Learning Disabilities Research and Practice, 20,* 24–30.

Pujol, J., Lopez-Sala, A., Sebastian-Galles, N., Deus, J., Cardoner, N., Soriano-Mas, C., Moreno, A., & Sans, A. (2004). Delayed myelination in children with developmental delay detected by volumetric MRI. *Neuroimage, 22,* 897–903.

Purcheco, S., & Hurtado, A. (2001). Media violence. In J. Worell (Ed.), *Encyclopedia of women and gender.* San Diego: Academic Press.

Putnam, S.P., Sanson, A.V., & Rothbart, M.K. (2002). Child temperament and parenting. In M.H. Bornstein (Ed.), *Handbook of parenting* (2nd ed.). Mahwah, NJ: Erlbaum.

Quadflieg, N., & Fichter, M.M. (2003). The course and outcome of bulimia nervosa. *European Child and Adolescent Psychiatry, 12* (Supplement 1), 1199–1209.

Quiggle, N.L., Garber, J., Panak, W.F., & Dodge, K.A. (1992). Social information processing in aggressive and depressed children. *Child Development, 63,* 1305–1320.

Quinn, P.C. (2004). Multiple sources of information and their integration, not dissociation, as an organizing framework for understanding infant concept formation. *Developmental Science, 7,* 511–513.

Quinn, P.C., & Eimas, P.D. (1996). Perceptual organization and categorization. In C. Rovee-Collier, & L.P. Lipsitt (Eds.), *Advances in infancy research* (Vol. 10, pp. 1–36). Norwood, NJ: Ablex.

Quintana, S.M. (2004). Ethnic identity development in Chicana/o youth. In R.J. Velasquez, B.W. McNeil, & L.M. Arellano (Eds.), *The handbook of Chicano psychology and mental health.* Mahwah, NJ: Erlbaum.

Qutub, M., Klapper, P., Vallely, P., & Cleator, G. (2001). Genital herpes in pregnancy: Is screening cost effective? *International Journal of STD and AIDS, 12,* 14–16.

Rabin, B.E., & Dorr, A. (1995, March). *Children's understanding of emotional events on family television series.* Paper presented at the meeting of the Society for Research in Child Development, Indianapolis.

Rabiner, D.L., Gordon, L., Klumb, D., & Thompson, L.B. (1991, April). *Social problem solving deficiencies in rejected children: Motivational factors and skill deficits.* Paper presented at the meeting of the Society for Research in Child Development, Seattle.

Radcliffe, D.J., Pliskin, J.S., Silvers, J.B., & Cuttler, L. (2004). Growth hormone therapy and quality of life in adults and children. *Pharmacoeconomics, 22,* 499–524.

Radke-Yarrow, M., Nottlemann, E., Martinez, P., Fox, M.B., & Belmont, B. (1992). Young children of affectively ill parents: A longitudinal study of psychosocial development. *Journal of the Academy of Child & Adolescent Psychiatry, 31,* 68–77.

Raffaelli, M., & Ontai, L.L. (2001). "She's sixteen years old and there's boys calling over to the house": An exploratory study of sexual socialization in Latino families. *Culture, Health, and Sexuality, 3,* 295–310.

Raffaelli, M., & Ontai, L.L. (2004). Gender socialization in Latino/a families: Results from two retrospective studies. *Sex Roles, 50,* 287–299.

Rainey, R. (1965). The effects of directed vs. nondirected laboratory work on high school chemistry achievement. *Journal of Research in Science Teaching, 3,* 286–292.

Ramacciotti, C.E., Coli, E., Paoli, R., Gabriellini, G., Schulte, F., Castrogiovanni, S., Dell'Osso, L., & Garfinkel, P.E. (2005). The relationship between binge eating disorder and non-purging bulimia nervosa. *Eating and Weight Disorders, 10,* 8–12.

Ramey, C.T., & Campbell, F.A. (1984). Preventive education for high-risk children: Cognitive consequences of the Carolina Abecedarian Project. *American Journal of Mental Deficiency, 88,* 515–523.

Ramey, C.T., & Ramey, S.L. (1998). Early prevention and early experience. *American Psychologist, 53,* 109–120.

Ramey, C.T., Ramey, S.L., & Lanzi, R.G. (2001). Intelligence and experience. In R.J. Sternberg & E.L. Grigorenko (Eds.), *Environmental effects on cognitive development.* Mahwah, NJ: Erlbaum.

Ramey, C.T., Ramey, S.L., & Lanzi, R.G. (2006). Children's health and education. In W. Damon & R. Lerner (Eds.), *Handbook of child psychology* (6th ed.). New York: Wiley.

Ramirez, M. (2004). Mestiza/o and Chicana/o: General issues. In R.J. Velasquez, B.W. McNeil, & L.M. Arellano (Eds.), *The handbook of Chicano psychology and mental health.* Mahwah, NJ: Erlbaum.

Rampage, C., Eovaldi, M., Ma, C., & Weigel-Foy, C. (2003). Adoptive families. In F. Walsh (Ed.), *Normal family processes: Growing diversity and complexity* (3rd ed.). New York: Guilford Press.

Ramphal, C. (1962). *A study of three current problems in education.* Unpublished doctoral dissertation, University of Natal, India.

Ramsey, P.S., Nuthalapaty, F.S., Lu, G., Ramin, S., Nuthalapaty, E.S., & Ramin, K.D. (2004). A survey of maternal-fetal medicine providers. *American Journal of Obstetrics and Gynecology, 191,* 1497–1502.

Ramus, F. (2004). Neurobiology of dyslexia: A reinterpretation of the data. *Trends in Neuroscience, 27,* 720–726.

Randolph, S., & Kochanoff, A. (2004). Child care research at the dawn of a new millennium. In J.G. Bremner & A. Fogel (Eds.), *Blackwell handbook of infant development.* Malden, MA: Blackwell.

Rankin, J.L., Lane, D.J., Gibbons, F.X., & Gerrard, M. (2004). Adolescents' self-consciousness: Longitudinal age changes and gender differences in two cohorts. *Journal of Research on Adolescence, 14,* 1–21.

Raphaelson, M. (2004). Stimulants and attention-deficit/hyperactivity disorder. *Journal of the American Medical Association, 292,* 2214.

Rappaport, N., & Thomas, C. (2004). Recent research findings on aggressive and violent behavior in youth: Implications for clinical assessment and intervention. *Journal of Adolescent Health, 35,* 260–277.

Raudenbush, S. (2001). Longitudinal data analysis. *Annual Review of Psychology* (Vol. 52). Palo Alto, CA: Annual Reviews.

Raven, P.H., Johnson, G.B., Singer, S., & Losos, J. (2005). *Biology* (7th ed.). New York: McGraw-Hill.

Reeves, G., & Schweitzer, J. (2004). Pharmacological management of attention deficit hyperactivity disorder. *Expert Opinions in Pharmacotherapy, 5,* 1313–1320.

Regalado, M., Sareen, H., Inkelas, M., Wissow, L.S., & Halfon, N. (2004). Parents' discipline of young children: Results from the National Survey of Early Childhood Health. *Pediatrics, 113,* 1952–1958.

Regev, R.H., Lusky, A., Dolfin, T., Litmanovitz, I., Arnon, S., Reichman, B., & the Israel Neonatal Network. (2003). Excess mortality and morbidity among small-for-gestational-age premature infants: A population-based study. *Journal of Pediatrics, 143,* 186–191.

Reid, P.T., & Zalk, S.R. (2001). Academic environments: Gender and ethnicity in U.S. higher education. In J. Worell (Ed.), *Encyclopedia of women and gender.* San Diego: Academic Press.

Reiner, W.G. (2001). Gender identity and sex reassignment. In L. King, B. Belman, & S. Kramer (Eds.), *Clinical pediatric urology* (3rd ed.). London: ISIS Medical.

Reiner, W.G., & Gearhart, J.P. (2004). Discordant sexual identity in some genetic males with cloacal exstrophy assigned to female sex at birth. *New England Journal of Medicine, 350,* 333–341.

Reis, O., & Youniss, J. (2004). Patterns of identity change and development in relationships with mothers and friends. *Journal of Adolescent Research, 19,* 31–44.

Renninger, K.A., & Sigel, I.E. (2006). Applying research to practice. In W. Damon & R. Lerner (Eds.), *Handbook of child psychology* (6th ed.). New York: Wiley.

Rest, J.R. (1986). *Moral development: Advances in theory and research.* New York: Praeger.

Rest, J.R. (1995). *Concerns for the social-psychological development of youth and educational strategies: Report for the Kaufmann Foundation.* Minneapolis: University of Minnesota, Department of Educational Psychology.

Rest, J.R., Narvaez, D., Bebeau, M.J., & Thomas, S.J. (1999). *Postconventional moral thinking.* Mahwah, NJ: Erlbaum.

Reuter, M., & Conger, R. (1995). Antecedents of parent-adolescent disagreements. *Journal of Marriage and the Family, 57,* 435–448.

Revelle, S.P. (2004). High standards + high-stakes = high achievement in Massachusetts. *Phi Delta Kappan, 85,* 591–597.

Reyna, V.F. (2004). How people make decisions that involve risk: A dual-process approach. *Current Directions in Psychological Science, 13,* 60–66.

Reyna, V.F., & Brainerd, C.J. (1995). Fuzzy-trace theory: An interim synthesis. *Learning and Individual Differences, 7,* 1–75.

Reynolds, A.J. (1999, April). *Pathways to long-term effects in the Chicago Child-Parent Center Program.* Paper presented at the meeting of the Society for Research in Child Development, Albuquerque.

Rhodes, J.E., Grossman, J.B., & Resch, N.L. (2000). Agents of change: Pathways through which mentoring relationships influence adolescents' academic adjustment. *Child Development, 71,* 1662–1671.

Richards, M.H., Larson, R., Miller, B.V., Luo, Z., Sims, B., Parrella, D.P., & McCauley, C. (2004). Risky and protective contexts and exposure to violence in urban African American young adolescents. *Journal of Clinical Child and Adolescent Psychology, 33,* 138–148.

Richards, M.H., Suleiman, L., Sims, B., & Sedeno, A. (1994, February). *Experiences of ethnically diverse young adolescents growing up in poverty.* Paper presented at the meeting of the Society for Research on Adolescence, San Diego.

Richardson, G.A., Ryan, C., Willford, J., Day, N.L., & Goldschmidt, L. (2002). Prenatal alcohol and marijuana exposure: Effects on neuropsychological outcomes at 10 years. *Neurotoxicology and Teratology, 24,* 309–320.

Richter, L. (2003). Poverty, underdevelopment, and infant mental health. *Journal of Pediatric and Child Health, 39,* 243–248.

Rickards, T., & deCock, C. (2003). Understanding organizational creativity: Toward a paradigmatic approach. In M.A. Runco (Ed.), *Creativity research handbook.* Creskill, NJ: Hampton Press.

Rideout, V., Roberts, D.F., & Foehr, U.G. (2005). *Generation M.* Menlo Park, CA: Kaiser Family Foundation.

Ridgeway, D., Waters, E., & Kuczaj, S.A. (1985). Acquisition of emotion-descriptive language: Receptive and productive vocabulary norms for ages 18 months to 6 years. *Developmental Psychology, 21,* 901–908.

Rieckmann, T.R., Wadsworth, M.E., & Deyhle, D. (2004). Cultural identity, explanatory style, and depression in Navajo adolescents. *Cultural Diversity & Ethnic Minority Psychology, 10,* 365–382.

Riesch, S.K., Gray, J., Hoefs, M., Keenan, T., Ertil, T., & Mathison, K. (2003). Conflict and conflict resolution: Parent and young teen perceptions. *Journal of Pediatric Health Care, 17,* 22–31.

Rietveld, M.J., Dolan, C.V., van Baal, G.C., & Boomsma, D.I. (2003). A twin study of differentiation of cognitive abilities in childhood. *Behavior Genetics, 33,* 367–381.

Righetti-Veltema, M., Conne-Perreard, E., Bousquest, A., & Manzano, J. (2002). Postpartum depression and mother-infant relationship at 3 months old. *Journal of Affective Disorders, 70,* 291–306.

Rinehart, S.D., Stahl, S.A., & Erickson, L.G. (1986). Some effects of summarization training on reading and studying. *Reading Research Quarterly, 21,* 422–438.

Rivera, C., & Collum, E. (Eds.). *State assessment policy and practice for English language learners.* Mahwah, NJ: Erlbaum.

Rob, G. (2004). Attending to the execution of a complex motor skill: Expertise differences. *Journal of Experimental Psychology: Applied, 10,* 42–54.

Robbins, G., Powers, D., & Burgess, S. (2005). *A wellness way of life* (6th ed.). New York: McGraw-Hill.

Roberts, D.F. (1993). Adolescents and the mass media: From "Leave It to Beaver" to "Beverly Hills 90210." In R. Takanishi (Ed.), *Adolescence in the 1990s.* New York: Teachers College Press.

Roberts, D.F., & Foehr, U.G. (2003). *Kids and media in America: Patterns of use at the millennium.* New York: Cambridge University Press.

Roberts, D.F., Foehr, U.G., Rideout, V.J., & Brodie, M. (1999). *Kids and media at the new millennium: A Kaiser Family Foundation Report.* Menlo Park, CA: Kaiser Family Foundation.

Roberts, D.F., Henriksen, L., & Foehr, U.G. (2004). Adolescents and the media. In R. Lerner and L. Steinberg (Eds.), *Handbook of adolescent psychology* (2nd ed.). New York: Wiley.

Roberts, W., & Strayer, J. (1996). Empathy, emotional expressiveness, and prosocial behavior. *Child Development, 67,* 471–489.

Robins, R.W., Trzesniewski, K.H., Tracy, J.L., Gosling, S.D., & Potter, J. (2002). Global self-esteem across the lifespan. *Psychology and Aging, 17,* 423–434.

Rode, S.S., Chang, P., Fisch, R.O., & Sroufe, L.A. (1981). Attachment patterns of infants separated at birth. *Developmental Psychology, 17,* 188–191.

Rogoff, B. (1990). *Apprenticeship in thinking.* New York: Oxford University Press.

Rogoff, B. (1998). Cognition as a collaborative process. In W. Damon (Ed.), *Handbook of child psychology* (5th ed., Vol. 2). New York: Wiley.

Rogoff, B. (2003). *The cultural nature of human development.* New York: Oxford University Press.

Rogoff, B., Turkanis, C.G., & Bartlett, L., (Eds.). (2001). *Learning together.* New York: Oxford University Press.

Rogol, A.D., Roemmrich, J.N., & Clark, P.A. (1998, September). *Growth at puberty.* Paper presented at the workshop Physical Development, Health Futures of Youth II: Pathways to Adolescent Health, Maternal and Child Health Bureau, Annapolis, MD.

Rohner, R.P., & Rohner, E.C. (1981). Parental acceptance-rejection and parental control: Cross-cultural codes. *Ethnology, 20,* 245–260.

Roisman, G.I., Masten, A.S., Coatsworth, J.D., & Tellegen, A. (2004). Salient and emerging developmental tasks in the transition to adulthood. *Child Development, 75,* 123–133.

Roosa, M.W., Dumka, L.E., Gonzales, N.A., & Knight, G.P. (2002). Cultural/ethnic issues and the prevention scientist in the 21st century. *Prevention & Treatment, 5,* 1–13.

Rose, A.J. (2002). Co-rumination in the friendships of girls and boys. *Child Development, 73,* 1830–1843.

Rose, A.J., & Asher, S.R. (1999, April). *Seeking and giving social support within a friendship.* Paper presented at the meeting of the Society for Research in Child Development Albuquerque.

Rose, A.J., & Asher, S.R. (1999). Children's goals and strategies in response to conflicts within a friendship. *Developmental Psychology, 35,* 69–79.

Rose, L.C., & Gallup, A.M. (2000). The 32nd annual Phi Delta Kappa/Gallup Poll of the public's attitude toward the public schools. *Phi Delta Kappan, 82* (10), 41–58.

Rose, M.R., & Mueller, L.D. (2006). *Evolution and ecology of the organism.* Upper Saddle River, NJ: Prentice Hall.

Rose, S., & Frieze, I.R. (1993). Young singles' contemporary dating scripts. *Sex Roles, 28,* 499–509.

Rose, S.A., Feldman, J.F., & Wallace, I.F. (1992). Infant information processing in relation to six-year cognitive outcomes. *Child Development, 63,* 1126–1141.

Rosenblith, J.F. (1992). *In the beginning* (2nd ed.). Newbury Park, CA: Sage.

Rosenblum, G.D., & Lewis, M. (2003). Emotional development in adolescence. In G. Adams & M. Berzonsky (Eds.), *Blackwell handbook of adolescence.* Malden, MA: Blackwell.

Rosenfield, R.L., Bachrach, L.K., Chernausek, S.D., & others. (2000). Current age of onset of puberty [Letters to the editor], *Pediatrics, 106,* 622.

Rosenkoetter, L.I., Rosenkoetter, S.E., Ozretich, R.A., & Acock, A.C. (2004). Mitigating the harmful effects of violent television. *Applied Developmental Psychology, 25,* 25–47.

Rosenstein, D., & Oster, H. (1988). Differential facial responses to four basic tastes in newborns. *Child Development, 59,* 1555–1568.

Rosenthal, R., & Jacobsen, L. (1968). *Pygmalion in the classroom.* Fort Worth: Harcourt Brace.

Rosenzweig, M.R. (1969). Effects of heredity and environment on brain chemistry, brain anatomy, and learning ability in the rat. In M. Monosevitz, G. Lindzey, & D.D. Thiessen (Eds.), *Behavioral genetics.* New York: Appleton-Century-Crofts.

Rosenzweig, M.R. (2000). Ethology. In A. Kazdin (Ed.), *Encyclopedia of psychology.* Washington, DC, & New York: American Psychological Association and Oxford University Press.

Rosnow, R.L., & Rosenthal, R. (1996). *Beginning behavioral research* (2nd ed.). Upper Saddle River, NJ: Prentice Hall.

Rosnow, R.L., & Rosenthal, R. (2005). *Beginning behavioral research* (5th ed.). Upper Saddle River, NJ: Prentice-Hall.

Rosselli, H.C. (1996, February/March). Gifted students. *National Association for Secondary School Principals,* pp. 12–17.

Rothbart, M.K. (2004). Temperament and the pursuit of an integrated developmental psychology. *Merrill-Palmer Quarterly, 50,* 492–505.

Rothbart, M.K., & Bates, J.E. (1998). Temperament. In W. Damon (Ed.), *Handbook of child psychology* (5th ed., Vol. 3). New York: Wiley.

Rothbart, M.K., & Bates, J.E. (2006). Temperament. In W. Damon & R. Lerner (Eds.), *Handbook of child psychology* (6th ed.). New York: Wiley.

Rothbart, M.K., & Putnam, S.P. (2002). Temperament and socialization. In L. Pulkkinen & A. Caspi (Eds.), *Paths to successful development.* New York: Cambridge University Press.

Rothbart, M.L.K. (1971). Birth order and mother-child interaction, *Dissertation Abstracts, 27,* 45–57.

Rothbaum, F., Pott, M., Azuma, H., Miyake, K., & Weisz, J. (2000). The development of close relationships in Japan and the United States: Paths of symbiotic harmony and generative tension. *Child Development, 71,* 1121–1142.

Rovee-Collier, C. (1987). Learning and memory in children. In J.D. Osofsky (Ed.), *Handbook of infant development* (2nd ed.). New York: Wiley.

Rovee-Collier, C. (2004). Infant learning and memory. In U. Goswami (Ed.), *Blackwell handbook of childhood cognitive development.* Malden, MA: Blackwell.

Rovee-Collier, C., & Barr, R. (2004). Infant learning and memory. In J.G. Bremner & A. Fogel (Eds.) *Blackwell handbook of infant development.* Malden, MA: Blackwell.

Rowe, D.L. (2005). Stimulant drug action in attention deficit hyperactivity disorder (ADHD): Inference of neurophysiological mechanisms via quantitative modeling. *Clinical Neurophysiology, 116,* 324–325.

Rowe, S.M., & Wertsch, J.V. (2004). Vygotsky's model of cognitive development. In U. Goswami (Ed.), *Blackwell handbook of childhood cognitive development.* Malden, MA: Blackwell.

Rowntree, D. (2004). *Statistics without tears.* Boston: Allyn & Bacon.

Rubenstein, D. (2004). Language games and natural resources. *Journal of the Theory of Social Behavior, 34,* 55–71.

Rubin, D. (2006). *Gaining word power* (7th ed.). Boston: Allyn & Bacon.

Rubin, D.H., Krasilnikoff, P.A., Leventhal, J.M., Weile, B., & Berget, A. (1986, August 23). Effect of passive smoking on birthweight. *The Lancet,* 415–417.

Rubin, K.H., Bukowski, W., & Parker, J.G. (2006). Peer interactions, relationships, and groups. In W. Damon & R. Lerner (Eds.), *Handbook of child psychology* (6th ed.). New York: Wiley.

Rubin, K.H., Mills, R.S.L., & Rose-Krasnor, L. (1989). Maternal beliefs and children's competence. In B. Schneider, G. Attili, J. Nadel, & R. Weissberg (Eds.), *Social competence in developmental perspective.* Amsterdam: Kluwer Academic.

Rubin, Z., & Mitchell, C. (1976). Couples research as couples counseling. *American Psychologist, 31,* 17–25.

Rubin, Z., & Sloman, J. (1984). How parents influence their children's friendships. In M. Lewis (Ed.), *Beyond the dyad.* New York: Plenum.

Ruble, D.N. (1983). The development of social comparison processes and their role in achievement-related self-socialization. In E. Higgins, D. Ruble, & W. Hartup (Eds.), *Social cognitive development: A social-cultural perspective.* New York: Cambridge University Press.

Ruble, D.N. (2000). Gender constancy. In A. Kazdin (Ed.), *Encyclopedia of psychology.* Washington, DC, and New York: American Psychological Association and Oxford University Press.

Ruble, D.N., Martin, C.L., & Berenbaum, S.A. (2006). Gender development. In W. Damon & R. Lerner (Eds.), *Handbook of child psychology* (6th ed.). New York: Wiley.

Ruddell, R.B. (2006). *Teaching children to read and write* (4th ed.). Boston: Allyn & Bacon.

Ruff, H.A., & Capozzoli, M.C. (2003). Development of attention and distractibility in the first four years of life. *Developmental Psychology, 39,* 877–890.

Ruff, H.A., & Rothbart, M.K. (1996). *Attention in early development.* New York: Oxford University Press.

Rumberger, R.W. (1995). Dropping out of middle school: A multilevel analysis of students and schools. *American Educational Research Journal, 3,* 583–625.

Runco, M.A. (2004). Creativity. *Annual Review of Psychology, 55.* Palo Alto, CA: Annual Reviews.

Rupp, R., Rosenthal, S.L., & Stanberry, L.R. (2005). Pediatrics and herpes simple virus vaccines. *Seminars in Pediatric Infectious Diseases, 16,* 31–37.

Rusak, B., Robertson, H.A., Wisden, W., & Hunt, S.P. (1990). Light pulses that shift rhythms induce gene expression in the suprachiasmatic nucleus. *Science, 248,* 1237–1240.

Rusen, I.D., Liu, S., Sauve, R., Joseph, K.S., & Kramer, M.S. (2004). Sudden infant death syndrome in Canada: Trends in rates and risk factors, 1985–1998. *Chronic Diseases in Canada, 25,* 1–6.

Russell, S.T., & Joyner, K. (2001). Adolescent sexual orientation and suicide risk: Evidence from a national study. *American Journal of Public Health, 91,* 1276–1281.

Rutter, M. (1979). Protective factors in children's response to stress and disadvantage. In M.W. Kent & J.E. Rolf (Eds.), *Primary prevention in psychopathology* (Vol. 3). Hanover, NH: University of New Hampshire Press.

Ryan, A.S. (1997). The resurgence of breastfeeding in the United States. *Pediatrics, 99,* E-12.

Ryan, A.S., Wenjun, Z., & Acosta, A. (2002). Breastfeeding continues to increase into the new millennium. *Pediatrics, 110,* 1103–1109.

Ryan, R., & Deci, E. (2000). Self-determination theory and the facilitation of intrinsic motivation, social development, and well-being. *American Psychologist, 55,* 68–78.

Ryan, S.D., Pearlmutter, S., & Groza, V. (2004). Coming out of the closet: Opening agencies to gay and lesbian adoptive parents. *Social Work, 49,* 85–95.

Rymer, R. (1992). *Genie.* New York: HarperCollins.

Saarni, C. (1999). *The development of emotional competence.* New York: Guilford.

Saarni, C. (2000). Emotional competence: A developmental perspective. In R. Bar-On & J.D. Parker (Eds.), *The handbook of emotional intelligence.* San Francisco: Jossey-Bass.

Saarni, C., Campos, J., Camras, L.A., & Witherington, D. (2006). Emotional development. Action, communication, & understanding. In W. Damon & R. Lerner (Eds.), *Handbook of child psychology* (6th ed.). New York: Wiley.

Sabol, W.J., Coulton, C.J., & Korbin, J.F. (2004). Building community capacity for violence prevention. *Journal of Interpersonal Violence, 19,* 322–340.

Sabol, W.J., Coulton, C.J., & Polousky, E. (2004). Measuring child maltreatment risk in communities: A life table approach. *Child Abuse and Neglect, 28,* 967–983.

Sachs-Ericsson, N., Blazer, D., Plant, A.E., & Arnow, B. (2005). Childhood sexual and physical abuse and the 1-year prevalence of medical problems in the National Comorbidity Study. *Health Psychology, 24,* 32–40.

Sackett, P.R., Hardison, C.M., & Cullen, M.J. (2004). On interpreting stereotype threat as accounting for African-American White differences in cognitive tests. *American Psychologist, 59,* 7–13.

Sadeh, A., Raviv, A., & Gruber, R. (2000). Sleep patterns and sleep disruptions in school-age children. *Developmental Psychology, 36,* 291–301.

Sadker, M.P., & Sadker, D.M. (2000). *Teachers, schools, and society* (5th ed.). New York: McGraw-Hill.

Sadker, M.P., & Sadker, D.M. (2005). *Teachers, schools, and society* (7th ed.). New York: McGraw-Hill.

Saffran, J.R., Werker, J.F., & Werner, L.A. (2006). The infant's auditory world: Hearing, speech, and the beginnings of language. In W. Damon & R. Lerner (Eds.), *Handbook of child psychology* (6th ed.). New York: Wiley.

Sagan, C. (1977). *The dragons of Eden.* New York: Random House.

Saigal, S., den Ouden, L., Wolke, D., Hoult, L., Paneth, N., Streiner, D.L., Whitaker, A., & Pinto-Martin, J. (2003). School-age outcomes in children who were extremely low birth weight from four international population-based cohorts. *Pediatrics, 112,* 943–950.

Salkind, N.J. (2003). *Exploring research* (5th ed.). Upper Saddle River, NJ: Prentice-Hall.

Salovey, P., & Mayer, J.D. (1990). Emotional intelligence. *Imagination, Cognition, and Personality, 9,* 185–211.

Salovey, P., & Pizarro, D.A. (2003). The value of emotional intelligence. In R.J. Sternberg, J. Lautrey, & T.I. Lubert (Eds.), *Models of intelligence: International perspectives.* Washington, DC: American Psychological Association.

Samaniego, R.Y., & Gonzales, N.A. (1999). Multiple mediators of the effects of acculturation status on delinquency for Mexican American adolescents. *American Journal of Community Psychology, 27,* 189–210.

Samour, P.Q., Helm, K.K., & Lang, C.E. (Eds.). (2000). *Handbook of pediatric nutrition* (2nd ed.). Aspen, CO: Aspen.

Sampson, R., Raudenbush, S., & Earls, F. (1997). Neighborhoods and violent crime: A multilevel study of collective efficacy. *Science, 277,* 918–924.

Samuels, M., & Samuels, N. (1996). *New well pregnancy book.* New York: Fireside.

Sanchez-Johnsen, L.A., Fitzgibbon, M.L., Martinovich, Z., Stolley, M.R., Dyer, A.R., & Van Horn, L. (2004). Ethnic differences in correlates of obesity between Latin-American and black women. *Obesity Research, 12,* 652–660.

Sanders, D., & Wills, F. (2005). *Cognitive therapy.* Thousand Oaks, CA: Sage.

Sandstrom, M.J., & Zakriski, A.L. (2004). Understanding the experience of peer rejection. In J.B. Kupersmidt & K.A. Dodge (Eds.), *Children's peer relations: From development to intervention.* Washington, DC: American Psychological Association.

Sanson, A., & Rothbart, M.K. (1995). Child temperament and parenting. In M.H. Bornstein (Ed.), *Handbook of parenting* (Vol. 4). Hillsdale, NJ: Erlbaum.

Santiago-Delefosse, M.J., & Delefosse, J.M.O. (2002). Three positions on child thought and language. *Theory and Psychology, 12,* 723–747.

Santrock, J.W. (2006a). *Educational psychology* (2nd ed., *Revised updated*). New York: McGraw-Hill.

Santrock, J.W. (2006b). *Life-span development* (10th ed.). New York: McGraw-Hill.

Santrock, J.W., Sitterle, K.A., & Warshak, R.A. (1988). Parent-child relationships in stepfather families. In P. Bronstein & C.P. Cowan (Eds.), *Fatherhood today: Men's changing roles in the family.* New York: Wiley.

Santrock, J.W., & Warshak, R.A. (1979). Father custody and social development in boys and girls. *Journal of Social Issues, 35,* 112–125.

Sarigiani, P.A., & Petersen, A.C. (2000). Adolescence: Puberty and biological maturation. In A. Kazdin (Ed.), *Encyclopedia of psychology.* Washington, DC, & New York: American Psychological Association and Oxford University Press.

Savage, R.S., Frederickson, N., Godowin, R., Patni, U., Smith, N., & Tuersley, L. (2005). Relationships among rapid digit naming, phonological processing, motor automaticity, and speech perception in poor, average, and good readers and spellers. *Journal of Learning Disabilities, 38,* 12–28.

Savin-Williams, R.C. (2001). *Mom, dad, I'm gay.* Washington, DC: American Psychological Association.

Savin-Williams, R.C., & Diamond, L. (2004). Sex. In R. Lerner & L. Steinberg (Eds.), *Handbook of adolescent psychology* (2nd ed.). New York: Wiley.

Sax, L.J., Hurtado, S., Lindholm, J.A., Astin, A.W., Korn, W.S., & Mahoney, K.M. (2004). *The American freshman: National norms for fall 2004.* Los Angeles: Higher Education Research Institute, UCLA.

Scafidi, F., & Field, T.M. (1996). Massage therapy improves behavior in neonates born to HIV-positive mothers. *Journal of Pediatric Psychology, 21,* 889–897.

Scarr, S.A. (1984, May). Interview. *Psychology Today,* pp. 59–63.

Scarr, S.A. (1993). Biological and cultural diversity: The legacy of Darwin for development. *Child Development, 64,* 1333–1353.

Scarr, S.A. (2000). Day care. In A. Kazdin (Ed.), *Encyclopedia of psychology.* Washington, DC, & New York: American Psychological Association and Oxford University Press.

Scarr, S.A., & Weinberg, R.A. (1983). The Minnesota adoption studies: Genetic differences and malleability. *Child Development, 54,* 182–259.

Schachter, D.L. (2001). *The seven sins of memory.* Boston: Houghton Mifflin.

Schachter, S.C., & Ransil, B.J. (1996). Handedness distributions in nine professional groups. *Perceptual and Motor Skills, 82,* 51–63.

Schaffer, H.R. (1996). *Social development.* Cambridge, MA: Blackwell.

Schauble, L. (1996). The development of scientific reasoning in knowledge-rich contexts. *Developmental Psychology, 32,* 102–119.

Schlegel, M. (2000). All work and play. *Monitor on Psychology, 31* (11), 50–51.

Schmidt, U. (2003). Aetiology of eating disorders in the 21st century: New answers to old questions. *European Child and Adolescent Psychiatry, 12* (Supplement 1), 1130–1137.

Schmitt, D.P., & Pilcher, J.J. (2004). Evaluating evidence of psychological adaptation: How do we know one when we see one? *Psychological Science, 15,* 643–649.

Schnake, E.M., Peterson, N.M., & Corden, T.E. (2005). Promoting water safety: The physician's role. *Wisconsin Journal of Medicine, 104,* 45–49.

Schneider, W. (2004). Memory development in children. In U. Goswami (Ed.), *Blackwell handbook of childhood cognitive development.* Malden, MA: Blackwell.

Schneider, W., Kron, V., Hunnerkopf, M., & Krajewski, K. (2004). The development of young children's memory strategies: First findings from the Wurzburg Longitudinal Memory Study. *Journal of Experimental Child Psychology, 88,* 193–209.

Schneider, W., & Pressley, M. (1997). *Memory development between two and twenty.* Mahwah, NJ: Erlbaum.

Schnorr, T.M., & others. (1991). Video-display terminals and the risk of spontaneous abortion. *New England Journal of Medicine, 324,* 727–733.

Schoon, I., Bynner, J., Joshi, H., Parsons, S., Wiggins, R.D., & Sacker, A. (2002). The influence of context, timing, and duration of risk experiences for the passage from childhood to midadulthood. *Child Development, 73,* 1486–1504.

Schoon, I., Parsons, S., & Sacker, A. (2004). Socioeconomic adversity, educational resilience, and subsequent levels of adult adaptation. *Journal of Adolescent Research, 19,* 383–404.

Schrag, S.G., & Dixon, R.L. (1985). Occupational exposure associated with male reproductive dysfunction. *Annual Review of Pharmacology and Toxicology, 25,* 467–592.

Schulte, M.J., Ree, M.J., & Carretta, T.R. (2004). Emotional intelligence: Not much more than g and personality. *Personality and Individual Differences, 37,* 1059–1068.

Schultz, R.T., Grelotti, D.J., & Pober, B. (2001). Genetics of childhood disorders: XXVI. Williams syndrome and brain-behavior relationships. *Journal of the American Academy of Child & Adolescent Psychiatry, 40,* 606–609.

Schunk, D.H. (1991). Self-efficacy and academic motivation. *Educational Psychologist, 25,* 71–86.

Schunk, D.H. (2004). *Learning theories* (4th ed.). Upper Saddle River, NJ: Prentice Hall.

Schunk, D.H., & Zimmerman, B.J. (2003). Self-regulation and learning. In I.B. Weiner (Ed.), *Handbook of psychology* (Vol. 7). New York: Wiley.

Schunn, C.D., & Anderson, J. (2001). Acquiring expertise in science. In K. Crowley, C.D. Schunn, & T. Okada (Eds.), *Designing for science.* Mahwah, NJ: Erlbaum.

Schwarz, S.P. (2004). A mother's story. Available at http://www.makinglifeeasier.com

Scott, L.D. (2003). The relation of racial identity and racial socialization to coping with discrimination among African American adolescents. *Journal of Black Studies, 33,* 520–538.

Scott-Jones, D. (1995, March). *Incorporating ethnicity and socioeconomic status in research with children.* Paper presented at the meeting of the Society for Research in Child Development, Indianapolis.

Scourfield, J., Van den Bree, M., Martin, N., & McGuffin, P. (2004). Conduct problems in children and adolescents: A twin study. *Archives of General Psychiatry, 61,* 489–496.

Search Institute. (1995). *Barriers to participation in youth programs.* Unpublished manuscript, the Search Institute, Minneapolis.

Sebanc, A.M., Pierce, S.L., Cheatham, C.L., & Gunnar, M.R. (2003). Gendered social worlds in preschool: Dominance, peer acceptance, and assertiveness skills in boys' and girls' peer groups. *Social Development, 12,* 91–106.

Secada, W.G. (2005). The mediation of contextual resources. In C.R. Cooper, C.T. Garcia Coll, W.T. Barko, H.M. Davis, & C. Chatham (Eds.), *Developmental pathways through middle childhood.* Mahwah, NJ: Erlbaum.

Seidenfeld, M.E., Sosin, E., & Rickert, V.I. (2004). Nutrition and eating disorders in adolescents. *Mt. Sinai Journal of Medicine, 71,* 155–161.

Seidman, E. (2000). School transitions. In A. Kazdin (Ed.), *Encyclopedia of psychology.* Washington, DC, & New York: American Psychological Association and Oxford University Press.

Seifer, R. (2001). Socioeconomic status, multiple risks, and development of intelligence. In R.J. Sternberg & E.L. Grigorenko (Eds.), *Environmental effects on cognitive abilities.* Mahwah, NJ: Erlbaum.

Seligman, M.E.P. (1975). *Learned helplessness.* San Francisco: W.H. Freeman.

Seligman, M.E.P. (1995). *The optimistic child.* Boston: Houghton Mifflin.

Selman, R.L. (1976). Social-cognitive understanding. In T. Lickona (Ed.), *Moral development and behavior.* New York: Holt, Rinehart & Winston.

Selman, R.L. (1980). *The growth of interpersonal understanding.* New York: Academic Press.

Selman, R.L., & Dray, A.J. (2006). Risk and prevention. In W. Damon & R. Lerner (Eds.), *Handbook of child psychology* (6th ed.). New York: Wiley.

Serpell, R. (1974). Aspects of intelligence in a developing country. *African Social Research, 17,* 576–596.

Serpell, R. (1982). Measures of perception, skills, and intelligence. In W.W. Hartup (Ed.), *Review of child development research* (Vol. 6.). Chicago: University of Chicago Press.

Serpell, R. (2000). Culture and intelligence. In A. Kazdin (Ed.), *Encyclopedia of psychology.* Washington, DC, & New York: American Psychological Association and Oxford University Press.

Shaddy, D.J., & Colombo, J. (2004). Developmental changes in infant attention to dynamic and static stimuli. *Infancy, 5,* 355–365.

Shanker, A.V., Sastry, J., Erande, A., Joshi, A., Suryawanshi, N., Phadke, M.A., & Bollinger, R.C. (2005). Making the choice: The translation of global HIV and infant feeding policy to local practice among mothers in Pune, India. *Journal of Nutrition, 135,* 960–965.

Sharma, A.R., McGue, M.K., & Benson, P.L. (1996). The emotional and behavioral adjustment of adopted adolescents: Part I: Age at adoption. *Children and Youth Services Review, 18,* 101–114.

Sharma, A.R., McGue, M.K., & Benson, P.L. (1998). The psychological adjustment of United States adopted adolescents and their nonadopted siblings. *Child Development, 69,* 791–802.

Sharma, V. (2002). Pharmacotherapy of postpartum depression. *Expert Opinions on Pharmacotherapy, 3,* 1421–1431.

Sharp, V. (1999). *Computer education for teachers* (3rd ed.). New York: McGraw-Hill.

Shatz, M., & Gelman, R. (1973). The development of communication skills: Modifications in the speech of young children as a function of the listener. *Monographs of the Society for Research in Child Development, 38* (Serial No. 152).

Shaw, D., Gilliom, M., Ingoldsby, E.M., & Nagin, D.S. (2003). Trajectories leading to school-age conduct problems. *Developmental Psychology, 39,* 189–200.

Shaw, G.M. (2001). Adverse human reproductive outcomes and electromagnetic fields. *Bioelectromagnetics, 5* (Supplement), S5–S18.

Shaw, S.M. (1988). Gender differences in the definition and perception of household labor. *Family Relations, 37,* 333–337.

Shea, A., Walsh, C., MacMillan, H., & Steiner, M. (2005). Child maltreatment and HPA axis dysregulation: Relationship to major depressive disorder and post traumatic stress disorder in females. *Psychoneuroendocrinology, 30,* 162–178.

Sheets, R.H. (2005). *Diversity pedagogy.* Upper Saddle River, NJ: Prentice-Hall.

Sheiner, E., Levy, A., Katz, M., & Mazor, M. (2005, in press). Short stature—an independent risk factor for Cesarean delivery. *European Journal of Obstetrics, Gynecology,*

Shi, L., & Stevens, G.D. (2005). Disparities in access to care and satisfaction among U.S. children: The roles of race/ethnicity and poverty status. *Public Health Reports, 120,* 431–441.

Shields, S.A. (1998, August). *What* Jerry Maguire *can tell us about gender and emotion.* Paper presented at the meeting of the International Society for Research on Emotions, Wurzburg, Germany.

Shields, S.A. (1991). Gender in the psychology of emotion: A selective research review. In K.T. Strongman (Ed.), *International review of studies on emotion* (Vol. 1). New York: Wiley.

Shulman, L.S., & Shulman, J.H. (2004). How and what teachers learn: A shifting perspective. *Journal of Curriculum Studies, 36,* 257–271.

Shweder, R., Goodnow, J., Hatano, G., LeVine, R.A., Markus, H., & Miller, P. (2006). The cultural psychology of development: One mind, many mentalities. In W. Damon & R. Lerner (Eds.), *Handbook of child psychology* (6th ed.). New York: Wiley.

Siega-Riz, A.M., Kranz, S., Blanchette, D., Hanies, P.S., Guilkey, D.K., & Popkin, B.M. (2004). The effect of participation in the WIC program on preschoolers' diets. *Journal of Pediatrics, 144,* 229–234.

Siegel, L.S. (2003). Learning disabilities. In I.B. Weiner (Ed.), *Handbook of psychology* (Vol. 7). New York: Wiley.

Siegel, L.S., & Wiener, J. (1993, Spring). Canadian special education policies: Children with disabilities in a bilingual and multicultural society. *Social Policy Report, Society for Research in Child Development, 7,* 1–16.

Siegler, R.S. (1976). Three aspects of cognitive development. *Cognitive Psychology, 8,* 481–520.

Siegler, R.S. (1998). *Children's thinking* (3rd ed.). Upper Saddle River, NJ: Prentice Hall.

Siegler, R.S. (2001). Cognition, instruction, and the quest for meaning. In S.M. Carver & D. Klahr (Eds.), *Cognition and instruction*. Mahwah, NJ: Erlbaum.

Siegler, R.S. (2004). Learning about learning. *Merrill-Palmer Quarterly, 50,* 353–368.

Siegler, R.S. (2006). Microgenetic analysis of learning. In W. Damon & R. Lerner (Eds.), *Handbook of child psychology* (6th ed.). New York: Wiley.

Siegler, R.S., & Alibali, M.W. (2005). *Children's thinking* (4th ed.). Upper Saddle River, NJ: Prentice Hall.

Sigman, M., Cohen, S.E., & Beckwith, I. (2000). Why does infant attention predict adolescent intelligence? In D. Muir & A. Slater (Eds.), *Infant development: Essential readings.* Malden, MA: Blackwell.

Signore, C. (2001). Rubella. *Primary Care Update in Obstetrics and Gynecology, 8,* 133–137.

Silberman, M. (2006). *Teaching actively.* Boston: Allyn & Bacon.

Silva, C., & Martins, M. (2003). Relations between children's invented spelling and children's phonological awareness. *Educational Psychology, 23,* 3–16.

Sim, T. (2000). Adolescent psychosocial competence: The importance and role of regard for parents. *Journal of Research on Adolescence, 10,* 49–64.

Sim, T.N., & Ong, L.P. (2005). Parent punishment and child aggression in a Singapore Chinese preschool sample. *Journal of Marriage and the Family, 67,* 85–99.

Simmons, A.M., & Avery, P.G. (in press). Civic life as conveyed in U.S. civics and history textbooks. *Journal of Social Education.*

Simons-Morton, B., Haynie, D.L., Crump, A.D., Eitel, P., & Saylor, K.E. (2001). Peer and parent influences on smoking and drinking among early adolescents. *Health Education and Behavior, 28,* 95–107.

Singer, D.G. (1993). Creativity of children in a changing world. In G.L. Berry & J.K. Asamen (Eds.), *Children and television: Images in a changing sociocultural world.* Newbury Park, CA: Sage.

Singer, L.T., Arendt, R., Fagan, J., Minnes, S., Salvator, A., Bolck, T., & Becker, M. (1999). Neonatal visual information processing in cocaine-exposed and non-exposed infants. *Infant Behavior and Development, 22,* 1–15.

Sizer, F., & Whitney, E. (2006). *Nutrition* (10th ed.). Belmont, CA: Wadsworth.

Skinner, B.F. (1938). *The behavior of organisms: An experimental analysis*. New York: Appelton-Century-Crofts.

Skinner, B.F. (1957). *Verbal behavior*. New York: Appleton-Century-Crofts.

Skinner, E.A., Wellborn, J.G., & Connell, J.P. (1990). What it takes to do well in school and whether I've got it. *Journal of Educational Psychology, 82,* 22–32.

Slade, E.P., & Wissow, L.S. (2004). Spanking in early childhood and later behavior problems: A prospective study. *Pediatrics, 113,* 1321–1330.

Slama, R., Bouyer, J. Windham, G., Fenster, L., Werwatz, A., & Swan, S.H. (2005). Influence of paternal age on the risk of spontaneous abortion. *American Journal of Epidemiology, 161,* 816–823.

Slater, A. (2004). Visual perception. In A. Fogel & G. Bremner (Eds.), *Blackwell handbook of infant development.* London: Blackwell.

Slater, A., Field, T., & Hernandez-Reif, M. (2002). The development of the senses. In A. Slater & M. Lewis (Eds.), *Introduction to infant development.* New York: Oxford University Press.

Slater, A., Morison, V., & Somers, M. (1988). Orientation discrimination and cortical function in the human newborn. *Perception, 17,* 597–602.

Slavin, R.E., Hurley, E.A., & Chamberlin, A. (2003). Cooperative learning and achievement theory and research. In I.B. Weiner (Ed.), *Handbook of psychology* (Vol. 7). New York: Wiley.

Slijper, F.M.E. (1984). Androgens and gender role behavior in girls with congenital adrenal hyperplasia (CAH). *Progress in Brain Research, 61,* 417–422.

Slobin, D. (1972, July). Children and language: They learn the same way around the world. *Psychology Today,* 71–76.

Slomkowski, C., Rende, R., Conger, K.J., Simons, R.L., & Conger, R.D. (2001). Sisters, brothers, and delinquency: Social influence during early and middle adolescence. *Child Development, 72,* 271–283.

Smetana, J.G. (2005). Social domain theory. In M. Killen & J.G. Smetana (Eds.), *Handbook of moral development.* Mahwah, NJ: Erlbaum.

Smetana, J.G., & Turiel, E. (2003). Moral development during adolescence. In G. Adams & M. Berzonsky (Eds.), *The Blackwell handbook of adolescence.* Malden, MA: Blackwell.

Smit, E.M. (2002). Adopted children. *Journal of Child and Adolescent Psychiatric Nursing, 15,* 143–150.

Smith, D.D. (2006). *Introduction to special education* (5th ed. Update). Boston: Allyn & Bacon.

Smith, F. (2004). *Understanding reading* (6th ed.). Mahwah, NJ: Erlbaum.

Smith, K. (2002). Who's minding the kids? Child care arrangements: Spring 1977. *Current Population Reports,* P70–P86. Washington, DC: U.S. Census Bureau.

Smith, L. (2004). Piaget's model. In U. Goswami (Ed.), *Blackwell handbook of childhood cognitive development.* Malden, MA: Blackwell.

Smith, L., Muir, D.W., & Kisilevsky, B. (2001, April). *Preterm infants' responses to auditory stimulation of varying intensity.* Paper presented at the meeting of the Society for Research in Child Development, Minneapolis.

Smith, L.B. (1999). Do infants possess innate knowledge structures? The con side. *Developmental Science, 2,* 133–144.

Smith, L.M., Chang, L., Yonekura, M.L., Gilbride, K., Kuo, J., Poland, R.E., Walot, I., & Ernst, T. (2001). Brain proton magnetic resonance spectroscopy and imaging in children exposed to cocaine in utero. *Pediatrics, 107,* 227.

Smith, T.E.C., Polloay, E.A., Patton, J.R., & Dowdy, C.A. (2006). *Teaching students with special needs in inclusive settings* (4th ed. Update). Boston: Allyn & Bacon.

Smitsman, A. (2004). Action in infancy: Development of reaching and grasping. In J.G. Bremner & A. Fogel (Eds.), *Blackwell handbook of infancy.* Malden, MA: Blackwell.

Smulian, J.C., Ananth, C.V., Vintzileos, A.M., Scorza, W.E., & Knuppel, R.A. (2002). Parental age difference and adverse perinatal outcomes in the United States. *Pediatric and Perinatal Epidemiology, 16,* 320–327.

Snarey, J. (1987, June). A question of morality. *Psychology Today,* pp. 6–8.

Snarey, J. (1993). *How fathers care for the next generation.* Cambridge, MA: Harvard University Press.

Snow, C.E., & Yang, J.Y. (2006). Becoming bilingual, biliterate, and bicultural. In W. Damon & R. Lerner (Eds.), *Handbook of child psychology* (6th ed.). New York: Wiley.

Snyder, H.N., & Sickmund, M. (1999, October). *Juvenile offenders and victims: 1999 national report.* Washington, DC: National Center for Juvenile Justice.

Solomon, D., Battistich, V., Watson, M., Schaps, E., & Lewis, C. (2000). A six-district study of educational change: Direct and mediated effects of the Child Development Project. *Social Psychology of Education, 4,* 3–51.

Soltero, S.W. (2004). *Dual language: Teaching and learning in two languages.* Boston: Allyn & Bacon.

Sommer, B.B. (1978). *Puberty and adolescence.* New York: Oxford University Press.

Soong, W.T., Chao, K.Y., Jang, C.S., & Wang, J.D. (1999). Long-term effect of increased lead absorption on intelligence of children. *Archives of Environmental Health, 54,* 297–301.

Sophian, C. (1985). Perseveration and infants' search: A comparison of two- and three-location tasks. *Developmental Psychology, 21,* 187–194.

Sorof, J., & Daniels, S. (2002). Obesity hypertension in children: A problem of epidemic proportions. *Hypertension, 40,* 441–447.

Sorokin, P. (2002). New agents and future directions in biotherapy. *Clinical Journal of Oncological Nursing, 6,* 19–24.

Sowell, E., & Jernigan, T. (1998). Further MRI evidence of late brain maturation: Limbic volume increases and changing asymmetries during childhood and adolescence. *Developmental Neuropsychology, 14,* 599–617.

Sowter, B., Doyle, L.W., Morley, C.J., Altmann, A., & Halliday, J. (1999). Is sudden infant death syndrome still more common in very low birth weight infants in the 1990s? *Medical Journal of Australia, 171,* 411–413.

Spafford, C.S., & Grosser, G.S. (2005). *Dyslexia and reading difficulties* (2nd ed.). Boston: Allyn & Bacon.

Spandel, V. (2004). *Creating young writers.* Boston: Allyn & Bacon.

Spandorfer, S.D., Davis, O.K., Barmat, L.I., Chung, P.H., & Rosenwaks, Z. (2004). Relationship between maternal age and aneuploidy in in vitro fertilization pregnancy loss. *Obstetrics and Gynecology Survey, 59,* 773–774.

Spear, L.P. (2000). Neurobehavioral changes in adolescence. *Current Directions in Psychological Science, 4,* 111–114.

Spear, L.P. (2004). Adolescent brain development and animal models. *Annals of the New York Academy of Sciences, 1021,* 23–26.

Spearman, C.E. (1927). *The abilities of man.* New York: Macmillan.

Spelke, E.S. (1979). Perceiving bimodally specified events in infancy. *Developmental Psychology, 5,* 626–636.

Spelke, E.S. (1991). Physical knowledge in infancy: Reflections on Piaget's theory. In S. Carey & R. Gelman (Eds.), *The epigenesis of mind: Essays on biology and cognition.* Hillsdale, NJ: Erlbaum.

Spelke, E.S. (2000). Core knowledge. *American Psychologist, 55,* 1233–1243.

Spelke, E.S., Breinlinger, K., Macomber, J., & Jacobson, K. (1992). Origins of knowledge. *Psychological Review, 99,* 605–632.

Spelke, E.S., & Hespos, S.J. (2001). Continuity, competence, and the object concept. In E. Dupoux (Ed.), *Language, brain, and behavior.* Cambridge, MA: Bradford/MIT Press.

Spelke, E.S., & Newport, E.L. (1998). Nativism, empiricism, and the development of knowledge. In W. Damon (Ed.), *Handbook of child psychology* (5th ed., Vol. 2). New York: Wiley.

Spelke, E.S., & Owsley, C.J. (1979). Intermodal exploration and knowledge in infancy. *Infant Behavior and Development, 2,* 13–28.

Spence, J.T., & Buckner, C.E. (2000). Instrumental and expressive traits, trait stereotypes, and sexist attitudes: What do they signify? *Psychology of Women Quarterly, 24,* 44–62.

Spence, J.T., & Helmreich, R. (1978). *Masculinity and femininity: Their psychological dimensions.* Austin: University of Texas Press.

Spence, M.J., & DeCasper, A.J. (1987). Prenatal experience with low-frequency maternal voice sounds influences neonatal perception of maternal voice samples. *Infant Behavior & Development, 10,* 133–142.

Spencer, J.P., Vereijken, B., Diedrich, F.J., & Thelen, E. (2000). Posture and the emergence of manual skills. *Developmental Science, 3,* 216–233.

Spencer, M.B. (1990). Commentary in Spencer, M.B., & Dornbusch, S. Challenges in studying ethnic minority youth. In S.S. Feldman & G.R. Elliott (Eds.), *At the threshold: The developing adolescent.* Cambridge, MA: Harvard University Press.

Spencer, M.B. (1999). Social and cultural influences on school adjustment: The application of an identity-focused cultural ecological perspective. *Educational Psychologist, 34,* 43–57.

Spencer, M.B. (2006). Phenomenology and ecological systems theory. In W. Damon & R. Lerner (Eds.), *Handbook of child psychology* (6th ed.). New York: Wiley.

Spencer, M.B., & Dornbusch, S.M. (1990). Challenges in studying minority youth. In S.S. Feldman & G.R. Elliott (Eds.), *At the threshold: The developing adolescent.* Cambridge, MA: Harvard University Press.

Spencer, M.B., & Harpalani, V. (2004). Nature, nurture, and the question of "how?" In C.G. Coll, E.L. Bearer & R.M. Lerner (Eds.), *Nature and nurture.* Mahwah, NJ: Erlbaum.

Spencer, M.B., Noll, E., Stoltzfuz, J., & Harpalani, V. (2001). Identity and school adjustment: Revisiting the "acting white" assumption. *Educational Psychologist, 36,* 21–30.

Speranza, M., Corcos, M., Loas, G., Stephan, P., Guilbaud, O., Perez-Diaz, F., Venisse, J.L., Bizouard, P., Halfon, O., Flament, M., & Jeammet, P. (2005). Depressive personality dimensions and alexithymia in eating disorders. *Psychiatry Research, 135,* 153–163.

Spitzer, A.R. (2005). Current controversies in the pathophysiology and prevention of sudden infant death syndrome. *Current Opinion in Pediatrics, 17,* 181–185.

Spring, J. (2005). *The American school* (6th ed.). New York: McGraw-Hill.

Spring, J. (2006). *American education* (12th ed.). New York: McGraw-Hill.

Springer, S.P., & Deutsch, G. (1985). *Left brain, right brain.* San Francisco: Freeman.

Sroufe, L.A. (2000, Spring). The inside scoop on child development: Interview. *Cutting through the hype.* Minneapolis: College of Education and Human Development, University of Minnesota.

Sroufe, L.A. (2002). From infant attachment to promotion of adolescent autonomy. In J.G. Borkowski, S.L. Ramey, & M. Bristol-Power (Eds.), *Parenting and the child's world.* Mahwah, NJ: Erlbaum.

Sroufe, L.A., Egeland, B., & Carlson, E.A. (1999). One social world: The integrated development of parent-child and peer relationships. In W.A. Collins & B. Laursen (Eds.), *Minnesota symposium on child psychology* (Vol. 31). Mahwah, NJ: Erlbaum.

Sroufe, L.A., Egeland, B., Carlson, E., & Collins, W.A. (2005). The place of early attachment in developmental context. In K.E. Grossman, K. Krossman, & E. Waters (Eds.), *The power of longitudinal attachment research: From infancy and childhood to adulthood.* New York: Guilford Press.

Sroufe, L.A., & Waters, E. (1976). The ontogenesis of smiling and laughter: A perspective on the organization of development in infancy. *Psychological Review, 83,* 173–198.

Sroufe, L.A., Waters, E., & Matas, L. (1974). Contextual determinants of infant affectional response. In M. Lewis & L. Rosenblum (Eds.), *Origins of fear.* New York: Wiley.

St. Pierre, R., Layzer, J., & Barnes, H. (1996). *Regenerating two-generation programs.* Cambridge, MA: Abt Associates.

Stahl, S. (2002, January). *Effective reading instruction in the first grade.* Paper presented at the Michigan Reading Recovery conference, Dearborn, MI.

Stanford University Medical Center. (2005). *Growth hormone deficiency.* Stanford, CA: Pituitary Center, Stanford University.

Stanhope, L., & Corter, C. (1993, March). *The mother's role in the transition to siblinghood.* Paper presented at the biennial meeting of the Society for Research in Child Development, New Orleans.

Stanovich, K.E. (2004). *How to think straight about psychology* (7th ed.). Boston: Allyn & Bacon.

Starr, C. (2005). *Biology today and tomorrow.* Pacific Grove, CA: Brooks Cole.

Starr, C. (2006). *Biology* (6th Ed.). Pacific Grove, CA: Brooks Cole.

Stattin, H., & Magnusson, D. (1990). *Pubertal maturation in female development: Paths through life* (Vol. 2). Hillsdale, NJ: Erlbaum.

Steele, C.M., & Aronson, J. (1995). Stereotype threat and the intellectual test performance of African-Americans. *Journal of Personality and Social Psychology, 69,* 797–811.

Steele, C.M., & Aronson, J.A. (2004). Stereotype threat does not live by Steele and Aronson (1995) alone. *American Psychologist, 59,* 47–48.

Steele, C.M., & Markus, H.R. (2003, November 14). *Stereotype threat and black college students.* Paper presented at the meeting of the Stanford Alumni Association, Palo Alto, CA.

Steer, C.R. (2005). Managing attention deficit hyperactivity disorder: Unmet needs and future directions. *Archives of Disease in Childhood, 90* (Suppl. 1), 19–25.

Stegelin, D.A. (2003). Application of Reggio Emilia approach to early childhood science curriculum. *Early Childhood Education Journal, 30,* 163–169.

Stein, M.T. (2004). ADHD: The diagnostic process from different perspectives. *Journal of Developmental and Behavioral Pediatrics, 25* (Suppl. 5), S54–S58.

Stein, M.T., Kennell, J.H., & Fulcher, A. (2003). *Journal of Developmental and Behavioral Pediatrics, 24,* 195–198.

Stein, M.T., & Perrin, J.M. (2003). Diagnosis and treatment of ADHD in school-age children in primary care settings: A synopsis of the AAP practice guidelines. *Pediatric Review, 24,* 92–98.

Steinberg, L.D. (1986). Latchkey children and susceptibility to peer pressure: An ecological analysis. *Developmental Psychology, 22,* 433–439.

Steinberg, L.D. (2004). Risk taking in adolescence: What changes, and why? *Annals of the New York Academy of Sciences, 1021,* 51–58.

Steinberg, L.D. (2005). Cognitive and affective development in adolescence. *Trends in Cognitive Science, 9,* 69–74.

Steinberg, L.D., & Cauffman, E. (2001). Adolescents as adults in court. *Social Policy Report of the Society for Research in Child Development, XV* (No. 4), 1–13.

Steinberg, L.D., & Levine, A. (1997). *You and your adolescent* (2nd ed.). New York: Harper Perennial.

Steinberg, L.D., & Silk, J.S. (2002). Parenting adolescents. In M. Bornstein (Ed.), *Handbook of parenting* (2nd ed., Vol. 1). Mahwah, NJ: Erlbaum.

Steiner, J.E. (1979). Human facial expressions in response to taste and smell stimulation. In H. Reese & L. Lipsitt (Eds.), *Advances in child development and behavior* (Vol. 13). New York: Academic Press.

Steinman, M.A., Landefeld, C.S., & Gonzales, R. (2003). Predictors of broad-spectrum antibiotic prescribing for acute respiratory infections in adult primary care. *Journal of the American Medical Association, 289,* 719–725.

Stephenson, J. (2004). FDA warns on mercury in tuna. *Journal of the American Medical Association, 291,* 171.

Stern, D.N., Beebe, B., Jaffe, J., & Bennett, S.L. (1977). The infant's stimulus world during social interaction: A study of caregiver behaviors with particular reference to repetition and timing. In H.R. Schaffer (Ed.), *Studies in mother-infant interaction.* London: Academic Press.

Sternberg, R.J., Castejón, J.L., Prieto, M.D., Hautamäki, J., & Grigorenko, E.L. (2001). Confirmatory factor analysis of the Sternberg triarchic abilities test in three international samples: An empirical test of the triarchic theory of intelligence. *European Journal of Psychological Assessment, 17* (1), 1–16.

Sternberg, R.J. (1986). *Intelligence applied.* Fort Worth: Harcourt Brace.

Sternberg, R.J. (1993). *Sternberg Triarchic Abilities Test (STAT).* Unpublished test, Department of Psychology, Yale University, New Haven, CT.

Sternberg, R.J. (1997). Educating intelligence: Infusing the triarchic theory into instruction. In R.J. Sternberg & E. Grigorenko (Eds.), *Intelligence, heredity, and environment.* New York: Cambridge University Press.

Sternberg, R.J. (1999). Intelligence. In M.A. Runco & S. Pritzker (Eds.), *Encyclopedia of creativity.* San Diego: Academic Press.

Sternberg, R.J. (2001). Is there a heredity-environment paradox? In R.J. Sternberg & E.L. Grigorenko (Eds.), *Environmental effects on cognitive abilities.* Mahwah, NJ: Erlbaum.

Sternberg, R.J. (2002). Intelligence: The triarchic theory of intelligence. In J.W. Guthrie (Ed.), *Encyclopedia of education* (2nd ed.). New York: Macmillan.

Sternberg, R.J. (2003). Contemporary theories of intelligence. In I.B. Weiner (Ed.), *Handbook of psychology* (Vol. 7). New York: Wiley.

Sternberg, R.J. (2004). Individual differences in cognitive development. In P. Smith & C. Hart (Eds.), *Blackwell handbook of cognitive development.* Malden, MA: Blackwell.

Sternberg, R.J. (2006). *Cognitive psychology* (4th ed.). Belmont, CA: Wadsworth.

Sternberg, R.J., & Grigorenko, E.L. (Eds.). (2001). *Environmental effects on cognitive abilities.* Mahwah, NJ: Erlbaum.

Sternberg, R.J., & Grigorenko, E.L. (Eds.). (2004). *Culture and competence.* Washington, DC: American Psychological Association.

Sternberg, R.J., Grigorenko, E.L., & Kidd, K.K. (2005). Intelligence, race, and genetics. *American Psychologist, 60,* 46–59.

Sternberg, R.J., Grigorenko, E.L., & Singer, J.L. (Eds.). (2004). *Creativity: From potential to realization.* Washington, DC: American Psychological Association.

Sternberg, R.J., Nokes, K., Geissler, P.W., Prince, R., Okatcha, F., Bundy, D.A., & Grigorenko, E.L. (2001b). The relationship between academic and practical intelligence: A case study in Kenya. *Intelligence, 29,* 401–418.

Sternberg, R.J., & O'Hara, L.A. (2000). Intelligence and creativity. In R.J. Sternberg (Ed.), *Handbook of intelligence.* New York: Cambridge University Press.

Sternglanz, S.H., & Serbin, L.A. (1974). Sex-role stereotyping in children's television programming. *Developmental Psychology, 10,* 710–715.

Stetsenko, A., & Arievitch, I.M. (2004). The self in cultural-historical activity theory: Reclaiming the unity of social and individual dimensions of human development. *Theory and Psychology, 14,* 475–503.

Stetsenko, A., Little, T.D., Gordeeva, T., Grasshof, M., & Oettingen, G. (2000). Gender effects in children's beliefs about school performance. *Child Development, 71,* 517–527.

Steur, F.B., Applefield, J.M., & Smith, R. (1971). Televised aggression and the interpersonal aggression of preschool children. *Journal of Experimental Child Psychology, 11,* 442–447.

Stevens, J.W. (2005). Lessons learned from poor urban African American youth. In M. Ungar (Ed.), *Handbook for working with children and youth.* Thousand Oaks, CA: Sage.

Stevenson, H.C. (1998). Raising safe villages: Cultural-ecological factors that influence the emotional adjustment of adolescents. *Journal of Black Psychology, 24,* 44–59.

Stevenson, H.W. (1995). Mathematics achievement of American students: First in the world by the year 2000? In C.A. Nelson (Ed.), *Basic and applied perspectives on learning, cognition, and development.* Minneapolis: University of Minnesota Press.

Stevenson, H.W. (2000). Middle childhood: Education and schooling. In A. Kazdin (Ed.), *Encyclopedia of psychology.* Washington, DC, & New York: American Psychological Association and Oxford University Press.

Stevenson, H.W., Hofer, B.K., & Randel, B. (1999). *Middle childhood: Education and schooling.* Unpublished manuscript, Dept. of Psychology, University of Michigan, Ann Arbor.

Stevenson, H.W., Lee, S., Chen, C., Stigler, J.W., Hsu, C., & Kitamura, S. (1990). Contexts of achievement. *Monograph of the Society for Research in Child Development, 55* (Serial No. 221).

Stevenson, H.W., Lee, S., & Stigler, J.W. (1986). Mathematics achievement of Chinese, Japanese, and American children. *Science, 231,* 693–699.

Stevenson, H.W., & Zusho, A. (2002). Adolescence in China and Japan: Adapting to a changing environment. In B.B. Brown, R.W. Larson, & T.S. Saraswathi (Eds.), *The world's youth.* New York: Cambridge University Press.

Stice, E. (2002). Risk and maintenance factors for eating pathology: A meta-analytic review. *Psychological Bulletin, 128,* 825–848.

Stice, E., Presnell, K., & Spangler, D. (2002). Risk factors for binge eating onset in adolescent girls: A 2-year prospective investigation. *Health Psychology, 21,* 131–138.

Stigler, J.W., Nusbaum, H.C., & Chalip, L. (1988). Developmental changes in speed of processing: Central limiting mechanism or skill transfer. *Child Development, 59,* 1144–1153.

Stipek, D.J. (1996). Motivation and instruction. In D.C. Berliner & R.C. Calfee (Eds.), *Handbook of educational psychology.* New York: Macmillan.

Stipek, D.J. (2002). *Motivation to learn* (4th ed.). Boston: Allyn & Bacon.

Stipek, D.J. (2005, February 16). Commentary in *USA Today,* p. 1D.

Stipek, D.J., Recchia, S., & McClintic, S. (1992). Self-evaluation in young children. *Monographs of the Society for Research in Child Development, 57* (Serial No. 226), 2–3.

Stocker, C., & Dunn, J. (1990). Sibling relationships in childhood: Links with friendships and peer relationships. *British Journal of Developmental Psychology, 8,* 227–244.

Stocker, C., & Dunn, J. (1991). Sibling relationships in adolescence. In R.M. Lerner, A.C. Petersen, & J. Brooks-Gunn (Eds.), *Encyclopedia of adolescence* (Vol. 2). New York: Garland.

Stolley, K.S. (1993). Statistics on adoption in the United States. *The Future of Children, 3,* 26–42.

Stouthamer-Loeber, M., Loeber, R., Wei, E., Farrington, D.P., & Wikstrom, P.H. (2002). Risk and promotive effects in the explanation of persistent serious delinquency in boys. *Journal of Consulting and Clinical Psychology, 70,* 111–123.

Strasburger, V.C., & Donnerstein, E. (1999). Children, adolescents, and the media: Issues and solutions. *Pediatrics, 103,* 129–137.

Strauss, M.A. (1991). Discipline and deviance: Physical punishment of children and violence and other crimes in adulthood. *Social Problems, 38,* 133–154.

Strauss, M.A., Sugarman, D.B., & Giles-Sims, J. (1997). Spanking by parents and subsequent anti-social behavior in children. *Archives of Pediatrics and Adolescent Medicine, 151,* 761–767.

Strauss, R.S. (2001). Environmental tobacco smoke and serum vitamin C levels in children. *Pediatrics, 107,* 540–542.

Streissguth, A.P., Martin, D.C., Sandman, B.M., Kirchner, G.L., & Darby, B.L. (1984). Intrauterine alcohol and nicotine exposure: Attention and reaction time in four-year-old children. *Developmental Psychology, 20,* 533–543.

Striegel-Moore, R.H., Silberstein, L.R., & Rodin, J. (1993). The social self in bulimia nervosa: Public self-consciousness, social anxiety, and perceived fraudulence. *Journal of Abnormal Psychology, 102,* 297–303.

Stringer, S., & Neal, C. (1993, March). *Scaffolding as a tool for assessing sensitive and contingent teaching: A comparison between high- and low-risk mothers.* Paper presented at the biennial meeting of the Society for Research in Child Development, New Orleans.

Suárez-Orozco, C. (2002). Afterword: Understanding and serving the children of immigrants. *Harvard Educational Review, 71,* 579–589.

Sue, S. (1990, August). *Ethnicity and culture in psychological research and practice.* Paper presented at the meeting of the American Psychological Association, Boston.

Sue, S., & Morishima, J.K. (1982). *The mental health of Asian Americans: Contemporary issues in identifying and treating mental problems.* San Francisco: Jossey-Bass.

Sullivan, H.S. (1953). *The interpersonal theory of psychiatry.* New York: W.W. Norton.

Sullivan, J.L. (2003). Prevention of mother-to-child transmission of HIV—what next? *Journal of Acquired Immune Deficiency Syndrome, 34* (Supplement 1), S67–S72.

Sullivan, K., & Sullivan, A. (1980). Adolescent-parent separation. *Developmental Psychology, 16,* 93–99.

Summers, A.M., Farrell, S.A., Huang, T., Meier, C., & Wyatt, P.R. (2004). Maternal serum screening in Ontario using the triple marker test. *Journal of Medical Screening, 10,* 107–111.

Sung, H-E., Richter, L., Vaughan, R., Johnson, P.B., & Thom, B. (2005). Nonmedical use of prescription opiods among teenagers in the United States: Trends and correlates. *Journal of Adolescent Health, 37,* 44–51.

Suomi, S.J., Harlow, H.F., & Domek, C.J. (1970). Effect of repetitive infant-infant separations of young monkeys. *Journal of Abnormal Psychology, 76,* 161–172.

Super, C., & Harkness, S. (1997). The cultural structuring of child development. In J.W. Berry, Y.H. Poortinga, & J. Pandey (Eds.), *Handbook of cross-cultural psychology: Vol. 2. Theory and method.* Boston: Allyn & Bacon.

Susman, E.J., Dorn, L.D., & Schiefelbein, V.L. (2003). Puberty, sexuality, and health. In I.B. Weiner (Ed.), *Handbook of psychology* (Vol. 6). New York: Wiley.

Susman, E.J., Finkelstein, J.W., Chinchilli, V.M., Schwab, J., Liben, L.S., & others. (1998). The effect of sex hormone replacement therapy on behavior problems and moods in adolescents with delayed puberty. *Journal of Pediatrics, 133* (4), 521–525.

Susman, E.J., & Rogol, A. (2004). Puberty and psychological development. In R. Lerner & L. Steinberg (Eds.), *Handbook of adolescent psychology.* New York: Wiley.

Swaab, D.F., Chung, W.C., Kruijver, F.P., Hofman, M.A., & Ishunina, T.A. (2001). Structural and functional sex differences in the human hypothalamus. *Hormones and Behavior, 40,* 93–98.

Swanson, J.M., & Volkow, N.D. (2002). Pharmacokinetic and pharmacodynamic properties of stimulants: Implications for the design of new treatments for ADHD. *Behavior and Brain Research, 130,* 73–80.

Swenne, I. (2004). Weight requirements for return of menstruations in teenage girls with eating disorders, weight loss, and secondary amenorrherea. *Acta Paediatrica, 93,* 1449–1455.

Swisher, R., & Whitlock, J. (2003). How neighborhoods matter for youth development. In S.F. Hamilton & M.A. Hamilton (Eds.), *The youth development handbook.* Thousand Oaks, CA: Sage.

Swisher, R., & Whitlock, J. (2004). How neighborhoods matter for youth development. In S.F. Hamilton & M.A. Hamilton (Eds.), *The youth development handbook.* Thousand Oaks, CA: Sage.

Sykes, C.J. (1995). *Dumbing down our kids: Why America's children feel good about themselves but can't read, write, or add.* New York: St. Martin's Press.

Szaflarski, J.P., Binder, J.R., Possing, E.T., McKiernan, K.A., Ward, B.D., & Hammeke, T.A. (2002). Language lateralization in left-handed and ambidextrous people: fMRI data. *Neurology, 59,* 238–244.

Tager-Flusberg, H. (2005). Putting words together: Morphology and syntax. In J. Berko Gleason (Ed.), *The development of language* (6th ed.). Boston: Allyn & Bacon.

Takahashi, K. (1990). Are the key assumptions of the "Strange Situation" procedure universal? A view from Japanese research. *Human Development, 33,* 23–30.

Tamis-LeMonda, C.S., & Cabrera, N. (1999). Perspectives on father involvement: Research and policy. *Social Policy Report, Society for Research in Child Development, 13* (2), 1–25.

Tang, M.P., Chon, H.C., Tsao, P.N., Tson, K.I., & Hsieh, W.S. (2004). Outcome of very low birth weight infants with sonographic enlarged occipital horn. *Pediatric Neurology, 30,* 42–45.

Tannen, D. (1990). *You just don't understand!* New York: Ballantine.

Tappan, M.B. (1998). Sociocultural psychology and caring psychology: Exploring Vygotsky's "hidden curriculum." *Educational Psychologist, 33,* 23–33.

Tarpley, T. (2001). Children, the Internet, and other new technologies. In D. Singer & J. Singer (Eds.), *Handbook of children and the media.* Thousand Oaks, CA: Sage.

Tasker, F.L., & Golombok, S. (1997). *Growing up in a lesbian family: Effects on child development.* New York: Guilford.

Tassell-Baska, J., & Stambaugh, T. (2006). *Comprehensive curriculum for gifted learners* (3rd ed.). Boston: Allyn & Bacon.

Taylor, H.G., Klein, N., & Hack, M. (1994). Academic functioning in <750 gm birthweight children who have normal cognitive abilities: Evidence for specific learning disabilities. *Pediatric Research, 35,* 289A.

Taylor, S.E. (2002). *The tending instinct.* New York: Times Books.

Teasdale, T.W., & Owen, D.R. (2001). Cognitive abilities in left-handers: Writing posture revisited. *Neuropsychologia, 39,* 881–884.

Teissedre, F., & Chabrol, H. (2004). Detecting women at risk for postnatal depression using the Edinburgh Postnatal Depression Scale at 2 to 3 days postpartum. *Canadian Journal of Psychiatry, 49,* 51–54.

Temple, C.A., Nathan, R., Temple, F., & Burris, N.A. (1993). *The beginnings of writing* (3rd ed.). Boston: Allyn & Bacon.

Temple, C.A., Ogle, D., Crawford, A.N., & Freppon, P. (2005). *All children read.* Boston: Allyn & Bacon.

Terman, D.L., Larner, M.B., Stevenson, C.S., & Behrman, R.E. (1996). Special education for students with disabilities: Analysis and recommendations. *The Future of Children, 6* (1), 4–24.

Terman, L. (1925). *Genetic studies of genius. Vol. 1: Mental and physical traits of a thousand gifted children.* Stanford, CA: Stanford University Press.

Terry, W.S. (2003). *Learning and memory* (2nd ed.). Boston: Allyn & Bacon.

Tershakovec, A.M., Kuppler, K.M., Zemel, B.S., Katz, L., Weinzimer, S., Harty, M.P., & Stallings, V.A. (2003). Body composition and metabolic factors in obese children and adolescents. *International Journal of Obesity and Related Metabolic Disorders, 27,* 19–24.

Teti, D.M. (2001). Retrospect and prospect in the psychological study of sibling relationships. In J.P. McHale & W.S. Grolnick (Eds.), *Retrospect and prospect in the psychological study of families.* Mahwah, NJ: Erlbaum.

Teti, D.M., Sakin, J., Kucera, E., Caballeros, M., & Corns, K.M. (1993, March). *Transitions to siblinghood and security of firstborn attachment: Psychosocial and psychiatric correlates of changes over time.* Paper presented at the biennial meeting of the Society for Research in Child Development, New Orleans.

Thapar, A., Fowler, T., Rice, F., Scourfield, J., Van Den Bree, M., Thomas, S., Harold, G., & Hay, D. (2003). Maternal smoking during pregnancy and attention deficit hyperactivity disorder symptoms in offspring. *American Journal of Psychiatry, 160,* 1985–1989.

Tharp, R.G. (1994). Intergroup differences among Native Americans in socialization and child cognition: An orthogenetic analysis. In P.M. Greenfield & R. Cocking (Eds.), *Cross-cultural roots of minority child development.* Mahwah, NJ: Erlbaum.

Tharp, R.G., & Gallimore, R. (1988). *Rousing minds to life: Teaching, learning, and schooling in social context.* New York: Cambridge University Press.

Thelen, E. (1995). Motor development: A new synthesis. *American Psychologist, 50,* 79–95.

Thelen, E. (2000). Perception and motor development. In A. Kazdin (Ed.), *Encyclopedia of psychology.* Washington, DC, & New York: American Psychological Association and Oxford University Press.

Thelen, E. (2001). Dynamic mechanisms of change in early perceptual-motor development. In J.L. McClelland & R.S. Siegler (Eds.), *Mechanisms of cognitive development.* Mahwah, NJ: Erlbaum.

Thelen, E., Corbetta, D., Kamm, K., Spencer, J.P., Schneider, K., & Zernicke, R.F. (1993). The transition to reaching: Mapping intention and intrinsic dynamics. *Child Development, 64,* 1058–1098.

Thelen, E., & Smith, L.B. (1998). Dynamic systems theory. In W. Damon (Ed.), *Handbook of child psychology* (5th ed., Vol. 1). New York: Wiley.

Thelen, E., & Smith, L.B. (2006). Dynamic development of action and thought. In W. Damon & R. Lerner (Eds.), *Handbook of child psychology* (6th ed.). New York: Wiley.

Thelen, E., & Whitmeyer, V. (2005). Using dynamic field theory to conceptualize the interface of perception, action, and cognition. In J.J. Rieser, J.J. Lockman, & C.A. Nelson (Eds.), *Action as an organizer of learning and development.* Mahwah, NJ: Erlbaum.

Thomas, A., & Chess, S. (1991). Temperament in adolescence and its functional significance. In R.M. Lerner, A.C. Petersen, & J. Brooks-Gunn (Eds.), *Encyclopedia of adolescence* (Vol. 2). New York: Garland.

Thomas, K. (1998, November 4). Teen cyberdating is a new wrinkle for parents, too. *USA Today,* p. 9D.

Thomas, R.M. (2005). *Comparing theories of child development* (6th ed.). Belmont, CA: Wadsworth.

Thomas, R.M. (2005). *High-stakes testing.* Mahwah, NJ: Erlbaum.

Thompson, J. (2005). Breastfeeding: Benefits and implications. Part one. *Community Practice, 78,* 183–184.

Thompson, P.M., Giedd, J.N., Woods, R.P., MacDonald, D., Evans, A.C., & Toga, A.W. (2000). Growth patterns in the developing brain detected by using continuum mechanical tensor maps. *Nature, 404,* 190–193.

Thompson, R.A. (1994). Emotion regulation: A theme in search of a definition. *Monographs of the Society for Research in Child Development, 59* (Serial No. 240), 2–3.

Thompson, R.A. (2006). The development of the person. In W. Damon & R. Lerner (Eds.), *Handbook of child psychology* (6th ed.). New York: Wiley.

Thompson, R.A., Easterbrooks, M.A., & Walker. L. (2003). Social and emotional development in infancy. In I.B. Weiner (Ed.), *Handbook of psychology* (Vol. 6). New York: Wiley.

Thompson, R.A., & Goodvin, R. (2005). The individual child: Temperament, emotion, self, and personality. In M.H. Bornstein & M.E. Lamb (Eds.), *Developmental psychology* (5th ed.). Mahwah, NJ: Erlbaum.

Thompson, R.A., McGinley, M., & Meyer, S. (2005). Understanding values in relationships. In M. Killen & J. Smetana (Eds.), *Handbook of moral development.* Mahwah, NJ: Erlbaum.

Thorne, C., & Newell, M.L. (2003). Mother-to-child transmission of HIV infection and its prevention. *Current HIV Research, 4,* 447–462.

Thornton, S.J. (2001, April). *Caring and competence: Nel Noddings' curriculum thought.* Paper presented at the meeting of the American Educational Reseach Association, Seattle.

Thung, S.F., & Grobman, W.A. (2005). The cost-effectiveness of routine antenatal screening for maternal herpes simplex virus-1 and -2 antibodies. *American Journal of Obstetrics and Gynecology, 192,* 483–488.

Thurstone, L.L. (1938). *Primary mental abilities.* Chicago: University of Chicago Press.

Tierney, R.J., & Readence, J.E. (2005). *Reading strategies and practice* (6th ed.). Boston: Allyn & Bacon.

Tobin, A.J., & Dusheck, J. (2005). *Asking about life* (3rd ed.). Pacific Grove, CA: Brooks Cole.

Tolan, P.H., Gorman-Smith, D., & Henry, D.B. (2003). The developmental ecology of urban males' youth violence. *Developmental Psychology, 39,* 274–291.

Tomasello, M. (2006). Acquiring linguistic constructions. In W. Damon & R. Lerner (Eds.), *Handbook of child psychology* (6th ed.). New York: Wiley.

Tomasello, M., & Slobin, D.I. (Eds.). (2004). *Beyond nature-nurture.* Mahwah, NJ: Erlbaum.

Tong, E.K., England, L., & Glantz, S.A. (2005). Changing conclusions on secondhand smoke in a sudden infant death syndrome review funded by the tobacco industry. *Pediatrics, 115,* e356–e366.

Torgesen, J.K. (1999). Reading disabilities. In R. Gallimore, L.P. Bernheimer, D.L. MacMillan, D.L. Speece, & S. Vaughn (Eds.), *Developmental perspectives on children with learning disabilities.* Mahwah, NJ: Erlbaum.

Tough, S.C., Newburn-Cook, C., Johnston, D.W., Svenson, L.W., Rose, S., & Belik, J. (2002). Delayed childbearing and its impact on population rate changes in lower birth weight, multiple birth, and preterm delivery. *Pediatrics, 109,* 399–403.

Tourangeau, R. (2004). Survey research and societal change. *Annual Review of Psychology, Vol. 55.* Palo Alto, CA: Annual Reviews.

Tozer, S.E., Senese, G., & Violas, P.C. (2005). *School and society* (5th ed.). New York: McGraw-Hill.

Trafimow, D., Triandis, H.C., & Goto, S.G. (1991). Some tests of the distinction between the private and collective self. *Journal of Personality and Social Psychology, 60,* 649–655.

Trappe, R., Laccone, F., Cobilanschi, J., Meins, M., Huppke, P., Hanefeld, F., & Engel, W. (2001). MECP2 mutations in sporadic cases of Rett syndrome are almost exclusively of paternal origin. *American Journal of Human Genetics, 68,* 1093–1101.

Trasler, J.M. (2000). Paternal exposures: Altered sex ratios. *Teratology, 62,* 6–7.

Trasler, J.M., & Doerksen, T. (2000, May). *Teratogen update: Paternal exposure-reproductive risks.* Paper presented at the joint meeting of the Pediatric Academic Societies and American Academy of Pediatrics, Boston.

Trautner, H.M., Ruble, D.N., Cyphers, L. Kirsten, B., Behrendt, R., & Hartmann, P. (2005 in press). Rigidity and flexibility of gender stereotypes in children: Developmental or differential? *Infant and Child Development, 14.*

Treffers, P.E., Eskes, M., Kleiverda, G., & van Alten, D. (1990). Home births and minimal medical interventions. *Journal of the American Medical Association, 246,* 2207–2208.

Trehub, S.E., Schneider, B.A., Thorpe, L.A., & Judge, P. (1991). Observational measures of auditory sensitivity in early infancy. *Developmental Psychology, 27,* 40–49.

Treuth, M.S., Sunehag, A.L., Trautwein, L.M., Bier, D.M., Haywood, M.W., & Butte, N.F. (2003). Metabolic adaptation to high-fat and high-carbohydrate diets in children and adolescents. *American Journal of Clinical Nutrition, 77,* 479–489.

Triandis, H.C. (1994). *Culture and social behavior.* New York: McGraw-Hill.

Triandis, H.C. (2001). Individualism and collectivism. In D. Matsumoto (Ed.), *Handbook of culture and psychology.* New York: Oxford University Press.

Trimble, J.E. (1989, August). *The enculturation of contemporary psychology.* Paper presented at the meeting of the American Psychological Association, New Orleans, LA.

Trinidad, D.R., & Johnson, C.A. (2002). The association between emotional intelligence and early adolescent tobacco and alcohol use. *Personality and Individual Differences, 32,* 95–105.

Tritten, J. (2004). Embracing midwives everywhere. *Practicing Midwife, 7,* 4–5.

Troiano, R.P., & Flegal, K.M. (1998). Overweight children and adolescents: Description, epidemiology, and demographics. *Pediatrics, 101,* 497–504.

Tsigos, C., & Chrousos, G.P. (2002). Hypothalamic-pituitary-adrenal axis, neuroendocrine factors, and stress. *Journal of Psychosomatic Research, 53,* 865–871.

Turiel, E. (1998). The development of morality. In N. Eisenberg (Ed.), *Handbook of child psychology* (5th ed., Vol. 3). New York: Wiley.

Turiel, E. (2003). *The culture of morality.* New York: Cambridge University Press.

Turiel, E. (2006). The development of morality. In W. Damon & R. Lerner (Eds.) *Handbook of child psychology* (6th ed.). New York: Wiley.

Twenge, J.M., & Campbell, W.K. (2001). Age and birth cohort differences in self-esteem: A cross-temporal meta-analysis. *Personality and Social Psychology Bulletin, 5,* 321–344.

Tyler, C., & Edman, J.C. (2004). Down syndrome, Turner syndrome, and Klinefelter syndrome: Primary care throughout the life span. *Primary Care, 31,* 627–648.

U.S. Bureau of the Census. (2004). *Poverty.* Washington, DC: Author.

U.S. Department of Education. (2000). *Trends in educational equity for girls and women.* Washington, DC: Author.

U.S. Department of Education. (2000). *To assure a free and appropriate public education of all children with disabilities.* Washington, DC: U.S. Office of Education.

U.S. Department of Energy. (2001). *The human genome project.* Washington, DC: U.S. Department of Energy.

U.S. Department of Health and Human Services. (1999). *Trends in the well-being of America's children and youth 1999.* Washington, DC: U.S. Government Printing Office.

U.S. Department of Health and Human Services. (2001). *Youth violence.* Rockville, MD: U.S. Department of Health and Human Services.

U.S. Department of Health and Human Services. (2003). *Child abuse and neglect statistics.* Washington, DC: U.S. Department of Health and Human Services.

U.S. Food and Drug Administration. (2004, March 19). *An important message for pregnant women and women of childbearing age who may become pregnant about the risk of mercury in fish.* Washington, DC: Author.

Udry, J.R. & others. (1985). Serum androgenic hormones motivate sexual behavior in adolescent boys. *Fertility and Sterility, 43,* 90–94.

Umana-Taylor, A.J. (2004). Ethnic identity and self-esteem: Examining the role of social contexts. *Journal of Adolescence, 27,* 139–146.

Umana-Taylor, A.J., & Fine, M.A. (2004). Examining ethnic identity among Mexican-origin adolescents living in the United States. *Hispanic Journal of Behavioral Sciences, 26,* 36–59.

Underwood, M.K. (2003). *Social aggression among girls.* New York: Guilford.

Underwood, M.K. (2004). Gender and peer relations. In J.B. Kupersmidt & K.B. Dodge (Eds.), *Children's peer relations.* Washington, DC: American Psychological Association.

Underwood, M.K., & Hurley, J.C. (1997, April). *Children's responses to angry provocation as a function of peer status and aggression.* Paper presented at the meeting of the Society for Research in Child Development, Washington, DC.

Underwood, M.K., Scott, B.L., Galperin, M.B., Bjornstad, G.J., & Sexton, A.M. (2004). An observational study of social exclusion under varied conditions: Gender and developmental differences. *Child Development, 75,* 1538–1555.

Unger, B., Kemp, J.S., Wilkins, D., Psara, R., Ledbetter, T., Graham, M., Case, M., & Thach, B.T. (2003). Racial disparity and modifiable risk factors among infants dying suddenly and unexpectedly. *Pediatrics, 111,* E127–E131.

UNICEF. (2001). *UNICEF statistics: Low birthweight.* Geneva, Switzerland: UNICEF.

UNICEF. (2003). *State of the world's children: 2003.* Geneva: Author.

UNICEF. (2004). *The state of the world's children: 2004.* Geneva: UNICEF.

UNICEF. (2005). *State of the world's children.* Geneva: UNICEF.

Urbano, M.T., & Tait, D.M. (2004). Can the irradiated uterus sustain a pregnancy? *Clinical Oncology, 16,* 24–28.

Urberg, K. (1992). Locus of peer influence: Social crowd and best friend. *Journal of Youth and Adolescence, 21,* 439–450.

Vacca, J.A.L., Vacca, R.T., Gove, M.K., Burkey, L.C., Lenhart, L.A., & McKeon, C.A. (2006). *Reading and learning to read* (6th ed.). Boston: Allyn & Bacon.

Valencia, R.R., & Suzuki, L.A. (2001). *Intelligence testing and minority students.* Thousand Oaks, CA: Sage.

Van Beveren, T.T. (2002). *Prenatal development and the newborn.* Unpublished manuscript, University of Texas at Dallas, Richardson.

Van Buren, E., & Graham, S. (2003). *Redefining ethnic identity: Its relationship to positive and negative school adjustment outcomes for minority youth.* Paper presented at the meeting of the Society for Research in Child Development, Tampa.

van den Boom, D.C. (1989). Neonatal irritability and the development of attachment. In G.A. Kohnstamm, J.E. Bates, & M.K. Rothbart (Eds.), *Temperament in childhood.* New York: Wiley.

Van Egeren, L.A., & Hawkins, D.P. (2004). Coming to terms with coparenting: Implications of definition and measurement. *Journal of Adult Development, 11,* 165–178.

van Goozen, S.H.M., Matthys, W., Cohen-Kettenis, P.T., Thisjssen, J.H.H., & van Engeland, H. (1998). Adrenal androgens and aggression in conduct disorder prepubertal boys and normal control. *Biological Psychiatry, 43,* 156–158.

van IJzendoorn, M.H., & Kroonenberg, P.M. (1988). Cross-cultural patterns of attachment: A meta-analysis of the Strange Situation. *Child Development, 59,* 147–156.

Vandell, D.L. (1985, April). *Relationship between infant-peer and infant-mother interactions: What have we learned?* Paper presented at the meeting of the Society for Research in Child Development, Toronto.

Vandell, D.L. (2004). Early child care: The known and unknown. *Merrill-Palmer Quarterly, 50,* 387–414.

Vandell, D.L., & Pierce, K.M. (2002). After-school programs and structured activities that support children's development. In R. Garner (Ed.), *Hanging out: Community-based after-school programs for children.* Westport CT: Greenwood.

Vandell, D.L., & Wilson, K.S. (1988). Infants' interactions with mother, sibling, and peer: Contrasts and relations between interaction systems. *Child Development, 48,* 176–186.

Vaughn, S., Mathes, P.G., Linan-Thompson, S., & Francis, D.J. (2005). Teaching English language learners at risk for reading disabilities to read: Putting research into practice. *Learning Disabilities Research and Practice, 20,* 58–67.

Ventura, S.J., Martin, J.A., Curtin, S.C., & Mathews, T.J. (1997, June 10). *Report of final natality statistics, 1995.* Washington, DC: National Center for Health Statistics.

Verma, S., & Saraswathi, T.S. (2002). Adolescence in India: Street urchins or Silicon Valley millionaires? In B.B. Brown, R.W. Larson, & T.S. Saraswathi (Eds.), *The world's youth.* New York: Cambridge University Press.

Vicari, S., Bellucci, S., & Carlesimo, G.A. (2001). Procedural learning deficit in children with Williams syndrome. *Neuropsychologia, 39,* 665–677.

Vidaeff, A.C., & Mastrobattista, J.M. (2003). In utero cocaine exposure: A thorny mix of science and mythology. *American Journal of Perinatology, 20,* 165–172.

Vidal, F. (2000). Piaget's theory. In A. Kazdin (Ed.), *Encyclopedia of psychology.* Washington, DC, & New York: American Psychological Association and Oxford University Press.

Villiani, S.L. (1997). *Motherhood at the crossroads.* New York: Plenum.

Vinckenbosch, E., Robichon, F., & Eliez, S. (2005). Gray matter alteration in dyslexia: Converging evidence from volumetric and voxel-by-voxel MRI analyses. *Neuropsychologia, 43,* 324–331.

Vintzileos, A.M., Guzman, E.R., Smulian, J.C., Scorza, W.E., & Knuppel, R.A. (2002). Second-trimester genetic sonography in patients with advanced maternal age and normal triple screen. *Obstetrics and Gynecology, 99,* 993–995.

Voeller, K.K. (2004). Attention-deficit hyperactivity disorder. *Journal of Child Neurology, 19,* 798–814.

Volling, B.L. (2002). Sibling relationships. In M.H. Bornstein, L. Davidson, C.L.M. Keyes, & K.A. Moore (Eds.), *Well-being.* Mahwah, NJ: Erlbaum.

Volterra, M.C., Caselli, O., Capirci, E., & Pizzuto, E. (2004). Gesture and the emergence and development of language. In M. Tomasello & D.I. Slobin (Eds.), *Beyond nature-nurture.* Mahwah, NJ: Erlbaum.

Votruba-Drzal, E., Coley, R.L., & Chase-Lansdale, P.L. (2004). Child care and low-income children's development: Direct and moderated effects. *Child Development, 75,* 296–312.

Vreugdenhil, H.J., Mulder, P.G., Emmen, H.H., & Weisglas-Kuperus, N. (2004). Effects of perinatal exposure to PCBs on neuropsychological functions in the Rotterdam cohort at 9 years of age. *Neuropsychology, 18,* 185–193.

Vygotsky, L.S. (1962). *Thought and language.* Cambridge, MA: MIT Press.

Wachs, T.D. (1994). Fit, context and the transition between temperament and personality. In C. Halverson, G. Kohnstamm, & R. Martin (Eds.), *The developing structure of personality from infancy to adulthood.* Hillsdale, NJ: Erlbaum.

Wachs, T.D. (2000). *Necessary but not sufficient.* Washington, DC: American Psychological Association.

Wadhwa, P.D. (2005). Psychoneuroendocrine processes in human pregnancy influence fetal development and health. *Psychoneuroendocrinology, 30,* 724–743.

Wadsworth, S.J., Olson, R.K., Pennington, B.F., & DeFries, J.C. (2004). Differential genetic etiology of reading disability as a function of IQ. *Journal of Learning Disabilities, 33,* 192–199.

Wagner, R.K. (1997). Intelligence, training, and employment. *American Psychologist, 52,* 1059–1069.

Wagner, R.K., & Sternberg, R.J. (1986). Tacit knowledge and intelligent functioning in the everyday world. In R.J. Sternberg & R.K. Wagner (Eds.), *Practical intelligence.* New York: Cambridge University Press.

Wainright, J.L., & Patterson, C.J. (2005, April). *Adjustment among adolescents living with same-sex couples: Data from the National Longitudinal Study of Adolescent Health.* Paper presented at the meeting of the Society for Research in Child Development, Atlanta.

Walden, T. (1991). Infant social referencing. In J. Garber & K. Dodge (Eds.), *The development of emotional regulation and dysregulation.* New York: Cambridge University Press.

Wales, A. (2004). Promoting character education. *School Arts, 103* (10), 28–29.

Walker, E.F. (2002). Adolescent neurodevelopment and psychopathology. *Current Directions in Psychological Science, 11,* 24–28.

Walker, H. (1998, May 31). Youth violence: Society's problem. *Eugene Register Guard,* p. 1C.

Walker, L. (1982). The sequentiality of Kohlberg's stages of moral development. *Child Development, 53,* 1130–1136.

Walker, L.J. (2002). Moral exemplarity. In W. Damon (Ed.), *Bringing in a new era of character education.* Stanford, CA: Hoover Press.

Walker, L.J. (2004). Bridging the judgment/action gap in moral functioning. In D.K. Lapsley & D. Narvaez (Eds.), *Moral development, self, and identity.* Mahwah, NJ: Erlbaum.

Walker, L.J., de Vries, B., & Trevethan, S.D. (1987). Moral stages and moral orientation in real-life and hypothetical dilemmas. *Child Development, 58,* 842–858.

Walker, L.J., & Hennig, K.H. (2004). Differing conceptions of moral exemplars: Just, brave, and caring. *Journal of Personality and Social Psychology, 86,* 629–657.

Walker, L.J., Hennig, K.H., & Krettenauer, T. (2000). Parent and peer contexts for children's moral development. *Child Development, 71,* 1033–1048.

Walker, L.J., & Pitts, R.C. (1998). Naturalistic conceptions of moral maturity. *Developmental Psychology, 34,* 403–419.

Walker, S.O., Petrill, S.A., & Plomin, R. (2005). A genetically sensitive investigation of the effects of the school environment and socioeconomic status on academic achievement in seven-year-olds. *Educational Psychology, 25,* 55–63.

Wallace Foundation. (2004). *Out-of-school learning: All work and no play.* New York City: Author.

Wallerstein, J.S., & Johnson-Reitz, L. (2004). Communication in divorced and single parent families. In A.L. Vaneglisti (Ed.), *Handbook of family communication.* Mahwah, NJ: Erlbaum.

Walsh, L.A. (2000, Spring). The inside scoop on child development: Interview. *Cutting through the hype.* Minneapolis: College of Education and Human Development, University of Minnesota.

Walsh, W.B., & Betz, N.E. (2001). *Tests and measurement* (4th ed.). Upper Saddle River, NJ: Prentice-Hall.

Walters, E., & Kendler, K.S. (1994). Anorexia nervosa and anorexia-like symptoms in a population based twin sample. *American Journal of Psychiatry, 152,* 62–71.

Waltman, P.A., Brewer, J.M., Rogers, B.P., & May, W.L. (2004). Building evidence for practice: A pilot study of newborn bulb suctioning at birth. *Journal of Midwifery and Women's Health, 49,* 32–38.

Wang, S.H., Baillargeon, R., & Paterson, S. (2005). Detecting continuity violations in infancy: A new account and new evidence from covering and tube events. *Cognition, 95,* 129–173.

Ward, B.M., Lambert, S.B., & Lester, R.A. (2001). Rubella vaccination in prenatal and postnatal women: Why not use MM? *Medical Journal of Australia, 174,* 311–312.

Ward, L.M. (1995). Talking about sex: Common themes about sexuality in the prime-time television programs children and adolescents view most. *Journal of Youth and Adolescence, 24,* 595–615.

Ward, L.M. (2002). Does television exposure affect emerging adults' attitudes and assumptions about sexual relationships? Correlational and experimental confirmation. *Journal of Youth and Adolescence, 31,* 1–15.

Ward, L.M. (2004). Wading through stereotypes: Positive and negative associations between media use and black adolescents' conceptions of self. *Developmental Psychology, 40,* 284–294.

Ward, L.M., Gorvine, B., & Cytron, A. (2002). Would that really happen? Adolescents' perceptions of sexual relationships according to prime-time television. In J.D. Brown, J.R. Steele, & K. Walsh-Childers (Eds.), *Sexual teens, sexual media.* Mahwah, NJ: Erlbaum.

Wardlaw, G.M. (2006). *Contemporary nutrition* (6th ed.). New York: McGraw-Hill.

Wark, G.R., & Krebs, D.L. (2000). The construction of moral dilemmas in everyday life. *Journal of Moral Education, 29,* 5–21.

Warrick, P. (1992, March 1). The fantastic voyage of Tanner Roberts. *Los Angeles Times,* pp. E1, 11, 12.

Warrington, M., & Younger, M. (2003). "We decided to give it a twirl": Single-sex teaching in English comprehensive schools. *Gender and Education, 15,* 339–350.

Warshak, R.A. (2004, January). Personal communication, Department of Psychology, University of Texas at Dallas, Richardson.

Wasik, B.H. (Ed.). (2004). *Handbook of family literacy*. Mahwah, NJ: Erlbaum.

Wassenaar, M., & Hagoort, P. (2005). Word-category violations in patients with Broca's aphasia. *Brain and Language, 92,* 117–137.

Watemberg, N., Silver, S., Harel, S., & Lerman-Sagie, T. (2002). Significance of microcephaly among children with developmental abilities. *Journal of Child Neurology, 17,* 117–122.

Waterman, A.S. (1985). Identity in the context of adolescent psychology. In A.S. Waterman (Ed.), *Identity in adolescence: Processes and contents.* San Francisco: Jossey-Bass.

Waterman, A.S. (1989). Curricula interventions for identity change: Substantive and ethical considerations. *Journal of Adolescence, 12,* 389–400.

Waterman, A.S. (1992). Identity as an aspect of optimal psychological functioning. In G.R. Adams, T.P. Gullotta, & R. Montemayor (Eds.), *Adolescent identity formation.* Newbury Park, CA: Sage.

Waterman, A.S. (1997). An overview of service-learning and the role of research and evaluation in service-learning programs. In A.S. Waterman (Ed.), *Service learning.* Mahwah, NJ: Erlbaum.

Waters, E. (2001, April). *Perspectives on continuity and discontinuity in relationships.* Paper presented at the meeting of the Society for Research in Child Development, Minneapolis.

Waters, E., Corcoran, D., & Anafara, M. (2005). Attachment, other relationships, and the theory that all good things go together. *Human Development, 48,* 85–88.

Waters, E., Kondo-Ikemura, K., Posada, G., & Richters, J.E. (1990). Learning to love: Mechanisms and milestones. In M. Gunnar & L.A. Sroufe (Eds.), *Minnesota symposia on child psychology, 23.* Mahwah, NJ: Erlbaum.

Watras, J. (2002). *The foundations of educational curriculum and diversity: 1565 to the present.* Boston: McGraw-Hill.

Watson, J.B. (1928). *Psychological care of infant and child.* New York: W.W. Norton.

Watson, J.B., & Rayner, R. (1920). Conditioned emotional reactions. *Journal of Experimental Psychology, 3,* 1–14.

Watson, M., Kash, K.M., Homewood, J., Ebbs, S., Murday, V., & Eeles, R. (2005). Does genetic counseling have any impact on management of breast cancer risk? *Genetic Testing, 9,* 167–174.

Waxman, S.R., & Lidz, J.L. (2006). Early word learning. In W. Damon & R. Lerner (Eds.), *Handbook of child psychology* (6th ed.). New York: Wiley.

Waylen, A., & Wolke, D. (2004). Sex 'n' rock 'n' roll: The meaning and social consequences of pubertal timing. *European Journal of Endocrinology, 151* (Supplement 3), U151–U159.

Weber, E. (2005). *MI strategies in the classroom and beyond.* Boston: Allyn & Bacon.

Wechsler, D. (1939). *The measurement of adult intelligence.* Baltimore: Williams & Wilkins.

Wegman, M.E. (1987). Annual summary of vital statistics—1986. *Pediatrics, 80,* 817–827.

Wehrens, X.H., Offermans, J.P., Snijders, M., & Peeters, L.L. (2004). Fetal cardiovascular response to large placental chorionangiomas. *Journal of Perinatal Medicine, 32,* 107–112.

Weikart, D.P. (1993). Long-term positive effects in the Perry Preschool Head Start program. Unpublished data, High Scope Foundation, Ypsilanti, MI.

Weincke, J.K., Thurston, S.W., Kelsey, K.T., Varkonyi, A., Wain, J.C., Mark, E.J., & Christiani, D.C. (1999). Early age at smoking initiation and tobacco carcinogen DNA damage in the lung. *Journal of the National Cancer Institute, 91,* 614–619.

Weiner, I.B. (1980). Psychopathology in adolescence. In J. Adelson (Ed.), *Handbook of adolescent psychology.* New York: Wiley.

Weinraub, M., Horvath, D.L., & Gringlas, M.B. (2002). Single parenthood. In M.H. Bornstein (Ed.), *Handbook of parenting* (2nd ed., Vol. 3). Mahwah, NJ: Erlbaum.

Weinstock, M. (2005). The potential influence of maternal stress hormones on development and mental health of the offspring. *Brain, Behavior, and Immunology, 19,* 296–308.

Weiss, H.B., Dearing, E., Mayer, H., Kreider, H., & McCartney, K. (2005). Family educational involvement: Who can afford it and what does it afford? In C.R. Cooper, C.T. Garcia Coll, W.T. Bartko, H.M. Davis, & C. Chatman (Eds.), *Developmental pathways through middle childhood.* Mahwah, NJ: Erlbaum.

Weiss, R.E. (2001). *Pregnancy and birth: Rh factor in pregnancy.* Available on the Internet at: http://www.about.com.

Weisz, A.N., & Black, B.M. (2002). Gender and moral reasoning: African American youth respond to dating dilemmas. *Journal of Human Behavior in the Social Environment, 5,* 35–52.

Weizmann, F. (2000). Bowlby, John. In A. Kazdin (Ed.), *Encyclopedia of psychology.* Washington, DC, & New York: American Psychological Association and Oxford University Press.

Wellman, H.M. (1997, April). *Ten years of theory of mind: Telling the story backwards.* Paper presented at the meeting of the Society for Research in Child Development, Washington, DC.

Wellman, H.M. (2000). Early childhood. In A. Kazdin (Ed.), *Encyclopedia of psychology.* Washington, DC, & New York: American Psychological Association and Oxford University Press.

Wellman, H.M. (2004). Understanding the psychological world: Developing a theory of mind. In U. Goswami (Ed.), *Blackwell handbook of childhood cognitive development.* Malden, MA: Blackwell.

Wellman, H.M., Cross, D., & Watson, J. (2001). Meta-analysis of theory-of-mind development: The truth about false belief. *Child Development, 72,* 655–684.

Welti, C. (2002). Adolescents in South America: Facing the future with skepticism. In B.B. Brown, R.W. Larson, & T.S. Saraswathi (Eds.), *The world's youth.* New York: Cambridge University Press.

Wentworth, R.A.L. (1999). *Montessori for the millennium.* Mahwah, NJ: Erlbaum.

Wentzel, K.R. (1997). Student motivation in middle school: The role of perceived pedagogical caring. *Journal of Educational Psychology, 89,* 411–419.

Wentzel, K.R., & Asher, S.R. (1995). The academic lives of neglected, rejected, popular, and controversial children. *Child Development, 66,* 754–763.

Wentzel, K.R., Barry, C.M., & Caldwell, K.A. (2004). Friendships in middle school: Influences on motivation and school adjustment. *Journal of Educational Psychology, 96,* 195–203.

Werth, J.L. (2004). The relationships among clinical depression, suicide, and other actions that may hasten death. *Behavioral Science and the Law, 22,* 627.

Wertheimer, M. (1945). *Productive thinking.* New York: Harper.

West, J.R., & Blake, C.A. (2005). Fetal alcohol syndrome: An assessment of the field. *Experimental Biology and Medicine, 230,* 354–356.

Whalen, C.K. (2001). ADHD treatment in the 21st century: Pushing the envelope. *Journal of Clinical Child Psychology, 30,* 136–140.

White, A.M. (2005). The changing adolescent brain. *Education Canada, 45* (No. 2), 4–7.

White, C.W., & Coleman, M. (2000). *Early childhood education.* Columbus, OH: Merrill.

White, J.W. (2001). Aggression and gender. In J. Worell (Ed.), *Encyclopedia of women and gender.* San Diego: Academic Press.

Whithause, C. (2005). *Teaching and evaluating writing in the age of computers and high-stakes testing.* Mahwah, NJ: Erlbaum.

Whiting, B.B., & Edwards, C.P. (1988). *Children of different worlds.* Cambridge, MA: Harvard University Press.

Whitley, B.E. (2002). *Principles of research in behavioral science* (2nd ed.). New York: McGraw-Hill.

Wickelgren, I. (1999). Nurture helps to mold able minds. *Science, 283,* 1832–1834.

Wiersma, W.W., & Jurs, S.G. (2005). *Research methods in education* (8th ed.). Boston: Allyn & Bacon.

Wigfield, A., & Eccles, J.S. (Eds.). (2002). *Development of achievement motivation*. San Diego: Academic Press.

Wigfield, A., Eccles, J.S., Schiefele, U., Roeser, R., & Davis-Kean, P. (2006). Development of achievement motivation. In W. Damon & R. Lerner (Eds.), *Handbook of child psychology* (6th ed.). New York: Wiley.

Wilens, T.E., & Dodson, W. (2004). A clinical perspective on attention-deficit/hyperactivity disorder into adulthood. *Journal of Clinical Psychiatry, 65,* 1301–1313.

Wiles, J.W. (2005). *Curriculum essentials* (2nd ed.). Boston: Allyn & Bacon.

Williams, C., & Bybee, J. (1994). What do children feel guilty about? Developmental and gender differences. *Developmental Psychology, 30,* 617–623.

Williams, C.R. (1986). *The impact of television: A natural experiment in three communities*. New York: Academic Press.

Williams, D.D., Yancher, S.C., Jensen, L.C., & Lewis, C. (2003). Character education in a public high school: A multi-year inquiry into unified studies. *Journal of Moral Education, 32,* 3–33.

Williams, J.E., & Best, D.L. (1982). *Measuring sex stereotypes: A thirty-nation study*. Newbury Park, CA: Sage.

Williams, J.E., & Best, D.L. (1989). *Sex and psyche: Self-concept viewed cross-culturally*. Newbury Park, CA: Sage.

Williams, W.M., Papierno, P.B., Makel, M.C., & Ceci, S.J. (2004). Thinking like a scientist about real-world problems: The Cornell Institute for Research on Children Science Education Program. *Applied Developmental Psychology, 25,* 107–126.

Wilson, B. (2001, April). *The role of television in children's emotional development and socialization*. Paper presented at the meeting of the Society for Research in Child Development, Minneapolis.

Wilson, C.C. (2003). *Racism, sexism, and the media*. Newbury Park, CA: Sage.

Wilson-Shockley, S. (1995). *Gender differences in adolescent depression: The contribution of negative affect*. M.S. Thesis, University of Illinois at Urbana-Champaign.

Windle, M., & Windle, R.C. (2003). Alcohol and other substance use and abuse. In G. Adams & M. Berzonsky (Eds.), *Blackwell handbook of adolescence*. Malden, MA: Blackwell.

Windle, W.F. (1940). *Physiology of the human fetus*. Philadelphia: W.B. Saunders.

Winkler, I., & Cowan, N. (2005). From sensory to long-term memory: Evidence from auditory memory reactivation studies. *Experimental Psychology, 52,* 3–20.

Winn, I.J. (2004). The high cost of uncritical teaching. *Phi Delta Kappan, 85,* 496–497.

Winner, E. (1986, August). Where pelicans kiss seals. *Psychology Today*, pp. 24–35.

Winner, E. (1996). *Gifted children: Myths and realities*. New York: Basic Books.

Winner, E. (2000). The origins and ends of giftedness. *American Psychologist, 55,* 159–169.

Winner, E. (2006). Development in the arts. In W. Damon & R. Lerner (Eds.), *Handbook of child psychology* (6th ed.). New York: Wiley.

Winsler, A., Carlton, M.P., & Barry, M.J. (2000). Age-related changes in preschool children's systematic use of private speech in a natural setting. *Journal of Child Language, 27,* 665–687.

Winsler, A., Caverly, S.L., Willson-Quayle, A., Carlton, M.P., & Howell, C. (2002). The social and behavioral ecology of mixed-age and same-age preschool classrooms: A natural experiment. *Journal of Applied Developmental Psychology, 23,* 305–330.

Winsler, A., Diaz, R.M., & Montero, I. (1997). The role of private speech in the transition from collaborative to independent task performance in young children. *Early Childhood Research Quarterly, 12,* 59–79.

Wintre, M.G., & Vallance, D.D. (1994). A developmental sequence in the comprehension of emotions: Intensity, multiple emotions, and valence. *Developmental Psychology, 30,* 509–514.

Wiseman, C.V., Sunday, S.R., & Becker, A.E. (2005). Impact of the media on adolescent body image. *Child and Adolescent Psychiatric Clinics of North America, 14,* 453–471.

Wisniewski, A.B., Migeon, C.J., Meyer-Bahlburg, H.F.L., Gearhart, J.P., Berkoyitz, G.D., Brown, T.R., & Money, J. (2000). Complete androgen insensitivity syndrome: Long-term medical, surgical, and psychosexual outcome. *The Journal of Clinical Endocrinology and Metabolism, 85,* 2664–2669.

Witkin, H.A., Mednick, S.A., Schulsinger, R., Bakkestrom, E., Christiansen, K.O., Goodenbough, D.R., Hirchhorn, K., Lunsteen, C., Owen, D.R., Philip, J., Ruben, D.B., & Stocking, M. (1976). Criminality in XYY and XXY men. *Science, 193,* 547–555.

Women's Sports Foundation. (2001). *The 10 commandments for parents and coaches in youth sports*. Eisenhower Park, NY: Author.

Wood, J.W. (2006). *Teaching students in inclusive settings* (5th ed.). Upper Saddle River, NJ: Prentice Hall.

Wood, M.D., Vinson, D.C., & Sher, K.J. (2001). Alcohol use and misuse. In A. Baum, T.A. Revenson, & J.E. Singer (Eds.), *Handbook of health psychology*. Mahwah, NJ: Erlbaum.

Wood, W., & Eagly, A.H. (2002). A cross-cultural analysis of the behavior of women and men: Implications for the origins of self differences. *Psychological Bulletin, 128,* 699–727.

Woodard, E. (2000). *Media in the Home 2000: The fifth annual survey of parents and children*. Philadelphia: The Annenberg Public Policy Center.

Woodhill, B.M., & Samuels, C.A. (2004). Desirable and undesirable androgyny: A prescription for the twenty-first century. *Journal of Gender Studies, 13,* 15–28.

Woodward, A.L., & Markman, E.M. (1998). Early word learning. In D. Kuhn & R.S. Siegler (Eds.), *Handbook of child psychology* (5th ed., Vol. 2). New York: Wiley.

Worden, J.W. (2002). *Grief counseling and grief therapy* (3rd ed.). New York: Springer.

Worku, B., & Kassie, A. (2005). Kangaroo mother care: A randomized controlled trial on effectiveness of early kangaroo care for the low birthweight infants in Addis Ababa, Ethiopia. *Journal of Tropical Pediatrics, 51,* 93–97.

World Health Organization. (February 2, 2000). *Adolescent health behavior in 28 countries*. Geneva: Author.

Worobey, J., & Belsky, J. (1982). Employing the Brazelton scale to influence mothering: An experimental comparison of three strategies. *Developmental Psychology, 18,* 736–743.

Wren, T., & Mendoza, C. (2004). Cultural identity and personal identity. In D. Lapsley & D. Narvaez (Eds.), *Moral development, self, and identity*. Mahwah, NJ: Erlbaum.

Wright, M.R. (1989). Body image satisfaction in adolescent girls and boys. *Journal of Youth and Adolescence, 18,* 71–84.

Wroblewski, R., & Huston, A.C. (1987). Televised occupational stereotypes and their effects on early adolescents: Are they changing? *Journal of Early Adolescence, 7,* 283–297.

Yang, S., & Sternberg, R.J. (1997). Taiwanese Chinese people's conceptions of intelligence. *Intelligence, 25,* 21–36.

Yang, Y., May, Y., Ni, L., Zhao, S., Li, L., Zhang, J., Fan, M., Liang, C., Cao, J., & Xu, L. (2003). Lead exposure through gestation-only caused long-term memory deficits in young adult offspring. *Experimental Neurology, 184,* 489–495.

Yasui, M., Dorham, C.L., & Dishion, T.J. (2004). Ethnic identity and psychological adjustment: A validity analysis for European American and African American adolescents. *Journal of Adolescent Research, 19,* 807–825.

Yates, M. (1995, March). *Community service and political-moral discussions among Black urban adolescents*. Paper presented at the meeting of the Society for Research in Child Development, Indianapolis.

Yekin, Y. (2002). Do environmental and hereditary factors affect the psychophysiology and left-right shift in left-handers? *International Journal of Neuroscience, 110,* 109–134.

Yeung, W.J., Sandberg, J.F., Davis-Kean, P.E., & Hofferth, S.L. (2001). Children's time with fathers in intact families. *Journal of Marriage and Family, 63,* 136–154.

Yin, Y., Buhrmester, D., & Hibbard, D. (1996, March). *Are there developmental changes in the influence of relationships with parents and friends on adjustment during early adolescence?* Paper presented at the meeting of the Society for Research on Adolescence, Boston.

Young, D. (2001). The nature and management of pain: What is the evidence? *Birth, 28,* 149–151.

Young, K.T. (1990). American conceptions of infant development from 1955 to 1984: What the experts are telling parents. *Child Development, 61,* 17–28.

Young, S.K., & Shahinfar, A. (1995, March). *The contributions of maternal sensitivity and child temperament to attachment status at 14 months.* Paper presented at the meeting of the Society for Research in Child Development, Indianapolis.

Youniss, J. (1980). *Parents and peers in the social environment: A Sullivan-Piaget perspective.* Chicago: University of Chicago Press.

Yu, V.Y. (2000). Developmental outcome of extremely preterm infants. *American Journal of Perinatology, 17,* 57–61.

Yussen, S.R. (1977). Characteristics of moral dilemmas written by adolescents. *Developmental Psychology, 13,* 162–163.

Zaffanello, M., Maffeis, C., & Zamboni, G. (2005). Multiple positive results during a neonatal screening program. *Journal of Perinatal Medicine. 33,* 246–251.

Zakriski, A.L., Wheeler, E., Burda, J., & Shields, A. (2005). Justifiable psychopharmacology or overzealous prescription? Examining parental reports of lifetime prescription histories of psychiatrically hospitalized children. *Child and Adolescent Mental Health, 10,* 16–22.

Zaslow, M. (2004). Child-care for low-income families: Problems and promises. In A.C. Crouter & A. Booth (Eds.), *Work-family challenges for low-income parents and their children.* Mahwah, NJ: Erlbaum.

Zdravkovic, T., Genbacev, O., McMaster, M.T., & Fisher, S.J. (2005). The adverse effects of maternal smoking on the human placenta: A review. *Placenta, 26, Suppl A:* S81–S86.

Zelazo, P.D., & Muller, U. (2004). Executive function in typical and atypical development. In U. Goswami (Ed.), *Blackwell handbook of cognitive development.* Malden, MA: Blackwell.

Zelazo, P.D., Muller, U., Frye, D., & Marcovitch, S. (2003). The development of executive function in early childhood. *Monographs of the Society for Research in Child Development, 68* (3, Serial No. 274).

Zentall, S.S. (2006). *ADHD and education.* Upper Saddle River, NJ: Prentice Hall.

Zeskind, P.S., Klein, L., & Marshall, T.R. (1992). Adults' perceptions of experimental modifications of durations and expiratory sounds in infant crying. *Developmental Psychology, 28,* 1153–1162.

Zielinksi, D.S., Campa, M.I., & Eckenrode, J.J. (2003, April). *Child maltreatment and the early onset of problem behaviors: A follow-up at 19 years.* Paper presented at the meeting of the Society for Research in Child Development, Tampa.

Zigler, E.F., & Styfco, S.J. (1994). Head Start: Criticisms in a constructive context. *American Psychologist, 49,* 127–132.

Zimmerman, B.J., Bonner, S., & Kovach, R (1996). *Developing self-regulated learners.* Washington, DC: American Psychological Association.

Zimmerman, B.J., & Schunk, D.H. (2004). Self-regulating intellectual processes and outcomes: A social cognitive perspective. In D.Y. Dai, & R.J. Sternberg (Eds.), *Motivation, emotion, and cognition.* Mahwah, NJ: Erlbaum.

Zimmerman, R.S., Khoury, E., Vega, W.A., Gill, A.G., & Warheit, G.J. (1995). Teacher and student perceptions of behavior problems among a sample of African American, Hispanic, and non-Hispanic White students. *American Journal of Community Psychology, 23,* 181–197.

Zinn, M.B., & Wells, B. (2000). Diversity within Latino families: New lessons for family social science. In D.M. Demo, K.R. Allen, & M.A. Fine (Eds.), *Handbook of family diversity.* New York: Oxford University Press.

Zukow-Goldring, P. (2002). Sibling caregiving. In M.H. Bornstein (Ed.), *Handbook of parenting* (2nd ed., Vol. 3). Mahwah, NJ: Erlbaum.

Zuzanek, J. (2000). *The effects of time use and time pressure on child parent relationships.* Waterloo, Ontario: Otium.

CREDITS

Text/Line Art Credits

Chapter 1

Figure 1.3 From Bradley et al., 2001, "The Home Environment of Children in the United States, Part I," *Child Development,* 72, 1844–1867. Reprinted with permission of the Society for Research in Child Development.

Chapter 2

Figure 2.5 From "Bronfenbrenner's Ecological Theory of Development," C.B. Kopp & J.B. Krakow, 1982, *Child Development in the Social Context,* p. 648. Addison-Wesley Longman, Inc. Reprinted by permission of Pearson Education, Inc. **Figure 2.6** From Santrock, *Life-Span Development,* Ninth Edition. Copyright © 2004 The McGraw-Hill Companies. Reproduced with permission of The McGraw-Hill Companies. **Figure 2.7** From Santrock, *Children,* Eighth Edition, Fig. 2.9. Copyright © 2005 The McGraw-Hill Companies. Reproduced with permission of The McGraw-Hill Companies. **Figure 2.8** From Crowley et al., 2001, "Parents Explain More to Boys Than Girls During Shared Scientific Thinking," *Psychological Science,* 12, 258–261. Reprinted by permission of Blackwell Publishers. **Figure 2.11** From Santrock, *Children,* Seventh Edition, Fig. 2.11. Copyright © 2003 The McGraw-Hill Companies. Reproduced with permission of The McGraw-Hill Companies. **Figure 2.12** From Santrock, *Children,* Eighth Edition, Fig. 2.13. Copyright © 2005 The McGraw-Hill Companies. Reproduced with permission of The McGraw-Hill Companies.

Chapter 3

Figure 3.1 Bonner, John T., *The Evolution of Culture in Animals.* Copyright © 1980 Princeton University Press. Reprinted by permission of Princeton University Press. **Figure 3.2** From Santrock, *Psychology,* Seventh Edition, Fig. 3.22. Copyright © 2003 The McGraw-Hill Companies. Reproduced with permission of The McGraw-Hill Companies. **Figure 3.5** From Santrock, *Life-Span Development,* Ninth Edition, Fig. Ch. 3. Copyright © 2004 The McGraw-Hill Companies. Reproduced with permission of The McGraw-Hill Companies. **Figure 3.6** From Santrock, *Life-Span Development,* Eighth Edition, Fig. 3.8. Copyright © 2002 The McGraw-Hill Companies. Reproduced with permission of The McGraw-Hill Companies. **Figure 3.7** From Santrock, *Children,* Seventh Edition, Fig. 3.9. Copyright © 2003 The McGraw-Hill Companies. Reproduced with permission of The McGraw-Hill Companies. **Figure 3.8** Centers for Disease Control and Prevention, Atlanta, 2000, Figure 2.6, CDC website. "Reproductive Health: Assisted Reproductive Technology Success Rates." **Figure 3.9** Reprinted with permission of the Society for Research in Child Development. **p. 92** From D.M. Brozinsky & E. Pinderhughes, 2002, "Parenting and Child Development in Adoptive Families," in M. Bornstein (Ed.), *Handbook of Parenting,* 2nd ed., Mahwah, NJ: Erlbaum, pp. 288–292. Reprinted by permission. **Figure 3.10** From Santrock, *Children,* Seventh Edition, Fig. 3.14. Copyright © 2003 The McGraw-Hill Companies. Reproduced with permission of The McGraw-Hill Companies.

Chapter 4

p. 104 From Pamela Warrick, "The Fantastic Voyage of Tanner Roberts," *Los Angeles Tribune,* Sunday, March 1, 1992, pp. E-1, E11, E12. Reprinted with permission from TMS Reprints. **Figure 4.1** From Charles Carroll & Dean Miller, *Health: The Science of Human Adaptation,* 5th ed. Copyright © 1991 Times Mirror Higher Education Group, Inc., Dubuque, Iowa. All Rights Reserved. Reprinted by permission. **Figure 4.4** Reprinted from K.L. Moore, *The Developing Human: Clinically Oriented Embryology,* 4th ed. with permission from Elsevier. **Figure 4.7** From Virginia Apgar, 1975, "A Proposal for a New Method of Evaluation of a Newborn Infant," *Anesthesia and Analgesia* (32), pp. 267–360. Reprinted by permission of Lippincott, Williams & Wilkins.

Chapter 5

Figure 5.1 From Santrock, *Children,* Seventh Edition, Fig. 6.1. Copyright © 2003 The McGraw-Hill Companies. Reproduced with permission of The McGraw-Hill Companies. **Figure 5.2** From Santrock, *Adolescence,* Eighth Edition, Fig. 3.4. Copyright © 2001 The McGraw-Hill Companies. Reproduced with permission of The McGraw-Hill Companies. **Figure 5.3** From J.M. Tanner et al., "Standards from Birth to Maturity for Height, Weight, Height Velocity: British Children," *Archives of Diseases in Childhood,* 41. Copyright © 1966. Used by permission of BMJ Publishing Group. **Figure 5.4** From J.M. Tanner, "Growing Up," *Scientific American,* September 1973. Copyright © 1973 by Scientific American, Inc. All rights reserved. **Figure 5.6** From Santrock, *Children,* Seventh Edition, Fig. 6.7. Copyright © 2003 The McGraw-Hill Companies. Reproduced with permission of The McGraw-Hill Companies. **Figure 5.7** From Santrock, *Child Development,* Ninth Edition. Copyright © 2001 The McGraw-Hill Companies. Reproduced with permission of The McGraw-Hill Companies. **Figure 5.8** From Santrock, *Children,* Seventh Edition, Fig. 9.3. Copyright © 2003 The McGraw-Hill Companies. Reproduced with permission of The McGraw-Hill Companies. **Figure 5.10** Reprinted by permission of the publisher from *Development of the Human Cerebral Cortex, Vols. I-VIII,* by Jesse LeRoy Conel, Cambridge, MA: Harvard University Press, Copyright © 1939, 1975 by the President and Fellows of Harvard College. **Figure 5.11** From Santrock, *Psychology,* Seventh Edition, p. 128. Copyright © 2003 The McGraw-Hill Companies. Reproduced with permission of The McGraw-Hill Companies. **Figure 5.13** Data from National Center for Health Statistics and Center for Disease Control & Prevention, Atlanta. **Figure 5.16** From Santrock, *Topical Life-Span,* Second Edition, Fig. 4.7. Copyright © 2005 The McGraw-Hill Companies. Reproduced with permission of The McGraw-Hill Companies.

Chapter 6

Figure 6.3 From W.K. Frankenburg & J.B. Dodds, "The Denver Development Screening Test," *Journal of Pediatrics,* 71, 181–191. Copyright © 1967. Used by permission of MOSBY, Inc., a Harcourt Health Sciences Company. **Figure 6.5** Adapted from Alexander Semenoick, in R.L. Fantz, "The Origin of Form Perception," *Scientific American,* 1961. **Figure 6.6** From Slater et al., 1988, "Orientation Discrimination and Cortical Function in the Human Newborn," *Perception,* 17, 597–602 (Figure 1 and Table 1). Reprinted with permission of Pion Ltd., London. **p. 186** From *Parents' Guide to Girls' Sports.* Reprinted by permission of the Women's Sports Foundation.

Chapter 7

p. 210 From J. Piaget, 1952, *The Origins of Intelligence,* excerpts from pp. 27, 159, 225, 273, 339, Routledge Publishing. **Figure 7.1** From Santrock, *Topical Life-Span Development,* Second Edition, Fig. 6.1. Copyright © 2005 The McGraw-Hill Companies. Reproduced with permission of The McGraw-Hill Companies. **Figure 7.4** Reprinted with permission of the Society for Research in Child Development. **Figure 7.6** From Santrock, *Children,* Seventh Edition, Fig. 10.1. Copyright © 2003 The McGraw-Hill Companies. Reproduced with permission of The McGraw-Hill Companies. **Figure 7.7** Reprinted courtesy of

D. Wolf and J. Nove. **Figure 7.8** From Santrock, *Children*, Seventh Edition, Fig. 10.4. Copyright © 2003 The McGraw-Hill Companies. Reproduced with permission of The McGraw-Hill Companies. **Figure 7.9** From Santrock, *Children*, Seventh Edition, Fig. 10.5. Copyright © 2003 The McGraw-Hill Companies. Reproduced with permission of The McGraw-Hill Companies. **Figure 7.10** From Santrock, *Children*, Seventh Edition, Fig. 13.1. Copyright © 2003 The McGraw-Hill Companies. Reproduced with permission of The McGraw-Hill Companies. **pp. 228–229** From E.C. Frede, "The Role of Program Quality in Producing Early Childhood Program Benefits," *The Future of Children*, Vol. 5, No. 3, p. 125, a publication of The David and Lucile Packard Foundation. Reprinted by permission.

Chapter 8

Figure 8.1 From Santrock, *Topical Life-Span Development*, Second Edition, Fig. 7.2. Copyright © 2005 The McGraw-Hill Companies. Reproduced with permission of The McGraw-Hill Companies. **Figure 8.2** From Santrock, *Child Development*, Tenth Edition, Fig. 8.1. Copyright © 2004 The McGraw-Hill Companies. Reproduced with permission of The McGraw-Hill Companies. **Figure 8.3** From Santrock, *Topical Life-Span Development*, Second Edition, Fig. 7.8. Copyright © 2005 The McGraw-Hill Companies. Reproduced with permission of The McGraw-Hill Companies. **Figure 8.4** From Chi, 1978, "Knowledge Structures and Memory Development," in R.S. Siegler (Ed.), *Children's Thinking*. Mahwah, NJ: Erlbaum. Reprinted by permission from Lawrence Erlbaum Associates. **p. 253** From M. Bruck & S.J. Ceci, 1999, "The Suggestibility of Children's Memories," *Annual Review of Psychology*, 50, pp. 429–430. Reprinted by permission. **Figure 8.9** From Robert S. Siegler, *Four Rules for Solving the Balance Scale Task*, Carnegie Mellon University Press. Copyright © Robert S. Siegler. Reprinted by permission.

Chapter 9

Figure 9.1 From Santrock, *Psychology*, Seventh Edition, Fig. 10.1. Copyright © 2003 The McGraw-Hill Companies. Reproduced with permission of The McGraw-Hill Companies. **Figure 9.6** From Raven's *Standard Progressive Matrices*, Item A5. Used by permission of Campbell Thomson and McLaughlin, Ltd. **Figure 9.7** From Santrock, *Psychology*, Seventh Edition, Fig. 10.6. Copyright © 2003 The McGraw-Hill Companies. Reproduced with permission of The McGraw-Hill Companies. **Figure 9.8** From Morton Hunt, 1982, *The Universe Within: A New Science Explores the Human Mind*. Copyright © 1982 by Morton Hunt. Reprinted by permission of American Association on Mental Retardation.

Chapter 10

Figure 10.1 "The Rule Systems of Language," from S.L. Haight, *Language Overview*. Reprinted by permission of Sherrel Haight, Central Michigan University. **Figure 10.3** From Santrock, *Children*, Seventh Edition, Fig. 7.6. Copyright © 2003 The McGraw-Hill Companies. Reproduced with permission of The McGraw-Hill Companies. **Figure 10.4** From Santrock, *Children*, Seventh Edition, Fig. 7.7. Copyright © 2003 The McGraw-Hill Companies. Reproduced with permission of The McGraw-Hill Companies. **Figure 10.5** From Jean Berko, 1958, "The Child's Learning of English Morphology," in *Word*, Vol. 14, p. 154. Reprinted with permission. **Figure 10.6** From J.S. Chall, 1979, "The Great Debate: Ten Years Later, With a Modest Proposal for Reading Stages," in L.B. Resnick & P.A. Weaver (Eds.), *Theory and Practice of Early Reading*, Vol. 1, pp. 29–55. Mahwah, NJ: Erlbaum. Reprinted by permission of Lawrence Erlbaum Associates. **p. 313** From Jean Berko Gleason, *The Development of Language*, 3/e. Published by Allyn & Bacon, Boston, MA. Copyright © 1992 by Pearson Education. Reprinted by permission of the publisher. **Figure 10.10** From Hart & Risley, 1995, *Meaningful Differences in the Everyday Experiences of Young American Children*, Baltimore: Paul H. Brookes Publishing Co. Reprinted by permission. **Figure 10.11** From Santrock, *Topical Life-Span Development*, Second Edition, Fig. 9.6. Copyright © 2005 The McGraw-Hill Companies. Reproduced with permission of The McGraw-Hill Companies. **Figure 10.12** With permission from Dr. Ursula Bellugi.

Chapter 11

Figure 11.3 Reprinted by permission of the publisher from *Infancy: Its Place in Human Development*, by Jerome Kagan, R.B. Kearsley and P.R. Zelazo, p. 107, Cambridge, MA: Harvard University Press, Copyright © 1978 by the President and Fellows of Harvard College. **Figure 11.7** From Santrock, *Adolescence*, Tenth Edition, p. 524. Copyright © 2005 The McGraw-Hill Companies. Reproduced with permission of The McGraw-Hill Companies. **Figure 11.8** Excerpts adapted from *The Optimistic Child: A Proven Program to Safeguard Children Against Depression and Build Lifelong Resilience*. Copyright © 1995 by Martin E.P. Seligman, Ph.D., Karen Reivich, M.A., Lisa Jaycox, Ph.D., and Jane Gilham, Ph.D. Reprinted with permission. **Figure 11.9** From Santrock, *Topical Life-Span Development*, First Edition, Fig. 10.3. Copyright © 2002 The McGraw-Hill Companies. Reproduced with permission of The McGraw-Hill Companies. **Figure 11.11** From A.T. Ainsworth, "The Development of Infant-Mother Attachment," *Review of Child Developmental Research*, Vol. 3. Reprinted with permission of the Society for Research in Child Development. **Figure 11.12** From M.H. van Ijzendoorn and P.M. Kroonenberg, 1998, "Cross-Cultural Patterns of Attachment: A Meta-Analysis of the Strange Situation," *Child Development*, 59, 147–156. Reprinted with permission of the Society for Research in Child Development.

Chapter 12

Figure 12.1 From M. Lewis & J. Brooks-Gunn, *Social Cognition and the Acquisition of the Self*, p. 64. Reprinted with kind permission from Springer Science and Business Media. **Figure 12.2** From Thomas E. Lickona (Ed.), *Moral Development and Behavior*. Copyright © 1976. Used by permission of Thomas E. Lickona. **p. 376** Reprinted from D. Oyserman, K. Terry & D. Bybee, 2002, "A Possible Selves Intervention to Enhance School Involvement," *Journal of Adolescence*, 25, 313–326, with permission from Elsevier. **Figure 12.4** From S. Harter, 1999, *The Construction of the Self*, Table 6.1. New York: The Guilford Press. Reprinted with permission. **Figure 12.5** From Santrock, *Children*, Eighth Edition, Fig. 17.2. Copyright © 2005 The McGraw-Hill Companies. Reproduced with permission of The McGraw-Hill Companies. **Figure 12.6** From Santrock, *Children*, Eighth Edition, Fig. 17.3. Copyright © 2005 The McGraw-Hill Companies. Reproduced with permission of The McGraw-Hill Companies. **Figure 12.7** From Santrock, *Children*, Seventh Edition, p. 542. Copyright © 2003 The McGraw-Hill Companies. Reproduced with permission of The McGraw-Hill Companies.

Chapter 13

pp. 397–398 From R. Lippa, 2002. *Gender, Nature and Nurture*, pp. 103–104, 114. Mahwah, NJ: Erlbaum. Reprinted by permission from Lawrence Erlbaum Associates. **Figure 13.6** From the *Bem Sex Role Inventory*, by Sandra Bem, 1978. Reprinted by permission of Mind Garden.

Chapter 14

Figure 14.1 From R.S. Selman, "Social-Cognitive Understanding," in Thomas Lickona (Ed.), *Moral Development and Behavior*, 1976. Reprinted by permission of Thomas Lickona. **Figure 14.2** From L. Kohlberg, 1969, "Stage and Sequence: The Cognitive-Developmental Approach to Socialization," in D.A. Goslin (Ed.), *Handbook of Socialization Theory and Research*. Chicago: Rand McNally. Reprinted with permission of D.A. Goslin. **Figure 14.3** From Colby et al., 1983, "A Longitudinal Study of Moral Judgment," *Monographs for the Society for Research in Child Development*, Serial #201. Reprinted with permission of the Society for Research in Child Development.

Chapter 15

pp. 456, 476 From *Multiple Sclerosis: 300 Tips for Making Life Easier* by Shelley Peterman Schwarz. Reprinted by permission of Shelley Peterman Schwarz. **Figure 15.3** From Santrock, *Child Development*, Ninth Edition. Copyright © 2001 The McGraw-Hill Companies. Reproduced with permission of The McGraw-Hill Companies.

Chapter 16

Figure 16.3 From Nansel et al., 2001, "Bullying Behaviors Among U.S. Youth," *Journal of the American Medical Association*, Vol. 285, pp. 2094–2100. **Figure 16.5** From Dexter C. Dunphy, "The Social Structure of Urban Adolescent Peer Groups," *Sociometry*, Vol. 26, 1963. American Sociological Association, Washington, DC. **Figure 16.6** "Age of Onset of Romantic Activity," from "Romantic

Development: Does Age at Which Romantic Involvement Starts Matter?" by Duane Buhrmester, April 2001. Paper presented at the meeting of the Society for Research in Child Development, Minneapolis, MN. Reprinted with permission.

Chapter 17

Figure 17.1 From "Learner-Centered Principles Work Group," *Learner-Centered Psychological Principles: A Framework for School Redesign and Reform*, 1997. Found at www.apa.org/ed/lcp.html. Copyright © 1997 by the American Psychological Association. Reproduced with permission. **Figure 17.2** From "Position Statement on Developmentally Appropriate Practice in Programs for 4- and 5-Year-Olds," *Young Children*, 41, 23–27. Copyright © 1986. Used by permission of the National Association for the Education of Young Children. **Figure 17.5** From K. Wentzel, 1997, "Student Motivation in Middle School: The Role of Perceived Pedagogical Caring," *Journal of Educational Psychology*, 89, 411–419. Copyright © 1997 by the American Psychological Association. Reproduced with permission.

Chapter 18

Figure 18.1 From Harry C. Triandis, *Making Basic Texts in Psychology More Culture-Inclusive and Culture-Sensitive*. Used by permission of the University of Illinois Press. **Figure 18.3** From R.W. Larson, 2001, "How U.S. Children and Adolescents Spend Time: What It Does (and Doesn't) Tell Us About Their Development," *Current Directions in Psychological Science*, 10/e, Table 1, pp. 160–164. Reprinted by permission of Blackwell Publishers. **Figure 18.4** From Santrock, *Child Development*, Tenth Edition, Fig. 18.4. Copyright © 2004 The McGraw-Hill Companies. Reproduced with permission of The McGraw-Hill Companies. **Figure 18.6** From V. Rideout, D.F. Roberts, & U.G. Foehr, 2005, *Generation M*, p. 7. Menlo Park, CA: Kaiser Family Foundation. Reprinted with permission. **p. 570** From "Harlem: A Dream Deferred" in *The Collected Poems of Langston Hughes*, by Langston Hughes. Copyright © 1994 by The Estate of Langston Hughes. Used by permission of Alfred A. Knopf, a division of Random House, Inc. and Harold Ober Associates.

Photo Credits

Section Openers

1: © Ariel Skelley/CORBIS; **2:** © Petit Format/Nestle/Photo Researchers; **3:** © Ariel Skelley/CORBIS; **4:** © Ariel Skelley/CORBIS; **5:** © Francisco Cruz/SuperStock

Chapter 1

Opener: © Ariel Skelley/The Stock Market/CORBIS; **p. 6** (top): © AP/Wide World Photos; **p. 6** (bottom): © AP/Wide World Photos; **1.1:** Photo: © Erich Lessing/Art Resource, NY/Painting by A.I.G. Velasquez, Infanta Margarita Teresa in white garb, Kunsthistorische Museum, Vienna, Austria; **1.2:** © Archives of the History of American Psychology; **p. 11:** © Luis Vargas; **p. 11:** Poster: National Association for the Education of Young Children, Robert Maust/Photo Agora; **p. 12:** © Nancy Agostini; **1.6** (left to right): Courtesy of Landrum Shettles; © John Santrock; © Chromosohn Media, Inc./The Image Works; © CORBIS website; © James L. Shaffer; **p. 20:** © PhotoDisc/Getty website; **p. 23:** Courtesy Valerie Pang; **p. 27:** Courtesy of Katherine Duchen Smith, Certified Pediatric Nurse Practitioner, Ft. Collins, Colorado

Chapter 2

Opener: © Ray Stott/The Image Works; **p. 39:** © Bettmann/CORBIS; **p. 42:** © Sarah Putnam/Index Stock; **p. 43:** © Yves deBraine/Black Star/Stock Photo; **p. 45:** A.R. Lauria/Dr. Michael Cole, Laboratory of Human Cognition, University of California, San Diego; **p. 46:** © Bettmann/CORBIS; **p. 47:** © Bettmann/CORBIS; **p. 48:** © Nina Leen/TimePix/AP/Wide World Photos; **p. 49:** Courtesy of Urie Bronfenbrenner; **2.6:** Freud: © Bettmann/CORBIS; Pavlov: © CORBIS; Piaget: © Yves deBraine/Black Star/Stock Photo; Vygotsky: A.R. Lauria/Dr. Michael Cole, Laboratory of Human Cognition, University of California, San Diego; Skinner: © Harvard University News Office; Erikson: © UPI/Bettmann/CORBIS; Bandura: © Bettmann/CORBIS; Bronfenbrenner: Courtesy of Urie Bronfenbrenner; **p. 53:** © Richard T. Nowitz/Photo Researchers; **p. 55:** © Sovereign/Phototake; **p. 56:** © Bettmann/CORBIS; **p. 60:** © McGraw-Hill Company, photographer John Thoeming; **p. 63** (left): © Kevin Fleming/CORBIS; **p. 63** (right): © Ed Honowitz/Stone/Getty Images; **p. 64:** © Pam Reid

Chapter 3

Opener: © Tom Rosenthal/SuperStock; **p. 76:** © Enrico Ferorelli; **3.3:** © Sundstrom/Gamma; **3.4** (left & right): © Biophoto Associates/Photo Researchers, Inc.; **p. 85:** © 1989 Joel Gordon Photography; **p. 86:** © Andrew Eccles/Janet Botaish Group; **p. 87:** © Holly Ishmael; **p. 88:** © J. Pavlovsky/Sygma/CORBIS; **p. 91:** © Sondra Dawes/The Image Works; **p. 94:** © Myrleen Ferguson Cate/Photo Edit

Chapter 4

Opener: Photo Lennart Nilsson/Albert Bonniers Forlag AB, *A Child is Born*, Dell Publishing Company; **p. 107:** © David Young-Wolff/Photo Edit; **4.3** (top): Photo Lennart Nilsson/Albert Bonniers Forlag AB, *A Child is Born*, Dell Publishing Company; (middle & bottom): © Petit Format/Nestle Science Source/Photo Researchers; **4.5:** Courtesy of Ann Streissguth from A.P. Streissguth et al., "Teratogenic Effects of Alcohol in Humans and Laboratory Animals" in *Science*, 209 (18): 353–361, 1980; **p. 112:** © John Chiasson/Liaison Agency/Getty Images; **p. 114:** © Betty Press/Woodfin Camp; **p. 115:** © 1990 Alan Reininger/Contact Press Images; **p. 116:** © R.I.A./Gamma; **p. 117:** © Rachel Thompson; **p. 118:** © Viviane Moos/CORBIS; **p. 120** (top): © SIU/Peter Arnold, Inc.; **p. 120** (bottom): © M. Shostak/Anthro-Photo; **p. 121:** © Roger Tully/Stone/Getty Images; **p. 122:** © Linda Pugh; **p. 123:** © Stephen Marks, Inc./The Image Bank/Getty Images; **p. 125:** © Charles Gupton/Stock Boston; **p. 126:** Courtesy of Dr. Susan Ludington; **p. 127:** © Dr. Tiffany Field; **p. 130:** © Michael Newman/Photo Edit

Chapter 5

Opener: © Eyewire Vol. EP049/Getty Images; **p. 140:** © Bob Daemmrich/The Image Works; **p. 145:** © David Young-Wolf/Photo Edit; **5.7:** Photo Lennart Nilsson/Albert Bonniers Forlag; **5.8:** © A. Glauberman/Photo Researchers; **5.9a & b:** Courtesy of Dr. Harry T. Chugani, Children's Hospital of Michigan; **p. 149:** © 1999 Kenneth Jarecke/Contact Press Images; **p. 155:** © SuperStock; **p. 156:** © Ron Hutchings/Photo Edit; **p. 159:** Courtesy of Sharon McLeod; **p. 160:** Courtesy of The Hawaii Family Support Center, Healthy Start Program; **p. 161:** © Vol. DV251 Digital Vision/Getty Images; **p. 162:** © Bob Daemmrich/The Image Works; **p. 165:** Courtesy of Barbara Deloin; **p. 166:** © Tony Freeman/Photo Edit

Chapter 6

Opener: © George Disario/The Stock Market/CORBIS; **p. 178** (top & bottom): © Reuters NewMedia Inc/CORBIS; **p. 179:** Courtesy of Esther Thelen; **p. 182** (left & right): © Dr. Karen Adolph, New York University; **p. 184** (top): © Michael Greenlar/The Image Works; **p. 184** (bottom): © Frank Baily Studios; **p. 186:** © Steve Prezant/CORBIS; **p. 187:** Courtesy Amy Needham; **p. 188:** © Vol. EP078/Eyewire/Getty Images; **6.5:** Adapted from "The Origin of Form and Perception" by R.L. Fantz © 1961 by *Scientific American*. Photo © by David Linton; **6.7** (all): Courtesy of Dr. Charles Nelson; **6.9:** © Enrico Ferorelli; 6.10a: © Michael Siluk; **6.10b:** © Dr. Melanie Spence, University of Texas; **6.11:** © Jean Guichard/Sygma/CORBIS; **6.12** (all): From D. Rosenstein & H. Oster, "Differential Facial Responses to Four Basic Tastes in Newborns," in *Child Development*, Vol. 59, 1988. Copyright © Society For Research in Child Development, Inc.

Chapter 7

Opener: © Gabe Palmer/CORBIS; **p. 211:** © Archives Jean Piaget, Universite De Geneve, Switzerland; **7.3** (left & right): © Doug Goodman/Photo Researchers; **p. 221:** © Paul Fusco/Magnum Photos; **p. 223:** © David Young-Wolff/Photo Edit; **p. 224:** © Stewart Cohen/Stone/Getty Images; **p. 226:** © Archives Jean Piaget, Universite De Geneve, Switzerland; **p. 227:** © M & E Bernheim/Woodfin Camp; **p. 228:** © Elizabeth Crews/The Image Works; **p. 229:** © James Wertsch/Washington University in St. Louis; **p. 231:** Courtesy Barbara Rogoff; **7.12** (left): A.R. Lauria/Dr. Michael Cole, Laboratory of Human Cognition, University of California, San Diego; **7.12** (right): © 1999 Yves deBraine/Black Star/Stock Photo

Chapter 8

Opener: © Ariel Skelley/The Stock Market/CORBIS; **p. 240:** Courtesy of Laura Bickford; **8.5:** Courtesy of Dr. Carolyn Rovee-Collier; **p. 252:** © 2005 James Kamp; **p. 256:** © Nita Winter Photography; **p. 257:** © Richard Hutchings/Photo Researchers; **p. 259:** Courtesy of Judy DeLoache; **p. 261:** © PhotoDisc Green/PunchStock

Chapter 9

Opener: © Cindy Charles/Photo Edit; **p. 272:** © Project Spectrum; **p. 274:** © The Bettmann Archive/CORBIS; **p. 278:** © Joe McNally; **p. 289:** Courtesy of John Santrock; **p. 291:** © Jill Cannefax; **p. 293:** Courtesy of Sterling C. Jones, Jr.

Chapter 10

Opener: © Anne Rippy/The Image Bank/Getty Images; **10.2:** © 2003 University of Washington, Institute for Learning and Brain Sciences (I-LABS); **p. 308:** © ABPL Image Library/Animals **p. 310:** © Roseanne Olson/Stone/Getty Images; **p. 314:** Courtesy of Salvador Tamayo; **p. 315:** © AFP/CORBIS; **p. 316:** © Tim Davis/CORBIS; **p. 317:** Reprinted from Curtis, *Genie: A Psycholinguitic Study of a Modern Day "Wild Child."* Copyright © 1977 with permission from Elsevier; **p. 321:** © John Carter/Photo Researchers

Chapter 11

Opener: © James Marcial/SuperStock; **p. 332:** © Andy Sacks/Stone/Getty Images; **11.2** (all) and **11.4:** © Michael Lewis, Institute for the Study of Child Development; **p. 344:** © Jim Smith/Photo Researchers, Inc.; **p. 348:** © AFP/CORBIS; **p. 352:** © Michel Tcherevkoff/Image Bank/Getty Images; **11.10:** © Martin Rogers/Stock Boston; **11.11:** © Daniel Grogan; **p. 359:** © Penny Tweedie/Stone/Getty Images; **p. 361:** Courtesy of Rashmi Nakhre

Chapter 12

Opener: © Roger Allyn Lee/SuperStock; **p. 370** (left): © AP/Wide World Photos; **p. 370** (right): Courtesy of Maxine Hong Kingston; **p. 375:** Courtesy of Compton-Drew Investigative Learning Center Middle School, St. Louis, MO; **p. 386:** Courtesy of Margaret Beale Spencer; **p. 387:** Courtesy of Armando Ronquillo

Chapter 13

Opener: © Michelle D. Bridwell/Photo Edit; **p. 396:** © Shooting Star; **13.2:** © Digital Stock; **p. 413:** © Catherine Gehm

Chapter 14

Opener: © Don Smetzer/Stone/Getty Images; **p. 427:** © Arthur Tilley/Taxi/Getty Images; **p. 429:** © Raghu-Rai/Magnum Photos; **p. 430:** © Keith Carter Photography; **p. 439:** © Ronald Cortes; **p. 445:** Courtesy of Rodney Hammond; **p. 446:** © Saba/CORBIS

Chapter 15

Opener: © Rick Gomez/CORBIS; **p. 456:** Courtesy of Shelley Peterson Schwarz, URL: www.MeetingLifesChallenges.com, Email: help@MeetingLifesChallenges.com; **p. 460:** © Tom & Dee Ann McCarthy/CORBIS; **p. 461:** © Franco Vogt/CORBIS; **p. 462:** Courtesy of Janis Keyser; **15.2:** © Peter Correz/Stone/Getty Images; **p. 471:** Courtesy of Darla Botkin; **p. 478:** © Ariel Skelley/CORBIS; **p. 484:** © Michael Newman/Photo Edit; **p. 485:** © Shelly Gazin/The Image Works; **p. 486:** © Karen Kasmauski/Woodfin Camp; **p. 489:** © Jim Craigmyle/CORBIS

Chapter 16

Opener: © Rolf Bruderer/CORBIS; **p. 499:** © SuperStock; **16.1:** © Erik Anderson/Stock Boston; **p. 507** (left): © AFP/CORBIS; **p. 507** (middle): © Dan Gair Photographic/Index Stock; **p. 507** (right): © AP/Wide World Photos; **p. 510:** © Richard Hutchings/Photo Edit; **p. 511:** © Bryan Peterson; **p. 512:** © Roy Morsch/The Stock Market/CORBIS; **p. 520:** © PhotoDisc/Getty Images

Chapter 17

Opener: © Charles Thatcher/Stone/Getty Images; **p. 528:** From "Open Window" © 1994 Municipality of Reggio Emilia Infant-toddler Centers and Preschools. Published by Reggio Children; **p. 532:** Courtesy of Yolanda Garcia; **17.2:** © Ken Fisher/Stone/Getty Images; **p. 535:** © Ronnie Kaufman/The Stock Market/CORBIS; **p. 536:** © David DeLossy/The Image Bank/Getty Images; **p. 537:** © Marc Antman/The Image Works; **p. 538:** Courtesy of "I Have a Dream," Houston, TX; **p. 540:** © Lonnie Harp; **p. 541:** © John S. Abbott; **p. 544:** © David Young-Wolff/Photo Edit; **p. 546:** © Richard Hutchings/Photo Researchers; **p. 553:** © Eiji Miyazawa/Black Star/Stock Photo

Chapter 18

Opener: © David Young-Wolff/Photo Edit; **p. 562:** © Marjorie Shostak/Anthro Photos; **p. 565:** © Daniel Laine; **p. 571:** Courtesy of Carola Suarez-Orozco and photographer Kris Snibble/Harvard News; Office: © 2003 President and Fellows of Harvard College; **p. 573:** © USA Today Library, photo by H. Darr Beiser; **p. 578:** © Bob Daemmrich/The Image Works

NAME INDEX

C

D

E

F

N

O

P

Q

R

S

T

D

SUBJECT INDEX

References to figures are in italics.

E

F

G

N

O

P

Q

R

S

T

U

V

W

X

Z